1989 Tax Rate Schedules

Schedule X—Single

If taxable income is: Over—	But not over—	The tax is:	of the amount over—
$0	$18,550	. . . . 15%	$0
18,550	44,900	$2,782.50 + 28%	18,550
44,900	93,130	10,160.50 + 33%	44,900
93,130	. . . .	Use **Worksheet** below to figure your tax.	

Schedule Z— Head of household

If taxable income is: Over—	But not over—	The tax is:	of the amount over—
$0	$24,850	. . . . 15%	$0
24,850	64,200	$3,727.50+ 28%	24,850
64,200	128,810	14,745.50 + 33%	64,200
128,810	. . . .	Use **Worksheet** below to figure your tax.	

Schedule Y-1—Married filing jointly or Qualifying widow(er)

If taxable income is: Over—	But not over—	The tax is:	of the amount over—
$0	$30,950	. . . . 15%	$0
30,950	74,850	$4,642.50 + 28%	30,950
74,850	155,320	16,934.50 + 33%	74,850
155,320	. . . .	Use **Worksheet** below to figure your tax.	

Schedule Y-2— Married filing separately

If taxable income is: Over—	But not over—	The tax is:	of the amount over—
$0	$15,475	. . . . 15%	$0
15,475	37,425	$2,321.25 + 28%	15,475
37,425	117,895	8,467.25 + 33%	37,425
117,895	. . . .	Use **Worksheet** below to figure your tax.	

Worksheet (Keep for your records)

1. If your filing status is:
   - Single, enter $26,076.40
   - Head of household, enter $36,066.80
   - Married filing jointly or Qualifying widow(er), enter $43,489.60
   - Married filing separately, enter $35,022.35   . . . . 1. _____

2. Enter your taxable income . . . . 2. _____

3. If your filing status is:
   - Single, enter $93,130
   - Head of household, enter $128,810
   - Married filing jointly or Qualifying widow(er), enter $155,320
   - Married filing separately, enter $117,895   . . . . . 3. _____

4. Subtract line 3 from line 2. Enter the result. (If the result is zero or less, use the schedule above for your filing status to figure your tax. DON'T use this worksheet.) . . . . . . 4. _____

5. Multiply the amount on line 4 by 28% (.28). Enter the result . . . . 5. _____

6. Multiply the amount on line 4 by 5% (.05). Enter the result . . . . 6. _____

7. Multiply $560 by the number of exemptions claimed. (If married filing separately, see Note below.) Enter the result . . . . 7. _____

8. Compare the amounts on lines 6 and 7. Enter the **smaller** of the two amounts . . . . . . 8. _____

9. **Tax.** Add lines 1, 5, and 8. . . . . 9. _____

Note: *If married filing separately and you did* **not** *claim an exemption for your spouse, multiply $560 by the number of exemptions claimed. Add $560 to the result and enter the total on line 7 above.*

1990 ANNUAL EDITION

WEST'S FEDERAL TAXATION:

INDIVIDUAL INCOME TAXES

1990 ANNUAL EDITION

WEST'S FEDERAL TAXATION:

INDIVIDUAL INCOME TAXES

GENERAL EDITORS

William H. Hoffman, Jr., J.D., Ph.D., C.P.A.

James E. Smith, Ph.D., C.P.A.

Eugene Willis, Ph.D., C.P.A.

CONTRIBUTING AUTHORS

D. Larry Crumbley, Ph.D., C.P.A.
Texas A & M University

Steven C. Dilley, J.D., Ph.D., C.P.A.
Michigan State University

Patrica C. Elliott, D.B.A., C.P.A.
University of New Mexico

William H. Hoffman, Jr., J.D., Ph.D., C.P.A.
University of Houston

Jerome S. Horvitz, J.D., LL.M. in Taxation
University of Houston

Marilyn Phelan, J.D., Ph.D., C.P.A.
Texas Tech University

William A. Raabe, Ph.D., C.P.A.
University of Wisconsin-Milwaukee

Boyd C. Randall, J.D., Ph.D.
Brigham Young University

W. Eugene Seago, J.D., Ph.D., C.P.A.
Virginia Polytechnic Institute and State University

James E. Smith, Ph.D., C.P.A.
College of William and Mary

Willis C. Stevenson, Ph.D., C.P.A.
University of Wisconsin-Madison

Eugene Willis, Ph.D., C.P.A.
University of Illinois at Urbana

ASSOCIATE EDITORS

David M. Maloney, Ph.D., C.P.A.
University of Virginia

Tonya K. Flesher, Ph.D., C.P.A.
University of Mississippi

WEST PUBLISHING COMPANY

St. Paul   New York   Los Angeles   San Francisco

Interior design: David Corona
Copyediting: Patricia Lewis
Cover design: Peter Thiel

Copyright © 1989
Copyright © 1978, 1979, 1980, 1981, 1982, 1983, 1984, 1985, 1986, 1987, 1988
By **West Publishing Co.**
50 West Kellogg Boulevard
P.O. Box 64526
St. Paul, MN 55164–1003

Library of Congress Cataloging in Publication Data

Main entry under title:
  West's Federal Taxation.
  Includes index.
  1. Income tax—United States—Law
I. Hoffman, William H. III. Willis, Eugene

ISBN 0–314–51415–5   KF6369.W47   343'.73'052   77–20656

ISSN 0272–0329

1990 ANNUAL EDITION

PREFACE

This text is intended as a basis for a first course in Federal taxation for undergraduate or graduate accounting, business, and law students. With certain modifications in the coverage of the materials, the text may be used in a survey course on Federal taxation for undergraduate or graduate students. The materials may also be valuable as a tool for self-study, since they contain numerous clarifying examples adaptable to such an approach.

Tax policy considerations and historical developments are introduced in the text only to the extent that they shed light on the reason for a particular rule. The many simple and straightforward examples further clarify the materials by showing how a particular tax rule applies in an actual situation.

Since the original edition was issued in 1978, we have followed a policy of annually revising the text material to reflect statutory, judicial, and administrative changes in the Federal tax law and to correct any errors or other shortcomings. The 1990 edition has been thoroughly revised to reflect the Technical and Miscellaneous Revenue Act of 1988 and related developments.

In the 1990 edition, we have made some structural changes to give more extensive coverage of the most important tax developments in recent years. Chapter 7 is now devoted to coverage of the passive loss rules and at-risk limitations. Chapter 12 is now concerned exclusively with expanded coverage of the alternative minimum tax.

Special Features

- Once knowledge of the tax law has been acquired, it needs to be used. The tax minimization process, however, normally requires careful planning. Because we recognize the importance of planning procedures, most chapters include a separate section (designated *Tax Planning Considerations*) illustrating the applications of such procedures to specific areas.

- We believe that any basic course in Federal taxation should offer the reader the opportunity to learn and utilize the methodology of tax research. Chapter 2 and Appendix E are devoted to this methodology. Also, most chapters contain *Research Problems* that require the use of research tools. The effectiveness of the text does not, however, depend on the coverage of tax research procedures. Consequently, the treatment of this subject may be omitted without impairing the continuity of the remaining textual materials.

- Most chapters contain one or more *Concept Summaries* that synthesize important concepts in chart or tabular form.

- Although it is not our purpose to approach the presentation and discussion of taxation from the standpoint of preparation of tax returns, some orientation to forms is necessary. Because 1989 forms will not be available until later in the year, most tax return problems in this edition are written for tax year 1988. The 1988 problems may be solved manually, or many may be solved using the tax return preparation software (WEST–TAX Preparer) that may be purchased by students who use this text.

- Appendix F contains three comprehensive tax return problems written for tax year 1988. Each of these problems lends itself for use as a term project because of the sophistication required for satisfactory completion. Solutions to the problems in Appendix F are contained in the Instructor's Guide.

- For the reader's convenience, Appendix B contains a full reproduction of most of the 1988 tax forms frequently encountered in actual practice.

- Most tax textbooks are published in the spring, long before tax forms for the year of publication are available from the government. We believe that students should be exposed to the most current tax forms. As a result, we update selected forms problems and provide adopters with reproducible copies of these problems, along with blank tax forms and solutions on the new forms. Shortly after the beginning of 1990, adopters will receive selected tax return problems, updated and solved on 1989 forms.

Software

The trend toward increased use of the computer as an essential tool in tax practice has accelerated. To insure that the West's Federal Taxation instructional package continues to set the pace in this important area, the following products are available to be used with the 1990 edition:

- **BNA Income Tax Spreadsheet** (Educational Version): A comprehensive, menu-driven individual tax computation and planning package.

- **WEST–TAX Preparer:** A program for use in preparing and printing Federal income tax returns for individuals.

- **WEST–TAX Planner:** A Lotus-based tax computation and planning spreadsheet template for individual taxpayers (available free to adopters).

- **V–P PLANNER PLUS:** A spreadsheet program that is compatible with Lotus 123 (Release 2). It can be used to run WEST–TAX PLANNER.

The outstanding features of all of these software products are that they are powerful, easy to learn, and easy to use. We believe that tax education can be raised to a higher level through the use of computers and well-designed software. These software packages take the drudgery out of performing the complex computations involved in solving difficult tax problems. This allows students to concentrate on applying concepts and interpreting results.

To enable students to take advantage of these new software products, the 1990 Edition contains numerous tax return and tax planning problems. The tax planning problems allow students to evaluate alternative tax planning strategies and calculate the effect of various alternatives on the taxpayer's liability. Problems that lend themselves to solutions using the software packages described above are identified by a computer symbol to the left of the problem number. The instructions for each of these problems identify which software packages are appropriate for solving the problems.

Supplements

Other products in our 1990 instructional package include the following:

- The *Instructor's Guide* contains an instructor's summary of each chapter, test questions and solutions (referenced to pages in the text), and additional materials for classroom use and discussion.

- A *Solutions Manual* that has been carefully checked to ensure that it is error-free. All problems are labeled by topical coverage and a matrix has been added indicating which problems are new, modified or unchanged in the new edition. The solutions are referenced to pages in the text.

- WESTEST, a microcomputer test generation program for IBM PC's and compatibles and the Apple II family of computers.

- A *Student Study Guide* prepared by Gerald E. Whittenburg, San Diego State University, includes a chapter review of key concepts, self-evaluation tests with solutions, and a selection of CPA and IRS examination questions.

- *Transparency Masters* for selected complex problems, with a larger typeface for greater readability.

- *Transparency Acetates* for selected cumulative problems.

- *WFT Practice Sets*, 1989–90 Edition, prepared by John B. Barrack, University of Georgia, is designed to cover all the common forms that would be used by a tax practitioner for the average client.

- Limited free use to qualified adopters of WESTLAW, a computer-assisted tax and legal research service that provides access to hundreds of valuable information sources.

- *West's Internal Revenue Code of 1986 and Treasury Regulations: Annotated and Selected: 1989 Edition* by James E. Smith, College of William and Mary. This provides the opportunity for the student to be exposed to the Code and the Regulations in a single volume book, which also contains useful annotations.

- *West's Federal Taxation Newsletter Update* will be mailed to adopters twice a year. It will focus on new tax legislation and updated information.

While the primary emphasis of the text is on the income taxation of individuals, chapter 20 is an overview of the Federal taxation of other forms of business organization (corporations and partnerships). This chapter could be of particular significance to students who do not plan to take a second course in Federal taxation. For others, chapter 20 may serve as a lead-in to *West's Federal Taxation: Corporations, Partnerships, Estates, and Trusts.*

Acknowledgements

We are most appreciative of the many suggestions that we have received for revising the text, many of which have been incorporated in past editions and in the 1990 edition. In particular, we would like to thank Professor Radie Bunn of Southwest Missouri State University for his suggestions for the 1990 edition. In addition, we would like to thank the following reviewers for their help with the 1990 edition: Richard F. Boes, Idaho State University; Diane J. Green, Sam Houston State University; Leslie Grow, Central Missouri State University; David Harris, University of Texas-El Paso; Joseph D. Kaderabek, Baldwin-Wallace College; Michael Kinney, University of Arizona; M. Clyde Letsinger, University of Tennessee; Frances McNair, Mississippi State University; Robert L. Peace, North Carolina State University; Mark B. Persellin, Florida Atlantic University; Nancy J. Stara, University of Nebraska-Lincoln; James P. Trebby, Marquette University; John H. Wilguess, Oklahoma State University.

Finally, this 1990 edition would not have been possible without the technical assistance of and manuscript review by Bonnie Hoffman, CPA, and Freda Mulhall, CPA. We are indebted to them for their efforts.

William H. Hoffman, Jr.
Eugene Willis
James E. Smith

April, 1989

CONTENTS IN BRIEF

TABLE OF CONTENTS

PART TWO	GROSS INCOME

4 GROSS INCOME: CONCEPTS AND INCLUSIONS 4–1

PART THREE   DEDUCTIONS

6   DEDUCTIONS AND LOSSES: IN GENERAL   6–1

9 DEPRECIATION, COST RECOVERY, AMORTIZATION, AND DEPLETION 9–1

10 DEDUCTIONS: EMPLOYEE EXPENSES 10–1

PART FOUR   SPECIAL TAX COMPUTATION METHODS, PAYMENT PROCEDURES, AND TAX CREDITS

12 ALTERNATIVE MINIMUM TAX   12–1

13   TAX CREDITS AND PAYMENT PROCEDURES   13–1

17   PROPERTY TRANSACTIONS: SECTION 1231 AND RECAPTURE PROVISIONS   17–1

PART SIX   **ACCOUNTING PERIODS, ACCOUNTING METHODS, AND DEFERRED COMPENSATION**

18 ACCOUNTING PERIODS AND METHODS   18–1

APPENDIXES

1990 ANNUAL EDITION

WEST'S FEDERAL TAXATION:

INDIVIDUAL INCOME TAXES

1

INTRODUCTION AND BASIC TAX MODEL

Part 1 provides an introduction to taxation in the United States. Although the primary orientation of this text is income taxation, other types of taxes are also discussed briefly. The purposes of the Federal tax law are examined, and the legislative, administrative, and judicial sources of Federal tax law, including their application to the tax research process, are analyzed. Part 1 concludes with the introduction of the basic tax model for the individual taxpayer.

CHAPTER

1

An Introduction to Taxation and Understanding the Federal Tax Law

CHAPTER

2

Working with the Tax Law

CHAPTER

3

Tax Determination; Personal and Dependency Exemptions; An Overview of Property Transactions

1

An Introduction to Taxation and Understanding the Federal Tax Law

OBJECTIVES

Provide a brief history, including trends, of the Federal income tax.

Describe some of the criteria for selecting a tax base.

Explain the different types of taxes existing in the United States at the Federal, state, and local levels.

Furnish an introduction to the Federal income tax as applicable to individuals and corporations.

Introduce the major employment taxes such as the Federal Insurance Contributions Act (FICA) and the Federal Unemployment Tax Act (FUTA).

Briefly review the audit process in connection with tax administration.

Discuss the statute of limitations applicable to assessments by the IRS and on refunds claimed by taxpayers.

Highlight the interest and penalty rules relating to taxpayer noncompliance.

Explain the causal factors that have led to our present income tax system.

Describe the economic, social, equity, and political considerations that justify various aspects of the tax law.

Review the role played by the IRS and the courts in the evolution of the Federal tax system.

The primary objective of this chapter is to provide an overview of the Federal tax system. In this regard, some of the topics covered include the following:

● A brief review of the historical aspects of the Federal income tax.

● A summary of the different types of taxes existing at the Federal, state, and local levels.

● Some highlights illustrating how the tax laws are administered.

● A discussion of tax concepts that help in understanding the reasons for various tax provisions.

Why would a text devoted primarily to the Federal individual income tax discuss state and local taxes? A simple illustration can show the importance of these non-Federal taxes.

EXAMPLE 1	T is employed by X Corporation in State A. Y Corporation offers him a higher salary that, if accepted, would require relocating to State B. □

Although T must consider many nontax factors before he decides on a job change, he should also evaluate the tax climate. How do the state and local income taxes compare? State and local sales taxes could affect the cost of living differential. If T plans to remain (or become) a homeowner, how do state and local property taxes vary? After resolving these questions, the higher salary that T was offered may no longer be attractive.

HISTORY OF U.S. TAXATION

Early Periods

The concept of an income tax can hardly be regarded as a newcomer to the Western Hemisphere. Although an income tax was first enacted in 1634 by the English colonists in the Massachusetts Bay Colony, this form of taxation was not adopted by the Federal government until 1861. In fact, both the Federal Union and the Confederate States of America used the income tax to provide funds to finance the Civil War. Although modest in its reach and characterized by broad exemptions and low rates, the income tax generated $376 million of revenue for the Federal government during the Civil War.

When the Civil War ended, the need for additional revenue disappeared and the income tax was repealed. As was true before the war, the Federal government was able to finance its operations almost exclusively from customs duties (tariffs). It is somewhat surprising that no one challenged the constitutionality of the income tax in effect during the Civil War.

When a new Federal income tax on individuals was enacted in 1894, its opponents were prepared to and did challenge its constitutionality. The U.S. Constitution provided that ". . . No Capitation, or other direct, Tax shall be laid, unless in Proportion to the Census or Enumeration herein before directed to be taken." In *Pollock v. Farmers' Loan and Trust Co.,* [1] the U.S. Supreme Court found that the income tax was a direct tax that was unconstitutional, since it was not apportioned among the states in proportion to their populations.

A Federal corporate income tax, enacted by Congress in 1909, fared better in the judicial system. The U.S. Supreme Court found this tax to be constitutional because it was treated as an excise tax.[2] In essence, it was a tax on the right to do business in the corporate form. As such, it was likened to a form of the franchise tax.[3] It should be noted that the corporate form of doing business was developed in the late nineteenth century and was an unfamiliar concept to the framers of the U.S. Constitution. Since a corporation is an entity created under law, jurisdictions possess the right to tax its creation and operation. Using this rationale, many states still impose franchise taxes on corporations.

The ratification of the Sixteenth Amendment to the U.S. Constitution sanctioned both the Federal individual and corporate income taxes and, as a consequence, neutralized the continuing effect of the *Pollock* decision.

Revenue Acts

Following ratification of the Sixteenth Amendment, Congress enacted the Revenue Act of 1913. Under this Act, a flat 1 percent tax was levied upon the income of corporations. Individuals paid a normal tax rate of 1 percent on taxable income after deducting a personal exemption of $3,000 for a single individual and $4,000 for a married taxpayer. Surtax rates of 1 to 6 percent were applied to high-income taxpayers.

Various revenue acts were passed during the period from 1913 to 1939. In 1939, all of these revenue laws were codified into the Internal Revenue Code of 1939. In 1954, a similar codification of the revenue law took place. The current law consists of the Internal Revenue Code of 1986, which largely carries over the provisions of the 1954 Code. To date, the Code has been amended twice since 1986.

Historical Trends

The income tax has proved to be a major source of revenue for the Federal government. Figure 1–1 contains a breakdown of the major revenue sources.[4] The importance of the income tax is demonstrated by the fact that estimated income tax collections from individuals and corporations amount to 47 percent of the total receipts.

The need for revenues to finance the war effort during World War II converted the income tax into a "mass tax." For example, in 1939, less than 6 percent of the U.S. population was subject to the Federal income tax. In 1945, over 74 percent of the population was subject to the Federal income tax.[5]

1. 3 AFTR 2602, 15 S.Ct. 912 (USSC, 1895). See chapter 2 for an explanation as to how judicial decisions are cited.
2. *Flint v. Stone Tracy Co.,* 3 AFTR 2834, 31 S.Ct. 342 (USSC, 1911).
3. See the discussion of state franchise taxes later in the chapter.
4. As proposed by the Executive Office of the President for fiscal year 1989. *Budget of the United States Government,* Office of Management and Budget (Washington, D.C., 1988).
5. Richard Goode, *The Individual Income Tax* (Washington, D.C.: The Brookings Institution, 1964), pp. 2–4.

FIGURE 1–1	Federal Budget Receipts—1989	
	Individual income taxes	38%
	Corporation income taxes	9
	Social insurance taxes and contributions	31
	Excise taxes	3
	Borrowing	15
	Other	4
		100%

Certain changes in the income tax law are of particular significance in understanding the Federal income tax. In 1943, Congress passed the Current Tax Payment Act, which provided for the first pay-as-you-go tax system. A pay-as-you-go feature of an income tax system compels employers to withhold for taxes a specified portion of an employee's wages. Persons with income from other than wages must make periodic (e.g., quarterly) payments to the taxing authority (the Internal Revenue Service) for estimated taxes due for the year.

One trend that has caused considerable concern among many persons and groups has been the increased complexity of the Federal income tax laws. Often, under the name of tax reform, Congress has added to this complexity through frequent changes in the tax laws. Increasingly, this has forced many taxpayers to seek the assistance of tax professionals. At this time, therefore, substantial support exists for tax law simplification.

CRITERIA USED IN THE SELECTION OF A TAX BASE

Adam Smith first identified certain "canons of taxation" that are still considered when evaluating a particular tax structure. These canons of taxation are as follows: [6]

- *Equality.* Each taxpayer enjoys fair or equitable treatment by paying taxes in proportion to his or her income level. Ability to pay a tax is the measure of how equitably a tax is distributed among taxpayers.

- *Convenience.* Administrative simplicity has long been valued in formulating tax policy. If a tax is easily assessed and collected and the costs of its administration are low, it should be favored. The withholding (pay-as-you-go) system has been advocated because of its convenience for taxpayers.

- *Certainty.* A "good" tax structure exists if the taxpayer can readily predict when, where, and how a tax will be levied. Individuals and businesses need to know the likely tax consequences of a particular type of transaction.

- *Economy.* A "good" tax system involves only nominal collection costs by the government and minimal compliance costs on the part of the taxpayer. Although the government's cost of collecting Federal taxes amounts to less than one-half of 1 percent of the revenue collected, the

---

6. *The Wealth of Nations,* Book V, Chapter II, Part II (New York: Dutton, 1910).

complexity of our existing tax structure imposes substantial taxpayer compliance costs.

THE TAX STRUCTURE

Tax Rates

Tax rates are applied to the tax base to determine a taxpayer's liability. The tax rates may be proportional or progressive. A tax is proportional if the rate of tax remains constant for any given income level.

EXAMPLE 2

T has $10,000 of taxable income and pays a tax of $3,000, or 30%. Y's taxable income is $50,000 and the tax on this amount is $15,000, or 30%. If this constant rate is applied throughout the rate structure, the tax is proportional. ☐

The Federal income tax, Federal gift and estate taxes, and most state income tax rate structures are progressive. In the case of the Federal income tax, a higher percentage rate of tax is applied as taxable income increases.

EXAMPLE 3

If T, a married individual filing jointly, has taxable income of $10,000, the tax for 1989 is $1,500 for an average tax rate of 15%. If, however, T's taxable income was $50,000, the tax would be $9,976.50 for an average tax rate of 19.953%. The tax is progressive, since higher rates are applied to greater amounts of taxable income. ☐

Adjustments to Tax Base and Incidence of Taxation

The degree to which the total tax burden is shared by various segments of society is difficult to assess. Assumptions must be made concerning who absorbs the burden for payment of the tax. For example, since dividend payments to shareholders are not deductible by a corporation and such amounts are generally taxable income to shareholders, a form of double taxation on the same income is being levied. Concern over double taxation is valid to the extent that corporations are *not* able to shift the corporate tax to the consumer through higher commodity prices. Many research studies have shown a high degree of shifting of the corporate income tax. Thus, when the corporate tax can be shifted, it becomes merely a consumption tax that is borne by the ultimate purchasers of goods.

The U.S. Federal income tax rate structure for individuals is becoming less progressive. For example, for 1986 there were 15 rates, ranging from 0 to 50 percent. The Tax Reform Act (TRA) of 1986 reduced 1989 rates to 15 percent and 28 percent. Because it eliminated many deductions and other tax savings procedures, Congress expects the lower rates to reach a larger base of taxable income.

MAJOR TYPES OF TAXES

Property Taxes

Normally referred to as *ad valorem* taxes because they are based on value, property taxes are a tax on wealth, or capital. In this regard, they have much in common with death taxes and gift taxes discussed later in the chapter. Although property taxes do not tax income, the income actually derived (or the potential for any such income) may be relevant insofar as it affects the value of the property being taxed.

Property taxes fall into two categories: those imposed on realty and those imposed on personalty. Both have added importance, since they usually generate a deduction for Federal income tax purposes (see chapter 11).

Ad Valorem Taxes on Realty.   Property taxes on realty are exclusively within the province of the states and their local political subdivisions (e.g., cities, counties, school districts). They represent a major source of revenue for local governments, but their importance at the state level has waned over the past few years.[7] The trend has been for the states to look to other types of taxes (e.g., sales, income, severance) to meet their fiscal needs. Most of the revenue derived from property taxes on realty is used to provide essential governmental services (e.g., police and fire protection, public education, waste disposal, utility sources).

Particularly in those jurisdictions that do not impose ad valorem taxes on personalty, what is included in the definition of realty could have an important bearing on which assets are or are not subject to tax. Primarily a question of state property law, realty generally includes real estate and any capital improvements thereto that comprise "fixtures." Simply stated, a fixture is something so permanently attached to the real estate that its removal will cause irreparable damage. A built-in bookcase might well be a fixture, whereas a movable bookcase would not. Certain items such as electrical wiring and plumbing when installed in a building have ceased to be personalty and have become realty.

Some of the characteristics of ad valorem taxes on realty are highlighted as follows:

- Property owned by the Federal government is exempt from tax. Similar immunity usually is extended to property owned by state and local governments and by certain charitable organizations.

- Some states provide for lower valuations on property dedicated to agricultural use or other special uses (e.g., wildlife sanctuaries).

- Some states partially exempt the homestead portion of property from taxation. Modern homestead laws normally operate to protect some or all of a personal residence (including a farm or ranch) from the actions of creditors pursuing claims against the owner.

- Lower taxes may apply to a residence owned by an elderly taxpayer (e.g., age 65 and older).

---

7. Some states have imposed freezes on upward revaluations of residential housing.

- When non-income-producing property (e.g., a personal residence) is converted to income-producing property (e.g., a rental house), typically the appraised value increases.

- Some jurisdictions extend immunity from tax for a specified period of time (a "tax holiday") to new or relocated businesses.

Unlike the ad valorem tax on personalty (see below), the tax on realty is difficult to avoid. Since real estate is impossible to hide, a high degree of taxpayer compliance is not surprising. The only avoidance possibility that is generally available lies with the assessed value of the property. For this reason, both the assessed value of the property and, particularly, a reassessed value upward are not without their share of controversy and litigation. For these purposes, at least, everyone is convinced that his or her property is worth less than that belonging to neighbors or near-neighbors.

The four methods currently in use for assessing the value of real estate are as follows:

1. Actual purchase or construction price.

2. Contemporaneous sales prices or construction costs of comparable properties.

3. Cost of reproducing a building, less allowance for depreciation and obsolescence from the time of actual construction.

4. Capitalization of income from rental property.

Because all of these methods suffer faults and lead to inequities, a combination of one or more is not uncommon. For example, because of rising real estate values and construction costs, the use of actual purchase or construction price (method 1) places the purchaser of a new home at a definite disadvantage compared with the owner who acquired similar property years before. As another illustration, if the capitalization of income (method 4) deals with property subject to rent controls, the property may be undervalued.

The history of the ad valorem tax on realty has been marked by inconsistent results in its application due to a lack of competent tax administration and definitive guidelines as to assessment procedures. In recent years, however, significant steps toward improvement have taken place. Some jurisdictions, for example, have computerized their valuation reassessment procedures so as to have an immediate effect on all property located within any jurisdiction.

Ad Valorem Tax on Personalty. Personalty can be defined as all assets that are not realty. At the outset, it may be helpful to distinguish between the classification of an asset (realty or personalty) and the use to which it is placed. Both realty and personalty can be either business use or personal use property. Examples of this distinction include a residence (realty that is personal use), an office building (realty that is business use), surgical instruments (personalty that is business use), and regular wearing apparel (personalty that is personal use).[8]

---

8. The distinction, important for ad valorem and for Federal income tax purposes, becomes confused when personalty is often referred to as "personal" property to distinguish it from "real" property. Such designation does not give a complete picture of what is involved. The description "personal" residence, however, is clearer, since one can identify a residence as being real-

Personalty can be also classified as tangible property or intangible property. For ad valorem tax purposes, intangible personalty includes stocks, bonds, and various other securities (e.g., bank shares).

Generalizations concerning the ad valorem tax on personalty are as follows:

- Particularly with personalty devoted to personal use (e.g., jewelry, household furnishings), taxpayer compliance ranges from poor to zero. In some jurisdictions, enforcement of the tax on these items is not even attempted. For automobiles devoted to personal use, many jurisdictions have converted from value as the tax base to arbitrary license fees based on the weight of the vehicle. Recently, some jurisdictions are taking into consideration the age factor (e.g., automobiles six years or older are not subject to the ad valorem tax as they are presumed to have little, if any, value).

- For personalty devoted to business use (e.g., inventories, trucks, machinery, equipment), taxpayer compliance and enforcement procedures are measurably better.

- Which jurisdiction possesses the authority to tax movable personalty (e.g., railroad rolling stock) always has been and continues to be a troublesome issue.

- The ad valorem tax on intangibles, although it still exists in some jurisdictions, largely has fallen into disfavor. Undoubtedly the lack of effective enforcement capability on the part of the taxing authorities has contributed to this decline in use.

Transaction Taxes

Characteristically imposed at the manufacturer's, wholesaler's, or retailer's level, transaction taxes cover a wide range of transfers. Like many other types of taxes (e.g., income taxes, death taxes, and gift taxes), transaction taxes usually are not peculiarly within the exclusive province of any level of taxing authority (Federal, state, local government). As the description implies, these levies place a tax on transfers of property and normally are determined by a percentage rate multiplied by the value involved.

Federal Excise Taxes.   Long one of the mainstays of the Federal tax system, Federal excise taxes had declined in relative importance until recently. In late 1982, Congress substantially increased the Federal excise taxes on such items as tobacco products, fuel and gasoline sales, telephone usage, and air travel passenger tickets. Other Federal excise taxes include the following:

- Manufacturers' excise taxes on trucks, trailers, tires, firearms, sporting equipment, coal, and the gas guzzler tax on automobiles.[9]

- Alcohol taxes.

- Miscellaneous taxes (e.g., the tax on wagering).

---

ty. What is meant, in this case, is realty that is personal use property.

9. The gas guzzler tax is imposed on the manufacturers of automobiles and progresses in amount as the mileage ratings per gallon of gas decrease.

The list of transactions covered, although seemingly impressive, has diminished over the years. At one time, for example, there was a Federal excise tax on admission to amusement facilities (e.g., theaters) and on the sale of such "luxury" items as leather goods, furs, jewelry, and cosmetics.

When reviewing the list of both Federal and state excise taxes, one should recognize the possibility that the tax laws may be trying to influence social behavior. For example, the gas guzzler tax is intended as an incentive for the automobile companies to build cars that are fuel efficient. Since alcohol and tobacco are considered by many to be harmful to a person's health, why not increase their cost with the imposition of excise taxes and thereby discourage their use? Unfortunately, mixed evidence exists to support a high level of correlation between the imposition of an excise tax and consumer behavior.

State Excise Taxes.   Many state and local excise taxes parallel the Federal version. Thus, all states tax the sale of gasoline, liquor, and tobacco products; however, the rates vary significantly. For gasoline products, for example, compare the 20.9 cents per gallon imposed by the state of Wisconsin with the 8 cents per gallon levied by the state of Wyoming. For tobacco sales, contrast the 2 cents per pack of cigarettes in effect in North Carolina with the 35 cents per pack applicable in California. In the latter situation, is it surprising that the smuggling of cigarettes from North Carolina for resale elsewhere is so widespread? Here might be a situation where an excise tax probably encourages criminal conduct more than it discourages consumer use.

Other excise taxes found at some state and local levels include those on admission to amusement facilities; hotel occupancy and the rental of various other facilities; and the sale of playing cards, oleomargarine products, and prepared foods. Most states impose a transaction tax on the transfer of property that requires the recording of documents (e.g., real estate sales).[10] Some extend the tax to the transfer of stocks and other securities.

General Sales Taxes.   The distinction between an excise tax and a general sales tax is easy to make. One is restricted to a particular transaction (e.g., the 9 cents per gallon Federal excise tax on the sale of gasoline), while the other covers a multitude of transactions (e.g., a 5 percent tax on *all* retail sales). In actual practice, however, the distinction is not always that clear. Some state statutes might exempt certain transactions from the application of the general sales taxes (e.g., sales of food to be consumed off the premises, sales of certain medicines and drugs). Also, it is not uncommon to find that rates vary depending on the commodity involved. In many states, for example, preferential rates are allowed for the sale of agricultural equipment, or different rates (either higher or lower than the general rate) apply to the sale of automobiles. With many of these special exceptions and classifications of rates, a general sales tax can take on the appearance of a collection of individual excise taxes.

Every state that imposes a general sales tax levied on the consumer also has a use tax. The states without either tax are Alaska, Delaware, Montana, New Hampshire, and Oregon. To prevent the avoidance of a sales tax, a use tax is a necessary complement.

---

10. This type of tax has much in common with the stamp tax levied by Great Britain on the American colonies during the pre-Revolutionary period in U.S. history.

EXAMPLE 4   T resides in a jurisdiction that imposes a 5% general sales tax but lives near a state that has no tax at all. T purchases an automobile for $10,000 from a dealer located in the neighboring state. Has T saved $500 in sales taxes? The state use tax is designed to pick up the difference between the tax paid in another jurisdiction and what would have been paid in the state where T resides. □

Because the use tax is difficult to enforce for many purchases, it is often avoided. In some cases, for example, it may be worthwhile to make purchases through an out-of-state mail-order business. In spite of shipping costs, the avoidance of the local sales tax that otherwise might be incurred could make the price of such products as computer components cheaper. Some states are taking steps to curtail this loss of revenue. As for items such as automobiles (refer to Example 4), the use tax probably will be collected when the purchaser registers the item in his or her home state.

Local general sales taxes, over and above those levied by the state, are common. It is not unusual to find taxpayers living in the same state who pay different general sales taxes due to the location of their residence.

EXAMPLE 5   R and S, two individuals, both live in a state that has a general sales tax of 3%. S, however, resides in a city that imposes an additional general sales tax of 2%. In spite of the fact that R and S live in the same state, one is subject to a rate of 3%, while the other pays a tax of 5%. □

Severance Taxes.   Severance taxes are an important source of revenue for many states. These transaction taxes are based on the notion that the state has an interest in its natural resources (e.g., oil, gas, iron ore, coal); therefore, their extraction is an occasion for the imposition of a tax.

Death Taxes

A death tax is a tax on the right to transfer property or to receive property upon the death of the owner. Consequently, a death tax falls into the category of an excise tax. If the death tax is imposed on the right to pass property at death, it is classified as an estate tax. If it taxes the right to receive property from a decedent, it is termed an inheritance tax. Typical of other types of excise taxes, the value of the property transferred measures the base for determining the amount of the death tax.

Of the two, inheritance tax and estate tax, the Federal government imposes only an estate tax. State governments, however, levy inheritance taxes, estate taxes, or both.

EXAMPLE 6   At the time of her death, D lived in a state that imposes an inheritance tax but not an estate tax. S, one of D's heirs, lives in the same state. D's estate would be subject to the Federal estate tax, and S would be subject to the state inheritance tax. □

The Federal Estate Tax. The Revenue Act of 1916 incorporated the estate tax into the tax law. Although never designed to generate a large source of revenue, its original purpose was to prevent large concentrations of wealth from being kept within the family for many generations. Whether this objective has been accomplished is debatable. Like the income tax, estate taxes can be reduced through various planning procedures.

The gross estate includes property the decedent owned at the time of death. It also includes life insurance proceeds when paid to the estate or when paid to a beneficiary other than the estate if the deceased-insured had any ownership rights in the policy. Quite simply, the gross estate represents property interests subject to Federal estate taxation.[11] All property included in the gross estate is valued as of the date of death or, if the alternate valuation date is elected, six months later.[12]

Deductions from the gross estate in arriving at the taxable estate include funeral and administration expenses, certain taxes, debts of the decedent, casualty losses [13] incurred during the administration of the estate, transfers to charitable organizations, and, in some cases, the marital deduction. The marital deduction is available for amounts actually passing to a surviving spouse (a widow or widower).

Once the taxable estate has been determined and certain taxable gifts have been added to it, the estate tax can be computed. From the amount derived from the appropriate tax rate schedules, various credits should be subtracted to arrive at what, if any, tax is due.[14] Although many other credits also are available, probably the most significant one is the unified transfer tax credit. The main reason for this credit is to eliminate or reduce the estate tax liability for modest estates. For deaths after 1986, the amount of the credit is $192,800. Based on the estate tax rates, the amount of the credit covers a tax base of $600,000.

EXAMPLE 7   D had never made any taxable gifts before his death in 1987. If D died with a taxable estate of $600,000 or less, no Federal estate tax will be due because of the application of the unified transfer tax credit. Under the tax law, the estate tax on a taxable estate of $600,000 is $192,800. ☐

State Death Taxes. As noted earlier, states usually levy an inheritance tax, an estate tax, or both. The two forms of death taxes differ according to whether the tax is imposed on the heir or on the estate.

Characteristically, an inheritance tax divides the heirs into classes based on their relationship to the decedent. The more closely related the heir, the lower the rates imposed and the greater the exemption allowed. Some states completely exempt from taxation amounts passing to a surviving spouse.

---

11. For further information on these matters, see *West's Federal Taxation: Corporations, Partnerships, Estates, and Trusts.*

12. See the discussion of the alternate valuation date in chapter 14.

13. For a definition of casualty losses, see the Glossary of Tax Terms in Appendix C.

14. For tax purposes it is always crucial to appreci-

ate the difference between a deduction and a credit. A credit is a dollar-for-dollar reduction of tax liability. A deduction, however, only benefits the taxpayer to the extent of his or her tax bracket. An estate in a 50% tax bracket, for example, would need $2 of deductions to prevent $1 of tax liability from developing. In contrast, $1 of credit neutralizes $1 of tax liability.

Gift Taxes

Like a death tax, a gift tax is an excise tax levied on the right to transfer property. In this case, however, the tax is directed to transfers made during the owner's life and not at death. Also, a gift tax applies only to transfers that are not supported by full and adequate consideration.

EXAMPLE 8

D sells to his daughter property worth $20,000 for $1,000. Although property worth $20,000 has been transferred, only $19,000 represents a gift, since this is the portion not supported by full and adequate consideration. □

The Federal Gift Tax.   First enacted in 1932, the Federal gift tax was intended to complement the estate tax. Without any tax applicable to lifetime transfers by gift, it would be possible to avoid the estate tax and escape taxation entirely.

Only taxable gifts are subject to the gift tax. For this purpose, a taxable gift is measured by the fair market value of the property on the date of transfer less the annual exclusion of $10,000 per donee and, in some cases, less the marital deduction, which allows tax-free transfers between spouses. Each donor is allowed an annual exclusion of $10,000 for each donee.[15]

EXAMPLE 9

On December 31, 1988, D (a widow) gives $10,000 to each of her four married children (and their spouses) and her eight grandchildren. On January 3, 1989, she repeats the same procedure. Although D transferred $160,000 [$10,000 × 16 (number of donees)] in 1988 and $160,000 [$10,000 × 16 (number of donees)] in 1989 for a total of $320,000 ($160,000 + $160,000), she has not made a taxable gift. □

A special election applicable to married persons allows one-half of the gift made by the donor-spouse to be treated as being made by the nondonor-spouse. The effect of this election to split the gifts of property made to third persons is to increase the number of annual exclusions available. Also, it allows the use of the nondonor-spouse's unified transfer tax credit and may lower the tax brackets that will apply.

For taxable gifts made after 1976, the gift tax rate schedule is the same as that applicable to the estate tax. The schedule is commonly referred to as "the unified transfer tax schedule."

The unified transfer tax credit is available for all taxable gifts made after 1976. As was true with the Federal estate tax, the amount of this credit after is $192,800. There is, however, only one unified transfer tax credit, and it applies both to taxable gifts and to the Federal estate tax. In a manner of speaking, therefore, once the unified transfer tax credit has been exhausted for Federal gift tax purposes, it is no longer available to insulate a decedent from the Federal estate tax.

15. The purpose of the annual exclusion is to avoid the need to report and pay a tax on "modest" gifts. Without the exclusion, the Internal Revenue Service could face a real problem of taxpayer noncompliance. ·

By now it should be apparent that taxable gifts made after 1976 and estates are subject to the same set of tax rates and the same unified transfer tax credit. Also, such gifts affect the computation of the estate tax liability, since they have to be added to the tax base.

State Gift Taxes.   The states imposing a state gift tax are Delaware, Louisiana, New York, North Carolina, South Carolina, Tennessee, and Wisconsin. Most of the laws provide for lifetime exemptions and annual exclusions. Like the Federal gift tax, the state taxes are cumulative in effect. But unlike the Federal version, the amount of tax depends on the relationship between the donor and the donee. Like state inheritance taxes, larger exemptions and lower rates apply when the donor and donee are closely related to each other.

Income Taxes

Income taxes are levied by the Federal government, most states, and some local governments. The trend in recent years has been to place greater reliance on this method of taxation. This trend is not consistent with what is happening in other countries, and in this sense, our system of taxation is somewhat different.

Income taxes generally are imposed on individuals, corporations, and certain fiduciaries (estates and trusts). Most jurisdictions attempt to assure their collection by requiring certain pay-as-you-go procedures (e.g., withholding requirements as to employees and estimated tax prepayments for other taxpayers).

On occasion, Congress has seen fit to impose additional taxes on income. Such impositions were justified either by economic considerations or by special circumstances resulting from wartime conditions. During World War II, the Korean conflict, and the Vietnam conflict, excess-profits taxes were imposed in addition to the regular Federal income tax. The taxes were aimed at the profiteering that occurs when the economy is geared to the production of war materials.

Another additional income tax is the surcharge approach. During the period from April 1, 1968, to July 1, 1970, for example, taxpayers were subject to a surcharge of 10 percent of the amount of their regular income tax liability. This led to the strange result that taxpayers had to pay, so to speak, an income tax on their income tax. The justification for the special tax was to place restraints on what was regarded as an overactive economy, to curtail inflation, and to reduce the Federal deficit.

In light of current budget deficits, the surcharge approach has its advocates in Congress and therefore may be of more than historical interest. The advantage of the surcharge approach is that it represents a temporary solution to the problem. Thus, the tax can be imposed on a one-shot basis without compelling Congress to modify the regular income tax rates or base.

Federal Income Taxes.   Chapters 3 through 19 deal with the application of the Federal income tax to individuals. The procedure for determining the Federal income tax applicable to individuals is summarized in Figure 1–2.

The standard deduction and personal and dependency exemptions are explained in chapter 3.

The rules for the application of the Federal corporate income tax do not require the computation of adjusted gross income and do not provide for the standard deduction and personal and dependency exemptions. All allowable

FIGURE 1–2	Formula for Federal Income Tax on Individuals	
	Income (broadly conceived)	$xx,xxx
	Less: Exclusions (income that is not subject to tax)	(x,xxx)
	Gross income (income that is subject to tax)	$xx,xxx
	Less: Certain business deductions (usually referred to as deductions *for* adjusted gross income)	(x,xxx)
	Adjusted gross income	$xx,xxx
	Less: The greater of certain personal and employee deductions (usually referred to as *itemized deductions* or as deductions *from* adjusted gross income) *or*	
	The standard deduction (including any additional standard deduction) *and*	(x,xxx)
	Less: Personal and dependency exemptions	(x,xxx)
	Taxable income	$xx,xxx
	Tax on taxable income (see Tax Rate Schedules in Appendix A)	$ x,xxx
	Less: Tax credits (including Federal income tax withheld and other prepayments of Federal income taxes)	(xxx)
	Tax due (or refund)	$ xxx

deductions of a corporation fall into the business-expense category. In effect, therefore, the taxable income of a corporation is the difference between gross income (net of exclusions) and deductions.

Chapter 20 summarizes the rules relating to corporations. For an in-depth treatment of the Federal income tax as it affects corporations, estates, and trusts, see *West's Federal Taxation: Corporations, Partnerships, Estates, and Trusts*, 1990 Edition, chapters 2 through 6, 9, and 16.

State Income Taxes.   All but the following states impose an income tax on individuals: Alaska, Florida, Nevada, South Dakota, Texas, Washington, and Wyoming. New Hampshire and Tennessee have an income tax, but its application is limited to dividend and interest income.

Some of the characteristics of state income taxes are summarized as follows:

* With few exceptions, all states require some form of withholding procedures.

* Most states use as the tax base the income determination made for Federal income tax purposes.

* A minority of states go even further and impose a flat rate upon adjusted gross income (AGI) as computed for Federal income tax purposes. Several apply a rate to the Federal income tax liability. This is often referred to as the piggyback approach to state income taxation. Although the term "piggyback" does not lend itself to precise definition, in this sense, it means making use, for state income tax purposes, of what was done for Federal income tax purposes.

* Because of the tie-in to the Federal return, notification to the state of any changes made by the IRS upon audit of a Federal return usually is required.

- Most states allow a deduction for personal and dependency exemptions. Some states substitute a tax credit for a deduction.

- A diminishing minority of states allow a deduction for Federal income taxes.

- Most states allow their residents some form of tax credit for income taxes paid to other states.

- The due date for filing generally is the same as that for the Federal income tax (the fifteenth day of the fourth month following the close of the tax year).

Nearly all states have an income tax applicable to corporations. It is difficult to determine those that do not, because a state franchise tax sometimes is based in part on the income earned by the corporation.[16]

Local Income Taxes.   Cities imposing an income tax include, but are not limited to, Baltimore, Cincinnati, Cleveland, Detroit, Kansas City (Mo.), New York, Philadelphia, and St. Louis.

Employment Taxes

Classification as an employee usually leads to the imposition of employment taxes and to the requirement that the employer withhold specified amounts for income taxes. The rules governing the withholding for income taxes are discussed in chapter 13. The material that follows concentrates on the two major employment taxes: FICA (Federal Insurance Contributions Act—commonly referred to as the Social Security tax) and FUTA (Federal Unemployment Tax Act). Both taxes can be justified by social and public welfare considerations: FICA offers some measure of retirement security, and FUTA provides a modest source of income in the event of loss of employment.

Employment taxes come into play only if two conditions are satisfied. First, is the individual involved an "employee" (as opposed to "self-employed")? The differences between an employee and a self-employed person are discussed in chapter 10.[17] Second, if the individual involved is an employee, is he or she covered under FICA or FUTA or both? The coverage of both of these taxes is summarized in Figure 13-2 in chapter 13.[18]

FICA Taxes.   The tax rates and wage base under FICA are not constant, and as Figure 1-3 indicates, the increases over the years have been quite substantial. There appears to be every reason to predict that the rate and base amount will continue to rise in the future. Also note that Figure 1-3 represents the employee's share of the tax. As the employer must match the employee's portion, the *total* cost of FICA becomes 15.02 percent for 1989.

In at least two situations it is possible for an employee to have paid excess FICA taxes.

---

16. See the discussion of franchise taxes later in the chapter.

17. See also Circular E, Employer's Tax Guide, issued by the IRS as Publication 15.

18. Chapter 13 deals with the self-employment tax (the Social Security version of FICA for self-employed persons).

| FIGURE 1-3 | FICA Rates and Base |

Year	Percent	Base Amount	Maximum Tax
1978	6.05%	$ 17,700	$1,070.85
1979	6.13%	22,900	1,403.77
1980	6.13%	25,900	1,587.67
1981	6.65%	29,700	1,975.05
1982	6.70%	32,400	2,170.80
1983	6.70%	35,700	2,391.90
1984	6.70%	37,800	2,532.60
1985	7.05%	39,600	2,791.80
1986	7.15%	42,000	3,003.00
1987	7.15%	43,800	3,131.70
1988	7.51%	45,000	3,379.50
1989	7.51%	48,000	3,604.80
1990 on	7.65%	—*	—**

* Not yet determined by Congress.

** Cannot be computed until the wage base is set by Congress.

EXAMPLE 10

During 1989, T changed employers in the middle of the year, and from each job he earned $30,000 (all of which was subject to FICA). As a result, each employer withheld $2,253 (7.51% × $30,000) for a total of $4,506. Since T has overpaid his share of the FICA taxes by $901.20 [$4,506 (amount paid) − $3,604.80 (maximum tax from Figure 1-3)], he should claim this amount as a tax credit when filing an income tax return for 1989. The effect of a tax credit would be to reduce any income tax T might owe or, possibly, to generate a tax refund. □

EXAMPLE 11

During 1989, E earned $40,000 from her regular job and $10,000 from a part-time job (all of which was subject to FICA). As a result, one employer withheld $3,004 (7.51% × $40,000), while the other employer withheld $751 (7.51% × $10,000) for a total of $3,755. Since E has overpaid her share of FICA by $150.20 ($3,755 − $3,604.80), she should claim this amount as a tax credit when filing an income tax return for 1989. □

In both Examples 10 and 11, the employee was subject to overwithholding. In both cases, however, the employee was able to obtain a credit for the excess withheld. The same result does not materialize as to the portion paid by the employer. Since this amount is not refundable, it leads to a situation where employers pay more FICA taxes than the covered employees.

The mere fact that a husband and wife both are employed does not, by itself, result in overwithholding of FICA taxes.

EXAMPLE 12

During 1989, H and W (husband and wife) both are employed and each earns wages subject to FICA of $30,000. Accordingly, each has FICA withheld of $2,253 [7.51% × $30,000 (wages earned)] for a total of $4,506. Since neither spouse paid FICA in excess of $3,379.50 (refer to Figure 1–3), there is no overwithholding. □

A spouse employed by another spouse is subject to FICA. However, exempted are children under the age of 18 who are employed in a parent's trade or business.

FUTA Taxes.   The purpose of FUTA is to provide funds that the states can use to administer unemployment benefits. This leads to the somewhat unusual situation of one tax being handled by both Federal and state governments. The end product of such joint administration is to compel the employer to observe a double set of rules. Thus, state and Federal returns must be filed and payments made to both governmental units.

FUTA applies at a rate of 6.2 percent on the first $7,000 of covered wages paid during the year to each employee. The Federal government allows a credit for FUTA paid (or allowed under a merit rating system) to the state. The credit cannot exceed 5.4 percent of the covered wages. Thus, the amount required to be paid to the IRS could be as low as 0.8 percent (6.2 percent − 5.4 percent).

States follow a policy of reducing the unemployment tax on employers who experience stability in employment. Thus, an employer with little or no turnover among employees might find that the state rate could drop to as low as 0.1 percent or, in some states, even to zero. The reason for the merit rating credit is obvious. Steady employment means the state will have lower unemployment benefits to pay.

FUTA is to be distinguished from FICA in the sense that the incidence of taxation falls entirely upon the employer. A few states, however, levy a special tax on employees either to provide disability benefits or supplemental unemployment compensation, or both.

Other Taxes

To complete the overview of the U.S. tax system, some missing links need to be covered that do not fit into the classifications discussed elsewhere in this chapter.

Federal Customs Duties.   One tax that has not yet been mentioned is the tariff on certain imported goods.[19] Generally referred to as customs duties or levies, this tax, together with selective excise taxes, provided most of the revenues needed by the Federal government during the nineteenth century. Considering present times, it is remarkable to note that tariffs and excise taxes alone paid off the national debt in 1835 and enabled the U.S. Treasury to pay a surplus of $28 million to the states.

In recent years, tariffs have served the nation more as an instrument for carrying out protectionist policies than as a means of generating revenue. Thus, a particular U.S. industry might be saved from economic disaster, so the argument goes, by placing customs duties on the importation of foreign goods that can be sold at lower prices. The protectionist would contend that the

---

19. Less-developed countries that place principal reliance on one or more major commodities (e.g., oil, coffee) are prone to favor *export* duties as well.

tariff therefore neutralizes the competitive edge held by the producer of the foreign goods.

Protectionist policies seem more appropriate for less-developed countries whose industrial capacity has not yet matured. In a world where a developed country should have everything to gain from the encouragement of international free trade, such policies may be of dubious value. History proves that tariffs often lead to retaliatory action on the part of the nation or nations affected.

Miscellaneous State and Local Taxes. Most states impose a franchise tax on corporations. Basically, a franchise tax is one levied on the right to do business in the state. The base used for the determination of the tax varies from state to state. Although corporate income considerations may come into play, this tax most often is based on the capitalization of the corporation (either with or without certain long-term indebtedness).

Closely akin to the franchise tax are occupational taxes applicable to various trades or businesses, such as a liquor store license, a taxicab permit, or a fee to practice a profession such as law, medicine, or accounting. Most of these are not significant revenue producers and fall more into the category of licenses than taxes. The revenue derived is used to defray the cost incurred by the jurisdiction in regulating the business or profession in the interest of the public good.

Value Added Taxes

At least in the Common Market countries of Western Europe, the value added tax (VAT) has gained acceptance as a major source of revenue. Although variously classified, a VAT resembles a national sales tax, since it taxes the increment in value as goods move through production and manufacturing stages to the marketplace. A VAT has its proponents in the United States as a partial solution to high Federal budget deficits and increases in employment taxes. Its incorporation as part of our tax system in the near future is problematical, however.

TAX ADMINISTRATION

Internal Revenue Service

The responsibility for administering the Federal tax laws rests with the Treasury Department. Administratively, the IRS is part of the Department of the Treasury and is responsible for enforcing the tax laws.

The Commissioner of Internal Revenue is appointed by the President. His responsibilities are to establish policy and to supervise the activities of the entire IRS organization. The National Office organization of the IRS includes a Deputy Commissioner and several Assistant Commissioners who have supervisory responsibility over field operations.

The field organization of the IRS consists of the following:

- Service Centers (10) that are primarily responsible for processing tax returns, including the selection of returns for audit.

- District Directors (63) who perform audit work and are responsible for the collection of delinquent taxes.

- Regional Commissioners (7) who are responsible for the settlement of administrative appeals of disputed tax deficiencies.

The Audit Process

Selection of Returns for Audit.   The IRS utilizes mathematical formulas and statistical sampling techniques to select tax returns that are most likely to contain errors and to yield substantial amounts of additional tax revenues upon audit.

Though the IRS does not openly disclose all of its audit selection techniques, the following observations may be made relative to the probability of selection for audit:

- Certain groups of taxpayers are subject to audit much more frequently than others. These groups include individuals with gross income in excess of $50,000, self-employed individuals with substantial business income and deductions, and taxpayers with prior tax deficiencies. Also vulnerable are cash businesses (e.g., cafes and small service businesses) where the potential for tax avoidance is high.

EXAMPLE 13   T owns and operates a liquor store on a cash-and-carry basis. As all of T's sales are for cash, T might well be a prime candidate for an audit by the IRS. Cash transactions are easier to conceal than those made on credit.   □

- If information returns (e.g., Form 1099, Form W–2) are not in substantial agreement with reported income, an audit can be anticipated.

- If an individual's itemized deductions are in excess of norms established for various income levels, the probability of an audit is increased.

- Filing of a refund claim by the taxpayer may prompt an audit of the return.

- Certain returns are selected on a random sampling basis under the Taxpayer Compliance Measurement Program (TCMP). TCMP is used to develop, update, and improve the mathematical formulas and statistical sampling techniques used by the IRS.

- Information obtained from other sources (e.g., informants, news items). The tax law permits the IRS to pay rewards to persons who provide information that leads to the detection and punishment of those who violate the tax laws. Such rewards may not exceed 10 percent of the taxes, fines, and penalties recovered as a result of such information.

EXAMPLE 14   After 15 years of service, F is discharged by her employer, Dr. T. Shortly thereafter, the IRS receives an anonymous letter informing it that Dr. T keeps two separate sets of books, one of which substantially understates his cash receipts. ☐

EXAMPLE 15

During a divorce proceeding it is revealed that T, a public official, kept large amounts of cash in a shoe box at home. Such information is widely disseminated by the news media and comes to the attention of the IRS. Needless to say, the IRS would be interested in knowing whether such amounts originated from a taxable source and, if so, whether they were reported on T's income tax returns. ☐

Types of Audits.   Once a return is selected for audit, the taxpayer is notified accordingly. If the issue involved is minor, it may be that the matter can be resolved simply by correspondence between the IRS and the taxpayer.

EXAMPLE 16

During 1987, T received $340 in dividend income from Z Corporation. In early 1988, Z Corporation reflected the payment on Form 1099–DIV (an information return for the reporting of dividend payments), the original being sent to the IRS and a copy to T. When preparing his income tax return for 1987, T apparently overlooked this particular Form 1099–DIV and failed to include the dividend on Schedule B, Interest and Dividend Income, of Form 1040. In 1989, the IRS sends a notice to T calling his attention to the omission and requesting a remittance of $110 in additional tax, interest, and penalty. T promptly mails a check to the IRS for $110, and the matter is closed. ☐

Other examinations generally fall into the classification of either office audits or field audits. An office audit usually is restricted in scope and is conducted in the facilities of the IRS. By way of contrast, a field audit involves an examination of numerous items reported on the return and is conducted on the premises of the taxpayer or the taxpayer's representative.

Upon the conclusion of the audit, the examining agent issues a Revenue Agent's Report (RAR) that summarizes the findings. The RAR will result in a refund (the tax was overpaid), a deficiency (the tax was underpaid), or a "no change" (the tax was correct) finding.

Settlement Procedures.   If an audit results in an assessment of additional tax and no settlement is reached with the IRS agent, the taxpayer may attempt to negotiate a settlement with the IRS. If an appeal is desired, an appropriate request must be made to the Appeals Division of the IRS. In some cases, a taxpayer may be able to obtain a percentage settlement or a favorable settlement of one or more disputed issues because the Appeals Division is authorized to settle all disputes based on the hazards of litigation (the probability of favorable resolution of the disputed issue or issues if litigated).

If a satisfactory settlement is not reached within the administrative appeal process, the taxpayer may wish to litigate the case in the Tax Court, a Federal District Court, or the Claims Court. It should be noted, however, that litigation should be recommended only as a last resort because of the legal costs involved and the uncertainties relative to the final outcome. Tax litigation considerations are discussed more fully in chapter 2.

Statute of Limitations

A statute of limitations is a provision in the law that offers a party a defense against a suit brought by another party after the expiration of a specified period of time. The purpose of a statute of limitations is to preclude parties from prosecuting stale claims. The passage of time makes the defense of such claims difficult, since witnesses may no longer be available or evidence may have been lost or destroyed. Found at the state and Federal levels, such statutes cover a multitude of suits, both civil and criminal.

For our purposes, the relevant statutes deal with the Federal income tax. The two categories involved cover both the period of limitations applicable to the assessment of additional tax deficiencies by the IRS and the period that deals with claims for refunds by taxpayers.

Assessment by the IRS.   Under the general rule, the IRS may assess (impose) an additional tax liability against a taxpayer within three years of the filing of the income tax return. If the return is filed early, the three-year period begins to run from the due date of the return (usually April 15 for a calendar year individual taxpayer).

There is no statute of limitations on assessments of tax if no return is filed or if a fraudulent return is filed.

Limitations on Refunds.   If a taxpayer believes that an overpayment of Federal income tax was made, a claim for refund should be filed with the IRS. A claim for refund, therefore, is a request to the IRS that it return to the taxpayer the excessive income taxes paid.[20]

A claim for refund generally must be filed within three years from the date the return was filed or within two years from the date the tax was paid, whichever is later. Income tax returns that are filed early are deemed to have been filed on the date the return was due.

Interest and Penalties

Interest rates are determined quarterly by the IRS based on a procedure that utilizes the existing Federal short-term rate. The rates for tax refunds (overpayments) are 1 percent below those applicable to assessments (underpayments). For the first quarter (January 1–March 31) of 1989, the rates were 10 percent for refunds and 11 percent for assessments.[21]

For assessments of additional taxes, the interest begins running on the unextended due date of the return. With refunds, however, no interest is allowed if the overpayment is refunded to the taxpayer within 45 days of the date the return is filed. For this purpose, returns filed early are deemed to have been filed on the due date.

The tax law provides various penalties for lack of compliance on the part of taxpayers. Some of these penalties are summarized as follows:

- For a *failure to file* a tax return by the due date (including extension—see chapter 3) a penalty of 5 percent per month (up to a maximum of 25 percent) is imposed on the amount of tax shown as due on the return. Any fraction of a month counts as a full month.

---

20. The forms to use in filing a claim for refund are discussed in chapter 3.

21. The rate applicable after March 31, 1989, was not available when this text went to press.

- A penalty for a *failure to pay* the tax due (as shown on the return) in the amount of 0.5 percent per month (up to a maximum of 25 percent). During any month in which both the failure to file penalty and the failure to pay penalty apply, the failure to file penalty is reduced by the amount of the failure to pay penalty.

EXAMPLE 17   T files his tax return 18 days after the due date of the return. Along with the return, he remits a check for $1,000, which is the balance of the tax he owed. Disregarding the interest element, T's total penalties are as follows:

Failure to pay penalty (0.5% × $1,000)		$ 5
Plus:		
Failure to file penalty (5% × $1,000)	$50	
Less failure to pay penalty for the same period	5	
Failure to file penalty		45
Total penalties		$50

Note that the penalties for one full month are imposed even though T was delinquent by only 18 days. Unlike the method used to compute interest, any part of a month is treated as a whole month. □

- A negligence penalty of 5 percent if any of the underpayment was for intentional disregard of rules and regulations without intent to defraud. The penalty applies to the full amount of the underpayment and not to just that portion attributable to the negligence.

EXAMPLE 18   T underpaid his taxes for 1988 in the amount of $20,000, of which $15,000 is attributable to negligence. T's negligence penalty is $1,000 (5% × $20,000) and not $750 (5% × $15,000). □

- Various fraud penalties. Fraud is a deliberate action on the part of the taxpayer evidenced by deceit, misrepresentation, concealment, etc. For possible fraud situations, refer to Examples 14 and 15. The burden of proving fraud is on the IRS. This is in contrast with the usual deficiency assessment made by the IRS, in which case the burden is on the taxpayer to show that he or she does not owe any additional tax.

UNDERSTANDING THE FEDERAL TAX LAW

The Federal tax law is a mosaic of statutory provisions, administrative pronouncements, and court decisions. Anyone who has attempted to work with this body of knowledge would have to admit to its complexity. For the person who has to trudge through a mass of rules to find the solution to a tax problem, it may be of some consolation to know that the law's complexity can generally be explained. Whether sound or not, there is a reason for the formulation of every rule. Knowing these reasons, therefore, is a considerable step toward understanding the Federal tax law.

At the outset one should recognize that the Federal tax law has as its major objective the raising of revenue. But although the fiscal needs of the government are important, other considerations exist that explain certain portions of the law. Economic, social, equity, and political factors also play a significant role. Added to these factors is the marked impact the Internal Revenue Service and the courts have had and will continue to have on the evolution of Federal tax law. These matters are treated in the remainder of the chapter, and wherever appropriate, the discussion is tied to subjects covered later in the text.

Revenue Needs

The foundation of any tax system has to be the raising of revenue to cover the cost of government operations. Ideally, annual outlays should not be expected to exceed anticipated revenues, thereby leading to a balanced budget with no resulting deficit. Many states have achieved this objective by passing laws or constitutional amendments precluding deficit spending. Unfortunately, the Federal government has no such conclusive prohibition, and mounting annual deficits have become an increasing concern for many.

When finalizing the Tax Reform Act (TRA) of 1986, a deficit-conscious Congress was guided by the concept of revenue neutrality. The concept means that the changes made will neither increase nor decrease the net result previously reached under the prior rules. Revenue neutrality does not mean that any one taxpayer's tax liability will remain the same, as this will depend upon the circumstances involved. Thus, one taxpayer's increased tax liability could be another's tax savings. Although revenue neutral tax reform does not reduce deficits, at least it does not aggravate the problem.

One can expect budget deficit considerations to play an ever-increasing role in shaping future tax policy. The most recent tax legislation enacted, the Technical and Miscellaneous Revenue Act of 1988, is a good exemple of the application of the concept of revenue neutrality. While extending some expiring tax benefits, Congress was careful not to add to the existing deficit. This was accomplished by curtailing or eliminating some tax benefits.

Economic Considerations

The use of the tax system in an effort to accomplish economic objectives has become increasingly popular in recent years. Generally, it involves utilization of tax legislation to amend the Internal Revenue Code (which is a compilation of Federal tax statutes) and looks toward measures designed to help control the economy or to encourage certain activities and businesses.

Control of the Economy.   Congress has made use of depreciation write-offs as a means of controlling the economy. Theoretically, shorter class lives and accelerated methods should encourage additional investment in depreciable property acquired for business use. Conversely, longer class lives and the required use of the straight-line method of depreciation dampen the tax incentive for capital outlays.

Compared with past law, TRA of 1986 generally cut back on faster write-offs for property acquired after 1986. Particularly hard hit was most depreciable real estate, where class lives were extended from 19 years to as long as 31½ years and the straight-line method was made mandatory. These changes were made in the interest of revenue neutrality and in the belief that the current economy is stable.

Of more immediate impact on the economy is a change in the tax rate structure. With lower tax rates, taxpayers are able to retain additional spendable funds. Although TRA of 1986 lowered tax rates for most taxpayers, with the reduction or elimination of many deductions and credits, lower rates may not lead to lower tax liabilities. Thus, only time will tell what effect the tax rate changes made by TRA of 1986 will have on the economy.

Encouragement of Certain Activities.   Without passing judgment on the wisdom of any such choices, it is quite clear that the tax law does encourage certain types of economic activity or segments of the economy. If, for example, one assumes that technological progress should be fostered, the favorable treatment allowed research and development expenditures can be explained. Under the tax law, such expenditures can be either deducted in the year incurred or capitalized and amortized over a period of 60 months or more. In terms of timing the tax savings, such options usually are preferable to a capitalization of the cost with a write-off over the estimated useful life of the asset created. If the asset developed has an indefinite useful life, no write-off would be available without the two options allowed by the tax law.

Recent legislation further recognized the need to stimulate technological progress through the use of the tax laws. In addition to the favorable write-off treatment just noted, certain research and development costs now qualify for a 20 percent tax credit (see chapter 13).

Is it desirable to encourage the conservation of energy resources? Considering the world energy situation and our own reliance on foreign oil, the answer to this question has to be yes. The concern over energy usage was a prime consideration that led to the enactment of legislation to make various tax savings for energy conservation expenditures available to taxpayers.

Are ecological considerations a desirable objective? If they are, it explains why the tax law permits a 60-month amortization period for costs incurred in the installation of pollution control facilities.

Is it wise to stimulate U.S. exports of goods and services abroad? Considering the pressing and continuing problem of a deficit in the U.S. balance of payments, the answer should be clear. Along this line, Congress has created a unique type of organization designed to encourage domestic exports of goods, called Foreign Sales Corporations (FSCs). The FSC provisions eliminate the U.S. income tax on a percentage of profits from export sales. Also in an international setting, Congress has deemed it advisable to establish incentives for those U.S. citizens who accept employment overseas. Such persons receive generous tax breaks through special treatment of their foreign-source income and certain housing costs.

Is saving desirable for the economy? Saving leads to capital formation and thereby makes funds available to finance home construction and industrial expansion. The tax law provides incentives to encourage saving through preferential treatment accorded to private retirement plans. Not only are contributions to Keogh (H.R. 10) plans and certain Individual Retirement Accounts (IRAs) deductible, but income from such contributions accumulates free of tax. As noted below, the encouragement of private sector pension plans can also be justified under social considerations.

Encouragement of Certain Industries.   No one can question the proposition that a sound agricultural base is necessary for a well-balanced national economy. Undoubtedly this can explain why farmers are accorded special treatment under the Federal tax system. Among these benefits are the election to expense rather than capitalize certain soil and water conservation expenditures and fertilizers and the election to defer the recognition of gain on the receipt of crop insurance proceeds.

Encouragement of Small Business.   At least in the United States, a consensus exists that what is good for small business is good for the economy as a whole. Whether valid or not, this assumption has led to a definite bias in the tax law favoring small business.

In the corporate tax area, several provisions can be explained by the motivation to benefit small business. One provision permits the shareholders of a small business corporation to make a special election that generally will avoid the imposition of the corporate income tax.[22] Furthermore, such an election enables the corporation to pass through to its shareholders any of its operating losses.

Social Considerations

Some of the tax laws can be explained by looking to social considerations. This is particularly the case when dealing with the Federal income tax of individuals. Notable examples and the rationale behind each are summarized as follows:

- Certain benefits provided to employees through accident and health plans financed by employers are nontaxable to employees. It would appear socially desirable to encourage such plans, since they provide medical benefits in the event of an employee's illness or injury.

- Most premiums paid by an employer for group term insurance covering the life of the employee are nontaxable to the employee. These arrangements can be justified on social grounds in that they provide funds for the family unit to help it adjust following the loss of wages caused by the employee's death.

- A contribution made by an employer to a qualified pension or profit sharing plan for an employee receives special treatment. The contribution and any income it generates will not be taxed to the employee until the funds are distributed. Such an arrangement also benefits the employer by allowing a tax deduction when the contribution is made to the qualified plan. Private retirement plans should be encouraged, since they supplement the subsistence income level the employee otherwise would have under the Social Security system.[23]

- A deduction is allowed for contributions to qualified charitable organizations.[24] The deduction attempts to shift some of the financial and administrative burden of socially desirable programs from the public (the government) to the private (the citizens) sector.

---

22. Known as the S election, it is discussed in chapter 20.

23. The same rationale explains the availability of similar arrangements for self-employed persons

(the H.R. 10, or Keogh, plan). See chapter 19.

24. The charitable contribution deduction is discussed in chapter 11.

- A tax credit is allowed for amounts spent to furnish care for certain minor or disabled dependents to enable the taxpayer to seek or maintain gainful employment.[25] Who could deny the social desirability of encouraging taxpayers to provide care for their children while they work?

- A tax deduction is not allowed for certain expenditures deemed to be contrary to public policy. This disallowance extends to such items as fines, penalties, illegal kickbacks, bribes to government officials, and gambling losses in excess of gains. Social considerations dictate that these activities should not be encouraged by the tax law. Permitting the deduction would supposedly encourage such activities.

Many other examples could be included, but the conclusion would be unchanged. Social considerations do explain a significant part of the Federal tax law.

Equity Considerations

The concept of equity is relative. Reasonable persons can, and often do, disagree about what is fair or unfair. In the tax area, moreover, equity is most often tied to a particular taxpayer's personal situation. To illustrate, compare the tax positions of those who rent their personal residences with those who own their homes. Renters receive no Federal income tax benefit from the rent they pay. For homeowners, however, a large portion of the house payments they make may qualify for the Federal interest and property tax deductions. Although it may be difficult for renters to understand this difference in tax treatment, the encouragement of home ownership can be justified on both economic and social grounds.

In the same vein, compare the tax treatment of a corporation with that of a partnership. Although the two businesses may be of equal size, similarly situated, and competitors in production of goods or services, they are not treated comparably under the tax law. The corporation is subject to a separate Federal income tax; the partnership is not. Whether the differences in tax treatment can be justified logically in terms of equity is beside the point. The point is that the tax law can and does make a distinction between these business forms.

Equity, then, is not what appears fair or unfair to any one taxpayer or group of taxpayers. It is, instead, what the tax law recognizes. Some recognition of equity does exist, however, and offers an explanation of part of the law. The concept of equity appears in tax provisions that alleviate the effect of multiple taxation and postpone the recognition of gain when the taxpayer lacks the ability or wherewithal to pay the tax. Equity considerations also mitigate the effect of the application of the annual accounting period concept and cope with the eroding results of inflation.

Alleviating the Effect of Multiple Taxation.   The income earned by a taxpayer may be subject to taxes imposed by different taxing authorities. If, for example, the taxpayer is a resident of New York City, income might generate Federal, state of New York, and city of New York income taxes. To compensate for this apparent inequity, the Federal tax law allows a taxpayer to claim a deduction for state and local income taxes. The deduction does not,

---

25. See chapter 13.

however, neutralize the effect of multiple taxation, since the benefit derived depends on the taxpayer's Federal income tax bracket. Only a tax credit, rather than a deduction, would eliminate the effects of multiple taxation on the same income.

Equity considerations can explain the Federal tax treatment of certain income from foreign sources. Since double taxation results when the same income is subject to both foreign and U.S. income taxes, the tax law permits the taxpayer to choose between a credit and a deduction for the foreign taxes paid.

The Wherewithal to Pay Concept. The wherewithal to pay concept recognizes the inequity of taxing a transaction when the taxpayer lacks the means with which to pay the tax. It is particularly suited to situations in which the taxpayer's economic position has not changed significantly as a result of the transaction.

An illustration of the wherewithal to pay concept is the provision of the tax law dealing with the treatment of gain resulting from the sale of a personal residence. If the proceeds are rolled over (reinvested) in another personal residence within a specified time period, the gain will not be taxed (see chapter 15).

EXAMPLE 19

T sold his personal residence (cost of $60,000) for $100,000 and moved to another city. Shortly thereafter, T purchased a new personal residence for $100,000. □

In Example 19, T had an economic gain of $40,000 [$100,000 (selling price) − $60,000 (cost of residence)]. It would be inequitable to force T to pay a tax on this gain for two reasons. First, without disposing of the property acquired (the new residence), T would be hard-pressed to pay the tax. Second, T's economic position has not changed significantly.

A warning is in order concerning the application of the wherewithal to pay concept. It applies only in those situations specified by the tax law. Otherwise, the absence of cash and no apparent change in economic position will not preclude a transaction from being taxed.

EXAMPLE 20

Assume the same facts as in Example 19 except that the sale and purchase involved rental houses and not personal residences. Now, the sale of the first rental house will result in a gain of $40,000 that will be subject to tax. The fact that T reinvested the $100,000 in another rental house is of no consequence. □

Reconciling the different results reached in Examples 19 and 20 may seem difficult. But simply stated, the tax law applies the wherewithal to pay concept to the rollover on the gain from the sale of a personal residence. It does not do so when a rental house is involved, as Example 20 illustrates.

Mitigating the Effect of the Annual Accounting Period Concept. For purposes of effective administration of the tax law, all taxpayers must report to and settle with the Federal government at periodic intervals. Otherwise, taxpayers would remain uncertain as to their tax liabilities, and the government would have difficulty judging revenues and budgeting expenditures. The period selected for final settlement of most tax liabilities, in any event an arbitrary determination, is one year. At the close of each year, therefore, a taxpayer's position becomes complete for that particular year. Referred to as the annual accounting period concept, its effect is to divide each taxpayer's life, for tax purposes, into equal annual intervals.

The finality of the annual accounting period concept could lead to dissimilarity in tax treatment for taxpayers who are, from a long-range standpoint, in the same economic position.

EXAMPLE 21

R and S are two sole proprietors and have experienced the following results during the past four years:

	Profit (or Loss)	
Year	R	S
1986	$50,000	$150,000
1987	60,000	60,000
1988	70,000	70,000
1989	50,000	(50,000)

Although R and S have the same profit of $230,000 over the period from 1986–1989, the finality of the annual accounting period concept places S at a definite disadvantage for tax purposes. The net operating loss procedure offers S some relief by allowing him to apply some or all of his 1989 loss to the earliest profitable years (in this case, 1986). Thus, he would be in a position with a net operating loss carryback to obtain a refund for some of the taxes he paid on the $150,000 profit reported for 1986. □

The same reasoning used to support net operating losses can be applied to explain the special treatment accorded by the tax law to excess capital losses and excess charitable contributions.[26] Carryback and carryover procedures help mitigate the effect of limiting a loss or a deduction to the accounting period in which it was realized. With such procedures, a taxpayer might be able to salvage a loss or a deduction that might otherwise be wasted.

The installment method of recognizing gain on the sale of property allows a taxpayer to spread tax consequences over the payout period.[27] The harsh effect of taxing all the gain in the year of sale is thereby avoided. The installment method can also be explained by the wherewithal to pay concept, since recognition of gain is tied to the collection of the installment notes received from the sale of the property. Tax consequences, then, tend to correspond to the seller's ability to pay the tax.

---

26. The tax treatment of these items is discussed in chapters 8, 11, and 16.
27. Under the installment method, each payment received by the seller represents both a return of basis (the nontaxable portion) and profit from the sale (the taxable portion).

Coping with Inflation.   Because of the progressive nature of the income tax, a wage adjustment to compensate for inflation can increase the income tax bracket of the recipient. Known as the bracket creep, the overall impact is an erosion of purchasing power. Congress recognized this problem and began to adjust various income tax components in 1985 through an indexation procedure. Indexation is based upon the rise in the consumer price index over the prior year.

Because TRA of 1986 significantly raised the amount of each exemption and the standard deduction (previously the zero bracket amount) and lowered the tax rates, the indexation procedure has been temporarily suspended. However, indexation is scheduled to resume as follows: beginning in 1989 as to dollar amounts of the tax brackets and the standard deduction and beginning in 1990 as to personal and dependency exemptions.

Political Considerations

A large segment of the Federal tax law is made up of statutory provisions. Since these statutes are enacted by Congress, is it any surprise that political considerations influence tax law? For purposes of discussion, the effect of political considerations on the tax law is divided into the following topics: special interest legislation, political expediency situations, and state and local government influences.

Special Interest Legislation.   There is no doubt that certain provisions of the tax law can largely be explained by looking to the political influence some pressure groups have had on Congress. Is there any other realistic reason that, for example, prepaid subscription and dues income are not taxed until earned while prepaid rents are taxed to the landlord in the year received?

Special interest legislation is not necessarily to be condemned if it can be justified on economic, social, or some other utilitarian grounds. At any rate, it is an inevitable product of our political system.

Political Expediency Situations.   Various tax reform proposals rise and fall in favor depending upon the shifting moods of the American public. That Congress is sensitive to popular feeling is an accepted fact. Therefore, certain provisions of the tax law can be explained on the basis of political expediency existing at the time of enactment.

Measures that deter more affluent taxpayers from obtaining so-called preferential tax treatment have always had popular appeal and, consequently, the support of Congress. Provisions such as the alternative minimum tax, the imputed interest rules, and the limitation on the deductibility of interest on investment indebtedness can be explained on this basis.[28]

Other changes partially founded on the basis of political expediency include the lowering of individual income tax rates, raising the amount of the dependency exemption, and increasing the earned income credit.

State and Local Influences.   Political considerations have played a major role in the nontaxability of interest received on state and local obligations. In view of the furor that has been raised by state and local political figures every time any kind of modification of this tax provision has been proposed, one might well regard it as next to sacred.

---

28. See chapters 11 and 12.

Somewhat less apparent has been the influence state law has had in shaping our present Federal tax law. Of prime import in this regard has been the effect of the community property system employed in some states.[29] At one time, the tax position of the residents of these states was so advantageous that many common law states actually adopted community property systems. Needless to say, the political pressure placed on Congress to correct the disparity in tax treatment was considerable. To a large extent this was accomplished in the Revenue Act of 1948, which extended many of the community property tax advantages to residents of common law jurisdictions. The major advantage extended was the provision allowing married taxpayers to file joint returns and compute the tax liability as if the income had been earned one-half by each spouse. This result is automatic in a community property state, since half of the income earned by one spouse belongs to the other spouse. The income-splitting benefits of a joint return are now incorporated as part of the tax rates applicable to married taxpayers. See chapter 3.

Influence of the Internal Revenue Service

The influence of the IRS is recognized in many areas beyond its role in the issuance of the administrative pronouncements that make up a considerable portion of our tax law. In its capacity as the protector of the national revenue, the IRS has been instrumental in securing the passage of much legislation designed to curtail the most flagrant tax avoidance practices (to close tax loopholes). In its capacity as the administrator of the tax laws, the IRS has sought and obtained legislation to make its job easier (to attain administrative feasibility).

The IRS as Protector of the Revenue.   Innumerable examples can be given of provisions in the tax law that stemmed from the direct influence of the IRS. Usually, such provisions are intended to preclude the use of a loophole as a means of avoiding the tax consequences intended by Congress. Working within the letter of existing law, ingenious taxpayers and their advisers devise techniques that accomplish indirectly what cannot be accomplished directly. As a consequence, legislation is enacted to close the loopholes that taxpayers have located and exploited. Some tax law can be explained in this fashion and is discussed in the chapters to follow.

In addition, the IRS has secured from Congress legislation of a more general nature that enables it to make adjustments based on the substance, rather than the formal construction, of what a taxpayer has done. One such provision permits the IRS to make adjustments to a taxpayer's method of accounting when the method used by the taxpayer does not clearly reflect income.[30]

---

29. The nine states with community property systems are Louisiana, Texas, New Mexico, Arizona, California, Washington, Idaho, Nevada, and Wisconsin. The rest of the states are classified as common law jurisdictions. The difference between common law and community property systems centers around the property rights possessed by married persons. In a common law system, each spouse owns whatever he or she earns. Under a community property system, one-half of the earnings of each spouse is considered owned by the other spouse. Assume, for example, H and W are husband and wife and their only income is the $40,000 annual salary H receives. If they live in New York (a common law state), the $40,000 salary belongs to H. If, however, they live in Texas (a community property state), the $40,000 salary is divided equally, in terms of ownership, between H and W.

30. See chapter 18.

EXAMPLE 22

T, an individual cash basis taxpayer, owns and operates a pharmacy. All drugs and other items acquired for resale (e.g., cosmetics) are charged to the purchases account and written off (expensed) for tax purposes in the year of acquisition. As this procedure does not clearly reflect income, it would be appropriate for the IRS to require that T establish and maintain an ending inventory account. □

Administrative Feasibility.   Some of the tax law is justified on the grounds that it simplifies the task of the IRS in collecting the revenue and administering the law. With regard to collecting the revenue, the IRS long ago realized the importance of placing taxpayers on a pay-as-you-go basis. Elaborate withholding procedures apply to wages, while the tax on other types of income may be paid at periodic intervals throughout the year. The IRS has been instrumental in convincing the courts that accrual basis taxpayers should pay taxes on prepaid income in the year received and not when earned. The approach may be contrary to generally accepted accounting principles, but it is consistent with the wherewithal to pay concept.

Of considerable aid to the IRS in collecting revenue are the numerous provisions that impose interest and penalties on taxpayers for noncompliance with the tax law. Provisions such as the penalties for failure to pay a tax or to file a return that is due, the negligence penalty for intentional disregard of rules and regulations, and various penalties for civil and criminal fraud serve as deterrents to taxpayer noncompliance.

One of the keys to an effective administration of our tax system is the audit process conducted by the IRS. To carry out this function, the IRS is aided by provisions that reduce the chance of taxpayer error or manipulation and therefore simplify the audit effort that is necessary. An increase in the amount of the standard deduction, for example, reduces the number of individual taxpayers who will choose the alternative of itemizing their personal deductions.[31] With fewer deductions to check, the audit function is thus simplified.[32]

The audit function of the IRS has been simplified by provisions of the tax law dealing with the burden of proof. Suppose, for example, the IRS audits a taxpayer and questions a particular deduction. Who has the burden of proving the propriety of the deduction? The so-called presumption of correctness that attaches in favor of any deficiency assessed by the IRS can be explained by considering the nature of our tax system. The Federal income tax is a self-assessed tax, which means that each taxpayer is responsible for rendering an accounting to the IRS of all of his or her transactions during the year. A failure to do so means that any doubts will be resolved in favor of the IRS. Only in the case of fraud (which could involve fines and penal sanctions) does the IRS carry the burden of proof.

---

31. For a discussion of the standard deduction, see chapter 3.
32. The same justification was given by the IRS when it proposed to Congress the $100 limitation on personal casualty and theft losses. Imposition of the limitation eliminated many casualty and theft loss deductions and, as a consequence, saved the IRS considerable audit time. Later legislation, in addition to retaining the $100 feature, limits deductible losses to those in excess of 10% of a taxpayer's adjusted gross income. See chapter 8.

Influence of the Courts

In addition to interpreting statutory provisions and the administrative pronouncements issued by the IRS, the Federal courts have influenced tax law in two other respects.[33] First, the courts have formulated certain judicial concepts that serve as guides in the application of various tax provisions. Second, certain key decisions have led to changes in the Internal Revenue Code. Understanding this influence helps to explain some of our tax law.

Judicial Concepts Relating to Tax.   A leading tax concept developed by the courts deals with the interpretation of statutory tax provisions that operate to benefit taxpayers. The courts have established the rule that these relief provisions are to be narrowly construed against taxpayers if there is any doubt about their application. Suppose, for example, T wants to treat an expenditure as deductible for income tax purposes but has not literally satisfied the statutory requirements covering the deduction. Because income tax deductions are relief provisions favoring taxpayers, chances are the courts will deny T this treatment.

Important in this area is the arm's length concept. Particularly in dealings between related parties, transactions may be tested by looking to whether the taxpayers acted in an "arm's length" manner. The question to be asked is, Would unrelated parties have handled the transaction in the same way?

EXAMPLE 23

T, the sole shareholder of X Corporation, leases property to X for a yearly rental of $6,000. To test whether the corporation should be allowed a rent deduction for this amount, the IRS and the courts will apply the arm's length concept. Would X Corporation have paid $6,000 a year in rent if the same property had been leased from an unrelated party (rather than from the sole shareholder)? Suppose it is determined that an unrelated third party would have paid an annual rental for the property of only $5,000. Under these circumstances, X Corporation will be allowed a deduction of only $5,000. The other $1,000 it paid for the use of the property represents a nondeductible dividend. Accordingly, T will be treated as having received rent income of $5,000 and dividend income of $1,000. □

Judicial Influence on Statutory Provisions.   Some court decisions have been of such consequence that Congress has incorporated them into statutory tax law. For example, many years ago the courts found that stock dividends distributed to the shareholders of a corporation were not taxable as income. This result was largely accepted by Congress, and a provision in the tax statutes now covers the issue.

On occasion, however, Congress has reacted in a negative manner with respect to judicial interpretations of the tax law.

---

33. A great deal of case law is devoted to ascertaining congressional intent. The courts, in effect, ask, What did Congress have in mind when it enacted a particular tax provision?

EXAMPLE 24   L leases unimproved real estate to T for 40 years. At a cost of $200,000, T erects a building on the land. The building is worth $100,000 when the lease terminates and L takes possession of the property. Does L have any income either when the improvements are made or when the lease terminates? In a landmark decision, a court held that L must recognize income of $100,000 upon the termination of the lease. □

Congress felt that the result reached in Example 24 was inequitable in that it was not consistent with the wherewithal to pay concept. Consequently, the tax law was amended to provide that a landlord does not recognize any income either when the improvements are made (unless made in lieu of rent) or when the lease terminates.

Summary

In addition to its necessary revenue-raising objective, the Federal tax law has developed in response to several other factors:

- *Economic considerations.* The emphasis here is on tax provisions that help regulate the economy and encourage certain activities and types of businesses.

- *Social considerations.* Some tax provisions are designed to encourage (or discourage) certain socially desirable (or undesirable) practices.

- *Equity considerations.* Of principal concern in this area are tax provisions that alleviate the effect of multiple taxation, recognize the wherewithal to pay concept, mitigate the effect of the annual accounting period concept, and recognize the eroding effect of inflation.

- *Political considerations.* Of significance in this regard are tax provisions that represent special interest legislation, reflect political expediency situations, and exhibit the effect of state and local law.

- *Influence of the IRS.* Many tax provisions are intended to aid the IRS in the collection of the revenue and in the administration of the tax law.

- *Influence of the courts.* Court decisions have established a body of judicial concepts relating to tax law and have, on occasion, led Congress to enact statutory provisions to either clarify or negate their effect.

These factors explain various tax provisions and thereby help in understanding why the tax law developed to its present state. The next step involves learning to work with the tax law.

PROBLEM MATERIALS

Discussion Questions

1. A tax protester refuses to pay the Federal income tax on the grounds that the tax is unconstitutional. Any comment?

2. Do you feel that the Federal government could continue to collect the same amount of tax from its taxpayers if the pay-as-you-go tax system were abolished? Why?

3. Discuss Adam Smith's canons of taxation. Are these criteria for a "good" tax system still appropriate in today's economy?

4. Several proposals have been introduced in Congress that would institute a Federal value added tax (VAT). Such proposals would impose a tax on the increment in value that is added at each stage of the manufacturing process and would be levied on the party adding such value. Evaluate a VAT in terms of Adam Smith's canons of taxation.

5. T's personal residence is subject to three separate ad valorem property taxes. How could this be possible?

6. The use of computers by state and local taxing authorities usually has made the application of the ad valorem tax more equitable. Why is this the case?

7. After T converts her personal residence into a rental house, she finds that the ad valorem taxes on the property increase. Why might this happen?

8. T buys a new home for $150,000, its cost of construction plus the usual profit margin for the builder. The new home is located in a neighborhood largely developed 10 years ago when the homes sold for approximately $50,000 each. Assuming the homes of his neighbors are worth (in current values) in the vicinity of $150,000, could T be at a disadvantage with regard to the ad valorem tax on realty?

9. Recently, one of your friends successfully challenged a reappraisal of his personal residence by the county board of real estate tax assessors. He remarks to you that this should place him "in good shape for the next five years." What does he mean?

10. In early 1987, T purchased a vacant industrial complex for $1,200,000 which at that time had an ad valorem tax assessment of $1,000,000. During 1988, T made substantial improvements to the property. In 1989, the property is reassessed by the real property taxing authority at $1,500,000.

    a. In view of the purchase price of $1,200,000 in 1987, how can the original $1,000,000 assessment be explained?

    b. How can the 1989 increase in the assessment be explained?

11. While out of town on business, U stays at a motel with an advertised room rate of $30 per night. When checking out, U is charged $33. What would be a plausible reason for the extra $3 U had to pay?

12. On a recent trip to a nearby supermarket, T spent $42.00, of which $2.00 was for general sales tax. If T lives in a jurisdiction that imposes a 6% general sales tax on foodstuffs, why was the bill not $42.40?

13. T, a resident of Wyoming (which imposes a general sales tax), goes to Montana (which does not impose a general sales tax) to purchase her automobile. Will T successfully avoid the Wyoming sales tax? Explain.

14. States that generate a large amount of revenue from severance taxes on oil and gas (e.g., Alaska, Oklahoma, and Texas) are very vulnerable to OPEC pricing and production policies. Explain.

15. The retail purchase price of cigarettes in North Carolina is lower than in other states. Why?

16. "There is no national general sales tax." Explain this statement.

17. Why might a person who purchases a product from an establishment located in jurisdiction X wish to take delivery in jurisdiction Y? Would it matter whether or not the person resided in jurisdiction X? Explain.

18. "There is no Federal inheritance tax." Do you agree or disagree with this statement?

19. During his life, T has accumulated considerable wealth as a result of personal service income. T is quite distressed when he learns that upon his death the wealth will be subject to death taxes. He feels this is unfair, since the wealth accumulated has already been subject to taxation (the income tax). Please comment.

20. A decedent who leaves all of his property to his surviving spouse and to qualified charitable organizations will not be subject to a Federal estate tax. Explain.

21. How much property can D, a widow, give to her three married children (and their spouses) and five grandchildren over a period of 12 years without making a taxable gift?

22. A married person might be able to give twice as much property to a donee without incurring a Federal gift tax. Explain this statement.

23. At a social function you attended in early March of 1989, you overhear a guest, the CEO of a corporation, remark, "Thank goodness this is the end of FICA for a while!" Interpret this remark.

 24. An employee who has more than one job during the year always will have excess FICA withholdings. Do you agree? Why or why not?

25. H and W are husband and wife, and both are employed by X Corporation. Wages earned during 1989 are as follows: $52,000 by W and $36,000 by H. How much FICA must they pay for 1989?

26. T, the owner and operator of a construction company that builds outdoor swimming pools, releases most of his construction personnel during the winter months. Should this hurt T's FUTA situation? Why or why not?

27. Compare FICA and FUTA in connection with each of the following:
    a. Incidence of taxation.
    b. Justification for taxation.
    c. Reporting and filing requirements.
    d. Rates and base involved.

28. T is an ardent member of a religion that advocates tithing (contributing 10% of annual income to the church). Presuming T complies with

this guideline, could it increase the chance that T's individual Federal income tax return will be selected for audit by the IRS? Why or why not?

29. T, the owner and operator of a cash-and-carry military surplus retail outlet, has been audited many times by the IRS. When T mentions this fact to his next-door neighbor, an employee with Ford Motor Company, he is somewhat surprised to learn that the neighbor has never been audited by the IRS. Is there any explanation for this apparent disparity in treatment?

30. While Dr. T and his family are out of town on vacation, their home is burglarized. Among the items stolen and reported to the police are $35,000 in cash and gold coins worth $80,000. Shortly after the incident, Dr. T is audited by the IRS. Could there be any causal connection between the burglary and the audit? Explain.

31. An IRS agent audits S's income tax return and, as a result, issues an RAR (Revenue Agent's Report). Does this mean that S owes additional taxes? Explain.

32. T files her income tax return 45 days after the due date of the return without obtaining an extension from the IRS. Along with the return, she remits a check for $3,000, which is the balance of the tax owed by T. Disregarding the interest element, what are T's penalties for failure to file and for failure to pay?

33. T overstated his deductions on a prior year's Federal income tax return. Upon audit by the IRS, it is determined that the overstatement was partially the result of negligence. As a result, T owes additional income taxes of $10,000 ($9,000 attributable to the negligence). What is T's penalty?

34. What is meant by revenue neutral tax reform?

35. In what manner does the tax law encourage technological progress?

36. Does the tax law provide any stimulus for the development of international trade? Explain.

37. What purpose is served by provisions in the tax law that encourage private sector pension plans?

38. Discuss the probable justification for the following provisions of the tax law:

    a. The election permitted certain corporations to avoid the corporate income tax.

    b. A provision that makes nontaxable certain benefits furnished to employees through accident and health plans financed by employers.

    c. Nontaxable treatment for an employee as to premiums paid by an employer for group term insurance covering the life of the employee.

d. The tax treatment to the employee of contributions made by an employer to qualified pension or profit sharing plans.

e. The deduction allowed for contributions to qualified charitable organizations.

39. What purpose is served by the credit allowed for certain child or disabled dependent care expenses?

40. What purpose is served by allowing a deduction for home mortgage interest and property taxes?

41. T owns and operates a trucking firm. During the year, his employees incur a substantial number of fines for violating the highway speed limit. T considers these fines a necessary expense of running the business, as he knows his firm cannot make a profit by observing the posted speed limit. Are these fines deductible for income tax purposes? Why or why not?

42. U and V are two individual cash basis taxpayers who are employed as salespersons by different companies. U receives a fixed salary of $42,000, and V receives a fixed salary of $30,000 plus a year-end bonus based on annual sales. The bonus is determined and paid in January of the following year. For services rendered in 1989, U and V received the following amounts:

	U	V
Fixed salary	$42,000	$30,000
Bonus (received in 1990)	–0–	12,000
Total	$42,000	$42,000

a. Will U and V be treated the same for tax year 1989 as to the $42,000 each earned? Why or why not?

b. Could there be some missing information that would change your answer as to the equality or inequality of tax treatment?

43. a. What is the purpose of the indexation procedure?

b. What is the current status of this procedure?

c. To what items is indexation applicable?

44. Give an example of how the community property system has affected the Federal tax law.

45. T, an individual taxpayer, files a Federal income tax return for the year in which he reports income on a cash basis and expenditures on an accrual basis.

a. What was T trying to accomplish in reporting as income only the amounts actually received while claiming deductions for amounts due but unpaid?

b. Does the IRS have any defense against T's approach? Explain.

46. Forcing accrual basis taxpayers to recognize prepaid income when received (as opposed to when earned) accomplishes what objective?

47. On her income tax return for the year, T claims as a deduction certain charitable contributions that she did not make. When you question her about this she responds:

   a. "How is the IRS going to prove that I did not make these contributions?"

   b. "Even if the IRS disallows the deductions, the worst that can happen is that I will owe the same amount of tax I would have paid anyway."

   Comment on T's misconceptions about the tax law.

48. Under current tax law, a donor generally can make a gift of up to $10,000 per year to a donee without having to file a Federal gift tax return and pay a Federal gift tax. How does this provision simplify the administrative responsibility of the IRS for enforcement of the tax laws?

49. T leases a building from L for 20 years. During the term of the lease, T makes significant capital improvements to the property that revert to L on the termination of the lease. Several years after the lease has terminated, L sells the building for a profit, a portion of which is attributable to the value of the improvements made by T.

   a. Should the improvements made by T be taxed to L?

   b. If so, when (at the time when made, on the termination of the lease, or on the sale of the property)?

2

WORKING WITH THE TAX LAW

TAX SOURCES

Understanding taxation requires a mastery of the sources of the *rules of tax law.* These sources include not only legislative provisions in the form of the Internal Revenue Code, but also Congressional Committee Reports, Treasury Department Regulations, other Treasury Department pronouncements, and court decisions. Thus, the *primary sources* of tax information include pronouncements from all three branches of government: legislative, executive, and judicial.

In addition to being able to read and interpret the sources of the tax law, a tax professional must understand the relative weight of authority within these three primary sources. The tax law is of little significance, however, until it is applied to a set of facts and circumstances. This chapter, therefore, both introduces the statutory, administrative, and judicial sources of tax law and explains how the law is applied to individual and business transactions. It also explains the application of research techniques and the effective use of planning procedures.

Statutory Sources of the Tax Law

Origin of the Internal Revenue Code.   Before 1939, the statutory provisions relating to Federal taxation were contained in the individual revenue acts enacted by Congress. Because of the inconvenience and confusion that resulted from dealing with many separate acts, in 1939 Congress codified all of the Federal tax laws. Known as the Internal Revenue Code of 1939, the codification arranged all Federal tax provisions in a logical sequence and placed them in a separate part of the Federal statutes. A further rearrangement took place in 1954 and resulted in the Internal Revenue Code of 1954, which continued in effect until the Internal Revenue Code of 1986. Although Congress did not recodify the law in the Tax Reform Act (TRA) of 1986, the magnitude of the changes made by TRA of 1986 do provide some rationale for renaming the Federal tax law the Internal Revenue Code of 1986.

The following observations will help clarify the significance of the codification procedure:

- With some exceptions, neither the 1939 nor the 1954 Code substantially changed the tax law existing on the date of its enactment. Much of the 1939 Code, for example, was incorporated into the 1954 Code; the major change was the reorganization and renumbering of the tax provisions.

- Although the 1986 Code resulted in substantial changes, only a minority of the statutory provisions were affected.[1]

- Statutory amendments to the tax law are integrated into the Code. For example, the Technical and Miscellaneous Revenue Act of 1988 became part of the Internal Revenue Code of 1986. Based on the tax legislation

---

1. This point is important in assessing judicial decisions interpreting provisions of the Internal Revenue Code of 1939 and the Internal Revenue Code of 1954. If the same provision was in- cluded in the Internal Revenue Code of 1986 and has not been subsequently amended, the decision has continuing validity.

enacted in the 1980s, it appears that the tax law will be amended frequently.[2]

The Legislative Process. Federal tax legislation generally originates in the House of Representatives where it is first considered by the House Ways and Means Committee. Tax bills originate in the Senate when they are attached as riders to other legislative proposals.[3] If acceptable to the House Ways and Means Committee, the proposed bill is referred to the entire House of Representatives for approval or disapproval. Approved bills are sent to the Senate, where they are referred to the Senate Finance Committee for further consideration.[4] The next step involves referral from the Senate Finance Committee to the entire Senate. Assuming no disagreement between the House and Senate, passage by the Senate results in referral to the President for approval or veto. If the bill is approved or if the President's veto is overridden, the bill becomes law and part of the Internal Revenue Code of 1986.

When the Senate version of the bill differs from that passed by the House,[5] the Joint Conference Committee, which includes members of both the House Ways and Means Committee and the Senate Finance Committee, is called upon to resolve these differences. The result, usually a compromise between the two versions, is then voted on by both the House and the Senate. If both bodies accept the bill, it is referred to the President for approval or veto.

Referrals from the House Ways and Means Committee, the Senate Finance Committee, and the Joint Conference Committee are usually accompanied by Committee Reports. Because these Committee Reports often explain the provisions of the proposed legislation, they are a valuable source in ascertaining the intent of Congress. What Congress has in mind when it considers and enacts tax legislation is, of course, the key to interpreting such legislation by taxpayers, the IRS, and the courts. Since Regulations normally are not issued immediately after a statute is enacted, taxpayers often look to legislative history materials to ascertain congressional intent.

The typical legislative process for dealing with tax bills is summarized as follows:

---

2. Some of the major law changes during this period include the Multi-Employer Plan Amendments Act of 1980, Economic Recovery Tax Act of 1981, Subchapter S Revision Act of 1982, Tax Equity and Fiscal Responsibility Act of 1982, Retirement Equity Act of 1984, Deficit Reduction Act of 1984, Tax Reform Act of 1986, Revenue Act of 1987, and the Technical and Miscellaneous Revenue Act of 1988.

3. The Tax Equity and Fiscal Responsibility Act of 1982 originated in the Senate, and its constitutionality was unsuccessfully challenged in the courts. The Senate version of the Deficit Reduction Act of 1984 was attached as an amendment to the Federal Boat Safety Act.

4. Some tax provisions are commonly referred to by the number of the bill designated in the House when first proposed or by the name of the member of Congress sponsoring the legislation. For example, the Self-Employed Individuals Tax Retirement Act of 1962 is popularly known as H.R. 10 (House of Representatives Bill No. 10) or as the Keogh Act (Keogh being one of the members of Congress sponsoring the bill).

5. This is frequently the case with major tax bills. One factor contributing to a different Senate version is the latitude each individual senator has to make amendments to a bill when the Senate as a whole is voting on a bill referred to it by the Senate Finance Committee. During the passage of the Tax Reform Act of 1986, Senate leaders tried to make the law *amendment proof* to avoid the normal amendment process. Less latitude is allowed in the House of Representatives. Thus, the entire House either accepts or rejects what is proposed by the House Ways and Means Committee, and changes from the floor are not commonplace.

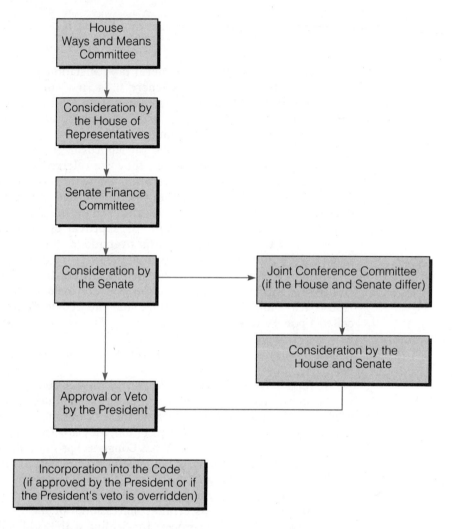

The role of the Joint Conference Committee indicates the importance of compromise in the legislative process. The practical effect of the compromise process can be illustrated by reviewing what happened to a new limitation on contributions by employees to their tax-sheltered annuities in the Tax Reform Act of 1986.

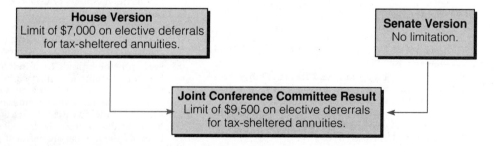

Arrangement of the Code. In working with the Code it helps to understand the format followed. Note, for example, the following partial table of contents:

Subtitle A. Income Taxes

Chapter 1. Normal Taxes and Surtaxes

Subchapter A. Determination of Tax Liability

Part I. Tax on Individuals

Sections 1–5

Part II. Tax on Corporations

Sections 11–12

* * *

In referring to a provision of the Code, the *key* is usually the Section number involved. In designating Section 2(a) (dealing with the status of a surviving spouse), for example, it would be unnecessary to include Subtitle A, Chapter 1, Subchapter A, Part I. Merely mentioning Section 2(a) will suffice, since the Section numbers run consecutively and do not begin again with each new Subtitle, Chapter, Subchapter, or Part. However, not all Code Section numbers are used. Notice that Part I ends with Section 5 and Part II starts with Section 11 (at present there are no Sections 6, 7, 8, 9, and 10).[6]

Tax practitioners commonly refer to some specific areas of income taxation by Subchapter designation. Some of the more common Subchapter designations include Subchapter C ("Corporate Distributions and Adjustments"), Subchapter K ("Partners and Partnerships"), and Subchapter S ("Tax Treatment of S Corporations and Their Shareholders"). In the last situation in particular, it is much more convenient to describe the subject of the applicable Code provisions (Sections 1361–1379) as S corporation status rather than as the "Tax Treatment of S Corporations and Their Shareholders."

Citing the Code.   Code Sections often are broken down into subparts.[7] Section 2(a)(1)(A) serves as an example.

Broken down as to content, § 2(a)(1)(A) becomes:

---

6. When the 1954 Code was drafted, the omission of Section numbers was intentional. This omission provided flexibility to incorporate later changes into the Code without disrupting its organization. When Congress does not leave enough space, subsequent Code Sections are given A, B, C, etc., designations. A good example is the treatment of §§ 280A through 280H.

7. Some Code Sections do not require subparts. See, for example, §§ 211 and 262.

8. Some Code Sections omit the subsection designation and use, instead, the paragraph designation as the first subpart. See, for example, §§ 212(1) and 1221(1).

§2 ─────────────────────────▶ Definitions and special rules (relating to the income tax imposed on individuals)

(a) ─────────────────────────▶ Definition of a surviving spouse

(1) ─────────────────────────▶ For purposes of §1 (the determination of the applicable rate schedule) a surviving spouse must meet certain conditions

(A) ─────────────────────────▶ One of the conditions necessary to qualify as a surviving spouse is that the taxpayer's spouse died during either of his or her two taxable years immediately preceding the present taxable year

Throughout the remainder of the text, references to the Code Sections are in the form given above. The symbols "§" and "§§" are used in place of "Section" and "Sections." Unless otherwise stated, all Code references are to the Internal Revenue Code of 1986. The format followed in the remainder of the text is summarized as follows:

Complete Reference	Text Reference
Section 2(a)(1)(A) of the Internal Revenue Code of 1986	§ 2(a)(1)(A)
Sections 1 and 2 of the Internal Revenue Code of 1986	§§ 1 and 2
Section 2 of the Internal Revenue Code of 1954	§ 2 of the Internal Revenue Code of 1954
Section 12(d) of the Internal Revenue Code of 1939 [9]	§ 12(d) of the Internal Revenue Code of 1939

Effect of Treaties.   The United States signs certain tax treaties with foreign countries to render mutual assistance in tax enforcement and to avoid double taxation. The Technical and Miscellaneous Revenue Act of 1988 provides that neither a tax law nor a tax treaty takes general precedence. Thus, the most recent item will take precedence. A taxpayer must disclose on the tax return any position where a treaty overrides a tax law.

Administrative Sources of the Tax Law

The administrative sources of the Federal tax law can be grouped as follows: Treasury Department Regulations, Revenue Rulings and Procedures, and other administrative pronouncements (see Concept Summary 2–1). All are issued either by the U.S. Treasury Department or by one of its instrumentalities [e.g., the Internal Revenue Service (IRS) or a District Director].

---

9. § 12(d) of the Internal Revenue Code of 1939 is the predecessor to § 2 of the Internal Revenue Code of 1954 and the Internal Revenue Code of 1986. Keep in mind that the 1954 Code super- seded the 1939 Code and the 1986 Code has su- perseded the 1954 Code. The reason for refer- ring to a provision of the 1939 or 1954 Code is set forth in Footnote 1 of this chapter.

CONCEPT SUMMARY 2–1

Administrative Sources

Source	Location	Authority
Regulations	Federal Register *	Force and effect of law.
Proposed Regulations	Federal Register * Internal Revenue Bulletin Cumulative Bulletin	Preview of final Regulations.
Temporary Regulations	Federal Register * Internal Revenue Bulletin Cumulative Bulletin	May be cited as a precedent.
Revenue Rulings Revenue Procedures	Internal Revenue Bulletin Cumulative Bulletin	Do not have the force and effect of law.
General Counsel's Memoranda Technical Memoranda Actions on Decisions	Tax Analysts' Tax Notes; P-H's Internal Memoranda of the IRS; CCH's IRS Position Reporter	May not be cited as a precedent.
Letter Ruling	Prentice-Hall and Commerce Clearing House loose-leaf services	Applicable only to taxpayer addressed. No precedential force.

* Finalized, proposed, and temporary Regulations are published in soft-cover form by several publishers.

Treasury Department Regulations.   Regulations are issued by the U.S. Treasury Department under authority granted by Congress.[10] Interpretative by nature, they provide taxpayers with considerable guidance on the meaning and application of the Code. Regulations may be issued in *proposed, temporary,* or *final* form. Although not issued by Congress, Regulations do carry considerable weight and are an important factor to consider in complying with the tax law.

Since Regulations interpret the Code, they are arranged in the same sequence. Regulations are, however, prefixed by a number that designates the type of tax or administrative, procedural, or definitional matter to which they relate. For example, the prefix 1 designates the Regulations under the income tax law. Thus, the Regulations under Code § 2 would be cited as Reg. § 1.2 with subparts added for further identification. These subparts often have no correlation in numbering pattern with the Code subsections. The prefix 20 designates estate tax Regulations; 25 covers gift tax Regulations; 31 relates to

10. § 7805.

employment taxes; and 301 refers to procedure and administration. This listing is not all-inclusive.

New Regulations and changes to existing Regulations are usually issued in proposed form before they are finalized. The time interval between the proposal of a Regulation and its finalization permits taxpayers and other interested parties to comment on the propriety of the proposal. Proposed Regulations under Code § 2, for example, would be cited as Prop.Reg. § 1.2. The Tax Court indicates that proposed Regulations carry no more weight than a position advanced in a written brief prepared by a litigating party before the Tax Court. *Finalized* Regulations have the force and effect of law.[11]

Sometimes *temporary* Regulations relating to elections and other matters where speed is important are issued by the Treasury. Such regulations are issued without the comment period required for proposed Regulations. Temporary Regulations have the same authoritative value as final Regulations and may be cited as precedents. Temporary Regulations are also issued as proposed Regulations and automatically expire within three years after the date of issuance.[12] For example, Temp. Reg. § 26.2662–1 deals with the generation-skipping transfer tax. The Treasury Department can be slow in finalizing temporary Regulations.

Proposed and final Regulations are published in the *Federal Register* and are reproduced in major tax services. Final Regulations are issued as Treasury Decisions (TDs).

Regulations may also be classified as *legislative, interpretative,* or *procedural.* Refer to the subsequent discussion of this classification scheme in Assessing the Validity of a Treasury Regulation.

Revenue Rulings and Revenue Procedures.   *Revenue Rulings* are official pronouncements of the National Office of the IRS.[13] Like Regulations, they are designed to provide interpretation of the tax law. However, they do not carry the same legal force and effect as Regulations and usually deal with more restricted problems. In addition, Regulations are approved by the Secretary of the Treasury, whereas Revenue Rulings are not. Both Revenue Rulings and Revenue Procedures serve an important function in that they afford *guidance* to both IRS personnel and taxpayers in handling routine tax matters.

Although letter rulings (discussed below) are not the same as Revenue Rulings, a Revenue Ruling often results from a specific taxpayer's request for a letter ruling. If the IRS believes that a taxpayer's request for a letter ruling deserves official publication because of its widespread impact, the holding will be converted into a Revenue Ruling. Names, identifying descriptions, and money amounts are changed to disguise the identity of the requesting taxpayer. The IRS will then issue what would have been a letter ruling as a Revenue Ruling for information and guidance of taxpayers, practitioners, and IRS personnel. In addition to arising from taxpayer requests, Revenue Rulings arise from technical advice to District Offices of the IRS, court decisions, suggestions from tax practitioner groups, and various tax publications.

Revenue Procedures are issued in the same manner as Revenue Rulings, but they deal with the internal management practices and procedures of the IRS. Familiarity with these procedures can increase taxpayer compliance and

---

11. *F.W. Woolworth Co.,* 54 T.C. 1233 (1970); *Harris M. Miller,* 70 T.C. 448 (1978); and *James O. Tomerlin Trust,* 87 T.C. 876 (1986).

12. § 7805(e).

13. § 7805(a).

assist the efficient administration of the tax laws by the IRS. The failure of a taxpayer to follow a Revenue Procedure can result in unnecessary delay or cause the IRS to decline to act in a discretionary situation on behalf of a taxpayer.

Revenue Rulings and Revenue Procedures are published weekly by the U.S. Government in the *Internal Revenue Bulletin* (I.R.B.). Semiannually, the bulletins for a six-month period are gathered together, reorganized by Code Section classification, and published in a bound volume called *Cumulative Bulletin* (C.B.).[14] The proper form for citing Rulings and Procedures depends on whether the item has been published in the *Cumulative Bulletin* or is available in I.R.B. form. Consider, for example, the following transition:

Temporary Citation
Rev.Rul. 87–57, I.R.B. No. 28, 7.
Explanation: Revenue Ruling Number 57, appearing on page 7 of the 28th weekly issue of the *Internal Revenue Bulletin* for 1987.

Permanent Citation
Rev.Rul. 87–57, 1987–2 C.B. 117.
Explanation: Revenue Ruling Number 57, appearing on page 117 of Volume 2 of the *Cumulative Bulletin* for 1987.

Since the second volume of the 1987 *Cumulative Bulletin* was not published until August of 1988, the I.R.B. citation must be used until that time. After the publication of the *Cumulative Bulletin*, the C.B. citation is proper. The basic portion of both citations (Rev.Rul. 87–57) indicates that this was the 57th Revenue Ruling issued by the IRS during 1987.

Revenue Procedures are cited in the same manner, except that "Rev. Proc." is substituted for "Rev.Rul." Some Revenue Procedures issued in 1988 had the following effects:

• Provided special procedures relating to the issuance of determination letters for retirement plans.

• Clarified depreciation rules for nonresidential property.

• Provided procedures for reducing withholding with respect to scholarship payments.

Letter Rulings. Individual (*letter*) rulings are issued upon a taxpayer's request and describe how the IRS will treat a proposed transaction for tax purposes. They apply only to the taxpayer who asks for and obtains the ruling.[15] Though this procedure may sound like the only real way to carry out effective tax planning, the IRS limits the issuance of individual rulings to

14. Usually only two volumes of the *Cumulative Bulletin* are published each year. However, when major tax legislation has been enacted by Congress, other volumes might be published containing the Congressional Committee Reports supporting the Revenue Act. See, for example, the two extra volumes for 1984 dealing with the Deficit Reduction Act of 1984. The 1984–3 *Cumulative Bulletin*, Volume 1, contains the text of the law itself; 1984–3, Volume 2, contains the Committee Reports. This makes a total of four volumes of the *Cumulative Bulletin* for 1984: 1984–1; 1984–2; 1984–3, Volume 1; and 1984–3, Volume 2.

15. In this regard, individual rulings differ from Revenue Rulings, which are applicable to *all* taxpayers. Individual rulings may later lead to the issuance of a Revenue Ruling if the holding involved affects many taxpayers. In its Agents' Manual, the IRS indicates that letter rulings may be used as a guide with other research materials in formulating a District Office position on an issue. The IRS is required to charge a taxpayer a fee for letter rulings, determination letters, etc.

restricted, preannounced areas of taxation. The main reason the IRS will not rule in certain areas is that such areas involve fact-oriented situations. Thus, it is not possible to obtain a ruling on many of the problems that are particularly troublesome for taxpayers.[16]

Both *mandatory* and *discretionary* letter rulings exist. A taxpayer must obtain a favorable ruling for certain changes in accounting procedures (e.g., a change in accounting period under § 442 or a change in accounting method under § 446). Such rulings are mandatory rulings. Discretionary rulings are not required by law; taxpayers request them at their own discretion. Further, the IRS issues these rulings at its discretion. For example, a taxpayer might request a ruling as to taxability of a corporate reorganization. In general, the IRS will rule on prospective transactions and on completed transactions where a return has not been filed for matters concerning income tax, gift tax, estate tax, generation-skipping transfer tax, and § 2032A ("Valuation of Certain Farm, Etc., Real Property").

The law now requires the IRS to make individual rulings available for public inspection after identifying details are deleted.[17] Published digests of private letter rulings can be found in *Private Letter Rulings* (published by Prentice-Hall), BNA *Daily Tax Reports*, and Tax Analysts & Advocates *Tax Notes*. *IRS Letter Rulings Reports* (published by Commerce Clearing House) contains both digests and full texts of all letter rulings.

Letter rulings are issued multi-digit file numbers, which indicate the year and week of issuance as well as the number of the ruling during that week. Consider, for example, Ltt. Rul. 8826052 dealing with the deductibility of interest expense:

88	26	052
Year 1988	26th week of issuance	Number of the ruling issued during 26th week

Other Administrative Pronouncements.   *Treasury Decisions* (TDs) are issued by the Treasury Department to promulgate new Regulations, amend or otherwise change existing Regulations, or announce the position of the Government on selected court decisions. Like Revenue Rulings and Revenue Procedures, TDs are published in the *Internal Revenue Bulletin* and subsequently transferred to the *Cumulative Bulletin*.

The IRS publishes other administrative communications in the *Internal Revenue Bulletin* such as Announcements, Notices, LRs (proposed Regulations), and Prohibited Transaction Exemptions.

The National Office of the IRS releases *Technical Advice Memoranda* (TAMs) weekly. Whereas letter rulings are responses to requests by taxpayers, TAMs are initiated by IRS personnel during IRS audits. A TAM gives the IRS's determination of an issue somewhat like a letter ruling. TAMs deal with

16. Rev.Proc. 89–3, I.R.B. No. 1, 29 contains a listing of areas in which the IRS will not issue advance rulings. From time to time, subsequent Revenue Procedures are issued that modify or amplify Rev.Proc. 89–3.

17. § 6110.

completed rather than proposed transactions and are often requested in relation to exempt organizations and employee plans. They are issued by the National Office of the IRS to the field personnel, whereas letter rulings are issued to taxpayers at their request. TAMs are not officially published and may not be cited or used as precedent.[18] The procedure for assigning file numbers to TAMs is the same as for letter rulings. For example, TAM 8834001 refers to the 1st TAM issued during the 34th week of 1988.

Like individual rulings, *determination letters* are issued at the request of taxpayers and provide guidance concerning the application of the tax law. They differ from individual rulings in that the issuing source is the District Director rather than the National Office of the IRS. Also, determination letters usually involve completed (as opposed to proposed) transactions. Determination letters are not published but are made known only to the party making the request.

The following examples illustrate the distinction between individual rulings and determination letters:

EXAMPLE 1

The shareholders of X Corporation and Y Corporation want assurance that the consolidation of the corporations into Z Corporation will be a nontaxable reorganization. The proper approach would be to request from the National Office of the IRS an individual ruling concerning the income tax effect of the proposed transaction. □

EXAMPLE 2

T operates a barber shop in which he employs eight barbers. To comply with the rules governing income tax and payroll tax withholdings, T wants to know whether the barbers working for him are employees or independent contractors. The proper procedure would be to request from the appropriate District Director a determination letter on the status of such persons. □

Several internal memoranda that constitute the working law of the IRS now must be released. These General Counsel's Memoranda (GCMs), Technical Memoranda (TMs), and Actions on Decisions (AODs) are not officially published, and the IRS indicates that they may not be cited as precedents by taxpayers. However, these working documents do explain the IRS's position on various issues.

Judicial Sources of the Tax Law

The Judicial Process in General.   After a taxpayer has exhausted some or all of the remedies available within the IRS (i.e., no satisfactory settlement has been reached at the agent or at the Appeals Division level), the dispute can be taken to the Federal courts. The dispute is first considered by a court of original jurisdiction (known as a trial court) with any appeal (either by the taxpayer or the IRS) taken to the appropriate appellate court. In most situations the taxpayer has a choice of any of *four trial courts*: a Federal District

---

18. § 6110(j)(3).

Court, the U.S. Claims Court, the U.S. Tax Court, or the Small Claims Division of the U.S. Tax Court. The trial and appellate court scheme for Federal tax litigation is illustrated in Figure 2–1.

The broken line between the U.S. Tax Court and the *Small Claims Division* indicates that there is no appeal from the Small Claims Division. The jurisdiction of the Small Claims Division is limited to cases involving amounts of $10,000 or less. The proceedings of the Small Claims Division are informal (e.g., no necessity for the taxpayer to be represented by a lawyer or other tax adviser). Commissioners rather then Tax Court judges preside over these proceedings. The decisions of the Small Claims Division are not precedents for any other court decision and are not reviewable by any higher court. Proceedings can be more timely and less expensive in the Small Claims Division.

American law, following English law, is frequently *made* by judicial decisions. Under the doctrine of *stare decisis*, each case (except in the Small Claims Division) has precedential value for future cases with the same controlling set of facts. Most Federal and state appellate court decisions and some decisions of trial courts are published. More than 3,000,000 judicial opinions have been published in the United States; over 30,000 cases are published each year.[19] Published court reports are organized by jurisdiction (Federal or state) and level of court (trial or appellate).

Trial Courts.   Differences between the various trial courts (courts of original jurisdiction) are summarized on the following pages.

FIGURE 2–1   Federal Judicial System

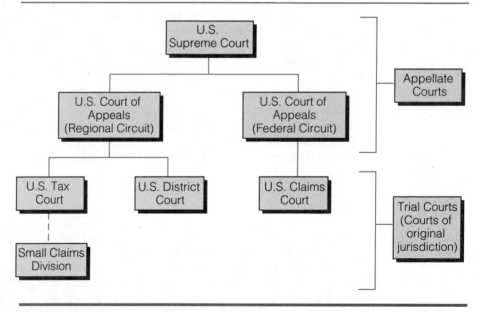

---

19. Jacobstein and Mersky, *Fundamentals of Legal Research*, 3rd Edition (Mineola, N.Y.: The Foundation Press, Inc., 1985).

- There is only one Claims Court and only one Tax Court, but there are many Federal District Courts. The taxpayer does not select the District Court that will hear the dispute but must sue in the one that has jurisdiction.

- Each District Court has only one judge, the Claims Court has 16 judges, and the Tax Court has 19 judges. In the case of the Tax Court, however, the entire court will decide a case (the court sits *en banc*) only when more important or novel tax issues are involved. Most cases will be heard and decided by one of the 19 judges.

- The Claims Court meets most often in Washington, D.C., whereas a District Court meets at a prescribed seat for the particular district. Since each state has at least one District Court and many of the more populous states have more, the inconvenience and expense of traveling for the taxpayer and his or her counsel (present with many suits in the Claims Court) is largely eliminated. Although the Tax Court is officially based in Washington, D.C., the various judges travel to different parts of the country and hear cases at predetermined locations and dates. Although this procedure eases the distance problem for the taxpayer, it could mean a delay before the case comes to trial and is decided.

- The Claims Court has jurisdiction in judgment upon any claim against the United States that is based upon the Constitution, any Act of Congress, or any regulation of an executive department.

- The Tax Court hears only tax cases. The Claims Court and District Courts hear nontax litigation as well. This difference, plus the fact that many Tax Court justices have been appointed from IRS or Treasury Department positions, has led some to conclude that the Tax Court has more expertise in tax matters.

- Some people believe that the Tax Court is more interested in protecting revenues than are the other trial courts. For example, IRS statistics show that for the years 1983 and 1984, taxpayers won in the Tax Court only 4.7 percent and 6.3 percent of the cases, respectively. During the same two years, taxpayers were successful 37 percent and 33.8 percent of the time in the District Courts and 50 percent and 46.3 percent of the time in the Claims Court.

- The only court in which a taxpayer can obtain a jury trial is a District Court. But since juries can only decide questions of fact and not questions of law, even those taxpayers who choose the District Court route often do not request a jury trial. In such event, the judge will decide all issues. Note that a District Court decision is controlling only in the district in which the court has jurisdiction.

- For the Claims Court or a District Court to have jurisdiction, the taxpayer must pay the tax deficiency assessed by the IRS and sue for a refund. A taxpayer who wins (assuming no successful appeal by the Government) recovers the tax paid plus appropriate interest thereon. For the Tax Court, however, jurisdiction is usually obtained without first paying the assessed tax deficiency. In the event the taxpayer loses in the Tax Court (and no appeal is taken or any such appeal is unsuccessful), the deficiency must be paid with appropriate interest.

- A taxpayer who selects the Tax Court may deposit a cash bond to stop the running of interest. The taxpayer must deposit both the amount of the tax and any accrued interest. If the taxpayer wins and the deposited amount is returned, the taxpayer will receive no interest from the Government on the deposit.

- The Claims Court does not have the power to fine or imprison for contempt of its order. Thus, a taxpayer will have to seek enforcement of the Claims Court's orders against nonparties in a District Court.

- Appeals from a District Court or a Tax Court decision are to the appropriate U.S. Court of Appeals. Appeals from the Claims Court go to the Court of Appeals for the Federal Circuit.

Appellate Courts.   The following listing indicates the Court of Appeals of appropriate jurisdiction for appeals from a trial court.

Jurisdiction of the Courts of Appeals

First	Fifth	California
Maine	Canal Zone	Hawaii
Massachusetts	Louisiana	Idaho
New Hampshire	Mississippi	Montana
Rhode Island	Texas	Nevada
Puerto Rico		Oregon
	Sixth	Washington
	Kentucky	Guam
Second	Michigan	
Connecticut	Ohio	Tenth
New York	Tennessee	Colorado
Vermont		Kansas
	Seventh	New Mexico
Third	Illinois	Oklahoma
Delaware	Indiana	Utah
New Jersey	Wisconsin	Wyoming
Pennsylvania		
Virgin Islands	Eighth	Eleventh
	Arkansas	Alabama
District of Columbia	Iowa	Florida
Washington, D.C.	Minnesota	Georgia
	Missouri	
	Nebraska	Federal [20]
Fourth	North Dakota	U.S. Claims Court
Maryland	South Dakota	
North Carolina		
South Carolina	Ninth	
Virginia	Alaska	
West Virginia	Arizona	

If the Government loses at the trial court level (District Court, Tax Court, or Claims Court), it need not (and frequently does not) appeal. The fact that an appeal is not made, however, does not indicate that the IRS agrees with the result and will not litigate similar issues in the future. There could be a number of reasons for the Service's failure to appeal. First, the current litiga-

---

20. The Court of Appeals for the Federal Circuit was created, effective October 1, 1982, by P.L. 97–164 (4/2/82) to hear decisions appealed from the Claims Court.

CONCEPT SUMMARY 2–2

Federal Judicial System: Trial Courts

Issue	U.S. Tax Court	U.S. District Court	U.S. Claims Court
Number of judges per court	19	1	16
Payment of deficiency before trial	No	Yes	Yes
Jury trial available	No	Yes	No
Types of disputes	Tax cases only	Most criminal and civil issues	Claims against the United States
Jurisdiction	Nationwide	Location of taxpayer	Nationwide
IRS acquiescence policy	Yes	No	No
Appeal route	U.S. Court of Appeals	U.S. Court of Appeals	U.S. Court of Appeals for the Federal Circuit

tion load may be heavy, and as a consequence, the IRS may decide that available personnel should be assigned to other, more important, cases. Second, the IRS may determine that this is not a good case to appeal. Such might be true if the taxpayer is in a sympathetic position or the facts are particularly strong in his or her favor. In such event, the IRS may wait to test the legal issues involved with a taxpayer who has a much weaker case. Third, if the appeal is from a District Court or the Tax Court, the Court of Appeals of jurisdiction could have some bearing on whether or not the decision is made to go forward with an appeal. Based on past experience and precedent, the IRS may conclude that the chance for success on a particular issue might be more promising in another Court of Appeals. The IRS will wait for a similar case to arise in a different appellate court.

With the establishment of the Federal Circuit at the appellate level, a taxpayer has an alternative forum to the Court of Appeals of his or her home circuit for the appeal. Appeals from both the Tax Court and the District Court go to a taxpayer's home circuit. Now, where a particular circuit has issued an adverse decision, the taxpayer may wish to select the Claims Court route, since any appeal will be to the Federal Circuit.

District Courts, the Tax Court, and the Claims Court must abide by the *precedents* set by the Court of Appeals of jurisdiction. A particular Court of Appeals need not follow the decisions of another Court of Appeals. All courts, however, must follow the decisions of the U.S. Supreme Court.

Because the Tax Court is a national court (it hears and decides cases from all parts of the country), the observation made in the previous paragraph has caused problems. For many years the Tax Court followed a policy of deciding cases based on what it thought the result should be, even though the appeal of its decision might have been to a Court of Appeals that had previously decided a similar case differently. A number of years ago this policy was changed in the *Golsen*[21] decision. Now the Tax Court will still decide a case as it feels the law should be applied *only* if the Court of Appeals of appropriate jurisdiction has not yet passed on the issue or has previously decided a similar case in accord with the Tax Court's decision. If the Court of Appeals of appropriate jurisdiction has previously held otherwise, the Tax Court will conform under the *Golsen* rule even though it disagrees with the holding.

EXAMPLE 3   Taxpayer T lives in Texas and sues in the Tax Court on Issue A. The Fifth Court of Appeals is the appellate court of appropriate jurisdiction. The Fifth Court of Appeals has already decided, in a case based on similar facts and involving a different taxpayer, that Issue A should be resolved against the Government. Although the Tax Court feels that the Fifth Court of Appeals is wrong, under its *Golsen* policy it will render judgment for T. Shortly thereafter, Taxpayer U, a resident of New York, in a comparable case, sues in the Tax Court on Issue A. Assume that the Second Court of Appeals, the appellate court of appropriate jurisdiction, has never expressed itself on Issue A. Presuming the Tax Court has not reconsidered its position on Issue A, it will decide against Taxpayer U. Thus, it is entirely possible for two taxpayers suing in the same court to end up with opposite results merely because they live in different parts of the country.

□

Appeal to the U.S. Supreme Court is by Writ of Certiorari. If the Court accepts jurisdiction, it will grant the Writ (*Cert. Granted*). Most often, it will deny jurisdiction (*Cert. Denied*). For whatever reason or reasons, the Supreme Court rarely hears tax cases. The Court usually grants certiorari to resolve a conflict among the Courts of Appeals (e.g., two or more appellate courts have assumed opposing positions on a particular issue). The granting of a Writ of Certiorari indicates that at least four members of the Supreme Court believe that the issue is of sufficient importance to be heard by the full court.

The *role* of appellate courts is limited to a review of the record of trial compiled by the trial courts. Thus, the appellate process usually involves a determination of whether or not the trial court applied the proper law in arriving at its decision. Rarely will an appellate court disturb a lower court's fact-finding determination.

Both the Code and the Supreme Court indicate that facts are binding on Federal courts of appeals unless clearly erroneous.[22] This appellate process is illustrated by a decision of the Court of Appeals for the District of Columbia involving whether a taxpayer was engaged in an activity for profit under § 183.[23] This appeals court specifically held that the "Tax Court's findings of facts are binding on Federal courts of appeals unless clearly erroneous." The

---

21. *Jack E. Golsen*, 54 T.C. 742 (1970).

22. §§ 7482(a) and (c). *Comm. v. Duberstein*, 60–2 USTC ¶9515, 5 AFTR2d 1626, 80 S.Ct. 1190 (USSC, 1960).

23. *Dreicer v. Comm.*, 81–2 USTC ¶9683, 48 AFTR2d 5884, 665 F.2d 1292 (CA-DC, 1981).

Court applauded the Tax Court for the thoroughness of its factual inquiry but could "not place the stamp of approval upon its eventual legal outcome." In reversing and remanding the decision to the Tax Court, the appellate court said that "the language of § 183, its legislative history and the applicable Treasury regulation combine to demonstrate that the court's [Tax Court's] standard is erroneous as a matter of law." The appeals court held that this taxpayer's claims of deductibility were to be evaluated by proper legal standards.

The result of an appeal could be any of a number of possibilities. The appellate court could approve (affirm) or disapprove (reverse) the lower court's finding, and it could also send the case back for further consideration (remand). When many issues are involved, it is not unusual to encounter a mixed result. Thus, the lower court could be affirmed (*aff'd*) on Issue A and reversed (*rev'd*) on Issue B, and Issue C could be remanded (*rem'd*) for additional fact finding.

When more than one judge is involved in the decision-making process, disagreement is not uncommon. In addition to the majority view, there could be one or more judges who concur (agree with the result reached but not with some or all of the reasoning) or dissent (disagree with the result). In any one case it is, of course, the majority view that controls. But concurring and dissenting views can have influence on other courts or, at some subsequent date when the composition of the court has changed, even on the same court.

Having concluded a brief description of the judicial process, it is appropriate to consider the more practical problem of the relationship of case law to tax research. As previously noted, court decisions are an important source of tax law. The ability to cite a case and to locate it is, therefore, a must in working with the tax law. The usual pattern for a judicial citation is as follows: case name, volume number, reporter series, page or paragraph number, and court (where necessary).

Judicial Citations—The U.S. Tax Court. A good starting point is with the Tax Court. The Court issues two types of decisions: Regular and Memorandum. The distinction between the two involves both substance and form. In terms of substance, *Memorandum* decisions deal with situations necessitating only the application of already established principles of law. *Regular* decisions involve novel issues not previously resolved by the Court. In actual practice, however, this distinction is not always preserved. Not infrequently, Memorandum decisions will be encountered that appear to warrant Regular status and vice versa. At any rate, do not conclude that Memorandum decisions possess no value as precedents. Both represent the position of the Tax Court and, as such, can be relied upon.

Another important distinction between the Regular and Memorandum decisions issued by the Tax Court involves their form. The Memorandum decisions are officially published in mimeograph form only, but Regular decisions are published by the U.S. Government in a series designated *Tax Court of the United States Reports*. Each volume of these *Reports* covers a six-month period (January 1 through June 30 and July 1 through December 31) and is given a succeeding volume number. But, as was true of the *Cumulative Bulletin*, there is usually a time lag between the date a decision is rendered and the date it appears in bound form. A temporary citation might be necessary to aid the researcher in locating a recent Regular decision. Consider, for example, the temporary and permanent citations for *Donald J. Porter*, a decision filed on March 5, 1987:

Temporary
Citation

{

Donald J. Porter, 88 T.C. ___, No. 28 (1987).
Explanation: Page number left blank because not yet known.

Permanent
Citation

{

Donald J. Porter, 88 T.C. 548 (1987).
Explanation: Page number now available.

Both citations tell us that the case will ultimately appear in Volume 88 of the *Tax Court of the United States Reports*. But until this volume is bound and made available to the general public, the page number must be left blank. Instead, the temporary citation identifies the case as being the twenty-eighth Regular decision issued by the Tax Court since Volume 87 ended. With this information, the decision can easily be located in either of the special Tax Court services published by Commerce Clearing House or Prentice-Hall. Once Volume 88 is released, the permanent citation can be substituted and the number of the case dropped.

Before 1943, the Tax Court was called the Board of Tax Appeals, and its decisions were published as the *United States Board of Tax Appeals Reports* (B.T.A.). These 47 volumes cover the period from 1924 to 1942. For example, the citation *Karl Pauli*, 11 B.T.A. 784 (1928) refers to the eleventh volume of the *Board of Tax Appeals Reports*, page 784, issued in 1928.

One further distinction between Regular and Memorandum decisions of the Tax Court involves the IRS procedure of *acquiescence* ("A" or "Acq.") or *nonacquiescence* ("NA" or "Nonacq."). If the IRS loses in a Regular decision, it will usually indicate whether it agrees or disagrees with the result reached by the Court. The acquiescence or nonacquiescence will be published in the *Internal Revenue Bulletin* and the *Cumulative Bulletin*. The procedure is not followed for Memorandum decisions or for the decisions of other courts. The IRS can retroactively revoke an acquiescence. The IRS sometimes issues an announcement that it will *or* will not follow a decision of another Federal court on similar facts. Such an announcement is not considered to be an acquiescence or nonacquiescence.

Most often the IRS issues nonacquiescences to Tax Court decisions that are not appealed. A nonacquiescence provides a warning to taxpayers that a similar case cannot be settled administratively. A taxpayer will incur fees and expenses even though the IRS may be unwilling to litigate a similar case.[24]

Although Memorandum decisions are not published by the U.S. Government, they are published by Commerce Clearing House (CCH) and Prentice-Hall (P-H). Consider, for example, the three different ways that *Jack D. Carr* can be cited:

Jack D. Carr, T.C. Memo. 1985–19
　　　　The 19th Memorandum decision issued by the Tax Court in 1985.

Jack D. Carr, 49 TCM 507
　　　　Page 507 of Vol. 49 of the *CCH Tax Court Memorandum Decisions*.

Jack D. Carr, P-H T.C.Mem.Dec. ¶85,019
　　　　Paragraph 85,019 of the *P-H T.C. Memorandum Decisions*.

---

24. G.W. Carter, "Nonacquiescence: Winning by Losing," *Tax Notes*, September 19, 1988, pp. 1301–1307.

Note that the third citation contains the same information as the first. Thus, ¶85,019 indicates the following information about the case: year 1985, 19th T.C.Memo. decision.[25] Although the Prentice-Hall citation does not indicate specifically a volume number, the paragraph citation does indicate that the decision can be found in the 1985 volume of the P-H Memorandum decision service.

Judicial Citations—The U.S. District Court, Claims Court, and Courts of Appeals. District Court, Claims Court, Court of Appeals, and Supreme Court decisions dealing with Federal tax matters are reported in both the CCH *U.S. Tax Cases* (USTC), and the P-H *American Federal Tax Reports* (AFTR) series.

Federal District Court decisions, dealing with *both* tax and nontax issues, also are published by West Publishing Company in its Federal Supplement Series. Examples of how a District Court case can be cited in three different forms appear as follows:

Simons-Eastern Co. v. U.S., 73–1 USTC ¶9279 (D.Ct.Ga., 1972).

Explanation: Reported in the first volume of the *U.S. Tax Cases* (USTC) published by Commerce Clearing House for calendar year 1973 (73–1) and located at paragraph 9279 (¶9279).

Simons-Eastern Co. v. U.S., 31 AFTR2d 73–640 (D.Ct.Ga., 1972).

Explanation: Reported in the 31st volume of the second series of the *American Federal Tax Reports* (AFTR2d) published by Prentice-Hall and beginning on page 640. The "73" preceding the page number indicates the year the case was published but is a designation used only in recent decisions.

Simons-Eastern Co. v. U.S., 354 F.Supp. 1003 (D.Ct.Ga., 1972).

Explanation: Reported in the 354th volume of the *Federal Supplement Series* (F.Supp.) published by West Publishing Company and commencing on page 1003.

In all of the preceding citations, note that the name of the case is the same (Simons-Eastern Co. being the taxpayer), as is the reference to the Federal District Court of Georgia (D.Ct.Ga.) and the year the decision was rendered (1972).[26] Decisions of the Claims Court and the Courts of Appeals are published in the USTCs, AFTRs, and a West Publishing Company reporter designated as the Federal Second Series (F.2d). However, beginning October 1982, the Claims Court decisions are published in another West Publishing Company reporter designated as the *Claims Court Reporter*. Illustrations of the different forms follow:

---

25. In this text, the Prentice-Hall citation for Memorandum decisions of the U.S. Tax Court is omitted. Thus, *Jack D. Carr* would be cited as: 49 TCM 507, T.C. Memo. 1985–19.

26. In this text, the case would be cited in the following form: *Simons-Eastern Co. v. U.S.*, 73–1 USTC ¶9279, 31 AFTR2d 73–640, 354 F.Supp. 1003 (D.Ct.Ga., 1972).

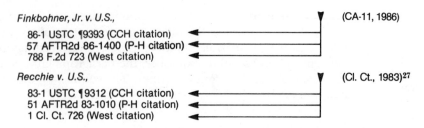

Finkbohner, Jr. v. U.S.,   (CA-11, 1986)

   86-1 USTC ¶9393 (CCH citation)
   57 AFTR2d 86-1400 (P-H citation)
   788 F.2d 723 (West citation)

Recchie v. U.S.,   (Cl. Ct., 1983)[27]

   83-1 USTC ¶9312 (CCH citation)
   51 AFTR2d 83-1010 (P-H citation)
   1 Cl. Ct. 726 (West citation)

Note that *Finkbohner, Jr.* is a decision rendered by the Eleventh Court of Appeals in 1986 (CA–11, 1986), while *Recchie* is one rendered by the Claims Court in 1983 (Cl.Ct., 1983).

Judicial Citations—The U.S. Supreme Court.   Like all other Federal tax cases (except those rendered by the Tax Court), Supreme Court decisions are published by Commerce Clearing House in the USTCs and by Prentice-Hall in the AFTRs. The U.S. Government Printing Office also publishes these decisions in the *United States Supreme Court Reports* (U.S.) as does West Publishing Company in its *Supreme Court Reporter* (S.Ct.) and the Lawyer's Co-Operative Publishing Company in its *United States Reports, Lawyer's Edition* (L.Ed.). The following illustrates the different ways the same decision can be cited:

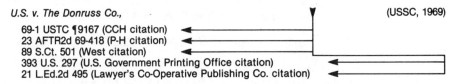

U.S. v. The Donruss Co.,   (USSC, 1969)

   69-1 USTC ¶9167 (CCH citation)
   23 AFTR2d 69-418 (P-H citation)
   89 S.Ct. 501 (West citation)
   393 U.S. 297 (U.S. Government Printing Office citation)
   21 L.Ed.2d 495 (Lawyer's Co-Operative Publishing Co. citation)

The parenthetical reference (USSC, 1969) identifies the decision as having been rendered by the U.S. Supreme Court in 1969. The citations given in this text for Supreme Court decisions will be limited to the CCH (USTC), P-H (AFTR), and the West (S.Ct.) versions. For a summary, see Concept Summary 2–3.

WORKING WITH THE TAX LAW—TAX RESEARCH

Tax research is the method whereby one determines the best available solution to a situation that possesses tax consequences. In other words, it is the process of finding a competent and professional conclusion to a tax problem. The problem might originate either from completed or proposed transactions. In the case of a completed transaction, the objective of the research would be to determine the tax result of what has already taken place. For example, was the expenditure incurred by the taxpayer deductible or not deductible for tax purposes? When dealing with proposed transactions, however, the tax research process is directed toward the determination of possible tax consequences. To the extent that tax research leads to a choice of alternatives or otherwise influences the future actions of the taxpayer, it becomes the key to effective tax planning.

Tax research involves the following procedures:

---

27. Before October 1, 1982, the Claims Court was
    called the Court of Claims.

CONCEPT SUMMARY 2–3

Judicial Sources

Court	Location	Authority
U.S. Supreme Court	S.Ct. Series (West) U.S. Series (U.S. Gov't.) L.Ed. (Lawyer's Co-Op.) AFTR (P-H) USTC (CCH)	Highest authority
U.S. Courts of Appeal	Federal 2nd (West) AFTR (P-H) USTC (CCH)	Next highest appel-late court
Tax Court (Regular decisions)	U.S. Govt. Printing Office PH/CCH separate services	Highest trial court *
Tax Court (Memoran-dum decisions)	P-H Memo TC (P-H) TCM (CCH)	Less authority than regular T.C. decision
U.S. Claims Court	Claims Court Report-er (West) AFTR (P-H) USTC (CCH)	Similar authority as Tax Court
U.S. District Courts	F.Supp. Series (West) AFTR (P-H) USTC (CCH)	Lowest trial court
Small Claims Divi-sion of Tax Court	Not published	No precedent value

* Theoretically, the Tax Court, Claims Court, and District Courts are on the same level of authority. But some people believe that since the Tax Court hears and decides tax cases from all parts of the country (it is a national court), its decisions may be more authoritative than a Claims Court or District Court decision.

- Identifying and refining the problem.
- Locating the appropriate tax law sources.
- Assessing the validity of the tax law sources.
- Arriving at the solution or at alternative solutions with due consideration given to nontax factors.
- Effectively communicating the solution to the taxpayer or the taxpayer's representative.
- Following up on the solution (where appropriate) in light of new developments.

These procedures are diagrammed in Figure 2–2. The broken lines reflect those steps of particular interest when tax research is directed towards proposed, rather than completed, transactions.

Identifying the Problem

Problem identification must start with a compilation of the relevant facts involved.[28] In this regard, *all* of the facts that might have a bearing on the problem must be gathered, because any omission could modify the solution to be reached. To illustrate, consider what appears to be a very simple problem.

EXAMPLE 4 · Early in December father, F, and mother, M, review their financial and tax situation with their son, S, and daughter-in-law, D. Both S and D are age 21. S is a student at a nearby university, and he owns some publicly traded stock that he inherited from his grandmother. S believes that the stock will decline significantly in value over the next several weeks and may never regain its current value. A current sale would result in approximately $7,000 of gross income. At this point, F and M provide about 55% of the support of S and D. Although neither is now employed, S has earned $960 and D has earned $900. The problem: Should the stock be sold, and would the sale prohibit F and M from claiming S and D as dependents? □

Refining the Problem

Initial reaction is that F and M in Example 4 could *not* claim S and D as dependents if the stock is sold, since S would then have earned more than the exemption amount under § 151(d). However, S is a full-time student, and § 151(c)(1)(B) allows a son or daughter who is a full-time student and who is under age 24 to earn more than the exemption amount without penalizing the parents with the loss of the dependency exemption. Thus, S could sell the stock without penalizing the parents with respect to the gross income test. However, the $7,000 income from the sale of the stock might cause the failure of the 50 percent support test, depending on how much S spends for his (or D's) support.

Assume, however, that further fact gathering reveals the following additional information:

- S does not really need to spend the proceeds from the sale of the stock.
- S receives a sizable portion of his own support from a scholarship.

With these new facts, additional research leads to § 152(d) and Reg. § 1.152–1(c), which indicate that a scholarship received by a student is not included for purposes of computing whether the parents furnished more than one-half of the child's support. Further, if S does not spend the proceeds from the sale of stock, such unexpended amount is not counted for purposes of the support test. Thus, it appears that the parents would not be denied the dependency exemptions for S and D.

28. For an excellent discussion of the critical role of facts in carrying out tax research, see Ray M. Sommerfeld and G. Fred Streuling, *Tax Re-* *search Techniques*, Tax Study No. 5 (New York: The American Institute of Certified Public Accountants, 1981), chapter 2.

FIGURE 2–2   Tax Research Process

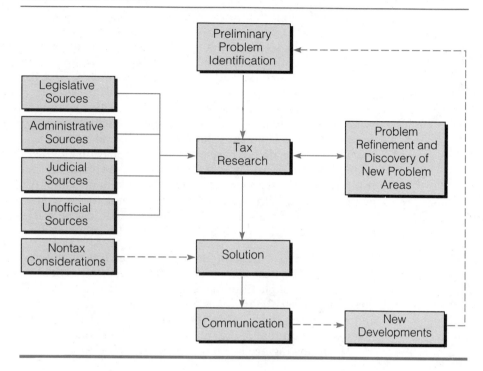

Locating the Appropriate Tax Law Sources

Once the problem is clearly defined, what is the next step? Although this is a matter of individual judgment, most involved tax research begins with the index volume of the tax service. If the problem is not that complex, the researcher may bypass the tax service and turn directly to the Internal Revenue Code and the Treasury Regulations. For the beginner, this procedure saves time and will solve many of the more basic problems. If the researcher does not have a personal copy of the Code or Regulations, resorting to the appropriate volume(s) of a tax service will be necessary.[29] The major tax services available are as follows:

Standard Federal Tax Reporter, Commerce Clearing House.

Federal Taxes, Prentice-Hall.

Mertens Law of Federal Income Taxation, Callaghan and Co.

Tax Coordinator, Research Institute of America.

Tax Management Portfolios, Bureau of National Affairs.

Rabkin and Johnson, *Federal Income, Gift and Estate Taxation*, Matthew Bender, Inc.

---

29. Several of the major tax services publish paperback editions of the Code and Treasury Regulations that can be purchased at modest prices. These editions are usually revised twice each year. For an annotated and abridged version of the Code and Regulations that is published annually, see James E. Smith, *West's Internal Revenue Code of 1986 and Treasury Regulations: Annotated and Selected* (St. Paul, Minnesota: West Publishing Company, 1989).

Working with the Tax Services.   In this text it is not feasible to teach the use of any particular tax service; this can be learned only by practice.[30] However, several important observations about the use of tax services cannot be overemphasized. First, never forget to check for current developments. The main text of any service is not revised frequently enough to permit reliance on that portion as the *latest* word on any subject. Where such current developments can be found depends, of course, on which service is being used. Both the Commerce Clearing House and Prentice-Hall services contain a special volume devoted to current matters. Second, when dealing with a tax service synopsis of a Treasury Department pronouncement or a judicial decision, remember there is no substitute for the original source.

To illustrate, do not base a conclusion solely on a tax service's commentary on *Simons-Eastern Co. v. U.S.*[31] If the case is vital to the research, look it up. It is possible that the facts of the case are distinguishable from those involved in the problem being researched. This is not to say that the case synopsis contained in the tax service is wrong; it might just be misleading or incomplete.

Tax Periodicals.   Additional sources of tax information are the various tax periodicals. The best means of locating a journal article pertinent to a tax problem is through Commerce Clearing House's *Federal Tax Articles*. This three-volume service includes a subject index, a Code Section number index, and an author's index. Also, the P-H tax service has a topical "Index to Tax Articles" section that is organized using the P-H paragraph index system.

The following are some of the more useful tax periodicals:

The Journal of Taxation
Warren, Gorham and Lamont
210 South Street
Boston, MA 02111

Tax Law Review
Warren, Gorham and Lamont
210 South Street
Boston, MA 02111

Trusts and Estates
Communication Channels, Inc.
6255 Barfield Road
Atlanta, GA 30328

Estate Planning
Warren, Gorham and Lamont
210 South Street
Boston, MA 02111

Taxation for Accountants
Warren, Gorham and Lamont
210 South Street
Boston, MA 02111

TAXES—The Tax Magazine
Commerce Clearing House, Inc.
4025 West Peterson Avenue
Chicago, IL 60646

National Tax Journal
21 East State Street
Columbus, OH 43215

The Tax Adviser
1211 Avenue of the Americas
New York, NY 10036

The Practical Accountant
1 Penn Plaza
New York, NY 10119

Journal of Corporate Taxation
Warren, Gorham and Lamont
210 South Street
Boston, MA 02111

Journal of Taxation for Individuals
Warren, Gorham and Lamont
210 South Street
Boston, MA 02111

30. The representatives of the various tax services are prepared to provide the users of their services with printed booklets and individual instruction on the utilization of such materials.

31. Refer to Footnote 26.

The Tax Executive
1300 North 17th Street
Arlington, VA 22209

Oil and Gas Tax Quarterly
Matthew Bender & Co.
235 East 45th Street
New York, NY 10017

The International Tax Journal
Panel Publishers
14 Plaza Road
Greenvale, NY 11548

The Tax Lawyer
American Bar Association
1800 M Street, N.W.
Washington, DC 20036

Journal of the American Taxation Association
American Accounting Association
5717 Bessie Drive
Sarasota, FL 33583

Tax Notes
6830 Fairfax Drive
Arlington, VA 22213

Assessing the Validity of the Tax Law Sources

Once a source has been located, the next procedure is to assess the source in light of the problem at hand. Proper assessment involves careful interpretation of the tax law with consideration as to its relevance and validity. In connection with validity, an important step is to check for recent changes in the tax law.

Interpreting the Internal Revenue Code.   The language of the Code can be extremely difficult to comprehend fully. For example, a subsection [§ 341(e)] relating to collapsible corporations contains *one* sentence of more than 450 words (twice as many as in the Gettysburg Address). Within this same subsection are two other sentences of 270 and 300 words. Research has shown that in one-third of the conflicts reaching the Tax Court, the Court could not discern the intent of Congress by simply reading the statute. Yet the overriding attitude of the Tax Court judges is that the statute comes first. Even when the statute is unworkable, the Court will not rewrite the law.[32] One author has noted 10 common pitfalls in interpreting the Code.[33]

1. Determine the limitations and exceptions to a provision. Do not permit the language of the Code Section to carry greater or lesser weight than was intended.

2. Just because a Section fails to mention an item does not necessarily mean that the item is excluded.

3. Read definitional clauses carefully.

4. Do not overlook small words such as *and* and *or*. There is a world of difference between these two words.

5. Read the Code Section completely; do not jump to conclusions.

6. Watch out for cross-referenced and related provisions, since many Sections of the Code are interrelated.

7. At times Congress is not careful when reconciling new Code provisions with existing Sections. Conflicts among Sections, therefore, do arise.

32. T. L. Kirkpatrick and W. B. Pollard, "Reliance by the Tax Court on the Legislative Interest of Congress," *The Tax Executive* (Summer 1986), pp. 358–359.

33. H. G. Wong, "Ten Common Pitfalls in Reading the Internal Revenue Code," *The Practical Accountant* (July–August 1972), pp. 30–33.

8. Be alert for hidden definitions; terms in a particular Code Section may be defined in the same Section *or in a separate Section.*

9. Some answers may not be found in the Code; therefore, a researcher may have to consult the Regulations and/or judicial decisions.[34]

10. Take careful note of measuring words such as *less than 50%, more than 50%,* and *at least 80%.*

Assessing the Validity of a Treasury Regulation.   It is often stated that Treasury Regulations have the force and effect of law. This statement is certainly true for most Regulations, but some judicial decisions have held a Regulation or a portion thereof invalid. The usual grounds for a court holding a Regulation invalid are that the Regulation is contrary to the intent of Congress upon the enactment of a particular Code Section. Most often the courts do not question the validity of Regulations because of the belief that "the first administrative interpretation of a provision as it appears in a new act often expresses the general understanding of the times or the actual understanding of those who played an important part when the statute was drafted." [35]

Keep the following observations in mind when assessing the validity of a Regulation:

- IRS agents must give the Code and the Regulations issued thereunder equal weight when dealing with taxpayers and their representatives.

- Proposed Regulations provide a preview of future final Regulations, but they are not binding on the IRS or taxpayers.

- In a challenge, the burden of proof is on the taxpayer to show that the Regulation is wrong. However, a court may invalidate a Regulation that varies from the language of the statute and has no support in the Committee Reports.

- If the taxpayer loses the challenge, the imposition of a negligence penalty can result.[36] This provision deals with the *disregard of rules or Regulations* on the part of the taxpayer. Of course, this negligence penalty may be imposed even where a taxpayer has relied on substantial authority in taking a position contrary to rules and Regulations.[37]

- Final Regulations tend to be legislative, interpretative, or procedural. *Procedural* Regulations neither establish tax laws nor attempt to explain tax laws. Procedural Regulations are *housekeeping type instructions* indicating information that taxpayers should provide the IRS as well as information about the internal management and conduct of the IRS itself.

- Some *interpretative* Regulations merely reprint or rephrase what Congress has stated in its Committee Reports issued in connection with the enactment of tax legislation. Such Regulations are *hard and solid* and

34. The Code is silent concerning the deductibility of education expenses. Such deductibility, however, falls under the general provision of § 162(a) (the allowance for "all the ordinary and necessary expenses paid or incurred during the taxable year in carrying on any trade or business . . ."). Guidelines for deductibility of education expenses can be found in Reg. § 1.162–5, and § 274(m)(2), which imposes a restriction on expenses for travel as a form of education. See chapter 10 for a more complete discussion.

35. *Augustus v. Comm.,* 41–1 USTC ¶9255, 26 AFTR 612, 118 F.2d 38 (CA–6, 1941).

36. § 6653(a).

37. *James O. Druker v. Comm.,* 1983–1 USTC ¶9116, 51 AFTR2d 83–436, 697 F.2d 46 (CA–2, 1983).

almost impossible to overturn, because they clearly reflect the intent of Congress. An interpretative Regulation is given less deference than a legislative Regulation, however. The Supreme Court has told lower courts to analyze Treasury Regulations carefully before accepting the Treasury's interpretation.[38]

- In some Code Sections, Congress has given to the *Secretary or his delegate* the authority to prescribe Regulations to carry out the details of administration or to otherwise complete the operating rules. Under such circumstances, it could almost be said that Congress is delegating its legislative powers to the Treasury Department. Regulations issued pursuant to this type of authority truly possess the force and effect of law and are often called *legislative* Regulations (e.g., consolidated return Regulations).

- Courts tend to apply a legislative re-enactment doctrine. A Regulation is assumed to have received Congressional approval if a particular Regulation was finalized many years earlier and Congress has not amended the Code Section pertaining to the Regulation.

Assessing the Validity of Other Administrative Sources of the Tax Law. Revenue Rulings issued by the IRS carry less weight than Treasury Department Regulations. Rulings are important, however, in that they reflect the position of the IRS on tax matters. In any dispute with the IRS on the interpretation of tax law, therefore, taxpayers should expect agents to follow the results reached in any applicable Rulings. A recent Tax Court decision, however, indicated that Revenue Rulings "typically do not constitute substantive authority for a position."[39] Most Revenue Rulings apply retroactively unless a specific statement indicates the extent to which a Ruling is to be applied without retroactive effect.[40]

Revenue Rulings further tell the taxpayer the IRS's reaction to certain court decisions. Recall that the IRS follows a practice of either acquiescing (agreeing) or nonacquiescing (not agreeing) with the *Regular* decisions of the Tax Court. This does not mean that a particular decision of the Tax Court is of no value if, for example, the IRS has nonacquiesced in the result. It does, however, indicate that the IRS will continue to litigate the issue involved.

Assessing the Validity of Judicial Sources of the Tax Law. The judicial process as it relates to the formulation of tax law has already been described. How much reliance can be placed on a particular decision depends upon the following variables:

- The level of the court. A decision rendered by a trial court (e.g., a Federal District Court) carries less weight than one issued by an appellate court (e.g., the Fifth Court of Appeals). Unless Congress changes the Code, decisions by the U.S. Supreme Court represent the last word on any tax issue.

38. *Vogel Fertilizer Co.*, 82–1 USTC ¶9134, 49 AFTR2d 82–491, 102 S.Ct. 821 (USSC, 1982); *National Muffler Dealers Assn., Inc.*, 79–1 USTC ¶9264, 43 AFTR2d 79–828, 99 S.Ct. 1304 (USSC, 1979).

39. *Nelda C. Stark*, 86 T.C. 243 (1986).
40. Rev.Proc. 87–1, 1987–1 C.B. 503.

- The legal residence of the taxpayer. If, for example, a taxpayer lives in Texas, a decision of the Fifth Court of Appeals means more than one rendered by the Second Court of Appeals. This result occurs because any appeal from a U.S. District Court or the Tax Court would be to the Fifth Court of Appeals and not to the Second Court of Appeals.[41]

- Whether the decision represents the weight of authority on the issue. In other words, is it supported by the results reached by other courts?

- The outcome or status of the decision on appeal. For example, was the decision appealed and, if so, with what result?

In connection with the last two variables, the use of a citator is invaluable to tax research.[42] Such use is illustrated in Appendix E.

Assessing the Validity of Other Sources. *Primary sources* of tax law include the Constitution, legislative history materials, statutes, treaties, Treasury Regulations, IRS pronouncements, and judicial decisions. The IRS considers only primary sources to constitute substantial authority. However, a researcher might wish to refer to *secondary materials* such as legal periodicals, treatises, legal opinions, general counsel memoranda, technical memoranda, and written determinations. In general, secondary sources are not authority. Reg. § 1.6661–3(b)(2) summarizes the opinion of the IRS as follows:

> In determining whether there is substantial authority . . . the following will be considered authority: Applicable provisions of the Internal Revenue Code and other statutory provisions; . . . regulations construing such statutes; court cases; administrative pronouncements (including revenue rulings and revenue procedures); tax treaties and regulations thereunder, and Treasury Department and other official explanations of such treaties; and Congressional intent as reflected in committee reports, . . . statements of managers. . . . Conclusions reached in treatises, legal periodicals, legal opinions or opinions rendered by other tax professionals, . . . general counsel memoranda . . ., technical memoranda, written determinations (except as provided in paragraph (b)(4)(i)) . . . are not authority. The authorities underlying such expressions of opinions where applicable to the facts of a particular case, however, may give rise to substantial authority for the tax treatment of an item.

An individual ruling or determination letter is substantial authority only to the taxpayer to whom it is issued.

Upon the completion of major tax legislation, the staff of the Joint Committee on Taxation (in consultation with the staffs of the House Ways and Means and Senate Finance Committees) often will prepare a General Explanation of the Act, commonly known as the bluebook because of the color of its cover. The IRS will not accept this detailed explanation as having legal effect. The bluebook does, however, provide valuable guidance to tax advisers and taxpayers until Regulations are issued, and some letter rulings and General Counsel's Memoranda of the IRS cite such explanations.

---

41. Before October 1, 1982, an appeal from the then named U.S. Court of Claims (the other trial court) was directly to the U.S. Supreme Court.

42. The major citators are published by Commerce Clearing House, Prentice-Hall, and Shepard's Citations, Inc.

Arriving at the Solution or at Alternative Solutions

In Example 4 the problem was whether dependency exemptions for a son and a daughter-in-law would be denied to a taxpayer if some stock were sold near the end of the year. A refinement of the problem added the additional information:

- S was a full-time student during four calendar months of the year.
- S and D anticipate filing a joint return.

Additional research leads to Reg. § 1.151–3(b), which indicates that to qualify as a student, S must be a full-time student during each of five calendar months of the year at an educational institution. Thus, proceeds from the sale of the stock by S would cause the loss of at least one dependency exemption for the parents because S's gross income would exceed the exemption amount. The parents still might be able to claim D as an exemption if the support test is met.

Section 151(c)(2) indicates that a supporting taxpayer is not permitted a dependency exemption for a married dependent if the married individual files a joint return. Initial reaction is that a joint return by S and D would be disastrous to the parents. However, more research uncovers two Revenue Rulings that provide an exception if neither the dependent nor the dependent's spouse is required to file a return but does so solely to claim a refund of tax withheld. The IRS asserts that each spouse must have gross income of less than the exemption amount.[43] Therefore, a sale of stock by S combined with filing a joint return would cause the loss of a dependency exemption for both S and D. If the stock is not sold until January, both exemptions may still be available to the parents. However, under § 151(d)(2) a personal exemption is not available to a taxpayer who can be claimed as a dependent by another taxpayer (whether actually claimed or not). Thus, if the parents can claim S and D as dependents, S and D would lose their personal exemptions.

Even if the stock is not sold until January, a refinement of the problem provides the additional information that D earned the $900 as a self-employed cosmetics sales-person. A self-employed individual with net earnings from a business of $400 or more must file a tax return regardless of his or her gross income. Not only is a return required, but D would be responsible for self-employment taxes. The IRS could argue that since D was required to file a tax return because her net earnings exceeded $400, the parents could not claim D as a dependent. D could no longer fall within the exception that she was merely filing a return to obtain a refund of tax withheld.

Communicating Tax Research

Once satisfied that the problem has been researched adequately, the researcher may need to prepare a memo setting forth the result. The form such a memo takes could depend on a number of considerations. For example, is any particular procedure or format recommended for tax research memos either by an employer or an instructor? Is the memo to be given directly to the client

---

43. Rev.Rul. 54–567, 1954–2 C.B. 108; Rev.Rul. 65–34, 1965–1 C.B. 86. An argument can be made that a return need not be filed unless their income exceeds the standard deduction for a married couple filing a joint return plus two exemption amounts.

or will it first pass to the researcher's employer? Whatever form it takes, a good research memo should contain the following elements:

- A clear statement of the issue.

- In more complex situations, a short review of the factual pattern that raises the issue.

- A review of the tax law sources (e.g., Code, Regulations, Rulings, judicial authority).

- Any assumptions made in arriving at the solution.

- The solution recommended and the logic or reasoning in its support.

- The references consulted in the research process.

In short, a good tax memo should tell the reader what was researched, the results of that research, and the justification for the recommendation made.[44]

Working with the Tax Law—Tax Planning

Tax research and tax planning are inseparable. The *primary* purpose of effective *tax planning* is to reduce the taxpayer's total tax bill. This does not mean that the course of action selected must produce the lowest possible tax under the circumstances. The minimization of tax liability must be considered in context with the legitimate business goals of the taxpayer.

A *secondary* objective of effective tax planning works toward a deferment or postponement of the tax. Specifically, this objective aims to accomplish any one or more of the following procedures: eradicating the tax entirely; eliminating the tax in the current year; deferring the receipt of income; converting ordinary income into capital gains; conversion of active to passive income; conversion of passive to active expense; proliferating taxpayers (i.e., forming partnerships and corporations or making lifetime gifts to family members); eluding double taxation; avoiding ordinary income; or creating, increasing, or accelerating deductions. However, this second objective should be accepted with considerable reservation. Although the maxim "A bird in the hand is worth two in the bush" has general validity, there are frequent cases in which the rule breaks down. For example, a tax election in one year, although it accomplishes a current reduction in taxes, could saddle future years with a disadvantageous tax position.

Nontax Considerations

There is an honest danger that tax motivations can take on a significance that is not in conformity with the true values involved. In other words, tax considerations can operate to impair the exercise of sound business judgment by the taxpayer. Thus, the tax planning process can become a medium through

---

44. See chapter 6 of the publication referred to in Footnote 28.

which to accomplish ends that are socially and economically objectionable. Ostensibly, a pronounced tendency exists for planning to go toward the opposing extremes of either not enough or too much emphasis on tax considerations. The happy medium—a balance that recognizes the significance of taxes, but not beyond the point at which planning serves to detract from the exercise of good business judgment—turns out to be the promised land that is seldom reached.

The remark is often made that a good rule to follow is to refrain from pursuing any course of action that would not be followed were it not for certain tax considerations. This statement is not entirely correct, but it does illustrate the desirability of preventing business logic from being *sacrificed at the altar of tax planning*. In this connection, the following comment is significant:

> The lure of a quick tax dollar is often the only justification for a transaction that might have been accomplished with much sounder economic results and equivalent tax savings if more careful and deliberate consideration had been given to the problem. Certainly in this atmosphere of the tax-controlled economy a very heavy obligation is cast upon the tax adviser to give serious consideration as to whether a proposed action achieves a desirable economic result apart from tax savings or whether the immediate tax advantages may be more than offset by later economic or personal disadvantage. We cannot afford to develop successful cures that are killing our patients.[45]

Tax Avoidance and Tax Evasion

A fine line exists between legal tax planning and illegal tax planning—tax avoidance versus tax evasion. *Tax avoidance* is merely tax minimization through legal techniques. In this sense, tax avoidance becomes the proper objective of all tax planning. Evasion, while also aimed at the elimination or reduction of taxes, connotes the use of subterfuge and fraud as a means to an end. Popular usage—probably because of the common goals that are involved—has linked these two concepts to the extent that any true distinctions have been obliterated in the minds of many. Consequently, the taint created by the association of tax avoidance and tax evasion has deterred some taxpayers from properly taking advantage of the planning possibilities. The now classic words of Judge Learned Hand in *Commissioner v. Newman* reflects the true values the individual should have:

> Over and over again courts have said that there is nothing sinister in so arranging one's affairs as to keep taxes as low as possible. Everybody does so, rich or poor; and all do right, for nobody owes any public duty to pay more than the law demands: taxes are enforced extractions, not voluntary contributions. To demand more in the name of morals is mere cant.[46]

---

45. Norris Darrell, "Some Responsibilities of the Tax Adviser in Regard to Tax Minimization Devices," *Proceedings of the New York University Eighth Annual Institute on Federal Taxation* (Albany, N.Y.: Matthew Bender & Co., 1950), pp. 988–989. For a more detailed discussion of tax planning, see Norwood, Chisholm, Burke, and Vaughn, *Federal Taxation: Research, Planning and Procedure* (Englewood Cliffs, N.J.: Prentice-Hall Inc., 1979), ch. 6.

46. *Comm. v. Newman*, 47–1 USTC ¶9175, 35 AFTR 857, 159 F.2d 848 (CA–2, 1947).

Follow-up Procedures

Because tax planning usually involves a proposed (as opposed to a completed) transaction, it is predicated upon the continuing validity of the advice based upon the tax research. A change in the tax law (either legislative, administrative, or judicial) could alter the original conclusion. Additional research may be necessary to test the solution in light of current developments (refer to one set of broken lines depicted in Figure 2–2).

Tax Planning—A Practical Application

Returning to the facts of Example 4, what could be done to protect the dependency exemptions for the parents? If S and D were to refrain from filing a joint return, both could be claimed by the parents. This result assumes that the stock is not sold.

An obvious tax planning tool is the installment method. Could the securities be sold using the installment method under § 453 and have most of the gain deferred into the next year? Under the installment method, certain gains may be postponed and recognized as the cash proceeds are received. The problem is that the installment method is not available for stock traded on an established securities market.[47]

A little more research, however, indicates that S can sell the stock and postpone the recognition of gain until the following year by selling short an equal number of substantially identical shares and covering the short sale in the subsequent year with the shares originally held. Selling short means that S sells borrowed stock (substantially identical) and repays the lender with the stock held on the date of the short sale. This *short against the box* technique would allow S to protect his $7,000 profit and defer the closing of such sale until the following year.[48] Further, if the original shares had been held for the required long-term holding period before the date of the short sale, S would be able to obtain long-term capital gain treatment.[49] Thus, some research and planning would reap tax savings for this family. Note the critical role of obtaining the correct facts in attempting to resolve the proper strategy for the taxpayers.

Throughout the text, most chapters include observations on Tax Planning Considerations. Such observations are not all-inclusive but are intended to illustrate some of the ways in which the material covered can be effectively utilized to minimize taxes.

Computer-Assisted Tax Research

The computer is being used more and more frequently in the day-to-day practice of tax professionals, students, and educators. Many software vendors offer tax return software programs for individual, corporate, partnership, and fiduciary returns. The use of computers, however, is not limited to the role of

47. Installment sales of real estate and casual sales of personal property are covered by § 453.
48. §§ 1233(a) and 1233(b)(2).
49. Long-term capital gains no longer receive pref-erential tax rate treatment. However, if S had capital losses from other transactions, the capital gains and capital losses could be offset.

batch-processed tax returns and computer timesharing for quantitative tax and problem-solving planning and calculations.

The microcomputer is becoming the revolutionary tool of the present—much as the electronic calculator did in the seventies. Electronic spreadsheets are being used to replace the 14-column worksheet. The electronic spreadsheet approach can be used for retirement planning, 1040 projections, real estate projections, partnership allocations, consolidated tax return problems, compensation planning—anytime projections and calculations are needed. Internally prepared tax-related programs are used by many public accounting firms. Software is available for the microcomputer for estate planning calculations.

LEXIS, a computerized legal data bank from Mead Data Central, has been available since 1973 as a complement to the conventional research approach (available in many of the more than 100 graduate tax programs). WESTLAW, a competitive system from West Publishing Company, has been operational since 1975. Prentice-Hall has a national computer network, called PHINet, which makes its loose-leaf service accessible by computer. Commerce Clearing House's legal data base is called ACCESS. WESTLAW, LEXIS, PHINet, and ACCESS are in actuality document retrieval systems that cannot interpret the law.

Users have access to these computerized data banks through special terminals and long-distance telephone lines. A user selects key words, phrases, or numbers and types the search request on the keyboard of the terminal. A display screen then shows the full text or portions of the various documents containing the words, phrases, or numbers in the search request. A printer can be used to obtain hard copy of any documents or portions of a document. For example, a researcher can obtain the decisions of a particular judge or court over a specified time period. It is also possible to access judicial opinions containing specific words or phrases of statutory language. These computer-assisted tax systems can be used as a citator by collecting all judicial decisions that have cited a particular decision or statute as well as all decisions that have a specific combination of two or more earlier decisions or statutes.

Computer-assisted tax research is useful in searching for facts because human indexing evolves around legal theories rather than fact patterns. Computer searching also is useful in finding new court decisions not yet in the printed indexes. Because computer searching probably does not find as many relevant cases as does manual searching, a combination of manual and computer searching can be quite effective.[50]

PROBLEM MATERIALS

Discussion Questions

(handwritten: if not supplemented amended yes?)

1. Judicial decisions interpreting a provision of the Internal Revenue Code of 1939 or 1954 are no longer of any value in view of the enact-

---

50. See p. 437 of the publication referred to in Footnote 19; Thomas and Weinstein, *Computer-Assisted Legal and Tax Research* (Paramus, N.J.: Prentice-Hall, 1986); and chapter 13 of W.A. Raabe, G.E. Whittenburg, and J. C. Bost, *West's Federal Tax Research*, 1st Edition (St. Paul: West Publishing Co., 1987).

ment of the Internal Revenue Code of 1986. Assess the validity of this statement.

2. The Technical and Miscellaneous Revenue Act of 1988 became part of the Internal Revenue Code of 1986. Explain this statement.

3. Trace through Congress the path usually followed by a tax bill.

4. Why are Committee Reports of Congress important as a source of tax law?

5. Why are certain Code Section numbers missing from the Internal Revenue Code (e.g., §§ 6, 7, 8, 9, 10)?

6. Suppose an international tax treaty between the United States and a foreign country conflicts with a Section of the Internal Revenue Code. Discuss.

7. Where may proposed Regulations first be found? How would a proposed Regulation under § 115 be cited?

8. Distinguish between legislative, interpretative, and procedural Regulations.

9. Distinguish between:
   a.   Treasury Regulations and Revenue Rulings.
   b.   Revenue Rulings and Revenue Procedures.
   c.   Revenue Rulings and individual (letter) rulings.
   d.   Individual (letter) rulings and determination letters.

10. Rank the following items from the highest authority to the lowest in the Federal tax law system:
   a.   Interpretative Regulation.
   b.   Legislative Regulation.
   c.   Letter ruling.
   d.   Revenue Procedure.
   e.   Internal Revenue Code.
   f.   Proposed Regulation.

11. Interpret each of the following citations:
   a.   Rev.Rul. 81–167, 1981–1 C.B. 45.
   b.   Rev.Proc. 85–41, 1985–2 C.B. 482.
   c.   Ltt.Rul. 8803020.

12. You find a 1989 letter ruling in which the factual situation is identical to the approach you wish to take. Can you rely on this letter ruling?

13. Discuss the two major types of letter rulings.

14. Identify the governmental unit that produces the following tax sources:
   a.   Proposed Regulations.
   b.   Revenue Procedures.
   c.   Letter rulings.

d. Determination letters.

e. Technical Advice Memoranda.

15. a. What are Treasury Decisions (TDs)?

b. What purpose do they serve?

c. Where are they published?

16. What are the major differences between individual rulings and determination letters?

17. Summarize the trial and appellate court system for Federal tax litigation.

18. Which of the following statements would be considered advantages of the Small Claims Division of the Tax Court?

a. Appeal to the Court of Appeals for the Federal Circuit is possible.

b. A hearing of a deficiency of $11,200 is considered on a timely basis.

c. Taxpayer can handle the litigation without using a lawyer or certified public accountant.

d. Taxpayer can use other Small Claims decisions for precedent value.

e. The actual hearing is held on an informal basis.

f. Travel time will probably be reduced.

19. List an advantage and a disadvantage of using the U.S. Tax Court as the trial court for Federal tax litigation.

20. List an advantage and a disadvantage of using a U.S. District Court as the trial court for Federal tax litigation.

21. List an advantage and a disadvantage of using the U.S. Claims Court as the trial court for Federal tax litigation.

22. A taxpayer lives in Michigan. In a controversy with the IRS, the taxpayer loses at the trial court level. Describe the appeal procedure under the following different assumptions:

a. The trial court was the Small Claims Division of the U.S. Tax Court.

b. The trial court was the U.S. Tax Court.

c. The trial court was a U.S. District Court.

d. The trial court was the U.S. Claims Court.

23. Suppose the U.S. Government loses a tax case in the U.S. District Court of Idaho but does not appeal the result. What does the failure to appeal signify?

24. Because the U.S. Tax Court is a national court, it always decides the same issue in a consistent manner. Assess the validity of this statement.

25. To what court are decisions of the following courts first appealed?

a. Small Claims Court.

b.   Federal District Court.

c.   U.S. Claims Court.

d.   U.S. Tax Court.

e.   Federal Court of Appeals.

26. A taxpayer from a U.S. District Court in which of the following states could appeal the decision to the Ninth Court of Appeals?

a.   Alaska.

b.   Arkansas.

c.   Arizona.

d.   Alabama.

e.   Maine.

f.   None of the above.

27. Explain the fact-finding determination of a Federal Court of Appeals.

28. What is the Supreme Court's policy on hearing tax cases?

29. In assessing the validity of a prior court decision, discuss the significance of the following on the taxpayer's issue:

a.   The decision was rendered by the U.S. District Court of Wyoming. Taxpayer lives in Wyoming.

b.   The decision was rendered by the U.S. Claims Court. Taxpayer lives in Wyoming.

c.   The decision was rendered by the Second Court of Appeals. Taxpayer lives in California.

d.   The decision was rendered by the U.S. Supreme Court.

e.   The decision was rendered by the U.S. Tax Court. The IRS has acquiesced in the result.

f.   Same as (e) except that the IRS has issued a nonacquiescence as to the result.

30. Where can a researcher locate a 1981 U.S. District Court decision?

31. What is the difference between a Regular and a Memorandum decision of the U.S. Tax Court?

32. The IRS may acquiesce or nonacquiesce to what court decisions? Can an acquiescence be withdrawn retroactively?

33. Interpret each of the following citations:

a.   54 T.C. 1514 (1970).

b.   408 F.2d 117 (CA–2, 1969).

c.   69–1 USTC ¶9319 (CA–2, 1969).

d.   23 AFTR2d 69–1090 (CA–2, 1969).

e.   293 F.Supp. 1129 (D.Ct., Miss., 1967).

f.   67–1 USTC ¶9253 (D.Ct., Miss., 1967).

g.   19 AFTR2d 647 (D.Ct., Miss., 1967).

h.   56 S.Ct. 289 (USSC, 1935).

    i.   36–1 USTC ¶9020 (USSC, 1935).

    j.   16 AFTR 1274 (USSC, 1935).

    k.   422 F.2d 1336 (Ct.Cls., 1970).

34. Explain the following abbreviations:

a.	CA–2	i.	USTC
b.	Cls.Ct.	j.	AFTR
c.	*aff'd.*	k.	F.2d
d.	*rev'd.*	l.	F.Supp.
e.	*rem'd.*		
f.	*Cert. denied*	m.	USSC
g.	*acq.*	n.	S.Ct.
h.	B.T.A.	o.	D.Ct.

35. Give the West Publishing Company's citation for the following courts:
    a. Small Claims Division of the Tax Court.
    b. Federal District Court.
    c. Supreme Court.
    d. U.S. Claims Court.

36. Where can you locate a published decision of the U.S. Claims Court?

37. Which of the following items probably can be found in the *Cumulative Bulletin*?
    a. Revenue Ruling.
    b. Small Claims Division of the U.S. Tax Court decision.
    c. Letter ruling.
    d. Revenue Procedure.
    e. Proposed Regulation.
    f. District Court decision.
    g. Senate Finance Committee Report.
    h. Acquiescences to Tax Court decisions.
    i. Tax Court Memorandum decision.
    j. Information Release (IR).

38. In the tax research process, what does problem identification involve?

39. Where can a researcher locate tax articles discussing a particular tax topic (e.g., alimony)?

40. In tax law, what has the highest tax authority or reliability?

41. Since a Regulation has the force and effect of tax law, can a Regulation be overturned by a court?

42. When might a researcher have a need to refer to a citator?

43. A student/friend majoring in sociology indicates that tax advisers are immoral since they merely help people cheat the government. Defend tax planning by tax advisers.

44. Which of the following would be considered differences between the Prentice-Hall and Commerce Clearing House *Citators*?

   a. Distinguishes between the various issues in a particular court decision.

   b. Lists all court decisions that cite the court decision being researched.

   c. Allows a researcher to determine the validity of a Revenue Ruling.

   d. Indicates whether a court decision is explained, criticized, followed, or overruled by a subsequent decision.

   e. Pinpoints the exact page on which one decision is cited by another case.

45. List the provider and the name of the four computer legal data bases.

Problems

46. T, an individual taxpayer, has just been audited by the IRS and, as a result, has been assessed a substantial deficiency (which has not yet been paid) in additional income taxes. In preparing his defense, T advances the following possibilities:

   a. Although a resident of Kentucky, T plans to sue in a U.S. District Court in Oregon that appears to be more favorably inclined towards taxpayers.

   b. If (a) is not possible, T plans to take his case to a Kentucky state court where an uncle is the presiding judge.

   c. Since T has found a B.T.A. decision that seems to help his case, he plans to rely on it under alternative (a) or (b).

   d. If he loses at the trial court level, T plans to appeal either to the U.S. Claims Court or to the U.S. Second Court of Appeals. The reason for this choice is the presence of relatives in both Washington, D.C., and New York. Staying with these relatives could save T lodging expense while his appeal is being heard by the court selected.

   e. Whether or not T wins at the trial court or appeals court level, he feels certain of success on an appeal to the U.S. Supreme Court.

   Evaluate T's notions concerning the judicial process as it applies to Federal income tax controversies.

47. Using the legend provided, classify each of the following statements (more than one answer per statement may be appropriate):

Legend

D = Applies to the U.S. District Court
T = Applies to the U.S. Tax Court
C = Applies to the U.S. Claims Court
A = Applies to the U.S. Court of Appeals
U = Applies to the U.S. Supreme Court
N = Applies to none of the above

a. Decides only Federal tax matters.

b. Decisions are reported in the F.2d Series.

c. Decisions are reported in the USTCs.

d. Decisions are reported in the AFTRs.

e. Appeal is by Writ of Certiorari.

f. Court meets most often in Washington, D.C.

g. A jury trial is available.

h. Trial courts.

i. Appellate courts.

j. Appeal is to the Federal Circuit and bypasses the taxpayer's particular circuit court.

k. Has a Small Claims Division.

l. The only trial court where the taxpayer does not have to pay the tax assessed by the IRS first.

48. Using the legend provided, classify each of the following tax sources:

Legend

P = Primary tax source
S = Secondary tax source
B = Both
N = Neither

a. Sixteenth Amendment to the Constitution.

b. Tax treaty between the United States and the United Kingdom.

c. Proposed Regulations.

d. Revenue Rulings.

e. General Counsel Memoranda.

f. Tax Court Memorandum decision.

g. *Yale Law Review* article.

h. Temporary Regulations.

i. Letter ruling.

j. District Court decision.

k. Small Claims Division of U.S. Tax Court decision.

l. Senate Finance Committee Report.

m. Technical Advise Memorandum.

49. You inherit a problem that was researched four months previously. You believe the answers are correct, but you wish to evaluate the reliability of the authority given in the research report. How do you determine the latest developments with respect to a research problem?

50. Using the legend provided, classify each of the following statements:

Legend

A = Tax avoidance
E = Tax evasion
N = Neither

a. T writes a $250 check as a charitable contribution on December 28, 1989, but does not mail the check to the charitable organization until January 10. T takes a deduction in 1989.

b. W decided not to report interest income from a bank because it was only $11.75.

c. T pays property taxes on his home in December 1989 rather than waiting until February 1990.

d. W switches her investments from taxable corporate bonds to tax-exempt municipal bonds.

e. T encourages his mother to save most of her Social Security benefits so that he will be able to claim her as a dependent.

Research Problems

Research Problem 1 Locate the following Internal Revenue Code citations and give a brief description of them:

a. § 118(a).

b. § 1231(c)(3).

c. § 4981A(c)(1).

Research Problem 2 Locate the following Regulation citations and give a brief description of them:

a. Reg. § 1.151–3(a).

b. Temp.Reg. § 18.1362–2(c).

c. Reg. § 1.1502–75(c)(2)(i).

Research Problem 3 What is the subject matter of the Revenue Procedure that begins on page 396 of the 1987–2 *Cumulative Bulletin*?

Research Problem 4

a. Using "Amortization of Intangibles" Tax Management Portfolio (TMP) 209–3rd, Bureau of National Affairs, determine the definition of "milk base."

b. Using "Mineral Properties Other Than Gas & Oil—Operation," Tax Management Portfolio (TMP) 90–6th, Bureau of National Affairs, determine a mineralogical definition of "quartzite."

Research Problem 5

    a.   What two famous performers are discussed on page 295 in Vol. 3B of *Mertens Law of Federal Income Taxation*, § 22.32?

    b.   According to *Mertens*, is clothing used by a baseball player or a professional golfer deductible as an ordinary and necessary business expense?

Research Problem 6   Determine the acquiescence/nonacquiescence position of the IRS with respect to the following:

    a.   *Woods Investment Co.*, 85 T.C. 274 (1985).

    b.   *Henry W. Schwartz Corp.*, 60 T.C. 728 (1973).

    c.   *Estate of Milton S. Lennard*, 61 T.C. 554 (1974).

Research Problem 7   Locate the following tax services in your library and indicate the name of the publisher and whether the service is organized by topic or Code Section:

    a.   *Federal Taxes.*

    b.   *Standard Federal Tax Reporter.*

    c.   *Tax Coordinator 2d.*

    d.   *Mertens Law of Federal Income Taxation.*

    e.   *Tax Management Portfolios.*

    f.   Rabkin & Johnson, *Federal Income, Gift & Estate Taxation.*

Research Problem 8   In the Tax Publications Matrix below, place an X if a court decision can be found in the publication. There may be more than one X along a row for a particular court decision.

Court	U.S. Govt. Printing Office	West Publishing Company				Prentice-Hall			Commerce Clearing House	
		Federal Supp.	Federal 2d	Claims Court Reporter	S.Ct	BTA Memo	TC Memo	AFTR	TC Memo	USTC
U.S. Supreme Court										
Court of Appeals										
Claims Court										
District Court										
Tax Court (regular decisions)										
Tax Court (memo decisions)										
Board of Tax Appeal										
BTA Memo										

Research Problem 9   Complete the following citations to the extent the research materials are available to you:

    a.   *U.S. v. Kirby Lumber Co.*, 2 USTC ___ (1931).

    b.   *U.S. v. Kirby Lumber Co.*, 10 AFTR ___ (1931).

    c.   *Comm. v. Anderson*, 371 F.2d ___ (___, 1966).

    d.   *James Soares*, 50 T.C. ___ (1968).

    e.   _____, 14 AFTR2d 64–5605 (___, ___).

  f. _____, 64–2 USTC ¶9743 (_____, ___).

  g. Rev.Rul. 86–58, 1986–__ C.B. ___.

  h. *R.M. Weyerhaeuser*, ___ B.T.A. ___ (1935).

  i. *Badias & Seijas*, T.C.Memo 1977–___.

  j. *Badias & Seijas*, 36 TCM ___ (1977).

  k. *King Enterprise, Inc. v. U.S.*, 24 AFTR2d ___, 69–2 USTC ___ (___, 1969).

Research Problem 10 By using the research materials available to you, answer the following questions:

  a. Has Prop. Reg. § 1.482–2 been finalized?

  b. What happened to *Golconda Mining Corp.*, 58 T.C. 736 (1972) on appeal?

  c. Does Rev.Rul. 69–185 still represent the position of the IRS on the issue involved?

Research Problem 11 Indicate the disposition of the following court decisions by the U.S. Supreme Court:

  a. *Comm. v. Anderson*, 371 F.2d 59 (CA–6, 1966).

  b. *Heard v. Comm.*, 326 F.2d 962 (CA–8, 1964).

  c. *Adolph Coors Co. v. Comm.*, 519 F.2d 1280 (CA–10, 1975).

  d. *Comm. v. Golonsky*, 200 F.2d 72 (CA–3, 1952).

Research Problem 12 Determine the reliability of the following items:

  a. *Simpson v. U.S.*, 261 F.2d 497 (CA–7, 1958).

  b. Rev.Proc. 83–78, 1983–2 C.B. 595.

  c. *Estate of Grace E. Lang*, 64 T.C. 404 (1975).

Research Problem 13 Determine the reliability of the following decisions:

  a. *Donald L. Wilkerson*, 70 T.C. 240 (1978).

  b. *David Rockefeller*, 76 T.C. 178 (1981).

  c. *Adolph B. Canelo*, 53 T.C. 217 (1969).

Research Problem 14 Determine the reliability of the following items:

  a. *Maid of The Mist Corp. v. Comm.*, T.C.Memo. 1977–263, 36 TCM 1068 (1977).

  b. *Lazisky v. Comm.*, 72 T.C. 495 (1979).

  c. *Farm Service Cooperative v. Comm.*, 70 T.C. 145 (1978).

  d. *Tufts v. Comm.*, 81–2 USTC ¶9754 (CA–5, 1981), rev'g 70 T.C. 756 (1978).

Research Problem 15 Find the decision *Barbados #6 Ltd.*, 85 T.C. 900 (1985).

  a. Who was the presiding judge?

  b. Was the decision reviewed by the full court? If so, who dissented from the majority opinion?

c. Who won?

d. Was the decision entered under the Rule of 155?

Research Problem 16   During 1989, T lived with and supported a 20-year-old woman who was not his wife. He resides in a state that has a statute that makes it a misdemeanor for a man and woman not married to each other to live together. May T claim his *friend* as a dependent assuming he satisfies the normal tax rules for the deduction? Should T consider moving to another state?

Partial list of research aids:

§ 152(b)(5).

John T. Untermann, 38 T.C. 93 (1962).

S.Rept. 1983, 85th Cong., 2d Sess., reprinted in the 1958 Code Cong. & Adm.News 4791, 4804.

Research Problem 17   Locate *New York University's Forty-Third Annual Institute on Federal Taxation.*

a. Turn to chapter 35, page 35–35, Chart III, and determine the present cost of an employer's obligation to pay an employee $20,000 in 10 years. Assume a 12% employer rate of return.

b. Turn to chapter 56, page 56–19, and determine what IRA fees are deductible.

3

TAX DETERMINATION; PERSONAL AND DEPENDENCY EXEMPTIONS; AN OVERVIEW OF PROPERTY TRANSACTIONS

OBJECTIVES

Explain how an individual's tax liability is determined.

Develop greater understanding of the standard deduction and other components of the tax formula for individuals.

Apply the rules for determining dependency exemptions and filing status.

Introduce the basic concepts of property transactions and their effect on taxable income.

Discuss several basic tax planning ideas for individual taxpayers.

Individuals are subject to Federal income tax based on taxable income. This chapter explains how an individual's income tax is determined.

To compute taxable income, it is necessary to understand the tax formula in Figure 3–1. Although the tax formula is rather simple, determination of an individual's taxable income can be quite complex. This complexity stems from the numerous provisions that govern the determination of gross income and allowable deductions.

After computing taxable income, the appropriate rates must be applied. This requires a determination of the individual's filing status since different rates apply for single taxpayers, married taxpayers, and heads of household. The basic tax rate structure is progressive, with a rate of 15 percent on taxable income up to specified amounts and 28 percent on additional taxable income.[1] In certain circumstances, the rate can go as high as 33 percent.

Once the individual's tax has been computed, prepayments and credits are subtracted to determine whether the taxpayer owes additional tax or is entitled to a refund.

When property is sold or otherwise disposed of, the result could affect the determination of income tax liability. Although property transactions are covered in detail in chapters 14–17, an understanding of certain basic concepts is helpful in working with some of the materials to follow. The concluding portion of this chapter furnishes an overview of the area, including the distinction between realized and recognized gain or loss, the classification of such gain or loss (ordinary or capital), and treatment for income tax purposes.

TAX FORMULA

Most individuals compute taxable income using the tax formula shown in Figure 3–1. Special provisions govern the computation of taxable income and the tax liability for certain minor children who have unearned income in excess of specified amounts. These provisions are discussed under Tax Deter-

FIGURE 3–1	Tax Formula	
	Income (broadly conceived)	$xx,xxx
	Less: Exclusions	(x,xxx)
	Gross income	$xx,xxx
	Less: Deductions *for* adjusted gross income	(x,xxx)
	Adjusted gross income	$xx,xxx
	Less: The greater of— Total itemized deductions *or* standard deduction	(x,xxx)
	Personal and dependency exemptions (number of exemptions × $2,000 in 1989)	(x,xxx)
	Taxable income	$xx,xxx

---

1. The 1989 Tax Table was not available from the IRS at the date of publication of this text. The Tax Table for 1988 and the Tax Rate Schedules for 1988 and 1989 are reproduced in Appendix A.

mination—Unearned Income of Minor Children Taxed at Parents' Rate later in the chapter.

Before illustrating the application of the tax formula, a brief discussion of the components of the formula is necessary.

Components of the Tax Formula

Income (Broadly Conceived). This includes all income, both taxable and nontaxable, of the taxpayer. Although it is essentially equivalent to gross receipts, it does not include a return of capital or receipt of borrowed funds.

Exclusions. For various reasons, Congress has chosen to exclude certain types of income from the income tax base. The principal income exclusions are discussed in chapter 5. A partial list of these exclusions is shown in Figure 3–2.

Gross Income. Gross income is defined broadly in the Code as "all income from whatever source derived."[2] It includes, but is not limited to, the items shown in the partial list in Figure 3–3. It does not include unrealized gains. Gross income is discussed in chapters 4 and 5.

EXAMPLE 1

L received the following amounts in 1989:

Salary	$30,000
Interest on savings account	900
Gift from her aunt	10,000
Prize won in state lottery	1,000
Alimony from ex-husband	12,000
Child support from ex-husband	6,000
Damages for injury in auto accident	25,000

Review Figures 3–2 and 3–3 to determine the amount L must include in the computation of taxable income and the amount she may exclude. After you have determined these amounts, check the answer in footnote 3.[3] □

Deductions for Adjusted Gross Income. Individual taxpayers have two categories of deductions: (1) deductions *for* adjusted gross income (deductions to arrive at adjusted gross income) and (2) deductions *from* adjusted gross income.

Deductions *for* adjusted gross income include ordinary and necessary expenses incurred in a trade or business, employee business expenses if such expenses are reimbursed by the employer, alimony paid, certain payments to an Individual Retirement Account, forfeited interest penalty for premature withdrawal of time deposits, the capital loss deduction, and others.[4] The prin-

---

2. § 61(a).
3. L must include $43,900 in computing taxable income ($30,000 salary + $900 interest + $1,000 lottery prize + $12,000 alimony). She

can exclude $41,000 ($10,000 gift from aunt + $6,000 child support + $25,000 damages).

4. § 62. See chapter 7 for details.

cipal deductions *for* adjusted gross income are discussed in chapters 7, 8, 9, and 10.

FIGURE 3–2   Partial List of Exclusions from Gross Income

Accident insurance proceeds

Annuities (to a limited extent)

Bequests

Child support payments

Compensatory damages

Cost-of-living allowance (for military)

Damages for personal injury or sickness

Death benefits (up to $5,000)

Disability benefits

Gifts

Group term life insurance, premium paid by employer (coverage not over $50,000)

Inheritances

Life insurance paid on death

Meals and lodging (furnished for employer's convenience)

Military allowances

Minister's dwelling rental value allowance

Railroad retirement benefits (to a limited extent)

Scholarship grants (to a limited extent)

Social Security benefits (to a limited extent)

Veterans' benefits

Welfare payments

Workers' compensation benefits

FIGURE 3–3   Partial List of Gross Income Items

Alimony

Annuities

Awards

Back pay

Bargain purchase from employer

Bonuses

Breach of contract damages

Business income

Clergy fees

Commissions

Compensation for services

Death benefits in excess of $5,000

Debts forgiven

Director's fees

Dividends

Embezzled funds

Employee awards (in certain cases)

Employee benefits (except certain fringe benefits)

Employee bonuses

Estate and trust income

Farm income

Fees

Gains from illegal activities

Gains from sale of property

Gambling winnings

Group term life insurance, premium paid by employer (coverage over $50,000)

Hobby income

Interest

Jury duty fees

Living quarters, meals (unless furnished for employer's convenience)

Mileage allowance

Military pay (unless combat pay)

Notary fees

Partnership income

Pensions

Prizes

Professional fees

Punitive damages

Reimbursement for moving expenses

Rents

Rewards

Royalties

Salaries

Severance pay

Strike and lockout benefits

Supplemental unemployment benefits

Tips and gratuities

Travel allowance

Wages

Adjusted Gross Income. This is an important subtotal that serves as the basis for computing percentage limitations on certain itemized deductions, such as medical expenses and charitable contributions. For example, medical expenses are deductible only to the extent they exceed 7.5 percent of adjusted gross income.

EXAMPLE 2

T earned a salary of $23,000 in 1989. He contributed $2,000 to his Individual Retirement Account (IRA) and sustained a $1,000 capital loss on the sale of XYZ Corporation stock. His adjusted gross income (AGI) is computed as follows:

Gross income		
Salary		$23,000
Less: Deductions *for* AGI		
IRA contribution	$2,000	
Capital loss	1,000	3,000
AGI		$20,000

□

EXAMPLE 3

Assume the same facts as in Example 2 except that T also had medical expenses of $1,800 in 1989. Medical expenses may be included in itemized deductions to the extent they exceed 7.5% of AGI. In computing his itemized deductions, T may include medical expenses of $300 [$1,800 medical expenses − $1,500 (.075 × $20,000 AGI)]. □

Itemized Deductions. As a general rule, personal expenditures are disallowed as deductions in arriving at taxable income. However, Congress has chosen to allow certain specified expenses as itemized deductions, such as medical expenses and charitable contributions, even though they are personal in nature. In addition, taxpayers are allowed to itemize expenses related to (1) the production or collection of income; (2) the management of property held for the production of income; and (3) the determination, collection, or refund of any tax.[5] Itemized deductions (discussed in chapter 11) include, but are not limited to, the expenses listed in Figure 3–4.

Standard Deduction. The standard deduction is a specified amount set by Congress and is dependent on the filing status of the taxpayer. The effect of the standard deduction is to exempt a taxpayer's income, up to the specified amount, from Federal income tax liability. In the past, Congress has attempted to set the tax-free amount represented by the standard deduction

5. § 212.

FIGURE 3–4	Partial List of Itemized Deductions

Medical expenses in excess of 7.5% of AGI

State and local income taxes

Real estate taxes

Personal property taxes

Interest on home mortgage

Investment interest (to a limited extent)

Charitable contributions

Casualty and theft losses in excess of 10% of AGI

Moving expenses

Miscellaneous expenses (to the extent such expenses exceed 2% of AGI)

    Union dues

    Professional dues and subscriptions

    Certain educational expenses

    Tax return preparation fee

    Investment counsel fees

    Unreimbursed employee business expenses (after 20% reduction for meals and entertainment)

approximately equal to an estimated poverty level,[6] but it has not always been consistent in doing so.

The standard deduction is the sum of two components: the basic standard deduction and the additional standard deduction.[7] Figure 3–5 lists the basic standard deduction allowed for taxpayers in each filing status. All taxpayers who are allowed a standard deduction will be entitled to the applicable amount listed in Figure 3–5. The standard deduction amounts are subject to adjustment for inflation each year.[8]

FIGURE 3–5	Basic Standard Deduction Amounts

Filing Status	Standard Deduction Amount	
	1989	1988
Single	$3,100	$3,000
Married, filing jointly	5,200	5,000
Surviving spouse	5,200	5,000
Head of household	4,550	4,400
Married, filing separately	2,600	2,500

6. S.Rep. No. 92–437, 92nd Cong., 1st Sess., 1971, p. 54. Another purpose of the standard deduction was discussed in chapter 1 under Influence of the Internal Revenue Service—Administrative Feasibility. The size of the standard deduction has a direct bearing on the number of taxpayers who are in a position to itemize deductions. A reduction of such taxpayers, in turn, requires less audit effort on the part of the IRS.

7. § 63(c)(1).

8. § 63(c)(4). In 1989, applying the "rounding down" provision of § 1(f)(6), the basic standard deduction was adjusted for inflation; the additional standard deduction was not.

A taxpayer who is age 65 or over *or* blind qualifies for an additional standard deduction. Two additional standard deductions are allowed for a taxpayer who is age 65 or over *and* blind. The additional standard deduction provisions apply for a qualifying spouse who is age 65 or over or blind, but not for dependents. The additional standard deduction amounts are listed in Figure 3–6.

FIGURE 3–6   Additional Standard Deduction Amounts

Filing Status	Amount of Each Additional Standard Deduction
Single	$750
Married, filing jointly	600
Surviving spouse	600
Head of household	750
Married, filing separately	600

The total standard deduction (the sum of the basic standard deduction and any additional standard deductions) is compared to total itemized deductions to determine whether or not the taxpayer will itemize. Taxpayers are allowed to deduct the greater of itemized deductions or the standard deduction. Taxpayers whose itemized deductions are less than the standard deduction will compute their taxable income using the standard deduction rather than itemizing.

EXAMPLE 4   T, who is single, is 66 years old. She had total itemized deductions of $3,600 during 1989. Her total standard deduction is $3,850 ($3,100 basic standard deduction plus $750 additional standard deduction). T will compute her taxable income for 1989 using the standard deduction ($3,850), since it exceeds her itemized deductions ($3,600). □

Exemptions.   Exemptions are allowed for the taxpayer, the taxpayer's spouse, and for each dependent of the taxpayer. The exemption amount is $1,950 in 1988 and $2,000 in 1989.

Application of the Tax Formula

The tax formula shown in Figure 3–1 is illustrated in Example 5.

EXAMPLE 5   J, age 25, is single and has no dependents. She is a high school teacher and earned an $18,000 salary in 1989. Her other income consisted of a $1,000 prize won in a sweepstakes contest she had entered and $500 interest on municipal bonds received as a graduation gift in 1986. During 1989, she sustained a deductible capital loss of $1,000. Her itemized deductions were $3,800. J's taxable income for the year is computed as follows:

Income (broadly conceived)		
Salary		$18,000
Prize		1,000
Interest on municipal bonds		500
		$19,500
Less: Exclusion—		
Interest on municipal bonds		(500)
Gross income		$19,000
Less: Deduction *for* adjusted gross income—		
Capital loss		(1,000)
Adjusted gross income		$18,000
Less: The greater of—		
Total itemized deductions	$3,800	
or standard deduction	$3,100	(3,800)
Personal and dependency exemptions (1 × $2,000)		(2,000)
Taxable income		$12,200

□

The structure of the individual income tax return (Form 1040, 1040A, or 1040EZ) differs somewhat from the tax formula in Figure 3–1. On the tax return, gross income generally is the starting point in computing taxable income. With few exceptions, exclusions are not reported on the tax return.

Individuals Not Eligible for the Standard Deduction

The following individual taxpayers are ineligible to use the standard deduction and must therefore itemize: [9]

- A married individual filing a separate return where either spouse itemizes deductions.
- A nonresident alien.
- An individual making a return for a period of less than 12 months because of a change in annual accounting period.

Special Limitations for Individuals Who Can Be Claimed as Dependents

Special rules apply to the standard deduction and personal exemption of an individual who can be claimed as a dependent on another person's tax return.

9. § 63(c)(6).

When filing his or her own tax return, a dependent's basic standard deduction is limited to the greater of $500 or the individual's earned income for the year.[10] However, if the individual's earned income exceeds the normal standard deduction, the standard deduction is limited to the appropriate standard deduction amount shown in Figure 3–5. These limitations apply only to the basic standard deduction. A dependent who is 65 or over or blind or both is also allowed the additional standard deduction amount (refer to Figure 3–6). These provisions are illustrated in Examples 6 through 12.

EXAMPLE 6	M, who is 17 years old and single, is claimed as a dependent on her parents' tax return. During 1989, she received $900 interest (unearned income) on a savings account. She also earned $400 from a part-time job. When M files her own tax return, her standard deduction is $500 (the greater of $500 or earned income of $400). □
EXAMPLE 7	Assume the same facts as in Example 6, except that M is 67 years old and is claimed as a dependent on her son's tax return. In this case when M files her own tax return, her standard deduction is $1,250 [$500 (the greater of $500 or earned income of $400) + $750 (the additional standard deduction allowed because M is 65 or over)]. □
EXAMPLE 8	K, who is 18 years old and single, is claimed as a dependent on his parents' tax return. During 1989, he received interest (unearned income) of $1,400 on a savings account. Since he did not work during 1989, he had no earned income. K's standard deduction is $500 (the greater of $500 or earned income). □
EXAMPLE 9	Assume the same facts as in Example 8, except that K is blind. On his own tax return, K's standard deduction is $1,250 [$500 (the greater of $500 or earned income) + $750 (the additional standard deduction allowed because K is blind)]. □
EXAMPLE 10	P, who is 16 years old and single, earned $1,000 from a summer job and had no unearned income during 1989. She is claimed as a dependent on her parents' tax return. Her standard deduction for 1989 is $1,000 (the greater of $500 or earned income). □
EXAMPLE 11	J, who is a 20-year-old, single, full-time college student, is claimed as a dependent on his parents' tax return. During 1989, he received interest

---

10. § 63(c)(5). Although the $500 amount is subject to adjustment for inflation each year, the amount was not adjusted for 1989 because of the "rounding down" provisions of § 1(f)(6).

(unearned income) of $1,000 on a savings account. He worked during the summer as a musician, earning $3,600. J's standard deduction is $3,100 (the greater of $500 or $3,600 earned income, but limited to the $3,100 standard deduction for a single taxpayer). □

EXAMPLE 12   Assume the same facts as in Example 11, except that J is blind. On his own tax return, J's standard deduction is $3,850 [$3,100 (the greater of $500 or $3,600 earned income, but limited to the $3,100 standard deduction for a single taxpayer) + $750 (the additional standard deduction allowed because J is blind)]. □

The taxpayer who claims an individual as a dependent is allowed to claim an exemption for the dependent. The dependent cannot claim a personal exemption on his or her own return.

PERSONAL AND DEPENDENCY EXEMPTIONS

The use of exemptions in the tax system is based in part on the concept that a taxpayer with a small amount of income should be exempt from income taxation. An exemption frees a specified amount of income from tax ($1,950 in 1988 and $2,000 in 1989).[11] An individual who is not claimed as a dependent by another taxpayer is allowed to claim his or her own personal exemption. In addition, a taxpayer may claim an exemption for each dependent.

EXAMPLE 13   B, who is single, supports her mother and father, who have no income of their own, and claims them as dependents on her tax return. B may claim a personal exemption for herself plus an exemption for each dependent. On her 1989 tax return, B may deduct $6,000 for exemptions ($2,000 per exemption × 3 exemptions). □

Personal Exemptions

The Code provides a personal exemption for the taxpayer and an additional exemption for the spouse if a joint return is filed. However, when separate returns are filed, a married taxpayer cannot claim an exemption for his or her spouse unless the spouse has no gross income and is not claimed as the dependent of another taxpayer.

The determination of marital status generally is made at the end of the taxable year, except when a spouse dies during the year. Spouses who enter into a legal separation under a decree of divorce or separate maintenance before the end of the year are considered to be unmarried at the end of the taxable year. The effect of death or divorce upon marital status is illustrated as follows:

11. Beginning in 1990, the exemption amount will be indexed (adjusted) for inflation.

	Marital Status for 1989
1. W is the widow of H who dies on January 3, 1989.	W and H are considered to be married for purposes of filing the 1989 return.
2. W and H entered into a divorce decree that is effective on December 31, 1989.	They are considered to be unmarried for purposes of filing the 1989 return.

Dependency Exemptions

As indicated in Example 13, the Code allows a taxpayer to claim a dependency exemption for each eligible individual. A dependency exemption may be claimed for each individual for whom the following five tests are met:

- Support.
- Relationship or member of the household.
- Gross income.
- Joint return.
- Citizenship or residency.

Support Test. Over one-half of the support of the individual must be furnished by the taxpayer. Support includes food, shelter, clothing, medical and dental care, education, etc. However, a scholarship received by a student is not included for purposes of computing whether the taxpayer furnished more than one-half of the child's support.[12]

EXAMPLE 14

H contributed $2,500 (consisting of food, clothing, and medical care) toward the support of his son, S, who earned $1,500 from a part-time job and received a $2,000 scholarship to attend a local university. Assuming that the other dependency tests are met, H may claim S as a dependent since he has contributed more than one-half of S's support. The $2,000 scholarship is not included as support for purposes of this test. □

If the individual does not spend funds that have been received from any source, such unexpended amounts are not counted for purposes of the support test. For example Social Security benefits received by the individual are not considered in applying the support test if such amounts are not spent on items considered *support*.

EXAMPLE 15

S contributed $2,000 toward his father's support during the year. His father received $1,800 in Social Security benefits and $300 of dividend income. All of these amounts were used for his support during the year.

12. Reg. § 1.152–1(c).

Since the Social Security payments expended for support are considered in the determination of whether the support test has been met, S cannot claim his father as a dependent because he has not contributed more than one-half of the total support. □

EXAMPLE 16

S contributed $3,000 to her father's support during the year. In addition, her father received $2,400 in Social Security benefits, $200 of interest, and wages of $600. The Social Security benefits, interest, and wages were deposited in the father's savings account and were not used for his support. Thus, the Social Security benefits, interest, and wages are not considered as support provided by S's father, and S may claim her father as a dependent if the other tests are met. ⊔

Capital expenditures for items such as furniture, appliances, and automobiles are included in total support if the item does, in fact, constitute support.[13]

EXAMPLE 17

F purchased a television set costing $150 and gave it to his minor daughter. The television set was placed in the child's bedroom and was used exclusively by her. F should include the cost of the television set in determining the support of his daughter. □

EXAMPLE 18

F paid $6,000 for an automobile that was titled and registered in his name. F's minor son is permitted to use the automobile equally with F. Since F did not give the automobile to his son, the $6,000 cost is not includible as a support item. However, the out-of-pocket operating expenses for the benefit of the child are includible as support.[14] □

One exception to the support test is based on the existence of a *multiple support agreement*. A multiple support agreement permits one of a group of taxpayers who furnish more than one-half of the support of an individual to claim a dependency exemption for that individual even if no one person provides more than 50 percent of the support.[15] Any person who contributed more than 10 percent of the support is entitled to claim the exemption if each person in the group who contributed more than 10 percent files a written consent. This provision frequently enables one of the children of aged dependent parents to claim an exemption when none of the children meets the 50 percent support test. Each person who is a party to the multiple support agreement must meet all other requirements (except the support requirement) for claiming the exemption. A person who does not meet the relationship or member of household requirement, for instance, cannot claim the

---

13. Rev.Rul. 57–344, 1957–2 C.B. 112; Rev.Rul. 58–419, 1958–2 C.B. 57.

14. *Your Federal Income Tax*, IRS Publication 17 (Rev. Nov. 88), p. 24.

15. § 152(c).

dependency exemption under a multiple support agreement, even though he or she contributes more than 10 percent of the individual's support.

EXAMPLE 19

M, who resides with her son, received $6,000 from various sources during 1989. This constituted her entire support for the year. The support was received from the following:

	Amount	Percentage of Total
A, a son	$2,880	48
B, a son	600	10
C, a daughter	1,800	30
D, a friend	720	12
	$6,000	100

If they file a multiple support agreement, either A or C may claim the dependency exemption for M. B may not claim M because he did not contribute more than 10% of her support, nor would B's consent be required in order for A and C to file a multiple support agreement. D does not meet the relationship or member of household test and therefore cannot be a party to the multiple support agreement. The decision as to who claims M will rest with A and C. It is possible for C to claim M, even though A furnished more of M's support. □

A second exception to the 50 percent support requirement can occur for a child of parents who are divorced or separated under a decree of separate maintenance. Under decrees executed after 1984, the custodial parent is allowed to claim the exemption unless that parent agrees in writing not to claim a dependency exemption for the child.[16.] Thus, claiming the exemption is dependent on whether or not a written agreement exists, not on meeting the support test.

EXAMPLE 20

H and W obtain a divorce decree in 1988. In 1989, their two children are in the custody of W. H contributed over half of the support for each child. Absent any written agreement relative to the dependency exemptions, W is entitled to the exemptions in 1989. However, H may claim the exemptions if W agrees in writing that he may do so. □

For the noncustodial parent to claim the exemption, the custodial parent must complete Form 8332 (Release of Claim to Exemption for Child of Divorced or Separated Parents). The release can apply to a single year, a number of specified years, or all future years. The noncustodial parent must attach a

---

16.   § 152(e).

copy of Form 8332 to his or her return. Form 8332 is not required, however, if there is a pre-1985 agreement that allows the noncustodial parent to claim the exemption and the noncustodial parent provides at least $600 of support for each child.

Relationship or Member of the Household Test.   To be a dependent, the individual must be either a relative of the taxpayer or a member of the taxpayer's household. The Code contains a detailed listing of the various blood and marriage relationships that qualify. Note, however, that the relationship test is met if the individual is a relative of either spouse and a relationship, once established by marriage, continues regardless of subsequent changes in marital status.

The following individuals may be claimed as dependents of the taxpayer if the other tests for dependency are met:[17]

1. A son or daughter of the taxpayer, or a descendant of either (grandchild).

2. A stepson or stepdaughter of the taxpayer.

3. A brother, sister, stepbrother, or stepsister of the taxpayer.

4. The father or mother of the taxpayer, or an ancestor of either (grand-parent).

5. A stepfather or stepmother of the taxpayer.

6. A son or daughter of a brother or sister (nephew or niece) of the tax-payer.

7. A brother or sister of the father or mother (uncle or aunt) of the tax-payer.

8. A son-in-law, daughter-in-law, father-in-law, mother-in-law, brother-in-law, or sister-in-law of the taxpayer.

9. An individual (other than an individual who at any time during the entire taxable year was the spouse of the taxpayer) who, for the entire taxable year of the taxpayer, has as his or her principal place of abode the home of the taxpayer and is a member of the taxpayer's household.

The following rules are also prescribed in the Code: [18]

*   A legally adopted child is treated as a natural child.

*   A foster child qualifies if the child has his or her principal place of abode in the taxpayer's household.

Gross Income Test.   The dependent's gross income must be less than the exemption amount ($2,000 in 1989) unless the dependent is a child of the taxpayer and is under 19 or a full-time student under the age of 24.[19] A parent

17. § 152(a). However, under § 152(b)(5), a taxpayer may not claim someone who is a member of his or her household as a dependent if their relationship is in violation of local law. For example, the dependency exemption was denied because the taxpayer's relationship to the person claimed as a dependent constituted *cohabitation*, a crime under applicable state law. *Cas-*

sius L. Peacock, III, 37 TCM 177, T.C. Memo. 1978–30.

18. § 152(b)(2).

19. § 151(c)(1) as amended by the Technical and Miscellaneous Revenue Act of 1988, effective for tax years beginning after 1988.

who provides over half of the support of a child who, at the end of the year, is under 19 or is a full-time student under 24 may claim a dependency exemption for such child. However, the dependent child may not claim a personal exemption on his or her own income tax return.

A child is defined as a son, stepson, daughter, stepdaughter, adopted son, or adopted daughter and may include a foster child.[20] For the child to qualify as a student for purposes of the dependency exemption, he or she must be a full-time student at an educational institution during some part of five calendar months of the year.[21] This exception to the gross income test for dependent children who are under 19 or full-time students under 24 permits a child or college student to earn money from part-time or summer jobs without penalizing the parent with the loss of the dependency exemption.

Joint Return Test.   If a dependent is married, the supporting taxpayer (e.g., the parent of a married child) is not permitted a dependency exemption if the married individual files a joint return with his or her spouse.[22] However, if neither the dependent nor the dependent's spouse is required to file a return but they file a joint return solely to claim a refund of all tax withheld and no tax liability would exist for either spouse on separate returns, the joint return rule does not apply.

EXAMPLE 21   P provides over half of the support of his son J. He also provides over half of the support of M, who is J's wife. In 1989, J had wages of $1,500, and M earned $1,800. J and M file a joint return for the year. Neither J nor M was required to file a return. P is allowed to claim both as dependents.

□

Citizenship or Residency Test.   To be a dependent, the individual must be either a U.S. citizen, resident, or national or a resident of Canada or Mexico for some part of the calendar year in which the tax year of the taxpayer claiming the exemption begins.

TAX DETERMINATION

Tax Table Method

Most taxpayers compute their tax using the Tax Table. Taxpayers who are eligible to use the Tax Table compute taxable income (as shown in Figure 3–1) and determine their tax by reference to the Tax Table. Certain taxpayers, however, may not use this method:

- An individual who files a short period return (see chapter 18).

- Individuals whose taxable income exceeds the maximum (ceiling) amount in the Tax Table. The 1988 Tax Table applies to taxable income below $50,000.

- An estate or trust.

---

20. Reg. § 1.151–3(a).
21. Reg. §§ 1.151–3(b) and (c).

22. § 151(c)(2).

The 1989 Tax Table was not available at the date of publication of this text. Therefore, the 1988 Tax Table will be used to illustrate the tax computation using the Tax Table method.

EXAMPLE 22

B, a single taxpayer, is eligible to use the Tax Table. For 1988, B had taxable income of $25,025. To determine B's tax using the Tax Table (see Appendix A), find the $25,000 to $25,050 income line. The first column to the right of the taxable income column is for single taxpayers. B's tax for 1988 is $4,687. □

Tax Rate Schedule Method

There are only two brackets for each filing status (15 percent and 28 percent). The 28 percent rate applies to taxable income above the following levels:

Filing Status	28% Rate Applies to Taxable Income Over
Single	$18,550
Head of household	24,850
Married, filing jointly	30,950
Married, filing separately	15,475

The 15 percent rate applies to taxable income less than or equal to these amounts. The 1989 Tax Rate Schedules are reproduced in Appendix A.

Use of the 1989 Tax Rate Schedule for a married couple filing jointly is illustrated in the following example.

EXAMPLE 23

B and D, who are married, file a joint return for 1989. They had taxable income of $35,950. Their tax is computed as follows:

Tax on $30,950 at 15%	$4,642.50
28% tax on $5,000 ($35,950 − $30,950)	1,400.00
Total tax liability	$6,042.50

The *marginal rate* (the highest rate applied in computing the tax) for B and D is 28%. Their *average rate* (the tax liability divided by taxable income) is 16.81% ($6,042.50/$35,950). □

Bracket Phase-Out.   Although the 1989 tax computation illustrated in Example 23 is quite simple, the computation can be much more complex for higher income taxpayers. This complexity arises because the benefit of the 15 percent bracket is phased out for taxpayers above specified income levels. The *bracket phase-out* is accomplished by imposing an additional tax liability (surtax) on the taxpayer. The additional tax is 5 percent of taxable income within the ranges specified in Figure 3–7.

FIGURE 3–7   1989 Phase-Out Ranges for 15% Bracket

	Filing Status			
	Single	Head of Household	Married, Joint *	Married, Separate
5% of taxable income from–to	$44,900– 93,130	$64,200– 128,810	$74,850– 155,320	$37,425– 117,895

* Also applies to surviving spouse.

The phase-out ranges are set so that the benefit from having the first level of income taxed at the 15 percent rate is phased out if taxable income is at the top of the range. The computation of the phase-out range for a single taxpayer is illustrated in Example 24.

EXAMPLE 24   A 28% bracket taxpayer saves 13% (28% − 15%) on all income taxed at 15%. This tax saving is recaptured through the bracket phase-out computation. The end point of the phase-out range for a single taxpayer is computed as follows:

Benefit of 15% bracket = .13 × $18,550 = $2,411.50
Taxable income to recapture benefit = $2,411.50/.05 = $48,230
$44,900 (bottom of range) + $48,230 = $93,130 (top of range)   □

Except for married taxpayers filing separately, taxpayers with taxable income that equals or exceeds the top of the phase-out range will pay a flat tax of 28 percent on all taxable income through the end of the bracket phase-out range.

EXAMPLE 25   H is single and has taxable income of $93,130 in 1989. This places her at the top of the bracket phase-out range. Her tax is computed as follows:

.15 × $18,550 =	$ 2,782.50
.28 × ($93,130 − $18,550) =	20,882.40
.05 × ($93,130 − $44,900) =	2,411.50
Total	$26,076.40

Double-check: $93,130 × .28 = $26,076.40

□

Note in Example 25 that all income in the phase-out range was taxed first at the 28 percent rate, with the additional 5 percent tax then added. Thus, the marginal tax rate on income in the bracket phase-out range is 33 percent. On taxable income beyond the top of the bracket phase-out range and exemption phase-out range (discussed below), the marginal rate drops back to 28 percent.

Exemption Phase-Out.   The exemption amounts deducted on a tax return are also subject to phase-out. The decrease in tax that results for each exemption claimed by a 28 percent bracket taxpayer is calculated in the following example.

EXAMPLE 26   Z, who is single, claims one exemption on her 1989 tax return. She has taxable income of $25,000 for the year. This places her in the 28% tax bracket. Therefore, as a result of deducting $2,000 for her exemption, she saves tax of $560 ($2,000 exemption × .28). ☐

The exemption phase-out begins once the bracket phase-out is completed (when taxable income exceeds $93,130 for single taxpayers, $128,810 for heads of household, $155,320 for married taxpayers filing jointly, and $117,895 for married taxpayers filing separately).

EXAMPLE 27   Assume the same facts as in Example 26. Because Z's taxable income does not exceed $93,130, the exemption phase-out is not required for Z. ☐

The exemption phase-out is accomplished by assessing an additional 5 percent tax on enough taxable income to recover the tax saved as a result of taking the exemption deduction. To phase out the benefit of the exemption deduction completely in 1989, it is necessary to assess additional tax of $560 (refer to Example 26). Therefore, $11,200 of taxable income ($11,200 × .05 exemption phase-out rate = $560 tax) is subject to the additional 5 percent tax for each exemption claimed.

EXAMPLE 28   Z, who is single, claims one exemption on her 1989 tax return. Z's taxable income in 1989 is $110,480. Because her taxable income exceeds $93,130, Z is subject to the exemption phase-out. Her tax for 1989 is computed as follows:

Tax on $18,550 at 15%	$ 2,782.50
Tax on ($110,480 − $18,550) at 28%	25,740.40
Bracket phase-out [($93,130 − $44,900) × .05]	2,411.50
Exemption phase-out ($11,200 × .05)	560.00
Total tax	$31,494.40

If Z had claimed two exemptions, the 5% exemption phase-out tax would have been applied to $17,350 ($110,480 − $93,130). ☐

Examination of Example 28 shows that the 5 percent exemption phase-out tax applies to the lesser of (1) $11,200 times the number of personal and dependency exemptions claimed or (2) taxable income minus the amount at the top of the bracket phase-out range.

In the case of married taxpayers filing separate returns, the additional tax liability because of the exemption phase-out is determined as if the taxpayer were allowed a personal exemption for his or her spouse.[23] This prevents married taxpayers from avoiding the full effect of the phase-out of personal exemptions by filing separate returns.

Computation of Net Taxes Payable or Refund Due

The pay-as-you-go feature of the Federal income tax system requires payment of all or part of the taxpayer's income tax liability during the year. These payments take the form of Federal income tax withheld by employers or estimated tax paid by the taxpayer or both. These amounts are applied against the tax from the Tax Table or Tax Rate Schedules to determine whether the taxpayer will get a refund or pay additional tax.

Employers are required to withhold income tax on compensation paid to their employees and to pay this tax over to the government. The employer notifies the employee of the amount of income tax withheld on Form W–2 (Wage and Tax Statement). The employee should receive this form by January 31 after the year in which the income tax is withheld.

Estimated tax must be paid by taxpayers who receive income that is not subject to withholding or income from which not enough tax is being withheld. These individuals must file Form 1040–ES (Estimated Tax for Individuals) and pay in quarterly installments the income tax and self-employment tax estimated to be due (see chapter 13 for a thorough discussion).

The income tax from the Tax Table or the Tax Rate Schedules is reduced first by the individual's tax credits. There is an important distinction between tax credits and tax deductions. Tax credits reduce the tax liability dollar-for-dollar. Tax deductions reduce taxable income on which the tax liability is based.

EXAMPLE 29

L is a taxpayer in the 28% tax bracket. As a result of incurring $1,000 in child care expenses (see chapter 13 for details), she is entitled to a $200 child care credit ($1,000 child care expenses × 20% credit rate). L also contributed $1,000 to the American Cancer Society and included this amount in her itemized deductions. The child care credit results in a $200 reduction of L's tax liability for the year. The contribution to the American Cancer Society reduces taxable income and results in a $280 reduction in L's tax liability ($1,000 reduction in taxable income × 28% tax rate). □

Tax credits are discussed in chapter 13. Several of the more common credits are as follows:

- Earned income credit.
- Credit for child and dependent care expenses.
- Credit for the elderly.
- Foreign tax credit.

23. § 1(g) as amended by the Technical and Miscellaneous Revenue Act of 1988.

Computation of an individual's net tax payable or refund due is illustrated in Examples 30 and 31.

EXAMPLE 30

Y, age 30, is a head of household taxpayer with two dependents. During 1989, Y had the following: taxable income, $30,000; income tax withheld, $4,100; estimated tax payments, $800; and credit for child care expenses, $200. Y's net tax payable is computed as follows:

Income tax (from 1989 Tax Rate Schedule, Appendix A, rounded)		$5,170
Less: Tax credits and prepayments—		
Credit for child care expenses	$ 200	
Income tax withheld	4,100	
Estimated tax payments	800	(5,100)
Net taxes payable or (refund due)		$ 70

□

EXAMPLE 31

Assume the same facts as in Example 30, except that income tax withheld was $4,300. Y's refund due is computed as follows:

Income tax		$5,170
Less: Tax credits and prepayments—		
Credit for child care expenses	$ 200	
Income tax withheld	4,300	
Estimated tax payments	800	(5,300)
Net taxes payable or (refund due)		$ (130)

□

Unearned Income of Minor Children Taxed at Parents' Rate

Before the Tax Reform Act (TRA) of 1986, a dependent child could claim an exemption on his or her own return even if claimed as a dependent by the parents.

EXAMPLE 32

In 1986, H and W established a savings account for their dependent child K, age 9. K, who had no other income, earned interest of $1,050 on the account during 1986. K's taxable income for 1986 was zero, because the interest of $1,050 was offset by K's exemption of $1,080 (the exemption amount applicable to 1986). □

Example 32 illustrates the pre-1987 use of a child's exemption to shelter unearned income from taxation. For pre-1987 years, an additional tax motivation existed for shifting income from parents to children. Although a child's unearned income in excess of the exemption amount was subject to tax, it was subject to tax at the child's rate.

EXAMPLE 33

Assume the same facts as in Example 32, except that K's interest income for 1986 was $5,000. Assume further that K's parents were in the 50% tax bracket (the top rate applicable to 1986). K's tax on the interest would have been $495. Had his parents kept the funds in their account, their tax would have been $2,500 ($5,000 interest × 50% tax rate). The income shifting procedure would have resulted in tax savings for the family of $2,005 ($2,500 tax at parents' rate minus $495 tax at child's rate). □

To reduce the tax savings that can result from shifting income from parents to children, the net unearned income (commonly called investment income) of certain minor children is taxed as if parent's income.[24] Unearned income includes such income as taxable interest, dividends, capital gains, rents, royalties, pension and annuity income, and income (other than earned income) received as the beneficiary of a trust. This provision, commonly referred to as the *kiddie tax*, applies to any child for any taxable year if the child has not reached age 14 by the close of the taxable year, has at least one living parent, and has unearned income of more than $1,000. The *kiddie tax* provision does not apply to a child 14 or older. However, the limitation on the use of the standard deduction and the unavailability of the personal exemption do apply to such child as long as the child is eligible to be claimed as a dependent by a parent.

The term *parent* is defined in the Senate Finance Committee Report as a parent or stepparent of the child. No statutory definition exists for the term.

Net Unearned Income. Net unearned income of a dependent child is computed as follows:

Unearned income

Less: $500

Less: The greater of

- $500 of the standard deduction *or*

- The amount of allowable itemized deductions directly connected with the production of the unearned income

Equals: Net unearned income

---

24. § 1(i) as amended by the Technical and Miscellaneous Revenue Act of 1988.

If net unearned income is zero (or negative), the child's tax is computed without using the parent's rate. If the amount of net unearned income (regardless of source) is positive, the net unearned income will be taxed at the parent's rate. The $500 amounts in the preceding formula are subject to adjustment for inflation each year (refer to footnote 10).

Election to Claim Certain Unearned Income on Parent's Return.   If all of the following requirements are met concerning a child under 14, the parent may elect to report the child's unearned income on the parent's own tax return. The child, then, is treated as having no gross income and is not required to file a tax return.

- Gross income is from interest and dividends only.

- Gross income is more than $500 and less than $5,000.

- No estimated tax has been paid in the name and Social Security number of the child and the child is not subject to backup withholding (see chapter 13).

The parent(s) must also pay an additional tax equal to the smaller of $75 or 15% of the child's gross income over $500. If any of the interest is from certain private activity bonds, that amount is a tax preference to the parents for purposes of the parent's alternative minimum tax (see chapter 12).

Tax Determination.   If a child under age 14 has net unearned income and the parental election either is not or cannot be made, the tax on the net unearned income (defined as "allocable parental tax") must be computed as though included in the parent's return and allocated to the child. Form 8615 (see Appendix B) is used to compute the tax. The steps required in this computation are illustrated in the following example.

EXAMPLE 34   H and W have two children, S (age 10) and D (age 8). In 1989, S received $2,500 of interest and dividend income, and D received $1,950 of interest and dividend income. Investment-related fees paid by S and D were $200 and $125, respectively. H and W had $69,450 of taxable income, not including their children's passive income. H and W do not make the parental election.

1. Determine net unearned income.

	S	D
Gross income	$2,500	$ 1,950
Less: $500	(500)	(500)
Less: The greater of		
• $500 or		
• Investment expense	(500)	(500)
Equals: Net unearned income	$1,500	$ 950

2. Determine allocable parental tax.

Parent's taxable income	$69,450
Plus: Net unearned income (S's $1,500 + D's $950)	2,450
Equals: Revised taxable income	$71,900
Tax (rounded)	$16,109
Less: Tax on parent's taxable income	(15,423)
Allocable parental tax	$ 686

3. Allocate parental tax.[25]

Son: $\frac{\$1,500}{\$2,450} \times \$686 = \underline{\$420}$

Daughter: $\frac{\$\ 950}{\$2,450} \times \$686 = \underline{\$266}$

4. Determine children's nonparental source tax.

	S	D
Adjusted gross income	$2,500	$1,950
Less: Standard deduction	(500)	(500)
Less: Personal exemption	(–0–)	(–0–)
Equals: Taxable income	$2,000	$1,450
Less: Net unearned income	(1,500)	(950)
Nonparental source taxable income	$ 500	$ 500
Equals: Tax ($500 × .15 rate)	$ 75	$ 75

5. Determine total tax liability.

	S	D
Nonparental source tax (Step 4)	$ 75	$ 75
Allocated parental tax (Step 3)	420	266
Total tax	$ 495	$ 341

□

EXAMPLE 35   Assume the same facts as in Example 34, except that the parents elect to claim on their own tax return the unearned income of S and D. The gross income in excess of $1,000 for each child amounts to $2,450 [$1,500 ($2,500 − $1,000) for S + $950 ($1,950 − $1,000) for D]. The parents include this amount in gross income. Their taxable income increases from $69,450 to $71,900, resulting in a tax liability of $686 more than would result on the parents' taxable income alone. These amounts are the same as those in Step 2 of Example 34. To their tax liability the parents

---

25. On Form 8615, the decimal for allocation of this tax among the children is carried to two places. Following the Form 8615 procedure would result in allocating $418 ($686 × .61) to S and $268 to D ($686 × .39).

must add for each child the lesser of $75 or 15% of gross income over $500. Thus, they must include $75 [the smaller of $75 or 15% of $2,000 ($2,500 − $500)] for S and $75 [the smaller of $75 or 15% of $1,450 ($1,950 − $500)] for D. The following total tax for the family unit results:

	Without Election	With Election
H and W	$15,423	$16,259*
S	495	–0–
D	341	–0–
	$16,259	$16,259

* $16,109 + $75 + $75.

Although in this case no tax saving results, the number of tax returns required to be filed is reduced from three to one. □

Other Provisions.   For children of divorced parents, the taxable income of the custodial parent is used to determine the allocable parental tax and this parent is the one who may elect to claim the child's unearned income. For married individuals filing separate returns, the individual with the greater taxable income is the applicable parent.

FILING CONSIDERATIONS

Under the category of filing considerations, the following questions need to be resolved:

- Is the taxpayer required to file an income tax return?
- If so, which form should be used?
- When and how should the return be filed?
- In computing the tax liability, which column of the Tax Table or which Tax Rate Schedule should be used?

The first three of these questions are discussed under Filing Considerations—Filing Requirements. The last question is treated under Filing Considerations—Filing Status.

Filing Requirements

General Rules.   An individual must file a tax return if certain minimum amounts of gross income have been received. The general rule is that a tax return is required for every individual who has taxable income that equals or exceeds the sum of the exemption amount plus the applicable standard deduction.[26] For example, a single taxpayer under age 65 must file a tax return in 1989 if gross income equals or exceeds $5,100 ($2,000 exemption plus $3,100 standard deduction).

Figure 3–8 lists the income levels [27] that require tax returns under the general rule, and also lists amounts that require tax returns under certain special rules.

The additional standard deduction for being 65 or older is taken into consideration in determining the gross income filing requirements. For example, note in Figure 3–8 that the 1989 filing requirement for a single taxpayer 65 or older is $5,850 ($3,100 basic standard deduction + $750 additional standard deduction + $2,000 exemption). However, the additional standard deduction for blindness is not taken into account. The 1989 filing requirement for a single taxpayer under 65 and blind is $5,100 ($3,100 basic standard deduction + $2,000 exemption).

Filing Requirements for Dependents. Computation of the gross income filing requirement for an individual who can be claimed as a dependent on another person's tax return is subject to more complex rules. Such an individual must file a return if he or she has either of the following:

- Earned income only and gross income that is more than the total standard deduction (including any additional standard deduction) that the individual is allowed for the year.

FIGURE 3–8   Filing Levels

Filing Status	1989 Gross Income	1988 Gross Income
Single		
Under 65 and not blind	$ 5,100	$ 4,950
Under 65 and blind	5,100	4,950
65 or older	5,850	5,700
Married filing joint return		
Both spouses under 65 and neither blind	$ 9,200	$ 8,900
Both spouses under 65 and one or both spouses blind	9,200	8,900
One spouse 65 or older	9,800	9,500
Both spouses 65 or older	10,400	10,100
Married filing separate return		
All—whether 65 or older or blind	$ 2,000	$ 1,950
Head of household		
Under 65 and not blind	$ 6,550	$ 6,350
Under 65 and blind	6,550	6,350
65 or older	7,300	7,100
Qualifying widow(er)		
Under 65 and not blind	$ 7,200	$ 6,950
Under 65 and blind	7,200	6,950
65 or older	7,800	7,550

---

26. The gross income amounts for determining whether a tax return must be filed will be adjusted for inflation each year.

27. § 6012(a)(1).

- Unearned income only and gross income of more than $500, plus any additional standard deduction that the individual is allowed for the year.

- Both earned and unearned income and gross income of more than the larger of earned income (but limited to the applicable basic standard deduction) or $500, plus any additional standard deduction that the individual is allowed for the year.

Thus, the filing requirement for a dependent who has no unearned income is the total of the basic standard deduction plus *any* additional standard deduction, which includes the additional deduction for blindness. For example, the 1989 filing requirement for a single dependent who is under 65 and not blind is $3,100, the amount of the basic standard deduction for 1989. The filing requirement for a single dependent under 65 and blind is $3,850 ($3,100 basic standard deduction + $750 additional standard deduction).

A self-employed individual with net earnings from a business or profession of $400 or more must file a tax return regardless of the amount of gross income.

Even though an individual's gross income is below the filing level amounts and he or she does not therefore owe any tax, the individual will have to file a return to obtain a tax refund of amounts that have been withheld. A return is also necessary to obtain the benefits of the earned income credit allowed to taxpayers with little or no tax liability. Chapter 13 discusses the earned income credit.

Selecting the Proper Form.   The 1989 tax forms had not been published at the date of publication of this text. The following comments apply to 1988 forms. It is possible that some provisions will change with respect to the 1989 forms.

Individual taxpayers file a return on either Form 1040, Form 1040A, or Form 1040EZ (see Appendix B). Form 1040A is a short form that is used by many taxpayers who have uncomplicated tax situations. In 1988, an individual was required to use Form 1040 rather than Form 1040A for any of the following reasons: [28]

- Taxable income was $50,000 or more.

- The taxpayer had income other than wages, salaries, tips, unemployment compensation, dividends, or interest.

- The taxpayer claimed credits other than credits for child or dependent care or the earned income credit.

- The taxpayer was required to use the Tax Rate Schedules.

- The taxpayer claimed any deductions other than the deduction for payments to an IRA.

Form 1040EZ is also a form for taxpayers with uncomplicated tax situations. In 1988, this form could be used by single taxpayers with no dependents who satisfied all of the following requirements:

28. *Your Federal Income Tax,* IRS Publication 17 (Rev. Nov. 88), p. 12.

- Was not 65 or over or blind.

- Had taxable income of less than $50,000.

- Had only wages, salaries, tips, and taxable scholarships and had interest income of $400 or less.

- Did not itemize deductions, claim any adjustments to income, or claim any tax credits.

Taxpayers who could not use Form 1040EZ used either Form 1040 or Form 1040A.

When and Where to File.   Tax returns of individuals are due on or before the fifteenth day of the fourth month following the close of the tax year. For the calendar year taxpayer, therefore, the usual filing date is on or before April 15 of the following year.[29] When the due date falls on a Saturday, Sunday, or legal holiday, the last day for filing falls on the next business day. If the return is mailed to the proper address with sufficient postage and is postmarked on or before the due date, it is deemed to be timely filed.

If a taxpayer is unable to file his or her return by the specified due date, a four-month extension of time can be obtained by filing Form 4868 (Application for Automatic Extension of Time to File U.S. Individual Income Tax Return).[30] Further extensions may be granted by the IRS upon a showing by the taxpayer of good cause. For this purpose, Form 2688 (Application for Extension of Time to File U.S. Individual Income Tax Return) should be used. An extension of more than six months will not be granted if the taxpayer is in the United States.

Although obtaining an extension excuses a taxpayer from a penalty for failure to file, it does not insulate against the penalty for failure to pay.[31] If more tax is owed, the filing of Form 4868 should be accompanied by an additional remittance to cover the balance due.

The return should be sent or delivered to the Regional Service Center of the IRS for the area where the taxpayer lives.[32]

If it is necessary to file an amended return (e.g., because of a failure to report income or to claim a deduction or tax credit), Form 1040X is filed by individual taxpayers. The form is generally filed within three years of the filing date of the original return or within two years from the time the tax was paid, whichever is later.

Filing Status

The amount of tax will vary considerably depending on which Tax Rate Schedule is used. This is illustrated in the following example.

EXAMPLE 36   The following amounts of tax are computed using the 1989 Tax Rate Schedule for a taxpayer (or taxpayers in the case of a joint return) with $40,000 of taxable income (see Appendix A).

---

29. § 6072(a).
30. Reg. § 1.6081–4.
31. For an explanation of these penalties, refer to chapter 1.

32. The Regional Service Centers and the geographical area each covers can be found on the back cover of *Your Federal Income Tax*, IRS Publication 17 (Rev. Nov. 88).

Filing Status	Amount of Tax (rounded)
Single	$8,789
Married, filing joint return	7,177
Married, filing separate return	9,188
Head of household	7,970

□

Rates for Single Taxpayers.   A taxpayer who is unmarried or separated from his or her spouse by a decree of divorce or separate maintenance and does not qualify for another filing status must use the rates for single taxpayers. Marital status is determined as of the last day of the tax year, except when a spouse dies during the year. In such a case, marital status is determined as of the date of death. State law governs whether a taxpayer is considered married, divorced, or legally separated.

Under a special relief provision, however, it is possible for married persons who live apart to qualify as single. Married taxpayers who are considered single under the *abandoned spouse rules* are allowed to use the head of household rates. See the discussion of this filing status under Abandoned Spouse Rules.

Rates for Married Individuals.   The joint return [Tax Rate Schedule Y, Code § 1(a)] was originally enacted in 1948 to establish equity between married taxpayers in common law states and those in community property states. Before enactment of the joint return rates, taxpayers in community property states were in an advantageous position relative to taxpayers in common law states.

EXAMPLE 37   A and B are husband and wife. A earns a salary of $40,000. B is not employed. Before enactment of the joint return provisions, their income tax would vary significantly depending on whether they lived in a common law state or a community property state. If they lived in a common law state, A would report $40,000 of income on his tax return. However, if they lived in a community property state, A and B would each report $20,000 of income. Because the rate structure is progressive (the higher the income, the higher the tax rate), the tax paid by A and B would be higher in a common law state than in a community property state. □

Under the joint return Tax Rate Schedule, the progressive rates are constructed based on the assumption that income is earned equally by the two spouses.

If married individuals elect to file separate returns, each reports only his or her own income, exemptions, deductions, and credits, and each must use the Tax Rate Schedule applicable to married taxpayers filing separately. It is generally advantageous for married individuals to file a joint return, since the combined amount of tax is lower. However, special circumstances (e.g., significant medical expenses incurred by one spouse subject to the 7.5 percent limitation) may warrant the election to file separate returns.

The Code places some limitations on deductions, credits, etc., when married individuals file separately. If either spouse itemizes deductions, the other spouse must also itemize. Married taxpayers who file separately cannot take either of the following:

- The credit for child and dependent care expenses (in most instances).
- The earned income credit.

The joint return rates also apply for two years following the death of one spouse, providing the surviving spouse maintains a household for a dependent child.[33] This filing status is commonly referred to as surviving spouse status.

EXAMPLE 38   H dies in 1988 leaving W with a dependent child. For the year of H's death (1988), W files a joint return with H (presuming the consent of H's executor is obtained). For the next two years (1989 and 1990), W, as a surviving spouse, may use the joint return rates. In subsequent years, W may use the head-of-household rates if she maintains a household as her home that is the domicile of the child. □

Rates for Heads of Household.   Unmarried individuals who maintain a household for a dependent (or dependents) are entitled to use the head-of-household rates.[34] The tax liability using the head-of-household rates falls between the liability using the joint return Tax Rate Schedule and the liability using the Tax Rate Schedule for single taxpayers.

To qualify for head-of-household rates, a taxpayer must pay more than half the cost of maintaining a household as his or her home. The household must also be the principal home of a dependent relative as defined in § 152(a).[35] As a general rule, the dependent must live in the taxpayer's household for over half the year.

The general rule has two exceptions. One exception is that an unmarried child (child also means grandchild, stepchild, or adopted child) need not be a dependent in order for the taxpayer to qualify as a head of household. This exception also applies to a married child if the child is claimed by the noncustodial parent as a result of a written agreement between the custodial parent and the noncustodial parent (refer to Example 20).

EXAMPLE 39   M maintains a household in which S, her nondependent unmarried son and she reside. Since S is not married, M qualifies for the head-of-household rates. □

Another exception to the general rule is that head-of-household status may be claimed if the taxpayer maintains a separate home for his or her parent or parents if at least one parent qualifies as a dependent of the taxpayer.[36]

---

33. § 2(a).
34. § 2(b).
35. § 2(b)(1)(A)(i).
36. § 2(b)(1)(B).

EXAMPLE 40   S, an unmarried individual, lives in New York City and maintains a household in Detroit for his dependent parents. S may use the favorable head-of-household rates even though his parents do not reside in his New York home. □

Abandoned Spouse Rules.   When married persons file separate returns, several unfavorable tax consequences result. For example, the taxpayer must use the Tax Rate Schedule for married taxpayers filing separately. To mitigate such harsh treatment, Congress enacted provisions commonly referred to as the abandoned spouse rules. These rules allow a married taxpayer to file as a head of household if all of the following conditions are satisfied:

- The taxpayer does not file a joint return.
- The taxpayer paid more than one-half the cost of maintaining his or her home for the tax year.
- The taxpayer's spouse did not live in the home during the last six months of the tax year.
- The home was the principal residence of the taxpayer's child, stepchild, or adopted child for more than half the year.
- The taxpayer could claim the child, stepchild, or adopted child as a dependent.[37]

GAINS AND LOSSES FROM PROPERTY TRANSACTIONS—IN GENERAL

Gains and losses from property transactions are discussed in detail in chapters 14 through 17. Because of their importance in the tax system, however, they are introduced briefly at this point.

On the sale or other disposition of property, gain or loss may result. Such gain or loss has an effect on the income tax position of the party making the sale or other disposition when the *realized* gain or loss is *recognized* for tax purposes. Without realized gain or loss, generally, there can be no recognized gain or loss. The concept of realized gain or loss can be expressed as follows:

$$\text{Amount realized from the sale} - \text{Adjusted basis of the property} = \text{Realized gain (or loss)}$$

The amount realized is the selling price of the property less any costs of disposition (e.g., brokerage commissions) incurred by the seller. Simply stated, adjusted basis of the property is determined as follows:

37. The dependency requirement does not apply, however, if the taxpayer could have claimed a dependency exemption except for the fact that the exemption was claimed by the noncustodial parent under a written agreement. Refer to Example 20 and related discussion.

Cost (or other original basis) at date of acquisition [38]

Add: Capital additions

Subtract: Depreciation (if appropriate) and other capital recoveries (see chapter 9)

Equals: Adjusted basis at date of sale or other disposition

All realized gains are recognizable (taxable) unless some specific provision of the tax law provides otherwise (see chapter 15 dealing with certain nontaxable exchanges). Realized losses may or may not be recognizable (deductible) for tax purposes, depending on the circumstances involved. Usually, losses realized from the disposition of personal use property (property neither held for investment nor used in a trade or business) are not recognizable.

EXAMPLE 41

During the current year, T sells his sailboat (adjusted basis of $4,000) for $5,500. T also sells one of his personal automobiles (adjusted basis of $8,000) for $5,000. T's realized gain of $1,500 from the sale of the sailboat is recognizable. On the other hand, the $3,000 realized loss on the sale of the automobile is not recognized and will not provide T with any deductible tax benefit. □

Once it has been determined that the disposition of property results in a recognizable gain or loss, the next step is to classify such gain or loss as capital or ordinary. Although ordinary gain is fully taxable and ordinary loss is fully deductible, the same may not hold true for capital losses.

GAINS AND LOSSES FROM PROPERTY TRANSACTIONS—CAPITAL GAINS AND LOSSES

Before 1987, preferential long-term capital gain treatment was accorded to the sale or exchange of capital assets that had been held for the appropriate long term holding period. Recognized gains and losses on capital assets are classified as long-term if the property is held for *more than one year.*

The favorable long-term capital gain rules applicable before 1987 provided for a deduction equal to 60 percent of net capital gain. The provisions were intended to encourage the formation of private capital investment. After 1987, net capital gain is taxed as ordinary income.

Definition of a Capital Asset

Capital assets are defined in the Code as any property held by the taxpayer *other than* property listed in § 1221. The list in § 1221 includes inventory, accounts receivable, and depreciable property or real estate used in a busi-

---

38. Cost usually means purchase price plus expenses incident to the acquisition of the property and incurred by the purchaser (e.g., broker- age commissions). For the basis of property acquired by gift or inheritance and other basis rules, see chapter 14.

ness. Thus, the sale or exchange of assets in these categories usually results in ordinary income or loss treatment (see chapter 17).

EXAMPLE 42

C owns a pizza parlor. During the current year, C sells two automobiles. The first automobile, which had been used as a pizza delivery car for three years, was sold at a loss of $1,000. Because this automobile is an asset used in his business (a § 1231 asset), C has an ordinary loss deduction of $1,000, rather than a capital loss deduction. The second automobile, which C had owned for two years, was C's personal car. It was sold for a gain of $800. The personal car is a capital asset. Therefore, C has a capital gain of $800. □

The principal capital assets held by an individual taxpayer include assets held for personal (rather than business) use, such as a personal residence or an automobile, and assets held for investment purposes (e.g., corporate securities and land).

Computation of Net Capital Gains and Losses

Short-term capital gains and losses (those on assets held for one year or less) are offset initially, and long-term capital losses are used to offset long-term capital gains. Any net short-term capital losses are used then to offset net long-term capital gains. The same offsetting process is used if a taxpayer has net long-term capital losses and net short-term capital gains.

EXAMPLE 43

In the current year, T has the following capital gains and losses: short-term losses of $4,000, short-term gains of $3,000, long-term gains of $6,000, and long-term losses of $2,000. T has net short-term capital losses of $1,000 ($4,000 − $3,000) and net long-term capital gains of $4,000 ($6,000 − $2,000). The $1,000 net short-term capital loss, is used to offset the $4,000 net long-term capital gain, resulting in an excess of net long-term capital gain over net short-term capital loss of $3,000. □

Capital Loss Limitation

Capital losses are first offset against capital gains. If an individual taxpayer has net capital losses, such losses are deductible as a deduction *for* adjusted gross income to a maximum of $3,000 per year. Any unused amounts are carried over for an indefinite period.

EXAMPLE 44

In 1989, T has $1,000 of net long-term capital losses and $2,000 of net short-term capital losses. T's other income is $100,000. T's capital loss deduction for 1989 is $3,000, which consists of $2,000 short-term capital loss and $1,000 long-term capital loss. □

When a taxpayer has both short-term and long-term capital losses, the short-term losses must be used first in absorbing the $3,000 limitation.

EXAMPLE 45   R has short-term capital losses of $2,500 and long-term capital losses of $5,000 in 1989. R's other income is $50,000. R uses the losses as follows:

Short-term loss	$2,500
Long-term loss	500
Maximum 1989 capital loss deduction	$3,000

The remaining long-term capital loss of $4,500 ($5,000 loss minus $500 used in 1989) may be carried over for an indefinite period. See chapter 16 for a detailed discussion of capital loss carryovers. ☐

Corporate taxpayers may offset capital losses only against capital gains. Capital losses in excess of capital gains may not be used to reduce ordinary income of a corporation. A corporation's unused capital losses are subject to a carryback and carryover. Capital losses are initially carried back three years and then carried forward five years to offset capital gains that arise in those years. See chapter 16 for a discussion of capital losses of individual and corporate taxpayers.

TAX PLANNING CONSIDERATIONS

Income of Minor Children

Taxpayers can use several strategies to avoid or minimize the effect of the new rules that tax the unearned income of certain minor children at the parents' rate. The new rules do not apply once a child reaches age 14. Parents should consider giving a younger child assets that defer taxable income until the child reaches age 14. For example, U.S. Government Series EE Savings Bonds can be used to defer income until the bonds are cashed in. This strategy won't work if a child already owns Series EE bonds and has elected to report each year's interest accrual as income in order to take advantage of his or her personal exemption and low rates in pre-1987 years. Once this election has been made, it cannot be changed.

Growth stocks typically pay little in the way of dividends. However, the profit on an astute investment may more than offset the lack of dividends. The child can hold the stock until he or she reaches age 14. If the stock is sold at a profit, the profit will be taxed at his or her low rates.

Taxpayers in a position to do so should employ their children in their business and pay them a reasonable wage for the work they actually perform (e.g., light office help, such as filing). The child's earned income will be sheltered by the standard deduction, and the parent's business is allowed a deduction for the wages. The under-age-14 rules have no effect on earned income, even if earned from the parents' business.

Alternating between Itemized Deductions and the Standard Deduction

When total itemized deductions are approximately equal to the standard deduction from year to year, it is possible for cash basis taxpayers to save taxes by proper timing of payments. To obtain a deduction for itemized deductions in one year and make use of the standard deduction in the next year, taxpayers should shift deductions from one year to the other. This will result in a larger benefit over the two-year period than otherwise would be available.

EXAMPLE 46

T, who is single, is a cash basis and calendar year taxpayer. For tax years 1988 and 1989, T's itemized deductions are as follows:

	1988	1989
Charitable contribution	$1,300	$1,300
Other itemized deductions (e.g., interest, taxes)	1,100	1,100
Total itemized deductions	$2,400	$2,400

As presently structured, in neither year will T be able to benefit from these itemized deductions, since they do not exceed the standard deduction applicable to a taxpayer claiming single status ($3,000 in 1988 and $3,100 in 1989). Thus, T's benefit for both years totals $6,100 ($3,000 + $3,100), all based on the standard deduction. □

EXAMPLE 47

Assume the same facts as in Example 46, except that in late 1988 T prepays the charitable contribution for 1989. With this change, T's position for both years becomes:

	1988	1989
Charitable contribution	$2,600	$ –0–
Other itemized deductions	1,100	1,100
Total itemized deductions	$3,700	$1,100

Under these circumstances, T would claim itemized deductions of $3,700 for 1988 and the standard deduction of $3,100 for 1989. A comparison of the total benefit of $6,800 ($3,700 + $3,100) with the result reached in Example 46 of $6,100 ($3,000 + $3,100) clearly shows the advantage of this type of planning. □

Dependency Exemptions

The Joint Return Test. For a taxpayer to be able to claim a married person as a dependent, such person must not file a joint return with his or her spouse. If a joint return has been filed, however, the damage might be undone if separate returns are substituted on a timely basis (on or before the due date of the return).

EXAMPLE 48

While preparing a client's 1988 income tax return on April 10, 1989, the tax practitioner discovered that the client's daughter filed a joint return with her husband in late January of 1989. Presuming the daughter otherwise qualifies as the client's dependent, the exemption will not be lost if she and her husband file separate returns on or before April 17, 1989. □

Keep in mind that the filing of a joint return will not be fatal to the dependency exemption if the parties are filing solely to recover all income tax withholdings, neither is required to file a return and no tax liability would exist on separate returns. The filing requirement for married persons filing separate returns applies. The application of these rules can be interesting when contrasting common law and community property jurisdictions.

EXAMPLE 49

In 1989, T furnished 80% of the support of his son (S) and daughter-in-law (D). During the year, D earned $2,100 from a part-time job. As a result, D and S filed a joint return to obtain a refund of all the income tax withheld. All parties reside in New York (a common law state). Presuming the joint return stands (refer to Example 48), T cannot claim either S or D as his dependent. Although D and S filed a joint return to recover D's withholdings, D was required to file (she had gross income of $2,000 or more). □

EXAMPLE 50

Assume the same facts as in Example 49, except that all parties reside in Arizona (a community property state). Under these circumstances, T may claim both S and D as dependents. Not only have they filed a joint return to recover all of D's withholdings, but neither was required to file. Recall that in a community property state (unless otherwise altered by agreement between spouses, if permitted by state law), half of the wages of a spouse are attributable to the other spouse. Thus, S and D will be treated as each having earned $1,050, which is less than the filing requirement for married persons filing separate returns. □

The Gross Income Test. The exception to the gross income test for a person under the age of 19 or a full-time student under the age of 24 applies only to a child of the taxpayer. The term "child" is limited to a son, stepson, daughter, stepdaughter, adopted son, or adopted daughter and may include a foster child.

EXAMPLE 51   Assume the same facts as in Example 49, except that S and D (the son and daughter-in-law) do not file a joint return. Further assume that D (the person who had gross income of $2,100) is a full-time student. Even though T may claim S as a dependent, D does not qualify, since she has gross income of $2,000 or more. The student exception to the gross income test does not apply, because D is not a "child" of T. □

As was true with Example 50, the residence of the parties in a common law or a community property state can produce different results.

EXAMPLE 52   In 1989, T furnishes 60% of the support of his son (S) and daughter-in-law (D), both over the age of 19. During the year, D earns $4,200 from a part-time job, while S is unemployed and not a full-time student. All parties reside in New Jersey (a common law state). T may claim S as a dependent, but D does not qualify because of the gross income test. □

EXAMPLE 53   Assume the same facts as in Example 52, except that all parties reside in Washington (a community property state). T may not claim either S or D as dependents because of the application of the gross income test. Each spouse is treated as having gross income of $2,100 (one-half of $4,200), which is not below the $2,000 restriction. □

The Support Test.   Adequate records of expenditures for support should be maintained in the event a dependency exemption is questioned on audit by the IRS. The maintenance of adequate records is particularly important for exemptions arising from multiple support agreements.

Relationship to the Deduction for Medical Expenses.   Generally, medical expenses are deductible only if they are paid on behalf of the taxpayer, his or her spouse, and their dependents. Since deductibility may rest on dependency status, planning becomes important in arranging multiple support agreements.

EXAMPLE 54   During 1989, M will be supported by her two sons (S_1 and S_2) and her daughter (D), each to furnish approximately one-third of the required support. If the parties decide that the dependency exemption should be claimed by the daughter under a multiple support agreement, any medical expenses incurred by M should be paid by D. □

In planning the decision under a multiple support agreement, one should take into account which of the parties is most likely to exceed the 7.5 percent limitation (see chapter 11). In Example 54, for instance, D might be a poor choice if she and her family do not expect to incur many medical and drug expenses of their own.

One exception exists to permit the deduction of medical expenses paid on behalf of someone who is not a spouse or a dependent. If the person could be claimed as a dependent *except* for the gross income or joint return test, the medical expenses are, nevertheless, deductible.

EXAMPLE 55

In 1989, T pays for all of the medical expenses of her uncle (U) and her married son (S). U otherwise qualifies as T's dependent, except that he had gross income of $2,500. Also, S otherwise qualifies as a dependent, except that he filed a joint return with his wife. Even though T may not claim dependency exemptions for U and S, she can claim the medical and drug expenses she paid on behalf of each. ☐

PROBLEM MATERIALS

Discussion Questions

1. Rearrange the following components to show the formula for arriving at the amount of Federal taxable income:

    a. Deductions *for* adjusted gross income. *aren't taxed, but on return.*

    b. The greater of the standard deduction or itemized deductions.

    c. Income (broadly conceived).

    d. Adjusted gross income. *:*

    e. Exclusions. *things not taxable - not on tax forms,*

    f. Personal and dependency exemptions.

    g. Gross income.

2. H earned a salary of $42,000 and made a deductible $2,000 contribution to his Individual Retirement Account in 1989. He incurred medical expenses of $3,500. He had other itemized deductions of $4,000. Compute H's total itemized deductions for 1989.

3. T, age 20 and a full-time student at Midwestern State University, is claimed as a dependent on his parents' tax return. During the summer of 1989, T earned $1,500 from a part-time job. T's only other income consisted of $1,200 in interest on a savings account. Compute T's tax liability for 1989.

4. Discuss the special limitations that apply to the personal exemption and standard deduction of an individual who can be claimed as a dependent of another taxpayer.

5. What tests must be met to qualify as a dependent of another person? Do any of these tests have exceptions? Explain.

6. If an individual who may qualify as a dependent does not spend funds that he or she has received (e.g., wages or Social Security benefits), are such unexpended amounts considered in applying the support test? Are such amounts included in applying the gross income test?

7. F contributed $2,100 toward the support of his son, S, who is 18 years old and a full-time college student. S earned $1,100 interest on a sav-

ings account and $900 working at a supermarket during the summer. S used all his earnings for his support. He also received a $1,000 scholarship from the college he attended. Can F claim S as a dependent? Explain.

8. M's only income was $2,200 in Social Security benefits she received during the year. She spent $1,700 of this amount towards her own support. M lives with her daughter D, who contributed $1,500 towards M's support. Can D claim M as a dependent? Explain.

9. M purchased a stereo system for her son G, age 16. The stereo was placed in G's room and used exclusively by G. M also purchased a new sports car, titled and registered in her own name, that was used 90% of the time by G. Should the cost of these items be considered as support in determining whether M may claim G as a dependent?

10. Z, who is a dependent of his parents, is a full-time student at Central City College. During 1989, Z, age 20, earned $1,500 from a part-time job. Because he is claimed as a dependent by his parents, Z will not be allowed to claim an exemption for himself when filing his own tax return. True or false? Explain.

11. D, age 18, was a full-time university student during 1989. D earned $1,500 from a part-time job during 1989 and received $1,300 in interest on money he inherited from his parents. D lives with his grandparents, who provided 80% of his support in 1989. D's grandparents can claim him as a dependent in 1989. True or false? Explain.

12. J's support is provided by her daughter (30%), her son (30%), and an unrelated friend (40%). Can J be claimed as a dependent by any of the individuals who contributed to her support? Explain.

13. H and W, who are the parents of C, a minor child, were divorced during 1986. W was awarded custody of C. H provided 70% of C's support in 1989, and W provided 30%. Who may claim the dependency exemption for C in 1989? Explain.

14. B, who is married, must use either (a) the rates for married taxpayers filing jointly or (b) the rates for married taxpayers filing separately. True or false? Explain.

15. B, who is unmarried, expects to have adjusted gross income of $22,000 in 1989. B does not itemize deductions. How much income tax can B save if N, his 10-year-old nephew, moves in with him and qualifies as his dependent in 1989?

16. A single individual age 65 or over and blind is required to file a Federal income tax return in 1989 if he or she has gross income of $5,850 or more (refer to Figure 3–8).

   a. Explain how the $5,850 filing requirement was computed.

   b. In general, explain the effect of the additional standard deduction on the determination of gross income requirements for filing.

17. T and S are engaged to be married. Each has gross income of $20,000 for 1989. Assume that they plan to make use of the standard deduction and have no dependency exemptions or tax credits. What is the overall

effect on the total Federal income taxes that would be paid if they marry before the end of 1989?

18. K, age 67 and blind, earned $4,500 of interest and received Social Security benefits of $7,200 in 1989. Is K required to file a tax return?

19. H, age 67, is married to W, who is age 62 and blind. H and W file a joint return. How much gross income can they earn before they are required to file an income tax return for 1989?

20. V, a high school student, earned $1,000 from a summer job in 1989. V is aware that this amount is below the income level that would require her to file a return and therefore does not plan to file. Do you have any advice for V?

21. What remedy is available to an individual who failed to claim a deduction or tax credit on a tax return that has been filed with the IRS?

22. During 1989, T had a $5,000 long-term capital gain on the sale of common stock he had held as an investment. In addition, he had a $2,000 loss on the sale of his personal automobile, which he had owned for a year. How do these transactions affect T's taxable income for 1989?

23. Ten years ago, T purchased a personal residence for $140,000. In the current year, she sells the residence for $105,000. T's friend tells her she has a recognizable loss of $35,000 from the sale. Do you agree with the friend's comment? Elaborate.

24. List some assets that are not capital assets.

25. Why is it important to determine whether an asset is an ordinary asset or capital asset?

26. If an individual has a salary of $30,000 and net long-term capital losses of $4,500, what amount is deductible?

27. If a corporation has net short-term capital losses of $20,000 and net long-term capital gains of $6,000, what amounts are deductible by the corporation? How are any unused losses treated?

Problems

28. Compute the taxpayer's taxable income for 1989 in each of the following cases:

    a. H is married and files a joint return with his wife W. H and W have two dependent children. They have adjusted gross income of $19,000 and $4,300 of itemized deductions.

    b. S is unmarried and has no dependents. He has adjusted gross income of $25,000 and itemized deductions of $2,200.

    c. G, age 22, is a full-time college student who is claimed as a dependent by her parents. She earned $2,500 from a part-time job and had interest income of $1,200. Her itemized deductions were $400.

d. M, age 20, is a full-time college student who is claimed as a dependent by his parents. He earned $1,500 from a part-time job and had interest income of $1,100. His itemized deductions were $700.

29. Determine the standard deduction and exemption amount as instructed for the following taxpayers:

a. S, age 35, is a single taxpayer with no dependents. What was the total of his standard deduction and exemption amount for 1988? What is it for 1989?

b. G, age 66, is a single taxpayer with no dependents. What was the total of his standard deduction and exemption amount for 1988? What is it for 1989?

c. M is a full-time college student, age 22, who is claimed as a dependent on her parents' Federal income tax return in 1989. She earned interest of $400 in 1989. What is the total of M's standard deduction and exemption amount for 1989?

d. Assume the same facts as in (c), except that M also earned $3,000 from a summer job in 1989. What is the total of her standard deduction and exemption amount in 1989?

e. B, age 21, is a full-time college student who was claimed as a dependent by her parents during 1989. She earned $400 interest plus $3,000 from a part-time job during 1989. What is the total of B's standard deduction and exemption amount for the year?

30. X, age 30, is single, and has no dependents. In 1989, X earned $22,000 and had itemized deductions of $2,100. Compute X's taxable income and tax before prepayments or credits for 1989.

31. T, who is single, earned $77,000 in 1989. He incurred a short-term capital loss of $5,000 and had total itemized deductions of $9,800. Compute T's taxable income and tax before prepayments and credits for 1989.

32. Determine the Federal income tax liability for the following taxpayers for 1989:

a. D, who is single and has no dependents, earned $35,640. She had total itemized deductions of $2,990.

b. H and W are married and file a joint return. They earned $36,680 and had total itemized deductions of $3,140.

c. B is a widow who qualifies as a head of household. She has a son, age 10, who qualifies as her dependent. She earned $36,680 and had total itemized deductions of $2,990.

d. H is married, files a separate return, and has no dependents. He earned $35,640 and had total itemized deductions of $2,370.

33. B, age 13, is a full-time student supported by his parents who claim him on their tax return for 1989. B's parents present you with the following information and ask that you prepare B's 1989 Federal income tax return:

Wages from summer job	$1,400
Interest on savings account at First National Bank	500
Interest on XYZ Corporation bonds B received as a gift from his grandfather two years ago	900
Dividend from Z Corporation	500

a. What is B's taxable income for 1989?

b. B's parents file a joint return for 1989 on which they report taxable income of $64,250. Compute B's 1989 tax liability.

34. Assume the same facts as in Problem 33, except that B earned no dividends and no interest from First National Bank. What is B's taxable income for 1989?

35. R is a wealthy executive who had taxable income of $200,000 in 1989. He is considering transferring title in a duplex he owns to his son S, age 6. S has no other income and is claimed as a dependent by R. Net rental income from the duplex is $4,000 a year, which S will be encouraged to place in a savings account. Will the family save income taxes in 1989 if R transfers title in the duplex to S? Explain.

36. Compute the 1989 tax liability for each of the following taxpayers:

a. E, age 24, is single and has no dependents. During 1989, he earned a salary of $36,000, had deductions *for* AGI of $2,000, and had itemized deductions of $3,100.

b. L, age 66, is single and has no dependents. She earned a salary of $28,000 in 1989 and had itemized deductions of $3,500.

37. H and J, both 40 years of age, are married and have no children. They file separate returns for 1989. H claims itemized deductions of $6,600, and J's itemized deductions total $1,700. Because her itemized deductions are less than the standard deduction, J intends to use the standard deduction for computing her taxable income. What is the amount of the standard deduction J may claim in 1989? Explain.

38. L, age 22, is single and lives with her parents, who provide 70% of her support. L, a part-time student at Parkland Community College, earned a salary of $8,000 in 1989 and had itemized deductions of $2,500. What is L's taxable income for 1989?

39. Compute the 1989 tax liability for each of the following taxpayers:

a. H and M, both age 46, are married, have two dependent children, and file a joint return. In 1989, their combined salaries totaled $110,000. They had deductions *for* AGI of $4,000 and total itemized deductions of $6,000.

b. D, age 45, is single and has no dependents. In 1989, he had a salary of $140,000, deductions *for* AGI of $3,000, and total itemized deductions of $12,000.

c. B and C, both age 65, are married, have no dependents, and file a joint return in 1989. Their combined salaries for 1989 were $220,000. They had deductions *for* AGI of $6,000 and itemized deductions of $20,000.

40. Compute the 1989 tax liability for each of the following taxpayers:

a. F, age 65, is single and has no dependents. In 1989, he earned $104,260, had deductions *for* AGI of $4,000, and had itemized deductions of $3,700.

b. J, who is single and has no dependents, has taxable income of $85,000 in 1989.

c. X, who is single and has no dependents, has taxable income of $95,000 in 1989.

d. N and P, both age 34, have one dependent child, L, age 10. In 1989, N and P have taxable income of $100,000. L receives interest income of $3,000 during the year. Compute L's 1989 tax liability.

41. T, age 12, is claimed as a dependent on his parents' 1989 Federal income tax return, on which they reported taxable income of $175,000. During the summer of 1989, T earned $1,800 from a job as a model. His only other income consisted of $1,200 in interest on a savings account. Compute T's taxable income and tax liability for 1989.

42. R, age 14, is claimed as a dependent on her parents' 1989 Federal income tax return, on which they reported $220,000 of taxable income. During 1989, R earned $3,000 of interest on a savings account. Compute R's taxable income and tax liability for 1989.

43. In each of the following independent cases, determine the number of personal and dependency exemptions T may claim for 1989. Assume any dependency test not mentioned has been met. Unless otherwise specified, T is unmarried.

Case 1. T provides 80% of the support of his nephew (age 17), who lives with him. During the year, the nephew has gross income of $2,200 and is a full-time student.

Case 2. Assume the same facts as in Case 1, except that the $2,200 was paid to the nephew as a scholarship to cover tuition at State University.

Case 3. T provides over 50% of the support of his son S and his son's wife D. S (age 22) is a full-time student at a university. During 1989, D earned $3,500 on which income taxes were withheld. On January 31, 1990, D filed a separate return for tax year 1989. All parties reside in New York.

Case 4. Assume the same facts as in Case 3, except that all parties reside in California.

Case 5. During 1989, T gave his father, F (age 68), cash of $1,000 and a used automobile (cost of $2,000). F's total expenditures for food, lodging, and clothing for 1989 amount to $3,000 ($1,000 received from T and $2,000 withdrawn from F's savings account). F dies on June 3, 1989.

Case 6. T and his two brothers each provide 15% of the support of their mother. The mother derives the remainder of her support from Social Security benefits of $1,300.

44. Determine the correct number of personal and dependency exemptions in each of the following situations:

    a.   T, age 66 and disabled, is a widower who maintains a home for his unmarried daughter who is 24 years old. The daughter earned $3,000 and attends college on a part-time basis. T provides more than 50% of her support.

    b.   T, a bachelor age 45, provides more than 50% of the support of his father, age 70. T's father had gross income of $900 from a part-time job.

    c.   T, age 45, is married and has two dependent foster children who live with him and are totally supported by T. One of the foster children, age 14, had $2,100 of gross income. T and his spouse file a joint return.

    d.   T, age 67, is married and has a married daughter, age 22. T's daughter attended college on a full-time basis and was supported by T. The daughter filed a joint return with her spouse. T filed a joint return with his spouse, age 62.

45. Compute the number of personal and dependency exemptions in the following independent situations:

    a.   T, a single individual, provides 60% of the support of his mother, age 69. T's mother received dividend income of $800 and $1,500 in Social Security benefits.

    b.   T, a married individual filing a joint return, provides 100% of the support of his son, age 21, who is a part-time student. T's son earned $2,300 during the year from part-time employment.

    c.   T, who is divorced, provides $2,000 of child support for his child who is living with her mother, who provides support of $2,500. An agreement executed in 1986 between T and his former wife provides that the noncustodial parent is to receive the dependency exemption. T's former wife provides him with a completed Form 8332.

46. Has T provided more than 50% support in the following situations?

    a.   T paid $6,000 for an automobile that was titled in his name. His 19-year-old son, S, uses the automobile approximately 50% of the time while attending a local college on a full-time basis. S earned $4,000 from a part-time job that was used to pay his college and living expenses. The value of S's room and board provided by T amounted to $1,200.

    b.   T contributed $4,000 to his mother's support during the year. His mother received $5,000 in Social Security benefits that she placed in her savings account for future use.

    c.   Assume the same facts as in (b), except that T's mother used the funds for her support during the year.

47. F contributed the following items toward the support of his son S:

Food, clothing, shelter	$2,300
Television set given to S as a Christmas present	300
Books for college	250

S, age 23, is a full-time student at the University of Georgia College of Law. In June, he married J, who is supported by her parents. S earned $3,300 during the summer and contributed the following items toward his own support:

Clothing	$ 600
Used car purchased for transportation to college	1,000
Insurance, maintenance, and operating expenses for car	800
Entertainment	420

S received a $2,000 scholarship from the University of Georgia. Which of the following statements is correct?

a.   F provided over half of S's support but cannot claim S as a dependent, because S's gross income exceeds the maximum amount allowable for a dependent.

b.   S's income will not prevent F from claiming S as a dependent. However, F cannot claim S as a dependent, because he provided less than half of S's support.

c.   F cannot claim S as a dependent for two reasons: F did not provide over half of S's support, and S's income exceeds the maximum amount allowable for a dependent.

d.   Based on the facts given, there is nothing that would prevent F from claiming S as a dependent. However, if S and J file a joint return, F will not be allowed to claim S as a dependent.

e.   None of the above.

48.   A, B, and C contribute to the support of their mother, M, age 67. M lives with each of the children for approximately four months during the year. Her total living costs amounted to $6,000 and were paid as follows:

From M's Social Security benefits	$1,700
By A	500
By B	1,300
By C	1,300
By T, M's unrelated friend	1,200
	$6,000

a.   Which, if any, of these individuals may claim M as a dependent (assume no multiple support agreement is filed)?

b.   If a multiple support agreement is filed, who must be a party to it, and who may claim the exemption for M under the agreement?

49.   Which of the following individuals are required to file a tax return for 1989? Should any of these individuals file a return even if such filing is not required? Why?

a.   T is married and files a joint return with his spouse, B. Both T and B are 47 years old. Their combined gross income was $9,000.

b. T is a dependent child under age 19 who received $1,000 in wages from a part-time job and $1,900 of dividend income.

c. T is single and is 67 years old. His gross income from wages was $5,800.

d. T is a self-employed single individual with gross income of $4,400 from an unincorporated business. Business expenses amounted to $3,900.

50. Can T use Tax Rate Schedule Z (head of household) in 1989?

a. T's wife died in 1988. T maintained a household for his two dependent children during 1989 and provided over one-half of the cost of the household.

b. T is unmarried and lives in an apartment. He supported his aged parents, who live in a separate home. T provides over one-half of the funds used to maintain his parents' home. T also claimed his parents as dependents, since he provided more than one-half of their support during the year.

c. T is unmarried and maintains a household (over one-half of the cost) for his 18-year-old married daughter and her husband. His daughter filed a joint return with her husband solely for the purpose of obtaining a refund of income taxes that were withheld. Neither T's daughter nor her husband was required to file a return.

51. Indicate in each of the following situations which of the Tax Rate Schedules T should use for calendar year 1989:

a. T, the mother and sole support of her three minor children, was abandoned by her husband in late 1988.

b. T is a widower whose wife died in 1988. T furnishes all of the support of his household, which includes two dependent children.

c. T furnishes all of the support of his parents, who live in their own home in a different city. T's parents qualify as his dependents. T is not married.

d. T's household includes an unmarried stepchild, age 18, who has gross income of $6,000 during the year. T furnishes all of the cost of maintaining the household. T is not married.

52. M, age 66, is a widow. Her husband died in 1987. M maintains a home in which she and her 28-year-old son reside. Her son G, who is blind, is a piano player at a local nightclub, where he earned $12,000 during 1989. G contributed $3,000 of his income toward household expenses and put the remainder in a savings account that he used to return to college full-time to pursue a master's degree in music starting in August 1989. M contributed $12,000 toward household expenses. What is the most favorable filing status available to M for 1989, and how many exemptions may M claim?

53. You are to solve this puzzle using your skills as a tax expert. Sam and Sally were contemplating marriage in December 1988. Sam's salary for 1988 was $12,000, and Sally's was $40,000. Sam had total itemized deductions of $1,900; Sally's itemized deductions totaled $2,800. Sam,

who earned interest of $2,000 on a savings account, made a deductible $2,000 contribution to his IRA. Sally made a deductible $1,000 contribution to her IRA. Sam and Sally planned to marry in December 1988 if marriage would save them any Federal income tax. Otherwise, they planned to marry in January 1989. Which of the following statements is correct?

a.   Sam and Sally married in December 1988.

b.   Sam and Sally married in January 1989.

54.   B, who is single and age 35, has adjusted gross income of $40,000 in 1988. He does not itemize deductions. N, his recently orphaned 10–year–old cousin, moved in with him in April, and B provided all of N's support during the remainder of 1988.

a.   Compute B's taxable income and tax liability for 1988.

b.   Assume that B has the same amount of adjusted gross income in 1989 and that N continues to reside with him through the end of the year. Compute B's taxable income and tax liability for 1989.

55.   H, age 65 and single, earned a salary of $42,000 and made a deductible $2,000 contribution to his Individual Retirement Account in 1989. He incurred medical expenses of $3,500 and had other itemized deductions of $3,000. Compute H's taxable income for 1989.

56.   In 1989, Della earned a salary of $30,000 and had a long-term loss of $4,000 on the sale of stock. She also had a $2,500 short-term loss on the sale of land held as an investment and a $1,500 gain on the sale of her personal automobile. She had owned the automobile for two years. Compute Della's adjusted gross income and capital loss carryover based on this information.

57.   K, age 39, is single. She maintains a household that is the residence of her two children, B, age 8, and G, age 11. The children are claimed as dependents by their father, who provides $2,000 child support for each of them. During 1989, K earned a salary of $48,000. Other items that affected her taxable income are as follows:

Total itemized deductions	$4,500
Capital gains	
Short-term	300
Long-term	3,500
Capital losses	
Short-term	(900)
Long-term	(700)
Interest income	650

K provides all the support for her mother, M, who lives in a nursing home. M qualifies as K's dependent.

a.   Compute K's adjusted gross income and taxable income for 1989.

b.   What is K's filing status for 1989?

58. H, single with no dependents, had a short-term capital loss of $2,600 in 1989. He earned a salary of $15,000 and had itemized. deductions of $2,100.

    a. Compute H's taxable income for 1989.

    b. Assume the same facts as in (a), except that H also had a $1,400 long-term capital loss in 1989. Compute H's taxable income and capital loss carryforward to 1990.

59. N, age 67, is married to H, age 65. N and H file a joint return for 1989. During 1989, N's salary was $92,000. N has an extensive portfolio of stock investments. During 1989, he engaged in several stock transactions, with the following results:

Capital gains	
Short-term	$3,700
Long-term	9,000
Capital losses	
Short-term	(2,500)
Long-term	(1,200)

    N and H had total itemized deductions of $9,400 during 1989. N received interest of $4,800 on City of Phoenix bonds.

    a. Compute taxable income for N and H for 1989.

    b. Assume the same facts as in (a), except that N's long-term capital gain was only $900.

60. T is a cash basis calendar year taxpayer. For the years 1988 and 1989, he expects adjusted gross income of $20,000 and the following itemized deductions:

Church pledge	$1,200
Interest on home mortgage	1,500
Property taxes	700

    Discuss the tax consequences of the following alternatives:

    a. In 1988, T pays his church pledge for 1988 and 1989 ($1,200 for each year).

    b. T does nothing different.

Cumulative Problems

61. John and Karen Sanders, both age 25, are married and file a joint return in 1988. They have one child, Linda, who was born on June 30, 1988. John's Social Security number is 266–77–2345, and Karen's is 467–33–1289. They live at 105 Bradley, Columbus, OH 43211.

    John, a computer programmer, earned $31,000, and his employer withheld $4,500. Karen, a medical student at Ohio State University, received $15,000 of income from a trust her father had established to pay for her education. This amount must be included in computing taxable income. In addition, Karen was awarded a $3,000 nontaxable scholarship by the medical school in 1988.

In examining their records, you find that John and Karen are entitled to the following itemized deductions:

State and local income taxes	$1,150
Real estate taxes	1,570
Home mortgage interest	3,840
Charitable contributions	620
Total	$7,180

John and Karen made estimated Federal tax payments of $1,200 in 1988.

Part 1—Tax Computation

Compute (a) adjusted gross income, (b) taxable income, and (c) net tax payable or refund due for John and Karen. Suggested software (if available): *WEST–TAX Preparer* for tax return solutions, *WEST–TAX Planner* or *BNA Individual Income Tax Spread Sheet* if tax return solutions are not desired.

Part 2—Tax Planning

Assume that all amounts from 1988 will be approximately the same in 1989 except for the following:

a.   John's salary will increase by 10%.

b.   John's employer will withhold $5,000 of Federal income tax.

How much additional estimated tax should the Sanders pay in 1989 so they will neither owe any tax nor receive any refund for 1989? Suggested software (if available): *WEST–TAX Planner* or *BNA Individual Income Tax Spread Sheet.*

 62. Henry and Wanda Black, 4030 Beachside Drive, Longboat Key, FL 33548, file a joint Federal income tax return for 1988. Henry, age 66, is a restaurant manager for Gourmet Tacos. His Social Security number is 344–99–7642. Wanda, who is 54, is a manager at Timothy's Beauty Salon. Her Social Security number is 654–33–7890. The Blacks come to you in early December 1988 seeking tax advice.

The Blacks have received or will receive the following amounts during 1988:

a.   Henry's salary, $38,000.

b.   Wanda's salary, $40,000.

c.   Proceeds from October 9, 1988, sale of XYZ Corporation stock (cost of $12,000) acquired on April 6, 1981, $26,000.

d.   Interest on bonds issued by the City of Sarasota, $900.

e.   Life insurance proceeds received on the death of Henry's mother, $75,000.

f.   Value of property inherited from Henry's mother, $130,000.

In examining the Blacks' records, you find the following items of possible tax consequence (all applicable to 1988):

g. The Blacks had other itemized deductions as follows:
   - Real estate taxes, $3,200.
   - Home mortgage interest, $4,500.
   - Charitable contributions (cash), $2,600.

h. Henry's employer withheld $6,800 of Federal income tax, and Wanda's employer withheld $7,000. In addition, they made estimated tax payments of $6,400.

Henry and Wanda's son Steven lived with the Blacks during 1988 except for nine months during which he was away at college. Steven, age 23, is a law student and plans to graduate in 1990. During the summer, Steven earned $2,100 and used the money he earned to pay for his college expenses. His parents contributed $3,000 toward his support.

Part 1—Tax Computation

Compute the following amounts for the Blacks if they file a joint return for 1988: gross income, adjusted gross income, taxable income, and net tax payable or refund due. Suggested software (if available): *WEST–TAX Preparer* for tax return solutions, *WEST–TAX Planner* or *BNA Individual Income Tax Spread Sheet* if tax return solutions are not desired.

Part 2—Tax Planning

The Blacks are contemplating a divorce and would prefer not filing jointly. They have asked you to compute their tax liabilities if they file separately rather than jointly. If they file separately, they will split itemized deductions and estimated tax payments equally, and each spouse will report one half of the capital gain, since they owned the XYZ Corporation stock jointly (refer to item c). Wanda will claim an exemption for Steven (assume he qualifies as her dependent). Will the Blacks have to pay more tax if they file separately? Explain. Suggested software (if available): *WEST–TAX Preparer* for tax return solutions, *WEST–TAX Planner* or *BNA Individual Income Tax Spread Sheet* if tax return solutions are not desired.

Research Problems

Research Problem 1   M, a foreign diplomat, was assigned to a post in India during 1986. J, his wife, lived in Maryland during 1986. M and J were married in 1977, separated in 1985, and divorced in 1988. In March 1986, J wrote a letter to M containing the following statement:

> "I have been trying to make arrangements for paying the 1985 income tax. I will examine and sign (if acceptable) a joint return if you prepare it and send the completed return and statements to me by June 1. Otherwise, I will file a separate return."

J did not receive the requested material and was advised by her attorney to file a separate 1985 return, which she filed on June 20, 1986. On this return, she reported $70 she had earned as a substitute teacher and $5 of interest on her savings account.

M requested an extension for filing his 1985 return, which he filed in January 1987. On this joint return, he claimed an exemption for J. He attached the following statement:

> "You will note that the return, a joint one since my wife and I are still legally married, bears only my signature. I am sending a copy to my lawyer in Washington in the hopes of having her sign it, a slim possibility since she, for reasons of her own, refused to sign the 1984 return."

Will the IRS accept M's return as a joint return? Will M be permitted to claim an exemption for J if he is required to amend and file a separate return?

Research Problem 2   B and L were married in 1959 and were divorced on November 15, 1981. B, who was employed as a long-haul truck driver, was awarded custody of the couple's seven children, who at that time ranged in age from 13 to 20 years.

After the divorce, L continued to live in the family home with B and their children. She held no outside employment during 1987 and 1988. B paid all personal, living, and household expenses for L, the children, and himself.

In 1988, B and L had another child.

For all years after the divorce, B filed as head of household. He claimed L and all of the children as dependents. The IRS disallowed B's exemption for L on B's 1987 and 1988 tax returns, arguing that B paid all of L's expenses in exchange for L's services of maintaining his household and raising their children. In effect, the IRS characterized the relationship between B and L as that of employer-employee.

Is B allowed to claim L as a dependent on his 1987 and 1988 tax returns?

PART

2

GROSS INCOME

Part 2 presents the income component of the basic tax model. Included in this presentation are the determination of what is income and the statutory exclusions that are permitted in calculating gross income. Because the taxpayer's accounting method and accounting period affect when income is reported, an introductory discussion of these topics is also included.

CHAPTER
4

Gross Income: Concepts and Inclusions

CHAPTER
5

Gross Income: Exclusions

4

GROSS INCOME: CONCEPTS AND INCLUSIONS

OBJECTIVES

Explain the all-inclusive concept of gross income and the underlying realization requirement.

Describe the cash and accrual methods of accounting for gross income.

Explain the principles applied to determine who is subject to tax on a particular item of income.

Analyze the Sections of the Internal Revenue Code that describe the determination of gross income from the following specific sources: alimony, below-market interest rate loans, annuities, prizes and awards, group term life insurance, unemployment compensation, and Social Security benefits.

Computation of the income tax liability of an individual or a corporation begins with the determination of gross income. Section 61 provides an all-inclusive definition of gross income and supplements it with a list of items (not all-inclusive) that are includible in gross income (e.g., compensation for services, rents, interest, dividends, alimony). Other Code Sections contain specific rules for particular types of income.

Congress has provided that certain items are exempt from taxation (e.g., interest on certain state and municipal bonds). The exemptions appear in §§ 101–150 of the Code and are discussed in chapter 5.

Gross Income—What Is It?

Definition

Section 61(a) of the Internal Revenue Code defines the term *gross income* as follows:

> Except as otherwise provided in this subtitle, gross income means all income from whatever source derived.

Since the sweeping scope of the definition is apparent, the Supreme Court has stated:

> The starting point in all cases dealing with the question of the scope of what is included in "gross income" begins with the basic premise that the purpose of Congress was to use the full measure of its taxing power.[1]

(The clause, "Except as otherwise provided in this subtitle," refers to Sections of the Code in which Congress has exempted certain types of income from the tax base. Such exclusions are discussed in chapter 5.)

Economic and Accounting Concepts

The term *income* is used in the Code but is not separately defined. Thus, early in the history of our tax laws, the courts were required to interpret "the commonly understood meaning of the term which must have been in the minds of the people when they adopted the Sixteenth Amendment to the Constitution."[2] In determining the definition of income, the Supreme Court rejected the economist's concept of income.

For the *economist*, economic income is measured by first determining the fair market value of the taxpayer's net assets at the beginning and end of the year. After this determination is made, economic income is defined as the sum of the taxpayer's change in net worth plus actual consumption of goods and services for the tax period. Economic income also includes imputed values for such items as the rental value of an owner-occupied home and the value of food a taxpayer might grow for personal consumption.[3]

---

1. *James v. U.S.*, 61–1 USTC ¶9449, 7 AFTR2d 1361, 81 S.Ct. 1052 (USSC, 1961).

2. *Merchants Loan and Trust Co. v. Smietanka*, 1 USTC ¶42, 3 AFTR 3102, 41 S.Ct. 386 (USSC, 1921).

3. See Henry C. Simons, *Personal Income Taxation* (University of Chicago Press, 1933), ch. 2–3.

EXAMPLE 1	T's economic income is calculated as follows:

Fair market value of T's assets on December 31, 1989	$220,000	
Less liabilities on December 31, 1989	(40,000)	
Net worth on December 31, 1989		$180,000
Fair market value of T's assets on January 1, 1989	$200,000	
Less liabilities on January 1, 1989	(80,000)	
Net worth on January 1, 1989		120,000
Increase in net worth		$ 60,000
Consumption		
Food, clothing, and other personal expenditures		25,000
Imputed rental value of T's home she owns and occupies		12,000
Economic income		$ 97,000

The need to value assets annually would make compliance with the law burdensome and would cause numerous controversies between the taxpayer and the IRS over valuation. In addition, using market values to determine income for tax purposes could result in liquidity problems. That is, the taxpayer's assets may increase in value even though they are not readily convertible into the cash needed to pay the tax (e.g., commercial real estate). Thus, the IRS, Congress, and the courts have rejected the economist's concept of income as impractical.

In contrast, the *accountant's concept of income* is founded on the realization principle.[4] According to this principle, income is not recognized until it is realized. Realization entails (1) an exchange of goods or services between the accounting entity and some independent, external group and (2) assets received in the exchange that are capable of being objectively valued. The mere appreciation in the market value of assets before a sale or other disposition is not sufficient to warrant income recognition. Also, imputed savings arising from the self-construction of assets to be used in one's own operations is not income, because there is no exchange.

---

4. See the American Accounting Association Committee Report on the "Realization Concept," *The Accounting Review* (April 1965), pp. 312–322.

The Supreme Court in *Eisner v. Macomber* [5] added the realization require-ment to a judicial definition of income that had been formulated in early cases:

> Income may be defined as the gain derived from capital, from labor, or from both combined, provided it is understood to include profit gained through a sale or conversion of capital assets. . . . Here we have the es-sential matter: not a gain accruing to capital; not a *growth* or *increment* of value *in* investment; but a gain, a profit, something of exchangeable value, *proceeding from* the property, *severed from* the capital, however, invested or employed, and *coming in*, being "*derived*"—that is, *received* or *drawn by* the recipient for his separate use, benefit and disposal—*that* is, income derived from the property.

Thus, the early Supreme Court definition of income can be simply restated as the gain realized from capital, from labor, or from a combination of the two.

As a result of cases subsequent to *Eisner v. Macomber*, the "from capital, from labor . . ." phrases can be deleted. For example, in *Glenshaw Glass Co.*,[6] the taxpayer received punitive damages from a supplier who had com-mitted fraud and violated Federal antitrust laws. Clearly, the damages were intended to be a punishment and therefore were not gain realized from capi-tal, from labor, or from both combined. Nevertheless, the Supreme Court held that the punitive damages received by Glenshaw were income:

> Here we have instances of undeniable accessions to wealth, clearly realized, and over which the taxpayers have complete dominion.

In other cases the Supreme Court reasoned similarly that proceeds from embezzlement [7] and extortion [8] were income.

In summary, *income* represents an increase in wealth recognized for tax purposes only upon realization.

Comparison of Accounting and Taxable Income

Although income tax rules frequently parallel financial accounting measure-ment concepts, differences do exist. Of major significance, for example, is the fact that unearned (prepaid) income received by an accrual basis taxpayer often is taxed in the year of receipt. For financial accounting purposes, such prepayments are not treated as income until earned.[9] Because of this and other differences, many corporations report financial accounting income that is substantially different from the amounts reported for tax purposes (see chapter 20, Reconciliation of Taxable Income and Accounting Income).

An explanation for some of the variations between accounting and taxa-ble income was given in a Supreme Court decision involving inventory and bad debt adjustments:[10] The relevant portion of the opinion follows:

---

5. 1 USTC ¶32, 3 AFTR 3020, 40 S.Ct. 189 (USSC, 1920).
6. 55–1 USTC ¶9308, 47 AFTR 162, 75 S.Ct. 473 (USSC, 1955).
7. *Supra*, Footnote 1.
8. *Rutkin v. U.S.*, 52–1 USTC ¶9260, 41 AFTR 596, 72 S.Ct. 571 (USSC, 1952).

9. Similar differences exist in the deduction area. Goodwill, for example, must be amortized for financial accounting purposes but cannot be de-ducted under the Federal income tax laws.
10. *Thor Power Tool Co. v. Comm.*, 79–1 USTC ¶9139, 43 AFTR2d 79–362, 99 S.Ct. 773 (USSC, 1979).

The primary goal of financial accounting is to provide useful information to management, shareholders, creditors, and others properly interested; the major responsibility of the accountant is to protect these parties from being misled. The primary goal of the income tax system, in contrast, is the equitable collection of revenue. . . . Consistently with its goals and responsibilities, financial accounting has as its foundation the principle of conservatism, with its corollary that 'possible errors in measurement [should] be in the direction of understatement rather than overstatement of net income and net assets.' In view of the Treasury's markedly different goals and responsibilities, understatement of income is not destined to be its guiding light.

. . . Financial accounting, in short, is hospitable to estimates, probabilities, and reasonable certainties; the tax law, with its mandate to preserve the revenue, can give no quarter to uncertainty.

In some instances, the tax law specifically permits rapid write-offs (e.g., limited expensing under § 179) and deferrals of income that are not available in financial accounting.[11] The student should note specific differences between tax accounting and financial accounting mentioned in the text.

Form of Receipt

Gross income is not limited to cash received. "It includes income realized in any form, whether in money, property, or services. Income may be realized [and recognized], therefore, in the form of services, meals, accommodations, stock or other property, as well as in cash."[12]

EXAMPLE 2

ABC Corporation allowed T, an employee, to use a company car for his vacation. T realized income equal to the rental value of the car for the time and mileage. □

EXAMPLE 3

M, an XYZ Corporation shareholder, bought property from the company for $10,000 when the property was worth $15,000. M realized income (a constructive dividend) of $5,000, the difference between the fair market value of the property and the price M paid. □

EXAMPLE 4

T owed $10,000 on a mortgage. The creditor accepted $8,000 in full satisfaction of the debt. T realized income of $2,000 from retiring the debt.[13]

□

---

11. In some of these cases, however, the tax law has a back-up provision in the form of the alternative minimum tax. For example, corporations may be required to pay a 20 percent minimum tax on one-half of the excess of pretax book income over taxable income. See chapter 12 for a discussion of the corporate alternative minimum tax.

12. Reg. § 1.61–1(a).

13. Reg. § 1.61–12. See *U.S. v. Kirby Lumber Co.*, 2 USTC ¶814, 10 AFTR 458, 52 S.Ct. 4 (USSC, 1931). Exceptions to this general rule are discussed in chapter 5.

Recovery of Capital Doctrine

The Constitution grants Congress the power to tax income but does not define the term. Because the Constitution does not define income, it would seem that Congress could simply tax gross receipts. Although Congress does allow certain deductions, none are constitutionally required. However, the Supreme Court has held that there can be no income subject to tax until the taxpayer has recovered the capital invested.[14]

> . . . We must withdraw from the gross proceeds an amount sufficient to restore the capital value that existed at the commencement of the period under consideration.

In its simplest application, the *recovery of capital doctrine* means a seller can reduce the gross receipts (selling price) by the adjusted basis in the property sold.[15] This net amount, in the language of the Code, is gross income. But the recovery of capital doctrine also has subtle implications.

EXAMPLE 5

B paid additional taxes of $5,000 because his accountant did not maintain proper documentation of expenses. B's loss was only temporary because he collected the $5,000 from the accountant after threatening a negligence suit. The $5,000 received from the accountant is not income because it merely replaces the capital taken by the tax collector as a result of the accountant's negligence.[16] B also lost one day's pay, $100, for time spent at the local office of the IRS protesting the additional taxes. The accountant reimbursed B for his loss of wages. The $100 is income rather than a recovery of capital because no capital was formed until either the income or its substitute (payment from the accountant) was received. □

EXAMPLE 6

Z Corporation recovered $150,000 as damages inflicted by a competitor on the goodwill of the corporation. The goodwill was the product of fast and efficient services to its customers, and no cost of the asset was reflected on the corporation's balance sheet. Because the company has no capital invested in its goodwill, the $150,000 is taxable.[17] □

EXAMPLE 7

C purchased an acre of land for $10,000. The following year X Electric Company paid C $1,000 for a permanent easement to run an underground cable across his property. The easement prevents C from making certain uses of his property (e.g., it affected where a house could be located and where trees could be planted), but C can still make some use of the property. The cost of the interest in the property C gave up for the $1,000 cannot be determined. Therefore, C may treat the $1,000 as a recovery of

---

14. *Doyle v. Mitchell Bros. Co.*, 1 USTC ¶17, 1 AFTR 235, 38 S.Ct. 467 (USSC, 1916).
15. For a definition of adjusted basis, see the Glossary of Tax Terms in Appendix C.
16. *Clark v. Comm.*, 40 B.T.A. 333 (1939).
17. *Raytheon Production Corp. v. Comm.*, 44–2 USTC ¶9424, 32 AFTR 1155, 144 F.2d 110 (CA–1, 1944).

his original cost of the property and reduce his basis to $9,000. If C later sells the property for more than $9,000, he will recognize a gain. ☐

Collections on annuity contracts and installment payments received from sales of property must be allocated between recovery of capital and income. Annuities are discussed in this chapter, and installment sales are discussed in chapter 18.

YEAR OF INCLUSION

Taxable Year

The annual accounting period is a basic component of our tax system.[18] Generally, a taxable entity may use a *calendar year* to report income. Those entities who keep adequate books and records generally may use a *fiscal year* (a period of 12 months ending on the last day of any month other than December) or a 52–53 week year that ends on the same day of the week nearest the last day of the same month each year.[19] A retailer considering a 52–53 week year might choose a year ending in January so that he or she can properly account for Christmas returns, and on a Saturday so that inventory can be taken on Sunday. Automobile dealers often select a fiscal year ending in September so that the taxable year corresponds with their natural business year (i.e., the change in car models).

Since the lifetime earnings of a taxable entity must be divided into these 12-month intervals and a progressive tax rate schedule must be applied to the taxable income for each interval, determining the period into which a particular item of income is allocated is often of more than just academic interest. Determining this period is important because (1) Congress may change the tax rate schedule, (2) the entity's income may rise or fall between years so that placing the income in a particular year may mean that the income is taxed at a different marginal rate, or (3) the entity may undergo a change in its status and a different tax rate schedule may apply (e.g., an individual might marry or a proprietorship might incorporate).

Several provisions in the Code contain limitations based on gross income or derivatives of gross income. For example, as discussed in chapter 3, generally a dependent's gross income cannot exceed the exemption amount ($2,000 in 1989), medical expenses are deductible (as an itemized deduction) only to the extent the expenses exceed 7.5 percent of the taxpayer's adjusted gross income, and miscellaneous expenses in excess of 2 percent of adjusted gross income are allowed as an itemized deduction. Thus, it is important to determine *when* the item of income is subject to taxation.

Accounting Methods

The year an item of income is subject to tax often depends upon which acceptable accounting method the taxpayer regularly employs.[20] Most individuals use the cash receipts and disbursements method of accounting, whereas

---

18. See Accounting Periods in chapter 18.
19. §§ 441(a) and (d). See Accounting Periods in chapter 18 for limitations on the ability to use a calendar or a fiscal year, including a 52–53 week year.
20. See Accounting Methods in chapter 18.

most corporations use the accrual method. The Regulations require the accrual method for determining purchases and sales when inventory is an income-producing factor.[21] Some businesses employ a hybrid method that is a combination of the cash and accrual methods of accounting. Generally, when a hybrid method is used, inventory is accounted for under the accrual method, and the cash method is used for all other income and expense items.

In addition to these overall accounting methods, a taxpayer may choose to spread the gain from the sale of property over the collection periods by electing the installment method of income recognition. Contractors may either spread profits from contracts over the periods in which the work is done (the percentage of completion method) or defer all profit until the year in which the project is completed (the completed contract method).[22]

The Commissioner has the power to prescribe the accounting method to be used by the taxpayer. Section 446(b) grants the Commissioner broad powers to determine if the accounting method used *clearly reflects income*:

> Exceptions—If no method of accounting has been regularly used by the taxpayer, or *if the method used does not clearly reflect income, the computation of taxable income shall be made under such method as, in the opinion of the Secretary or his delegate, does clearly reflect income.*

A change in the method of accounting requires the consent of the Commissioner.[23]

Cash Receipts Method.   Under the *cash receipts method*, property or services received are included in the taxpayer's gross income in the year of actual or constructive receipt by the taxpayer or agent, regardless of whether the income was earned in that year.[24] The receipt of income need not be reduced to cash in the same year. All that is necessary for income recognition is that property or services received have a fair market value—a cash equivalent.[25] Thus, if a cash basis taxpayer receives a note in payment for services, he or she has income in the year of receipt equal to the fair market value of the note. However, a creditor's mere promise to pay (e.g., an account receivable), with no supporting note, is not usually considered to have a fair market value.[26] Thus, the cash basis taxpayer defers income recognition until the account receivable is collected.

EXAMPLE 8   D, an accountant, reports his income by the cash method. In 1989, he performed an audit for X and billed the client for $5,000, which was collected in 1990. In 1989, D also performed an audit for Y. Because of Y's precarious financial position, D required Y to issue an $8,000 secured negotiable note in payment of the fee. The note had a fair market value of

21. Reg. § 1.446–1(c)(2)(i). See the Glossary of Tax Terms in Appendix C for a discussion of the terms "accrual method," "accounting method," and "accounting period." Other circumstances for which the accrual method must be used are presented in chapter 18.

22. §§ 453(a) and (b), § 453A, and Reg. § 1.451–3. See chapter 18 for limitations on the use of the installment method and the completed contract method.

23. § 446(e). See chapter 18.

24. *Julia A. Strauss*, 2 B.T.A. 598 (1925). See the Glossary of Tax Terms in Appendix C for a discussion of the terms "cash equivalent doctrine" and "constructive receipt."

25. Reg. §§ 1.446–1(a)(3) and (c)(1)(i).

26. *Bedell v. Comm.*, 1 USTC ¶359, 7 AFTR 8469, 30 F.2d 622 (CA–2, 1929).

$6,000. D collected $8,000 on the note in 1990. D's gross income for the two years is as follows:

	1989	1990
Fair market value of note received from Y	$6,000	
Cash received		
From X on account receivable		$5,000
From Y on note receivable		8,000
Less: Recovery of capital		(6,000)
Total gross income	$6,000	$7,000

□

Accrual Method.   Under *accrual accounting*, an item is generally included in the gross income for the year in which it is earned, regardless of when the income is collected. The income is earned when (1) all the events have occurred that fix the right to receive such income and (2) the amount thereof can be determined with reasonable accuracy.[27]

Generally, the taxpayer's rights to the income accrue when title to property passes to the buyer or the services are performed for the customer or client.[28] If the rights to the income have accrued but are subject to a potential refund claim (e.g., under a product warranty), the income is reported in the year of sale and a deduction is allowed in subsequent years when actual claims accrue.[29]

Where the taxpayer's rights to the income are being contested (e.g., a contractor who fails to meet specifications), the year in which the income is subject to tax depends upon whether payment has been received. If payment has not been received, no income is recognized until the claim has been settled. Only then is the right to the income established.[30] However, if the payment is received before the dispute is settled, the court-made *claim of right doctrine* requires the taxpayer to recognize the income in the year of receipt.[31]

EXAMPLE 9

A contractor completed a building in 1989 and presented a bill to the customer. The customer refused to pay the bill and claimed that the contractor had not met specifications. A settlement with the customer was not reached until 1990. Assuming the customer had a valid claim, no income would accrue to the contractor until 1990. If the customer paid for the work and then filed suit for damages, the contractor could not defer the income (the income would be taxable in 1989). □

27. Reg. § 1.451–1(a).
28. *Lucas v. North Texas Lumber Co.*, 2 USTC ¶484, 8 AFTR 10276, 50 S.Ct. 184 (USSC, 1929).
29. *Brown v. Helvering*, 4 USTC ¶1223, 12 AFTR 128, 54 S.Ct. 356 (USSC, 1933).
30. *Burnet v. Sanford and Brooks*, 2 USTC ¶636, 9 AFTR 603, 51 S.Ct. 150 (USSC, 1931).
31. *North American Oil Consolidated Co. v. Burnet*, 3 USTC ¶943, 11 AFTR 16, 52 S.Ct. 613 (USSC, 1932). See the Glossary of Tax Terms in Appendix C for a discussion of the term "claim of right doctrine."

The measure of accrual basis income is generally the amount the taxpayer has a right to receive. Unlike the cash basis, the fair market value of the customer's obligation is irrelevant in measuring accrual basis income.

EXAMPLE 10   Assume the same facts as in Example 8, except D is an accrual basis taxpayer. D must recognize $13,000 ($8,000 + $5,000) income in 1989, the year his rights to the income accrued. □

Exceptions Applicable to Cash Basis Taxpayers

Constructive Receipt.   Income that has not actually been received by the taxpayer is taxed as though it had been received—the income is *constructively received*—under the following conditions:

- The amount is made readily available to the taxpayer.
- The taxpayer's actual receipt is not subject to substantial limitations or restrictions.[32]

The rationale for the constructive receipt doctrine is that if the income is available, the taxpayer should not be allowed to postpone the income recognition. For instance, a taxpayer is not permitted to defer income for December services by refusing to accept payment until January. However, determining whether the income is *readily available* and whether *substantial limitations or restrictions exist* necessitates a factual inquiry that leads to a judgment call.[33] Some examples of the application of the constructive receipt doctrine follow:

EXAMPLE 11   P received a salary check on December 31 but after banking hours. P must recognize income on December 31 because the funds were made available to him on that date.[34] □

EXAMPLE 12   T is a member of a barter club. In 1989, T performed services for other club members and earned 1,000 points. Each point entitles him to $1 in goods and services sold by other members of the club, and the points can be used at any time. In 1990, T exchanged his points for a new color TV. T must recognize $1,000 income in 1989 when the 1,000 points were credited to his account.[35] □

EXAMPLE 13   On December 31, an employer issued a bonus check to an employee but asked him to hold it for a few days until the company could make deposits to cover the check. The income was not constructively received on Decem-

---

32. Reg. § 1.451–2(a).
33. *Baxter v. Comm.*, 87–1 USTC ¶ 9315, 59 AFTR2d 87–1068, 816 F.2d 493 (CA–9, 1987).
34. *C. F. Kahler*, 18 T.C. 31 (1952).
35. Rev.Rul. 80–52, 1980–1 C.B. 100.

ber 31, since the issuer did not have sufficient funds in its account to pay the debt.[36] ☐

EXAMPLE 14 R owned interest coupons that matured on December 31. The coupons could be converted to cash at any bank at maturity. Thus, the income is constructively received on December 31.[37] ☐

EXAMPLE 15 GM Company mails dividend checks on December 31, 1989. The checks will not be received by shareholders until January. The shareholders do not realize income until 1990. ☐

The constructive receipt doctrine does not reach income that the taxpayer is not yet entitled to receive even though he or she could have contracted to receive the income at an earlier date.

EXAMPLE 16 X offered to pay Y $100,000 for land in December 1989. Y refused but offered to sell the land to X on January 1, 1990, when Y would be in a lower tax bracket. If X accepted Y's offer, the gain would be taxed in 1990 when the sale was completed.[38] ☐

EXAMPLE 17 T is a professional athlete and reports his income by the cash method. In negotiating a contract, the club owner made two alternative offers to T:

1. $1,000,000 cash upon signing in 1989.

2. $100,000 per year plus 10% interest for 10 years.

T accepted the second offer. The income is taxed according to the amount he actually receives ($100,000 per year plus interest). The $1,000,000 T could have contracted to receive in 1989 is not constructively received in that year because he accepted the alternative offer.[39] If the final contract had provided that T could receive either the lump sum or installment payments, the $1,000,000 would have been constructively received in 1989. ☐

Income set apart or made available is not constructively received if its actual receipt is subject to *substantial restrictions*. The life insurance industry has used substantial restrictions as a cornerstone for designing life insurance contracts with favorable tax features. Ordinary life insurance policies provide (1) current protection—an amount payable in the event of death—and (2) a savings feature—a cash surrender value payable to the policyholder if he or she terminates the policy during his or her life. The annual increase in cash

36. *L. M. Fischer*, 14 T.C. 792 (1950).
37. Reg. § 1.451–2(b).
38. *Cowden v. Comm.*, 61–1 USTC ¶9382, 7 AFTR2d 1160, 289 F.2d 20 (CA–5, 1961).
39. Rev.Rul. 60–31, 1960–1 C.B. 174, discussed further in chapter 19.

surrender value is not taxable because the policyholder must cancel the policy to actually receive the increase in value. Because the cancellation requirement is a substantial restriction, the policyholder does not constructively receive the annual increase in cash surrender value.[40] Employees often receive from their employers property subject to substantial restrictions. Generally, no income is recognized until the restrictions lapse.[41]

EXAMPLE 18

C is a key employee of T, Inc. The corporation gave stock with a value of $10,000 to C. The stock could not be sold, however, for five years. C will not be required to recognize income until the restrictions lapse at the end of five years. □

Original Issue Discount.   Lenders frequently make loans that require a payment at maturity of more than the amount of the original loan. The difference between the amount due at maturity and the amount of the original loan is actually interest but is referred to as *original issue discount.* Under the general rules of tax accounting, the cash basis lender would not report the original issue discount as interest income until the year the amount is collected, although an accrual basis borrower would deduct the interest as it accrues. However, the Code puts the lender and borrower on parity by requiring that the original issue discount be reported when it accrues, regardless of the taxpayer's accounting method.[42]

EXAMPLE 19

On July 1, 1989, T, a cash basis taxpayer, paid $84,232 for an 18-month certificate of deposit with a maturity value of $100,000. The effective interest rate on the certificate was 12%. T must report $5,054 interest income for 1989:

$$(.12 \times \$84,232)(\tfrac{1}{2} \text{ year}) = \underline{\$5,054}$$ □

The original issue discount rules do not apply to U.S. savings bonds (discussed in the following paragraphs) or to obligations with a maturity date of one year or less from the date of issue.[43] See chapter 16 for additional discussion of the tax treatment of original issue discount.

Series E and Series EE Bonds.   Certain U.S. government savings bonds (Series E before 1980 and Series EE after 1979) are issued at a discount and are redeemable for fixed amounts that increase at stated intervals. No interest payments are actually made. The difference between the purchase price and the amount received on redemption is the bondholder's interest income from the investment.

The income from these savings bonds is generally deferred until the bonds are redeemed or mature. Furthermore, Series E bonds can be exchanged within one year of their maturity date for Series HH bonds, and the interest on the Series E bonds can be further deferred until maturity of the

---

40. *Theodore H. Cohen*, 39 T.C. 1055 (1963).

41. § 83(a). See also the discussion of Restricted Property Plans in chapter 19.

42. §§ 1272(a)(3) and 1273(a).

43. § 1272(a)(2).

Series HH bonds.[44] Thus, U.S. savings bonds have attractive income deferral features not available with corporate bonds and certificates of deposit issued by financial institutions.

Of course, the deferral feature of government bonds issued at a discount is not an advantage if the investor has insufficient income to be subject to tax as the income accrues. In fact, the deferral may work to the investor's disadvantage if he or she has other income in the year the bonds mature or the bunching of the bond interest into one tax year creates a tax liability. Fortunately, U.S. government bonds have a provision for these investors. A cash basis taxpayer can elect to include in gross income the annual increment in redemption value.[45]

When the election is made to report the income from the bonds on an annual basis, it applies to all such obligations the taxpayer owns at the time of the election and all such securities acquired subsequent to the election. A change in the method of reporting the income from the bonds requires permission from the IRS.

Amounts Received under an Obligation to Repay. The receipt of funds with an obligation to make repayment in the future is the essence of borrowing. Because the taxpayer's assets and liabilities increase by the same amount, no income is realized when the borrowed funds are received. Because amounts paid to the taxpayer by mistake and customer deposits are often classified as borrowed funds, receipt of the funds is not a taxable event.

EXAMPLE 20	A customer erroneously paid a utility bill twice. The utility company does not recognize income from the second payment because it has a liability to the customer.[46] □

EXAMPLE 21	A lessor received a damage deposit from a tenant. No income is recognized by the lessor before forfeiture of the deposit because the lessor has an obligation to repay the deposit if no damage occurs.[47] However, if the deposit is in fact a prepayment of rent, it is taxed in the year of receipt. □

Exceptions Applicable to Accrual Basis Taxpayers

Prepaid Income. For financial reporting purposes, advance payments received from customers are reflected as prepaid income and as a liability of the seller. However, for tax purposes, the prepaid income often is taxed in the year of receipt.

---

44. Treas. Dept. Circulars No. 1–80 and No. 2–80, 1980–1 C.B. 714, 715. Note that interest is paid at semiannual intervals on the Series HH bonds and must be included in income as received. Refer to chapter 5 for the discussion of the savings bond interest exclusion.

45. § 454(a).

46. *Comm. v. Turney*, 36–1 USTC ¶9168, 17 AFTR 679, 82 F.2d 661 (CA–5, 1936).

47. *John Mantell*, 17 T.C. 1143 (1952).

EXAMPLE 22 In December 1989, a tenant paid his January 1990 rent of $1,000. The accrual basis landlord must include the $1,000 in his 1989 income for tax purposes, although the unearned rent income is reported as a liability on the landlord's December 31, 1989, balance sheet. □

Taxpayers have repeatedly argued that deferral of income until it is actually earned properly matches revenues and expenses. Moreover, a proper matching of income with the expenses of earning the income is necessary to clearly reflect income, as required by the Code. The Commissioner responds that § 446(b) grants him broad powers to determine whether an accounting method clearly reflects income. He further argues that generally accepted financial accounting principles should not dictate tax accounting for prepaid income because of the practical problems of collecting Federal revenues. Collection of the tax is simplest in the year the taxpayer receives the cash from the customer or client.

Over a 40-year period of litigation, the Commissioner has been only partially successful in the courts. In cases involving prepaid income from services to be performed at the demand of customers (e.g., dance lessons to be taken at any time in a 24-month period), the Commissioner's position has been upheld.[48] In such cases, the taxpayer's argument that deferral of the income was necessary to match the income with expenses was not persuasive because the taxpayer did not know precisely when each customer would demand services and, thus, when the expenses would be incurred. However, taxpayers have had some success in the courts when the services were performed on a fixed schedule (e.g., a baseball team's season-ticket sales).[49] In some cases involving the sale of goods, taxpayers have successfully argued that the prepayments were mere deposits[50] or in the nature of loans.[51]

Against this background of mixed results in the courts, Congressional intervention, and taxpayers' strong resentment of the IRS's position, in 1971 the IRS modified its prepaid income rules, as explained in the following paragraphs.

Generally, a taxpayer can elect to defer recognition of income from *advance payments for goods* if the taxpayer's method of accounting for the sale is the same for tax and financial reporting purposes.[52]

EXAMPLE 23 B Company will ship goods only after payment for the goods has been received. In December 1989, B received $10,000 for goods that were not

48. *Automobile Club of Michigan v. U.S.*, 57–1 USTC ¶9593, 50 AFTR 1967, 77 S.Ct. 707 (USSC, 1957); *American Automobile Association v. U.S.*, 61–2 USTC ¶9517, 7 AFTR2d 1618, 81 S.Ct. 1727 (USSC, 1961); *Schlude v. Comm.*, 63–1 USTC ¶9284, 11 AFTR2d 751, 83 S.Ct. 601 (USSC, 1963).

49. *Artnell Company v. Comm.*, 68–2 USTC ¶959, 22 AFTR2d 5590, 400 F.2d 981 (CA–7, 1968). See also *Boise Cascade Corp. v. U.S.*, 76–1 USTC ¶9286, 37 AFTR 76–696, 530 F.2d 1367 (Ct. Cls., 1976).

50. *Vernstra & DeHavaan Coal Co.*, 11 T.C. 964 (1948).

51. *Consolidated-Hammer Dry Plate & Film Co. v. Comm.*, 63–1 USTC ¶9494, 11 AFTR2d 1518, 317 F.2d 829 (CA–7, 1963).

52. Reg. § 1.451–5(b). See Reg. § 1.451–5(c) for exceptions to this deferral opportunity. The financial accounting conformity requirement is not applicable to contractors who use the completed contract method.

shipped until January 1990. The company can elect to report the income for tax purposes in 1990, assuming the company reports the income in 1990 for financial reporting purposes. ☐

Deferral of Advance Payments for Services.   Revenue Procedure 71–21[53] permits an accrual basis taxpayer to defer recognition of income for *advance payments for services* to be performed by the end of the tax year following the year of receipt. No deferral is allowed if the taxpayer might be required to perform any services, under the agreement, after the tax year following the year of receipt of the advance payment.

EXAMPLE 24

X Corporation, an accrual basis taxpayer, sells its services under 12-month, 18-month, and 24-month contracts. The corporation provides services to each customer every month. In April of 1989, X Corporation sold the following customer contracts:

Length of Contract	Total Proceeds
12 months	$6,000
18 months	3,600
24 months	2,400

Fifteen hundred dollars of the $6,000 may be deferred ($3/12 \times \$6,000$) and $1,800 of the $3,600 may be deferred ($9/18 \times \$3,600$) because those amounts will not be earned until 1990. However, the entire $2,400 received on the 24-month contracts is taxable in the year of receipt (1989), since a part of the income will still be unearned by the end of the tax year following the year of receipt. ☐

Revenue Procedure 71–21 does *not apply* to prepaid rent, prepaid interest, or amounts received under guarantee or warranty contracts. Thus, the income will still be taxed in the year of receipt if collected before the income is actually earned. However, there is a special condition on the definition of the term *rent*:

"Rent" does not include payments for the use or occupancy of rooms or other space where significant services are also rendered to the occupant. . . .

The effect of the definition is to allow hotels, motels, tourist homes, and convalescent homes to defer the recognition of income under the rules discussed above.

In summary, Revenue Procedure 71–21 will result in conformity of tax and financial accounting in a very limited number of prepaid income cases. It is not apparent why prepaid rents and interest may not be deferred, why revenues under some service contracts may be spread over two years, and

53. 1971–2 C.B. 549.

why revenues under longer service contracts must be reported in one year. Although Revenue Procedure 71–21 has reduced the number of controversies involving prepaid income, a consistent policy has not yet evolved.

INCOME SOURCES

Personal Services

It is a well-established principle of taxation that income from personal services must be included in the gross income of the person who performs the services. This principle was first established in a Supreme Court decision, *Lucas v. Earl*.[54] Mr. Earl entered into a binding agreement with his wife under which Mrs. Earl was to receive one-half of Mr. Earl's salary. Justice Holmes used the celebrated *fruit* and *tree* metaphor to explain that the fruit (income) must be attributed to the tree from which it came (Mr. Earl's services). A mere assignment of income does not shift the liability for the tax.

In the case of a child, the Code specifically provides that amounts earned from personal services must be included in the child's gross income. This result applies even though the income is paid to other persons (e.g., the parents).[55]

Income from Property

Income from property (interest, dividends, rent) must be included in the gross income of the *owner* of the property. If a father clips interest coupons from bonds shortly before the interest payment date and gives the coupons to his son, the interest will still be taxed to the father. A father who assigns rents from rental property to his daughter will be taxed on the rent, since he retains ownership of the property.[56]

Who is to pay the tax on income accrued at the time of the transfer of income-producing property, and when does the income accrue? The position of the IRS is that in the case of a gift, interest accrues on a daily basis. However, the cash basis donor does not recognize the income until it is collected by the donee.[57]

EXAMPLE 25   F, a cash basis taxpayer, gave S bonds with a face amount of $10,000 and an 8% stated rate of interest. The gift was made on November 30, and the interest is payable each January 1. When S collects the interest in January, F must recognize $732 in interest income (8% × $10,000 × 334/365). S will recognize $68 in interest income ($800 − $732). □

When property that has accrued interest is sold, a portion of the selling price is treated as interest and is taxed to the seller in the year of sale.

54. 2 USTC ¶496, 8 AFTR 10287, 50 S.Ct. 241 (USSC, 1930).
55. § 73.
56. *Galt v. Comm.*, 54–2 USTC ¶9457, 46 AFTR 633, 216 F.2d 41 (CA–7, 1954); *Helvering v. Horst*, 40–2 USTC ¶9787, 24 AFTR 1058, 61 S.Ct. 144 (USSC, 1940).
57. Rev.Rul. 72–312, 1972–1 C.B. 22.

EXAMPLE 26 Assume the same facts as in Example 25, except that F sold the bonds on November 30 to an unrelated party for $10,000 plus accrued interest of $732. F must recognize $732 in interest income when the bonds are sold. □

Dividends, unlike interest, do not accrue on a daily basis because the declaration of the dividend is at the discretion of the board of directors of the corporation. Generally, dividends are taxed to the person who is entitled to receive them—the shareholder of record as of the corporation's record date.[58] However, the Tax Court has held that a donor does not shift dividend income to the donee if a gift of stock is made after the date of declaration but before the date of record.[59] The *fruit* has sufficiently ripened as of the declaration date to tax the dividend to the donor of the stock.

EXAMPLE 27 On June 20, 1989, the board of directors of Z Corporation declares a $10 per share dividend. The dividend is payable on June 30, 1989, to shareholders of record on June 25, 1989. As of June 20, 1989, M owned 200 shares of Z Corporation's stock. On June 21, 1989, M sold 100 of the shares to N for their fair market value and gave 100 of the shares to S. Assume both N and S are shareholders of record as of June 25, 1989. N (the purchaser) will be taxed on $1,000, since he is entitled to receive the dividend. However, M (the donor) will be taxed on the $1,000 received by S (the donee) because the gift was made after the declaration date of the dividend. □

Income from Partnerships, S Corporations, Trusts, and Estates

A *partnership* is not a separate taxable entity. Rather, the partnership merely files an information return (Form 1065), which serves to provide the data necessary for determining the character and amount of each partner's distributive share of the partnership's income and expenses. Each partner must then report his or her distributive share of the partnership's income and deductions for the partnership's tax year ending within or with his or her tax year. The income must be reported by each partner as if earned, even if such amounts are not actually distributed. Because a partner pays tax on income as the partnership earns it, a distribution by the partnership to the partner is treated under the recovery of capital rules.[60]

EXAMPLE 28 T owned a one-half interest in the capital and profits of T & S Company (a partnership). For tax year 1989, the partnership earned revenue of $150,000 and had operating expenses of $80,000. During the year, T withdrew from his capital account $2,500 per month (for a total of $30,000).

58. Reg. § 1.61–9(c). The record date is the cutoff for determining the shareholders who are entitled to receive the dividend.

59. *M. G. Anton*, 34 T.C. 842 (1960).

60. § 706(a) and Reg. § 1.706–1(a)(1). For further discussion see chapter 20.

For 1989, T must report $35,000 as his share of the partnership's profits [½ × ($150,000 − $80,000)] even though he received a distribution of only $30,000. □

A *small business corporation* may elect to be taxed similarly to a partnership. Thus, the shareholders pay the tax on the corporation's income.[61] The electing corporation is referred to as an *S corporation.* Generally, the shareholder reports his or her proportionate share of the corporation's income and deductions for the year, whether or not any distributions are actually made by the corporation.

EXAMPLE 29   Assume the same facts as in Example 28, except that T & S Company is an S corporation. T's income for the year is his share of the net taxable income earned by the corporation ($35,000) rather than the amount actually distributed to him. □

The *beneficiaries* of *estates and trusts* generally are taxed on the income earned by the estates or trusts that is actually distributed or required to be distributed to them.[62] Any income not taxed to the beneficiaries is taxable to the estate or trust.

Income in Community Property States

General Rules.   State law in Louisiana, Texas, New Mexico, Arizona, California, Washington, Idaho, Nevada, and Wisconsin is based upon a community property system. All other states have a common law property system. The basic difference between common law and community property systems centers around the property rights of married persons.

Under a *community property* system, all property is deemed to be either separately owned by the spouse or belonging to the marital community. Property may be held separately by a spouse if it was acquired before marriage or received by gift or inheritance following marriage. Otherwise, any property is deemed to be community property. For Federal tax purposes, each spouse is taxed on one-half of the income from property belonging to the community.

The laws of Texas, Louisiana, and Idaho distinguish between separate property and the income it produces. In these states, the income from separate property belongs to the community. Accordingly, for Federal income tax purposes, each spouse is taxed on one-half of the income. In the remaining community property states, separate property produces separate income that the owner-spouse must report on his or her Federal income tax return.

What appears to be income, however, may really represent a recovery of capital. A recovery of capital and gain realized on separate property retains its identity as separate property. Items such as nontaxable stock dividends, royalties from mineral interests, and gains and losses from the sale of property take on the same classification as the assets to which they relate.

---

61. §§ 1361(a) and 1366. For further discussion see chapter 20.
62. §§ 652(a) and 662(a). For further discussion of the taxation of income from partnerships, S corporations, trusts, and estates, see *West's Federal Taxation: Corporations, Partnerships, Estates, and Trusts,* chapters 7, 8, 9, and 16.

EXAMPLE 30   H and W are husband and wife and reside in a community property state. Among other transactions during the year, the following occurred:

- Nontaxable stock dividend received by W on stock that was given to her by her mother after her marriage.

- Gain of $10,000 on the sale of unimproved land purchased by H before his marriage.

- Oil royalties of $15,000 from a lease W acquired after marriage with her separate funds.

Since the stock dividend was distributed on stock held by W as separate property, it also is her separate property. The same result occurs as to the oil royalties W receives. All of the proceeds from the sale of unimproved land (including the gain of $10,000) are H's separate property. □

Income from personal services (salaries, wages, income from a professional partnership) is generally treated as one-half earned by each spouse in all community property states.

EXAMPLE 31   H and W are married but file separate returns. H received $25,000 salary and $300 taxable interest on a savings account he established in his name. The deposits to the savings account were made from H's salary earned since the marriage. W collected $2,000 taxable dividends on stock she inherited from her father. W's gross income is computed as follows under three assumptions as to the state of residency of the couple:

	California	Texas	Common Law States
Dividends	$ 2,000	$ 1,000	$2,000
Salary	12,500	12,500	–0–
Interest	150	150	–0–
	$14,650	$13,650	$2,000

□

Community Property Spouses Living Apart.   The general rules for taxing the income from services performed by residents of community property states can create complications and even inequities for spouses who are living apart.

EXAMPLE 32   C and D were married but living apart for the first nine months of 1989 and were divorced as of October 1, 1989. In December 1989, C married E, who was married but living apart from F before their divorce in June 1989. C and F had no income from personal services in 1989.

C brought into the C–E marriage a tax liability on one-half of D's earnings for the first nine months of the year. However, E left with F a tax liability on one-half of E's earnings for the first six months of 1989. □

In circumstances such as those depicted in Example 32, the accrued tax liability could be factored into a property division being negotiated at a time when the parties did not need further complications. In other cases, an abandoned spouse could be saddled with a tax on income earned by a spouse whose whereabouts are unknown.

In 1980, Congress developed a simple solution to the many tax problems of community property spouses living apart. A spouse (or former spouse) will be taxed only on his or her actual earnings from personal services if the following conditions are met:[63]

- The individuals live apart for the entire year.

- They do not file a joint return with each other.

- No portion of the earned income is transferred between the individuals.

EXAMPLE 33

H and W reside in a community property state, and both are gainfully employed. On July 1, 1989, they separated, and on June 30, 1990, they were divorced. Assuming their only source of income is wages, one-half of such income for each year is earned by June 30, and they did not file a joint return for 1989, each should report the following gross income:

	H's Separate Return	W's Separate Return
1989	One-half of H's wages	One-half of H's wages
	One-half of W's wages	One-half of W's wages
1990	All of H's wages	All of W's wages

The results would be the same if H or W married another person in 1990, except the newlyweds would probably file a joint return. □

It should be noted that the exception does not apply to income from community property.

EXAMPLE 34

Assume the same facts as in Example 33, except that W had established a savings account with her earnings received while married to H. Because the savings account is community property, H and W must each report interest income from the account as follows:

	H's Separate Return	W's Separate Return
1989	One-half	One-half
Through June 30, 1990	One-half	One-half
After June 30, 1990	None	All

☐

The Commissioner may absolve from liability an *innocent spouse* who does not live apart for the entire year and files a separate return but omits his or her share of the community income received by the other spouse. To qualify for the innocent spouse relief, the taxpayer must not know or must have no reason to know of the omitted community income.

ITEMS SPECIFICALLY INCLUDED IN GROSS INCOME

The general principles of gross income determination (discussed in the previous sections) as applied by the IRS and the courts have on occasion yielded results Congress found unacceptable. Consequently, Congress has set forth more specific rules for determining the gross income from certain sources. Some of these special rules appear in §§ 71–89 of the Code.

Alimony and Separate Maintenance Payments

When a married couple divorce or become legally separated, state law generally requires a division of the property accumulated during the marriage. In addition, one spouse may have a legal obligation to support the other spouse. The Code distinguishes between the support payments (alimony or separate maintenance) and the property division in terms of the tax consequences.

Alimony and separate maintenance payments are *deductible* by the party making the payments and are *includible* in the gross income of the party receiving the payments.[64] Thus, income is shifted from the income earner to the income beneficiary, who is better able to pay the tax on the amount received.

EXAMPLE 35

H and W were divorced, and H was required to pay W $15,000 of alimony each year. H earns $31,000 a year. The tax law presumes that because W received the $15,000, she is more able than H to pay the tax on that amount. Therefore, W must include the $15,000 in her gross income, and H is allowed to deduct $15,000 from his gross income. ☐

64. §§ 71 and 215.

A transfer of property other than cash to a former spouse under a divorce decree or agreement is not a taxable event. The transferee's cost basis in the asset is the same as the transferor's basis.[65]

EXAMPLE 36   H transfers stock to W as part of a 1989 divorce settlement. The cost of the stock to H is $12,000, and the stock's value at the time of the transfer is $15,000. W later sells the stock for $16,000. H is not required to recognize gain from the transfer of the stock to W, and W has a realized and recognized gain of $4,000 ($16,000 − $12,000) when she sells the stock.

□

In the case of cash payments, however, it is often difficult to distinguish payments under a support obligation (alimony) and payments for the other spouse's property (property settlement). In 1984 Congress developed objective rules to classify the payments.

Post-1984 Agreements and Decrees.   Cash payments made under post-1984 agreements and decrees are classified as alimony only if the following conditions are satisfied:

1. The agreement or decree does not specify that the cash payments are not alimony.

2. The payor and payee are not members of the same household at the time the payments are made.

3. There is no liability to make the payments for any period after the death of the payee.[66]

Requirement 1 allows the parties to determine by agreement whether or not the payments will be alimony. The prohibition on cohabitation—requirement 2—is aimed at assuring the alimony payments are associated with duplicative living expenses (maintaining two households).[67] Requirement 3 is an attempt to prevent alimony treatment from being applied to what is, in fact, a payment for property rather than a support obligation. That is, a seller's estate generally will receive payments for property due after the seller's death. Such payments after the death of the payee could not be for the payee's support.

Front-Loading.   As a further safeguard against a property settlement being disguised as alimony, special rules apply to post-1986 agreements if payments in the first or second year exceed $15,000. If the change in the amount of the payments exceeds statutory limits, *alimony recapture* results to the extent of the excess alimony payments. In the *third* year, the payor must include the excess alimony payments for the first and second years in gross income, and

---

65. § 1041, added to the Code in 1984 to repeal the rule of *United States v. Davis,* 62–2 USTC ¶ 9509, 9 AFTR2d 1625, 82 S.Ct. 1190 (USSC, 1962). Under the Davis rule, which was applicable to pre–1985 divorces, a transfer incident to divorce was a taxable event.

66. § 71(b)(1).

67. *Alexander Washington,* 77 T.C. 601 (1981) at 604.

the payee is allowed a deduction for these excess alimony payments. The recaptured amount is computed as follows: [68]

$$R = D + E$$

$$D = B - (C + \$15{,}000)$$

$$E = A - \left(\frac{B - D + C}{2} + \$15{,}000\right)$$

R = amount recaptured in Year 3

D = recapture from Year 2

E = recapture from Year 1

A, B, C = payments in the first (A), second (B), and third (C) calendar years of the agreement or decree, where $D \geq 0, E \geq 0$

The recapture formula provides an objective technique for determining alimony recapture. Thus, at the time of the divorce, the taxpayers can ascertain the tax consequences. The general concept is that if the alimony payments decrease by over \$15,000 between years in the first three years, there will be alimony recapture with respect to the decrease in excess of \$15,000 each year. For the change between Year 2 and Year 3, this is the rule that is applied. However, rather than making the same calculation for Year 2 payments versus Year 1 payments, the Code requires that the *average* of the payments in Years 2 and 3 be compared with the Year 1 payments. For this purpose, revised alimony for Year 2 (alimony deducted for Year 2 minus the alimony recapture for Year 2) is used.

EXAMPLE 37

H and W were divorced in 1989. Under the agreement, W was to receive \$50,000 in 1989, \$20,000 in 1990, and nothing thereafter. The payments were to cease upon W's death or remarriage. In 1991, H must include an additional \$32,500 in gross income, and W is allowed a deduction for the same amount.

$$D = \$20{,}000 - (\$0 + \$15{,}000) = \$5{,}000$$

$$E = \$50{,}000 - \left(\frac{\$20{,}000 - \$5{,}000 + \$0}{2} + \$15{,}000\right) = \$27{,}500$$

$$R = \$5{,}000 + \$27{,}500 = \$32{,}500$$

If \$50,000 were paid in 1989 and nothing is paid for the following years, \$35,000 would be recaptured in 1991.

$$D = \$0 - (\$0 + \$15{,}000) = -\$15{,}000, \text{ but D must be } \geq \$0$$

$$E = \$50{,}000 - \left(\frac{\$0 - \$0 + \$0}{2} + \$15{,}000\right) = \$35{,}000$$

$$R = \$0 + \$35{,}000 = \$35{,}000$$

☐

---

68. § 71(f).

For 1985 and 1986 agreements and decrees, alimony recapture is required during the second and third years if payments decrease by more than $10,000. A special formula is applied to compute the recapture amounts.[69]

Recapture is not required if the decrease in payments is due to death of either spouse or remarriage of the payee. In addition, the recapture rules do not apply to contingent payments (e.g., a percentage of income from certain property or a percentage of the payor spouse's compensation) that are to be made over a period of three years or longer (unless death, remarriage, or other contingency occurs) and the contingencies are beyond the payor's control.[70]

EXAMPLE 38

Under a 1989 divorce agreement, H was to receive an amount equal to one-half of W's income from certain rental properties for 1989–1992. Payments were to cease upon the death of H or W or upon the remarriage of H. H received $50,000 in 1989 and $50,000 in 1990; however in 1991, the property was vacant, and H received nothing. W, who deducted alimony in 1989 and 1990, is not required to recapture any alimony in 1991 because the payments were contingent. □

Pre-1985 Agreements and Decrees.   Because payments will continue to be made under pre-1985 agreements for many years, these provisions are briefly reviewed here. The requirements for alimony treatment under pre-1985 agreements are as follows:

1. The payments must be made pursuant to either (a) a court order (a decree of divorce, separate maintenance decree, or decree of support) or (b) a written separation agreement (in short, the payments cannot be voluntary).

2. The payments must be either (a) for a period of more than 10 years or (b) subject to a contingency (e.g., the death of either spouse, remarriage of the recipient, or change in the economic status of either spouse).

3. The payments must be in "discharge of a legal obligation arising from the marital or family obligations."[71]

The third requirement presents numerous problems because the *legal obligation* is determined under state law. Many states require that a spouse be paid for his or her *fair share* of the property that has been accumulated during the marriage but retained by the other spouse. Additionally, a state may impose a support obligation on the spouse. Only payments under the support obligation satisfy the marital obligation requirement (3). Thus, a cash payment may be (1) solely for support, (2) solely for property, or (3) in part for support and in part for property. Moreover, the labels the spouses attach to the payments (by pre-1985 agreement) do not control.

Child Support.   A taxpayer does not realize income from the receipt of child support payments made by his or her former spouse. This is true be-

---

69. See § 421 of the Deficit Reduction Act of 1984 and § 1843(c)(2) of the Tax Reform Act of 1986.

70. §§ 71(f)(5)(A) and (C).

71. §§ 71(a) and (b) prior to amendment by § 422 of the Deficit Reduction Act of 1984.

cause the money is received subject to the duty to use the money for the child's benefit.

In many cases, it is difficult to determine whether an amount received is alimony or child support. Under pre-1985 decrees and agreements, according to the Supreme Court, if the decree or agreement does not specifically provide for child support, none of the payments will be treated as such.[72]

EXAMPLE 39

A pre-1985 divorce agreement provides that H is required to make periodic alimony payments of $500 per month to W. However, when H and W's child reaches age 21, marries, or dies (whichever occurs first), the payments will be reduced to $300 per month. W has custody of the child. Although it is reasonable to infer that $200 ($500 − $300) is for child support because no payments are specified as child support, the entire $500 is alimony. □

In 1984, Congress changed the results in Example 39 but only as to post-1984 agreements and decrees. Under the revision, if the amount of the payments would be reduced upon the happening of a contingency related to a child (e.g., the child attains age 21 or dies), the amount of the future reduction in the payment will be deemed child support.[73]

EXAMPLE 40

The facts are the same as in Example 39 except that the agreement is a post-1984 agreement. Child support payments are $200 each month and alimony is $300 each month. □

Imputed Interest on Below-Market Loans

As discussed earlier in the chapter, generally no income is recognized unless it is realized. Realization generally occurs when the taxpayer performs services or sells goods and thus becomes entitled to a payment from the other party. It follows that no income is realized if the goods or services are provided at no charge. Under this interpretation of the realization requirement, before 1984, interest-free loans were used to shift income between taxpayers.

EXAMPLE 41

D (daughter) is in the 20% tax bracket and has no investment income. F (father) is in the 50% tax bracket and has $200,000 in a money market account earning 10% interest. F would like D to receive and pay tax on the income earned on the $200,000. Because F would also like to have access to the $200,000 should he need the money, he does not want to make an outright gift of the money, nor does he want to commit the money to a trust.

---

72. *Comm. v. Lester*, 61–1 USTC ¶9463, 7 AFTR2d 1445, 81 S.Ct. 1343 (USSC, 1961).

73. § 71(c)(2). Pre-1985 agreements can be amended so that the revision will apply [§ 422(e) of the Deficit Reduction Act of 1984].

Before 1984, F could achieve his goals as follows. F could transfer the money market account to D in exchange for D's $200,000 noninterest-bearing note, payable on F's demand. As a result, D would receive the income, and the family's taxes would be decreased by $6,000.

Decrease in F's tax— (.10 × $200,000) .50 =	($10,000)
Increase in D's tax— (.10 × $200,000) .20 =	4,000
Decrease in the family's taxes	($6,000)

Concept Summary 4–1

Tax Treatment of Payments and Transfers Pursuant to Post–1984 Divorce Agreements and Decrees

	Payor	Recipient
Alimony	Deduction from gross income.	Included in gross income.
Alimony recapture	Included in gross income of the third year.	Deducted from gross income of the third year.
Child support	Not deductible.	Not includible in income.
Property settlement	No income or deduction.	No income or deduction; basis for the property is the same as the transferor's basis.

Under the 1984 amendments to the Code, F in Example 41 is required to recognize imputed interest income.[74] Also, D is deemed to have incurred interest expense equal to F's imputed interest income. D's interest may be deductible on her return as portfolio interest if she itemizes deductions (see chapter 11). To complete the fictitious series of transactions, F is then deemed to have given D the amount of the imputed interest D did not pay. The gift received by D is not subject to income tax (see chapter 5), although F may be subject to the unified transfer tax on the amount deemed given to D (refer to chapter 1).

Imputed interest is calculated using the rate the Federal government pays on new borrowings and is compounded semiannually. This Federal rate is adjusted monthly and is published by the IRS.[75] Actually, there are three

74. § 7872(a)(1).

75. §§ 7872(b)(2) and (f)(2).

Federal rates: short-term (not over three years and including demand loans), mid-term (over three years but not over nine years), and long-term (over nine years).

EXAMPLE 42

Assume the Federal rate applicable to the loan in Example 41 is 12% through June 30 and 13% from July 1 through December 31. F made the loan on January 1, and the loan is still outstanding on December 31. F must recognize interest income of $25,780, and D has interest expense of $25,780. F is deemed to have made a gift of $25,780 to D.

Interest calculations	
January 1–June 30—	
.12 ($200,000) (½ year)	$12,000
July 1–December 31—	
.13 ($200,000 + $12,000) (½ year)	13,780
	$25,780

☐

If interest is charged on the loan but is less than the Federal rate, the imputed interest is the difference between the amount that would have been charged at the Federal rate and the amount actually charged.

EXAMPLE 43

Assume the same facts as in Example 42, except that F charged 6% interest, compounded annually.

Interest at the Federal rate	$ 25,780
Less interest charged	
(.06 × $200,000)	(12,000)
Imputed interest	$ 13,780

☐

The imputed interest rules apply to the following *types* of below-market loans: [76]

1. Gift loans (made out of love, affection, or generosity, as in Example 41).

2. Compensation-related loans (employer loans to employees).

3. Corporation-shareholder loans (a corporation's loans to its shareholders).

---

76. § 7872(c).

4. Tax avoidance loans and other loans that significantly affect the bor-
    rower's or lender's Federal tax liability (discussed in the following
    paragraphs).

The effects of the first three types of loans on the borrower and lender are
summarized in Concept Summary 4–2.

Tax Avoidance and Other Below-Market Loans.   In an effort to close any
possible loopholes, Congress provided catchall provisions that apply to tax
avoidance and other below-market loans. The Conference Report provides the
following example of an arrangement that might be subject to the imputed
interest rules: [77]

EXAMPLE 44   Annual dues for the XY Health Club are $400. In lieu of paying dues, a
                    member can make a $4,000 deposit, refundable at the end of one year.
                    The club can earn $400 interest on the deposit.

                        If interest were not imputed, an individual with $4,000 could, in
                    effect, earn tax-exempt income on the deposit. That is, rather than invest
                    the $4,000, earn $400 in interest, pay tax on the interest, and then pay
                    $400 in dues, the individual could avoid tax on the interest by making the
                    deposit. Thus, income and expenses are imputed as follows: interest in-
                    come and nondeductible health club fees for the club member; income
                    from fees and interest expense for the club. □

Exceptions and Limitations.   No interest is imputed on total outstanding
gift loans of $10,000 or less between individuals, unless the loan proceeds are
used to purchase income-producing property.[78] This exemption eliminates
from these complex provisions immaterial amounts that do not result in
apparent shifts of income.

On loans of $100,000 or less between individuals, the imputed interest
cannot exceed the borrower's net investment income for the year.[79] The rationale for this limitation is that the loan cannot cause a shift of more income
(from lender to borrower) than was earned by the borrower. As a further
limitation, or exemption, if the borrower's net investment income for the year
does not exceed $1,000, no interest is imputed on loans of $100,000 or less.
However, these limitations for loans of $100,000 or less do not apply if a
principal purpose of a loan is tax avoidance. According to the Senate Report,
if a principal purpose of a loan is to shift income to a taxpayer in a lower tax
bracket (as illustrated in Example 41), the purpose is a proscribed one. Therefore, in such a case interest is imputed, and the imputed interest is not limited
to the borrower's net investment income.[80]

---

77. H. Rep. No. 98–861, 98th Cong., 2d Sess., 1984,
     p. 1023.
78. § 7872(c)(2).
79. § 7872(d).

80. *Deficit Reduction Tax Bill of 1984: Explanation
     of the Senate Finance Committee* (April 2, 1984),
     p. 484.

CONCEPT SUMMARY 4–2

Effect of Certain Below-Market Loans on the Lender and Borrower

Type of Loan		Lender	Borrower
Gift	Step 1	Interest income	Interest expense
	Step 2	Gift made	Gift received
Compensation-related	Step 1	Interest income	Interest expense
	Step 2	Compensation expense	Compensation income
Corporation to shareholder	Step 1	Interest income	Interest expense
	Step 2	Dividend paid	Dividend income

EXAMPLE 45

F made interest-free gift loans as follows:

Borrower	Amount	Borrower's Net Investment Income	Purpose
S	$ 8,000	$ 1,000	Education
D	9,000	500	Purchase of stock
B	25,000	–0–	Purchase of a business
M	60,000	15,000	Purchase of a residence
O	120,000	–0–	Purchase of a residence

Assume that tax avoidance is not a principal purpose of any of the loans. The S loan is not subject to the imputed interest rules because the $10,000 exception applies. The $10,000 exemption does not apply to the D loan because the proceeds were used to purchase income-producing assets. However, under the $100,000 exception, the imputed interest is limited to D's investment income ($500). Since the $1,000 exception also applies to this loan, no interest will be imputed.

No interest is imputed on the B loan because the $100,000 exception applies. Interest will be imputed on the M loan based on the lesser of (1) the lender's $15,000 net investment income or (2) the interest as calculated by applying the Federal rate to the outstanding loan. None of the exceptions apply to the O loan. ☐

As with gift loans, there is a $10,000 exemption for compensation-related loans and corporation-shareholder loans. However, the $10,000 exception does not apply if tax avoidance is one of the principal purposes of a loan.[81] This vague tax avoidance standard makes practically all compensation-related

---

81. § 7872(c)(3).

and corporation-shareholder loans suspect. Nevertheless, the $10,000 exception should apply when an employee's borrowing was necessitated by personal needs (e.g., to meet unexpected expenses) rather than tax considerations.

Measuring Income.   The measurement of the gift, compensation, or dividend resulting from a loan depends upon whether the loan is (1) a *demand loan* payable at the demand of the lender or (2) a *term loan* due as of a specific date. In the case of a demand loan, the interest is calculated using the short-term rate, and the forgone interest is the measure of the gift, compensation, or dividend. In the case of a term loan, the difference between the face amount of the loan and its present value at the date of the loan is the measure of the gift, compensation, or dividend.[82] The interest income is computed by applying the imputed interest rate to the balance of the loan. For both the demand loan and the term loan, semiannual compounding is required.

EXAMPLE 46   R, the employer, loaned $100,000 interest-free to E, an employee, on January 1 of the current tax year. The loan was due in five years, and the Federal *mid-term* rate was 10.7% compounded semiannually (the equivalent of 11% with annual compounding).

R's compensation expense and E's compensation income for the current tax year are computed as follows:

Face amount	$100,000
Less present value of $100,000 due in 5 years, i=11%	(59,345)
Original issue discount	$ 40,655

R's interest income and E's interest expense are computed as follows:

Year	Beginning Balance	Applicable Interest @ 11%	Ending Balance
1989	$ 59,345 *	$ 6,528	$ 65,873
1990	65,873	7,246	73,119
1991	73,119	8,043	81,162
1992	81,162	8,928	90,090
1993	90,090	9,910	100,000
		$40,655	

*   Beginning loan balance equals $100,000 face amount minus $40,655 original issue discount.

82. Joint Committee of Taxation, *Tax Reform Act of 1984: General Explanation of the Revenue Provisions*, p. 532.

For income tax purposes (but not for gift tax purposes), term gift loans are treated as demand loans.

EXAMPLE 47

Assume the same facts as in Example 46, except that the $100,000 was received by E as a gift loan. Further assume that the Federal *short-term* rate was 9.76% compounded semiannually (the equivalent of 10% with annual compounding). The amount of the gift is $40,655 (calculated using the *mid-term* rate) but R's interest income and E's interest expense are equal to the Federal *short-term* rate times the amount of the loan (.10 × $100,000 = $10,000). □

The apparent rationale for treating all gift loans as demand loans is that as a practical matter, the lender could receive his or her principal at any time at his or her demand.

Income from Annuities

Annuity contracts generally require the purchaser (the annuitant) to pay a fixed amount for the right to receive a future stream of payments.[83] Typically, the issuer of the contract is an insurance company and will pay the annuitant a cash value if the annuitant cancels the contract. The insurance company invests the amounts received from the annuitant, and the income earned serves to increase the cash value of the policy. No income is recognized at the time the cash value of the annuity increases because the taxpayer has not actually received any income. The income is not constructively received because, generally, the taxpayer must cancel the policy to receive the increase in value (the increase in value is subject to substantial restrictions).

EXAMPLE 48

T, age 50, paid $30,000 for an annuity contract that is to pay him $500 per month beginning when he reaches age 65 and continuing until his death. If T should cancel the policy after one year, he would receive $30,200. The $200 increase in value is not includible in the gross income of T, as long as T does not actually receive the $200. □

The tax accounting problem associated with receiving payments under an annuity contract is one of apportioning the amounts received between recovery of capital and income.

EXAMPLE 49

In 1989, T purchased for $15,000 an annuity intended as a source of retirement income. In 1991, when the cash value of the annuity was $17,000, T collected $1,000 on the contract. Is the $1,000 gross income, recovery of capital, or a combination of recovery of capital and income?

□

---

83. See the Glossary of Tax Terms in Appendix C for a definition of the term "annuity."

The statutory solution to this problem depends upon whether the payments began before or after the annuity starting date and upon when the policy was acquired.

Collections before the Annuity Starting Date.   Generally an annuity contract specifies a date on which monthly or annual payments will begin—the annuity starting date. Often the contract will also allow the annuitant to collect a limited amount before the starting date. The amount collected may be characterized as either an actual withdrawal of the increase in cash value or a loan on the policy. In 1982, Congress changed the rules applicable to these withdrawals and loans.

Collections (including loans) equal to or less than the post-August 13, 1982, increases in cash value must be included in gross income. Amounts received in excess of post-August 13, 1982, increases in cash value are treated as a recovery of capital until the taxpayer's cost has been entirely recovered. Additional amounts are included in gross income.[84] The taxpayer may also be subject to a penalty on early distributions of 10 percent of the income recognized. The penalty generally applies if the amount is received before the taxpayer reaches age 59½ or is disabled.[85]

EXAMPLE 50   T, age 50, purchased an annuity policy for $30,000 in 1989. In 1991, when the cash value of the policy has increased to $33,000, T withdraws $4,000. T must recognize $3,000 of income ($33,000 cash value − $30,000 cost) and must pay a penalty of $300 ($3,000 × 10%). □

The 1982 rules were enacted because Congress perceived abuse of the recovery of capital rule. Formerly, individuals could purchase annuity contracts that guaranteed an annual increase in cash value and withdraw the equivalent of interest on the contract but recognize no income. This is no longer possible. In addition, the individual must recognize income from borrowing on the contract (e.g., pledging the contract as security for a loan) as well as from an actual distribution.

Collections on and after the Annuity Starting Date.   The annuitant can exclude from income (as a recovery of capital) the proportion of each payment that the investment in the contract bears to the expected return under the contract. The *exclusion amount* is calculated as follows:

$$\frac{\text{Investment}}{\text{Expected return}} \quad \times \quad \text{Annuity payment} \quad = \quad \text{Exclusion amount}$$

The *expected return* is the annual amount to be paid to the annuitant multiplied by the number of years the payments will be received. The payment period may be fixed (a *term certain*) or for the life of one or more individuals. When payments are for life, the taxpayer must use the annuity

---

84.   § 72(c)(3); Reg. § 1.72–9.   85.   § 72(q).

table published by the IRS to determine the expected return (see Figure 4–1). This is an actuarial table that contains life expectancies.[86] The expected return is calculated by multiplying the appropriate multiple (life expectancy) by the annual payment.

FIGURE 4–1	Ordinary Life Annuities: One Life–Expected Return Multiples				
Age	**Multiple**	**Age**	**Multiple**	**Age**	**Multiple**
5	76.6	42	40.6	79	10.0
6	75.6	43	39.6	80	9.5
7	74.7	44	38.7	81	8.9
8	73.7	45	37.7	82	8.4
9	72.7	46	36.8	83	7.9
10	71.7	47	35.9	84	7.4
11	70.7	48	34.9	85	6.9
12	69.7	49	34.0	86	6.5
13	68.8	50	33.1	87	6.1
14	67.8	51	32.2	88	5.7
15	66.8	52	31.3	89	5.3
16	65.8	53	30.4	90	5.0
17	64.8	54	29.5	91	4.7
18	63.9	55	28.6	92	4.4
19	62.9	56	27.7	93	4.1
20	61.9	57	26.8	94	3.9
21	60.9	58	25.9	95	3.7
22	59.9	59	25.0	96	3.4
23	59.0	60	24.2	97	3.2
24	58.0	61	23.3	98	3.0
25	57.0	62	22.5	99	2.8
26	56.0	63	21.6	100	2.7
27	55.1	64	20.8	101	2.5
28	54.1	65	20.0	102	2.3
29	53.1	66	19.2	103	2.1
30	52.2	67	18.4	104	1.9
31	51.2	68	17.6	105	1.8
32	50.2	69	16.8	106	1.6
33	49.3	70	16.0	107	1.4
34	48.3	71	15.3	108	1.3
35	47.3	72	14.6	109	1.1
36	46.4	73	13.9	110	1.0
37	45.4	74	13.2	111	.9
38	44.4	75	12.5	112	.8
39	43.5	76	11.9	113	.7
40	42.5	77	11.2	114	.6
41	41.5	78	10.6	115	.5

---

86. The life expectancies in Figure 4–1 apply for annuity investments made on or after July 1, 1986. See *Pension and Annuity Income*, IRS Publication 575 (Rev. Nov. 87), pp. 22–24 for the IRS table to use for investments made before July 1, 1986.

EXAMPLE 51   The taxpayer, age 54, purchased an annuity from an insurance company for $90,000. He was to receive $500 per month for life. His life expectancy (from Figure 4–1) is 29.5 years from the annuity starting date. Thus, his expected return is $500 × 12 × 29.5 = $177,000, and the exclusion amount is $3,051 [($90,000 investment/$177,000 expected return) × $6,000 annual payment]. The $3,051 is a nontaxable return of capital, and $2,949 is included in gross income. ☐

The exclusion ratio applies until the annuitant has recovered his or her investment in the contract. Once the investment is recovered, the entire amount of subsequent payments is taxable. If the annuitant dies before recovering his or her investment, the unrecovered cost is deductible in the year the payments cease (usually the year of death).[87]

EXAMPLE 52   Assume the taxpayer in Example 51 received annuity payments for 30.5 years (366 months). For the last 12 months [366 − (12 × 29.5) = 12], the taxpayer would include $500 each month in gross income. If instead the taxpayer died after 36 months, he is eligible for a $80,847 deduction on his final tax return.

Cost of the contract	$90,000
Cost previously recovered $90,000/$177,000 × 36 ($500) =	(9,153)
Deduction	$80,847

☐

Prizes and Awards

Before 1954, there was uncertainty relative to the taxability of prizes and awards. Taxpayers often sought to treat prizes and awards as nontaxable gifts. In many situations, it was difficult to determine whether the prize or award was in the nature of a gift. In 1954, Congress added § 74 to eliminate this uncertainty.

The fair market value of prizes and awards (other than scholarships exempted under § 117, to be discussed subsequently) must be included in income. Therefore, TV giveaway prizes, door prizes, and awards from an employer to an employee in recognition of performance are fully taxable to the recipient.

An exception is provided if the award is received in recognition of religious, charitable, scientific, educational, artistic, literary, or civic achievement and the recipient transfers the award to a qualified governmental unit or nonprofit organization. In such cases, the recipient must be selected without any action on his or her part to enter a contest or proceeding, and the recipient must not be required to render substantial future services as a

87. § 72(b).

condition for receiving the prize or award.[88] Thus, the benefit of the exclusion appears to be to allow the recipient to avoid any annual limitation on the charitable contributions deduction (see chapter 11).

Another exception is provided for certain employee achievement awards in the form of tangible personal property (e.g., a gold watch). The awards must be made in recognition of length of service or safety achievement. Generally, the ceiling on the excludible amount is $400. However, if the award is a qualified plan award, the ceiling on the exclusion is $1,600.[89]

Group Term Life Insurance

Before 1964, the IRS did not attempt to tax the value of life insurance protection provided to an employee by the employer. Some companies took undue advantage of the exclusion by providing large amounts of insurance protection for executives. Therefore, Congress enacted § 79, which created a limited exclusion. Current law allows an exclusion for premiums on the first $50,000 of group term life insurance protection.

The benefits of this exclusion are available only to employees. Proprietors and partners are not considered employees. Moreover, the Regulations generally require broad-scale coverage of employees to satisfy the *group* requirement (e.g., shareholder-employees would not constitute a qualified group). The exclusion applies only to term insurance (protection for a period of time but with no cash surrender value) and not to ordinary life insurance (lifetime protection plus a cash surrender value that can be drawn upon before death).

As mentioned, the exclusion applies to the first $50,000 of group term life insurance protection. For each $1,000 coverage in excess of $50,000, the employee must include the following amounts in gross income.[90]

Uniform Premiums for $1,000 of Group Term Life Insurance Protection	
Attained Age Last Day of the Employee's Tax Year	Cost Per $1,000 of Protection for One-Month Period
Under 30	8 cents
30–34	9 cents
35–39	11 cents
40–44	17 cents
45–49	29 cents
50–54	48 cents
55–59	75 cents
60–64	$1.17

EXAMPLE 53	XYZ Corporation has a group term life insurance policy with coverage equal to the employee's annual salary. Mr. A, age 52, is president of the

---

88. § 74(b).
89. §§ 74(c) and 274(j).

90. Reg. § 1.79–3(d)(2).

corporation and receives an annual salary of $75,000. Mr. A must include $144 in gross income from the insurance protection for the year.

$$\left(\frac{\$75,000 - \$50,000}{\$1,000}\right) \times (.48) \times (12 \text{ months}) = \$144 \qquad \square$$

Generally, the amount that must be included in income, computed from the above table, is much less than the price an individual would pay for the same amount of protection. Thus, even the excess coverage provides some tax-favored income for employees when group term life insurance coverage in excess of $50,000 is desirable. However, if the plan discriminates in favor of certain key employees (e.g., officers), the key employees are not eligible for the exclusion. In such a case, the key employees must include in gross income the greater of actual premiums paid by the employer or the amount calculated from the Uniform Premiums table. The other employees are still eligible for the $50,000 exclusion and continue to use the Uniform Premiums table to compute the income from excess insurance protection.[91]

Unemployment Compensation

In a series of rulings over a period of 40 years, the IRS exempted unemployment benefits from tax. These payments were considered social benefit programs for the promotion of the general welfare. As previously discussed, the scope of § 61, gross income, is probably broad enough to include unemployment benefits (since an increase in wealth is realized when the payments are received). Nevertheless, the IRS had chosen to exclude such benefits.

In 1978, Congress addressed the unemployment compensation issue and provided that unemployment benefits are taxable only if the recipient's adjusted gross income exceeds certain levels. In 1986, Congress readdressed the issue by providing that all unemployment compensation benefits are includible in gross income.[92]

Social Security Benefits

If a taxpayer's income exceeds a specified base amount, as much as one-half of Social Security retirement benefits must be included in gross income. The taxable amount of Social Security benefits is the *lesser* of the following:[93]

* .50 (Social Security benefits)
* .50 [modified adjusted gross income + .50 (Social Security benefits) − base amount]

Modified adjusted gross income is, generally, the taxpayer's adjusted gross income from all sources (other than Social Security), plus the foreign earned income exclusion and any tax-exempt interest received. The *base amount* is as follows:

---

91. § 79(d).
92. § 85.

93. § 86.

- $32,000 for married taxpayers who file a joint return.

- $0 for married taxpayers who do not live apart for the entire year but file separate returns.

- $25,000 for all other taxpayers.

EXAMPLE 54

A married couple with adjusted gross income of $40,000, no tax-exempt interest, and $11,000 of Social Security benefits who file jointly must include one-half of the benefits in gross income. This works out as the lesser of the following:

1. .50 ($11,000) = $5,500
2. .50 [$40,000 + .50 ($11,000) − $32,000] = .50 ($13,500) = $6,750

If the couple's adjusted gross income were $15,000 and Social Security benefits totaled $5,000, none of the benefits would be taxable, since .50 [$15,000 + .50 ($5,000) − $32,000] = $0. □

TAX PLANNING CONSIDERATIONS

The materials in this chapter focused on the all-inclusive concept of gross income. Not much was discussed concerning ways to minimize taxable income. However, a few observations can be made with regard to timing the recognition of income and shifting income to relatives.

Tax Deferral

General. Since deferred taxes are tantamount to interest-free loans from the government, the deferral of taxes is a worthy goal of the tax planner. However, the tax planner must also consider the tax rates for the years the income is shifted from and to. For example, a one-year deferral of income from a year in which the taxpayer's tax rate was 15 percent to a year in which the tax rate will be 28 percent would not be advisable if the taxpayer expects to earn less than a 13 percent after-tax return on the deferred tax dollars.

The taxpayer can often defer the recognition of income from appreciated property by postponing the event triggering realization (the final closing on a sale or exchange of property). If the taxpayer needs cash, obtaining a loan by using the appreciated property as collateral may be the least costly alternative. When the taxpayer anticipates reinvesting the proceeds, a sale may be inadvisable.

EXAMPLE 55

T owns 100 shares of XYZ Company common stock with a cost of $10,000 and a market value of $50,000. Although the stock's value has increased substantially in the past three years, T thinks the growth days are over. If he sells the XYZ stock, T will invest the proceeds from the sale in other common stock. Assuming T is in the 28% marginal tax bracket, he will have only $38,800 [$50,000 − .28 ($50,000 − $10,000)] to reinvest. The alternative investment must substantially outperform XYZ in the future in order for the sale to be beneficial. □

Selection of Investments. Because no tax is due until a gain has been recognized, the law favors investments that yield appreciation rather than annual income.

EXAMPLE 56

S can buy a corporate bond or an acre of land for $10,000. The bond pays $1,000 of interest (10%) each year, and S expects the land to increase in value 10% each year for the next 10 years. She is in the 40% (combined Federal and state) tax bracket. Assuming the bond would mature or the land would be sold in 10 years and S would reinvest the interest at a 10% before-tax return, she would accumulate the following amount at the end of 10 years.

		Bonds	**Land**
Original investment		$10,000	$10,000
Annual income	$ 1,000		
Less tax	(400)		
	$ 600		
Compound amount reinvested for 10 years at 6% after-tax	× 13.18	7,908	
		$17,908	
Compound amount, 10 years at 10%			× 2.59
			$25,900
Less tax on sale: 40% ($25,900 − $10,000)			(6,360)
			$19,540

Therefore, the value of the deferral that results from investing in the land rather than in the bond is $1,632 ($19,540 − $17,908). □

Series E and EE bonds can also be purchased for long-term deferrals of income. As discussed in the chapter, Series E bonds can be exchanged for new Series HH bonds to further postpone the tax. In situations where the taxpayer's goal is merely to shift income one year into the future, bank certificates of deposit are useful tools. If the maturity period is one year or less, all interest is reported in the year of maturity. Time certificates are especially useful for a taxpayer who realizes an unusually large gain from the sale of property in one year (and thus is in a high tax bracket) but expects his or her income to be less the following year.

Cash Basis. The timing of income from services can often be controlled through the use of the cash method of accounting. Although taxpayers are somewhat constrained by the constructive receipt doctrine (they cannot turn their backs on income), seldom will customers and clients offer to pay before they are asked. The usual lag between billings and collections (e.g., December's billings collected in January) will result in a continuous deferring of some income until the last year of operations. A salaried individual approaching retirement may contract with his or her employer before the services are rendered to receive a portion of compensation in the lower tax bracket retirement years.

Prepaid Income. For the accrual basis taxpayer who receives advance payments from customers, the transactions should be structured to avoid payment of tax on income before the time the income is actually earned. Revenue Procedure 71–21 provides the guidelines for deferring the tax on prepayments for services, and Reg. § 1.451–5 provides the guidelines for deferrals on sales of goods. In addition, with respect to both the cash and accrual basis taxpayer, income can sometimes be deferred by stipulating that the payments are deposits rather than prepaid income. For example, a landlord should require an equivalent damage deposit rather than require prepayment of the last month's rent under the lease.

Shifting Income to Relatives

The tax liability of a family can be minimized by shifting income from higher- to lower-bracket family members. This can be accomplished through gifts of income-producing property. Furthermore, in many cases, the shifting of income can be accomplished with no negative effect on the family's investment plans.

EXAMPLE 57

B, who is in the 28% tax bracket, would like to save for his children's education. All of the children are under 14 years of age. Mr. B could transfer income-producing properties to the children, and the children could each receive income of up to $500 each year with no tax liability. The next $500 would be taxed at the child's tax rate. After a child has more than $1,000 income, there is no tax advantage to shifting more income to the child (because the income will be taxed at the parents' rate) until the child is 14 years old (when all income will be taxed according to the child's tax rate). □

The Uniform Gifts to Minors Act, a model law adopted by all states (but with some variations among the states), facilitates income shifting. Under the Act, a gift of intangibles (e.g., bank accounts, stocks, bonds, life insurance contracts) can be made to a minor but with an adult serving as custodian. Usually, a parent who makes the gift is also named as custodian. The state laws allow the custodian to sell or redeem and reinvest the principal and to accumulate or distribute the income, practically at the custodian's discretion provided there is no commingling of the child's income with the parent's property. Thus, the parent can give appreciated securities to the child, and the donor custodian can then sell the securities and reinvest the proceeds, thereby shifting both the gain and annual income to the child. Such planning is limited by the tax liability calculation provision for a child under the age of 14 (refer to chapter 3).

U.S. government bonds (Series E and EE) can be purchased by the parent for his or her children. When this is done, the children generally should file a return and elect to report the income on the accrual basis.

EXAMPLE 58

F (father) pays $7,500 for Series EE bonds in 1989 and immediately gives them to S (son), who will enter college the year of original maturity of the bonds. The bonds have a maturity value of $10,000. S elects to report the annual increment in redemption value as income for each year the bonds are held. The first year the increase is $250, and S includes that amount in his gross income. If S has no other income, no tax will be due on the $250 bond interest, since such amounts will be more than offset by S's available standard deduction. The following year, the increment is $260, and S includes this amount in income. Thus, over the life of the bonds, S will include $2,500 in income ($10,000 − $7,500), none of which will result in a tax liability, assuming S has no other income. However, if the election had not been made, S would be required to include $2,500 in income on the bonds in the year of original maturity, if redeemed as planned. This amount of income might result in a tax liability. □

In some cases, it may be advantageous for the child not to make the accrual election. For example, a child under age 14 with investment income of more than $1,000 each year and parents in the 28 percent tax bracket would probably benefit from deferring the tax on the savings bond interest. The child would also benefit from the use of the usually lower tax rate (rather than subjecting the income to his or her parents' tax rate) if the bonds mature after the child is age 14 or older.

Accounting for Community Property

The classification of income as community or separate property becomes important when either of two events occurs:

- Husband and wife, married taxpayers, file separate income tax returns for the year.

- Husband and wife obtain a divorce and therefore have to file separate returns for the year (refer to chapter 3).

For planning purposes, it behooves married persons to keep track of the source of income (community or separate). To be in a position to do this effectively when income-producing assets are involved, it may be necessary to distinguish between separate and community property.[94]

---

94. Being able to distinguish between separate and community property is crucial to the determination of a property settlement incident to a divorce. It also is vital in the estate tax area (re-fer to chapter 1), since the surviving wife's or husband's share of the community property is not included in the gross estate of the deceased spouse.

Alimony

The person making the alimony payments favors a divorce settlement that includes a provision for deductible alimony payments. On the other hand, the recipient prefers that the payments do not qualify as alimony. If the payor is in a higher tax bracket than the recipient, both parties may benefit by increasing the payments and structuring them so that they qualify as alimony.

EXAMPLE 59

H and W are negotiating a divorce settlement. H has offered to pay W $10,000 each year for 10 years, but payments would cease upon W's death. W is willing to accept the offer, if the agreement will specify that the cash payments are not alimony. H is in the 33 percent tax bracket, and W's marginal rate is 15 percent.

If H and W agree that H would pay W $12,000 of alimony each year, W as well as H would have improved after-tax cash flows.

	Annual Cash Flows	
	H	W
Non-alimony payments	$(10,000)	$10,000
Alimony payments	$(12,000)	$12,000
Tax effects		
.33 ($12,000)	3,960	
.15 ($12,000)		(1,800)
After-tax cash flows	$ (8,040)	$10,200
Benefit of alimony option	$ 1,960	$ 200

Both parties benefit at the government's expense if the $12,000 alimony option is used. □

PROBLEM MATERIALS

Discussion Questions

1. What are some of the differences between accounting, tax, and economic concepts of income?

2. Which of the following would be considered "income" for the current year by an economist but would not be gross income for tax purposes? Explain.

   a. Securities acquired two years ago for $10,000 had a value at the beginning of the current year of $12,000 and a value at the end of the year of $13,000.

   b. An individual lives in the home he owns.

    c.   A corporation obtained a loan from a bank.

    d.   A shareholder paid a corporation $3,000 for property valued at $5,000.

    e.   An individual owned property that was stolen. The cost of the property three years ago was $2,000, and an insurance company paid the owner $6,000 (the value of the property on the date of theft).

    f.   At the end of the current year a shareholder sold stock for 200% of all dividends to be paid on the stock from the date of sale until the shareholder's death.

    g.   An individual found a box of seventeenth century Spanish coins while diving off the Virginia coast.

    h.   An individual received a $200 rebate from the manufacturer upon the purchase of a new car.

3.   Evaluate the arguments in favor of deferring the recognition of income until a sale or exchange occurs in the following cases:

    a.   A farmer owns appreciated land.

    b.   A corporation owns appreciated inventory.

    c.   An investor owns appreciated stock listed on the New York Stock Exchange.

4.   T had owned a tract of land for several years when the local government decided to build an airport near the property. T's cost of the property was $50,000. The local government paid T $10,000 for invasion of his airspace. What is T's gross income from the receipt of the $10,000?

5.   T is in the 28% tax bracket. He has the following alternative uses of his time: (1) T can work and earn $600 (before tax), or (2) T can stay at home and paint his house. If T selects (1), he must pay $500 to have his house painted. Which alternative would our tax laws encourage T to select?

6.   Comment on the following: "Our tax laws encourage the taxpayer to hold appreciated assets and to sell assets that have declined in value."

7.   Under what conditions must the taxpayer use the accrual method of accounting?

8.   A corporation pays all of its monthly salaried employees on the last Friday in each month. What would be the tax consequences to the employees if the date of payment were changed to the first Monday of the following month?

9.   T believes that his tax rates will be lower in 1990 than in 1989. To take advantage of the lower rates, T instructs his employer to wait until January 1990 to give him his salary check for December 1989. In the past, T has always received his December check on or before December 31. Evaluate T's tax planning strategy.

10.   T is a cash basis attorney. On December 31, 1989, a client was on the way to T's office to pay T a $5,000 fee. T met the client on the elevator,

and the client offered T $5,000 cash. As T reached for the cash, the elevator came to an abrupt halt, causing T to fall against a railing, bump his head, and lose consciousness. On January 1, 1990, T awoke in the hospital to the sound of the persistent client stuffing $5,000 into T's pajama pocket. When should T report the $5,000 as income?

11. M, an accrual basis taxpayer, performed services for a client in 1989. The charge for the service was $450, but the customer paid only $200 in 1989 because he claimed that M did not adequately perform the service. M and the client negotiated a settlement in 1990, and the client paid an additional $150. What is M's 1989 income from the contract?

12. In 1989, T, an accrual basis taxpayer, rendered services for a customer with a poor credit rating. T's charge for the service was $1,000. T sent a bill to the customer for $1,000 but reported only $500 of income. He justified reporting only $500 as follows: "I'm being generous reporting $500. I'll be lucky if I collect anything." How much should T include as gross income from the contract in 1989.

13. In January 1989, T, a cash basis taxpayer, purchased for $2,000 a five-year Series EE U.S. government bond with a maturity value of $3,000. He also purchased for $2,000 a three-year bank certificate of deposit with a maturity value of $2,500. Is T required to recognize any interest income in 1989?

14. Compare the accounting and tax treatment of income collected by an accrual basis taxpayer before it is earned.

15. M is in the wholesale hardware business. His customers pay for the goods at the time they place the order. Often, M is out of stock on particular items and must back order the goods. When this occurs, he usually retains the customer's payment, orders the goods from the manufacturer, and ships the goods to the customer within a month. At the end of the year there were several unfilled orders. Is it possible for M to defer the recognition of income from the receipt of advance payments on the unfilled orders?

16. F (father) paid $200 for an automobile that needed repairs. He worked nights and weekends to restore the car. Several individuals offered to purchase the car for $2,800. F gave the car and a list of potential buyers to S (son), whose college tuition was due in a few days. S sold the car for $2,800 and paid his tuition. Does F have any taxable income from the transaction?

17. F, a cash basis taxpayer, sold a bond for $10,250 with accrued interest of $750. F's basis in the bond was $9,000. Compute F's income from this transaction.

18. Father gave Son 100 shares of X Corporation stock on June 20. X Corporation had declared a $1 per share dividend on the stock on June 15, payable on June 30 to holders of record as of June 25. Who must report the dividend income, Father or Son?

19. P transferred rental properties to a corporation. P's objective was to minimize his liability for injuries that may occur on the property. The

tenants continued to pay rents to P. Who must include the rents in gross income?

20. Who pays the tax on undistributed income of (a) an S corporation and (b) an estate?

21. H and W were residents of a community property state. In 1989, H left W for parts unknown. H and W were still married at year-end. How will H's absence complicate W's 1989 tax return?

22. What is the purpose of the front-loading rules?

23. A post-1984 divorce agreement between H and W provides that H is to pay W $500 per month for 13 years. H and W have a child who is eight years old. Termination of the monthly payments will coincide with the child's attaining age 21. Can the monthly payments qualify as alimony?

24. H and W were divorced. They jointly owned a home in the mountains with a basis of $50,000 and a fair market value of $80,000. According to the terms of the divorce, W gave H $40,000 for his one-half interest in the mountain home. W later sold the house for $85,000. What is W's gain from the sale?

25. On January 1, when the applicable Federal rate was 12%, Father made a $50,000 interest-free loan to Daughter, who used the money to retire a 14% mortgage on her personal residence. Daughter's only income for the year was $20,000 in salary. What are the effects of the interest-free loan on Father's and Daughter's gross income for the current tax year, assuming there are no other outstanding loans between them?

26. T received an interest-free loan from his employer. He received $24,200 on January 1, 1989, and signed a note for that amount due on December 31, 1990. At the time of the loan, the applicable Federal rate was 10% (compounded annually). What are the effects of the loan on T's 1989 taxable income?

27. T purchased an annuity for $12,000. The annuity will pay $500 per month until T's death. T reasons that he should not report any income until the third year, after he has recovered his capital. The local Internal Revenue Service agent thinks T should report all receipts as income, except the last $12,000 collected on the contract. Who is correct?

28. R's employer provided him with group term life insurance protection equal to his wages for the previous year, $30,000. The employer's cost of the coverage was $300, and the Uniform Premium amount was $270. The plan was declared discriminatory because officers received insurance equal to three times their annual salaries. What is R's gross income from the insurance protection?

29. When a taxpayer is receiving Social Security benefits, could a $1,000 increase in income from services cause the taxpayer's adjusted gross income to increase by more than $1,000?

30. Why do you suppose that no more than one-half of a recipient's Social Security benefits are taxable?

Problems

31. Does the taxpayer realize gross income from the following events:
    a. T bought a used piano for $50. When he started repairing the piano, he discovered it was stuffed with Confederate notes with a face amount of $10,000. T knows that collectors will pay him $30 for the Confederate notes.
    b. Same as (a), except the notes have a value of $500.
    c. T also discovered oil on his property during the year, and the value of the land increased from $10,000 to $5,000,000.

32. Determine the taxpayer's income for tax purposes in each of the following cases:
    a. In the current year, RST Corporation purchased $1,000,000 par value of its own bonds and paid the bondholders $950,000 plus $50,000 of accrued interest. The bonds had been issued 10 years ago at par and were to mature 25 years from the date of issue. Does the corporation recognize income from the purchase of the bonds?
    b. A shareholder of a corporation sold property to the corporation for $60,000 (the shareholder's cost). The value of the property on the date of sale was $50,000. Does the taxpayer have any taxable income from the sale?
    c. T was a football coach at a state university. Because of his disappointing record, he was asked to resign and accept one-half of his pay for the remaining three years of his contract. The coach resigned, accepting $75,000.

33. Which of the following investments will yield the greater after-tax value assuming the taxpayer is in the 40% tax bracket (combined Federal and state) in all years and the investments will be liquidated at the end of five years?
    a. Land that will increase in value by 10% each year.
    b. A taxable bond yielding 10% before tax, and the interest can be reinvested at 10% before tax.
    c. Common stock that will increase in value at the rate of 5% (compounded) each year and pays dividends equal to 5% of the year-end value of the stock. The dividends can be reinvested at 10% before tax.
    d. A tax-exempt state government bond yielding 8%. The interest can be reinvested at a before-tax rate of 10%, and the bond matures in 10 years.

    Given: Compound amount of $1 at the end of five years:

Interest Rate	Factor
6%	1.33
8%	1.47
10%	1.61

Compound value of annuity payments at the end of five years:

Interest Rate	Factor
6%	5.64
8%	5.87
10%	6.11

34. Determine the taxpayer's income for tax purposes in each of the following cases:

   a. R borrowed $30,000 from the First National Bank. R was required to deliver to the bank stocks with a value of $30,000 and a cost of $10,000. The stocks were to serve as collateral for the loan.

   b. P owned a lot on Sycamore Street that measured 100 feet by 100 feet. His cost of the lot is $10,000. The city condemned a 10-foot strip of the land so that it could widen the street. P received a $2,000 condemnation award.

   c. M owned land zoned for residential use only. The land cost $5,000 and had a market value of $7,000. M spent $500 and several hundred hours petitioning the county supervisors to change the zoning to A–1 commercial. The value of the property immediately increased to $20,000 when the county approved the zoning change.

35. X Inc. is a dance studio that sells dance lessons for cash, on open account, and for notes receivable. The company also collects interest on bonds held as an investment. The company's cash receipts for 1989 totaled $160,000:

Cash sales	$ 50,000
Collections on accounts receivable	70,000
Collections on notes receivable	35,000
Interest on bonds	5,000
	$160,000

The balances in accounts receivable, notes receivable, and accrued interest on bonds at the beginning and end of the year were as follows:

	1–1–89	12–31–89
Accounts receivable	$25,000	$22,000
Notes receivable	12,000	11,000
Accrued interest on bonds	3,000	4,000
	$40,000	$37,000

The fair market value of the notes is equal to 80% of their face amount. There were no bad debts for the year, and all notes were for services performed during the year.

Compute the corporation's gross income:

   a. Using the cash basis of accounting.

   b. Using the accrual basis of accounting.

   c. Using a hybrid method—accrual basis for lessons and cash basis for interest income.

36. Discuss the tax effects of the following transactions on a cash basis employee:

    a. The employer's computer made an error and printed two payroll checks for T for the week ending December 28, 1989. The checks were automatically deposited to T's bank account on December 29, 1989. T discovered the error in January 1990, informed the employer of the mistake, and paid the company the excess amount received.

    b. On December 31, an employee received a $500 advance for estimated traveling expenses for the following January. The employee actually spent $480 in January and retained the $20 to apply to February expenses.

37. M owns a life insurance policy. The cash surrender value of the policy increased $1,500 during the year. He purchased a certificate of deposit on June 30 of the current year for $37,600. The certificate matures in three years when its value will be $50,000 (interest rate of 10%). However, if M redeems the certificate before the end of the first year, he receives no interest. M also purchased a Series EE U.S. government savings bond for $6,000. The maturity value of the bond is $10,000 in six years (yield of 9%), and the redemption price of the bond increased by $400 during the year. M has owned no other savings bonds. What is M's current year gross income from the above items?

38. R is an accrual basis taxpayer. Determine his 1989 gross income from the following transactions:

    a. In December 1989, R sold goods under terms that specified that the customer owned the product but could return it within 30 days of purchase if not completely satisfied. In January 1990, goods sold in December for $20,000 (cost of $12,000) were returned by dissatisfied customers.

    b. R performed services in 1989 and sent his customer a bill for $5,000. The customer placed a $5,000 check in the mail on December 31, 1989, but R did not receive the check until January 3, 1990.

    c. In 1989, R collected $4,000 from the sale of a product that cost R $2,800. The customer claimed the product was defective and filed a suit in 1989 for refund. In 1990 (before R filed his 1989 return), the court awarded the customer damages of $2,000.

    d. R sold goods that cost $3,500 for $5,000. The customer gave R a note for $5,000. However, the customer was a poor credit risk, and the fair market value of the note was only $2,000.

39. P is a cash basis taxpayer. Determine her 1989 gross income from the following transactions:

    a. In 1987, P negotiated her 1988 salary. The employer offered to pay P $200,000 in 1988. P countered that she wanted $10,000 each month in 1988 and the remaining $80,000 in January 1989. P wanted the $80,000 income shifted to 1989 because she expected her 1989 tax rates to be lower. The employer agreed to P's terms.

b. In 1988, P was running short of cash and needed money for Christmas. Her employer loaned her $20,000 in November 1988. P signed a note for $20,000 plus 10% interest, the applicable Federal rate. In January 1989, the employer subtracted the $20,000 and $333 interest from the $80,000 due P and paid P $59,667.

c. On December 31, 1989, Z offered to buy land from P for $30,000 (P's basis was $8,000). P refused to sell in 1989, but at that time, P contracted to sell the land to Z in 1990 for $30,000.

40. Discuss the tax effects of the following transactions on an accrual basis taxpayer:

a. On December 15, 1989, B signed a contract to purchase land from T. Payment for the land was to be made on closing, January 15, 1990. During the interval between the contract and the closing dates, B's attorney was to verify that T had good title to the land. The closing was completed on January 15, 1990.

b. M collected $1,500 for services rendered the client in 1989. Late in 1989, the client complained that the work was not done in accordance with contract specifications. Also in 1989, the parties agreed to allow an arbitrator to settle the dispute. In January 1990, the arbitrator ordered M to refund $500 to the client.

41. The Z Apartments requires its new tenants to pay the rent for the first and last months of the annual lease and a $300 damage deposit, all at the time the lease is signed. In December 1989, a tenant paid $600 for January 1990 rent, $600 for December 1990 rent, and $300 for the damage deposit. In January 1991, Z refunded the tenant's damage deposit. What are the effects of these payments on Z's taxable income for 1989, 1990, and 1991?

a. Assume Z is a cash basis taxpayer.

b. Assume Z is an accrual basis taxpayer.

42. G purchased Series EE U.S. government savings bonds for S, his son, and A and B, his grandsons. S is in the 28% tax bracket. A is 21 years old and is a senior in college. He has no income for the current year but will become an officer in the family-owned business and will earn $40,000 per year soon after he graduates from college. B is six years old and has no other income. Each bond had an original cost of $6,000, and the final maturity value is $10,000 in eight years. The donees have never owned any other U.S. bonds. When should the donees report their $4,000 ($10,000 − $6,000) interest income from the bonds?

43. a. T is a cash basis taxpayer. On December 1, 1989, T gave a corporate bond to his son, S. The bond had a face amount of $10,000 and paid $1,200 each January 31. Also on December 1, 1989, T gave common stocks to his daughter, D. Dividends totaling $720 had been declared on the stocks on November 30, 1989, and were payable on January 15, 1990. D became the shareholder of record in time to collect the dividends. What is T's 1990 gross income from the bond and stocks?

b. In 1989, T's mother was unable to pay her bills as they came due. T, his employer, and his mother's creditors entered into an arrangement whereby T's employer would withhold $500 per month from T's salary and the employer would pay the $500 to the creditors. In 1989, $3,000 was withheld from T's salary and paid to the creditors. Is T required to pay tax on the $3,000?

c. F is considering purchasing a zero coupon (no interest is paid until maturity) corporate bond for himself and for his minor son, S (age 4). The bonds have an issue price of $300 and pay $1,000 at the end of 10 years. F is in the 28% tax bracket, and S has no other taxable income. Would the zero coupon bond be an equally suitable investment for F and S?

44. a. An automobile dealer has several new cars in inventory but often does not have the right combination of body style, color, and accessories. In some cases, the dealer makes an offer to sell a car at a certain price, accepts a deposit, and then orders the car from the manufacturer. When the car is received from the manufacturer, the sale is closed, and the dealer receives the balance of the sales price. At the end of the current year, the dealer has deposits totaling $8,200 for cars that have not been received from the manufacturer. When is the $8,200 subject to tax?

b. T Corporation, an exterminating company, is a calendar year taxpayer. It contracts to service homeowners once a month under a one-year or a two-year contract. On April 1 of the current year, the company sold a customer a one-year contract for $60. How much of the $60 is taxable in the current year if the company is an accrual basis taxpayer? If the $60 is payment on a two-year contract, how much is taxed in the year the contract is sold?

c. X, an accrual basis taxpayer, owns an amusement park whose fiscal year ends September 30. To increase business during the fall and winter months, X sold passes that would allow the holder to ride free during the months of October through March. During the month of September, $6,000 was collected from the sale of passes for the upcoming fall and winter. When will the $6,000 be taxable to X?

d. The taxpayer is in the office equipment rental business and uses the accrual basis of accounting. In December, he collected $5,000 in rents for the following January. When is the $5,000 taxable?

45. T owns 100% of the stock of T, Inc., an S corporation. For 1989, the corporation earned $100,000 taxable income but paid only $30,000 in dividends to T. T is also a beneficiary of a trust. The trustee can distribute or withhold income according to the needs of the beneficiary. In 1989, the trust earned $20,000 but distributed only $5,000 to T because T had adequate income from other sources. What is T's taxable income from the S corporation and trust for 1989?

46. H and W lived together for part of the year but were divorced on December 31, 1989. H earned $30,000 salary from his employer during the year. W's salary was $16,000. W also received $8,000 in taxable dividends from stock held as separate property.

If H and W reside in Texas, how much income should be reported by each on their separate tax returns for 1989?

b. If amounts are withheld from their salaries, how are these amounts reported on H and W's separate returns?

c. If H and W reside in a common law state, how much income should be reported by each on their separate returns?

47. H and W were married on June 30, 1989, and resided in Dallas, Texas. On December 31, 1989, they separated, and on March 31, 1990, they were divorced. On July 1, 1990, H moved to Grundy, Virginia, and re-married in December 1990. W did not remarry. H's and W's incomes for the relevant periods were as follows:

Salary	H	W
January 1–June 30, 1989	$23,000	$15,000
July 1–December 31, 1989	24,000	16,000
January 1–March 31, 1990	25,000	18,000
April 1–December 31, 1990	40,000	20,000

In addition to the salaries listed, on January 31, 1990, H received $2,400 interest on savings certificates acquired on February 1, 1989. What is W's gross income for 1989 and 1990 as computed on separate returns?

48. H and W were divorced on July 1 of the current year after 10 years of marriage. Their current year's income received before the divorce was as follows:

H's salary	$20,000
W's salary	25,000
Rent on apartments purchased by W 15 years ago	6,000
Dividends on stock H inherited from his mother 4 years ago	1,200
Interest on a savings account in W's name funded with her salary	600

Allocate the income to H and W assuming they live in:

a. California.

b. Texas.

49. Mr. and Mrs. X are in the process of negotiating their divorce agreement. What would be the tax consequences to Mr. X and Mrs. X if the following, considered individually, become part of the agreement:

a. Mrs. X is to receive $1,000 per month until she dies or remarries. She also is to receive $500 per month for 12 years for her one-half interest in their personal residence. She paid for her one-half interest out of her earnings.

b. Mrs. X is to receive a principal sum of $100,000. Of this amount, $50,000 is to be paid in the year of the divorce and $5,000 per year will be paid to her in each of the following 10 years or until Mrs. X's death.

c. Mrs. X is to receive the family residence (value of $120,000 and basis of $75,000). The home was jointly owned by Mr. and Mrs. X. In exchange for the residence, Mrs. X relinquished all of her rights to property accumulated during the marriage. She also is to receive $1,000 per month until her death or remarriage but for a period of not longer than 10 years.

50. Under the terms of a post-1986 divorce agreement, W is to receive payments from H as follows: $50,000 in Year 1, $40,000 in Year 2, and $20,000 each year for Years 3 through 10. W is also to receive custody of their minor son. The payments will decrease by $5,000 per year if the son dies or when he attains age 21 and will cease upon W's death.

    a. What will be W's taxable alimony in Year 1?

    b. What will be the effect of the Years 2 and 3 payments on W's taxable income?

51. Under the terms of their divorce agreement, H is to transfer common stocks (cost of $25,000, market value of $60,000) to W in satisfaction of W's property rights. W is also to receive $15,000 per year until her death or remarriage. W originally asked for $9,000 alimony and $5,000 child support. It was the understanding between H and W that W would use $5,000 of the amount received for the support of the children. How will the terms of the agreement affect H's taxable income?

52. a. M (mother) is in the 28% tax bracket, and S (son) is in the 15% tax bracket. M loans S $50,000, and S invests the money in a bond that yields a 10% return. If M had not made the loan, she would have purchased the bond. The relevant Federal rate is 12%. There are no other loans between the family members. What is the effect of the preceding transactions on M's and S's combined tax for the year?

    b. T, an individual, had outstanding interest-free loans receivable as follows:

Borrower	Amount of Loan	Use of the Loan Proceeds
S, T's son	$ 15,000	Medical school tuition
D, T's daughter	25,000	Start of an unincorporated business
R, T's employee	2,000	Payment of medical bills
B, T's brother	110,000	Payment of attorney fees

    S had $1,500 net investment income for the year. D's income was $5,000 earned by the business and $1,500 of dividends. R's only income was his $12,000 salary. B is in prison serving 145 years to life and has no income.

    All loans were outstanding for the entire year, and the Federal rate is 12% compounded semiannually (12.36% effective annual rate).

    Compute T's imputed interest income.

53. On June 30, 1989, T borrowed $50,000 from his employer. On July 1, 1989, T used the money as follows:

Interest-free loan to T's controlled corporation (operated by T on a part-time basis)	$21,000
Interest-free loan to S (T's son)	9,000
National Bank of Grundy 9% certificate of deposit ($15,260 due at maturity, June 30, 1990)	14,000
National Bank of Grundy 10% certificate of deposit ($7,260 due at maturity, June 30, 1991)	6,000
	$50,000

T's employer did not charge him interest. The applicable Federal rate was 12% throughout the relevant period. S had investment income of $800 for the year, and he used the loan proceeds to pay medical school tuition. There were no other outstanding loans between T and S. What are the effects of the preceding transactions on T's taxable income for 1989?

54. Mr. Z is the sole shareholder of Z, Inc. He is also employed by the corporation. On June 30, 1988, Z borrowed $8,000 from Z, Inc., and on July 1, 1989, he borrowed an additional $3,000. Both loans were due on demand. No interest was charged on the loans and the Federal rate was 10% for all relevant dates. Z used the money to purchase stock, and he had no investment income. Determine the tax consequences to Z and Z, Inc. in each of the following situations.

    a. The loans are considered employer-employee loans.

    b. The loans are considered corporation-shareholder loans.

55. T purchased an annuity from an insurance company for $12,000 on January 1, 1989. The annuity was to pay him $1,500 per year for life. At the time he purchased the contract, his life expectancy was 10 years.

    a. Determine T's taxable income from the annuity in the first year.

    b. Assume T lives 20 years after purchasing the contract. What would be T's taxable income in the nineteenth year?

    c. Assume T died in 1992, after collecting a total of $6,000. What will be the effect of the annuity on his 1992 gross income?

56. In 1989, R purchased an annuity for $50,000. He was 59 at the time he purchased the contract. Payments were to begin when R attained age 62. In 1990, when the cash surrender value had increased to $51,000, R exercised a right to receive $1,500 and accept reduced payments after age 62. In 1992, when he had a life expectancy of 18 years, R received his first annual $3,000 payment under the contract.

    a. What is R's income from the contract in 1990?

    b. Compute R's taxable collections under the annuity contract in 1992.

57. Indicate whether or not the following items result in taxable income to the recipient. If the item is not taxable, explain why.

    a. S won the Miss Centerville beauty contest and received a $1,000 cash prize.

    b.   L won the master's mile run. As the winner, L received a $1,000 cash prize paid by a philanthropist who sponsored the race to encourage running.

    c.   Mr. and Mrs. D are married and file a joint return. They had adjusted gross income of $19,000 before considering unemployment benefits of $1,800.

58. T does not think she has an income tax problem but would like to discuss her situation with you just to make sure she will not get hit with an unexpected tax liability. Base your suggestions on the following relevant financial information:

    a.   T's share of the SAT Partnership income is $40,000, but none of the income can be distributed, because the partnership needs the cash for operations.

    b.   T's Social Security benefits totaled $8,400, but T loaned the cash received to her nephew.

    c.   T assigned to a creditor the right to collect $1,200 interest on some bonds she owned.

    d.   T and her husband lived together in California until September, when they separated. T has heard rumors that her husband had substantial gambling winnings since they separated.

59. M and W are married and file a joint return. In 1989, they received $9,600 in Social Security benefits and $29,000 taxable pension benefits, interest, and dividends.

    a.   Compute the couple's adjusted gross income on a joint return.

    b.   If M works part-time and earns $5,000, how much would M and W's adjusted gross income increase?

    c.   Assume W cashed certificates of deposit that had paid $8,000 in interest each year and purchases State of Virginia bonds that pay $6,000 in interest each year. How much would M and W's adjusted gross income decrease? (Assume W had no gain or loss from cashing the certificates.)

60. In the following problems, assume the unmarried taxpayer has no tax-exempt interest income and receives $6,000 per year in Social Security benefits:

    a.   Compute the maximum adjusted gross income from other sources the taxpayer can receive without including any of the Social Security benefits in adjusted gross income.

    b.   How much adjusted gross income from other sources must the taxpayer receive before $3,000 in Social Security benefits are included in adjusted gross income?

61. The LMN Partnership has a group term life insurance plan. Each partner has $100,000 protection, and each employee has protection equal to twice his or her annual salary. Employee V (age 34) had $80,000 insurance under the plan and partner N (age 46) had $100,000 coverage. The cost of V's coverage for the year was $110, and the cost of N's protection was $380.

a.   Assuming the plan was nondiscriminatory, how much must V and N include in gross income from the insurance?

b.   Assuming the plan is discriminatory, how much must N include in his gross income from the insurance?

Cumulative Problems

 62.   Thomas R. Rucker, age 42, is single and is employed as a plumber for Ajax Plumbing Company. Tom's Social Security number is 262–06–3814. Tom lives at 252 Mason Place, Grand View, WV 22801. His salary was $38,000, and his employer withheld Federal income tax of $7,600.

Tom's mother, Sue Rucker, age 68, lives in a small house Tom bought for her in Florida. She has no income of her own and is totally dependent on Tom for her support. To provide his mother with some spending money, Tom assigned to her the income from some XYZ Corporation bonds he owns. The interest received by Tom's mother was $1,050. Tom retained ownership of the bonds but surrendered all rights to the interest on the bonds.

Over the years, Tom and his physician, Joe Zorn, have become good friends. During 1989, Tom incurred doctor bills of $350. Instead of paying Zorn in cash, Tom did the plumbing work for a new bar Zorn had installed in his basement in September 1989. Tom and Zorn agreed that the value of Tom's services was equal to the $350 in medical bills.

On September 5, 1989, Tom sold 100 shares of ABC Corporation stock for $3,100. He had acquired the stock on May 2, 1981, for $1,600.

Tom's itemized deductions for 1989 were as follows:

State income tax withheld	$ 900
Real estate taxes paid	600
Home mortgage interest (paid to Grand View Savings and Loan)	2,800
Cash contributions to First Church	800

Part 1—Tax Computation

Compute Tom's 1989 Federal income tax payable (or refund due).

Part 2—Tax Planning

For 1990, assume that all items of income and expense will be approximately the same as in 1989, except for the following:

●   Tom expects a 10% increase in salary and taxes withheld beginning January 1, 1990.

●   He does not expect to incur any medical expenses.

●   His real estate taxes will increase to $800.

●   He expects to contribute $1,200 to First Church.

●   He does not expect to have any capital gains or losses in 1990.

Tom plans to marry in June 1990. His fiancée, Sarah, plans to quit her job in Pittsburgh and move to Grand View to be with Tom. She does not plan to seek employment after the move. Sarah earned $18,000 through May 1990. Her employer withheld Federal income tax of $3,600, state income tax of $900, and FICA of $1,352.

Compute the estimated total tax liability for the Ruckers for 1990. Should Tom ask his employer to withhold more or less than the amount withheld last year? How much?

63. Dan and Freida Butler, husband and wife, file a joint return. The Butlers live at 625 Oak Street, Corbin, KY 27521. Dan's Social Security number is 482–61–1231, and Freida's is 162–79–1245.

During 1989, Dan and Freida furnished over half of the total support of each of the following individuals:

   a. Gina, their daughter, age 22, who was married on December 21, 1989, has no income of her own, and for 1989 files a joint return with her husband, who earned $8,000 during 1989.

   b. Sam, their son, age 17, who had gross income of $2,500 and who dropped out of high school in February 1989.

   c. Ben Brow, Freida's brother, age 27, who is a full-time college student with gross income of $2,100.

Dan, a radio announcer for WJJJ, earned a salary of $32,000 in 1989. Freida was employed part-time as a real estate salesperson by Corbin Realty and was paid commissions of $18,000 in 1989. She incurred automobile expenses of $900 while showing property to her clients. She was not reimbursed by her employer for these expenses. Freida sold a house on December 30, 1989, and will be paid a commission of $1,500 (not included in the $18,000) on the January 10, 1990, closing date.

Dan and Freida own 500 shares of stock in Q Corporation. Q declared a dividend of $2 per share on the stock on December 15, 1989, and mailed dividend checks on December 31. Dan and Freida received their dividend check on January 4, 1990.

Dan and Freida had itemized deductions as follows:

State income tax withheld	$1,500
Real estate taxes paid	880
Interest on home mortgage (paid to Corbin Savings and Loan)	4,800
Cash contributions to the Boy Scouts	340

Their employers withheld Federal income tax of $8,600 (Dan $5,100, Freida $3,500), and the Butlers paid estimated tax of $800.

Part 1—Tax Computation

Compute Dan and Freida's 1989 Federal income tax payable (or refund due).

Part 2—Tax Planning

Dan plans to reduce his work schedule and work only halftime for WJJJ in 1990. He has been writing songs for several years and wants to devote more time to developing a career as a songwriter. Because of the uncertainty in the music business, however, he would like you to make all computations assuming he will have no income from song-writing in 1990. To make up for the loss of income, Freida plans to increase the amount of time she spends selling real estate. She estimates she will be able to earn $33,000 in 1990 and will incur unreimbursed expenses of $1,500. Assume all other income and expense items will be approximately the same as they were in 1989. Will the Butlers have more or less disposable income (after Federal income tax) in 1990?

64. Sam T. Seymour would like to forget 1988 (and almost did as a result of his drinking problem). Although he received a salary of $65,800 and $380 of interest income, a divorce nearly brought him to financial ruin. The divorce was final on February 28, 1988. Under the agreement, Sam was required to do the following:

- Pay his minor daughter Pam's private school tuition of $10,800.

- Pay his ex-wife, Patricia Ann Seymour, a $40,000 lump-sum payment on March 1, 1988, and $2,000 each month thereafter through February 1995. The payments are to cease upon Patricia's death.

- Transfer to Patricia stock acquired in 1984 for $40,000 that now has a market value of $82,000.

Patricia retained custody of Pam but spent only $4,000 for Pam's support in 1988. The divorce agreement was silent as to whether Sam could claim Pam as a dependent and as to whether the cash payments to Patricia would constitute alimony.

Sam paid the tuition and made the $40,000 lump-sum payment but, because he was dismissed from his job in August 1988, was able to make only seven of the monthly payments to Patricia.

On November 1, 1988, when the applicable Federal rate was 10%, Sam was compelled to borrow $35,000 from his mother (Mollie Seymour). He gave her a noninterest-bearing second mortgage on his residence. There were no other loans outstanding between Sam and his mother.

Other information relevant to Sam's 1988 return is as follows:

a. Sam's disabled brother, Fred Seymour, lived with Sam from April through December 1988. Fred's only income was $3,600 of Social Security disability payments, and Sam contributed $4,000 towards Fred's support. No one else contributed to Fred's support. Fred's Social Security number is 245–99–4444.

b. Sam's only deductible items were home mortgage interest, $2,080; state income tax, $2,380; county property taxes, $3,000; charitable contributions, $200.

c. Sam's employer withheld $16,337 of Federal income tax.

d. Sam is 47 years old, his Social Security number is 215–71–1041, and he lives at 170 Ford Street, Gretna, TN 37929.

e. Patricia Ann Seymour's Social Security number is 712–15–9701.

Compute Sam's 1988 Federal income tax payable (or refund due). If you use tax forms for your computations, you will need Form 1040 and Schedule A.

Research Problems

Research Problem 1   T is the vice president of a large publicly held corporation. As an officer, T has participated in the company's bonus plan for several years. In a previous year, the bonuses given were in the form of annuity contracts purchased from an insurance company. The contracts were nontransferable, and payments did not begin until the employee reached age 65. T's return was examined, and the revenue agent contended that T should include the purchase price of the annuity in income in the year the contract was received. Since the annuity is nontransferable and T does not have the option to receive cash, T does not think income should be recognized until collection on the annuity contract begins. The taxpayer asks your opinion on the matter.

Research Problem 2   On December 31, 1989, T, a cash basis taxpayer, received a telephone call from a client. T was advised that if she went to the client's office, T could collect a $10,000 check due to her for services. The client's office was 40 miles away, T was busy, and her bank would not give her credit for the deposit until January 1990. T therefore told the client to mail her the check. The IRS agent examining T's return has determined that the $10,000 was 1989 income. Do you agree?

Research Problem 3   Mr. A is a commissioned agent for a large insurance company. During the year he purchased a policy on his life and the lives of his children and received a commission. Mr. A treated the commission on these policies as a reduction in cost rather than as income. However, during an audit the revenue agent indicates that Mr. A must include the commission in his gross income. The taxpayer seeks your assistance in resolving the matter with the agent.

> *Partial list of research aids:*
>
> *Ostheimer v. U.S.*, 59–1 USTC ¶9300, 3 AFTR2d 886, 264 F.2d 789 (CA–3, 1959).
>
> Rev.Rul. 55–273, 1955–1 C.B. 221.

Research Problem 4   The Great Electric Company requires new customers to make a $100 deposit to secure future payments for electricity. After the customer has established a good payment record (usually within two years), the company refunds the deposit to the customer. If the services are terminated before refund, the deposit is usually applied against the final bill. The IRS agent insists that the company must include the deposits in gross income for the year the deposits are received. Can you find authority for excluding the deposits from income?

5

Gross Income: Exclusions

ITEMS SPECIFICALLY EXCLUDED FROM GROSS INCOME

Chapter 4 discussed the concepts and judicial doctrines that affect the determination of gross income. If an income item is within the all-inclusive definition of gross income, the item can be excluded only if the taxpayer can locate specific authority for doing so. Chapter 5 focuses on the exclusions Congress has authorized.

STATUTORY AUTHORITY

Sections 101 through 150 provide the authority for excluding specific items from gross income. In addition, other exclusions are scattered throughout the Code. Each exclusion has its own legislative history and reason for enactment. Certain exclusions are intended as a form of indirect welfare payments. Other exclusions prevent double taxation of income or provide incentives for socially desirable activities (e.g., nontaxable scholarships for educational activities).

In some cases, exclusions have been enacted by Congress to rectify the effects of judicially imposed decisions. For example, § 109 was enacted to exclude the value of improvements made by a lessee from the lessor's income upon termination of the lease. Previously, the Supreme Court held that such amounts were includible in gross income.[1] In this court decision, the lessor was required to include the fair market value of the improvements in gross income upon the termination of the lease despite the fact that there had been no sale or disposition of the property. Congress provided relief in this situation by enacting § 109, which defers taxing the value of the improvements until the property is sold.[2]

Section 123 was enacted to counter a District Court's decision in *Arnold v. U.S.*[3] In *Arnold*, the court included in gross income the insurance proceeds paid to the taxpayer as reimbursement for temporary housing expenses incurred as a result of a fire in the taxpayer's home. Similar payments made by a government agency to families displaced by urban renewal projects had been held nontaxable in a previous Revenue Ruling. Dissatisfied with the results in *Arnold*, Congress exercised its authority by exempting from tax the insurance proceeds received in circumstances similar to that case.

CONCEPT SUMMARY 5-1

Summary of Principal Exclusions from Gross Income

1. Donative items

     Gifts, bequests, inheritances, and employee death benefits [§§ 102 and 101(b)]

     Life insurance proceeds paid by reason of death (§ 101)

     Scholarships (§ 117)

1. *Helvering v. Bruun*, 40-1 USTC ¶9337, 24 AFTR 652, 60 S.Ct. 631 (USSC, 1940).
2. If the improvements were made by the tenant in lieu of rent, the value of the improvements is not eligible for exclusion.
3. 68-2 USTC ¶9590, 22 AFTR2d 5661, 289 F.Supp. 206 (D.Ct.N.Y., 1968).

2. Personal and welfare items

    Injury or sickness payments (§ 104)

    Public assistance payments (Rev.Rul. 71–425, 1971–2 C.B. 76)

    Amounts received under insurance contracts for certain living expenses (§ 123)

    Reimbursement for the costs of caring for a foster child (§ 131)

3. Wage and salary supplements

  a. Fringe benefits

    Accident and health benefits (§§ 105 and 106)

    Lodging and meals furnished for the convenience of the employer (§ 119)

    Rental value of parsonages (§ 107)

    Employee achievement awards [§ 74(c)]

    Employer contributions to employee group term life insurance (§ 79)

    Cafeteria plans (§ 125)

    Child or dependent care (§ 129)

    Services provided to employees at no additional cost to the employer (§ 132)

    Employee discounts (§ 132)

    Working condition and de minimis fringes (§ 132)

    Athletic facilities provided to employees (§ 132)

    Tuition reductions granted to employees of educational institutions (§ 117)

  b. Military benefits

    Combat pay (§ 112)

    Mustering-out pay (§ 113)

    Housing, uniforms, and other benefits (§ 134)

  c. Foreign earned income (§ 911)

4. Investor items

    Interest on state and local government obligations (§ 103)

    Improvements by lessee to lessor's property (§ 109)

5. Benefits for the elderly

    Social Security benefits (except in the case of certain higher income taxpayers)

    Gain from the sale of personal residence by elderly taxpayers (§ 121)

6. Other benefits

    Income from discharge of indebtedness (§ 108)

    Recovery of a prior year's deduction that yielded no tax benefit (§ 111)

    Educational savings bonds (§ 135)

GIFTS AND INHERITANCES

Beginning with the Income Tax Act of 1913 and continuing to the present, Congress has allowed the recipient of a gift to exclude the value of the property from gross income. The exclusion applies to gifts made during the life of the donor (*inter vivos* gifts) and transfers that take effect upon the death of the donor (bequests and inheritances).[4] However, as discussed in chapter 4, the recipient of a gift of income-producing property is subject to tax on the income subsequently earned from the property. Also, as discussed in chapter 1, the donor or the decedent's estate may be subject to gift or estate taxes on the transfer.

In numerous cases, gifts are made in a business setting. For example, a salesperson gives a purchasing agent free samples; an employee receives cash from his or her employer on retirement; a corporation makes payments to employees who were victims of a natural disaster; a corporation makes a cash payment to a former employee's widow. In these and similar instances, it is frequently unclear whether a gift was made or the payments represent compensation for past, present, or future services.

The courts have defined a *gift* as "a voluntary transfer of property by one to another without adequate [valuable] consideration or compensation therefrom."[5] If the payment is intended to be for services rendered, it is not a gift, even though the payment is made without legal or moral obligation and the payor receives no economic benefit from the transfer. To qualify as a gift, the payment must be made "out of affection, respect, admiration, charity or like impulses."[6] Thus, the cases on this issue have been decided on the basis of the donor's intent.

In a landmark case, *Comm. v. Duberstein,*[7] the taxpayer (Duberstein) received a Cadillac from a business acquaintance. Duberstein had supplied the businessman with the names of potential customers with no expectation of compensation. The Supreme Court concluded:

> . . . despite the characterization of the transfer of the Cadillac by the parties [as a gift] and the absence of any obligation, even of a moral nature, to make it, it was at the bottom a recompense for Duberstein's past service, or an inducement for him to be of further service in the future.

Duberstein was therefore required to include the fair market value of the automobile in gross income.

Similarly, a bequest may be taxable if it represents a disguised form of compensation for services.[8]

EXAMPLE 1   T agreed to perform services for D. In exchange for the services, D promised to bequeath specific securities to T. The value of the securities on the date of D's death must be included in T's gross income. □

4. § 102.

5. *Estate of D. R. Daly,* 3 B.T.A. 1042 (1926).

6. *Robertson v. U.S.,* 52–1 USTC ¶9343, 41 AFTR 1053, 72 S.Ct. 994 (USSC, 1952).

7. 60–2 USTC ¶9515, 5 AFTR2d 1626, 80 S.Ct. 1190 (USSC, 1960).

8. *Wolder v. Comm.,* 74–1 USTC ¶9266, 33 AFTR2d 74–813, 493 F.2d 608 (CA-2, 1974).

LIFE INSURANCE PROCEEDS

Generally, insurance proceeds paid to the beneficiary by reason of the death of the insured are exempt from income tax.[9] Congress chose to exempt life insurance proceeds for the following reasons:

- For family members, life insurance proceeds serve much the same purpose as a nontaxable inheritance.

- In a business context (as well as in a family situation), life insurance proceeds replace an economic loss suffered by the beneficiary.

EXAMPLE 2

X Corporation purchased a life insurance policy to cover its key employee. If the proceeds were taxable, the corporation would require more insurance coverage to pay the tax as well as to cover the economic loss of the employee. □

Thus, in general, Congress concluded that making life insurance proceeds exempt from income tax was a good policy. It should be noted, however, that life insurance proceeds are subject to the Federal estate tax.

The income tax exclusion applies only when the insurance proceeds are received by reason of the death of the insured. If the owner cancels the policy and receives the cash surrender value, the owner must recognize gain (amount received less the cost of the policy). Also, if the beneficiary receives the insurance proceeds in payment of an amount due from the decedent, the amount is paid by reason of the liability rather than by reason of death. Thus, the insurance proceeds are taxable.[10]

EXAMPLE 3

T sold property to D, who agreed to pay the purchase price in installments. T reported his gain by the installment method (gain is prorated on the basis of collections). D pledged his life insurance as security for the debt. T collected on the insurance policy when D died. The insurance proceeds are taxed to T the same as if D had paid his liability. □

Another exception to exclusion treatment applies if the insurance contract has been transferred for valuable consideration. The insurance proceeds are includible in the gross income of the transferee to the extent the insurance proceeds received exceed the amount paid for the policy by the transferee plus any subsequent premiums paid.

EXAMPLE 4

A pays premiums of $500 for an insurance policy in the face amount of $1,000 upon the life of B and subsequently transfers the policy to C for $600. C receives the proceeds of $1,000 on the death of B. The amount that

---

9. § 101(a).
10. *Landfield Finance Co. v. U.S.,* 69–2 USTC ¶9680, 24 AFTR2d 69–5744, 418 F.2d 172 (CA–7, 1969).

C can exclude from gross income is limited to $600 plus any premiums paid by C subsequent to the transfer. ☐

The Code, however, provides exceptions to the rule illustrated in the preceding example. The four exceptions include transfers to the following:

1. A partner of the insured.
2. A partnership in which the insured is a partner.
3. A corporation in which the insured is an officer or shareholder.
4. A transferee whose basis in the policy is determined by reference to the transferor's basis.

The first three exceptions facilitate the use of insurance contracts to fund buy-sell agreements.

EXAMPLE 5   R and S are equal partners who have an agreement that allows either partner to purchase the interest of a deceased partner for $50,000. Neither partner has sufficient cash to actually buy the other partner's interest, but each has a life insurance policy on his own life in the amount of $50,000. R and S could exchange their policies (usually at little or no taxable gain), and upon the death of either partner, the surviving partner could collect tax-free insurance proceeds. The proceeds could then be used to purchase the decedent's interest in the partnership. ☐

The fourth exception applies to policies that were transferred pursuant to a tax-free exchange (e.g., a transfer of insurance policies to a corporation by its controlling shareholders in exchange for the corporation's stock or securities).[11]

Interest on Life Insurance Proceeds

Investment earnings arising from the reinvestment of life insurance proceeds are generally subject to income tax. Often the beneficiary will elect to collect the insurance proceeds in installments. The annuity rules (discussed in chapter 4) are used to apportion the installment payment between the principal element (excludible) and the interest element (includible).[12]

EMPLOYEE DEATH BENEFITS

Frequently an employer makes payments to a deceased employee's surviving spouse, children, or other beneficiaries. If the payments are made out of a legal obligation (e.g., the decedent's accrued salaries), the amounts are generally taxable to the recipient just the same as if the employee had lived and collected on the obligation. But where the employer makes voluntary payments, the gift issue arises. Generally, the IRS considers such payments to be

---

11. § 351. See chapter 20.   12. Reg. §§ 1.72–7(c)(1) and 1.101–7T.

compensation for prior services rendered by the deceased employee.[13] However, some courts have held that payments to an employee's surviving spouse or other beneficiaries are gifts if the following are true: [14]

- The payments were made to the surviving spouse and children rather than to the employee's estate.

- The employer was not obligated to pay any additional compensation to the deceased.

- The employer derived no benefit from the payments.

- The surviving spouse and children performed no services for the employer.

- The decedent had been fully compensated for services rendered.

- Compensation payments were made pursuant to a board of directors' resolution that followed a general company policy of providing such payments for families of deceased employees (but not exclusively for families of shareholder-employees).

These factors, together, indicate whether the payment was made as an *act of affection or charity*. A widow's case for exclusion is greatly strengthened if the payment is made in *light of her financial needs*.[15]

Section 101(b) attempts to eliminate or reduce controversy in this area by providing an automatic exclusion of the first $5,000 paid by the employer to the employee's beneficiaries by reason of the death of the employee. The $5,000 exclusion must be apportioned among the beneficiaries on the basis of each beneficiary's percentage of the total death benefits received. When the employer's payments exceed $5,000, the beneficiaries may still be able to exclude the entire amount received as a gift if they are able to show gratuitous intent on the part of the employer.

EXAMPLE 6

When H died, his employer paid his accrued salary of $3,000 to W, H's widow. The employer's board of directors also authorized payments to W ($4,000), H's daughter ($2,000), and H's son ($2,000) "in recognition of H's many years of service to the company."

The $3,000 accrued salary is compensation for past services and was owed to H at the time of his death. Therefore, the $3,000 is includible in gross income. The additional payments to the widow and children were not owed to H. However, because the payments were made in recognition of H's past service, under the *Duberstein* decision, the payments are not gifts. The employee death benefit exclusion enables the widow and children to exclude the following amounts:

---

13. Rev.Rul. 62–102, 1962–2 C.B. 37.

14. *Estate of Sydney J. Carter v. Comm.*, 72–1 USTC ¶9129, 29 AFTR2d 332, 453 F.2d 61 (CA–2, 1972), and cases cited therein.

15. *Simpson v. U.S.*, 58–2 USTC ¶9923, 2 AFTR2d 6036, 261 F.2d 497 (CA–7, 1958), *cert. denied*, 79 S.Ct. 724 (USSC, 1958).

Widow	$\dfrac{\$4,000}{\$8,000}$	$\times\ \$5,000\ =$	$2,500
Daughter	$\dfrac{\$2,000}{\$8,000}$	$\times\ \$5,000\ =$	1,250
Son	$\dfrac{\$2,000}{\$8,000}$	$\times\ \$5,000\ =$	1,250
			$5,000

□

Besides avoiding the gift issue in many cases, the employee death benefit exclusion is intended to allow a substitute for tax-exempt life insurance proceeds.

SCHOLARSHIPS

Payments or benefits received by a student at an educational institution may be (1) compensation for services, (2) a gift, or (3) a scholarship. If the payments or benefits are received as compensation for services (past or present), the fact that the recipient is a student generally does not render the amounts received nontaxable.[16]

EXAMPLE 7

State University waives tuition for all graduate teaching assistants. The tuition waived is intended as compensation for services and is therefore included in the graduate assistant's gross income. □

As discussed earlier, gifts are not includible in gross income.

The scholarship rules are intended to provide exclusion treatment for education-related benefits that cannot qualify as gifts but are not compensation for services. According to the Regulations, "a scholarship is an amount paid or allowed to, or for the benefit of, an individual to aid such individual in the pursuit of study or research."[17] The recipient must be a candidate for a degree at an educational institution.[18]

EXAMPLE 8

T entered a contest sponsored by a local newspaper. Under the contest rules, each contestant would submit an essay on local environmental issues. The contest prize was one year's tuition at State University. T won the contest. The newspaper had a legal obligation to T (as contest winner). Thus, the benefits are not a gift. However, since the tuition payment aided the individual in pursuing his studies, the payment is a scholarship. □

---

16. Reg. § 1.117–2(a). See *C. P. Bhalla*, 35 T.C. 13 (1960), for a discussion of the distinction between a scholarship and compensation. See also *Bingler v. Johnson*, 69–1 USTC ¶9348, 23 AFTR2d 1212, 89 S.Ct. 1439 (USSC, 1969).

17. Prop.Reg. § 1.117–6(a)(3)(i).
18. § 117(a).

A scholarship recipient may exclude from gross income the amount used for tuition and related expenses (fees, books, supplies, and equipment required for courses), provided the conditions of the grant do not require that the funds be used for other purposes.[19] Amounts received for room and board are not excludible and are treated as earned income for purposes of calculating the standard deduction.[20]

EXAMPLE 9

T received a scholarship from State University of $9,500 to be used to pursue a bachelor's degree. T spent $4,000 on tuition, $3,000 on books and supplies, and $2,500 for room and board. T may exclude $7,000 ($4,000 + $3,000) from gross income. The $2,500 spent for room and board is includible in T's gross income.

The scholarship was T's only source of income. Her parents provided more than 50% of T's support and claimed T as a dependent. T's standard deduction will equal her $2,500 gross income. Thus, she has no taxable income. □

Timing Issues. Frequently, the scholarship recipient is a cash basis taxpayer who receives the money in one tax year but pays the educational expenses in a subsequent year. The amount eligible for exclusion may not be known at the time the money is received. In that case, the transaction is held *open* until the educational expenses are paid.[21]

EXAMPLE 10

In August 1989, T received $10,000 as a scholarship for the academic year 1989–1990. T's expenditures for tuition, books, and supplies were as follows:

August–December 1989	$3,000
January–May 1990	4,500
	$7,500

T's gross income for 1990 would include $2,500 ($10,000 − $7,500) that is not excludible as a scholarship. □

Disguised Compensation. Some employers make scholarships available solely to the children of key employees. The tax objective of these plans is to provide a nontaxable fringe benefit to the executives by making the payment to the child in the form of an excludible scholarship. However, the IRS has ruled that the payments are generally includible in the gross income of the parent-employee.[22]

---

19. § 117(b).
20. Prop.Reg. § 1.117–6(h).
21. Prop.Reg. § 1.117–6(b)(2).

22. Rev.Rul. 75–448, 1975–2 C.B. 55. *Richard T. Armantrout*, 67 T.C. 996 (1977).

COMPENSATION FOR INJURIES AND SICKNESS

Damages

A person who suffers harm caused by another is often entitled to compensatory damages. The tax consequences of the receipt of damages depend on the type of harm the taxpayer has experienced. The taxpayer may seek recovery for a loss of income, expenses incurred, property destroyed, or personal injury.

Generally, reimbursement for a loss of income is taxed the same as the income replaced. A recovery of expenses is generally taxable under the broad concept of gross income (but the expenses paid may be deductible, as discussed in subsequent chapters). A payment for damaged or destroyed property is treated as an amount received in a sale or exchange of the property. Thus, the taxpayer has a realized gain if the damage payments received exceed the property's basis. Damages for personal injuries receive special treatment under the Code.

Personal Injury.   The legal theory of personal injury damages is that the amount received is intended "to make the plaintiff [the injured party] whole as before the injury." [23] It follows that if the damage payments received were subject to tax, the after-tax amount received would be less than the actual damages incurred and the injured party would not be "whole as before the injury."

Congress has specifically excluded from gross income the amount of any damage payments received (whether by suit or agreement) on account of personal injuries or sickness. The courts have applied the exclusion to any personal wrong committed against the taxpayer (e.g., breach of promise to marry, invasion of privacy, libel, slander, assault, battery). The exclusion also applies to compensation for loss of income (ordinarily taxable, as previously discussed) and recovery of expenses (except medical expenses deducted by the taxpayer) resulting from the personal injury. [24]

In libel and slander cases, a single event can cause both a personal injury and damage to a business reputation. The measurement of damages to the business reputation is based on the estimated loss of income. Taxpayers argue that the amounts received for loss of income in these cases is no different from other personal injury cases and thus should be excluded. According to the IRS, however, the business reputation damages are separate from the personal injury and are taxable. [25]

EXAMPLE 11   P, a television announcer, was dissatisfied with the manner in which R, an attorney, was defending the television station in a libel case. P stated on television that R was botching the case. R sued P for slander. The damages R claimed were for loss of income from clients and potential

---

23. *C. A. Hawkins*, 6 B.T.A. 1023 (1928).

24. § 104(a)(2) and Rev.Rul. 85–97, 1985–2 C.B. 50.

25. Rev.Rul. 85–143, 1985–2 C.B. 55, in which the IRS announced it would not follow the Ninth Court of Appeals decision in *Roemer v. Comm.*, 83–2 USTC ¶9600, 52 AFTR2d 83–5954, 716 F.2d 693 (CA–9, 1983). See also *Wade E. Church*, 80 T.C. 1104 (1983).

clients who heard P's statement. R's claim is for damages to his business reputation, and the amounts received are taxable.

R collected on the suit against P and was on his way to a party to celebrate his victory when a negligent driver, N, drove his truck into R's automobile, injuring R. R filed suit for the personal injuries and claimed as damages the loss of income for the period he was unable to work as a result of the injury. All amounts received by R from N, including the reimbursement for lost income, are nontaxable, because the claims are based on a personal injury. □

Punitive Damages. In addition to seeking *compensatory* damages, the injured party may seek *punitive* damages, which are often awarded to punish the defendant for gross negligence or the intentional infliction of harm. Punitive damages are taxable under the broad concept of gross income.[26] In addition, according to the IRS, the personal injury exclusion does not apply, because the amounts are awarded on account of the defendant's egregious behavior rather than the plaintiff's personal injury.[27]

Lump-Sum Awards. Often the court will award an individual a lump sum for all of the various types of damages claimed, or the injured party may settle with an insurance company for a lump sum. The tax problem of a lump-sum award is that the amount must be allocated among the various types of damages previously discussed. According to the IRS, the amount received must first be allocated to the claims that are based on objective evidence. Any remaining amounts will be allocated among claims of a speculative nature (e.g., pain and suffering and punitive damages) on the basis of the relative amounts of the claims.[28]

EXAMPLE 12

T was injured in an automobile accident caused by D, who was driving 50 miles per hour in a school zone while under the influence of alcohol. T filed suit against D. In the suit, T requested the following:

Payment of medical expenses	$ 5,000
Personal injury (pain and suffering)	25,000
Loss of income	20,000
Punitive damages	50,000
	$100,000

T had deducted $1,500 of the medical expenses as an itemized deduction on his tax return for the previous year. The loss of income is salary that T did not receive while he was recovering from the injury.

Before trial, T settled with D's insurance company for $49,000. T's medical expenses and the lost income are based on objective evidence of

26. *Glenshaw Glass v. Comm.*, 55–1 USTC ¶9308, 47 AFTR 162, 75 S.Ct. 473 (USSC, 1955).

27. Rev.Rul. 84–108, 1984–2 C.B. 32.

28. Rev.Rul. 85–98, 1985–2 C.B. 51.

values. Therefore, T must allocate $5,000 of the amount received to the medical expense claim and $20,000 to the loss of income. The remaining $24,000 is allocated between pain and suffering and punitive damages based on the relative amount of the claims.

$$\text{Pain and suffering} = \frac{\$25,000}{\$75,000} \times \$24,000 = \underline{\$8,000}$$

$$\text{Punitive damages} = \frac{\$50,000}{\$75,000} \times \$24,000 = \underline{\$16,000}$$

T would recognize income as follows:

Reimbursement of previously deducted expenses	$ 1,500
Punitive damages	16,000
Total	$17,500

□

Workers' Compensation

State workers' compensation laws require the employer to pay fixed amounts for specific job-related injuries. The state laws were enacted so that the employee will not have to go through the ordeal of a lawsuit (and possibly not collect damages because of some defense available to the employer) to recover the damages. Although the payments are intended, in part, to compensate for a loss of future income, Congress has specifically exempted workers' compensation benefits from inclusion in gross income.[29]

Accident and Health Insurance Benefits

The income tax treatment of accident and health insurance benefits depends on whether the policy providing the benefits was purchased by the taxpayer or the taxpayer's employer. Benefits collected under an accident and health insurance policy *purchased by the taxpayer* are excludible. In this case, benefits collected under the taxpayer's insurance policy are excluded even though the payments are a substitute for income.[30]

EXAMPLE 13

B purchased a medical and disability insurance policy. The insurance company paid B $200 per week to replace wages he lost while in the hospital. Although the payments serve as a substitute for income, the amounts received are tax-exempt benefits collected under B's insurance policy. □

---

29. § 104(a)(1).   30. § 104(a)(3).

EXAMPLE 14

J's injury resulted in a partial paralysis of his left foot. He received $5,000 from his accident insurance company, under a policy he had purchased, for the injury. The $5,000 accident insurance proceeds are tax-exempt.

□

A different set of rules applies if the accident and health insurance protection was *purchased by the individual's employer*, as discussed in the following section.

EMPLOYER-SPONSORED ACCIDENT AND HEALTH PLANS

Congress encourages employers to provide employees, retired former employees, and their dependents with accident and health and disability insurance plans. The premiums are deductible by the employer and excluded from the employee's income.[31] Although § 105(a) provides the general rule that the employee has includible income when he or she collects the insurance benefits, two exceptions are provided.

Section 105(b) excludes payments received for medical care of the employee, spouse, and dependents except to the extent such amounts relate to medical expenses that were deducted by the taxpayer in a prior year.

EXAMPLE 15

D incurred $3,000 of medical expenses in 1989. D claimed the medical expenses as an itemized deduction on his 1989 return. D's adjusted gross income for 1989 was $30,000, and he had no other medical expenses. Because only medical expenses in excess of 7.5% of adjusted gross income may be claimed as an itemized deduction on D's 1989 return, the expense reduced taxable income by only $750 [$3,000 − .075($30,000) = $750]. In 1990, D received a $2,000 reimbursement from his employer-sponsored health insurance plan. The general rule of § 105(b) excludes the $2,000 from D's income. However, because D deducted the medical expenses on his return, the exception in § 105(b) applies. D is required to include in 1990 gross income the $750 deducted on his 1989 return. □

Section 105(c) excludes payments for the permanent loss or the loss of the use of a member or function of the body or the permanent disfigurement of the employee, spouse, or a dependent. Payments that are a substitute for salary (e.g., related to the period of time absent) are includible.

EXAMPLE 16

E lost an eye in an automobile accident unrelated to his work. As a result of the accident, E incurred $2,000 of medical expenses, which he deducted on his return. He collected $10,000 from an accident insurance policy carried by his employer. The benefits were paid according to a schedule of amounts that varied with the part of the body injured (e.g., $10,000 for loss of an eye, $20,000 for loss of a hand). Because the payment was for

---

31. § 106, Reg. § 1.106–1, and Rev.Rul. 82–196, 1982–1 C.B. 106.

loss of a *member or function of the body*, § 105(c) applies and the $10,000 is excluded from income. E was absent from work for a week as a result of the accident. His employer provided him with insurance for the loss of income due to illness or injury. E collected $500, which is includible in gross income. □

Medical Reimbursement Plans

In lieu of, and in some cases in addition to, providing the employee with insurance coverage for hospital and medical expenses, the employer may agree to reimburse the employee for these expenses. The amounts received through the insurance coverage (insured plan benefits) are excluded from income under § 105 (as previously discussed). Unfortunately in terms of cost considerations, the insurance companies that issue this type of policy usually require a broad coverage of employees. An alternative is to have a plan that is not funded with insurance (a self-insured arrangement). The benefits received under a self-insured plan can be excluded from the employee's income, if the plan does not discriminate in favor of highly compensated employees.

MEALS AND LODGING

Furnished for the Convenience of the Employer

As discussed in chapter 4, income can take any form, including meals and lodging. However, § 119 excludes from income the value of meals and lodging provided to the employee and the employee's spouse and dependents under the following conditions: [32]

- The meals and/or lodging are *furnished* by the employer, on the employer's *business premises*, for the *convenience of the employer*.

- In the case of lodging, the employee is *required* to accept the lodging as a condition of employment.

Each of these requirements has been strictly construed by the courts.
  At least two questions have been raised with regard to the *furnished by the employer* requirement:

- Who is considered an *employee* ?

- What is meant by *furnished* ?

  The IRS and some courts have reasoned that because a partner is not an employee, the exclusion does not apply to a partner. However, the Tax Court and the Fifth Court of Appeals have ruled in favor of the taxpayer on this issue.[33]

---

32. § 119(a). The meals and lodging are also excluded from FICA and FUTA tax. *Rowan Companies, Inc. v. U.S.*, 81–1 USTC ¶9749, 48 AFTR2d 81–5115, 101 S.Ct. 2288 (USSC, 1981).

33. Rev.Rul. 80, 1953–1 C.B. 62; *Comm. v. Doak*, 56–2 USTC ¶9708, 49 AFTR 1491, 234 F.2d 704 (CA–4, 1956); *Comm. v. Moran*, 56–2 USTC ¶9789, 50 AFTR 64, 236 F.2d 595 (CA–8, 1956);

Robinson v. U.S., 60–1 USTC ¶9152, 5 AFTR2d 315, 273 F.2d 503 (CA–3, 1960); *Briggs v. U.S.*, 56–2 USTC ¶10020, 50 AFTR 667, 238 F.2d 53 (CA–10, 1956), but see *G. A. Papineau*, 16 T.C. 130 (1956); *Armstrong v. Phinney*, 68–1 USTC ¶9355, 21 AFTR2d 1260, 394 F.2d 661 (CA–5, 1968).

The Supreme Court held that a cash meal allowance was ineligible for the exclusion because the employer did not actually furnish the meals.[34] Similarly, one court denied the exclusion where the employer paid for the food and supplied the cooking facilities but the employee prepared the meal.[35]

The *on the employer's business premises* requirement, applicable to both meals and lodging, has resulted in much litigation. The Regulations define business premises as simply "the place of employment of the employee."[36] Thus, the Sixth Court of Appeals held that a residence, owned by the employer and occupied by an employee, two blocks from the motel that the employee managed was not part of the business premises.[37] However, the Tax Court considered an employer-owned house across the street from the hotel that was managed by the taxpayer to be on the business premises of the employer.[38] Perhaps these two cases can be reconciled by comparing the distance from the lodging facilities to the place where the employer's business was conducted. The closer the lodging to the business operations, the more likely the convenience of the employer is served.

The *convenience of the employer* test is intended to focus on the employer's motivation for furnishing the meals and lodging rather than on the benefits received by the employee. If the employer furnishes the meals and lodging primarily to enable the employee to perform his or her duties properly, it does not matter that the employee considers these benefits to be a part of his or her compensation.

The Regulations give the following examples in which the tests for excluding meals are satisfied:[39]

- A waitress is required to eat her meals on the premises during the busy lunch and breakfast hours.
- A bank furnishes a teller meals on the premises to limit the time the employee is away from his or her booth during the busy hours.
- A worker is employed at a construction site in a remote part of Alaska. The employer must furnish meals and lodging due to the inaccessibility of other facilities.

The *employee required* test applies to lodging. If the employee's use of the housing would serve the convenience of the employer, but the employee is not required to use the housing, the exclusion is not available.

EXAMPLE 17   U, a utilities company, has all of its service personnel on 24-hour call for emergencies. The company encourages its employees to live near the plant so that the employees can respond quickly to emergency calls. Company owned housing is available rent-free. Only 10 of the employees live in the company housing because it is not suitable for families.

34. *Comm. v. Kowalski*, 77–2 USTC ¶9748, 40 AFTR2d 6128, 98 S.Ct. 315 (USSC, 1977).

35. *Tougher v. Comm.*, 71–1 USTC ¶9398, 27 AFTR2d 1301, 441 F.2d 1148 (CA–9, 1971).

36. Reg. § 1.119–1(c)(1).

37. *Comm. v. Anderson*, 67–1 USTC ¶9136, 19 AFTR2d 318, 371 F.2d 59 (CA–6, 1966).

38. *J.B. Lindeman*, 60 T.C. 609 (1973).

39. Reg. § 1.119–1(f).

Although the company-provided housing serves the convenience of the employer, it is not required. Therefore, the employees who live in the company housing cannot exclude its value from gross income. □

In addition, if the employee has the *option* of cash or lodging, the *required* test is not satisfied.

EXAMPLE 18

T is the manager of a large apartment complex. The employer gives T the option of rent-free housing (value of $6,000 per year) or an additional $5,000 per year. T selects the housing option. Therefore, he must include $6,000 in gross income. □

Other Housing Exclusions

An employee of an educational institution may be able to exclude the value of campus housing provided by the employer. Generally, the employee does not recognize income if he or she pays annual rents equal to or greater than 5 percent of the appraised value of the facility. If the rent payments are less than 5 percent of the value of the facility, the excess must be included in gross income.[40]

EXAMPLE 19

X University provides on-campus housing for its full-time faculty during the first three years of employment. The housing is not provided for the convenience of the employer. Professor B pays $3,000 annual rent for the use of a residence with an appraised value of $100,000 and an annual rental value of $12,000. Professor B must recognize $2,000 gross income [.05($100,000) − $3,000 = $2,000] for the value of the housing provided to him. □

Ministers of the gospel can exclude (1) the rental value of a home furnished as compensation or (2) a rental allowance paid to them as compensation, to the extent the allowance is used to rent or provide a home.[41] The housing or housing allowance must be provided as compensation for the conduct of religious worship, the administration and maintenance of religious organizations, or the performance of teaching and administrative duties at theological seminaries.

EXAMPLE 20

Pastor B is allowed to live rent-free in a house owned by the congregation. The annual rental value of the house is $6,000 and is provided as part of the pastor's compensation for ministerial services. Assistant Pastor C is paid a $4,500 cash housing allowance. He uses the $4,500 to pay rent and utilities on a home he and his family occupy. Neither Pastor B nor Assistant Pastor C is required to recognize gross income associated with the housing or housing allowance. □

---

40. § 119(d).   41. § 107 and Reg. § 1.107–1.

Military personnel are allowed housing exclusions under various circumstances. Authority for these exclusions is found in Federal laws that are not part of the Internal Revenue Code.[42]

OTHER EMPLOYEE FRINGE BENEFITS

Specific Benefits

In recent years, Congress has enacted exclusions to encourage employers to (1) finance and make available child care facilities, (2) provide athletic facilities for employees, and (3) finance certain employees' basic education. These provisions are summarized as follows:

- The employee does not have to include in gross income the value of child and dependent care services paid for by the employer and incurred to enable the employee to work. The exclusion cannot exceed $5,000 per year ($2,500 if married and filing separately). For a married couple, the annual exclusion cannot exceed the earned income of the spouse who has the lesser amount of earned income. For an unmarried taxpayer, the exclusion cannot exceed the taxpayer's earned income.[43]

- The value of the use of a gymnasium or other athletic facilities by employees, their spouses, and their dependent children may be excluded from an employee's gross income. The facilities must be on the employer's premises, and substantially all of the use of the facilities must be by employees and their family members.[44]

- An employee (including retired and disabled former employees) of a nonprofit educational institution can exclude undergraduate tuition reductions granted to the employee and his or her spouse and dependents. The exclusion extends to undergraduate tuition reductions granted by any nonprofit educational institution to employees (and their families) of any other nonprofit educational institution.[45]

EXAMPLE 21   University Y allows the dependent children of University X employees to attend University Y with no tuition charged. University X grants reciprocal benefits to the children of University Y employees. Also, the dependent children can attend tuition-free the university where their parents are employed. Employees who take advantage of these benefits are not required to recognize gross income. □

Until recently, if an employee was granted a choice between cash and a nontaxable fringe benefit, the better view was that having the option of cash made the fringe benefit taxable. However, in 1981, Congress enacted the *cafeteria plan rules*, which allow the employee to choose nontaxable benefits

---

42. § 134. See H. Rep. No. 99–841, 99th Cong., 2d Sess., p. 548 (1986).

43. § 129. The exclusion applies to the same types of expenses that, if they were paid by the employee (and not reimbursed by the employer), would be eligible for the Credit for Child and Dependent Care Expense, discussed in chapter 13.

44. § 132(h)(5).

45. § 117(d).

(e.g., group term life insurance, health and accident protection, and child care) rather than cash compensation. The rules also provide for such benefits to remain nontaxable.[46] Cafeteria plans provide tremendous flexibility in tailoring the employee-pay package to fit individual needs. Some employees (usually the younger group) prefer cash, while others (usually the older group) will opt for the fringe benefit program.

EXAMPLE 22

Y Corporation offers its employees (on a nondiscriminatory basis) a choice of any one or all of the following benefits:

	Cost
Group term life insurance	$ 200
Hospitalization insurance for family members	2,400
Child care payments	1,800
	$4,400

If a benefit is not selected, the employee receives cash equal to the cost of the benefit. T, an employee, has a spouse who works for another employer that provides hospitalization insurance but no child care payments. T elects to receive the group term life insurance, the child care payments, and $2,400 of cash. Only the $2,400 must be included in T's gross income. □

General Classes of Excluded Benefits

An employer can confer numerous forms and types of economic benefits on employees. Under the all-inclusive concept of income, the benefits are taxable unless one of the provisions previously discussed specifically excludes the item from gross income. The income is the fair market value of the benefit. This reasoning can lead to results that Congress considers unacceptable, as illustrated in the following example.

EXAMPLE 23

T is employed in New York as a ticket clerk for Trans National Airlines. He has a sick mother in Miami, Florida. T has no money. Trans National has daily flights from New York to Miami that often leave with empty seats. The cost of a ticket is $400, and T is in the 28% tax bracket. If Trans National allows T to fly without charge to Miami, under the general gross income rules, T has income equal to the value of a ticket. Therefore, T must pay $112 tax (.28 × $400) on a trip to Miami. Because T does not have $112, he cannot visit his mother, and the airplane flies with another empty seat. □

---

46. § 125.

If Trans National in Example 23 will allow employees to use resources that would otherwise be wasted, why should the tax laws interfere with the employee's decision to take advantage of the available benefit? Thus, to avoid the undesirable results that occur in Example 23 and in similar situations as well as to create uniform rules for fringe benefits, Congress established four broad classes of nontaxable employee benefits: [47]

- No-additional-cost services.
- Qualified employee discounts.
- Working condition fringes.
- De minimis fringes.

No-Additional-Cost Services. Example 23 illustrates this type of fringe benefit. To qualify as nontaxable, the service must be offered to customers in the ordinary course of the business in which the employee works and the employer must not incur substantial additional costs (including forgone revenues) in providing the service to the employee. Therefore, T in Example 23 would not be required to recognize income from the flight on the company plane.

Note that if T were employed in a hotel owned by Trans National, the receipt of the airline ticket would be taxable, because T did not work in that line of business. However, the Code allows the exclusion for reciprocal benefits offered by employers in the same line of business.

EXAMPLE 24   T is employed as a desk clerk for Plush Hotels, Inc. The company and Chain Hotels, Inc., have an agreement that allows any of their employees to stay without charge in either company's resort hotels during the off-season. T would not be required to recognize income from taking advantage of the plan by staying in a Chain Hotel. □

The no-additional-cost exclusion extends to the employee's spouse and dependent children and to retired and disabled former employees. In Temporary Regulations, the IRS has conceded that partners who perform services for the partnership are employees for purposes of the exclusion.[48] (As discussed earlier in the chapter, the IRS contends that partners are not employees for purposes of the § 119 meals and lodging exclusion.) However, the exclusion is not allowed to highly compensated employees unless the availability of the benefit is not discriminatory.

Qualified Employee Discounts. When the employer sells goods or services (other than no-additional-cost benefits just discussed) to the employee for a price that is less than the price charged regular customers, the employee realizes income equal to the discount. However, § 132(c) allows the employee to exclude the discount from income. Of course, the exclusion is subject to limitations:

- The exclusion is not available for real property (e.g., a house) or for personal property of the type commonly held for investment (e.g., common stocks).

---

47. See, generally, § 132.   48. Temp.Reg. § 1.132–1T(b).

- The property or services must be from the same line of business in which the employee works.

- In the case of property, the exclusion is limited to the *gross profit component* of the price to customers.

- In the case of services, the exclusion is limited to 20 percent of the customer price.

EXAMPLE 25

X Corporation, which operates a department store, sold a television set to a store employee for $300. The regular customer price is $500, and the gross profit rate is 25%. The corporation also sold the employee a service contract for $120. The regular customer price on the contract is $150. The employee must recognize $75 income.

Customer price for property	$500
Less: Gross profit (25%)	(125)
	$375
Employee price	300
Income	$ 75
Customer price for service	$150
Less: 20 percent	(30)
	$120
Employee price	120
Income	$–0–

EXAMPLE 26

Assume the same facts as in Example 25, except the employee is a clerk in a hotel operated by X Corporation. Because the line of business requirement is not met, the employee must recognize $200 income ($500 − $300) from the purchase of the television and $30 income ($150 − $120) from the service contract. □

As in the case of no-additional-cost benefits, the exclusion applies to employees (including service partners), employees' spouses and dependent children, and retired and disabled former employees. However, the exclusion does not apply to highly compensated individuals unless the availability of the discount is not discriminatory.

Working Condition Fringes.   The general rule of § 132(d) is that an employee is not required to include in gross income the cost of property or services provided by the employer if the employee could deduct the cost of those items if he or she had actually paid for them.

EXAMPLE 27

T is a certified public accountant employed by an accounting firm. The employer pays T's annual dues to professional organizations. T is not required to include the payment of the dues in gross income, because if he had paid the dues, he would have been allowed to deduct the amount as an employee business expense (as discussed in chapter 10). □

In many cases, this exclusion merely avoids reporting income and an offsetting deduction. However, in three specific situations, the working condition fringe benefit rules allow an exclusion where the expense would not be deductible if paid by the employee:

1. The value of parking space provided to an employee may be excluded even though parking is ordinarily a nondeductible commuting expense (see chapter 10).

2. Automobile salespeople are allowed to exclude the value of certain personal use of company demonstrators (e.g., commuting to and from work).

3. The employee business expense would be eliminated by the 2 percent floor on miscellaneous deductions under § 67 (see chapter 11).

De Minimis Fringes. As the term suggests, de minimis fringe benefits are so small that accounting for them is impractical. The House Report contains the following examples of de minimis fringes:

- The typing of a personal letter by a company secretary, occasional personal use of a company copying machine, monthly transit passes provided at a discount not exceeding $15, occasional company cocktail parties or picnics for employees, occasional supper money or taxi fare for employees because of overtime work, and certain holiday gifts of property with a low fair market value are excluded.

- Subsidized eating facilities operated by the employer are excluded if located on or near the employer's business premises, if revenue equals or exceeds direct operating costs, and if nondiscrimination requirements are met.[49]

When taxpayers venture beyond the specific examples contained in the House Report, there is obviously much room for disagreement as to what is de minimis.

Plan Requirements for Employer–Sponsored Benefits

Throughout the history of the tax law, Congress has guarded against the use of employee benefits plans that primarily benefit a chosen few—the highly compensated employees. Therefore, the Code sets forth stringent notice and coverage requirements for the benefits discussed in this chapter (as well as group term life insurance discussed in chapter 4).[50]

49. H. Rep. No. 98–432, 98th Cong., 2d Sess., p. 1592 (1984).

50. §§ 89(a) and (k). See the discussion of the term "highly compensated employee" in chapter 19.

1. The plan must be in writing.

2. The employees' rights under the plan must be legally enforceable.

3. The plan must be established with the intention of being maintained indefinitely.

4. Employees must be provided with reasonable notice of benefits available under the plan.

5. The plan must be maintained for the exclusive benefit of employees (or spouses and dependents).

6. The plan must not discriminate in favor of highly compensated employees.

Failure to satisfy any one of the first five tests will mean that all employees must include their benefits in gross income. Failing the sixth test, however, can produce different tax consequences depending on the particular type of fringe benefit. For some benefits, all participants are taxed on the value of the benefits received from a discriminatory plan. For other benefits, only the highly compensated employees must recognize income. In the latter case, the income recognized by the highly compensated employees may be the total value of the benefits received, or only the value of benefits received in excess of the benefits received by other employees. These rules are summarized in Concept Summary 5–2.

CONCEPT SUMMARY 5–2

Income from Discriminatory Employee Benefits Plans [51]

Type of Benefits	Highly Compensated Employees	Other Employees
Dependent care, subsidized eating facilities.	Income equal to the value of benefits.	Same as highly compensated.
Accident and health insurance (including medical reimbursement and disability), group term life insurance.	Income equal to the value of excess benefits (benefits in excess of those received by *other* employees).	No income.
Cafeteria plans, no-additional-cost fringes, employee discounts, tuition reduction plans.	Income equal to value of benefits received.	No income.
Working condition and de minimis fringes.	No income.	No income.

---

51. §§ 89(a) and (k) and 129(d).

EXAMPLE 28

M Corporation has health insurance and employee discount plans that are written, enforceable, and permanent. The employees are aware of the benefits, and the plans are maintained for the exclusive benefit of employees. The company also owns a beach condominium that is used to entertain customers. Employees are allowed to use the beach facility at no charge during the winter months, but they have no enforceable rights (the use is at the employer's discretion). The health insurance plan is discriminatory in that the spouses of highly compensated employees are covered but not the spouses of other employees. The employee discounts are 15% of list price for highly compensated employees and 10% for all other employees.

T, a highly compensated employee, received health insurance protection with a value of $1,800. The value of the protection provided for his wife was $1,200. He used the beach house for one week with the rental value being $800. T also enjoyed $1,500 in employee discounts for the year. T must recognize income as follows:

Insurance protection for his wife	$1,200
Rental value of house	800
Employee discounts	1,500
	$3,500

Although the beach house might otherwise qualify as a no-additional-cost fringe, the use of the house is taxable because the employees have no enforceable rights. Although T would have been allowed to exclude a 10% employee discount, the entire $1,500 is taxable because the plan favors highly compensated employees. ☐

The rationale for these differing results of discrimination is as follows. Generally, the discriminatory plans that result in income only for the highly compensated employee are the types that are tailored to produce varying benefits. For example, hospitalization coverage may provide a semi-private room for some employees and a private room for others. Congress does not intend to make the typical employee (with semi-private coverage) subject to tax on the benefit simply because the highly compensated employee (with private room coverage) received superior benefits. However, in other cases (e.g., dependent care), Congress concluded that the only way to assure broad scale coverage was to use an *all or nothing* approach.

Finally, note that the six requirements set forth above do not apply to working condition and de minimis fringe benefits. Generally, these benefits arise in a context in which it is not feasible to satisfy a nondiscrimination requirement. Imposing a nondiscrimination requirement would be tantamount to repealing the exclusion.

EXAMPLE 29

R Corporation's officers are allowed to have personal letters typed by company secretaries. On the average, a secretary will spend one hour each month on the letters. The benefit is de minimis, which means accounting for the cost is impractical in view of the small amount of money involved. If the costs are too small to be of concern, whether the benefits are discriminatory is also immaterial. ☐

EXAMPLE 30   R Corporation's offices are located in the center of a large city. The company pays for parking spaces to be used only by the company's officers. The parking space rental qualifies as a working condition fringe and may be excluded from gross income even though the plan is discriminatory. ☐

Taxable Fringe Benefits

If the fringe benefits cannot qualify for any of the specific exclusions or do not fit into any of the general classes of excluded benefits, the taxpayer must recognize gross income equal to the fair market value of the benefits. Obviously, problems are frequently encountered in determining values. The IRS has issued extensive Regulations addressing the valuation of personal use of an employer's automobiles and meals provided at an employer-operated eating facility.[52]

FOREIGN EARNED INCOME

A U.S. citizen is generally subject to U.S. tax on his or her income regardless of the income's geographic origin. The income may also be subject to tax in the foreign country, and thus the taxpayer must carry a double tax burden. Out of a sense of fairness and to encourage U.S. citizens to work abroad (so that exports might be increased), Congress has provided alternative forms of relief from taxes on foreign earned income. The taxpayer can elect *either* (1) to include the foreign income in his or her taxable income and then claim a credit for foreign taxes paid or (2) to exclude the foreign earnings from his or her U.S. gross income.[53] The foreign tax credit option is discussed in chapter 13, but as is apparent from the following discussion, most taxpayers will choose the exclusion.

Foreign earned income consists of the earnings from the individual's personal services rendered in a foreign country (other than as an employee of the U.S. government). To qualify for the exclusion, the taxpayer must either be a bona fide resident of the foreign country or be present in the country for at least 330 days during any 12 consecutive months.[54]

EXAMPLE 31   T's trips to and from a foreign country in connection with his work were as follows:

---

52. Reg. § 1.61–2 T(j). Generally, the income from the personal use of the employer's automobile is based on the lease value of the automobile (what it would have cost the employee to lease the automobile). Meals are valued at 150% of the employer's direct costs (e.g., food and labor) of preparing the meals.

53. § 911(a).

54. § 911(d). For the definition of resident, see Reg. § 1.871–2(b). Under the Regulations, a taxpayer is not a resident if he or she is there for a definite period (e.g., until completion of a construction contract).

Arrived in Foreign Country	Arrived in United States
March 10, 1989	February 1, 1990
March 7, 1990	June 1, 1990

During the 12 consecutive months ending on March 10, 1990, T was present in the foreign country for at least 330 days (365 days less 28 days in February and 7 days in March 1990). Therefore, all income earned in the foreign country through March 10, 1990, is eligible for the exclusion. The income earned from March 11, 1990, through May 31, 1990, is also eligible for the exclusion, because T was present in the foreign country for 330 days during the 12 consecutive months ending on May 31, 1990. □

The exclusion is *limited* to $70,000 per year. For married persons, both of whom have foreign earned income, the exclusion is computed separately for each spouse. Community property rules do not apply (the community property spouse is not deemed to have earned one-half of the other spouse's foreign earned income). A taxpayer who is present in the country for less than the entire year must compute the maximum exclusion on a daily basis ($70,000 divided by the number of days in the entire year and multiplied by the number of days present in the foreign country during the year).

In addition to the exclusion for foreign earnings, the reasonable housing costs incurred by the taxpayer and the taxpayer's family in a foreign country in excess of a base amount may be excluded from gross income. The base amount is 16 percent of the U.S. government pay scale for a GS–14 (Step 1) employee, which varies from year to year.[55]

As previously mentioned, the taxpayer may elect to include the foreign earned income in Federal adjusted gross income and claim a credit (an offset against U.S. tax) for the foreign tax paid. The credit alternative may be advantageous if the individual's foreign earned income far exceeds the excludible amount so that the foreign taxes paid exceed the U.S. tax on the amount excluded. However, once an election is made, it applies to all subsequent years, unless affirmatively revoked. A revocation is effective for the year of the change and the four subsequent years.

INTEREST ON CERTAIN STATE AND LOCAL GOVERNMENT OBLIGATIONS

At the time the Sixteenth Amendment was ratified by the states, there was some question as to whether the Federal government possessed the constitutional authority to tax interest on state and local government obligations. Taxing the interest on these obligations was thought to violate the doctrine of intergovernmental immunity in that the tax would impair the state and local governments' ability to finance their operations.[56] Thus, interest on state and

---

55. § 911(c).

56. *Pollock v. Farmer's Loan & Trust Co.*, 3 AFTR 2557, 15 S.Ct. 912 (USSC, 1895).

local government obligations was specifically exempted from Federal income taxation.[57] However, the Supreme Court recently concluded that there is no constitutional prohibition against levying a nondiscriminatory Federal income tax on state and local government obligations. Nevertheless, currently the statutory exclusion still exists.[58]

Obviously, the exclusion of the interest reduces the cost of borrowing for state and local governments. A taxpayer in the 28 percent tax bracket requires only a 5.76 percent yield on a tax-exempt bond to obtain the same after-tax income as a taxable bond paying 8 percent interest [$5.76\% \div (1 - .28) = 8\%$].

The lower cost for the state and local governments is more than offset by the revenue loss of the Federal government. Also, tax-exempt interest is considered to be a substantial loophole for the very wealthy. For this reason, bills have been proposed to Congress calling for Federal government subsidies to those state and local governments that voluntarily choose to issue taxable bonds. Under the proposals, the tax-exempt status of existing bonds would not be eliminated.

The current exempt status applies solely to state and local government bonds. Thus, income received from the accrual of interest on an overpayment of state income tax is fully taxable.[59] Nor does the exemption apply to gains on the sale of tax-exempt securities.

EXAMPLE 32

T purchases State of Virginia bonds for $10,000 on July 1, 1989. The bonds pay $400 interest each June 30th and December 31st. On March 31, 1990, T sells the bonds for $10,500 plus $200 accrued interest. T must recognize a $500 gain ($10,500 − $10,000), but the $200 accrued interest is exempt from taxation. □

During recent years, state and local governments have developed sophisticated financial schemes to attract new industry. For example, local municipalities have issued bonds to finance the construction of plants to be leased to private enterprise. Because the financing could be arranged with low interest rate municipal obligations, the plants could be leased at a lower cost than the private business could otherwise obtain. However, Congress has placed limitations on the use of tax-exempt securities to finance private business.[60]

DIVIDENDS

General Information

A *dividend* is a payment to a shareholder with respect to his or her stock. Dividends to shareholders are taxable only to the extent the payments are made from *either* the corporation's *current earnings and profits* (in many cases the same as net income per books) or its *accumulated earnings and*

---

57. § 103(a).

58. *South Carolina v. Baker III*, 88–1 USTC ¶9284, 61 AFTR2d 88–102, 108 S.Ct. 1355 (USSC, 1988).

59. *Kieselbach v. Comm.*, 43–1 USTC ¶9220, 30 AFTR 370, 63 S.Ct. 303 (USSC, 1943); *U.S. Trust*

Co. of New York v. Anderson, 3 USTC ¶1125, 12 AFTR 836, 65 F.2d 575 (CA–2, 1933).

60. See § 103(b).

profits (in many cases the same as retained earnings per books).[61] Distributions that exceed earnings and profits are treated as a nontaxable recovery of capital and reduce the shareholder's basis in the stock. Once the shareholder's basis is reduced to zero, any subsequent distributions in excess of the corporation's earnings and profits are taxed as capital gains (see chapter 14).[62]

Some payments are frequently referred to as dividends but are not considered dividends for tax purposes.

- Dividends received on deposits with savings and loan associations, credit unions, and banks are actually interest (a contractual rate paid for the use of money).

- Patronage dividends paid by cooperatives (e.g., for farmers) are rebates made to the users and are considered reductions in the cost of items purchased from the association. The rebates are usually made after year-end (after the cooperative has determined whether it has met its expenses) and are apportioned among members on the basis of their purchases.

- Mutual insurance companies pay dividends on unmatured life insurance policies that are considered rebates of premiums.

- Shareholders in a mutual investment fund are allowed to report as capital gains their proportionate share of the fund's gains realized and distributed. The capital gain and ordinary income portions are reported on the Form 1099 that the fund supplies its shareholders each year.

Stock Dividends

When a corporation issues a simple stock dividend (e.g., common stock issued to common shareholders), the shareholder has merely received additional shares to represent the same total investment. Thus, the shareholder does not realize income.[63] However, if the shareholder has the *option* of receiving either cash or stock in the corporation, the individual realizes gross income whether he or she receives stock or cash.[64] A taxpayer who elects to receive the stock could be deemed to be in constructive receipt of the cash he or she has rejected.[65] However, the amount of the income in this case is the value of the stock received, rather than the cash the shareholder has rejected. See chapter 14 for a detailed discussion of stock dividends.

TAX BENEFIT RULE

Generally, if a taxpayer obtains a deduction for an item in one year and later recovers a portion of the prior deduction, the recovery is included in gross income in the year received.[66]

---

61. § 316(a).

62. § 301(c). See chapter 3, *West's Federal Taxation: Corporations, Partnerships, Estates, and Trusts*, for a detailed discussion of corporate distributions.

63. *Eisner v. Macomber*, 1 USTC ¶32, 3 AFTR 3020, 40 S.Ct. 189 (USSC, 1920); § 305(a).

64. § 305(b).

65. Refer to the discussion of constructive receipt in chapter 4.

66. § 111(a). See the Glossary of Tax Terms in Appendix C for a discussion of the term "tax benefit rule."

EXAMPLE 33   A taxpayer deducted as a loss a $1,000 receivable from a customer when it appeared the amount would never be collected. The following year, the customer paid $800 on the receivable. The taxpayer must report as income the $800 in the year it is received. □

However, § 111 provides that no income is recognized upon the recovery of a deduction, or the portion of a deduction, that did not yield a tax benefit in the year it was taken. If the taxpayer in Example 33 had no tax liability in the year of the deduction (e.g., the itemized deductions and personal exemptions exceeded adjusted gross income), the recovery would be partially or totally excluded from income in the year of the recovery.[67]

EXAMPLE 34   Before deducting a $1,000 loss from an uncollectible receivable in 1988, T had adjusted gross income of $5,150. Because T's standard deduction and personal exemption for the year totaled $4,950, the $1,000 loss yielded only $200 in tax benefits ($5,150 − $4,950 = $200). If the customer makes payments on the debt in a subsequent year, the first $200 collected will be taxable as a recovery of a prior deduction, and any additional amounts collected would be nontaxable, because only $200 of the loss yielded a reduction in taxable income. □

INCOME FROM DISCHARGE OF INDEBTEDNESS

A transfer of appreciated property in satisfaction of a debt is an event that triggers the realization of income. The transaction is treated as a sale of the appreciated property followed by payment of the debt.[68] Foreclosure by a creditor is also treated as a sale or exchange of the property.[69]

EXAMPLE 35   T owed the State Bank $100,000 on an unsecured note. The note was satisfied by T when he transferred to the bank common stock with a basis of $60,000 and a fair market value of $100,000. T must recognize $40,000 gain on the transfer. T also owed the bank $50,000 on a note secured by land. When T's basis in the land was $20,000 and the land's fair market value was $50,000, the bank foreclosed on the loan and took title to the land. T must recognize a $30,000 gain on the foreclosure. □

In some cases, a creditor will not exercise his or her right of foreclosure and will even forgive a portion of the debt to assure the vitality of the debtor. In such cases, the debtor realizes income from discharge of indebtedness.

---

67. Itemized deductions are discussed in chapter 11.

68. Reg. § 1.1001–2(a).

69. *Estate of Delman v. Comm.*, 73 T.C. 15 (1979).

EXAMPLE 36 X Corporation is unable to meet the mortgage payments on its factory building. Both the corporation and the mortgage holder are aware of the depressed market for industrial property in the area. Foreclosure would only result in the creditor's obtaining unsalable property. To improve X Corporation's financial position and thus improve X's chances of obtaining the additional credit from other lenders necessary for survival, the creditor agrees to forgive all amounts past due and to reduce the principal amount of the mortgage. □

Generally, the income realized by the debtor from the forgiveness of a debt is taxable.[70] A similar debt discharge (produced by a different creditor motivation) associated with personal use property is illustrated in Example 37.

EXAMPLE 37 In 1985, T borrowed $60,000 from National Bank to purchase her personal residence. T agreed to make monthly principal and interest payments for 15 years. The interest rate on the note was 8%. In 1989, when the balance on the note had been reduced through monthly payments to $48,000, the bank offered to accept $45,000 in full settlement of the note. The bank made the offer because interest rates had increased to 12%. T accepted the bank's offer. As a result, T must recognize $3,000 ($48,000 − $45,000) income.[71] □

The following discharge of indebtedness situations are subject to special treatment:[72]

1. Creditors' gifts.
2. Discharges under Federal bankruptcy law.
3. Discharges that occur when the debtor is insolvent.
4. A solvent farmer whose farm debt is discharged.
5. A seller's cancellation of the buyer's indebtedness.
6. A shareholder's cancellation of the corporation's indebtedness.
7. Forgiveness of loans to students.

If the creditor reduces the debt as an act of *love, affection or generosity*, the debtor has simply received a nontaxable gift (situation 1). Rarely will a gift be found to have occurred in a business context. A businessperson may settle a debt for less than the amount due, but as a matter of business expediency (e.g., high collection costs or disputes as to contract terms) rather than generosity.[73]

In situations 2, 3, and 4, the Code allows the debtor to reduce his or her basis in assets by the realized gain from the discharge.[74] Thus, the realized gain is merely deferred until the assets are sold (or depreciated). Similarly, in

70. *U.S. v. Kirby Lumber Co.*, 2 USTC ¶814, 10 AFTR 458, 52 S.Ct. 4 (USSC, 1931), codified in § 61(a)(12).
71. Rev.Rul. 82–202, 1982–1 C.B. 35.
72. §§ 108 and 1017.

73. *Comm. v. Jacobson*, 49–1 USTC ¶9133, 37 AFTR 516, 69 S.Ct. 358 (USSC, 1949).
74. §§ 108(a), (e), and (g). Note that § 108(b) provides that other tax attributes (e.g., net operating loss) will be reduced by the realized gain

situation 5 (a price reduction), the debtor reduces the basis in the specific assets financed by the seller.[75]

A shareholder's cancellation of the corporation's indebtedness to him or her (the sixth exception) usually is considered a contribution of capital to the corporation. Thus, the corporation's paid-in capital is increased and its liabilities are decreased by the same amount.[76]

Many states make loans to students on the condition that the loan will be forgiven if upon completion of study the student will practice a profession in the state. The amount of the loan that is forgiven is excluded from gross income.[77]

EDUCATIONAL SAVINGS BONDS

The Technical and Miscellaneous Revenue Act of 1988 has created a new exclusion associated with the funding of higher education.[78] The effective date of this provision is for taxable years beginning after December 31, 1989.

The provision allows the taxpayer to exclude from gross income the interest earned on certain Series EE U.S. government savings bonds that are redeemed to pay qualified higher education expenses. The exclusion applies only to the following savings bonds:

- Savings bonds issued after December 31, 1989.

- Savings bonds issued to an individual who was at least 24 years old at the time of issuance.

The exclusion is not available for a married couple who file separate returns.

The redemption proceeds must be used to pay qualified higher education expenses. *Qualified higher education expenses* consist of tuition and fees paid to an eligible education institution for the taxpayer, spouse, or dependent. If the redemption proceeds (both principal and interest) exceed the qualified higher education expenses, only a pro rata portion of the interest will qualify for exclusion treatment.

EXAMPLE 38   T's redemption proceeds from qualified savings bonds during the taxable year were $6,000 (principal of $4,000 and interest of $2,000). T's qualified higher education expenses were $5,000. Since the redemption proceeds exceed the qualified higher education expenses, only $1,667 ($5,000/$6,000 × $2,000) of the interest is excludible. □

The exclusion is limited by the application of the wherewithal to pay concept. That is, once the modified adjusted gross income exceeds $40,000 ($60,000 on a joint return), the phase-out of the exclusion commences. The exclusion is completely phased-out once the modified adjusted gross income reaches $55,000 ($90,000 on a joint return). The otherwise excludible interest is reduced by the amount calculated as follows:

---

from the debt discharge prior to the basis adjustment unless the taxpayer elects to apply the basis adjustment first.

75. § 108(e)(5).

76. § 108(e)(6).

77. § 108(f).

78. § 135.

$$\frac{\text{Modified AGI} -- \$40,000}{\$15,000} \times \begin{array}{c}\text{Excludible interest} \\ \text{before phase-out}\end{array} = \begin{array}{c}\text{Reduction in} \\ \text{excludible interest}\end{array}$$

On a joint return, $60,000 is substituted for the $40,000 and $30,000 is substituted for the $15,000. The phase-out amounts are to be indexed for inflation.

EXAMPLE 39

Assume the same facts as in Example 38, except that T's modified adjusted gross income is $50,000. The phase-out provision will result in T's interest exclusion being reduced by $1,111 [($50,000 − $40,000)/$15,000 × $1,667)]. Therefore, T's exclusion is $556 ($1,667 − $1,111). □

Modified adjusted gross income is adjusted gross income prior to the § 911 foreign earned income exclusion and the educational savings bond exclusion.

TAX PLANNING CONSIDERATIONS

The present law excludes certain types of economic gains from taxation. Therefore, tax planning techniques may be useful to assist taxpayers in obtaining the maximum benefits from the exclusion of such gains. Following are some of the tax planning opportunities made available by the exclusions described in this chapter.

Life Insurance

Life insurance offers several favorable tax attributes. As discussed in chapter 4, the annual increase in the cash surrender value of the policy is not taxable (because no income has been actually or constructively received). By borrowing on the policy's cash surrender value, the owner can actually receive in cash the increase in value of the policy but without recognition of income.

Employee Benefits

Generally, employees view accident and health insurance, as well as life insurance, as necessities. Employees can obtain group coverage at much lower rates than individuals would have to pay for the same protection. Premiums paid by the employer can be excluded from the employees' gross income. Because of the exclusion, employees will have a greater after-tax and after-insurance income if the employer pays a lower salary but also pays the insurance premiums.

EXAMPLE 40

Individual A receives a salary of $30,000. The company has group insurance benefits, but A was required to pay his own premiums as follows:

Hospitalization and medical insurance	$1,400
Term life insurance ($30,000)	200
Disability insurance	400
	$2,000

To simplify the analysis, assume A's tax rate on income is 28%. After paying taxes of $8,400 (.28 × $30,000) and $2,000 for insurance, A has $19,600 ($30,000 − $8,400 − $2,000) for his other living needs.

If A's employer reduced A's salary by $2,000 (to $28,000) but paid A's insurance premiums, A's tax liability would be only $7,840 ($28,000 × .28). Thus, A would have $20,160 ($28,000 − $7,840) to meet his other living needs. The change in the compensation plan would save $560 ($20,160 − $19,600). □

Similarly, employees must often incur expenses for child care and parking. The employee can have more income for other uses if the employer pays these costs for the employee but reduces the employee's salary by the cost of the benefits.

The meals and lodging exclusion enables the employee to receive from his or her employer what he or she ordinarily must purchase with after-tax dollars. Although the requirements that the employee live and take his or her meals on the employer's premises limit the tax planning opportunities, in certain situations, the exclusion is an important factor in the employee's compensation (e.g., hotels, motels, restaurants, farms, and ranches).

The employees' discount provision is especially important for manufacturers and wholesalers. Employees of manufacturers can avoid tax on the manufacturer's, wholesaler's, and retailer's markups. The wholesaler's employees can avoid tax on an amount equal to the wholesale and retail markups.

It should be recognized that the exclusion of benefits is generally available only to employees. Proprietors and partners must pay tax on the same benefits their employees receive tax-free. By incorporating and becoming an employee of the corporation, the former proprietor or partner can also receive these tax-exempt benefits. Thus, the availability of employee benefits is a consideration in the decision to incorporate.

Problem Materials

Discussion Questions

1. What are the possible tax consequences to an owner of land when a tenant constructs a permanent building on the property?

2. Who pays the income tax on a gift of the income from a certain piece of property—the donee or the donor?

3. a. A served as chairman of the local school board. Upon completion of his term in office, the organization awarded him a silver serving tray in recognition of his outstanding service to the organization.

The value of the tray is $200. Is A required to include the value of the tray in his income?

    b.   Assume the employees took up a collection and purchased the tray for A.

4. T was driving down a road when he saw that B was having trouble changing a tire. T stopped and helped B. As B was leaving, he gave T $20 and thanked him. Is T required to include the $20 in gross income?

5. Friends In Need is an unincorporated organization of individuals who have pledged to help one another. The Friends have a burial fund whereby a participant contributes $1 each month. If a member or a member's spouse or child dies during the month, the member or his or her estate will receive $300 to help with burial expenses. T's wife died during the year, and T collected $300 from the burial fund to which he had contributed $48. Is T required to include the $300 in gross income?

6. M Corporation purchased a $1,000,000 insurance policy on the life of the company's president. The company paid $100,000 of premiums, the president died, and the company collected the face amount of the policy. How much must M Corporation include in gross income?

7. Under what conditions can payments to the family of a deceased employee be excluded from gross income?

8. Company A provides its employees with $10,000 group term life insurance. Company B does not provide insurance but generally gives the family of a deceased employee $10,000. Compare the tax consequences of the insured and uninsured plans.

9. T received an academic scholarship to State University. Under the scholarship agreement, he received tuition ($1,500), books ($400), and room and board ($5,000). What is T's gross income from the scholarship?

10. X Company has a scholarship program for children of its employees. Employees with more than four years of service can receive up to $1,000 as reimbursement of college tuition paid by the employee. Are the payments excludible as scholarships?

11. V was injured in an accident unrelated to his employment. While V was away from work, he collected his regular salary of $4,500 and $3,600 on his accident and health income continuation insurance he had purchased for $900. What is V's income from the payments?

12. R and T were traveling together in a defectively manufactured automobile. As a result of the defects, the automobile ran off the road and crashed into a tree. R and T each broke an arm in the accident. R was a baseball pitcher and was unable to pitch for one year as a result of the accident. He received a $400,000 damage award in a suit against the automobile manufacturer. T was a 65-year-old retiree and received $25,000 as an award for damages. The difference in the damage awards was largely due to R's greater loss of earnings. Is R taxed on any of the $400,000 received?

13. What nontaxable benefits can a company provide its retired former employees?

14. What nontaxable fringe benefits are available to employees that are not available to partners and proprietors?

15. How does one determine if the meals and lodging supplied by the employer are to serve a valid business purpose? Is the tax treatment of meals and lodging affected if the employer advertises that the meals and lodging provided are one of the employees' fringe benefits?

16. P, a full-time employee of State University, is allowed to use the university's tennis courts when they are not being used by the tennis team and physical education classes. Does P derive gross income from the use of the tennis courts?

17. The management of X Life Insurance Company believes it is good business to encourage employees to exercise and stay healthy. Therefore, the company built a gymnasium in the basement of the main office building and made the facility available to all of the company's 1,200 employees. Z Life Insurance Company has only 30 employees. It is not feasible for Z Company to maintain its own gymnasium, but the company would like to encourage employees to exercise. Therefore, Z Company has offered to pay membership fees for any employee who wishes to join the health club located in the adjoining building. Compare the tax treatment of the health facility benefits provided the employees of the two companies.

18. T is employed by X, Inc., an automobile manufacturing company. X sold T a new automobile at company cost of $8,400. The price charged a dealer would have been $10,000, and the retail price of the automobile was $11,500. What is T's gross income from the purchase of the automobile?

19. Z Company provides the same types of benefits to all employees. However, the highly compensated employees receive superior benefits for the following:

    a. A subsidized eating facility is available only to managers and officers.

    b. Managers and officers have private room hospitalization insurance coverage whereas other employees have semi-private room coverage.

    c. Managers and officers get free parking, but other employees do not.

    Do the superior benefits affect the highly compensated (managers and officers) and other employees' gross income?

20. Z Corporation is opening a branch in Kazonbi, an African country that does not levy an income tax on citizens of foreign countries. T, a U.S. citizen, is considering two offers from his employer, Z Corporation. He can work for 6 months in Kazonbi and 6 months in the United States and receive a salary of $4,000 per month, or he can work in Kazonbi for 12 months at the same monthly salary. T would prefer to spend as much time in the United States as possible and prefers the first alter-

native. However, he asks your advice as to how income taxes might affect his decision.

21. T owns 100 shares of stock in XYZ Corporation. The corporation declares a dividend that gives T the option of receiving 10 additional shares of XYZ stock or $200 cash. T elects to receive 10 additional shares of stock. What are the tax consequences to T?

22. X, a cash basis taxpayer, was in a contract dispute with Y. In 1989 X performed services for Y, but Y would not pay. X had no gross income and $6,000 of itemized deductions and personal exemptions in 1989. In 1990 the dispute was settled, and X received $10,000. Can X exclude any of the $10,000 under the tax benefit rule?

23. In 1989, F received a $400 factory rebate on supplies purchased and deducted as a business expense in 1988. In 1989, S received a $400 factory rebate on a personal automobile purchased in December 1988. Both F and S had over $10,000 of taxable income in 1988 and 1989. Is the receipt of $400 taxable to F or S?

24. How does the tax treatment of a corporation's income generated by the retirement of bonds for less than book value (issue price plus amortized discount or less amortized premium) differ from the income derived from a shareholder's forgiveness of the corporation's indebtedness?

25. In 1981, R purchased real estate for $50,000. By 1988, the property had appreciated to $150,000. In 1988, R borrowed $120,000 and gave a mortgage on the property as security for the debt. In 1989, when the value of the property equaled the balance on the mortgage ($120,000), R transferred the property to the mortgagee in satisfaction of the debt. Did R realize income from discharge of indebtedness?

Problems

26. Determine whether the following may be excluded from gross income as gifts, bequests, scholarships, prizes, or life insurance proceeds:

    a. Uncle told Nephew, "Come live with me and take care of me in my old age and you can have all my property after my death." Nephew complied with Uncle's request. Uncle's will made Nephew sole beneficiary of the estate.

    b. Uncle told Nephew, "If you study hard and make the dean's list this year, I will pay your tuition for the following year." Nephew made the dean's list, and Uncle paid the tuition.

    c. Uncle told Nephew, "If you make the dean's list this year, I will pay you $500." Nephew made the dean's list, and Uncle paid the $500.

    d. D cashed in her life insurance contract and collected $10,000. She had paid premiums totaling $7,000.

27. Determine the taxable life insurance proceeds in the following cases:

    a. B purchased a sports franchise and player contracts from S. As part of the transaction, B purchased a life insurance contract on a key player from S for $50,000. One month later, the player was killed in an automobile accident, and B collected $500,000 on the life insurance contract.

    b. P and R formed a partnership and agreed that upon the death of either partner, the surviving partner would purchase the decedent's partnership interest. P purchased a life insurance policy on R's life and paid $5,000 in premiums. Upon R's death, P collected $100,000 on the life insurance policy and used the proceeds to purchase R's interest in the partnership.

    c. Same as (b), except the partnership was incorporated and P and R owned all the stock. Upon incorporation, P and R transferred their life insurance policies to the corporation in exchange for stock. When R died, the corporation redeemed (purchased) R's stock, using the $100,000 life insurance proceeds.

28. Determine the effect on Z's gross income of the following:

    a. Z Company sells furniture to customers on credit. Customers are required to purchase credit life insurance, with the proceeds payable to Z. The company collected $3,000 when a customer died.

    b. A, a major shareholder in Z Company, transferred his life insurance policy to the corporation in exchange for additional stock. A had paid $6,000 in premiums. When A died, the company collected the face amount of the policy of $25,000. During the time it held the policy, Z Company paid additional premiums of $1,000.

    c. Z Company also purchased an insurance policy on the life of the company president, B. The company had paid $10,000 in premiums, and the cash surrender value of the policy was $10,500 when B died. The company collected $25,000, which was the face amount of the policy.

29. T died at age 35. He was married and had six minor children. His employer, XYZ Plumbing Company, made payments to Mrs. T as follows:

T's accrued salary at date of death	$1,200
Family death benefits under long-standing company policy ($3,000 is paid to the spouse and $1,000 is paid to each child of a deceased employee)	3,000
A payment authorized by the board of directors to help Mrs. T pay debts accumulated by T	1,500

T and Mrs. T filed a joint return in the year of T's death. Determine the amounts from above that must be included in their gross income.

30. F was awarded an academic scholarship to State University. He received $5,000 in August and $5,000 in December 1989. F had enough personal savings to pay all expenses as they came due. F's expenditures for the relevant period were as follows:

Tuition, August 1989	$2,500
Tuition, December 1989	2,800
Books and educational supplies	
August–December 1989	600
January–May 1990	650
Room and board	
August–December 1989	3,000
January–May 1990	2,400

Determine the effect on F's gross income for 1989 and 1990.

31. Which of the following payments for damages would be taxable:

    a. A corporation received $100,000 from a competitor for infringement of its patent rights.

    b. A woman is paid $60,000 because her personal files were incorporated in a biography without her consent.

    c. A client is paid $12,000 by an investment counselor as reimbursement for a loss resulting from the counselor's poor advice.

32. Coach Z intentionally hit M, a basketball referee, after M called a technical foul on Z. M had actual damages as follows:

Medical expenses	$18,000
Loss of income	9,000
	$27,000

    M threatened Z with a lawsuit for actual damages, plus $25,000 as compensation for M's pain and suffering and $200,000 for punitive damages. Z admitted liability and has offered to settle for $40,000. M's hospitalization insurance paid for all of his medical expenses, and M did not deduct any medical expenses on his tax return. Determine the tax consequences to M if he accepts Z's offer under the following conditions:

    a. M had filed suit for damages as described above, and M and Z settled for $40,000 one hour before the trial was to begin. The settlement agreement did not allocate the $40,000 amount among the various claims.

    b. M did not file suit, but Z's insurance company paid M $40,000, and M signed an agreement that allocated $27,000 for medical expenses and loss of income and $13,000 for pain and suffering. The insurance company was not liable for punitive damages.

33. R was injured in an accident that was not related to his employment. He incurred $10,000 in medical expenses and collected $7,500 on a medical insurance policy he purchased. He also collected $9,500 in medical benefits under his employer's group plan. Originally the doctor diagnosed R's injury as requiring no more than 3 months of disability. Because of subsequent complications, R was unable to return to work until 14 months after the accident. While away from the job, R collected $200 per week on his employer's wage continuation plan. R also owned an insurance policy that paid him $100 per week while he

was disabled. What are the tax consequences to R of the receipt of the following:

a. $17,000 medical benefits.

b. $300 per week to replace R's wages.

34.   T, age 45, is an officer of XYZ Company, which provided T with the following fringe benefits in 1989:

    a.   Hospitalization insurance for T and his dependents. The cost of coverage for T was $450, and the additional cost for T's dependents was $400.

    b.   Reimbursement of $700 from an uninsured medical reimbursement plan available to all employees.

    c.   Group term life insurance protection of $120,000. (Each employee received coverage equal to twice his or her annual salary.)

    d.   Salary continuation payments of $2,600 while T was hospitalized for an illness.

In addition, T was covered by his employer's workers' compensation insurance policy. Premiums on the policy were $2 per $1000 salary ($120 for T's coverage). While T was ill, he collected $1,600 on a salary continuation insurance policy he had purchased.

Determine the amounts T must include in gross income.

35.   T served as the manager of an orphanage in 1989. In this connection, he had the following transactions:

    a.   He received no salary from his job but was given room and board (valued at $3,600) on the premises. No other person was employed by the orphanage, which is a tax-exempt organization.

    b.   The orphanage paid $300 in tuition for a night course T took at a local university. The course was in the field of philosophy and dealt with the meaning of life. The payment was authorized by the orphanage's trustees in a written resolution.

    c.   The orphanage paid $500 of the premiums on T's life insurance policy and all of his medical expenses of $1,800. Again, the payment was made pursuant to a resolution approved by the trustees.

Determine the effect of these transactions on T's gross income.

36.   A, age 40, is an officer of the XYZ Company, which provided the following nondiscriminatory fringe benefits in 1989:

    a.   Group term life insurance protection of $80,000.

    b.   Group hospitalization insurance, $1,080.

    c.   Reimbursement of $2,800 from an uninsured medical reimbursement plan maintained exclusively for highly compensated employees.

    d.   Salary continuation payments for $3,000 while A was hospitalized for an illness.

In addition, A collected $1,800 from a wage continuation policy he had purchased.

Which items are includible in gross income?

37. Determine the taxpayer's gross income for each of the following:

   a. T is the manager of a plant. The company owns a house one mile from the plant (rental value of $6,000) that T is allowed to occupy.

   b. M works for an insurance company that allows employees to eat in the cafeteria for $.50 a meal. Generally, the cost to the insurance company of producing a meal is $5.00, and a comparable meal could be purchased for $4.00. M ate 150 meals in the cafeteria during the year.

   c. Z is a Methodist minister and receives a housing allowance of $600 per month from his church. Z is buying his home and uses the $600 to make house payments ($450) and to pay utilities ($150).

   d. P is a college professor and lives in campus housing. He is not charged rent. The value of the house is $100,000, and the annual rental value is $7,200.

38. Does the taxpayer recognize gross income in the following situations?

   a. A is a registered nurse working in a community hospital. She is not required to take her lunch on the hospital premises, but she can eat in the cafeteria at no charge. The hospital adopted this policy to encourage employees to stay on the premises and be available in case of emergencies. During the year, A ate most of her meals on the premises. The total value of those meals was $750.

   b. J is the manager of a hotel. His employer will allow him to live in one of the rooms rent free or to receive a $200 per month cash allowance for rent. J elected to live in the hotel.

   c. S is a forest ranger and lives in his employer's cabin in the forest. He is required to live there, and because there are no restaurants nearby, the employer supplies S with groceries that he cooks and eats on the premises.

   d. T is a partner in the ABC Ranch (a partnership). He is the full-time manager of the ranch. ABC has a business purpose for T's living on the ranch.

39. T is employed by F Bowling Lanes, Inc. Determine T's gross income in each of the following situations:

   a. T's children are allowed to use the lanes without charge. Each child can also bring a friend without charge. This benefit is available to all employees. During the year, the children bowled 200 games, and the usual charge was $1.50 per game. Friends of T's children bowled 150 games.

   b. The company has a lunch counter. T is allowed to take home the leftover donuts each night. The company's cost was $400, and the value of the donuts T took home was $150.

   c. The company pays T's subscription to *Bowling Lanes Management*, a monthly journal.

40. X Corporation would like you to review its employee fringe benefits program with regard to the effects of the plan on the company's president (P), who is also the majority shareholder:

    a. All employees receive free tickets to State University football games. P is seldom able to attend the games and usually gives his tickets to his nephew. The cost of P's tickets for the year was $75.

    b. The company pays all parking fees for its officers but not for other employees. The company paid $1,200 for P's parking for the year.

    c. Employees are allowed to use the copy machine for personal purposes as long as the privilege is not abused. P is president of a trade association and made extensive use of the copy machine to prepare mailings to members of the association. The cost of the copies was $900.

    d. The company is in the household moving business. Employees are allowed to ship goods without charge whenever there is excess space on a truck. P purchased a dining room suite for his daughter. Company trucks delivered the furniture to the daughter. Normal freight charges would have been $600.

    e. The company has a storage facility for household goods. Officers are allowed a 20% discount on charges for storing their goods. All other employees are allowed a 10% discount. P's discounts for the year totaled $400.

41. Which of the following benefits are excludible from an employee's gross income even though provided on a discriminatory basis (they favor higher paid employees)?

    a. Occasional use of the employer's typewriter to type a personal letter.

    b. A 10% discount on merchandise.

    c. Parking.

    d. Meals provided in a subsidized eating facility.

42. R is a U.S. citizen and a production manager for XYZ Company. On May 1, 1988, he was temporarily assigned to the Monterrey, Mexico, plant. On August 6, 1988, he returned to the United States for medical treatment. On September 1, 1988, he returned to his duties in Monterrey. Except for a two-week period in the United States (December 16–31, 1988), he worked in Monterrey until December 1, 1989, when he was transferred to Boston, Massachusetts. R's salary was $4,000 per month in 1988 and $5,000 per month in 1989. His housing expense did not exceed the base amount. Compute R's foreign earned income exclusion in 1988 and 1989.

43. Determine T's gross income from the following receipts for the year:

Interest on U.S. government savings bonds	$ 500
Sale of State of Virginia bonds (basis of $9,000)	10,000
Interest on Virginia tax refund	1,500
Interest on Pulaski County school bonds	800
Sale of Augusta County bonds (basis of $4,000)	3,500
Patronage dividend from the Good Life Food Cooperative (a health food store)	200

44. During the current year, H (husband) and W (wife) had dividends and other receipts from investments as follows:

July 2   W received two shares of M Sales Corporation common stock as a stock dividend. The stock had a fair market value of $160 at the time of receipt. W elected to receive the stock rather than $150 cash.

December 15   H and W received $90 cash dividends from B Manufacturing Company on jointly owned common stock.

December 31   H received $130 dividends from DC Company, a Canadian corporation.

December 31   W received notice that $140 in dividends on her First Savings & Loan Association savings account had been credited and the amount was available for withdrawal.

Compute the gross income for H and W on a joint return.

45. How does the tax benefit rule apply in the following cases:

   a. In 1988, T paid X $5,000 for locating a potential client. The deal fell through, and in 1989, X refunded the $5,000 to T.

   b. In 1988, T paid an attorney $300 for services in connection with a title search. Because the attorney was negligent, T incurred some additional costs in acquiring the land. In 1989, the attorney refunded his $300 fee to T.

   c. In 1989, T received a $90 dividend with respect to 1989 premiums on her life insurance policy.

   d. In 1989, a cash basis farmer received a $400 patronage dividend with respect to 1988 purchases of cattle feed.

46. T, who is in the 28% tax bracket, recently collected $100,000 on a life insurance policy she carried on her father. She currently owes $120,000 on her personal residence and $120,000 on business property. National Bank holds the mortgage on both pieces of property and has agreed to accept $100,000 in complete satisfaction of either mortgage. The interest rate on the mortgages is 8%, and both mortgages are payable over 10 years. T can also purchase Montgomery County school bonds yielding 8%. What would be the tax consequences of each of the following alternatives, assuming T presently deducts the mortgage interest on her tax return:

   a. Retire the mortgage on the residence.

   b. Retire the mortgage on the business property.

   c. Purchase tax-exempt bonds but not pay off either mortgage.

   Which alternative should T select?

47. T had total assets of $100,000 and liabilities of $150,000; it was apparent that T could not meet his liabilities as they came due. Determine the consequences of the following agreements T reached with his creditors.

a.   The State Bank agreed to extend the due date for an additional year on a $30,000 note due in exchange for an increase in the interest rate.

b.   T's older brother, Z, forgave T's $10,000 debt. When asked about why he did it, Z responded, "T's my brother."

c.   An equipment supplier agreed to reduce the amount T owed for equipment by $5,000 "to help a good customer stay in business."

Cumulative Problems

48.   Oliver W. Hand was divorced from Sandra D. Hand on May 12, 1988. On September 6, 1989, Oliver married Beulah Crane. Oliver and Beulah will file a joint return for 1989. Oliver's Social Security number is 262–60–3814. Beulah's number is 259–68–4184, and she will adopt "Hand" as her married name. The Hands live at 210 Mason Drive, Atlanta, GA 30304. Sandra's Social Security number is 219–74–1361.

Oliver is 49 and is employed by Atom, Inc., as an electrical engineer. His salary for 1989 was $48,200. Beulah is 30 and earned $24,000 as a marriage counselor in 1989. She was employed by Family Counselors, Inc.

The decree of divorce required Oliver to pay Sandra $1,000 per month for 132 months. Oliver was also required to pay $200 a month in support of Daisy Hand, his 11-year-old daughter. Sandra was granted custody of Daisy and can document that she provided $2,000 of support for Daisy. Oliver made 12 payments in 1989.

Oliver's employer provided him with group term life insurance coverage in the amount of $90,000 in 1989.

Beulah's employer provided Beulah with free parking in a parking garage adjacent to the office building where Beulah works. The monthly charge to the general public is $50.

Oliver received dividends of $40 on Z Corporation stock he owned before marriage, and Beulah received dividends of $50 on her separately owned M Corporation stock. They received dividends of $100 on jointly owned B Corporation stock, which they acquired after marriage. Oliver and Beulah live in a common law state.

Combined itemized deductions for Oliver and Beulah in 1989 were as follows:

State income taxes withheld		
Oliver	$810	
Beulah	430	$1,240
Real estate taxes on residence		820
Home mortgage interest		
(paid to Atlanta Federal Savings and Loan)		4,020
Cash contributions to church		900

In 1989, Beulah received a refund of 1988 state income taxes of $250. She had deducted state income taxes withheld as an itemized deduction on her 1988 return.

Additional information:

- Oliver's employer withheld Federal income tax of $7,200 and $3,605 of FICA (Social Security) tax. Beulah's employer withheld $2,800 of Federal income tax and $1,802 of FICA tax.

Part 1—Tax Computation

Compute the Hands' net tax payable (or refund due) for 1989. Suggested software (if available): *WEST–TAX Planner* or *BNA Individual Income Tax Spreadsheet.*

Part 2—Tax Planning

Assume the Hands came to you in early December of 1989 seeking tax planning advice for 1989 and 1990. They provide you with the following information:

a. All the facts previously presented will be essentially the same in 1990 except for the items described in (b), (c), (d), and (e).

b. Oliver inherited $100,000 from his mother on December 1. He will use part of his inheritance to pay off the mortgage on the Hands' residence on January 3, 1990. Consequently, there will be no mortgage interest expense in 1990.

c. Oliver expects a 6% salary increase in 1990, and Beulah expects a 10% increase.

d. The Hands have pledged to contribute $2,400 to their church in 1990 (as opposed to $900 contributed in 1989). However, they could use Oliver's inherited funds to pay the pledge before the end of 1989 if you advise them to do so to achieve an overall tax savings.

e. The Hands acquired 100 shares of ABC Corporation stock on July 5, 1989, at a total cost of $2,000. The value of the stock has increased rapidly, and it is now worth $5,000. The Hands plan to sell the stock and ask whether they should sell it in 1989 or wait until 1990.

Advise the Hands as to the appropriate tax planning strategy for 1989 and 1990. Support your recommendations by computing their tax liabilities for 1989 and 1990 considering the various available alternatives. Suggested software (if available): *WEST–TAX Planner* or *BNA Individual Income Tax Spreadsheet.*

 49. Archie S. Monroe (Social Security number 363–33–1411) is married to Annie B. Monroe (Social Security number 259–68–4284). The Monroes live at 215 Adams Dr., Thor, VA 24317. They file a joint return and have two dependent children (Barry and Betty). In 1989, Archie and Annie had the following transactions:

a. Salary received by Archie from Allen Steel Company (Archie is vice president).	$65,000
b. Interest received on jointly owned State of Nebraska bonds.	8,000
c. Group term life insurance premiums paid by Archie's employer (coverage of $40,000).	80
d. Annual increment in the value of Series E government savings bonds (the Monroes have not previously included the accrued amounts in gross income).	400
e. Taxable dividends received from Allen Steel Company, a U.S. corporation (the stock was jointly owned). Of the $5,900 in dividends, $1,000 was mailed on December 31, 1989, and received by Archie and Annie on January 4, 1990.	5,900
f. Alimony payments to Archie's former wife (Rosa T. Monroe, Social Security number 800–60–2580) under a divorce decree.	9,000
g. Itemized deductions.	
State income tax	1,600
Real estate tax on residence	600
Interest on personal residence (paid to Thor Federal Savings)	3,000
Cash contribution to church	700
h. Federal income tax withheld.	11,976

Part 1—Tax Computation

Compute the Monroes' net tax payable (or refund due) for 1989. Suggested software (if available): *WEST–TAX Planner* or *BNA Individual Income Tax Spreadsheet.*

Part 2—Tax Planning

The Monroes plan to sell 200 shares of stock they purchased on July 12, 1980, at a cost of $18,000. The stock is worth $10,000 in December 1989, and the Monroes' broker predicts a continued decline in value. Annie plans to resume her career as a model in 1990, and her earnings will move the Monroes into the top tax bracket. How much Federal income tax will the Monroes save for 1989 if they sell the stock in 1989? Should they sell the stock in 1989 or 1990? Suggested software (if available): *WEST–TAX Planner* or *BNA Individual Income Tax Spreadsheet.*

Research Problems

Research Problem 1   S was asked by the M County School Board to resign her position as superintendent of public schools. She refused and submitted to the board a list of grievances. She also alleged that the board had damaged her professional reputation. S was later fired, but after threatening suit she was paid $20,000 by the board. S has supplied a doctor's testimony clearly showing that the dispute with the board caused her to become physically and mentally ill. Is the $20,000 taxable?

Research Problem 2   E was recently hired as manager of Fertile Farm, Inc. E is required to live in the employer's house on the farm. E and the employer are trying to decide how to arrange terms with the electric company. The employer would like E to have the account with the utility in E's name, but the employer would reimburse E $200 each month. The $200 should be adequate to cover all charges. The employer requests this ar-

rangement because the previous manager established the account in the company's name and left town without paying the bill.
E has asked your tax advice on the matter.

Research Problem 3   The taxpayer is a physician employed by Middle State Hospital. He is on call at all hours and is required to live on the hospital grounds. The hospital furnishes the housing but withholds $500 each month, the fair rental value of the property, from the taxpayer's salary. Can the $500 withheld each month be excluded from the taxpayer's gross income?

Research Problem 4   Z sold real estate but was not to collect the selling price for 90 days. Until then, Z needed $100,000 to meet other commitments. He owns tax-exempt securities with a value of $100,000, but he wants to keep them. An officer of C Bank suggested that the bank purchase the securities for $100,000, but Z would have a 120-day option to repurchase them. Z and the bank executed the agreement, and Z exercised his option to repurchase the securities. C Bank collected $2,500 interest while it held the securities. The IRS contends that the substance of the transaction was a loan from the bank to Z and that the interest the bank collected on the securities was taxable interest from Z. Can you find authority to support the bank's position that the interest is tax-exempt?

3

DEDUCTIONS

Part 3 presents the deduction component of the basic tax model. Deductions are classified as business versus nonbusiness, "for" versus "from," employee versus employer, active versus passive, and reimbursed versus unreimbursed. The effect of each of these classifications is analyzed. The presentation includes not only the deductions that are permitted, but also limitations and disallowances associated with deductions. Because deductions can exceed gross income, the treatment of losses is also included.

6

DEDUCTIONS AND LOSSES: IN GENERAL

OBJECTIVES   Explain the importance of deductions *for* and *from* adjusted gross income.
Classify the deductions *for* and *from* adjusted gross income.
Define the meaning of "ordinary," "necessary," and "reasonable" in relation to deductible business expenses.
Explain the differences between cash basis and accrual basis.
Discuss the following disallowance possibilities: public policy limitations, political activities, investigation of business opportunities, hobby losses, vacation home rentals, payment of expenses of others, personal expenditures, unrealized losses, capital expenditures, and transactions between related parties.
Explain the substantiation requirements that must be met to take a deduction.
Examine the nondeductibility of expenses and interest related to tax-exempt income.
Describe various tax planning techniques concerning the time value of deductions, unreasonable compensation, shifting deductions, hobby losses, and substantiation requirements.

CLASSIFICATION OF DEDUCTIBLE EXPENSES

As discussed in chapters 5 and 6, § 61 provides an all-inclusive definition of gross income. Deductions, however, must be specifically provided for by law. The courts have established the doctrine that an item is not deductible unless a specific provision in the tax law allows its deduction. Whether and to what extent deductions shall be allowed depends on legislative grace.[1]

It is important to classify deductible expenses as deductions *for* adjusted gross income (deductions subtracted from gross income in calculating adjusted gross income) or deductions *from* adjusted gross income (AGI). Deductions *for* AGI can be taken whether or not the taxpayer itemizes. Deductions *from* AGI result in a tax benefit only if they exceed the taxpayer's standard deduction. If itemized deductions (*from* AGI) are less than the standard deduction, they are of no tax benefit.

EXAMPLE 1

T is married and files a joint return with his spouse in 1989. He and his wife have adjusted gross income of $30,000 and have $4,000 of itemized deductions during the year. In December, T asks you whether he should prepay his real estate taxes of $400 in December or wait until the due date in January 1990. The standard deduction for 1989 is $5,000 and the real estate taxes are deductible only as itemized deductions. T would therefore obtain no tax benefit from prepaying the real estate taxes in December and should make the payment in January of 1990. Recall from chapter 3 the tax planning opportunities in timing these deductions. □

Deductions *for* AGI are also important in determining the *amount* of itemized deductions, because many itemized deductions (e.g., medical expenses and personal casualty losses) are limited to amounts in excess of specified percentages of AGI. Itemized deductions that are deductible only to the extent that they exceed a specified percentage of AGI are increased when AGI is decreased (by deductions *for* AGI). Likewise, when AGI is increased, such itemized deductions are decreased.

EXAMPLE 2

T, who earns a salary of $20,000 and has no other income, itemizes deductions in 1989. His medical expenses for the year were $1,800. Since medical expenses are deductible only to the extent they exceed 7.5% of AGI, T's medical expense deduction is $300 [$1,800 − (.075 × $20,000)]. If T had a $2,000 deduction *for* AGI, his medical expense deduction would be $450 [$1,800 − (.075 × $18,000)]. If the $2,000 deduction was *from* AGI, his medical expense deduction would remain $300, since AGI would be unchanged. □

A deduction *for* adjusted gross income is also more valuable to the taxpayer who lives in a state that begins its tax computation with Federal AGI rather

---

1. *New Colonial Ice Co. v. Helvering*, 4 USTC ¶1292, 13 AFTR 1180, 54 S.Ct. 788 (USSC, 1934).

than with Federal taxable income. A lower base of Federal AGI will result in lower state income taxes.

Deductions for Adjusted Gross Income

To understand how deductions of individual taxpayers are classified, it is necessary to understand the role of § 62. Section 62 merely classifies various deductions as deductions *for* adjusted gross income. It does not provide the authority for taking the deduction. For example, § 212 allows individuals to deduct expenses attributable to income-producing property. Section 62(a)(4) classifies § 212 expenses that are attributable to rents or royalties as deductions *for* AGI. Likewise, a deduction for trade or business expenses is allowed by § 162; such expenses are classified as deductions *for* AGI by § 62(a)(1).

If a deduction is not listed in § 62, it is *not* a deduction for AGI; it is an itemized deduction. Following is a list of the items classified as deductions *for* AGI by § 62.

1. Expenses attributable to a trade or business carried on by the taxpayer, if such trade or business does not consist of the performance of services by the taxpayer as an employee.

2. Expenses incurred by a taxpayer in connection with the performance of services as an employee if such expenses are reimbursed, an adequate accounting is made to the employer, and the employee is not allowed to keep any excess reimbursements.

3. Deductions that result from losses on the sale or exchange of property by the taxpayer.

4. Deductions attributable to property held for the production of rents and royalties.

5. The deduction for payment of alimony allowed by § 215.

6. Certain contributions to pension, profit sharing, and annuity plans of self-employed individuals.

7. The deduction for certain retirement savings allowed by § 219.

8. A certain portion of lump-sum distributions from pension plans taxed under § 402(e).

9. Penalties forfeited because of premature withdrawal of funds from time savings accounts or deposits.

10. Trade or business expenses of a *qualified performing artist* incurred in connection with the performance of services as an employee in the performing arts.

11. The deduction for certain required repayments of supplemental unemployment compensation benefits.

12. Depreciation and depletion deductions allowed to a life tenant of property; an income beneficiary of property held in trust; or an heir, legatee, or devisee of an estate.

13. The deduction for reforestation expenses allowed by § 194.

Items 1 through 8 are covered in detail in various chapters throughout the text. Although items 9 through 13 are not covered in detail in the text, they are included here to provide a complete list of deductions covered by § 62.

Itemized Deductions

Section 63(f) defines itemized deductions as the deductions allowed other than "the deductions allowable in arriving at adjusted gross income"; that is, deductions that are not deductions *for* adjusted gross income are itemized deductions.

Section 212 allows deductions for ordinary and necessary expenses paid or incurred for the following:

- The production or collection of income.

- The management, conservation, or maintenance of property held for the production of income.

- Expenses paid in connection with the determination (including tax return preparation), collection, or refund of any tax.

Section 62(a)(4) classifies § 212 expenses that are related to rent and royalty income as deductions *for* AGI. All other § 212 expenses are itemized deductions (deductions *from* AGI).[2]

Investment-related expenses (e.g., safe deposit box rentals) are deductible[3] as itemized deductions attributable to the production of investment income.

Taxpayers are also allowed to deduct certain expenses that are primarily personal in nature. These expenses, which are not generally related to the production of income, are deductions *from* AGI (itemized deductions). Some of the more frequently encountered deductions in this category include the following:

- Contributions to qualified charitable organizations (not to exceed 50 percent of AGI).

- Medical expenses (in excess of 7.5 percent of AGI).

- State and local taxes (e.g., real estate taxes and state and local income taxes).

- Personal casualty losses (in excess of an aggregate floor of 10 percent of AGI and a $100 floor per casualty).

- Certain personal interest (e.g., mortgage interest on a personal residence).

Certain miscellaneous itemized deductions are deductible only to the extent that in the aggregate they exceed 2 percent of adjusted gross income. Other miscellaneous itemized deductions are fully deductible. Itemized deductions are discussed in detail in chapter 11.

---

2. §§ 62(5) and 62(a)(4).   3. Reg. § 1.212–1(g).

Trade or Business Expenses

Section 162(a) permits a deduction for all ordinary and necessary expenses paid or incurred in carrying on a trade or business, including reasonable salaries paid for services and expenses for the use of business property. Such expenses are deducted *for* AGI.

It is sometimes difficult to determine whether an expenditure is deductible as a trade or business expense. The term "trade or business" is not defined in the Code or Regulations, and the courts have not provided a satisfactory definition. Therefore, it is usually necessary to ask one or more of the following questions to determine whether an item qualifies as a trade or business expense:

- Was the use of the particular item related to a business activity? For example, if funds are borrowed for use in a business, the interest is deductible as a business expense (as a deduction *for* AGI).

- Was the expenditure incurred with the intent to realize a profit or to produce income? For example, expenses in excess of the income from raising horses would not be deductible if the activity were classified as a personal hobby rather than a trade or business.

- Were the taxpayer's operation and management activities extensive enough to indicate the carrying on of a trade or business?

Section 162 excludes the following items from classification as trade or business expenses:

- Charitable contributions or gifts.
- Illegal bribes and kickbacks and certain treble damage payments.
- Fines and penalties.

A bribe paid to a domestic official is not deductible if it is illegal under the laws of the United States. Foreign bribes (sometimes referred to as grease payments) are deductible unless they are unlawful under the Foreign Corrupt Practices Act of 1977.[4]

Ordinary and Necessary Requirement.   The terms "ordinary" and "necessary" are found in both §§ 162 and 212. Section 162 governs the deductibility of trade or business expenses, and § 62(a)(1) classifies trade or business expenses of individuals as deductions *for* AGI. To be deductible under § 162, any trade or business expense must be ordinary and necessary. In addition, compensation for services must be "reasonable" in amount.

Many expenses that are necessary are *not* ordinary. The words "ordinary and necessary" are not defined in the Code or Regulations. However, the courts have held that an expense is necessary if a prudent businessperson would incur the same expense and the expense is expected to be appropriate and helpful in the taxpayer's business.[5]

---

4. § 162(c)(1).
5. *Welch v. Helvering*, 3 USTC ¶1164, 12 AFTR 1456, 54 S.Ct. 8 (USSC, 1933).

EXAMPLE 3   T purchased a manufacturing concern that had just been adjudged bankrupt. Because the business had a poor financial rating, T satisfies some of the obligations incurred by its former owners. Although there was no legal obligation to pay these debts, T felt this was the only way to reestablish a source of credit for future inventory purchases. The Supreme Court found that such payments were necessary in that they were both appropriate and helpful[6] However, the Court held that such payments were *not* ordinary but were in the nature of capital expenditures to build a reputation. Therefore, no deduction was allowed. □

An expense is ordinary if it is normal, usual, or customary in the type of business conducted by the taxpayer and is not capital in nature.[7] However, the courts have also held that an expense need not be recurring to be deductible as ordinary.[8]

EXAMPLE 4   T engaged in a mail-order business. The post office judged that his advertisements were false and misleading. Under a fraud order, the post office stamped "fraudulent" on all letters addressed to T's business and returned them to the senders. T spent $30,000 on legal fees in an unsuccessful attempt to force the post office to stop. The legal fees (though not recurring) were ordinary business expenses because such fees were normal, usual, or customary in the circumstances.[9] □

The Regulations under § 212 require that expenses bear a reasonable and proximate relationship to the production or collection of income or to the management, conservation, or maintenance of property held for the production of income.[10]

EXAMPLE 5   W owns a small portfolio of investments, including 10 shares of T, Inc., common stock worth $1,000. W incurred $350 in travel expenses to attend the annual shareholders' meeting at which she voted her 10 shares against the current management group. No deduction is permitted, because a 10-share investment is insignificant in value in relation to the travel expenses incurred.[11] □

Reasonableness Requirement.   The Code refers to reasonableness solely with respect to salaries and other compensation for services.[12] The courts,

6. *Dunn and McCarthy, Inc. v. Comm.*, 43–2 USTC ¶9688, 31 AFTR 1043, 139 F.2d 242 (CA–2, 1943).

7. *Deputy v. DuPont*, 40–1 USTC ¶9161, 23 AFTR 808, 60 S.Ct. 363 (USSC, 1940).

8. *Supra*, note 6.

9. S.B. Heininger, 44–1 USTC ¶ 9109, 31 AFTR 783, 64 S.Ct. 249 (USSC, 1943).

10. Reg. § 1.212–1(d).

11. *J. Raymond Dyer*, 36 T.C. 456 (1961); Reg. § 1.212–1(d).

12. § 162(a)(1).

however, have held that for any business expense to be ordinary and necessary it must also be reasonable in amount.[13]

What constitutes reasonableness is a question of fact. If an expense is unreasonable, the excess amount is not allowed as a deduction. The question of reasonableness generally arises with respect to closely held corporations where there is no separation of ownership and management. In such cases, transactions between the shareholders and the company may result in the disallowance of deductions for excessive salaries and rent expense paid by the corporation. However, an unusually large salary will be viewed by the courts in light of all relevant circumstances, and such a salary may be found reasonable despite its size.[14] If excessive payments for salaries and rents bear a close relationship to the percentage of stock ownership of the recipients, such amounts are generally treated as dividends to the shareholders and are not deductible by the corporation.[15] However, deductions for reasonable salaries will not be disallowed solely because the corporation has paid insubstantial portions of its earnings as dividends to its shareholders.[16]

EXAMPLE 6   XYZ Corporation is closely held in equal ownership interests by X, Y, and Z. The company has been highly profitable for several years and has not paid dividends. X, Y, and Z are key officers of the company, and each receives a salary of $200,000. Salaries for similar positions in comparable companies average only $100,000. Amounts paid to X, Y, and Z in excess of $100,000 may be deemed unreasonable, and a total of $300,000 in salary deductions may be disallowed. The excess amounts may be treated as dividends rather than salary income to X, Y, and Z, because such amounts are proportional to stock ownership. Salaries are deductible by the corporation but dividends are not. □

Business and Nonbusiness Losses

Section 165 provides for a deduction for losses not compensated for by insurance. As a general rule, deductible losses of individual taxpayers are limited to those incurred in a trade or business or in a transaction entered into for profit. However, individuals are also allowed to deduct losses that are the result of a casualty. Casualty losses include, but are not limited to, fire, storm, shipwreck, and theft (see chapter 8 for a further discussion of this topic). Deductible personal casualty losses are reduced by $100 per casualty and the aggregate of all casualty losses is reduced by 10 percent of adjusted gross income. A personal casualty loss is an itemized deduction.

---

13. *Comm. v. Lincoln Electric Co.*, 49–2 USTC ¶9388, 38 AFTR 411, 176 F.2d 815 (CA–6, 1949).

14. *James D. Kennedy, Jr. v. Comm.*, 82–1 USTC ¶9186, 49 AFTR2d 82–628, 671 F.2d 167 (CA–6, 1982), Rev'g 72 T.C. 793 (1979).

15. Reg. § 1.162–8.

16. Rev.Rul. 79–8, 1979–1 C.B. 92.

Deductions and Losses—Timing of Expense Recognition

A taxpayer's method of accounting is a major factor in determining taxable income. The method used determines when an item is includible in income and when an item is deductible on the tax return. Usually the taxpayer's regular method of recordkeeping is used for income tax purposes.[17] The taxing authorities do not require uniformity among all taxpayers, but they do require that the method used clearly reflect income and that items be handled consistently.[18] The most common methods of accounting are the cash method and the accrual method.

Cash Method Requirements

The expenses of cash basis taxpayers are deductible only when they are actually paid with cash or other property. Promising to pay or issuing a note does not satisfy the "actually paid" requirement.[19] However, the payment can be made with borrowed funds. Thus, at the time taxpayers charge expenses on their bank credit cards, they are allowed to claim the deduction because they are deemed to have simultaneously borrowed money from the credit card issuer and constructively paid the expenses.[20]

Although the cash basis taxpayer must have actually or constructively paid the amount, payment does not assure a current deduction. Cash basis as well as accrual basis taxpayers cannot take a current deduction for capital expenditures, except through amortization or depreciation over the life of the asset. The Regulations set forth the general rule that an expenditure that creates an asset having a useful life that extends substantially beyond the end of the tax year must be capitalized.[21]

EXAMPLE 7   T, a cash basis taxpayer, rents property from L. On July 1, 1989, T paid $2,400 rent for the 24 months ending June 30, 1991. The prepaid rent extends 18 months—substantially beyond the year of payment. Therefore, T must capitalize the prepaid rent and amortize the expense on a monthly basis. His deduction for 1989 is $600. □

The Tax Court and the IRS took the position that an asset that would expire or would be consumed by the end of the tax year following the year of payment had a life that extended substantially beyond the year of payment and had to be prorated. However, the Ninth Circuit Court held that such expenditures are currently deductible, and the Supreme Court apparently concurs.[22]

---

17. § 446(a).

18. §§ 446(b) and (e); Reg. § 1.446–1(a)(2).

19. *Page v. Rhode Island Trust Co., Exr.*, 37–1 USTC ¶9138, 19 AFTR 105, 88 F.2d 192 (CA–1, 1937).

20. Rev.Rul. 78–39, 1978–1 C.B. 73. See also Rev. Rul. 80–335, 1980–2 C.B. 170, which applies to pay-by-phone arrangements.

21. Reg. § 1.461–1(a).

22. *Martin J. Zaninovich v. Comm.*, 80–1 USTC ¶9342, 45 AFTR2d 80–1442, 616 F.2d 429 (CA–9, 1980), reversing 69 T.C. 605 (1978). Cited by the Supreme Court in *Hillsboro National Bank v. Comm.*, 83–1 USTC ¶9229, 51 AFTR2d 83–874, 103 S.Ct. 1134 (1983).

EXAMPLE 8   Assume the same facts as in Example 7, except that T was required to pay only 12 months rent in 1989. T paid $1,200 on July 1, 1989. The entire $1,200 would be deductible in 1989. □

The payment, however, must be required (and not a voluntary prepayment) to obtain the current deduction under the one-year rule.[23]

To obtain a current deduction for an asset, the taxpayer also must demonstrate that an allowance of the current deduction will not result in a material distortion of income. Generally, the deduction will be allowed if the item is recurring (e.g., rent) or was made for a business purpose (rather than to manipulate income).[24] Deduction of prepaid interest is disallowed by § 461(g).

Limitations on Who Can Use the Cash Method.   In the cash method of accounting, possibilities exist for the manipulation of taxable income between years. The tax law lessens these possibilities by prohibiting the use of the cash method by the following taxpayers: [25]

- Corporations (other than S corporations).

- Partnerships where one of the partners is a corporation (other than an S corporation), except in certain specified cases.

- Trusts subject to tax under § 511(b) with respect to activities of the trust constituting an unrelated trade or business.

- Tax shelters, regardless of income level.

Exceptions are provided for small businesses, farms, certain personal service corporations, and entities not fitting into one of the four classifications just listed.

Small businesses whose average annual gross income for the preceding three years does not exceed $5 million are allowed to use the cash method.

Farms include any business engaged in the growing, raising, managing, or training of crops or livestock. Nurseries, sod farms, ornamental and Christmas tree operations, and fruit or nut tree operations are included in the definition of farms. Other tree-raising or harvesting operations (e.g., timber) are not defined as farms.

A personal service corporation can use the cash method provided both a function test and an ownership test [26] are met. The function test is met if at least 95 percent of the corporation's activities are the performance of services in the fields of health, law, engineering, architecture, accounting, actuarial science, performing arts, or consulting.

The ownership test is met if substantially all of the value of the outstanding stock of the corporation is owned by any of the following:

- Employees performing services for the corporation in a field satisfying the function test.

---

23. *Bonaire Development Co. v. Comm.*, 82–2 USTC ¶9428, 50 AFTR2d 82–5167, 679 F.2d 159 (CA–9, 1982).

24. *Stephen A. Keller v. Comm.*, 84–1 USTC ¶9428, 53 AFTR2d 84–660, 725 F.2d 1173 (CA–8, 1984),

affirming 79 T.C. 7 (1982).

25. § 448.

26. § 448(d)(2).

- Retired individuals who performed services for the corporation or its predecessor(s) in such field.

- The estate of such an individual.

- Any person who acquired his or her ownership interest as a result of the death of such an individual within the prior 24 months (disregarding community property laws).

Accrual Method Requirements

The period in which an accrual basis taxpayer can deduct an expense is determined by applying the economic performance test.[27] The economic performance test is met only when the service, property, or use of property giving rise to the liability is actually performed for, provided to, or used by the taxpayer.[28]

EXAMPLE 9

On December 15, 1989, a rusted water main broke and flooded the business premises of T, an accrual basis calendar year taxpayer. An outside firm surveyed the damage and estimated the cleanup fee at $6,000. T signed a contract (paying 20% down) on December 20, 1989. Because of the holidays, the cleanup crew did not start work until January 2, 1990. T cannot deduct the $1,200 until 1990, when the services are performed. □

An exception to the economic performance requirements provides that certain recurring items may be deducted if the following conditions are met:

- Such items are treated consistently.

- Either they are not material in amount or such accrual results in better matching of income and expenses.

- The all-events test is met.

- Economic performance occurs within a reasonable period but not more than 8½ months after year-end.[29] The all-events test is met when all the events have occurred that determine the fact of the liability and the amount of the liability can be determined with reasonable accuracy.[30]

EXAMPLE 10

T, an accrual basis calendar year taxpayer, entered into a monthly maintenance contract during the year. T makes a monthly accrual at the end of every month for this service and pays the fee sometime between the first and fifteenth of the following month when services are performed. The amount involved is immaterial, and all other tests are met. The December 1989 accrual is deductible even though the service is performed on January 12, 1990. □

---

27. § 461(h)(1).
28. §§ 461(h)(2)(A) and (B).

29. § 461(h)(3)(A).
30. Reg. § 1.461–1(a)(2).

EXAMPLE 11   T, an accrual basis calendar year taxpayer, shipped merchandise sold on December 30, 1989, via Greyhound Van Lines on January 2, 1990, and paid the freight charges at that time. Since she reported the sale of the merchandise in 1989, the shipping charge should also be deductible in 1989, since that results in a better matching of income and expenses. □

Reserves for estimated expenses that are frequently employed for financial accounting purposes generally are not allowed for tax purposes, because the economic performance test cannot be satisfied.

EXAMPLE 12   T Airlines is required by Federal law to conduct tests of its engines after 3,000 flying hours. Aircraft cannot return to flight until the tests have been conducted. An unrelated garage does all of the company's tests for $1,500 per engine. For financial reporting purposes, the company accrues an expense based upon $.50 per hour of flight and credits an allowance account. The actual amounts paid to the garage are offset against the allowance account. However, for tax purposes, the economic performance test is not satisfied until the work has been done. □

DISALLOWANCE POSSIBILITIES

The tax law provides for the disallowance of certain types of expenses. Without specific restrictions in the tax law, taxpayers might attempt to deduct certain items that in reality are personal, nondeductible expenditures. For example, specific tax rules are provided to determine whether an expenditure is for trade or business purposes and therefore deductible, or related to a personal hobby and therefore nondeductible.

Certain disallowance provisions represent a codification or extension of prior court decisions. For example, the courts had denied deductions for payments deemed to be in violation of public policy. Thus, the tax law was changed to provide specific authority for the disallowance of such deductions. Detailed discussions of specific disallowance provisions in the tax law follow.

Public Policy Limitation

Justification for Denying Deductions.   The courts developed the principle that a payment that is in violation of public policy is not a necessary expense and therefore is not deductible.[31]

A bribe or fine, for example, may be appropriate, helpful, and even contribute to the profitability of an activity. The courts have held that to allow such expenses would frustrate sharply defined public policy. A deduction would dilute the effect of the penalty since the government would be indirectly subsidizing a taxpayer's wrongdoing.

---

31. *Tank Truck Rentals, Inc. v. Comm.*, 58–1 USTC ¶9366, 1 AFTR2d 1154, 78 S.Ct. 507 (USSC, 1958).

The IRS and the courts were always free to restrict deductions if, in their view, the expenses were contrary to public policy. It was often necessary for taxpayers to go to court to determine if their expense violated public policy.

Recognizing that the public policy doctrine could be arbitrarily applied in cases where no governmental body had clearly defined such a policy, Congress enacted legislation in an attempt to limit the use of the doctrine. The legislation identifies and limits disallowance of deductions to certain types of expenditures that are considered contrary to public policy. Deductions are disallowed for the following expenses:

- Bribes and kickbacks (in the case of foreign bribes and kickbacks, only if the payments violate the U.S. Foreign Corrupt Practices Act of 1977).

- Fines and penalties paid to a government for violation of law.

EXAMPLE 13

Y Corporation, a moving company, consistently loads its trucks with weights in excess of the limits allowed by state law because the additional revenue more than offsets the fines levied. Because the fines are in violation of public policy, they are not deductible. ☐

- Two thirds of the treble damage payments made to claimants resulting from violation of the antitrust law.[32]

Section 162(c) states that no deduction is permitted for a kickback that is illegal under state law (if such state law is generally enforced) and that subjects the payor to a criminal penalty or the loss of license or privilege to engage in a trade or business.

EXAMPLE 14

During the year T, an insurance salesman, paid $5,000 to U, a real estate broker. The payment represented 20% of the commissions earned by T from policies referred by U. Under state law, the splitting of commissions by an insurance salesperson is an act of misconduct that could warrant a revocation of the salesperson's license. Thus, the payments of $5,000 by T to U are not deductible provided the state law is generally enforced. ☐

Legal Expenses Incurred in Defense of Civil or Criminal Penalties. Generally, legal expenses are deductible *for* adjusted gross income as ordinary and necessary business expenses if incurred in connection with a trade or business activity. Legal expenses may also be deductible *for* adjusted gross income as expenses incurred in conjunction with rental property held for the production of income. Legal expenses are deductible *from* adjusted gross income if they are for fees for tax advice relative to the preparation of the taxpayer's income tax returns. These tax-related legal fees are itemized deductions (discussed more fully in chapter 10) that are deductible only to the extent that they exceed 2 percent of adjusted gross income.

Personal legal expenses are not deductible. Legal fees incurred in connection with a criminal defense are deductible if the crime is associated with the taxpayer's trade or business activity.[33] To deduct legal expenses, the taxpayer

---

32. §§ 162(c), (f), and (g).
33. *Comm. v. Tellier*, 66–1 USTC ¶9319, 17 AFTR2d

633, 86 S.Ct. 1118 (USSC, 1966).

must be able to show that the origin and character of the claim are directly related to a trade or business or an income-producing activity. Otherwise, the legal expenses are personal and nondeductible.

EXAMPLE 15

T, a financial officer of X Corporation, incurred legal expenses in connection with the defense in a criminal indictment for evasion of X Corporation's income taxes. T may deduct her legal expenses because she is deemed to be in the trade or business of being an executive, and such legal action impairs her ability to conduct this business activity.[34] □

Expenses Relating to an Illegal Business.   The usual expenses of operating an illegal business (e.g., a numbers racket) are deductible. However, § 162 disallows a deduction for fines, bribes to public officials, illegal kickbacks, and other illegal payments.[35]

EXAMPLE 16

S owns and operates an illegal gambling establishment. In connection with this activity, he had the following expenses during the year:

Rent	$ 60,000
Payoffs to the police	40,000
Depreciation on equipment	100,000
Wages	140,000
Interest	30,000
Criminal fines	50,000
Illegal kickbacks	10,000
Total	$430,000

All of the usual expenses (rent, depreciation, wages, and interest) are deductible, payoffs, fines, and kickbacks are not deductible. Of the $430,000 spent, therefore, $330,000 is deductible and $100,000 is not. □

An exception applies to expenses incurred with regard to illegal trafficking in drugs.[36] Drug dealers are not allowed a deduction for ordinary and necessary business expenses incurred in such a business. However, a deduction for cost of goods sold is allowed.

Political Contributions and Lobbying Activities

Political Contributions.   Generally, no business deduction is permitted for direct or indirect payments for political purposes.[37] Historically, the government has been reluctant to grant favorable tax treatment to business expendi-

---

34. Rev.Rul. 68–662, 1968–2 C.B. 69.
35. *Supra*, note 32.
36. § 280E.
37. § 276.

tures for political purposes because of the possible abuses and the need to prevent undue influence upon the political process.

Lobbying Expenditures.   A deduction is allowed for certain expenses incurred to influence legislation, provided that the proposed legislation is of direct interest to the taxpayer.[38] A direct interest exists if the legislation is of such a nature that it will, or may reasonably be expected to, affect the trade or business of the taxpayer.[39] Dues and expenses paid to an organization that consists of individuals with a common direct interest in proposed legislation are deductible in proportion to the organization's legislative activity.[40] A common direct interest exists where an organization consists of persons with the same direct interests in legislation or proposed legislation. However, no deduction is allowed for any expenses incurred to influence the public on legislative matters or for any political campaign.

EXAMPLE 17

T, a contractor, drove to his state capitol to testify against proposed legislation that would affect building codes. T believes that the proposed legislation is unnecessary and not in the best interest of his company. The expenses are deductible, because the legislation is of direct interest to T's company. If T later journeyed to another city to make a speech concerning the legislation at a Lion's Club meeting, his travel expenses would not be deductible, because the expenses were incurred to influence the public on legislative matters. □

Investigation of a Business

Investigation expenses are those expenses paid or incurred to determine the feasibility of entering a new business or expanding an existing business. They include such costs as travel, engineering and architectural surveys, marketing reports, and various legal and accounting services. How such expenses are treated for tax purposes depends on a number of variables, including the following:

• The current business, if any, of the taxpayer.

• The nature of the business being investigated.

• The extent to which the investigation has proceeded.

• Whether or not the acquisition actually takes place.

If the taxpayer is in a business the same as or similar to that being investigated, all expenses in connection therewith are deductible in the year paid or incurred.[41] The tax result would be the same whether or not the taxpayer acquired the business being investigated.[42]

---

38. § 162(e)(1)(A).

39. Reg. § 1.162–20(c)(2)(ii)(b)(1). A proposed amendment to Reg. § 1.162–20 establishes a three-factor test for determining whether an attempt to influence the public is made.

40. § 162(e)(1)(B) and Prop.Reg. § 1.162–20(c)(3).

41. Throughout the portions of the Code dealing with deductions, the phrase "paid or incurred" is used. "Paid" has reference to the cash basis taxpayer who gets a deduction only in the year of payment. "Incurred" concerns the accrual basis taxpayer who obtains the deduction in the year in which the liability for the expense becomes certain (refer to chapter 5).

42. *York v. Comm.*, 58–2 USTC ¶9952, 2 AFTR2d 6178, 261 F.2d 421 (CA–4, 1958).

EXAMPLE 18   T, an accrual basis sole proprietor, owns and operates three motels in Georgia. In 1989, T incurs expenses of $8,500 in investigating the possibility of acquiring several additional motels located in South Carolina. The $8,500 is deductible in 1989 whether or not T acquires the motels in South Carolina. □

When the taxpayer is not in a business that is the same as or similar to the one being investigated, the tax result usually depends on whether the new business is acquired. If the business is not acquired, all investigation expenses generally become nondeductible.[43]

EXAMPLE 19   R, a retired merchant, incurs expenses in traveling from Rochester, New York, to California to investigate the feasibility of acquiring several auto care centers. If no acquisition takes place (the project is abandoned), none of the expenses are deductible. □

If a taxpayer is in a business that is not the same as or similar to the business being investigated, and the investigation effort actually leads to the acquisition of a new business, the expenses must be capitalized. At the election of the taxpayer, such expenses may be amortized over a period of 60 months or more.[44]

Hobby Losses

Deductions for business or investment expenses are permitted only if the taxpayer can show that the business or investment activity was entered into for the purpose of making a profit. Certain activities may have profit-seeking or personal attributes, depending upon individual circumstances (e.g., raising horses and operating a farm used as a weekend residence). Personal losses are not deductible, although losses attributable to profit-seeking activities may be deducted and used to offset a taxpayer's other income. For this reason, provisions that limit the deductibility of hobby losses are necessary.

General Rules.   If a taxpayer (an individual or an S corporation) can show that an activity has been conducted with the intent to earn a profit, any losses from the activity are fully deductible and § 183 is not applicable. The hobby loss rules apply only if the activity is not engaged in for profit. Hobby expenses are deductible only to the extent of hobby income.[45]
    The Regulations stipulate the following relevant factors to be considered in determining whether an activity is profit-seeking or a hobby:[46]

- Whether the activity is conducted in a businesslike manner.

- The expertise of the taxpayers or their advisers.

- The time and effort expended.

- The expectation that the assets of the activity will appreciate in value.

---

43. Rev.Rul. 57–418, 1957–2 C.B. 143; *Morton Frank*, 20 T.C. 511 (1953); and *Dwight A. Ward*, 20 T.C. 332 (1953).

44. § 195.

45. § 183(b)(2).

46. Reg. §§ 1.183–2(b)(1) through (9).

- The previous success of the taxpayer in the conduct of similar activities.
- The history of income or losses from the activity.
- The relationship of profits earned to losses incurred.
- The financial status of the taxpayer (e.g., if the taxpayer does not have substantial amounts of other income, this fact may indicate that the activity is engaged in for profit).
- Elements of personal pleasure or recreation in the activity.

Presumptive Rule of § 183.   The Code provides a rebuttable presumption that an activity is profit-seeking if it shows a profit in at least three of any five consecutive years (two of seven years for activities involving horses) ending with the taxable year in question.[47] If these profitability tests are met, the activity is presumed to be a trade or business rather than a personal hobby. In effect, the IRS bears the burden of proving that the activity is personal rather than trade or business related.

EXAMPLE 20   N, an executive for a large corporation, is paid a salary of $200,000. His wife is a collector of antiques. Several years ago she opened an antique shop in a local shopping center and spends most of her time buying and selling antiques. She occasionally earns a small profit from this activity but more frequently incurs substantial losses. If such losses are business related, they are fully deductible against N's salary income if a joint return is filed.

- As a tax adviser you should initially determine if the antique "business" has met the three-out-of-five years profit test.
- If the presumption is not met, the activity may nevertheless qualify as a business if the taxpayer can show that the intent is to engage in a profit-seeking activity. It is not necessary to show actual profits.
- Attempts should be made to fit the operation within the nine criteria prescribed in the Regulations and previously listed. These criteria are the factors considered in trying to rebut the § 183 presumption. □

If an activity is deemed to be a hobby, the expenses are deductible only to the extent of the income from the hobby. These expenses must be deducted in the following order:

- Amounts deductible under other Code sections without regard to the nature of the activity, such as property taxes.
- Amounts deductible under other Code sections had the activity been engaged in for profit, but only if those amounts do not affect adjusted basis (e.g., maintenance).
- Amounts deductible under other Code sections had the activity been engaged in for profit, which affects adjusted basis (e.g., depreciation).[48]

---

47. § 183(d).

48. § 183(b)(2) and Reg. § 1.183–1(b)(1).

These deductions are deductible *from* adjusted gross income (as itemized deductions to the extent they exceed 2 percent of adjusted gross income.)[49]

EXAMPLE 21

T, the vice president of an oil company, has AGI of $80,000. He decides to pursue painting in his spare time. He used a home studio, comprising 10% of the home's square footage. During the current year, T incurs the following expenses:

Correspondence study course	$ 350
Art supplies	300
Fees paid to models	1,000
Home studio expenses:	
Total property taxes	900
Total home mortgage interest	10,000
Depreciation on studio furnishings	900
Depreciation on 10% of home	500
Total home maintenance and utilities	3,600

During the year, T sold paintings for a total of $3,200. If the activity is held to be a hobby, T is allowed deductions as follows:

Gross income		$3,200
Deduct: Taxes and interest (10% of $10,900)		1,090
Remainder		$2,110
Deduct: Study course	$ 350	
Art supplies	300	
Models' fees	1,000	
Maintenance and utilities (10%)	360	2,010
Remainder		100
Depreciation ($500, but limited to $100)		100
Net income		$ –0–

T includes the $3,200 of income in AGI, making his AGI $83,200. The taxes and interest are itemized deductions, deductible in full. The remaining $2,110 of expenses are reduced by 2% of T's AGI ($1,664) so the net deduction is $446. Since the property taxes and home mortgage interest are deductible anyway, the net effect is a $2,754 ($3,200 less $446) increase in taxable income. ☐

EXAMPLE 22

If T's activity in Example 21 is held to be a business, he could have deducted expenses totalling $2,510 ($2,010 plus $500 of depreciation) *for*

---

49. § 183(b) and Rev.Rul. 75-14, 1975-1 C.B. 90.

AGI, in addition to the $1,090 of taxes and interest. All expenses would be trade or business expenses deductible *for* AGI. His reduction in AGI would be as follows:

Gross income		$3,200
Less: Taxes and interest	$1,090	
Other business expenses	2,010	
Depreciation	500	3,600
Reduction in AGI		$ (400)

□

Rental of Vacation Homes

Restrictions on the deductions allowed for part-year rentals of personal residences (including vacation homes) were written into the law to prevent taxpayers from deducting essentially personal expenses as rental losses. Before these restrictions were added, many taxpayers who had vacation homes tried to treat the homes as rental property and generate rental losses as deductions *for* adjusted gross income. For example, a summer cabin would be rented (or held out for rent) for 2 months per year, used for vacationing for 1 month, and left vacant the rest of the year. The taxpayer would then deduct 11 months' depreciation, maintenance, etc., as rental expenses, resulting in a rental loss. Section 280A eliminates this treatment by allowing deductions on residences used primarily for personal purposes only to the extent of income generated. Thus, only a break-even situation is allowed; no losses can be deducted.

There are three possible tax treatments for residences used for both personal and rental purposes. The treatment is dependent upon the relative time the residence is used for personal purposes versus rental use.

Primarily Personal Use.   If the residence is rented for less than 15 days per year, it is treated as a personal residence. The rental income is excluded from income, and mortgage interest and real estate taxes are allowed as itemized deductions, as with any personal residence.[50] No other expenses (e.g., depreciation, utilities, maintenance) are deductible.

EXAMPLE 23   T owns a vacation cottage on the lake. During 1989, she rented it for $1,600 for two weeks, lived in it two months, and left it vacant the remainder of the year. The year's expenses amounted to $6,000 interest expense, $500 property taxes, $1,500 utilities and maintenance, and $2,400 depreciation. Since the property was not rented for at least 15 days, the income is excluded, the interest and property tax expenses are itemized deductions, and the remaining expenses are nondeductible personal expenses. □

Primarily Rental Use.   If the residence is not used for personal use for the greater of more than 14 days or more than 10 percent of the total days rented, the residence is treated as rental property.[51] The expenses must be allocated between personal and rental days if there are any personal use days during

---

50.   § 280A(g).

51.   § 280A(d) and Prop.Reg. § 1.280A–3(c).

the year. In such a case, the deduction of the expenses allocated to rental days can exceed rental income and result in a rental loss, which may be deductible under the passive loss rules (discussed in chapter 7).

EXAMPLE 24   Assume T in Example 23 had rented the cottage for 120 days. The cottage would be primarily rental if she did not use it for personal purposes for more than 14 days. □

EXAMPLE 25   Assume T in Example 23 had rented the cottage for 200 days. She could use it for personal use for no more than 20 days (10% of the rental days) for it to be primarily rental. □

EXAMPLE 26   Assume that T in Example 23 used the cottage for 12 days and rented it for 48 days for $4,800. Since she did not use the cottage for more than 14 days, the expenses must be allocated between personal and rental days, and the cottage is treated as rental property.

	Rental	Personal
Percentage of use	80%	20%
Income	$4,800	$ -0-
Expenses		
Interest ($6,000)	$4,800	$1,200
Property taxes ($500)	400	100
Utilities and Maintenance ($1,500)	1,200	300
Depreciation ($2,400)	1,920	480
Total expenses	$8,320	$2,080
Rental loss	($3,520)	$ -0-

T deducts the $3,520 rental loss for AGI (assuming she meets the passive loss rules, discussed in chapter 7). She also has itemized interest of $1,200 and taxes of $100. The portion of utilities and maintenance and depreciation attributable to personal use is not deductible. □

Personal Rental Use.   If the residence is rented for 15 or more days *and* is used for personal purposes for the greater of (1) more than 14 days or (2) more than 10 percent of the rental days, it is treated as a personal/rental residence and expenses are allowed only to the extent of income.

EXAMPLE 27   Assume that T in Example 23 had rented the property for 30 days and lived in it for 30 days. The residence is classified as personal/rental property since T used it more than 14 days and rented it for more than 14 days. The expenses must be allocated, and the rental expenses are allowed only to the extent of rental income. □

If a residence is classified as personal/rental property, the expenses that are deductible anyway (e.g., real estate taxes) must be deducted first. If a positive net income results, otherwise nondeductible expenses (e.g., maintenance, utilities, insurance) are allowed next. Finally, depreciation is allowed if any positive balance remains.

Expenses must be allocated between personal and rental days before the limits are applied. The courts have held that taxes and interest, which accrue ratably over the year, are allocated on the basis of 365 days.[52] The IRS, however, disagrees and allocates taxes and interest on the basis of total days of use.[53] Other expenses (utilities, maintenance, depreciation, etc.) are allocated on the basis of total days used.

EXAMPLE 28

S rents her vacation home for 60 days and lives in the home for 30 days. The limitations applicable to personal/rental residences apply. S's gross rental income is $10,000. For the entire year, the real estate taxes are $2,190; S's mortgage interest expense is $10,220; utilities and maintenance expense equals $2,400; and depreciation is $9,000. Using the IRS approach, these amounts are deductible in this specific order:

Gross income	$10,000
Deduct: Taxes and interest (60/90 × $12,410)	8,273
Remainder to apply to rental operating expenses and depreciation	$ 1,727
Deduct: Utilities and maintenance (60/90 × $2,400)	1,600
Balance	$ 127
Deduct: Depreciation (60/90 × $9,000 = $6,000 but limited to above balance)	127
Net income	$ –0–

The nonrental use portion of taxes and interest ($4,137 in this case) is deductible if the taxpayer elects to itemize (see chapter 11). The personal use portion of utilities, maintenance, and depreciation is not deductible in any case. Also note that the basis of the property is not reduced by the $5,873 depreciation not allowed ($6,000 − $127) because of the above limitation. (See chapter 14 for discussion of the reduction in basis for depreciation allowed or allowable.) □

EXAMPLE 29

Using the court's approach in allocating property taxes and interest, S, in Example 28, would have this result:

---

52. *Dorance D. Bolton v. Comm.*, 82–2 USTC ¶9699, 51 AFTR2d 83–305, 694 F.2d 556 (CA–9, 1982).

53. Prop.Reg. § 1.280A–3(d)(4).

Gross income	$10,000
Deduct: Taxes and interest (60/365 × $12,410)	2,040
Remainder to apply to rental operating expenses and depreciation	$ 7,960
Deduct: Utilities and maintenance (60/90 × $2,400)	1,600
Balance	$ 6,360
Deduct: Depreciation (60/90 × $9,000, but limited to $6,360)	6,000
Net rental income	$ 360

S can deduct $10,370 ($12,410 paid − $2,040 deducted as expense in computing rental income) of personal use interest and taxes. ☐

Note the contrasting results in Examples 28 and 29. Using the IRS's approach (Example 28) results in no rental gain or loss and an itemized deduction for taxes and interest of $4,137. In Example 29, S has net rental income of $360 and $10,370 of itemized deductions. The court's approach decreases her taxable income by $10,010 ($10,370 itemized deductions less $360 net rental income). The IRS's approach reduces her taxable income by only $4,137.

EXAMPLE 30   Assume that S in Example 28 had not lived in the home at all during the year. The property is a rental property. The rental loss is calculated as follows:

Gross income	$10,000
Expenses	
Taxes and interest	$12,410
Utilities and maintenance	2,400
Depreciation	9,000
Total expenses	$23,810
Rental loss	($13,810)

Whether any of the rental loss would be deductible would depend upon whether S actively participated in the rental activity and met the other requirements for passive losses (discussed in chapter 7). ☐

Section 280A(d) resolves the problem of whether or not a taxpayer's primary residence is subject to the preceding rules if it is converted to rental property. The deduction for expenses of the property incurred during a qualified rental period is not subject to the personal use test of the vacation home rules. A qualified rental period is a consecutive period of 12 or more months.

The period begins or ends in the taxable year in which the *residence* is rented or held for rental at a fair rental price. The residence must not be rented to a related party [as defined in § 267(c)(4)]. If the property is sold before 12 months, the qualified rental period is the actual time rented.

See Concept Summary 6–1 on page 6–23 for a summary of the vacation home rules.

Expenditures Incurred for Taxpayer's Benefit or Taxpayer's Obligation

Generally, an expense must be incurred for the taxpayer's benefit or arise from the taxpayer's obligation. An individual cannot claim a tax deduction for the payment of the expenses of another individual.

EXAMPLE 31

During the current year, F pays the interest on his son, T's, home mortgage. Neither F nor T can take a deduction for the interest paid, because the obligation is not F's and F's son did not pay the interest. The tax result would have been more favorable had F made a cash gift to T and let him pay the interest. The interest then could have been deducted by the son, and (depending upon other gifts and the amount involved) F might not have been liable for any gift taxes. A deduction would have been created with no cash difference to the family. □

One exception to this rule is the payment of medical expenses for a dependent. Such expenses are deductible by the payor.[54]

Disallowance of Personal Expenditures

Section 262 states that "except as otherwise expressly provided in this chapter, no deduction shall be allowed for personal, living, or family expenses." Thus, to justify a deduction an individual must be able to identify a particular Section of the Code that sanctions the deductibility of an otherwise nondeductible personal expenditure (e.g., charitable contributions, § 170; medical expenses, § 213; moving expenses, § 217). Sometimes the character of a particular expenditure is not easily determined.

EXAMPLE 32

During the current year, H pays $1,500 in legal fees and court costs to obtain a divorce from his wife, W. Involved in the divorce action is a property settlement that concerns the disposition of income-producing property owned by H. In a similar situation, the Tax Court[55] held that H could not deduct any of the $1,500 costs. "Although fees primarily related to property division concerning his income-producing property, they weren't ordinary and necessary expenses paid for conservation or maintenance of property held for production of income. Legal fees incurred in defending against claims that arise from a taxpayer's

---

54. § 213(a).   1970–27.
55. *Harry H. Goldberg*, 29 TCM 74, T.C.Memo.,

marital relationship aren't deductible expenses regardless of possible consequences on taxpayer's income-producing property." □

CONCEPT SUMMARY 6–1

Vacation/Rental Home

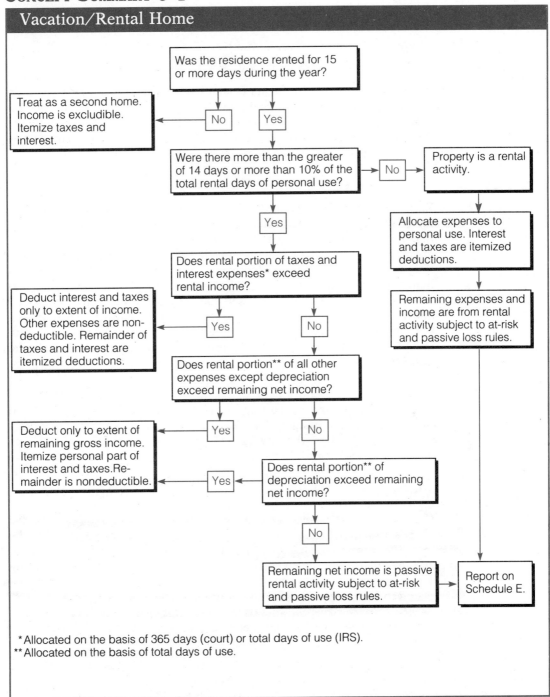

*Allocated on the basis of 365 days (court) or total days of use (IRS).
**Allocated on the basis of total days of use.

The IRS has clarified the issue of the deduction of legal fees incurred in connection with a divorce.[56] To be deductible, an expense must relate solely to tax advice in a divorce proceeding. For example, legal fees attributable to the determination of dependency exemptions of children, the creation of a trust to make periodic alimony payments, or determination of the tax consequences of a property settlement are deductible if the fees are distinguishable from the general legal fees incurred in obtaining a divorce. Therefore, it is advisable to request an itemization of attorney's fees to substantiate a deduction for the tax-related amounts.

Disallowance of Deductions for Unrealized Losses

One of the basic concepts in the tax law is that a deduction can be taken only when a loss has actually been realized. For example, a drop in the market price of securities held by the taxpayer does not result in a loss until the securities are actually sold or exchanged at the lower price. Furthermore, any deductible loss is limited to the taxpayer's basis in the asset.

EXAMPLE 33   Early this year, T purchased a home in a new residential subdivision for $80,000. Shortly thereafter, heavy spring rains led to severe flooding, indicating that the subdivision's drainage facilities were inadequate. Because the subdivision now has a reputation for poor drainage, T estimates that he could receive only $50,000 on the sale of his home. He has the written appraisal reports of several reputable real estate brokers to support the $30,000 loss in value. Although § 165 allows a deduction for casualty losses, such deduction is based on actual physical loss and not the decline in value that might be a "fluctuation in market value not attributable to any actual physical depreciation."[57] □

In one case,[58] the court held that a loss in fair market value due to permanent buyer resistance resulting from flood damage to the neighborhood would be allowed as a casualty loss. The value of the property permanently decreased as a result of the changed character of the neighborhood. See Chapter 8 for a discussion of casualty losses.

Disallowance of Deductions for Capital Expenditures

The Code specifically disallows a deduction for "any amount paid out for new buildings or for permanent improvements or betterments made to increase the value of any property or estate."[59] The Regulations further define capital expenditures to include those expenditures that add to the value or prolong the life of property or adapt the property to a new or different use.[60] Incidental repairs and maintenance of the property are not capital expenditures and can be deducted as ordinary and necessary business expenses. Repairing a roof is a deductible expense, but replacing a roof is a capital expenditure

56. Rev.Rul. 72–545, 1972–2 C.B. 179.
57. *Joe B. Thornton*, 47 T.C. 1 (1966).
58. *Finkbohner, Jr. v. U.S.*, 86–1 USTC ¶9393, 57

AFTR2d 86, 788 F.2d 723 (CA–11, 1986).
59. § 263(a)(1).
60. Reg. § 1.263(a)–1(b).

subject to depreciation deductions over its useful life. The tune-up of a delivery truck is an expense; a complete overhaul is probably a capital expenditure.

Exceptions. There are several exceptions to the general rule regarding capitalization of expenditures. Taxpayers can elect to expense certain mineral developmental costs and intangible drilling costs.[61] Certain farm capital expenditures (such as soil and water conservation) and certain research and experimental expenditures may be immediately expensed.[62]

In addition, § 179 permits an immediate write-off of certain amounts of depreciable property. These provisions are discussed more fully in chapter 9.

Capitalization versus Expense. When an expenditure is capitalized rather than expensed, the deduction is at best deferred and at worst lost forever. Although an immediate tax benefit for a large cash expenditure is lost, the cost can be deducted in increments over a longer period of time. If the expenditure is for some improvement that has an ascertainable life, it can be capitalized and depreciated or amortized over that life. Costs that can be amortized include copyrights and patents. However, there are many other expenditures, such as land and payments made for goodwill, that cannot be amortized or depreciated. Goodwill has an indeterminate life, and land is not a depreciable asset, since its value generally does not decline.

EXAMPLE 34

T purchased a prime piece of land located in an apartment-zoned area. T paid $500,000 for the property, which had an old but usable apartment building on it. T immediately had the building demolished at a cost of $100,000. The $500,000 purchase price and the $100,000 demolition costs must be capitalized, and the basis of the land is $600,000. Since land is a nondepreciable asset, no deduction is allowed. More favorable tax treatment might result if T rented the apartments in the old building for a period of time to attempt to establish that there was no intent to demolish the building. If T's attempt is successful, it might be possible to allocate a substantial portion of the original purchase price of the property to the building (a depreciable asset). When the building is later demolished, any remaining adjusted basis can be deducted as an ordinary (§ 1231) loss. (See chapter 17 for a discussion of the treatment of § 1231 assets.) □

In some cases, a taxpayer might prefer to capitalize rather than expense a particular item if the property is depreciable. An immediate deduction could create a net operating loss that expires in 15 years (unless utilized). No tax benefit (or a smaller tax benefit) would be derived from an immediate deduction. The same expenditure, if capitalized and depreciated over a longer future period, could be offset against taxable income later (or against higher tax bracket income in future years) resulting in a greater tax benefit.

Capitalization Elections. Because of the tax avoidance possibilities inherent in allowing elective "capitalize or expense" decisions, the treatment of most expenditures, by law, is not elective. However, in certain cases, it is permissible to elect to capitalize *or* to expense immediately a particular item.

61. §§ 263(c) and 616. 62. §§ 174, 175, and 180.

For example, § 266 allows some taxpayers (but not individuals, S corporations, or personal holding companies) an opportunity to capitalize certain "taxes and carrying charges." This election applies to carrying charges, interest on indebtedness, and certain taxes (such as property and employer-paid payroll taxes) paid during the construction period on realty or personalty. It does not matter whether the property is business or nonbusiness in nature.[63] A taxpayer may elect to capitalize some expenditures and not others. For example, one could elect to capitalize property taxes and expense interest on the construction indebtedness. A new election may be made for each project. One could elect to capitalize expenditures on a factory being constructed and expense the same type of items on a constructed machine. On unimproved and unproductive real estate (land held for later sale, for example) a new election must be made for each year.

Section 189 requires individuals, S corporations, and personal holding companies to capitalize construction period interest and taxes, subject to specific rules for amortizing such amounts (see chapter 9). This Code Section was intended both to match expenses with income in accordance with the traditional accounting principle and to restrict tax shelter opportunities for individuals.

Transactions between Related Parties

The Code places restrictions on the recognition of gains and losses between related parties. Because of relationships created by birth, marriage, and business, there would be endless possibilities for engaging in various types of financial transactions that would produce tax savings with no real economic substance or change. For example, a wife could sell property to her husband at a loss and deduct the loss on their joint return, and her husband could hold the asset indefinitely. This illustrates the creation of an artificial loss. Such "sham" transactions have resulted in a complex set of laws designed to eliminate these abuses.

Losses.   Section 267 provides for the disallowance of any "losses from sales or exchanges of property . . . directly or indirectly" between related parties.[64] Upon the subsequent sale of such property to a nonrelated party, any gain recognized is reduced by the loss that was previously disallowed.

EXAMPLE 35   F sells common stock with a basis of $1,000 to his son, T, for $800. T sells the stock several years later for $1,100. F's $200 loss is disallowed upon the sale to T, and only $100 of gain is taxable to T upon the subsequent sale. □

EXAMPLE 36   F sells common stock with a basis of $1,000 to his son, T, for $800. T sells the stock to an unrelated party for $900. T's gain of $100 is not recognized because of F's previously disallowed loss of $200. Note that the offset may result in only partial tax benefit upon the subsequent sale. If the property had not been transferred to T, F could have recognized a $100 loss upon

---

63. Reg. § 1.266–1(b).   64. § 267(a)(1).

the subsequent sale to the unrelated party ($1,000 basis − $900 selling price). □

EXAMPLE 37

F sells common stock with a basis of $1,000 to an unrelated third party for $800. F's son repurchased the same stock in the market on the same day for $800. The $200 loss is not allowed, because the transaction is an indirect sale between related parties.[65] □

Unpaid Expenses and Interest. Section 267 also prevents related taxpayers from engaging in tax avoidance schemes in which one related taxpayer uses the accrual method of accounting and the other is on the cash basis. For example, an accrual basis closely held corporation could borrow funds from a cash basis individual shareholder. At the end of the year, the corporation would accrue and deduct the interest, but the cash basis lender would not recognize interest income, since no interest had been paid. Section 267 specifically defers the deduction of the accruing taxpayer until the recipient taxpayer must include it in income (when actually paid to the cash basis taxpayer).[66] This rule applies to interest as well as other expenses, such as salaries and bonuses.

Relationships and Constructive Ownership. Section 267 operates to disallow losses and defer deductions only between related parties. Losses or deductions generated by similar transactions with an unrelated party are allowed. Related parties include the following: [67]

- Siblings and half-siblings, spouses, ancestors (parents, grandparents) and lineal descendants (children, grandchildren) of the taxpayer.

- A corporation owned more than 50 percent (directly or indirectly) by the taxpayer.

- Two corporations that are members of a controlled group.

- A series of other complex relationships between trusts, corporations, and individual taxpayers.

The law provides that constructive ownership rules are applied to determine whether the taxpayers are related. [68] Constructive ownership rules state that stock owned by certain relatives or related entities is deemed to be owned by the taxpayer for purposes of applying the loss and expense deduction disallowance rules. For example, a taxpayer is deemed to own not only his or her stock but the stock owned by his or her lineal descendants, ancestors, brothers and sisters or half-brothers and half-sisters, and spouse. The taxpayer is also deemed to own his or her proportionate share of stock owned by any partnership, corporation, estate, or trust of which he or she is a member. Additionally, an individual is deemed to own any stock owned, directly or indirectly, by his or her partner. However, constructive ownership by an individual of the partnership's and the other partner's shares does not extend to the individual's spouse or other relatives.

65. *McWilliams v. Comm.*, 47–1 USTC ¶9289, 35 AFTR 1184, 67 S.Ct. 1477 (USSC, 1947).

66. § 267(a)(2).

67. § 267(b).

68. § 267(c).

EXAMPLE 38   The stock of V Corporation is owned 20% by T, 30% by T's father, 30% by T's mother, and 20% by T's sister. On July 1 of the current year, T loaned $10,000 to V Corporation at 11% annual interest, principal and interest payable on demand. For tax purposes, V Corporation uses the accrual basis and T uses the cash basis. Both are on a calendar year. Since T is deemed to own the 80% owned by her parents and sister, she constructively owns 100% of V Corporation. If the corporation accrues but does not pay the interest within the taxable year, no deduction can be taken until payment is made to T. □

Substantiation Requirements

The tax law is built on a voluntary system. Taxpayers file their tax returns, report income and take deductions to which they are entitled, and pay their taxes through withholding or estimated tax payments during the year. The taxpayer carries the burden of proof for substantiating expenses deducted on his or her return and thus must retain adequate records for such substantiation. Upon audit, the function of the Internal Revenue Service is to disallow any undocumented or unsubstantiated deductions. As can be imagined, this relationship has resulted in numerous conflicts between taxpayers and the IRS.

Some events throughout the year should be documented as they occur. For example, it is generally advisable to receive a pledge payment statement from one's church, in addition to a cancelled check, for proper documentation of a charitable contribution. Other types of deductible expenditures may require receipts or some other type of support.

Some types of deductible expenditures, such as business entertainment, gifts, and travel, have been subject to abuse. To prevent such abuse, the law provides that no deduction will be allowed for any travel, entertainment, or business gift expenditure unless properly substantiated by adequate records. Such records should contain the following information: [69]

- The amount of the expense.
- The time and place of travel or entertainment (or date of gift).
- The business purpose of such expense.
- The business relationship of the taxpayer to the person entertained (or receiving the gift).

This means that taxpayers must maintain an account book or diary in which the above information is recorded at the time of the expenditure. Documentary evidence, such as itemized receipts, is required to support all expenditures for lodging while traveling away from home and for any other expenditure of $25 or more.[70] If a taxpayer fails to keep adequate records, each expense must be established by a written or oral statement of the exact details of the expense and by other corroborating evidence.[71]

---

69. § 274(d).
70. Reg. §§ 1.274–5(c)(2)(iii)(a) and (b).
71. Reg. § 1.274–5(c)(3).

| EXAMPLE 39 | B had entertainment expenses substantiated only by credit card receipts. The receipts established the time, place, and amount of the expenditure. Because neither the business relationship nor the business purpose was established, the deduction will be disallowed.[72] □ |

| EXAMPLE 40 | D had entertainment expenses substantiated by a diary showing the time, place, amount of the expenditure, business relationship, and business purpose. However, since he had no receipts, any expenditures of $25 or more will be disallowed.[73] □ |

Specific rules for deducting travel and entertainment expenses are discussed in chapter 10. Certain mixed-use (both personal and business) property is also subject to the adequate records requirement (discussed in chapter 9).

Expenses and Interest Relating to Tax-Exempt Income

Certain income, such as interest on municipal bonds, is tax-exempt, and § 212 allows the taxpayer to deduct expenses incurred for the production of income. If it were not for the disallowance provisions of § 265, it might be possible to make money at the expense of the government by excluding interest income and deducting interest expense.

CONCEPT SUMMARY 6–2

Classification of Expenses

Expense Item	Deductible For AGI	Deductible From AGI	Not Deductible	Applicable Code §
Investment expenses				
Rent and royalty	X			§ 62(a)(4)
All other investments		X[4]		§ 212
Employee expenses				
Commuting expenses			X	§ 262
Travel and transportation[1]		X[4,5]		§ 162(a)(2)
Reimbursed expenses[1]	X			§ 62(a)(2)(A)
Moving expenses		X		§ 217
Entertainment[1]		X[4,5]		§ 212
All other employee expenses[1]		X[4,5]		§ 212
Certain expenses of performing artists	X			§ 62(a)(2)(B)
Trade or business expenses	X			§ 162

---

72. *Frank J. Borsody*, 35 TCM 214, T.C.Memo. 1976–47.

73. *Quen W. Young*, 37 TCM 131, T.C.Memo. 1978–19.

Expense Item	Deductible For AGI	Deductible From AGI	Not Deductible	Applicable Code §
Casualty losses				
Business	X			§ 165(c)(1)
Personal		X [6]		§ 165(c)(3)
Tax determination				
Collection, or				
Refund expenses		X [4]		§ 212
Bad debts	X			§ 166
Medical expenses		X [7]		§ 213
Charitable contributions		X		§ 170
Taxes				
Trade or business	X			§ 162
Personal Taxes				
Real property		X		§ 164(a)(1)
Personal property		X		§ 164(a)(2)
State and local income		X		§ 164(a)(3)
Investigation of a business [2]	X			§ 162
Interest				
Business	X			§ 162
Personal [3]		X		§ 163(a)
All other personal expenses			X	§ 262

1. Unless reimbursed and an adequate accounting made.
2. Provided certain criteria are met.
3. Subject to the excess investment interest provisions and consumer interest phase-out.
4. Subject (in the aggregate) to a 2%-of-AGI floor imposed by § 67.
5. Only 80% of meals and entertainment are deductible.
6. Subject to a 10%-of-AGI floor and a $100 floor.
7. Subject to a 7.5%-of-AGI floor.

EXAMPLE 41

P, a taxpayer in the 28% bracket, purchased $100,000 of 6% municipal bonds. At the same time, she used the bonds as collateral on a bank loan of $100,000 at 8% interest. A positive cash flow would result from the tax benefit as follows:

Cash paid out on loan	($8,000)
Cash received from bonds	6,000
Tax savings from deducting interest expense (28% of $8,000 interest expense)	2,240
Net positive cash flow	$ 240

□

To eliminate the possibility illustrated in Example 41, § 265 specifically disallows as a deduction the expenses of producing tax-exempt income. Interest on any indebtedness incurred or continued to purchase or carry tax-exempt obligations is disallowed under § 265. There are special rules for nonbanking financial institutions.[74]

Judicial Interpretations.   It is often difficult to show a direct relationship between borrowings and investment in tax-exempt securities. Suppose, for example, that a taxpayer borrows money, adds it to existing funds, buys inventory and stocks, then later sells the inventory and buys municipal bonds. A series of transactions such as these can completely obscure any relationship between the loan and the tax-exempt investment. One solution would be to disallow interest on any debt to the extent that the taxpayer held any tax-exempt securities. This approach would preclude individuals from deducting part of their home mortgage interest if they owned any municipal bonds. However, the law was not intended to go to such extremes. As a result, judicial interpretations have tried to show reasonableness in the disallowance of interest deductions under § 265.

In one case,[75] a company used municipal bonds as collateral on short-term loans to meet seasonal liquidity needs. The Court disallowed the interest deduction on the grounds that the company could predict its seasonal liquidity needs and therefore knew it would have to borrow the money to continue to carry the tax-exempt securities. The same company *was* allowed an interest deduction on a building mortgage, even though tax-exempt securities it owned could have been sold to pay off the mortgage. The Court reasoned that short-term liquidity needs would have been impaired if the tax-exempt securities were sold. Furthermore, the Court ruled that carrying the tax-exempt securities bore no relationship to the long-term financing of a construction project.

In another case,[76] the Court disallowed an interest deduction to a company that refused to sell tax-exempt securities it had received from the sale of a major asset. The company's refusal to sell the tax-exempt securities necessitated large borrowings to finance company operations. The Court found that the primary reason that the company would not sell its bonds to reduce its bank debt was the tax savings, even though other business reasons existed for holding the municipal bonds. Moreover, there was a direct relationship between the bonds and the debt, because they both arose from the same transaction.

EXAMPLE 42   In January of the current year, T borrowed $100,000 at 8% interest. She used the loan proceeds to purchase 5,000 shares of stock in P Corporation. In July, she sold the stock for $120,000 and reinvested the proceeds in City of Denver bonds, the income from which is tax-exempt. Assuming the $100,000 loan remained outstanding throughout the entire year, the interest attributable to the period in which the bonds were held cannot be deducted. ☐

---

74. § 265(b).
75. *The Wisconsin Cheeseman, Inc. v. U.S.,* 68–1 USTC ¶9145, 21 AFTR2d 383, 388 F.2d 420 (CA–7, 1968).

76. *Illinois Terminal Railroad Co. v. U.S.,* 67–1 USTC ¶9374, 19 AFTR2d 1219, 375 F.2d 1016 (Ct.Cls., 1967).

TAX PLANNING CONSIDERATIONS

Time Value of Tax Deductions

Cash basis taxpayers often have the ability to make early payments for their expenses at the end of the tax year. This permits such payments to be deducted currently instead of in the following tax year. Because of the time value of money, a tax deduction this year may be worth more than the same deduction next year. Before employing this strategy, the taxpayer must consider next year's expected income and tax rates and whether a cash flow problem may develop from early payments.

The time value of money as well as tax rate changes must be taken into consideration when an expense can be paid and deducted in either of two years.

EXAMPLE 43

T pledged $1,000 to her church's special building fund. She can make the contribution in December 1989 or January 1990. T is in the 33% tax bracket in 1989 because of the 15% bracket phase-out, and in the 28% bracket in 1990. She itemizes in both years. If she takes the deduction in 1989, she saves $71 ($330 − $259), due to the decrease in the tax rates and the time value of money.

	1989	1990
Contribution	$1,000	$1,000
Tax bracket	.33	.28
Tax savings	$ 330	$ 280
Discounted @ 8%	1.0	.926
Savings in present value	$ 330	$ 259

☐

EXAMPLE 44

Assume the same facts as in Example 43, except that T is in the 28% bracket in both 1989 and 1990. T's savings by taking the deduction in 1989 is $21 ($280 − $259), due to the time value of money.

	1989	1990
Contribution	$1,000	$1,000
Tax bracket	.28	.28
Tax savings	$ 280	$ 280
Discounted @ 8%	1.0	.926
Savings in present value	$ 280	$ 259

☐

Unreasonable Compensation

In substantiating the reasonableness of a shareholder-employee's compensation, an internal comparison test is sometimes useful. If it can be shown that employees who are nonshareholders receive the same (or more) compensation as shareholder-employees in comparable positions, it is evident that compensation is not unreasonable.

Another possibility is to demonstrate that the shareholder-employee has been underpaid in prior years. For example, the shareholder-employee may have agreed to take a less-than-adequate salary during the unprofitable formative years of the business, provided this "postponed" compensation will be paid in later, more profitable years. This agreement should be documented, if possible, in the corporate minutes.

It is important to keep in mind that in testing for reasonableness, it is the *total* pay package that must be taken into account. One must look at all fringe benefits or perquisites, such as contributions by the corporation to a qualified pension plan (even though those amounts are not immediately available to the covered employee-shareholder).

Shifting Deductions

Taxpayers should manage their obligations to avoid the loss of a deduction. Deductions can be shifted among family members, depending upon who makes the payment. For example, a father buys a car for his daughter and both sign the note. The taxpayer who makes the payment gets the deduction for the interest. If the note is signed by the daughter only and her father makes the payment, neither is entitled to a deduction.

Hobby Losses

To demonstrate that an activity has been entered into for the purpose of making a profit (it is not a hobby), a taxpayer should treat the activity as a business. The business should engage in advertising, use business letterhead stationery, and maintain a business phone.

If a taxpayer's activity earns a profit in three out of five consecutive years, the presumption is that the activity is engaged in for profit. It may be possible for a cash basis taxpayer to meet these requirements by timing the payment of expenses or the receipt of revenues. The payment of certain expenses incurred before the end of the year might be made in the following year, or the billing of year-end sales might be delayed so that collections are received in the following year.

It should be kept in mind that the three-out-of-five-years rule under § 183 is not absolute. All it does is shift the presumption. If a profit is not made in three out of five years, the losses may still be allowed if the taxpayer can show that such losses are due to the nature of the business. For example, success in artistic or literary endeavors can take a long time. Also, due to the present state of the economy, full-time farmers and ranchers are often unable to show a profit; how can one expect a part-time farmer or rancher to do so?

Merely satisfying the three-out-of-five-year rules does not guarantee that one is automatically home free. If the three years of profits are insignificant relative to the losses of other years, or if the profits are not from the ordinary operation of the business, the Internal Revenue Service may still be able to establish that the taxpayer is not engaged in an activity for profit. If a taxpayer in such a situation can show conformity with the factors enumerated in the

Regulations[77] or can show evidence of business hardships (e.g., injury, death, or illness), the government cannot override the presumptive rule of § 183.[78]

EXAMPLE 45

A taxpayer had the following gains and losses in an artistic endeavor:

1985	($50,000)
1986	(65,000)
1987	400
1988	200
1989	125

Under these circumstances, the IRS would try to overcome the presumptive rule, proving that the operation is *not* a bona fide business. □

Substantiation Requirements

One relatively painless method of meeting the substantiation requirements for business meals or entertainment would be to pay the bill by credit card. The time, place, and amount of the expenditure are substantiated. At the same time, the taxpayer should write on the back of the receipt the name and relationship of the person entertained and a notation of what business was discussed. This would meet the rest of the requirements specified by § 274(d).

PROBLEM MATERIALS

Discussion Questions

1. "All income must be reported and all deductions are allowed unless specifically disallowed in the Code." True or false? Discuss.

2. T, who had adjusted gross income of $30,000, had deductions of $5,000. Would it matter to T whether they were *for* or *from* AGI? Why or why not?

3. If a taxpayer is audited and $1,000 of income is added to his adjusted gross income, will his tax increase (ignoring penalties and interest) be equal to $1,000 multiplied by his tax bracket? Discuss.

4. Are the following items deductible *for* adjusted gross income, deductible *from* adjusted gross income, or nondeductible personal items?

   a. Unreimbursed travel expenses of an employee.

   b. Alimony payments. *before   for.*

---

77. Reg. §§ 1.183–2(b)(1) through (9).
78. *Hunter Faulconer, Sr.,* 45 TCM 1084, T.C.Memo.
1983–165; rev'd, 84–2 USTC ¶9955, 55 AFTR2d 85–302, 748 F.2d 890 (CA–4, 1984).

    c.   Charitable contributions.

    d.   Medical expenses.   } *from*

    e.   Safe deposit box rentals.

    f.   Repairs made on a personal residence. *No deduct*

    g.   Expenses related to tax-exempt municipal bonds. *No deduct.*

5. Are the following expenditures deductible *for* AGI, deductible *from* AGI, nondeductible personal items, or capital expenditures?

    a.   Repairs made to a rental property.

    b.   State income taxes.

    c.   Investment advice subscriptions.

    d.   Child support payments.

    e.   New roof on rental property.

    f.   New roof on personal residence.

    g.   Mortgage interest on personal residence.

6. Define and contrast the "ordinary" and "necessary" tests for business expenses.

7. T, a cash basis taxpayer, decides to reduce his taxable income for 1989 by buying $10,000 worth of supplies on December 28, 1989. The supplies will be used up in 1990. Can T deduct this expenditure in 1989? Would your answer differ if T bought the supplies because a supplier was going out of business and had given T a significant discount on the supplies?

8. T, a cash basis taxpayer, borrowed $20,000 on December 18, 1989, for two years at 12% interest. As a condition of the loan, the lender wanted T to prepay the two years' interest. T, who had heard that he could deduct no more than one year's interest, convinced the lender to accept prepayment of only one year's interest in December and the rest in January 1990 so that he could deduct the rest of the interest in 1990. T then deducted $2,400 interest in 1989 and in 1990. Can he do this?

9. What is the significance of the economic performance test?

10. What is the "actually paid" requirement for the deduction of an expense by a cash basis taxpayer? Does actual payment insure a deduction?

11. Which of the following businesses must use the accrual method of accounting?

    a.   A corporation with annual gross receipts of $12 million from equipment rentals.

    b.   A partnership (not a tax shelter) engaged in farming that has annual gross receipts of $8 million.

    c.   A corporation that acts as an insurance agent. Annual gross receipts are $1 million.

    d.   A manufacturer with annual gross receipts of $600,000.

    e.   A retailer with annual gross receipts of $250,000.

12. T operates a drug-running operation. Which of the following expenses incurred by T are deductible?

    a. Bribes paid to border guards.

    b. Salaries to employees.

    c. Price paid for drugs purchased for resale.

    d. Kickbacks to police.

    e. Rent on an office.

13. When Mr. Jones died, he left equal shares of stock to his four children, although he made it clear that he wanted Jill and John (the two children who were interested in his business) to run the business. This was quite all right with the other two children, who were to receive $100,000 each per year from the company and were free to pursue their own interests. Jill and John each received reasonable salaries of $250,000 and $210,000 respectively. They paid the other two siblings salaries of $100,000 each. What were they trying to accomplish from a tax standpoint? Will it work? If not, what are the tax consequences to the corporation and to the other two siblings?

14. T is an executive in X Corporation. She used insider information to buy X Corporation stock just before public announcement of the discovery of huge oil reserves on company-owned property. She was caught and incurred legal expenses and treble damage payments. Can she deduct either expense?

15. How are expenses (e.g., travel, meals, and lodging) incurred in connection with the investigation of a new business opportunity treated if the new business is acquired? If the new business is *not* acquired?

16. If a taxpayer is unable to meet the requirements of § 183 relative to earning a profit in at least three of five consecutive years, is it possible to qualify the activity as a business? Why or why not?

17. If a taxpayer meets the requirements of § 183 relative to earning a profit in at least three of five consecutive years, is it still possible for the IRS to treat the activity as a hobby of the taxpayer? Why or why not?

18. T was transferred from Phoenix to North Dakota on March 1 of the current year. He immediately put his home in Phoenix up for rent. The home was rented May 1 to November 30 and was vacant during the month of December. It was rented again on January 1 for six months. What expenses, if any, can T deduct on his return? Which deductions are *for* AGI and which ones are *from* AGI?

19. Contrast the differing results obtained in a personal/rental situation by allocating property taxes and interest on the IRS's basis and the court's basis. Which method would the taxpayer prefer?

20. Discuss the tax treatment of the rental of a vacation home if it is:

    a. Rented 10 days during the year. No treatment.

    b. Rented 130 days during the year; used personally for 12 days.

    c. Rented for 250 days; used personally for 40 days.

21. Is it ever possible to deduct expenditures incurred for another individual's benefit? Explain.

22. T repaired the roof on his factory at a cost of $1,500 in the current year. During the same year, S replaced the roof on her small rental house for $1,500. Both taxpayers are on the cash basis. Are their expenditures treated the same on their tax returns? Why or why not?

23. Would anyone ever *want* to capitalize (rather than expense) an item? Explain.

24. T owns 20% of X Corporation; 20% of X's stock is owned by S, T's mother; 15% is owned by R, T's brother; the remaining 45% is owned by unrelated parties. T is on the cash basis, and X Corporation is on the accrual basis. On December 31, 1989, X accrued T's salary of $5,000 and paid it on April 4, 1990. Both are on a calendar year. What is the tax effect to T and X?

25. Discuss the reasons for the disallowance of losses between related parties. Would it make any difference if a parent sold stock to an unrelated third party and the child repurchased the same number of shares of the stock in the market the same day?

26. T sold 100 shares of XYZ Company stock to F, her brother, for $8,000. She had originally paid $7,100 for the stock. F later sold the stock for $6,000 on the open market. What are the tax consequences to T and F?

27. Would your answer to Question 26 differ if T had sold the stock to F for $6,500?

28. The Acme Corporation is owned as follows:

T	20%
P, T's wife	20%
S, T's mother	15%
R, T's father	25%
Q, an unrelated party	20%

T and P each loaned the Acme Corporation $10,000 out of their separate funds. On December 31, 1989, Acme accrued interest at 12% on both loans. The interest was paid on February 4, 1990. Acme is on the accrual basis, and T and P are on the cash basis. What is the tax treatment of this interest expense/income to T, P, and Acme?

29. Discuss the substantiation requirements for deductible expenditures, particularly those for travel and entertainment.

30. Would a record of the past year's travel expenses meet the substantiation requirements if the record were compiled at the time the tax return for that year was prepared? Explain.

31. Discuss the tracing problems encountered in the enforcement of the restrictions of § 265 that disallow a deduction for the expenses of producing tax-exempt income.

Problems

32. P, who is single, has a sole proprietorship and keeps her books on the cash basis. Following is a summary of her receipts, disbursements, and other items related to her business account for 1989:

Receipts

Sales	$28,000
Dividend received from AT&T	300
Interest on savings account	450
Long-term capital gain on sale of stock	1,200

Disbursements

Rent on building used 75% for business and 25% for living quarters	6,000
Salary paid to part-time secretary	3,000

Taxes

Sales tax on personal purchases	280
Gross receipts tax on sales	840
State income taxes	750
Estimated Federal income tax payments	2,500
Charitable contributions	1,400
Purchase of delivery truck on December 31, 1989, received and placed in service on January 8, 1990	9,200
Insurance on business property (policy runs from October 1, 1989, to September 30, 1990)	1,200
Depreciation on business equipment	1,000
Business supplies	980

Calculate P's adjusted gross income for 1989.

33. T, a cash basis taxpayer, rented a building from J on October 1, 1989, paying $12,000 (one full year's rent) in advance and a $10,000 deposit. The lease is for 15 years. T adds improvements costing $40,000 that have a 20-year life and that will revert to J upon termination of the lease.

    a.   How much rent can T deduct in 1989?

    b.   How much does J include in income if he is an accrual basis taxpayer? A cash basis taxpayer?

    c.   How is the deposit of $10,000 treated by both?

    d.   How are the improvements treated by both T and J?

34. T traveled to a neighboring state to investigate the purchase of two restaurants. His expenses included travel, legal, accounting, and miscellaneous expenses. The total was $12,000. He incurred the expenses in March and April 1989.

    a.   What can he deduct in 1989 if he was in the restaurant business and did not acquire the two restaurants?

    b.   What can he deduct in 1989 if he was in the restaurant business and acquired the two restaurants and began operating them on July 1, 1989?

    c.   What can he deduct in 1989 if he did not acquire the two restaurants and was not in the restaurant business?

d. What can he deduct in 1989 if he acquired the two restaurants but was not in the restaurant business when he acquired them?

35. L is a housewife who makes pottery items at home for sale to friends. She had the following income and expenses for the year:

Sales	$1,000
Expenses	
Materials	400
Advertising	250
Travel	350
Classes in ceramics	500
	$1,500
Net loss	$ (500)

How much must L include in income? What can she deduct, assuming AGI of $30,000?

36. T, an executive with an adjusted gross income of $100,000 before consideration of income or loss from his horse business, also raises miniature horses. His income comes from winning horse shows, stud fees, and sales of yearlings. His home is on 20 acres, 18 of which he uses to pasture the horses and upon which he has erected stables, paddocks, fences, tack houses, and so forth.

He uses an office in his home that is 10% of the square footage of the home. He uses the office exclusively for keeping records of breeding lines, histories, and show and veterinary records. His records show the following income and expenses for 1989:

Income from fees, prizes, and sales	$22,000
Expenses:	
Entry fees	1,000
Feed and veterinary bills	4,000
Supplies	900
Publications and dues	500
Travel to horse shows	2,300
Salaries and wages of employees	8,000
Depreciation on horse equipment	3,000
Depreciation on horse farm improvements	7,000
Depreciation on 10% of home	1,000
Total home mortgage interest	24,000
Total property taxes on home	2,200
Total property taxes on horse farm improvements	800

The mortgage interest is only on his home. The horse farm improvements are not mortgaged.

How must T treat the income and expenses of the operation if the minature horse activity is held to be a hobby?

37. How would your answer in Problem 36 differ if the horse operation was held to be a business?

38. J is a promoter, real estate developer, and investor. Because he has inherited wealth, he can afford to be somewhat of a wheeler-dealer. He is single, age 41. During 1989, J incurred expenses in traveling to the

state capitol to testify against proposed legislation for a green belt around the city because it interfered with some of his development plans. The expenses amounted to $900. He also spent $300 traveling to various locations to speak to civic groups against the proposed legislation.

J also incurred $1,600 of expense investigating the purchase of a computer franchising operation. He did not purchase the operation, because he felt that his lack of expertise in that type of business was too big an obstacle to overcome.

J was involved in a promoting scheme with a legislator and took as his fee a parcel of land worth $18,000. The scheme resulted in the newspaper's making defamatory remarks about J, who sued and was awarded $50,000 for slander and damage to his business reputation.

J's other income and expenses for the year were as follows:

Income	
Interest	$ 80,000
Dividends	160,000
Short-term capital loss	(50,000)
Long-term capital gains	175,000
Other fees	24,000
Expenses	
Office expenses	17,000
Expenses incurred on land held for resale	6,000
Tax advice	5,000
All other itemized deductions	34,000

Calculate J's taxable income for 1989.

39. T and S are married, filing a joint return. Both are under age 65, and they have one child, who is blind. T is a full-time student and received a scholarship (tuition waiver) for $5,000 during the year and G.I. benefits of $7,200. S is an executive in state government and earned a salary of $48,000. In her spare time she makes macramé animals. She sold $700 worth of the animals during the year. Her expenses were as follows:

Supplies	$250
Interest on business loan	600
Advertising	50

S also won a prize of $600 playing bingo. T and S received dividends of $230 and had interest of $310 credited to their savings account during the year. Calculate their adjusted gross income for 1989.

40. During 1989, P's vacation home was used as follows: 30 days of occupancy by P, 120 days of rental to unrelated parties, and 215 days of vacancy. Further information concerning the property is summarized as follows:

Rental income	$4,500
Expenses	
Real estate taxes	$1,095
Interest on mortgage	2,555
Utilities and maintenance	1,200
Repairs	400
Landscaping	1,700
Depreciation	3,000

Compute P's net rental income or loss and the amounts that P can itemize on her income tax return.

41. Would your answer differ in Problem 40 if P had used the home for 5 days instead of 30? Explain, showing computations if needed.

42. Would your answer to Problem 40 differ if P had rented the home for 10 days instead of 120? Explain, showing computations if needed.

43. T, single, age 40, had the following income and expenses in 1989:

Income	
Salary	$43,000
Rental of vacation home (rented 60 days, used personally 60 days, vacant 245 days)	4,000
Municipal interest	2,000
Dividend from General Motors	400
Expenses	
Interest	
On home mortgage	8,400
On vacation home	4,745
On loan used to buy municipal bonds	3,100
On various credit cards	600
Taxes	
State and local sales tax	700
Property tax on home	2,200
Property tax on vacation home	1,095
State income tax	3,300
Charitable contributions	1,100
Tax return preparation fee	300
Utilities and maintenance on vacation home	2,600
Depreciation on rental 50% of vacation home	3,500

Calculate T's taxable income for 1989.

44. R is single, and her adjusted gross income for 1989 is $20,000. Calculate R's itemized deductions for 1989, given the following information.

Medical expenses		
R's personal medical expenses	$1,400	
R's dependent daughter's medical expenses	800	
R's mother's medical expenses (her mother is not her dependent)	600	
Taxes		
No Real estate taxes on rental property for .	500	
Real estate taxes on R's personal residence	900 ~	900
No Real estate taxes on daughter's personal residence	850	
R's state income taxes deduct.	630 —	630
No R's state and local sales tax	310	1530

Interest
    On rental property mortgage Not itemized,   6,200
    On R's personal residence mortgage itemized.   8,500 —
    On daughter's personal residence mortgage No   7,200
    On business loans Not itemized,   1,600
Charitable contributions   950 —
Depreciation on rental property   3,000
Utilities and maintenance
    On rental property   2,600
    On R's home   2,900
    On daughter's home   2,100
Depreciation on auto used in R's business   1,800
Depreciation on R's personal auto   2,300
Depreciation on daughter's personal auto   1,960

45. J sold stock (basis of $20,000) to her brother, B, for $16,000.

    a. What are the tax consequences to J?

    b. What are the tax consequences to B if he later sells the stock for
        $21,000? For $14,000? For $18,000?

46. What is R's constructive ownership of X Corporation, given the follow-
    ing information:

Shares owned by R	900
Shares owned by S, R's uncle	600
Shares owned by T, R's partner	30
Shares owned by U, a partnership owned by R and T equally	300
Shares owned by V, R's granddaughter	570
Shares owned by unrelated parties	600

47. T was divorced on November 1, 1989, after separating from her hus-
    band H, on June 1, 1989. Her 21-year-old daughter, D, who is a full-
    time student, lives with her. T provides over one-half of D's support. T
    is 43 years of age. T, H, and D all live in Texas.

    During the year, the following income items were noted by T:

T's salary	$12,000
H's salary	36,000
D's salary	2,500
Municipal bond interest earned in December	300
General Motors dividend received during the marriage	180
Alimony received	1,000
FMV of land received in divorce settlement	18,000
Original cost of land received in divorce settlement	10,000

The following expenses were paid by T:

Cost of leveling the land received in the divorce settlement	$1,500
Interest paid	
On loan incurred to invest in municipal bonds	320
On T's share of home mortgage	3,100
On D's auto loan	1,600
All other itemized deductions	2,000

a.   Calculate T's taxable income for 1989.

b.   What is T's filing status?

Cumulative Problems

 48.   Thomas J. Smith, age 36, is single and lives at 1648 South Mill Road, Chicago, Illinois, 60609. His Social Security number is 623–33–9281. He does not want to designate $1 to the Presidential Election Campaign.

Thomas, who is employed as an executive, earned $60,000 during the year. His employer withheld $8,500 in Federal income tax, $1,100 in state income tax and the appropriate amount of FICA (Social Security) tax.

Thomas was divorced in 1984 and is entitled to a dependency exemption for Susan, his 8-year-old daughter who lives with her mother. Susan's Social Security number is 623–84–6144. Her mother, Joan, is 31, and her Social Security number is 666–44–8888. Thomas paid $5,000 for Susan's support and $6,000 in alimony to Joan. He sold 100 shares of General Co. stock on April 18, 1988, for $5,000. He had purchased them on September 4, 1985, for $3,000. He sold 300 shares of U.S. United Co. stock on July 8, 1988, for $6,000. He had acquired them on April 17, 1988, for $10,000. Thomas had the following interest and dividend items in 1988:

Interest credited to his savings account at State Street Savings	$400
Dividends from General Co. stock	300
Dividends from U.S. United Co. stock*	200
Dividends from AT & T stock	400
Interest on City of Denver general obligation bonds	300

Other items that may have tax consequences are:

a.   Thomas paid $600 for tax return preparation, $50 for a safe deposit box, and $320 for investment advice.

b.   He made charitable contributions of $2,600 during the year, $500 of which was charged on his MasterCard.

c.   Thomas paid the following expenses for Susan, in addition to child support:

Dental and medical bills	$1,400
Piano lessons	300
Private school fees	1,200

    d.   He incurred unreimbursed medical expenses (doctor and hospital) of $800, personal property taxes of $200, $460 additional state income taxes paid in 1988 upon filing his 1987 state income tax return, and $300 in credit card interest.

    e.   His home expenses included home mortgage interest of $8,400 (he bought the home in 1983 and the interest is on the original mortgage), real property taxes of $450, and utilities and maintenance of $2,400.

Calculate the net tax payable (or refund due) for 1988. If you use tax forms in your solution, you will need Form 1040 and Schedules A, B, and D. Suggested software (if available): *WEST–TAX Preparer* for tax return solutions, *WEST–TAX Planner* or *BNA Individual Income Tax Spreadsheet* if tax return solutions are not desired.

49.   John and Mary Jane are married, filing jointly. They are both under age 65 and are expecting their first child in early 1990. John's salary in 1989 was $60,000, from which $12,000 of Federal income tax and $3,200 of state income tax were withheld. Mary Jane made $30,000 and had $5,000 of Federal income tax withheld and $2,000 of state income tax withheld.

They had $400 of savings account interest and $800 of dividends during the year.

They made charitable contributions of $2,000 during the year and paid an additional $200 in state income taxes in 1989 upon filing their 1988 state income tax return. Their deductible home mortgage interest was $8,200, and their property taxes came to $1,600. They had no other deductible expenses.

    a.   Calculate their tax (or refund) due for 1989. Suggested software (if available): *WEST–TAX Planner.*

    b.   Assume that they had come to you for advice in December 1989. John had learned that he was to receive a $20,000 bonus. He wants to know if he should take it in December 1989 or in January 1990. Mary Jane will quit work in January to stay home with the baby. Their itemized deductions will decrease by $2,000 because Mary Jane will not have state income taxes withheld. Suggested software (if available): *WEST–TAX Planner.*

Research Problems

Research Problem 1   Taxpayer sold his unmortgaged home for $150,000 cash. He made a down payment on a new home of $50,000 and acquired a mortgage of $135,000. He invested the remaining $100,000 of the sales proceeds in municipal bonds. Is he prohibited under § 265 from deducting the interest on $100,000 of the home mortgage?

Research Problem 2   Taxpayer, a certified public accountant, gave the wrong advice to a client. As a result, the client incurred an additional $75,000 of costs. The CPA reimbursed the client and, although he had malpractice insurance, failed to file a claim for fear of either having his insurance cancelled or having the premiums drastically increased. Can the taxpayer deduct the $75,000 as a loss incurred in a trade or business under § 165(c) or as an ordinary and necessary business expense under § 162 of the Code?

Research Problem 3   D is a graduate student working on her Ph.D. in microbiology. She attended the university under the G.I. bill, which pays her tuition and books in full. The G.I. benefits are not taxable. She was appointed to a research team, and the university paid her a monthly stipend of $450 for the year. She was required to register and pay tuition for the semesters she was on the research team. Her tuition was still paid for by the V.A. Can she deduct the tuition as a business expense?

Research aids:

§ 265

Rev.Rul. 88–3, 1983–1 CB 72

Research Problem 4   S is a self-employed lawyer. One of his hobbies is songwriting. He had one song published in 1986. Over the next three years, S spent a considerable amount of time writing songs and meeting with producers. He has not shown a profit. He maintains a separate room in his house for the sole purpose of writing music, and he deducted a pro rata share of the utility bills and other home expenses. He incurred other expenses amounting to $4,000. Will his expenses for this endeavor be disallowed as a hobby loss?

Research aid:

§ 183

7

PASSIVE ACTIVITY LOSSES

THE TAX SHELTER PROBLEM

Before Congress enacted legislation to reduce or eliminate their effectiveness, *tax shelters* were popular investments for tax avoidance purposes. The ability of taxpayers to avoid or reduce the tax bite through tax shelter investments has been limited greatly by the *at-risk limitations* and the *passive loss rules.*

The first major provision aimed at the tax shelter strategy was the at-risk limitation enacted in 1976. The objective of the at-risk rules was to limit a taxpayer's tax shelter deductions to the amount *at risk*; that is, the amount the taxpayer stood to lose if the investment turned out to be a financial disaster. Before the at-risk rules were enacted, tax shelter promoters sold tax shelters with the promise of write-offs equal to some multiple of the taxpayer's investment. These multiple write-offs were generally made possible through the use of *nonrecourse debt* to acquire assets for the tax shelter. Nonrecourse debt is an obligation for which the endorser is not personally liable. An example of nonrecourse debt is a mortgage on real estate acquired by a partnership without the assumption of any liability for the mortgage by the partnership or any of the partners. The acquired property generally is pledged as collateral for the loan.

EXAMPLE 1	T invested $20,000 for a 10% interest in a tax shelter. Through the use of $800,000 of nonrecourse financing, the partnership acquired property worth $1,000,000. Depreciation, interest, and other deductions related to the property resulted in a loss of $400,000, of which T's share was $40,000. Because T has only $20,000 at risk, he cannot deduct more than $20,000 of the loss. The deduction may be limited further by the passive loss rules. □

The passive loss rules, enacted in the Tax Reform Act of 1986, have nearly made the term *tax shelter* obsolete. Now such investments are generally referred to as passive investments, or *passive activities,* rather than tax shelters.

Passive activities include certain rental activities and any trade or business in which the investor does not *materially participate.* Losses from such investments are referred to as passive losses. The passive loss rules require that income and deductions be classified as *active, portfolio,* or *passive.* Passive losses cannot be offset against active income or portfolio income, only against passive income.

EXAMPLE 2	K, a physician, earned $150,000 from his practice in 1985 (before the passive loss rules were enacted). He also received $10,000 in dividends and interest on various portfolio investments. During the year, he acquired a 20% interest in a tax shelter investment that produced a $100,000 loss. Assume the loss is not subject to the at-risk limitation. In 1985, K would have been allowed to deduct his $20,000 share of the tax shelter loss, resulting in adjusted gross income of $140,000 ($150,000 salary + $10,000 dividends and interest − $20,000 tax shelter loss). □

EXAMPLE 3	Assume the same facts as in Example 2, except that the year is 1989 and that K does not materially participate in the operations of the activity. K's $20,000 share of the loss is a *passive loss* and is not deductible in 1989. It is treated as a *suspended loss,* which is carried over to the future. If K has passive income from this investment, or other passive investments, in the future, the suspended loss can be offset against that passive income. If K does not have passive income against which he can offset the suspended loss in the future, he will be allowed to offset the loss against other types of income upon eventual disposition of the passive activity. K's adjusted gross income in 1989 is $160,000 ($150,000 salary + $10,000 portfolio income), compared to $140,000 based on the same set of facts in 1985. ☐

AT-RISK RULES

The at-risk provisions limit the deductibility of losses from business and income-producing activities. These provisions, which apply to individuals and closely held corporations, are designed to prevent a taxpayer from deducting losses in excess of the actual economic investment in an activity.

Under the at-risk rules, a taxpayer's deductible losses from an activity for any taxable year are limited to the amount the taxpayer has placed at risk (the amount the taxpayer could actually lose) in the activity. The initial amount considered at risk is generally the sum of the following: [1]

- The adjusted basis of property (including cash) contributed to the activity.

- Amounts borrowed for use in the activity for which the taxpayer has personal liability or has pledged as security property not used in the activity.

This amount generally is increased each year by the taxpayer's share of income and is decreased by the taxpayer's share of losses and withdrawals from the activity.

A taxpayer generally is not considered at risk with respect to borrowed amounts if either of the following is true:

- The taxpayer is not personally liable for repayment of the debt (nonrecourse loans).

- The lender has an interest (other than as a creditor) in the activity (except to the extent provided in Treasury Regulations).

The taxpayer also is not considered at risk with respect to amounts for which he or she is protected against loss by guarantees, stop-loss arrangements, insurance (other than casualty insurance), or a similar arrangement.

Any losses disallowed for any given taxable year by the at-risk rules may be deducted in the first succeeding year in which the rules do not prevent the deduction.

---

1. § 465(b)(1).

EXAMPLE 4   In 1989, T invests $40,000 in an oil partnership that, by the use of nonrecourse loans, spends $60,000 on intangible drilling costs applicable to T's interest. Since T has only $40,000 of capital at risk, he cannot deduct more than $40,000 against his other income. The nondeductible loss of $20,000 can be carried over to 1990. □

EXAMPLE 5   Assume that in 1990, T has taxable income from oil of $20,000. He can deduct the carried-over loss against the $20,000 of income. □

EXAMPLE 6   Assume that in 1990, T has an additional loss from the oil venture of $5,000 but he has increased his at-risk capital by $20,000. He can deduct the $5,000 plus $15,000 of the loss carried over from 1989. □

Recapture of previously allowed losses occurs to the extent the at-risk amount is reduced below zero.[2] This rule applies if the amount at risk is reduced below zero by distributions to the taxpayer, by changes in the status of indebtedness from recourse to nonrecourse, or by the commencement of a guarantee or other similar arrangement that affects the taxpayer's risk of loss.

Generally, a taxpayer's amount at risk is separately determined with respect to separate activities. Nevertheless, activities are treated as one activity (aggregated) if the activities constitute a trade or business and either of the following is true:

- The taxpayer actively participates in the management of that trade or business.

- In the case of a trade or business carried on by a partnership or an S corporation, 65 percent or more of the entity's losses is allocable to persons who actively participate in the management of the trade or business.

PASSIVE LOSS RULES

Before the enactment of the passive loss rules, taxpayers were able, by investing in activities in which they did not participate (passive investments), to create tax losses that did not cause actual (or potential) economic losses.

The classic example of a tax shelter that created noneconomic tax losses is a limited partnership owning rental property, because the at-risk limitation did not apply to real estate before 1987. An individual could buy an interest in a limited partnership, which in turn would buy rental property with a large nonrecourse mortgage. Since the entire cost (including the mortgage) attributable to the building could be depreciated and the interest paid on the mortgage could be expensed, tax losses were generated. There was no real *economic loss*, however, since the rental income generated was sufficient to make the mortgage payments and the real estate in most cases, was appreciating on the open market. Furthermore, the individual limited partners were not personally liable for the mortgage.

<table>
<tr><td>EXAMPLE 7</td><td>T invested $20,000 for a 10% interest in a limited partnership. The partnership paid $200,000 down and negotiated a 10–year nonrecourse mortgage of $800,000 at 9% interest to acquire a $1,000,000 building to be used for rental purposes. The building was placed in service in January 1984, and the 15–year depreciation schedule applicable to 1984 was used (see chapter 9). The depreciation deduction was 12% in the first year, 10% in the second year, and 9% in the third year. Total depreciation for the 3–year period was $310,000 ($1,000,000 × .31). Interest was $72,000 in the first year ($800,000 × .09), $64,800 in the second year [($800,000 − $80,000 payment on principal) × .09], and $57,600 in the third year [($800,000 − $80,000 − $80,000) × .09]. Total interest was $194,400 ($72,000 + $64,800 + $57,600). The partnership's rental income was $390,000 during the 3–year period, and taxes, insurance, and other expenses totaled $120,000. The partnership's loss for the 3–year period is computed as follows:</td></tr>
</table>

Rental income		$390,000
Expenses		
Interest	$194,400	
Taxes, insurance, other	120,000	
Depreciation	310,000	624,400
Partnership's loss		$234,400
T's 10% share of loss		$23,440

At the end of three years, T would have deducted $23,440, or $3,440 more than he invested. From an economic perspective, however, T did not lose $23,440. The value of his partnership interest could have increased because of appreciation of the building (on which $310,000 of depreciation was taken), increased rents, or other factors. □

Some tax shelters offered write-offs in the first year of two or more times the amount of the initial investment. These write-offs were deducted against the investor's other income, such as salary and interest. To eliminate these tax shelter losses, the passive loss rules were added to the law, effective in 1987.

Overview of the Passive Loss Rules

The passive loss rules require classification of income and losses into three categories: (1) active (e.g., salaries), (2) passive (e.g., income or loss from limited partnership interests), and (3) portfolio (e.g., interest and dividends). Losses generated by passive activities cannot offset income from the other two sources.[3] Tax credits from passive activities can be offset only against the

3. § 469(a)(1)(A).

tax attributable to passive income.[4] The unused losses and credits are carried over and may be used to offset future passive income or deducted when a taxpayer disposes of his or her entire interest in the passive activity in a fully taxable transaction. Credits can be lost forever if a taxable disposition does not result in sufficient tax to offset the credits.

Special rules apply in the case of (1) a passive activity that is converted to an active activity, (2) the death of a taxpayer owning an interest in a passive activity, (3) the installment sale of such an interest, and (4) the gift of a passive activity. Transfers of passive activities at death and by gift are covered later in the chapter under Dispositions of Passive Interests.

Taxpayers Subject to the Passive Loss Rules

The passive loss rules apply to individuals, estates, trusts, closely held C corporations, and personal service corporations.[5] Passive income or loss from investments in S corporations or partnerships flows through to the owners (see chapter 20), and the passive loss rules are applied at the owner level.

Application of the passive loss limitation to personal service corporations is intended to prevent taxpayers from sheltering personal service income by creating personal service corporations and acquiring passive activities at the corporate level.

EXAMPLE 8   Six attorneys, who earn a total of $1,000,000 a year in their individual practices, form a personal service corporation. Shortly after its formation, the corporation invests in a passive activity that produces a $200,000 loss during the year. Because the passive loss rules apply to personal service corporations, the $200,000 loss is not deductible by the corporation. □

Determination of whether a corporation is a *personal service corporation* is based on rather broad definitions. A personal service corporation is a corporation that meets *both* the following conditions:

- The principal activity is the performance of personal services.

- Such services are substantially performed by owner-employees.

Personal service corporations include those in the fields of health, law, engineering, architecture, accounting, actuarial science, performing arts, and consulting.[6] A corporation is treated as a personal service corporation if more than 10 percent of the stock (by value) is held by owner-employees.[7] A shareholder is treated as an owner-employee if he or she is an employee or shareholder on *any day* during the testing period.[8] For these purposes, shareholder status and employee status do not even have to occur on the same day.

Application of the passive loss rules to closely held (non-personal service) corporations also is intended to prevent individuals from incorporating to avoid the passive loss limitation. A corporation is classified as a closely held

---

4. § 469(a)(1)(B).
5. § 469(a).
6. § 448(d).

7. § 469(j)(2).

8. § 269A(b)(2).

corporation if, at any time during the taxable year, more than 50 percent of the value of its outstanding stock is owned, directly or indirectly, by or for not more than five individuals. Closely held corporations may offset passive losses against *active* income, but not against portfolio income.

EXAMPLE 9

Y Corporation, a closely held corporation, has $500,000 of passive losses from a rental activity, $400,000 of active business income, and $100,000 of portfolio income. The corporation may offset $400,000 of the $500,000 passive loss against the $400,000 of active business income, but may not offset the remainder against the $100,000 of portfolio income. □

Application of the passive loss limitation as illustrated in Example 9 prevents taxpayers from transferring their portfolio investments to closely held corporations for the purpose of offsetting passive losses against portfolio income.

Individual taxpayers are not allowed to offset passive losses against *either* active or portfolio income.

Disallowed Passive Losses

The passive loss rules disallow 100 percent of losses on passive activities acquired after October 22, 1986. However, under transition rules the disallowance provisions for losses on passive activities acquired before October 23, 1986, are phased in over five years. If a taxpayer has a loss on a passive activity acquired before October 23, 1986 (the date of enactment of TRA of 1986), a percentage of the loss may be deducted under the transition rules. Congress enacted the phase-in schedule to provide some relief to taxpayers who had committed their investment funds to passive activities prior to enactment of the passive loss limitations. The applicable percentages are shown in the following table.

Taxable Years Beginning in	Losses and Credits Allowed	Losses and Credits Disallowed
1987	65%	35%
1988	40%	60%
1989	20%	80%
1990	10%	90%
1991	0%	100%

EXAMPLE 10

T acquired a passive activity in 1984. In 1989, a loss of $10,000 was realized on this activity. Under the transition rules, $2,000 (20% of $10,000) is deductible in 1989. That is, $2,000 can be deducted against active and/or portfolio income in 1989. The $8,000 disallowed loss is suspended. A suspended loss can be carried forward and deducted against passive income in later years. If T has no passive income in later years, the suspended loss is deducted when the passive activity is disposed of (see Example 46). If the passive activity had been acquired after October 22, 1986, no deduction would be allowed in 1989, and the entire $10,000 would be suspended. □

A suspended loss on a pre-enactment passive activity is not added to a following year's loss in calculating that year's disallowed loss.

EXAMPLE 11

Assume the taxpayer in Example 10 had another loss of $2,000 on the pre-enactment passive activity in 1990. Under the transition rules, 10% of a pre-enactment passive activity loss is deductible in 1990 and 90% of the loss is disallowed. This disallowance percentage is applied to the $2,000 loss in 1990. It is not applied to the $8,000 suspended loss from 1989, because that loss already has been reduced by the percentage applicable to 1989. Therefore, $8,000 of the 1989 loss and $1,800 (90% of $2,000) of the 1990 loss are carried over to 1991. □

If a taxpayer has both pre-enactment and post-enactment activities, the transition percentage is applied to the lesser of (1) the pre-enactment passive activity loss, or (2) the net passive loss from pre-enactment and post-enactment activities.

EXAMPLE 12

T has two passive activity investments. Investment A was purchased in 1985 and Investment B was purchased in 1987. In 1989, Investment A generated a $10,000 loss and Investment B generated an $8,000 gain. The net passive loss is $2,000. The allowable deduction is $400 (20% of $2,000). The remaining $1,600 is suspended and carried over. □

EXAMPLE 13

In Example 12, if Investment A had generated income of $10,000 and Investment B had generated an $8,000 loss, the net passive gain of $2,000 would be included in income. □

EXAMPLE 14

In Example 12, assume Investment A had generated a loss of $10,000 and Investment B had generated a loss of $8,000. The net passive loss is $18,000. Only $2,000 (20% of $10,000) could be deducted in 1989. The remaining $16,000 ($8,000 plus 80% of $10,000) would be suspended and carried over to 1990. □

Passive Activities Defined

Code § 469(c) provides a broad definition of the term *passive activity*, but it is necessary to examine the Temporary Regulations [9] to understand how the

---

9. The Temporary Regulations are also Proposed Regulations. Temporary Regulations have the same effect as Final Regulations. Refer to chap-ter 2 for a discussion of the different categories of regulations.

definition is to be applied. According to the Code, the following activities are to be treated as passive activities:

- Any *trade or business* in which the taxpayer does not *materially participate.*
- Any *rental activity.*
- Any *limited partnership* activity.

This definition was contained in TRA of 1986, which was enacted in October 1986. Application of the definition raised some difficult questions:

- What constitutes material participation?
- Are all kinds of rental businesses to be treated as rental activities?
- Are all limited partnership investments to be treated as passive activities?

Not until February 1988 did the Treasury Department issue Temporary Regulations to help taxpayers cope with these questions. These Temporary Regulations provide guidelines for answering the three questions listed above.

The original Code definition of passive activities is illustrated in Examples 15 through 18. The Temporary Regulations are discussed immediately thereafter.

EXAMPLE 15

T invested in a *limited partnership* that engaged in cattle-feeding operations. The investment is a passive activity. T cannot deduct losses from this passive activity against his active and portfolio income unless he materially participates in the activity. (The material participation tests for limited partners were added by the Temporary Regulations.) □

EXAMPLE 16

T invested in a *general partnership* that engaged in cattle-feeding operations. If T materially participates in the activity, such activity is not a passive activity, and any losses generated can be deducted against T's active or portfolio income. □

EXAMPLE 17

T in Example 16 is a college professor who did not materially participate in the cattle-feeding operation. Although the activity is not a limited partnership, it is still a passive activity to T, because T did not materially participate in the activity. T cannot deduct losses against his salary and portfolio income. □

EXAMPLE 18

T owns a triplex. He lives in one unit and rents the other two. The two rented units constitute a passive activity. T may be able to deduct losses from the two units, subject to specified limits, if he qualifies for the rental exception (discussed later in the chapter). □

Material Participation

If a taxpayer materially participates in a nonrental activity, any loss from that activity will be treated as an active loss that can be offset against active income. On the other hand, if a taxpayer does not materially participate, the loss will be treated as a passive loss, which can only be offset against passive income. Therefore, controlling whether a particular activity is treated as active or passive is an important part of the tax strategy of a taxpayer who owns an interest in one or more businesses. Consider the following examples.

EXAMPLE 19

T, a corporate executive, earns a salary of $200,000 per year. In addition, T owns a separate business, acquired in 1988, in which he participates. The business produces a loss of $100,000 in 1989. If T materially participates in the business, the $100,000 loss is an active loss that may be offset against his active income from his corporate employer. If he does not materially participate, the loss is passive and is suspended. T may use the suspended loss in the future only if he has passive income or disposes of the activity. □

EXAMPLE 20

K, an attorney, earns $250,000 a year in her law practice. In 1988, she acquired interests in two activities, A and B, in which she participates in 1989. Activity A, in which she does *not* materially participate, produces a loss of $50,000. K has not yet met the material participation standard for Activity B, which produces income of $80,000. However, K can meet the material participation standard if she spends an additional 50 hours in Activity B during the year. Should K attempt to meet the material participation standard for Activity B? If she continues working in the activity and becomes a material participant, the $80,000 income from the activity is active, and the $50,000 passive loss from Activity A must be suspended. A more favorable tax strategy would be for K to *not meet* the material participation standard for Activity B, thus making the income from that activity passive. This would enable her to offset the $50,000 passive loss from Activity A against the passive income from Activity B. □

It would be possible to devise numerous scenarios in which the taxpayer could control the tax outcome by increasing or decreasing his or her participation in different activities. Examples 19 and 20 demonstrate some of the possibilities. The conclusion reached in most analyses of this type will be that taxpayers will benefit by having profitable activities classified as passive, so that any passive losses can be used to offset passive income. On the other hand, if the activity produces a loss, the taxpayer will benefit if it is classified as active so the loss will not be subject to the passive loss limitations.

As discussed above, a nonrental trade or business in which a taxpayer owns an interest must be treated as a passive activity unless the taxpayer materially participates. The Staff of the Joint Committee on Taxation explained the importance of the material participation standard as follows: [10]

---

10. *General Explanation of the Tax Reform Act of 1986 ("Blue Book")*, prepared by The Staff of the Joint Committee on Taxation, May 4, 1987, H.R. 3838, 99th Cong., p. 212.

Congress believed that there were several reasons why it was appropriate to examine the materiality of a taxpayer's participation in an activity in determining the extent to which such taxpayer should be permitted to use tax benefits from the activity. A taxpayer who materially participated in an activity was viewed as more likely than a passive investor to approach the activity with a significant nontax economic profit motive, and to form a sound judgment as to whether the activity had genuine economic significance and value. A material participation standard identified an important distinction between different types of taxpayer activities. It was thought that, in general, the more passive investor seeks a return on capital invested, including returns in the form of reductions in the taxes owed on unrelated income, rather than an ongoing source of livelihood. A material participation standard reduced the importance, for such investors, of the tax-reduction features of an investment, and thus increased the importance of the economic features in an investor's decision about where to invest his funds.

The Code provides that material participation requires the taxpayer to be involved in the operations of the activity on a *regular, continuous,* and *substantial* basis.[11] The Temporary Regulations provide more specific tests for determining whether a taxpayer is a material participant.

Code § 469(c)(2) provides that rental activities are treated as passive activities. Under the Temporary Regulations, however, some rental activities are treated as passive activities and some are not. The Temporary Regulations provide guidelines for identifying rental activities that are not automatically treated as passive activities. These rules are discussed later in the chapter under Rental Activities. If a rental activity is not automatically treated as a passive activity, it is treated as a business, subject to the seven material participation rules discussed below.

A special exception exists under which a taxpayer might be allowed to deduct a limited amount of a loss on rental real estate, even though the activity is classified as passive. This provision is covered under Exceptions to the Passive Loss Rules.

Tests Based on Current Participation.   Material participation is achieved by meeting any one of seven tests provided in the Regulations. The first four tests are quantitative tests that require measurement, in hours, of the taxpayer's participation in the activity during the year.

Rule 1.   The individual participates in the activity for more than 500 hours during the year.

The purpose of the 500–hour requirement is to restrict deductions from the types of trade or business activities Congress intended to treat as passive activities. The 500–hour standard for material participation was adopted for the following reasons: [12]

● Few investors in traditional tax shelters devote more than 500 hours a year to such an investment.

---

11. § 469(h)(1).
12. Preamble to Temp. and Prop.Regs. § 1.469T, p. 58.

- The IRS believes that income from an activity in which the taxpayer participates for more than 500 hours a year should not be treated as passive.

Rule 2. *The individual's participation in the activity for the taxable year constitutes substantially all of the participation in the activity of all individuals (including non-owner employees) for the year.*

EXAMPLE 21   T, a physician, operates a separate business in which he participates for 80 hours during the year. He is the only participant and has no employees in the separate business. T meets the material participation standards of Rule 2. If T had employees, it would be difficult to apply Rule 2, because the Temporary Regulations do not define the term *substantially all.* □

Rule 3. *The individual participates in the activity for more than 100 hours during the year, and the individual's participation in the activity for the year is not less than the participation of any other individual (including non-owner employees) for the year.*

EXAMPLE 22   J, a college professor, owns a separate business in which she participates 110 hours during the year. She has an employee who works 90 hours during the year. J meets the material participation under Rule 3, but probably would not meet it under Rule 2 because her participation is only 55 percent of the total participation. It is not likely that 55 percent would meet the *substantially all* requirement of Rule 2. □

Rules 2 and 3 are included because the IRS recognizes that the operation of some activities does not require more than 500 hours of participation during the year.

Rule 4. *The activity is a significant participation activity for the taxable year, and the individual's aggregate participation in all significant participation activities during the year exceeds 500 hours. A significant participation activity is one in which the individual's participation exceeds 100 hours during the year.*

The *significant participation* rule treats taxpayers whose aggregate participation in several significant participation activities exceeds 500 hours as material participants. Rule 4 thus accords the same treatment to an individual who devotes an aggregate of more than 500 hours to several significant participation activities as to an individual who devotes more than 500 hours to a single activity.

EXAMPLE 23   T owns five different businesses. His participation in each activity during the year was as follows:

Activity	Hours of Participation
A	110
B	140
C	120
D	150
E	100

Activities A, B, C, and D are significant participation activities, and T's aggregate participation in those activities is 520 hours. Therefore, Activities A, B, C, and D are not treated as passive activities. Activity E is not a significant participation activity (not more than 100 hours), so it is not included in applying the 500–hour test. Activity E will be treated as a passive activity, unless T meets one of the other material participation tests with respect to Activity E. □

EXAMPLE 24   Assume the same facts as in the previous example, except that Activity A does not exist. All of the activities would be treated as passive. Activity E is not counted in applying the more than 500–hour test, so T's aggregate participation in significant participation activities is 410 hours (140 in Activity B + 120 in Activity C + 150 in Activity D). T could meet the significant participation test for Activity E by participating for one more hour in the activity. This would cause Activities B, C, D, and E to be treated as nonpassive activities. Before deciding whether to participate for at least one more hour in Activity E, T should assess the overall effect such participation would have on his tax liability. □

Tests Based on Prior Participation.   The tests in Rules 5 and 6 are based on material participation in prior years. Under these rules, a taxpayer who is no longer a material participant in an activity can continue to be *classified* as a material participant. The IRS takes the position that material participation in a trade or business for a long period of time is likely to indicate that the activity represents the individual's principal livelihood, rather than a passive investment.[13] Consequently, withdrawal from the activity, or reduction of participation to the point where it is not material, does not change the classification of the activity from active to passive.

Rule 5.   The individual materially participated in the activity for any five taxable years (whether consecutive or not) during the ten taxable years that immediately precede the taxable year.

Rule 1 (the 500–hour rule) is the only test that can be used in determining whether a taxpayer was a material participant in an activity for any taxable year beginning before 1987. Rules 2 through 7 are irrelevant for this purpose.[14]

---

13. Ibid., p. 60.

14. Temp. and Prop.Regs. § 1.469–5T(j).

EXAMPLE 25   D, who owns a 50% interest in a restaurant, was a material participant in the operations of the restaurant from 1984 through 1988. He retired at the end of 1988 and is no longer involved in the restaurant except as an investor. D will be treated as a material participant in the restaurant in 1989. Even if he does not become involved in the restaurant as a material participant again, he will continue to be treated as a material participant in 1990, 1991, 1992, and 1993. In 1994 and later years, D's share of income or loss from the restaurant will be classified as passive. □

Rule 6.   The activity is a personal service activity, and the individual materially participated in the activity for any three preceding taxable years (whether consecutive or not).

As indicated above, the material participation standards differ for personal service activities and other businesses. An individual who was a material participant in a personal service activity for *any three years* prior to the taxable year continues to be treated as a material participant after withdrawal from the activity.

EXAMPLE 26   E, a CPA, retires from the EFG partnership after working full time in the partnership for 30 years. As a retired partner, he will continue to receive a share of the profits of the firm for the next 10 years, even though he will not participate in the firm's operations. E also owns an interest in a passive activity that produces a loss for the year. E continues to be treated as a material participant in the EFG partnership, and his income from the partnership is active income. He will not be allowed to offset the loss from his passive investment against the income from the EFG partnership. □

Facts and Circumstances Test.   Rule 7 provides a facts and circumstances test to determine whether the taxpayer has materially participated. The Code criteria of regular, continuous, and substantial participation are used in applying the test.

Rule 7.   Based on all the facts and circumstances, the individual participates in the activity on a regular, continuous, and substantial basis during the year.

The Temporary Regulations do not define what constitutes regular, continuous, and substantial participation. However, a part of the Temporary Regulations has been reserved for further development of this test. Presumably, additional guidelines will be issued in the future. For the time being, taxpayers should rely on Rules 1 through 6 in making the determination as to the nature of an activity.

Participation generally includes any work done by an individual in an activity that he or she owns. Participation does not include work if it is of a type not customarily done by owners and if one of the principal purposes of such work is to avoid the disallowance of passive losses or credits. Also, work done in an individual's capacity as an investor (e.g., reviewing financial reports in a non-managerial capacity) is not counted in applying the material participation tests. Participation by an owner's spouse counts as participation by the owner.[15]

EXAMPLE 27

T, who is a partner in a CPA firm, owns a computer store that has operated at a loss during the year. In order to offset this loss against the income from his CPA practice, T would like to avoid having the computer business classified as a passive activity. Through December 15, he has worked 400 hours in the business in management and selling activities. During the last two weeks of December, he works 80 hours in management and selling activities and 30 hours doing janitorial chores. Also during the last two weeks in December, T's wife participates 40 hours as a salesperson. She has worked as a salesperson in the computer store in prior years, but has not done so during the current year. If any of T's work is of a type not customarily done by owners *and* if one of the principal purposes of such work is to avoid the disallowance of passive losses or credits, it is not counted in applying the material participation tests. It is likely that T's 480 hours of participation in management and selling activities would count as participation, but the 30 hours spent doing janitorial chores would not. However, the 40 hours of participation by T's wife would count, and T would qualify as a material participant under the more than 500 hour rule (480 + 40 = 520). □

Generally, a *limited partner* is not deemed to participate materially unless the partner qualifies under Rule 1, 5, or 6 in the above list. However, a *general partner* may qualify as a material participant by meeting any of the seven material participations tests. If an unlimited, or general, partner also owns a limited interest in the same limited partnership, all interests are treated as a general interest.[16]

Rental Activities

According to the Code, any rental activity is to be treated as a *passive activity*.[17] A *rental activity* is defined as any activity where payments are received principally for the use of tangible property.[18] The Temporary Regulations hold that an activity *generally* is a rental activity if

- tangible property held in connection with the activity is used by customers or held for use by customers, *and*

- the expected gross income from the activity represents payments principally for the use of such property.[19]

However, the Temporary Regulations provide six exceptions to the general definition of rental activity. An activity that is treated as a *nonrental activity* under any of the six exceptions will not automatically be classified as passive. Instead, the activity will be treated as an activity that is subject to the *material participation standards*. If the taxpayer materially participates in the activity,

---

15. Temp. and Prop.Regs. § 1.469–5T(f)(3).
16. Temp. and Prop.Regs. § 1.469–5T(e)(3)(iii).
17. § 469(b)(2).
18. § 469(j)(8).
19. Temp. and Prop.Regs. § 1.469–1T(e)(3)(i).

any income or loss from the activity will be active. Otherwise, the income or loss will be passive. The six exceptions are discussed below.

1. *The average period of customer use for such property is seven days or less.*

   Under this exception, activities involving the short-term use of tangible property such as automobiles, videocassettes, tuxedos, tools, and other such property will not be treated as rental activities. The provision also applies to short-term rentals of hotel or motel rooms.

   This exception is based on the presumption that a person who rents property for seven days or less is generally required to provide *significant services* to the customer. Providing such services supports a conclusion that the person is engaged in a service business rather than a rental business.

2. *The average period of customer use for such property is 30 days or less, and significant personal services are provided by the owner of the property.*

   For longer term rentals, the presumption that significant services are provided is not automatic, as it is in the case of the seven-day exception. Instead, the taxpayer must be able to *prove* that significant personal services are rendered in connection with the activity. Therefore, an understanding of what constitutes significant personal services is necessary in order to apply this rule.

   Significant personal services include only services provided by *individuals*. This provision excludes such items as telephone and cable television services. Four additional categories of *excluded services* are not considered significant personal services: [20]

   • Services necessary to permit the lawful use of the property.

   • Services performed in connection with the construction of improvements to property.

   • Services performed in connection with the performance of repairs that extend the property's useful life for a period substantially longer than the average period for which such property is used by customers.

   • Services similar to those commonly provided in connection with long-term rentals of high-grade commercial or residential real property (including cleaning and maintenance of common areas, routine repairs, trash collection, elevator service, and security at entrances or perimeters).

3. *Extraordinary personal services are provided by the owner of the property without regard to the average period of customer use.*

   Extraordinary personal services are services provided by individuals where the use by customers of the property is incidental to their receipt of such services. For example, a patient's use of a hospital bed is incidental to his use of medical services. Another example would be the use of a boarding school's dormitory, which is incidental to the scholastic services received.

---

20. Temp. and Prop.Regs. § 1.469–1T(e)(3)(iv).

4. *The rental of such property is treated as incidental to a nonrental activity of the taxpayer.*

Rentals of real property incidental to a nonrental activity are not considered a passive activity. The Temporary Regulations provide that the following rentals are not passive activities:[21]

- *Property held primarily for investment.* This occurs where the principal purpose for holding the property is the expectation of gain from the appreciation of the property and the gross rental income is less than 2 percent of the lesser of (1) the unadjusted basis or (2) the fair market value of the property.

EXAMPLE 28

A taxpayer invests in vacant land for the purpose of realizing a profit on its appreciation. He leases the land during the period he holds it. The unadjusted basis is $250,000 and its fair market value is $350,000. The lease payments are $4,000 per year. Because gross rental income is less than 2% of $250,000, the activity is not a rental activity. ☐

- *Property used in a trade or business.* This occurs where the property is owned by a taxpayer who is an owner of the trade or business using the rental property. Also it is required that the property was used in the trade or business during the year or during at least two of the five preceding taxable years. The 2 percent test above is also applied.

EXAMPLE 29

A farmer owns land with an unadjusted basis of $250,000 and a fair market value of $350,000. He used it for farming purposes in 1986 and 1987. In 1988 he leased the land to another farmer for $4,000. The activity is not a rental activity. ☐

- *Property held for sale to customers.* If property is held for sale to customers and rented during the year, the rental of the property is not a rental activity.

EXAMPLE 30

An automobile dealer rents automobiles held for sale to customers to persons who are having their own cars repaired. The activity is not a rental activity. ☐

EXAMPLE 31

A taxpayer acquires land upon which to construct a shopping center. Before beginning construction, he rents it to a business for use as a parking lot. Since the land was not acquired as an investment, nor used in his trade or business, nor held for sale to customers, the rental is a rental activity. ☐

---

21. Temp. and Prop.Regs. §§ 1.469–1T(e)(3)(vi)(B) and (E).

- Lodging rented for the convenience of an employer. If an employer provides lodging for an employee incidental to the employee's performance of services in the employer's trade or business, no rental activity exists.

EXAMPLE 32

Taxpayer has a farming business. He rents houses on his property to migrant workers during the harvest season. He does not have a rental activity. □

- A partner who rents property to a partnership that is used in the partnership's trade or business does not have a rental activity.

EXAMPLE 33

The owner of a business incorporates the business, retaining the land and building as his separate property. He then rents the property to the business. He does not have a rental activity. □

The rules above were written to prevent taxpayers from converting active or portfolio income into a passive activity for the purpose of offsetting other passive losses.

In other cases, passive activity income is reclassified as nonpassive activity income. Such cases include significant participation activities, rentals of nondepreciable property, net investment income from passive equity-financed lending activities, net income from certain property rented incidental to development activities, and property rented to a nonpassive activity.[22]

5. *The taxpayer customarily makes the property available during defined business hours for nonexclusive use by various customers.*

EXAMPLE 34

P is the owner-operator of a public golf course. Some customers pay daily greens fees each time they use the course, while others purchase weekly, monthly, or annual passes. The golf course is open every day from sunrise to sunset, except on certain holidays and on days when the course is closed due to weather conditions. P is not engaged in a rental activity, regardless of the average period of use of the course by customers. □

6. *The property is provided for use in an activity conducted by a partnership, S corporation, or joint venture in which the taxpayer owns an interest.*

EXAMPLE 35

B, a partner in the ABC Partnership, contributes the use of a building to the partnership. The partnership has net income of $30,000 during the year, of which B's share is $10,000. Unless the partnership is engaged in a rental activity, none of B's income from the partnership is income from a rental activity. □

---

22. Temp. and Prop.Regs. §§ 1.469–2T(f)(2)
    through (7).

Calculation of Passive Losses

A passive activity loss is defined in the Code as the amount (if any) by which aggregate losses from all passive activities exceed the aggregate income from all passive activities for the year.[23] The Temporary Regulations, on the other hand, define passive loss as the amount (if any) by which passive activity deductions for the taxable year exceed the passive activity gross income for the taxable year.[24]

While the passive loss definitions in the Code and Temporary Regulations appear very similar, there is an important difference. The Code definition implies that there are two steps in determining the amount of a passive loss:

- Compute the passive loss or passive income for each separate passive activity.

- Offset net passive income from profitable activities against net passive losses from unprofitable activities.

The approach specified in the Temporary Regulations requires subtracting the *expenses* from all passive activities from the *income* from all passive activities. If expenses exceed income, the net result is a passive loss.

Until the disparity between the Code and Temporary Regulations is resolved, taxpayers should follow the Code, since it is a higher ranking source of authority. In addition, the Code requires any suspended passive losses to be allocated among different activities of the taxpayer (see Example 45). This cannot be done unless the Code approach to computing passive losses is followed. The Code definition of passive loss is illustrated in Example 36.

EXAMPLE 36

A taxpayer participates in two activities deemed to be passive activities. Both activities were acquired in 1987. Activity A has generated passive income of $5,500. Activity B has generated a passive loss of $8,500. The $5,500 of passive income is sheltered by $5,500 of the passive loss. However, the net passive loss of $3,000 ($8,500 less $5,500) may not be applied against other nonpassive income. The loss may be carried forward to the succeeding year and applied against any passive income of that year. Such losses are called *suspended losses*. □

Identification of Passive Activity

It is difficult to apply the passive loss rules because the authorities have not yet issued an explanation of what constitutes an activity. The only guidance on this question is contained in IRS Notice 88–94.[25] At issue is whether a taxpayer must construe a business with several parts as a single activity, or whether each part of the business can be construed as a separate activity.

EXAMPLE 37

T owns a business with two separate departments. Department A produces a $95,000 loss, and Department B produces $80,000 of income. Assume

---

23. § 469(d)(1).
24. Temp. and Prop.Regs. § 1.469–2T(a).

25. 1988–35 I.R.B. 25.

Department A is a passive activity but Department B is not. If T is required to treat his business as a single activity, it is necessary to make a determination as to whether both departments, when considered as one activity, constitute a passive or nonpassive activity. This will require an application of the material participation standards, and the treatment of the net loss of $15,000 will depend on the outcome. □

EXAMPLE 38

Assume the same facts as in the previous example. If T disposes of Department A, and if he is allowed to treat the two departments as separate activities, he will be allowed to utilize the passive loss from Department A. The loss can be offset against any gain from the disposition. If any loss remains after the suspended loss is offset against gain from the disposition, the remaining loss may be offset against nonpassive income. However, if T is required to treat the two departments as a single activity, he will not be allowed to utilize the passive loss when he disposes of Department A, because he has not disposed of the entire *single* activity. □

The two examples above illustrate the importance of the definition of what constitutes a separate activity. It appears that Notice 88–94 gives a taxpayer considerable flexibility as to how such operations are to be treated. Regulations dealing with this definition are to be issued in the future. Until then, considerable uncertainty will exist.

Income Not Treated as Passive.   Certain items of income and deduction are not taken into account in computing passive activity losses.[26] Some of these income items are discussed in this section. Others are beyond the scope of this text. Deductions that are not treated as passive are covered in the following section.

Portfolio income of an activity is not included in computing the passive income or loss from the activity. This provision negates any tax benefit taxpayers would otherwise achieve by transferring assets that produce portfolio income to an activity that produces a passive loss. Thus, it is possible that an activity might produce a passive loss *and* portfolio income in the same year.

EXAMPLE 39

K owns an activity that produces a passive loss of $15,000 during the year. He transfers to the activity corporate stock that produces portfolio income of $15,000. The passive loss cannot be offset against the portfolio income. K must report a passive loss of $15,000 and portfolio income of $15,000 from the activity. □

Portfolio income includes interest, annuities, royalties, dividends, and other items. However, such income is excluded from the passive loss computation if it is *not derived* in the ordinary course of business.[27] For example, interest earned on loans made in the ordinary course of a trade or business of lending money would not be treated as portfolio income. In addition, interest on accounts receivable arising from the performance of services or the sale of

---

26. Temp. and Prop.Regs. § 1.469–2T(a)(2).   27. Temp. and Prop.Regs. § 1.469–2T(c)(3).

property would not be treated as portfolio income if credit is customarily offered to customers by the business.

Gains on dispositions of portfolio assets are also treated as portfolio income. The rules for determining whether other gain is to be treated as portfolio income are very complex and are beyond the scope of this text. Refer to the Temporary and Proposed Regulations for additional information.[28]

Compensation paid to or on behalf of an individual for services performed or to be performed is not treated as passive activity gross income.[29]

EXAMPLE 40

T owns 50% of the stock of X, Inc., an S corporation that owns rental real estate. X pays T a $10,000 salary for services he performs for the corporation in connection with management of the rental real estate. The corporation has a $30,000 passive loss on the property during the year. T must report compensation income of $10,000 and a passive loss of $15,000 ($30,000 × .50). □

Some of the other income items that are specifically excluded from the passive loss computation are listed below: [30]

- Gross income of an individual from intangible property (such as a patent, copyright, or literary, musical, or artistic composition) if the taxpayer's personal efforts significantly contributed to the creation of the property.

- Gross income attributable to a refund of any state, local, or foreign income, war profits, or excess profits tax.

- Gross income of an individual for a covenant not to compete.

Deductions Not Treated as Passive.   The general rule is that a deduction is treated as a passive activity deduction if and only if the deduction arises in connection with the conduct of an activity that is a passive activity. The Temporary Regulations list several items that are not to be treated as passive activity deductions: [31]

- Any deduction for an expense that is clearly and directly allocable to portfolio income.

- Any deduction for a loss from the disposition of property of a type that produces portfolio income.

- Any deduction with respect to a dividend if the dividend is not included in passive activity gross income.

- Any deduction for qualified residence interest or interest that is capitalized pursuant to a capitalization provision.

- Any miscellaneous itemized deduction that is disallowed by operation of the 2 percent floor.

- Any deduction allowed under § 170 for a charitable contribution.

---

28. Temp. and Prop.Regs. § 1.469–2T(c)(2).
29. Temp. and Prop.Regs. § 1.469–2T(c)(4).
30. Temp. and Prop.Regs. § 1.469–2T(c)(7).
31. Temp. and Prop.Regs. § 1.469–2T(d).

- Any net operating loss carryforward allowed under § 172.

- Any capital loss carryforward allowed under § 1212(b).

Suspended Losses

The determination of whether a loss is suspended under the passive loss rule is made after the application of the at-risk rules as well as other provisions relating to the measurement of taxable income. A loss that would not be allowed for the year because the taxpayer is not at risk with respect to it is suspended under the at-risk provision and not under the passive loss rule.

A taxpayer's basis is reduced by deductions (e.g., depreciation) even if the deductions are not currently usable because of the passive loss rule.

EXAMPLE 41

T's adjusted basis in a passive activity is $10,000 at the beginning of 1991. His loss from the activity in 1991 is $4,000. Since T had no passive activity income, the $4,000 cannot be deducted. At year-end, T has an adjusted basis of $6,000 in the activity and a suspended loss of $4,000. □

EXAMPLE 42

T in Example 41 had a loss in the activity in 1992 of $9,000. Since the $9,000 exceeds T's at-risk amount ($6,000) by $3,000, that $3,000 loss is disallowed by the at-risk rules. If T has no passive activity income, the remaining $6,000 cannot be deducted. At year-end, T has a $3,000 unused loss under the at-risk rules, $10,000 of suspended passive losses, and an adjusted basis in the activity of zero. □

EXAMPLE 43

T in Example 42 realized a $1,000 gain in 1993. Because the $1,000 increases his at-risk amount, $1,000 of the $3,000 unused loss can be reclassified as a passive loss. If T has no other passive income, the $1,000 income is offset against $1,000 of suspended passive losses. At the end of 1993, T has no taxable passive income, $2,000 ($3,000 − $1,000) of unused losses under the at-risk rules, $10,000 ($10,000 + $1,000 of reclassified unused at-risk losses − $1,000 of passive losses offset against passive gains), and an adjusted basis in the activity of zero. □

EXAMPLE 44

In 1994, T had no gain or loss from the activity in Example 43. He contributed $5,000 more to the passive activity. Because the $5,000 increases his at-risk amount, the $2,000 of unused losses under the at-risk rules is reclassified as a passive loss. T gets no passive loss deduction in 1994. At year-end, he has no unused losses under the at-risk rules, $12,000 of suspended passive losses ($10,000 + $2,000 of reclassified unused at-risk losses), and an adjusted basis of $3,000 ($5,000 additional investment − $2,000 of reclassified losses). □

Interest deductions attributable to passive activities are treated as passive activity deductions but are not treated as investment interest. (See chapter 11 for a detailed discussion of investment interest.) As a result, these interest deductions are subject to limitation under the passive loss rule and not under the investment interest limitation.

Carryovers of Suspended Losses.　　To determine the suspended loss for an activity, passive activity losses must be allocated among all activities in which the taxpayer has an interest. The allocation is made to the activity by multiplying the disallowed passive activity loss from all activities by a fraction, the numerator of which is the loss from the activity and the denominator of which is the sum of the losses for the taxable year from all activities having losses.

EXAMPLE 45

T has investments in three passive activities (acquired in 1989) with the following income and losses for that year:

Activity A	($30,000)
Activity B	(20,000)
Activity C	25,000
Net passive loss	($25,000)
Allocated to:	
A ($25,000 × $30,000/$50,000)	$15,000
B ($25,000 × $20,000/$50,000)	10,000
Total suspended losses	($25,000)

☐

Suspended losses are carried over indefinitely and are deducted from the activities to which they relate in the immediately succeeding taxable year.[32]

EXAMPLE 46

Assume the same facts as in Example 45. In 1990, the disallowed loss from 1989 of $15,000 for Activity A is treated as a deduction from Activity A. Likewise, the disallowed loss of $10,000 from Activity B is treated as a deduction from Activity B. ☐

Upon the taxable disposition of a passive activity, the suspended passive losses from that activity can be offset against the taxpayer's nonpassive and portfolio income. See Dispositions of Passive Interests later in the chapter.

Calculation of Passive Credits.　　Credits arising from passive activities are limited much like passive losses. They can be utilized only against regular tax attributable to passive income,[33] which is calculated by comparing the tax on all income (including passive income) with the tax on income excluding passive income.

32.　§ 469(b).　　　　　　　　33.　§ 469(d)(2).

EXAMPLE 47   A taxpayer owes $50,000 of tax, disregarding net passive income, and $80,000 of tax, considering both net passive and other taxable income (disregarding the credits in both cases). The amount of tax attributable to the passive income is $30,000.

Tax due (before credits) including net passive income	$80,000
Less: Tax due (before credits) without including net passive income	(50,000)
Tax attributable to passive income	$30,000

☐

In the preceding example, a maximum of $30,000 of passive activity credits can be claimed; the excess credits are carried over. These passive activity credits (such as the jobs credit, low-income housing credit, research activities credit, and rehabilitation credit) can be used against the *regular* tax attributable to passive income only. If a taxpayer has a net loss from passive activities during a given year, no credits can be used. Likewise, if a taxpayer has net passive income but the alternative minimum tax applies to that year, no passive activity credits can be used. (The alternative minimum tax is discussed in chapter 12.) In addition, the unused passive losses are carried over.

When the passive activity that generates tax credits fits under the exception for rental real estate activities (discussed subsequently under Exceptions to the Passive Loss Rules), such credits must be converted into deduction equivalents. The deduction equivalent is the deduction necessary to reduce one's tax liability by an amount equal to the credit. A taxpayer with $5,000 of credits and a tax bracket of 28 percent would have a deduction equivalent of $17,857 ($5,000 divided by 28 percent). See the subsequent discussion under the rental real estate exception for examples calculating deduction equivalents.

Carryovers of Passive Credits.   Tax credits attributable to passive activities can be carried forward indefinitely much like suspended passive losses. Unlike passive losses, however, passive credits can be lost forever when the activity is disposed of in a taxable transaction.

EXAMPLE 48   T sold a passive activity for a gain of $10,000. The activity had suspended losses of $40,000 and suspended credits of $15,000. The $10,000 gain is offset by $10,000 of the suspended losses, and the remaining $30,000 of suspended losses is deductible against T's active and portfolio income. The suspended credits are lost forever, because no tax was generated by the sale of the activity. This is true even if T has a positive taxable income or if she is subject to the alternative minimum tax. ☐

EXAMPLE 49

If T in Example 48 had realized a $100,000 gain on the sale of the passive activity, the $15,000 of suspended credits could have been used to the extent of regular tax attributable to the net passive income.

Gain on sale	$100,000
Less: Suspended losses	40,000
Net gain	$ 60,000

If the tax attributable to the net gain of $60,000 is $15,000 or more, the entire $15,000 of suspended credits can be used. If the tax attributable to the gain is less than $15,000, the excess of the suspended credit over the tax attributable to the gain is lost forever. □

When there is adequate regular tax liability from passive activities to trigger the use of suspended credits, such credits lose their character as passive credits. They are reclassified as regular tax credits and made subject to the same limits as other credits (discussed in chapter 13).

This reclassification of passive credits can occur when they cannot be used in the year of reclassification because the taxpayer is subject to the alternative minimum tax (discussed in chapter 12). Tax credits cannot reduce the tax calculated under the alternative minimum tax rules; the credits are carried over under the general rules for tax credits.

EXAMPLE 50

During the year, T had the following regular tax, alternative minimum tax, and credits:

Activity	Regular Tax	Alternative Minimum Tax	Tax Credits	Carried Over As Passive	Carried Over As Regular
Passive	$ 50	$150	$150	$100	$ 50
Active	500	450	150	—	150
	$550	$600	$300	$100	$200

Even though T has to pay the alternative minimum tax of $600 because it exceeds the regular tax of $550, he can reclassify $50 of the suspended passive credits as regular credits because of the $50 of regular tax generated by passive income. He has suspended passive credits of $100 left over for use against future passive income tax. The $50 of reclassified credits can be used in a future year (together with the $150 of active credits) against tax attributable to active and portfolio income. The entire $200 of regular tax credit carryovers is subject to the general rules governing credits. (See chapter 13.) □

Exceptions to the Passive Loss Rules.   The passive loss rules do not apply to working interests in any oil or gas property. In addition, a transitional exception exists for investors in low-income housing. The most significant exception, however, is for rental real estate activities. Generally, up to $25,000 of losses on rental real estate activities of an individual may be deducted against nonpassive or portfolio income.[34] The annual $25,000 deduction is reduced by 50 percent of the taxpayer's AGI in excess of $100,000. Thus, the entire deduction is phased out at $150,000. If married individuals file separately, the $25,000 deduction is reduced to zero unless they lived apart for the entire year. If they lived apart for the entire year, the loss amount is $12,500 each, and the phase-out begins at $50,000. AGI for purposes of the phase-out is calculated without regard to IRA deductions, Social Security benefits, and net losses from passive activities.

To qualify for the $25,000 exception, a taxpayer must meet the following requirements: [35]

- Actively participate in the rental real estate activity.

- Own 10 percent or more (in value) of all interests in the activity during the entire taxable year (or shorter period during which the taxpayer held an interest in the activity).

The difference between active participation and material participation is that the former can be satisfied without regular, continuous, and substantial involvement in operations as long as the taxpayer participates in the making of management decisions in a significant and bona fide sense. Management decisions that are relevant in this context include such decisions as approving new tenants, deciding on rental terms, and approving capital or repair expenditures.

The $25,000 allowance is available after all active participation rental losses and gains are netted and applied to other passive income.

EXAMPLE 51   K, who has $90,000 of AGI before considering rental activities, has $85,000 of losses from a rental real estate activity in which she actively participates. She also actively participates in another rental real estate activity from which she has $25,000 of income. She has other passive income of $36,000. The net rental loss of $60,000 is offset by the $36,000 of passive income, leaving $24,000 that can be deducted against other income. □

The $25,000 offset allowance is an aggregate of both deductions and credits in deduction equivalents. The deduction equivalent of a passive activity credit is the amount of deductions that would reduce the tax liability for the taxable year by an amount equal to the credit.[36] If the total deduction and deduction equivalent exceed $25,000, the taxpayer must allocate on a pro rata basis, first among the losses (including real estate rental activity losses suspended in prior years) and then to credits.

---

34. § 469(i).
35. § 469(i)(6).

36. § 469(j)(5).

EXAMPLE 52

T is an active participant in a real estate rental activity that produces $8,000 of income, $26,000 of deductions, and $1,500 of credits. T, who is in the 28% tax bracket, may deduct the net passive loss of $18,000 ($8,000 less $26,000). As a result, he has an available deduction equivalent of $7,000 ($25,000 less $18,000 passive loss). Therefore, the maximum amount of credits that may be claimed by T is $1,960 ($7,000 × .28). Since the actual credits are less than this amount, the entire $1,500 credit is claimed. □

EXAMPLE 53

B who is in the 28% tax bracket is an active participant in three separate rental real estate activities. She has $20,000 of losses from Activity A, $10,000 of losses from Activity B, and $4,200 of passive credits from Activity C. B's deduction equivalent from the credits is $15,000 ($4,200 ÷ .28). Total passive deductions and deduction equivalents are $45,000 ($20,000 + $10,000 + $15,000) and therefore exceed the maximum allowable amount of $25,000. The taxpayer must allocate pro rata first from among losses and then from among credits. Deductions from Activity A are limited to $16,667 ($25,000 × [$20,000 ÷ ($20,000 + $10,000)], and deductions from Activity B are limited to $8,333 ($25,000 × [$10,000 ÷ ($20,000 + $10,000)]).

Since the amount of passive deductions exceeds the $25,000 maximum, the deduction balance of $5,000 and passive credit of $4,200 must be carried forward.

The suspended losses and credits by activity are as follows:

	Total	Activity A	B	C
Allocated losses	$30,000	$20,000	$10,000	$ –0–
Allocated credits	4,200	–0–	–0–	4,200
Utilized losses	25,000	(16,667)	(8,333)	
Suspended losses	5,000	3,333	1,667	–0–
Suspended credits	4,200	-0-	-0-	4,200

□

Further complications arise when both losses and credits are generated by passive rental activities. Recall that the phase-out of rental losses begins when the taxpayer's AGI reaches $100,000. For each two dollars by which AGI exceeds $100,000, one dollar of the $25,000 loss is disallowed. When the taxpayer's AGI reaches $150,000, no real estate rental loss is allowed.

Where real estate rental activities generate rehabilitation and low-income housing credits, the phase-out range is between $200,000 and $250,000 of AGI.

EXAMPLE 54

T has a net passive activity loss attributable to a low-income housing investment. If her AGI is $175,000, she cannot deduct a loss on the activity, because her AGI exceeds the upper limit of the loss phase-out range of $150,000. She could use up to $25,000 of deduction equivalents ($7,000 of credits) of a low-income housing credit, because that phase-out does not begin until AGI reaches $200,000. □

Dispositions of Passive Interests

When a taxpayer disposes of his or her entire interest in a passive activity, the actual economic gain or loss on the investment finally can be determined. As a result, under the passive loss rule, upon a fully taxable disposition, any overall loss from the activity realized by the taxpayer is recognized and allowed against any income. Special rules apply to dispositions of certain property that disallow their classification as passive income. Included in these rules are dispositions of partnership interests and S corporation stock, partial interests in property, property used in more than one activity, and substantially appreciated property formerly used in a nonpassive activity.[37]

Since the purpose of the disposition rule is to allow the taxpayer's real economic losses to be deducted, credits (which are not related to the measurement of such loss) are not allowable specially by reason of a disposition. Credits will be allowed only when there is sufficient tax on passive income to absorb such credits.

A fully taxable disposition generally includes a sale of the property to a third party at arm's length and thus, presumably, for a price equal to the property's fair market value. Gain recognized upon a transfer of an interest in a passive activity generally is treated as passive and is first offset by the suspended losses from that activity.

EXAMPLE 55

T sold an apartment house with an adjusted basis of $100,000 for $180,000. In addition, T has suspended losses associated with that specific apartment house of $60,000. The total gain, $80,000, and the taxable gain, $20,000, are calculated as follows:

Net sales price	$ 180,000
Less: Adjusted basis	(100,000)
Total gain	$ 80,000
Less: Suspended losses	(60,000)
Taxable gain (passive)	$ 20,000

□

If current and suspended losses of the passive activity exceed the gain realized or if the sale results in a realized loss, the sum of:

---

37. Temp. and Prop.Regs. §§ 1.469–2T(c)(2)(i) and (ii).

- Any loss from the activity for the tax year (including losses suspended in the activity disposed of), plus

- Any loss realized on the disposition

in excess of

- Net income or gain for the tax year from all passive activities (without regard to the activity disposed of)

is treated as a loss that is not from a passive activity.

EXAMPLE 56

T sold an apartment house with an adjusted basis of $100,000 for $150,000. In addition, T has current and suspended losses associated with that specific apartment house of $60,000 and has no other passive activities. The total gain, $50,000, and the deductible loss, $10,000, are calculated as follows:

Net sales price	$ 150,000
Less: Adjusted basis	(100,000)
Total gain	$ 50,000
Less: Suspended losses	(60,000)
Deductible loss	$(10,000)

The $10,000 deductible loss is offset against the taxpayer's ordinary income and portfolio income. ☐

Disposition of a Passive Activity at Death. A transfer of a taxpayer's interest in an activity by reason of the taxpayer's death results in suspended losses being allowed (to the decedent) to the extent they exceed the amount, if any, of the step-up in basis allowed.[38] Suspended losses are lost to the extent of the amount of the basis increase. The losses allowed generally would be reported on the final return of the deceased taxpayer.

EXAMPLE 57

A taxpayer dies with passive activity property having an adjusted basis of $40,000, suspended losses of $10,000, and a fair market value at the date of the decedent's death of $75,000. The heir's basis for the property is $75,000, which is fair market value at the date of death (see chapter 14). The basis increase would be $35,000 (fair market value at date of death in excess of adjusted basis). None of the $10,000 suspended loss would be deductible by either the decedent or the beneficiary. The total of adjusted basis ($40,000) and the suspended losses ($10,000) did not exceed the fair market value of the property ($75,000). ☐

---

38. § 469(g)(2).

EXAMPLE 58

A taxpayer dies with passive activity property having an adjusted basis of $40,000, suspended losses of $10,000, and a fair market value at the date of the decedent's death of $45,000. Since the basis increase under § 1014 would be only $5,000 ($45,000 − $40,000), the suspended losses allowed are limited to $5,000 ($10,000 suspended loss at time of death − $5,000 increase in basis). The $5,000 loss available to the decedent would be reported on the decedent's last income tax return. □

Disposition of a Passive Activity by Gift.   In a disposition of a taxpayer's interest in a passive activity by a gift, the suspended losses are added to the basis of the property.[39]

EXAMPLE 59

A taxpayer makes a gift of passive activity property having an adjusted basis of $40,000, suspended losses of $10,000, and a fair market value at the date of the gift of $100,000. The taxpayer cannot deduct the suspended losses in the year of the disposition. The suspended losses transfer with the property and are added to the adjusted basis of the property. □

If less than 100 percent of the interest is transferred by gift, an allocable portion of the suspended losses is added to the basis of the gift. The remaining losses remain suspended in the hands of the donor.

EXAMPLE 60

A taxpayer makes a gift of a 50% interest in passive activity property having an adjusted basis of $40,000, suspended losses of $10,000, and a fair market value at the date of the gift of $45,000. The carryover basis would be $20,000 (donor's adjusted basis × 50%). The $5,000 of suspended losses ($10,000 × 50%) is added to the basis of the property immediately before the transfer. This transaction results in a basis to the donee of $25,000.

The donor's basis in his remaining 50% interest is $20,000 ($40,000 adjusted basis × 50%). The $5,000 of suspended losses transferred to the donee cannot be used to offset the income produced by the property in the future. The $5,000 of suspended losses remaining can be used to offset the donor's income in the future. □

Installment Sale of a Passive Activity.   An installment sale of a taxpayer's entire interest in a passive activity triggers the recognition of the suspended losses.[40] The losses are allowed in each year of the installment obligation in the ratio that the gain recognized in each year bears to the total gain on the sale.

EXAMPLE 61

T sold his entire interest in a passive activity for $100,000. His adjusted basis in the property was $60,000. If T uses the installment method, his gross profit ratio is 40% ($40,000/$100,000). If T received a $20,000 down

39. § 469(j)(6).   40. § 469(g)(3).

payment, he would recognize a gain of $8,000 (40% of $20,000). If the activity had a suspended loss of $25,000, T would deduct $5,000 [($8,000 ÷ $40,000) × $25,000] of the suspended loss in the first year. □

Passive Activity Changes to Active.   If a formerly passive activity becomes an active one, suspended losses are allowed against income from the now active business.[41] The activity must continue to be the same activity.

Nontaxable Exchange of a Passive Activity.   In a nontaxable exchange of a passive investment, the taxpayer keeps the suspended losses, which generally become deductible when the acquired property is sold. If the activity of the old and new property are the same, suspended losses can be used.

EXAMPLE 62   A taxpayer exchanged a duplex for a limited partnership interest using a § 721 nonrecognition transaction (see chapter 20 for details). The suspended losses from the duplex will not be deductible until the limited partnership interest is sold. Two separate activities exist: a rental real estate activity and a limited partnership activity. If the taxpayer had continued to own the duplex and the duplex had future taxable income, the suspended losses would have become deductible before the time of disposition. □

EXAMPLE 63   In a § 1031 nontaxable exchange (see chapter 15 for details), a taxpayer exchanged a duplex for an apartment house. The suspended losses from the duplex will be deductible against future taxable income of the apartment house. The same activity exists. □

TAX PLANNING CONSIDERATIONS

Utilizing Passive Losses

Taxpayers who have passive activity losses should adopt a strategy of generating passive activity income that can be sheltered by existing passive losses. One approach is to buy an interest in any passive activity that is generating income.

Losses from passive activities acquired after October 22, 1986, are not covered by the phase-in rules. From a tax perspective, it would be foolish to buy a loss-generating passive activity after that date unless one has other passive income to shelter or the activity is rental real estate that can qualify for the $25,000 exception.

A taxpayer with existing passive losses might consider buying rental property. If a large down payment is made and the straight-line method of ACRS (discussed in chapter 9) is elected, a positive net income could be realized. The income would be sheltered by other passive losses, depreciation expense would be spread out evenly and preserved for future years, and depreciation

41. § 469(f).

recapture (discussed in chapter 17) is avoided upon the sale of the property. Future gain realized upon the sale of the rental property could be sheltered by existing suspended passive losses.

Taxpayers with passive losses should consider all other trades or businesses in which they have an interest. If they show that they do not materially participate in the activity, the activity becomes a passive activity. Any income generated could be sheltered by existing passive losses and suspended losses. Family partnershps in which certain members do not materially participate would qualify. The silent partner in any general partnership engaged in a trade or business would also qualify.

PROBLEM MATERIALS

Discussion Questions

1. Discuss tax shelters and how taxpayers used such investments to reduce, defer, or eliminate income taxes.

2. What does "at risk" mean? What is its significance?

3. Explain how the at-risk limitation and the passive loss rules have reduced the effectiveness of tax shelter investments.

4. What is nonrecourse debt? How was it used to generate large tax shelter deductions?

5. What constitutes a taxpayer's initial at-risk amount, and what causes increases and decreases in the amount at risk?

6. T invested $10,000 in a cattle-feeding operation that used nonrecourse notes to purchase $100,000 in feed, which was fed to the cattle and expensed. T's share of the expense was $18,000. How much can he deduct?

7. What is a passive activity?

8. Under the passive loss rules, taxpayers must classify income and losses into three categories. Name these three categories and discuss each category briefly.

9. Describe the limitations that apply to passive activity losses and passive activity credits.

10. Passive losses and credits for any particular year may be suspended. When can suspended losses and credits be used?

11. Distinguish between the passive loss limitations that apply to pre-enactment activities and those that apply to post-enactment activities.

12. In 1989, T incurred a $100,000 loss on a passive activity that he acquired in 1985 and a $40,000 loss on a passive activity he acquired in 1988. How much may he deduct?

13. In 1989, T incurred a $100,000 loss on a passive activity that he acquired in 1985 and had $40,000 of income on a passive activity he acquired in 1988. How much may he deduct?

14. Discuss whether the passive loss rules apply to the following: individuals, closely held C corporations, S corporations, partnerships, and personal service corporations.

15. Define *passive activity,* and discuss the difficult questions raised by the Code definition of the term.

16. What is the significance of the term *material participation?* Why is the extent of a taxpayer's participation in an activity important in determining whether a loss from the activity is deductible or nondeductible?

17. T owns an interest in an activity that produces a $100,000 loss during the year. Would T generally prefer to have the activity classified as active or passive? Discuss.

18. T owns an interest in an activity that produces $100,000 of income during the year. Would T generally prefer to have the activity classified as active or passive? Discuss.

19. Why did the IRS adopt the more-than-500-hour standard for material participation?

20. K, a physician, operates a separate business that he acquired in 1985. He participated for 90 hours in the business in 1989, and the business incurred a loss of $20,000. Under what circumstances would the loss be deductible as an ordinary loss?

21. J, an attorney, operates a separate business that he acquired in 1985. He has one part-time employee in the business. J participated for 130 hours in the business in 1989, and the business incurred a loss of $20,000. Under what circumstances would the loss be deductible as an ordinary loss?

22. Z, a professor, operates three separate businesses, all acquired in 1985. She participates for less than 500 hours in each business. Each business incurs a loss during the year. Are there any circumstances under which Z may treat the losses as active?

23. In 1988, P retired as a partner in a CPA firm he founded 30 years ago. He continues to share in the profits, although he no longer participates in the activities of the firm. P also owns an interest in a passive activity that he acquired in 1984. The passive activity produced a loss of $50,000 in 1989. Can P offset the loss against his income from the CPA firm?

24. Some types of work are counted in applying the material participation standards, and some types are not counted. Discuss and give examples of each type.

25. Some rental activities automatically are treated as passive activities, and others are treated as passive only if the owner does not meet the material participation standards. How can one differentiate between the two categories?

26. What are *significant personal services,* and what is the importance of such services in determining whether a rental activity is treated as a passive activity?

27. What are *extraordinary personal services,* and what is the importance of such services in determining whether a rental activity is treated as a passive activity?

28. Discuss which types of services are treated as significant personal services. Which types are not treated as significant personal services?

29. Discuss the following issues in connection with the calculation of passive losses:
    a. What constitutes a passive activity?
    b. What types of income are not treated as passive income?
    c. What types of deductions are not treated as passive deductions?

30. What is a suspended loss? Why is it important to allocate suspended losses in cases where a taxpayer has interests in more than one passive activity?

31. Suspended credits may be lost upon the disposition of a passive activity, whereas suspended losses are generally usable. Explain.

32. In connection with passive activities, what is a *deduction equivalent?* How is a deduction equivalent computed?

33. What is the difference between material participation and active participation with regard to the passive loss rules?

34. Upon the taxable disposition of a passive activity, what happens to the suspended losses? The suspended credits?

35. Is a hobby loss ever treated as a passive loss? Why or why not?

Problems

36. In 1988, T invested $100,000 in a limited partnership that has a working interest in an oil well. In 1988, his share of the losses of the partnership was $45,000. In 1989, his share of the losses was $95,000. In 1990, his share of partnership income was $10,000, and he invested an additional $15,000 in the venture. How much can T deduct in 1988? In 1989? In 1990?

37. Taxpayer has an investment in a passive limited partnership purchased in 1985 and incurred losses from it of $100,000 in both 1989 and 1990. Assuming he has enough at risk to deduct the losses, how much can he deduct in 1989 and 1990?

38. Taxpayer has investments in four passive activity partnerships purchased in 1984. In 1989, the income and losses were as follows:

Partnership	Income (Loss)
A	$ 60,000
B	(60,000)
C	(30,000)
D	(10,000)

In 1990, he sold all three interests as follows:

Partnership	Gain (Loss) on Sale *	1990 Income (Loss)
A	$ 80,000	$ 20,000
B	(20,000)	4,000
C	(17,000)	(9,000)
D	20,000	(3,000)

    * Before suspended losses. (None before 1989).

a. Calculate taxpayer's deductible loss, if any, in 1989.

b. Calculate taxpayer's gain or loss on the sale of each of the partnerships and how the gains or losses are treated.

39. H and W are married with no dependents and live together in Ohio, which is not a community property state. Since W has large medical expenses, H and W seek your advice about filing separately to save taxes. Their income and expenses for 1989 are as follows:

H's salary	$ 60,000
W's salary	20,000
Dividends and interest (joint)	1,500
Rental loss from actively managed units (joint)	(22,000)
W's medical expenses	5,800
All other itemized deductions:*	
H	8,000
W	2,000

    * None subject to limitations.

Would H and W pay less in taxes if they filed jointly or separately for 1989?

40. T is active in three separate rental real estate activities and is in the 28% tax bracket. She had $12,000 of losses from Activity A, $18,000 of losses from Activity B, and income of $10,000 from Activity C. She also had $2,100 of tax credits from Activity A. Calculate her deductions and credits allowed and the suspended losses and credits.

41. T died owning an interest in a passive activity property with an adjusted basis of $80,000, suspended losses of $8,000, and a fair market value of $85,000. What can be deducted on her final income tax return?

42. In 1989, T gave her son a passive activity with an adjusted basis of $100,000. Fair market value of the activity was $180,000, and the activity had suspended losses of $25,000. In 1990, the son realized income from the passive activity of $12,000. What is the effect on T and T's son in 1989 and 1990?

43. T invested $150,000 in a passive activity in 1982. On January 1, 1989, his adjusted basis in the activity was $30,000. His share of the losses in the activity were as follows:

Year	Gain (Loss)
1989	($40,000)
1990	(30,000)
1991	50,000

How much can T deduct in 1989 and 1990? What is T's taxable income from the activity in 1991? Keep in mind the at-risk rules as well as the passive loss rules.

44. Would your answer to Problem 43 differ if T had purchased the activity in 1987?

45. T acquired a passive activity in 1989 that generated tax credits of $2,000 and income of $4,000. The regular tax attributable to the income was $1,120. However, T paid taxes of $80,000 under the alternative minimum tax provisions. In 1990, the activity generated $1,000 of income upon which $280 of regular tax was due. T paid regular taxes that year of $40,000. When and how can he take the $2,000 of credits?

46. T sold a passive activity in 1990 for $150,000. His adjusted basis was $50,000. T used the installment method of reporting the gain. The activity had suspended losses of $12,000. T received $60,000 in the year of sale. What is his gain? How much of the suspended losses can T deduct?

47. If T in Problem 46 had no suspended losses, was in the 28% tax bracket, and had $10,000 of tax credits attributable to the acitivity, how much of the credits could he use in 1990?

Research Problems

Research Problem 1   H is a married individual who files a separate return for the taxable year. He is employed full-time as an attorney. H, who also owns an interest in a minor league baseball team, does no work in connection with the activity during the year. He anticipates that the activity will result in a loss for the taxable year. H pays his wife to work as an office receptionist in connection with the activity for an average of 20 hours a week during the year. Will H be allowed to deduct his share of the loss from the activity?

Research Problem 2   On October 22, 1986, K owned a 10% interest in a passive activity. In 1988, she acquired an additional 5% interest in the activity. In 1989, the activity produced a loss of $100,000. How much of the loss can K deduct in 1989?

Research Problem 3   J owns interests in three business activities, X, Y, and Z. J does not materially participate in any of the activities considered separately, but he does participate for 110 hours in Activity X, 160 hours in Activity Y, and 125 hours in Activity Z. J does not own interests in any other businesses. J's net passive income (loss) for the taxable year from Activities X, Y, and Z is as follows:

	X	**Y**	**Z**
Gross income	$600	$700	$900
Deductions	(200)	(1,000)	(300)
Net income (loss)	$400	($300)	$600

How much of the gross income from the three activities is treated as income that is not from a passive activity?

8

DEDUCTIONS AND LOSSES: CERTAIN BUSINESS EXPENSES AND LOSSES

OBJECTIVES

Determine the amount of a bad debt deduction.

Distinguish between business and nonbusiness bad debts and recognize the tax consequences of the distinction.

Examine the tax treatment for worthless securities and § 1244 stock.

Calculate the amount of loss for business use property.

Define the term "casualty" and compute the amount of casualty and theft losses.

Recognize the alternative tax treatments for research and experimental expenditures.

Determine the amount of net operating loss.

Recognize the impact of the carryover of a net operating loss.

Working with the tax formula for individuals requires the proper classification of items that are deductible *for* adjusted gross income (AGI) and items that are deductions *from* AGI (itemized deductions). Business expenses and losses, discussed in this chapter, are reductions of gross income to arrive at the taxpayer's adjusted gross income. Expenses and losses incurred in connection with a transaction entered into for profit and expenses attributable to rents and royalties are deducted for AGI. All other expenses and losses incurred in connection with a transaction entered into for profit are deducted from AGI. Losses on personal use property are deducted as an itemized deduction. Itemized deductions are deductions from AGI.

Bad Debts

If a taxpayer sells goods or provides services on credit and the account receivable subsequently becomes worthless, a bad debt deduction is permitted only if income arising from the creation of the account receivable was previously included in income.[1] No deduction is allowed, for example, for a bad debt arising from the sale of a product or service when the taxpayer is on the cash basis, because no income is reported until the cash has been collected. A bad debt deduction for a cash basis taxpayer would amount to a double deduction, because the expenses of the product or service rendered are deducted when payments are made to suppliers and to employees.

EXAMPLE 1

T, an individual engaged in the practice of accounting, performed accounting services for X for which he charged $8,000 ($7,700 for services and $300 for materials). X never paid the bill, and his whereabouts are unknown.

If T is an accrual basis taxpayer, the $8,000 would be included in income when the services were performed. The $300 would be a business expense when the costs were incurred. When it is determined that X's account will not be collected, the $8,000 will be expensed as a bad debt.

If T is a cash basis taxpayer, the $8,000 would not be included in income until payment is received. However, the $300 would be a business expense at the time the expense was incurred. When it is determined that X's account will not be collected, the $8,000 will not be a bad debt expense, since it was never recognized as income. □

Specific Charge-Off Method

For tax years beginning after 1986, taxpayers (other than certain financial institutions) may use only the specific charge-off method in accounting for bad debts. The reserve method for computing deductions for bad debts is allowed for certain financial institutions.

A taxpayer using the specific charge-off method may claim a deduction when a specific business debt becomes either partially or wholly worthless or when a specific nonbusiness debt becomes wholly worthless.[2] The taxpayer

---

1. Reg. § 1.166–1(e).   2. § 166(a) and Reg. § 1.166.

must satisfy the IRS that a debt is partially worthless and must demonstrate the amount of worthlessness.

If a business debt previously deducted as partially worthless becomes totally worthless in a future year, only the remainder not previously deducted can be written off.

In the case of total worthlessness, a deduction is allowed for the entire amount in the year the debt becomes worthless. The amount of the deduction depends on the taxpayer's basis in the bad debt. If the debt arose from the sale of services or products and the face amount was previously included in income, that amount is deductible. If the taxpayer purchased the debt, the deduction is equal to the amount the taxpayer paid for the debt instrument.

One of the more difficult tasks is determining if and when a bad debt is worthless. The loss is deductible only in the year of partial or total worthlessness for business debts and only in the year of total worthlessness for nonbusiness debts. Legal proceedings need not be initiated against the debtor when the surrounding facts indicate that such action will not result in collection.

EXAMPLE 2

In 1987, J loaned $1,000 to K, who agreed to repay the loan in two years. In 1989, K disappeared after the note became delinquent. If a reasonable investigation by J indicates that he cannot find K or that a suit against K would not result in collection, J can deduct the $1,000 in 1989. ☐

Bankruptcy is generally an indication of at least partial worthlessness of a debt. Bankruptcy may create worthlessness before the settlement date. If this is the case, the deduction must be taken in the year of worthlessness, not in the later year upon settlement.

EXAMPLE 3

In Example 2, assume K filed for personal bankruptcy in 1988. At that time, J learned that unsecured creditors (including J) were expected to receive ultimately 20¢ on the dollar. In 1989, settlement is made and J receives only $150. He should deduct $800 ($1,000 loan less $200 expected settlement) in 1988 and $50 in 1989 ($200 balance less $150 proceeds). J is not permitted to wait until 1989 to deduct the entire $850. ☐

Reserve Method.   As a result of the repeal of the reserve method, the balance in any reserve for bad debts is includible in income ratably over a period of four years. This inclusion begins with the first tax year beginning after December 31, 1986.

Business versus Nonbusiness Bad Debts

A nonbusiness bad debt is a debt unrelated to the taxpayer's trade or business either when it was created or when it became worthless. The nature of a debt depends on whether the lender was engaged in the business of lending money or if there is a proximate relationship between the creation of the debt and the lender's trade or business. The use to which the borrowed funds are put by the debtor is of no consequence. Loans to relatives or friends are the most common type of nonbusiness bad debt.

CONCEPT SUMMARY 8–1

	Specific Charge-off Method
Expense deduction and account write-off	The expense arises and the write-off takes place when a specific business account becomes either partially or wholly worthless or when a nonbusiness account becomes wholly worthless.
Recovery of accounts previously written off	If the account recovered was written off during the current taxable year, the write-off entry is reversed. If the account recovered was written off during a previous taxable year, income is created subject to the tax benefit rule.

EXAMPLE 4

J loaned his friend, S, $1,500. S used the money to start a business, which subsequently failed. Even though proceeds of the loan were used in a business, the loan is a nonbusiness bad debt, because the business was S's, not J's. □

The distinction between a business bad debt and a nonbusiness bad debt is important. A business bad debt is deductible as an ordinary loss in the year incurred, whereas a nonbusiness bad debt is always treated as a short-term capital loss. Thus, regardless of the age of a nonbusiness bad debt, the deduction may be of limited benefit due to the capital loss limitations on deductibility in any one year. The maximum amount of a net short-term capital loss that an individual can deduct against ordinary income in any one year is $3,000 (see chapter 16 for a detailed discussion). Although no deduction is allowed when a nonbusiness bad debt is partially worthless, the taxpayer is entitled to deduct the net amount of the loss upon final settlement.

The following examples are illustrations of business bad debts adapted from the Regulations.[3]

EXAMPLE 5

In 1988, L sold his business but retained a claim (note or account receivable) against B. The claim became worthless in 1989. L's loss is treated as a business bad debt, because the debt was created in the conduct of L's former trade or business. Business bad debt treatment is accorded to L despite the fact that he was holding the note as an investor and was no longer in a trade or business when the claim became worthless. □

EXAMPLE 6

In 1987, L died and left his business assets to his son, S. One of the business assets inherited by S was a claim against B that became worthless in S's hands in 1989. S's loss is a business bad debt, since the loss is

3. Reg. § 1.166–5(d).

sustained as a proximate incident to the conduct of the trade or business in which S is engaged at the time the debt becomes worthless. ☐

The nonbusiness bad debt provisions are not applicable to corporations. It is assumed that any loans made by a corporation are related to its trade or business.

Loss of Deposits in Insolvent Financial Institutions

Qualified individuals can elect to deduct losses on deposits in qualified financial institutions as personal casualty losses in the year in which the amount of the loss can be reasonably estimated. If the election is made to treat a loss on a deposit as a personal casualty loss, no bad debt deduction for the loss will be allowed.[4] As a personal casualty loss, the loss would be subject to the $100 per event floor and the 10 percent of AGI aggregate floor. Both floors limiting casualty losses are explained later in the chapter.

The amount of loss to be recognized under the election is the difference between (1) the taxpayer's basis in the deposit and (2) a reasonable estimate of the amount to be received. Election of this casualty loss treatment is effective with respect to losses incurred in tax years beginning after 1982.

A qualified individual is any individual other than:

- An owner of 1 percent or more of the value of the stock of the institution in which the loss was sustained.

- An officer of such institution.

- Certain relatives and other persons who are tax-related to such owners and officers.

A qualified financial institution is a commercial bank, a thrift institution, an insured credit union, or any similar institution chartered and supervised under Federal or state law. A deposit, for purposes of this provision, is any deposit, withdrawal certificate, or withdrawable or repurchasable share of or in a qualified financial institution.

Loans between Related Parties

Loans between related parties (especially family members) raise the issue of whether the loan was bona fide or was a gift. The Regulations state that a bona fide debt arises from a debtor-creditor relationship based on a valid and enforceable obligation to pay a fixed or determinable sum of money. Thus, individual circumstances must be examined to determine whether advances between related parties are gifts or loans. Some considerations are these: Was a note properly executed? Is there collateral? What collection efforts were made? What was the intent of the parties?

EXAMPLE 7 | L loans $2,000 to his widowed mother for an operation. L's mother owns no property and is not employed, and her only income consists of Social

---

4. § 165(l).

Security benefits. No note is issued for the loan, no provision for interest is made, and no repayment date is mentioned. In the current year, L's mother dies leaving no estate. Assuming the loan is not repaid, L cannot take a deduction for a nonbusiness bad debt, because the facts indicate that no debtor-creditor relationship existed. □

CONCEPT SUMMARY 8–2

Bad Debt Deductions

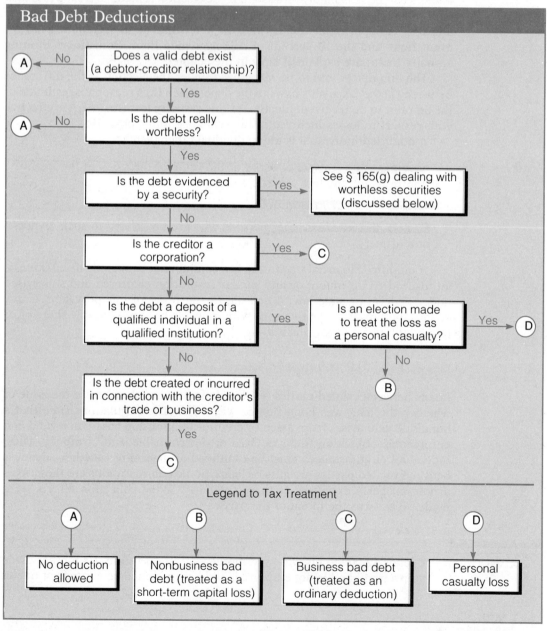

Legend to Tax Treatment

A	B	C	D
No deduction allowed	Nonbusiness bad debt (treated as a short-term capital loss)	Business bad debt (treated as an ordinary deduction)	Personal casualty loss

WORTHLESS SECURITIES

A loss is allowed under § 165 for a security that becomes worthless during the year.[5] Such securities are shares of stock or some form of indebtedness. The losses generated are usually treated as capital losses deemed to have occurred on the last day of the taxable year. Capital losses may be of limited benefit due to the $3,000 capital loss limitation.

EXAMPLE 8	T, a calendar year taxpayer, owns stock in X Corporation (a publicly held company). The stock was acquired as an investment on November 30, 1988, at a cost of $5,000. On April 1, 1989, the stock became worthless. Since the stock is deemed to have become worthless as of December 31 of 1989, T has a capital loss from an asset held for 13 months (a long-term capital loss). ☐

Securities in Affiliated Corporations

If securities of an affiliated corporation become worthless during the taxable year, the corporate taxpayer's loss will be treated as an ordinary loss rather than a capital loss. A corporation is treated as an affiliated corporation to the parent if two requirements are satisfied. First, the corporate shareholder must own at least 80 percent of the voting power of all classes of stock and at least 80 percent of each class of nonvoting stock of the affiliated company. Second, more than 90 percent of the gross receipts of the affiliate must be from sources other than royalties, rents, dividends, interest, annuities, and gains from sales or exchanges of stocks and securities.[6]

Small Business Stock

The general rule is that shareholders receive capital gain or loss treatment upon the sale or exchange of stock. However, it is possible to receive an ordinary loss deduction if the loss is sustained on small business stock— § 1244 stock. Only individuals[7] who acquired the stock from the corporation are eligible to receive ordinary loss treatment under § 1244, and the loss is limited to $50,000 ($100,000 for married individuals filing jointly) per year. The corporation must meet certain qualifications for the worthlessness of § 1244 stock to be treated as an ordinary—rather than a capital—loss. The major qualification is that the total amount of money and other property received by the corporation for stock as a contribution to capital (or paid-in surplus) does not exceed $1,000,000. Section 1244 stock can be common or preferred stock.

EXAMPLE 9	On July 1, 1987, T, a single individual, purchased 100 shares of X Corporation common stock for $100,000. The X stock qualified as § 1244 stock. On June 20, 1989, T sold all of the X stock for $20,000. Because the X

---

5. § 165(g).

6. § 165(g)(3).

7. The term "individuals" includes a partnership but not a trust or an estate.

stock is § 1244 stock, T would have $50,000 of ordinary loss and $30,000 of long-term capital loss. □

LOSSES OF INDIVIDUALS

An individual may deduct the following losses under § 165(c):

- Losses incurred in a trade or business.
- Losses incurred in a transaction entered into for profit.
- Losses caused by fire, storm, shipwreck, or other casualty or by theft.

A taxpayer suffering losses from damage to nonbusiness property can deduct only those losses attributable to fire, storm, shipwreck, or other casualty or theft. Although the meaning of the terms "fire, storm, shipwreck, and theft" is relatively free from dispute, the term "other casualty" needs further clarification. It means casualties analogous to fire, storm, or shipwreck. The term also includes accidental loss of property provided the loss qualifies under the same rules as any other casualty. These rules are that the loss must result from an event that is (1) identifiable; (2) damaging to property; and (3) sudden, unexpected, and unusual in nature. A sudden event is one that is swift and precipitous and not gradual or progressive. An unexpected event is an event that is ordinarily unanticipated and occurs without the intent of the one who suffers the loss. An unusual event is one that is extraordinary and non-recurring, that does not commonly occur during the activity in which the taxpayer was engaged when the destruction occurred.[8] Examples include hurricanes, tornadoes, floods, storms, shipwrecks, fires, auto accidents, mine cave-ins, sonic booms, and vandalism. Weather that causes damages (drought, for example) must be unusual and severe for the particular region. Damage must be to the taxpayer's property to qualify as a casualty loss.

The deduction for a casualty loss from an automobile accident can be taken only if the damage was not caused by the taxpayer's willful act or willful negligence.

EXAMPLE 10 T parks her car on a hill and fails to set the brake properly and to curb the wheels. As a result of T's negligence, the car rolls down the hill and is damaged. The repairs to T's car should qualify for casualty loss treatment, since T's act of negligence appears to be simple rather than willful. □

Events That Are Not Casualties

Not all acts of God are treated as casualty losses for income tax purposes. Because a casualty must be sudden, unexpected, and unusual, progressive deterioration (such as erosion due to wind or rain) is not a casualty, because it does not meet the suddenness test.

Examples of nonsudden events that do not qualify as casualties include disease and insect damages. In the past, some courts have held that termite

---

8. Rev.Rul. 72–592, 1972–2 C.B. 101.

damage over periods of up to 15 months after infestation constituted a sudden event and was, therefore, deductible as a casualty loss.[9] On the other hand, when the damage was caused by termites over periods of several years, some courts have disallowed a casualty loss deduction.[10] Despite the existence of some judicial support for the deductibility of termite damage as a casualty loss, the current position of the IRS is that termite damage is not deductible.[11]

Other examples of events that are not casualties are losses resulting from a decline in value rather than an actual loss of the property. No loss was allowed where the taxpayer's home declined in value as a result of a landslide that destroyed neighboring homes but did no actual damage to the taxpayer's home.[12] Similarly, a taxpayer was allowed a loss for the actual flood damage to his property but not for the decline in market value due to the property's being flood-prone.[13]

The Eleventh Circuit Court has stated that loss of present value generated by a fear of future damage cannot be factored into the fair market value of the property. However, the Court has held that permanent buyer resistance, as evidenced by changes made to the neighborhood surrounding the taxpayer's home following a flood, does affect the fair market value and may be included in a determination as to what the fair market value is after the disaster.[14]

Theft Losses

Theft includes, but is not necessarily limited to, larceny, embezzlement, and robbery.[15] Theft does not include misplaced items.[16]

Theft losses are computed like other casualty losses (discussed in the following section), but the timing for recognition of the loss differs. A theft loss is deducted in the year of discovery, not the year of the theft (unless, of course, the discovery occurs in the same year as the theft). If, in the year of the discovery, a claim exists (e.g., against an insurance company) and there is a reasonable expectation of recovering the fair market value of the asset from the insurance company, no deduction is permitted.[17] If, in the year of settlement, the recovery is less than the asset's fair market value, a partial deduction may be available.

EXAMPLE 11   J's new sailboat was stolen from the storage marina in December 1988. He discovered the loss on June 3, 1989, and filed a claim with his insurance company that was settled on January 30, 1990. Assuming there is a reasonable expectation of full recovery, no deduction is allowed in 1989. A partial deduction may be available in 1990 if the actual insurance

9. *Rosenberg v. Comm.*, 52–2 USTC ¶9377, 42 AFTR 303, 198 F.2d 46 (CA–8, 1952); *Shopmaker v. U.S.*, 54–1 USTC ¶9195, 45 AFTR 758, 119 F.Supp. 705 (D.Ct.Mo., 1953).

10. *Fay v. Helvering*, 41–2 USTC ¶9494, 27 AFTR 432, 120 F.2d 253 (CA–2, 1941); *U.S. v. Rogers*, 41–1 USTC ¶9442, 27 AFTR 423, 120 F.2d 244 (CA–9, 1941).

11. Rev.Rul. 63–232, 1963–2 C.B. 97.

12. *H. Pulvers v. Comm.*, 69–1 USTC ¶9222, 23 AFTR2d 69–678, 407 F.2d 838 (CA–9, 1969).

13. *S. L. Solomon*, 39 TCM 1282, T.C.Memo 1980–87.

14. *Finkbohner, Jr. v. U.S.*, 86–1 USTC ¶9393, 57 AFTR2d 86–1400, 788 F.2d 723 (CA–11, 1986).

15. Reg. § 1.165–8(d).

16. *Mary Francis Allen*, 16 T.C. 163 (1951).

17. Reg. §§ 1.165–1(d)(2) and 1.165–8(a)(2).

proceeds are less than the fair market value of the asset. (Loss measurement rules are discussed later in this chapter.) □

When to Deduct Casualty Losses

Generally, a casualty loss is deducted in the year the loss occurs. However, no casualty loss is permitted if a reimbursement claim with a "reasonable prospect of [full] recovery" exists.[18] If the taxpayer has a partial claim, only part of the loss can be claimed in the year of the casualty, and the remainder is deducted in the year the claim is settled.

EXAMPLE 12   G's new sailboat was completely destroyed by fire in 1989. Its cost and fair market value was $10,000. G's only claim against the insurance company was on a $7,000 policy that was not settled by year-end. The following year, 1990, G settled with the insurance company for $6,000. G is entitled to a $3,000 deduction in 1989 and a $1,000 deduction in 1990. If the sailboat were held for personal use, the $3,000 deduction in 1989 would be reduced first by $100 and then by 10% of G's 1989 adjusted gross income. The $1,000 deduction in 1990 would be reduced by 10% of G's 1990 adjusted gross income (see the following discussion). □

If a taxpayer receives reimbursement for a casualty loss sustained and deducted in a previous year, an amended return is not filed for that year. Instead, the taxpayer must include the reimbursement in gross income on the return for the year in which it is received to the extent that the previous deduction resulted in a tax benefit.

An exception is allowed for casualties sustained in an area designated as a disaster area by the President of the United States.[19] In such cases, the taxpayer may elect to treat the loss as having occurred in the taxable year immediately preceding the taxable year in which the disaster actually occurred. The rationale for this exception is to provide immediate relief to disaster victims in the form of accelerated tax benefits.

If the due date, plus extensions, for the prior year's return has not passed, a taxpayer makes the election to claim the disaster area loss on the prior year's tax return. If the disaster occurs after the prior year's return has been filed, it is necessary to file either an amended return or a refund claim. In any case, the taxpayer must show clearly that such an election is being made.

Disaster loss treatment also applies in the case of a personal residence that has been rendered unsafe for use as a residence because of a disaster. This provision applies when, within 120 days after the President designates the area as a disaster area, the state or local government where the residence is located orders the taxpayer to demolish or relocate the residence.[20]

---

18. Reg. § 1.165–1(d)(2)(i).
19. § 165(h).
20. § 165(k).

Measuring the Amount of Loss

The rules for determining the amount of a loss depend in part on whether business use or personal use property was involved. Another factor that must be considered is whether the property was partially or completely destroyed.

If business property or property held for the production of income (e.g., rental property) is completely destroyed, the loss is always equal to the adjusted basis of the property at the time of destruction.

EXAMPLE 13

T's automobile, which was used only for business, was destroyed by fire. T had unintentionally allowed his insurance coverage to expire. The fair market value of the automobile was $9,000 at the time of the fire, and its adjusted basis was $10,000. T is allowed a loss deduction of $10,000 (the basis of the automobile). The $10,000 loss is a deduction for AGI. □

A different measurement rule applies for partial destruction of business property and property held for the production of income, and for partial or complete destruction of personal use property. In these situations, the loss is the lesser of the following:

1. The adjusted basis of the property.

2. The difference between the fair market value of the property before the event and the fair market value immediately after the event.

EXAMPLE 14

K's automobile, which is used only for business purposes, was damaged in a wreck. At the date of the wreck, the fair market value of the automobile was $12,000, and its adjusted basis was $9,000. After the wreck, the value of the automobile was appraised at $4,000. K's loss deduction is $8,000 (the lesser of adjusted basis or the decrease in fair market value). The $8,000 loss is a deduction for AGI. □

The deduction for the loss of property that is part business and part personal must be computed separately for the business portion and the personal portion.

Any insurance recovery reduces the loss for business, production of income, and personal use losses. In fact, a taxpayer may realize a gain if the insurance proceeds exceed the amount of the loss. Chapter 17 discusses the treatment of net gains and losses on business property and property held for the production of income.

A taxpayer will not be permitted to deduct a casualty loss for damage to insured personal use property unless he or she files a timely insurance claim with respect to the damage to the property. This rule applies to the extent that any insurance policy provides for full or partial reimbursement for the loss.[21]

The amount of the loss for personal use property must be further reduced by a $100 per event floor and a 10 percent of AGI aggregate floor.[22] The $100 floor applies separately to each casualty and applies to the entire loss from each casualty (e.g., if a storm damages both a taxpayer's residence and auto-

---

21. § 165(h)(4)(E).

22. § 165(c)(3).

mobile, only $100 is subtracted from the total amount of the loss). The losses are then added together, and the total is reduced by 10 percent of the taxpayer's adjusted gross income. The resulting loss is the taxpayer's itemized deduction for casualty and theft losses.

EXAMPLE 15

G, who had AGI of $30,000, was involved in a motorcycle accident. His motorcycle, which had a fair market value of $12,000 and a basis of $9,000, was completely destroyed. He received $5,000 from his insurance company. G's casualty loss deduction is $900 [$9,000 basis — $5,000 insurance — $100 floor — $3,000 (.10 × $30,000 AGI)]. The $900 casualty loss is an itemized deduction (from AGI). □

The rules for computing loss deductions where there are multiple losses are explained in Examples 16 and 17.

EXAMPLE 16

During the year, T had the following losses:

Asset	Adjusted Basis	Fair Market Value of Asset Before the Casualty	After the Casualty	Insurance Recovery
A	$900	$200	$ -0-	$400
B	300	800	250	100

Assets A and B were used in T's business at the time of the casualty. The following losses are allowed:

Asset A: $500. The complete destruction of a business asset results in a deduction of the adjusted basis of the property (reduced by any insurance recovery) regardless of the asset's fair market value.

Asset B: $200. The partial destruction of a business (or personal) asset results in a deduction equal to the lesser of the adjusted basis ($300) or the loss in value ($550), reduced by any insurance recovery ($100).

Both Asset A and Asset B losses are deductions for adjusted gross income. The $100 floor and the 10% of AGI floor do not apply, because the assets are business assets. □

EXAMPLE 17

During the year, T had adjusted gross income of $20,000 and the following separate casualty losses:

Asset	Adjusted Basis	Fair Market Value of Asset		Insurance Recovery
		Before the Casualty	After the Casualty	
A	$ 900	$ 600	$ -0-	$200
B	2,500	4,000	1,000	-0-
C	800	400	100	250

Assets A, B, and C were held for personal use, and the losses to these three assets are from three different casualties. The computation of the loss to each asset is as follows:

Asset A: $300. The lesser of the adjusted basis of $900 or the $600 loss in value, reduced by the insurance recovery of $200, minus the $100 floor.

Asset B: $2,400. The lesser of the adjusted basis of $2,500 or the $3,000 loss in value, minus the $100 floor.

Asset C: $ -0-. The lesser of the adjusted basis of $800 or the $300 loss in value, reduced by the insurance recovery of $250, minus the $100 floor.

T's itemized casualty loss deduction for the year is $700:

Asset A loss	$ 300
Asset B loss	2,400
Asset C loss	-0-
Total loss	$2,700
Less: 10% of AGI (10% × $20,000)	(2,000)
Itemized casualty loss deduction	$ 700

□

When a nonbusiness casualty loss is spread between two taxable years because of the "reasonable prospect of recovery" doctrine, the loss in the second year is not reduced by the $100 floor, because this floor is imposed per event and has already reduced the amount of the loss in the first year. However, the loss in the second year is still subject to the 10 percent floor based on the taxpayer's second year adjusted gross income (refer to Example 12).

Taxpayers who suffer qualified disaster area losses can elect to deduct such losses in the year preceding the year of occurrence. The disaster loss will be treated as having occurred in the preceding taxable year, and hence, the 10 percent of AGI floor will be determined by using the adjusted gross income of the year for which the deduction is claimed.[23]

23.   § 165(i).

Generally, an appraisal before and after the casualty is needed to measure the amount of the loss. However, the cost of repairs to the damaged property is acceptable as a method of establishing the loss in value provided the following criteria are met:

- The repairs are necessary to restore the property to its condition immediately before the casualty.

- The amount spent for such repairs is not excessive.

- The repairs do not extend beyond the damage suffered.

- The value of the property after the repairs does not, as a result of the repairs, exceed the value of the property immediately before the casualty.[24]

Statutory Framework for Deducting Losses of Individuals

Casualty and theft losses incurred by an individual in connection with a trade or business are deductible *for* adjusted gross income.[25] These losses are not subject to the $100 per event and the 10 percent of AGI limitations.

Losses incurred by an individual in a transaction entered into for profit are not subject to the $100 per event and the 10 percent of AGI limitations. If these losses are attributable to rents or royalties, the deduction is *for* AGI.[26] However, if these losses are not connected with property held for the production of rents and royalties, they are deductions *from* AGI. More specifically, these losses are classified as other miscellaneous itemized deductions. An example of this type of loss would be a theft of a security. The aggregate of certain miscellaneous itemized deductions is subject to a 2 percent of AGI floor (explained in chapter 10).

Casualty and theft losses attributable to personal use property are subject to the $100 per event and 10 percent of AGI limitations. These losses are itemized deductions, but they are not subject to the 2 percent of AGI floor.[27]

Casualty Gains and Losses

If a taxpayer has personal casualty and theft gains as well as losses, a special set of rules applies for determining the tax consequences. The term "personal casualty gain" means the recognized gain from a casualty or theft. A *personal casualty loss* for this purpose is a casualty or theft loss after the application of the $100 floor. A taxpayer who has both gains and losses for the taxable year must first net (offset) the personal casualty gains and personal casualty losses. If the gains exceed the losses, the gains and losses will be treated as gains and losses from the sale of capital assets. The capital gains and losses will be short term or long term, depending on the period the taxpayer held each of the assets.

EXAMPLE 18   During the year, T had the following casualty gains and losses (after deducting the $100 floor):

---

24. Reg. § 1.165–7(a)(2)(ii).
25. § 62(a)(1).

26. § 62(a)(4).
27. § 67(b)(3).

Asset	Holding Period	Gain or (Loss)
A	Three months	($ 300)
B	Three years	(2,400)
C	Two years	3,200

T would compute the tax consequences as follows:

Personal casualty gain	$3,200
Personal casualty loss ($300 + $2,400)	(2,700)
Net personal casualty gain	$ 500

T would treat all of the gains and losses as capital gains and losses and would have the following:

Short-term capital loss (Asset A)	$ 300
Long-term capital loss (Asset B)	2,400
Long-term capital gain (Asset C)	3,200

☐

If personal casualty losses exceed personal casualty gains, all gains and losses are treated as ordinary items. The gains—and the losses to the extent of gains—will be treated as ordinary income and ordinary loss in computing adjusted gross income. Losses in excess of gains are deducted as itemized deductions to the extent such losses exceed 10 percent of adjusted gross income.[28]

EXAMPLE 19

During the year, T had adjusted gross income of $20,000 and the following casualty gain and loss (after deducting the $100 floor):

Asset	Holding Period	Gain or (Loss)
A	Three years	($2,700)
B	Four months	200

T would compute the tax consequences as follows:

28. § 165(h).

Personal casualty loss	($2,700)
Personal casualty gain	200
Net personal casualty loss	($2,500)

T would treat the gain and the loss as ordinary items. The $200 gain and $200 of the loss would be included in computing adjusted gross income. T's itemized deduction for casualty losses would be computed as follows:

Casualty loss in excess of gain ($2,700 − $200)	$ 2,500
Less: 10% of AGI (10% × $20,000)	(2,000)
Itemized deduction	$ 500

☐

CONCEPT SUMMARY 8–3

Casualty Gains and Losses

	Business Use or Production of Income Property	Personal Use Property
Event creating the loss	Any event.	Casualty or theft loss.
Amount	The lesser of the decline in fair market value or the adjusted basis, but always the adjusted basis if the property is totally destroyed.	The lesser of the decline in fair market value or the adjusted basis.
Insurance	Insurance proceeds received reduce the amount of the loss.	Insurance proceeds received (or for which there is an unfiled claim) reduce the amount of the loss.
$100 floor	Not applicable.	Applicable per event.
Gains and losses	Gains and losses are netted (see detailed discussion in chapter 17).	Personal casualty and theft gains and losses are netted.
Gains exceeding losses		The gains and losses are treated as gains and losses from the sale of capital assets.

	Business Use or Production of Income Property	Personal Use Property
Losses exceeding gains		The gains—and the losses to the extent of gains—are treated as ordinary items in computing adjusted gross income. The losses in excess of gains, to the extent they exceed 10% of adjusted gross income, are itemized deductions.

RESEARCH AND EXPERIMENTAL EXPENDITURES

Section 174 sets forth the treatment accorded to "research and experimental expenditures." The Regulations define research and experimental expenditures as follows:

> . . .all such costs incident to the development of an experimental or pilot model, a plant process, a product, a formula, an invention, or similar property, and the improvement of already existing property of the type mentioned. The term does not include expenditures such as those for the ordinary testing or inspection of materials or products for quality control or those for efficiency surveys, management studies, consumer surveys, advertising, or promotions.[29]

Expenses in connection with the acquisition or improvement of land or depreciable property are not research and experimental expenditures. Rather, they increase the basis of the land or depreciable property. However, depreciation on a building used for research may be a research and experimental expense.

The law permits three alternatives for the handling of research and experimental expenditures. These expenditures may be expensed in the year paid or incurred, or they may be deferred and amortized. If neither of these two methods is elected, the research and experimental costs must be capitalized. If the costs are capitalized, a deduction may not be available until the research project is abandoned or is deemed worthless. Since many products resulting from research projects do not have a definite and limited useful life, a taxpayer should ordinarily elect to write off the expenditures immediately or to defer and amortize them. It is generally preferable to elect an immediate write-off of the research expenditures because of the time value of the tax deduction.

The law also provides for a research activities credit. The credit amounts to 20 percent of certain research and experimental expenditures made before 1989.[30] (The credit is discussed more fully in chapter 13.)

---

29. Reg. § 1.174–2(a)(1).   30. § 41.

Expense Method

A taxpayer can elect to expense all of the research and experimental expenditures incurred in the current year and all subsequent years. The consent of the IRS is not required if the method is adopted for the first taxable year in which such expenditures were paid or incurred. Once such an election is made, the taxpayer must continue to expense all qualifying expenditures unless a request for a change is made to the IRS. In certain instances, a taxpayer may incur research and experimental expenditures before actually engaging in any trade or business activity. In such instances, the Supreme Court has applied a liberal standard of deductibility and permitted a deduction in the year of incurrence.[31]

Deferral and Amortization Method

The deferral and amortization method is allowed for the treatment of research and experimental expenditures if the taxpayer makes an election.[32] Under the election, research and experimental expenditures are amortized ratably over a period of not less than 60 months. A deduction is allowed beginning with the month in which the taxpayer first realizes benefits from the experimental expenditure. The election is binding, and a change requires permission from the IRS.

The option to treat research and experimental expenditures as deferred expense is usually employed when a company does not have sufficient income to offset the research and experimental expenses. Rather than create net operating loss carryovers that might not be utilized because of the 15-year limitation on such carryovers, the deferral and amortization method may be used.

NET OPERATING LOSSES

The requirement that every taxpayer file an annual income tax return (whether on a calendar year or a fiscal year) may result in certain inequities for taxpayers who experience cyclical patterns of income or expense. Inequities result from the application of a progressive rate structure to amounts of taxable income determined on an annual basis. A net operating loss in a particular tax year would produce no tax benefit if the Code did not include provisions for the carryback and carryforward of such losses to profitable years.

EXAMPLE 20

J has a business that realizes the following taxable income or loss over a five-year period: 19X1, $50,000; 19X2, ($30,000); 19X3, $100,000; 19X4, ($200,000); and 19X5, $380,000. She is married and files a joint return. P, on the other hand, has a taxable income pattern of $60,000 every year. He, too, is married and files a joint return. Note that both J and P have total taxable income of $300,000 over the five-year period. Assume there is no

31. *Snow v. Comm.*, 74–1 USTC ¶9432, 33 AFTR2d 74–1251, 94 S.Ct. 1876 (USSC, 1974).

32. § 174(b)(2).

provision for carryover of net operating losses. A comparison of their five-year tax bills follows:

Year	J's Tax	P's Tax
1	$ 9,977	$12,777
2	-0-	12,777
3	25,234	12,777
4	-0-	12,777
5	107,520	12,777
	$142,731	$63,885

The computation of tax is made without regard to any net operating loss benefit. Rates applicable to 1989 are used to compute the tax.

Even though J and P realized the same total income ($300,000) over the five-year period, J had to pay taxes of $142,731, while P paid taxes of $63,885. □

To provide partial relief from this inequitable tax treatment, a deduction is allowed for net operating losses.[33] This provision permits the offset of net operating losses for any one year against taxable income of other years. A net operating loss is intended as a relief provision for business income and losses. Thus, only losses from the operation of a trade or business (or profession), casualty and theft losses, or losses from the confiscation of a business by a foreign government can create a net operating loss. In other words, a salaried individual with itemized deductions and personal exemptions in excess of income is not permitted to deduct such excess amounts as a net operating loss. On the other hand, a personal casualty loss is treated as a business loss and can therefore create (or increase) a net operating loss for a salaried individual.

Carryback and Carryover Periods

A net operating loss must be applied initially to the three taxable years preceding the year of the loss (unless an election is made not to carry the loss back at all). It is carried first to the third prior year, then to the second prior year, then to the immediately preceding tax year (or until used up). If the loss is not fully used in the carryback period, it must be carried forward to the first year after the loss year, and then forward to the second, third, etc., year after the loss year. The carryover period is 15 years. If a loss is sustained in 1989, it is used in this order: 1986, 1987, 1988, 1990 through 2004.

A taxpayer can irrevocably elect not to carry back a net operating loss to any of the three prior years. In such case, the loss is available as a carryover for 15 years. A taxpayer would make the election if it is to his or her tax advantage. For example, a taxpayer might be in a low marginal tax bracket in the carryback years but expect to be in a high marginal tax bracket in future

---

33. § 172.

years. Therefore, it would be to the taxpayer's advantage to use the net operating loss to offset income in years when the tax rate is high rather than use it when the tax rate is relatively low.

If the loss is being carried to a preceding year, an amended return is filed on Form 1040X or a quick refund claim is filed on Form 1045. In any case, a refund of taxes previously paid is requested. When the loss is carried forward, the current return shows a net operating loss deduction for the prior year's loss.

Where there are net operating losses in two or more years, the rule is always to use the earliest year's loss first until it is completely absorbed. The later years' losses can then be used until they also are absorbed or lost. Thus, one year's return could show net operating loss carryovers from two or more years. Each loss is computed and applied separately.

Computation of the Net Operating Loss

Since the net operating loss provisions apply solely to business-related losses, certain adjustments must be made to reflect a taxpayer's "economic" loss. The required adjustments for corporate taxpayers are usually insignificant, because a corporation's tax loss is generally similar to its economic loss. However, in computing taxable income, individual taxpayers are allowed deductions for such items as personal and dependency exemptions and itemized deductions that do not reflect actual business-related economic losses.

To arrive at the net operating loss (economic loss) for an individual, taxable income must be adjusted by adding back the following items: [34]

1. No deduction is allowed for personal and dependency exemptions. These amounts do not reflect economic, or business, outlays and hence must be added back.

2. The net operating loss carryover or carryback from another year is not allowed in the computation of the current year's net operating loss.

3. Capital losses and nonbusiness deductions are limited in determining the current year's net operating loss. These limits are as follows:

    a. The excess of nonbusiness capital losses over nonbusiness capital gains must be added back.

    b. The excess of nonbusiness deductions over the sum of nonbusiness income and *net* nonbusiness capital gains must be added back. Net nonbusiness capital gains are the excess of nonbusiness capital gains over nonbusiness capital losses. Nonbusiness income includes such passive items as dividends and interest. It does not include such items as salaries, rents, and gains and losses on the sale or exchange of business assets. Nonbusiness deductions are total itemized deductions less personal casualty losses.

        A taxpayer who does not itemize deductions computes the excess of nonbusiness deductions over nonbusiness income by substituting the taxpayer's standard deduction for total itemized deductions.

---

34. § 172(d); Reg. § 1.172–3(a).

    c.   The excess of business capital losses over the sum of business capital gains and the excess of nonbusiness income and net nonbusiness capital gains over nonbusiness deductions must be added back.

    d.   The add-back for net nonbusiness capital losses and excess business capital losses does not include net capital losses not included in the current year computation of taxable income because of the capital loss limitation provisions (discussed in chapter 16).

The capital loss and nonbusiness deduction limits are illustrated in Examples 21 through 24.

EXAMPLE 21

For 1989, taxpayer and spouse have $6,000 of nonbusiness capital losses and $4,000 of nonbusiness capital gains. They must add back $2,000 ($6,000 − $4,000) in determining the excess of nonbusiness capital losses over nonbusiness capital gains. □

EXAMPLE 22

For 1989, taxpayer and spouse have $2,000 of nonbusiness capital gains, $1,000 of nonbusiness capital losses, $2,000 of interest income, and no itemized deductions. They must add back $2,000 ($5,000 standard deduction − [$2,000 interest income + $1,000 ($2,000 − $1,000) net nonbusiness capital gains]). Note that, in this example, there is no excess of nonbusiness capital losses over nonbusiness capital gains. □

EXAMPLE 23

For 1989, taxpayer and spouse have $2,000 of nonbusiness capital gains, $1,000 of nonbusiness capital losses, $6,000 of interest income, $5,500 of itemized deductions (none of which are personal casualty losses), $5,000 of business capital losses, and $1,000 of business capital gains. They must add back $2,500 ($5,000 business capital losses − [$1,000 business capital gains + ($6,000 nonbusiness income + $1,000 net nonbusiness capital gains − $5,500 nonbusiness deductions)]). Note that, in this example there is no excess of nonbusiness capital losses over nonbusiness capital gains, nor is there an excess of nonbusiness deductions over the sum of nonbusiness income and net nonbusiness capital gains. □

EXAMPLE 24

For 1989, taxpayer and spouse have $2,000 of nonbusiness capital gains, $3,000 of nonbusiness capital losses, $6,000 of interest income, $7,000 of itemized deductions (none of which are personal casualty losses), $8,000 of business capital losses, and $4,000 of business capital gains. They must add back $1,000 ($7,000 − $6,000), the excess of nonbusiness deductions over nonbusiness income, and $3,000, the excess of combined capital losses. Because of the capital loss limitations, only $3,000 of the loss would have been used in computing taxable income for the year. □

Example 25 illustrates the computation of a net operating loss.

EXAMPLE 25   T began the operation of a retail store in 1988 and experienced a net operating loss of $185 for that year. T had no taxable income for 1985, 1986, or 1987. T is married, has no dependents, and files a joint return. For 1989, T and his wife had the following taxable income:

Gross income from the business	$67,000	
Less: Business expenses	71,000	($4,000)
Salary from a part-time job		875
Interest on savings account		525
Nonbusiness long-term capital gain		1,000
NOL carryover from 1988		(185)
Net loss on rental property		(100)
Adjusted gross income		($1,885)
Less: Itemized deductions		
Interest expense	$ 3,000	
Taxes	4,300	
Casualty loss	2,000	
Total itemized deductions		(9,300)
Exemptions (2 × $2,000)		(4,000)
Taxable income		($15,185)

T's net operating loss is computed as follows:

Taxable income				($15,185)
Add:				
Net operating loss from 1988			$ 185	
Personal exemptions (2)			4,000	
Excess of nonbusiness deductions over nonbusiness income				
Total itemized deductions		$ 9,300		
Less: Casualty loss		(2,000)		
		$ 7,300		
Less: Interest	$ 525			
Less: Long-term capital gain	1,000	(1,525)	5,775	9,960
Net operating loss				($ 5,225)

The economic loss can be thought of as follows:

Business loss	($4,000)
Rental loss	(100)
Casualty loss	(2,000)
Salary income	875
Net economic (operating) loss	($5,225)

□

CONCEPT SUMMARY 8-4

Computation of Net Operating Loss

Taxable income shown on the return
Add back:

1. Personal and dependency exemptions.

2. Net operating loss carryover or carryback from another year.

3. The excess of nonbusiness capital losses over nonbusiness capital gains.

4. The excess of nonbusiness deductions over the sum of nonbusiness income plus *net* nonbusiness capital gains.

5. The excess of business capital losses over the sum of business capital gains plus the excess of nonbusiness income and *net* nonbusiness capital gains over nonbusiness deductions. The add-back from the total of items 3 and 5 will not exceed $3,000 because of the capital loss limitation rules.

Equals the net operating loss.

Recomputation of Tax Liability for Year to Which Net Operating Loss Is Carried

When a net operating loss is carried back to a nonloss year, the taxable income and income tax for the carryback year must be recomputed by including the net operating loss as a deduction for adjusted gross income. Several deductions (such as medical expenses) are based on the amount of adjusted gross income. When a net operating loss is carried back, all such deductions except the charitable contributions deduction must be recomputed on the basis of the new adjusted gross income after the net operating loss has been applied. The deduction for charitable contributions would be determined without regard to any net operating loss carryback but with regard to any other modification affecting adjusted gross income. Furthermore, any tax credits limited by or based upon the tax must be recomputed, based on the recomputed tax.

EXAMPLE 26	J sustained a net operating loss of $11,000 in 1990. Because J had no taxable income in 1987 or 1988, the loss is carried back to 1989. For 1989, his income tax return was as follows:

Salary income		$10,000
Dividends		2,000
Net long-term capital gain		1,400
Adjusted gross income		$13,400
Itemized deductions		
Charitable contributions	$1,700	
Interest	2,800	
Taxes	1,420	(5,920)
Exemptions (2 × $2,000)		(4,000)
Taxable income		$ 3,480
Tax (married filing jointly)		$ 522

J's new tax liability for the carryback year is computed as follows:

Adjusted gross income		$ 13,400
Less: Net operating loss		(11,000)
Recomputed adjusted gross income		$ 2,400
Itemized deductions		
Charitable contributions	$1,700	
Interest	2,800	
Taxes	1,420	(5,920)
Exemptions (2 × $2,000)		(4,000)
Recomputed taxable income		$ (7,520)
Tax		$ -0-
Tax originally paid and refund claim		$ 522

☐

After computing the amount of refund claim for the initial carryback year, it is then necessary to determine the extent to which any loss remains to carry over to future years. The amount of this carryover loss is the excess of the net operating loss over the taxable income of the year to which the loss is being applied. However, the taxable income of the year to which the loss is being applied must be determined with the following modifications:

- No deduction is allowed for excess capital losses over capital gains.

- No deduction is allowed for the 60 percent long-term capital gains deduction (applicable to pre–1987 years).

- No deduction is allowed for the net operating loss that is being carried back. However, deductions are allowed for net operating losses occurring before the loss year.

- Any deductions claimed that are based on or limited by adjusted gross income must be determined after making the preceding adjustments. However, charitable contributions do not take into account any net operating loss carryback.

- No deduction is allowed for exemptions.

EXAMPLE 27

Referring to the facts in Example 26, the net operating loss carryover from 1989 available for future years would be ($3,520), computed as follows:

Salary income		$10,000
Dividends		2,000
Net long-term capital gain		1,400
Adjusted gross income		$13,400
Itemized deductions		
Charitable contributions	$1,700	
Interest	2,800	
Taxes	1,420	(5,920)
Exemptions (not allowed)		–0–
Modified taxable income		$ 7,480
Net operating loss		($11,000)
Modified taxable income		7,480
Net operating loss to carry forward		($ 3,520)

Since the ending figure is negative, it represents the net operating loss remaining to carry over to 1991 or later years. □

TAX PLANNING CONSIDERATIONS

Documentation of Related-Taxpayer Loans, Casualty Losses, and Theft Losses

Since non-bona fide loans between related taxpayers may be treated as gifts, adequate documentation is needed to substantiate a bad debt deduction if the loan subsequently becomes worthless. Documentation should include proper execution of the note (legal form) and the establishment of a bona fide purpose for the loan. In addition, it is desirable to stipulate a reasonable rate of interest and a fixed maturity date.

Since a theft loss is not permitted for misplaced items, a loss should be documented by a police report and evidence of the value of the property (e.g., appraisals, pictures of the property, newspaper clippings). Similar documentation of the value of property should be provided to support a casualty loss deduction, because the amount of loss is measured by the decline in fair market value of the property.

Casualty loss deductions must be reported on Form 4684 (see Appendix B).

Small Business Stock

Because § 1244 limits the amount of loss classified as ordinary loss on a yearly basis, a taxpayer might maximize the benefits of § 1244 by selling the stock in more than one taxable year. The result could be that the losses in any one taxable year would not exceed the § 1244 limits on ordinary loss.

Casualty Losses

A special election is available for taxpayers who sustain casualty losses in an area designated by the President as a disaster area. This election affects only the timing, not the calculation, of the deduction. The deduction can be taken in the year before the year in which the loss occurred. Thus, an individual can take the deduction on the 1988 return for a loss occurring between January 1 and December 31, 1989. The benefit, of course, is a faster refund (or reduction in tax). It will also be advantageous to carry the loss back if the taxpayer's tax rate in the carryback year is higher than the tax rate in the year of the loss.

To find out if an event qualifies as a disaster area loss, one can look in any of the major tax services or in the Weekly Compilation of Presidential Documents or the Internal Revenue Bulletin.

Net Operating Losses

In certain instances, it may be advisable for a taxpayer to elect not to carry back a net operating loss. For an individual, the benefits from the loss carryback could be scaled down or lost due to the economic adjustments that must be made to taxable income for the year to which the loss is carried. For example, a taxpayer should attempt to minimize the number of taxable years to which a net operating loss is carried. The more years to which the net operating loss is applied, the more lost benefits from items such as exemptions and long-term capital gains.

The election to not carry back the loss might also be advantageous if there is a disparity in marginal tax rates applicable to different tax years.

EXAMPLE 28

T sustained a net operating loss of $10,000 in Year 4. His marginal tax bracket in Year 1 was 15%. In Year 5, however, he expects his bracket to be 28% due to a large profit he will make on a business deal. If T carries his loss back, his refund will be $1,500 (i.e., 15% × $10,000). If he elects not to carry it back to Year 1 but chooses, instead, to carry it forward, his savings will be $2,800 (28% × $10,000). Even considering the time value of an immediate tax refund, T appears to be better off by using the carryover approach. □

PROBLEM MATERIALS

Discussion Questions

1. Dr. T, an individual, cash basis taxpayer, is engaged in the general practice of dentistry. Dr. T performed extensive bridge and crown work on Mr. S, for which he charged $3,500 ($2,500 for services and $1,000 for materials and lab work). Since Mr. S never paid the bill and has left for parts unknown, Dr. T feels that he is entitled to a bad debt deduction of $3,500. Comment on Dr. T's tax position on this matter.

2. Under what circumstances may a taxpayer take a deduction for partial worthlessness of a bad debt?

3. Discuss the difference between business and nonbusiness bad debts. How is the distinction determined? How is each treated on the return?

4. What factors are to be considered in determining whether a bad debt arising from a loan between related parties is, in fact, a bad debt?

5. Discuss a taxpayer's options as to the tax treatment of a loss incurred on a deposit in a qualified financial institution. Also note the consequences of each option.

6. Discuss the tax treatment of any remaining balance in a reserve for bad debts account.

7. Discuss whether a bond that is worthless is a worthless security or a bad debt.

8. Compare the tax treatment of losses on § 1244 stock with the usual treatment of losses on capital stock.

9. What acts of God give rise to a casualty loss? Which ones do not? Discuss.

10. How are thefts treated differently from acts of God for casualty loss purposes?

11. How is a personal casualty loss computed? A business casualty loss? What effect do insurance proceeds have on both types of losses?

12. When casualty losses exceed casualty gains, the amount of the casualty loss subject to the 10% of AGI floor is only the casualty loss in excess of casualty gains. Discuss the significance of netting losses against gains in this manner rather than having the entire casualty loss subject to the 10% of AGI floor.

13. Discuss the use of repair costs as a measure for the amount of a casualty loss.

14. Discuss whether an individual taxpayer may take a deduction for a loss for termite damage to a building used in the taxpayer's business.

15. What is a disaster area loss? Why might a taxpayer benefit from making the disaster area loss election?

16. Discuss the tax consequences of not making an insurance claim when insured personal use property is subject to a casualty or theft loss.

17. May an individual take a deduction for a loss on business property if it is not clear whether the property was stolen or simply misplaced?

18. Is it generally advantageous for a taxpayer to spread a casualty loss between two years under the reasonable prospect of recovery doctrine?

19. Discuss whether a loss in connection with a transaction entered into for profit is a deduction *for* adjusted gross income or *from* adjusted gross income.

20. Why do most taxpayers elect to write off research and experimental expenditures rather than capitalize and amortize such amounts? Are there some situations in which the capitalization approach would be preferable?

21. If a business does not elect to expense or amortize research expenditures, what is the possibility of writing off such expenditures?

22. Why can the sale of small business stock (§ 1244 stock) at a loss create or increase a net operating loss?

23. What is the rationale behind the net operating loss deduction? Who benefits from this provision?

24. Why are such items as nonbusiness deductions and personal and dependency exemptions not allowed in computing the net operating loss?

25. Discuss the periods to which net operating losses may be carried. Can the taxpayer elect not to carry a net operating loss back to any one year? What possible benefit might result from not carrying a loss back to a particular year?

26. Discuss the recomputation of a tax liability for the year to which a net operating loss is applied.

27. Discuss the treatment of nonbusiness capital gains in excess of nonbusiness capital losses in the computation of a net operating loss.

Problems

28. M loaned T $10,000 on April 1, 1988. In 1989 T filed for bankruptcy. At that time, it was revealed that T's creditors could expect to receive 60¢ on the dollar. In February 1990, final settlement was made and M received $3,000. How much loss can M deduct and in which year? How is it treated on M's return?

29. X Company had employed the allowance method for computing its bad debts for tax purposes through the year 1986. At the beginning of 1989, the credit balance in the allowance account was $120,000. During 1989, X identified $70,000 of accounts as worthless. Determine the tax consequences to X associated with the allowance for bad debts and the bad debt expense for 1989.

30. T, a single taxpayer, bought stocks for $65,000 on December 27, 1988. On May 15, 1989, the company went bankrupt and the stock became worthless.

    a. Does the taxpayer have a deduction?

    b. When?

    c. What is the character of the loss?

    d. If the stock qualified as § 1244 stock, when is the taxpayer allowed the deduction, what is the amount of the loss, and what is the character of the loss?

31. A, a single taxpayer, had the following items for the current year:

    • A business bad debt of $2,000.

    • A nonbusiness bad debt of $5,000.

    • Stock acquired on November 15 of last year for $10,000 that became worthless on March 5 of the current year.

    • Loss of $20,000 on the sale of § 1244 stock that A acquired two years ago for $50,000.

    • Salary of $70,000.

    Determine A's adjusted gross income for the current year.

32. When J returned from a vacation in Hawaii on November 8, 1989, she discovered that a burglar had stolen her silver, stereo, and color television. In the process of removing these items, the burglar damaged some furniture that originally cost $1,400. J's silver cost $3,640 and was valued at $6,500; the stereo system cost $8,400 and was valued at $6,200; the television cost $840 and was worth $560. J filed a claim with her insurance company and was reimbursed in the following amounts on December 20, 1989:

Silver	$2,800
Stereo	5,600
Television	490

    The insurance company disputed the reimbursement claimed by J for the damaged furniture, but she protested and was finally paid $280 on January 30, 1990. The repairs to the furniture totaled $448. J's adjusted gross income for 1989 was $12,000, and it was $15,000 for 1990. How much can J claim as a casualty loss? In which year?

33. K owned three acres of land in Kansas upon which he had his home, two rental houses, an apartment building, and his construction company. A tornado hit the area and destroyed one of the rental houses, damaged the apartment building, and destroyed some of K's construction equipment. The tenant of K's other rental house moved out for fear of another tornado, and K lost $450 in rent. Other losses were as follows:

Item	Adjusted Basis	FMV Before	FMV After	Insurance Proceeds
Rental house #1	$ 34,500	$ 43,500	$ -0-	$30,000
Apartment building	100,000	225,000	180,000	31,500
Equipment	90,000	112,500	-0-	75,000

   a. How much is K's casualty loss before applying any limitation?

   b. Assuming the loss occurred on March 3, 1990, and that the area was designated by the President as a disaster area, what options are open to K with respect to the timing of the loss deduction?

34. On January 7 of the current year, T dropped off to sleep while driving home from a business trip. Luckily, she was only slightly injured in the resulting accident, but her car was completely destroyed.

T had purchased the car new two years ago and had driven it 64,000 miles at the time of the accident. Of these miles, 28,000 were business miles; the remaining miles were personal miles. The car cost $7,200 new. T has taken $1,985 of depreciation for the business use of the car. She carried $1,000 deductible collision insurance on the car. Her insurance company settled her claim by paying her $2,400 for the car (fair market value before the wreck was $3,400).

After T's release from the hospital the day after the accident, she could not find her purse (cost $65, fair replacement value $30) or its contents, which included $350 in cash and $500 in traveler's checks. The traveler's checks were replaced by the issuing company. She also was unable to locate the stone from her diamond engagement ring. The stone cost her husband $2,500 when purchased nine years ago and was worth $6,400 at the time of the loss.

   a. Determine the amount of T's deductible loss *for* adjusted gross income.

   b. Determine the amount of the loss deductible *from* adjusted gross income, assuming adjusted gross income for the year is $25,000.

35. On June 15, 1989, T was involved in an accident with his personal automobile. T had purchased the car new two years ago for $14,000. At the time of the accident, the car was worth $10,000. After the accident, the car was appraised at $3,000. T had an insurance policy that had a 20% deductible clause. Because T was afraid that the policy would be cancelled, he made no claim against the insurance policy for the damages to the car.

On September 17, 1989, T was involved in an accident with his business automobile. The automobile had a fair market value of $12,000 before the accident, and it was worthless after the accident. T had a basis in the car of $15,000 at the time of the accident. This car was covered by an insurance policy that had a 10 percent deductible clause. T made no claim against this policy. T earned a salary of $50,000 and had other itemized deductions of $8,000 for the year. Determine taxable income for T and his wife, who file a joint return for 1989.

36. In 1988, W deposited $10,000 with a commercial bank. On September 1, 1989, W was notified that the bank was insolvent and that he would receive only 20% of his deposit. W had adjusted gross income of $30,000 for 1989. Determine W's possible deductions with respect to his lost deposit.

37. H and W, who file a joint return, had the following items for their 1989 tax return:

    - H's salary—$18,000.

    - W's salary—$20,000.

    - Interest income from City of New York bonds—$4,000.

    - Gross dividends from domestic corporations—$800.

    - Many years ago, H loaned $4,000 to a friend. The friend has never repaid any of the amount, and now that the friend has filed for bankruptcy, there is no prospect of recovering any of the amount.

    - During the year, a fire completely destroyed H and W's personal residence and an antique car used by W for personal use. The home was uninsured at the time of the fire. It was worth $150,000, with H and W having a basis in the home of $80,000. The car was insured for its fair market value, and H and W received $10,000. Their basis in the car was $4,000.

    - H and W have other miscellaneous deductions (subject to the 2% of AGI floor) of $5,000.

    a. What is H and W's taxable income for 1989?

    b. What is H and W's net operating loss for 1989?

38. During 1989, H and W, married with three dependent children, had the following items of income and expense:

Gross receipts from business	$85,000
Business expenses	97,000
W's salary	13,000
Gain on sale of stock purchased three years ago	2,000
Interest from bank account	1,000

    a. Determine the amount of H and W's 1989 taxable income.

    b. Determine the amount of the 1989 net operating loss.

39. G, who is married and files a joint return, owns a grocery store. In 1989, his gross sales were $286,000 and operating expenses were $310,000. Other items on his 1989 return were as follows:

Nonbusiness capital gains (short-term)	$10,000
Nonbusiness capital losses (long-term)	9,000
Itemized deductions	10,000
Ordinary nonbusiness income	4,000
Salary from part-time job	10,000

During the years 1986 and 1987, G had no taxable income. In 1988, G had taxable income of $25,300 computed as follows:

Net business income		$60,000
Interest income		2,000
Adjusted gross income		$62,000
Less: Itemized deductions		
Charitable contributions of $40,000, limited to 50% of AGI	$31,000	
Medical expenses of $6,550, limited to the amount in excess of 7.5% of AGI ($6,550–$4,650)	1,900	
Total itemized deductions		(32,900)
Exemptions (2 × $1,950)		(3,900)
Taxable income		$25,200

a. What is G's 1989 net operating loss?

b. Determine G's recomputed taxable income for 1988.

40. During 1989 T, married with one dependent child, had the following items of income, expense, and loss to report:

Gross receipts from business	$250,000
Business expenses	274,000
Interest received from State of Utah bonds	8,000
Interest received from bank savings account	2,000
Wife's salary from part-time work	6,000
Long-term capital gain on sale of stock held as an investment	9,000
Short-term capital loss on sale of State of Utah bonds	8,000
Itemized deductions	2,700

a. Assuming T files a joint return, what is T's taxable income for 1989?

b. What is the amount of T's net operating loss for 1989?

41. Assume that in addition to the information in Problem 40, T had no taxable income for the years 1986 and 1987 and $5,850 of taxable income for 1988 computed as follows:

Salary		$25,000
Capital loss		(1,000)
Adjusted gross income		$24,000
Less: Itemized deductions		
Charitable contributions of $20,000, limited to 50% of AGI	$12,000	
Medical expenses of $2,100, limited to the amount in excess of 7.5% of AGI ($2,100–$1,800)	300	
Total itemized deductions		(12,300)
Exemptions (3 × $1,950)		(5,850)
Taxable income		$ 5,850

Determine the amount of T's 1989 net operating loss to be carried forward to 1990.

42. H is married, has two dependent children, and files jointly. He had the following income and deductions for 1989:

Salary	$36,000
Dividends from domestic corporations	600
Interest received from bank savings account	6,000
1988 net operating loss carried to 1989	6,000
Itemized deductions	5,000
Business capital gains	7,000
Business capital losses	5,000

In addition to the above information, H's uninsured personal residence was damaged by fire during the year. The home had a value of $240,000 before the fire, but it was worth only $80,000 after the fire. H's basis in the home was $200,000.

a. What is H's taxable income for 1989?

b. What is H's net operating loss for 1989?

43. S, single and age 32, had the following items for the tax year 1989:

- Salary of $40,000.
- Interest income from U.S. government bonds of $2,000.
- Dividends from a foreign corporation of $500.
- Sale of small business § 1244 stock on October 20, 1989, for $10,000. The stock had been acquired two years earlier for $65,000.
- Business bad debt of $3,000.
- Nonbusiness bad debt of $5,000.
- Sale of small business § 1244 stock on November 12, 1989, for $4,000. The stock had been acquired on June 5, 1989, for $800.
- Sale of common stock on December 4, 1989, for $40,000. The stock was acquired four years ago for $18,000.
- Total itemized deductions of $8,000.

Determine S's net operating loss for 1989.

44. W, single and age 38, had the following income and expense items in 1989:

Nonbusiness bad debt	$ 6,000
Business bad debt	2,000
Nonbusiness long-term capital gain	4,000
Nonbusiness short-term capital loss	3,000
Salary	40,000
Interest income	1,000

Determine W's adjusted gross income for 1989.

45. Assume that in addition to the information in Problem 44, W had the following items in 1989:

| Personal casualty gain on an asset held for four months | $10,000 |
| Personal casualty loss on an asset held for two years | 1,000 |

Determine W's adjusted gross income for 1989.

46. Assume that in addition to the information in Problems 44 and 45, W had the following items in 1989:

| Personal casualty loss on an asset held for five years | $50,000 |
| Interest expense on home mortgage | 3,000 |

Determine W's taxable income and net operating loss for 1989.

47. F Corporation, a manufacturing company, decided to develop a new line of fireworks. Because of the danger involved, F purchased an isolated parcel of land for $50,000 and constructed a building for $400,000. The building was to be used for research and experimentation in creating the new fireworks. The project was begun in 1989 with no projection as to the length of time for completion of the project. F Corporation had the following expenses in 1989 in connection with the project:

Salaries	$45,000
Utilities	3,000
Materials	12,000
Insurance	6,000
Cost of market survey study to determine profit potential for new fireworks line	5,000
Depreciation on the building	8,000

If F Corporation elects to expense research and experimental expenditures, determine the amount to be expensed in 1989.

Cumulative Problems

48. Ned Wilson, age 60, single, and retired, has no dependents. Ned lives at 231 Wander Lane, Salt Lake City, UT 84201. Ned's Social Security number is 985–12–3774. During 1989, Ned had the following income and expense items:

a. On January 27, 1988, Ned deposited $8,000 in a savings account at the ABC Financial Company. The savings account bore interest at 15%, compounded semiannually. Ned received a $600 interest payment on July 27, 1988, but received no interest payments thereafter. The finance company filed for bankruptcy on January 12, 1989. Ned received a $710 check in final settlement of his account from the bankruptcy trustee on December 20, 1989.

b. On January 1, 1989, a fire severely damaged a two-story building owned by Ned, who occupied the second story of the building as a residence and had recently opened a hardware store on the ground level. The following information is available with respect to the incident:

	Adjusted Basis	Fair Market Value	
		Before	After
Building	$64,000	$130,000	$50,000
Inventory	35,000	55,000	None
Store equipment	3,000	1,800	None
Home furnishings	12,600	6,000	800
Personal auto	8,900	7,800	7,600

Ned's fire insurance policy paid the following amounts for damages covered by:

Building	$50,000	(policy maximum)
Inventory	33,000	
Store equipment	None	
Home furnishings	1,000	(policy maximum)
Personal auto	None	

Assume all of the destroyed property was acquired on December 15, 1988.

c. On March 1, 1984, Ned loaned a neighboring businessman $15,000. The debtor died of a heart attack on June 21, 1989. Ned had no security and was unable to collect anything from the man's estate.

d. Ned received $72,000 of interest income from Salt Lake City Bank.

e. On March 2, 1989, Ned sold a piece of real estate he had been holding for speculation for $90,000. Ned had bought the land July 18, 1974, for $52,800.

f. Ned made a charitable contribution of $3,000.

g. Ned made four quarterly estimated tax payments of $5,000 each.

Part 1—Tax Computation

Compute Ned's 1989 Federal income tax payable (or refund due), assuming he deducts the lost deposit as a bad debt. Suggested software (if available): *WEST-TAX Planner* or *BNA Individual Income Tax Spreadsheet.*

Part 2—Tax Planning

Determine whether Ned should elect to treat the deposit in ABC Financial Company as a casualty loss rather than as a bad debt. Suggested software (if available): *WEST-TAX Planner* or *BNA Individual Income Tax Spreadsheet.*

49. Sam Sampson, age 55, is single and has no dependents. He is employed by Acme Corporation as an internal auditor. Sam lives at 2135 Rosebud Avenue, Denver, CO 23106. Sam's Social Security number is 222-33-7077. During 1989, Sam had the following income and expense items:

a. Sam sold X Corporation stock on January 21, 1989, for $6,000. He had purchased the stock on July 6, 1983, for $4,000.

b.   On September 1, 1989, Sam learned that Bart Smugg had been sentenced to jail in a foreign country for 20 years. Sam had loaned Bart $20,000 on June 1, 1988. The loan was due on June 1, 1989, and Sam has not been able to collect.

c.   On August 15, 1989, Sam's broker informed him that the Y Corporation stock he owned was completely worthless. Sam had purchased the stock on December 23, 1988, for $3,000.

d.   On April 15, 1989, Sam sold W Corporation stock to an unrelated party for $12,000. Sam's basis in the stock was $17,000. Sam had organized W Corporation on March 7, 1984, but the business never really got off the ground. The stock was § 1244 stock.

e.   Sam sold D Corporation stock on May 11, 1989, for $11,000. He had purchased the stock on November 21, 1980, for $3,000.

f.   Sam's salary from Acme Corporation was $60,000.

g.   Acme Corporation withheld Federal income tax of $13,000.

Compute Sam's 1989 Federal income tax payable (or refund due). Suggested software (if available): *WEST–TAX Planner* or *BNA Individual Income Tax Spreadsheet*.

50.   Jane Smith, age 40, is single and has no dependents. She is employed part-time as a legal secretary by Legal Services, Inc. She owns and operates Typing Services located near the campus of San Jose State University at 1986 Campus Drive. She is a cash basis taxpayer. Jane lives at 2020 Oakcrest Road, San Jose, CA 95134. Jane's Social Security number is 123–89–6666. Jane indicates that she wishes to designate $1 to the Presidential Election Campaign Fund. During 1988, Jane had the following income and expense items:

a. $10,000 salary from Legal Services, Inc.

b. $32,000 gross receipts from her typing services business.

c. $300 cash dividend from Buffalo Mining Company, a Canadian corporation.

d. $1,000 Christmas bonus from Legal Services, Inc.

e. $10,000 life insurance proceeds on the death of her sister.

f. $5,000 check given to her by her wealthy aunt.

g. $100 won in a bingo game.

h.   Expenses connected with the typing service:

Office rent	$5,000
Supplies	2,400
Utilities and telephone	3,680
Wages to part-time typists	4,000
Payroll taxes	600
Equipment rentals	3,000

i. $3,000 interest expense on a home mortgage (paid to San Jose Savings and Loan).

j. $5,000 fair market value of silverware stolen from her home by a burglar on October 12, 1988. Jane had paid $4,000 for the silverware on July 1, 1979. She was reimbursed $1,500 by her insurance company.

k. Jane had loaned $2,100 to a friend, Joan Jensen, on June 3, 1985. Joan declared bankruptcy on August 14, 1988, and was unable to repay the loan.

l. Legal Services, Inc., withheld Federal income tax of $400 and FICA tax of $670.

m. Jane made four quarterly estimated tax payments of $1,250 each.

Part 1—Tax Computation

Compute Jane Smith's 1988 Federal income tax payable (or refund due). If you use tax forms for your computations, you will need Forms 1040 and 4684 and Schedules A, C, D, and SE. Suggested software (if available): *WEST–TAX Preparer* for tax return solutions, *WEST–TAX Planner* or *BNA Individual Income Tax Spreadsheet* if tax solutions are not desired.

Part 2—Tax Planning

In 1989, Jane plans to quit her part-time job with Legal Services, Inc. Therefore, items a, d, and l will not recur in 1989. Jane plans to work full-time in her typing services business (refer to item b) and expects gross receipts of $50,000. She projects that all business expenses (refer to item h) will increase by 10%, except for office rent, which, under the terms of her lease, will remain the same as in 1988. Items e, f, g, j, and k will not recur in 1989. Items c and i will be approximately the same as in 1988.

Jane would like you to compute the minimum amount of estimated tax (refer to item m) she will have to pay for 1989 so that she will not have to pay any additional tax upon filing her 1989 Federal income tax return. Suggested software (if available): *WEST–TAX Planner* or *BNA Individual Income Tax Spreadsheet.*

Research Problems

Research Problem 1   A and B have a winter home in Park City, Utah, where they take frequent skiing vacations. In the spring of the current year, after an unusually wet winter and a record-setting thaw, a mudslide came through the subdivision. The slide damaged the garage of the home. If adequate support had been given to the hill, the slide would likely have been avoided. The mudslide also caused damage to neighboring homes, resulting in a drop in value of all the homes in the area. The damage to the garage was $10,000, and the home decreased in value by $20,000. How much, if any, of the damage and/or the loss in value can be deducted as a § 165 casualty loss?

Research Problem 2   Samuel Yancey made deductible alimony payments of $80,000 for the year. The payments were deductible for AGI under § 62(10). Because of the large deduction, Samuel has a negative taxable income for the year. Discuss the possibility of Samuel having a net operating loss for the year as a result of the alimony payment.

Research Problem 3   John Smith was engaged to be married to Nancy Brown. In contemplation of marriage, John deposited $10,000 in a bank account for Nancy, to be used after their marriage. Sometime thereafter, the engagement was broken off, and Nancy used the $10,000 for herself. John has attempted to collect the $10,000 from Nancy without success, and now Nancy has filed for bankruptcy. Discuss the possibility of John's claiming the $10,000 as a nonbusiness bad debt.

9

DEPRECIATION, COST RECOVERY, AMORTIZATION, AND DEPLETION

The Internal Revenue Code provides for a deduction for the consumption of the cost of an asset through depreciation, cost recovery, amortization, or depletion. Before discussing each cost consumption method, however, it is beneficial to review the difference between the classification of an asset (realty or personalty) and the use to which it is placed (business or personal). Personalty can be defined as all assets that are not realty.[1] Both realty and personalty can be either business use or personal use property. Examples of this distinction include a residence (realty that is personal use), an office building (realty that is business use), a dump truck (personalty that is business use), and regular wearing apparel (personalty that is personal use).

A further distinction is made between tangible and intangible property. Tangible property is any property with physical substance (e.g., equipment, buildings), while intangible property lacks such substance (e.g., goodwill, patents).

A write-off of the cost (or other adjusted basis) of an asset is known as depreciation, cost recovery, depletion, or amortization. Depreciation and cost recovery relate to tangible property, depletion involves certain natural resources (e.g., oil, coal, gravel), and amortization concerns intangible property. As noted later, a write-off for income tax purposes is not allowed when an asset lacks a determinable useful life (e.g., land, goodwill) or when it is not business use property.

The depreciation rules were completely overhauled by the Economic Recovery Tax Act of 1981 (ERTA). Hence, *most* property placed in service after December 31, 1980, is subject to the accelerated cost recovery system (ACRS). However, property acquired before January 1, 1981, that is still in use, as well as *certain* property acquired after December 31, 1980, is subject to the pre-ERTA depreciation rules. The Tax Reform Act (TRA) of 1986 completely revised the ACRS rules for property placed in service after December 31, 1986. Therefore, a knowledge of all of the depreciation and cost recovery rules may be needed as Example 1 illustrates.

EXAMPLE 1   ABC owns equipment purchased in 1980. The equipment has a 10–year useful life. The business also owns several trucks purchased in 1986. In 1988, the business purchased a computer. To compute the depreciation and cost recovery for 1989, ABC will use the pre-ERTA depreciation rules for the equipment, the pre-TRA of 1986 cost recovery rules for the trucks, and the post-TRA of 1986 cost recovery rules for the computer. □

This chapter first discusses the pre-ERTA depreciation rules, including the amortization rules not changed by ERTA, and then discusses the pre-TRA and post-TRA of 1986 ACRS rules.[2]

---

1. Refer to chapter 1 for a further discussion.
2. Depreciation is covered in § 167, and ACRS appears in § 168.

DEPRECIATION AND AMORTIZATION

Section 167 permits a depreciation deduction in the form of a reasonable allowance for the exhaustion, wear and tear, and obsolescence of business property and property held for the production of income (e.g., rental property held by an investor).[3] Obsolescence refers to normal technological change due to reasonably foreseeable economic conditions. If rapid or abnormal obsolescence occurs, a taxpayer may change to a shorter estimated useful life if there is a "clear and convincing basis for the redetermination."

The taxpayer must adopt a reasonable and consistent plan for depreciating the cost or other basis of assets over the estimated useful life of the property (e.g., the taxpayer cannot arbitrarily defer or accelerate the amount of depreciation from one year to another). The basis of the depreciable property must be reduced by the depreciation allowed and not less than the allowable amount.[4] The *allowed* depreciation is the depreciation actually taken, whereas the *allowable* depreciation is the amount that could have been taken under the applicable depreciation method. For example, if the taxpayer does not claim any depreciation on property during a particular year, the basis of the property still must be reduced by the amount of depreciation that should have been deducted.

EXAMPLE 2

On January 1, T paid $6,000 for a truck to be used in his business. He chose a four-year estimated useful life, no salvage value, and straight-line depreciation. Thus, the allowable depreciation deduction was $1,500 per year. However, depreciation actually taken (allowed) was as follows:

Year 1	$1,500
Year 2	-0-
Year 3	-0-
Year 4	1,500

The adjusted basis of the truck must be reduced by the amount of allowable depreciation of $6,000 ($1,500 × 4 years) despite the fact that T claimed only $3,000 depreciation during the four-year period. Therefore, if T sold the truck at the end of Year 4 for $1,000, a $1,000 gain would be recognized, since the adjusted cost basis of the truck is zero. □

Qualifying Property

As mentioned earlier, the use rather than the character of property determines whether a depreciation deduction is permitted. Property must be used in a trade or business or held for the production of income to qualify as depreciable.

---

3. § 167(a) and Reg. § 1.167(a)–1.

4. § 1016(a)(2) and Reg. § 1.167(a)–10(a).

CONCEPT SUMMARY 9–1

Depreciation and Cost Recovery: Relevant Time Periods

System	Date Property is Placed in Service
§ 167 depreciation	Before January 1, 1981 and *certain* property placed in service after December 31, 1980.
Pre-TRA of 1986 ACRS	After December 31, 1980, and before January 1, 1987.
Post-TRA of 1986 ACRS	After December 31, 1986.

EXAMPLE 3

T is a self-employed CPA who uses her automobile for both personal and business purposes. A depreciation deduction is permitted only for the business use part. Assume the automobile was acquired at a cost of $12,000 and T's mileage during the year was 10,000 miles, of which 3,000 miles were for business. Only 30% of the cost, or $3,600, would be subject to depreciation. □

The basis for depreciation generally is the adjusted cost basis used to determine gain if the property is sold or disposed of.[5] However, if personal use assets are converted to business or income-producing use, the basis for depreciation and for loss is the *lower* of the adjusted basis or fair market value when the property is converted.[6]

EXAMPLE 4

T acquires a personal residence for $30,000. Four years later, he converts the property to rental use when the fair market value is only $25,000. The basis for depreciation is $25,000, since the fair market value is less than the adjusted basis. The $5,000 decline in value is deemed to be personal (since it occurred while the property was held for personal use) and therefore nondeductible. □

The Regulations provide that tangible property is depreciable only to the extent that the property is subject to wear and tear, decay or decline from natural causes, exhaustion, and obsolescence.[7] Thus, land and inventory are not depreciable, but land improvements are depreciable (e.g., paved surfaces, fences, landscaping).

Amortization of intangible property is not permitted unless the property has a definite and limited useful life. For example, patents and copyrights have a definite and limited legal life and are therefore eligible for amortization. Goodwill is not amortizable, since its life extends for an unlimited period.

---

5. § 167(g).
6. Reg. § 1.167(g)–1.

7. Reg. § 1.167(a).

Other Depreciation Considerations

For property subject to depreciation under § 167, taxpayers generally must take into account the *salvage value* (assuming there is a salvage value) of an asset in calculating depreciation. An asset cannot be depreciated below its salvage value. However, the Code permits a taxpayer to disregard salvage value for amounts up to 10 percent of the basis in the property. This rule applies to tangible personal property (other than livestock) with an estimated useful life of three years or more.[8]

EXAMPLE 5

The XYZ Company acquired a machine for $10,000 in 1980 with an estimated salvage value of $3,000 after 10 years. The company may disregard salvage value to the extent of $1,000 and compute the machine's depreciation based upon a cost of $10,000 less $2,000 salvage. The adjusted basis may be reduced to $2,000 (depreciation of $8,000 may be taken) despite the fact that the actual salvage value is $3,000. □

This rule was incorporated into the law to reduce the number of IRS and taxpayer disputes relative to the salvage value that should be used.

Another consideration is the *choice of depreciation methods* from among the several allowed. The Code provides for the following alternative depreciation methods for property placed into service before January 1, 1981, and for *certain* property placed in service after December 31, 1980:[9]

- The straight-line method (cost basis less salvage ÷ estimated useful life).

- The declining-balance method (DB) using a rate not to exceed twice the straight-line rate. Common methods included 200 percent DB (double-declining balance), 150 percent DB, and 125 percent DB. Salvage value is not taken into account under any of the declining-balance methods. However, no further depreciation can be claimed once net book value (cost minus depreciation) and salvage value are the same.

- The sum-of-the-years digits' method (SYD).

- Any other consistent method that does not result in greater total depreciation being claimed during the first two-thirds of the useful life than would have been allowable under the double-declining balance method. Permissible methods include machine-hours and the units-of-production method.

EXAMPLE 6

On January 1, 1980, T acquired a new automobile to be used in his business. The asset cost $10,000 with an estimated salvage value of $2,000 and a four-year estimated useful life. The following amounts of depreciation could be deducted, depending on the method of depreciation used [note that pre-ERTA rules (depreciation calculated under § 167) continue to apply for the entire useful life of assets acquired before 1981]:

---

8. § 167(f) and Reg. § 1.167(a)–1(c).   9. § 167(b).

	1980	1981	1982	1983
Straight-line				
$10,000 cost less ($2,000 salvage value reduced by 10% of cost) ÷ 4 years	$2,250	$2,250	$2,250	$2,250
Double-declining balance				
a. $10,000 × 50% (twice the straight-line rate)	5,000			
b. ($10,000 − $5,000) × 50%		2,500		
c. ($10,000 − $5,000 − $2,500) × 50%			1,250	
d. ($10,000 − $5,000 − $2,500 − $1,250) × 50%				250 [10]
Sum-of-the-years' digits *: $10,000 cost less ($2,000 salvage value reduced by 10% of cost) or $9,000				
a. $9,000 × 4/10	3,600			
b. $9,000 × 3/10		2,700		
c. $9,000 × 2/10			1,800	
d. $9,000 × 1/10				900

* The sum-of-the-years' digits (SYD) method formula is

$$\text{Cost minus salvage value} \times \frac{\text{Remaining life at the beginning of the year}}{\text{Sum-of-the-years' digits of the estimated life}}$$

In this example, the denominator for SYD is $1 + 2 + 3 + 4$, or 10. The numerator is 4 for Year 1 (the number of years left at the beginning of Year 1), 3 for Year 2, etc. The denominator can be calculated by the following formula:

$$S = \frac{Y(Y + 1)}{2} \text{ where } Y = \text{estimated useful life}$$

$$S = \frac{4(4 + 1)}{2} = 10 \qquad \square$$

EXAMPLE 7

Using the depreciation calculations in Example 6, the depreciation reserve (accumulated depreciation) and book value at the end of 1983 are as follows:

---

10. Total depreciation taken cannot exceed cost minus estimated salvage value ($1,000 in this example).

	Cost	− Depreciation	= Net Book Value *
Straight-line	$10,000	$9,000	$1,000
Double-declining balance	10,000	9,000	1,000
Sum-of-the-years' digits	10,000	9,000	1,000

* Note that an asset may not be depreciated below its salvage value even when a declining-balance method is used.

In 1969, Congress placed certain restrictions on the use of accelerated methods for new and used realty that are subject to the depreciation rules under § 167. These restrictions were imposed to reduce the opportunities for using real estate investments as tax shelters. The use of accelerated depreciation frequently resulted in the recognition of ordinary tax losses on economically profitable real estate ventures.

The following methods were permitted for residential and nonresidential real property: [11]

	Nonresidential Real Property (commercial and industrial buildings, etc.)	Residential Real Property (apartment buildings, etc.)
New property acquired after July 24, 1969, and generally before January 1, 1981	150% DB, SL	200% DB, SYD, 150% DB, or SL
Used property acquired after July 24, 1969, and generally before January 1, 1981	SL	125% DB if estimated useful life is 20 years or greater or SL

Restrictions on the use of accelerated methods were not imposed on new tangible personalty (e.g., machinery, equipment, and automobiles). However, the 200 percent declining-balance and sum-of-the-years' digits methods were not permitted for used tangible personal property. The 150 percent declining-balance method was permitted for used tangible personalty that had a useful life of at least three years. Since the acquisition of used property did not result in any net addition to gross private investment in our economy, Congress chose not to provide as rapid accelerated depreciation for used property. It should be noted that accelerated methods (200 percent declining-balance and sum-of-the-years' digits) were permitted for new residential rental property. Presumably, the desire to stimulate construction of new housing units justified the need for such accelerated methods.

11. § 167(j). See the Glossary of Tax Terms in Appendix C for the definition of residential rental property.

The determination of a *useful life* for a depreciable asset often led to disagreement between taxpayers and the IRS. One source of information was the company's previous experience and policy with respect to asset maintenance and utilization. Another source was the guideline lives issued by the IRS.[12] In 1971, the IRS guideline life system was modified and liberalized by the enactment of the Asset Depreciation Range (ADR) system.[13]

ACCELERATED COST RECOVERY SYSTEM (ACRS)

General Considerations

The depreciation rules before ERTA were designed to allocate depreciation deductions over the period the asset was used in business so that the deductions for the cost of an asset were matched with the income produced by the asset (the so-called matching concept). Often this led to controversies between taxpayers and the IRS concerning the estimated useful life of an asset, and it delayed the tax benefit to be derived from the recoupment of a capital investment in the form of a deduction for depreciation.

One way to resolve the estimated useful life problem was to utilize the Asset Depreciation Range (ADR) system, which specified ranges for particular assets. Taxpayers could select a useful life for an asset within the specified range for that particular asset. However, many assets were not eligible for ADR, or taxpayers saw fit not to elect the system. In such cases, useful lives were determined according to the facts and circumstances pertaining to each asset or by agreement between the taxpayer and the IRS.

For property placed in service after December 31, 1980, the ADR system and depreciation calculated under § 167 have generally been replaced by the § 168 accelerated cost recovery system (ACRS). Under ACRS, the cost of an asset is recovered over a predetermined period that is generally shorter than the useful life of the asset or the period the asset is used to produce income. The change was designed to encourage investment, improve productivity, and simplify the law and its administration. However, the pre-ACRS depreciation rules will continue to apply in the following situations:

- Property placed in service after 1980 whose life is not based on years (e.g., units-of-production method).

- The remaining depreciation on property placed in service by the taxpayer before 1981.

- Personal property acquired after 1980 if the property was owned or used during 1980 by the taxpayer or a related person (antichurning rule)[14].

- Property that is amortized (e.g., leasehold improvements).

For property placed in service after December 31, 1986, ACRS has been revised by TRA of 1986. However, the pre-TRA of 1986 ACRS rules still apply to property placed in service before January 1, 1987.

---

12. Rev.Proc. 72–10, 1972–1 C.B. 721, superseded by Rev.Proc. 83–35, 1983–1 C.B. 745.
13. Reg. § 1.167(a)–11.
14. § 168(f). The antichurning rules could also re- quire the use of pre-TRA of 1986 ACRS rules on property placed in service after December 31, 1986.

Eligible Property under ACRS

Assets used in a trade or business or for the production of income are depreciable if they are subject to wear and tear, decay or decline from natural causes, or obsolescence. Assets that do not decline in value on a predictable basis or that do not have a determinable useful life (e.g., land, goodwill, stock, antiques) are not depreciable.

New or used tangible depreciable property (real or personal) placed in service after December 31, 1980 (except for the four exceptions noted above), is subject to the ACRS rules. Property placed in service before January 1, 1987, is subject to pre-TRA of 1986 ACRS rules, and property placed in service after December 31, 1986, is subject to post-TRA of 1986 ACRS rules.

Personalty: Recovery Periods and Methods

Classification of Property: Pre-TRA of 1986. Pre-TRA of 1986 ACRS provides that the cost of eligible personalty (and certain realty) is recovered over 3, 5, 10, or 15 years. The classification of property by recovery period is as follows:

3 years	Autos, light-duty trucks, R & D equipment, racehorses over 2 years old and other horses over 12 years old, and personalty with an ADR midpoint life of 4 years or less.[15]
5 years	Most other equipment except long-lived public utility property. Also includes single-purpose agricultural structures and petroleum storage facilities, which are designated as § 1245 property under the law.
10 years	Public utility property with an ADR midpoint life greater than 18 but not greater than 25 years, burners and boilers using coal as a primary fuel if used in a public utility power plant and if replacing or converting oil- or gas-fired burners or boilers, railroad tank cars, mobile homes, and realty with an ADR midpoint life of 12.5 years or less (e.g., theme park structures).
15 years	Public utility property with an ADR midpoint life exceeding 25 years (except certain burners and boilers using coal as a primary fuel).

Taxpayers have the choice of using (1) the straight-line method over the regular or optional (see below) recovery period or (2) a prescribed accelerated method over the regular recovery period. These two methods are both part of the ACRS system. However, a convenient name is not provided for either of the two methods. Hereafter, the straight-line method will be referred to as the *optional (or elective) straight-line method.* The method using percentages prescribed in the Code will be referred to as the *statutory percentage method.*

---

15. Rev.Proc. 83–35, 1983–1 C.B. 745, is the source for the ADR midpoint lives.

The rates to be used in computing the deduction under the statutory percentage method are shown in Table 9–1 (all tables are located at the end of the chapter prior to the Problem Materials) and are based on the 150 percent declining-balance method, using the half-year convention [16] and an assumption of zero salvage value.

EXAMPLE 8

In December 1982, T buys the following business assets: $34,000 of machinery, $6,000 of office furniture, and $16,000 of light-duty trucks. The machinery and office furniture are five-year properties, and the trucks are three-year properties. T's depreciation deductions using the statutory percentage method are as follows:

1982	
25% of $16,000 (trucks)	$ 4,000
15% of $40,000 (machinery and furniture)	6,000
	$10,000
1983	
38% of $16,000	$ 6,080
22% of $40,000	8,800
	$14,880
1984	
37% of $16,000	$ 5,920
21% of $40,000	8,400
	$14,320
1985	
21% of $40,000	$ 8,400
1986	
21% of $40,000	$ 8,400

□

Note that in 1982, T got a half-year's depreciation deduction (since the half-year convention is reflected in the percentages in Table 9–1) although she held the property only one month.

In the year that personal property is disposed of, no cost recovery is allowed.

---

16. The half-year convention assumes all property is placed in service at mid-year and thus provides for a half-year's cost recovery.

EXAMPLE 9   Assume the same facts as in Example 8. If T sold the trucks on December 1, 1983, T would only have cost recovery of $8,800 for the machinery and furniture. T would have no cost recovery for the trucks even though they were held for 11 months. □

Reduction of Basis for Investment Tax Credit.   For personalty placed in service after 1982 and before January 1, 1986, the basis of the property for the ACRS write-off must be reduced by one-half the amount of the investment tax credit taken on the property.[17] Investment credit is not allowed on realty. (See chapter 13 for details.)

EXAMPLE 10   On January 1, 1985, T purchases a machine, which is five-year ACRS property, for $10,000. T takes a $1,000 investment tax credit on the property (10% of $10,000). The basis of the property must be reduced by $500 (½ of the $1,000 investment tax credit). Thus, T's cost recovery allowance will be based on $9,500 [$10,000 (cost) − $500 (reduction for investment tax credit)]. T's cost recovery deduction for 1985 will be $1,425 (15% of $9,500). □

As an alternative to reducing the basis of the property, a taxpayer may elect to take a reduced investment tax credit. Under this election, the investment tax credit is 8 percent (rather than 10 percent) for recovery property that is not three-year property and 4 percent (instead of 6 percent) for three-year property.

TRA of 1986 repealed the investment tax credit for property placed in service after December 31, 1985. Therefore, the reduction of basis for the investment tax credit is not a concern for such property.

Classification of Property: Post-TRA of 1986.   The general effect of TRA of 1986 is to lengthen asset lives. Post-TRA of 1986 ACRS provides that the depreciation basis of eligible personalty (and certain realty) is recovered over 3, 5, 7, 10, 15, or 20 years. The classification of property by recovery period is as follows: [18]

3-year 200% class . . . . . ADR midpoints of 4 years and less.[19] Excludes automobiles and light trucks. Includes horses that are racehorses more than 2 years old and other horses more than 12 years old.

---

17. § 48(q).
18. § 168(e).

19. Rev.Proc. 87–56, 1987–2 C.B. 674 is the source for the ADR midpoint lives.

5-year 200% class . . . . . ADR midpoints of more than 4 years and less than 10 years, adding automobiles, light trucks, qualified technological equipment, renewable energy and biomass properties that are small power production facilities, research and experimentation property, semiconductor manufacturing equipment, and computer-based central office switching equipment.

7-year 200% class . . . . . ADR midpoints of 10 years and more and less than 16 years, adding single-purpose agricultural or horticultural structures and property with no ADR midpoint not classified elsewhere. Includes railroad track.

10-year 200% class . . . . . ADR midpoints of 16 years and more and less than 20 years.

15-year 150% class . . . . . ADR midpoints of 20 years and more and less than 25 years, including sewage treatment plants, and telephone distribution plants and comparable equipment used for the two-way exchange of voice and data communications.

20-year 150% class . . . . . ADR midpoints of 25 years and more, other than real property with an ADR midpoint of 27.5 years and more, and including sewer pipes.

Accelerated depreciation is allowed for these six ACRS classes of property. Two hundred percent declining-balance is used for the 3-, 5-, 7-, and 10-year classes, with a switchover to straight-line depreciation when it yields a larger amount. One hundred and fifty percent declining-balance is allowed for the 15- and 20-year classes, with an appropriate straight-line switchover.[20]

The property in these accelerated depreciation classes may be depreciated using straight-line depreciation if an election is made. Certain property is not eligible for accelerated depreciation and must be depreciated under an alternative depreciation system (ADS). Both the straight-line election and ADS are discussed later in the chapter.

The original ACRS system gave the taxpayer a half-year of depreciation for the tax year he or she placed an asset in service but allowed the taxpayer to recover the balance of the depreciable basis over the years remaining in the property's recovery period. No recovery allowance existed for the year of disposition or retirement. Thus, conceptually, the taxpayer was considered to have placed property in service at the beginning of the recovery period but was allowed only a half-year's worth of depreciation for the placed-in-service year. By contrast, the new system views property as placed in service in the middle of the first year.[21] Thus, for example, the statutory recovery period for three-year property begins in the middle of the year an asset is placed in service and ends three years later. In practical terms, the new rule means that taxpayers must wait an extra year to recover the cost of depreciable assets. That is, the actual write-off periods are 4, 6, 8, 11, 16, and 21 years. The new system also allows for a half-year of cost recovery in the year of disposition or retirement.

---

20. § 168(b).   21. § 168(d)(4)(A).

CONCEPT SUMMARY 9–2

Cost Recovery Periods: Post–TRA of 1986

Class of Property	Examples
3–year	Tractor units for use over-the-road.
	Any horse that is not a racehorse and is more than 12 years old at the time it is placed in service.
	Any racehorse that is more than 2 years old at the time it is placed in service.
	Breeding hogs.
	Special tools used in the manufacturing of motor vehicles such as dies, fixtures, molds, and patterns.
5–year	Automobiles and taxis.
	Light and heavy general-purpose trucks.
	Buses.
	Trailers and trailer-mounted containers.
	Typewriters, calculators, and copiers.
	Computers and peripheral equipment.
	Breeding and dairy cattle.
7–year	Office furniture, fixtures, and equipment.
	Breeding and work horses.
	Agricultural machinery and equipment.
	Single-purpose agricultural or horticultural structures.
10–year	Vessels, barges, tugs, and similar water transportation equipment.
	Assets used for petroleum refining, manufacture of grain and grain mill products, manufacture of sugar and sugar products, and manufacture of vegetable oils and vegetable oil products.
15–year	Land improvements.
	Assets used for industrial steam and electric generation and/or distribution systems.
	Assets used in the manufacture of cement.
	Railroad track.
	Assets used in pipeline transportation.
	Electric utility nuclear production plant.
	Municipal wastewater treatment plant.
20–year	Farm buildings except single-purpose agricultural and horticultural structures.
	Gas utility distribution facilities.
	Water utilities.
	Municipal sewer.

The methodology for computing the cost recovery is the same as under the original ACRS method. The depreciation basis is multiplied by the percentages that reflect the applicable depreciation method and the applicable convention. The percentages are shown in Table 9–2.

EXAMPLE 11

T acquires a five-year class asset on April 10, 1989, for $30,000. T's cost recovery deduction for 1989 is $6,000 [$30,000 × .20 (Table 9–2)]. □

EXAMPLE 12

Assume the same facts as in Example 11, except that T disposes of the asset on March 5, 1991. T's cost recovery deduction for 1991 is $2,880 [$30,000 × ½ × .192 (Table 9–2)]. □

Under the original ACRS rules for personal property, the half-year convention was used no matter what the pattern of acquisitions was during the year. Thus, if a substantial dollar amount of assets was acquired late in the tax year, the half-year convention still applied. The law now contains a provision to curtail the benefits of such tax planning. If more than 40 percent of the value of property other than eligible real estate (see Realty: Recovery Periods and Methods: Post-TRA of 1986, for a discussion of eligible real estate) is placed in service during the last quarter of the year, a *mid-quarter convention* applies.[22] Property acquisitions are then grouped by the quarter they were acquired and depreciated accordingly. Acquisitions during the first quarter would receive 10.5 months of depreciation; the second quarter, 7.5 months; the third quarter, 4.5 months; and the fourth quarter, 1.5 months. The percentages are shown in Table 9–3.

EXAMPLE 13

X Corporation acquires the following five-year class property:

Property Acquisition Dates	Cost
February 15	$ 200,000
July 10	400,000
December 5	600,000
Total	$1,200,000

If X Corporation uses statutory percentage ACRS, the cost recovery for the first two years would be computed as indicated below. Since 50% ($600,000/$1,200,000) of the acquisitions are in the last quarter, the mid-quarter convention applies.

---

22. § 168(d)(3).

Year 1

February 15	[$200,000 × .35 (Table 9–3)]	$ 70,000
July 10	($400,000 × .15)	60,000
December 5	($600,000 × .05)	30,000
Total		$160,000

Year 2

February 15	[$200,000 × .26 (Table 9–3)]	$ 52,000
July 10	($400,000 × .34)	136,000
December 5	($600,000 × .38)	228,000
Total		$416,000

□

Realty: Recovery Periods and Methods

Pre-TRA of 1986. Under the original version of ACRS, realty is assigned a 15-year recovery period. Component depreciation generally is no longer allowed.[23]

Real property other than low-income housing can be depreciated using the 175 percent declining-balance method, changing to the straight-line method to maximize acceleration. Low-income housing is depreciated using the 200 percent declining-balance method, changing to straight-line. In either case, an assumption of zero salvage value is made. Statutory percentages for real property are shown in Table 9–4, which contains rates for low-income housing as well as for other 15-year real estate.

Since the half-year convention does not apply to 15-year real property, Table 9–4 is structured differently from Tables 9–1 and 9–2. The cost recovery deduction for 15-year real property is based on the month the asset is placed in service rather than on the half-year convention.

EXAMPLE 14

T purchased a warehouse for $100,000 on January 1, 1984. The first year's cost recovery allowance using the statutory percentage method is $12,000 (12% of $100,000). Cost recovery deductions for 1985, 1986, and 1987 are, respectively, $10,000, $9,000, and $8,000. (Refer to Table 9–4 for percentages.) □

EXAMPLE 15

Assume the same facts as in Example 14, except the property is low-income housing. Cost recovery deductions for 1984 through 1987 are $13,000, $12,000, $10,000, and $9,000. □

---

23. See the Glossary of Tax Terms in Appendix C for a definition of component depreciation.

The Deficit Reduction Act of 1984 changed the recovery period for real property to 18 years. This applies generally to property placed in service after March 15, 1984. However, the 15-year recovery period is retained for low-income housing as well as for real property placed in service before March 16, 1984.

Eighteen-year real property placed in service after June 22, 1984, is subject to a mid-month convention.[24] This means that real property placed in service at any time during a particular month is treated as if it were placed in service in the middle of such month. This allows for one-half month's cost recovery for the month the property is placed in service. If the property is disposed of before the end of the recovery period, one-half month's cost recovery is permitted for the month of disposition regardless of the specific date of disposition. Statutory percentages for 18-year real property with a mid-month convention are shown in Table 9–5.

EXAMPLE 16

T purchased a building for $300,000 and placed it in service on August 21, 1984. The first year's cost recovery using the statutory percentage method is $12,000 (4% × $300,000). (See Table 9–5 for percentages.) □

EXAMPLE 17

Assume the same facts as in Example 16 and that T disposes of the building on May 3, 1990. The cost recovery in the year of disposition is $6,750 ($300,000 × 6% × 4.5/12). □

Public Law 99–121 extended the minimum recovery period for real property (except low-income housing) from 18 years to 19 years. This applies to property placed in service after May 8, 1985. Statutory percentages for 19-year real property are shown in Table 9–6. Because the percentages are determined using a mid-month convention, the computation of cost recovery is mechanically the same as illustrated with respect to 18-year property with the mid-month convention.

Post-TRA of 1986.   Residential rental real estate is given a recovery period of 27.5 years and is depreciated using the straight-line method. *Residential rental real estate* includes property for which 80 percent or more of the gross rental revenues are from nontransient dwelling units (e.g., an apartment building). Hotels, motels, and similar establishments are not residential rental property. Low-income housing is classified as residential rental real estate. Nonresidential real estate has a recovery period of 31.5 years and is depreciated using the straight-line method.[25]

Note that some items of real property are not real estate for purposes of the revised ACRS. Single-purpose agricultural structures are in the seven-year ACRS class. Land improvements are in the 15-year ACRS class.

All eligible real estate is depreciated using the mid-month convention. Regardless of when during the month the property is placed in service, it is

---

24. A transitional rule, which provides for a full-month convention, is effective for property placed in service after March 15, 1984, and be-   fore June 23, 1984.

25. §§ 168(b) and (c).

deemed to have been placed in service at the middle of the month. In the year of disposition, a mid-month convention is also used.

Depreciation is computed by multiplying the applicable rate (Table 9–7) by the depreciation basis.

EXAMPLE 18

T acquired a building on April 1, 1989, for $800,000. If the building is classified as residential rental real estate, the cost recovery for 1989 would be $20,608 (.02576 × $800,000). If the building is classified as nonresidential real estate, the 1989 cost recovery would be $17,992 (.02249 × $800,000). ☐

Straight-Line Election under ACRS

Pre-TRA of 1986.   Taxpayers may *elect* to write off an asset using the straight-line method rather than the statutory percentage method. The straight-line recovery period may be equal to the prescribed recovery period under the statutory percentage method, or it may be a longer period. Allowable straight-line recovery periods for each class of property are summarized as follows:

3-year property . . . . 3, 5, or 12 years

5-year property . . . . 5, 12, or 25 years

10-year property . . . . 10, 25, or 35 years

15-year property . . . . 15, 35, or 45 years

18-year real property and low-income housing (placed in service after March 15, 1984) . . . . 18, 35, or 45 years

19-year real property and low-income housing (placed in service after May 8, 1985) 19, 35, or 45 years

---

If the straight-line option is elected, the half-year convention is applied in computing the cost recovery deduction for property other than 15-year, 18-year, or 19-year real property. The effect of electing the straight-line method for personal property is to extend the stated statutory recovery period by one year (e.g., three to four and five to six years). There is no cost recovery deduction in the year of disposition of property other than 15-year, 18-year, or 19-year real property. This rule is applicable to both the statutory percentage method and the optional straight-line method.

EXAMPLE 19

J acquired a light-duty truck (three-year property) on March 1, 1986, at a cost of $10,000. J elects to write off the cost of the truck using the optional straight-line method with a recovery period of five years. Because the half-year convention applies, J can deduct only $1,000 [($10,000 ÷ 5) × ½] in 1986. ☐

EXAMPLE 20   Assume the same facts as in Example 19. If J disposes of the truck at any time during 1987, no cost recovery deduction is allowed for 1987, the year of disposition. □

The half-year convention does not apply for 15-year, 18-year, or 19-year real property for which the straight-line option is elected. Nor is the cost recovery deduction disallowed in the year of disposition. The first year's deduction and the deduction for the year of disposition are computed on the basis of the number of months the property was in service during the year. Examples 21 and 22 illustrate the calculations for 15-year real property.

EXAMPLE 21   K acquired a store building on October 1, 1983, at a cost of $150,000. K elects the straight-line method using a recovery period of 15 years. K's cost recovery deduction for 1983 is $2,500 [($150,000 ÷ 15) × 3/12].

□

EXAMPLE 22   Assume the same facts as in Example 21 and that K disposes of the asset on September 30, 1985. K's cost recovery deduction for 1985 would be $7,500 [($150,000 ÷ 15) × 9/12]. □

If the straight-line option is elected for 18-year or 19-year real property, the cost recovery allowances in the year the property is placed in service and in the year of disposition are computed the same (except for the use of different rates) as under statutory percentage cost recovery. Table 9-8 contains the applicable percentages to be used if the straight-line option is elected for 19-year real property. (The tables that contain the percentages for 18-year real property using the straight-line method over 18, 35, and 45 years and 19-year real property using the straight-line method over 35 and 45 years are not reproduced in this text.)

For each class of property other than 15-year, 18-year, or 19-year real estate, the straight-line election applies to *all* assets in a *particular class* that are placed in service during the year for which the election is made and later to the entire recovery period for those vintage assets. The election may be changed for property of the same class placed in service in other taxable years. By contrast, the straight-line election for 15-year, 18-year, or 19-year real property may be made on a *property-by-property* basis within the same year.

Post-TRA of 1986.   Although straight-line depreciation is required for all eligible real estate as previously discussed, the taxpayer may elect to use the straight-line method for personal property.[26] The property is depreciated using the class life (recovery period) of the asset with a half-year convention or a mid-quarter convention, whichever is applicable. The election is available on a class-by-class and year-by-year basis. The percentages for the straight-line election with a half-year convention appear in Table 9-9.

---

26. § 168(b)(5).

EXAMPLE 23   T acquired a 10-year class asset on August 4, 1989, for $100,000. T's cost recovery deduction for 1989 is $5,000 ($100,000 × .050). T's cost recovery deduction for 1990 is $10,000 ($100,000 × .100). □

Election to Expense Assets

Section 179 (Election to Expense Certain Depreciable Business Assets) permits an election to write-off up to $10,000 of the acquisition cost of tangible personal property used in a trade or business.[27]   Such amounts that are expensed may not be capitalized and depreciated. The election is an annual election and applies to the acquisition cost of property placed in service that year.[28]

EXAMPLE 24   T acquires machinery (five-year class) on February 1, 1989, at a cost of $40,000 and elects to expense $10,000 under § 179. T's statutory percentage cost recovery deduction for 1989 is $6,000 [($40,000 cost − $10,000 expensed) × .200]. T's total deduction for 1989 is $16,000 ($10,000 + $6,000). □

Section 179 has two additional limitations. First, the ceiling amount on the deduction is reduced dollar-for-dollar when property (other than eligible real estate) placed in service during the taxable year exceeds $200,000. Second, the amount expensed under § 179 cannot exceed the aggregate amount of taxable income derived from the conduct of any trade or business by the taxpayer. Taxable income of a trade or business is computed without regard to the amount expensed under § 179. Any expensed amount in excess of taxable income is carried forward to future taxable years and added to other amounts eligible for expensing (i.e., it is subject to the ceiling rules for the future years).[29]

EXAMPLE 25   T owns a computer service and operates it as a sole proprietorship. In 1989, she will net $5,000 before considering any § 179 deduction. If T spends $204,000 on new equipment, her § 179 expense deduction would be computed as follows:

---

27. From 1982 through 1986, the write-off amount was limited to $5,000.

28. § 179(b). The amount shown is per taxpayer, per year. On a joint return, the statutory amounts apply to the couple. If the taxpayers are married and file separate returns, each spouse is eligible for 50% of the statutory amount.

29. § 179(b). These two limitations apply to property placed in service after December 31, 1986.

§ 179 deduction before adjustment	$10,000
Less: Dollar limitation reduction ($204,000 − $200,000)	(4,000)
Remaining § 179 deduction	$ 6,000
Business income limitation	$ 5,000
§ 179 deduction allowed	$ 5,000
§ 179 deduction carryforward ($6,000 − $5,000)	$ 1,000

□

The basis of the property for purposes of cost recovery is reduced by the § 179 amount after it is adjusted for property in excess of $200,000. This adjusted amount does not reflect any business income limitation. This is illustrated in Example 26.

EXAMPLE 26

Assume the same facts as in Example 25 and that the new equipment is five-year class property. T's statutory percentage cost recovery deduction for 1989 is $39,600 [($204,000 − $6,000) × .200]. □

Conversion of the expensed property to personal use at any time results in recapture income (see chapter 17). A property is converted to personal use if it is not used predominantly in a trade or business. Regulations provide for the mechanics of the recapture.[30]

ACRS Antichurning Rules

Pre-TRA of 1986. Generally, the ACRS deduction may be larger than the depreciation deduction under pre-1981 rules. Thus, there was concern that some taxpayers might engage in transactions that did not result in an actual ownership change in an attempt to change pre-1981 property into post-1980 recovery property. To prevent this, the original ACRS provisions contain antichurning rules that prevent the use of ACRS on personal property acquired after 1980 if the property was owned or used during 1980 by the taxpayer or a related person (it is *churned* property). Therefore, the taxpayer must use pre-1981 depreciation rules on churned property.

EXAMPLE 27

T began renting a tractor to use in his farming business in 1979. T used the tractor until 1982, at which time he purchased it. T is not entitled to use ACRS because he used the tractor in 1980. Instead, he must use the pre-1981 depreciation rules. □

---

30. Reg. § 1.179–1(e).

In addition, ACRS does not apply to real property if any of the following is true:

- The property was owned by the taxpayer or a related person at any time during 1980.

- The taxpayer leases the property to a person or anyone related to such person who owned the property at any time during 1980.

- The property is acquired in nonrecognition transactions, such as certain like-kind exchanges or involuntary conversions (see chapter 15). However, this applies only to the extent that the basis of the property includes an amount representing the adjusted basis of other property owned by the taxpayer or a related person during 1980.

EXAMPLE 28

In 1986, J made a nontaxable like-kind exchange. He gave an apartment building, held since 1978, with an adjusted basis of $300,000 and a fair market value of $400,000. He also gave $200,000 in cash. In exchange, J received an apartment building worth $600,000. The basis of the new building is $500,000 [$300,000 (basis of old building) + $200,000 (cash paid)], but only $200,000 of the basis is subject to the ACRS rules. The $300,000 carryover basis is subject to the pre-ACRS rules. □

A person is considered related to a previous user or owner if a family or fiduciary relationship exists or if ownership of 10 percent of a corporation or partnership exists.

Post-TRA of 1986.   TRA of 1986 contains antichurning rules similar to those just discussed in connection with the original ACRS provisions. Hence, taxpayers are prevented from depreciating personal property placed in service by the taxpayer or a related person before 1987 under the revised ACRS rules.[31]

Business and Personal Use of Automobiles and Other Listed Property

Generally effective for property placed in service after June 18, 1984, limits exist on ACRS deductions and investment tax credits with respect to business and personal use of automobiles and other listed property. If the listed property *is predominantly used* for business, the taxpayer is allowed to take the investment tax credit and use statutory percentage ACRS to recover cost. In cases where the property is *not predominantly used* for business, cost is recovered using a straight-line recovery, and no investment tax credit can be taken.

TRA of 1986 repealed the investment tax credit for property placed in service after December 31, 1985. Therefore, the issue of whether investment tax credit can be taken is relevant only through 1985. (Because of the repeal of the investment tax credit, the credit is not discussed further in this section.)

Automobiles and Other Listed Property Used Predominantly in Business. For listed property to be considered as predominantly used in business, the

---

31. § 168(f)(5).

percentage of use for business must exceed 50 percent.[32] The use of listed property for production of income does not qualify as business use for purposes of the more-than-50 percent test. However, if the more-than-50 percent test is met, production of income and business use percentages are used to compute the ACRS deduction.

EXAMPLE 29

On September 1, 1989, T places in service listed five-year recovery property. The property cost $10,000. If T uses the property 40% for business and 25% for the production of income, the property will not be considered as predominantly used for business. The cost would be recovered using straight-line cost recovery. If, however, T uses the property 60% for business and 25% for the production of income, the property will be considered as used predominantly for business. T's cost recovery for the year would be $1,700 ($10,000 × .200 × 85%). □

The base for determining the percentage of business usage for listed property is determined under the Regulations. The Regulations provide that for automobiles a mileage-based percentage is to be used. Other listed property is to use the most appropriate unit of time (e.g., hours) the property is actually used (rather than available for use).[33]

The more-than-50 percent business use test applies to all *listed property*, which includes the following:

- Any passenger automobile.

- Any other property used as a means of transportation.

- Any property of a type generally used for purposes of entertainment, recreation, or amusement.

- Any computer or peripheral equipment, with the exception of equipment used exclusively at a regular business establishment, including a qualifying home office.

- Any other property specified in the Regulations.[34]

The law places special limitations on statutory percentage ACRS recovery for passenger automobiles. These statutory dollar limits were imposed on passenger automobiles because of the belief that the tax system was being used to underwrite automobiles whose cost and luxury far exceeded what was needed for their business use.

A *passenger automobile* is any four-wheeled vehicle manufactured for use on public streets, roads, and highways with an unloaded gross vehicle weight rating of 6,000 pounds or less.[35] This definition specifically excludes vehicles used directly in the business of transporting people or property for compensation such as taxicabs, ambulances, hearses, and trucks and vans as prescribed by the Regulations.

The limits placed on the amounts of ACRS statutory percentage recovery for passenger automobiles are as follows: [36]

---

32. § 280F(b)(4).
33. Reg. § 1.280F-6T(e).
34. § 280F(d)(4).

35. § 280F(d)(5).

36. § 280F(a)(2).

Year	Recovery Limitation
1	$2,560
2	4,100
3	2,450
Succeeding years until the cost is recovered	1,475

However, these limits are imposed before any percentage reduction for personal use. In addition, the limitation in the first year includes any amount the taxpayer elects to expense under § 179.[37] If the passenger automobile is used partly for personal use, the personal use percentage is ignored for the purpose of determining the unrecovered cost available for deduction in later years.

EXAMPLE 30

On July 1, 1989, T places in service an automobile that cost $20,000. The car is always used 80% for business and 20% for personal use. The cost recovery for the automobile would be as follows:

1989—$2,048   [$20,000 × 20% (limited to $2,560) × 80%]

1990—$3,280   [$20,000 × 32% (limited to $4,100) × 80%]

1991—$1,960   [$20,000 × 19.2% (limited to $2,450) × 80%]

1992—$1,180   [$20,000 × 11.52% (limited to $1,475) × 80%]

1993—$1,180   [$20,000 × 11.52% (limited to $1,475) × 80%]

1994—$ 922   [$20,000 × 5.76% (limited to $1,475) × 80%]

1995—$1,180   [$6,788 unrecovered cost ($20,000 − $13,212 *), therefore $1,475 × 80%]

1996—$1,180   [$5,313 unrecovered cost ($20,000 − $14,687), therefore $1,475 × 80%]

1997—$1,180   [$3,838 unrecovered cost ($20,000 − $16,162), therefore $1,475 × 80%]

1998—$1,180   [$2,363 unrecovered cost ($20,000 − $17,637), therefore $1,475 × 80%]

1999—$ 710   [$888 unrecovered cost ($20,000 − $19,112), therefore $888 × 80%]

*   [$2,560 + $4,100 + $2,450 + $1,475 + $1,475 + ($20,000 × 5.76%)].

The total cost recovery for the years 1989–1999 is $16,000 (80% business usage × $20,000). □

The cost recovery limitations are maximum amounts. If the ACRS percentages produce a lesser amount of cost recovery, the lesser amount is used.

---

37. § 280F(d)(1).

EXAMPLE 31

On April 2, 1989, T places in service an automobile that cost $10,000. The car is always used 70% for business and 30% for personal use. The cost recovery for 1989 would be $1,400 ($10,000 × 20% × 70%). ☐

Note that the cost recovery limitations apply *only* to passenger automobiles and not to other listed property.

Automobiles and Other Listed Property Not Used Predominantly in Business. The cost of listed property that does not pass the more-than-50 percent business usage test in the year the property is placed in service must be recovered using the straight-line method.[38] Under TRA of 1986, the straight-line method to be used is that required under the alternative depreciation system (ADS) (explained later in the chapter). This system requires a straight-line recovery period of five years for automobiles. However, even though the straight-line method is used, the cost recovery allowance for passenger automobiles cannot exceed the limitations.

EXAMPLE 32

On July 27, 1989, T places in service an automobile that cost $20,000. The auto is used 40% for business and 60% for personal use. The cost recovery allowance for 1989 is $800 [$20,000 × 10% (Table 9-11) × 40%]. ☐

EXAMPLE 33

Assume the same facts as in Example 32, except that the auto cost $50,000. The cost recovery allowance for 1989 is $1,024 [$50,000 × 10% = $5,000 (limited to $2,560) × 40%]. ☐

If the listed property fails the more-than-50 percent business usage test, the straight-line method must be used for the remainder of the property's life. This applies even if at some later date the business usage of the property increases to more than 50 percent. However, even though the straight-line method must continue to be used, the amount of cost recovery will reflect the increase in business usage.

EXAMPLE 34

Assume the same facts as in Example 32, except that in 1990, T uses the auto 70% for business and 30% for personal use. T's cost recovery allowance for 1990 is $2,800 [$20,000 × 20% (Table 9-11) × 70%]. ☐

Change from Predominantly Business Use. If the business use percentage of listed property falls to 50 percent or lower after the year the property is placed in service, the property is subject to *cost recovery recapture*. The amount required to be recaptured and included in the taxpayer's return as ordinary income is the excess depreciation.

Excess depreciation is the excess of the ACRS percentage deduction taken in prior years over the amount that would have been allowed if the straight-line method had been used since the property was placed in service.[39]

---

38. § 280F(b)(2).   39. § 280F(b)(3).

EXAMPLE 35

T purchased a car on January 22, 1989, at a cost of $20,000. Business usage was 80% in 1989, 70% in 1990, 40% in 1991, and 60% in 1992. ACRS deductions in 1989 and 1990 are $2,048 (80% × $2,560) and $2,870 (70% × $4,100), respectively. T's excess depreciation to be recaptured as ordinary income in 1991 is $518, calculated as follows:

1989

ACRS allowance	$2,048
Straight-line ($20,000 × 10% × 80%)	(1,600)
Excess	$ 448

1990

ACRS allowance	$2,870
Straight-line ($20,000 × 20% × 70%)	(2,800)
1990 excess	$ 70
1989 excess	448
Total excess	$ 518

☐

After the business usage of the listed property drops below the more-than-50 percent level, the straight-line method must be used for the remaining life of the property.

EXAMPLE 36

Assume the same facts as in Example 35. T's cost recovery allowance for the years 1991 and 1992 would be $980 and $885, computed as follows:

1991—$980 [($20,000 × 20%) limited to $2,450 × 40%]

1992—$885 [($20,000 × 20%) limited to $1,475 × 60%]

☐

Substantiation Requirements. Listed property is now subject to the substantiation requirements of § 274. This means that business usage must be proven as to the amount of expense or use, the time and place of use, the business purpose for the use, and the business relationship to the taxpayer of persons using the property. Substantiation will require adequate records or sufficient evidence corroborating the taxpayer's statement. However, these substantiation requirements do not apply to vehicles that, by reason of their nature, are not likely to be used more than a de minimis amount for personal purposes.[40]

Alternative Depreciation System (ADS)

TRA of 1986 provides for an *alternative depreciation system (ADS)*,[41] which must be used for the following:

- To calculate the portion of depreciation treated as a tax preference item for purposes of the corporate and individual alternative minimum tax (see chapter 12).

- To compute depreciation allowances for property for which any of the following is true:

  - Used predominantly outside the United States.

  - Leased or otherwise used by a tax-exempt entity.

  - Financed with the proceeds of tax-exempt bonds.

  - Imported from foreign countries that maintain discriminatory trade practices or otherwise engage in discriminatory acts.

- To compute depreciation allowances for earnings and profits purposes (see chapter 20).

In general, depreciation is computed using straight-line recovery without regard to salvage value. However, for purposes of the alternative minimum tax, depreciation of personal property is computed using the 150 percent declining-balance method with an appropriate switch to the straight-line method.

The Technical and Miscellaneous Revenue Act of 1988 allows taxpayers to *elect* to use the 150 percent declining-balance method to compute the regular tax rather than the 200 percent declining-balance method which is available for personal property. Hence, there will be no difference between the cost recovery for computing the regular tax and the alternative minimum tax. However, taxpayers that make this election must use the ADS recovery periods in computing the cost recovery for the regular tax.

The taxpayer must use the half-year or the mid-quarter convention, whichever is applicable, for all property other than eligible real estate. The mid-month convention is used for eligible real estate. The applicable depreciation rates are found in Tables 9–10, 9–11, and 9–12.

The recovery periods under the alternative depreciation system are as follows:[42]

- The ADR midpoint life for property that does not fall into any of the following listed classes.

- Five years for qualified technological equipment, automobiles, and light-duty trucks.

- Twelve years for personal property with no class life.

40. §§ 274(d) and (i).

41. § 168(g).

42. The class life for certain properties described in § 168(e)(3) are specially determined under § 168(g)(3)(B).

● Forty years for all residential rental property and all nonresidential real property.

In lieu of depreciation under the regular ACRS method, taxpayers may *elect* straight-line under ADS for property that qualifies for the regular ACRS method. The election is available on a class-by-class and year-by-year basis for property other than eligible real estate. The election for eligible real estate is on a property-by-property basis. One reason for making this election is to avoid a difference between deductible depreciation and earnings and profits depreciation.

EXAMPLE 37

T acquires an apartment building on March 17, 1989, for $700,000. T takes the maximum cost recovery for determining taxable income. T's cost recovery for computing 1989 taxable income would be $20,153 [$700,000 × .02879 (Table 9-7)]. However, T's cost recovery for computing T's earnings and profits would be only $13,853 [$700,000 × .01979 (Table 9-12)]. □

DEPLETION

In developing an oil or gas well, four types of expenditures must be made by the producer. The first type is the payment for the natural resource (the oil under the ground). Because natural resources are physically limited, these costs are recovered through depletion. The second type occurs when the property is made ready for drilling: the cost of labor in clearing the property, erecting derricks, and drilling the hole. These costs, called intangible drilling and development costs, generally have no salvage value and are a lost cost if the well is dry. The third type of cost is for tangible assets such as tools, pipes, and engines. Such costs are capital in nature and must be capitalized and recovered through depreciation. Finally, there are costs that are incurred after the well is producing, including such items as labor, fuel, and supplies. They are clearly operating expenses that are deductible currently when incurred (on the accrual basis) or when paid (on the cash basis).

The expenditures for depreciable assets and operating expenses pose no unusual problems for producers of natural resources. The tax treatment of depletable costs and intangible drilling and development costs is quite a different matter.

Intangible Drilling and Development Costs (IDC)

Intangible drilling and development costs can be handled in one of two ways at the option of the taxpayer. They can be *either* charged off as an expense in the year in which they are incurred or capitalized and written off through depletion. The election is made in the first year that such expenditures are incurred either by taking a deduction on the return or by adding them to the depletable basis. No formal statement of intent is required. Once made, the election is binding on both the taxpayer and the Internal Revenue Service for all such expenditures in the future. If the taxpayer fails to make the election to expense such costs on the original timely filed return the first year such expenditures are incurred, an automatic election to capitalize them has been made and is irrevocable.

As a general rule, it is more advantageous to expense intangible drilling and development costs. The obvious benefit of an immediate write-off (as opposed to a deferred write-off through depletion) is not the only advantage. Since a taxpayer can use percentage depletion, which is calculated without reference to basis (see Example 41), the intangible drilling and development costs may be completely lost as a deduction if they are capitalized.

Depletion Methods

Wasting assets (e.g., oil, gas, coal, gravel) are subject to depletion, which simply is a form of depreciation applicable to natural resources. Land generally cannot be depleted.

The owner of an interest in the wasting asset is entitled to deduct depletion. An owner is one who has an economic interest in the property.[43] An economic interest requires the acquisition of an interest in the minerals in place and the receipt of income from the extraction or severance of such minerals. Like depreciation, depletion is a deduction *for* adjusted gross income.

There are two methods of calculating depletion: cost and percentage. Cost depletion can be used on any wasting asset (and is the only method allowed for timber). Percentage depletion is subject to a number of limitations, particularly as to oil and gas deposits. Depletion should be calculated both ways, and generally the method that results in the *largest* deduction is used. The choice between cost and percentage depletion is an annual election.

Cost Depletion.   *Cost depletion* is determined by using the adjusted basis of the asset.[44] Such basis is divided by the estimated recoverable units of the asset (e.g., barrels, tons) to arrive at the depletion per unit. The depletion per unit then is multiplied by the number of units sold (*not* the units produced) during the year to arrive at the cost depletion allowed. Cost depletion, therefore, resembles the units-of-production method of calculating depreciation.

EXAMPLE 38   On January 1, 1989, T purchased the rights to a mineral interest for $1,000,000. At that time, the remaining recoverable units in the mineral interest were estimated to be 200,000. Under these circumstances, the depletion per unit becomes $5 [$1,000,000 (adjusted basis) ÷ 200,000 (estimated recoverable units)]. If during the year 60,000 units were mined and 25,000 were sold, the cost depletion would be $125,000 [$5 (depletion per unit) × 25,000 (units sold)]. □

If later it is discovered that the original estimate was incorrect, the depletion per unit for future calculations must be redetermined based on the revised estimate.[45]

EXAMPLE 39   Assume the same facts as in Example 38. In 1990, T realizes that an incorrect estimate was made. The remaining recoverable units now are

---

43. Reg. § 1.611–1(b).   45. § 611(a).
44. § 612.

determined to be 400,000. Based on this new information, the revised depletion per unit becomes $2.1875 [$875,000 (adjusted basis) ÷ 400,000 (estimated recoverable units)]. Note that the adjusted basis is the original cost ($1,000,000) reduced by the depletion claimed in 1989 ($125,000). If 30,000 units are sold in 1990, the depletion for the year would be $65,625 [$2.1875 (depletion per unit) × 30,000 (units sold)]. □

Percentage Depletion.   *Percentage depletion* (also referred to as statutory depletion) is a specified percentage provided for in the Code. The percentage varies according to the type of mineral interest involved. A sample of these percentages is shown in Figure 9–1. The rate is applied to the gross income from the property, but in no event may percentage depletion exceed 50 percent of the taxable income from the property before the allowance for depletion.[46]

EXAMPLE 40

Assuming gross income of $100,000, a depletion rate of 22%, and other expenses relating to the property of $60,000, the depletion allowance is determined as follows:

Gross income	$100,000
Less: Other expenses	(60,000)
Taxable income before depletion	$ 40,000
Depletion allowance [the lesser of $22,000 (22% × $100,000) or $20,000 (50% × $40,000)]	(20,000)
Taxable income after depletion	$ 20,000

The adjusted basis of the property would be reduced by $20,000, the depletion allowed. If the other expenses had been only $55,000, the full $22,000 could have been deducted, and the adjusted basis would have been reduced by $22,000. □

Note that percentage depletion is based on a percentage of the gross income from the property and makes no reference to cost. When percentage depletion is used, it is therefore possible to deduct more than the original cost of the property. If percentage depletion is used, however, the adjusted basis of the property (for computing cost depletion) must be reduced by the amount of percentage depletion taken until basis reaches zero.

Effect of Intangible Drilling Costs on Depletion.   The treatment of intangible drilling and development costs has an effect on the depletion deduction in two ways. If the costs are capitalized, the basis for cost depletion is increased. As a consequence, the cost depletion is increased. If intangible drilling and development costs are expensed, they reduce the taxable income from

---

46. § 613(a). Special rules apply for certain oil and
gas wells under § 613A (e.g., the 50% ceiling is
replaced with a 65% ceiling).

FIGURE 9–1   Sample of Percentage Depletion Rates

22% Depletion

Cobalt	Sulfur
Lead	Tin
Nickel	Uranium
Platinum	Zinc

15% Depletion

Copper	Oil and gas
Gold	Oil shale
Iron	Silver

14% Depletion

Borax	Magnesium carbonates
Calcium carbonates	Marble
Granite	Potash
Limestone	Slate

10% Depletion

| Coal | Perlite |
| Lignite | Sodium chloride |

5% Depletion

| Gravel | Pumice |
| Peat | Sand |

the property. This reduction may result in application of the provision that limits depletion to 50 percent of taxable income before deducting depletion.

EXAMPLE 41

J purchased the rights to an oil interest for $1,000,000. The recoverable barrels were estimated to be 200,000. During the year, 50,000 barrels were sold for $2,000,000. Regular expenses amounted to $800,000, and intangible drilling and development costs were $650,000. If the intangible drilling and development costs are capitalized, the depletion per unit is $8.25 ($1,000,000 plus $650,000 divided by 200,000 barrels), and the following taxable income results:

Gross income	$2,000,000
Less: Expenses	(800,000)
Taxable income before depletion	$1,200,000
Cost depletion ($8.25 × 50,000) = $412,500	
Percentage depletion (15% × $2,000,000) = $300,000	
Greater of cost or percentage depletion	(412,500)
Taxable income	$ 787,500

If the costs are expensed, the taxable income becomes $275,000, as follows:

Gross income	$2,000,000
Less: Expenses, including IDC	(1,450,000)
Taxable income before depletion	$ 550,000
Cost depletion [($1,000,000 ÷ 200,000 barrels) × 50,000 barrels] = $250,000	
Percentage depletion (15% of $2,000,000, limited to 50% of $550,000 taxable income before depletion) = $275,000	
Greater of cost or percentage depletion	(275,000)
Taxable income after depletion	$ 275,000

For further restrictions on the use or availability of the percentage depletion method, see § 613.

REPORTING PROCEDURES

Sole proprietors engaged in a business should file a Schedule C, Profit or (Loss) from Business or Profession, to accompany Form 1040. Schedule C for 1988 is presented because the 1989 form was not yet available.

The top part of page 1 requests certain key information about the taxpayer (e.g., name, address, Social Security number) and the business methods involved (e.g., accounting method and inventory method used). Part I provides for the reporting of items of income. If the business requires the use of inventories and the computation of cost of goods sold (see chapter 18 for when this is necessary), Part III must be completed and the cost of goods sold amount transferred to line 2 of Part 1.

Part II allows for the reporting of deductions. Some of the deductions discussed in chapters 8 and 9 and their location on the form are bad debts (line 7), depletion (line 11), and depreciation (line 12). Other expenses (line 29) include those items not already covered (see lines 6–28). An example would be research and experimental expenditures.

If depreciation is claimed, it should be supported by completing Form 4562. Form 4562 for 1988 is presented because the 1989 form was not yet available. The amount listed on line 12 of Form 4562 is then transferred to line 12 of Part II of Schedule C.

EXAMPLE 42

Thomas Andrews, Social Security number 123–45–6789, was employed as an accountant until July 1987, when he opened his own practice. His address is 279 Mountainview, Ogden, UT 84201. Andrews keeps his books on the accrual basis and had the following revenue and business expenses in 1988:

a. Revenue from accounting practice, $80,000.

b. Bad debts, $2,000.

c. Automobile expenses, $3,000.

d. Insurance, $800.

e. Office supplies, $4,000.

f. Rent, $12,000.

g. Furniture and fixtures acquired on July 15, 1987, for $8,000. Andrews used the ACRS statutory percentage cost recovery method.

h. Business automobile acquired on May 20, 1987, for $10,000. Andrews used the ACRS statutory percentage cost recovery method. The automobile, which was driven 12,000 miles during 1988, was used only for business purposes.

i. Microcomputer acquired on May 7, 1988, for $14,000. Andrews elects § 179 and uses the ACRS statutory percentage cost recovery method.

Andrews would report the above information on Schedule C and Form 4562 as illustrated on the following pages. □

Form **4562**	**Depreciation and Amortization**	OMB No. 1545-0172
Department of the Treasury Internal Revenue Service	▶ See separate instructions. ▶ Attach this form to your return.	**1988** Attachment Sequence No. **67**

Name(s) as shown on return	Identifying number
Thomas Andrews	123-45-6789

Business or activity to which this form relates

Accounting Services

Part I **Depreciation** (*Use Part III for automobiles, certain other vehicles, computers, and property used for entertainment, recreation, or amusement.*)

Section A.—Election To Expense Depreciable Assets (Section 179)

(a) Description of property	(b) Date placed in service	(c) Cost	(d) Expense deduction
1 5-Year Class Prop.-Microcomputer	5/7/88	14,000	10,000

2 Listed property—Enter total from Part III, Section A, column (h) . . . .

3 Total (add lines 1 and 2, but do not enter more than $10,000) . . . . | 10,000

4 Enter the amount, if any, by which the cost of all section 179 property placed in service during this tax year is more than $200,000 . . . .

5 Subtract line 4 from line 3. If less than zero, enter zero. (See instructions for other limitations.) . . . . . | 10,000

Section B.—Depreciation

(a) Class of property	(b) Date placed in service	(c) Basis for depreciation (Business use only—see instructions)	(d) Recovery period	(e) Method of figuring depreciation	(f) Deduction
6 Modified Accelerated Cost Recovery System (MACRS) (see instructions): For assets placed in service ONLY during tax year beginning in 1988					
a 3-year property					
b 5-year property		4,000	5-YR	PRE	800
c 7-year property					
d 10-year property					
e 15-year property					
f 20-year property					
g Residential rental property					
h Nonresidential real property					

7 Alternative Depreciation System (ADS)

8 Listed property—Enter total from Part III, Section A, column (g) . . . . | 3,200

9 MACRS deduction for assets placed in service prior to 1988 (see instructions) . . . . | 1,959

Section C.—ACRS and/or Other Depreciation

10 Property subject to section 168(f)(1) election (see instructions) . . . .

11 ACRS and/or other depreciation (see instructions) . . . .

Section D.—Summary

12 Total (add deductions on lines 5 through 11). Enter here and on the Depreciation line of your return (Partnerships and S corporations—Do NOT include any amounts entered on line 5.) . . . . | 15,959

13 For assets above placed in service during the current year, enter the portion of the basis attributable to section 263A costs. (see instructions). . . . .

Part II **Amortization**

(a) Description of property	(b) Date acquired	(c) Cost or other basis	(d) Code section	(e) Amortization period or percentage	(f) Amortization for this year
1 Amortization for property placed in service **only** during tax year beginning in 1988					

2 Amortization for property placed in service prior to 1988 . . . .

3 Total. Enter here and on Other Deductions or Other Expenses line of your return . . . .

See Paperwork Reduction Act Notice on page 1 of the separate instructions.   Form **4562** (1988)

Form 4562 (1988)   Page **2**

Part III **Automobiles, Certain Other Vehicles, Computers, and Property Used for Entertainment, Recreation, or Amusement (Listed Property).**

If you are using the standard mileage rate or deducting vehicle lease expense, complete columns (a) through (d) of Section A, all of Section B, and Section C if applicable.

Section A.—Depreciation (If automobiles and other listed property placed in service after June 18, 1984, are used 50% or less in a trade or business, the section 179 deduction is not allowed and depreciation must be taken using the straight line method over 5 years. For other limitations, see instructions.)

Do you have evidence to support the business use claimed?   ☒ **Yes** ☐ **No** If "Yes," is the evidence written? ☒ **Yes** ☐ **No**

(a) Type of property (list vehicles first)	(b) Date placed in service	(c) Business use percentage (%)	(d) Cost or other basis (see instructions for leased property)	(e) Basis for depreciation (Business use only—see instructions)	(f) Depreciation method and recovery period	(g) Depreciation deduction	(h) Section 179 expense
VEHICLE	5/20/87	100	10,000	10,000	PRE, 5-YR	3,200	

Total (Enter here and on line 2, page 1.) . . . .

Total (Enter here and on line 8, page 1.) 3,200

Section B.—Information Regarding Use of Vehicles

Complete this section as follows, if you deduct expenses for vehicles:
- *Always complete this section for vehicles used by a sole proprietor, partner, or other more than 5% owner or related person.*
- *If you provided vehicles to employees, first answer the questions in Section C to see if you meet an exception to completing this section for those items.*

	Vehicle 1		Vehicle 2		Vehicle 3		Vehicle 4		Vehicle 5		Vehicle 6	
1 Total miles driven during the year . . .	12,000											
2 Total business miles driven during the year	12,000											
3 Total commuting miles driven during the year.	-0-											
4 Total other personal (noncommuting) miles driven	-0-											
	Yes	No	Yes	No	Yes	No	Yes	No	Yes	No	Yes	No
5 Was the vehicle available for personal use during off-duty hours?		X										
6 Was the vehicle used primarily by a more than 5% owner or related person? . . .		X										
7 Is another vehicle available for personal use?.	X											

Section C.—Questions for Employers Who Provide Vehicles for Use by Employees.
(Answer these questions to determine if you meet an exception to completing Section B. **Note:** *Section B must always be completed for vehicles used by sole proprietors, partners, or other more than 5% owners or related persons.)*

	Yes	No
8 Do you maintain a written policy statement that prohibits all personal use of vehicles, including commuting, by your employees?		
9 Do you maintain a written policy statement that prohibits personal use of vehicles, except commuting, by your employees? (See instructions for vehicles used by corporate officers, directors, or 1% or more owners.)		
10 Do you treat all use of vehicles by employees as personal use?		
11 Do you provide more than five vehicles to your employees and retain the information received from your employees concerning the use of the vehicles?		
12 Do you meet the requirements concerning qualified automobile demonstration use (see instructions)?		
Note: *If your answer to 8, 9, 10, 11, or 12 is "Yes," you need not complete Section B for the covered vehicles.*		

SCHEDULE C	**Profit or Loss From Business**	OMB No. 1545-0074

SCHEDULE C
(Form 1040)

Department of the Treasury
Internal Revenue Service

Profit or Loss From Business
(Sole Proprietorship)
Partnerships, Joint Ventures, Etc., Must File Form 1065.
▶ **Attach to Form 1040, Form 1041, or Form 1041S.**   ▶ **See Instructions for Schedule C (Form 1040).**

OMB No. 1545-0074

1988
Attachment Sequence No. **09**

Name of proprietor	Social security number (SSN)
Thomas Andrews	123 : 45 : 6789

A Principal business or profession, including product or service (see Instructions)
Accounting Services

B Principal business code (from Part IV) ▶ | 7 | 6 | 5 | 8 |

C Business name and address ▶ Andrews Accounting Services
279 Mountain View, Ogden, UT 84201

D Employer ID number (Not SSN)

E Method(s) used to value closing inventory:
   (1) ☐ Cost   **(2)** ☐ Lower of cost or market   **(3)** ☐ Other (attach explanation)

		Yes	No
F Accounting method: **(1)** ☐ Cash **(2)** ☒ Accrual **(3)** ☐ Other (specify) ▶			
G Was there any change in determining quantities, costs, or valuations between opening and closing inventory? (If "Yes," attach explanation.)			X
H Are you deducting expenses for business use of your home? (If "Yes," see Instructions for limitations.)			X
I Did you "materially participate" in the operation of this business during 1988? (If "No," see Instructions for limitations on losses.) . . .		X	

J If this schedule includes a loss, credit, deduction, income, or other tax benefit relating to a tax shelter required to be registered, check here . . ▶ ☐
   If you check this box, you MUST attach **Form 8271.**

Part I Income

1a Gross receipts or sales	**1a**	80,000
b Less: Returns and allowances	**1b**	
c Subtract line 1b from line 1a. Enter the result here . . .	**1c**	80,000
2 Cost of goods sold and/or operations (from Part III, line 8)	**2**	
3 Subtract line 2 from line 1c and enter the **gross profit** here	**3**	80,000
4 Other income (including windfall profit tax credit or refund received in 1988)	**4**	
5 Add lines 3 and 4. This is the **gross income** . . . . ▶	**5**	80,000

Part II Deductions

6 Advertising	**6**		**23** Repairs	**23**	
7 Bad debts from sales or services (see Instructions)	**7**	2,000	**24** Supplies (not included in Part III)	**24**	
8 Bank service charges	**8**		**25** Taxes	**25**	
9 Car and truck expenses . . .	**9**	3,000	**26** Travel, meals, and entertainment:		
10 Commissions	**10**		**a** Travel	**26a**	
11 Depletion	**11**		**b** Meals and entertainment .		
12 Depreciation and section 179 deduction from Form 4562 (not included in Part III)	**12**	15,959	**c** Enter 20% of line 26b subject to limitations (see Instructions) . .		
13 Dues and publications . . .	**13**		**d** Subtract line 26c from 26b . . .	**26d**	
14 Employee benefit programs .	**14**		**27** Utilities and telephone	**27**	
15 Freight (not included in Part III) .	**15**		**28a** Wages		
16 Insurance	**16**	800	**b** Jobs credit . . .		
17 Interest:			**c** Subtract line 28b from 28a . .	**28c**	
a Mortgage (paid to banks, etc.) .	**17a**		**29** Other expenses (list type and amount):		
b Other	**17b**		....		
18 Laundry and cleaning . . .	**18**		....		
19 Legal and professional services .	**19**		....		
20 Office expense	**20**	4,000	....		
21 Pension and profit-sharing plans .	**21**		....		
22 Rent on business property . .	**22**	12,000		**29**	

30 Add amounts in columns for lines 6 through 29. These are the **total deductions** . . . . ▶	**30**	37,759
31 Net profit or (loss). Subtract line 30 from line 5. If a profit, enter here and on Form 1040, line 12, and on Schedule SE, line 2. If a loss, you MUST go on to line 32. (Fiduciaries, see instructions.).	**31**	42,241

32 If you have a loss, you MUST check the box that describes your investment in this activity (see Instructions) . . . .
   32a ☐ All investment is at risk.
   32b ☐ Some investment is not at risk.

   If you checked 32a, enter the loss on Form 1040, line 12, and Schedule SE, line 2. If you checked 32b, you MUST attach **Form 6198.**

For Paperwork Reduction Act Notice, see Form 1040 Instructions.   **Schedule C (Form 1040) 1988**

Page **2**

Part III	Cost of Goods Sold and/or Operations (See Schedule C Instructions for Part III)		
1	Inventory at beginning of year. (If different from last year's closing inventory, attach explanation.)	**1**	
2	Purchases less cost of items withdrawn for personal use	**2**	
3	Cost of labor. (Do not include salary paid to yourself.)	**3**	
4	Materials and supplies	**4**	
5	Other costs	**5**	
6	Add lines 1 through 5	**6**	
7	Less: Inventory at end of year	**7**	
8	**Cost of goods sold and/or operations.** Subtract line 7 from line 6. Enter the result here and in Part I, line 2. .	**8**	

TAX PLANNING CONSIDERATIONS

Depreciation and ACRS

Depreciation schedules should be reviewed annually for possible retirements, abandonments, obsolescence, and changes in estimated useful lives.

EXAMPLE 43

An examination of the depreciation schedule of X Company reveals the following:

- Asset A was abandoned when it was discovered that the cost of repairs would be in excess of the cost of replacement. Asset A had an adjusted basis of $3,000.

- Asset D was being depreciated over a period of 10 years, but a revised estimate showed that its estimated remaining life is only 2 years. Its original cost was $60,000, and it had been depreciated under the straight-line method for 3 years. It was a pre-ERTA asset and was not subject to ACRS provisions.

- Asset J had become obsolete this year, at which point, its adjusted basis was $8,000.

The depreciation expense on Asset D should be $21,000 [$60,000 (cost) − $18,000 (accumulated depreciation) = $42,000 ÷ 2 (remaining estimated useful life)]. Assets A and J should be written off for an additional expense of $11,000 ($3,000 + $8,000). □

Because of the deductions for depreciation, interest, and ad valorem property taxes, investments in real estate can be highly attractive. In figuring the economics of such investments, one should be sure to take into account any tax savings that result.

EXAMPLE 44

In early January 1989, T (an individual in the 28% tax bracket) purchased residential rental property for $170,000 (of which $20,000 was allocated to the land and $150,000 to the building). T made a down payment of $25,000 and assumed the seller's mortgage for the balance. Under the mortgage agreement, monthly payments of $1,000 are required and are applied toward interest, taxes, insurance, and principal. Since the property was already occupied, T continued to receive from the tenant rent of

$1,200 per month. T actively participates in this activity and hence comes under the special rule for a rental real estate activity with respect to the limitation on passive activity losses.

During the first year of ownership, T's expenses were as follows:

Interest	$10,000
Taxes	800
Insurance	1,000
Repairs and maintenance	2,200
Depreciation ($150,000 × .03485)	5,228
Total	$19,228

The deductible loss from the rental property is computed as follows:

Rental income ($1,200 × 12 months)	$14,400
Less expenses (see above)	(19,228)
Net loss	$(4,828)

But what is T's overall position for the year when the tax benefit of the loss is taken into account? Considering just the cash intake and outlay, it is summarized as follows:

Intake—		
Rental income	$14,400	
Tax savings [28% (income tax bracket) × $4,828 (loss from the property)]	1,352	$15,752
Outlay—		
Mortgage payments ($1,000 × 12 months)	$12,000	
Repairs and maintenance	2,200	(14,200)
Net cash benefit		$ 1,552

☐

It should be noted, however, that should T cease being an active participant in the rental activity, the passive loss rules would apply, and T could lose the current period benefit of the loss.

Depletion

Since the election to use the cost or percentage depletion method is an annual election, a taxpayer can use cost depletion (if higher) until the basis is exhausted and then switch to percentage depletion in the following years.

EXAMPLE 45   Assume the following facts for T:

Remaining depletable basis	$ 11,000
Gross income (10,000 units)	100,000
Expenses (other than depletion)	30,000

Since cost depletion is limited to the basis of $11,000 and if the percentage depletion is $22,000 (assume a 22% rate), T would choose the latter. His basis is then reduced to zero. In future years, however, he can continue to take percentage depletion, since percentage depletion is taken without reference to the remaining basis. □

The election to expense intangible drilling and development costs is a one-time election. Once the election is made to either expense or capitalize the intangible drilling and development costs, it is binding on all future expenditures. The permanent nature of the election makes it extremely important for the taxpayer to determine which treatment will provide the greatest tax advantage. (Refer to Example 41 for an illustration of the effect of using the two different alternatives for a given set of facts.)

TABLES

TABLE 9–1   ACRS Statutory Percentages for Property Other Than 15-Year Real Property, 18-Year Real Property, or 19-Year Real Property

For Property Placed in Service after December 31, 1980, and before January 1, 1987

The applicable percentage for the class of property is:

Recovery Year	3-Year	5-Year	10-Year	15-Year Public Utility
1	25	15	8	5
2	38	22	14	10
3	37	21	12	9
4		21	10	8
5		21	10	7
6			10	7
7			9	6
8			9	6
9			9	6
10			9	6
11				6
12				6
13				6
14				6
15				6

TABLE 9–2   Accelerated Depreciation for Personal Property Assuming
Half-Year Convention

For Property Placed in Service after December 31, 1986

Recovery Year	3-Year (200% DB)	5-Year (200% DB)	7-Year (200% DB)	10-Year (200% DB)	15-Year (150% DB)	20-Year (150% DB)
1	33.33	20.00	14.29	10.00	5.00	3.750
2	44.45	32.00	24.49	18.00	9.50	7.219
3	14.81*	19.20	17.49	14.40	8.55	6.677
4	7.41	11.52*	12.49	11.52	7.70	6.177
5		11.52	8.93*	9.22	6.93	5.713
6		5.76	8.92	7.37	6.23	5.285
7			8.93	6.55*	5.90*	4.888
8			4.46	6.55	5.90	4.522
9				6.56	5.91	4.462*
10				6.55	5.90	4.461
11				3.28	5.91	4.462
12					5.90	4.461
13					5.91	4.462
14					5.90	4.461
15					5.91	4.462
16					2.95	4.461
17						4.462
18						4.461
19						4.462
20						4.461
21						2.231

* Switchover to straight-line depreciation.

TABLE 9–3   Accelerated Depreciation for Personal Property Assuming Mid-Quarter
Convention

For Property Placed in Service after December 31, 1986
(Partial Table *)

3-Year

Recovery Year	First Quarter	Second Quarter	Third Quarter	Fourth Quarter
1	58.33	41.67	25.00	8.33
2	27.78	38.89	50.00	61.11

5-Year

Recovery Year	First Quarter	Second Quarter	Third Quarter	Fourth Quarter
1	35.00	25.00	15.00	5.00
2	26.00	30.00	34.00	38.00

* The figures in this table are taken from the official tables that appear in Rev.Proc. 87–57, 1987–2 C.B. 687. Because of their length, the complete tables are not presented.

TABLE 9–4   ACRS Statutory Percentages for 15-Year Real Property

For Property Placed in Service after December 31, 1980, and before January 1, 1987
15-Year Real Property: Low-Income Housing

Year	Month Placed in Service											
	1	2	3	4	5	6	7	8	9	10	11	12
1	13%	12%	11%	10%	9%	8%	7%	6%	4%	3%	2%	1%
2	12%	12%	12%	12%	12%	12%	12%	13%	13%	13%	13%	13%
3	10%	10%	10%	10%	11%	11%	11%	11%	11%	11%	11%	11%
4	9%	9%	9%	9%	9%	9%	9%	9%	10%	10%	10%	10%
5	8%	8%	8%	8%	8%	8%	8%	8%	8%	8%	8%	9%
6	7%	7%	7%	7%	7%	7%	7%	7%	7%	7%	7%	7%
7	6%	6%	6%	6%	6%	6%	6%	6%	6%	6%	6%	6%
8	5%	5%	5%	5%	5%	5%	5%	5%	5%	5%	6%	6%
9	5%	5%	5%	5%	5%	5%	5%	5%	5%	5%	5%	5%
10	5%	5%	5%	5%	5%	5%	5%	5%	5%	5%	5%	5%
11	4%	5%	5%	5%	5%	5%	5%	5%	5%	5%	5%	5%
12	4%	4%	4%	5%	4%	5%	5%	5%	5%	5%	5%	5%
13	4%	4%	4%	4%	4%	4%	5%	4%	5%	5%	5%	5%
14	4%	4%	4%	4%	4%	4%	4%	4%	4%	5%	4%	4%
15	4%	4%	4%	4%	4%	4%	4%	4%	4%	4%	4%	4%
16	—	—	1%	1%	2%	2%	2%	3%	3%	3%	4%	4%

For Property Placed in Service after December 31, 1980, and before March 16, 1984
15-Year Real Property (other than low-income housing)

Year	Month Placed in Service											
	1	2	3	4	5	6	7	8	9	10	11	12
1	12%	11%	10%	9%	8%	7%	6%	5%	4%	3%	2%	1%
2	10%	10%	11%	11%	11%	11%	11%	11%	11%	11%	11%	12%
3	9%	9%	9%	9%	10%	10%	10%	10%	10%	10%	10%	10%
4	8%	8%	8%	8%	8%	8%	9%	9%	9%	9%	9%	9%
5	7%	7%	7%	7%	7%	7%	8%	8%	8%	8%	8%	8%
6	6%	6%	6%	6%	7%	7%	7%	7%	7%	7%	7%	7%
7	6%	6%	6%	6%	6%	6%	6%	6%	6%	6%	6%	6%
8	6%	6%	6%	6%	6%	6%	6%	6%	6%	6%	6%	6%
9	6%	6%	6%	6%	5%	6%	5%	5%	5%	6%	6%	6%
10	5%	6%	5%	6%	5%	5%	5%	5%	5%	5%	6%	5%
11	5%	5%	5%	5%	5%	5%	5%	5%	5%	5%	5%	5%
12	5%	5%	5%	5%	5%	5%	5%	5%	5%	5%	5%	5%
13	5%	5%	5%	5%	5%	5%	5%	5%	5%	5%	5%	5%
14	5%	5%	5%	5%	5%	5%	5%	5%	5%	5%	5%	5%
15	5%	5%	5%	5%	5%	5%	5%	5%	5%	5%	5%	5%
16	—	—	1%	1%	2%	2%	3%	3%	4%	4%	4%	5%

TABLE 9–5 ACRS Cost Recovery Table for 18-Year Real Property

**For Property Placed in Service after June 22, 1984, and before May 9, 1985
18-Year Real Property (18-Year 175% Declining Balance)
(Assuming Mid-Month Convention)**

If the recovery year is:	And the month in the first recovery year the property is placed in service is:											
	1	2	3	4	5	6	7	8	9	10	11	12
	The applicable percentage is (use the column for the month in the first year the property is placed in service):											
1	9	9	8	7	6	5	4	4	3	2	1	0.4
2	9	9	9	9	9	9	9	9	9	10	10	10.0
3	8	8	8	8	8	8	8	8	9	9	9	9.0
4	7	7	7	7	7	8	8	8	8	8	8	8.0
5	7	7	7	7	7	7	7	7	7	7	7	7.0
6	6	6	6	6	6	6	6	6	6	6	6	6.0
7	5	5	5	5	6	6	6	6	6	6	6	6.0
8	5	5	5	5	5	5	5	5	5	5	5	5.0
9	5	5	5	5	5	5	5	5	5	5	5	5.0
10	5	5	5	5	5	5	5	5	5	5	5	5.0
11	5	5	5	5	5	5	5	5	5	5	5	5.0
12	5	5	5	5	5	5	5	5	5	5	5	5.0
13	4	4	4	5	4	4	5	4	4	4	5	5.0
14	4	4	4	4	4	4	4	4	4	4	4	4.0
15	4	4	4	4	4	4	4	4	4	4	4	4.0
16	4	4	4	4	4	4	4	4	4	4	4	4.0
17	4	4	4	4	4	4	4	4	4	4	4	4.0
18	4	3	4	4	4	4	4	4	4	4	4	4.0
19		1	1	1	2	2	2	3	3	3	3	3.6

TABLE 9–6   ACRS Cost Recovery Table for 19-Year Real Property

**For Property Placed in Service after May 8, 1985, and before January 1, 1987
19-Year Real Property (19-Year 175% Declining Balance)
(Assuming Mid-Month Convention)**

If the recovery year is:	And the month in the first recovery year the property is placed in service is:											
	1	2	3	4	5	6	7	8	9	10	11	12
	The applicable percentage is (use the column for the month in the first year the property is placed in service):											
1	8.8	8.1	7.3	6.5	5.8	5.0	4.2	3.5	2.7	1.9	1.1	0.4
2	8.4	8.5	8.5	8.6	8.7	8.8	8.8	8.9	9.0	9.0	9.1	9.2
3	7.6	7.7	7.7	7.8	7.9	7.9	8.0	8.1	8.1	8.2	8.3	8.3
4	6.9	7.0	7.0	7.1	7.1	7.2	7.3	7.3	7.4	7.4	7.5	7.6
5	6.3	6.3	6.4	6.4	6.5	6.5	6.6	6.6	6.7	6.8	6.8	6.9
6	5.7	5.7	5.8	5.9	5.9	5.9	6.0	6.0	6.1	6.1	6.2	6.2
7	5.2	5.2	5.3	5.3	5.3	5.4	5.4	5.5	5.5	5.6	5.6	5.6
8	4.7	4.7	4.8	4.8	4.8	4.9	4.9	5.0	5.0	5.1	5.1	5.1
9	4.2	4.3	4.3	4.4	4.4	4.5	4.5	4.5	4.5	4.6	4.6	4.7
10	4.2	4.2	4.2	4.2	4.2	4.2	4.2	4.2	4.2	4.2	4.2	4.2
11	4.2	4.2	4.2	4.2	4.2	4.2	4.2	4.2	4.2	4.2	4.2	4.2
12	4.2	4.2	4.2	4.2	4.2	4.2	4.2	4.2	4.2	4.2	4.2	4.2
13	4.2	4.2	4.2	4.2	4.2	4.2	4.2	4.2	4.2	4.2	4.2	4.2
14	4.2	4.2	4.2	4.2	4.2	4.2	4.2	4.2	4.2	4.2	4.2	4.2
15	4.2	4.2	4.2	4.2	4.2	4.2	4.2	4.2	4.2	4.2	4.2	4.2
16	4.2	4.2	4.2	4.2	4.2	4.2	4.2	4.2	4.2	4.2	4.2	4.2
17	4.2	4.2	4.2	4.2	4.2	4.2	4.2	4.2	4.2	4.2	4.2	4.2
18	4.2	4.2	4.2	4.2	4.2	4.2	4.2	4.2	4.2	4.2	4.2	4.2
19	4.2	4.2	4.2	4.2	4.2	4.2	4.2	4.2	4.2	4.2	4.2	4.2
20	0.2	0.5	0.9	1.2	1.6	1.9	2.3	2.6	3.0	3.3	3.7	4.0

TABLE 9–7	Straight-Line Depreciation for Real Property Assuming Mid-Month Convention*

For Property Placed in Service after December 31, 1986
27.5-Year Residential Real Property

The applicable percentage is (use the column for the
month in the first year the property is placed in service):

Recovery Year(s)	1	2	3	4	5	6	7	8	9	10	11	12
1	3.485	3.182	2.879	2.576	2.273	1.970	1.667	1.364	1.061	0.758	0.455	0.152
2–18	3.636	3.636	3.636	3.636	3.636	3.636	3.636	3.636	3.636	3.636	3.636	3.636
19–27	3.637	3.637	3.637	3.637	3.637	3.637	3.637	3.637	3.637	3.637	3.637	3.637
28	1.970	2.273	2.576	2.879	3.182	3.485	3.636	3.636	3.636	3.636	3.636	3.636
29	0.000	0.000	0.000	0.000	0.000	0.000	0.152	0.455	0.758	1.061	1.364	1.667

31.5-Year Nonresidential Real Property

The applicable percentage is (use the column for the
month in the first year the property is placed in service):

Recovery Year(s)	1	2	3	4	5	6	7	8	9	10	11	12
1	3.042	2.778	2.513	2.249	1.984	1.720	1.455	1.190	0.926	0.661	0.397	0.132
2–19	3.175	3.175	3.175	3.175	3.175	3.175	3.175	3.175	3.175	3.175	3.175	3.175
20–31	3.174	3.174	3.174	3.174	3.174	3.174	3.174	3.174	3.174	3.174	3.174	3.174
32	1.720	1.984	2.249	2.513	2.778	3.042	3.175	3.175	3.175	3.175	3.175	3.175
33	0.000	0.000	0.000	0.000	0.000	0.000	0.132	0.397	0.661	0.926	1.190	1.455

* The official tables contain a separate row for each year. For ease of presentation, certain years are grouped in these two tables. In some instances, this will produce a difference of .001 for the last digit when compared with the official tables.

TABLE 9–8   ACRS Cost Recovery Table for 19-Year Real Property: Optional Straight-Line

For Property Placed in Service after May 8, 1985, and before January 1, 1987 19-Year Real Property for Which an Optional 19-Year Straight-Line Method Is Elected (Assuming Mid-Month Convention)

If the recovery year is:	And the month in the first recovery year the property is placed in service is:											
	1	2	3	4	5	6	7	8	9	10	11	12
	The applicable percentage is (use the column for the month in the first year the property is placed in service):											
1	5.0	4.6	4.2	3.7	3.3	2.9	2.4	2.0	1.5	1.1	.7	.2
2	5.3	5.3	5.3	5.3	5.3	5.3	5.3	5.3	5.3	5.3	5.3	5.3
3	5.3	5.3	5.3	5.3	5.3	5.3	5.3	5.3	5.3	5.3	5.3	5.3
4	5.3	5.3	5.3	5.3	5.3	5.3	5.3	5.3	5.3	5.3	5.3	5.3
5	5.3	5.3	5.3	5.3	5.3	5.3	5.3	5.3	5.3	5.3	5.3	5.3
6	5.3	5.3	5.3	5.3	5.3	5.3	5.3	5.3	5.3	5.3	5.3	5.3
7	5.3	5.3	5.3	5.3	5.3	5.3	5.3	5.3	5.3	5.3	5.3	5.3
8	5.3	5.3	5.3	5.3	5.3	5.3	5.3	5.3	5.3	5.3	5.3	5.3
9	5.3	5.3	5.3	5.3	5.3	5.3	5.3	5.3	5.3	5.3	5.3	5.3
10	5.3	5.3	5.3	5.3	5.3	5.3	5.3	5.3	5.3	5.3	5.3	5.3
11	5.3	5.3	5.3	5.3	5.3	5.3	5.3	5.3	5.3	5.3	5.3	5.3
12	5.3	5.3	5.3	5.3	5.3	5.3	5.3	5.3	5.3	5.3	5.3	5.3
13	5.3	5.3	5.3	5.3	5.3	5.3	5.3	5.3	5.3	5.3	5.3	5.3
14	5.2	5.2	5.2	5.2	5.2	5.2	5.2	5.2	5.2	5.2	5.2	5.2
15	5.2	5.2	5.2	5.2	5.2	5.2	5.2	5.2	5.2	5.2	5.2	5.2
16	5.2	5.2	5.2	5.2	5.2	5.2	5.2	5.2	5.2	5.2	5.2	5.2
17	5.2	5.2	5.2	5.2	5.2	5.2	5.2	5.2	5.2	5.2	5.2	5.2
18	5.2	5.2	5.2	5.2	5.2	5.2	5.2	5.2	5.2	5.2	5.2	5.2
19	5.2	5.2	5.2	5.2	5.2	5.2	5.2	5.2	5.2	5.2	5.2	5.2
20	.2	.6	1.0	1.5	1.9	2.3	2.8	3.2	3.7	4.1	4.5	5.0

TABLE 9–9   Straight-Line Depreciation for Personal Property Assuming Half-Year Convention *

For Property Placed in Service after December 31, 1986

ACRS Class	% First Recovery Year	Other Recovery Years		Last Recovery Year	
		Years	%	Year	%
3-Year	16.67	2–3	33.33	4	16.67
5-Year	10.00	2–5	20.00	6	10.00
7-Year	7.14	2–7	14.29	8	7.14
10-Year	5.00	2–10	10.00	11	5.00
15-Year	3.33	2–15	6.67	16	3.33
20-Year	2.50	2–20	5.00	21	2.50

* The official table contains a separate row for each year. For ease of presentation, certain years are grouped in this table. In some instances, this will produce a difference of .01 for the last digit when compared with the official table.

TABLE 9–10   Alternative Minimum Tax: 150% Declining-Balance Assuming Half-Year Convention

**For Property Placed in Service after December 31, 1986
(Partial Table*)**

Recovery Year	3-Year 150%	5-Year 150%	9-Year 150%	10-Year 150%
1	25.00	15.00	8.33	7.50
2	37.50	25.50	15.28	13.88
3	25.00**	17.85	12.73	11.79
4	12.50	16.66**	10.61	10.02
5		16.66	9.65**	8.74**
6		8.33	9.64	8.74
7			9.65	8.74
8			9.64	8.74
9			9.65	8.74
10			4.82	8.74
11				4.37

* The figures in this table are taken from the official table that appears in Rev.Proc. 87–57, 1987–2 C.B. 687. Because of its length, the complete table is not presented.

** Switchover to straight-line depreciation.

TABLE 9–11   ADS Straight-Line for Personal Property Assuming Half-Year Convention

**For Property Placed in Service after
December 31, 1986
(Partial Table*)**

Recovery Year	5-Year Class	9.5-Year Class	12-Year Class
1	10.00	5.26	4.17
2	20.00	10.53	8.33
3	20.00	10.53	8.33
4	20.00	10.53	8.33
5	20.00	10.52	8.33
6	10.00	10.53	8.33
7		10.52	8.34
8		10.53	8.33
9		10.52	8.34
10		10.53	8.33
11			8.34
12			8.33
13			4.17

* The figures in this table are taken from the official table that appears in Rev.Proc. 87–57, 1987–2 C.B. 687. Because of its length, the complete table is not presented. The tables for the mid-quarter convention also appear in Rev.Proc. 87–57.

TABLE 9–12   ADS Straight-Line for Real Property Assuming Mid-Month Convention

For Property Placed in Service after December 31, 1986

Recovery Year	Month Placed in Service											
	1	2	3	4	5	6	7	8	9	10	11	12
1	2.396	2.188	1.979	1.771	1.563	1.354	1.146	0.938	0.729	0.521	0.313	0.104
2–40	2.500	2.500	2.500	2.500	2.500	2.500	2.500	2.500	2.500	2.500	2.500	2.500
41	0.104	0.312	0.521	0.729	0.937	1.146	1.354	1.562	1.771	1.979	2.187	2.396

PROBLEM MATERIALS

Discussion Questions

1. What is the difference between the terms "depreciation" and "amortization"?

2. If a taxpayer does not claim depreciation in one year, can an excess amount be claimed during a subsequent year? How is the basis for depreciable property affected by the failure to claim depreciation during any one year?

3. If a personal use asset is converted to business use, why is it necessary to compute depreciation on the lower of fair market value or adjusted basis at the date of conversion?

4. Discuss the difference in the tax treatment of patents and goodwill with respect to amortization.

5. When can a taxpayer disregard salvage value on property acquired before 1981?

6. What depreciation methods can be used for the following assets that were acquired after 1969 and before January 1, 1981:
   a. Used machinery and equipment used in the business.
   b. New apartment building held for investment.
   c. Land held for business use.
   d. Used apartment building held for investment.
   e. New factory used for business.
   f. New automobile used in the business.

7. Discuss the half-year convention as it is used in the post-TRA of 1986 ACRS rules.

8. Discuss the mid-month convention as it is used in the post-TRA of 1986 ACRS rules.

9. Discuss the different ACRS recovery periods for ACRS real property depending on when the property is placed in service.

10. Why would a taxpayer elect the optional straight-line method for an asset acquired after 1986?

11. Discuss the applicable conventions if a taxpayer elects to use straight-line cost recovery for property placed in service after December 31, 1986.

12. Why is the basis of an asset reduced by the § 179 amount before the amount of the cost recovery allowance is computed?

13. Discuss the limitation on the § 179 amount that can be expensed and its impact on the basis of the property.

14. Discuss the tax consequences of listed property passing or failing the more-than-50% business usage test.

15. What are the tax consequences of using listed property for the production of income?

16. Should a taxpayer make the § 179 election with respect to passenger automobiles?

17. Discuss the tax consequences that result when a passenger automobile, which satisfied the more-than-50% business usage test during the first two years, fails the test for the third year.

18. Discuss the extent to which the 150% declining-balance method can be used under the alternative depreciation system.

19. Briefly discuss the differences between cost depletion and percentage depletion.

Problems

20. On January 1, 1979, X Company acquired an automobile for use in its business for $9,000. No depreciation was taken in 1979 or 1980, since the company had net operating losses and wanted to "save" the deductions for later years. In 1981, the company claimed a three-year life for the automobile (and no salvage value) and deducted $3,000 of depreciation using a straight-line rate. On January 1, 1982, the automobile was sold for $4,500. Calculate the gain or loss on the sale of the automobile in 1982.

21. X acquired a personal residence in 1978 for $60,000. In January 1980, he converted the residence to rental property when the fair market value was $64,000.

    a. Calculate the amount of depreciation that can be taken in 1980, assuming that the straight-line rate is used, there is no salvage value, and the residence has a 30-year estimated useful life.

    b. What would your answer be if the property were worth only $40,000 in 1980?

22. T, who is single, acquired a new machine for $42,000 on January 1, 1979. Calculate the total depreciation deduction allowed in the first year if the estimated useful life is 10 years (salvage value of $5,200) under each of the following methods:

   a.   200% declining-balance.

   b.   Sum-of-the-years' digits.

   c.   150% declining-balance.

   d.   Straight-line.

23. Taxpayer acquired a building for $250,000 (exclusive of land) on January 1, 1984. Calculate the depreciation using the statutory percentage method for 1984 and 1985 if:

    a. The real property is low-income housing.

    b. The real property is a factory building.

24. U acquires a warehouse on March 1, 1984, at a cost of $2,000,000 and does not elect the straight-line recovery method. On August 30, 1991, U sells the warehouse.

    a. Calculate U's cost recovery allowance for 1984.

    b. Calculate U's cost recovery allowance for 1991.

25. On December 2, 1984, W purchased and placed in service a warehouse. The warehouse cost $800,000. W used the ACRS statutory percentage cost recovery method. On July 7, 1989, W sold the warehouse.

    a. Determine W's cost recovery for 1984.

    b. Determine W's cost recovery for 1989.

26. Assume the same facts as in Problem 25, except that the warehouse was purchased on December 2, 1986, and sold on June 7, 1991.

    a. Determine W's cost recovery for 1986.

    b. Determine W's cost recovery for 1991.

27. T, who is single, acquired a new copier (five-year class property) on March 2, 1989, for $28,000. What is the maximum amount that T can deduct in 1989 assuming the following:

    a. The taxable income derived from T's trade or business (without regard to the amount expensed under § 179) is $100,000.

    b. The taxable income derived from T's trade or business (without regard to the amount expensed under § 179) is $3,000.

28. H owns a small business that he operates as a sole proprietor. In 1989, H will net $9,000 of business income before consideration of any § 179 deduction. H spends $205,000 on new equipment in 1989. If H also has $3,000 of § 179 deduction carryforwards from 1988, determine his § 179 expense deduction for 1989 and the amount of any carryforward.

29. K acquired a machine on June 5, 1989, for $100,000. The machine is a five-year class asset. Calculate K's deduction for 1989 assuming the following:

    a. K elects the straight-line method over the five-year recovery period and does not elect immediate expensing under § 179.

    b. K elects immediate expensing under § 179 and does not elect the straight-line method.

30. Q is the proprietor of a small business. In 1989, his business income, before consideration of any § 179 deduction, is $5,000. Q spends $203,000 on new equipment and furniture for 1989. If Q elects to take the § 179 deduction on a desk that cost $15,000 (included in the $203,000), determine Q's total cost recovery for 1989 with respect to the desk.

31. During May 1989, T bought the following business assets:

Factory machinery (seven-year class property)	$50,000
Light-duty truck (five-year class property)	20,000

    Calculate T's cost recovery allowances for 1989 using the statutory percentage method, assuming T does not make the § 179 election.

32. On March 10, 1989, T purchased three-year class property for $20,000. On December 15, 1989, T purchased five-year class property for $50,000.

    a. Calculate T's cost recovery for 1989, assuming T does not make the § 179 election or use straight-line depreciation.

    b. Calculate T's cost recovery for 1989, assuming T does elect to use § 179 and does not elect to use straight-line depreciation.

33. T acquired a building for $250,000 (exclusive of land) on January 1, 1989. Calculate the cost recovery for 1989 and 1990 if the real property is residential rental property. Nonresidential real property.

34. U acquires a warehouse on March 1, 1989, at a cost of $2,000,000. On September 30, 1996, U sells the warehouse. Calculate U's cost recovery for 1989. For 1996.

35. On July 1, 1989, A places in service a computer (five-year class property). The computer cost $20,000. A used the computer 45% for business and 30% for the production of income. The remainder of the time, A used the computer for personal purposes. If A does not elect § 179, determine her cost recovery deduction for the computer for 1989.

36. On February 16, 1989, T purchased and placed into service a new car. The purchase price was $18,000. T drove the car 12,000 miles during the remainder of the year, 9,000 miles for business and 3,000 miles for personal use. T used the statutory percentage method of cost recovery. Calculate the total deduction T may take for 1989 with respect to the car.

37. On June 5, 1989, R purchased and placed in service a $15,000 car. The business use percentage for the car is always 100%. Compute R's cost recovery deduction in 1995.

38. On May 7, 1989, S purchased and placed in service a $30,000 car. The business use percentage for the car is always 40% . Compute S's cost recovery deduction in 1989.

39. On June 20, 1989, T purchased and placed in service a new car. The purchase price was $30,000. The car was used 30% for business, 30% for the production of income, and 40% for personal use. Determine the total deduction T may take for 1989 with respect to the car.

40. On June 14, 1989, T purchased and placed in service a new car. The purchase price was $13,000. The car was used 75% for business and 25% for personal use in both 1989 and 1990. In 1991, the car was used 40% for business and 60% for personal use. Compute the cost recovery allowance for the car in 1991 and the cost recovery recapture.

41. In 1989 R purchased a computer (five-year property) for $120,000. The computer was used 60% for business, 20% for income production, and 20% for personal use. In 1990 the usage changed to 40% for business, 30% for income production, and 30% for personal use. Compute the cost recovery for 1990 and any cost recovery recapture. Assume R did not make a § 179 election on the computer in 1989.

42. On March 5, 1989, T purchased office furniture and fixtures for $40,000. The assets are seven-year class property and have an ADS midpoint of 9.5 years. Determine T's cost recovery deduction for 1989 using the alternative depreciation system assuming T does not make a § 179 election.

43. In 1989 L purchased a light-duty truck for $12,000. The truck is used 100% for business. L did not make a § 179 election with respect to the truck. If L uses statutory percentage ACRS, determine L's cost recovery for 1989 for computing taxable income and for computing L's alternative minimum tax.

44. T acquired a mineral interest during the year for $5,000,000. A geological survey estimated that 250,000 tons of the mineral remained in the deposit. During the year, 70,000 tons were mined and 45,000 tons were sold for $6,000,000. Other expenses amounted to $4,000,000. Assuming the mineral depletion rate is 22%, calculate T's lowest taxable income.

45. T purchased an oil interest for $2,000,000. Recoverable barrels were estimated to be 500,000. During the year, 120,000 barrels were sold for $3,840,000, regular expenses (including depreciation) were $1,240,000, and IDC were $1,000,000. Calculate the taxable income under the expensing and capitalization methods of handling IDC.

Cumulative Problems

46. John Smith, age 31, is single and has no dependents. At the beginning of 1989, John started his own excavation business and named it Earth Movers. John lives at 1045 Center Street, Lindon, UT, and his business is located at 381 State Street, Lindon, UT. The zip code for both addresses is 84059. John's Social Security number is 321–09–6456, and the business identification number is 98–1234567. John is a cash basis taxpayer. During 1989, John had the following items in connection with his business:

Fees for services	$120,000
Building rental expense	12,000
Office furniture and equipment rental expense	2,400
Office supplies	500
Utilities	1,000
Salary for secretary	15,000
Salary for equipment operators	55,000
Payroll taxes	7,000
Fuel and oil for the equipment	10,000
Purchase of a front-end loader on January 15, 1989, for $50,000. John made the election under § 179.	50,000
Purchase of a new dump truck on January 18, 1989	30,000

During 1989, John had the following additional items:	
Interest income from First National Bank	$ 8,000
Dividends from Exxon	500
Quarterly estimated tax payments	1,000

Assuming John does not itemize his deductions, compute his Federal income tax payable (or refund due).

47. Bob Brown, age 30, is single and has no dependents. He was employed as a barber until May 1988 by Hair Cuts, Inc. In June 1988, Bob opened his own styling salon, the Style Shop, located at 465 Willow Drive, St. Paul, MN 55455. Bob is a cash basis taxpayer. He lives at 1021 Snelling Avenue, St. Paul, MN 55455. His Social Security number is 821–56–7102. Bob does not wish to designate $1 to the Presidential Election Campaign Fund. During 1988, Bob had the following income and expense items:

   a. $10,800 salary from Hair Cuts, Inc.

   b. $920 Federal income tax withheld by Hair Cuts, Inc.

   c. $350 cash dividend from General Motors.

   d. $3,600 gross receipts from his own hair styling business.

   e. Expenses connected with Bob's hair styling business:

   - $100 laundry and cleaning

   - $2,400 rent

   - $700 supplies

   - $500 utilities and telephone

   f. Bob purchased and installed a fancy barber chair on June 3, 1988. The chair cost $6,400. Bob did not make the § 179 election.

   g. Bob had no itemized deductions.

   Compute Bob Brown's 1988 Federal income tax payable (or refund due). If you use tax forms for your computations, you will need Forms 1040 and 4562 and Schedules C and SE. Suggested software (if available): *WEST–TAX Preparer* for tax return solutions, *WEST–TAX Planner* or *BNA Individual Income Tax Spreadsheet* if tax return solutions are not desired.

Research Problems

Research Problem 1   H, who is one of your clients, is considering building a golf course in the resort area of Sun River, Oregon. Because the land is unimproved, all of the sand traps, greens, fairways, and tees will need to be constructed. Advise H as to whether any deductions can be taken on these landscaping improvements.

Research Problem 2   DJ operated several garbage dumps throughout the Chicago area. In 1989, DJ purchased a tract of land for $150,000. This land contained a pit that could accommodate 2,500,000 cubic yards of garbage. In 1989, the value of the land was reasonably estimated to be worth $55,000 without the pit. The sellers indicated that they had charged a premium for the land because they knew that DJ needed land with a pit for dumping garbage in that area. At the end of 1989 and several years thereafter, DJ had the property surveyed to determine the amount of space filled and the amount remaining. In 1989, 2,300,000 cubic yards remained to be filled. Discuss whether DJ would be able to depreciate the value of the air space that is now being reduced by the dumping of the garbage.

Research Problem 3   D, a dentist, purchased five paintings for a total of $17,000. D displayed the paintings on her business premises as part of the office decor. Discuss whether D can depreciate the paintings using ACRS with the paintings being classified as five-year property.

Research Problem 4   On May 1, 1978, John Woods purchased a condominium in Hawaii for $140,000. John lived in the condominium until January 1, 1989, at which time he moved to San Francisco and converted the condominium to rental property. On January 1, 1989, the condominium was worth $200,000. During 1989, the unit was rented for 200 days and John returned to live in the condominium for 30 days. Income and expenses for the condominium were as follows:

Rental income	$20,000
Taxes and interest	12,000
Utilities and maintenance	5,000

Discuss and determine the maximum amount of depreciation John can take with respect to the condominium for 1989. Assume the condominium has a useful life of 30 years from January 1, 1989, and an estimated salvage value of zero.

10

DEDUCTIONS: EMPLOYEE EXPENSES

OBJECTIVES

Discuss factors that determine whether an individual is self-employed or an employee.

Distinguish between self-employment and employee business expenses.

Determine which employee business expenses are deductions *for* adjusted gross income and which are deductions *from* adjusted gross income.

Identify miscellaneous itemized deductions subject to the 2 percent floor.

Distinguish between travel and transportation expenses.

Examine the requirements for deducting moving expenses and the limitations on the amount deductible.

Discuss when and how education expenses can be deducted.

Discuss the limitations on the deductibility of entertainment expenses.

Develop tax planning ideas related to employee business expenses.

10–1

Employees frequently incur expenses in connection with employment activities. Some of these expenses are deductible and some are not. Certain deductible expenses are subject to specific reductions and limitations. After determining which expenses are deductible and applying any limitations, the expenses must be classified as deductions *for* or deductions *from* AGI.

The rules for computing and classifying expenses incurred by self-employed individuals sometimes differ from those applicable to employees. Therefore, it is important to determine whether an individual is an employee or is self-employed. Guidelines for making this determination are discussed in the following section. This discussion is followed by coverage of the rules for computing and classifying employee business expenses.

CLASSIFICATION OF EMPLOYMENT-RELATED EXPENSES

Self-Employed versus Employee Status

In many instances it is difficult to distinguish between an individual who is self-employed and one who is performing services as an employee. Expenses of self-employed individuals are deductible as trade or business expenses (*for* adjusted gross income).

EXAMPLE 1   N, a self-employed CPA, incurred transportation expenses of $1,000 in connection with his business. The transportation expenses are deductions *for* AGI, because they are expenses incurred by a self-employed individual. □

Expenses incurred by an employee in an employment relationship are subject to limitations. Only reimbursed employee expenses are deductible *for* adjusted gross income. All other deductible employee expenses are deducted *from* adjusted gross income.

EXAMPLE 2   K, a CPA employed by N, incurred unreimbursed transportation expenses of $1,000 in connection with his employment activities. Because K is an employee, the transportation expenses are deductions *from* adjusted gross income (subject to a 2% floor discussed in Example 7). □

EXAMPLE 3   G, a CPA employed by N, incurred entertainment expenses of $1,000 in connection with his employment activities. N reimbursed G for these entertainment expenses. G must include the $1,000 reimbursement in gross income, and he may take a $1,000 deduction *for* AGI. (See Example 21). □

As the preceding examples illustrate, because of the differences in the treatment of expenses, it is important to determine when an employer-employee relationship exists.

Generally, an employer-employee relationship exists when the employer has the right to specify the end result and the ways and means by which the end result is to be attained.[1] Thus, an employee is subject to the will and control of the employer with respect not only to what shall be done but also to how it shall be done. If the individual is subject to the direction or control of another only to the extent of the end result (e.g., the preparation of a taxpayer's return by an independent CPA) and not as to the means of accomplishment, an employer-employee relationship does not exist.

Certain factors may indicate an employer-employee relationship. They include the right to discharge without legal liability the person performing the service, the furnishing of tools or a place to work, and payment based on time spent rather than the task performed. However, each case is tested on its own merits, and the right to control the means and methods of accomplishment is the definitive test. Generally, physicians, lawyers, dentists, contractors, subcontractors, and others who offer services to the public are not classified as employees.

| EXAMPLE 4 | D is a lawyer whose major client accounts for 60% of her billings. She does the routine legal work and income tax returns at the client's request. She is paid a monthly retainer in addition to amounts charged for extra work. D is a self-employed individual. Even though most of her income is from one client, she still has the right to determine how the end result of her work is attained. ☐ |

| EXAMPLE 5 | E is a lawyer hired by D to assist D in the performance of services for the client mentioned in Example 4. E is under D's supervision; D reviews E's work and D pays E an hourly fee. E is an employee of D. ☐ |

| EXAMPLE 6 | F is a practical nurse who works as a live-in nurse. She is under the supervision of the patient's doctor and is paid by the patient. F is not an employee of either the patient (who pays her) or the doctor (who supervises her). The ways and means of attaining the end result (care of the patient) are under her control. ☐ |

Real estate agents and direct sellers are classified as self-employed persons if two conditions are met. The first condition is that substantially all of their income for services must be directly related to sales or other output. The second condition is that their services must be performed under a written contract that specifies that they are not to be treated as employees for tax purposes.[2] The Internal Revenue Service may not issue any rulings or regulations dealing with classification as employees or independent contractors until Congress enacts legislation clarifying the issue.

A self-employed individual is required to file Schedule C of Form 1040, and all related allowable expenses are deductions *for* adjusted gross income.[3]

---

1. Reg. § 31.3401(c)–(1)(b).
2. § 3508(b).

3. §§ 62(a)(2) and 162(a). See Appendix B for a reproduction of Schedule C.

Deductions for or from AGI

The Code specifies that reimbursed employee expenses are deductible *for* adjusted gross income.[4] All unreimbursed employee expenses are deductions *from* adjusted gross income (AGI) and can be deducted only if the employee-taxpayer itemizes deductions. Partially reimbursed expenses require an apportionment between these two categories (*for* and *from* AGI).

The distinction between deductions *for* and deductions *from* AGI is important. No benefit is received for an item that is deductible *from* AGI if a taxpayer's itemized deductions are less than the standard deduction. Refer to chapter 6 for a detailed discussion of deductions *for* versus deductions *from* AGI.

Limitations on Itemized Deductions

Many itemized deductions, such as medical expenses and charitable contributions, are subject to limitations expressed as a percentage of AGI. These limitations may be expressed as floors or ceilings. For example, medical expenses are deductible only to the extent they exceed 7.5 percent of AGI (there is a 7.5 percent floor). Charitable contributions in excess of 50 percent of AGI are not deductible in the year of the contribution. In other words, there is a 50 percent ceiling on the deductibility of charitable contributions. These limitations are discussed more fully in chapter 11.

Miscellaneous Itemized Deductions Subject to the 2 Percent Floor. Certain miscellaneous itemized deductions, including unreimbursed employee business expenses, must be aggregated and then reduced by 2 percent of AGI. Expenses subject to the 2 percent floor include the following:

- All § 212 expenses, except expenses of producing rent and royalty income (refer to chapter 6).
- All unreimbursed employee expenses (after 20 percent reduction, if applicable).
- Professional dues and subscriptions.
- Union dues and work uniforms.
- Employment-related education expenses.
- Malpractice insurance premiums.
- Expenses of job hunting (including employment agency fees and resumé-writing expenses).
- Home office expenses of an employee or outside salesperson.
- Legal, accounting, and tax return preparation fees.
- Hobby expenses (up to hobby income).
- Investment expenses, including investment counsel fees, subscriptions, and safe deposit box rental.
- Custodial fees relating to income-producing property or an IRA or a Keogh plan.

4. § 67.

- Any fees paid to collect interest or dividends.
- Appraisal fees establishing a casualty loss or charitable contribution.

All miscellaneous itemized deductions subject to the 2 percent floor are added together and reduced by 2 percent of AGI. Only the excess is deductible.

EXAMPLE 7

T, who has AGI of $20,000, has the following miscellaneous itemized deductions:

Gambling losses (to extent of gains)	$1,200
Tax return preparation fees	300
Unreimbursed employee transportation	200
Professional dues and subscriptions	260
Safe deposit box rental	30

T's itemized deductions are as follows:

Deduction not subject to 2% floor (gambling losses)		$1,200
Deductions subject to 2% floor ($300 + $200 + $260 + $30)	$ 790	
Less 2% of AGI	(400)	390
Total miscellaneous itemized deductions		$1,590

If T's AGI were $40,000, the floor would be $800 (2% of $40,000), and T could not deduct any expenses subject to the 2% floor. □

Miscellaneous Itemized Deductions Not Subject to the 2 Percent Floor. Certain miscellaneous itemized deductions, including the following, are not subject to the 2 percent floor:

- Impairment-related work expenses of handicapped individuals.[5]
- Federal estate tax on income in respect of a decedent.[6]
- Certain adjustments when a taxpayer restores amounts held under a claim of right.[7]
- Amortizable bond premium.[8]
- Gambling losses to the extent of gambling winnings.[9]

---

5. § 67(d).
6. § 691(c).
7. § 1341.
8. § 171.
9. § 165(d).

- Deductions allowable in connection with personal property used in a short sale.
- Certain terminated annuity payments.[10]
- Certain costs of cooperative housing corporations.[11]

Percentage Reduction for Meals and Entertainment Expenses

Deductions for meals and entertainment (including entertainment facilities) are limited to 80 percent of allowable expenditures.[12]

EXAMPLE 8

T spends $100 for deductible business entertainment. He is not reimbursed by his employer. Only $80 is allowed as a deduction. This $80 is combined with other miscellaneous itemized deductions subject to the 2 percent floor, and the total is reduced by 2% of AGI. □

The 80 percent limit applies to the following: [13]

- Any expense for food or beverages.
- Any expense that constitutes entertainment, amusement, or recreation (or expense related to a facility used in connection with these activities).

Transportation expenses are not affected by this provision—only meals and entertainment.

EXAMPLE 9

T pays a $20 cab fare to meet her client for dinner at The Ritz. The meal costs $90, and T leaves a $15 tip. T's deduction is $104 [($90 + $15) × 80% + $20 cab fare]. □

The 80 percent rule applies to taxes and tips relating to meals and entertainment. Cover charges, parking fees at an entertainment location, and room rental fees for a meal or cocktail party are also subject to the 80 percent rule.

EXAMPLE 10

S incurs the following expenses for a business meal:

Cost of meal	$50
Tax on meal	2
Tip	8
Total	$60

S's deduction is limited to $48 (80% of $60). □

---

10. § 72(b)(3).
11. § 216.

12. § 274(n).
13. § 274(n)(1).

The 80 percent rule is applied after determining the allowable amount of the expenditure. In other words, "lavish or extravagant" expenses are excluded before the application of the 80 percent rule.

EXAMPLE 11

T consumed a meal while in travel status. Of his $100 expenditure, $30 is disallowed as lavish or extravagant. His deduction is limited to $56 (80% of $70). □

EXAMPLE 12

S, who is self-employed, purchased two tickets to an entertainment event from a scalper and used the tickets to entertain a client. She paid $200 and the face value of the tickets was $100. S's deduction cannot exceed $80 (80% of $100). □

The 80 percent rule is applied before application of the 2 percent floor previously discussed.

EXAMPLE 13

T incurs unreimbursed meal and entertainment expenses of $1,000 in the course of his job as a salesman. His AGI is $20,000, and he has no other expenses subject to the 2 percent floor. If T itemizes, his deduction is limited to $400, as follows:

Expenses	$1,000
Less: 20%	(200)
Amount subject to 2% of AGI floor	$ 800
Less 2% of AGI	(400)
Deductible	$ 400

□

It does not matter where or how meal and entertainment expenses are incurred. Only 80 percent of meals incurred in the course of travel away from home, in connection with moving expenses, or in connection with education expenses are deductible. In addition, the cost of meals furnished by an employer to employees on the employer's premises is subject to the 80 percent rule in computing the employer's deduction.

Exceptions for Luxury Water Travel.   If meals and entertainment incurred in the course of luxury water travel are not separately stated, the 80 percent rule does not apply. If meals and entertainment are separately stated or are clearly identifiable, the 80 percent rule is applied before the limitation on luxury water travel expenses (discussed later in the chapter).

Exceptions to the 80 Percent Rule.   The 80 percent rule has eight exceptions. Exceptions one and two apply where the full value of meals or entertainment is included in the compensation of employees [14] or the income of independent contractors.[15]

EXAMPLE 14

T won an all-expense-paid pleasure trip to Europe for selling the most insurance in her company during the year. X, T's employer, included the fair market value of the trip on T's W–2 (Wage and Tax Statement). X need not allocate any of the cost to meals or entertainment. X deducts the entire amount, and T receives no deduction. □

The third exception applies to meals and entertainment in a subsidized eating facility or where the *de minimis* fringe benefit rule is met (refer to chapter 5).[16]

EXAMPLE 15

General Hospital has an employee cafeteria on the premises for doctors, nurses, and other employees. Such employees need to be available during meal breaks for emergencies. The cafeteria operates at a loss and is subsidized by the hospital. The 80% rule does not apply to such subsidy. □

EXAMPLE 16

Y Company gives a ham, a fruitcake, and a bottle of wine to each employee at year-end. Y's costs for these items are not subject to the percentage reduction rule. The *de minimis* fringe benefit exclusion applies to business gifts of packaged foods and beverages. □

Exception four applies to fully reimbursed employee business meals and entertainment expenses. The 80 percent rule applies to the person making the reimbursement.[17]

EXAMPLE 17

T is a salesman who paid for lunch with a customer. He made an adequate accounting to his employer, Y, who reimbursed T. T omits both the reimbursement and the expense on his return. Y (the employer) can deduct only 80% of the expenditure on his return. □

Exception five relates to traditional employer-paid recreation expenses for employees.[18]

EXAMPLE 18

X Company provides a yearly Christmas party and an annual spring picnic for its employees and their families. X's reasonable costs for these events are fully deductible. □

The sixth exception is applicable to items such as samples and promotional activities made available to the general public.[19]

---

14. § 274(e)(2).
15. § 274(e)(9).
16. § 274(n)(2)(B).

17. § 274(e)(3).
18. § 274(e)(4).
19. § 274(e)(7).

EXAMPLE 19	The owner of a hardware store advertises that tickets to a baseball game will be provided to the first 50 people who purchase a lawn mower from the store during a sale. The full amount of the face value of the tickets is deductible by the owner. ☐

EXAMPLE 20	A wine merchant permits potential customers to sample wine that he is offering for sale. The merchant can deduct in full the cost of wine used as a sample, along with reasonable costs associated with the wine tasting. For example, food that is provided with the wine to demonstrate the suitability of the wine for particular types of meals is deductible in full. ☐

The seventh exception applies to expenses for attendance at a sports event meeting certain charitable fund-raising requirements. This is discussed later in the chapter under Entertainment Expenses.[20]

Exception number eight is a rather obvious one. The cost of providing meals or entertainment is fully deductible if the meals or entertainment are sold by the taxpayer in a bona fide transaction.[21] A restaurant, for example, may deduct the full amount of its ordinary and necessary expenses in providing meals to paying customers.

Reimbursed Expenses

Reimbursements are included in an employee's gross income. Since reimbursements are income, an offsetting deduction *for* adjusted gross income is allowed in certain circumstances.

When reimbursements are present, there are three distinct possibilities:

- The expenses and the reimbursement are equal.
- The reimbursement exceeds the expenses.
- The expenses exceed the reimbursement.

The reporting treatment of these possibilities depends on whether the employee has made an *adequate accounting* to the employer.

An adequate accounting means that the employee has submitted a record (with receipts and other substantiation) to the employer. The following pertinent facts are required: amount, place, and date of expenditure and the business purpose and business relationship of the expenditure.[22]

Many companies reduce their paperwork by adopting a policy of reimbursing employees a flat dollar amount per day of business travel. Such per diem allowances, if reasonable, constitute an adequate accounting unless the employer and employee are related. The use of a mileage allowance (currently 24 cents per mile) also constitutes an adequate accounting.

Any employee who does not adequately account to his or her employer must submit a detailed statement with his or her return showing expense categories, reimbursements, etc. Employee expenses are reported on Form

20. § 274(n)(2)(C).
21. § 274(e)(8).

22. Reg. § 1.162–17(b)(4).

2106 (see the 1988 Form 2106 in Appendix A). The following situations may be encountered:

- *Expenses and reimbursements are equal.* If an adequate accounting has been made, the employee may omit both the reimbursement and the expenses from the tax return. If an adequate accounting has not been made, the reimbursements are included in income. Until 1989, the expenses were deductible *for* AGI, and the 2 percent floor did not apply. After 1988, such expenses are miscellaneous itemized deductions subject to the 2 percent floor. See the discussion below.

EXAMPLE 21

M, an employee of an unrelated corporation, incurred the following expenses, which were carefully documented and submitted for complete reimbursement:

Travel	
Transportation	$1,600
Meals	180
Lodging	800
Other	
Dues and subscriptions	70
Entertainment	350
Total reimbursed	$3,000

M can ignore both the reimbursement and the expenditures on her tax return, because she made an adequate accounting to her employer. Only 80% of the meals and entertainment expenses can be deducted by the employer. If M had not made an adequate accounting, reimbursements would be included in income. Expenses would be itemized subject to the 2 percent floor. □

- *Reimbursements exceed expenses.* Until 1989, an employee who made an adequate accounting could report the excess reimbursements as miscellaneous income. The expenses and the reimbursements up to the amount of the expenses could be ignored.

In 1988, the Welfare Reform Act added new § 62(c), which requires employees to include reimbursements in income and to itemize the expenses if either of the following occurs:

1. Employees do not make an adequate accounting to their employers.
2. Employees make an adequate accounting, but the company allows them to keep all or part of the reimbursements that are not spent.

The effect of the new law, effective in 1989, is to force employees in either of the two situations above to itemize deductions. These deductions are subject to the 80 percent rule and the 2 percent floor.

EXAMPLE 22

Assume the same facts as in Example 21, except that M received $4,000 in reimbursements *in 1988.* M can ignore the first $3,000 of reimbursements and expenses (because of the adequate accounting) and report $1,000 as additional compensation. Her employer can deduct only 80% of the meals and entertainment expenses. □

EXAMPLE 23

Assume the same facts as in Example 21, except that the year is 1989, M's AGI is $50,000, and she received $4,000 in reimbursements. She must include $4,000 in income. The $3,000 of expenses are miscellaneous itemized deductions. After the 2 percent floor, her deduction is only $2,000 ($3,000 less 2% of $50,000). Instead of a net $1,000 increase in income, she has a net $2,000 increase ($4,000 of reimbursements less the $2,000 deduction). □

- *Expenses exceed reimbursements.* Regardless of whether an adequate accounting is made to the employer, a statement of all expenses (by category) and all reimbursements must be attached to the income tax return.[23] The excess expenses are deductible.

The reimbursed portion of all expenses is deductible *for* AGI, since the reimbursements are included in income. The unreimbursed part is deductible *from* AGI. The unreimbursed meals and entertainment are subject to the 80 percent rule, and all unreimbursed employee expenses are subject to the 2 percent floor. Together with all other miscellaneous expenses subject to the 2 percent floor, unreimbursed expenses are reduced by 2 percent of AGI.

EXAMPLE 24

Assume the same facts as in Example 21, except that the reimbursement was $2,250. The ratio of reimbursement is 75% ($2,250/$3,000). M's deductions are as follows:

For AGI:

Income	$2,250
Reimbursed expenses (75%)	(2,250)
Net	$ –0–

From AGI:

Unreimbursed meals and entertainment [($180 + $350) × 25%]	$132.50
Less: 20%	(26.50)
Net	$106.00
Plus: Other expenses [25% × ($1,600 + $800 + $70)]	617.50
Total	$723.50

---

23. Reg. §§ 1.162–17(b)(1), (2), and (3).

The $723.50 is added to other miscellaneous deductions subject to the 2 percent floor, and the total is reduced by 2% of AGI. If M's AGI is $15,000 and she has no other miscellaneous itemized deductions subject to the 2 percent floor, her deduction is $423.50 [$723.50 − (2% × $15,000)]. □

TRANSPORTATION EXPENSES

Qualified Expenditures

An employee may deduct unreimbursed employment-related transportation expenses as miscellaneous itemized deductions (*from* AGI, subject to the 2 percent floor). Transportation expense includes only the cost of transporting the employee from one place to another when the employee is not away from home *in travel status*. Such costs include taxi fares, automobile expenses, tolls, and parking.

Commuting from home to one's place of employment is a personal, nondeductible expense. The fact that one employee drives 30 miles to work and another employee walks six blocks is of no significance.[24]

EXAMPLE 25   G is employed by X Corporation. He drives 22 miles each way to work. One day G drove to a customer's office from his place of work. The drive was a 14-mile round trip to the customer's office. G can take a deduction for 14 miles of business transportation. The remaining 44 miles are a nondeductible commuting expense. □

Exceptions to Disallowance of Commuting Expenses.   The general rule that disallows a deduction for commuting expenses has several exceptions. An employee who uses an automobile to transport heavy tools to work and who otherwise would not drive to work will be allowed a deduction. However, the deduction is allowed only for the additional costs incurred to transport work implements. Additional costs are those exceeding the cost of commuting by the same mode of transportation without the tools. For example, the rental of a trailer for transporting tools is deductible, but the expenses of operating the automobile are not deductible.[25] The Supreme Court has held that a deduction is permitted only if the taxpayer can show that he or she would not have used the automobile were it not necessary to transport tools or equipment.[26]

Another exception is provided for an employee who has a second job. The expenses of getting from one job to another are deductible. If the employee goes home between jobs, the deduction is based on the distance between jobs.

EXAMPLE 26   In the current year, T holds two jobs, a full-time job with B Corporation and a part-time job with C Corporation. During the 250 days that she works (adjusted for weekends, vacation, and holidays), T customarily leaves home at 7:30 A.M. and drives 30 miles to the B Corporation plant, where she works until 5:00 P.M. After dinner at a nearby cafe, T drives 20

24. *Tauferner v. U.S.*, 69–1 USTC ¶ 9241, 23 AFTR2d 69–1025, 407 F.2d 243 (CA–10, 1969).
25. Rev.Rul. 75–380, 1975–2 C.B. 59.
26. *Fausner v. Comm.*, 73–2 USTC ¶ 9515, 32 AFTR2d 73–5202, 93 S.Ct. 2820 (USSC, 1973).

miles to C Corporation and works from 7:00 to 11:00 P.M. The distance from the second job to T's home is 40 miles. Her deduction is based on 20 miles (the distance between jobs). □

It is sometimes difficult to distinguish between a nondeductible commuting expense and a deductible transportation expense necessary to the taxpayer's business. If the taxpayer is required to incur a transportation expense to travel between work stations, that expense is deductible. However, the commuting costs from home to the first work station and from the last work station to home are not deductible.

EXAMPLE 27	V works for a firm in downtown Denver and commutes to work. V occasionally works in a customer's office. On one such occasion, he drove directly to the customer's office, a round-trip distance from his home of 40 miles. He did not go into his office, which is a 52-mile round-trip. None of his mileage is deductible. □
EXAMPLE 28	T, a general contractor, drove from his home to his office, then drove to three building sites to perform his required inspections, and finally drove home. The costs of driving to his office and driving home from the last inspection site are nondeductible commuting expenses. The other transportation costs are deductible. □

Also deductible is the reasonable travel cost between the general working area and a temporary work station outside that area. What constitutes the general working area depends on the facts and circumstances of each situation. For example, a bank manager who must spend an occasional day at a remote branch office in the suburbs can deduct transportation expenses (or mileage) as an employee expense. If an employee is permanently reassigned to a new location, however, the assignment is deemed to be for an indefinite period, and the expenses are nondeductible commuting expenses. Furthermore, if an employee customarily works on several temporary assignments in a localized area, that localized area becomes the regular place of employment. Transportation from home to these locations becomes a personal, nondeductible commuting expense.

EXAMPLE 29	S, a building inspector in Minneapolis, regularly inspects buildings for building code violations for his employer, a general contractor. During one busy season, the St. Paul inspector became ill, and S was required to inspect several buildings in St. Paul. The expenses for transportation for the trips within Minneapolis and St. Paul are deductible. □

Computation of Automobile Expenses

A taxpayer has two choices in computing automobile expenses. The actual operating cost, which includes depreciation, gas, oil, repairs, licenses, and insurance, may be used. Records must be kept that detail the automobile's personal and business use. Only the percentage (based upon the ratio of business miles to total miles) allocable to business transportation and travel is allowed as a deduction. Complex rules for the computation of depreciation (discussed in chapter 9) apply if the actual expense method is used.

Use of the automatic mileage method is the second alternative. The deduction is based upon 24 cents per mile for the first 15,000 business miles driven. Eleven cents per mile is allowed for any miles in excess of 15,000.[27] Parking fees and tolls are allowed in addition to expenses computed using the automatic mileage method.[28]

Generally, a taxpayer may elect either method for any particular year. However, the following restrictions apply:

- If two or more vehicles are in use (for business purposes) at the *same* time (not alternately), a taxpayer may not use the automatic mileage method.

- A basis adjustment is required if the taxpayer changes from the automatic mileage method to the actual operating cost method. The cost basis of the automobile must be reduced by the amount of straight-line depreciation that would have been allowed had the automatic mileage method not been used. Use of the standard mileage rate in the first year the auto is placed in service is considered an election to exclude the auto from the ACRS method of depreciation (discussed in chapter 9).[29]

- A taxpayer may not switch to the automatic mileage method if the ACRS statutory percentage method or expensing under § 179 has been used.

- Once an automobile has been fully depreciated, the standard mileage rate of 11 cents per mile is used for all miles thereafter.

EXAMPLE 30   W uses her automobile 60% for business and 40% for pleasure. During 1989, she drove a total of 40,000 miles. W purchased the automobile for $8,000 on January 1, 1985, and has depreciated it on the straight-line method over its three-year useful life. She can use the automatic mileage method, but because the automobile has been fully depreciated, she is limited to 11 cents per mile, or $2,640 (.11 × 40,000 × 60%). □

Any reimbursement for auto expenses must be reported on the tax return to reduce the deduction if the automatic mileage method is used. If an employee is reimbursed, it may still be possible to claim an additional miscellaneous itemized deduction subject to the 2 percent floor. If there is an excess of actual expenses over the reimbursed amounts, the excess is deductible. Also, if the standard mileage rate (24 cents) exceeds the reimbursed rate (e.g., 15 cents), the taxpayer is entitled to a deduction for the difference when the optional method is elected. Frequently, taxpayers discover that actual automobile expenses, such as for depreciation, gas, oil, and repairs, exceed the amount of expense calculated under the standard mileage rate prescribed by the IRS.

---

27. *Your Federal Income Tax*, IRS Publication 17 (Rev. Nov. 88), p. 108.
28. Rev.Rul. 73–91, 1973–1 C.B. 71.
29. Rev.Proc. 82–61, 1982–2 C.B. 849.

TRAVEL EXPENSES

Definition of Travel Expenses

An itemized deduction is allowed for unreimbursed travel expenses related to a taxpayer's employment, subject to the 2 percent floor. Travel expenses are more broadly defined in the Code than are transportation expenses. Travel expenses include transportation expenses and meals and lodging while away from home in the pursuit of a trade or business. Meals cannot be lavish or extravagant under the circumstances. Transportation expenses are deductible even though the taxpayer is not away from home. A deduction for travel expenses is available only if the taxpayer is away from his or her tax home. Travel expenses also include reasonable laundry and incidental expenses. To the extent that travel expenses are reimbursed, they are deductible *for* adjusted gross income; the unreimbursed part is a miscellaneous itemized deduction subject to the 2 percent floor. Unreimbursed meals and entertainment expenses are subject to the 80 percent rule.

Away-from-Home Requirement

The crucial test for the deductibility of travel expenses is whether or not the employee is away from home overnight. "Overnight" need not be a 24-hour period, but it must be a period substantially longer than an ordinary day's work and must require rest, sleep, or a relief-from-work period.[30] A one-day or intracity business trip is not travel, and meals and lodging for such a trip are not deductible.

The employee must be away from home for a temporary period. If the taxpayer-employee is reassigned to a new post for an indefinite period of time, that new post becomes his or her tax home. *Temporary* indicates that the assignment's termination is expected within a reasonably short period of time. The position of the IRS is that the tax home is the business location, post, or station of the taxpayer. Thus, travel expenses are not deductible if a taxpayer is reassigned for an indefinite period and does not move his or her place of residence to the new location.

EXAMPLE 31

T's employer opened a branch office in San Diego. T was assigned to the new office for three months to train a new manager and to assist in setting up the new office. T tried commuting from his home in Los Angeles for a week and decided that he could not continue driving several hours a day. He rented an apartment in San Diego, where he lived during the week. He spent weekends with his wife and children at their home in Los Angeles. T's rent, meals, laundry, incidentals, and automobile expenses in San Diego are deductible. The transportation expense related to his weekend trips home is personal and is limited to what the cost of meals and lodging in San Diego would have been. □

30. *U.S. v. Correll,* 68–1 USTC ¶ 9101, 20 AFTR2d 5845, 88 S.Ct. 445 (USSC, 1967); Rev.Rul. 75–168, 1975–1 C.B. 58.

EXAMPLE 32	Assume that T in Example 31 was transferred to the new location to become the new manager permanently. T's wife and children continued to live in Los Angeles until the end of the school year. T is no longer "away from home," because the assignment is not temporary. T's travel expenses are not deductible. ☐

Determining the Tax Home.   Under ordinary circumstances, there is no problem in determining the location of a taxpayer's tax home and whether or not the taxpayer is on a temporary work assignment away from that tax home. Under other circumstances, however, this is a controversial problem that has found the IRS and various courts in conflict.[31] An example of this problem is the situation in which a construction worker cannot find work in the immediate area and takes work several hundred miles away, with the duration of that work uncertain. The IRS has published criteria for determining whether a work assignment is temporary rather than permanent or indefinite.[32]

In general, the IRS regards a work assignment of less than a year as temporary. A work assignment of more than two years is regarded as indefinite or permanent, regardless of the facts and circumstances. The nature of a work assignment expected to last between one and two years will be determined on the basis of the facts and circumstances of the specific case.

The following objective factors are to be used in determining whether the home that the taxpayer claims to be away from is the taxpayer's actual tax home:

- Whether the taxpayer has used the claimed home for lodging purposes while performing work in the vicinity thereof immediately before the current job.

- Whether the taxpayer continues to maintain bona fide work contacts (such as job seeking, leave of absence, ongoing business) in the area during the alleged temporary employment.

- Whether the taxpayer's living expenses at the claimed home are duplicated because work requires the taxpayer to be away from home.

- Whether the taxpayer has a family member or members (marital or lineal only) currently residing at the claimed home or currently continues to use the claimed home frequently for the purposes of his or her own lodging.

Travel expenses are disallowed unless the taxpayer clearly demonstrates a realistic expectation as to the temporary nature of the job and satisfies all four of the above requirements. If the taxpayer clearly demonstrates the expectation that the job is of a temporary nature and satisfies two of the above requirements, the deductibility question will be decided on the basis of all the facts and circumstances of the case. If it is determined that the assignment is indefinite rather than temporary, no deduction will be allowed for the traveling expenses.

If an employee establishes a new home as the result of a work assignment or if there is no established tax home, living expenses are of a personal nature and are therefore nondeductible.

---

31. Rev.Rul. 73–529, 1973–2 C.B. 37.   32. Rev.Rul. 83–82, 1983–1 C.B. 45.

EXAMPLE 33

H is employed as a long-haul truck driver. He stores his clothes and other belongings at his parents' home and stops there for periodic visits. The rest of the time, H is on the road, sleeping in his truck and in motels. His meals, lodging, laundry, and incidental expenses are not deductible, because he has no tax home from which he can be absent.[33] □

Disallowed and Limited Travel Expenses

The possibility always exists that taxpayers will attempt to treat vacation or pleasure travel as deductible business travel. To prevent such abuses, the law contains limitations for certain travel expenses.

Nonbusiness Conventions.   One tactic taxpayers used in an attempt to deduct the cost of vacations was to attend a tax or financial seminar at a vacation resort. They then took the travel expenses as a deduction under § 212, which allows deductions related to the production of income or determination of taxes.

A further refinement was that the seminar or convention promoters would videotape the lectures and supply a copy to the participants. Many participants did not attend any lectures but would take the videotapes home and view them later. In the meantime, the taxpayer would enjoy several days of vacation at the resort and deduct the expenses.

In an attempt to prevent such abuses, the law disallows all deductions related to attending a convention, seminar, or similar meeting unless the expenses are related to a trade or business of the taxpayer.[34] The restriction does not apply to trade or business conventions and seminars. For example, a CPA who is an employee of an accounting firm can deduct the expenses of attending a tax seminar. A stockbroker can deduct the cost of attending a convention regarding investments. A physician attending either the tax or the investment meeting can deduct nothing. If the lectures are videotaped, both the CPA and the stockbroker must attend convention sessions to view the videotaped materials along with other participants. This requirement does not disallow deductions for costs (other than travel, meals, and entertainment) of renting or using videotaped materials related to business.

EXAMPLE 34

A CPA is unable to attend a convention at which current developments in taxation are discussed. She paid $200 for videotapes of the lectures that she viewed at home later. The $200 is a miscellaneous itemized deduction (subject to the 2 percent floor) if the CPA is an employee. If she is self-employed, the $200 is a deduction *for* AGI. □

Luxury Water Travel.   Limits are placed on the deductibility of travel by water.[35] The deduction is limited to twice the highest amount generally allowable for a day of travel for Federal employees serving in the United States.

---

33. *Moses Mitnick*, 13 T.C. 1 (1949).
34. § 274(h)(1).

35. § 274(m)(1).

EXAMPLE 35	During the taxable year, the highest Federal per diem rate is $136. T took a six-day trip from New York to London on the *Queen Mary II* to meet with customers. The maximum deduction related to the water travel is $1,632 [($136 × 2) × 6 days]. □

If the expenses of luxury water travel include separately stated amounts for meals or entertainment, those amounts must be reduced by 20 percent before the application of this per diem limitation. If the meals and entertainment are not separately stated (or otherwise clearly identifiable), the 20 percent reduction does not apply.

The per diem rule does not apply to any expense allocable to a convention, seminar, or other meeting held on any cruise ship.[36] The deduction for such a meeting is limited to $2,000 per individual per year. This deduction is restricted to ships registered in the United States and sailing to ports of call located within the United States or its possessions (e.g., Puerto Rico).[37] Thus, a cruise on a ship of U.S. registry sailing to Bermuda would not qualify. A cruise on the same ship from Florida to Puerto Rico would qualify.

Educational Travel.   No deduction is allowed for travel that by itself is deemed by the taxpayer to be educational.[38] This does not apply to a deduction claimed for travel that is necessary to engage in an activity that gives rise to a business deduction relating to education.

EXAMPLE 36	M, a German teacher, travels to Germany to maintain general familiarity with the language and culture. No travel expense deduction is allowed. □

EXAMPLE 37	J, a scholar of French literature, travels to Paris to do specific library research that cannot be done elsewhere and to take courses that are offered only at the Sorbonne. The travel costs are deductible, assuming that the other requirements for deducting education expenses (discussed later in the chapter) are met. □

Combined Business and Pleasure Travel

To be deductible, travel expenses need not be incurred in the performance of specific job functions. Travel expenses incurred in attending a professional convention are deductible by an employee if attendance is connected with services as an employee. For example, an employee of a CPA firm could deduct travel expenses incurred in attending a meeting of the American Institute of Certified Public Accountants.

Travel deductions have been abused in the past by persons who claimed a tax deduction for what was essentially a personal vacation. As a result, several provisions have been enacted to govern deductions associated with combined business and pleasure trips. If the business/pleasure trip is from one point in

---

36. § 274(m)(1)(B)(i).

37. §§ 274(h)(1) and (2). See § 274(h)(3)(B) for the definition of "cruise ship."

38. § 274(m)(2).

the United States to another point in the United States, the transportation expenses are deductible only if the trip is *primarily for business*.[39] If the trip is primarily for pleasure, no transportation expenses can be taken as a deduction. However, even though a trip is primarily for pleasure (or other personal reasons), any expenses incurred at the destination that are properly allocable to business are deductible.

EXAMPLE 38

J traveled from Seattle to New York on a combined business and pleasure trip. She spent five days conducting business and three days sightseeing and attending shows. Her plane and taxi fare amounted to $560. Her meals amounted to $100 per day, and lodging and incidental expenses were $150 per day. She can deduct the transportation charges of $560, since the trip was primarily for business (five days of business versus three days of sightseeing). Meals are limited to $400 [5 days × ($100 × 80%)], and other expenses are limited to $750 (5 days × $150). All the travel expenses are miscellaneous itemized deductions subject to the 2 percent floor. □

EXAMPLE 39

Assume the same facts as in the previous example except that J conducted business for two days and vacationed the remaining six days. Since the trip is then primarily personal, no transportation expenses are deductible. Lodging and incidental expenses for two days ($300) and 80 percent of the meals for two days ($160) are deductible as miscellaneous itemized deductions subject to the 2 percent floor. □

The incremental costs paid for travel of a taxpayer's relative cannot be deducted unless that person's presence has a bona fide business purpose. Incidental services performed by family members do not constitute a bona fide business purpose.

When the trip is outside the United States, special rules apply.[40] If the taxpayer is away from home for seven days or less or if less than 25 percent of the time was for personal purposes, no allocation of transportation expenses need be made. No allocation is required if the taxpayer has no substantial control over arrangements for the trip or the desire for a vacation is not a major factor in taking the trip. If the trip is primarily for pleasure, no transportation charges are deductible. In all other cases, all travel expenses must be allocated between business and personal expenses. Days devoted to travel are considered as business days. Weekends, legal holidays, and intervening days are considered business days, provided that both preceding and succeeding days were business days.

EXAMPLE 40

K took a trip from New York to Japan primarily for business purposes. He was away from home from June 10 through June 19. He spent three days vacationing and seven days conducting business (including two travel days). K's air fare was $2,500, his meals amounted to $100 per day, and lodging and incidental expenses were $160 per day. Since K was away

---

39. Reg. § 1.162–2(b)(1).

40. § 274(c) and Reg. § 1.274–4.

from home for more than seven days and more than 25% of his time was devoted to personal purposes, only 70% (7 days business/10 days total) of the travel is deductible. His deductions are as follows:

Transportation (70% × $2,500)		$1,750
Lodging ($160 × 7)		1,120
Meals ($100 × 7)	$700	
Less: 20%	(140)	560
Total		$3,430

Note that the $3,430 is a miscellaneous itemized deduction subject to the 2 percent floor. □

EXAMPLE 41

L, a fashion buyer for a large department store, travels to London primarily to view the spring collections. She is gone 10 days (including 2 days of travel). She spends 8 days (including travel time) engaged in business and 2 days sightseeing. Since less than 25% of the total time is spent vacationing, all her transportation expenses and all but 2 days of meals and lodging are deductible. The meals are reduced by 20%, and all the expenses are miscellaneous itemized deductions subject to the 2 percent floor. □

EXAMPLE 42

Assume L in Example 41 had spent six days vacationing, two days traveling, and two days conducting business. The trip probably would be primarily for pleasure, and none of the transportation expenses would be deductible. Two days of meals and lodging expenses would be deductible, subject to the same limitations. □

Foreign Convention Expenses

Certain restrictions are imposed on the deductibility of expenses paid or incurred to attend conventions located outside the North American area. For this purpose, the North American area includes the United States, its possessions (including the Trust Territory of the Pacific Islands), Canada, and Mexico. The expenses will be disallowed unless it is established that the meeting is directly related to a trade or business of the taxpayer. Disallowance will also occur unless the taxpayer shows that it is as reasonable for the meeting to be held in a foreign location as within the North American area.

The foreign convention rules will not operate to bar a deduction to an employer if the expense is compensatory in nature. For example, a trip to Paris won by a top salesperson is included in the gross income of the employee and is fully deductible by the employer.

MOVING EXPENSES

Moving expenses are deductible for moves in connection with the commencement of work (either as an employee or as a self-employed individual) at a new principal place of work.[41] Reimbursement from employers must be included in gross income. Moving expenses are itemized deductions but are *not* subject to the 2 percent floor. Meals included as moving expenses are subject to the 80 percent rule. To be eligible for a moving expense deduction, a taxpayer must meet two basic tests: distance and time.

Distance Test

The distance test requires that the taxpayer's new job location must be at least 35 miles farther from the taxpayer's old residence than the old residence was from the former place of employment. In this regard, the location of the new residence is not relevant. This eliminates a moving deduction for taxpayers who purchase a new home in the same general area without changing their place of employment. Those who accept a new job in the same general area as the old job location are also eliminated. If a new job does not necessitate moving or if the move is for personal reasons (e.g., a better neighborhood), the taxpayer is not permitted a tax deduction.

EXAMPLE 43

J was permanently transferred to a new job location. The distance from J's former home to his new job (80 miles) exceeds the distance from his former home to his old job (30 miles) by more than 35 miles. J has met the distance requirements for a moving expense deduction. (See the following diagram.)

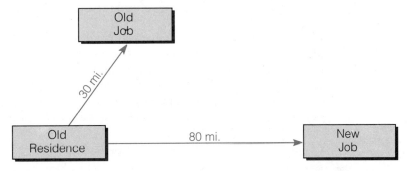

If J was not employed before the move, his new job must be at least 35 miles from his former residence. In this instance, the distance requirements would be met if J had not been previously employed. □

Time Requirements

To be eligible for a moving expense deduction, an employee must be employed on a full-time basis at the new location for 39 weeks in the 12-month period following the move. If the taxpayer is a self-employed individual, he or she must work in the new location for 78 weeks during the next two years. The first 39 weeks must be in the first 12 months. The taxpayer can work either as a self-employed individual or as an employee. The time requirement is suspended if the taxpayer dies, becomes disabled, or is discharged or transferred by the new employer through no fault of the employee.

41. § 217(a).

It is obvious that an employee might not be able to meet the 39-week requirement by the end of the tax year. For this reason, two alternatives are allowed. The taxpayer can take the deduction in the year the expenses were incurred, even though the 39-week test has not been met. If the taxpayer later fails to meet the test, the income of the following year must be increased by an amount equal to the deduction previously claimed for moving expenses. The second alternative is to wait until the test is met and then file an amended tax return for the prior year.

When Deductible

The general rule is that expenses of a cash basis taxpayer are deductible only in the year of payment. However, if reimbursement is received from the employer, an election may be made to deduct the moving expenses in the year subsequent to the move in the following circumstances:

- The moving expenses are incurred and paid in 1989, and the reimbursement is received in 1990.

- The moving expenses are incurred in 1989 and are paid by the employee in 1990 (on or before the due date including extensions for filing the 1989 return), and the reimbursement from the employer is received in 1990.

The election to deduct moving expenses in the year the reimbursement is received is made by claiming the deduction on the return or filing an amended return or claim for refund for the taxable year the reimbursement is received.

The moving expense deduction is allowed regardless of whether the employee is transferred by the existing employer or is employed by a new employer. Also, it is allowed if the employee moves to a new area and obtains employment or switches from self-employed status to employee status (and vice versa). In addition, the moving expense deduction is allowed if an individual is unemployed before obtaining employment in a new area.

Classification of Moving Expenses

There are five classes of moving expenses,[42] and different limitations and qualifications apply to each class.[43] Direct moving expenses include the following:

1. *The expense of moving household and personal belongings.* This class includes fees paid to a moving company for packing, storing, and moving possessions and the rental of a truck if the taxpayer moves his or her own belongings. Also included is the cost of moving household pets. Reasonableness is the only limit on these direct expenses. Such expenses as refitting rugs or draperies and losses on the disposal of club memberships are not deductible as moving expenses.

2. *Travel to the new residence.* This includes the cost of transportation, meals, and lodging of the taxpayer and the members of the taxpayer's household en route. It does not include the cost of moving servants or

---

42. § 217(b)(1)(A).

43. §§ 217(b)(1)(B), (C), (D), and (E).

others who are not members of the household. The taxpayer can elect to take actual auto expenses (no depreciation is allowed) or the automatic mileage method. In this case, moving expense mileage is limited to nine cents per mile for each car. These expenses are also limited by the reasonableness standard. For example, if one moves from Texas to Florida via Maine and takes six weeks to do so, the transportation, meals, and lodging must be allocated between personal and moving expenses.

Indirect moving expenses include the following:

3. *House-hunting trips.* Expenses of traveling (including meals and lodging) to the new place of employment to look for a home are deductible only if the job has been secured in advance of the house-hunting trip. The dollar limitation is explained below.

4. *Temporary living expenses.* Meals and lodging expenses incurred while living in temporary quarters in the general area of the new job while waiting to move into a new residence are deductible. (The dollar limits are discussed below.) These living expenses are limited to any consecutive 30-day period beginning after employment is secured.

5. *Certain residential buying and selling expenses.* Buying and selling expenses include those that would normally be offset against the selling price of a home and those expenses incurred in buying a new home. Examples are commissions, escrow fees, legal expenses, points paid to secure a mortgage, transfer taxes, and advertising. Also deductible are costs involved in settling an old lease or acquiring a new lease or both. Fixing-up expenses, damage deposits, prepaid rent, and the like are not deductible.

Buying and selling expenses of any asset normally increase the basis or reduce the selling price of that asset. Such expenses on the sale or purchase of a personal residence can be considered in computing basis or selling price or as a moving expense under class 5. Any buying or selling expenses claimed as a moving expense deduction cannot be added to the basis of a new home or subtracted from the amount realized on the sale of an old home. This restriction eliminates any possible double benefit of deducting the costs at both points. Generally, since the taxpayer can defer the gain on the sale of a personal residence, the election to take the maximum amount as a moving expense deduction will be preferable. (The dollar limits are discussed below.)

Example 44	T, an executive in the 28% tax bracket, incurred commission expenses of $5,000 on the sale of his personal residence when he was transferred to another state. He can deduct $3,000 (the dollar limitation on class 5 moving expenses) of the commission as a moving expense, which will save him $840 in taxes. The remaining $2,000 will reduce the realized gain on the sale of his home. If T buys a new home, the gain on the sale of the old one will be deferred if certain requirements are met resulting in no current tax (see chapter 15). □

Indirect moving expenses are limited to a total of $3,000. Furthermore, house-hunting and temporary living expenses may not exceed

$1,500 in the aggregate. Direct moving expenses, as discussed previously, are unlimited.

Moving Expense Limits

Classes 1 [44] + 2	=	No limit
Classes 3 + 4	=	$1,500 limit
Classes 3 + 4 + 5	=	$3,000 limit

Generally, the above dollar limitations apply regardless of filing status. If both spouses change jobs and file separate returns, the limitations are $750 (instead of $1,500) and $1,500 (instead of $3,000). If only one spouse makes a job change, the spouse who makes the change is allowed the full amount. If both change jobs, do not live together, and work at job sites at least 35 miles apart, each spouse applies the $1,500 and the $3,000 limits. It does not matter whether they file jointly or separately.

EXAMPLE 45

T, an employee of X Corporation, is hired by Y Corporation at a substantial increase in salary. T is hired in February 1989 and is to report for work in March 1989. The new job requires a move from Los Angeles to New York City. In connection with the move, T incurs the following expenses:

February 1989 house-hunting trip (no meals)	$ 650
Temporary living expenses in New York City incurred by T and family from March 10–30, 1989, while awaiting the renovation of their new apartment (including $400 of meals)	1,000
Penalty for breaking lease on Los Angeles apartment	2,400
Charge for packing and moving household goods	4,200
Transportation and lodging expenses during move (March 5–10)	700
Meal expense during move	300

T can deduct the following amount:

---

44. The numbers refer to the types of moving expenses outlined on pages 10–22 and 10–23.

Moving household goods		$4,200
Transportation and lodging		700
Meals ($300 less 20%)		240
House-hunting trip	$ 650	
Temporary living expenses [$600 plus ($400 cost of meals × 80%)]	920	
	$1,570	
Limited to	$1,500	
Lease penalty	2,400	
	$3,900	
Limited to		3,000
Total itemized moving expense deduction		$8,140

☐

Form 3903 is used to report the detailed calculations of the ceiling limitations, reimbursements, and change in job locations. If the employee is reimbursed for the move, such reimbursement is included in salary income on line 7 of Form 1040. If the reimbursement is less than the moving expenses, the excess expenses are an itemized deduction. The meal expenses are reduced by 20 percent, but the moving expenses are not subject to the 2 percent floor. An over-reimbursement will result in a net increase in taxable income.

EDUCATION EXPENSES

General Requirements

An employee may deduct expenses incurred for education as ordinary and necessary business expenses provided such items were incurred for either of two reasons:

1. To maintain or improve existing skills required in the present job.
2. To meet the express requirements of the employer or the requirements imposed by law to retain his or her employment status.

Education expenses are not deductible if the education is for either of the following purposes:

1. To meet the minimum educational standards for qualification in the taxpayer's existing job.
2. To qualify the taxpayer for a new trade or business.[45]

Thus, fees incurred for professional qualification exams (the bar exam, for example) and fees for review courses (such as a CPA review course) are not deductible.[46] A partial deduction may be allowed for non-accounting courses that also maintain and improve an accountant's existing skills in a present·job.[47] If the education incidentally results in a promotion or raise, the

45. Reg. §§ 1.162–5(b)(2) and (3).
46. Reg. § 1.212–1(f) and Rev.Rul. 69–292, 1969–1 C.B. 84.
47. *Howard Sherman Cooper*, 38 TCM 955, T.C. Memo. 1979–241.

deduction can still be taken as long as the education maintained and improved existing skills and did not qualify a person for a new trade or business. A change in duties is not always fatal to the deduction if the new duties involve the same general work. For example, the IRS has ruled that a practicing dentist's education expenses incurred to become an orthodontist are deductible.[48]

Requirements Imposed by Law or by the Employer for Retention of Employment

Teachers qualify under the provision that permits the deduction of education expenses if additional courses are required by the employer or are imposed by law. Many states require a minimum of a bachelor's degree and a specified number of additional courses to retain a teaching job. In addition, some public school systems have imposed a master's degree requirement and have required teachers to make satisfactory progress toward a master's degree in order to keep their positions. An instructor with a master's degree who is teaching at a college where the minimum degree for a permanent post is a doctorate is not permitted to deduct the expenses of obtaining a Ph.D., since the instructor is obtaining the minimum education required for that position.[49]

Maintaining or Improving Existing Skills

The "maintaining or improving existing skills" requirement in the Code has been difficult for both taxpayers and the courts to interpret. For example, a business executive may be permitted to deduct the costs of obtaining an M.B.A. on the grounds that the advanced management education is undertaken to maintain and improve existing management skills. If the business executive incurred the expenses to obtain a law degree, the expenses would not be deductible, because they constitute training for a new trade or business. The Regulations deny the deduction by a self-employed accountant of expenses relating to law school.[50] In addition, several courts have disallowed deductions to IRS agents for the cost of obtaining a law degree, since the degree was not required to retain employment and the education qualified the agent for a new profession.[51] Clearly, the executive mentioned previously would be eligible to deduct the costs of specialized, nondegree management courses that were taken for continuing education or to maintain or improve existing skills.

Classification of Specific Items

Education expenses include books, tuition, typing, and transportation (e.g., from the office to night school) and travel (e.g., meals and lodging while away from home at summer school).

EXAMPLE 46   T, who holds a bachelor of education degree, is a secondary education teacher in the Los Angeles, California, school system. The school board

---

48. Rev.Rul. 74–78, 1974–1 C.B. 44.

49. Reg. § 1.162–5(b)(2)(iii) Example (2); *Kenneth C. Davis*, 65 T.C. 1014 (1976).

50. Reg. § 1.162–5(b)(3)(ii) Example (1).

51. *J.L. Weiler*, 54 T.C. 398 (1970).

recently changed its minimum education requirement for new teachers by prescribing five years of college training instead of four. Under a grandfather clause, teachers who have only four years of college would continue to qualify if they show satisfactory progress toward a graduate degree. T enrolls at the University of Southern California and takes three graduate courses. T's unreimbursed expenses for this purpose are as follows:

Books and tuition	$ 250
Lodging while in travel status (June–August)	1,150
Meals while in travel status	800
Laundry while in travel status	220
Transportation	600

T has a miscellaneous itemized deduction subject to the 2% floor as follows:

Books and tuition	$ 250
Lodging	1,150
Meals (80% of $800)	640
Laundry	220
Transportation	600
	$2,860

☐

ENTERTAINMENT EXPENSES

Many taxpayers attempt to deduct personal entertainment expenses as business expenses. In response to these abuses by taxpayers, Code § 274 restricts the deductibility of entertainment expenses. The law contains strict record-keeping requirements and provides restrictive tests for the deduction of certain types of entertainment expenses.

Classification of Expenses

Entertainment expenses can be categorized as follows: those *directly related* to business and those *associated with* business.[52] Directly related expenses are related to an actual business meeting or discussion. These expenses can be contrasted with entertainment expenses that are incurred to promote goodwill. To obtain a deduction for directly related entertainment, it is not necessary to show that actual benefit resulted from the expenditure as long as there was a reasonable expectation of benefit. To qualify as directly related, the

---

52. § 274(a)(1)(A).

expense should be incurred in a clear business setting. If there is little possibility of engaging in the active conduct of a trade or business due to the nature of the social facility, it may be difficult to qualify the expenditure as directly related to business.

Expenses associated with, rather than directly related to, business entertainment must serve a specific business purpose, such as obtaining new business or continuing existing business. These expenditures qualify only if the expenses directly precede or follow a bona fide business discussion. Entertainment occurring on the same day as the business discussion meets the test.

Restrictions upon Deductibility

Business Meals.   Any business meal is deductible only if the following are true: [53]

- The meal is directly related to or associated with the active conduct of a trade or business.
- The expense is not lavish or extravagant under the circumstances.
- The taxpayer (or an employee) is present at the meal.

A business meal with a business associate or customer is not deductible unless business is discussed. This requirement is not intended to disallow the deduction for a meal consumed while away from home on business.

EXAMPLE 47   T travels to San Francisco for a business convention. She pays for dinner with three colleagues and is not reimbursed by her employer. They do not discuss business. She can deduct 80% of the cost of her meal. However, she cannot deduct the cost of her colleagues' meals. □

The *clear business purpose* test requires that meals be directly related to or associated with the active conduct of a business. A meal is not deductible if it serves no business purpose.

EXAMPLE 48   T decides what stocks to add to or remove from his portfolio on the basis of advice from his stockbroker. If T takes his stockbroker to lunch to discuss his portfolio, he cannot deduct the meal's cost, because his investment activities are not considered a business. Similarly, there's no deduction if he has dinner with his tax adviser to discuss ways to reduce his income tax liability. □

The taxpayer or an employee must be present at the business meal for the meal to be deductible.[54]

EXAMPLE 49   T reserved a table (and picked up the tab) for a business meal. Although business was discussed, neither T nor an employee attended. A deduction

---

53. § 274(k).   54. § 162(k)(3).

for the meal expense is disallowed. T can take a deduction for a business gift, but such gifts are limited to $25 per person per year. ☐

EXAMPLE 50   T, a party to a contract negotiation, buys dinner for other parties to the negotiation but does not attend the dinner. No deduction is allowed. ☐

An independent contractor who renders significant services to the taxpayer is treated as an employee.

EXAMPLE 51   In Example 50, if T's attorney (who negotiates contracts for T) had attended the meal, T would be allowed a deduction. ☐

The attendance requirement does not apply where there is a transfer for business purposes, such as a holiday gift of a ham or a bottle of wine.

Entertainment Facilities.   Deducting the cost of maintaining an entertainment facility (e.g., a hunting lodge, fishing camp, yacht, country club) lends itself to taxpayer abuse, since such a facility could be used for personal vacations and entertainment. For this reason, the law allows deductions only for "dues or fees to any social, athletic, or sporting club or organization" [55] and imposes stringent recordkeeping requirements.

To obtain a deduction for the dues paid or incurred to maintain a club membership, a primary use test is imposed. Unless it can be shown that over 50 percent of the use of the facility was for business purposes, no deduction is permitted. In meeting the primary use test, the following rules govern:

- Consider only the days the facility is used. Thus, days of nonuse do not enter into the determination.
- A day of both business and personal use counts as a day of business use.
- Business use includes entertainment that is associated with or directly related to business.

Even if the primary use test is satisfied, only the portion of the dues attributable to the directly related entertainment qualifies for the deduction.

EXAMPLE 52   T, the sales manager of an insurance agency, is expected to incur entertainment expenses in connection with the sale of insurance. None of these expenses are reimbursed by his employer. During the year, T paid the following amounts to the Leesville Country Club:

---

55. §§ 274(a)(2)(A) and (C).

Membership fee (refundable upon termination of membership)	$2,000
Annual dues	1,200
Meals relating to business use	900
Meals and other charges relating to personal use	400
Other charges relating to business use	200

The club was used 120 days for purposes directly related to business and 80 days for personal use. The club was not used at all during the remaining days of the year. Since the facility was used for business more than 50% of the time (120 days out of 200 days), the primary use test is satisfied. The portion of the annual dues that can be deducted is $720 (120/200 = 60% × $1,200). None of the membership fee is deductible, since it is refundable. The total deduction allowed is as follows:

Annual dues	$ 720
Business meals	900
Other business charges	200
Total	$1,820
Less 20%	(364)
Deductible	$1,456

Note that the $1,456 is a miscellaneous itemized deduction subject to the 2 percent floor. □

Ticket Purchases for Entertainment. A deduction for the cost of a ticket for an entertainment activity is limited to the face value of the ticket.[56] This limitation is applied before the 80 percent rule. The face value of a ticket includes any tax. Under this rule, the excess payment to a scalper for a ticket is not deductible. Similarly, the fee to a ticket agency for the purchase of a ticket is not deductible.

An exception exists for expenses of a sports event meeting certain charitable fund-raising requirements. The exception applies to the entire ticket package (e.g., parking, meals, seating). The full amount is deductible if the event:

- Is organized for the primary purpose of benefiting a tax-exempt charitable organization [described in § 501(c)(3)].
- Contributes 100 percent of the net proceeds to the charity.
- Uses volunteers for substantially all work performed in carrying out the event.

Expenditures for the rental or use of a luxury skybox at a sports arena in excess of the face value of regular tickets are disallowed as deductions. If a luxury skybox is used for entertainment that is directly related to or associated with business, the deduction is limited to the face value of nonluxury box

56. § 274(i).

seats. All seats in the luxury skybox are counted, even when some seats are unoccupied.

The disallowance of the excess cost was phased in over three years: one-third was disallowed in 1987, two-thirds in 1988, and 100 percent in 1989 and future years.[57]

The taxpayer may also deduct stated charges for food and beverages under the general rules for business entertainment. The deduction for skybox seats, food, and beverages is limited to 80 percent of cost.

EXAMPLE 53

In 1989, AW, Inc., pays $6,000 to rent a 10-seat skybox at City Stadium for three football games. Nonluxury box seats at each event range in cost from $25 to $35 a seat. In March, an AW representative and five clients of AW use the skybox for the first game. The entertainment follows a bona fide business discussion, and AW spends $85 for food and beverages during the game. AW computes its deduction for the first sports event as follows:

Food and beverages	$ 85
Deduction for seats ($35 × 10 seats)	350
Total entertainment expense	$ 435
80% limitation	×.80
Deduction	$ 348

Note that 100% of the excess cost is disallowed in 1989 and future years.

□

Recordkeeping Requirements.   Section 274(d) provides that no deduction is permitted unless the taxpayer substantiates, by adequate records or by sufficient evidence corroborating the taxpayer's statements, the following:

- The amount of the expense.
- The time and place of the expense.
- The business purpose.
- The business relationship.

If reimbursements equal expenses and the employee makes an adequate accounting to the employer, both the reimbursements and the expenses can be omitted from the tax return. The employee is required only to state on the return that the reimbursements did not exceed the allowable expenses.[58] In all other cases, the employee must submit a statement with the return. When the reimbursements exceed the allowable expenses, the excess must be included in income. If expenses exceed the reimbursements, the taxpayer must detail both on the return to deduct the excess. Where an employee owns more than 10 percent of the employer corporation's stock, a statement of the expenses

---

57. § 273(i)(2)(B).   58. Reg. §§ 1.162–17(b)(1) and 1.274–5(e)(2).

must accompany the return. The last requirement applies to all reimbursements and expenses of the shareholder-employee.[59]

Business Gifts. Business gifts are deductible to the extent of $25 per donee per year. An exception is made for gifts costing $4 or less (e.g., pens with the employee's or company's name on them) or promotional materials. Such items are not treated as business gifts subject to the $25 limitation. In addition, incidental costs such as engraving of jewelry and nominal charges for giftwrapping, mailing, and delivery are not included in the cost of the gift in applying the limitation. The $25 limitation applies to both direct and indirect gifts. A gift is indirect if it is made to a person's spouse or other family member or to a corporation or partnership on behalf of the individual. All such gifts must be aggregated in applying the $25 limit. Excluded from the $25 limit are gifts or awards to employees, such as for length of service, that are under $400.[60] Gifts to superiors and employers are not deductible.

It is necessary to maintain records substantiating the gifts. These substantiation requirements are similar to the rules applying to entertainment expenses previously discussed.

Business gifts made by employees are deductible *for* AGI if they are reimbursed. If unreimbursed, they are miscellaneous itemized deductions subject to the 2 percent floor.

OTHER EMPLOYEE EXPENSES

Office in the Home

Employees and self-employed individuals are not allowed a deduction for expenses of an office in the home unless a portion of the residence is used exclusively on a regular basis as either:

- The principal place of business for any trade or business of the taxpayer.
- A place of business used by clients, patients, or customers.

Employees must meet an additional test: The use must be for the convenience of the employer rather than merely being "appropriate and helpful."[61]

The exclusive use requirement means that a specific part of the home must be used solely for business purposes. A deduction, if permitted, will require an allocation of total expenses of operating the home between business and personal use based on floor space or number of rooms.

Even if the taxpayer meets the above requirements, the allowable home office expenses may not exceed the gross income from the business less all other business expenses attributable to the activity. Furthermore, the home office expenses that must be deducted first are those that would be allowable as itemized deductions anyway (e.g., mortgage interest and real estate taxes). All home office expenses of an employee are miscella-

59. Reg. §§ 1.274–5(e)(2)(ii) and (iii) and Rev.Rul. 73–191, 1973–1 C.B. 151.
60. § 274(b)(1)(C). § 274(b)(3)(C) allows a deduction for gifts to employees of up to $1,600 under a *qualified plan* as long as the average cost of all awards under the qualified plan does not exceed $400. Qualified plans are described in § 274(b)(3).
61. § 280A(c)(1).

neous itemized deductions subject to the 2 percent floor, except those (such as interest) that qualify as other personal itemized deductions. Home office expenses of a self-employed individual are trade or business expenses and are deductible *for* AGI.

Any disallowed home office expenses can be carried forward and used in future years subject to the same limitations.

EXAMPLE 54

T is a certified public accountant employed by a regional CPA firm as a tax manager. He operates a separate business in which he refinishes furniture in his home. For this business, he uses two rooms in the basement of his home exclusively and regularly. The floor space of the two rooms constitutes 10% of the floor space of his residence. Gross income from the business totals $8,000. Expenses of the business (other than home office expenses) are $6,500. The following home office expenses are incurred:

Real property taxes on residence	$4,000
Interest expense on residence	7,500
Operating expenses of residence	2,000
Depreciation on residence (based on 10% business use)	250

T's deductions are determined as follows:

Business income		$8,000
Less: Other business expenses		(6,500)
		$1,500
Less: Allocable taxes ($4,000 × 10%)	$400	
Allocable interest ($7,500 × 10%)	750	(1,150)
		$ 350
Allocable operating expenses of the residence ($2,000 × 10%)		(200)
		$ 150
Allocable depreciation ($250, limited to remaining income)		(150)
		$ –0–

T has a carryover of $100 (the unused excess depreciation). Because T is self-employed, the allocable taxes and interest ($1,150), the other deductible office expenses ($200 + $150), and $6,500 of other business expenses are deductible *for* AGI. □

EXAMPLE 55

T, an accountant for the XYZ Corporation, maintains an office in her home. She uses the office primarily for reading professional journals, and her family uses the office for personal reasons. T occasionally brings home work relating to XYZ Corporation and uses the office at home on weekends and during the evenings. Her outside consulting activities are limited to the preparation of a few tax returns from which she received $1,000 gross income during 1989. Mortgage interest and real estate taxes allocable to the office amounted to $1,500. An allocable portion of other household expenses, including utilities and depreciation, was $1,000. The $1,500 mortgage interest and real estate taxes are deductible *from* adjusted gross income as itemized deductions. None of the other expenses are deductible, because the office in T's home is not used exclusively and on a regular basis by T as a place of business. In addition, an employee must show that the office is used for the convenience of the employer. It appears that T's office is merely appropriate and helpful in the performance of her duties as an employee. This situation does not permit a deduction.

□

The home office limitation cannot be circumvented by leasing part of one's home to an employer, using it as a home office, and deducting the expenses as a rental expense under § 212.

Miscellaneous Employee Expenses

Some miscellaneous employee expenses that are deductible are special clothing and its upkeep, union dues, and professional expenses. Others are professional dues, professional meetings, and employment agency fees for seeking employment in the same trade or business, whether or not a new job is secured. These deductions are *for* adjusted gross income only if the expenses are reimbursed. In all other cases, they are miscellaneous itemized deductions subject to the 2 percent floor.

To be deductible, special clothing must be both specifically required as a condition of employment and not generally adaptable for regular wear. For example, a police officer's uniform is not suitable for off-duty activities. An exception is clothing used to the extent that the clothing takes the place of regular clothing (e.g., military uniforms).

The current position of the IRS is that expenses incurred in seeking employment are deductible if the taxpayer is seeking employment in the same trade or business. The deduction is allowed whether or not the attempts to secure employment are successful. An unemployed taxpayer can take a deduction providing there has been no substantial lack of continuity between the last job and the search for a new one. No deduction is allowed for persons seeking their first job or seeking employment in a new trade or business (whether or not successful).

Other employee expenses that are not deductible are commuting expenses and any other expenditures of a personal nature.

Expenses of Employees Working Outside the United States

The U.S. income tax applies to the worldwide income of its citizens and residents. Since most other countries also have an income tax, expatriates (Americans working abroad) were at the distinct disadvantage of having to pay two income taxes on foreign earned income. The increased cost of living in some foreign countries plus the scarcity of adequate housing in less-developed countries made working abroad even more disadvantageous to Americans. To induce U.S. citizens and residents to accept employment or relocation overseas, U.S. companies were compelled to offer various cost differentials and tax equalization assurances. This increased their labor costs and placed U.S. concerns at an economic disadvantage with their foreign competitors. To mitigate the problem, Congress passed favorable legislation for foreign earned income.

The expatriate has the option of a flat-dollar exclusion (discussed in chapter 5), a considerably simplified excess housing allowance, or both. The new provisions are summarized as follows:

- To qualify, the taxpayer must satisfy either the bona fide residence test or the physical presence test—330 full days of foreign residency out of 12 consecutive months. An exception to the 330-day rule is provided for expatriates who are forced to leave a country because of civil unrest or similar conditions, such as the widespread civil disorder in Lebanon.

- In addition to electing the foreign earned income exclusion, an expatriate may elect to exclude an amount determined on the basis of housing costs incurred. For this purpose, the housing cost amount consists of reasonable housing costs, including rent, insurance, and utilities. Housing costs do not include interest and taxes that are independently deductible. The amount to be excluded is the excess of these costs over 16 percent of the salary of a government employee holding grade GS–14. For those expatriates who are not reimbursed for housing costs, a special rule substitutes a deduction for the exclusion.

- Deductions or credits for foreign taxes attributable to the excluded income are not allowable. Consequently, the expatriate is placed in a position of having to forgo the foreign tax credit in order to obtain the exclusion.

- The exclusions are elective. Taxpayers are able to elect the income and housing-reimbursement exclusions separately, together, or not at all. Once elected, however, the exclusions are binding upon subsequent years unless affirmatively revoked. Revocation places the taxpayer in a five-year holding period during which the exclusions cannot be reelected.

The exclusion rule for expatriates is generally advantageous for those working in countries with low, if any, income taxes. If, on the other hand, the country imposes a high income tax, it may be preferable not to elect the exclusions and to use the foreign tax credit route to reduce or eliminate U.S. income taxes.

Contributions to Individual Retirement Accounts

An important and popular deduction *for* adjusted gross income is the amount contributed to an Individual Retirement Account (IRA). This amount may be as great as $2,000 per year for an individual. IRAs are covered in detail in chapter 19.

CONCEPT SUMMARY 10–1

Determining the Deductibility of Employee Business Expenses

	If the expense is	The 20% reduction applies to	And is deductible	And is
1.	Any allowable employee business expense (fully reimbursed and adequate accounting made).	None.	*for* AGI	Omitted from the return, as are all reimbursements.[1,2]
2.	Any allowable employee business expense (fully reimbursed and no adequate accounting made).	All.	*from* AGI	A miscellaneous deduction subject to the 2% floor.
3.	Any partially reimbursed allowable business expense (whether or not adequate accounting made).	Unreimbursed part of meals and entertainment only.	Reimbursed portion is *for* AGI and unreimbursed is *from* AGI.	Unreimbursed part is a miscellaneous deduction subject to the 2% floor.[3]

Unreimbursed Expenses

	If the expense is	The 20% reduction applies to	And is deductible	And is
4.	Transportation expenses.	None.	*from* AGI	A miscellaneous deduction subject to the 2% floor.[3]
5.	Travel expenses.			
	a. meals.	All.	*from* AGI	A miscellaneous deduction subject to the 2% floor.[3]
	b. lodging.	None.	*from* AGI	A miscellaneous deduction subject to the 2% floor.[3]
	c. incidentals.	None.	*from* AGI	A miscellaneous deduction subject to the 2% floor.[3]

If the expense is	The 20% reduction applies to	And is deductible	And is
6. Education expenses.	Only meal expenses.	*from* AGI	A miscellaneous deduction subject to the 2% floor.[3]
7. Moving expenses.	Only meal expenses.	*from* AGI	A miscellaneous deduction not subject to the 2% floor.[4]
8. A deductible IRA.	None.	*for* AGI	N/A
9. Home office expenses.	None.	*from* AGI	Interest and property taxes are not subject to the 2% floor, all others are.[3]
10. Professional or union dues.	None.	*from* AGI	A miscellaneous deduction subject to the 2% floor.[3]
11. Uniforms.	None.	*from* AGI	A miscellaneous deduction subject to the 2% floor.[3]
12. Job-hunting expenses (if in same field).	Only meal and entertainment expenses.	*from* AGI	A miscellaneous deduction subject to the 2% floor.[3]
13. Entertainment expenses.	All.	*from* AGI	A miscellaneous deduction subject to the 2% floor.[3]
14. An outside salesperson's expenses.	Only meals and entertainment expenses.	*from* AGI	A miscellaneous deduction subject to the 2% floor.[3]

1. If reimbursements exceed expenses, the reimbursements are included in income; expenses are itemized, subject to the 2% floor.
2. Employer can deduct only 80% of meals and entertainment.
3. Miscellaneous deductions are added together and reduced by 2% of AGI.
4. Moving expenses are itemized, whether or not reimbursed.

TAX PLANNING CONSIDERATIONS

Self-Employed Individuals

Some taxpayers have the flexibility to be classified as either employees or self-employed individuals (e.g., real estate agents or direct sellers). Such taxpayers should not automatically assume that the latter is better until all factors are considered.

It is advantageous to deduct one's business expenses *for* adjusted gross income and avoid the 2 percent floor. However, a self-employed individual may have higher expenses, such as local gross receipts taxes, license fees, franchise fees, personal property taxes, and occupation taxes. The recordkeeping and filing requirements can be quite burdensome.

One of the most expensive considerations is the Social Security tax versus the self-employment tax. In 1989, for example, the Social Security tax rate for an employee is 7.51 percent, while a self-employed individual is subject to a self-employment tax rate of 13.02 percent. Both are levied on the first $48,000.

After analyzing all these factors, a taxpayer may decide that employee status is preferable to self-employed status.

Shifting Deductions between Employer and Employee

An employee can avoid the 2 percent floor for employee business expenses. Typically, an employee incurs travel and entertainment expenses in the course of employment. The corporation gets the deduction if it reimburses the employee, and the employee gets the deduction *for* AGI. An adequate accounting must be made, and excess reimbursements cannot be kept.

Transportation and Travel Expenses

Adequate detailed records should be kept of all transportation and travel expenses. Since the regular mileage allowance is 24 cents per mile, a new, expensive automobile used primarily for business may generate a higher expense based on actual cost. The election to expense part of the cost of the automobile under § 179, ACRS depreciation, insurance, repairs and maintenance, automobile club dues, and interest on the auto loan may result in automobile expenses greater than the automatic mileage allowance.

If a taxpayer wishes to sightsee or vacation on a business trip, it would be beneficial to schedule business on both a Friday and a Monday to turn the weekend into business days for allocation purposes. It is especially crucial to schedule appropriate business days when foreign travel is involved.

Unreimbursed Employee Business Expenses

The 2 percent floor for unreimbursed employee business expenses offers a tax planning opportunity for married couples. If one spouse has high miscellaneous expenses subject to the floor, it may be beneficial for the couple to file separate returns. If they file jointly, the 2 percent floor will be based on the incomes of both. Filing separately will lower the reduction to 2 percent of only one spouse's income.

Other provisions of the law should be considered, however. For example, filing separately could cost a couple losses of up to $25,000 from self-managed rental units under the passive loss rules (discussed in chapter 7).

Another possibility is to negotiate a salary reduction with one's employer in exchange for the 100 percent reimbursement of employee expenses. The employee would be better off, because the 2 percent floor would not apply. The employer would be better off, because expense reimbursements are not subject to Social Security and other payroll taxes.

Moving Expenses

Reimbursements of moving expenses must be included in gross income, and certain moving expenses may not be deductible because of the ceiling limitations. As a result, an employee may be required to pay additional income tax because of an employment-related move. Some employers reimburse their employees for these additional taxes, which are estimated and included in the employee's reimbursement.

Persons who retire and move to a new location incur personal nondeductible moving expenses. However, if the retired person accepts a full-time job in the new location before moving, the moving expenses become deductible.

Education Expenses

Education expenses are treated as nondeductible personal items unless the individual is employed or is engaged in a trade or business. A temporary leave of absence for further education is one way to reasonably assure that the taxpayer is still qualified, even if a full-time student. It has been held that an individual could deduct education expenses even though he resigned from his job, returned to school full time for two years, and accepted another job in the same field upon graduation. The Court held that the student had merely suspended active participation in his field.[62] In another instance, a nurse had been inactive in her field for 13 years and returned to school to study biology. She was not in a trade or business, and her expenses were not deductible.[63] To secure the deduction, an individual should be advised to arrange his or her work situation to preserve employee or business status.

Entertainment Expenses

Proper documentation of expenditures is essential because of the strict recordkeeping requirements and the restrictive tests that must be met. For example, credit card receipts as the sole source of documentation may be inadequate to substantiate the business purpose and business relationship.[64] Taxpayers should be advised to maintain detailed records of amounts, time, place, business purpose, and business relationships. A credit card receipt details the place, date, and amount of the expense. A notation made on the receipt of the names of the person(s) attending, the

---

62. *Stephen G. Sherman,* 36 TCM 1191, T.C.Memo. 1977–301.

63. *Geraldine G. Cannon,* 36 TCM 1130, T.C.Memo. 1977–283; *John M. Cannon,* 40 TCM 541, T.C.

Memo. 1980–224, affirmed by court order (CA–7, 1981).

64. *George L. Gee,* 36 TCM 327, T.C.Memo. 1977–72.

business relationship, and the topic of discussion should constitute proper documentation.

Associated with or goodwill entertainment is not deductible unless a business discussion is conducted immediately before or after the entertainment. Furthermore, a business purpose must exist for such entertainment. Taxpayers should be advised to arrange for a business discussion before or after such entertainment. They must provide documentation of the business purpose (e.g., to obtain new business from a prospective customer).

Since a 50 percent test is imposed for the deductibility of country club dues, it may be necessary to accelerate business use or reduce personal use of a club facility. The 50 percent test is made on a daily use basis, and detailed records should therefore be maintained to substantiate business versus personal use.

EXAMPLE 56

T confers with his CPA on December 5 and finds that he has used the country club 30 days for business and 33 days for personal use. On the advice of his CPA, T schedules four business lunches between December 5 and December 31 and refrains from using the club for personal purposes until January of the following year. Because of this action, T will meet the 50% test and will be permitted a deduction for a portion of the club dues. □

Unreimbursed meals and entertainment are subject to the 80 percent rule in addition to the 2 percent floor. Negotiating a salary reduction, as previously discussed under Unreimbursed Employee Business Expenses, is even more valuable to the taxpayer.

PROBLEM MATERIALS

Discussion Questions

1. What difference does it make if an individual's expenses are classified as employment-related expenses or as expenses from self-employment?

2. Discuss the factors that may indicate an employer-employee relationship. What is the definitive test?

3. What are the requirements for a real estate agent or a direct seller to be classified as a self-employed individual?

4. Why might a real estate agency prefer that its real estate agents be classified as self-employed persons rather than employees?

5. How does the tax treatment of meals and entertainment differ from the treatment of other employee business expenses? Does the treatment differ if the expenses are reimbursed?

6. What § 212 expenses are subject to the 2 percent floor?

7. Why is a taxpayer permitted to take a deduction *for* adjusted gross income for reimbursed expenses that would otherwise be treated as itemized deductions if no reimbursement were received?

8. What constitutes an adequate accounting to an employer? Why does the IRS allow an employee to ignore both the expense and the reimbursement if they are equal and if an adequate accounting is made?

9. What tax return reporting procedures must be followed by an employee under the following circumstances:
   a. Expenses and reimbursements are equal, and an adequate accounting is made to the employer.
   b. Reimbursements exceed expenses, and an adequate accounting is made to the employer.
   c. Expenses exceed reimbursements, and no accounting is made to the employer.

10. T received a reasonable per diem allowance while out of town on business for his employer. By staying at the YMCA and eating at fast-food restaurants, his actual expenses were less than his per diem allowance. What are the tax consequences to T?

11. A taxpayer has two jobs. He drives 40 miles to his first job. The distance from the first job to the second is 32 miles. During the year he worked 200 days at both jobs. On 150 days, he drove from his first job to the second job. On the remaining 50 days, he drove home (40 miles) and then to the second job (42 miles). How much can he deduct?

12. What expenses are subject to the 80 percent rule? What are the exceptions?

13. Discuss the deductibility of travel related to educational activities.

14. Can an employee who receives a reimbursement of 15 cents per mile for job-related automobile expenses deduct any excess expense amounts on his or her tax return?

15. What are the limitations on the deduction of expenses for luxury water travel?

16. Distinguish between transportation expenses and travel expenses.

17. J incurred travel expenses while away from home on company business. These expenses were not reimbursed by his employer. Can J deduct the travel expenses? If so, where and how are they deducted?

18. T accepts a three-year work assignment in another city. Are the rental payments and meal expenses incurred because of that work assignment deductible as travel expenses?

19. J takes a combined business and pleasure trip to Hawaii. What portion of the expenses is deductible?

20. G took a combined business and pleasure trip to Europe. She traveled to London from New York on Friday, vacationed on Saturday and Sunday, conducted business on Monday, got snowed in at the airport on Tuesday, traveled to Paris on Wednesday, relaxed on Thursday (a legal holiday), conducted business on Friday, went sightseeing on Saturday and Sunday, picked up business samples and papers on Monday and flew back to New York on Tuesday. What portion of her air fare can she deduct?

21. Discuss the restrictions on nonbusiness conventions for tax purposes.

22. What are the distance requirements for moving expenses?

23. What are a taxpayer's two alternatives if she moves in November and cannot meet the 39-week test by December 31? Which alternative is financially preferable if she meets the test in the following year? If she does not meet the test?

24. Distinguish between direct moving expenses and indirect moving expenses. Why is it important to classify such items properly?

25. What limits are imposed on the deduction of expenses for tickets purchased for business entertainment? How are such expenses treated on an employee's return if they are reimbursed? Not reimbursed?

26. What difference does it make if a taxpayer is improving existing skills or acquiring new ones for the purpose of the education deduction? Under what general tax principle does the justification for this rule lie?

27. Discuss the requirements for the deductibility of business meals.

28. Discuss the difference between entertainment that is *directly related to* business and entertainment that is *associated with* business.

29. J, a stockbroker, buys his CPA's lunch, over which they discuss J's tax problems. Can J deduct the cost of the meal? Could the CPA get the deduction if he pays for the meal?

30. F asks your advice on December 1 regarding the tax deductibility of his country club dues. To date, the club has been used 40 days for purposes directly related to business use, 42 days for purposes associated with business use, and 84 days for personal use. During December, members of F's family have planned to use the facility four more days for personal parties. No business use is planned in December. What would you advise F to do?

31. To what extent may a taxpayer take a deduction for business gifts to a business associate? To an employee? To a superior?

32. How are deductible home office expenses treated for tax purposes? Is the deduction *for* or *from* AGI?

33. P took a cruise in the Hawaiian Islands on a ship of U.S. registry to attend a business-related seminar. The cost was $3,000. What, if anything, can she deduct?

Problems

34. B incurred the following expenses on a trip that was 100% for business and that required him to be away from home overnight:

Airfare	$1,082
Taxi	30
Meals	75
Room	105
Entertainment	40
Laundry	25

The expenses are not reimbursed by B's employer. How much can B deduct, and is the deduction *for* or *from* AGI?

35. T is a professor who consults on the side. She uses one-fifth of her home exclusively for her consulting business, and clients regularly meet her there. T is single and under 65. Her AGI (before considering consulting income) is $40,000. Other relevant data follows:

Income from consulting business	$3,600
Consulting expenses other than home office	1,100
Total costs relating to home	
Interest and taxes	8,000
Utilities	1,400
Maintenance and repairs	900
Depreciation (based on ⅕ business use)	1,200

Calculate T's AGI for 1989.

36. D, a professor of French history, went to France during the year to research documents available only in France. His time on the trip was spent entirely on business. No vacation days were involved, and D kept adequate records. D received no reimbursements for the following carefully documented expenses:

Airfare and other transportation	$1,600
Hotels	1,200
Meals	900

   a. What can D deduct in 1989 if he has AGI of $30,000 and no other miscellaneous itemized deductions? Are the deductions *for* or *from* AGI?

   b. Would your answer differ if D had gone to France to soak up the culture and brush up on his French?

37. J, an executive, traveled to England to confer with branch office officials of his company. Because an inner-ear birth defect prevents him from flying, he traveled to England on the *Queen Elizabeth II*. The journey, which took six days and cost $1,800, was sold as a package deal with no breakdown of costs. How much can J deduct in 1989, assuming the U.S. government per diem amount is $100? Would your answer differ if the cost were broken down between transportation ($800) and meals and entertainment ($1,000)?

38. T, a manager with X Corporation, owns 25% of the company's stock. He made an adequate accounting for the following business expenses and was fully reimbursed:

Transportation	$1,500
Meals	800
Lodging	1,600
Entertainment	1,200

   How should T treat these expenses on his tax return for 1989? Would your answer differ if T had not made an adequate accounting?

39. T incurred the following employee expenses:

Travel while away from home (including meals of $500)	$2,000
Transportation	1,000
Entertainment of customers	900
Professional dues	600
Telephone for business use	500

T's employer paid T a $3,500 allowance to cover all of these expenses. T made an adequate accounting. Calculate T's deductions *for* and *from* adjusted gross income. His AGI was $25,000.

40. S received reimbursements of $3,300 after adequately accounting to his employer. His expenses were as follows:

Airfare, taxi, and auto mileage	$2,000
Meals while away from home	600
Lodging while away from home	1,400
Entertainment while away from home	1,000
Dues, subscriptions, and books	500

What are S's deductions *for* and *from* adjusted gross income? Assume an AGI of $50,000.

41. K received $4,400 in reimbursements after she had made an adequate accounting to her employer. Her expenses were as follows:

Transportation expenses	$3,200
Meals while away from home	1,400
Lodging and incidentals	2,300
Dues, phone, and subscriptions	100
Entertainment	1,000

How much can K deduct *for* and *from* AGI? Assume K had AGI of $50,000 and no other miscellaneous itemized deductions.

42. P, an executive with X Corporation, incurred the following employee business expenses:

Lodging	$2,000
Meals	1,600
Transportation	2,400
Entertainment	1,500
Phone	500

P received $5,600 to cover the above expenses. He made an adequate accounting. In addition to incurring the above expenses, P incurred expenses in attending a seminar on communications for executives. He paid $500 in transportation, $100 in meals, and $300 in fees and books. He was not reimbursed.

P's salary was $50,000. He made a deductible contribution of $2,000 to his IRA. His only other income was interest of $800. He is 47 and single.

Calculate P's AGI and itemized employee expenses.

43. N took a business trip of 10 days. Seven days were spent on business (including travel time) and 3 days were personal. His unreimbursed expenses were as follows:

Airfare	$1,500
Lodging (per day)	200
Meals (per day)	100
Entertainment of clients	300

a. How much can N deduct if the trip is within the United States?

b. How much can N deduct if the trip is outside the United States?

44. P took a trip from Los Angeles to Tokyo, primarily on business for the company of which she is president. She spent eight days on business and two days sightseeing. P's travel expenses were as follows:

Airfare	$1,200
Meals	750
Lodging	950
Incidental expenses	100

What travel expenses may P deduct? Are P's expenses deductible *for* or *from* AGI?

45. M took a business trip from Seattle to Chicago. He spent two days in travel, conducted business for four days, and visited friends for four days. He incurred the following expenses:

Airfare	$ 700
Lodging	2,000
Meals	1,600
Entertainment of clients	500

M received no reimbursements. What can M deduct? Are the deductions *for* or *from* AGI?

46. T, who is age 42 and single, earned a salary of $60,000. She had other income consisting of interest of $2,000, dividends of $1,600, and long-term capital gains of $4,000.

T loaned a friend $5,000 two years ago. In the current year the friend died, leaving no assets. T will not receive any repayments on the loan.

T adequately accounted to her employer and received a reimbursement of $3,000. She incurred the following expenses during the year:

Transportation	$2,300
Meals	1,600
Dues and subscriptions	800
Entertainment of clients	300
Total	$5,000

Calculate J's AGI and itemized employee business expenses.

47. H, an investment counselor, attended a conference on the impact of the new tax law on investment choices. His unreimbursed expenses were as follows:

Airfare	$250
Lodging	500
Meals	300
Tuition and fees	400

a. How much can H deduct on his return? Are the expenses *for* or *from* AGI?

b. Would your answer differ if H were a self-employed physician?

48. T incurred the following expenses when she was transferred from San Francisco to Dallas:

Loss on the sale of old residence	$7,000
Moving company's charges	2,100
House-hunting trip	1,200
Temporary living expenses for 60 days (including meals of $1,000)	3,000
Broker's fees on residence sold	5,000
Charges for fitting drapes in new residence	800

a. How much can T deduct? Is the deduction *for* or *from* AGI?

b. What would be T's tax consequences if the employer reimbursed her for all of the expenses?

49. D, a resident of Vermont, graduated from a college in Boston and was hired by a St. Louis CPA firm. She incurred the following moving expenses:

Apartment-hunting trip to St. Louis (including meals of $200)	$1,200
Loss of damage deposit because of ruined carpet in Boston apartment	200
Expense of renting and driving a truck with household goods	2,200
Lodging in St. Louis for one week before apartment was ready	350
Meals for one week before apartment was ready	210
Cost of shipping pet cat to St. Louis	150
Payment to real estate firm that located a suitable apartment in St. Louis	75
Cost of refitting drapes for St. Louis apartment	125

How much can D deduct? Are the expenses deductible *for* or *from* AGI?

50. D belongs to a country club that she uses for entertaining clients of her employer as well as for personal use. She incurred charges as follows:

Initiation fee (nonrefundable)	$5,000
Annual dues	3,600
Business meals	4,000
Other business charges	800
Personal meals and charges	3,100

D kept careful records, which revealed the following use:

Days *associated with* business	60
Days *directly related* to business	50
Days for personal use	80

Forty of the personal use days occurred on the same days that the club was used for entertainment directly related to business.

a. How much can D deduct if she received no reimbursements?

b. Would your answer differ if she made an adequate accounting and received a $3,000 reimbursement?

51. T belongs to a country club that he uses for both business and personal purposes. Assuming none of his expenses are reimbursed, how much can he deduct on his tax return in the following two cases:

Annual dues	$5,000
Meals *directly related* to business	400
Meals *associated with* business	300
"Quiet business meals" (business was not discussed)	350
Personal meals and charges	2,000

Case (a) Days directly related to business	110
Days associated with business	30
Days for personal use	150
Case (b) Days directly related to business	70
Days associated with business	80
Days for personal use	75

52. M is an executive with a large manufacturing firm. He is 54 and married and has two children. His compensation was $126,000. His wife is not employed.

    M took a trip from New York to London primarily for business. He was away from home 12 days, spending 8 days conducting business and 4 days vacationing. He incurred transportation expenses of $3,000, lodging expenses of $200 per day, meals of $60 per day, and expenses while entertaining clients of $500.

    M belonged to a country club that he used for both personal and business entertainment. His records reveal that he used the facility 57 days for purposes directly related to business, 14 days for purposes associated with business, and 93 days for personal use during the year. Expenses were as follows:

Annual dues	$6,000
Business meals	1,800
Business entertainment	965
Personal meals and charges	3,100

    M received $8,600 in dividends and $3,400 in interest during the year. He paid $18,000 in alimony to his former wife.

    Calculate M's adjusted gross income.

53. J is an accountant with XYZ Company. He is also a self-employed tax consultant with several clients and earns $12,000 per year from his outside consulting. He has an office in his home that he uses exclusively for meeting with his consulting clients and for work he performs for his clients. Based on square footage, he estimates that total expenses amount to $3,500, including $1,500 of taxes and interest on his home mortgage.

    a. Can J take a deduction for an office in the home? If so, how does he report it and how much can he deduct?

    b. If the office was also used for work J brought home from his regular job, how would your answer to (a) differ? Assume J used the office 80% for his consulting business and 20% for his regular job.

54. C is a self-employed wholesale jobber who had sales of $80,000 in 1989. He keeps meticulous business income and expense records.

    His business expenses included an office in his home, used exclusively for his business. Expenses allocated to the home office on the basis of square footage were as follows:

Taxes and interest	$1,300
Utilities and maintenance	620
Office depreciation	1,200
Office supplies	380
Office furniture depreciation	700

C incurred the following business expenses:

Transportation	$6,000
Business meals	1,400
Business entertainment	900
Telephone, dues, and books	1,500
Other business expenses	2,000

C paid $20,000 to his former wife, of which $8,000 was child support and $12,000 was alimony. He made a $2,000 deductible contribution to his IRA. C received interest of $2,000 and dividends of $1,000 during the year. Calculate his AGI for 1989.

55. T is a single, 37-year-old executive who earned $60,000 in 1989. He also earned $2,000 in dividends and had interest of $1,800 credited to his savings account. A former friend skipped town, owing T $1,500 and leaving him with no possibility of collecting this bona fide personal loan. An examination of T's records revealed the following:

   • T paid $5,000 in alimony and $3,000 in child support to his former wife.

   • T incurred education expenses to maintain and improve his existing skills. Tuition and books cost $580, transportation expenses amounted to $960, and parking fines totaled $80.

   • T paid $1,200 in country club dues and $920 for meals for clients. The club was used 200 days for business and 50 days for personal use.

   • T took a business trip to London. He flew there on a Thursday, conducted business on Friday, went sightseeing on Saturday and Sunday, conducted business on Monday and Tuesday, and flew home on Wednesday. His unreimbursed expenses amounted to $2,100 for airfare, $500 for meals, and $1,400 for lodging.

   Calculate T's adjusted gross income and his itemized employee deductions.

56. T and S are married and file a joint return. T is a manager and earned a salary and bonus of $31,000 in 1989. He incurred employee business expenses of $800 for transportation and $400 for meals and entertainment. He made an adequate accounting to his employer and was fully reimbursed. He took a combined business and pleasure trip to New York. He spent five days conducting business and three days sightseeing. His airfare and taxi expense amounted to $1,200, meals averaged $60 per day, and lodging was $80 per day. He was not reimbursed. He made a $2,000 contribution to his IRA.

   S is a self-employed court reporter who works out of the home. One room is used regularly and exclusively for her business. She had receipts of $12,000 and incurred office expenses of $1,000 for depreciation, $300 for utilities and phone, and $500 for repairs and maintenance. She earned $200 in interest on her savings account and incurred other business expenses of $2,300. She made a payment of $2,000 to her IRA.

Calculate taxable income for T and S on a joint return, assuming all other itemized deductions totaled $4,100.

57. T is a single saleswoman who earned $38,000 in 1989. Her employer gave her a $5,000 expense account intended to cover all her employee expenses. She incurred expenses of $3,000 for transportation; $2,000 for meals and entertainment; and $2,200 for dues, subscriptions, phone, and gifts (none of which exceeded $25).

She sold some stocks, realizing a $6,000 long-term capital gain. She had dividend income of $650 and earned interest of $900, of which $250 was on municipal bonds. During the year, she was awarded $10,000 from a competitor for defamation of character.

In November, she spent her vacation cruising the Hawaiian Islands on a ship of U.S. registry. Daily lectures and seminars on improving selling techniques were conducted. She can prove that the cruise, which cost her $3,500, was directly related to her job.

Calculate T's adjusted gross income and deductible itemized employee expenses.

Cumulative Problems

58. Sam Diamond is 38 and single with no dependents. His salary was $34,000, from which $3,800 was withheld for Federal income tax. The proper amount of FICA (Social Security) taxes and state income taxes of $1,400 were also withheld. Examination of his 1989 records revealed the following:

a. Sam had other receipts as follows:

Dividends on AT & T stock	$370
Interest credited to savings account	92
State income tax refund (he itemized in 1988)	268

b. Sam's other deductions were as follows:

Home mortgage interest	$7,900
Property taxes	620
Charitable contributions	580

c. Sam paid his former wife $2,200 for support of their child, Mary, who lives with her mother.

d. Sam received $5,000 in settlement of a damage claim resulting from a personal automobile accident.

e. He took a business trip during 1989 and was reimbursed $1,500 by his employer. His expenses were as follows:

Transportation	$ 850
Meals	160
Lodging and incidentals	340
	$1,350

f. He drove a total of 8,000 business miles and uses the standard mileage rate to compute his automobile expense.

g. Sam incurred the following unreimbursed employee business expenses:

Business meals	$500
Publications and dues	250
Phone and miscellaneous	60
Business entertainment	290
Tuition and books for course at local college	612

Compute Sam's Federal income tax payable (or refund due) for 1989. Suggested software (if available): *WEST–TAX Planner* or *BNA Individual Income Tax Spreadsheet.*

59. Robert T. Washington is 40 years old and divorced. He is a wholesale broker for General Suppliers, Inc. His commissions and salary amounted to $104,000 in 1989. His employer withheld $21,000 in Federal income taxes. Robert lives in a state that has no state income tax. Examination of Robert's 1989 records revealed the following:

a. Robert paid his former wife Jean $12,000, of which $7,000 was alimony and $5,000 support for their daughter, Brenda, age 6. His ex-wife, who has custody of Brenda, can document that she spent $2,000 on her daughter's support. She has signed an agreeement that Robert gets the exemption.

b. Robert received dividends from Acme Company of $1,000 and interest on his money market account at Citizen's Federal of $3,200. His favorite uncle gave him $10,000 as a Christmas gift, which he invested in municipal bonds that earned $75 interest in 1989.

c. Since General Suppliers, Inc., has no offices (only a warehouse), Robert works out of a home office that constitutes 20% of his home's floor space. His expenses in connection with his home were as follows:

Depreciation (on office space only)	$ 600
Property taxes	1,800
Interest on home mortgage	12,000
Cleaning, repairs, and maintenance	1,300
Utilities	2,600

His local telephone service cost $300, of which 50% was business. His long-distance business calls totaled $800. His office furniture has been fully depreciated.

d. Robert belongs to a country club that he uses for business purposes. He used the club 80 days for purposes directly related to business and 120 days for personal use. His carefully kept records reveal that his dues amounted to $2,400, business-related meals were $1,560, and personal charges were $2,300.

e. Robert also had the following well-documented business expenses:

Magazines and dues	$160
Gifts to customers: (5 @ $50)	250
(10 @ $20)	200
Entertainment of customers	800
Cleaning and maintenance of business suits and silk ties	400

f. Business mileage on Robert's fully depreciated auto was 5,000 miles. Total mileage for the year on the car, which was placed in service on 1–1–84, was 30,000 miles.

g. Robert took a combined business and pleasure trip to San Francisco in June. He spent eight days conducting business and four days visiting museums. His airfare and taxi expense was $500; meals cost $50 per day; and lodging and incidentals amounted to $200 per day.

h. Other expenses included the following:

Contribution to United Negro College Fund	$1,000
Contribution to Methodist Church	1,200
Expenses of traveling to Olympia to speak to the Elks Club against proposed legislation regarding wholesalers	300
Personal doctor and dentist bills	2,600
Dentist bills for daughter	3,000
Tax preparation fee	350
Investment periodicals	50
Other itemized deductions	6,900

Compute Robert Washington's Federal income tax payable or refund due for 1989. Suggested software (if available): *WEST–TAX Planner* or *BNA Individual Income Tax Spreadsheet*.

60. George M. and Martha J. Jordan have no dependents and are both under age 65. George is an outside salesman for Consolidated Jobbers, and his Social Security number is 682–99–444. Martha is an executive with General Corporation, and her Social Security number is 741–88–6642. The Jordans live at 321 Oak Street, Lincoln, NE 68024. They both want to contribute to the Presidential Election Campaign Fund.

In 1988, George earned $32,000 in commissions. His employer withholds FICA but not Federal income taxes. George paid $6,000 in estimated taxes. Martha earned $62,000, from which $10,508 was withheld for Federal income taxes. Neither George nor Martha received any expense reimbursements. Nebraska has no state income tax.

George uses his two-year-old car on sales calls and keeps a log of all miles driven. In 1988, he drove 36,000 miles, 25,000 of them for business. He made several out-of-state sales trips, incurring transportation costs of $1,600, meals of $800, and lodging costs of $750. He also spent $1,400 during the year taking customers to lunch.

Martha incurred the following expenses related to her work: taxi fares of $125, business lunches of $615, and a yearly commuter train ticket of $800. During the year, Martha received $1,200 in interest from the employees' credit union, $100,000 life insurance proceeds upon the death of her mother in December, and $500 in dividends from General Motors. She contributed $2,000 to her Individual Retirement Account. Neither George nor Martha is covered by an employee retirement plan. Martha gave a gift valued at $500 to the president of her firm upon his promotion to that position.

The Jordans had additional expenditures as follows:

Charitable contributions (cash)	$ 800
Medical and dental expenses	1,400
Real property taxes	1,200
Home mortgage interest	9,381
Charge account interest	193
Tax return preparation fee	150

Part 1—Tax Computation

Compute the Jordans' Federal income tax payable or refund due, assuming they file a joint income tax return for 1988. You will need Form 1040, two copies of Form 2106, and Schedules A and B. Suggested software (if available): *WEST–TAX Preparer* for tax return solutions, *WEST–TAX Planner* or *BNA Individual Income Tax Spreadsheet* if tax return solutions are not desired.

Part 2—Tax Planning

Martha and George ask your help in deciding what to do with the $100,000 Martha inherited in 1988. They are considering three conservative investment alternatives: Suggested software (if available): *WEST–TAX Planner* or *BNA Individual Income Tax Spreadsheet.*

- Invest in 8% long-term U.S. bonds.
- Invest in 7% Series EE bonds and elect to defer the interest earned.
- Invest in 6% municipal bonds.

a. Calculate the best alternative for next year. Assume that Martha and George will have the same income and deductions in 1989, except for the income from the investment they choose.

b. What other factors should the Jordans take into account?

Research Problems

Research Problem 1   Phil Johnson retired after a long, fruitful career as an executive with Ajax Corporation. He joined a group known as SCORE, an organization in which retired executives provide consulting services for small start-up businesses. Phil did not receive any compensation but incurred out-of-pocket expenses. He claimed these expenses on his tax return as trade or business expenses. Was he correct?

Research Problem 2   T, a heart specialist, left his job in Texas to accept a position in a California medical center. In addition to seeing patients, he was required to work on the hospital's heart transplant project under the supervision of Dr. H. Dr. H was an impossible boss, who had already had two other doctors removed from the team. After 35 weeks of employment, Dr. H had T terminated from the project. Will T be able to deduct his moving expenses?

Research aid:

§ 217(c)(2)

Research Problem 3   M and F are husband and wife. M owns a small company that manufactures business machines. Many of the machine parts are made in Japan. On average, M spends three months in Japan on business each year. In 1988, M and F took a 63–day trip to Japan to discuss a new contract. Fifteen days were spent vacationing. F did not participate in the business meetings. Can M deduct any of F's expenses? Must he allocate expenses between business and personal days?

Research aid:

§ 274(c)(2)(B)

11

DEDUCTIONS AND LOSSES: CERTAIN ITEMIZED DEDUCTIONS

OBJECTIVES Distinguish between deductible and nondeductible personal expenses.
Define medical expenses and compute the medical expense deduction.
Contrast deductible taxes and nondeductible fees, licenses, etc.
Discuss rules relating to the Federal tax treatment of state income taxes.
Determine whether various types of interest are deductible.
Define charitable contributions and discuss related measurement problems and percentage limitations.
Enumerate the business and personal expenditures that are deductible either as miscellaneous itemized deductions or as other itemized deductions.

General Classification of Expenses

Personal expenditures are specifically disallowed as deductions by § 262. Personal expenses can be contrasted with business expenses that are incurred in the production or expectation of profit. Business expenditures are deductions from gross income in arriving at adjusted gross income and are reported on Schedule C of Form 1040. Certain nonbusiness expenses are also deductible in arriving at adjusted gross income (e.g., expenses attributable to rents and royalties and forfeited interest on a time savings deposit).

This chapter is principally concerned with expenses that are essentially personal in nature but that are deductible because of legislative grace (e.g., charitable contributions, medical expenses, and certain state and local taxes). If the Code does not specifically state that a personal type of expense is deductible, no deduction is permitted. Allowable personal expenses are deductible *from* adjusted gross income in arriving at taxable income if the taxpayer elects to itemize them. A taxpayer would so elect if the total of the itemized deductions exceeds the standard deduction [1] based on the taxpayer's filing status. Chapter 3 described the situations in which a taxpayer is not eligible for the standard deduction. At this point, it may be helpful to review the computation in the tax formula for individuals that appears in chapters 1 and 3.

Medical Expenses

General Requirements

Medical expenses paid for the care of the taxpayer, spouse, and dependents are allowed as an itemized deduction to the extent the expenses are not reimbursed. The medical expense deduction is limited to the amount by which such expenses exceed 7.5 percent of the taxpayer's adjusted gross income.

Medical Expenses Defined

The term *medical care* includes expenditures incurred for the "diagnosis, cure, mitigation, treatment, or prevention of disease, or for the purpose of affecting any structure or function of the body." [2] A partial list of deductible and nondeductible medical items is shown in Figure 11–1.

A medical expense does not have to relate to a particular ailment to be deductible. Since the definition of medical care is broad enough to cover preventive measures, the cost of periodic physical and dental exams would qualify even for a taxpayer in good health.

The deductibility of nursing home expenses depends on the medical condition of the patient and the nature of the services rendered.[3] If an individual enters a home for the aged for personal or family considerations and not

---

1. The total standard deduction is the sum of the basic standard deduction and the additional standard deduction.

2. § 213(d)(1)(A).

3. Reg. § 1.213–1(e)(1)(v).

FIGURE 11–1	Deductible and Nondeductible Medical Expenses	

Deductible	**Nondeductible**
Medical (including dental, mental, and hospital) care	Funeral, burial, or cremation expenses
Prescription drugs	Nonprescription drugs (except insulin)
Special equipment	Bottled water
Wheelchairs	Toiletries, cosmetics
Crutches	Diaper service, maternity clothes
Artificial limbs	Programs for the general improvement of health
Eyeglasses (including contact lenses)	Weight reduction
Hearing aids	Health spas
Transportation for medical care	Stop-smoking clinics
Medical and hospital insurance premiums	Social activities (e.g., dancing and swimming lessons)

because he or she requires medical or nursing attention, deductions are allowed only for the costs attributable to the medical and nursing care.

EXAMPLE 1

T has a chronic heart ailment. His family has decided to place T in a nursing home equipped to provide medical and nursing care facilities. Total nursing home expenses amount to $15,000 per year. Of this amount, $4,500 is directly attributable to medical and nursing care. Since T is in need of significant medical and nursing care and is placed in the facility primarily for this purpose, all $15,000 of the nursing home costs are deductible (subject to the 7.5% floor). ☐

EXAMPLE 2

Assume the same facts as in Example 1, except that T does not have a chronic heart ailment. T enters the nursing home because he and his family feel that all of them would be more comfortable with this arrangement. Under these circumstances, only $4,500 of the expenses would be deductible because the move was primarily for personal considerations.

☐

Tuition expenses of a dependent at a special school may be deductible as a medical expense. The cost of medical care could include the expenses of a special school for a mentally or physically handicapped individual. The deduction will be allowed if the individual's condition is such that the resources of the school for alleviating such infirmities are a principal reason for the individual's presence there. If this is the case, the cost of meals and lodging, in addition to the tuition, is a proper medical expense deduction.[4]

---

4. *Donald R. Pfeifer*, 37 TCM 817, T.C.Memo. 1978–189. Also see Rev.Rul. 78–340, 1978–2 C.B. 124.

EXAMPLE 3

T's daughter D attended public school through the seventh grade. Because D was a poor student, she was examined by a psychiatrist who diagnosed an organic problem that created a learning disability. Upon the recommendation of the psychiatrist, D is enrolled in a private school so that she can receive individual attention. If the school has no special program for students with learning disabilities and does not provide special medical treatment, the expenses related to D's attendance would not be deductible as medical expenses. The cost of any psychiatric care, however, would qualify as a medical expense. □

Example 3 shows that the recommendation of a physician does not make the expenditure automatically deductible.

Capital Expenditures for Medical Purposes

Capital expenditures normally are adjustments to basis and are not deductible. However, both a capital expenditure for a permanent improvement and expenditures made for the operation or maintenance of the improvement may qualify as medical expenses. If a capital expenditure qualifies as a medical expense, the allowable cost is deductible in the year incurred. The tax law makes no provision for depreciating medical expenses as it does for other capital expenditures.

Some examples of capital expenditures for medical purposes are swimming pools if the taxpayer does not have access to a neighborhood pool and air conditioners if they do not become permanent improvements (e.g., window units).[5] Other examples include dust elimination systems,[6] elevators,[7] and a room built to house an iron lung. These expenditures are medical in nature if they are incurred as a medical necessity upon the advice of a physician, the facility is used primarily by the patient alone, and the expense is reasonable. A capital improvement that ordinarily would not have a medical purpose qualifies as a medical expense if it is directly related to prescribed medical care and is deductible to the extent that the expenditure exceeds the increase in value of the related property. Appraisal costs would also be deductible but not as medical expenses. Such amounts are expenses incurred in the determination of the taxpayer's tax liability.[8]

EXAMPLE 4

T is advised by his physician to install an elevator in his residence so that T's wife, who is afflicted with heart disease, will not be required to climb the stairs. The cost of installing the elevator is $3,000, and the increase in the value of the residence is determined to be only $1,700. Therefore, $1,300 is deductible as a medical expense. Additional utility costs to operate the elevator and maintenance costs are deductible as medical expenses as long as the medical reason for the capital expenditure continues to exist. □

5. Rev.Rul. 55–261, 1955–1 C.B. 307, modified by Rev.Rul. 68–212, 1968–1 C.B. 91.
6. *F.S. Delp*, 30 T.C. 1230 (1958).
7. *Riach v. Frank*, 62–1 USTC ¶ 9419, 9 AFTR2d 1263, 302 F.2d 374 (CA–9, 1962).
8. § 212(3).

To enable a physically handicapped individual to live independently and productively, the full cost of certain home-related capital expenditures incurred qualifies as a medical expense. These expenditures are subject to the 7.5 percent floor only, and the increase in the home's value is deemed to be zero. Qualifying costs include expenditures for constructing entrance and exit ramps to the residence, widening hallways and doorways to accommodate wheelchairs, installing support bars and railings in bathrooms and other rooms, and adjusting electrical outlets and fixtures.[9]

Transportation and Lodging Expenses for Medical Treatment

Payments for transportation to and from a point of treatment for medical care are deductible as medical expenses (subject to the 7.5 percent floor). Transportation expenses for medical care include bus, taxi, train, or plane fare, charges for ambulance service, and out-of-pocket expenses for the use of an automobile. A mileage allowance of nine cents per mile [10] may be used instead of actual out-of-pocket automobile expenses. A deduction is also allowed for the transportation expenses of a parent who must accompany a child who is receiving medical care or for a nurse or other person giving medical assistance to a person who is traveling to get medical care and cannot travel alone.

A deduction is allowed for lodging while away from home for medical expenses if the following requirements are met: [11]

- The lodging is primarily for and essential to medical care.
- Medical care is provided by a doctor in a licensed hospital or a similar medical facility (e.g., a clinic).
- The lodging is not lavish or extravagant under the circumstances.
- There is no significant element of personal pleasure, recreation, or vacation in the travel away from home.

Lodging expenses included as medical expenses cannot exceed $50 per night for each person. The deduction is allowed not only for the patient but also for a person who must travel with the patient (e.g., a parent traveling with a child who is receiving medical care).

EXAMPLE 5

T was advised by his doctor to receive specialized medical care that could be rendered only in a hospital in Boston. T resides in Columbus, Ohio, and incurred transportation costs of $300 to reach the Boston hospital. The transportation costs of $300 qualify as medical expenses because the expenditure was primarily for and essential to medical care. □

Amounts Paid for Medical Insurance Premiums

Medical insurance premiums are included with other medical expenses subject to the 7.5 percent floor. If amounts are paid under an insurance contract

---

9. For a complete listing of the items that qualify, see Rev.Rul. 87–106, 1987–2 C.B. 67.

10. Rev.Proc. 85–49, 1985–2 C.B. 716.

11. § 213(d)(2).

to cover loss of life, limb, sight, etc., no amount can be deducted unless the coverage for medical care is separately stated in the contract.

Medical insurance premiums paid by the taxpayer under a group plan or an individual plan are included as medical expenses. If an employer pays all or part of the taxpayer's medical insurance premiums, the amount paid is not included in gross income by the employee and is not included in the employee's medical expenses.

If a taxpayer is self-employed, special rules apply regarding medical insurance premiums. Up to 25 percent of the premiums are deductible as a business expense (*for* AGI). Any excess can be claimed as a medical expense. For this special treatment to apply, the following conditions must be satisfied:

- The taxpayer must not be covered under a medical plan of an employer or of a spouse's employer.

- The plan must meet the nondiscrimination rules that apply to all employer plans (see chapter 19).

The business deduction cannot exceed the net profit from the self-employment activity.[12]

EXAMPLE 6

During 1989, T was a self-employed real estate broker with no employees. For the year, he had $45,000 net profit from real estate transactions and paid $2,000 in medical insurance premiums. T may deduct $500 (25% × $2,000) of the premiums as a business expense. The balance of $1,500 ($2,000 − $500) qualifies as a medical expense. □

Medical Expenses Incurred for Dependents

In computing the medical expense deduction, a taxpayer may include medical expenses for a person who was a dependent at the time the expenses were paid or incurred. Also includible are medical expenses incurred for a person who could be claimed by the taxpayer as a dependent except that the person did not meet the gross income or the joint return tests (see chapter 3).

EXAMPLE 7

T (age 22) is married and a full-time student at a university. During 1989, T incurred medical expenses that were paid by M (T's mother). M provided more than half of T's support for the year. Even if T files a joint return with his wife, M may claim those medical expenses she paid. M would combine such expenses with her own in applying the 7.5% floor. □

Medical expenses paid on behalf of a former spouse are deductible if the parties were married when the expenditures were incurred. Also, medical expenses can be incorporated in the divorce decree and consequently may be deductible as alimony payments (*for* AGI).[13]

For divorced persons with children, a special rule applies to the noncustodial parent. The noncustodial parent may claim any medical expenses he or

---

12. § 162(m). This provision expires after December 31, 1989.

13. This assumes the conditions of § 215 are met.

she pays even though the custodial parent claims the children as dependents. This rule applies if the dependency exemptions could have been shifted to the noncustodial parent by the custodial parent's waiver (refer to chapter 3).

EXAMPLE 8

F and M are divorced in 1988, and M is awarded custody of their child C. During 1989, F makes the following payments to M: $3,600 for child support and $2,500 for C's medical bills. Together, F and M provide more than one-half of C's support. Even though M claims C as a dependent, F can combine C's medical expenses with his own. □

Year of Deduction

Regardless of a taxpayer's method of accounting, medical expenses are deductible only in the year paid. In effect, therefore, this places all individual taxpayers on a cash basis as far as the medical expense deduction is concerned. One exception, however, is allowed for deceased taxpayers. If the medical expenses are paid within one year from the day following the day of death, they can be treated as being paid at the time they were *incurred*.[14] Thus, such expenses may be reported on the final income tax return of the decedent or on earlier returns if incurred before the year of death.

No deduction will be allowed for payment of medical care to be rendered in the future unless the taxpayer is under an obligation to make the payment.[15] The IRS does allow a deduction for the portion of a lump-sum prepayment allocable to medical care made to a retirement home under a life care plan.[16]

Reimbursements

If medical expenses are reimbursed in the same year as paid, no problem arises. The reimbursement merely reduces the amount that would otherwise qualify for the medical expense deduction. But what happens if the reimbursement is received in a later year than the expenditure? Unlike casualty losses where reasonable prospect of recovery must be considered (refer to chapter 8), the expected reimbursement is disregarded in measuring the amount of the deduction. Instead, the reimbursement is accounted for separately in the year in which it occurs.

As a general rule, when a taxpayer receives an insurance reimbursement for medical expenses deducted in a previous year, the reimbursement must be included in gross income in the year of receipt. However, taxpayers are not required to report more than the amount previously deducted as medical expenses. Thus, a taxpayer who did not itemize deductions in the year the expenses were incurred is not required to include a reimbursement in gross income.

The tax benefit rule applies to reimbursements if the taxpayer itemized deductions in the previous year. In this case, the taxpayer may be required to report some or all of the medical expense reimbursement in income in the year the reimbursement is received. Under the tax benefit rule, the taxpayer

---

14. § 213(c).

15. *Robert S. Basset*, 26 T.C. 619 (1956).

16. Rev.Rul. 75–302, 1975–2 C.B. 86.

may exclude the reimbursement from income up to the amount of the deductions that did not decrease income tax in the earlier year.

EXAMPLE 9

T has adjusted gross income of $20,000 for 1988. He was injured in a car accident and paid $1,300 for hospital expenses and $700 for doctor bills. T also incurred medical expenses of $600 for his dependent child. In 1989, T was reimbursed $600 by his insurance company for his car accident. His deduction for medical expenses in 1988 is computed as follows:

Hospitalization	$1,300
Bills for doctor's services	700
Medical expenses for dependent	600
Total	$2,600
Less: 7.5% of $20,000	(1,500)
Medical expense deduction (assuming T itemizes his deductions)	$1,100

Assume that T would have elected to itemize his deductions even if he had no medical expenses in 1988. If the reimbursement for medical care had occurred in 1988, the medical expense deduction would have been only $500 [$2,000 ($2,600 total medical expenses − $600 reimbursement) − $1,500 floor], and T would have paid more income tax.

Since the reimbursement was made in a subsequent year, T would include $600 in gross income for 1989. If T had not itemized in 1988, he would not include the $600 reimbursement in 1989 gross income, because he received no tax benefit in 1988. □

TAXES

The deduction of certain state and local taxes paid or accrued by a taxpayer is permitted by § 164. The deduction was created to relieve the burden of multiple taxes upon the same source of revenue.

Deductibility as a Tax

One must make a distinction between a tax and a fee, since fees are not deductible unless incurred as an ordinary and necessary business expense or as an expense in the production of income.

The IRS has defined a tax as follows:

A tax is an enforced contribution exacted pursuant to legislative authority in the exercise of taxing power, and imposed and collected for the purpose of raising revenue to be used for public or governmental purposes, and not as payment for some special privilege granted or service rendered. Taxes are, therefore, distinguished from various other contributions and charges imposed for particular purposes under particular powers or functions of the government. In view of such distinctions, the question whether a particular contribution or charge is to be regarded as a tax depends upon its real nature.[17]

Thus, in accordance with the above definition, fees for dog licenses, automobile inspection, automobile titles and registration, hunting and fishing licenses, bridge and highway tolls, drivers' licenses, parking meter deposits, postage, etc., are not considered to be deductible. These items, however, could be deductible if incurred as a business expense or for the production of income. Deductible and nondeductible taxes are summarized in Figure 11–2.[18]

Property Taxes, Assessments, and Apportionment of Taxes

Property Taxes.   State, local, and foreign taxes on real and personal property are generally deductible only by the person against whom the tax is imposed. Cash basis taxpayers may deduct these taxes in the year of actual payment, and accrual basis taxpayers may deduct them in the year that fixes the right to deductibility.

Deductible personal property taxes must be ad valorem (assessed in relation to the value of the property). Therefore, a motor vehicle tax based on weight, model, year, and horsepower is not an ad valorem tax. However, a tax based on value and other criteria may qualify in part.

EXAMPLE 10   State X imposes a motor vehicle registration tax on 4% of the value of the vehicle plus 40 cents per hundredweight. B, a resident of the state, owns a car having a value of $4,000 and weighing 3,000 pounds. B pays an annual registration fee of $172. Of this amount, $160 (4% of $4,000) would be

---

FIGURE 11–2   Deductible and Nondeductible Taxes

Deductible	Nondeductible
State, local, and foreign real property taxes	Federal income taxes
State and local personal property taxes	FICA taxes imposed on employees
State, local, and foreign income taxes	Employer FICA taxes paid on domestic household workers
The crude oil windfall profit tax	Estate, inheritance, and gift taxes
The environmental tax	General sales taxes
	Federal, state, and local excise taxes (e.g., gasoline, tobacco, spirits)
	Foreign income taxes if the taxpayer chooses the foreign tax credit option
	Taxes on real property to the extent such taxes are to be apportioned and treated as imposed on another taxpayer

---

17. Rev.Rul. 57–345, 1957–2 C.B. 132, and Rev.Rul. 70–622, 1970–2 C.B. 41.

18. Most deductible taxes are contained in § 164, while the nondeductible items are included in § 275.

deductible as a personal property tax. The remaining $12, based on the weight of the car, would not be deductible. ☐

Assessments for Local Benefits.   As a general rule, real property taxes do not include taxes assessed for local benefits, since such assessments tend to increase the value of the property (e.g., special assessments for streets, sidewalks, curbing, and other like improvements). A taxpayer cannot deduct the cost of a new sidewalk (relative to a personal residence), even though the construction was required by the city and the sidewalk may have provided an incidental benefit to the public welfare.[19] Such assessments are added to the adjusted basis of the taxpayer's property.

Assessments for local benefits are deductible as a tax if they are made for maintenance or repair or for meeting interest charges with respect to such benefits. In such cases, the burden is on the taxpayer to show the allocation of the amounts assessed for the different purposes. If the allocation cannot be made, none of the amount paid is deductible.

Apportionment of Real Property Taxes between Seller and Purchaser. Real estate taxes for the entire year are apportioned between the buyer and seller on the basis of the number of days the property was held by each in the year of sale. This apportionment is required without regard to whether the tax is paid by the buyer or the seller or is prorated pursuant to the purchase agreement. The rationale for apportioning the taxes between the buyer and seller is based on the administrative convenience of the IRS in determining who is entitled to deduct the real estate taxes in the year of sale. In making the apportionment, the assessment date and the lien date are disregarded.

EXAMPLE 11   The real property tax year in County R is April 1 to March 31. S, the owner on April 1, 1989, of real property located in County R, sells the real property to B on June 30, 1989. B owns the real property from June 30, 1989, through March 31, 1990. The tax for the real property tax year April 1, 1989, through March 31, 1990, is $730. The portion of the real property tax treated as imposed upon S, the seller, is $180 (90/365 × $730, April 1 through June 29, 1989), and $550 (275/365 × $730, June 30, 1989 through March 31, 1990) of the tax is treated as imposed upon B, the purchaser. Note that the allocable part of the real estate tax year applicable to the seller ends on the day before the sale, and the date of sale is included in the part of such year applicable to the purchaser. ☐

If the actual real estate taxes are not prorated between the buyer and seller as part of the purchase agreement, adjustments are required. The adjustments are necessary in order to determine the amount realized by the seller and the adjusted cost basis of the property to the buyer. If the buyer pays the entire amount of the tax, he or she has, in effect, paid the seller's portion of the real estate tax and has therefore paid more for the property than the actual purchase price. Thus, the amount of real estate tax that is apportioned to the seller (for Federal income tax purposes) is added to the buyer's cost

19. *Erie H. Rose*, 31 TCM 142, T.C.Memo. 1972–39; Reg. § 1.164–4(a).

basis. The seller must increase the amount realized on the sale by the same amount.

EXAMPLE 12

S sells real estate on October 3, 1989, for $50,000. The buyer, B, pays the real estate taxes of $1,095 for the calendar year, which is the real estate property tax year. Of the real estate taxes, $825 is apportioned to and is deductible by the seller, S, and $270 of the taxes is deductible by B. The buyer has, in effect, paid S's real estate taxes of $825 and has therefore paid $50,825 for the property. B's basis is increased to $50,825, and the amount realized by S from the sale is increased to $50,825. □

The opposite result occurs if the seller (rather than the buyer) pays the real estate taxes. In this case, the seller reduces the amount realized from the sale by the amount that has been apportioned to the buyer. The buyer is required to reduce his or her adjusted basis by a corresponding amount.

EXAMPLE 13

S sells property for $50,000 on October 3, 1989. While S held the property, he paid the real estate taxes for the calendar year, which is the real estate property tax year, in the amount of $1,095. Although S paid the entire $1,095 of real estate taxes, $270 of that amount is apportioned to B and is therefore deductible by B. The effect is that the buyer, B, has paid only $49,730 for the property. The amount realized by S, the seller, is reduced by $270, and B reduces his cost basis in the property to $49,730. □

Income Taxes

It is the position of the IRS that state and local income taxes imposed upon an individual are deductible only as itemized deductions even if the taxpayer's sole source of income is from a business, rents, or royalties.

Cash basis taxpayers are entitled to deduct state income taxes withheld by the employer in the year such amounts are withheld. In addition, estimated state income tax payments are deductible in the year the payment is made by cash basis taxpayers even if the payments relate to a prior or subsequent year.[20] If the taxpayer overpays state income taxes because of excessive withholdings or estimated tax payments, the refund that is received must be included in gross income of the following year to the extent that the deduction reduced the tax liability in the prior year.

EXAMPLE 14

T is a cash basis unmarried taxpayer who had $800 of state income tax withheld during 1989. Additionally in 1989, T paid $100 that was due when she filed her 1988 state income tax return and made estimated payments of $300 on her 1989 state income tax. When T filed her 1989 Federal income tax return in April 1990, she elected to itemize deduc-

20. Rev.Rul. 71–190, 1971–1 C.B. 70. See also Rev. Rul. 82–208, 1982–2 C.B. 58, wherein a deduction is not allowed when the taxpayer cannot, in good faith, reasonably determine that there is additional state income tax liability.

tions, which amounted to $5,500, including the $1,200 of state income tax payments and withholdings, all of which reduced her tax liability.

As a result of overpaying her 1989 state income tax, T received a refund of $200 early in 1990 that would be included in T's 1990 gross income in computing her Federal income tax whether T received a check from the state for $200 or applied the $200 toward her 1990 state income tax. □

INTEREST

A deduction for interest has been allowed since enactment of the income tax law in 1913. Despite its long history of Congressional acceptance, the interest deduction continues to be one of the most controversial areas in the tax law.

The controversy has centered around the propriety of allowing the deduction of interest charges for the purchase of consumer goods and services and interest on borrowings used to acquire investments (investment interest). TRA of 1986 effectively put an end to this controversy by phasing out the deduction for personal interest and further limiting the deduction for investment interest after 1990. Even when interest is allowed as a deduction, limits are imposed on the deductibility of prepaid interest. In addition, no deduction is permitted for interest on debt incurred to purchase or carry tax-exempt securities.

Disallowed and Allowed Items

Interest has been defined by the Supreme Court as compensation for the use or forbearance of money.[21] The general rule permits a deduction for all interest paid or accrued within the taxable year on indebtedness.[22] This general rule is modified by other Code provisions that disallow or restrict certain interest deductions.

Personal (Consumer) Interest.   Personal interest is any interest allowable as a deduction, with some exceptions as follows:

- Trade or business interest.
- Investment interest.
- Interest on passive activities.
- Home mortgage interest to a limited extent if it is qualified residence interest.

For this purpose, trade or business interest does not include interest on indebtedness to finance employee business expenses; such interest is personal interest. Personal, or consumer, interest also includes finance charges on department store and bank credit card purchases and on gasoline credit cards.[23] The term also includes late payment charges on utility bills [24] as well as interest on income tax deficiencies and assessments.

---

21. *Old Colony Railroad Co. v. Comm.*, 3 USTC ¶ 880, 10 AFTR 786, 52 S.Ct. 211 (USSC, 1936).

22. § 163(a).

23. Rev.Rul. 73–136, 1973–1 C.B. 68.

24. Rev.Rul. 74–187, 1974–1 C.B. 48.

Personal interest is no longer fully deductible. The phase-out of the deduction takes place over a five-year period as shown in Figure 11–3. The deduction is the percentage allowed times the total personal interest expense. Thus, for the tax years 1987–1990, some deduction may be allowed for personal interest.

Investment Interest. Taxpayers frequently borrow funds that they then use to acquire investment assets. When the interest expense is large relative to the income from the investments, substantial tax benefits could result. Congress has therefore placed limitations on the deductibility of interest when funds are borrowed for the purpose of purchasing or continuing to hold investment property.

Prior to 1987, investment interest expense was deductible to the extent of $10,000 [25] plus net investment income. Under TRA of 1986, investment interest expense is limited to net investment income for the year.[26] This rule will be fully in effect in 1991. For the four years 1987–1990, investment interest expense in excess of net investment income is allowed based on the prior-law amount of $10,000, using the percentages in Figure 11–3. The computation is illustrated in Example 16.

Investment income is gross income from interest, dividends, annuities, and royalties not derived in the ordinary course of a trade or business. It also includes net gain attributable to the disposition of property producing the types of income just enumerated or held for investment. Income from a passive activity and income from a real estate activity in which the taxpayer actively participates are not included in investment income.

Net investment income is the excess of investment income over investment expenses. Investment expenses are those deductible expenses directly connected with the production of investment income. Investment expenses do not include interest expense. Some investment expenses may fall into the category of other miscellaneous deductions and be subject to the 2 percent floor (discussed later in the chapter).

EXAMPLE 15   T has AGI of $80,000, which includes dividends and interest income of $18,000. Besides investment interest expense, she had the following in-

FIGURE 11–3   Personal Interest Phase-out Percentages

Taxable Year Beginning in	Percentage Disallowed	Percentage Allowed
1987	35%	65%
1988	60%	40%
1989	80%	20%
1990	90%	10%
1991 and after	100%	–0–

25. $5,000 for a married individual filing a separate return; zero for a trust.   26. § 163(d).

vestment expenses in connection with her portfolio of stocks and bonds and had other pertinent itemized deductions as follows:

Safe deposit box rental (to hold investment securities)	$ 120
Investment counsel fee	1,200
City ad valorem property tax on stocks and bonds	3,000
Unreimbursed business travel	850
Uniforms	600

Before T can determine her investment expenses for purposes of calculating net investment income, those miscellaneous expenses that are not investment expenses are disallowed before any investment expenses are disallowed, under the 2% of AGI floor:

Total disallowed (2% of AGI)	$1,600
Less: Unreimbursed business travel	(850)
Uniforms	(600)
Balance of disallowance represents disallowed investment expense	$ 150

T's investment expenses are calculated as follows:

Miscellaneous deductions investment expense ($120 + $1,200)	$1,320
Less: Disallowed portion (see above)	150
Deductible miscellaneous deductions investment expense	$1,170
Plus: Ad valorem tax on investment property	3,000
Total investment expenses	$4,170

T's net investment income is $13,830 ($18,000 investment income − $4,170 investment expenses). □

After net investment income is determined, deductible investment interest expense can be calculated. Investment interest expense does not include qualified residence interest (see below) or interest taken into account in computing income or loss from a passive activity (see chapter 7). Also, it does not include interest that is otherwise nondeductible (e.g., interest on amounts borrowed to purchase or carry tax-exempt securities).

EXAMPLE 16

For 1989, T is a single person employed by a law firm. His investment activities for the year are as follows:

Net investment income	$30,000
Investment interest expense	44,000

T's investment interest deduction for 1989 is $32,000 as determined below:

Investment interest expense to the extent of net investment income	$30,000
Allowable excess as per Figure 11–3 (20% × $10,000)	2,000
Total interest allowed	$32,000

The amount of investment interest disallowed is carried over to future years. In Example 16, therefore, the amount that is carried over to 1990 is $12,000 ($44,000 investment interest expense—$32,000 allowed). No limit is placed on the carryover period.

The investment interest expense deduction is determined by completing Form 4952.

Qualified Residence Interest.   As previously stated, personal interest does not include qualified residence interest (interest on a home mortgage). Qualified residence interest is interest paid or accrued during the taxable year on indebtedness (subject to limitations) *secured* by any property that is a qualified residence of the taxpayer.

A qualified residence means the taxpayer's principal residence and one other residence of the taxpayer or spouse. The principal residence is one that meets the requirement for nonrecognition of gain upon sale under § 1034 (see chapter 15). The "one other residence," or second residence, refers to one that is used as a residence if not rented or, if rented, meets the requirements for personal residence under the rental of vacation home rules (refer to chapter 6). A taxpayer who has more than one second residence can make the selection each year as to which one is the qualified second residence. A residence includes, in addition to a house in the ordinary sense, cooperative apartments, condominiums, and mobile homes and boats that have living quarters (sleeping accommodations and toilet and cooking facilities).

Although in most cases, interest paid on a home mortgage would be fully deductible, there are limitations.[27] If the indebtedness is acquisition indebtedness, interest paid or accrued during the tax year on aggregate indebtedness of $1,000,000 ($500,000 for married persons filing separate returns) or less is qualified residence interest. *Acquisition indebtedness* refers to amounts in-

---

27. § 163(h)(3).

curred in acquiring, constructing, or substantially improving a qualified residence of the taxpayer. In addition, interest on aggregate home equity indebtedness that does not exceed $100,000 ($50,000 for married persons filing separate returns) is qualified residence interest. Home equity indebtedness is such debt, other than acquisition indebtedness, that does not exceed the fair market value of the qualified residence reduced by the amount of acquisition indebtedness. The use of the proceeds from this home equity indebtedness is of no consequence; the interest is qualified residence interest even if the proceeds are used for personal purposes.

Any indebtedness incurred on or before October 13, 1987, and secured by a qualified residence at all times thereafter before interest is paid or accrued is treated as acquisition indebtedness and is not subject to the $1,000,000 limitation.

Any interest paid on a mortgage secured by a third or more residences or paid on indebtedness that exceeds the allowable amounts is deductible according to the use of the proceeds. If the proceeds are used for personal purposes, the interest is nondeductible, subject to the disallowance phase-in rules; if used for business, the interest is fully deductible. Interest on such proceeds used for investment purposes or in passive activities is subject to the limitations applicable to those activities.

Interest Paid for Services.   It is common practice in the mortgage loan business to charge a fee for finding, placing, or processing a mortgage loan. Such fees are often called points and are expressed as a percentage of the loan amount. In periods of tight money, it may be necessary to pay points to obtain the necessary financing. To qualify as deductible interest, the points must be considered compensation to a lender solely for the use or forbearance of money. The points cannot be a form of service charge or payment for specific services if they are to qualify as deductible interest.[28] Points are required to be capitalized and are amortized and deductible ratably over the life of the loan. A special exception permits the purchaser of a personal residence to deduct qualifying points in the year of payment.[29] The exception also covers points paid to obtain funds for home improvements. However, points paid to refinance an existing home mortgage cannot be immediately expensed but must be capitalized and amortized as interest expense over the life of the new loan.[30]

Points paid by the seller are not deductible, because the debt on which they are paid is not the debt of the seller. Points paid by the seller are treated as a reduction of the selling price of the property.

Prepayment Penalty.   When a mortgage or loan is paid off in full in a lump sum before its term (early), the lending institution may require an additional payment of a certain percentage applied to the unpaid amount at the time of prepayment. This is known as a prepayment penalty and is considered to be interest (e.g., personal, qualified residence, investment) in the year it is paid.

Related Parties.   Nothing prevents the deduction of interest paid to a related party as long as the payment actually took place and the interest meets the requirements for deductibility as previously stated. Recall from chapter 6 that

---

28. Rev.Rul. 67–297, 1967–2 C.B. 87.

29. § 461(g)(2).

30. Rev.Rul. 87–22, 1987–1 C.B. 146.

a special rule for related taxpayers applies when the debtor uses the accrual basis and the related creditor is on the cash basis. If this rule is applicable, interest that has been accrued but not paid at the end of the debtor's tax year is not deductible until payment is made and the income is reportable by the cash basis recipient.

Tax-Exempt Securities. Section 265 provides that no deduction is allowed for interest on debt incurred to purchase or carry tax-exempt securities. A major problem has been for the courts to determine what is meant by the words "to purchase or carry." Refer to chapter 6 for a detailed discussion of these issues.

Restrictions on Deductibility and Timing Considerations

Taxpayer's Obligation. Allowed interest is deductible if the related debt represents a bona fide obligation for which the taxpayer is liable.[31] Thus, a taxpayer may not deduct interest paid on behalf of another individual. For interest to be deductible, both debtor and creditor must intend that the loan be repaid. Intent of the parties can be especially crucial between related parties such as a shareholder and a closely held corporation. A shareholder may not deduct interest paid by the corporation on his or her behalf.[32] Likewise, a husband may not deduct interest paid on his wife's property if he files a separate return, except in the case of qualified residence interest. If both husband and wife consent in writing, either the husband or the wife may deduct the allowed interest on the principal residence and one other residence.

Time of Deduction. Generally, interest must be paid to secure a deduction unless the taxpayer uses the accrual method of accounting. Under the accrual method, interest is deductible ratably over the life of the loan.

EXAMPLE 17

In November 1989, T borrows $1,000 to purchase appliances for a rental house. The loan is payable in 90 days at 12% interest. On the due date in February 1990, T pays the $1,000 note and interest amounting to $30. T can deduct the accrued portion ($2/3 \times \$30 = \$20$) of the interest in 1989 only if he is an accrual basis taxpayer. Otherwise, the entire amount of interest ($30) is deductible in 1990. □

Prepaid Interest. Accrual method reporting is imposed on cash basis taxpayers relative to interest prepayments that extend beyond the end of the taxable year.[33] Such payments must be allocated to the tax years to which the interest payments relate. These provisions were intended to prevent cash basis taxpayers from "manufacturing" tax deductions before the end of the year by entering into prepayment of interest agreements.

---

31. *Arcade Realty Co.*, 35 T.C. 256 (1960).

32. *Continental Trust Co.*, 7 B.T.A. 539 (1927).

33. § 461(g)(1).

Classification of Interest Expense

Whether interest is deductible *for* adjusted gross income or as an itemized deduction depends on whether the indebtedness has a business, investment, or personal purpose. If the indebtedness is incurred in relation to a business (other than performing services as an employee) or for the production of rent or royalty income, the interest is deductible *for* adjusted gross income. However, if the indebtedness is incurred for personal use, such as consumer interest or qualified residence interest, any deduction allowed is reported on Schedule A of Form 1040 if the taxpayer elects to itemize. If the taxpayer is an employee who incurs debt in relation to his or her employment, the interest is considered to be personal, or consumer, interest. Business expenses appear on Schedule C of Form 1040, and expenses related to rents or royalties are reported on Schedule E.

For classification purposes, the IRS has issued complex tracing rules[34] to establish the use to which borrowed funds are put.

Interest on amounts borrowed in excess of $50,000 in total on life insurance policies purchased after June 20, 1986, covering the life of a self-employed taxpayer or an officer or employee of a corporation is nondeductible even though the borrowed funds are used in a trade or business.

CHARITABLE CONTRIBUTIONS

Section 170 permits the deduction of contributions made to qualified domestic organizations by individuals and corporations. Contributions to qualified charitable organizations serve certain social welfare needs and therefore relieve the government of the cost of providing these needed services to the community.

The charitable contribution provisions are among the most complex in the tax law. To determine the amount deductible as a charitable contribution, several important questions must be answered:

- What constitutes a charitable contribution?

- Was the contribution made to a qualified organization?

- When is the contribution deductible?

- What special rules apply to contributions of property that has increased in value?

- What percentage limitations apply to the charitable contribution deduction?

- What recordkeeping and reporting requirements apply to charitable contributions?

These questions are addressed in the sections that follow.

---

34. T.D. 8145, 1987–2 C.B. 47, which contains Reg.
    § 1.163–8T.

Criteria for a Gift

Section 170(c) defines "charitable contribution" as a gift made to a qualified organization. The major elements needed to qualify a contribution as a gift are a donative intent, the absence of consideration, and acceptance by the donee. Consequently, the taxpayer has the burden of establishing that the transfer was made from motives of "disinterested generosity" as established by the courts.[35] As one can imagine, this test is quite subjective and has led to problems of interpretation.

To the extent a tangible benefit is derived from a contribution, the value of such benefit cannot be deducted.

EXAMPLE 18	R purchases a ticket at $100 for a special performance of the local symphony (a qualified charity). If the price of a ticket to a symphony concert is normally $15, R is allowed only $85 as a charitable contribution. ☐

An exception to this benefit provides for the deduction of an automatic percentage of the amount paid for the right to purchase athletic tickets from colleges and universities.[36] Under this exception, 80 percent of the amount paid to or for the benefit of the institution qualifies as a charitable contribution deduction.

EXAMPLE 19	T donates $500 to State University's athletic department. The amount guarantees that T will have preferred seating on the 50-yard line. Subsequently, T buys four $35 game tickets. Under the exception to the benefit rule, however, T is allowed a $400 (80% of $500) charitable contribution deduction for the taxable year. If, however, T's $500 donation includes four $35 tickets, that portion [$140 ($35 × 4)] and the remaining portion of $360 ($500 − $140) are treated as sepqrate amounts. Thus, T is allowed a charitable contribution deduction of $288 (80% of $360). ☐

The following items may not be deducted as charitable contributions:

- Dues, fees, or bills paid to country clubs, lodges, fraternal orders, or similar groups.
- Cost of raffle, bingo, or lottery tickets.
- Cost of tuition.
- Value of time or services.
- Value of blood given to a blood bank.
- Donations to homeowners associations.
- Gifts to individuals.
- Rental value of property used by a qualified charity.

---

35. *Comm. v. Duberstein*, 60–2 USTC ¶ 9515, 5 AFTR2d 1626, 80 S.Ct. 1190 (USSC, 1960).

36. § 170(m).

Qualified Organizations

To be deductible, a contribution must be made to one of the following organizations: [37]

- A state or possession of the United States or any subdivisions thereof.

- A corporation, trust, or community chest, fund, or foundation that is situated in the United States and is organized and operated exclusively for religious, charitable, scientific, literary, or educational purposes or for the prevention of cruelty to children or animals.

- A veterans' organization.

- A fraternal organization operating under the lodge system.

- A cemetery company.

The IRS publishes a list of organizations that have applied for and received tax-exempt status under § 501 of the Code.[38] This publication is updated frequently and may be helpful to determine if a gift has been made to a qualifying charitable organization.

Because gifts made to needy individuals are not deductible, a deduction will not be permitted if a gift is received by a donee in an individual capacity rather than as a representative of a qualifying organization.

Time of Payment

A charitable contribution generally is deducted in the year the payment is made. This rule applies to both cash and accrual basis individuals. An accrual basis corporation, however, is permitted a deduction if the board of directors authorizes such payment during the taxable year and the contribution is made within two and one-half months after the close of the taxable year.

A contribution is ordinarily deemed to have been made on the delivery of the property to the donee. For example, if a gift of securities (properly endorsed) is made to a qualified charitable organization, the gift is considered complete on the day of delivery or mailing. However, if the donor delivers the certificate to his or her bank or broker or to the issuing corporation, the gift is considered complete on the date the stock is transferred on the books of the corporation.

A contribution made by check is considered delivered on the date of mailing. Thus, a check mailed on December 31, 1989, is deductible on the taxpayer's 1989 tax return. If the contribution is charged on a bank credit card, the date the charge is made determines the year of deduction. For a pay-by-phone account, the date shown on the statement issued by the financial institution is the date of payment.

---

37. § 170(c).
38. Although this *Cumulative List of Organizations,* IRS Publication 78 (available by purchase from the Superintendent of Documents, U.S. Government Printing Office, Washington, DC 20402), may be helpful, it is not required that a qualified organization be listed. Not all organizations that qualify are listed in this publication (e.g., American Red Cross, University of Cleveland).

Recordkeeping and Valuation Requirements

Recordkeeping Requirements. Cash contributions must be substantiated by one of the following: [39]

- A cancelled check.

- A receipt, letter, or other written communication from the charitable organization (showing the name of the organization, the date, and the amount of the contribution).

- Other reliable written records (contemporaneous records or other evidence, such as buttons and tokens, given to contributors by the donee organization).

If a cash contribution of $3,000 or more is given to any one organization, the name of the organization and the amount of the contribution must be reported on the taxpayer's return.

The records required for noncash contributions vary depending on the amount of the contribution. If the value of the contribution is $500 or less, it must be evidenced by a receipt from the charitable organization. The receipt must show the following:

- The name of the charitable organization.

- The date and location of the charitable contribution.

- A reasonably detailed description of the contributed property.

Generally, charitable organizations do not attest to the fair market value of the donated property. Nevertheless, the taxpayer must maintain reliable written evidence of the following information concerning the donation:

- The fair market value of the property and how that value was determined.

- The amount of the reduction in the value of the property (if required) for certain appreciated property and how that reduction was determined.

- Terms of any agreement with the charitable organization dealing with the use of the property and potential sale or other disposition of the property by the organization.

- A signed copy of the appraisal if the value of the property was determined by appraisal. Only for a contribution of art with an aggregate value of $20,000 or more must the appraisal be attached to the taxpayer's return.

Additional information is required if the value of the donated property is over $500 but not over $5,000. Also, the taxpayer must file Section A of Form 8283 (Noncash Charitable Contributions) for such contributions.

For noncash contributions with a claimed value in excess of $5,000 ($10,000 in the case of nonpublicly traded stock), the taxpayer must file Section B of Form 8283. This schedule must show a summary of the appraisal

39. *Your Federal Income Tax,* IRS Publication 17 (Rev. Nov. 88), p. 139.

and must be attached to the taxpayer's return. Failure to comply with these reporting rules may result in disallowance of the charitable contribution deduction. Additionally, significant overvaluation exposes the taxpayer to rather stringent penalties.

Valuation Requirements.   Property donated to a charity is generally valued at fair market value at the time the gift is made. The Code and Regulations give very little guidance on the measurement of the fair market value except to say, "The fair market value is the price at which the property would change hands between a willing buyer and a willing seller, neither being under any compulsion to buy or sell and both having reasonable knowledge of relevant facts."

Limitations on Charitable Contribution Deductions

In General.   Charitable contributions made by individuals are subject to specified percentage of adjusted gross income limitations: 50 percent, 30 percent, or 20 percent. The percentage depends on the type of property contributed and the type of charity to which the contribution is made. To understand the complex rules for computing the amount of a charitable contribution, it is necessary to understand the distinction between capital gain property and ordinary income property. In addition, it is necessary to understand when the 50 percent, 30 percent, and 20 percent limitations apply. If a taxpayer's contributions for the year exceed the applicable percentage limitations, the excess contributions may be carried forward and deducted during a five-year carryover period. These topics are discussed in the sections that follow.

Corporations are subject to an overall limitation of 10 percent of taxable income computed without regard to the contributions made and certain other adjustments. The rules applicable to contributions by corporations are discussed in detail in chapter 20.

Ordinary Income Property.   Ordinary income property is any property that, if sold, will result in the recognition of ordinary income. The term includes inventory for sale in the taxpayer's trade or business, a work of art created by the donor, and a manuscript prepared by the donor. It also includes a capital asset held by the donor for less than the required holding period for long-term capital gain treatment. Property that results in the recognition of ordinary income due to the recapture of depreciation is ordinary income property. If ordinary income property is contributed, the deduction is equal to the fair market value of the property less the amount of ordinary income that would have been reported if the property were sold. In most instances, the deduction is limited to the cost basis of the property to the donor.

EXAMPLE 20   T owned stock in EC Corporation that he donated to a local university on May 1, 1989. T had purchased the stock for $2,500 on March 3, 1989, and the stock had a value of $3,600 when he made the donation. Since the property had not been held for a sufficient period to meet the long-term capital gain requirements, a short-term capital gain of $1,100 would have been recognized had the property been sold. Since short-term capital gain property is treated as ordinary income property, T's charitable contribution deduction is limited to the property's cost of $2,500. □

Capital Gain Property. Capital gain property is any property that would have resulted in the recognition of long-term capital gain or § 1231 gain if the property had been sold by the donor. As a general rule, the deduction for a contribution of capital gain property is equal to the fair market value of the property.

Two major exceptions preclude the deductibility of the appreciation on long-term capital gain property. One exception concerns private foundations. Private foundations are organizations that traditionally do not receive their funding from the general public (e.g., the Ford Foundation). Generally, foundations fall into two categories: operating and nonoperating. A private *operating* foundation is one that spends substantially all of its income in the active conduct of the charitable undertaking for which it was established.[40] Other private foundations are *nonoperating* foundations. However, if a nonoperating private foundation distributes the contributions it receives according to special rules within two and one-half months following the year of the contribution, the organization is treated the same as public charities and private operating foundations. Often, only the private foundation knows its status (operating or nonoperating) for sure, and such status can change from year to year.

If capital gain property is contributed to a private nonoperating foundation, the taxpayer must reduce the contribution by the long-term capital gain that would have been recognized if the property had been sold at its fair market value. The effect of this provision is to limit the deduction to the property's basis.

EXAMPLE 21	T purchases stock for $800 on January 1, 1975, and donates it to a private nonoperating foundation on June 21, 1989, when it is worth $2,000. T's charitable contribution is $800, the stock's basis. □

Example 22	Assume the same facts as in Example 21, except that the donation is to a private operating foundation. Now, T's charitable contribution is $2,000. □

A second exception applying to capital gain property relates to tangible personalty.[41] If tangible personalty is contributed to a public charity such as a museum, church, or university, the charitable deduction is reduced by the long-term capital gain if the property is put to an unrelated use. A taxpayer in this instance must establish that the property is not in fact being put to an unrelated use by the donee. The taxpayer must also establish that at the time of the contribution it was reasonable to anticipate that the property would not be put to an unrelated use. For a contribution of personalty to a museum, if the work of art is the kind of art normally retained by the museum, it will be

---

40. § 4942.

41. Tangible personalty is all property that is not realty (land and buildings) and does not include intangible property such as stock or securities.

reasonable for a donor to anticipate that the work of art will not be put to an unrelated use. This will be the case even if the object is later sold or exchanged by the museum.[42]

EXAMPLE 23

T contributes a Picasso painting, for which he paid $20,000, to a local museum. It had a value of $30,000 at the time of the donation. The painting was displayed by the museum for a period of two years and subsequently sold for $50,000. The charitable contribution is not reduced by the unrealized appreciation, since the painting was put to a related use even though it was later sold by the museum. □

As noted in chapter 12, for purposes of the alternative minimum tax, the net untaxed appreciation on charitable contributions is a tax preference item.

Contribution of Services.   No deduction is allowed for a contribution of one's services to a qualified charitable organization. However, unreimbursed expenses related to the services rendered may be deductible. For example, the cost of a uniform (without general utility) that is required to be worn while performing services may be deductible, as are certain out-of-pocket transportation costs [43] incurred for the benefit of the charity. Deductions are permitted for transportation, reasonable expenses for lodging, and 80 percent of the cost of meals while away from home incurred in performance of the donated services. Also there must be no significant element of personal pleasure, recreation, or vacation in such travel.[44]

EXAMPLE 24

M, a delegate representing her church in Miami, Florida, travels to a two-day national meeting in Denver, Colorado, in February. After the meeting, M spends two weeks at a nearby ski resort. Under these circumstances, none of the transportation, meals, or lodging would be deductible, since there is a significant element of personal pleasure, recreation, or vacation. □

Fifty Percent Ceiling.   Contributions made to public charities may not exceed 50 percent of an individual's adjusted gross income for the year. Excess contributions may be carried over to the next five years. The 50 percent ceiling on contributions applies to the following types of public charities:

- A church or a convention or association of churches.

- An educational organization that maintains a regular faculty and curriculum.

- A hospital or medical school.

- An organization supported by the government that holds property or investments for the benefit of a college or university.

---

42. Reg. § 1.170A–4(b)(3)(ii)(b).

43. In lieu of these out-of-pocket costs for an automobile, § 170(j) specifies a standard mileage rate of 12 cents per mile.

44. § 170(k).

- A governmental unit that is Federal, state, or local.

- An organization normally receiving a substantial part of its support from the public or a governmental unit.

The 50 percent ceiling also applies to contributions to the following organizations:

- All private operating foundations.

- Certain private nonoperating foundations that distribute the contributions they receive to public charities and private operating foundations within two and one-half months following the year they receive the contribution.

- Certain private nonoperating foundations in which the contributions are pooled in a common fund and the income and principal sum are paid to public charities.

Thirty Percent Ceiling. A 30 percent ceiling applies to contributions of cash and ordinary income property to private nonoperating foundations. The 30 percent ceiling also applies to contributions of appreciated capital gain property to 50 percent organizations unless the taxpayer elects to reduce the contribution by the appreciation in order to raise the ceiling to 50 percent. This is referred to as the reduced deduction election. This election generally would be made only when there is little appreciation in the property or when there will be no benefit from a carryover. This latter situation could occur regarding the final income tax return of a deceased taxpayer.

Contributions in excess of the 30 percent ceiling may be carried forward for five years and are subject to the 30 percent ceiling in the carryover year. If the election is made to reduce the contribution by the appreciation in order to raise the ceiling to 50 percent, there is no carryforward of any amount that is nondeductible in the current year.

Twenty Percent Ceiling. A 20 percent ceiling applies to contributions of appreciated long-term capital gain property to certain private nonoperating foundations. Contributions in excess of the 20 percent ceiling may be carried forward for five years.

MISCELLANEOUS ITEMIZED DEDUCTIONS

According to § 262, no deduction is allowed for personal, living, or family expenses. However, there are a number of expenditures that one may incur that are related to employment. If an employee or outside salesperson incurs unreimbursed business expenses, including travel and transportation, the expenses are deductible as miscellaneous deductions.[45] Beyond unreimbursed employee expenses and those of an outside salesperson, certain other expenses fall into the special category of miscellaneous itemized deductions. They are deductible only if, in total, they exceed 2 percent of the taxpayer's adjusted gross income. Miscellaneous itemized deductions include (but are not limited to) the following:

---

45. Actors and performing artists who meet certain requirements are not subject to this rule.

- Professional dues to membership organizations.

- Uniforms or other clothing that cannot be used for normal wear.

- Fees incurred for the preparation of one's tax return or fees incurred for tax litigation before the IRS or the courts.

- Job-hunting costs.

- Fee paid for a safe deposit box used to store papers and documents relating to taxable income-producing investments.

- Investment expenses that are deductible under § 212 as discussed in chapter 6.

- Appraisal fees to determine the amount of a casualty loss or the fair market value of donated property.

- Hobby losses up to the amount of hobby income, see chapter 6.

Employee business expenses that are reimbursed are not itemized but are deducted *for* adjusted gross income. Employee business expenses are discussed in depth in chapter 10.

OTHER ITEMIZED DEDUCTIONS

Certain expenses and losses do not fall into any category of itemized deductions already discussed (medical, taxes, interest, charitable, and miscellaneous) but are nonetheless deductible.

- Moving expenses that meet the requirements for deductibility, discussed in chapter 10.

- Casualty and theft losses, discussed in chapter 9.

- Gambling losses up to the amount of gambling winnings.

- Impairment-related work expenses of a handicapped person.

- The unrecovered investment in an annuity contract when the annuity ceases by reason of death, discussed in chapter 8.

The amount of each expense that is allowable as a deduction may be limited by the rules within a particular category (casualty and theft losses, moving expenses, gambling losses).

Although these other itemized deductions are not miscellaneous itemized deductions by Code definition,[46] the IRS has chosen to make no such distinction. Except for moving expenses and casualty and theft losses, which are separate line items on Schedule A (Form 1040), these other itemized deductions are categorized as "Miscellaneous deductions not subject to 2% AGI limit."

Comprehensive Example of Schedule A.   Harry and Jean Brown, married filing jointly, had the following transactions for the current year:

---

46. § 67(b).

- Medicines that required a prescription $ 430
- Doctor and dentist bills paid and not reimbursed   2,120
- Medical insurance premium payments   1,200
- Contact lenses   175
- Transportation for medical purposes (425 miles × 9 cents/mile + $4.75 parking)   43
- State income tax withheld   620
- Real estate taxes   1,580
- Interest paid on qualified residence mortgage   2,840
- Finance charges paid on credit cards   34
- Interest on loan to purchase personal auto   265
- Charitable contributions in cash   860
- Transportation in performing charitable services (860 miles × 12 cents/mile + $15.80 parking and tolls)   119
- Unreimbursed employee expenses (from a Form 2106)   870
- Tax return preparation   150
- Professional expenses (dues and publications)   135
- Safe deposit box (used for keeping investment documents and tax records)   35

The Browns' adjusted gross income is $40,000. The completed Schedule A for 1988 reports itemized deductions totaling $7,497.

TAX PLANNING CONSIDERATIONS

Effective Utilization of Itemized Deductions

Since an individual may use the standard deduction in one year and itemize deductions in another year, it is frequently possible to obtain maximum benefit by shifting itemized deductions from one year to another. For example, if a taxpayer's itemized deductions and the standard deduction are approximately the same for each year of a two-year period, the taxpayer should use the standard deduction in one year and shift itemized deductions (to the extent permitted by law) to the other year. The individual could, for example, prepay a church pledge for a particular year or avoid paying end-of-the-year medical expenses to shift the deduction to the following year.

Utilization of Medical Deductions

When a taxpayer anticipates that his or her medical expenses will approximate the percentage floor, much might be done to generate a deductible excess. Any of the following procedures can help build a deduction by the end of the year:

SCHEDULES A&B (Form 1040)
Department of the Treasury
Internal Revenue Service

Schedule A—Itemized Deductions
(Schedule B is on back)
► Attach to Form 1040. ► See Instructions for Schedules A and B (Form 1040).

OMB No. 1545-0074
1988
Attachment Sequence No. 07

Name(s) as shown on Form 1040: Harry and Jean Brown
Your social security number: 371 : 30 : 3987

Medical and Dental Expenses (Do not include expenses reimbursed or paid by others.) (See Instructions on page 23.)

- 1a Prescription medicines and drugs, insulin, doctors, dentists, nurses, hospitals, medical insurance premiums you paid, etc. — **1a** 3,750
- b Other (list—include hearing aids, dentures, eyeglasses, transportation and lodging, etc.) ► Contacts 175 Transportation and Lodging 43 — **1b** 218
- 2 Add lines 1a and 1b, and enter the total here — **2** 3,968
- 3 Multiply the amount on Form 1040, line 32, by 7.5% (.075) — **3** 3,000
- 4 Subtract line 3 from line 2. If zero or less, enter -0-. **Total medical and dental** ► **4** 968

Taxes You Paid (See Instructions on page 23.)

- 5 State and local income taxes — **5** 620
- 6 Real estate taxes — **6** 1,580
- 7 Other taxes (list—include personal property taxes) ► — **7**
- 8 Add the amounts on lines 5 through 7. Enter the total here. **Total taxes** ► **8** 2,200

Interest You Paid (See Instructions on page 24.)

Note: New rules apply to the home mortgage interest deduction. See Instructions.

- 9a Deductible home mortgage interest you paid to financial institutions (report deductible points on line 10) — **9a** 2,840
- b Deductible home mortgage interest you paid to individuals (show that person's name and address) ► — **9b**
- 10 Deductible points. (See Instructions for special rules.) — **10**
- 11 Deductible investment interest (see page 24) — **11**
- 12a Personal interest you paid (see page 24) . **12a** 299
- b Multiply the amount on line 12a by 40% (.40). Enter the result . **12b** 120
- 13 Add the amounts on lines 9a through 11, and 12b. Enter the total here. **Total interest** ► **13** 2,960

Gifts to Charity (See Instructions on page 25.)

- 14 Contributions by cash or check. (If you gave $3,000 or more to any one organization, show to whom you gave and how much you gave.) ► — **14** 979
- 15 Other than cash or check. (You must attach Form 8283 if over $500.) — **15**
- 16 Carryover from prior year — **16**
- 17 Add the amounts on lines 14 through 16. Enter the total here. **Total contributions** ► **17** 979

Casualty and Theft Losses

- 18 Casualty or theft loss(es) (attach Form 4684). (See page 25 of the Instructions.) ► **18**

Moving Expenses

- 19 Moving expenses (attach Form 3903 or 3903F). (See page 26 of the Instructions.) ► **19**

Job Expenses and Most Other Miscellaneous Deductions (See page 26 for expenses to deduct here.)

- 20 Unreimbursed employee expenses—job travel, union dues, job education, etc. (You MUST attach Form 2106 in some cases. See Instructions.) ► — **20** 870
- 21 Other expenses (investment, tax preparation, safe deposit box, etc.). List type and amount ► Tax Prep. 150 Prof. Dues 135 Safety Dep. Box 35 — **21** 320
- 22 Add the amounts on lines 20 and 21. Enter the total. — **22** 1,190
- 23 Multiply the amount on Form 1040, line 32, by 2% (.02). Enter the result here — **23** 800
- 24 Subtract line 23 from line 22. Enter the result (if zero or less, enter zero) ► **24** 390

Other Miscellaneous Deductions

- 25 Other (from list on page 26 of Instructions). Enter type and amount ► **25**

Total Itemized Deductions

- 26 Add the amounts on lines 4, 8, 13, 17, 18, 19, 24, and 25. Enter the total here. Then enter on Form 1040, line 34, the LARGER of this total or your standard deduction from page 17 of the Instructions. ► **26** 7,497

For Paperwork Reduction Act Notice, see Form 1040 Instructions.   Schedule A (Form 1040) 1988

- Incur the obligation for or have carried out needed dental work.[47] Orthodontic treatment, for example, may have been recommended for a member of the taxpayer's family.

- Have elective remedial surgery that may have been postponed from prior years (e.g., tonsillectomies, vasectomies, correction of hernias, hysterectomies).

47. Prepayment of medical expenses does not generate a deduction unless the taxpayer is under an obligation to make such payment.

- Incur the obligation for capital improvements to taxpayer's personal residence recommended by a physician (e.g., an air filtration system to alleviate a respiratory disorder).

As an aid to taxpayers who might experience temporary cash-flow problems at the end of the year, the use of bank credit cards is deemed to be payment for purposes of timing the deductibility of charitable and medical expenses.

EXAMPLE 25

On December 12, 1989, T (a calendar year taxpayer) purchases two pairs of prescription contact lenses and one pair of prescribed orthopedic shoes for a total of $305. These purchases are separately charged to T's credit card. On January 6, 1990, T receives his statement containing these charges and makes payment shortly thereafter. The purchases are deductible as medical expenses in the year charged (1989) and not in the year the account is settled (1990). □

Recognizing which expenditures qualify for the medical deduction also may be crucial to exceeding the percentage limitations.

EXAMPLE 26

T employs E (an unrelated party) to care for her incapacitated and dependent mother. E is not a trained nurse but spends approximately one-half of the time performing nursing duties (e.g., administering injections and providing physical therapy) and the rest of the time doing household chores. An allocable portion of E's wages that T pays (including the employer's portion of FICA taxes) qualifies as a medical expense. □

To assure a deduction for the entire cost of nursing home care for an aged dependent, it is helpful if the transfer of the individual to the home is for medical reasons and recommended by a doctor. In addition, the nursing home facilities should be adequate to provide the necessary medical and nursing care. To assure a deduction for all of the nursing care expenses, it is necessary to show that the individual was placed in the home for required medical care rather than for personal or family considerations.

Proper documentation is required to substantiate medical expenses. The taxpayer should keep all receipts for credit card or other charge purchases of medical services and deductible drugs as well as all cash register receipts. In addition medical transportation mileage should be recorded.

If a taxpayer or a dependent of the taxpayer must be institutionalized in order to receive adequate medical care, it may be good tax planning to make a lump-sum payment that would cover medical treatment for future periods. It is advised that a contract be negotiated with the institution so that the expense is fixed and the payment is not a mere deposit.

Protecting the Interest Deduction

Although the deductibility of prepaid interest by a cash basis taxpayer has been severely restricted, a notable exception allows a deduction for points paid to obtain financing for the purchase or improvement of a principal residence in the year of payment. However, such points must actually be paid by the taxpayer obtaining the loan and must represent a charge for the use of money. It has been held that points paid from the mortgage proceeds do not satisfy the payment requirement.[48] Also, the portion of the points attributable to service charges does not represent deductible interest.[49] For taxpayers financing home purchases or improvements, planning usually should be directed toward avoiding these two hurdles to immediate deductibility.

In rare instances, a taxpayer may find it desirable to forgo the immediate expensing of points in the year paid. Instead, it could prove beneficial to capitalize such points and write them off as interest expense over the life of the mortgage.

EXAMPLE 27

X purchases a home on December 15, 1989, for $95,000 with $30,000 cash and a 15-year mortgage of $65,000 financed by the Greater Metropolis National Bank. X pays two points in addition to interest allocated to the period from December 15 until December 31, 1989, at an annual rate of 10%. Since X does not have enough itemized deductions to exceed the standard deduction for 1989, she should elect to capitalize the interest expense by amortizing the points over 15 years. In this instance, X would deduct $86.67 for 1990, as part of her qualified residence interest expense [$1,300 (two points) divided by 15 years], if she elects to itemize that year.

□

Because the deductibility of personal (consumer) interest will disappear after 1990 (see Figure 11–3 earlier in the chapter), taxpayers should consider making use of home equity indebtedness. Called *home equity loans,* these loans utilize the personal residence of the taxpayer as security. Since the tracing rules do not apply to home equity indebtedness, the funds from these loans can be used for personal purposes (e.g., auto loans, education). By making use of home equity loans, therefore, what would have been nondeductible consumer interest becomes deductible qualified residence interest.

However, home equity loans are limited to the lesser of:

- The fair market value of the residence, reduced by acquisition indebtedness, or

- $100,000 ($50,000 for married persons filing separate returns).

EXAMPLE 28

T owns a personal residence with a fair market value of $150,000 and an outstanding first mortgage of $100,000. T issues a lien on the residence and in return borrows $15,000 to purchase a new family automobile. All interest on the $115,000 debt is treated as qualified residence interest. □

---

48. *Alan A. Rubnitz,* 67 T.C. 621 (1977).   49. *Donald L. Wilkerson,* 70 T.C. 240 (1978).

Assuring the Charitable Contribution Deduction

For a charitable contribution deduction to be available, the recipient must be a qualified charitable organization. Sometimes the mechanics of how the contribution is carried out can determine whether or not a deduction results.

EXAMPLE 29

T wants to donate $5,000 to her church's mission in Seoul, Korea. In this regard, she considers three alternatives:

1. Send the money directly to the mission.

2. Give the money to her church with the understanding that it is to be passed on to the mission.

3. Give the money directly to the missionary in charge of the mission who is currently in the United States on a fund-raising trip.

If T wants to obtain a deduction for the contribution, she would be well advised to choose alternative 2. A direct donation to the mission (alternative 1) would not be deductible because the mission is a foreign charity. A direct gift to the missionary (alternative 3) does not comply, since an individual cannot be a qualified charity for income tax purposes.[50] □

When making donations of other than cash, the type of property chosen can have decided implications in measuring the amount, if any, of the deduction.

EXAMPLE 30

T wants to give $60,000 in value to her church in some form other than cash. In this connection, she considers four alternatives:

1. Stock held as an investment with a cost basis of $100,000 and a fair market value of $60,000.

2. Stock held for five years as an investment with a cost basis of $10,000 and a fair market value of $60,000.

3. The rent-free use for a year of a building that normally leases for $5,000 a month.

4. A valuable stamp collection held as an investment and owned for ten years with a cost basis of $10,000 and a fair market value of $60,000. The church plans to sell the collection if and when it is donated.

Alternative 1 is ill-advised as the subject of the gift. Even though T would obtain a deduction of $60,000, she would forgo the potential loss of $40,000 that would be recognized if the property were sold.[51] Alternative 2 makes good sense, since the deduction still is $60,000 and none of the $50,000 of appreciation that has occurred must be recognized as income.

---

50. *Thomas E. Lesslie,* 36 TCM 495, T.C.Memo. 1977–111.

51. *LaVar M. Withers,* 69 T.C. 900 (1978).

Alternative 3 yields no deduction at all and would not, therefore, appear to be a wise choice. Alternative 4 involves tangible personalty that the recipient does not plan to use. As a result, the amount of the deduction would be limited to $10,000, the stamp collection's basis.[52] ☐

For property transfers (particularly real estate), the ceiling limitations on the amount of the deduction allowed in any one year (50 percent, 30 percent, or 20 percent of adjusted gross income, as the case may be) could be a factor to take into account. With proper planning, donations can be controlled to stay within the limitations and therefore avoid the need for a carryover of unused charitable contributions.

EXAMPLE 31

T wants to donate a tract of unimproved land held as an investment to the University of Maryland (a qualified charitable organization). The land has been held for six years and has a current fair market value of $300,000 and a basis to T of $50,000. T's adjusted gross income for the current year is estimated to be $200,000, and he expects much the same for the next few years. In the current year he deeds (transfers) an undivided one-fifth interest in the real estate to the university. ☐

What has T in Example 31 accomplished for income tax purposes? In the current year, he will be allowed a charitable contribution deduction of $60,000 (⅕ × $300,000), which will be within the applicable limitation of adjusted gross income (30% × $200,000). Presuming no other charitable contributions for the year, T has avoided the possibility of a carryover. In future years, T can arrange donations of undivided interests in the real estate to stay within the bounds of the percentage limitations. The only difficulty with this approach is the necessity of having to revalue the real estate each year before the donation, since the amount of the deduction is based on the fair market value of the interest contributed at the time of the contribution.

It may be wise to avoid a carryover of unused charitable contributions, if possible, because that approach may be dangerous in several respects. First, the carryover period is limited to five years. Depending on the taxpayer's projected adjusted gross income rather than actual adjusted gross income, some of the amount carried over may expire without tax benefit after the five-year period has ended. Second, unused charitable contribution carryovers do not survive the death of the party making the donation and as a consequence are lost.

PROBLEM MATERIALS

Discussion Questions

1. X has a history of heart disease. Upon the advice of his doctor, he installs an elevator in his residence so he does not have to climb stairs.

---

52. No reduction of appreciation is necessary in alternative 2, since stock is intangible property and not tangible personalty. As noted in chapter 12, however, the untaxed appreciation is a tax preference item for purposes of the alternative minimum tax.

Is this a valid medical expense? If it is, how much of the expense is deductible?

2. T, a self-employed individual taxpayer, prepared his own income tax return for the past year and asked you to check it over for accuracy. Your review indicates that T failed to claim certain business entertainment expenses.

   a. Would the correction of this omission affect the amount of medical expenses T can deduct? Explain.

   b. Would it matter if T were employed rather than self-employed?

3. If T's medical expense deduction was $500 in 1989 and the amount reduced T's tax liability, how would a $300 insurance reimbursement be treated if received in 1990? Received in 1989? What if T had not itemized deductions in 1989 and received the $300 reimbursement in 1990?

4. Discuss what medical expenses of a dependent are deductible. What if there is a multiple support agreement (refer to chapter 3) regarding the medical expenses of a dependent?

5. T is employed as an accountant in New Orleans, Louisiana. One of T's friends, Dr. D, practices general dentistry in Hot Springs, Arkansas. Once a year during the deer hunting season, T travels to Hot Springs for his annual dental checkup. While there, T makes use of Dr. D's deer lodge for hunting purposes. Do any of T's travel expenses for the trip to Arkansas qualify for the medical expense deduction? Why or why not?

6. T's son is performing poorly in public school. Not only is he failing most subjects but he responds negatively to constructive criticism from his teachers. Upon the recommendation of a child psychiatrist, T enrolls his son in X Academy, a private school that has a better teacher-to-student ratio and more personalized instruction. Is the tuition T pays to X Academy deductible as a medical expense? Explain.

7. What is an ad valorem tax? Why should a distinction be made between an ad valorem tax (based on value) and a tax based on other factors such as weight, year, and model?

8. Why is it necessary to make an apportionment of real estate taxes between the buyer and the seller of a home in the year of sale? What effect does the apportionment have upon the adjusted basis of the property to the buyer if the seller pays the real estate taxes?

9. If a taxpayer overpays his or her state income tax due to excessive withholdings or estimated tax payments, how is the refund check treated when received in the subsequent year? Are the excess amounts paid deductible in the current year?

10. The city of Galveston, Texas, assessed beachfront property owners for the construction of jetties to protect shorelines from the destructive effects of the ocean. Is this assessment deductible?

11. How can home equity loans be used to avoid the nondeductibility of interest on amounts borrowed to finance the purchase of consumer goods?

12. As to the deductibility of "points," comment on the following:
    a. Those paid by the seller.
    b. Those paid to finance the purchase of a rental house.
    c. Those relating to the rendering of personal services.
    d. When capitalization and amortization might be advisable.
    e. Points paid from the mortgage proceeds.

13. Discuss the special problems that arise with respect to the deductibility of interest on a debt between related parties. How does § 267 of the Code relate to this problem?

14. If a taxpayer pays interest on behalf of another, is the payment deductible?

15. How and why does the tax treatment of interest expense differ when borrowed funds are used for business versus personal purposes?

16. Why has Congress imposed limitations on the deductibility of interest when funds are borrowed for the purpose of purchasing or continuing to hold investment property?

17. Why is it necessary for a charitable organization to receive qualified status under § 501 of the Code?

18. What is ordinary income property? If inventory with an adjusted cost basis of $60 and fair market value of $100 is contributed to a public charity, how much is deductible?

19. What is capital gain property? What tax treatment is required if capital gain property is contributed to a private nonoperating foundation? To a public charity? What difference does it make if the contribution is tangible personalty and it is put to a use unrelated to the donee's business?

20. An accountant normally charges $100 an hour when preparing financial statements for clients. If the accountant performs accounting services for a church without charge, can the value of the donated services be deducted on his or her tax return?

21. Discuss the recordkeeping and reporting requirements for contributions of property in excess of $500. For contributions of property with a claimed value in excess of $5,000.

22. Name some of the miscellaneous deductions that are reported on Schedule A. What happens to these deductions if the taxpayer does not itemize?

23. Which employee expenses are deductible as itemized deductions? Are there any limitations?

Problems

24. H and W are married and together have adjusted gross income of $24,000. They have no dependents, and they filed a joint return in

1989. Each pays $450 for hospitalization insurance. During the year, they paid the following amounts for medical care: $1,900 in doctor and dentist bills and hospital expenses and $310 for prescribed medicine and drugs. An insurance reimbursement for hospitalization was received in December 1989 for $700. Determine the deduction allowable for medical expenses paid in 1989.

25. X lives in Arkansas and discovers that he has a rare disease that can be treated only with surgery by a surgeon in France. X incurs $1,500 in air fare, $200 in meals taken at the medical facility, and $800 in lodging expenses for eight nights of lodging related to his medical care in France. What amount, if any, of these expenses is deductible?

26. H and W, who have a dependent child, C, were both under 65 years of age at the close of calendar year 1989 and filed a joint return for that year. During the year 1989, H's mother, M, attained the age of 65 and qualified as a dependent of H. The adjusted gross income in 1989 of H and W was $14,000. During the year, H and W paid the following amounts for medical care: $700 for doctors and hospital expenses and $145 for prescribed medicine and drugs for themselves, $375 for doctors and hospital expenses and $70 for prescribed medicine and drugs for C, and $500 for doctors and hospital expenses and $125 for prescribed medicine and drugs for M. No insurance reimbursements were received for these expenses. How much is allowed as a deduction for medical expenses for the taxable year 1989?

27. Upon the advice of his physician, T, a heart patient, installs an elevator in his personal residence at a cost of $8,000. The elevator has a cost recovery period of five years. A neighbor who is in the real estate business charges T $40 for an appraisal that places the value of the residence at $50,000 before the improvement and $55,000 after. The value increases because T lives in a region where many older people retire and therefore would find the elevator an attractive feature in a home. As a result of the operation of the elevator, T noticed an increase of $55 in his utility bills for the current year. Disregarding percentage limitations, which of the above expenditures qualify as a medical deduction?

28. J, who had adjusted gross income of $20,000, incurred the following medical expenses during 1989: $2,000 for doctor and hospital bills, $1,200 for medical insurance premiums, and $300 for drugs and medicines that require a prescription. He was reimbursed for $1,500 of the doctor and hospital bills by his insurance company. Also, J is physically handicapped and spent $2,500 constructing entrance and exit ramps to his personal residence. The value of the home was increased by $1,400 as a result of these expenditures. Compute J's medical expense deduction for 1989.

29. The city of Houston adopted a zoning ordinance that requires a minimum number of off-street parking spaces for each building. To finance the parking lots, the city levied an assessment of $1,000 against each commercial property in each district. These funds were used to construct off-street parking for the commercial property. Is the $1,000 assessment deductible?

30. T uses the cash method of accounting and lives in a state that imposes an income tax (including withholding from wages). On April 14, 1989, he files his state return for 1988, paying an additional $500 in income taxes. During 1989, his withholdings for state income tax purposes amount to $2,750. On April 13, 1990, T files his state return for 1989 claiming a refund of $125. The refund is received by T on August 3, 1990.

    a. If T itemizes his deductions, how much may he claim as a deduction for state income taxes on his Federal return for calendar year 1989 (filed in April 1990)?

    b. How will the refund of $125 received in 1990 be treated for Federal income tax purposes?

31. In County Z the real property tax year is the calendar year. The real property tax becomes a personal liability of the owner of real property on January 1 in the current real property tax year 1989. The tax is payable on July 1, 1989. On May 1, 1989, A sells his house to B, who uses the cash method of accounting, but B reports his income on the basis of a fiscal year ending July 31. On July 1, 1989, B pays the entire real estate tax for the year ending December 31, 1989. How much of the real estate tax for 1989 is considered to be imposed on B?

32. In 1989, M has $8,000 of investment income and the following miscellaneous deductions:

Unreimbursed employee business expenses (meals included at 80%)	$1,000
Tax return preparation fee	150
Investment expenses	600

    For purposes of the investment interest expense limitation, what is the total of M's net investment income in each of the following independent situations:

    a. AGI of $30,000.

    b. AGI of $70,000.

    c. AGI of $100,000.

33. X is married and files a joint tax return for 1989. X has investment interest expense of $95,000 for a loan made to him in 1989 to purchase a parcel of unimproved land. His income from investments (dividends and interest) totaled $15,000. After reducing his miscellaneous deductions by the applicable 2% floor, the deductible portion of investment expenses amounted to $2,500. X also has $3,000 as a net long-term capital gain from the sale of another parcel of unimproved land. Calculate X's investment interest deduction for 1989.

34. E borrowed $200,000 to acquire a parcel of land to be held for investment purposes. During 1989, she paid interest of $20,000 on the loan. She had adjusted gross income of $50,000 in 1989. Other 1989 items related to E's investments include the following:

Investment income	$10,200
Long-term gain on sale of stock	4,000
Investment counsel fees	1,500

E is unmarried and elected to itemize her deductions. She had no miscellaneous deductions other than the investment counsel fees. Determine E's investment interest deduction for 1989.

35. R and H, married taxpayers filing a joint return, incurred the following items of interest expense during 1989:

Interest on personal residence	$7,200
Interest on bank loan used to acquire an automobile	1,300
Interest on credit cards	700

They acquired the residence in 1988 at a cost of $100,000 (20,000 cash + $80,000 mortgage). The residence is worth $200,000. Compute the deduction for interest expense for R and H for 1989.

36. In 1989 T borrows $120,000 to purchase an airplane (to be used for pleasure purposes) by placing a lien on his personal residence. At this time the first mortgage on the residence has a balance of $300,000, and the residence has a fair market value of $600,000. How should T determine his interest deduction for 1989?

37. T and his wife W own a personal residence in the city. For many years, they have owned a beach house 50 miles away. They do not rent out the beach house because they spend every weekend there. Last year, they purchased a condominium in Boulder, Colorado, for their son to live in while he attends college. During 1989, they paid the following mortgage interest (each mortgage is secured by the respective property): $7,800 on their personal residence, $5,500 on the beach house, and $9,000 on the condominium. How much can T and W deduct for the year as qualified residence interest?

38. A, B, and C are equal owners in the X Corporation. All three shareholders make loans to X Corporation in 1989 and receive interest-bearing notes. A and B are brothers, and C is their uncle. All three owners are on the cash method of accounting, while X Corporation is on the accrual method. A, B, C, and X Corporation use a calendar year for tax purposes. Can X Corporation deduct the interest payments made to A, B, and C on April 1, 1990, for 1989?

39. Dr. X, a famous heart surgeon practicing in Chicago, performs heart surgery in charitable hospitals around the state during one day of each week. He incurs $250 per week in travel and related expenses pursuant to the rendition of these services. He receives no compensation for the services, nor is he reimbursed for the travel expenses. Assume his professional fees average $3,000 per operation and that he normally performs two operations each day. Based on these facts, what is Dr. X's charitable contribution deduction for the year?

40. Taxpayer's child attends a parochial school operated by the church the family attends. Taxpayer made a donation of $300 to the church in lieu of the normal registration fee of $100 for children of nonmem-

bers. In addition, the regular tuition of $75 per week is paid to the school. Based on this information, what is the taxpayer's charitable contribution?

41. Determine the amount of the charitable deduction allowed in each of the following situations:

  a. Donation of X Corporation stock (a publicly traded corporation) to taxpayer's church. The stock cost the taxpayer $2,000 four months ago and has a fair market value of $3,000 on the date of the donation.

  b. Donation of a painting to the Salvation Army. The painting cost the taxpayer $2,000 five years ago and has a fair market value of $3,500 on the date of the donation.

  c. The local branch of the American Red Cross uses a building rent-free for half of the current year. The building normally rents for $500 a month.

  d. Donation by a cash basis farmer to a church of a quantity of grain worth $900. The grain was raised by the farmer in the preceding year at a cost of $650, all of which was deducted for income tax purposes.

42. T, an individual with an adjusted gross income of $60,000 in 1989, contributed 300 shares of IBM stock to a local college. The adjusted basis of the IBM stock was $90 per share, and the stock's fair market value was $150 per share on the date of the gift. The stock was acquired in 1985 and contributed to the college in 1989.

  a. Calculate the amount of the gift that qualifies for the charitable contribution deduction.

  b. How are excess amounts, if any, treated?

43. X is a single parent, and his son resided with him during 1989. X has $250 in interest expense, $375 in medical expenses after applying the 7.5% limitation, and $700 in charitable contributions. Can X deduct any of these expenditures?

44. On December 30, 1989, T purchased four tickets to a charity ball sponsored by the city of Mobile and for the benefit of underprivileged children. Each ticket cost $100 and had a fair market value of $25. On the same day of the purchase, T gave the tickets to the minister of her church for personal use by his family. At the time of the gift of the tickets, T pledged $1,000 to the building fund of her church. The pledge was satisfied by check dated December 31, 1989, but not mailed until January 3, 1990.

  a. Presuming T is a cash basis and calendar year taxpayer, how much can be deducted as a charitable contribution for 1989?

  b. Would the amount of the deduction be any different if T is an accrual basis taxpayer? Explain.

45. In 1989 T pays $500 to become a charter member of State University's Athletic Council. The membership ensures that T will receive choice seating at all of State's home football games. Also in 1989, T pays $120

(the regular retail price) for season tickets for himself and his wife. As to these items, how much qualifies as a charitable contribution?

46. Classify each of the following independent expenditures as nondeductible (ND) items, business (*dfor*) deductions, or itemized (*dfrom*) deductions. (*Note:* In many cases it may be necessary to refer to the materials from earlier chapters of the text.)

    a. Interest allowed on home mortgage accrued by a cash basis taxpayer. ND

    b. State income taxes paid by a sole proprietor of a business. from

    c. Subscription to *The Wall Street Journal* paid by a vice president of a bank and not reimbursed by her employer. from

    d. Automobile mileage for attendance at weekly church services. ND

    e. Street-paving assessment paid to the county by a homeowner.

    f. Speeding ticket paid by the owner-operator of a taxicab. ND

    g. Interest and taxes paid by the owner of residential rental property. for

    h. Business entertainment expenses (properly substantiated) paid by a self-employed taxpayer. for

    i. State and Federal excise taxes on tobacco paid by a self-employed taxpayer who gave his clients cigars as Christmas presents. The business gifts were properly substantiated and under $25 each. for

    j. State and Federal excise taxes on cigarettes purchased by a heavy smoker for personal consumption. ND

    k. Federal excise taxes (nine cents per gallon) on the purchase of gasoline for use in the taxpayer's personal automobile. ND

    l. Theft loss of personal jewelry worth $300 but which originally cost $75. from   ND not enough.

    m. Maternity clothing purchased by a taxpayer who is pregnant. ND

    n. Medical expenses paid by an employer on behalf of an employee. for

    o. Qualified residence interest paid by a taxpayer on a loan obtained to build an artist studio in his personal residence. Assume that taxpayer's art activities are classified as a hobby. from

    p. Assume the same facts as in (o) except that the art activities are classified as a trade or business. for

47. V had adjusted gross income of $30,000 in 1989. V's itemized deductions totaled $8,000, including $1,000 of miscellaneous itemized deductions (determined before considering the 2% floor). Determine V's allowable itemized deductions for 1989.

Cumulative Problems

48. Sally and Bob Smith are married taxpayers, age 44 and 42, respectively, who file a joint return. In 1988, Bob was employed as an assistant manager for Shoe-A-Rama at a salary of $26,000. Sally is a high school teacher and earned $16,000. Sally has two children, Joe and Sue, ages

13 and 15, from a previous marriage. The children reside with Sally and Bob throughout the school year and reside with Bill, Sally's former husband, during the summer. Pursuant to the divorce decree (which was executed in 1983), Bill pays $100 per month per child for each of the nine months during which Sally has custody of the children, but the decree is silent as to which parent may claim the exemptions. Bill claims that he spends $200 a month supporting each child during the three summer months when the children live with him. Sally can document that she and Bob provided support of $1,600 for each child in 1988.

In August, Bob and Sally decided to add a "mother-in-law" suite to their home to provide more comfortable accommodations for Mary Berry, Sally's mother who had moved in with them the preceding February after the death of Sally's father. Not wanting to borrow the money for this addition Bob and Sally sold 400 shares of Amalgamated Corporation stock for $30 per share on May 9, 1988, and used the $12,000 to cover construction costs. They had purchased the stock on August 7, 1986, for $20 a share. They received dividends of $100 on the jointly owned stock before the sale.

Mary Berry is 66 years old and received $3,600 in Social Security benefits during the year, of which she gave Bob and Sally $1,200 to use toward household expenses and deposited $2,400 in her personal savings account. Bob and Sally determine that they spent $1,500 of their own money for food, clothing, medical expenses, and other items for Mary, not counting the rental value of the portion of the house she occupies.

Bob and Sally received $1,600 interest on city of Toledo bonds they had bought in 1988. Bob had heard from a friend that municipal bonds were paying good rates and that municipal bond interest was not taxable. To finance the purchase of the bonds, he borrowed $20,000 from the bank at 10% interest, figuring the deduction for interest would save him enough income tax to make the investment worthwhile. He paid the bank $2,000 interest during 1988. Other interest paid during the year included $3,530 on their home mortgage (paid to a Federal savings & loan) and $106 on various charge accounts.

Sally's favorite uncle died in February and willed Sally 50 shares of Disney stock worth $60 per share. Sally received dividends of $20 on the stock during the year.

In December 1988, Bob was riding a snowmobile he had just acquired for $4,200. In his eagerness to try it out, he neglected two things. First, he had forgotten to insure it. Second, he had not taken time to read the operating instructions. As a result of his lack of familiarity with the snowmobile, he lost control of it as he was headed toward a large, concrete barn. Fortunately, Bob was able to jump off before the crash and escaped injury. The barn was not damaged. The snowmobile, however, was demolished. Bob sold it back to the dealer for parts for $200.

Bob and Sally paid doctor and hospital bills of $2,800 and were reimbursed by their insurance company for $1,400. Prescription medicines and drugs cost them $600, and premiums on their health insurance policy were $450. Included in the amounts paid for hospital bills was $800 for Mary Berry, and of the $600 spent for medicines and drugs, $300 was for Mary.

Taxes paid during the year included $1,120 property taxes on their home and state income taxes (withheld) of $850. In March 1988, Bob and Sally received a refund on their 1987 state income taxes of $140. They had itemized deductions on their 1987 return and had received a tax benefit for the full amount of state income taxes reported.

Bob and Sally contribute $20 a week to the First United Church and have cancelled checks for these contributions totaling $1,040. In addition, Bob's employer withheld $260 from his check, per his instructions, as a contribution to United Way. Bob and Sally also have a receipt from the Salvation Army for some used clothing the family had contributed. Bob and Sally estimated the value of the clothes at $200.

Bob and Sally had $4,103 ($2,292 for Bob, $1,811 for Sally) of Federal income tax withheld in 1988 and paid no estimated Federal income tax.

Compute net tax payable or refund due for Bob and Sally Smith for 1988. Suggested software (if available): *WEST–TAX Preparer* for tax return solutions, *WEST–TAX Planner* or *BNA Individual Income Tax Spreadsheet* if tax return solutions are not desired.

49. Sam Worthing, age 45, is married and has two dependent children. In 1989, he incurred the following:

Salary received from his employer, Geophysics, Inc.	$60,000
Cost of art supplies. Sam took up painting as a hobby and plans to sell the paintings to friends and art galleries but had no willing purchasers during 1989.	1,000
Contribution of shares of IBM stock to his church (fair market value of $1,000, cost of $400, and acquired in 1976).	1,000
Sam's wife, Irene, had a diamond ring that was stolen in April 1989. A police report was filed, but her ring was not recovered. It is not covered by insurance. The ring had recently been appraised at $2,000, which was also its original cost.	2,000
Travel (meals included at 80%) and auto expenses incurred in connection with Sam's employment (none of which was reimbursed).	2,500

Sam and his family moved from Nashville to Boston during the year and incurred the following unreimbursed expenses:

Moving van	$2,500	
House-hunting expenses (meals included at 80%)	1,800	
Sales commissions on the former house	3,500	7,800

Sam incurred and paid the following personal expenses:	
Medical and dental bills for the family	1,500
State and local income and property taxes	4,500

Determine the Worthings' adjusted gross income and taxable income for 1989, assuming that a joint return is filed and that there are no other items of income or expense. Suggested software (if available): *WEST–TAX Planner* or *BNA Individual Income Tax Spreadsheet.*

Research Problems

Research Problem 1   Taxpayer's son suffered from emotional difficulties that resulted in a learning disability. The boy's psychiatrist recommended a private boarding school, such school's stated goal being to educate the underachiever. A tutorial system and special remedial assistance were provided by the teachers. However, because no psychiatrist or psychologist was on the staff, the students did not receive any type of psychiatric or psychological therapy or counseling. Further, taxpayer and his wife were divorced during this time, and the family court categorized the school costs as an extraordinary medical expense in determining the amount of child support that taxpayer was required to pay. Can these school costs of the son be deducted as medical expenses by the taxpayer?

Research Problem 2   T suffers from a degenerative spinal disorder. Her physician recommended the installation of a swimming pool at her residence for her use to prevent the onset of permanent paralysis. T's residence had a market value of approximately $500,000 before the swimming pool was installed. The swimming pool was built, and an appraiser estimated that the value of T's home increased by $98,000 because of the addition.

> The pool cost $194,000, and T claimed a medical deduction on her tax return of $172,000. Upon audit of the return, the IRS determined that an adequate pool should have cost $70,000 and would increase the property value by only $31,000. Thus, the IRS claims that T should be entitled to a deduction of only $39,000.
>
> a.   Is there any ceiling limitation on the amount deductible as a medical expense?
>
> b.   Can capital expenses be deducted as medical expenses?
>
> c.   What is the significance of a "minimum adequate facility"? Should aesthetic or architectural qualities be considered in this determination?

Research Problem 3   The taxpayer suffered from hypoglycemia, a condition caused by abnormally low blood sugar in the body. The taxpayer's doctor prescribed frequent feedings of a high protein diet as the major treatment for the condition. Taxpayer compared her food bills with those of her friends and estimated that the cost of her food with high protein supplements was much greater than that of ordinary food bought at the grocery store. In the current year, taxpayer paid $3,483 for food and estimated that 30% of this sum was attributable to extra protein required to treat her condition. Is this extra sum deductible as a medical expense?

Research Problem 4   Several years ago, R, a cash basis taxpayer, obtained a mortgage from State Bank to purchase a personal residence. In December 1989, $9,500 of interest was due on the mortgage, but R had only $75 in his checking account. On December 31, 1989, R borrowed $9,500 from State Bank, evidenced by a note, and the proceeds were deposited in R's checking account. On the same day, R issued a check in the identical amount of $9,500 to State Bank for the interest expense due. Is this interest expense deductible for the tax year 1989?

Partial list of research aids:

§ 163(h)(3).

William M. Roberts, 53 TCM 787, T.C.Memo. 1987–235.

Research Problem 5 In 1989 T pledges $400,000 to her church, which is conducting a fund-raising campaign to construct a new sanctuary. To satisfy her pledge, she sells land (worth $500,000) to the church for $100,000. The land had been held by T for many years as an investment and had an adjusted basis to her of $100,000. T chose the sale approach in order to recoup her original investment in the property. Discuss the tax ramifications of this transaction.

4

SPECIAL TAX COMPUTATION METHODS, PAYMENT PROCEDURES, AND TAX CREDITS

Part 4 presents several topics that relate to the theme of tax liability determination. The taxpayer must calculate the tax liability in accordance with the basic tax formula and also in accordance with the tax formula for the alternative minimum tax (AMT). The basic tax formula was presented in Part 1, and the AMT formula is covered in Part 4. Tax credits reduce the amount of the calculated tax liability. The specific procedures for the timing of the payment of the tax liability are also discussed.

SPECIAL TAX COMPUTATION METHODS, PAYMENT PROCEDURES, AND TAX CREDITS

12

ALTERNATIVE MINIMUM TAX

OBJECTIVES
Examine the rationale for the individual alternative minimum tax.

Apply the formula for computing alternative minimum taxable income.

Discuss the role of adjustments in the computation of the alternative minimum tax and explain the adjustments required.

Differentiate tax preferences from alternative minimum tax adjustments and discuss specific tax preferences.

Expand the formula for computation of alternative minimum taxable income to arrive at the alternative minimum tax.

Describe the role of the alternative minimum tax credit in the alternative minimum tax structure.

Introduce the corporate alternative minimum tax.

Once gross income has been determined (refer to chapters 4 and 5) and various deductions accounted for (refer to chapters 6–11), the income tax liability can be computed. Generally the computation procedure requires only familiarity with use of the Tax Table or Tax Rate Schedules. Some taxpayers, however, may be subject to taxes in addition to the regular income tax. One such additional tax is the alternative minimum tax. Any taxpayer who is subject to the regular income tax may be subject to the alternative minimum tax. This chapter explains the provisions of the alternative minimum tax and the determination of tax liability under its terms.

INDIVIDUAL ALTERNATIVE MINIMUM TAX

The tax law contains many incentives that are intended to influence the economic and social behavior of taxpayers (refer to chapter 1). Some of the more prominent incentives to influence *economic* behavior permit rapid write-offs of certain costs, including the following:

- Accelerated depreciation write-offs for realty (buildings) and personalty (e.g., machinery and equipment).
- Immediate expensing of intangible drilling costs, circulation expenditures, mining exploration and development costs, and research and development expenditures.

Tax incentives designed to provide relief for taxpayers also include provisions that allow for deferral of income. These deferral provisions include use of the installment method and the completed contract method for reporting income.

Other tax incentives that are intended to influence social or economic behavior include the following:

- Charitable contribution deductions based on the fair market value of appreciated long-term capital gain property.
- Deduction of certain personal expenditures, including consumer interest and state and local taxes.
- Exclusion of interest on debt obligations of state and local governmental units.

Statistical data compiled by the Department of the Treasury revealed that some taxpayers with large economic incomes were able to minimize or even avoid the payment of income tax by taking advantage of the incentive provisions that Congress had enacted.

Although taxpayers were reducing taxes legally through various investments that resulted in preferential treatment for income tax purposes, Congress was distressed by the resulting inequity. This point is made clear in the following extract from the Report by the Ways and Means Committee of the House of Representatives on the Tax Reform Act of 1969:

This is obviously an unfair situation. In view of the tax burden on our citizens, at this time, it is particularly essential that our taxes be distributed in a fair manner.

Your committee believes that no one should be permitted to avoid his fair share of the tax burden—to shift his tax load to the backs of other taxpayers.[1]

To ensure that taxpayers who benefit from such special provisions pay at least a minimum amount of tax, Congress enacted a special tax, called the *alternative minimum tax* (*AMT*), that applies to corporations, individuals, trusts, and estates. Because it is referred to as a *minimum* tax, it is easy to misinterpret the nature of the tax. The AMT is *not* beneficial to taxpayers. Instead of saving (or minimizing) tax dollars through special computation procedures, it could result in additional tax liability.

Originally, the minimum tax was a special tax of 10 percent levied against specified items of tax preference in excess of $30,000 and was added on to the regular income tax; thus, it was commonly referred to as the add-on minimum tax. The present AMT, however, applies only if it exceeds the regular income tax.

In expanding the scope of the AMT in TRA of 1986, Congress reaffirmed the position taken in enacting the original minimum tax in 1969.

[T]he minimum tax should serve one overriding objective: to ensure that no taxpayer with substantial economic income can avoid significant tax liability by using exclusions, deductions, and credits. Although these provisions may provide incentives for worthy goals, they become counterproductive when taxpayers are allowed to use them to avoid virtually all tax liability. The ability of high-income taxpayers to pay little or no tax undermines respect for the entire tax system and, thus, for the incentive provisions themselves. In addition, even aside from public perceptions . . . it is inherently unfair for high-income taxpayers to pay little or no tax due to their ability to utilize tax preferences.[2]

Overview of the Alternative Minimum Taxable Income (AMTI) Computation

The original minimum tax and previous versions of the AMT were based on tax preferences. For example, if a taxpayer deducted percentage depletion in excess of the basis of a mineral property, the excess depletion was treated as a tax preference and became a part of the minimum tax base. The *current* AMT is based on preferences *and* adjustments to regular taxable income.

The concept of *AMT adjustments* to taxable income was introduced in TRA of 1986. Adjustments arise because Congress has prescribed AMT treatment for certain income and deduction items that differs from the regular income tax treatment of these items. The alternative minimum taxable income (AMTI) computation starts with taxable income and makes adjustments to reflect these differences between income tax and AMT treatment of the specified items. Tax preferences are then added and the total is labeled AMTI. The first step in the calculation of the AMT is the determination of AMTI:

Taxable income
Plus: Positive AMT adjustments
Minus: Negative AMT adjustments

1. 1969–3 C.B. 249.

2. *General Explanation of the Tax Reform Act of 1986 ("Blue Book"),* prepared by The Staff of the Joint Committee on Taxation, May 4, 1987, H.R. 3838, 99th Cong., pp. 432–433.

Plus: Tax preferences
Equals: Alternative minimum taxable income

In order to comprehend the structure of the AMT, it is important to understand the nature of adjustments and preferences.

Adjustments.   As shown in the AMTI formula above, taxable income is increased by *positive adjustments* and decreased by *negative adjustments*. Many of the positive adjustments arise as a result of timing differences related to deferral of income or acceleration of deductions. When these timing differences reverse, *negative adjustments* are made.

Adjustments to taxable income that arise as a result of timing differences related to the acceleration of deductions for regular tax purposes include the following:

- Difference between modified ACRS depreciation deducted for income tax purposes and ADS (alternative depreciation system) depreciation deductible for AMT purposes.

- Difference between the amount allowed under *immediate expensing* provisions applicable for income tax purposes and the amount that would be allowed if the expenditures were *amortized* as prescribed for AMT purposes.

In addition, there are timing differences that relate to deferrals allowed for regular tax purposes but not for AMT purposes. Included in this category of adjustments is the difference between income reported under the completed contract method for income tax purposes and income that would be reported under the percentage of completion method prescribed for AMT purposes.

There are several other adjustments that do not relate to timing differences. The "adjustments" in question are more like preferences than adjustments in that they are always positive, never negative (they always increase and never decrease AMTI). Included in this category of adjustments are the following:

- Itemized deductions allowed for regular tax purposes but not for AMT purposes (e.g., consumer interest and state and local taxes).

- The standard deduction if the taxpayer does not itemize.

- The deduction for personal and dependency exemptions.

These adjustments, and their effect on AMTI, are discussed in detail under AMT Adjustments.

Preferences.   Some deductions allowed to taxpayers for regular income tax purposes provide extraordinary tax savings. Congress has chosen to single out these items, which are referred to as tax preferences. The AMT is designed to take back the tax benefits derived through the use of preferences in the computation of taxable income for regular income tax purposes. This is why taxable income, which is the starting point in computing AMTI, is increased by tax preference items. The effect of adding these preference items is to disallow for alternative minimum tax purposes those preferences that were allowed in the regular income tax computation. Tax preferences include the following items:

- Percentage depletion in excess of the property's adjusted basis.

- Intangible drilling costs in excess of 65 percent of the net income from oil, gas, and geothermal properties.

- Net appreciation on contributed long-term capital gain property.

- Interest on certain private activity bonds.

- Excess of the fair market value of incentive stock options exercised during the year over the option price.

- Excess of accelerated over straight-line depreciation on real property placed in service before 1987.

- Excess of accelerated over straight-line depreciation on leased personal property placed in service before 1987.

- Excess of amortization allowance over depreciation on pre–1987 certified pollution control facilities.

These preferences are discussed in detail under AMT Preferences.

AMT Adjustments

Circulation Expenditures.   For income tax purposes, circulation expenditures, other than those the taxpayer elects to charge to a capital account, may be expensed in the year incurred.[3] Such expenditures include those made to establish, maintain, or increase the circulation of a newspaper, magazine, or other periodical.

Circulation expenditures are not deductible in the year incurred for AMT purposes. In computing AMTI, these expenditures must be capitalized and amortized ratably over the three-year period beginning with the year in which the expenditures were made.[4]

The AMT adjustment for circulation expenditures is the amount expensed for income tax purposes minus the amount that can be amortized for AMT purposes. The adjustment can be either positive or negative, as shown in Example 1 below. The *nature* of AMT adjustments can be understood by examining the adjustments required for circulation expenditures.

EXAMPLE 1   In 1989, T incurs $24,000 of deductible circulation expenditures. This amount is deducted for income tax purposes. For AMT purposes, the circulation expenditures must be deducted over a three-year period. This results in a deduction for AMT purposes of $8,000 ($24,000 ÷ 3). T's schedule of adjustments is shown on the following page:

---

3. § 173(a).   4. § 56(b)(2)(A)(i).

Year	Income Tax Deduction	AMT Deduction	AMT Adjustment
1989	$24,000	$ 8,000	+$16,000
1990	–0–	8,000	–8,000
1991	–0–	8,000	–8,000
Total	$24,000	$24,000	$ –0–

□

The AMT adjustments can be avoided if the taxpayer elects to write off the circulation expenditures over a 3-year period for regular income tax purposes.[5]

Depreciation of Post-1986 Real Property.   For real property placed in service after 1986, AMT depreciation is computed under the alternative depreciation system, which uses the straight-line method over a 40-year life. The depreciation lives for regular tax purposes are 27.5 years for residential rental property and 31.5 years for all other real property. The difference between AMT depreciation and regular tax depreciation is treated as an adjustment in computing the AMT. The differences will be positive during the regular tax life of the asset, because the asset is written off over a shorter period for regular tax purposes. For example, during the first 31.5 years in the life of nonresidential real property, the regular tax depreciation will exceed the AMT depreciation, because AMT depreciation is computed over a 40-year period. Therefore, the required adjustment will be positive. In the remaining 8.5 years of the asset's AMT life, regular tax depreciation will be zero, and AMT depreciation will be larger than zero. Therefore, the adjustment will be negative during the final 8.5 years. Over the 40-year AMT life of the asset, total depreciation will be the same for both regular and AMT purposes, and the cumulative balance of the positive and negative adjustments will be zero.

EXAMPLE 2

In 1988, V placed in service a nonresidential building costing $126,000. Depreciation for regular tax purposes in 1989 is $4,000 ($126,000 ÷ 31.5 years). Depreciation for AMT purposes in 1989 (using the alternative depreciation method) is $3,150 ($126,000 ÷ 40 years). This results in a positive AMT adjustment for 1989 of $850 ($4,000 regular depreciation – $3,150 alternative depreciation). □

EXAMPLE 3

Assume the same facts as in the previous example, except that it is the thirty-fifth year in the life of the building. Depreciation for regular tax purposes is zero, since the building was fully depreciated over 31.5 years. However, depreciation for AMT purposes is $3,150 ($126,000 ÷ 40). This results in a negative AMT adjustment of $3,150 ($0 – $3,150). □

---

5. § 59(e)(2)(A).

For real property and leased personal property placed in service before 1987, the difference between accelerated depreciation for regular income tax and straight-line depreciation for the AMT results in a tax preference rather than an AMT adjustment. These situations are explained later in the chapter under AMT Preferences.

Depreciation of Post–1986 Personal Property.   For most personal property placed in service after 1986, the modified ACRS (MACRS) deduction for regular income tax purposes is based on the 200 percent declining balance method with a switch to straight-line when that method produces a larger depreciation deduction for the asset. For AMT purposes, the taxpayer must use the alternative depreciation system (ADS). This method is based on the 150 percent declining balance method with a similar switch to straight-line for all personal property. Refer to chapter 9 for a detailed discussion of the MACRS and ADS methods.

All property placed in service after 1986 may be taken into consideration in computing one net adjustment. Using this netting process, the AMT adjustment for a tax year is the difference between the total MACRS depreciation for all personal property computed for regular tax purposes and the total ADS depreciation computed for AMT purposes. When the total of MACRS deductions exceeds the total of ADS deductions, the amount of the adjustment is positive. When the total of ADS deductions exceeds the total of MACRS deductions, the adjustment for AMTI is negative.

The MACRS deduction for personal property will be larger than the ADS deduction in the early years of an asset's life, but the ADS deduction will be larger in the later years. This is so because ADS lives (based on class life) are longer than MACRS lives (based on recovery period).[6] Over the ADS life of the asset, the same amount of depreciation will be deducted for both regular tax and AMT purposes. In the same manner as other timing adjustments, the AMT adjustments over the ADS life of the asset will net to zero.

The taxpayer may elect to use ADS for regular income tax purposes.[7] If this election is made, no AMT adjustment is required because the depreciation deduction will be the same for regular tax and for the AMT.

Pollution Control Facilities.   For regular tax purposes, the cost of certified pollution control facilities may be amortized over a period of 60 months. For AMT purposes, the cost of these facilities placed in service after 1986 must be depreciated under the ADS over the appropriate class life, determined as explained above for depreciation of post–1986 property. The required adjustment (either positive or negative) for AMTI is equal to the difference between the amortization deduction allowed for regular tax and the depreciation deduction computed under ADS.

In the case of pre–1987 facilities, a similar calculation results in an AMT preference, as discussed later in the chapter.

Mining Exploration and Development Costs.   In computing taxable income, taxpayers are allowed to deduct certain mining exploration and development expenditures. The deduction is allowed for expenditures paid or incurred during the taxable year for exploration [8] (ascertaining the existence,

6. Class lives and recovery periods are established for all assets in Rev.Proc. 87–56, 1987–2 C.B. 674.

7. § 168(g)(7).

8. § 617(a).

location, extent, or quality of a deposit or mineral) and for development of a mine or other natural deposit, other than an oil or gas well. Mining development expenditures are those paid or incurred after the existence of ores and minerals in commercially marketable quantities has been disclosed.[9]

For AMT purposes, however, mining exploration and development costs must be capitalized and amortized ratably over a 10-year period.[10] The AMT adjustment for mining exploration and development costs that are expensed is equal to the amount expensed minus the allowable expense if the costs had been capitalized and amortized ratably over a 10-year period. This provision does not apply to costs relating to an oil or gas well.

EXAMPLE 4

In 1989, M incurs $150,000 of mining exploration expenditures. This amount is deducted for regular income tax purposes. For AMT purposes, these mining exploration expenditures must be amortized over a 10–year period. M must make a positive adjustment for AMTI of $135,000 [$150,000 (allowed for regular tax) − $15,000 (for AMT)] for 1989, the first year. In each of the next nine years for AMTI, M is required to make a negative adjustment of $15,000 [$0 (allowed for regular tax) − $15,000 (for AMT)]. □

To avoid the AMT adjustments for mining exploration and development costs, a taxpayer may elect to write off the expenditures over a 10–year period for regular income tax purposes.[11]

Research and Experimentation Expenditures.   For income tax purposes, research and experimentation expenditures (see chapter 8) may be deducted by the taxpayer in the year paid or incurred.[12] However, for AMT purposes, such expenditures must be capitalized and amortized ratably over a 10-year period.[13] For research and experimentation expenditures that are expensed, the AMT adjustment is equal to the amount expensed minus the amount that would have been allowed if the expenditures had been capitalized and amortized ratably over a 10-year period. The AMT adjustment for research and experimentation expenditures can be avoided if the taxpayer elects to write the expenditures off over a 10-year period.

EXAMPLE 5

T incurred research and experimentation expenditures of $100,000 in 1989 and elected to expense that amount for regular tax purposes. Since research and experimentation expenditures must be amortized over a 10-year period for AMT purposes, T's AMT deduction is $10,000 each year ($100,000 ÷ 10 years) for 1989 and the succeeding nine years. T has a positive adjustment for 1989 of $90,000 ($100,000 allowed for regular tax − $10,000 allowed for AMT purposes). The adjustment reverses in each of the following nine years ($0 deduction for regular tax − $10,000 for AMT purposes = $10,000 negative adjustment). □

---

9. § 616(a).
10. § 56(a)(2).
11. §§ 59(e)(2)(D) and (E).
12. § 174(a).
13. § 56(b)(2)(A)(ii).

If, in 1989, T in Example 5 elects to claim a tax credit of 20 percent of the research and experimentation expenditures (see chapter 13), the amount expensed currently must be reduced by one-half of the credit.[14] Thus, in this situation, T would be allowed a current deduction of $90,000 [$100,000 (amount of expenditures) − $10,000 (one-half of the $20,000 credit taken)] for regular tax purposes. For AMTI, T has a positive adjustment for 1989 of $81,000 [$90,000 allowed for regular tax − $9,000 ($90,000 ÷ 10 years) for AMT purposes]. In each of the next nine years, the AMT adjustment is a negative $9,000 [$0 (deduction for regular tax) − $9,000 (for AMT)].

Although the research and experimentation expenditures tax credit cannot be used in the year of election if T is liable for the AMT, the credit is subject to the general rules applicable to unused business tax credits. Thus, the benefit of the credit will be realized in a year when T is liable for the regular tax instead of the AMT.

Passive Activity Losses.   Losses on passive activities acquired *after* October 22, 1986, are not deductible in computing either the income tax or the AMT.[15] However, for income tax purposes, losses incurred on passive activities acquired *before* October 23, 1986, are deductible as follows: 65 percent in 1987, 40 percent in 1988, 20 percent in 1989, 10 percent in 1990, and 0 percent thereafter. These percentages are referred to as transition percentages. Rules for the deductibility of passive losses are summarized below.

Date Activity Acquired	AMT Deduction	Income Tax Deduction
After 10/22/86	Zero	Zero
Before 10/23/86	Zero	Amount allowed under transition percentages

Passive activity losses on pre-October 23, 1986, passive activities that are deducted for income tax purposes are not deductible in arriving at alternative minimum taxable income (AMTI).[16] Consequently, an AMT adjustment is required.

EXAMPLE 6

In 1989, W has a $100,000 loss on a passive activity that she acquired in 1985. Assume that none of the loss is attributable to adjustments or preferences. Under the transition rules, 20% of the passive activity loss is allowed, so W may deduct $20,000 for income tax purposes. For AMT purposes, the entire passive activity loss is disallowed in 1989. As a result, W has a positive adjustment to AMTI of $20,000. □

The passive loss that can be used to offset passive income for income tax purposes may be different from the passive loss used to offset passive income for AMT purposes, as it is in Example 6. Consequently, the suspended passive

---

14. § 280C(c).

15. §§ 469(a) and 58(b)(3).

16. § 58(b)(3).

loss for income tax purposes may be different from the suspended passive loss for AMT purposes. In Example 6, the suspended passive loss for regular income tax is $80,000 ($100,000 − $20,000 used). For AMT purposes, the suspended passive loss is $100,000 ($100,000 − $0 used).

The passive loss limitations of § 469 apply in computing AMTI,[17] except that in applying these limitations:

1. The AMT adjustments to taxable income apply.

2. Any deduction, to the extent such deduction is an item of tax preference for AMT purposes, is not taken into account.

Due to the lack of Regulations or other IRS pronouncements, there is considerable uncertainty as to how the AMT passive loss provisions are to be interpreted. The only guidance at this point appears in the material prepared by the Staff of the Joint Committee on Taxation, as reflected in Example 7.[18]

EXAMPLE 7

A taxpayer has $200,000 of salary income and $50,000 of gross income from passive activities. The taxpayer's deductions with respect to the passive activities equal $120,000 for regular [income] tax purposes and $80,000 for minimum tax purposes. [Assume all passive activities were acquired after October 22, 1986.] For regular tax purposes, the taxpayer has income of $200,000 [salary] and a suspended passive loss in the amount of $70,000 [$50,000 gross income from passive activities − $120,000 deductions from passive activities]. For minimum tax purposes, the taxpayer has income of $200,000 [salary] and a suspended passive loss of $30,000 [$50,000 income from passive activities − $80,000 deductions from passive activities]. □

The Staff of the Joint Committee on Taxation provides another clue as to the interpretation of the provisions related to AMT passive losses:

. . . where a Code provision refers to a 'loss' of the taxpayer from an activity, for purposes of the alternative minimum tax the existence of a loss is determined with regard to the items that are includable and deductible for minimum tax, not regular tax, purposes. . . . With respect to the passive loss provision, for example, section 58 provides expressly that, in applying the limitation for minimum tax purposes, all minimum tax adjustments to income and expense *are made* and regular tax deductions that are items of tax preference *are disregarded.*

Until regulations are issued, Example 7, along with the language of § 58(b) and the above explanation by the Staff of the Joint Committee, leads to the interpretations in Examples 8 and 9.

---

17. §§ 58(b)(1) and (2).
18. *General Explanation of the Tax Reform Act of 1986 ("Blue Book"),* prepared by The Staff of the Joint Committee on Taxation, May 4, 1987,

H.R. 3838, 99th Cong., p. 448. The example is quoted verbatim, except for the material enclosed within brackets [ ].

EXAMPLE 8

T acquired two passive activities in 1989. Activity A had net passive income of $10,000, and there were no AMT adjustments or preferences in connection with the activity. Activity B had gross income of $28,000 and operating expenses (not affected by AMT adjustments or preferences) of $20,000. T claimed MACRS depreciation of $20,000 for Activity B; depreciation under the alternative depreciation system (ADS) would have been $15,000. In addition, T deducted $10,000 of percentage depletion in excess of basis. The following comparison illustrates the differences in the computation of the passive loss for income tax and AMT purposes.

	Income Tax	AMT
Gross income	$28,000	$28,000
Deductions:		
Operating expenses	$20,000	$20,000
Depreciation	20,000	15,000
Depletion	10,000	–0–
Total deductions	$50,000	$35,000
Passive loss	$22,000	$ 7,000

Because the adjustment for depreciation ($5,000) applies and the preference for depletion ($10,000) is not taken into account in computing AMTI, the regular tax passive activity loss of $22,000 for Activity B must be reduced by these amounts, resulting in a passive activity loss for AMT purposes of $7,000, as shown. □

For income tax purposes, T would offset the $10,000 of net passive income from Activity A with $10,000 of the passive loss from Activity B. For AMT purposes, T would offsct the $10,000 of net passive income from Activity A with the $7,000 passive activity loss allowed from Activity B, resulting in passive activity income of $3,000. Thus, in computing AMTI, T must make a positive passive loss adjustment of $3,000 [$10,000 (passive activity loss allowed for regular tax) − $7,000 (passive activity loss allowed for the AMT)]. To avoid duplication, the AMT adjustment for depreciation and the preference for depletion are *not* separately reported. They are accounted for in determining the AMT passive loss adjustment.

EXAMPLE 9

Assume the same facts as in the previous example. For regular tax purposes, T has a suspended passive loss of $12,000 [$22,000 (amount of loss) − $10,000 (used in 1989)]. This suspended passive loss can offset passive income in the future or can offset active or portfolio income when T disposes of the loss activity (see chapter 7). For AMT purposes, T's suspended passive loss is $0 [$7,000 (amount of loss) − $7,000 (amount used in 1989)]. □

Passive Farm Losses. A passive farm loss is defined as any loss from a tax shelter farming activity (a farming syndicate or any other activity consisting of farming unless the taxpayer materially participates in the activity). For regular tax purposes, losses from passive farm activities are subject to the phase-in rules for passive losses (refer to chapter 7).

The limitations for passive farm losses are more severe than the limitations for passive losses in general. Each farming activity is treated separately for purposes of applying the limitation, and there is no netting of passive losses from one farming activity against passive income from a different farming activity. For AMT purposes, the passive farm loss limitations are applied before application of the general passive loss limitations. Thus, even though passive income from a farming activity cannot be offset by passive losses from other farming activities, such income can be offset by passive loss from nonfarm activities.[19]

If a farm passive activity results in a suspended loss, the suspended loss can offset income only from the same activity in a subsequent year for AMTI. This rule does not apply, however, in the year of termination of the taxpayer's entire interest in the farm shelter activity. In this case, the amount of loss is allowed in determining AMTI and is not treated as a loss from a farm tax shelter activity.[20]

If a taxpayer is insolvent at the end of the taxable year, the amount of recomputed passive activity loss (both farm and nonfarm) for AMTI is reduced by the amount of insolvency. For this purpose, the taxpayer is insolvent to the extent that liabilities exceed the fair market value of assets.

Use of Completed Contract Method of Accounting. For any long-term contract entered into after March 1, 1986, taxpayers are required to use the percentage of completion method for AMT purposes. However, in limited circumstances, taxpayers can use the completed contract method for regular tax purposes.[21] Thus, a different amount of income will be recognized for regular tax purposes than is recognized for AMT purposes. The resulting AMT adjustment is equal to the difference between income reported under the percentage of completion method and the amount reported using the completed contract method. The adjustment can be either positive or negative, depending on the amount of income recognized under the different methods.

An AMT adjustment on long-term contracts can be avoided by using the percentage of completion method for regular income tax purposes rather than the completed contract method.

Incentive Stock Options. The exercise of an incentive stock option does not increase regular taxable income.[22] However, for AMT purposes, the excess of the fair market value of stock over the exercise price is treated as an adjustment in the first taxable year in which the rights in the stock are freely transferable or are not subject to a substantial risk of forfeiture. The basis of such stock for AMT purposes is equal to the fair market value taken into account in determining the adjustment.

---

19. *General Explanation of the Tax Reform Act of 1986 ("Blue Book")*, prepared by The Staff of the Joint Committee on Taxation, May 4, 1987, H.R. 3838, 99th Cong., pp. 446–447.

20. § 58(c)(2).

21. See chapter 18 Accounting Periods and Methods for a detailed discussion of the completed contract and percentage of completion methods of accounting.

22. § 421(a).

EXAMPLE 10

In 1989, M exercised an incentive stock option that had been granted by his employer, X Corporation. M acquired 1,000 shares of X Corporation stock for the option price of $20 per share. The stock is freely transferable. The fair market value of the stock at the date of exercise was $50 per share. For AMT purposes, M has a positive gain or loss adjustment (see below) for 1989 of $30,000 ($50,000 fair market value − $20,000 option price). The transaction does not affect regular taxable income. For income tax purposes, the basis of the stock is $20,000, the amount M paid for the stock. The AMT basis, however, is $50,000, the fair market value of the stock at the exercise date. As a result of these different bases, upon sale of the stock, AMT gain (loss) will be different from income tax gain (loss). □

Adjusted Gain or Loss.   When property is sold during the year or a casualty occurs to business or income-producing property, gain or loss reported for regular income tax may be different than gain or loss determined for the AMT. This is so because the adjusted basis of the property for AMT purposes must reflect any current and prior AMT adjustments for the following:

- Depreciation
- Circulation expenditures
- Research and experimentation expenditures
- Mining exploration and development costs
- Amortization of certified pollution control facilities.

If the gain computed for AMT purposes is less than the gain computed for regular income tax *or* if the loss for AMT purposes is more than the loss for regular tax purposes *or* if a loss is computed for AMT purposes and a gain for regular tax, the difference is a negative gain or loss adjustment in determining AMTI. Otherwise, the AMT gain or loss adjustment is positive.

Alternative Tax Net Operating Loss Deduction.   In computing taxable income, taxpayers are allowed to deduct net operating loss (NOL) carryovers and carrybacks (refer to chapter 8). The income tax NOL must be modified, however, in computing AMTI. The starting point in computing the alternative tax NOL is the regular NOL computed for income tax purposes. The AMT NOL, however, is determined by applying AMT adjustments and ignoring tax preferences. Thus, preferences that have been deducted in computing the income tax NOL will be added back, thereby reducing or eliminating the AMT NOL.

EXAMPLE 11

In 1989, T incurred a net operating loss of $100,000. T had no AMT adjustments, but his deductions included tax preferences of $18,000. His AMT NOL carryover to 1990 will be $82,000 ($100,000 regular tax NOL − $18,000 tax preferences deducted in computing the NOL). □

In Example 11, if the adjustment was not made to the income tax NOL, the $18,000 in tax preference items deducted in 1989 would have the effect of reducing AMTI in the year the 1989 NOL is utilized. This would weaken the entire concept of the AMT.

If a taxpayer has an alternative tax NOL that is carried back or over to another year, such alternative tax NOL must be used against AMTI in the carryback or carryover year even if the regular tax, rather than the alternative minimum tax, applies.

EXAMPLE 12   K's alternative tax NOL for 1990 (carried over from 1989) is $10,000. AMTI before considering the alternative tax NOL is $25,000. If K's regular income tax exceeds the AMT, the AMT does not apply. Nevertheless, K's alternative tax NOL of $10,000 is "used up" in 1990 and is not available for carryover to a later year. □

Itemized Deductions.   Two categories of itemized deductions that are allowed in computing taxable income are not allowed in computing AMTI: taxes (state, local, foreign income, and property taxes) and miscellaneous itemized deductions that are subject to the 2 percent of AGI floor. A positive AMT adjustment in the total amount for each is required. Moreover, if the taxpayer's gross income includes the recovery of any tax deducted as an itemized deduction, a negative AMT adjustment in the amount of the recovery is allowed for AMTI. This is so even though the deduction occurred in a prior tax year.

Itemized deductions that are allowed for AMT purposes include the following:

- Casualty losses.
- Gambling losses.
- Charitable contributions.
- Medical expenses in excess of 10 percent of AGI.
- Estate tax on income in respect of a decedent.
- Qualified interest.

The rules for determining the AMT deductions for medical expenses are sufficiently complex to require further explanation.

For income tax purposes, medical expenses are deductible to the extent they exceed 7.5 percent of AGI. However, for AMT purposes, medical expenses are deductible only to the extent they exceed 10 percent of AGI.

EXAMPLE 13   K, who had AGI of $100,000 in 1989, incurred medical expenses of $12,000 during the year. For income tax purposes, K can deduct $4,500 [$12,000 medical expenses − .075($100,000 AGI)]. In computing the AMT, K can deduct only $2,000 [$12,000 medical expenses − .10($100,000 AGI)]. Because taxable income is the starting point in computing AMTI, K must make a positive adjustment of $2,500 ($4,500 income tax deduction − $2,000 AMT deduction). □

The AMT itemized deduction allowed for interest expense includes only qualified housing interest and investment interest to the extent of net investment income that is included in the determination of AMTI.

In computing regular taxable income, taxpayers who itemize can deduct the following types of interest (refer to chapter 11):

- Personal (consumer) interest, subject to the transition rules.

- Qualified residence interest.

- Investment interest, subject to the investment interest limitations.

For AMT purposes, personal (consumer) interest is not deductible. Therefore, taxpayers who deduct the limited amount of personal interest allowed under transition rules for regular income tax purposes are required to make a positive AMT adjustment in that amount in computing AMTI.

Under current income tax rules, taxpayers who itemize can deduct qualified residence interest on up to two residences. However, the deduction is limited to interest on acquisition indebtedness up to $1,000,000 and home equity indebtedness up to $100,000. Acquisition indebtedness is debt incurred in acquiring, constructing, or substantially improving a qualified residence of the taxpayer and secured by the residence of the taxpayer. Home equity indebtedness is indebtedness secured by a qualified residence of the taxpayer, but does not include acquisition indebtedness.

The mortgage interest deduction for AMT purposes is limited to *qualified housing interest,* rather than *qualified residence interest.* Qualified housing interest includes only interest incurred to acquire, construct, or substantially improve the taxpayer's principal residence. It also includes such interest on one other dwelling used for personal purposes. Upon refinancing a loan, interest paid will be deductible as qualified housing interest for AMT purposes only if:

- The proceeds are used to acquire or substantially improve a qualified residence.

- Interest on the prior loan was qualified housing interest.

- The amount of the loan was not increased.

Further, a special rule applies to indebtedness incurred before July 1, 1982, and secured at that time by a qualified residence. Qualified housing interest includes interest on all such debt even if it does not fall under the definition of acquisition indebtedness.

A positive AMT adjustment is required in the amount of the difference between qualified *residence* interest allowed as an itemized deduction for regular tax purposes and qualified *housing* interest allowed in the determination of AMTI.

Investment interest is deductible for income tax purposes to the extent of net investment income plus the lesser of excess investment interest or $10,000 multiplied by the applicable transition percentage. Excess investment interest is the excess of investment interest incurred over net investment income before deducting investment interest.

EXAMPLE 14
In 1989, J had net investment income of $15,000 before deducting investment interest. She incurred investment interest expense of $30,000 during the year. Her investment interest deduction is $17,000 [$15,000 net investment income + .20($10,000)]. □

The investment interest deduction for AMT purposes does not include interest deductible under the transition rules ($2,000 in Example 14). Therefore, J in Example 14 would make a positive adjustment of $2,000 in computing AMTI.

If a taxpayer pays or incurs interest expense on an investment in specified private activity bonds,[23] such interest expense is not deductible for regular tax purposes because the income from these bonds is not included in taxable income. For AMT purposes, though, the interest income is a preference item (explained later in the chapter); thus it is included in net investment income for AMT purposes, as are other related AMT adjustments and preferences. This results in an allowable itemized deduction in determining AMTI for the interest expense related to this investment.

The AMT deduction for investment interest may be larger than for regular income tax purposes because of the inclusion in AMTI of preferences, such as the interest income from specified private activity bonds.

EXAMPLE 15
Assume the same facts as in Example 14, except that J also has $10,000 of interest income from specified private activity bonds. She has no interest expense or other deductions related to the bonds. J's itemized deduction for investment interest expense for regular tax purposes remains the same ($17,000) as in Example 14. For AMT purposes, the itemized deduction allowed for investment interest expense now becomes $25,000, the amount of net investment income ($15,000 + $10,000). In determining AMTI, J would make a negative adjustment of $8,000 [$17,000 (amount allowed for regular tax) − $25,000 (amount allowed for the AMT)]. □

The AMT deduction for qualified interest includes qualified housing interest plus other interest to the extent of qualified net investment income included in the alternative minimum tax base.

Qualified net investment income is the excess of qualified investment income over qualified investment expenses. Qualified investment income includes the following to the extent that such amounts are not derived from the conduct of a trade or business:

• Gross income from interest, dividends, rents, and royalties.

• Any net gain attributable to the disposition of property held for investment.

Qualified investment expenses include deductions directly connected with the production of qualified net investment income to the extent that such deductions are allowable in computing adjusted gross income and are not items of tax preference.

23.   § 57(a)(5).

Other Adjustments. The standard deduction is not allowed as a deduction in computing AMTI. Although it would be rare for a person who does not itemize to be subject to the AMT, it is possible. In such a case, the taxpayer would be required to enter a positive adjustment for the standard deduction in computing the AMT.

The exemption amount deducted for income tax purposes is not allowed in computing AMT.[24] Therefore, taxpayers must enter a positive AMT adjustment for the exemption amount claimed in computing the income tax. A separate exemption (discussed below) is allowed for AMT purposes. To allow both the income tax exemption amount and the AMT exemption amount would result in extra benefits for taxpayers.

EXAMPLE 16

T, who is single, has no dependents and does not itemize deductions. He earned a salary of $105,100 in 1989. Based on this information, T's taxable income for 1989 is $100,000 ($105,100 − $3,100 standard deduction − $2,000 exemption). □

EXAMPLE 17

Assume the same facts as in Example 16. In addition, assume T's tax preferences for the year totaled $150,000. T's AMTI is $255,100 ($100,000 taxable income + $3,100 adjustment for standard deduction + $2,000 adjustment for exemption + $150,000 tax preferences). □

AMT Preferences

Percentage Depletion. Congress originally enacted the percentage depletion rules to provide taxpayers with incentives to invest in the development of specified natural resources. Percentage depletion is computed by multiplying a rate specified in the Code times the gross income from the property (refer to chapter 9). The percentage rate is based on the type of mineral involved. The basis of the property is reduced by the amount of percentage depletion taken until the basis reaches zero. However, once the basis of the property reaches zero, it is possible to continue taking percentage depletion deductions. Thus, over the life of the property, depletion deductions may greatly exceed the cost of the property.

The percentage depletion preference is equal to the excess of the regular tax deduction for percentage depletion over the adjusted basis of the property at the end of the taxable year. Basis is determined without regard to the depletion deduction for the taxable year.

EXAMPLE 18

T owns a mineral property that qualifies for a 22% depletion rate. The basis of the property at the beginning of 1989 was $10,000. Gross income from the property in 1989 was $100,000. For regular tax purposes, T's percentage depletion deduction (assume it is not limited by taxable income from the property) is $22,000. For AMT purposes, T has a tax preference of $12,000 ($22,000 − $10,000). □

24. § 56(b)(1)(E).

Intangible Drilling Costs.   In computing the income tax, taxpayers are allowed to deduct certain intangible drilling and development costs in the year incurred, although such costs are normally capital in nature.[25] The deduction is allowed for costs incurred in connection with oil and gas wells and geothermal wells. A geothermal deposit is defined as a geothermal reservoir consisting of natural heat that is stored in rock or in an aqueous liquid or vapor.[26]

For AMT purposes, excess intangible drilling costs (IDC) for the year are treated as a preference. The preference for excess IDC is computed as follows:

Intangible drilling costs expensed in the year incurred
Minus: Deduction if IDC were capitalized and amortized over 10 years
Equals: Excess of IDC expense over amortization
Minus: 65% of net oil and gas income
Equals: Tax preference item

EXAMPLE 19

J, who incurred IDC of $50,000 in 1989, elected to expense that amount. J's net oil and gas income for the year was $60,000. J's tax preference for IDC for 1989 is $6,000 [($50,000 IDC − $5,000 amortization) − (.65 × $60,000 income)]. □

Charitable Contributions of Appreciated Property.   For income tax purposes, taxpayers who contribute appreciated long-term capital gain property to a qualified charity are allowed to compute their itemized deduction based on the fair market value of the property (refer to chapter 11). This can result in a generous tax benefit if the property is greatly appreciated, because the unrealized appreciation is not taxable.

EXAMPLE 20

T contributed X Corporation stock to the United Fund, a qualified charitable organization. T's basis in the stock was $5,000, and its fair market value at the date of contribution was $100,000. T's charitable contribution deduction is based on the $100,000 fair market value, even though the $95,000 of appreciation has never been included in income. □

For AMT purposes the contribution of appreciated long-term capital gain property to charity results in a tax preference item. Unrealized gain on such property is offset by unrealized loss on other long-term capital gain property contributed to charity. Thus, only the net amount of appreciation on all long-term capital gain properties contributed to charity becomes a preference.

EXAMPLE 21

H made two contributions of long-term capital gain property to charity during 1989. Asset A had a fair market value of $60,000 and an adjusted basis of $25,000. Asset B had a fair market value of $40,000 and an adjusted basis of $56,000. H's tax preference on the contributions is

---

25. § 263(c).   26. § 613(e).

$19,000 ($35,000 appreciation on Asset A − $16,000 decline in value on Asset B). □

It is interesting to note that Congress first considered including unrealized appreciation on contributed property (as well as tax-exempt interest discussed below) as tax preference items in 1969.[27] However, it was not until TRA of 1986 that these items were treated as preferences. Thus, a proposal is not necessarily dead if it is not enacted when originally considered by Congress. The Code contains numerous examples of proposals that were enacted many years after they no longer appeared to be a threat.

Interest on Private Activity Bonds. An important theme underlying TRA of 1986 was a broadening of the base for the AMT. Congress concluded that certain items not treated as tax preferences under pre-1986 law should be added to the AMT base. Such action was necessary so that the AMT could serve its intended purpose of requiring taxpayers with substantial incomes to pay some tax.

One of the items added to the AMT base is tax-exempt interest on newly issued private activity bonds. For income tax purposes, the interest on these specified private activity bonds is exempt under § 103. For AMT purposes, interest on these bonds is treated as a tax preference if the bonds were issued on or after August 7, 1986. The relevant date for bonds that would not have been industrial development bonds under prior law is September 1, 1986. Section 141 of the Code contains a lengthy, complex definition of private activity bonds.[28] In general, private activity bonds are bonds where more than 10 percent of the proceeds are used for private business use and certain other tests under §§ 141(b)(2) and (c) are met.

Although the interest on private activity bonds is treated as an AMT preference, it continues to be tax-exempt for income tax purposes. In addition, expenses related to purchasing or carrying tax-exempt private activity bonds are treated differently for AMT purposes and income tax purposes. Such expenses continue to be disallowed for income tax purposes, but they are allowed in computing AMT. Therefore, the required adjustment is equal to the interest on private activity bonds minus any deduction that would have been allowed for income tax purposes if the interest had been included in gross income.

Depreciation. For real property and leased personal property placed in service before 1987, there is an AMT preference for the excess of accelerated depreciation over straight-line depreciation. The following discussion will focus on leased personal property, rather than real property, to illustrate the nature of this depreciation preference.

Accelerated depreciation on pre–1987 leased personal property was computed using specified ACRS percentages. Percentages for five-year cost recovery property (refer to Figure 9–1, chapter 9) were as follows: 15 percent, 22 percent, 21 percent, 21 percent, and 21 percent. For AMT purposes, depreciation on pre–1987 leased personal property that was five-year property under ACRS was computed over an AMT life of eight years using the straight-line method. As a result, in the early years of the life of the asset, the cost recovery allowance used in computing income tax was greater than the straight-line

27. Treasury Tax Reform Studies and Proposals (Part 2), pp. 132 and 142 (1969).

28. Before TRA of 1986, private activity bonds were known as industrial development bonds.

depreciation deduction allowed in computing AMT. The excess depreciation was treated as a tax preference item.

EXAMPLE 22   P acquired personal property on January 1, 1986, at a cost of $10,000. The property, which was placed in service as leased personal property on January 1, was five-year ACRS property. P's 1986 depreciation deduction for regular tax purposes was $1,500 ($10,000 cost × 15% rate). For AMT purposes, the asset was depreciated over the AMT life of eight years using the straight-line method. Thus, AMT depreciation for 1986 was $625 [($10,000 ÷ 8) × ½ year convention]. P's tax preference for 1986 was $875 ($1,500 − $625). ACRS depreciation for 1989 is $2,100 ($10,000 × .21 ACRS rate), and straight-line depreciation is $1,250 ($10,000 ÷ 8). Therefore, the tax preference for 1989 is $850 ($2,100 − $1,250). P's tax preferences for excess depreciation are summarized below:

Year	ACRS Allowance	AMT Deduction	Preference
1986	$1,500	$ 625	$875
1987	2,200	1,250	950
1988	2,100	1,250	850
1989	2,100	1,250	850
1990	2,100	1,250	850

□

Amortization of Certified Pollution Control Facilities.   Section 169 of the Code provides an election that allows taxpayers to amortize the cost of certified pollution control facilities over a period of 60 months. For pre-1987 facilities, excess amortization is a tax preference item. Excess amortization equals the amortization deducted by the taxpayer minus the amount that would have been deducted if the asset were depreciated over its longer useful life or cost recovery period. A similar calculation for certified pollution control facilities placed in service *after* 1986, is treated as an *adjustment*, discussed in a prior section of the chapter.

Other Components of the AMT Formula

Alternative minimum taxable income is a somewhat confusing term. For income tax purposes, once taxable income has been computed, it is possible to compute the income tax. However, after AMTI has been computed, it is not possible to compute the AMT until the *AMT base* has been determined. An additional step is necessary to arrive at the AMT base. This procedure is shown in the AMT formula in Figure 12–1.

Exemption Amount.   The exemption amount is $40,000 for married taxpayers filing joint returns, $30,000 for single taxpayers, and $20,000 for mar-

---

FIGURE 12–1   Alternative Minimum Tax Formula

Regular taxable income
Plus or minus: Adjustments
Plus: Tax preferences
Equals: Alternative minimum taxable income
Minus: Exemption
Equals: Alternative minimum tax base
Times: 21% rate
Equals: Tentative minimum tax before foreign tax credit
Minus: Alternative minimum tax foreign tax credit
Equals: Tentative minimum tax
Minus: Regular tax liability *
Equals: Alternative minimum tax (if amount is positive)

* This is the regular tax liability for the year reduced by any allowable foreign tax credit. It does not include any tax on lump-sum distributions from pension plans, any investment tax credit recapture, or any low-income credit recapture. See § 55(c).

---

ried taxpayers filing separate returns. Phase-out of the exemption begins when AMTI exceeds specified levels:

- $112,500 for single taxpayers.
- $150,000 for married taxpayers filing jointly.
- $75,000 for married taxpayers filing separately.

The exemption is phased out at a rate of 25 cents on the dollar. The following table shows the beginning and end of the AMT exemption phase-out range for each filing status.

Status	Exemption	Phase-out Begins at	Phase-out Ends at
Married, joint	$40,000	$150,000	$310,000
Single or Head of household	30,000	112,500	232,500
Married, separate	20,000	75,000	155,000

To preclude the tax saving that might result when married taxpayers file separate returns, a special rule applies to these taxpayers. The AMTI of a married person filing a separate return is increased by the lesser of:

- 25 percent of the AMTI that exceeds $155,000 (the amount at which the exemption phases out on a separate return), or
- $20,000 (the maximum exemption amount of the taxpayer's spouse).

The following example explains the calculation of the phase-out of the AMT exemption.

EXAMPLE 23   G, who is single, has AMTI of $192,500 in 1989. Her $30,000 exemption is reduced by $20,000 [($192,500 − $112,500) × .25 phase-out rate]. G's AMT exemption for 1989 is $10,000 ($30,000 exemption − $20,000 reduction). □

AMT Rate.   The rate for the AMT is a flat 21 percent.

Illustration of the AMT Computation

The provisions for computation of the AMT are illustrated in the following example.

EXAMPLE 24   T, who is single, had taxable income for 1989 as follows:

Salary		$192,000
Interest		8,000
Adjusted gross income		$200,000
Less itemized deductions:		
Medical expenses ($35,000 − 7.5% of $200,000 AGI) [a]	$20,000*	
State income taxes	12,520	
Interest [b]		
Home mortgage (for qualified housing)	30,000*	
Investment interest	5,300*	
Contributions	7,000*	
Casualty losses	4,000*	(78,820)
		$121,180
Less exemption		(2,000)
Taxable income		$119,180

[a] Total medical expenses were $35,000, reduced by 7.5% of AGI, resulting in an itemized deduction of $20,000. However, for AMT purposes, the reduction is 10%, which leaves an AMT itemized deduction of $15,000 ($35,000 − 10% of $200,000 AGI). Therefore, an adjustment of $5,000 is required for medical expenses disallowed for AMT purposes.

[b] In this illustration, all interest is deductible in computing alternative minimum taxable income. Qualified housing interest is deductible. Investment interest ($5,300) is deductible to the extent of net investment income included in the minimum tax base. For this purpose, the $8,000 of interest income is treated as net investment income.

Deductions marked by an asterisk are allowed as *alternative tax itemized deductions.* Alternative minimum taxable income is computed as follows (assume T had exclusion preferences of $150,000):

Taxable income	$119,180
Plus: Adjustments	
State income taxes	12,520
Medical expenses	5,000
Personal exemption	2,000
Plus: Tax preferences	150,000
Equals: Alternative minimum taxable income	$288,700
Minus: AMT exemption (phased down to zero)	0
Equals: Minimum tax base	$288,700
Times: AMT rate	.21
	$ 60,627
Minus: Regular tax on taxable income	(33,930)
Equals: Alternative minimum tax	$ 26,697

□

AMT Credit

As discussed previously, timing differences will give rise to adjustments to the minimum tax base. In later years, the timing differences will reverse, as was illustrated in several of the preceding examples. To provide equity for the taxpayer when timing differences reverse, the regular tax liability may be reduced by a tax credit for prior years' minimum tax liability attributable to timing differences. The minimum tax credit may be carried over indefinitely. Therefore, there is no need to keep track of when the minimum tax credit arose.

EXAMPLE 25

Assume the same facts as in Example 1. Also assume that in 1988, T paid AMT as a result of the $16,000 adjustment arising from the circulation expenditures. In 1989, $8,000 of the timing difference reverses, resulting in regular taxable income that is $8,000 greater than AMTI. Because T has already paid AMT as a result of the write-off of circulation expenditures, he is allowed an AMT credit in 1989. □

The AMT credit is applicable only for the AMT that results from timing differences. It is not available in connection with the adjustment for itemized deductions or with exclusion preferences. Exclusion preferences include excess percentage depletion, the charitable contribution preference, and the specified private activity bond interest preference.

EXAMPLE 26

D, who is single, has zero taxable income in 1989. He also has positive timing adjustments of $300,000 and exclusion preferences of $100,000. His AMTI is $400,000, because his AMT exemption is phased out completely due to the level of AMTI. D's AMT is $84,000 ($400,000 × 21% AMT rate). □

To determine the amount of AMT credit to carry over, the AMT must be recomputed reflecting only the exclusion preferences and the AMT exemption amount.

EXAMPLE 27   Assume the same facts as in the previous example. If there had been no positive timing adjustments in 1989, D's AMT liability would have been $14,700 [($100,000 exclusion preferences − $30,000 exemption) × 21% AMT rate]. D may carry over an AMT credit of $69,300 ($84,000 AMT − $14,700 related to exclusion preferences). □

Concept Summary 12–1 presents an expanded version of the AMT formula, with brief descriptions of the components of the formula. Form 8801 should be used to calculate the credit for prior year minimum tax.

CONCEPT SUMMARY 12–1

Expanded Alternative Minimum Tax Formula

Taxable income

Plus or minus: Adjustments to taxable income that are required to compute AMTI, including the following:

Excess of ACRS over alternative depreciation on real property placed in service after 1986 [AMT alternative period is 40 years vs. regular tax periods of 27.5 years for residential rental property and 31.5 years for all other real property].

Excess of ACRS depreciation over alternative depreciation on all personal property placed in service after 1986 (AMT requires 150% declining-balance method, switching to straight-line over the asset's ADR midpoint or class life).

Deductions for circulation expenditures (AMT requires amortization over three years vs. immediate expensing allowed for regular tax).

Deductions for mining and exploration expenditures (AMT requires amortization over 10 years vs. immediate expensing allowed for regular tax).

Deductions for research and experimentation expenditures (AMT requires amortization over 10 years vs. immediate expensing allowed for regular tax).

Passive activity losses deductible for regular tax purposes under the phase-in of the disallowance rules.

Passive farm losses if the taxpayer does not materially participate in the farming activity.

Deferral of income for regular tax purposes using the completed contract method.

Excess of the fair market value of incentive stock options exercised during the year over the option price in the tax year in which the stock is freely transferable or not subject to substantial risk of forfeiture.

Itemized deductions allowed for regular tax but not for AMT (including consumer interest, certain mortgage interest, certain investment interest, state and local taxes, and medical expenses, except to the extent such medical expenses exceed 10% of AGI).

Standard deduction (if taxpayer did not itemize).

Personal exemptions.

Plus: Preferences that must be added to compute alternative minimum taxable income (AMTI), including the following:

Percentage depletion in excess of the property's adjusted basis.

Intangible drilling costs (IDC) in excess of 65% of the net income from oil, gas, and geothermal properties (AMT requires amortization over 120 months vs. immediate expensing of IDC allowed for regular tax).

Net appreciation on contributed long-term capital gain property (considering all contributions, whether the property has appreciated or declined in value).

Interest on certain private activity bonds.

Excess of accelerated over straight-line depreciation on real property placed in service before 1987.

Excess of accelerated over straight-line depreciation on leased personal property placed in service before 1987.

Excess of amortization allowance over depreciation on pre-1987 certified pollution control facilities.

Minus: The allowable alternative tax net operating loss (which cannot offset more than 90% of alternative minimum taxable income).

Equals: Alternative minimum taxable income.

Minus: Exemption ($40,000 for married joint, $30,000 for single or head of household, $20,000 for married separate, subject to the phase-out rules).

Equals: Alternative minimum tax base.

Times: 21% rate.

Equals: Tentative minimum tax before foreign tax credit.

Minus: AMT foreign tax credit (may not reduce tentative minimum tax before foreign tax credit by more than 90%).

Equals: Tentative minimum tax.

Minus: Regular tax.

Equals: Alternative minimum tax.

CORPORATE ALTERNATIVE MINIMUM TAX

The AMT applicable to corporations is quite similar to that applicable to individuals. Many of the adjustments and tax preference items necessary to arrive at AMTI are the same. The rates and exemptions are different, but the objective is identical: to force taxpayers who are more profitable than their taxable income reflects to pay additional income taxes.

The formula for determining the AMT liability of corporate taxpayers appears in Figure 12–2 and follows the format of Form 4626 (Alternative Minimum Tax—Corporations).

FIGURE 12–2   AMT Formula for Corporations

	Regular taxable income before NOL deduction
Plus or minus:	AMT adjustments
Plus:	Tax preferences
Equals:	Alternative minimum taxable income (AMTI) before AMT NOL deduction
Minus:	AMT NOL deduction (limited to 90% of AMTI)
Equals:	Alternative minimum taxable income (AMTI)
Minus:	Exemption
Equals:	Alternative minimum tax base
Times:	20% rate
Equals:	AMT before AMT foreign tax credit
Minus:	AMT foreign tax credit (limited to 90% of credit)
Equals:	Tentative alternative minimum tax
Minus:	Regular tax liability before credits minus regular foreign tax credit
Equals:	Alternative minimum tax (AMT)

AMT Adjustments

As Figure 12–2 indicates, the starting point for computing AMTI is the taxable income of the corporation before any net operating loss deduction. Certain adjustments must be made to this amount. Unlike tax preference items, which are always additions, the adjustments may either increase or decrease taxable income to arrive at AMTI.

Although net operating losses are separately stated in Figure 12–2, they are, in fact, negative adjustments. They are separately stated in Figure 12–2 and Form 4626 because they may not exceed 90 percent of AMTI. Thus, this adjustment cannot be determined until all other adjustments and tax preference items are considered. This 90 percent limitation on NOLs is to assure that each corporate taxpayer pays at least a minimum tax of not less than 2 percent of its AMTI each year (10% times 20% rate). However, this 2 percent AMTI figure may be reduced by the exemption amount and credits, so that a corporation may pay no AMT. Other *adjustments* include the following:

- A portion of accelerated depreciation on property placed in service after 1986. For realty, the adjustment amount is the difference between accelerated depreciation and straight-line using a 40-year life. For personalty, the adjustment is the excess of accelerated depreciation over the amount determined using the 150 percent declining balance method switching to straight-line.

- Passive activity losses of certain closely held corporations and personal service corporations.

- The excess of mining exploration and development costs over what would have resulted if the costs had been capitalized and written off over 10 years.

- For contracts entered into on or after March 1, 1986, the percentage of completion method must be used for AMTI purposes. Thus, corporations using the completed contract method must make the appropriate adjustment.

- A portion of business untaxed reported profits.

Business Untaxed Reported Profits

An additional adjustment is included in determining AMTI with respect to those corporations whose taxable income differs from that used for financial accounting purposes. Because of the notoriety occasioned by the news that some large corporations were able to enjoy large book profits but paid little, if any, Federal income tax, Congress decided to make sure some of these book profits would be subject to tax. At least for 1987 through 1989, this is done by making one-half of the excess of pretax adjusted net book income over AMTI a positive adjustment. Adjusted net book income refers to the net income or loss as set forth on the taxpayer's applicable financial statements, subject to several adjustments.[29] This business untaxed reported profits adjustment is treated as a timing adjustment even if it clearly relates to a permanent exclusion.

EXAMPLE 28

Z Corporation's pretax book income is $1,000,000, and its AMTI (before including this adjustment) is $200,000. The adjustment for untaxed reported profits is $400,000 [50% $\times$ ($1,000,000 $-$ $200,000)]. Thus, total AMTI is $600,000 ($200,000 + $400,000). $\square$

For the determination of adjusted net book income, Congress provided an order of priority (if item 1 exists, it is to be used), summarized as follows:

1. Financial statements filed with the Securities and Exchange Commission.

2. Certified audited financial statements prepared for nontax purposes (e.g., reporting to shareholders).

3. Financial statements that must be filed with any Federal or other governmental agency (e.g., state railroad commission).

4. Financial statements used for credit purposes.

5. Financial statements provided to shareholders.

6. Financial statements used for other substantial nontax purposes.

7. The corporation's earnings and profits for the year.

Many accountants are fearful that the motivation to reduce book income to avoid the AMT may lead to manipulation of sound accounting standards for financial reporting. If this fear is justified, using book income as the base for any tax may be an undesirable approach in the long run.

After 1989, the use of pretax book income is to be replaced by a concept based on adjusted earnings and profits. However, the corporation presently must use current adjusted earnings and profits in determining the business untaxed reported profits adjustment if it does not have any of the financial statements listed in items 1 through 6. If the corporation does not have any of the financial statements listed in items 1 through 3 but does have one or more of the financial statements listed in items 4

---

29. § 56(f)(2)(A) and Temp. Reg. § 1.56–IT(b)(2)(i).

through 6, it may elect to use current earnings and profits. Such an election is irrevocable, but it may be attractive where the earnings and profits amount is closer to AMTI than to pretax book income.

Tax Preferences

AMTI includes designated tax preference items. In some cases, this has the effect of subjecting nontaxable income to the AMT. Some of the more common tax preferences include the following:

- Amortization claimed on certified pollution control facilities.

- Accelerated depreciation on real property (placed in service before 1987) in excess of straight-line.

- Tax-exempt interest on state and local bonds where the generated funds are not used for an essential function of the government (specified private activity bonds).

- Percentage depletion claimed in excess of the adjusted basis of the property.

- The excess of intangible drilling costs over 10-year amortization to the extent such excess is greater than 65 percent of net oil and gas income.

- Untaxed appreciation on property donated to charity.

EXAMPLE 29   For 1989, W Corporation (a calendar year taxpayer) had the following transactions:

Taxable income	$200,000
Mining exploration costs	50,000
Percentage depletion claimed (the property has a zero adjusted basis)	70,000
Donation of land held since 1980 as an investment (basis of $40,000 and fair market value of $50,000) to a qualified charity	50,000
Interest on City of Elmira (Michigan) bonds. The proceeds were used for nongovernmental purposes	20,000

W Corporation's AMTI for 1989 is determined as follows:

Taxable income		$200,000
Adjustments:		
Excess mining exploration costs [$50,000 (amount expensed) − $5,000 (amount allowed over a 10-year amortization period)]		45,000
Tax preferences:		
Excess depletion	$ 70,000	
Untaxed appreciation on charitable contribution ($50,000 − $40,000)	10,000	
Interest on bonds	20,000	100,000
AMTI		$345,000

☐

Exemption

The tentative AMT is 20 percent of AMTI that exceeds the corporation's exemption amount. The exemption amount for a corporation is $40,000 reduced by 25 percent of the amount by which AMTI exceeds $150,000.

EXAMPLE 30

Y Corporation has AMTI of $180,000. Since the exemption amount is reduced by $7,500 [25% × ($180,000 − $150,000)], the amount remaining is $32,500 ($40,000 − $7,500). Thus, Y Corporation's alternative minimum tax base (refer to Figure 12–2) is $147,500 ($180,000 − $32,500). ☐

Note that the exemption phases out entirely when AMTI reaches $310,000.

Other Aspects of the AMT

Investment tax credit carryovers and other general business credits under the regular tax can offset 25 percent of AMT liability. Only 90 percent of foreign tax credits can be applied against AMT liability.

The AMT credit carryover is determined in a manner similar to that for individual taxpayers.

EXAMPLE 31

In Example 29, the AMTI exceeds $310,000, so there is no exemption amount. The tentative minimum tax would be $69,000 (20% of $345,000). Assuming the regular tax liability in 1989 is $68,000 (34% of $200,000), the AMT liability is $1,000 ($69,000 − $68,000). ☐

To determine the minimum tax credit carryover, the AMT must be recomputed reflecting only the exclusion preference of $100,000. This results in no AMT, since the regular tax of $68,000 exceeds the tentative minimum tax of $60,000 (without considering the timing preferences of $45,000). Thus, the amount of the minimum tax credit carryover is $1,000, which is all of the current year's AMT.

TAX PLANNING CONSIDERATIONS

Avoiding Preferences and Adjustments

Several strategies and elections are available that enable taxpayers to avoid having preferences and adjustments.

- A taxpayer who is in danger of incurring AMT liability should not invest in tax-exempt private activity bonds unless such strategy makes good investment sense. Any AMT triggered by interest on private activity bonds will reduce the yield on an investment in these bonds. Other tax-exempt bonds or taxable corporate bonds might yield a better after-tax return.

- A taxpayer may elect to expense certain costs in the year incurred or to capitalize and amortize the costs over some specified period. The decision should be based on the present discounted value of after-tax cash flows under the available alternatives. Costs subject to elective treatment include circulation expenditures, mining exploration and development costs, and research and experimentation expenditures.

Controlling the Timing of Preferences and Adjustments

The AMT exemption often will keep items of tax preference from being subject to the AMT. To use the AMT exemption effectively, taxpayers should avoid bunching preferences and positive adjustments in any one year. To avoid bunching of preferences and adjustments, taxpayers should attempt to control the timing of such items when possible. For example, the contribution of appreciated long-term capital gain property will result in a tax preference item. The timing of such a contribution is usually subject to the control of the taxpayer. Before making a substantial contribution of such property, the taxpayer should assess his or her position relative to the AMT.

Taking Advantage of the AMT/Regular Tax Rate Differential

A taxpayer who cannot avoid triggering the AMT in a given year can usually save taxes by taking advantage of the rate differential between the AMT and the regular tax.

EXAMPLE 32   T, who expects to be in the 28% tax bracket in 1989, is subject to the AMT in 1988. He is considering the sale of a parcel of land at a gain of $100,000. If he sells the land in 1989, he will have to pay tax of $28,000 ($100,000 gain × .28 regular tax rate). However, if he sells the land in 1988, he will pay tax of $21,000 ($100,000 gain × .21 AMT rate). Thus, accelerating the sale into 1988 will save T $7,000 in tax. □

EXAMPLE 33   B, who expects to be in the 28% tax bracket in 1989, is subject to the AMT in 1988. He is going to contribute $10,000 in cash to his alma mater, State University. If he makes the contribution in 1989, he will save tax of $2,800 ($10,000 contribution × .28 regular tax rate). However, if he makes the contribution in 1988, he will save tax of $2,100 ($10,000 contribution × .21 AMT rate). Thus, deferring the contribution until 1989 will save B $700 in tax. ☐

This deferral/acceleration strategy should be considered with regard to any income or expenses for which the taxpayer can control the timing.

PROBLEM MATERIALS

Discussion Questions

1. List and discuss the tax preferences and adjustments subject to the alternative minimum tax.

2. A wealthy acquaintance of yours is concerned about the alternative minimum tax on tax preference items and is thinking about selling all of his municipal bonds to prevent the interest from being subject to the tax. What advice should you give him?

3. Why did Congress enact the alternative minimum tax?

4. M, a corporate executive, plans to exercise an incentive stock option granted by his employer to purchase 1,000 shares of the corporation's stock for an option price of $50 per share. The stock is currently selling for $125 per share. Explain the possible consequences of this action on M's regular tax and alternative minimum tax.

5. Two elements in the alternative minimum tax formula are tax preferences and alternative minimum tax adjustments. Explain how these elements differ.

6. Adjustments that are considered in computing the alternative minimum tax can be either positive or negative. Give an example of such an adjustment, including amounts. Explain the rationale behind the concept of positive and negative adjustments.

7. How can a taxpayer avoid having an alternative minimum tax adjustment for research and experimentation expenditures?

8. What is a passive farm loss? How is it treated for regular tax purposes? How is it treated for alternative minimum tax purposes?

9. T, an equipment dealer who will be subject to the alternative minimum tax in 1989, has an opportunity to make a large sale of equipment in December 1989. Discuss tax planning strategies T should consider in connection with the sale.

10. Certain taxpayers have the option of using either the percentage of completion method or the completed contract method for reporting

profit on long-term contracts. What impact could the alternative minimum tax have on this decision?

11. Does computation of the alternative minimum tax ever require an adjustment for the standard deduction?

12. Does computation of the alternative minimum tax ever require an adjustment for personal and dependency exemptions?

13. Are all itemized deductions that are allowed in computing taxable income also allowed in computing alternative minimum taxable income? Explain any differences.

14. In computing the alternative tax itemized deduction for interest, it is possible that some interest allowed as an itemized deduction for income tax purposes will not be allowed. Explain.

15. The net operating loss for computing taxable income differs from the alternative tax net operating loss. Explain.

16. As it relates to the alternative minimum tax, what purpose does the business untaxed profits serve?

17. Discuss tax planning strategies for minimizing the alternative minimum tax.

Problems

18. T, who is single, has no dependents and does not itemize. She has the following items relative to her tax return for 1989:

Bargain element from the exercise of an incentive stock option (no restrictions apply to the stock)	$ 50,000
Accelerated depreciation on real estate investments acquired before 1987 (straight-line depreciation would have yielded $60,000)	80,000
Percentage depletion in excess of property's adjusted basis	90,000
Taxable income for regular tax purposes	150,000

   a.   Determine the items of tax preference T has for 1989.

   b.   Calculate the alternative minimum tax (if any) for 1989.

19. B, who is single, has the following items for 1989:

Income	
Salary	$ 150,000
Interest from bank	5,000
Interest on corporate bonds	10,000
Dividends	4,000
Short-term capital gain	12,000
Long-term capital gain	20,000

Expenses:

Unreimbursed employee business expenses (no meals or entertainment)	3,000
Total medical expenses	40,000
State income taxes	8,000
Real property taxes	7,000
Home mortgage interest (for qualified housing)	5,000
Casualty loss on vacation home	
Decline in value	20,000
Adjusted basis	70,000
Insurance proceeds	12,000
Tax preferences	100,000

Compute B's tax liability for 1989 before credits or prepayments.

20. In 1989, T incurred a net operating loss of $40,000. He deducted total tax preference items of $16,000 in arriving at the NOL and elected to carry the NOL forward. Compute T's alternative minimum tax net operating loss carryover.

21. During the course of your interview with Jim, who is one of your tax clients, you obtain the following information:

a. Jim, age 52, is single and has no dependents. He is independently wealthy and lives in Aspen, Colorado. In 1989, he earned $18,000 as a ski instructor.

b. Jim's savings account at First National Bank was credited with $45,000 of interest during the year. In addition, he received $126,000 of dividends from General Motors.

c. On March 15, 1989, Jim sold 10,000 shares of Widgets, Inc., stock for $45 per share. He had acquired 15,000 shares of Widgets stock on April 1, 1982, at a cost of $35 per share.

d. An examination of Jim's personal financial documents yields the following information:

- IRA contribution, $2,000 (Jim is not covered by his employer's pension plan).
- State income taxes withheld and estimated payments, $2,500.
- Real estate taxes on his residence, $8,800.
- Home mortgage interest, $45,500.
- Credit card interest, $900.
- Cash contributions to qualified (50% limit) charities, $10,000.
- Professional dues and subscriptions, $500.
- Tax return preparation fee, $2,500.

e. Jim owns several condominiums at Snowmass Ski Resort. Throughout the year, the condominiums are rented to vacationers for short periods on a weekly or monthly basis. Jim acquired the condos in 1983. Accelerated depreciation on these units in 1989 was $180,000. Straight-line depreciation for 1989 would have been $120,000. There was a net loss on the condos of $180,000 in 1989. Jim is not involved in the management of the condos. He pays

Snowmass Property Management, Inc., to handle all management aspects of the properties.

f.   In 1985, Jim invested in an equipment leasing deal. Income from this investment was $140,000 in 1989. The following expenses were incurred: interest, $50,000; management fees, $21,000; equipment expenses, $33,000; and accelerated depreciation, $225,000 (straight-line depreciation would have been $185,000).

g.   In 1985, Jim acquired an Aspen apartment complex, which he manages. Rental income in 1989 was $240,000. Expenses were $275,000, including accelerated depreciation of $90,000. Straight-line depreciation would have been $72,000.

h.   In 1989, Jim invested in MNO Realty, a limited partnership. His share of the partnership's loss in 1989 was $300,000. His share of the partnership's excess depreciation (the excess of accelerated over straight-line) was $40,000.

i.   Jim's employer withheld $3,500 of Federal income tax in 1989. In addition, Jim made estimated payments of $45,000.

Analyze Jim's tax information and compute his tax liability for 1989. Suggested software (if available): *WEST–TAX Planner* or *BNA Individual Income Tax Spreadsheet.*

22.   For 1989, P Corporation (a calendar year taxpayer) had the following transactions:

Taxable income	$100,000
Accelerated depreciation on realty in excess of straight-line (placed in service in 1988)	150,000
Amortization of certified pollution control facilities	10,000
Tax-exempt interest on municipal bonds (funds were used for nongovernmental purposes)	30,000
Untaxed appreciation on property donated to charity	8,000
Percentage depletion in excess of the property's basis	60,000

a.   Determine P Corporation's AMTI for 1989.

b.   Determine the alternative minimum tax base (refer to Figure 12–2).

c.   Determine the tentative minimum tax.

d.   What is the amount of the AMT?

23.   In each of the following independent situations, determine the tentative alternative minimum tax:

	AMTI (before the exemption amount)
Q Corporation	$150,000
R Corporation	160,000
T Corporation	320,000

24.   U Corporation's pretax book income is $1,100,000, and its AMTI (before including business untaxed reported profits) is $300,000. What is U Corporation's total AMTI?

Cumulative Problems

25. X, who is single and age 46, has no dependents. In 1989, he earned a salary of $150,000 as vice president of ABC Manufacturing Corporation. Over the years, he has invested wisely and owns several thousand shares of stock, an apartment complex, and mineral property.

    In January 1989, X sold 500 shares of stock for a gain of $50,000. He had owned the stock for 12 years. X received dividends of $15,000 on the stock he retained.

    On May 20, 1989, X exercised his rights under ABC's incentive stock option plan. For an option price of $26,000, he acquired stock worth $53,000. The stock is freely transferrable.

    Gross rental income from the apartment complex, which was acquired in 1982, was $140,000. Deductible expenses for the complex were $240,000. X does not participate in management of the complex.

    X received net income of $60,000 from an interest in a mineral property acquired in 1980.

    X received $10,000 interest on corporate bonds in 1989. His itemized deductions were as follows: state and local income taxes, $3,300; property taxes on residence, $3,200; mortgage interest on home (qualified housing), $18,000; cash contributions to public charities, $12,000.

    Compute X's lowest legal tax liability, before prepayments or credits, for 1989.

26. R, age 38, is single and has no dependents. He is independently wealthy as a result of having inherited sizable holdings in real estate and corporate stocks and bonds. R is a minister at First Methodist Church, but he accepts no salary from the church. However, he does reside in the church's parsonage free of charge. The rental value of the parsonage is $400 a month. The church also provides R a cash grocery allowance of $50 a week. Examination of R's financial records provides the following information for 1989:

    a. On January 16, 1989, R sold 2,000 shares of stock for a gain of $100,000. The stock was acquired four years ago.

    b. R received gross rental income of $160,000 from an apartment complex he owns and manages.

    c. Expenses related to the apartment complex, which he acquired in 1983, were $145,000, including declining-balance depreciation of $68,000 (straight-line depreciation would have been $41,000).

    d. R's dividend and interest income was $40,000.

    e. R had the following itemized deductions *from* adjusted gross income:

       - $7,000 contribution to Methodist church.

       - $2,000 interest on consumer purchases.

       - $8,500 state and local income taxes.

       - $9,000 medical expenses.

- $1,000 casualty loss (in excess of the $100 limitation and the 10% limitation).

Compute R's tax, including alternative minimum tax if applicable, before prepayments or credits, for 1989. Suggested software (if available): *BNA Individual Income Tax Spreadsheet.*

27. Tim Wulf, age 33, is single and has no dependents. His Social Security number is 232–44–4411, and he is employed by Scottsdale Contractors, Inc., as an engineer. He lives at 2511 Camelback Road, Scottsdale, AZ 85251.

   a. Tim's salary for 1989 was $85,000. In addition, he received a year-end bonus of $8,000. Both amounts were reported on his Form W–2, along with a moving expense reimbursement (see item c). His employer withheld Federal income tax of $28,000, state income tax of $2,500, and FICA tax (Social Security) of $3,380.

   b. He received interest of $2,400 from Scottsdale Savings and Loan and dividends of $900 from ABC Corporation.

   c. Scottsdale Contractors paid Tim a $6,000 reimbursement for expenses he incurred in moving from Minneapolis, Minnesota, to Scottsdale on January 3, 1989. Tim incurred the following expenses in connection with the move:

House-hunting expenses	$ 800
Temporary living expenses including meals of $200 (15 days)	900
Expenses of locating new apartment	400
Travel in moving from old residence (including meals of $100)	700
Transportation of furniture, etc.	5,800

   d. On December 12, Tim sold 100 shares of ABC Corporation stock for $15 per share. He had acquired the stock on September 8, 1989 at a cost of $7 per share.

   e. On October 16, Tim sold 10 acres of property he had held as an investment. He purchased the property for $20,000 on May 14, 1978. He received $50,000 for the property, less a 6% real estate broker's commission.

   f. Tim purchased 100 shares of DEF Corporation stock on February 9 for $45 per share. On August 6, he sold the stock for $31 per share.

   g. GHI Corporation filed for bankruptcy on November 11, and GHI stock became worthless on that date. Tim had acquired 50 shares of the stock on July 7 for $52 per share.

   h. Tim used his personal automobile to inspect various building projects during the year. His employer reimbursed him for 8,000 business miles at the rate of 15 cents per mile. He did not keep records of actual automobile expenses incurred.

   i. On March 15, 1989, Tim contributed $2,000 to his Individual Retirement Account for 1988. He is not yet covered by his new employer's pension plan.

   j. Tim's former wife, Jane (Social Security number 711–33–4444), was granted a divorce from Tim in 1984. She was awarded alimony of $500 per month, and in 1989, Tim made 12 such payments.

In addition, Tim paid child support of $600 per month for his son Samuel, age 9. There was no agreement in the divorce decree as to who could claim Samuel as a dependent.

k. Tim paid 1988 state income tax of $500 on April 10, 1989, when he filed his 1988 state income tax return. In addition, he paid a penalty of $10 and interest of $20.

l. On December 29, Tim paid the final installment on his estimated state income tax for 1989. This installment, which was not due until January 15, 1990, was $450.

m. Tim paid real estate taxes of $1,925 in 1989.

n. A statement from Arizona Federal Savings and Loan indicates that Tim paid mortgage interest on his residence of $8,500 during 1989.

o. Interest on credit cards totaled $660.

p. Tim contributed $100 per month to various charities.

q. Tim paid a $400 fee for preparation of his 1988 tax return on April 10, 1989.

Compute Tim Wulf's 1989 Federal income tax liability. Suggested software (if available): *WEST–TAX Preparer* for tax return solutions, *WEST–TAX Planner* or *BNA Individual Income Tax Spreadsheet* if tax return solutions are not desired.

28. Michael Young, a 36-year-old architect, is single and has no dependents. He lives at 8685 Midway Road, Kent, OH 44240. His Social Security number is 857–97–2873.

Michael reported adjusted gross income of $100,000 and taxable income of $84,500 on Form 1040 for 1988. His itemized deductions reported on Schedule A included the following:

- Total medical expenses, $12,000.
- State and local income taxes, $3,400.
- Real property taxes on personal residence, $2,500.
- Interest on charge accounts ($1,000 total × .40 allowed), $400.
- Miscellaneous itemized deductions in excess of 2% floor, $800.

In November 1988, Michael exercised an incentive stock option and acquired 1,000 shares of his employer's stock for the option price of $20 per share. The fair market value of the stock at the date of exercise was $85 per share. The stock is freely transferrable.

Michael acquired private activity bonds on January 2, 1988. He earned interest of $4,000 on the bonds during 1988.

Determine whether Michael is subject to the alternative minimum tax. Use Form 6251, Alternative Minimum Tax—Individuals, for your computations.

Research Problem

Research Problem 1   T is a full-time gambler whose only source of income is money that he wins from his gambling activities. IRS contends that T's gambling losses should be treated as itemized deductions for purposes of computing the alternative minimum tax. T argues that the gambling losses should be treated as trade or business expenses. Who is correct, T or the IRS?

13

TAX CREDITS AND PAYMENT PROCEDURES

Tax credits are an important factor in determining the final amount of tax that must be paid or the amount of refund a taxpayer receives. This chapter first examines the tax credits that enter into the calculation of one's tax liability. Then, treated separately under Payment Procedures, the significant tax credit dealing with wage withholding is explained. Included in this discussion is a review of the various procedures to be followed in calculating the amount that should be withheld and the special problems of self-employed persons.

Some tax credits are refundable if they exceed the taxpayer's tax liability. The amount of the credit is paid to the taxpayer even if he or she has no tax liability. Others are nonrefundable. In some cases, even though the allowed nonrefundable credit is not paid directly to the taxpayer, the portion not used up in the current year may reduce tax liability for other years, first for prior years or for future years. In other situations, the credit is wasted if it exceeds tax liability. The refundable or nonrefundable nature of tax credits is covered later in the chapter under Priority of Credits.

TAX POLICY CONSIDERATIONS

Congress has generally used tax credits to achieve social or economic objectives or to provide equity for different types of taxpayers. For example, the investment tax credit was introduced in 1962. It was expected to encourage growth in the economy, improve the competitive position of American industry at home and abroad, and help alleviate the nation's balance of payments problem.[1] However, the investment tax credit has been repealed for property placed in service after December 31, 1985. This is in line with Congress's new objective of removing or reducing the effect of taxes as a factor in business decisions.

A tax credit should not be confused with an income tax deduction. Certain expenditures of individuals are permitted as deductions from gross income in arriving at adjusted gross income (e.g., business expenses or certain reimbursed employee expenses). Additionally, individuals are allowed to deduct certain nonbusiness personal and investment-related expenses *from* adjusted gross income. Whereas the tax benefit received from a tax deduction is dependent on the tax rate, a tax credit is not affected by the tax rate of the taxpayer.

EXAMPLE 1   Assume Congress wishes to encourage a certain type of expenditure. One way to accomplish this objective would be to allow a tax credit of 25% for such expenditures. Another way to accomplish this objective would be to allow an itemized deduction for the expenditures. Assume taxpayer A's tax rate is 15%, while taxpayer B's rate is 28%. The tax benefits available to each taxpayer, for a $1,000 expenditure, are summarized as follows:

1. Summary of remarks of the Secretary of the Treasury, quoted in S.Rept. 1881, 87th Cong.,   2nd Sess., reported in 1962–3 C.B. 707.

	Taxpayer A	Taxpayer B
Tax benefit if a 25% credit is allowed	$250	$250
Tax benefit if an itemized deduction is allowed	150	280

These results make it clear that tax credits provide benefits on a more equitable basis than do tax deductions. This is even more apparent considering the fact that the deduction approach will benefit only those taxpayers who itemize deductions, while the credit approach benefits all taxpayers who make the specified expenditure. ☐

For many years, Congress made liberal use of the tax credit provisions of the Code in implementing tax policy. Although existing tax credits still carry out this objective, budget constraints and economic considerations have dictated the repeal of some credits (e.g., investment tax credit, political contributions credit). Nevertheless, such credits as those applicable to jobs for certain disadvantaged persons, child and dependent care, and expenses related to qualified low-income housing still reflect social policy considerations. Other credits, such as those applicable to research activities, have been retained based on economic considerations.

SPECIFIC BUSINESS-RELATED TAX CREDIT PROVISIONS

The business-related tax credits that form a single general business credit include the investment tax credit, jobs credit, research activities credit, and low-income housing credit. Each is determined separately under its own set of rules and is explained here in the order listed.

Investment Tax Credit

Since its original enactment in 1962, the investment tax credit (ITC) has been suspended, reinstated, repealed, and reenacted in response to varying economic conditions and political pressures. These changes in the tax laws have created a nightmare for tax practitioners. This phenomenon continued with the TRA of 1986 provisions related to the ITC. Although this act repealed the regular credit for most property placed in service after 1985, the ITC is still allowed for certain types of property under transitional rules (discussed below). In addition, practitioners will have to deal with carryover and recapture provisions related to the ITC for many years in the future. Because of all of these provisions, a basic understanding of the pre-1986 ITC is necessary.

The ITC has three components: the regular ITC[2], the credit for rehabilitation expenditures, and the business energy credit. The regular ITC was allowed before 1986 for most tangible personal property and is still allowed for transition property (discussed under Transition Property). The rehabilitation credit is allowed for exenditures to rehabilitate (1) industrial and commercial

2. It is still necessary to know how to compute the regular ITC for transition property.

buildings originally placed in service before 1936 and (2) certified historic structures. The third component of the ITC, the business energy credit, is allowed to a limited extent for expenditures by businesses for certain energy conservation equipment. The latter two components of the ITC are discussed later in the chapter under Tax Credit for Rehabilitation Expenditures and Business Energy Credits.

Qualifying Property.   The ITC was allowed for most tangible personal property (e.g., automobiles, machinery, and furniture) and was not allowed for most real property (e.g., land and buildings). Both categories had exceptions. It was sometimes difficult to determine whether an item was tangible personal property that was eligible for the ITC or whether such property was a structural component of a building that was not eligible for the ITC. An item is generally considered to be tangible personal property if it can be removed without causing structural damage to the building.

Upon premature disposition of property on which the ITC has been taken, all or part of the credit that was taken is subject to recapture. Therefore, upon the disposition of property, it will continue to be necessary to determine whether the ITC was taken on the property if the recapture provisions apply.

Transition Property.   The ITC is still allowed for certain property placed in service after 1985 if the property qualifies as transition property.[3] An asset qualifies as *transition property* only if the taxpayer had, on December 31, 1985, a written, binding contract to acquire, construct, or reconstruct the asset. If this provision is satisfied, an additional requirement provides that the property must be placed in service by a specified date. The specified dates for *acquired* property are based on the asset depreciation range (ADR) midpoint lives of the assets. The following table shows the specified dates:

ADR Midpoint Life	Must Be Placed in Service Before
Less than 5 years	7/1/86
At least 5 but less than 7 years	1/1/87
At least 7 but less than 20 years	1/1/89
20 or more years	1/1/91

In addition to the preceding rules for acquired property, a complex set of rules for constructed or reconstructed property exists.

Computation of Qualified Investment.   Because of the recapture provisions and the carryover provisions applicable to the ITC, it is necessary to understand how the credit was computed. The ITC was based on the aggregate amount, without limit, of qualifying new property that was placed in service during the year. In addition, although used ITC property was included in the calculation of the ITC, the maximum includible cost for used property was $125,000 per year ($150,000 in tax years after 1987).

---

3. § 49(e).

EXAMPLE 2

In 1985, T acquired used machinery (which was five-year recovery property) for use in his business. The cost of such property was $200,000. Only $125,000 of the machinery qualified for the ITC because of the limitation on used property. □

That part of the cost of property that was deducted under the election to expense certain depreciable business assets could not be used for the credit computation.[4]

Amount of the Credit. The credit was based on the recovery period under ACRS (refer to chapter 9 for details). To avoid a basis reduction, the taxpayer could elect a reduced ITC rate. Rates for the full credit and the reduced credit were as follows:

Recovery Period (in years)	Full Credit Rate	Reduced Credit Rate
3	6%	4%
5, 10, or 15	10%	8%

EXAMPLE 3

In 1985, T acquired and placed in service the following new assets: automobile, $9,000; light-duty truck, $12,000; office furniture, $2,500; and airplane, $120,000. T's tentative ITC (using the full credit rates) was computed as follows:

Qualifying Property	Cost	Recovery Period	Rate of Credit	Investment Tax Credit
Automobile	$ 9,000	3 years	6%	$ 540
Light-duty truck	12,000	3 years	6%	720
Office furniture	2,500	5 years	10%	250
Airplane	120,000	5 years	10%	12,000
Tentative investment tax credit				$13,510

□

The amount computed in Example 3 is described as the tentative investment tax credit because the allowable credit for any year was subject to a ceiling limitation based on tax liability. Any ITC unused under this rule could first be carried back, then carried forward, as explained later in the chapter under Priority of Credits.

Taxpayers could compute the ITC using the full credit rate or a reduced credit rate. Taxpayers who used the full ITC rate were required to reduce the

4. § 179.

basis of the property (for property placed in service after 1982) by one-half of the ITC taken. No basis reduction was required if the ITC was computed using the reduced rate. The basis of transition property must be reduced by the full amount of any credit taken on the property.

EXAMPLE 4

In 1985, T purchased a machine, which was five-year ACRS property, for $10,000. T took a $1,000 ITC on the property (10% of $10,000). The basis of the property had to be reduced by $500 [½ of $1,000 (ITC)]. Thus, T's cost recovery allowance was based on $9,500 [$10,000 (cost) − $500 (reduction for ITC)]. If the property was transition property placed in service in 1986, the basis would have to be reduced by $1,000, the full amount of the ITC. □

For purposes of this rule requiring a reduction in basis, the full rate for transition property placed in service in 1988 and later is 6½ percent. See Example 6. For 1987, the 10 percent rate was adjusted based on the number of months in the tax year remaining after June 1987. See Example 7.

Recapture of Investment Tax Credit.   The amount of the ITC is based on the recovery period of the qualifying property (refer to Example 3). However, if property is disposed of (or ceases to be qualified ITC property) before the end of the recovery period, the taxpayer must recapture all or a portion of the ITC originally taken.[5] The amount of the ITC that is recaptured in the year of premature disposition (or disqualification as ITC property) is added to the taxpayer's regular tax liability for the recapture year (except for purposes of computing the alternative minimum tax).

The portion of the credit recaptured is a specified percentage of the credit that was taken by the taxpayer. This percentage is based on the period the ITC property was held by the taxpayer, as shown in Figure 13–1.

FIGURE 13–1   ITC Recapture

If the Property Is Held for	**The Recapture Percentage Is**	
	For 15-Year, 10-Year, and 5-Year Property	**For 3-Year Property**
Less than 1 year	100	100
One year or more but less than 2 years	80	66
Two years or more but less than 3 years	60	33
Three years or more but less than 4 years	40	0
Four years or more but less than 5 years	20	0
Five years or more	0	0

---

5.   § 47(a)(5).

EXAMPLE 5   T acquired office furniture (five-year recovery property) on January 3, 1985, at a cost of $5,000. T's ITC on the office furniture was $500 (10% of $5,000). T sold the furniture in June 1989. Since T held the furniture more than four years but less than five, he is required to recapture ITC of $100 (20% of $500). The effect of the recapture is to increase T's 1989 tax liability by the $100 of ITC recaptured. □

Recapture of the ITC generally is triggered by the following: [6]

- Disposition of property through sale, exchange, or sale-and-leaseback transactions.
- Retirement or abandonment of property or conversion to personal use.
- Gifts of ITC property.
- Transfers to partnerships and corporations unless certain conditions are met.
- Like-kind exchanges (certain exceptions are provided).

Exceptions are provided for in the Code to prevent inequities. The following transactions illustrate some situations to which the recapture provisions are not applicable:

- A transfer of property to an estate by reason of death.
- A transfer pursuant to certain tax-free reorganizations.
- A liquidation of a subsidiary corporation where the assets are transferred to the parent without receiving a change in basis.
- A transfer of property between spouses or incident to divorce.

Reduction of Investment Tax Credit.   In general, a 35 percent reduction of the ITC is required for ITC earned on transition property *and* for carryovers of the ITC from pre-1986 years. The full 35 percent reduction applies for taxable years beginning after July 1, 1987.[7]

EXAMPLE 6   In 1989, T placed in service qualified transition property that cost $54,000. The ITC of $5,400 (10% of $54,000) must be reduced by 35%. This reduction amount of $1,890 (35% of $5,400) is not allowed as a credit for any other year. The 35 percent reduction results in an effective rate of $6\frac{1}{2}$ percent [10% − (35% of 10%)]. T is allowed a reduced regular ITC in the amount of $3,510 [$5,400 − $1,890 (reduction amount)] or $6\frac{1}{2}\% \times$ $54,000. □

A partial reduction applied to taxpayers having a taxable year that straddled July 1, 1987 (e.g., 1987 calendar year). For any year straddling July 1, 1987, the 35 percent reduction was prorated based on the number of months in the taxable year after June 30, 1987.

---

6. Reg. § 1.47–2.
7. The reduction does not apply to qualified tim-   ber property. § 49(c)(5)(ii).

EXAMPLE 7   Assume the same facts as in Example 6, except that the year was 1987 and T was a *calendar year* taxpayer. The 35% reduction was prorated based on the number of months of the tax year remaining after June 1987 (6 months in this case). T was required to reduce the regular ITC by 17.5% [35% − (35% × ⁶⁄₁₂)]. Thus, the reduction amount was $945 (17.5% of $5,400), and the reduced ITC allowed was $4,455 ($5,400 − $945). For purposes of basis reduction, the full credit was 8.25% [10% − (35% of 10%) × ⁶⁄₁₂]. □

The 35 percent reduction also applies to *carryforwards* of the regular ITC, regardless of when the property was placed in service. Thus, any carryforwards from pre–1987 years were carried through 1987 in the manner described in Example 7. If any carryforwards remain, they are subject to the full 35 percent reduction in 1988 and subsequent years. Based on tax liability (specially defined later in the chapter under Priority of Credits), one of three situations develops:

1. If the taxpayer is able to use all of the reduced amount of carryforwards in the tax year, that is the end of the matter. None of the 35 percent reduction amount can be carried to any other year.

2. If only a portion of the reduced ITC carryforwards can be used, the unused portion *and* a corresponding portion of the reduction amount are carried forward to the next year. Assume that the taxpayer is able to use 20 percent of the reduced carryforwards. The other 80 percent, *and* 80 percent of the reduction amount, are carried forward.

3. If the taxpayer is not able to use any of the allowed ITC carryforward, the entire amount [both the reduced amount and the reduction amount] are carried forward to the next year.

Sooner or later, either in the current tax year or in a carryforward year, the entire reduction amount is lost permanently.

Tax Credit for Rehabilitation Expenditures

Taxpayers are allowed a tax credit for expenditures to rehabilitate industrial and commercial buildings and certified historic structures. This credit was introduced in 1978, as an extension of the ITC, to discourage the relocation of businesses from older, economically distressed areas (e.g., innercity) to newer locations and to preserve historic structures. Thus, no credit is allowed for the rehabilitation of personal use property.

The rates of credit and the structures to which the credit applies have been changed by Congress from time to time to ensure that the credit accomplishes its intended purpose. Currently, the operating features of this credit are summarized as follows: [8]

---

8. § 46(a)(3).

Rate of the Credit for Rehabilitation Expenses	Nature of the Property
10%	Nonresidential buildings, other than certified historic structures, originally placed in service before 1936
20%	Residential and nonresidential certified historic structures

To qualify for the credit, a taxpayer is required to depreciate the costs of the rehabilitation using the straight-line method (refer to chapter 9 for details on depreciation provisions). The basis of a rehabilitated building must reflect the full rehabilitation credit that is allowed.[9]

EXAMPLE 8

T spent $50,000 to rehabilitate a building that had originally been placed in service in 1932. T is allowed a credit of $5,000 (10% of $50,000) for rehabilitation expenditures. T then increases the basis of the building by $45,000 [$50,000 (rehabilitation expenditures) − $5,000 (credit allowed)] and must depreciate these capitalized expenditures using the straight-line method. □

To qualify for the credit, buildings must be substantially rehabilitated. A building has been substantially rehabilitated if qualified rehabilitation expenditures exceed the greater of (1) the adjusted basis of the property before the rehabilitation or (2) $5,000. Qualified rehabilitation expenditures do not include the cost of acquiring a building, the cost of facilities related to a building (such as a parking lot), and the cost of enlarging an existing building. Stringent rules apply concerning the retention of internal and external walls.

The rehabilitation credit must be recaptured if the rehabilitated property is disposed of prematurely or if it ceases to be qualifying property. The amount recaptured is based on a holding period requirement of five years.

EXAMPLE 9

On March 15, 1986, M placed in service $20,000 of rehabilitation expenditures on a building qualifying for a 15% credit (the rate in effect at that time). A credit of $3,000 ($20,000 × 15%) was allowed, and the basis of the building was increased by $17,000 ($20,000 − $3,000). The building was sold on December 15, 1989. M must recapture a portion of the rehabilitation credit based on the schedule in Figure 13–1. Because M held the rehabilitated property for more than three years but less than four, 40% of the credit, or $1,200, must be added to T's 1989 tax liability. Also, the adjusted basis of the rehabilitation expenditures is increased by the $1,200 recaptured amount. □

9. § 48(q)(3).

For tax years after 1986, the amount of credit allowed in a tax year may be limited by the passive activity rules. Refer to chapter 7.

Business Energy Credits

Since 1978, a business energy credit has been allowed to encourage the conservation of natural resources and to develop alternative energy sources (to oil and natural gas). Most of these credits have now expired. Three remain through December 31, 1989: the credit for solar energy property (at a 10% rate), geothermal property (10%), and ocean thermal property (15%). Except that only new property is eligible for the credit, the rules regarding the regular ITC apply to these credits as well. In the case of recapture, however, if the property ceases to be energy property but still qualifies for the regular ITC, only the energy credit portion is affected. This is so because the business energy credit was allowed in addition to the regular ITC.

Reporting the ITC involves one or all of several forms:

- Form 3468, Computation of Investment Credit, is used for determining the amount of current year credit for all three components. Schedule B of the form is used for calculating the business energy credit.

- Form 4255, Recapture of Investment Credit (Including Energy Investment Credit), is used to determine the increase in tax from recapture.

- If the taxpayer also has any of the other business credits (e.g., jobs credit, research credit), Form 3800, General Business Credit, consolidates these for purposes of determining the current year amount allowed. This form is also used when the taxpayer has carrybacks or carryforwards of general business credits from other years.

Jobs Credit

The jobs credit (also referred to as the targeted jobs credit) was enacted to encourage employers to hire individuals from one or more of the following target groups traditionally subject to high rates of unemployment: [10]

- Vocational rehabilitation referrals.
- Economically disadvantaged youths (age 18 to 22).
- Economically disadvantaged Vietnam-era veterans.
- Recipients of certain Social Security supplemental security income benefits.
- General assistance recipients.
- Youths (age 16 to 19) participating in cooperative education programs.
- Economically disadvantaged ex-convicts.
- Eligible work incentive employees.
- Qualified summer youth employees (age 16 and 17).

---

10. § 51.

The jobs credit is not available for wages paid to certain related parties. The credit is available for first-year wages paid to employees who started work on or before December 31, 1989.

Computation of the regular jobs credit differs from the computation of the credit for qualified summer youth employees only in the amount of wages eligible for the credit.

Computation of the Regular Jobs Credit.   The regular jobs credit is equal to 40 percent of the first $6,000 of wages (per eligible employee) for the first year of employment. The employer's tax deduction for wages is reduced by the amount of the credit. For an employer to qualify for the credit, an unemployed individual must be certified by a local jobs service office of a state employment security agency.

Wages will be taken into account in computing the regular jobs credit only if paid to an individual who is employed for at least 90 days or has completed 120 hours of work. The equivalent thresholds for qualified summer youth employees are 14 days or 20 hours.

EXAMPLE 10

In 1989, T Company hires four handicapped individuals (certified to be eligible employees for the jobs credit). Each of these employees is paid wages of $7,000 during 1989. T Company's jobs credit is $9,600 [($6,000 × 40%) × 4 employees]. If the tax credit is taken, T Company must reduce its deduction for wages paid by $9,600. No credit is available for wages paid to these employees after the first year of employment. □

EXAMPLE 11

On October 1, 1989, M, a calendar year taxpayer, hired a member of a targeted group and obtained the required certification. During the last three months of 1989, this employee is paid $2,500. M is allowed a jobs credit of $1,000 ($2,500 × 40%). The employee continues to work for M in 1990 and is paid $7,000 through September 30. Because up to $6,000 of first-year wages are eligible for the credit, M is also allowed a 40% credit on $3,500 [$6,000 − $2,500 (wages paid in 1989)] of wages paid in 1990, or $1,400 ($3,500 × 40%). None of this employee's wages paid after September 30, the end of the first year of employment, are eligible for the jobs credit. Likewise, no credit is allowed for wages paid to persons newly hired after December 31, 1989. □

Computation of the Jobs Credit for Qualified Summer Youth Employees. The credit for qualified summer youth employees is allowed on wages for services during any 90-day period between May 1 and September 15. A qualified summer youth employee generally must be age 16 or 17 on the hiring date. The maximum wages eligible for the credit are $3,000 per summer youth employee. Thus, the maximum credit per employee for 1989 is $1,200 ($3,000 × 40%[11]). If the employee continues employment after the 90-day period as a member of another targeted group, the amount of wages subject to the regular jobs credit must be reduced by the wages paid to the employee as a qualified summer youth employee.

---

11. For eligible summer hires before 1989, the rate of credit was 85%.

EXAMPLE 12   X Corporation employs T as a qualified summer youth employee beginning May 1, 1989. After 90 days, T continues his employment as a member of a second targeted group. T was paid $2,000 as a qualified summer youth employee. As a member of the second targeted group, T is paid another $5,000. Of the $7,000 total paid to T, only $6,000 qualifies for the jobs credit. This amount consists of the $2,000 wages paid under the qualified summer youth employee program plus $4,000 ($6,000 − $2,000) paid to T as a member of the other targeted group. X Corporation's jobs credit for 1989 will be 40% of $6,000 ($2,000 + $4,000), or $2,400. □

Research Activities Credit

To encourage research and experimentation, usually described as research and development (R & D), a credit is allowed for certain qualifying expenditures paid or incurred through 1989. The research activities credit has two components: an incremental credit and a basic research credit.[12]

Incremental Research Activities Credit.   The incremental research activities credit applies only to the extent that the qualifying expenditures for the current year exceed the average amount of research expenditures in a base period. The base period consists of the preceding three taxable years.

For expenses to be treated as *qualified research expenditures*, the research must meet the following tests:

● The expenditures must qualify for treatment as expenses under § 174 of the Code.

● The research must be for the purpose of discovering information technological in nature.

● Application of the research must be intended to be useful in the development of a new or improved business component of the taxpayer.

A business component is any product, process, computer software, technique, formula, or invention that is to be held for sale, lease, or license or used by the taxpayer in a trade or business of the taxpayer.

In general, research expenditures qualify if the research relates to a new or improved function, performance, reliability, or quality. Such expenses are not subject to a percentage limitation if the research is performed in-house (by the taxpayer or employees). If, however, the research is conducted by persons outside the taxpayer's business (under contract), only 65 percent of the amount paid qualifies for the credit.[13]

EXAMPLE 13   M incurs the following research expenditures for the tax year.

In-house wages, supplies, computer time	$50,000
Paid to XY Scientific Foundation for research	30,000

M's qualified research expenditures amount to $69,500 [$50,000 + ($30,000 × 65%)]. □

---

12. § 41.   13.   § 41(b)(3)(A).

Beyond giving the general guidelines discussed above, the Code does not give specific examples of qualifying research. However, the credit is *not* allowed for research that falls into any of the following categories: [14]

- Research conducted after the beginning of commercial production of the business component.

- Research related to the adaptation of an existing business component to a particular customer's requirement or need.

- Research related to the reproduction of an existing business component (in whole or in part) from a physical examination of the business component itself or from plans, blueprints, detailed specifications, or publicly available information with respect to such business component.

- Surveys and studies such as market research, testing, and routine data collection.

- Research on computer software developed by or for the benefit of the taxpayer primarily for internal use by the taxpayer (unless the software relates to a research activity that is qualified).

- Research conducted outside the United States.

- Research in the social sciences, arts, or humanities.

- Research to the extent funded by any grant or contract or otherwise by another person or government entity.

Qualified research and experimentation expenditures not only are eligible for the 20 percent credit but also can be expensed in the year incurred (or amortized over 60 months or more if the taxpayer chooses).[15] If the choice is the expense deduction, the amount of the expense must be reduced by 50 percent of the credit.[16]

EXAMPLE 14

X Corporation incurred incremental research and experimentation expenditures of $100,000. Assume X Corporation is in the 34% tax bracket and elects to expense the amounts paid. The $100,000 must be reduced by $10,000 (50% of the credit allowed), resulting in an expense deduction of $90,000. The corporation will receive a $50,600 tax benefit for the incremental research and experimentation costs as follows:

Research activities credit ($100,000 × 20%)	$20,000
Tax savings from deduction ($90,000 × 34%)	30,600
Total tax benefit	$50,600

---

14. § 41(d).

15. § 174. Also refer to discussion of rules for deduction of research and development expendi-

tures in chapter 8.

16. § 280C, effective for tax years after 1988.

Incremental research expenditures are defined as the excess of qualified research expenses for the year over the base period research expenses. Generally the term *base period research expense* means the average of qualified research expenditures for the three years immediately preceding the taxable year for which the computation is being made.

EXAMPLE 15

Y incurs qualified research and experimentation expenditures as follows: $70,000 in 1989, $50,000 in 1988, $40,000 in 1987, and $30,000 in 1986. Incremental research expenses for 1989 are computed as follows:

Expenses in 1989	$70,000
Minus: Average base period expenses [($50,000 + $40,000 + $30,000) ÷ 3]	40,000
Incremental expenses	$30,000

Y would be entitled to a maximum credit of $6,000 (20% of $30,000) in 1989. □

A special rule limits the credit available for taxpayers who have incurred small amounts of research and experimentation costs during the base period. The rule provides that in no event shall the base period research expenses be treated as less than 50 percent of research expenses in the determination year.

EXAMPLE 16

Assume the same facts as in Example 15, except that qualified research and experimentation expenses in 1989 were $100,000. Incremental research and experimentation expenditures eligible for the credit are computed as follows:

Expenses in 1989	$100,000
Minus: Base period expenses (50% of $100,000, since average expenses for the base period are less than 50% of the 1989 expenses)	50,000
Incremental expenses	$ 50,000

□

For individuals, this credit is limited to the taxpayer's interest in the business generating the credit.

EXAMPLE 17

Assume the same facts as in Example 15 and that Y has total taxable income of $80,000, of which $45,000 is attributable to the business that incurred the research activities credit. Y's tax credit of $6,000 is limited to $3,375 for the tax year:

$$\$6,000 \times \frac{\$45,000 \text{ (income attributable to this business)}}{\$80,000 \text{ (total taxable income)}} = \$3,375$$

☐

The calculation is made similarly for each separate business and pass-through entity in which the taxpayer has an interest.

Basic Research Credit.   Corporations (but not S corporations or personal service corporations) are allowed an additional 20 percent credit for basic research payments in excess of a base amount. *Basic research payments* are defined as amounts paid in cash (property transfers do not qualify) to a qualified basic research organization. However, two requirements must be met for the payments to qualify. First, such payments must be made pursuant to a written agreement between the corporation and the qualified organization. Second, basic research is to be performed by the qualified organization. These requirements exist because Congress wanted to provide increased tax incentives for corporate cash expenditures for university basic research but did not want the expenditures to represent a switching of donations from general university giving.

Basic research is defined generally as any original investigation for the advancement of scientific knowledge not having a specific commercial objective. However, the definition excludes basic research conducted outside the United States and basic research in the social sciences, arts, or humanities. This reflects the intent of Congress to encourage high-tech research in the United States.

The calculation of this additional credit for basic research expenditures is complex and is based on the amount of such expenditures in excess of a limited specially defined base amount.[17] This amount in turn may be subject to cost of living adjustments.

Furthermore, the amount of these basic research expenditures that is eligible for this additional credit does not enter into the calculation of the incremental research expenditures credit. Thus, the portion of these basic research expenditures that does not exceed the base amount is not eligible for this additional credit, but does become a component of the regular credit for increasing research activities.

EXAMPLE 18	Y Corporation, a qualifying corporation, pays $75,000 to a university for basic research. Assume that Y Corporation's specially calculated base amount is $50,000. The basic research activities credit allowed is $5,000 [($75,000 − $50,000) × 20%]. The $50,000 of current year basic research expenditures that are not eligible for the credit because they do not exceed the base amount are treated as contract research expenses for purposes of the regular incremental research activities credit. ☐

17. § 41(e).

Low-Income Housing Credit

A credit is available to owners of qualified low-income housing projects.[18] The purpose of this low-income housing credit is to encourage building owners to make affordable housing available for low-income individuals.

This particular credit, more than any other, is influenced by many nontax factors. First, certification of the property by the appropriate state or local agency authorized to provide low-income housing credits is required. These are issued based on a nationwide allocation. Once issued, however, they remain in effect for the entire credit period. Additional units require new certification based on allocations in effect at that subsequent time.

The amount of credit is based on the qualified basis of the property. The qualified basis depends on the number of units rented to low-income tenants. Low-income tenants are those whose income is a percentage of the area median gross income. Area median gross income is determined under the United States Housing Act of 1937. These special rules are seemingly endless.

Once declared eligible, the property must meet the required conditions continuously throughout a 15–year compliance period, although the credit itself is allowed over a 10–year period. The amount of the credit varied in 1987 from 9 percent for newly constructed property and rehabilitated property to 4 percent on Federally subsidized projects. Since 1987, the credit amount is determined monthly by the IRS. Once determined, though, the percentage remains constant for that property.

The *qualified basis* is that portion of the basis of the entire property (eligible basis) that is rented to qualifying low-income tenants. The amount of credit is determined by multiplying the qualified basis by the applicable percentage.

EXAMPLE 19   C spends $100,000 to build a qualified low-income housing project completed January 1, 1989. The entire project is rented to low-income families. If the rate is 9%, C may claim a credit of $9,000 ($100,000 × 9%) in 1989 and in each of the following nine years. Generally, first-year credits are prorated based on the date the project is placed in service. A full year's credit is taken in each of the next nine years, and any remaining first-year credit is claimed in the eleventh year. □

Recapture of a portion of the credit may be required if the number of units set aside for low-income tenants falls below a minimum threshold, if the taxpayer disposes of the property or the interest in it, or if the taxpayer's amount at risk decreases. No credits will be authorized after 1989 unless 10 percent or more of the cost of the project has been incurred before 1989. In this case, the property must be placed in service before 1991.

Finally, the passive activity rules (see chapter 7) as applied to rental property may further limit the amount of this credit for a particular year.

18. § 42.

OTHER TAX CREDITS

Earned Income Credit

Taxpayers whose income is below a specified level may be eligible for an earned income credit.[19] In 1989, if an individual's adjusted gross income is $10,240 or less, the earned income credit is 14 percent of earned income not exceeding $6,500, for a maximum credit of $910. If an individual's adjusted gross income is greater than $10,240, the maximum earned income credit of $910 (14% times $6,500) is reduced by 10 percent of the amount of adjusted gross income (or, if greater, earned income) that exceeds $10,240. The credit is reduced to zero when either earned income or adjusted gross income reaches $19,340.

EXAMPLE 20

In 1989, T who otherwise qualifies for the earned income credit, receives wages of $11,220 and has no other income. T's earned income credit is $910 (14% × $6,500 of earned income) reduced by $98 [($11,220 − $10,240) × 10%]. Thus, T's earned income credit is $812 ($910 − $98) for 1989. □

The phase-out levels of $10,240 and $19,340, along with the income base eligible for the credit, are adjusted annually for inflation.

It is not necessary to compute the credit as was done in Example 20. As part of the tax simplification process, the IRS issues an Earned Income Credit Table for the determination of the appropriate amount of the earned income credit. This table, along with a worksheet, is included in the instructions to both Form 1040 and Form 1040A.

To be *eligible* for the credit, the taxpayer must meet one of the following filing statuses:

- Married and entitled to a dependency exemption for a child.

- Surviving spouse with a child who qualifies as a dependent.

- Head of household with an unmarried (need not be a dependent) child, stepchild, or grandchild or with a married (must be a dependent[20]) child, stepchild, or grandchild.

Such child, stepchild, or grandchild must reside with the taxpayer in the United States for more than six months of the tax year (the entire tax year in the case of a surviving spouse). Married individuals must file a joint return to receive the benefits of the credit.

The earned income credit is a form of negative income tax (a refundable credit for taxpayers who do not have a tax liability). An eligible individual may elect to receive advance payments of the earned income credit from his or her employer (rather than to receive the credit from the IRS upon filing of

---

19. § 32.

20. § 32(c)(1). The credit can also be claimed by a custodial parent who is not entitled to a dependency exemption for a child. This situation de-velops when the exemption is released through a written agreement or in a pre-1985 divorce or separation.

the tax return). If this election is made, the taxpayer must file a certificate of eligibility (Form W–5) with his or her employer and *must* file a tax return for the year the income is earned.

Tax Credit for Elderly or Disabled Taxpayers

The credit for the elderly was originally enacted in 1954 as the retirement income credit to provide tax relief for those who were not receiving substantial benefits from tax-free Social Security payments.[21]

EXAMPLE 21

X is a retired taxpayer who received $8,000 of Social Security benefits as his only income in 1989. X's Social Security benefits are excluded from gross income. Therefore, his income tax is $0. In 1989, Y, a single taxpayer 66 years of age, has $8,000 of income from a pension plan funded by his former employer. Assuming Y has no itemized deductions or deductions *for* adjusted gross income, his income tax for 1989 (before credits) is $323 (rounded). The retirement income credit was enacted to mitigate this inequity. □

The credit for the elderly rules apply to taxpayers age 65 or over and to individuals under age 65 who are retired with a permanent and total disability and who have disability income from a public or private employer on account of the disability.

The *maximum* allowable credit is $1,125 (15% × $7,500 of qualifying income), but this amount is reduced for taxpayers who receive Social Security benefits as well as for taxpayers whose adjusted gross income exceeds specified amounts. Many taxpayers receive Social Security benefits or adjusted gross income high enough to reduce the base for the credit to zero.

The eligibility requirements and the tax computation are somewhat complicated. Because of this complexity, an individual may elect to have the IRS compute his or her tax and the amount of the tax credit.

The credit is based on an initial amount (referred to as the *base amount*) of $5,000 for a single taxpayer. The base amount is also $5,000 for married taxpayers filing a joint return when only one spouse is 65 or older. This increases to $7,500 for married taxpayers filing jointly when both spouses are 65 or older. For married individuals filing separately, the base amount is $3,750. To qualify for the credit, married taxpayers generally must file a joint return. However, if the married individuals live apart, under certain conditions they may each claim a maximum base for the tax credit of $3,750 on separate returns. For taxpayers under age 65 who are retired on permanent and total disability, the base amounts could be less than those stated because such amounts are limited to taxable disability income.

This initial base amount is *reduced* by (1) Social Security, Railroad Retirement, and certain excluded pension benefits and (2) one-half of the taxpayer's adjusted gross income in excess of $7,500 for a single taxpayer, a head of household, or a surviving spouse. The adjusted gross income factor is increased to $10,000 for married taxpayers filing jointly. It is generally $5,000

---

for married taxpayers filing separately. The credit is equal to 15 percent of the base amount after subtracting the adjustments just described.

EXAMPLE 22

H and his wife W are both over 65 and received Social Security benefits of $2,000 in 1989. On a joint return, H and W reported adjusted gross income of $12,000.

Base amount		$7,500
Less: Social Security benefits	$2,000	
One-half of the excess of adjusted gross income of $12,000 over $10,000	1,000	(3,000)
Balance subject to credit		$4,500
Tax credit allowed ($4,500 × 15 percent)		$ 675

□

The credit for the elderly is reduced by any alternative minimum tax. Schedule R of Form 1040 is used to calculate and report the credit.

Foreign Tax Credit

Both individual taxpayers and corporations may claim a tax credit for foreign income tax paid on income earned and subject to tax in another country or a U.S. possession.[22] As an alternative, a taxpayer may claim a deduction instead of a credit.[23] In most instances the tax credit is advantageous, since it is a direct offset against the tax liability.

The purpose of the foreign tax credit is to mitigate double taxation, since income earned in a foreign country is subject to both U.S. and foreign taxes. However, the operation of the ceiling limitation formula may result in some form of double taxation or taxation at rates in excess of U.S. rates when the foreign tax rate is in excess of U.S. rates. This is a distinct possibility because U.S. tax rates have recently been lowered whereas many foreign countries have not reduced their rates. In addition, recent changes in the law now place added restrictions upon the benefits of the credit.

Computation.   Taxpayers are required to compute the foreign tax credit based upon an overall limitation.[24] The foreign tax credit is the *lesser* of the foreign taxes imposed or the overall limitation.

EXAMPLE 23

In 1989, T, a calendar year taxpayer, has $10,000 of income from Country Y, which imposes a 15% tax, and $20,000 from Country Z, which imposes a 50% tax. T has taxable income of $70,000 from within the United States.

---

22. Section 27 provides for the credit, but the qualifications and calculation procedure for the credit are contained in §§ 901–908.

23. § 164.

24. § 904.

Assume that the U.S. tax on $100,000 of taxable income before the credit is $28,344. Overall limitation:

$$\frac{\text{Foreign income}}{\text{Total worldwide taxable income}} = \frac{\$30,000}{\$100,000} \times \$28,344 = \$8,503$$

In this case, $8,503 is the amount allowed as the foreign tax credit because this amount is less than the $11,500 of foreign taxes imposed [$1,500 (Country Y) + $10,000 (Country Z)]. □

Thus, the overall limitation results in some of the foreign income being subjected to double taxation. Unused foreign tax credits may be carried back two years and forward five years. Form 1116, Computation of Foreign Tax Credit, is used to compute the limitation on the amount of foreign tax credit.

Only foreign income taxes, war profits taxes, and excess profits taxes (or taxes paid in lieu of such taxes) qualify for the credit. In determining whether or not the tax is an income tax, U.S. criteria are applied. Thus, value added taxes (VAT), severance taxes, property taxes, and sales taxes do not qualify, because they are not regarded as taxes on income. Such taxes may be deductible, however.

The foreign earned income exclusion was discussed in chapter 5, and expenses of employees working outside the United States were discussed in chapter 10.

Credit for Child and Dependent Care Expenses

A credit is allowed to taxpayers who incur employment-related expenses for child or dependent care.[25] The credit is a specified percentage of expenses incurred to enable the taxpayer to work or to seek employment. Expenses on which the credit is based are subject to limitations.

Eligibility.   An individual must maintain a household for either of the following:

- A dependent [26] under age 13.[27]

- A dependent or spouse who is physically or mentally incapacitated.

   Generally, married taxpayers must file a joint return to obtain the credit.

Eligible Employment-Related Expenses.   Eligible expenses include amounts paid for household services and care of a qualifying individual that are incurred to enable the taxpayer to be employed. Child and dependent care expenses include expenses incurred in the home, such as payments for a housekeeper. Out-of-the-home expenses that qualify for the credit include those for the care of a dependent under the age of 13 and those incurred for an older dependent or spouse who is physically or mentally incapacitated as long as he or she regularly spends at least eight hours each day in the taxpayer's household. This makes the credit available to taxpayers who keep handicapped or older children and elderly relatives in the home instead of institu-

---

25. § 21.

26. The credit may also be claimed by the custodial parent for a nondependent child under age 13 if the noncustodial parent is allowed to claim the child as a dependent under a pre-1985 divorce agreement or under a waiver in the case of a post-1984 agreement.

27. For years prior to 1989, the age was under 15.

tionalizing them. Out-of-the-home expenses incurred for services provided by a dependent care center will qualify only if the center complies with all applicable laws and regulations of a state or unit of local government.

Child care payments to a relative are eligible for the credit unless the relative is a dependent of the taxpayer or the taxpayer's spouse or is a child (under age 19) of the taxpayer.

EXAMPLE 24

M is an employed mother of an eight-year-old child. M pays her mother, G, $1,500 per year to care for the child after school. M does not claim G as a dependent. M pays her daughter D, age 17, $900 for the child's care during the summer. Of these amounts, only the $1,500 paid to G qualifies as employment-related child care expenses. □

The total for qualifying employment-related expenses is limited to an individual's earned income. For married taxpayers, this limitation applies to the spouse with the *lesser* amount of earned income. Special rules are provided for taxpayers with nonworking spouses who are disabled or are full-time students. If a nonworking spouse is physically or mentally disabled or is a full-time student, such spouse is *deemed* to have earned income. The deemed amount is $200 per month if there is one qualifying individual in the household or $400 per month if there are two or more qualifying individuals in the household.

Allowable Amounts. In general, the credit is equal to a percentage of unreimbursed employment-related expenses up to $2,400 for one qualifying individual and $4,800 for two or more individuals. The rate is 30 percent, reduced 1 percent for each $2,000 (or fraction thereof) of additional adjusted gross income in excess of $10,000 (but not below 20 percent). The following chart shows the applicable percentage for taxpayers with adjusted gross income greater than $10,000:

Adjusted Gross Income in Excess of	Applicable Rate of Credit
$10,000	29%
12,000	28%
14,000	27%
16,000	26%
18,000	25%
20,000	24%
22,000	23%
24,000	22%
26,000	21%
28,000	20%

EXAMPLE 25   H and W are married and file a joint return. They have two children under age 13 and incurred $6,000 of child care expenses (for a housekeeper) during the year. H and W were fully employed, with H earning $10,000 and W earning $3,000. They have no other income or deductions *for* AGI. The maximum amount of child care expenses for two or more dependents is $4,800, but this amount is further limited by the earned income of W (the spouse with the lesser amount). In this case, the amount allowed as child care expenses would be $3,000 (earned income of W). H and W have combined AGI of $13,000, which reduces their applicable rate of credit to 28% (see chart above). H and W would be entitled to a tax credit of $840 (28% × $3,000) for the tax year. □

EXAMPLE 26   W, who has two children under age 13, worked full-time while her spouse, H, was attending college for 10 months during the year. W earned $10,000 and incurred $5,000 of child care expenses. H is deemed to be fully employed and to have earned $400 for each of the 10 months (or a total of $4,000). Since H and W have adjusted gross income of $10,000, they will not have to make an adjustment to the maximum credit rate of 30%. H and W are limited to $4,000 in qualified child care expenses (the lesser of $4,800 or $4,000). They are entitled to a tax credit of $1,200 (30% × $4,000) for the year. □

Dependent Care Assistance Program.   Recall from chapter 5 that an exclusion from gross income is allowed for a limited amount reimbursed to the taxpayer for child or dependent care expenses. The taxpayer is not allowed both an exclusion from income and a child and dependent care credit on the same amount. The allowable child and dependent care expenses are reduced dollar for dollar by the amount of reimbursement.

EXAMPLE 27   Assume the same facts as in Example 25, except that of the $6,000 paid for child care, H was reimbursed $3,000 by his employer under a qualified dependent care assistance program. The maximum amount of child care expenses for two or more dependents of $4,800 is reduced by the $3,000 reimbursement, resulting in a tax credit of $504 [28% × ($4,800 − $3,000)]. □

In any case, the child and dependent care credit will not be allowed unless, at the time the credit is claimed, the taxpayer reports the correct name, address, and tax identification number (either Social Security Number or Employer Identification Number) of the care provider. If the care provider is a tax-exempt organization, the name and address but not the tax identification number are required.

The credit is claimed by completing and filing Form 2441, Credit for Child and Dependent Care Expenses. A copy of this form appears in Appendix B.

Credit for Mortgage Interest Paid

Qualified home buyers are allowed to claim a tax credit for a portion of mortgage interest paid.[28] Under this program, qualified first-time home buyers are issued *mortgage credit certificates*. Such certificates can be issued only by state or local political subdivisions with authority to issue qualified mortgage bonds to provide funds for home financing. The mortgage credit certificate specifies both the portion of the debt that qualifies for the credit and the percentage rate for the credit.

The taxpayer's credit is the product of the certificate credit rate and the mortgage interest paid during the year on the certified indebtedness amount. The certificate credit rate must be at least 10 percent but not more than 50 percent. However, if the credit rate exceeds 20 percent, the credit may not exceed $2,000 per year. The interest deduction on the qualifying mortgage is reduced by the amount of the credit claimed. The mortgage interest credit is nonrefundable, but excess credits may be carried over for three years.

EXAMPLE 28   W, who holds a mortgage credit certificate specifying a 50% credit rate, paid qualifying mortgage interest of $4,400 during the year. Because the credit rate exceeds 20%, W's credit is limited to $2,000, and his interest deduction is $2,400 ($4,400 interest paid − $2,000 mortgage interest credit). □

The authority of qualified governmental units to issue mortgage credit certificates expires after 1989. In any event, a mortgage credit certificate, once issued, remains in effect as long as the residence being financed continues to be the certificate recipient's principal residence.

PRIORITY OF CREDITS

Refundable versus Nonrefundable Credits

Certain credits are refundable; others are nonrefundable. Refundable credits include taxes withheld on wages (§ 31), the earned income credit (§ 32), tax withheld at the source on nonresident aliens and foreign corporations (§ 33), and the credit for certain uses of gasoline and special fuels (§ 34). *Refundable credits* are refunded to the taxpayer even if the amount of the credit (or credits) exceeds the taxpayer's tax liability.

EXAMPLE 29   T, who is single, had taxable income of $27,000 in 1989. His income tax from the 1989 Tax Rate Schedule is $5,149. During 1989, T's employer withheld income tax of $5,349. T is entitled to a refund of $200, since the credit for tax withheld on wages is a refundable credit. □

---

28. § 25.

Nonrefundable credits are not refunded if they exceed the taxpayer's tax liability.

EXAMPLE 30   T is single, age 67, and retired. T's taxable income for 1989 is $1,320, and the tax on this amount is $198. T's tax credit for the elderly is $225. This credit can be used to reduce T's net tax liability to zero, but it will not result in a refund, even though the credit ($225) exceeds the tax liability ($198). This result occurs because the tax credit for the elderly is a nonrefundable credit. □

Some nonrefundable credits, such as the foreign tax credit, are subject to carryover provisions if they exceed the amount allowable as a credit in a given year. Other nonrefundable credits, such as the tax credit for the elderly (refer to Example 30), are not subject to carryover provisions and are lost if they exceed the limitations. Because some credits are subject to carryover provisions while others are not, it is important to determine the order in which credits are offset against the tax liability. The Code provides that nonrefundable credits are to be offset against a taxpayer's income tax liability in the following order:

- Nonrefundable personal credits:

  - Child and dependent care credit.
  - Credit for the elderly and disabled.
  - Mortgage certificate credit.

- Foreign tax credit.
- Orphan drugs testing credit.
- Nonconventional source fuel credit.
- General business credit, which is the sum of the following:

  - Investment tax credit.
  - Jobs credit.
  - Alcohol fuels credit.
  - Research activities credit.
  - Low-income housing credit.

General Business Credit

Two special rules apply to the general business credit. First, any unused credit must first be carried back 3 years, then forward 15 years. Second, for any tax year, the general business credit is limited.[29] The components of the ceiling amount are defined below:

---

29. § 38(c).

Regular tax liability. The tax liability determined from the appropriate tax table or tax rate schedule, based on taxable income. The following are *not* included in regular tax liability:

- Alternative minimum tax (see chapter 12).
- Additional taxes imposed on excess benefits and premature distributions from retirement plans and from IRAs (see chapter 19).
- Pass-through taxes of S corporations (see chapter 20).

Net regular tax liability. The regular tax liability reduced by the following nonrefundable tax credits:

- Child and dependent care expenses credit.
- Credit for the elderly and the permanently and totally disabled.
- Credit for mortgage interest paid.
- Foreign tax credit.
- Orphan drug testing credit.
- Credit for producing fuel from nonconventional sources.

Net income tax. The regular tax liability plus the alternative minimum tax reduced by the nonrefundable tax credits that enter into the calculation of net regular tax liability.

Tentative minimum tax. The tentative minimum tax minus the foreign tax credit allowed for this purpose.

With the above definitions clearly in mind, the general business credit is limited to the taxpayer's *net income tax* reduced by the greater of:

- The *tentative minimum tax.*
- 25 percent of *net regular tax liability* that exceeds $25,000.[30]

EXAMPLE 31

T's general business credit for 1989 is $70,000, consisting of $30,000 regular ITCs and $40,000 of other general business credits. His net income tax is $130,000, tentative minimum tax is $80,000, and net regular tax liability is $50,000. He has no other tax credits. The computation of T's general business credit allowed for the tax year is computed as follows:

---

30. This amount is $12,500 for married taxpayers filing separately unless one of the spouses is not entitled to the general business credit.

Net income tax	$130,000
Less: The greater of	
• $80,000 (tentative minimum tax)	
• $6,250 [25% × ($50,000 − $25,000)]	80,000
Amount of general business credit allowed for tax year	$ 50,000

T then has $20,000 ($70,000 − $50,000) of unused general business credits. ☐

Treatment of Unused General Business Credits

Unused credits are initially carried back three years (to the earliest year in the sequence) and are applied to reduce tax during these years. Thus, the taxpayer may receive a refund of tax from the benefits of such carryback. Any remaining unused credits are then carried forward 15 years.[31] A FIFO method is applied to the carryovers, carrybacks, and utilization of credits earned during a particular year. The oldest credits are used first in determining the amount of the general business credit.

The FIFO method minimizes the potential for loss of a general business credit benefit because of the expiration of credit carryovers, since the earliest years are used before the current credit for the taxable year.

EXAMPLE 32

This example illustrates the use of general business credit carryovers.

General business credit carryovers		
1986	$ 4,000	
1987	6,000	
1988	2,000	
Total carryovers	$12,000	
1989 general business credit		$40,000
Total credit allowed in 1989 (based on tax liability)	$50,000	
Less: Utilization of carryovers		
1986	(4,000)	
1987	(6,000)	
1988	(2,000)	
Remaining credit allowed	$38,000	
Applied against		
1989 general business credit		(38,000)
1989 unused amount carried forward to 1990		$ 2,000

☐

---

31. § 39(a)(1).

CONCEPT SUMMARY 13–1

Tax Credits

Credit	Computation	Comments
Tax withheld on wages (§ 31)	Amount is reported to employee on W–2 form.	Refundable credit.
Earned income (§ 32)	Amount is determined by reference to Earned Income Credit Table published by IRS. Computations underlying amounts in Earned Income Credit Table are illustrated in Example 20. $910 maximum credit in 1989.	Refundable credit. A form of negative income tax to assist low-income taxpayers. Earned income and AGI must be less than $19,340 in 1989. Child (must be dependent in most cases) must live with taxpayer.
Child and dependent care (§ 21)	Rate ranges from 20% to 30% depending on AGI. Maximum base for credit is $2,400 for one qualifying individual, $4,800 for two or more.	Nonrefundable personal credit. No carryback or carryforward. Benefits taxpayers who incur employment-related child or dependent care expenses in order to work or seek employment. Eligible dependents include children under age 13 or dependent (any age) or spouse who is physically or mentally incapacitated.
Elderly and disabled (§ 22)	15% of sum of base amount minus reductions for (a) Social Security and other nontaxable benefits and (b) excess AGI. Base amount is fixed by law (e.g., $5,000 for a single taxpayer).	Nonrefundable personal credit. No carryback or carryforward. Provides relief for taxpayers not receiving substantial tax-free retirement benefits.
Mortgage certificate (§ 25)	Specified certificate rate (from 10% to 50%) times qualified interest paid. Limited to $2,000 if credit rate exceeds 20%.	Nonrefundable personal credit. Unused credits may be carried forward three years. Provides tax break for qualified first-time home buyers.
Foreign tax (§ 27)	Foreign income/total worldwide taxable income × U.S. tax = overall limitation. Lesser of foreign taxes imposed or overall limitation.	Nonrefundable credit. Unused credits may be carried back two years and forward five years. Purpose is to prevent double taxation on foreign income.
General business (§ 38)	May not exceed net income tax minus the greater of tentative minimum tax or 25% of net regular tax liability that exceeds $25,000.	Nonrefundable credit. Components include investment tax credit, jobs credit, alcohol fuels credit, research activities credit, and low-income housing credit.

Credit	Computation	Comments
		Unused credit may be carried back 3 years and forward 15 years. FIFO method applies to carryovers, carrybacks, and credits earned during current year.
Investment (§ 46)	Qualifying investment times regular percentage, energy percentage, or rehabilitation percentage, depending on type of property. Part of general business credit and subject to limitations thereon.	Nonrefundable credit. Part of general business credit and therefore subject to same carryback, carryover, and FIFO rules. Regular percentage applies to transition property. Energy percentages range from 10% to 15%. Regular rehabilitation rate is 10%; rate for certified historic structures is 20%.
Jobs credit (§ 51)	Regular credit is 40% of first $6,000 of wages paid to each eligible employee. Qualified summer youth employee (QSYE) credit is 40% of first $3,000 of wages paid to QSYE.	Nonrefundable credit. Part of general business credit and therefore subject to same carryback, carryover, and FIFO rules. Purpose is to encourage employment of specified groups. QSYE generally must be age 16 or 17 on hiring date.
Research activities (§ 41)	Incremental credit is 20% of excess of computation year expenditures minus average base period expenditures. Basic research credit is allowed to certain corporations for 20% of cash payments to qualified organizations that exceed a specially calculated base amount.	Nonrefundable credit. Part of general business credit and therefore subject to same carryback, carryover, and FIFO rules. Purpose is to encourage high-tech research in the United States.
Low-income housing (§ 42)	Appropriate rate times eligible basis (portion of project attributable to low-income units).	Nonrefundable credit. Part of general business credit and therefore subject to same carryback, carryover, and FIFO rules. Credit is available each year for 10 years. Recapture applies unless 15-year compliance period requirements are met.

PAYMENT PROCEDURES

The tax law contains elaborate rules that require the prepayment of various Federal taxes. Consistent with the pay-as-you-go approach to the collection of taxes, these rules carry penalties for lack of compliance.[32] Prepayment procedures fall into two major categories: those applicable to employers and those applicable to self-employed persons. For employers, both payroll taxes (FICA and FUTA) and income taxes may be involved. With self-employed taxpayers, the focus is on the income tax and the self-employment tax.

Procedures Applicable to Employers

As noted in chapter 1, *employment taxes* include FICA (Federal Insurance Contributions Act) and FUTA (Federal Unemployment Tax Act). The employer usually is responsible for withholding the employee's share of FICA (commonly referred to as Social Security tax) and appropriate amounts for income taxes. In addition, the employer must match the FICA portion withheld and fully absorb the cost of FUTA. The sum of the employment taxes and the income tax withholdings must be paid to the IRS at specified intervals.

The key to employer compliance in this area involves the resolution of the following points:

- Ascertaining which employees and wages are covered by employment taxes and are subject to withholding for income taxes.

- Arriving at the amount to be withheld.

- Reporting and paying employment taxes and income taxes withheld to the IRS on a timely basis through the use of proper forms.

Coverage Requirements.   Circular E (Employer's Tax Guide), Publication 15, issued by the IRS contains a complete list of which employees and which wages require withholdings for income taxes and employment taxes. Figure 13–2 extracts a portion of this list and is reproduced on page 13–31. In working with Figure 13–2, consider the following observations:

- The designation "Exempt" in the income tax withholding column does not mean that the amount paid is nontaxable to the employee. It merely relieves the employer from having to withhold.

EXAMPLE 33	T works for X Corporation and has the type of job where tips are not common but do occur. If the total tips T receives are less than $20 per month, X Corporation need not withhold Federal income taxes on these amounts. Nevertheless, T must include the tips in his gross income. □

---

32. See, for example, § 3403 (employer liable for any taxes withheld and not paid over to the IRS), § 6656 (10% penalty on amounts with- held and not paid over and 25% penalty for overstated deposit claims), and § 6654 (penalty for failure to pay estimated income taxes).

- In some cases, income tax withholding is not required but is voluntary. This is designated "Exempt (taxable if both employer and employee voluntarily agree)."

EXAMPLE 34   T is employed as a gardener by a wealthy family. In the past, he has encountered difficulty in managing his finances so as to be in a position to pay the income tax due every April 15. To ease the cash flow problem that develops in April, T requests that the employer withhold income taxes from his wages. □

- The FICA (Social Security) column refers to the employer's share. The same is true of the Federal Unemployment column (FUTA) since the employee does not contribute to this tax.

Amount of Withholding.   In the case of FICA, withholdings from employees must continue until the base amount is reached (refer to Figure 1–3 in chapter 1). In tax year 1989, for example, FICA withholding would cease once the employee has earned wages subject to FICA in the amount of $48,000.

Arriving at the amount to be withheld for income tax purposes is not so simple. It involves three basic steps: [33]

- Have the employee complete Form W–4 or W–4A, Employee's Withholding Allowance Certificate.
- Determine the employee's payroll period.
- Compute the amount to be withheld, usually using either the wage-bracket tables or the percentage method.

Form W–4 reflects the employee's marital status and withholding allowances. Generally, it need not be filed with the IRS and is retained by the employer as part of the payroll records.[34] The employer need not verify the number of exemptions claimed. Any misinformation contained therein will be attributed to the employee. However, if the employer has reason to believe that the employee made a false statement, the IRS District Director should be notified. In the meantime, the Form W–4 should be honored.

Employees are subject to both civil and criminal penalties for filing false withholding statements. These penalties were instituted because many employees (particularly tax protestors) were claiming excessive withholding allowances. The civil penalty for filing false information with respect to wage withholding is $500.

On Form W–4 an employee may claim withholding allowances for the following: personal exemptions for self and spouse (unless either is claimed as a dependent of another person) and dependency exemptions. One *special withholding allowance* may be claimed if the employee is single and has only one job, if the employee is married and has only one job and spouse is not employed, or if

---

33. The withholding provisions are contained in §§ 3401 and 3402. These Sections will not be referenced specifically in the discussion that follows.
34. Filing a copy of Form W–4 with the IRS is nec-essary if the employee claims more than 10 exemptions or, in certain cases, claims exempt status. The IRS is aware that some employees deliberately avoid income tax withholding through the use of either of these procedures.

wages from a second job or a spouse's wages (or both) are $2,500 or less. An employee who plans to itemize deductions or claim adjustments to income (e.g., alimony, deductible IRA contributions) should use the worksheet provided on page 3 of Form W–4 to determine the correct number of additional allowances.

FIGURE 13–2   Withholding Classifications

Special Classes of Employment and Special Types of Payments	Treatment under Different Employment Taxes		
	Income Tax Withholding	**Social Security**	**Federal Unemployment**
Dismissal or severance pay	Taxable	Taxable	Taxable
Family employees			
a. Son or daughter under 18 employed by parent (or by partnership consisting only of parents).	Taxable	Exempt	Exempt
b. Spouse employed by spouse.	Taxable	Taxable	Exempt
c. Parent employed by a son or daughter.	Taxable	Taxable if in course of the son's or daughter's business. For household work in private home of employer, refer to section 14 in Circular E.	Exempt
Household workers (domestic service in private homes; farmers, see Circular A).	Exempt (taxable if both employer and employee voluntarily agree).	Taxable if paid $50 or more in cash in quarter.	Taxable if employer paid cash wages of $1,000 or more in any calendar quarter in the current or preceding year.
Interns working in hospitals	Taxable	Taxable	Exempt
Meals and lodging including those furnished at a bargain charge to the employee.	a. Meals—taxable unless furnished for employer's convenience and on the employer's premises. b. Lodging—taxable unless furnished on employer's premises, for the employer's convenience, and as a condition of employment.		
Ministers of churches performing duties as such.	Exempt (taxable if both employer and employee voluntarily agree).	Exempt	Exempt
Moving expenses			
a. Reimbursement for moving expenses you reasonably believe are deductible by employee.	Exempt	Exempt	Exempt
b. Reimbursement for moving expenses you believe are not deductible by employee.	Taxable	Taxable	Taxable
Newspaper carrier under age 18 delivering to customers.	Exempt (taxable if both employer and employee voluntarily agree).	Exempt	Exempt
Tips, if less than $20 in a month.	Exempt from withholding. Taxable to employee.	Exempt	Exempt
Workmen's compensation.	Exempt	Exempt	Exempt

To avoid having too little tax withheld, some employees may find it necessary to reduce their withholding allowances. Such might be the case for an employee who is single and has more than one job. Likewise, a married employee who has a working spouse or more than one job might wish to claim fewer allowances.

If both spouses of a married couple are employed, they may allocate their total allowances between themselves as they see fit. The same allocation procedure is required if a taxpayer has more than one job. In no event should the same allowance be claimed more than once at the same time. It is permissible to declare *fewer* allowances than the taxpayer is entitled to in order to increase the amount of withholding. Doing so, however, does not affect the number of exemptions allowable on the employee's income tax return. Also, provision is made to permit an employee to have the employer withhold a certain dollar amount in addition to the required amount. This additional dollar amount can be arbitrary or calculated in accordance with a worksheet and tables on page 3 of Form W–4.

EXAMPLE 35

H, who earns $15,000, is married to W, who earns $25,000. They have three dependent children and will claim the standard deduction. Together they should be entitled to five allowances [2 (for personal exemptions) + 3 (for dependency exemptions)]. The special withholding allowance is not available, since both spouses earn more than $2,500. If H were the spouse first employed and his Form W–4 reflects five allowances, W's Form W–4 should claim none. They could, however, reallocate their allowances between them as long as the total claimed does not exceed five. □

EXAMPLE 36

Assume the same facts as in Example 35, except that W is not employed. H, however, has a full-time job (from which he has wages of $30,000) and a part-time job (from which he earns $5,000). If H's Form W–4 filed with his full-time employer reflects five allowances, he should claim none as to the part-time job. In this case, the special withholding allowance is not available, since H has two jobs at the same time and his wages from his second job are more than $2,500. □

The period of service for which an employee is paid is known as the *payroll period*. Daily, weekly, biweekly, semimonthly, and monthly periods are the most common arrangements. If an employee has no regular payroll period, he or she is considered to be paid on a daily basis.

Once the allowances are known (as reflected on Form W–4) and the payroll period determined, the amount to be withheld for Federal income taxes can be computed. The computation usually is made through the use of the wage-bracket tables or by the percentage method.

Wage-bracket tables are available for daily, weekly, biweekly, semimonthly, and monthly payroll periods as to single (including heads of household) and married taxpayers. An extract of the tables dealing with married persons on a monthly payroll period is reproduced in Figure 13–3.

The table in Figure 13–3 is for the period after December 1988. The use of withholding tables is illustrated in Example 37.

FIGURE 13–3 Withholding Table

MARRIED Persons–MONTHLY Payroll Period
(For Wages Paid After December 1988)

And the wages are–		And the number of withholding allowances claimed is–										
At least	But less than	0	1	2	3	4	5	6	7	8	9	10
		The amount of income tax to be withheld shall be–										
$2,640	$2,680	$359	$334	$309	$284	$259	$234	$209	$184	$159	$134	$109
2,680	2,720	365	340	315	290	265	240	215	190	165	140	115
2,720	2,760	371	346	321	296	271	246	221	196	171	146	121
2,760	2,800	377	352	327	302	277	252	227	202	177	152	127
2,800	2,840	383	358	333	308	283	258	233	208	183	158	133
2,840	2,880	391	364	339	314	289	264	239	214	189	164	139
2,880	2,920	402	370	345	320	295	270	245	220	195	170	145
2,920	2,960	413	376	351	326	301	276	251	226	201	176	151
2,960	3,000	424	382	357	332	307	282	257	232	207	182	157
3,000	3,040	436	389	363	338	313	288	263	238	213	188	163
3,040	3,080	447	400	369	344	319	294	269	244	219	194	169
3,080	3,120	458	411	375	350	325	300	275	250	225	200	175
3,120	3,160	469	423	381	356	331	306	281	256	231	206	181
3,160	3,200	480	434	387	362	337	312	287	262	237	212	187
3,200	3,240	492	445	398	368	343	318	293	268	243	218	193
3,240	3,280	503	456	410	374	349	324	299	274	249	224	199
3,280	3,320	514	467	421	380	355	330	305	280	255	230	205
3,320	3,360	525	479	432	386	361	336	311	286	261	236	211
3,360	3,400	536	490	443	396	367	342	317	292	267	242	217
3,400	3,440	548	501	454	408	373	348	323	298	273	248	223
3,440	3,480	559	512	466	419	379	354	329	304	279	254	229
3,480	3,520	570	523	477	430	385	360	335	310	285	260	235
3,520	3,560	581	535	488	441	395	366	341	316	291	266	241
3,560	3,600	592	546	499	452	406	372	347	322	297	272	247
3,600	3,640	604	557	510	464	417	378	353	328	303	278	253
3,640	3,680	615	568	522	475	428	384	359	334	309	284	259
3,680	3,720	626	579	533	486	439	393	365	340	315	290	265
3,720	3,760	637	591	544	497	451	404	371	346	321	296	271
3,760	3,800	648	602	555	508	462	415	377	352	327	302	277
3,800	3,840	660	613	566	520	473	426	383	358	333	308	283
3,840	3,880	671	624	578	531	484	438	391	364	339	314	289
3,880	3,920	682	635	589	542	495	449	402	370	345	320	295
3,920	3,960	693	647	600	553	507	460	413	376	351	326	301
3,960	4,000	704	658	611	564	518	471	424	382	357	332	307
4,000	4,040	716	669	622	576	529	482	436	389	363	338	313
4,040	4,080	727	680	634	587	540	494	447	400	369	344	319
4,080	4,120	738	691	645	598	551	505	458	411	375	350	325
4,120	4,160	749	703	656	609	563	516	469	423	381	356	331
4,160	4,200	760	714	667	620	574	527	480	434	387	362	337
4,200	4,240	772	725	678	632	585	538	492	445	398	368	343
4,240	4,280	783	736	690	643	596	550	503	456	410	374	349
4,280	4,320	794	747	701	654	607	561	514	467	421	380	355
4,320	4,360	805	759	712	665	619	572	525	479	432	386	361
4,360	4,400	816	770	723	676	630	583	536	490	443	396	367
4,400	4,440	828	781	734	688	641	594	548	501	454	408	373
4,440	4,480	839	792	746	699	652	606	559	512	466	419	379
4,480	4,520	850	803	757	710	663	617	570	523	477	430	385
4,520	4,560	861	815	768	721	675	628	581	535	488	441	395
4,560	4,600	872	826	779	732	686	639	592	546	499	452	406
4,600	4,640	884	837	790	744	697	650	604	557	510	464	417
4,640	4,680	895	848	802	755	708	662	615	568	522	475	428
4,680	4,720	906	859	813	766	719	673	626	579	533	486	439
4,720	4,760	917	871	824	777	731	684	637	591	544	497	451
4,760	4,800	928	882	835	788	742	695	648	602	555	508	462
4,800	4,840	940	893	846	800	753	706	660	613	566	520	473
4,840	4,880	951	904	858	811	764	718	671	624	578	531	484
4,880	4,920	962	915	869	822	775	729	682	635	589	542	495
4,920	4,960	973	927	880	833	787	740	693	647	600	553	507
4,960	5,000	984	938	891	844	798	751	704	658	611	564	518
5,000	5,040	996	949	902	856	809	762	716	669	622	576	529
5,040	5,080	1,007	960	914	867	820	774	727	680	634	587	540
5,080	5,120	1,018	971	925	878	831	785	738	691	645	598	551
5,120	5,160	1,029	983	936	889	843	796	749	703	656	609	563
5,160	5,200	1,040	994	947	900	854	807	760	714	667	620	574
5,200	5,240	1,052	1,005	958	912	865	818	772	725	678	632	585

$5,240 and over   Use Table 4(b) for a **MARRIED person** on page 22. Also see the instructions on page 20.

EXAMPLE 37   T is married and has three dependent children and no additional allowances for itemized deductions, adjustments to income, or child care credit. In his job with X Corporation, T earns $2,770 in May 1989. Presuming T's wife is not employed and all available allowances are claimed on Form W–4, X Corporation should withhold $227 a month from T's wages.

This amount is taken from the six allowances column in the wage bracket of $2,760–$2,800. The six allowances result from personal exemptions (two) plus the special withholding allowance (one) plus dependency exemptions (three). □

Although the wage-bracket table requires few, if any, calculations, the percentage method is equally acceptable and sometimes is used by employers. Its use may be necessary for payroll periods where no wage-bracket tables are available (quarterly, semiannual, and annual payroll periods) and where wages paid exceed the amount allowed for use of the wage-bracket tables. The percentage method is particularly useful when payroll computations are computerized. The use of this method, however, requires the use of a conversion chart based on one withholding allowance. That is, the amount of one allowance is equal to the exemption amount divided by the number of payroll periods in a year. For example, the amount of one allowance for a taxpayer who is paid weekly is $38.46 ($2,000/52 payroll periods).

Payroll Period	Amount of One Allowance
Daily	$ 7.69
Weekly	38.46
Biweekly	76.92
Semimonthly	83.33
Monthly	166.67
Quarterly	500.00
Semiannual	1,000.00
Annual	2,000.00

To use under the percentage method, proceed as follows:

Step 1. Multiply the amount of one allowance (as specified in the conversion chart) by the employee's total allowances (taken from Form W–4).

Step 2. Subtract the product reached in step 1 from the employee's wages. The remainder is called "amount of wages."

Step 3. Using the result derived in step 2, compute the income tax withholding under the proper percentage-method table.

The table used in applying the percentage method for those with monthly payroll periods is reproduced in Figure 13–4.

An illustration of the percentage method follows:

EXAMPLE 38

Assume the same facts as in Example 37, except that T's income tax withholding is determined using the percentage method.

Step 1. $166.67 (amount of one allowance for a monthly payroll period) × 6 (total allowances) = $1,000.02.

Step 2. $2,770 (monthly salary) − $1,000.02 (step 1) = $1,769.98 (amount of wages).

Step 3. Referring to Figure 13–4: 15% $\times$ $1,502.98 (excess of step 2 amount over $267) = $225.45. □

By way of comparison, the wage-bracket tables yield an amount for income tax withholding of $227 (refer to Example 37) while the percentage method results in $225.45 (refer to Example 38). The difference is explained by the fact that the wage-bracket table amounts are derived by computing the withholding on the median wage within each bracket.

Reporting and Payment Procedures. Proper handling of employment taxes and income tax withholdings requires considerable compliance effort on the part of the employer. Among the Federal forms that will have to be filed are the following:

Form Designation	Title
SS–4	Application for Employer Identification Number
W–2	Wage and Tax Statement
W–3	Transmittal of Income and Tax Statements
940	Employer's Annual Federal Unemployment Tax Return
941	Employer's Quarterly Federal Tax Return

Form SS–4 is the starting point, since it provides the employer with an identification number that must be used on all of the other forms filed with the IRS and the Social Security Administration. The number issued (usually in about 10 days after the filing of Form SS–4) consists of nine digits and is hyphenated between the second and third digits (e.g., 72–1987316).

Form W–2 furnishes essential information to employees concerning wages paid, FICA, and income tax withholdings. The multiple copies of Form W–2 are distributed as follows: Copy A is sent by the employer to the Social Security Administration office that services the area, Copy B goes to the employee and is to be attached to his or her income tax return, Copy C also

---

FIGURE 13–4   Table for Percentage Method of Withholding [35]

TABLE 4—If the Payroll Period With Respect to an Employee Is Monthly

(a) SINGLE person—including head of household:			(b) MARRIED person—		
If the amount of wages (after subtracting withholding allowances) is:	*The amount of income tax to be withheld shall be:*		*If the amount of wages (after subtracting withholding allowances) is:*	*The amount of income tax to be withheld shall be:*	
Not over $92 0			Not over $267 0		
Over—	*But not over—*	*of excess over—*	*Over—*	*But not over—*	*of excess over—*
$92	—$1,638 . . . .15%	—$92	$267	—$2,846 . . . .15%	—$267
$1,638	—$3,833 . . . $231.90 plus 28%	—$1,638	$2,846	—$6,504 . . . $386.85 plus 28%	—$2,846
$3,833	—$8,786 . . . $846.50 plus 33%	—$3,833	$6,504	—$16,010 . . . $1,411.09 plus 33%	—$6,504
$8,786 . . . . $2,480.99 plus 28%		—$8,786	$16,010 . . . . $4,548.07 plus 28%		—$16,010

---

35. This table is for wages paid after December 1988.

goes to the employee for retention in personal records, and Copy D is kept by the employer as part of the usual payroll records. Extra copies of Form W–2 may have to be prepared for state and local use. An employee, for example, who lives in New York City, would require additional copies of Form W–2 for state and city income tax purposes. Form W–2 must be furnished to an employee not later than January 31 of the following year. If an employee leaves a place of employment before the end of the year, Form W–2 can be given to that employee at any time after employment ends. However, if the terminated employee asks for Form W–2, it must be given to him or her within 30 days after the request or the final wage payment, whichever is later.

Form W–3 must accompany the Copies A of Forms W–2 filed by the employer. Its basic purpose is to summarize and reconcile the amounts withheld for FICA and income taxes from *all* employees.

Form 940 constitutes the employer's annual accounting for FUTA purposes. It must be filed on or before January 31 of the following year and must be accompanied by the payment of any undeposited FUTA due the Federal government.

Regardless of whether or not monthly deposits are required (see below) each employer must settle his or her employment taxes every quarter. To do this, Form 941 must be filed on or before the last day of the month following the end of the quarter. Due dates for the filing of Form 941 for each quarter are as follows:

Quarter	End of Quarter	Due Date
January, February, March	March 31	April 30
April, May, June	June 30	July 31
July, August, September	September 30	October 31
October, November, December	December 31	January 31

Form 941 lists the wages subject to FICA, provides for the computation of the tax, and summarizes the income tax withholdings. Any balance due over prior deposits must be remitted with the form.

The frequency with which an employer must make payments to the IRS depends on the monthly total of three items: the income tax withheld from the employees, the FICA taxes withheld from the employees, and the employer's share of FICA. When the cumulative total of these three items is $500 or more but less than $3,000 for any month, the amount generally must be deposited within 15 days after the close of the month.[36]

EXAMPLE 39   E, an employer, had total taxes (amounts withheld plus employer's portion of FICA) of $450 on wages paid in October and $550 on wages paid in November. No deposit is required for October, but the total amount of $1,000 ($450 + $550) must be deposited by December 15. ☐

---

36. Circular E, *Employer's Tax Guide,* IRS Publication 15 (Rev. Jan. 89), p. 9.

The payment should be sent or taken to any commercial bank qualified as a depository for Federal taxes or to the nearest Federal Reserve bank. The mailing date on which the deposit is received by the depository or Federal Reserve bank determines the timeliness of the deposit. A deposit under $20,000 received by the bank after the due date will be considered timely if the employer can show that it was mailed on or before the second day before the due date. Since proof of mailing should be available, certified or registered mail should be used. To be considered timely, a deposit of $20,000 or more must be received by the depository by the due date.

As soon as the cumulative total of FICA and income taxes withheld is $3,000 or more in any eighth-monthly period, the employer must deposit the taxes within three banking days after the close of the period. An *eighth-monthly period* is the period that ends on the 3rd, 7th, 11th, 15th, 19th, 22nd, 25th, and the last day of each month. The monthly or eighth-monthly period deposit, when required, must be accompanied by a coupon from Form 8109 (Federal Tax Deposit Coupon Book) with the type of tax and the tax period appropriately entered. When the employer files Form 941, he or she will claim the deposit payments as a reduction of tax due.

EXAMPLE 40

T, an employer, withheld $3,500 in taxes from wages paid from the first through the third of May. T must deposit these taxes within three banking days after May 3. □

For those employers who are not required to make deposits, the payment of payroll taxes and income tax withholdings is postponed to the time of filing Form 941 if the balance due is less than $500. If the balance due is $500 or more, the entire amount must be deposited on or before the fifteenth day of the first month following the close of the quarter.

Withholding on Pensions

Withholding is required for pension payments unless the taxpayer affirmatively *elects* to have *no* tax withheld. Part of the reason for this provision is to ease the burden on the retiree of filing and paying quarterly estimated tax payments.

The amount of the withholding depends on whether the payments are periodic (e.g., an annuity) or nonperiodic (e.g., a lump-sum distribution). If periodic, the payments are treated as wages and the regular payroll withholding procedures apply to the taxable portion. The payee informs the payor concerning his or her marital status and exemptions by filing Form W–4P, Withholding Certificate for Pension or Annuity Payments. A payee who does not furnish any information or furnishes inadequate information concerning his or her tax status will be treated by the payor as being married with three withholding allowances. A 10 percent rate of withholding generally applies to pension distributions that are not periodic unless the payment is a qualified total distribution. Optional withholding tables apply for total distributions from a qualified pension, profit sharing, stock bonus, or annuity plan.[37] Re-

37. Alternative Tax Withholding Methods and Tables, IRS Publication 493 (Rev. Jan. 89).

cipients may elect to have no income tax withheld on pension or annuity payments. However, such taxpayers may be required to make estimated tax payments on the amounts received.

Backup Withholding

Some types of payments made to individuals by banks or businesses are now subject to backup withholding under certain conditions. Backup withholding is designed to insure that income tax is collected on interest and other payments reported on a Form 1099. If backup withholding applies, the payor must withhold 20 percent of the amount paid. Backup withholding applies in the following situations:

- The taxpayer does not give the business or bank his or her identification number in the required manner.

- The taxpayer is required, but fails, to certify that he or she is not subject to backup withholding.

- The Internal Revenue Service notifies the bank or business that the taxpayer gave an incorrect identification number.

- The Internal Revenue Service notifies the bank or business to start withholding on the interest or dividends or other payments it pays the taxpayer because the taxpayer has not reported such items on his or her tax return.

Taxpayers who give false information to avoid backup withholding are subject to a $500 civil penalty. Conviction on a criminal penalty subjects the taxpayer to a fine of up to $1,000, imprisonment up to one year, or both.

Procedures Applicable to Self-Employed Persons

Although the discussion to follow largely centers on self-employed taxpayers, some of the procedures may be applicable to employed persons. In many cases, for example, employed persons may be required to pay estimated tax if they have income other than wages that is not subject to withholding. An employee may have a second trade or business conducted in a self-employment capacity. Depending on the circumstances, the second job may require the payment of a self-employment tax. Taxpayers whose income consists primarily of rentals, dividends, or interest (this list is not all-inclusive) may be required to pay estimated tax.

Estimated Tax for Individuals.   *Estimated tax* is the amount of tax (including alternative minimum tax and self-employment tax) an individual expects to owe for the year after subtracting tax credits and income tax withheld. Any individual who has estimated tax for the year of $500 or more *and* whose withholding does not equal or exceed the required annual payment (discussed below) must make quarterly payments.[38] Otherwise, a penalty may be assessed. No quarterly payments are required (no penalty will apply on an underpayment) if the taxpayer's estimated tax is under $500. No penalty will apply if the taxpayer had no tax liability for the preceding tax year *and* the

---

38.   § 6654(c)(1).

preceding tax year was a taxable year of 12 months *and* the taxpayer was a citizen or resident for the entire preceding tax year. In this regard, having no tax liability is not the same as having no additional tax to pay.

The required annual payment must first be computed. This is the *smallest* of the following amounts:

- Ninety percent of the tax shown on the current year's return.

- One hundred percent of the tax shown on the preceding year's return (such return must cover the full 12 months of the preceding year).

- Ninety percent of the tax determined by placing taxable income, alternative minimum taxable income, and adjusted self-employment income on an annualized basis.

One-fourth of this required annual payment is due on April 15, June 15, and September 15 of the tax year and January 15 of the following year. If no estimated tax was due on April 15 of the tax year but, because of a change in income, estimated tax was due after April 15, one-half of the estimated tax is due on June 15, one-fourth on September 15, and one-fourth on January 15. Likewise, if estimated tax becomes due after June 15, three-fourths must be paid on September 15 and one-fourth on January 15. And if estimated tax first becomes due after September 15, 100 percent of the estimated tax is due on January 15. If the taxpayer files his or her return on or before January 31 following the tax year and pays the full amount shown as payable, no penalty applies with respect to any underpaid fourth-quarter required installment.

An equal part of withholding is deemed paid on each due date. Thus, the quarterly installment of the required annual payment reduced by the applicable withholding is the estimated tax to be paid. Payments are to be accompanied by the payment voucher for the appropriate date from Form 1040–ES. A Form 1040–ES is generally mailed to each taxpayer who paid estimated tax during the prior year and to those who should have paid estimated tax in the prior year. First-time filers obtain the form from the IRS.

Married taxpayers may make joint estimated tax payments even though a joint income tax return is not subsequently filed. In such event, the estimated tax payments may be applied against the separate return liability of the spouses as they see fit. If a husband and wife cannot agree on a division of the estimated tax payments, the Regulations provide that the payments are to be allocated in proportion to the tax liability on the separate returns.

Penalty on Underpayments.   A nondeductible penalty is imposed on the amount of underpayment of estimated tax. The rate for this penalty is the same as the rate for underpayments of tax and is adjusted quarterly to reflect changes in the average prime rate. A special rule applicable only to underpayments of estimated tax extends the first-quarter rate to the first 15 days in April.[39]

An *underpayment* occurs when any installment (the sum of estimated tax paid and income tax withheld) is less than 25 percent of the required annual payment. The penalty is applied to the amount of the underpayment for the period of the underpayment.[40]

---

39. § 6621(b)(2)(B).   40. § 6654(b)(2).

EXAMPLE 41   T made the following payments of estimated tax during 1989 and had no income tax withheld:

April 15, 1989	$1,400
June 15, 1989	2,300
September 15, 1989	1,500
January 15, 1990	1,800

T's actual tax for 1989 is $8,000 and tax in 1988 was $10,000. Therefore, each installment should have been at least $1,800 [($8,000 × 90%) × 25%]. Of the payment on June 15, $400 will be credited to the unpaid balance of the first quarterly installment due on April 15,[41] thereby effectively stopping the underpayment penalty for the first quarterly period. Of the remaining $1,900 payment on June 15, $100 is credited to the September 15 payment, resulting in this third quarterly payment being $200 short. Then $200 of the January 15 payment is credited to the September 15 shortfall, ending the period of underpayment for that portion due. The January 15, 1990, installment is now underpaid by $200, and a penalty will apply from January 15, 1990, to April 15, 1990 (unless paid sooner). T's underpayments for the periods of underpayment are as follows:

1st installment due:	$400 from April 15–June 15
2nd installment due:	paid in full
3rd installment due:	$200 from September 15, 1989–January 15, 1990
4th installment due:	$200 from January 15–April 15, 1990

□

If a possible underpayment of estimated tax is indicated, Form 2210 should be filed to compute the penalty due or to justify that no penalty applies.

Supplemental Medicare Premium.   Elderly and certain disabled individuals are required to pay additional tax (a surtax) if the following conditions exist:

• Are eligible for more than 6 months of the tax year for Medicare Part A benefits.

• Have income tax liability of $150 or more.

This supplemental premium is determined by dividing the individual's adjusted income tax liability for the year by $150, then multiplying that amount by the premium rate. (Adjusted income tax is total tax reduced by self-employment tax, if any.) The supplemental premium is limited to a ceil-

---

41. Payments are credited to unpaid installments in the order in which such installments are re-   quired to be paid. § 6654(b)(3).

ing amount each year. The premium rates and ceiling amounts are set for 5 years as follows:

Tax years beginning in	Supplemental premium rate	Ceiling amount
1989	$22.50	$ 800
1990	37.50	850
1991	39.00	900
1992	40.50	950
1993	42.00	1,050

After 1993, the premium rate will be indexed.

If the taxpayer is married and filing a joint return and both spouses are Medicare eligible for more than 6 full months in 1989, the ceiling amount is $1,600. If only one spouse meets the eligibility requirements, the adjusted tax is halved for purposes of determining the supplemental premium for the eligible spouse.

To simplify the calculation, the IRS issues a Premium Table based on $50 increments of income tax. The supplemental premium is not added to the taxpayer's regular tax for purposes of allowing tax credits or for determining alternative minimum tax. Also, the supplemental premium is not deductible as a medical expense for those who itemize deductions.

For the tax year 1989, the supplemental premium must be paid when the 1989 return is filed (due April 15, 1990). Beginning with the tax year 1990, the supplemental premium must be included in each estimated tax payment.

Self-Employment Tax. The tax on self-employment income is levied to provide Social Security benefits for self-employed individuals. Individuals with net earnings from self-employment of $400 or more are subject to the self-employment tax.[42] For 1989, the self-employment tax is 15.02 percent on self-employment income up to $48,000. However, the self-employed taxpayer is allowed a credit of 2 percent of self-employment income up to $48,000, resulting in a net rate of 13.02 percent.

The self-employment tax rate increases to 15.30 percent for 1990 and later years. Beginning in 1990, there will be no credit, but self-employed taxpayers will be allowed an income tax deduction for one-half the amount of self-employment taxes paid.

If an individual also receives wages in 1989 subject to FICA tax, the $48,000 ceiling amount upon which the self-employment tax is computed is reduced. Thus, no self-employment tax is due if a self-employed individual also receives FICA wages of $48,000.

EXAMPLE 42

In 1989, T had $33,000 of net earnings from the conduct of a bookkeeping service (trade or business activity). He also received wages as an employee amounting to $18,000 during the year. T's taxable self-employment

42. § 6017.

income for the year is $30,000 [$48,000 (maximum subject to FICA) − $18,000 (wages)]. □

Net earnings from self-employment include gross income from a trade or business less allowable trade or business deductions, the distributive share of any partnership income or loss derived from a trade or business activity, and net income from the rendering of personal services as an independent contractor. Gain or loss from the disposition of property (including involuntary conversions) is excluded from the computation of self-employment income unless the property involved is inventory.

The IRS has ruled that director's fees, which are paid to a nonemployee, are self-employment income because a director is considered to be engaged in a trade or business activity.[43] Such director's fees are deemed subject to self-employment tax when earned regardless of when actually paid.

EXAMPLE 43

P, a former treasurer, is retired from X Company but is retained as a corporate director. She performs these duties in 1989 under a deferred arrangement whereby she will be paid $12,000 in 1991, at which time she will be 70 years old. (At age 70, a retired individual's Social Security benefits are not reduced by earned income.) In 1989, the year earned, the $12,000 of director's fees will be subject to self-employment tax and may also reduce any Social Security benefits she may be receiving. For income tax purposes, however, the $12,000 of director's fees will be subject to tax in 1991, the year received. □

EXAMPLE 44

Assume the same facts as in Example 43, except that P is not retired. In addition to the director's fees, she is paid a salary of $70,000 in her capacity as treasurer of the company. Because her salary exceeds the wage base ($48,000) for FICA tax purposes, the director's fees are not subject to self-employment tax. The deferred arrangement works to P's advantage in this case. The director's fees are subject to income tax in 1991 when received, but they will not reduce her Social Security benefits in that year because she will be age 70. □

An employee who performs services on a part-time basis as an independent contractor or an employee who is engaged in a separate trade or business activity may be subject to the self-employment tax.

TAX PLANNING CONSIDERATIONS

Research Activities Credit

Recall that the incremental research activities credit applies only to the extent that the qualifying expenditures for the current year exceed the average for a base period. The base period usually is the past three years.

---

43. Rev.Rul. 57–246, 1957–1 C.B. 388, and Rev.Rul. 68–595, 1968–2 C.B. 378.

Because research activities often are discretionary for the taxpayer, proper timing of the expenditures may generate a credit that otherwise might not materialize. The key would be to concentrate the routine expenditures (either past or present) into one given year where the credit is desired.

EXAMPLE 45

T, a calendar year taxpayer, operates a sole proprietorship that manufactures sun screen lotion that is sold under her own label in a three-state area. In the past, T has routinely spent $100,000 a year on research devoted to the development of new products. In 1989, T decides to anticipate the research she will conduct in 1990 in developing a new line of skin care products and, as a result, spends $200,000 instead of the usual $100,000. Presuming the average base period expenses to be $100,000, T has generated a credit of $20,000 for 1989, determined as follows:

Expenses in 1989	$200,000
Minus average base period expenses	100,000
Incremental expenses	$100,000
Credit rate	20%
Amount of credit	$ 20,000

Several observations must be made regarding Example 45. First, T has just barely avoided the base period adjustment required when the incremental expenses are unduly large (see Example 16). Second, T's actions are particularly wise if the credit is not extended by Congress beyond 1989. As the law currently stands, the same procedure would not work in 1990 because the credit will have expired. Third, 50 percent of the credit ($10,000) will not be available for amortization, expensing, or capitalization. Thus, only $190,000 of the $200,000 spent will qualify. In retrospect, had the same procedure been carried out in 1988, no 50 percent adjustment would have been necessary.

Foreign Tax Credit

A U.S. citizen or resident working abroad (commonly referred to as an *expatriate*) may elect to take either a foreign tax credit or the foreign earned income exclusion. In cases where the income tax of a foreign country is higher than the U.S. income tax, the credit choice usually is preferable. If, however, the reverse is true, election of the foreign earned income exclusion probably reduces the overall tax burden.

Unfortunately, the choice between the credit and the earned income exclusion is not without some limitations. The election of the foreign earned income exclusion, once made, can be revoked for a later year. However, once revoked, the earned income exclusion will not be available for a period of five years unless the IRS consents to an earlier date. This will create a dilemma for expatriates whose job assignments over several years shift between low and high bracket countries.

EXAMPLE 46

In 1987, T, a calendar year taxpayer, is sent by his employer to Saudi Arabia (a low-tax country). For 1987, therefore, T elects the foreign earned income exclusion. In 1988, T's employer transfers him to France (a high-tax country). Accordingly, T revokes the foreign earned income exclusion for 1988 and chooses instead to use the foreign tax credit. If T is transferred back to Saudi Arabia (or any other low-tax country) within five years, he no longer has access to the foreign earned income exclusion. □

Credit for Child and Dependent Care Expenses

A taxpayer might incur employment-related expenses that also qualify as medical expenses (e.g., a nurse is hired to provide in-the-home care for an ill and incapacitated dependent parent). Such expenses may be either deducted as medical expenses (subject to the 7.5 percent limitation) or utilized in determining the child and dependent care credit. If the choice is to take the dependent care credit and the employment-related expenses exceed the limitation ($2,400, $4,800, or earned income, as the case may be), the excess may be considered a medical expense. If, however, the choice is made to deduct such qualified employment-related expenses as medical expenses, any portion that is not deductible because of the 7.5 percent limitation may not be used in computing the child and dependent care credit.

EXAMPLE 47

T, a single individual, has the following tax position for tax year 1989:

Adjusted gross income		$30,000
Itemized deductions *from* adjusted gross income—		
Other than medical expenses	$2,500	
Medical expenses	6,000	$ 8,500

All of T's medical expenses were incurred to provide nursing care for her disabled father while she was working. The father lives with T and qualifies as T's dependent. □

What should T do in this situation? One approach would be to use $2,400 of the nursing care expenses to obtain the maximum dependent care credit allowed of $480 (20% × $2,400). The balance of these expenses should be claimed as medical expenses. After a reduction of 7.5 percent of adjusted gross income, this would produce a medical expense deduction of $1,350 [$3,600 (remaining medical expenses) − (7.5% × $30,000)].

Another approach would be to claim the full $6,000 as a medical expense and forgo the dependent care credit. After the 7.5 percent adjustment of $2,250 (7.5% × $30,000), a deduction of $3,750 remains.

The choice, then, is between a credit of $480 plus a deduction of $1,350 and a credit of $0 plus a deduction of $3,750. Which is better, of course, depends upon the relative tax savings involved.

Adjustment to Increase Withholding

The penalty for underpayment of estimated tax by individuals is computed for each quarter of the tax year. A taxpayer can play *catch-up* to a certain extent. Each quarterly payment is credited to the unpaid portion of any previous required installment. Thus, the penalty stops on that portion of the underpayment for the previous quarter. Since income tax withheld is assumed to have been paid evenly throughout the year and is allocated equally among the four installments in computing any penalty, a taxpayer who would otherwise be subject to a penalty for underpayment should increase withholdings late in the year. This can be done by changing the number of allowances claimed on Form W–4 or by special arrangement with the employer to increase the amount withheld.

A similar way to avoid (or reduce) a penalty for underpayment is to have the employer continue Social Security withholding beyond the base amount.

EXAMPLE 48

T, a calendar year taxpayer, earns $72,000 from her job. In late August of 1989, T realizes that she will be subject to a penalty for underpayment of estimated tax due to income from outside sources. Consequently, she instructs her employer to continue FICA withholdings for the rest of 1989. If this is done, an extra $24,000 [$72,000 (annual salary) − $48,000 (base amount for 1989)] will be subject to 7.51% (the employee's FICA rate for 1989). Thus, T generates an additional $1,802.40 (7.51% × 24,000) that will be deemed withheld ratably during 1989. □

Adjustments to Avoid Overwithholding

Publication 505, Tax Withholding and Estimated Tax, contains worksheets that taxpayers may use to take advantage of special provisions for avoiding overwithholding. Extra exemptions for withholding purposes are allowed if the taxpayer has unusually large itemized deductions, deductions *for* adjusted gross income, or tax credits. Net losses from Schedules C, D, E, and F may be considered in computing the number of extra withholding exemptions. Net operating loss carryovers may also be considered in the computation. A taxpayer who is entitled to extra withholding exemptions for any of these reasons should file a new Form W–4, Employee's Withholding Allowance Certificate, with his or her employer.

PROBLEM MATERIALS

Discussion Questions

1. Would an individual taxpayer receive greater benefit from deducting an expenditure or from taking a credit equal to 25% of the expenditure?

2. If investment credit property is prematurely disposed of or ceases to be qualified property, how is the tax liability affected in the year of the disposition?

3. The regular investment tax credit was repealed for property placed in service after December 31, 1985. Is there any way a taxpayer can benefit from unused ITC related to investment tax credit property placed in service on or before that date? Explain.

4. The investment tax credit is still allowed for transition property. What requirements must be met for property to qualify as transition property?

5. Discuss the basis reduction provisions relating to pre-1986 property on which the investment tax credit was taken. How do these provisions differ from the basis reduction provisions applicable to transition property?

6. R, a calendar year business taxpayer, had unexpired investment tax credits (carryovers) at the beginning of 1986. Early in December, R billed customers so that they could pay by year-end. In addition to accelerating income in this manner, R postponed business deductions. These procedures generated enough tax liability so that R was able to absorb all of the carryovers. Disregarding any effect of lower tax rates in 1987 and later years, did R act wisely?

7. At the beginning of 1987, T, a calendar year taxpayer, had unused regular investment tax credits of $20,000. Based on tax liability, T was able to use $4,125 of these credits in 1987.

    a. Explain how these carryforwards were handled as they passed through the 1987 tax year.

    b. How much was carried forward to 1988?

    c. If T was able to use $5,000 of these credits in 1988, how much was carried forward to 1989?

8. V is considering the purchase and renovation of an old building. He has heard about the tax credit for rehabilitation expenditures but does not know the specific rules applicable to the credit. He has asked you to explain the most important details to him. What will you tell V?

9. On August 1, 1989, Z hired C, who is certified as a member of a targeted group for purposes of the jobs credit. C was paid $900 per month. He worked for eight months. How much is Z's jobs credit for wages paid to C during 1989? For 1990?

10. What credit provisions in the tax law were enacted to encourage technological development in the United States?

11. The research activities credit has two components: the incremental research credit and the basic research credit. What types of expenditures are eligible for the incremental research credit? What types of expenditures are eligible for the basic research credit?

12. Which of the following taxpayers are eligible for the earned income credit?

a. H and W are married and have a dependent child. H earned $7,600 and W earned $7,000 during 1989.

b. A, who is divorced from B, maintains a household for her son J. Under a pre-1985 divorce agreement, J is claimed as a dependent by B, his father, who contributes $2,000 toward his support. A earns $14,000 and has no other income.

c. P, an unmarried taxpayer, earns $12,000 in 1989 and has no other income. He claims a dependency exemption for his aunt under a multiple support agreement.

13. Individuals who receive substantial Social Security benefits are usually not eligible for the tax credit for the elderly because these benefits effectively eliminate the base upon which the credit is computed. True or false? Explain.

14. Discuss the requirements for obtaining a tax credit for child and dependent care expenses.

15. Some employers sponsor a child care assistance program. If an unmarried taxpayer pays $6,000 for the care of one child under the age of 13 and receives $4,000 in reimbursement from a qualified program, how is the child care credit affected? What if the $6,000 covers the care of three children under age 13?

16. Do child care payments to relatives qualify for the child care credit?

17. J and K are married and have a dependent child eight years of age. J earned $15,000 during 1989. K, a full-time student for the entire year, was not employed. J and K believe they are not entitled to the credit for child and dependent care because K was not employed. Is this correct? Explain your answer.

18. Discuss the underlying rationale for the enactment of the following tax credits:

a. Low-income housing credit.

b. Foreign tax credit.

c. Tax credit for the elderly or disabled.

d. Earned income credit.

e. Credit for child and dependent care expenses.

f. Jobs credit.

19. What is a refundable credit? Give examples. What is a nonrefundable credit? Give examples.

20. In determining the maximum amount of general business credit allowed an individual taxpayer for a tax year, net income tax, tentative minimum tax, and net regular tax liability are important concepts.

a. Define each term.

b. Using these terms, state the general business credit limitation for an individual taxpayer for 1989.

21. The FIFO method is applied to general business credit carryovers, carrybacks, and the utilization of credits generated during a particular

year. What effect does the FIFO method have on the utilization of general business credit carryovers?

22. Discuss the order in which credits are offset against the tax liability. Why is the order in which credits are utilized important?

23. Under what circumstances will the special withholding allowance be allowed for purposes of determining income tax withholding?

24. Although T is entitled to four allowances, she claimed just one on her Form W–4.

    a.   Why would T claim fewer allowances than she is entitled to?

    b.   Is this procedure permissible?

    c.   Will this affect the number of exemptions T can claim on her Federal income tax return?

25. At a social function you hear a guest comment: "I quit paying Social Security taxes in March of this year." Interpret this statement.

26. If the employer is not required to withhold income taxes on an item of income paid to an employee, does this mean that the item is nontaxable? Explain.

27. If the computation of income tax withholding for employers is to be done manually, the use of the wage-bracket tables is to be preferred over the percentage method. Why?

28. When comparing the use of the wage-bracket tables and the percentage method on the same wage, the amount of the income tax to be withheld may not be the same.

    a.   Is there an explanation for this variation in results? Elaborate.

    b.   Make up a hypothetical salary between $2,760 and $2,800 where both approaches will yield the same amount of withholding (refer to Figures 13–3 and 13–4 in this chapter).

29. T, an employee of Z Corporation, has an annual salary of $80,000. Frequently, T turns down offers for outside consulting on the grounds that he does not wish to incur a self-employment tax. Does T's reasoning make sense? Please explain.

30. E, an employee of R Corporation, has an annual salary of $25,000. Until 1989, E's withholdings for income tax purposes always approximated her income tax liability (either a slight refund resulted or a slight amount of tax was due). In early 1989, however, E inherits $300,000 from an uncle. For tax year 1989, will E have a problem in terms of the estimated tax? Why or why not?

Problems

31. M, a calendar year taxpayer, entered into a written contract, binding on December 31, 1985, to purchase new industrial equipment. This property cost $150,000 and had a class life of 22 years. Compute M's tentative regular investment credit and determine the basis of the

equipment for purposes of cost recovery if the equipment is placed in service.

    a.   In 1986.

    b.   In 1987.

    c.   In 1989.

32. B claimed the investment tax credit on the following property acquired in 1985:

Asset	Recovery Period	Cost
Truck	3 years	$20,000
Machinery	5 years	80,000

    a.   Compute B's maximum tentative investment tax credit for 1985.

    b.   Assume B sells both assets in 1989 after holding them for four full years. What is the amount of investment tax credit B must recapture in 1989?

33. T acquired an office building that had originally been placed in service in 1930. The building cost $50,000, and T spent $60,000 to rehabilitate it. The building was placed in service on July 1, 1989. Compute T's credit for rehabilitation expenditures, basis in the building, and cost recovery allowance for 1989.

34. Z Corporation acquired an office building for $100,000 in 1989. The building originally had been placed in service in 1930. Z spent $50,000 for qualified rehabilitation expenditures. Compute Z's rehabilitation credit for 1989.

35. On August 1, 1984, R acquired and placed in service a pre–1936 office building. The cost was $250,000, of which $50,000 applied to the land. The building is 18–year real property. In order to keep tenants, R spent $140,000 renovating the building in 1989. The expenses were of the type that qualify for the rehabilitation credit. These improvements were placed in service on May 1.

    a.   Compute R's rehabilitation tax credit for 1989.

    b.   Determine cost recovery for the year.

    c.   What is R's basis in the property at the end of 1989?

36. X Company hired six handicapped individuals (qualifying X Company for the jobs credit) in 1989. Each of these individuals received wages of $7,000 during 1989.

    a.   Calculate the amount of the jobs credit for 1989.

    b.   Assume X Company paid total wages of $120,000 to its employees during the year. How much of this amount is deductible in 1989 if the jobs credit is elected?

37. On May 15, 1989, Y Corporation hired four individuals (A, B, C, and D), all of whom qualified Y Corporation for the jobs credit. A and B also were certified as qualified summer youth employees. D moved out of state in September, quitting his job after earning $4,000 in wages. A,

B, and C all continued as employees of Y Corporation. During 1989 C earned $6,500. A and B each earned $3,500 during their first 90 days of employment. Beginning on August 15, A and B were certified for participation in the company's cooperative education program. In this capacity, A earned $2,000 to December 31 and $2,500 to the end of school on May 15, 1990. B also earned an additional $2,000 to December 31, at which time he quit school and left the program. Compute Y Corporation's jobs credit, without regard to the tax liability ceiling limitation, for 1989. Also compute Y's deduction for wages paid to A, B, C, and D during 1989. Will Y receive any benefit in 1990?

38. In 1989, X Corporation hired two handicapped workers who qualify as targeted employees for purposes of the jobs credit. Each employee was paid $10,000 in 1989. Compute X's allowable jobs credit for 1989 with respect to these two employees.

39. P incurred research and experimentation expenses (not including expenditures for basic research) as follows:

1989	$100,000
1988	80,000
1987	60,000
1986	40,000

    a. Compute P's incremental research activities credit for 1989.

    b. Assume the same facts as above, except that P incurs $160,000 of research and experimentation expenses in 1989. Compute P's incremental research activities credit for 1989.

40. Which of the following individuals qualify for the earned income credit for 1989?

    a. T is single and has no dependents. His income consisted of $6,000 wages and taxable interest of $1,000. T's adjusted gross income is $7,000.

    b. T maintains a household for a dependent unmarried child and is eligible for head-of-household tax rates. Her income consisted of $7,000 salary and $500 taxable interest.

    c. T is married and files a joint return with his wife. T and his wife have no dependents. Their combined income consisted of $8,000 salary and $600 taxable interest. Adjusted gross income is $8,600.

41. T, a widower, lives in an apartment with his three minor children whom he supports. T earned $16,600 during 1989. He contributed $1,000 to an IRA and uses the standard deduction. Calculate the amount, if any, of T's earned income credit.

42. H, age 67, and W, age 66, are married retirees who received the following income and retirement benefits during 1989:

Fully taxable pension from H's former employer	$10,000
Dividends and interest	2,000
Social Security benefits	4,000
	$16,000

Assume H and W file a joint return and have no deductions *for* adjusted gross income and do not itemize. Are they eligible for the tax credit for the elderly? If so, calculate the amount of the credit, assuming the credit is not limited by their tax liability.

43. H, age 67, and W, age 66, are married retirees who received the following income and retirement benefits during 1989:

Fully taxable pension from H's former employer	$ 5,000
Dividends and interest	8,000
Social Security benefits	1,750
	$14,750

   Assume H and W file a joint return, have no deductions *for* adjusted gross income, and do not itemize. Are they eligible for the tax credit for the elderly? If so, calculate the amount of the credit assuming their actual tax liability (before credits) is $390.

44. X, a U.S. citizen, had taxable income of $50,000 from sources within the United States and $10,000 of foreign income from investments in France. X paid a tax of $1,200 to the French government. X files a joint return with his wife. X and his wife have two minor children, use the standard deduction, and have no other income or deductions. Compute the net tax payable if X elects to take the foreign tax credit in 1989.

45. XYZ Corporation is a U.S. corporation that has foreign operations (a division) in England. XYZ had U.S. taxable income of $100,000, which included $50,000 from the foreign division. XYZ paid foreign taxes of $30,000. XYZ's U.S. tax liability was $22,250 before deducting any foreign tax credit. Compute the amount of XYZ Corporation's foreign tax credit for 1989.

46. H and W are married and have two dependent children under age 13. W worked full time and earned $27,000 during 1989 (and had no deductions *for* AGI) while her husband attended college on a full-time basis for the entire year. H and W incurred child care expenses of $4,000 during the year, filed a joint return, and used the standard deduction. Calculate the amount, if any, of their child care credit for 1989.

47. In 1989, W hired a domestic worker to enable her to work on a full-time basis. W made salary payments of $7,000 to the housekeeper during the year and earned $6,000 from her employer. W's husband earned $58,000 from his employer. W and her husband have two dependent children under age 13, elected the standard deduction, and filed a joint return. Compute the amount of child and dependent care credit, if any, for 1989.

48. H and W maintain a household for two minor children, age 10 and 14. H is employed on a full-time basis; W held a part-time job during the entire year. H's gross earned income was $30,000, and W earned $3,500. H and W incurred $7,000 of child care expenses. H and W file a joint return for 1989 and have itemized deductions of $6,000. Calculate the amount, if any, of the credit for child care expenses.

49. F spends $500,000 to build a qualified low-income housing project in 1987. He financed the project partly from savings and partly from funds borrowed from First National Bank. All units are rented to families that qualify on the basis of income. Compute F's low-income housing credit for all relevant years.

50. Assume the same facts as in Problem 49, except that the project was financed with the borrowed proceeds from tax-exempt government bonds. What is the total amount of the low-income housing credit that G will be able to claim?

51. B has a tentative general business credit of $110,000 for 1989. B's net regular tax liability before the general business credit is $125,000; tentative minimum tax is $100,000. Compute B's allowable general business credit for 1989.

52. In each of the following independent situations, determine the maximum withholding allowances permitted T (an employee) on Form W–4:

    a. T is single with no dependents.

    b. T is married to a nonemployed spouse, and they have no dependents.

    c. T is married to S, an employed spouse, and they have three dependent children. On the Form W–4 that she filed with the employer, S claimed zero allowances.

    d. Assume the same facts as in (c), except that T and S fully support T's mother, who lives with them. The mother (age 70 and blind) qualifies as their dependent. (Refer to chapter 3.)

    e. T is single with no dependents but works for two employers, one on a full-time basis and the other on a part-time basis. The Form W–4 filed with the first employer (the full-time job) reflects two withholding exemptions. The wages from each job exceed $2,500.

    f. Assume the same facts as in (e), except that T is married to a nonemployed spouse.

53. T is married to a nonemployed spouse and has four dependents. T is employed by Z Corporation and is paid a monthly salary of $3,000 ($36,000 per year). Using these facts, determine the amount to be withheld by Z Corporation for Federal income tax purposes under the wage-bracket tables and under the percentage method.

54. H and W are married and file a joint return for 1989. Both are eligible for Medicare for more than 6 months of the tax year.

    a. Determine their supplemental Medicare premium if their tax liability is $9,825.

    b. Determine their premium if their tax liability is $19,825.

55. During 1989, T, the owner of a store, had the following income and expenses:

Gross profit on sales	$36,000
Income from part-time job (subject to FICA)	14,000
Business expenses (related to store)	15,000
Fire loss on store building	1,200
Dividend income	200
Long-term capital gain on the sale of a stock investment	2,000

Compute T's self-employment tax.

Cumulative Problems

56. H and W, ages 38 and 36, are married and file a joint return. Their household includes S, their 10-year-old son, and F, who is H's 76-year-old father. F is very ill and has been confined to bed for most of the year. He has no income of his own and is fully supported by H and W. H and W had the following income and expenses during 1989:

H's wages	$ 9,800
W's salary	17,200
Interest from First National Bank	250
Unemployment compensation received by H, who was laid off for five months during the year	4,000
Dividends received on January 3, 1990; the corporation mailed the check on December 31, 1989	250
Amounts paid to N, H's niece, for household help and caring for S and F while H and W were working	3,000
Unreimbursed travel expenses (including meals of $200) incurred by W in connection with her job	750
Total itemized deductions (not including any potential deductions mentioned elsewhere in the problem)	4,600
Federal income taxes withheld by their employers	2,300

Compute net tax payable or refund due for H and W for 1989. Suggested software (if available): *WEST–TAX Planner.*

57. H and W are married and file a joint return. They have two dependent children, S and D, ages 12 and 16, respectively. H is a self-employed businessman (sole proprietor of an unincorporated business), and W is a corporate executive. H has the following income and expenses from his business:

Gross income	$280,000
Business expenses (including accelerated depreciation in excess of straight-line on real property of $26,000)	166,000

Records related to W's employment provide the following information:

Salary	$130,000
Unreimbursed travel expenses (including $200 of meals)	1,000
Unreimbursed entertainment expenses	600

Other pertinent information relating to 1989 is as follows:

Proceeds from sale of stock acquired on July 15, 1989 (cost of $10,000), sold on August 1	$ 8,000
Proceeds from sale of stock acquired in 1976 (cost of $6,000)	4,800
Wages paid to full-time domestic worker for housekeeping and child supervision	10,000
Dividends ($6,000) and interest ($2,000) received	8,000
Total itemized deductions (not including any potential deductions above)	26,900
Federal income tax withheld	27,000
Estimated payments on Federal income tax	34,000

Compute the lowest net tax payable or highest refund due for H and W for 1989. Suggested software (if available): *WEST–TAX Planner.*

 58. Joseph Miller (Social Security number 268–71–5670) lives at 328 Indian Creek, Freeland, MI 48462. He is a sole proprietor owner of a barber shop. Joseph is not married. His unmarried son Harry, age 22, lives with him. Harry is not in college and works full-time. Except for providing living quarters, Joseph does not otherwise support Harry. Harry claims his own personal exemption on his income tax return.

For 1989, Joseph provides the following information concerning the operations of Joseph's Barber Shop, located at 8925 State Street.

Gross income	$29,352
Advertising	860
Operating supplies	1,950
Rent paid	4,800
Utilities	2,400
Magazines and newspapers	320
Depreciation	1,060
Salaries	10,000
Employer's share of FICA tax	750

Joseph has an unused regular investment tax credit of $1,000 from 1985, the year he began this business. He had no Federal income tax liability in each of the intervening years.

The following amounts of income and expenditures relate to the 1989 tax year:

- Dividends received from a Canadian corporation, $1,700, after the company withheld $300 for Canadian income tax.

- Medical expenses (Joseph does not have hospitalization insurance), $400.

- Real estate taxes on personal residence, $2,042.

- Interest on personal residence, $3,660.

- Charitable contributions, $400.

- Contribution to his IRA, $1,500.

Based on the self-employment tax he paid in 1988, Joseph made estimated tax payments of $1,110 in 1989. Determine the amount of tax due (or refund) for 1989. Suggested software (if available): *WEST–TAX Planner* or *BNA Individual Income Tax Spreadsheet.*

59. James R. Jordan lives at 2322 Branch Road, Mesa, AZ 85202. He is a tax accountant with Mesa Manufacturing Company. He also writes computer software programs for tax practitioners and has a part-time tax practice. James, age 35, is single and has no dependents. His Social Security number is 111–35–2222. He wants to contribute one dollar to the Presidential Election Campaign Fund.

During 1988, James earned a salary of $45,680 from his employer. He received interest of $890 from Home Federal Savings and Loan and $435 from Home State Bank. He received dividends of $620 from Acme Corporation, $470 from Jason Corporation, and $360 from General Corporation.

James received a $1,600 income tax refund from the state of Arizona on May 12, 1988. On his 1987 Federal income tax return, he reported total itemized deductions of $6,700, which included $2,000 of state income tax withheld by his employer.

Fees earned from his part-time tax practice in 1988 totaled $4,200. He paid $500 to have the tax returns processed by a computerized tax return service.

On February 1, 1988, James bought 500 shares of Acme Corporation common stock for $17.60 a share. On July 16, James sold the stock for $15 a share.

James bought a used pickup truck for $3,000 on June 5, 1988. He purchased the truck from his brother-in-law, who was unemployed and was in need of cash. On November 2, 1988, he sold the truck to a friend for $3,400.

On January 2, 1976, James acquired 100 shares of Jason Corporation common stock for $30 a share. He sold the stock on December 19, 1988, for $75 a share.

During 1988, James received royalties of $15,000 on a software program he had written. James incurred the following expenditures in connection with his software writing activities:

Cost of microcomputer (100% business use)	$ 8,000
Cost of printer (100% business use)	2,000
Supplies	650
Fee paid to computer consultant	3,500

James elected to expense the maximum portion of the cost of the microcomputer and printer allowed under the provisions of § 179.

Although his employer suggested that James attend a convention on current developments in corporate taxation, James was not reimbursed for the travel expenses of $1,360 he incurred in attending the convention. The $1,360 included $200 for the cost of meals.

On December 15, 1988, James opened an Individual Retirement Account, in which he deposited $2,000. He is covered by Mesa Manufacturing Company's pension plan.

During 1988, James paid $300 for prescription medicines and $2,875 in doctor bills, hospital bills, and medical insurance premiums. His employer withheld state income tax of $1,954. James paid real property taxes of $1,766 on his home. Interest on his home mortgage was $3,845, and interest to credit card companies was $320. James contributed $20 each week to his church and $10 each week to the United Way. Professional dues and subscriptions totaled $350.

James's employer withheld Federal income taxes of $9,672 during 1988. James paid estimated taxes of $1,600. What is the amount of James Jordan's net tax payable or refund due for 1988? If James has a tax refund due, he wants to have it credited toward his 1989 income tax. If you use tax forms for your solution, you will need Forms 1040, 2106, and 4562 and Schedules A, B, C, D, and SE. Suggested software (if available): *WEST–TAX Preparer* for tax return solutions, *WEST–TAX Planner* or *BNA Individual Income Tax Spreadsheet* if tax return solutions are not desired.

Research Problems

Research Problem 1   T is a CPA employed by an international accounting firm. In 1984, the accounting firm asked T to transfer to its Paris office. As part of the inducement to get T to accept the transfer, the accounting firm agreed to reimburse him for all expenses incurred in the move. The firm also agreed to pay all of T's moving expenses on his eventual return to the United States. Reimbursement of moving expenses for the return move was not contingent on T's continued employment by the firm. In 1989, T returned to the United States and was assigned to the firm's New York office. T properly included the reimbursement in gross income in 1989. In computing his foreign tax credit, T treated the reimbursement as income earned from personal services performed outside the United States. The IRS treated the income as earned from services performed within the United States and reduced T's foreign tax credit. Should T contest the IRS treatment of the moving expense reimbursement?

Research Problem 2   In 1989 T, who is single, paid $1,500 in child care expenses for the care of her son, age 10. T lives in a state that reimburses eligible parents for child care expenses. T was reimbursed by the state agency for $1,200 of the child care expenses incurred in 1989. T properly excluded this reimbursement from gross income on her 1989 tax return, on which she claimed a credit for child care expenses based on the $1,500 expenditure. The IRS disallowed the child care credit for $1,200 of the expenses, allowing a credit only for the $300 not reimbursed by the state agency. T has asked your advice as to whether she should challenge this action by the IRS. What advice will you give her?

Research Problem 3   P was hired as an air traffic controller at a major airport in 1983. The FAA did not require either flight training or pilot experience as a condition of P's employment. P was provided with classroom and on-the-job training by the FAA. In 1985, P received her journeyman's rating from the FAA. This rating provided her with job security as an air traffic controller.

P's duties included (a) providing flight data to pilots, (b) managing aircraft on the ground from arrival to terminal or from the terminal to departure, (c) issuing commuting clearance orders and related information to pilots, and (d) clearing landings and take-offs.

In late 1985, P purchased a used, single-engine airplane. On her 1985 Federal income tax return, she deducted over $4,000 of expenses on the plane (including depreciation) as education expenses. In addition, she claimed an investment tax credit of approximately $1,600 on the plane. The IRS denied the deductions and the ITC related to the plane P acquired. Was the IRS correct in denying these tax benefits?

Partial list of research aids:
§ 162(a)
Reg. § 1.162–5

Research Problem 4   From 1978 through 1982, T was an assistant professor at State University. In January of 1980, she signed a contract with X Publishing Company to co-author the fifth edition of a textbook entitled *Textiles*. She completed the task in 1981, and the text was published shortly thereafter. During each of the next five years, T received royalties of approximately $4,500 each year from X Publishing Company.

Until her venture with X Publishing Company, T had never engaged in commercial authorship. At no time during the royalty period was T under any obligation to continue her authorship activities. Must T pay self-employment tax on the royalties she received? Explain.

Partial list of research aids:
Comm. v. Groetzinger, 87–1 USTC ¶ 9191, 59 AFTR2d 87–532, 107 S.Ct. 980 (USSC, 1987).

5

PROPERTY TRANSACTIONS

Part 5 presents the tax treatment of sales, exchanges and other dispositions of property. Included are the determination of the realized gain or loss, recognized gain or loss, and the classification of the recognized gain or loss as capital or ordinary. The topic of basis is evaluated both in terms of its effect on the calculation of the gain or loss and in terms of the determination of the basis of any contemporaneous or related subsequent acquisitions of property.

14

PROPERTY TRANSACTIONS: DETERMINATION OF GAIN OR LOSS AND BASIS CONSIDERATIONS

OBJECTIVES

Explain the computation of realized gain or loss on property dispositions.
Define the terms "amount realized" and "adjusted basis."
Distinguish between realized and recognized gain or loss.
Discuss the recovery of capital doctrine.
Explain how basis is determined for various methods of asset acquisition.
Present various loss disallowance provisions.
Identify tax planning opportunities related to selected property transactions.

OUTLINE

This chapter and the following three chapters are concerned with the income tax consequences of property transactions (the sale or other disposition of property). The following questions are to be considered with respect to the sale or other disposition of property:

- Is there a realized gain or loss?
- If so, is the gain or loss recognized?
- If the gain or loss is recognized, is it ordinary or capital?
- What is the basis of replacement property, if any, that is acquired?

Chapters 14 and 15 are concerned with the determination of realized and recognized gain or loss and the basis of property. Chapters 16 and 17 are concerned with the classification of the recognized gain or loss as ordinary or capital.

DETERMINATION OF GAIN OR LOSS

Realized Gain or Loss

Realized gain or loss is measured by the difference between the amount realized from the sale or other disposition of property and the property's adjusted basis on the date of disposition. If the amount realized exceeds the property's adjusted basis, the result is a realized gain. Conversely, if the property's adjusted basis exceeds the amount realized, the result is a realized loss.[1]

EXAMPLE 1

T sells X Corporation stock with an adjusted basis of $3,000 for $5,000. T's realized gain is $2,000. If T had sold the stock for $2,000, he would have had a $1,000 realized loss. ☐

Sale or Other Disposition.   The term *sale or other disposition* is defined broadly in the tax law and includes virtually any disposition of property. Thus, transactions such as trade-ins, casualties, condemnations, thefts, and bond retirements are treated as dispositions of property. The most common disposition of property arises from a sale or exchange.[2] The key factor in determining whether a disposition has taken place usually is whether an identifiable event has occurred [3] as opposed to a mere fluctuation in the value of the property.[4]

---

1. § 1001(a) and Reg. § 1.1001–1(a).
2. Certain transactions are treated as deemed sales or exchanges. For example, a taxpayer who makes a charitable contribution of property for which the associated mortgage exceeds the property's adjusted basis is deemed to have a sale or exchange to the extent of the excess (*Leo G. Ebben*, 45 TCM 1283, T.C.Memo. 1983–200). Likewise, if a donor makes a gift of property with the condition that the donee pay the gift

tax, the donor has realized gain to the extent the gift tax paid exceeds the donor's adjusted basis for the property [*Diedrich v. Comm.*, 82–1 USTC ¶9419, 50 AFTR2d 82–5054, 102 S.Ct. 2414 (USSC, 1982)].

3. Reg. § 1.1001–1(c)(1).

4. *Lynch v. Turrish*, 1 USTC ¶18, 3 AFTR 2986, 38 S.Ct. 537 (USSC, 1918).

EXAMPLE 2

T owns X Corporation stock that cost $3,000. The stock has appreciated in value by $2,000 since T purchased it. T has no realized gain, since mere fluctuation in value is not a disposition or identifiable event for tax purposes. Nor would T have a realized loss had the stock declined in value by $2,000. □

Amount Realized.   The *amount realized* from a sale or other disposition of property is the sum of any money received plus the fair market value of other property received. The amount realized also includes amounts representing real property taxes treated as imposed on the seller if such amounts are to be paid by the buyer.[5] The reason for including these taxes in the amount realized is that their payment by the purchaser is, in effect, an additional amount paid to the seller of the property.

The amount realized also includes any liability on the property disposed of, such as a mortgage debt, if the buyer assumes the mortgage or the property is sold subject to the mortgage.[6] The amount of such liability is included in the amount realized even if the debt is nonrecourse and the amount of the debt is greater than the fair market value of the mortgaged property.[7]

EXAMPLE 3

T sells property on which there is a mortgage of $20,000 to U for $50,000 cash. T's amount realized from the sale is $70,000 if the mortgage is assumed by U or if U takes the property subject to the mortgage. □

The *fair market value* of property received in a sale or other disposition has been defined by the courts as the price at which property will change hands between a willing seller and a willing buyer when neither is compelled to sell or buy.[8] Fair market value is determined by considering the relevant factors in each case.[9] An expert appraiser is often required to evaluate these factors in arriving at fair market value. When the fair market value of the property received cannot be determined, the value of the property surrendered may be used.[10]

In calculating the amount realized, selling expenses such as advertising, commissions, and legal fees relating to the disposition are deducted. The amount realized is the net amount received directly or indirectly by the taxpayer from the disposition of property regardless of whether it is in the form of cash.

Adjusted Basis.   The *adjusted basis* of property disposed of is the property's original basis adjusted to the date of disposition.[11] Original basis is the cost or other basis of the property on the date the property is acquired by the

---

5. § 1001(b) and Reg. § 1.1001-1(b). Refer to chapter 11 for a discussion of this subject.

6. *Crane v. Comm.*, 47-1 USTC ¶9217, 35 AFTR 776, 67 S.Ct. 1047 (USSC, 1947). Although a legal distinction exists between the direct assumption of a mortgage and taking property subject to a mortgage, the tax consequences in calculating the amount realized are the same.

7. *Tufts v. Comm.*, 83-1 USTC ¶9328, 51 AFTR2d 83-1132, 103 S.Ct. 1826 (USSC, 1983).

8. *Comm. v. Marshman*, 60-2 USTC ¶9484, 5 AFTR2d 1528, 279 F.2d 27 (CA-6, 1960).

9. *O'Malley v. Ames*, 52-1 USTC ¶9361, 42 AFTR 19, 197 F.2d 256 (CA-8, 1952).

10. *U.S. v. Davis*, 62-2 USTC ¶9509, 9 AFTR2d 1625, 82 S.Ct. 1190 (USSC, 1962).

11. § 1011(a) and Reg. § 1.1011-1.

taxpayer. *Capital additions* increase and *recoveries of capital* decrease the original basis so that on the date of disposition the adjusted basis reflects the unrecovered cost or other basis of the property.[12] Adjusted basis is determined as follows:

Cost (or other adjusted basis) on date of acquisition
+ Capital additions
− Capital recoveries
= Adjusted basis on date of disposition

Capital Additions. Capital additions include the cost of capital improvements and betterments made to the property by the taxpayer. These expenditures are distinguishable from expenditures for the ordinary repair and maintenance of the property that are neither capitalized nor added to the original basis (refer to chapter 6). The latter expenditures are deductible in the current taxable year if they are related to business or income-producing property. Amounts representing real property taxes treated as imposed on the seller but paid or assumed by the buyer are part of the cost of the property.[13] Any liability on property that is assumed by the buyer is also included in the buyer's original basis of the property. The same rule applies if property is acquired subject to a liability. Amortization of the discount on bonds increases the adjusted basis of the bonds.[14]

Capital Recoveries. The following are examples of capital recoveries:

1. *Depreciation and Cost Recovery Allowances.* The original basis of depreciable property is reduced by the annual depreciation charges (or cost recovery allowances) while the property is held by the taxpayer. The amount of depreciation that is subtracted from the original basis is the greater of the *allowed* or *allowable* depreciation on an annual basis.[15] In most circumstances, the allowed and allowable depreciation amounts are the same (refer to chapter 9).

2. *Investment Tax Credit.* For property placed in service after 1982 and before 1986, the taxpayer may be required to reduce the adjusted basis of the property by 50 percent of the available investment tax credit. Such reduction in the adjusted basis of the property is required unless the taxpayer has elected to take a reduced investment tax credit (refer to chapters 9 and 13).[16]

3. *Casualties and Thefts.* A casualty or theft may result in the reduction of the adjusted basis of property.[17] The adjusted basis is reduced by the amount of the deductible loss. In addition, the adjusted basis is reduced by the amount of insurance proceeds received. However, the receipt of insurance proceeds may result in a recognized gain rather than in a deductible loss. Such gain increases the adjusted basis of the property.[18]

12. § 1016(a) and Reg. § 1.1016–1.
13. Reg. §§ 1.1001–1(b)(2) and 1.1012–1(b). Refer to chapter 11 for a discussion of this subject.
14. §§ 1232(a)(2)(A) and 1232A(a) and (c)(5). See chapter 16 for a discussion of bond discount and the related amortization.
15. § 1016(a)(2) and Reg. § 1.1016–3(a)(1)(i). Basis is reduced for allowable depreciation only to the extent of any tax benefit that would result.
16. §§ 48(q)(1) and (4) and 1016(a)(22).
17. Refer to chapter 8 for the discussion of casualties and thefts.
18. Reg. § 1.1016–6(a).

EXAMPLE 4

An insured truck used in a trade or business is destroyed in an accident. The adjusted basis is $8,000, and the fair market value is $6,500. Insurance proceeds of $6,500 are received. The amount of the casualty loss is $1,500 ($6,500 insurance proceeds − $8,000 adjusted basis). The adjusted basis is reduced by the $1,500 casualty loss and the $6,500 of insurance proceeds received. □

EXAMPLE 5

An insured truck used in a trade or business is destroyed in an accident. The adjusted basis is $6,500, and the fair market value is $8,000. Insurance proceeds of $8,000 are received. The amount of the casualty gain is $1,500 ($8,000 insurance proceeds − $6,500 adjusted basis). The adjusted basis is increased by the $1,500 casualty gain and is reduced by the $8,000 of insurance proceeds received ($6,500 basis before casualty + $1,500 casualty gain − $8,000 insurance proceeds = $0 basis). □

4. *Certain Corporate Distributions.* A corporate distribution to a shareholder that is not taxable is treated as a return of capital, and it reduces the basis of the shareholder's stock in the corporation.[19] For example, if a corporation makes a cash distribution to its shareholders and has no earnings and profits, such distributions are treated as a return of capital. If the corporation does have earnings and profits but makes a distribution in excess of such earnings and profits, the excess distribution is treated as a return of capital. Once the basis of the stock is reduced to zero, the amount of any subsequent distributions is a capital gain if the stock is a capital asset.

EXAMPLE 6

U Corporation has accumulated earnings and profits of $140,000 at the beginning of 1989. For 1989, U Corporation generates current earnings and profits of $30,000. During 1989, U Corporation makes cash distributions to its only shareholder, T, in the amount of $200,000. T's basis for his U Corporation stock is $20,000. Of the $200,000 cash distributed to T, $170,000 is classified as dividend income (to the extent of current earnings and profits of $30,000 and beginning accumulated earnings and profits of $140,000). The next $20,000 is treated as a return of capital and reduces T's basis for his U Corporation stock to zero. The remaining $10,000 is a capital gain. □

5. *Amortizable Bond Premium.* The basis in a bond purchased at a premium is reduced by the amortizable portion of the bond premium.[20] Investors in taxable bonds may *elect* to amortize the bond premium, but the premium on tax-exempt bonds *must be* amortized.[21] The amount of the amortized premium on taxable bonds is permitted as an interest deduc-

---

19. § 1016(a)(4) and Reg. § 1.1016–5(a). See chapter 20 for further discussion of corporate distributions.

20. § 1016(a)(5) and Reg. § 1.1016–5(b). The accounting treatment of bond premium amortiza-

tion is the same as for tax purposes. The amortization results in a decrease in the bond investment account.

21. § 171(c).

tion. Therefore, the election produces the opportunity for an annual interest deduction to offset ordinary income in exchange for a larger capital gain or smaller capital loss on the disposition of the bond. No such interest deduction is permitted for tax-exempt bonds.

The amortization deduction is allowed for taxable bonds because the premium is viewed as a cost of earning the taxable interest from the bonds. The reason the basis of taxable bonds is reduced is that the amortization deduction is a recovery of the cost or basis of the bonds. The basis of tax-exempt bonds is reduced even though the amortization is not allowed as a deduction. No amortization deduction is permitted on tax-exempt bonds, since the interest income is exempt from tax and the amortization of the bond premium merely represents an adjustment of the effective amount of such income.

EXAMPLE 7

T purchases S Corporation taxable bonds with a face value of $100,000 for $110,000, thus paying a premium of $10,000. The annual interest rate is 7%, and the bonds mature 10 years from the date of purchase. The annual interest income is $7,000 (7% × $100,000). If T elects to amortize the bond premium, the $10,000 premium is deducted over the 10–year period. T's basis for the bonds is reduced each year by the amount of the amortization deduction. Note that if the bonds were tax-exempt, amortization of the bond premium and the basis adjustment would be mandatory. However, no deduction would be allowed for the amortization. ☐

Recognized Gain or Loss

Recognized gain is the amount of the realized gain included in the taxpayer's gross income.[22] A *recognized loss*, on the other hand, is the amount of a realized loss that is deductible for tax purposes.[23] As a general rule, the entire amount of a realized gain or loss is recognized.[24]

Concept Summary 14–1 summarizes the realized gain or loss and recognized gain or loss concepts.

Nonrecognition of Gain or Loss

In certain cases, a realized gain or loss is not recognized upon the sale or other disposition of property. One of the exceptions to the recognition of gain or loss involves nontaxable exchanges, which are covered in chapter 15. Additional exceptions include losses realized upon the sale, exchange, or condemnation of personal use assets (as opposed to business or income-producing property) and gains realized upon the sale of a residence by taxpayers 55 years of age or older (see chapter 15). In addition, realized losses from the sale or exchange of business or income-producing property between certain related parties are not recognized.[25]

Sale, Exchange, or Condemnation of Personal Use Assets.   A realized loss from the sale, exchange, or condemnation of personal use assets (e.g., a

22. § 61(a)(3) and Reg. § 1.61–6(a).
23. § 165(a) and Reg. § 1.165–1(a).
24. § 1001(c) and Reg. § 1.1002–1(a).
25. § 267(a)(1).

personal residence or an automobile not used at all for business or income-producing purposes) is not recognized for tax purposes. An exception exists for casualty or theft losses from personal use assets (see chapter 8). In contrast, any gain realized from the sale or other disposition of personal use assets is, generally, fully taxable. The following examples illustrate the tax consequences of the sale of personal use assets.

EXAMPLE 8   T sells an automobile, which is held exclusively for personal use, for $6,000. The adjusted basis of the automobile is $5,000. T has a realized and recognized gain of $1,000. □

EXAMPLE 9   T sells the automobile in Example 8 for $4,000. T has a realized loss of $1,000, but the loss is not recognized. □

CONCEPT SUMMARY 14–1

Recognized Gain or Loss

Recovery of Capital Doctrine

Doctrine Defined.   The *recovery of capital doctrine* pervades all the tax rules relating to property transactions and is very significant with respect to these transactions. The doctrine derives its roots from the very essence of the income tax—a tax on income. Therefore, as a general rule, a taxpayer is entitled to recover the cost or other original basis of property acquired and is not taxed on that amount.

The cost or other original basis of depreciable property is recovered through annual depreciation deductions. The basis is reduced as the cost is recovered over the period the property is held. Therefore, when property is sold or otherwise disposed of, it is the adjusted basis (unrecovered cost or other basis) that is compared to the amount realized from the disposition to determine realized gain or loss.

Relationship of the Recovery of Capital Doctrine to the Concepts of Realization and Recognition.   If a sale or other disposition results in a realized gain, the taxpayer has recovered more than the adjusted basis of the property. Conversely, if a sale or other disposition results in a realized loss, the taxpayer has recovered less than the adjusted basis.

The general rules for the relationship between the recovery of capital doctrine and the realized and recognized gain and loss concepts are summarized as follows:

Rule 1.   A realized gain that is *never recognized* results in the *permanent recovery* of more than the taxpayer's cost or other basis for tax purposes. For example, all or a portion of the realized gain on the sale of a personal residence by taxpayers 55 years of age or older can be excluded from gross income under § 121.

Rule 2.   A realized gain on which *recognition is postponed* results in the *temporary recovery* of more than the taxpayer's cost or other basis for tax purposes. For example, an exchange of like-kind property under § 1031, an involuntary conversion under § 1033, or a replacement of a personal residence under § 1034 are all eligible for postponement treatment.

Rule 3.   A realized loss that is *never recognized* results in the *permanent recovery* of less than the taxpayer's cost or other basis for tax purposes. For example, a loss on the sale of an automobile held for personal use is not deductible.

Rule 4.   A realized loss on which *recognition is postponed* results in the *temporary recovery* of less than the taxpayer's cost or other basis for tax purposes. For example, the realized loss on the exchange of like-kind property under § 1031 is postponed.

These rules are illustrated in discussions to follow in this and the next chapter.

BASIS CONSIDERATIONS

Determination of Cost Basis

The basis of property is generally the property's cost. Cost is the amount paid for the property in cash or other property.[26] This general rule follows logically from the recovery of capital doctrine; that is, the cost or other basis of property is to be recovered tax-free by the taxpayer.

A *bargain purchase* of property is an exception to the general rule for determining basis. A bargain purchase may result when an employer transfers property to an employee at less than the property's fair market value (as compensation for services) or when a corporation transfers property to a shareholder at less than the property's fair market value (a dividend). The basis of property acquired in a bargain purchase is the property's fair market value.[27] If the basis of the property were not increased by the bargain amount, the taxpayer would be taxed on this amount again at disposition.

---

26.   § 1012 and Reg. § 1.1012–1(a).   27.   Reg. §§ 1.61–2(d)(2)(i) and 1.301–1(j).

EXAMPLE 10   T buys a machine from her employer for $10,000 on December 30, 1989. The fair market value of the machine is $15,000. T must include the $5,000 difference between cost and the fair market value of the machine in gross income for the taxable year 1989. The bargain element represents additional compensation to T. T's basis for the machine is $15,000, the machine's fair market value. ☐

Identification Problems.   Cost identification problems are frequently encountered in securities transactions. For example, the Regulations require that the taxpayer adequately identify the particular stock that has been sold.[28] A problem arises when the taxpayer has purchased separate lots of stock on different dates or at different prices and cannot adequately identify the lot from which a particular sale takes place. In this case, the stock is presumed to come from the first lot or lots purchased (a FIFO presumption).[29] When securities are left in the custody of a broker, it may be necessary to provide specific instructions and receive written confirmation as to which securities are being sold.

EXAMPLE 11   T purchases 100 shares of S Corporation stock on July 1, 1987, for $5,000 ($50 a share) and another 100 shares of the same stock on July 1, 1988, for $6,000 ($60 a share). She sells 50 shares of the stock on January 2, 1989. The cost of the stock sold, assuming T cannot adequately identify the shares, is $50 a share, or $2,500. This is the cost T will compare to the amount realized in determining the gain or loss from the sale. ☐

Allocation Problems.   When a taxpayer acquires multiple assets in a lump-sum purchase, it is necessary to allocate the total cost among the individual assets.[30] Allocation is necessary because some of the assets acquired may be depreciable (e.g., buildings) and others not (e.g., land). In addition, only a portion of the assets acquired may be sold, or some of the assets may be capital or § 1231 assets that receive special tax treatment upon subsequent sale or other disposition. A lump-sum cost is allocated on the basis of the fair market values of the individual assets acquired.

EXAMPLE 12   T purchases a building and land for $800,000. Because of the depressed nature of the industry in which the seller was operating, T was able to negotiate a very favorable purchase price. Appraisals of the individual assets indicate that the fair market value of the building is $600,000 and that of the land is $400,000. T's basis for the building is $480,000 ($600,000/$1,000,000 × $800,000), and the basis for the land is $320,000 ($400,000/$1,000,000 × $800,000). ☐

If a business is purchased and *goodwill* is involved, a special allocation rule applies. Initially, the purchase price is assigned to the assets, excluding

---

28. Reg. § 1.1012–1(c)(1).   30. Reg. § 1.61–6(a).
29. *Kluger Associates, Inc.,* 69 T.C. 925 (1978).

goodwill, to the extent of the total fair market value of the assets. This assigned amount is then allocated among these assets on the basis of the fair market value of the individual assets acquired. Goodwill is then assigned the residual amount of the purchase price. The resultant allocation is applicable to both the buyer and the seller.[31]

EXAMPLE 13

T sells his business to P. T and P agree that the values of the individual assets are as follows:

Inventory	$ 50,000
Building	500,000
Land	200,000
Goodwill	150,000

Negotiations conducted by T and P result in a sales price of $1 million. The application of the residual method with respect to goodwill results in the following allocation of the $1 million purchase price:

Inventory	$ 50,000
Building	500,000
Land	200,000
Goodwill	250,000

The residual method requires that all of the excess of the purchase price over the fair market value of the assets ($1,000,000 − $900,000 = $100,000) be allocated to goodwill. Absent this requirement, the purchaser could allocate the excess pro rata to all of the assets, including goodwill, based on their respective fair market values. This would have resulted in only $166,667 [$150,000 + ($150,000 ÷ $900,000 × $100,000)] being assigned to goodwill. □

In the case of *nontaxable stock dividends*, the allocation depends upon whether the dividend is a common stock dividend on common stock or a preferred stock dividend on common stock. If the dividend is common on common, the cost of the original common shares is allocated to the total shares owned after the dividend.[32]

EXAMPLE 14

T owns 100 shares of S Corporation common stock for which he paid $1,100. He receives a 10% common stock dividend, giving him a new total of 110 shares. Before the stock dividend, T's basis was $11 per share

---

31. § 1060.
32. §§ 305(a) and 307(a). The holding period of the new shares includes the holding period of the

old shares. § 1223(5) and Reg. § 1.1223–1(e). See chapter 16 for a discussion of the importance of the holding period.

($1,100 divided by 100 shares). The basis of each share after the stock dividend is $10 ($1,100 divided by 110 shares). ☐

If the dividend is preferred stock on common, the cost of the original common shares is allocated between the common and preferred shares on the basis of their relative fair market values on the date of distribution.[33]

EXAMPLE 15

S owns 100 shares of X Corporation common stock for which she paid $1,000. She receives a stock dividend of 50 shares of preferred stock on her common stock. The fair market values on the date of distribution of the preferred stock dividend are $30 a share for common stock and $40 a share for preferred stock. Thus, the total fair market value is $3,000 ($30 × 100) for common stock and $2,000 ($40 × 50) for preferred stock. The basis of S's common stock after the dividend is $600, or $6 a share ($3,000/$5,000 × $1,000), and the basis of the preferred stock is $400, or $8 a share ($2,000/$5,000 × $1,000). ☐

In the case of *nontaxable stock rights*, the basis of the rights is zero unless the taxpayer elects or is required to allocate a portion of the cost of the stock to the rights. If the fair market value of the rights is 15 percent or more of the fair market value of the stock, the taxpayer is required to allocate. If the value of the rights is less than 15 percent of the value of the stock, the taxpayer may elect to allocate.[34] The result is that either the rights will have no basis or the cost of the stock on which the rights are received will be allocated between the stock and rights on the basis of their relative fair market values.

EXAMPLE 16

T receives nontaxable stock rights with a fair market value of $1,000. The fair market value of the stock on which the rights were received is $8,000 (cost $10,000). T does not elect to allocate. The basis of the rights is zero. If the rights are exercised, the basis of the new stock will be the exercise (subscription) price. ☐

EXAMPLE 17

Assume the same facts as in Example 16, except the fair market value of the rights is $3,000. T must allocate, because the value of the rights is 15% or more of the value of the stock ($3,000/$8,000 = 37.5%). The basis of the rights is $2,727 ($3,000/$11,000 × $10,000), and the basis of the stock is $7,273 ($8,000/$11,000 × $10,000). If the rights are exercised, the basis of the new stock will be the exercise (subscription) price plus the basis of the rights. If the rights are sold, gain or loss is recognized. This allocation rule applies only when the rights are exercised or sold. Therefore, if the rights are allowed to lapse (expire), the rights have no basis, and the basis of the original stock is the stock's cost, $10,000. ☐

The holding period of nontaxable stock rights includes the holding period of the stock on which the rights were distributed. However, if the rights are

---

33. Reg. § 1.307–1(a).   34. § 307(b).

exercised, the holding period of the newly acquired stock begins with the date the rights are exercised.[35] The significance of the holding period for capital assets is discussed in chapter 16.

Gift Basis

When a taxpayer receives property as a gift, there is no cost to the recipient. Thus, under the cost basis provision, the donee's basis would be zero. However, this would violate the statutory intent that gifts are not subject to the income tax. With a zero basis, a sale by the donee would result in all of the amount realized being treated as realized gain. Therefore, a basis is assigned to the property received depending on the date of the gift, the basis of the property to the donor, the amount of gift tax paid, and the fair market value of the property.[36]

Gifts Prior to 1921.   If property was acquired by gift before 1921, its basis for income tax purposes is its fair market value on the date of the gift.[37]

Gift Basis Rules if No Gift Tax Is Paid.   Property received by gift can be referred to as *dual basis* property; that is, the basis for gain and the basis for loss might not be the same amount. The present basis rules for gifts of property can be described as follows:

- If the donee subsequently disposes of gift property in a transaction that results in a gain, the basis to the donee is the same as the donor's adjusted basis.[38] The donee's basis in this case is referred to as the *gain basis*. Therefore, a *realized gain* results if the amount realized from the disposition exceeds the donee's gain basis.

EXAMPLE 18   T purchased stock in 1988 for $10,000. He gave the stock to his son, S, in 1989, when the fair market value was $15,000. Assuming no gift tax was paid on the transfer and the property is subsequently sold by S for $15,000, S's basis would be $10,000, and S would have a realized gain of $5,000. □

- If the donee subsequently disposes of gift property in a transaction that results in a loss, the basis to the donee is the lower of the donor's adjusted basis or fair market value on the date of the gift. The donee's basis in this case is referred to as the *loss basis*. Therefore, a *realized loss results* if the amount realized from the disposition is less than the donee's loss basis.

EXAMPLE 19   T purchased stock in 1988 for $10,000. T gave the stock to his son, S, in 1989, when the fair market value was $7,000. S later sold the stock for

---

35. § 1223(5) and Reg. §§ 1.1223–1(e) and (f).

36. § 102(a). See the Glossary of Tax Terms in Appendix C for a definition of the term "gift."

37. § 1015(c) and Reg. § 1.1015–3(a).

38. § 1015(a) and Reg. § 1.1015–1(a)(1). See Reg. § 1.1015–1(a)(3) for cases in which the facts necessary to determine the donor's adjusted basis are unknown. Refer to Example 24 for the effect on depreciation deductions by the donee.

$6,000. S's basis would be $7,000 (fair market value is less than donor's adjusted basis of $10,000), and the loss from the sale would be $1,000 ($6,000 amount realized − $7,000 basis). □

The amount of the loss basis will differ from the amount of the gain basis only if at the date of the gift the adjusted basis of the property exceeds the property's fair market value. Note that the loss basis rule prevents the donee from receiving a tax benefit from the decline in value while the donor held the property. Therefore, in Example 19, S had a loss of only $1,000 rather than a loss of $4,000. The $3,000 difference represents the decline in value while T held the property. It is perhaps ironic, however, that the gain basis rule may eventually result in the donee's being subject to income tax on the appreciation that occurs while the donor held the property, as illustrated in Example 18.

If the amount realized from sale or other disposition is between the basis for loss and the basis for gain, no gain or loss is realized.

EXAMPLE 20   Assume the same facts as in Example 19, except that S sold the stock for $8,000. The application of the gain basis rule produces a loss of $2,000 ($8,000 − $10,000). The application of the loss basis rule produces a gain of $1,000 ($8,000 − $7,000). Therefore, neither a gain nor a loss is recognized because the amount realized is between the gain basis and the loss basis. □

Adjustment for Gift Tax.   If gift taxes are paid by the donor, the donee's gain basis may exceed the adjusted basis of the property to the donor. This will occur only if the fair market value of the property at the date of the gift is greater than the donor's adjusted basis (the property has appreciated in value). The portion of the gift tax paid that is related to the appreciation is added to the donor's basis in calculating the donee's gain basis for the property. In this circumstance, the formula for calculating the donee's gain basis is as follows: [39]

$$\text{Donee's gain basis} = \text{Donor's adjusted basis} + \left(\frac{\text{Unrealized appreciation}}{\text{Fair market value at date of gift}} \times \text{Gift tax paid} \right)$$

EXAMPLE 21   F made a gift of stock to S in 1989, when the fair market value of the stock was $40,000. F had purchased the stock in 1978 for $10,000. Because the unrealized appreciation is $30,000 ($40,000 fair market value less $10,000 adjusted basis) and the fair market value is $40,000, three-fourths ($30,000/$40,000) of the gift tax paid is added to the basis of the property. If the gift tax is $4,000, S's basis in the property is $13,000 [$10,000 + $3,000 (¾ of the $4,000 gift tax)]. □

---

39. § 1015(d)(6).

EXAMPLE 22   F made a gift of stock to S in 1989, when the fair market value of the stock was $40,000. Gift tax of $4,000 was paid by F, who had purchased the stock in 1978 for $45,000. Because there is no unrealized appreciation at the date of the gift, none of the gift tax paid is added to the donor's basis in calculating the donee's gain basis. Therefore, the donee's gain basis is $45,000. □

For *gifts made before 1977*, the full amount of the gift tax paid is added to the donor's basis. However, the ceiling on this total is the fair market value of the property at the date of the gift. Thus, in Example 21, if the gift was made before 1977, the basis of the property would be $14,000 ($10,000 + $4,000). In Example 22, the basis would still be $45,000 ($45,000 + $0).

Holding Period.   The *holding period* for property acquired by gift begins on the date the property was acquired by the donor if the gain basis rule applies.[40] The holding period starts on the date of the gift if the loss basis rule applies.[41] The significance of the holding period for capital assets is discussed in chapter 16.

The following example summarizes the basis and holding period rules for gift property:

EXAMPLE 23   T acquires 100 shares of X Corporation stock on December 30, 1978, for $40,000. On January 3, 1989, when the stock has a fair market value of $38,000, T gives it to S. Gift tax of $4,000 is paid by the donor. There is no increase in basis for a portion of the gift tax paid because the property had not appreciated in value at the time of the gift. Therefore, S's gain basis is $40,000. S's basis for determining loss is $38,000 (fair market value) because the fair market value on the date of the gift is less than the donor's adjusted basis.

- If S sells the stock for $45,000, he has a recognized gain of $5,000. The holding period for determining whether the capital gain is short term or long term begins on December 30, 1978, the date the property was acquired by the donor.

- If S sells the stock for $36,000, he has a recognized loss of $2,000. The holding period for determining whether the capital loss is short term or long term begins on January 3, 1989, the date of the gift.

- If S sells the property for $39,000, there is no gain or loss, since the amount realized is less than the gain basis of $40,000 and more than the loss basis of $38,000. □

Basis for Depreciation.   The basis for depreciation on depreciable gift property is the donee's gain basis.[42] This rule is applicable even if the donee later sells the property at a loss and uses the loss basis rule in calculating the amount of the realized loss.

40. § 1223(2) and Reg. § 1.1223–1(b).
41. Rev.Rul. 59–86, 1959–1 C.B. 209.

42. §§ 1011 and 167(g) and Reg. §§ 1.1011–1 and 1.167(g)–1.

EXAMPLE 24	F gave a machine to D in 1989, when the adjusted basis was $32,000 (cost of $40,000 — accumulated depreciation of $8,000) and the fair market value was $26,000. No gift tax was paid. D's gain basis at the date of the gift is $32,000, and D's loss basis is $26,000. During 1989, D deducts depreciation (cost recovery) of $10,240 ($32,000 × 32%). Therefore, at the end of 1989, D's gain basis is $21,760 ($32,000 − $10,240), and D's loss basis is $15,760 ($26,000 − $10,240). ☐

Property Acquired from a Decedent

General Rules.   The basis of property acquired from a decedent is generally the property's fair market value at the date of death (referred to as the *primary valuation amount*).[43] The property's basis is the fair market value six months after the date of death if the executor or administrator of the estate *elects* the alternate valuation date for estate tax purposes. This amount is referred to as the *alternate valuation amount*. If an estate tax return does not have to be filed because the estate is below the threshold amount for taxability, the alternate valuation date and amount are not available. Even if an estate tax return is filed and the executor elects the alternate valuation date, the six months after death date is available only for property that the executor has not distributed before this date. Any property distributed or otherwise disposed of during this six-month period will have an adjusted basis equal to the fair market value on the date of distribution or other disposition.[44]

For inherited property, both unrealized appreciation and decline in value are taken into consideration in determining the basis of the property for income tax purposes. Contrast this with the carryover basis rules for property received by gift.

The alternate valuation date can be elected only if the election results in the reduction of both the value of the gross estate and the estate tax liability below the amounts they would have been if the primary valuation date had been used. Thus, the planning opportunity of increasing the basis of the property to the beneficiary for income tax purposes by electing the alternate valuation amount while not increasing the estate tax liability is negated.[45]

EXAMPLE 25	D inherited property from her father, who died in 1989. Her father's adjusted basis for the property at date of death was $35,000. The property's fair market value at date of death was $50,000. The alternate valuation date was not elected. D's basis for income tax purposes is $50,000. This is commonly referred to as a *stepped-up basis*. ☐

---

43. § 1014(a).

44. § 2032(a)(1) and Rev.Rul. 56–60, 1956–1 C.B. 443.

45. § 2032(c). For the estates of individuals dying before July 19, 1984, an election was available regardless of whether the gross estate was increased or decreased. Note that increasing the value of the gross estate did not result in a greater estate tax liability if the increase was offset with available estate tax deductions or credits.

EXAMPLE 26

Assume the same facts as in Example 25, except the property's fair market value at date of death was $20,000. D's basis for income tax purposes is $20,000. This is commonly referred to as a *stepped-down basis.* □

EXAMPLE 27

D inherited property from her father, who died in 1989. Her father's adjusted basis for the property at date of death was $35,000. The property's fair market value was $250,000 at date of death and was $260,000 six months after death. The alternate valuation date cannot be elected because the value of the gross estate has increased during the six-month period. D's basis for income tax purposes is $250,000. □

EXAMPLE 28

Assume the same facts as in Example 27, except the property's fair market value six months after death was $245,000. If the executor elects the alternate valuation date, D's basis for income tax purposes is $245,000.

□

EXAMPLE 29

Assume the same facts as in the previous example, except the property is distributed four months after the date of the decedent's death. At the distribution date, the property's fair market value is $247,500. Since the executor elected the alternate valuation date, D's basis for income tax purposes is $247,500. □

The Code contains a provision designed to eliminate a tax avoidance technique referred to as *deathbed gifts.* If the time period between the date of the gift of appreciated property and the date of the donee's death is not greater than one year, the usual basis rule (stepped-up basis) for inherited property will not apply. The adjusted basis of such property inherited by the donor or his or her spouse from the donee shall be the same as the decedent's adjusted basis for the property rather than the fair market value at the date of death or the alternate valuation date.[46]

EXAMPLE 30

N gives stock to his uncle, U, in 1989. N's basis for the stock is $1,000, and the fair market value is $9,000. No gift tax is paid. Eight months later, N inherits the stock from U. At the date of U's death, the fair market value of the stock is $12,000. N's adjusted basis for the stock is $1,000. □

Survivor's Share of Property.   Both the decedent's share and the survivor's share of *community property* have a basis equal to fair market value on the date of the decedent's death.[47] This result applies to the decedent's share of the community property because the property flows to the surviving spouse from the estate (fair market value basis for inherited property). Likewise, the surviving spouse's share of the community property is deemed to be acquired

---

46. § 1014(e).   47. § 1014(b)(6).

by bequest, devise, or inheritance from the decedent. Therefore, it will also have a basis equal to fair market value.

EXAMPLE 31

H and W reside in a community property state. H and W own community property (200 shares of XYZ stock) that was acquired in 1973 for $100,000. Assume that H dies in 1989, when the securities are valued at $300,000. One-half of the XYZ stock is included in H's estate. If W inherits H's share of the community property, the basis for determining gain or loss is:

> $300,000 [$150,000 (W's share of one-half of the community proper-ty) plus $150,000 ($\frac{1}{2} \times$ $300,000, the value of XYZ stock at date of death)] for the 200 shares of XYZ stock. □

In a *common law* state, only one-half of jointly held property of spouses (tenants by the entirety or joint tenants with rights of survivorship) is includible in the estate.[48] In such a case, no adjustment of the basis is permitted for the excluded property interest.

EXAMPLE 32

Assume the same facts as in the previous example, except that the property is jointly held by H and W who reside in a common law state. Also assume that H purchased the property and made a gift of one-half of the property when the stock was acquired, with no gift tax being paid. Only one-half of the XYZ stock is included in H's estate, and W's basis for determining gain or loss in the excluded half is not adjusted upward for the increase in value to date of death. Therefore, W's basis would be $200,000 ($50,000 + $150,000). □

Holding Period of Property Acquired from a Decedent. The holding peri-od of property acquired from a decedent is *deemed to be long term* (held for the required long-term holding period). This provision is applicable regardless of whether the property is disposed of at a gain or a loss.[49]

Disallowed Losses

Related Taxpayers. Section 267 provides that realized losses from sales or exchanges of property, directly or indirectly, between certain related parties are not recognized. This loss disallowance provision applies to several types of related-party transactions. The most common involve (1) members of a fami-ly and (2) transactions between an individual and a corporation in which the individual owns, directly or indirectly, more than 50 percent in value of the corporation's outstanding stock. Section 707 provides a similar loss disallow-ance provision if the related parties are a partner and a partnership in which the partner owns, directly or indirectly, more than 50 percent of the capital interests or profits interests in the partnership. The rules governing the rela-tionships covered by § 267 were discussed in chapter 6. See chapter 15 for the

---

48. § 2040(a).   49. § 1223(11).

discussion of the special rules under § 1041 for property transfers between spouses or incident to divorce.

If income-producing or business property is transferred to a related taxpayer and a loss is disallowed, the basis of such property to the recipient is the property's cost to the transferee. However, if a subsequent sale or other disposition of the property results in a realized gain, the amount of gain is reduced by the loss that was previously disallowed.[50] This *right of offset* is not applicable if the original sale involved the sale of a personal use asset (e.g., the sale of a personal residence between related taxpayers). Likewise, this right of offset is available only to the original transferee (the related-party buyer).

Example 33

F sells business property with an adjusted basis of $50,000 to his daughter, D, for its fair market value of $40,000.

- F's realized loss of $10,000 is not recognized.

- How much gain will D recognize if she sells the property for $52,000? D recognizes a $2,000 gain. Her realized gain is $12,000 ($52,000 less her basis of $40,000), but she can offset F's $10,000 loss against the gain.

- How much gain will D recognize if she sells the property for $48,000? D recognizes no gain or loss. Her realized gain is $8,000 ($48,000 less her basis of $40,000), but she can offset $8,000 of F's $10,000 loss against the gain. Note that F's loss can only offset D's gain. It cannot create a loss for D.

- How much loss will D recognize if she sells the property for $38,000? D recognizes a $2,000 loss, the same as her realized loss ($38,000 less $40,000 basis). F's loss does not increase D's loss. F's loss can be offset only against a gain. Since D had no gain, F's loss cannot be used and is never recognized. Of course, it is assumed in this example that the property is business or income producing to D. If not, D's $2,000 loss would be personal and would not be recognized. □

The loss disallowance rules are designed to achieve two objectives. First, the rules prevent a taxpayer from directly transferring an unrealized loss to a related taxpayer in a higher tax bracket who could receive a greater tax benefit from the recognition of the loss. Second, the rules eliminate a substantial administrative burden on the Internal Revenue Service in terms of the appropriateness of the selling price (fair market value or not). The loss disallowance rules are applicable even in those cases where the selling price is equal to fair market value and can be validated (e.g., listed stocks).

The holding period of the buyer for the property is not affected by the holding period of the seller; that is, the buyer's holding period includes only the period of time he or she has held the property.[51]

Wash Sales.   Section 1091 stipulates that in certain cases, a realized loss on the sale or exchange of stock or securities is not recognized. Specifically, if a taxpayer sells or exchanges stock or securities and within 30 days before or

---

50. § 267(d) and Reg. § 1.267(d)–1(a).

51. §§ 267(d) and 1223(2) and Reg. § 1.267(d)–1(c)
        (3).

after the date of such sale or exchange acquires substantially identical stock or securities, any loss realized from the sale or exchange is not recognized.[52] The term *acquire* means acquire by purchase or in a taxable exchange and includes an option to purchase substantially identical securities. *Substantially identical* means the same in all important particulars. Corporate bonds and preferred stock are normally not considered substantially identical to the corporation's common stock. However, if the bonds and preferred stock are convertible into common stock, they may be considered substantially identical under certain circumstances.[53] Attempts to avoid the application of the wash sales rules by having a related taxpayer repurchase the securities have been unsuccessful.[54] These wash sales provisions do not apply to gains.

Recognition of the loss is disallowed because the taxpayer is considered to be in substantially the same economic position after the sale and repurchase as before the sale and repurchase. However, this rule does not apply to taxpayers engaged in the business of buying and selling securities.[55] Investors, however, are not allowed to create losses through wash sales to offset income for tax purposes.

Realized loss that is not recognized is added to the basis of the substantially identical stock or securities whose acquisition resulted in the nonrecognition of loss.[56] In other words, the basis of the replacement stock or securities is increased by the amount of the unrecognized loss. If the loss were not added to the basis of the newly acquired stock or securities, the taxpayer would never recover the entire basis of the old stock or securities.

The basis of the new stock or securities includes the unrecovered portion of the basis of the formerly held stock or securities. Therefore, the holding period of the new stock or securities begins on the date of acquisition of the old stock or securities.[57]

EXAMPLE 34

T owns 100 shares of A Corporation stock (adjusted basis of $20,000), 50 shares of which she sells for $8,000. Ten days later, T purchases 50 shares of the same stock for $7,000. T's realized loss of $2,000 ($8,000 less $10,000 adjusted basis of 50 shares) is not recognized because it resulted from a wash sale. T's basis in the newly acquired stock is $9,000 ($7,000 purchase price plus $2,000 unrecognized loss from the wash sale). □

The taxpayer may acquire less than the number of shares sold in a wash sale. In this case, the loss from the sale is prorated between recognized and unrecognized loss on the basis of the ratio of the number of shares acquired to the number of shares sold.[58]

Tax Straddles. Before the enactment of § 1092, it was possible to use commodity tax straddles to shelter income through the recognition of losses and the deferral of unrealized gains. With only a six-month holding period requirement at that time, it was likely that the unrealized gain, when eventually realized, would be taxed as favorable long-term capital gain.[59]

52. § 1091(a) and Reg. §§ 1.1091–1(a) and (f).
53. Rev.Rul. 56–406, 1956–2 C.B. 523.
54. *McWilliams v. Comm.*, 47–1 USTC ¶9289, 35 AFTR 1184, 67 S.Ct. 1477 (USSC, 1947).
55. Reg. § 1.1091–1(a).
56. § 1091(d) and Reg. § 1.1091–2(a).
57. § 1223(4) and Reg. § 1.1223–1(d).
58. § 1091(b) and Reg. § 1.1091–1(c).
59. This was the position of the taxpayer and not necessarily that of the Internal Revenue Service. For example, see the position to the contrary taken in Rev.Rul. 77–185, 1977–1 C.B. 48.

Section 1092 was enacted to negate the beneficial results presented in the previous paragraph. However, in the interim period, subsequent legislation has repealed favorable tax treatment for long-term capital gains. Despite this, § 1092 is still needed to negate the beneficial straddle result of recognition of losses and the deferral of unrealized gains.

A *straddle* is defined as offsetting positions with respect to personal property (e.g., buy and sell orders in the same commodity or a sell order with physical possession of the commodity).[60] Although a fluctuation in the market price may leave the taxpayer's economic position unchanged, an unrealized loss occurs on one position and an unrealized gain on the other. The liquidation of the loss position by the taxpayer would produce realized loss (probably a short-term capital loss). The unrealized gain would not be realized until a subsequent taxable year when the taxpayer closed that position (probably resulting in long-term capital gain).

As a general rule, the recognition of any loss with respect to one or more positions is limited in any taxable year by § 1092. The amount of the recognized loss that is permitted is equal to the excess of the realized loss over any unrealized gain on offsetting positions to the loss position. Nonrecognized losses under this provision are treated as having occurred in the following taxable year and are subject to the deferral rule for that taxable year.[61]

EXAMPLE 35	T purchases two gold futures contracts, one to buy and the other to sell, for $10,000 each in November 1989. T's position is a straddle because he has offsetting positions. When the market fluctuates, one position shows a gain and the other a loss. Before the end of 1989, T liquidates one position and realizes a $1,000 loss. At the same time, he has an unrealized gain of $1,000 on the offsetting position, which he does not liquidate. T's recognized loss is limited to the excess of the realized loss over the unrealized gain with respect to the offsetting position. In this example, T has no recognized loss (realized loss of $1,000 less unrealized gain of $1,000). ☐

The straddle limitations apply to certain positions in stock and most stock options. The limitations also apply to stock that is part of a straddle for which at least one of the offsetting positions is stock of a corporation formed or availed of for the purpose of taking offsetting positions to those taken by any shareholder.

Conversion of Property from Personal Use to Business or Income-Producing Use

As discussed previously, losses from the sale of personal use assets are not recognized for tax purposes, but losses from the sale of business and income-producing assets are deductible. Can a taxpayer convert a personal use asset that has declined in value to business use and then sell the asset to recognize a business loss? The law prevents this by requiring that the *original basis for loss* on personal use assets converted to business or income-producing use is the lower of the property's adjusted basis or fair market value on the date of conversion.[62] The gain basis for converted property is the property's adjusted

---

60. § 1092(c).

61. §§ 1092(a)(1)(A) and (B).

62. Reg. § 1.165–9(b)(2).

basis on the date of conversion. The law is not concerned with gains on converted property because gains are recognized regardless of whether property is business, income producing, or personal use.

EXAMPLE 36

T's personal residence has an adjusted basis of $75,000 and a fair market value of $60,000. T converts the personal residence to rental property. His basis for loss is $60,000 (lower of $75,000 adjusted basis and fair market value of $60,000). The $15,000 decline in value is a personal loss and can never be recognized for tax purposes. T's basis for gain is $75,000. □

The basis for loss is also the basis for depreciating the converted property.[63] This is an exception to the general rule that provides that the basis for depreciation is the gain basis (e.g., property received by gift). This exception prevents the taxpayer from recovering a personal loss indirectly through depreciation of the higher original basis. After the property is converted, both its basis for loss and its basis for gain are adjusted for depreciation deductions from the date of conversion to the date of disposition. These rules apply only if a conversion from personal to business or income-producing use has actually occurred.

EXAMPLE 37

At a time when her personal residence (adjusted basis of $40,000) is worth $50,000, T converts one-half of it to rental use. The property is not ACRS recovery property. At this point, the estimated useful life of the residence is 20 years and there is no estimated salvage value. After renting the converted portion for five years, T sells the property for $44,000. All amounts relate only to the building; the land has been accounted for separately. T has a $2,000 realized gain from the sale of the personal use portion of the residence and a $7,000 realized gain from the sale of the rental portion. These gains are computed as follows:

	Personal Use	Rental
Original basis for gain and loss—adjusted basis on date of conversion (fair market value is greater than the adjusted basis)	$20,000	$20,000
Depreciation—five years	None	5,000
Adjusted basis—date of sale	$20,000	$15,000
Amount realized	22,000	22,000
Realized gain	$ 2,000	$ 7,000

□

---

63. Reg. § 1.167(g)–1.

As discussed in chapter 15, T may be able to defer recognition of part or all of the $2,000 gain from the sale of the personal use portion of the residence under § 1034. The $7,000 gain from the business portion is recognized.

EXAMPLE 38

Assume the same facts as in the previous example, except that the fair market value on the date of conversion is $30,000 and the sales proceeds are $16,000. T has a $12,000 realized loss from the sale of the personal use portion of the residence and a $3,250 realized loss from the sale of the rental portion. These losses are computed as follows:

	Personal Use	Rental
Original basis for loss—fair market value on date of conversion (fair market value is less than the adjusted basis)	*	$15,000
Depreciation—five years	None	3,750
Adjusted basis—date of sale	$20,000	$11,250
Amount realized	8,000	8,000
Realized loss	$12,000	$ 3,250

* Not applicable.

The $12,000 loss from the sale of the personal use portion of the residence is not recognized. The $3,250 loss from the business portion is recognized. □

Additional Complexities in Determining Realized Gain or Loss

Amount Realized. The calculation of the amount realized may appear to be one of the least complex areas associated with property transactions. However, because of the numerous positive and negative adjustments that may be required in calculating this amount, the calculation can be complex and confusing. In addition, the determination of the fair market value of the items received by the taxpayer can be a difficult task. The following example provides insight into various items that can have an impact on the amount realized.

EXAMPLE 39

T sells an office building and the associated land on October 1, 1989. Under the terms of the sales contract, T is to receive $600,000 in cash. The purchaser is to assume T's mortgage of $300,000 on the property. To enable the purchaser to obtain adequate financing to pay the $600,000, T is to pay the $15,000 in points charged by the lender. The broker's commission on the sale is $45,000. The purchaser agrees to pay the property taxes for the entire year of $12,000. The amount realized by T is calculated as follows:

Selling price		
Cash	$600,000	
Mortgage assumed by purchaser	300,000	
Seller's property taxes paid by purchaser ($12,000 × 9/12)	9,000	$909,000
Less		
Broker's commission	$ 45,000	
Points paid by seller	15,000	60,000
Amount realized		$849,000

□

Adjusted Basis.   Three types of items tend to complicate the determination of adjusted basis. First, the applicable tax provisions for calculating the adjusted basis are dependent on how the property was acquired (e.g., purchase, taxable exchange, nontaxable exchange, gift, inheritance). Second, if the asset is subject to depreciation, cost recovery, or amortization, adjustments must be made to the basis during the time period the asset is held by the taxpayer. Upon disposition of the asset, the taxpayer's records for both of these items may be deficient. For example, the donee does not know the amount of the donor's basis or the amount of gift tax paid by the donor, or the taxpayer does not know how much depreciation he or she has deducted. Third, the same type of problem encountered in calculating the amount realized of various positive and negative adjustments is also encountered in calculating the adjusted basis.

EXAMPLE 40   P purchased a personal residence in 1987. The purchase price and the related closing costs were as follows:

Purchase price	$125,000
Recording costs	140
Title fees and title insurance	815
Survey costs	115
Attorney's fees	750
Appraisal fee	60

Other relevant tax information for the house during the time it was owned by P is as follows:

- Constructed a swimming pool for medical reasons. The cost was $10,000, of which $3,000 was deducted as a medical expense.

- Added a solar heating system. The cost was $15,000.

- Deducted home office expenses of $6,000. Of this amount, $3,200 was for depreciation.
- None of the closing costs were deducted as moving expenses.

The adjusted basis for the house is calculated as follows:

Purchase price	$125,000
Recording costs	140
Title fees and title insurance	815
Survey costs	115
Attorney's fees	750
Appraisal fee	60
Swimming pool ($10,000 − $3,000)	7,000
Solar heating system	15,000
	$148,880
Less: Depreciation deducted on home office	3,200
Adjusted basis	$145,680

□

Summary of Basis Adjustments

Some of the more common items that either increase or decrease the basis of an asset appear in Concept Summary 14–2.

CONCEPT SUMMARY 14–2

Adjustments to Basis

Item	Effect	Refer to Chapter	Explanation
Amortization of bond discount.	Increase	16	Amortization is mandatory for certain taxable bonds and elective for tax-exempt bonds.
Amortization of bond premium.	Decrease	14	Amortization is mandatory for tax-exempt bonds and elective for taxable bonds.
Amortization of covenant not to compete.	Decrease	16	Covenant must be for a definite and limited time period.
Amortization of intangibles.	Decrease	9	Not all intangibles can be amortized (e.g., goodwill).
Assessment for local benefits.	Increase	11	To the extent not deductible as taxes (e.g., assessment for streets and sidewalks that increase the value of the property versus one for maintenance or repair or for meeting interest charges).

Item	Effect	Refer to Chapter	Explanation
Bad debts.	Decrease	8	Only the specific charge-off method is permitted.
Capital additions.	Increase	14	Certain items, at the taxpayer's election, can be capitalized or deducted (e.g., selected indirect moving expenses and medical expenses).
Casualty.	Decrease	8	For a casualty loss, the amount of the adjustment is the summation of the deductible loss and the insurance proceeds received. For a casualty gain, the amount of the adjustment is the insurance proceeds received reduced by the recognized gain.
Cost recovery.	Decrease	9	§ 168 is applicable to tangible assets placed in service after 1980 whose useful life is expressed in terms of years.
Condemnation.	Decrease	15	See casualty explanation.
Depletion.	Decrease	9	Use the greater of cost or percentage depletion. Percentage depletion can still be deducted when the basis is zero.
Depreciation.	Decrease	9	§ 167 is applicable to tangible assets placed in service before 1981 and to tangible assets not depreciated in terms of years.
Easement.	Decrease		If no use of the land is retained by the taxpayer, all of the basis is allocable to the easement transaction. However, if only part of the land is affected by the easement, only part of the basis is allocable to the easement transaction.
Improvements by lessee to lessor's property.	Increase	5	Adjustment occurs only if the lessor is required to include the fair market value of the improvements in gross income under § 109.
Imputed interest.	Decrease	18	Amount deducted is not part of the cost of the asset.
Inventory: lower of cost or market.	Decrease	18	Not available if the LIFO method is used.
Investment tax credit.	Decrease	13	Amount is 50% of the investment tax credit. If the election to reduce the investment tax credit is made, no adjustment is required.
Investment tax credit recapture.	Increase	13	Amount is 50% of the investment tax credit recaptured. If the election to reduce the investment tax credit was made, no adjustment is required.
Limited expensing under § 179.	Decrease	9	Occurs only if the taxpayer elects § 179 treatment.

Item	Effect	Refer to Chapter	Explanation
Medical capital expenditure permitted as a medical expense.	Decrease	11	Adjustment is the amount of the deduction (the effect on basis is to increase it by the amount of the capital expenditure net of the deduction).
Moving capital expenditure permitted as a moving expense.	Decrease	10	Adjustment is for the amount the taxpayer elects to deduct as an indirect moving expense (the effect on basis is to increase it by the amount of the capital expenditure net of the deduction).
Real estate taxes; apportionment between the buyer and seller.	Increase or Decrease	11	To the extent the buyer pays the seller's pro rata share, the buyer's basis is increased. To the extent the seller pays the buyer's pro rata share, the buyer's basis is decreased.
Rebate from manufacturer.	Decrease		Since the rebate is treated as an adjustment to the purchase price, it is not included in the buyer's gross income.
Stock dividend.	Decrease	5	Adjustment occurs only if the stock dividend is nontaxable.
Stock rights.	Decrease	14	Adjustment occurs only for nontaxable stock rights and only if the fair market value of the rights is at least 15% of the fair market value of the stock or, if less than 15%, the taxpayer elects to allocate the basis between the stock and the rights.
Theft.	Decrease	8	See casualty explanation.

In discussing the topic of basis, a number of specific techniques for determining basis have been presented. Although the various techniques are responsive to and mandated by transactions occurring in the marketplace, they do possess enough common characteristics to be categorized as follows:

- The basis of the asset may be determined by reference to the asset's cost.

- The basis of the asset may be determined by reference to the basis of another asset.

- The basis of the asset may be determined by reference to the asset's fair market value.

- The basis of the asset may be determined by reference to the basis of the asset to another taxpayer.

TAX PLANNING CONSIDERATIONS

Cost Identification and Documentation Considerations

The allocation of the contract price for multiple assets acquired in a single transaction is needed for several reasons. First, some of the assets may be depreciable although others are not. From the different viewpoints of the buyer and the seller, this may produce a tax conflict that will need to be resolved. That is, the seller will prefer a high allocation for nondepreciable assets, whereas the purchaser will prefer a high allocation for depreciable assets (see chapters 16 and 17). Second, the seller will need to know the amount realized on the sale of the capital assets and the ordinary income assets to classify the recognized gains and losses as capital or ordinary. For example, whether the allocation is to goodwill or a covenant not to compete (see chapters 16 and 17) will produce different tax consequences to the seller. Third, the buyer will need the adjusted basis of each asset to calculate the realized gain or loss on the sale or other disposition of each asset.

Selection of Property for Making Gifts

A donor can achieve several tax advantages by making gifts of appreciated property. Income tax on the unrealized gain that would have occurred had the donor sold the property is avoided by the donor. A portion of this amount can be permanently avoided as the result of the donee's adjusted basis being increased by a part of the gift tax paid by the donor. Even absent this increase in basis, the income tax liability on the sale of the property by the donee can be less than the income tax liability that would have resulted from the donor's sale of the property. Such reduced income tax liability will occur if the donee is in a lower tax bracket than the donor. In addition, any subsequent appreciation during the time the property is held by the lower tax bracket donee will result in a tax savings on the sale or other disposition of the property. Such gifts of appreciated property can be an effective tool in family tax planning.

Taxpayers should generally not make gifts of depreciated property (property that, if sold, would produce a realized loss) because the donor does not receive an income tax deduction for the unrealized loss element. In addition, the donee will receive no benefit from this unrealized loss upon the subsequent sale of the property because of the loss basis rule. The loss basis rule provides that the donee's basis is the lower of the donor's basis or fair market value at the date of the gift. If the donor anticipates that the donee will sell the property upon receiving it, the donor should sell the property and take the loss deduction, assuming the loss is deductible. The donor can then give the proceeds from the sale to the donee.

Selection of Property for Making Bequests

A decedent's will should generally make bequests of appreciated property. Doing so enables income tax to be avoided by the decedent and the inheritor of the property on the unrealized gain because the recipient takes the fair market value as his or her basis.

Taxpayers generally should not make bequests of depreciated property (property that, if sold, would produce a realized loss) because the decedent does not receive an income tax deduction for the unrealized loss element. In addition, the inheritor will receive no benefit from this unrealized loss upon the subsequent sale of the property.

EXAMPLE 41

On the date of her death, W owned land held for investment purposes. The land had an adjusted basis of $600,000 and a fair market value of $100,000. If W had sold the property before her death, the recognized loss would have been $500,000. If H inherits the property and sells it for $50,000, the recognized loss will be $50,000 (the decline in value since W's death). In addition, regardless of the period of time the property is held by H, the holding period is long term (see chapter 16). □

From an income tax perspective, it is preferable to transfer appreciated property as a bequest rather than as a gift.[64] This results from the step-up in basis for inherited property, whereas for property received by gift, the donee has a carryover basis.

Disallowed Losses

Section 267 Disallowed Losses.   Taxpayers should be aware of the desirability of avoiding transactions that activate the loss disallowance provisions for related parties. This is so even in light of the provision that permits the related-party buyer to offset his or her realized gain by the related-party seller's disallowed loss. Even with this offset, several inequities exist. First, the tax benefit associated with the disallowed loss ultimately is realized by the wrong party (the related-party buyer rather than the related-party seller). Second, the tax benefit of this offset to the related-party buyer does not occur until the buyer disposes of the property. Therefore, the longer the time period between the purchase and disposition of the property by the related-party buyer, the less will be the economic benefit. Third, if the property does not appreciate to at least its adjusted basis to the related-party seller during the time period the related-party buyer holds it, part or all of the disallowed loss will be permanently lost. Fourth, since the right of offset is available only to the original transferee (the related-party buyer), all of the disallowed loss will be permanently lost if the original transferee subsequently transfers the property by gift or bequest.

EXAMPLE 42

T sells property with an adjusted basis of $35,000 to B, his brother, for $25,000, the fair market value of the property. The $10,000 realized loss to T is disallowed by § 267. If B subsequently sells the property to an unrelated party for $37,000, B will have a recognized gain of $2,000 (realized gain of $12,000 reduced by disallowed loss of $10,000). Therefore, from the perspective of the family unit, the original $10,000 realized loss ultimately is recognized. However, if B sells the property for $29,000, he will have a recognized gain of $0 (realized gain of $4,000 reduced by disal-

---

64. Consideration must also be given to the estate tax consequences of the bequest versus the gift tax consequences of the gift.

lowed loss of $4,000 necessary to offset the realized gain). From the perspective of the family unit, $6,000 of the realized loss of $10,000 is permanently wasted ($10,000 realized loss minus $4,000 offset permitted). □

Wash Sales.   The wash sales provisions can be avoided if the security is replaced within the statutory time period with a similar rather than a substantially identical security. For example, the sale of Bethlehem Steel common stock and a purchase of Inland Steel common stock would not be treated as a wash sale. Such a procedure can enable the taxpayer to use an unrealized capital loss to offset a recognized capital gain. The taxpayer can sell the security before the end of the taxable year, offset the recognized capital loss against the capital gain, and invest the sales proceeds in a similar security.

Because the wash sales provisions do not apply to gains, it may be desirable to engage in a wash sale before the end of the taxable year. This recognized capital gain may be used to offset capital losses or capital loss carryovers from prior years.

PROBLEM MATERIALS

Discussion Questions

1. When will a property transaction result in a realized gain? A realized loss?

2. What is included in the amount realized from a sale or other disposition of property?

3. If a taxpayer sells property for cash, the amount realized consists of the net proceeds from the sale. For each of the following, indicate the effect on the amount realized:
   a. The property is sold on credit.
   b. A mortgage on the property is assumed by the buyer.
   c. The taxpayer makes a gift of property, and the donee pays the gift tax.
   d. The taxpayer contributes the property to charity, and the charity assumes the mortgage on the property.

4. T is negotiating to buy some land. Under the first option, T will give S $70,000 and assume S's mortgage on the land for $30,000. Under the second option, T will give S $100,000, and S will immediately pay off the mortgage. T would like for his basis for the land to be as high as possible. Given this objective, which option should T select?

5. If the buyer of property assumes the seller's mortgage, why is the amount of the mortgage included in the amount realized by the seller? What effect does the mortgage assumption have on the seller's (a) adjusted basis for the mortgaged property and (b) realized gain or loss?

6. The taxpayer owns land and a building with an adjusted basis of $50,000 and a fair market value of $250,000. The property is subject to a mortgage of $400,000. Since the taxpayer is in arrears on the mort-

gage payments, the creditor is willing to accept the property in return for cancelling the amount of the mortgage.

    a. How can the adjusted basis of the property be less than the amount of the mortgage?

    b. If the creditor's offer is accepted, what are the effects on the amount realized, the adjusted basis, and the realized gain or loss?

    c. Does it matter in (b) if the mortgage is recourse or nonrecourse?

7. Distinguish between the effect on the basis for a machine of depreciation under § 167 and cost recovery under § 168.

8. C and D each own an automobile that each uses exclusively in his respective trade or business. The adjusted basis of each automobile is $10,000, and the fair market value is $9,000. Both automobiles are destroyed in accidents. C's automobile is insured, and C receives insurance proceeds of $9,000. D's automobile is uninsured. Explain how the adjusted basis for each automobile is reduced to zero, even though one is insured and the other is uninsured.

9. T owns stock in X Corporation and Y Corporation. He receives a $1,000 distribution from both corporations. The instructions from X Corporation state that the $1,000 is a dividend. The instructions from Y Corporation state that the $1,000 is not a dividend. What could cause the instructions to differ as to the tax consequences?

10. Why does the amortization of the discount on a bond increase the adjusted basis for the bond and the amortization of the premium on a bond decrease the adjusted basis for the bond? At what point does the amortization of the discount or premium stop?

11. A taxpayer who acquires a taxable bond at a discount is required to amortize the discount, whereas a taxpayer who acquires a tax-exempt bond at a discount may elect to amortize the discount. What effect does the amortization have on the adjusted basis for the bonds? Why is the amortization for the taxable bond mandatory whereas for the tax-exempt bond it is elective?

12. A taxpayer who acquires a taxable bond at a premium may elect to amortize the premium, whereas a taxpayer who acquires a tax-exempt bond at a premium must amortize the premium. Why would a taxpayer make the amortization election for taxable bonds? What effect does the mandatory amortization of tax-exempt bonds have on taxable income?

13. Why are gains from the sale or exchange of personal use assets recognized when such losses are never recognized?

14. T's building is condemned and his realized loss is $5,000. U's building is condemned and her realized loss is $6,000. U deducts her realized loss of $6,000 on her tax return whereas T is unable to deduct his realized loss of $5,000 on his tax return. Explain why only U is permitted to deduct her realized loss.

15. Discuss the relationship between the recovery of capital doctrine and the receipt of a dividend distribution.

16. E owns a life insurance policy that will pay $100,000 to R, his spouse, on his death. At the date of E's death, the total premiums E had paid on the policy were $65,000. In accordance with § 101(a)(1), R excludes the $100,000 of insurance proceeds. Discuss the relationship, if any, between the § 101 exclusion and the recovery of capital doctrine.

17. When, as a general rule, does a taxpayer recover more than cost? Less than cost? Give some examples.

18. T owns 300 shares of Z Corporation stock. He acquired the shares as follows:

    On February 16, he purchased 100 shares.

    On June 3, he inherited 100 shares.

    On October 12, he received 100 shares as a gift.

    T decides to sell 200 shares prior to the end of the year. How will he determine the adjusted basis for the 200 shares sold?

19. How is cost allocated for lump-sum purchases?

20. Discuss the differences in tax treatment for allocating basis to nontaxable stock dividends when the form of the dividend is a common stock dividend on common stock versus a preferred stock dividend on common stock.

21. Discuss the differences in tax treatment when stock rights are allocated a cost basis and when stock rights have no cost basis. When does each of these situations occur?

22. Under what circumstances is it possible to recognize no gain or loss on the sale of an asset previously received as a gift?

23. Why does the Code contain both a gain basis rule and a loss basis rule for gift property? Under what circumstances will both rules produce the same basis amount?

24. How do gift taxes paid by the donor affect the income tax rules for gift property?

25. Outline the rules concerning depreciation (or cost recovery allowance) and the holding period for gift property. Why are these rules important?

26. Discuss the differences in tax treatment between property sold before death and inherited property. Why is this important?

27. T acquires or receives the following property during the taxable year:

    Purchases a warehouse.

    Inherits land from his deceased aunt.

    Receives 100 shares of stock as a birthday present from his aunt.

    Which of the properties has a carryover basis and which has a new basis?

28. R makes a gift of an appreciated building to E. E dies three months later, and R inherits the building from E. During the period that E held the building, he deducted depreciation and made a capital expen-

diture. What effect might these items have on R's basis for the inherited building?

29. Immediately before his death in 1989, H sells securities (adjusted basis of $100,000) for their fair market value of $20,000. The sale was not to a related party. The securities were community property, and H is survived by his wife, W.

   a.   Did H act wisely? Why or why not?

   b.   Suppose the figures are reversed (sale for $100,000 of property with an adjusted basis of $20,000). Would the sale be wise? Why or why not?

30. The alternate valuation date can be elected by the executor of an estate only if the election results in reducing both the value of the gross estate (the fair market value of the property declines during the six-month period after death) and the estate tax liability.

   a.   From an estate tax perspective, why would the executor make the election if such election did not reduce the value of the gross estate?

   b.   From an income tax perspective, what is the benefit of the election if the property has appreciated during the six-month period after death?

   c.   What is the congressional justification for this limitation?

31. What are related-party transactions, and why are they important?

32. What is a wash sale? Why isn't a realized loss recognized on a wash sale? How is the recovery of capital doctrine maintained?

33. R owns 100 shares of stock in Z Corporation. His adjusted basis for the stock is $5,000. On December 21, R sells the stock in the marketplace for $12,000. R purchases 100 shares of stock in Z Corporation in the marketplace on January 5 of the following year for $12,200.

   a.   What is R trying to achieve from a tax perspective?

   b.   Will he succeed?

   c.   Using the same data, except that R's adjusted basis for the stock is $15,000, respond to (a) and (b).

34. What is the basis for property converted from personal use to business or income-producing use when there is a loss? When there is a gain? Why is there a difference? How does conversion affect depreciation and why?

35. For both property received by gift and property converted from personal use to business or income-producing use, it may be necessary to calculate the basis under two different formulas. Discuss the similarities and differences as they relate to the basis for gain, loss, and depreciation.

Problems

36. A sold her home for $350,000 in 1989. She had purchased it in 1985 for $190,000. During the period of ownership, A had:

- Deducted $57,500 office-in-home expenses ($17,500 depreciation). (Refer to chapter 10.)

- Deducted a casualty loss to residential trees from a hurricane. The total loss was $12,000 (after the $100 floor and the 10% of adjusted gross income floor), and A's insurance company reimbursed A for $10,500. (Refer to chapter 8.)

- Paid street paving assessment of $5,000 and added sidewalks for $7,000.

- Installed an elevator for medical reasons. The total cost was $20,000, and A deducted $9,000 as medical expenses. (Refer to chapter 11.)

- Paid legal expenses in connection with the move to the home in 1985 of $3,000. A deducted these expenses as moving expenses. (Refer to chapter 10.)

- Received $5,500 from a utility company for an easement to install underground utility lines across the property.

What is A's realized gain?

37. R bought a rental house at the beginning of 1984 for $80,000, of which $10,000 is allocated to the land and $70,000 to the building. Early in 1986, he had a tennis court built in the backyard at a cost of $5,000. R has deducted $32,200 for depreciation on the house and $1,300 for depreciation on the court. At the beginning of 1989, R sells the house and tennis court for $125,000 cash.

    a. What is R's realized gain or loss?

    b. If an original mortgage of $20,000 is still outstanding and the buyer assumes the mortgage in addition to the cash payment, what is R's realized gain or loss?

    c. If the buyer takes the property subject to the mortgage, what is R's realized gain or loss?

38. T is negotiating the sale of a tract of his land to P. Use the following classification scheme to classify each of the items contained in the proposed sales contract:

Legend

DART = Decreases amount realized by T.
IART = Increases amount realized by T.
DABT = Decreases adjusted basis to T.
IABT = Increases adjusted basis to T.
DABP = Decreases adjusted basis to P.
IABP = Increases adjusted basis to P.

a. T is to receive cash of $50,000.

b. T is to receive P's note payable for $25,000, payable in three years.

c. P assumes T's mortgage of $5,000 on the land.

d. P agrees to pay the realtor's sales commission of $8,000.

e. P agrees to pay the property taxes on the land for the entire year. If each party paid his or her respective share, T's share would be $1,000, and P's share would be $3,000.

f. P pays legal fees of $500.

g. T pays legal fees of $750.

39. D's residence, with a basis of $80,000 and a fair market value of $100,000, is damaged by fire. After the fire, the fair market value is $45,000. D receives insurance proceeds of $55,000. His adjusted gross income is $40,000.

a. What effect does the casualty have on the adjusted basis?

b. What effect does the casualty have on the adjusted basis if the residence is uninsured?

40. T's warehouse, which has an adjusted basis of $250,000, is destroyed by a hurricane. T receives insurance proceeds of $400,000. Because T has excess warehouse space in his business, he invests the $400,000 in X Corporation stock.

a. Calculate T's realized gain or loss.

b. Calculate T's recognized gain or loss.

c. Calculate T's basis for the X Corporation stock.

41. C owns all of the stock of a corporation. The earnings and profits of the corporation are $25,000. C's adjusted basis for his stock is $40,000. He receives a cash distribution of $50,000 from the corporation.

a. What effect does the distribution have on the adjusted basis of C's stock?

b. What effect would the distribution have on the adjusted basis of C's stock if the earnings and profits of the corporation were $80,000?

42. B paid $270,000 for bonds with a face value of $250,000 at the beginning of 1985. The bonds mature in 10 years and pay 9% interest per year.

a. If B sells the bonds for $255,000 at the beginning of 1989, does she have a realized gain or loss? If so, how much?

b. If B trades the bonds at the beginning of 1990 for stock worth $262,500, does she have a realized gain or loss? If so, how much?

43. Which of the following would definitely result in a recognized gain or loss?

a. K sells his lakeside cabin, which has an adjusted basis of $10,000, for $15,000.

b. A sells his personal residence, which has an adjusted basis of $15,000, for $10,000.

c. C's personal residence is on the site of a proposed airport and is condemned by the city. C receives $55,000 for the house, which has an adjusted basis of $65,000.

d. B sells his personal residence, which has an adjusted basis of $80,000, for $90,000.

e. J gives stock to his niece. J's adjusted basis is $3,000, and the fair market value is $5,000.

44. R makes the following purchases and sales of stock:

Transaction	Date	No. of Shares	Company	Price per Share
Purchase	1–1–87	300	MDG	$ 75
Purchase	6–1–87	150	RU	300
Purchase	11–1–87	60	MDG	70
Sale	12–3–87	180	MDG	70
Purchase	3–1–88	120	RU	375
Sale	8–1–88	90	RU	330
Sale	1–1–89	150	MDG	90
Sale	2–1–89	75	RU	500

Assuming that R is unable to identify the particular lots that are sold with the original purchase, what is the realized gain or loss on each type of stock as of:

a. 7–1–87

b. 12–31–87

c. 12–31–88

d. 7–1–89

45. P purchases the assets of a sole proprietorship from S. The adjusted basis of each of the assets on S's books and the fair market value of each asset as agreed to by P and S are as follows:

Asset	S's Adjusted Basis	FMV
Accounts receivable	$ –0–	$ 10,000
Notes receivable	15,000	20,000
Machinery and equipment	85,000	100,000
Building	100,000	300,000
Land	200,000	350,000

The purchase price is $900,000. Determine P's basis for each of the assets of the sole proprietorship.

46. During the year, F received the following dividends on her stock portfolio:

a. Five shares of common stock in U Company on 10 shares of common stock she already owns. F paid $30 a share for the original 10 shares.

b. Twenty shares of preferred stock in X Company on 200 shares of common stock for which F paid $10,000. The fair market value of the preferred stock on the date of distribution was $40, and the fair market value of the common stock was $60.

What is the basis per share for each of the common shares and the preferred shares?

47. K receives nontaxable stock rights with a fair market value of $1,900. The fair market value of the stock on which the rights were received is $12,000. The cost of the stock was $11,000. What is the basis of the rights for purposes of exercise or sale?

48. J owns 1,000 shares of Y Corporation stock with a basis of $10,000 and a fair market value of $14,000. She receives nontaxable stock rights to purchase additional shares. The rights have a fair market value of $2,000.

    a. What is the basis of the stock and the basis of the stock rights?

    b. What is the recognized gain or loss if the stock rights are sold for $2,000?

    c. What is the recognized gain or loss if the stock rights are allowed to lapse?

49. T received various gifts over the years. He has decided to dispose of the following assets that he received as gifts:

    a. In 1923, he received land worth $20,000. The donor's adjusted basis was $24,000. T sells the land for $150,000 in 1989.

    b. In 1935, he received stock in G Company. The donor's adjusted basis was $1,000. The fair market value on the date of the gift was $2,000. T sells the stock for $2,500 in 1989.

    c. In 1920, he received a Rolls Royce worth $22,000. The donor's adjusted basis for the auto was $16,000. T sells the auto for $35,000 in 1989.

    d. In 1951, he received land worth $12,000. The donor's adjusted basis was $15,000. T sells the land for $4,000 in 1989.

What is the realized gain or loss from each of the preceding transactions? Assume in each of the gift transactions that no gift tax was paid.

50. A received a car from Z as a gift. Z paid $7,000 for the car. She had used it for business purposes and had deducted $2,000 for depreciation up to the time she gave the car to A. The fair market value of the car is $3,500.

    a. Assuming A uses the car for business purposes, what is his basis for depreciation?

    b. If the estimated useful life is two years (from the date of the gift), what is his depreciation deduction for each year? Use the straight-line method.

    c. If A sells the car for $800 one year after receiving it, what is his gain or loss?

    d. If A sells the car for $4,000 one year after receiving it, what is his gain or loss?

51. R receives a gift of property (after 1976) that has a fair market value of $100,000 on the date of gift. The donor's adjusted basis for the property was $60,000. Assume the donor paid gift tax of $16,000 on the gift.

    a. What is R's basis for gain and loss and for depreciation?

    b. If R had received the gift of property before 1977, what would his basis be for gain and loss and for depreciation?

52. L receives a gift of income-producing property that has an adjusted basis of $20,000 on the date of the gift. The fair market value of the property on the date of the gift is $18,000. Gift tax amounting to $400 was paid by the donor. L later sells the property for $19,000. Determine L's recognized gain or loss.

53. U is going to make a gift to N, his daughter, who is age 16. U is undecided as to whether he should give N $10,000 in cash or give her stock worth $10,000. The adjusted basis of the stock is $13,000. U anticipates that N will sell the stock.

    a. Should U make a gift of the stock, or should he sell the stock and give the cash proceeds to N?

    b. If the fair market value of the stock is $15,000, what factors are relevant to U's decision as to whether he should make a gift of the stock or sell the stock and give the cash proceeds to N?

    c. Assume the stock is family corporation stock and that N is not expected to sell it. The fair market value is $10,000. What are the tax consequences to U if he gives N $10,000 in cash and then sells the stock to N for $10,000.

54. T is planning to make a charitable contribution of stock worth $20,000 to the Boy Scouts. The stock T is considering contributing has an adjusted basis of $15,000. A friend has suggested that T sell the stock and contribute the $20,000 in proceeds rather than contribute the stock.

    a. Should T follow the friend's advice? Why?

    b. Assume the fair market value is only $13,000. In this case, should T follow the friend's advice? Why?

    c. Rather than make a charitable contribution to the Boy Scouts, T is going to make a gift to N, his niece. Advise T regarding (a) and (b).

55. D receives a house as a gift from F in 1985. F had inherited the house from G in 1960. G had purchased the house in 1945 for $20,000 and had used it as his personal residence. The fair market value of the house at the date of G's death in 1960 was $95,000. F also had used the house as his principal residence. During the periods that G and F owned the property, they incurred the following expenditures:

	G	F
Mortgage interest	$13,000	$ -0-
Property taxes	3,000	12,000
Capital expenditures	4,000	10,000
Repairs	2,500	6,000
Utilities	5,000	25,000
Insurance	1,500	3,500

Since both G and F were accountants, they had maintained meticulous records supporting these expenditures. When D received the property in 1985, the fair market value was $150,000. F paid gift tax on the transfer of $35,800. D occupied the house as his personal residence for 14 months, at which time he converted the property to rental housing. The fair market value of the property at the date of conversion was $120,000. The decline in value was primarily due to a zoning change that allowed a mobile home park to be located across the street.

After renting the property for two years, D sells it for $108,000 and incurs selling expenses of $6,000. During the period that D owned the property, he incurred the following expenditures:

	Residence Period	Rental Period
Property taxes	$ 1,400	$ 2,400
Capital expenditures	12,000	1,000
Repairs	500	1,500
Utilities	2,100	-0-
Insurance	300	-0-
Depreciation	0	16,000

a. Calculate G's adjusted basis for the property immediately before his death.

b. Calculate F's basis for the property at the time he inherits it.

c. Calculate F's adjusted basis for the property immediately before his gift of it to D.

d. Calculate D's basis for the property at the time he receives it as a gift.

e. Calculate D's adjusted basis for the property at the date of the conversion for purposes of calculating depreciation.

f. Calculate D's realized and recognized gain or loss on the sale.

56. Q's estate includes the following assets available for distribution to R, one of Q's beneficiaries:

	Decedent's Adjusted Basis	FMV at Date of Death	FMV at Alternate Valuation Date
Cash	$10,000	$ 10,000	$ 10,000
Stock	40,000	125,000	60,000
Apartment building	60,000	300,000	325,000
Land	75,000	100,000	110,000

The fair market value of the stock six months after Q's death was $60,000. However, believing that the stock would continue to decline in value, the executor of the estate distributed the stock to R one month after Q's death. R immediately sold the stock for $85,000.

a. Determine R's basis for the assets if the primary valuation date and amount apply.

b. Determine R's basis for the assets if the executor elects the alternate valuation date and amount.

57. C inherited land from her grandfather, whose basis in the land was $150,000. At the date of the grandfather's death, the fair market value of the land was $200,000. Six months thereafter the land had appreciated to $220,000. According to the executor, $4,000 of the estate tax payable is allocable to the land. In filing the estate tax return, the executor is willing to make any elections that will produce beneficial income tax consequences to the taxpayer.

a. What is C's basis in the inherited property?

b. What is C's basis in the inherited property if the grandfather's basis was $300,000?

c. What is C's basis in the inherited property if the fair market value of the land on the date of the grandfather's death was $220,000 and the fair market value six months thereafter was $200,000?

58. T makes a gift of 100 shares of appreciated stock to his uncle, G, on January 5, 1989. The basis of the stock is $3,150, and the fair market value is $5,250. G dies on October 8, 1989. During the period that G held the stock, he received a 5% nontaxable stock dividend. Under the provisions of G's will, T inherits 100 shares of the stock. The value of the stock for Federal estate tax purposes is $55 per share.

a. What is the basis of the inherited stock to T?

b. What is the basis of the inherited stock to T if T had given the stock to G on January 5, 1988?

59. H sells to his brother, B, two city lots for $35,000 with an adjusted basis for determining loss to him of $42,000.

a. Is the loss allowable as a deduction to H?

b. If B sells the city lots for $39,000, what is his realized gain or loss? His recognized gain or loss?

60. B sells stock to his sister S for $36,000. B's adjusted basis for the stock is $25,000, and the fair market value of the stock is $36,000. Calculate B's realized and recognized gain and S's basis for the stock.

61. T owns a 60% capital and profits interest in TS Partnership, which sells property to T for $75,000. The partnership's adjusted basis for the property is $90,000.

a. Calculate the realized and recognized loss to the partnership.

b. Calculate the basis of the property to T.

c. If T subsequently sells the property for $87,000, calculate T's realized and recognized gain or loss.

d. If T gives the property to his daughter D, who subsequently sells it for $87,000, calculate D's realized and recognized gain or loss. Assume no gift tax is paid on the gift and the fair market value on the date of the gift is $80,000.

e. Determine the tax consequences in (a) through (d) if T is a shareholder and TS is a corporation.

62. M owns land with an adjusted basis of $30,000. M sells the land to her sister Q for the land's fair market value of $26,000. Q makes a gift of the land to her nephew N. Q pays gift tax of $1,000. At the date of the gift, the fair market value of the land is $29,000.

a. What is the realized and recognized gain or loss to N if he sells the land for $36,000?

b. What is the realized and recognized gain or loss to N if he sells the land for $23,000?

c. How would the results in (a) and (b) differ if N had inherited the property from Q?

63. On September 15, 1989, S decides to revise his stock holdings as follows:

Date	Company	No. of Shares	Trans-action	Price	Cost
9–10–89	Pan Am	100	Buy	$25/share	
9–15–89	Kodak	120	Sell	20/share	$25/share
9–15–89	Ford	70	Sell	25/share	20/share
9–15–89	IBM	95	Sell	5/share	10/share
9–15–89	Xerox	220	Sell	8/share	5/share
9–15–89	Pan Am	100	Sell	20/share	30/share
10–4–89	Ford	100	Buy	20/share	
10–8–89	ABC	120	Buy	7/share	
10–25–89	Kodak	95	Buy	30/share	
10–14–89	American	50	Buy	4/share	

a. What is the recognized gain or loss for each of the stocks sold on September 15?

b. Explain why the gain or loss is or is not recognized on each sale.

64. W purchased 50 shares of A Corporation common stock for $2,500 on May 12, 1989. On August 12, 1989, W purchased 25 additional shares for $1,375; on August 27, 1989, W purchased 10 additional shares for $500. On September 3, 1989, he sold the 50 shares purchased on May 12, 1989, for $2,000.

a. What is W's realized gain or loss on September 3, 1989?

b. What is W's recognized gain or loss?

c. What is the basis of W's remaining shares after the sale on September 3?

65. J purchases two wheat futures contracts, one to buy and one to sell, for $7,000 each in August 1989. In November 1989, J liquidates the po-

sition, showing a loss of $1,000. At the same time, the offsetting position is showing a gain of $975.

a. What is J's recognized loss?

b. Would liquidating the offsetting position in November 1989 affect the recognized loss?

66. A retires from a public accounting firm to enter private practice. He had bought a home two years earlier for $40,000. Upon beginning his business, he converts one fourth of his home into an office. The fair market value of the home on the date of conversion (January 1, 1985) is $75,000. The adjusted basis is $56,000 (ignore land). A lives and works in the home for five years (after converting it to business use) and sells it at the end of the fifth year. A deducted $6,440 of cost recovery using the statutory percentage method.

a. How much gain or loss is recognized if A sells the property for $44,000?

b. If he sells the property for $70,000?

67. D purchased residential property in 1982 as a personal residence. The residential property was acquired at a cost of $75,000, of which $45,000 is allocable to the building. D uses the property as his personal residence until January 1, 1986, at which time the property's fair market value is $66,000, of which $36,000 is allocable to the building. D rents the property from January 1, 1986, until January 1, 1989, at which time he sells it for $108,000. D deducted $9,032 of cost recovery using the statutory percentage method.

a. What is D's realized gain or loss from the sale?

b. What is D's recognized gain or loss?

68. T, age 93, has accumulated substantial assets during his life. Among his many assets are the following, which he is considering giving to G, his grandson.

Assets	Adjusted Basis	Fair Market Value
X Corporation stock	$ 50,000	$700,000
Y Corporation stock	70,000	71,000
Z Corporation stock	200,000	50,000

T has been in ill health for the past five years. His physician has informed him that he probably will not live for more than six months. Advise T which of the stocks should be transferred as gifts and which as bequests.

Cumulative Problems

69. Ada Johnson, age 28, is single and has no dependents. Her Social Security number is 444–11–3333, and she resides at 210 Avenue G, Kentwood, LA 70444. Her salary in 1989 was $25,000. She incurred unreimbursed expenses of $800 for travel and $500 for entertainment in

connection with her job as an assistant personnel director. In addition, she had the following items of possible tax consequence in 1989:

a. Itemized deductions (not including any potential deductions mentioned previously), $5,800.

b. Proceeds from the October 8, 1989, sale of land inherited from her father on June 15, 1989 (fair market value on June 15 was $35,000; her father's adjusted basis was $15,000), $38,000.

c. Proceeds from the November 1, 1989, sale of 50 shares of X Corporation stock received as a gift from her father on October 5, 1976, when the fair market value of the stock was $6,000 (her father's adjusted basis in the stock was $5,500, and he paid gift tax of $800 on the transfer), $7,500.

d. Proceeds from the November 5, 1989, sale of her personal automobile, for which she had paid $4,500 in 1982, $3,100.

e. Proceeds from the December 3, 1989, sale of 10 shares of Y Corporation stock to her brother (she had paid $85 per share for the stock on February 7, 1989), $600.

f. Dividends received from a domestic corporation, $120.

Part 1—Tax Computation

Ada's employer withheld Federal income tax of $3,880. Compute Ada's net tax payable or refund due for 1989. Suggested software (if available): *WEST–TAX Planner* or *BNA Individual Income Tax Spreadsheet.*

Part 2—Tax Planning

As of the beginning of 1990, Ada is promoted to the position of personnel director. The promotion will result in a salary increase. Her new position will result in an estimated increase in her expenses for travel from $800 to $3,000 and in her expenses for entertainment from $500 to $4,000. Her employer has offered her the following options.

a. Salary increase of $20,000.

b. Salary increase of $12,000 and reimbursement for all travel and entertainment expenses not in excess of $7,000.

Ada estimates that her itemized deductions (excluding any potential deductions for travel and entertainment) will remain at $5,800. She anticipates that no dividends will be received and no proceeds from asset sales will be received.

Calculate Ada's tax liability for 1990 under both option (a) and option (b) so she can decide which option to select. Suggested software (if available): *WEST–TAX Planner* or *BNA Individual Income Tax Spreadsheet.*

70. Kenneth Cloud, age 67, is married and files a joint return with his wife, Sarah, age 65. Kenneth and Sarah are both retired. In 1989, they received Social Security benefits of $2,400. Kenneth's Social Security number is 666–55–1111, and Sarah's is 555–66–2222. They reside at 405 College Drive, Hammond, LA 70408.

Kenneth, who retired on January 1, 1989, receives benefits from a qualified pension plan of $600 a month for life. His total contributions to the plan were $18,000. Kenneth's life expectancy at the annuity starting date on January 1, 1989, was 14 years.

Sarah, who retired on December 31, 1988, started receiving benefits of $800 a month on January 1, 1989. Her life expectancy was 18 years from the annuity starting date, and her investment in the qualified pension plan was $57,600.

On September 27, 1989, Kenneth and Sarah received a 10% stock dividend on 50 shares of stock they owned. They had paid $11 a share for the stock in 1976. On December 16, 1989, they sold the five shares received as a stock dividend for $30 a share.

On January 10, 1989, Sarah sold the car she had used in commuting to and from work. She paid $5,000 for the car in 1983 and sold it for $2,000. Kenneth and Sarah received a gift of 100 shares of stock from their son Thomas in 1976. Thomas's basis in the stock was $30 a share, and the fair market value at the date of gift was $25 a share. No gift tax was paid. Kenneth and Sarah sold the stock on October 8, 1989, for $15 a share.

Kenneth and Sarah paid estimated Federal income tax of $200 and had itemized deductions of $6,300.

Compute their net tax payable or refund due for 1989. Suggested software (if available): *WEST–TAX Planner.*

 71. Tom Hanks, age 52, and Carol Hanks, age 33, are going to file a joint return for 1988. Tom's Social Security number is 111–60–1234, and Carol's is 222–50–4326. Tom and Carol reside at 200 Hall, Charleston, WV 25302. Tom, an executive vice president for X Corporation, received a salary of $125,000. In addition, he received the following benefits from X Corporation.

- Group term life insurance (maturity value of $200,000, premiums paid by X Corporation of $1,100).

- Payments under an uninsured medical reimbursement plan of $2,500. Such payments are available only to executives at the vice president level or higher.

- Tuition, room, and board of $14,000 for Tom's daughter, Alice, to attend Y University. Such payments are available to all children of executives at the vice president level or higher. Alice's Social Security number is 333–40–0001.

- Carol is an outside salesperson. Her sales commissions amounted to $45,000. She incurred and paid the following related expenses during 1988:

- Automobile operating expenses of $5,500 (the car was furnished by her employer and was used 100% for business).

- $1,400 for entertainment of clients.

During 1988, Tom and Carol had the following asset transactions:

- On January 8, Tom and Carol exchanged with Z jointly owned stock in B Corporation for stock in C Corporation. The adjusted basis of the stock in B Corporation was $23,000, and the fair market value of the C Corporation stock was $22,000. Tom and Carol had purchased the stock three years earlier.

- On January 1, Tom sold a rental house that he had inherited on June 12, 1979. The fair market value of the property at the date of the decedent's death was $93,000. During the period that Tom owned the house, he deducted depreciation of $20,000 (using the straight-line method). The selling price was $80,000, and selling expenses of $6,000 were incurred.

- On March 19, Tom sold for $9,000 an automobile that had been used exclusively for personal purposes. The car, which Tom acquired on July 8, 1984, had cost $14,500.

- On January 6, Carol purchased 100 shares of D Corporation stock for $1,000. In February, she purchased an additional 100 shares for $1,200. On December 2, she sold 150 shares for $3,000.

- Carol received a five-unit apartment building by gift on January 3, 1984. At the date of the gift, the donor's adjusted basis was $315,000 and the fair market value was $285,000. The donor paid gift taxes of $16,000. During the period that Carol owned the property, she deducted depreciation (using the straight-line method) of $84,000. On December 31, she sold the property, net of selling expenses, for $204,000.

Revenues and expenses associated with the rental property were as follows:

Revenues	$47,000
Expenses	
Interest	$ 8,000
Repairs and maintenance	1,800
Depreciation	21,000
Property taxes	5,200
Miscellaneous	500
	$36,500

In addition, Tom and Carol paid the following during 1988:

Charitable contributions	$2,100
Medical and dental expenses, less $2,500 reimbursed by Tom's medical plan	1,400
State income taxes	5,300
Real property taxes (excluding taxes on rental properties)	1,200
Personal property taxes	275
Home mortgage interest	5,100

- Carol received life insurance proceeds of $100,000 on the death of her father. Although the insurance company offered her a 10-year payout with interest, she requested and received the proceeds of $100,000 during 1988.

Compute Tom and Carol's lowest net tax payable or refund due for 1988. Withholdings for Federal income taxes for Tom were $45,500 and for Carol were $7,400. In addition, Tom and Carol made estimated tax payments of $8,000. If you use tax forms for your computations, you will need Forms 1040 and 2106 and Schedules A, D, and E. Suggested software (if available): *WEST–TAX Preparer* for tax return solutions, *WEST–TAX Planner if tax return solutions are not desired.*

Research Problems

Research Problem 1   On January 1, 1989, X, a major shareholder in H Corporation, purchases land from the company for $300,000. The fair market value of the land is $1,200,000, and the adjusted basis in the hands of the corporation is $400,000.

   a.   What are the possible tax consequences to X?

   b.   What is the basis of the land to X?

   c.   What is the tax consequence to H Corporation?

Research Problem 2   T owns real estate with an adjusted basis of $600,000 and a fair market value of $1,100,000. The amount of the nonrecourse mortgage on the property is $2,500,000. Because of substantial past and projected future losses associated with the real estate development (occupancy rate of only 37% after three years), T deeds the property to the creditor.

   a.   What are the tax consequences to T?

   b.   Assume the data are the same, except the fair market value of the property is $2,525,000. Therefore, T also receives $25,000 from the creditor when he deeds the property to the creditor. What are the tax consequences to T?

Partial list of research aids:

Rev.Rul. 76–111, 1976–1 C.B. 214.

Crane v. Comm., 47 USTC ¶9217, 35 AFTR 776, 67 S.Ct. 1047 (USSC, 1947).

Research Problem 3   O gives stock worth $400,000 to G. O's adjusted basis in the stock is $50,000. The gift taxes due are $118,400. As a condition for receiving the gift of stock, G agrees to pay the gift tax. The stock is transferred to G on February 5, 1989.

   a.   What are the income tax consequences to O?

   b.   What are the income tax consequences to O if the gift was made on February 5, 1981?

Research Problem 4   L is leasing an office building from O. Under the provisions of the lease, L is obligated to repair the roof of the leased premises. The estimated cost of such repairs is $500,000. Before making such repairs, L sells all of his assets, including the leasehold, to P for $4 million. P assumes L's obligation to make the repairs.

   a.   Determine the amount realized on the asset sale by L.

   b.   Determine the tax effect to O of the asset sale.

15

PROPERTY TRANSACTIONS: NONTAXABLE EXCHANGES

OBJECTIVES

Discuss the rationale for nonrecognition (postponement) of gain in certain property transactions.

Identify the different types of nontaxable exchanges.

Explain the nonrecognition provisions and basis determination rules for like-kind exchanges.

Examine the nonrecognition provisions available on the involuntary conversion of property.

Describe the provisions for postponing recognition of gain on the sale and replacement of a personal residence.

Discuss the provisions for permanent exclusion of gain on the sale of a personal residence applicable to taxpayers age 55 and older.

Identify tax planning opportunities related to the nonrecognition provisions discussed in the chapter.

A taxpayer who is going to replace a productive asset (e.g., machinery) used in a trade or business might structure the transactions as a sale of the old asset and the purchase of a new asset. Under this circumstance, any realized gain on the asset sale is recognized. The basis of the new asset is its cost. Conversely, the taxpayer may be able to trade the old asset for the new asset. This exchange of assets may qualify for nontaxable exchange treatment.

The tax law recognizes that nontaxable exchanges result in a change in the *form* but not in the *substance* of the taxpayer's relative economic position. The replacement property received in the exchange is viewed as substantially a continuation of the old investment.[1] Additional justification for nontaxable exchange treatment is that this type of transaction does not provide the taxpayer with the wherewithal to pay the tax on any realized gain. The nonrecognition provisions do not apply to realized losses from the sale or exchange of personal use assets. Such losses are not recognized because they are personal in nature and not because of any nonrecognition provision.

In a *nontaxable exchange*, realized gains or losses are not recognized. However, the nonrecognition is usually temporary. The recognition of gain or loss is merely *postponed* (deferred) until the property received in the nontaxable exchange is subsequently disposed of in a taxable transaction. This is accomplished by assigning a carryover basis to the replacement property.

EXAMPLE 1

T exchanges property with an adjusted basis of $10,000 and a fair market value of $12,000 for property with a fair market value of $12,000. The transaction qualifies for nontaxable exchange treatment. T has a realized gain of $2,000 ($12,000 amount realized − $10,000 adjusted basis). His recognized gain is $0. His basis in the replacement property is a carryover basis of $10,000. Assume the replacement property is nondepreciable. If T subsequently sells the replacement property for $12,000, his realized and recognized gain will be the $2,000 gain that was postponed (deferred) in the nontaxable transaction. If the replacement property is depreciable, the carryover basis of $10,000 is used in calculating depreciation. □

In some nontaxable exchanges, only part of the property involved in the transaction will qualify for nonrecognition treatment. If the taxpayer receives cash or other nonqualifying property, part or all of the realized gain from the exchange is recognized. In these instances, gain is recognized because the taxpayer has changed or improved his or her relative economic position and has the wherewithal to pay income tax to the extent of cash or other property received.

It is important to distinguish between a nontaxable disposition, as the term is used in the statute, and a tax-free transaction. First, a direct exchange is not required in all circumstances (e.g., replacement of involuntarily converted property or sale and replacement of a personal residence). Second, as previously mentioned, the term *nontaxable* refers to postponement of recognition via a carryover basis. In a tax-free transaction, the nonrecognition is permanent (e.g., see the discussion later in the chapter of the § 121 election by a taxpayer age 55 or over to exclude gain on the sale of a residence).

---

1. Reg. § 1.1002–1(c).

Therefore, the basis of any property acquired is not dependent on that of the property disposed of by the taxpayer.

Like-Kind Exchanges—§ 1031

Section 1031 provides for nontaxable exchange treatment if the following requirements are satisfied: [2]

- The form of the transaction is an exchange.
- Both the property transferred and the property received are held either for productive use in a trade or business or for investment.
- The property is like-kind property.

Like-kind exchanges include business for business, business for investment, investment for business, or investment for investment property. Property held for personal use, inventory, and partnership interests (both limited and general) do not qualify under the like-kind exchange provisions. Securities, even though held for investment, do not qualify for like-kind exchange treatment.

The nonrecognition provision for like-kind exchanges is *mandatory* rather than elective. That is, a taxpayer who wants to recognize a realized gain or loss will have to structure the transaction in a form that does not satisfy the statutory requirements for a like-kind exchange. This topic is discussed further under Tax Planning Considerations.

Like-Kind Property

"The words 'like-kind' refer to the nature or character of the property and not to its grade or quality. One kind or class of property may not . . . be exchanged for property of a different kind or class." [3]

Although the term *like-kind* is intended to be interpreted very broadly, two categories of exchanges are not included in this broad definition. First, livestock of different sexes do not qualify as like-kind property. Second, real estate can be exchanged only for other real estate, and personalty can be exchanged only for other personalty. For example, the exchange of a machine (personalty) for an office building (realty) is not a like-kind exchange. *Real estate* includes principally rental buildings, office and store buildings, manufacturing plants, warehouses, and land. It is immaterial whether real estate is improved or unimproved. Thus, unimproved land can be exchanged for an apartment house. *Personalty* includes principally machines, equipment, trucks, automobiles, furniture, and fixtures.

Example 2	T made the following exchanges during the taxable year:
	a. Inventory for a machine used in business.
	b. Land held for investment for a building used in business.

---

2. § 1031(a) and Reg. § 1.1031(a)–1(a).   3. Reg. § 1.1031(a)–1(b).

   c.   Stock held for investment for equipment used in business.

   d.   A business truck for a business machine.

   e.   An automobile used for personal transportation for a machine used in business.

   f.   Livestock for livestock of a different sex. □

Exchanges (b), investment real property for business real property, and (d), business personalty for business personalty, qualify as exchanges of like-kind property. Exchanges (a), inventory; (c), stock; (e), personal use automobile (not held for business or investment purposes); and (f), livestock of different sexes, do not qualify.

Exchange Requirement

The transaction must actually involve a direct exchange of property to qualify as a like-kind exchange. Thus, the sale of old property and the purchase of new property, even though like-kind, is generally not an exchange. However, if the two transactions are mutually dependent, the IRS may treat the two interdependent transactions as a like-kind exchange. For example, if the taxpayer sells an old business machine to a dealer and purchases a new one from the same dealer, like-kind exchange treatment could result.[4]

    The taxpayer might want to avoid nontaxable exchange treatment. Recognition of gain gives the taxpayer a higher basis for depreciation (see Example 27). To the extent that such gains would, if recognized, be passive activity income that could offset passive activity losses, it may be preferable to avoid the nonrecognition provisions through an indirect exchange transaction. For example, a taxpayer may sell property to one individual and follow the sale with a purchase of similar property from another individual. The taxpayer may also want to avoid nontaxable exchange treatment so that a realized loss can be recognized.

Boot *(handwritten: generally its cash.)*

If the taxpayer in a like-kind exchange gives or receives some property that is not like-kind property, recognition may occur. Property that is not like-kind property, including cash, is referred to as *boot.*

    The receipt of boot will trigger recognition of gain if there is realized gain. The amount of the recognized gain is the *lesser* of the boot received or the realized gain (realized gain serves as the ceiling on recognition).

EXAMPLE 3   T and S exchange machinery, and the exchange qualifies as like-kind under § 1031. Since T's machinery (adjusted basis of $20,000) is worth $24,000 and S's machine has a fair market value of $19,000, S also gives T cash of $5,000. T's recognized gain is $4,000, the lesser of the realized gain ($24,000 amount realized − $20,000 adjusted basis = $4,000) or the fair market value of the boot received ($5,000). □

---

4. Rev.Rul. 61–119, 1961–1 C.B. 395.

EXAMPLE 4

Assume the same facts as in the previous example, except that S's machine is worth $21,000 (not $19,000). Under these circumstances, S gives T cash of $3,000 to make up the difference. T's recognized gain is $3,000, the lesser of the realized gain ($24,000 amount realized − $20,000 adjusted basis = $4,000) or the fair market value of the boot received ($3,000). □

The receipt of boot does not result in recognition if there is realized loss.

EXAMPLE 5

Assume the same facts as in Example 3, except the adjusted basis of T's machine is $30,000. T's realized loss is $6,000 ($24,000 amount realized − $30,000 adjusted basis = $6,000 realized loss). The receipt of the boot of $5,000 does not trigger recognition. Therefore, the recognized loss is $0. □

The giving of boot usually does not trigger recognition. If the boot given is cash, any realized gain or loss will not be recognized.

EXAMPLE 6

T and S exchange equipment in a like-kind exchange. T receives equipment with a fair market value of $25,000. T transfers equipment worth $21,000 (adjusted basis of $15,000) and cash of $4,000. T's realized gain is $6,000 ($25,000 amount realized − $15,000 adjusted basis − $4,000 cash). However, none of the realized gain is recognized. □

If, however, the boot given is appreciated or depreciated property, gain or loss is recognized to the extent of the differential between the adjusted basis and the fair market value of the boot. For this purpose, *appreciated or depreciated property* is defined as property for which the adjusted basis is not equal to the fair market value.

EXAMPLE 7

Assume the same facts as in the previous example, except that T transfers equipment worth $10,000 (adjusted basis of $12,000) and boot worth $15,000 (adjusted basis of $9,000). T's realized gain appears to be $4,000 ($25,000 amount realized − $21,000 adjusted basis). Since realization previously has served as a ceiling on recognition, it appears that the recognized gain is $4,000 (lower of realized gain of $4,000 or amount of appreciation on boot of $6,000). However, the recognized gain actually is $6,000 (full amount of the appreciation on the boot). In effect, T must calculate the like-kind and boot parts of the transaction separately. That is, the realized loss of $2,000 on the like-kind property is not recognized ($10,000 fair market value − $12,000 adjusted basis), and the $6,000 realized gain on the boot is recognized ($15,000 fair market value − $9,000 adjusted basis). □

One other similar circumstance exists in which realization does not serve as a ceiling on recognition.

EXAMPLE 8

T and S exchange equipment in a like-kind exchange. T receives from S like-kind equipment with a fair market value of $25,000 and boot with a fair market value of $6,000. T gives up like-kind equipment with an adjusted basis of $12,000 and boot with an adjusted basis of $8,000. Although T's realized gain appears to be $11,000 ($25,000 + $6,000 − $12,000 − $8,000), T must report the like-kind and boot elements separately. It is therefore necessary to know the fair market value of the like-kind property and the boot transferred by T. Assume the fair market value of the like-kind equipment given up by T is $9,000 and that of the boot is $22,000. The realized loss of $3,000 on the like-kind property is not recognized ($9,000 fair market value − $12,000 adjusted basis), and the $14,000 realized gain on the boot is recognized ($22,000 fair market value − $8,000 adjusted basis). □

Basis of Property Received

If an exchange does not qualify as nontaxable under § 1031, gain or loss is recognized, and the basis of property received in the exchange is the property's fair market value. If the exchange qualifies for nonrecognition, the basis of property received must be adjusted to reflect any postponed (deferred) gain or loss. The *basis* of *like-kind property* received in the exchange is the property's fair market value less postponed gain or plus postponed loss. If the exchange partially qualifies for nonrecognition (if there is recognition associated with boot), the basis of like-kind property received in the exchange is the property's fair market value less postponed gain or plus postponed loss. The *basis* of any *boot* received is the boot's fair market value.

If there is a postponed loss, nonrecognition creates a situation in which the taxpayer has recovered *less* than the cost or other basis of the property exchanged in an amount equal to the unrecognized loss. If there is a postponed gain, the taxpayer has recovered *more* than the cost or other basis of the property exchanged in an amount equal to the unrecognized gain.

EXAMPLE 9

T exchanges a building (used in his business) with an adjusted basis of $30,000 and fair market value of $38,000 for land with a fair market value of $38,000. The land is to be held as an investment. The exchange qualifies as like-kind (an exchange of business real property for investment real property). Thus, the basis of the land is $30,000 (the land's fair market value of $38,000 less the $8,000 postponed gain on the building). If the land is later sold for its fair market value of $38,000, the $8,000 postponed gain will be recognized. □

EXAMPLE 10

Assume the same facts as in the previous example, except that the building has an adjusted basis of $48,000 and fair market value of only $38,000. The basis in the newly acquired land is $48,000 (fair market value of $38,000 plus the $10,000 postponed loss on the building). If the land is later sold for its fair market value of $38,000, the $10,000 postponed loss will be recognized. □

The Code provides an alternative approach for determining the basis of like-kind property received:
Adjusted basis of like-kind property surrendered

+ Adjusted basis of boot given
+ Gain recognized
− Fair market value of boot received
− Loss recognized
= Basis of like-kind property received

This approach is logical in terms of the recovery of capital doctrine. That is, the unrecovered cost or other basis is increased by additional cost (boot given) or decreased by cost recovered (boot received). Any gain recognized is included in the basis of the new property. The taxpayer has been taxed on this amount and is now entitled to recover it tax-free. Any loss recognized is deducted from the basis of the new property. The taxpayer has received a tax benefit on that amount.

The *holding period* of the property surrendered in the exchange carries over and *tacks on* to the holding period of the like-kind property received.[5] The logic of this rule is derived from the basic concept of the new property as a continuation of the old investment. For the boot received, there will be a new holding period (from the date of exchange) rather than a carryover holding period.

Depreciation recapture potential also carries over to the property received in a like-kind exchange.[6] See chapter 17 for a discussion of this topic.

The following comprehensive example illustrates the like-kind exchange rules.

EXAMPLE 11

T exchanged the following old machines for new machines in five independent like-kind exchanges:

Exchange	Adjusted Basis of Old Machine	Fair Market Value of New Machine	Adjusted Basis of Boot Given	Fair Market Value of Boot Received
1	$4,000	$9,000	$ –0–	$ –0–
2	4,000	9,000	3,000	–0–
3	4,000	9,000	6,000	–0–
4	4,000	9,000	–0–	3,000
5	4,000	3,500	–0–	300

T's realized and recognized gains and losses and the basis of each of the like-kind properties received are as follows:

---

5. § 1223(1) and Reg. § 1.1223–1(a). For this carryover holding period rule to apply to like-kind exchanges after March 1, 1954, the like-kind property surrendered must have been either a capital asset or § 1231 property. See chapters

16 and 17 for the discussion of capital assets and § 1231 property.

6. §§ 1245, 1250, 1245(a)(2), and 1250(b)(3) and Reg. §§ 1.1245–2(a)(4) and 1.1250–2(d)(1).

	Realized Gain (Loss)	Recognized Gain (Loss)	New Basis Calculation									
Exchange			Old Adj. Basis	+	Boot Given	+	Gain Recognized	–	Boot Received	=	New Basis
1	$5,000	$ –0–	$4,000	+	$ –0–	+	$ –0–	–	$ –0–	=	$ 4,000 *
2	2,000	–0–	4,000	+	3,000	+	–0–	–	–0–	=	7,000 *
3	(1,000)	–(0)–	4,000	+	6,000	+	–0–	–	–0–	=	10,000 **
4	8,000	3,000	4,000	+	–0–	+	3,000	–	3,000	=	4,000 *
5	(200)	–(0)–	4,000	+	–0–	+	–0–	–	300	=	3,700 **

* Basis may be determined in gain situations under the alternative method by subtracting the gain not recognized from the fair market value of the new property, i.e.,

> $9,000 – $5,000 = $4,000 for exchange 1.
> $9,000 – $2,000 = $7,000 for exchange 2.
> $9,000 – $5,000 = $4,000 for exchange 4.

** In loss situations, basis may be determined by adding the loss not recognized to the fair market value of the new property, i.e.,

> $9,000 + $1,000 = $10,000 for exchange 3.
> $3,500 + $200 = $3,700 for exchange 5.

The basis of the boot received is the boot's fair market value.

☐

If the taxpayer either assumes a liability or takes property subject to a liability, the amount of the liability is treated as boot received. Example 12 illustrates the effect of such a liability. In addition, the example illustrates the tax consequences for both parties involved in the like-kind exchange.

EXAMPLE 12

X and Y exchange real estate investments. X gives up property with an adjusted basis of $250,000 (fair market value $400,000) that is subject to a mortgage of $75,000 (assumed by Y). In return for this property, X receives property with a fair market value of $300,000 (adjusted basis $200,000) and cash of $25,000.

- X's realized gain is $150,000. X gave up property with an adjusted basis of $250,000. X received $400,000 from the exchange ($300,000 fair market value of like-kind property plus $100,000 boot received). The boot received consists of the cash of $25,000 received from Y and X's mortgage of $75,000 that is assumed by Y.

- X's recognized gain is $100,000. The realized gain of $150,000 is recognized to the extent of boot received.

- X's basis in the real estate received from Y is $250,000. This basis can be computed by subtracting the postponed gain ($50,000) from the fair market value of the real estate received ($300,000). It can also be computed by adding the recognized gain ($100,000) to the adjusted basis of the real estate given up ($250,000) and subtracting the boot received ($100,000).

- Y's realized gain is $100,000. Y gave up property with an adjusted basis of $200,000 plus boot of $100,000 ($75,000 mortgage assumed plus $25,000 cash) or a total of $300,000. Y received $400,000 from the exchange (fair market value of like-kind property received).

- Y has no recognized gain because he did not receive any boot. The entire gain of $100,000 is postponed.

- Y's basis in the real estate received from X is $300,000. This basis can be computed by subtracting the postponed gain ($100,000) from the fair market value of the real estate received ($400,000). It can also be computed by adding the boot given ($75,000 mortgage assumed by Y plus $25,000 cash) to the adjusted basis of the real estate given up ($200,000).[7] □

INVOLUNTARY CONVERSIONS—§ 1033

General Scheme

Don't worry about.

Section 1033 provides that a taxpayer who suffers an involuntary conversion of property may postpone recognition of *gain* realized from the conversion. The objective of this provision is to provide relief to the taxpayer who has suffered hardship and who does not have the wherewithal to pay the tax on any gain realized from the conversion. Postponement of realized gain is permitted to the extent that the taxpayer reinvests the amount realized from the conversion in replacement property. The rules for nonrecognition of gain are as follows:

- If the amount reinvested in replacement property *equals or exceeds* the amount realized, realized gain is *not recognized.*

- If the amount reinvested in replacement property is *less than* the amount realized, realized gain *is recognized* to the extent of the deficiency.

If a *loss* occurs on an involuntary conversion, § 1033 does not modify the normal rules for loss recognition. That is, if realized loss otherwise would be recognized, § 1033 does not change the result.

Involuntary Conversion Defined

An *involuntary conversion* results from the destruction (complete or partial), theft, seizure, requisition or condemnation, or the sale or exchange under threat or imminence of requisition or condemnation of the taxpayer's property.[8] To prove the existence of a threat or imminence of condemnation, the taxpayer must obtain confirmation that there has been a decision to acquire the property for public use. In addition, the taxpayer must have reasonable grounds to believe the property will be taken.[9] The property does not have to be sold to the authority threatening to condemn it to qualify for § 1033

---

7. Example (2) of Reg. § 1.1031(d)–2 illustrates a special situation where both the buyer and the seller transfer liabilities that are assumed or property is acquired subject to a liability by the other party.

8. § 1033(a) and Reg. §§ 1.1033(a)–1(a) and –2(a).
9. Rev.Rul. 63–221, 1963–2 C.B. 332, and *Joseph P. Balistrieri*, 38 TCM 526, T.C.Memo. 1979–115.

postponement. The taxpayer can sell the property to another party if he or she satisfies the previously mentioned confirmation and reasonable grounds requirements.[10] Likewise, the sale of property to a condemning authority by a taxpayer who acquired the property from its former owner with the knowledge that the property was under threat of condemnation also qualifies as an involuntary conversion under § 1033.[11] A voluntary act, such as an act of arson by a taxpayer involving his or her own property, is not an involuntary conversion.[12]

Although most involuntary conversions are casualties or condemnations, some special situations are included within the definition. Involuntary conversions, for example, include livestock destroyed by or on account of disease or exchanged or sold because of disease or solely on account of drought.

Computing the Amount Realized

The amount realized from the condemnation of property usually includes only the amount received as compensation for the property.[13] Any amount received that is designated as severance damages by both the government and the taxpayer is not included in the amount realized. Severance awards usually occur when only a portion of the entire property is condemned (e.g., a strip of land is taken to build a highway). Severance damages are awarded because the value of the taxpayer's remaining property has declined as a result of the condemnation. Such damages reduce the basis of the property. However, if either of the following requirements is satisfied, the nonrecognition provision of § 1033 applies to the severance damages.

- Severance damages are used to restore the usability of the remaining property.
- The usefulness of the remaining property is destroyed by the condemnation, and the property is sold and replaced at a cost equal to or exceeding the sum of the condemnation award, severance damages, and sales proceeds.

Replacement Property

The requirements for replacement property generally are more restrictive than those for like-kind property under § 1031. The basic requirement is that the replacement property be similar or related in service or use to the involuntarily converted property.[14]

Different interpretations of the phrase *similar or related in service or use* apply if the involuntarily converted property is held by an *owner-user* rather than an *owner-investor* (e.g., lessor). The taxpayer who uses the property in his or her trade or business is subject to a more restrictive test in terms of acquiring replacement property. For the owner-user, the *functional use test* applies, and for the owner-investor, the *taxpayer use test* applies.

Taxpayer Use Test.   The taxpayer use test for owner-investors provides the taxpayer with more flexibility in terms of what qualifies as replacement prop-

10. Rev.Rul. 81–180, 1981–2 C.B. 161.
11. Rev.Rul. 81–181, 1981–2 C.B. 162.
12. Rev.Rul. 82–74, 1982–1 C.B. 110.

13. *Pioneer Real Estate Co.*, 47 B.T.A. 886 (1942), *acq.* 1943 C.B. 18.
14. § 1033(a) and Reg. § 1.1033(a)–1.

erty than does the functional use test for owner-users. Essentially, the properties must be used by the taxpayer (the owner-investor) in similar endeavors. For example, rental property held by an owner-investor will qualify if replaced by other rental property, regardless of the type of rental property involved. This test would be met if an investor replaced a manufacturing plant with a wholesale grocery warehouse if both properties were held for the production of rental income.[15] A rental residence replaced by a personal residence does not meet this test.[16]

Functional Use Test.   This test requires that the taxpayer's use of the replacement property and of the involuntarily converted property be the same. A rental residence replaced by a personal residence does not meet this test. A manufacturing plant replaced by a wholesale grocery warehouse, whether rented or not, does not meet this test; but as indicated above, the IRS applies the taxpayer use test to owner-investors. However, the functional use test still applies to owner-users (e.g., a manufacturer whose manufacturing plant is destroyed by fire is required to replace the plant with another facility of similar functional use).

Special Rules.   Under one set of circumstances, the broader replacement rules for like-kind exchanges are substituted for the narrow replacement rules normally used for involuntary conversions. This beneficial provision applies if business real property or investment real property is condemned. Therefore, the taxpayer has substantially more flexibility in terms of his or her selection of replacement property. For example, improved real property can be replaced with unimproved real property. Another special rule provides that proceeds from the involuntary conversion of livestock due to soil or other environmental contamination need be expended only for any property to be used for farming, including real property. Finally, another special rule permits an indirect replacement approach. Under this rule, the taxpayer can acquire controlling interest (80 percent) in a corporation that owns property that qualifies as replacement property in lieu of purchasing the replacement property directly. However, the aforementioned special rule that substitutes the broader replacement rules for like-kind exchanges cannot be used in conjunction with this indirect replacement approach.

The rules concerning the nature of replacement property are illustrated in Concept Summary 15–1.

Time Limitation on Replacement

The taxpayer has a two-year period after the close of the taxable year in which any gain is realized from the involuntary conversion to replace the property.[17] This rule affords as much as three years from the date of realization of gain to replace the property if the realization of gain took place on the first day of the taxable year.[18] If the form of the involuntary conversion is the condemnation of real property used in a trade or business or held for investment, a three-year period is substituted for the normal two-year period. Thus, the taxpayer

---

15. *Loco Realty Co. v. Comm.*, 62–2 USTC ¶ 9657, 10 AFTR2d 5359, 306 F.2d 207 (CA–8, 1962).

16. Rev.Rul. 70–466, 1970–2 C.B. 165.

17. §§ 1033(a)(2)(B) and (g)(4) and Reg. §§ 1.1033(a)–2(c)(3) and (f)–1(b).

18. The taxpayer can apply for an extension of this time period anytime before its expiration [Reg. § 1.1033(a)–2(c)(3)]. Also, the period for filing the application for extension can be extended if the taxpayer shows reasonable cause.

CONCEPT SUMMARY 15–1

Replacement Property Tests			
Type of Property and User	**Like-Kind Test**	**Taxpayer Use Test**	**Functional Use Test**
Land used by a manufacturing company is condemned by a local government authority.	X		
Apartment and land held by an investor are sold due to the threat or imminence of condemnation.	X		
An investor's rented wholesale grocery warehouse is destroyed by fire; the warehouse may be replaced by other rental properties (e.g., an apartment building).		X	
A manufacturing plant is destroyed by fire; replacement property must consist of another manufacturing plant that is functionally the same as the property converted.			X
Personal residence of taxpayer is condemned by a local government authority; replacement property must consist of another personal residence.			X

could actually have as much as four years from the date of realization of gain to replace the property in this case.

EXAMPLE 13 T's warehouse is destroyed by fire on December 16, 1989. The adjusted basis is $325,000. Proceeds of $400,000 are received from the insurance company on January 10, 1990. T is a calendar year taxpayer. The latest date for replacement is December 31, 1992 (the end of the taxable year in which realized gain occurred plus two years). The critical date is not the date the involuntary conversion occurred, but rather the date of gain realization. ☐

EXAMPLE 14 Assume the same facts as in the previous example, except T's warehouse is condemned. The latest date for replacement is December 31, 1993 (the end of the taxable year in which realized gain occurred plus three years). ☐

The earliest date for replacement typically is the date the involuntary conversion occurs. However, if the property is condemned, it is possible to replace the condemned property before this date. In this case, the earliest date is the date of the threat or imminence of requisition or condemnation of the property. The purpose of this provision is to enable the taxpayer to make an orderly replacement of the condemned property.

Nonrecognition of Gain

Nonrecognition of gain can be either mandatory or elective, depending upon whether the conversion is direct (into replacement property) or into money.

Direct Conversion.   If the conversion is directly into replacement property rather than into money, nonrecognition of realized gain is *mandatory*. In this case, the basis of the replacement property is the same as the adjusted basis of the converted property. Direct conversion is rare in practice and usually involves condemnations. The following example illustrates the application of the rules for direct conversions.

EXAMPLE 15

T's property with an adjusted basis of $20,000 is condemned by the state. T receives property with a fair market value of $50,000 as compensation for the property taken. Since the nonrecognition of realized gain is mandatory for direct conversions, T's realized gain of $30,000 is not recognized, and the basis of the replacement property is $20,000 (adjusted basis of the condemned property). ☐

Conversion into Money.   If the conversion is into money, "at the election of the taxpayer the gain shall be recognized only to the extent that the amount realized upon such conversion . . . exceeds the cost of such other property or such stock." [19] This is the usual case, and nonrecognition (postponement) is *elective.*

The basis of the replacement property is the property's cost less postponed (deferred) gain.[20] The holding period of the replacement property, if the election to postpone gain is made, includes the holding period of the converted property.

Section 1033 applies *only to gains* and *not to losses*. Losses from involuntary conversions are recognized if the property is held for business or income-producing purposes. Personal casualty losses are recognized, but condemnation losses related to personal use assets (e.g., a personal residence) are neither recognized nor postponed.

Examples 16 and 17 illustrate the application of the involuntary conversion rules.

EXAMPLE 16

T's building (used in his trade or business), with an adjusted basis of $50,000, is destroyed by fire in 1989. T is a calendar year taxpayer. In 1989, T receives an insurance reimbursement for the loss in the amount of $100,000. T invests $75,000 in a new building.

- T has until December 31, 1991, to make the new investment and qualify for the nonrecognition election.

---

19. § 1033(a)(2)(A) and Reg. § 1.1033(a)–2(c)(1).   20. § 1033(b).

- T's realized gain is $50,000 ($100,000 insurance proceeds less $50,000 adjusted basis of old building).

- Assuming the replacement property qualifies as similar or related in service or use, T's recognized gain is $25,000. T reinvested $25,000 less than the insurance proceeds ($100,000 proceeds minus $75,000 reinvested). Therefore, his realized gain is recognized to that extent.

- T's basis in the new building is $50,000. This is the building's cost of $75,000 less the postponed gain of $25,000 (realized gain of $50,000 less recognized gain of $25,000).

- The computation of realization, recognition, and basis would apply even if T were a real estate dealer and the building destroyed by fire were part of his inventory. Section 1033 does not generally exclude inventory, as does § 1031. □

EXAMPLE 17   Assume the same facts as in the previous example, except that T receives only $45,000 (instead of $100,000) of insurance proceeds. T would have a realized and recognized loss of $5,000. The basis of the new building would be the building's cost of $75,000. If the building destroyed were held for personal use, the recognized loss would be subject to other limitations.[21] The loss of $5,000 would be limited to the decline in fair market value of the property, and the amount of the loss would be reduced first by $100 and then by 10% of adjusted gross income (refer to chapter 8). □

Although the previous discussion describes an indirect conversion as a conversion into money, § 1033 refers to indirect conversions as conversions "into money or other property not similar or related in service or use to the converted property. . . ."[22] An indirect conversion into other than money would be rare, but it could occur and is treated the same as a conversion into money.

Involuntary Conversion of a Personal Residence

The tax consequences of the involuntary conversion of a personal residence depend upon whether the conversion is a casualty or condemnation and whether a realized loss or gain results.

Loss Situations.   If the conversion is a condemnation, the realized loss is not recognized. Loss from the condemnation of a personal use asset is never recognized. If the conversion is a casualty (a loss from fire, storm, etc.), the loss is recognized subject to the personal casualty loss limitations.

Gain Situations.   If the conversion is a condemnation, the gain may be postponed under either § 1033 or § 1034. That is, the taxpayer may elect to treat the condemnation as a sale under the deferral of gain rules relating to the sale of a personal residence under § 1034 (presented subsequently). If the

---

21. § 165(c)(3) and Reg. § 1.165–7.   22. § 1033(a)(2).

conversion is a casualty, the gain can be postponed only under the involuntary conversion provisions.

Reporting Considerations

An election to postpone gain normally is made on the return for the taxable year in which gain is realized. The taxpayer should attach to the return a statement that includes supportive details. If the property has not been replaced before filing the tax return, the taxpayer should also attach a supporting statement to the return for the taxable year in which the property is replaced.

If the property either is not replaced within the prescribed period or is replaced at a cost less than anticipated, an amended return must be filed for the taxable year in which the election was made. A taxpayer who has elected § 1033 postponement and makes an appropriate replacement may not later revoke the election. In addition, once the taxpayer has designated qualifying property as replacement property, he or she cannot later change the designation.[23] If no election is made on the return for the taxable year in which gain is realized, an election may still be made within the prescribed time period by filing a claim for credit or refund.[24]

Involuntary conversions from casualty and theft are reported first on Form 4684, Casualties and Thefts. Casualty and theft losses on personal use property for the individual taxpayer are carried from Form 4684 to Schedule A of Form 1040. For other casualty and theft items, the Form 4684 amounts are generally reported on Form 4797, Supplemental Schedule of Gains and Losses, unless Form 4797 is not required. In the latter case, the amounts are reported directly on the tax return involved.

Except for personal use property, recognized gains and losses from involuntary conversions other than by casualty and theft are reported on Form 4797. As stated previously, if the property involved in the involuntary conversion (other than by casualty and theft) is personal use property, any loss is not recognized. Any gain is treated as gain on a voluntary sale.

SALE OF A RESIDENCE—§ 1034

A realized loss from the sale of a personal residence is not recognized because the residence is personal use property. A realized gain is, however, subject to taxation. There are two provisions in the tax law whereby all or part of the realized gain is either postponed or excluded from taxation. The first of these, § 1034, is discussed below. The second, § 121, is discussed later in the chapter.

Section 1034 provides for the *mandatory* nonrecognition of gain from the sale or exchange of a personal residence if the sales proceeds are reinvested in a replacement residence within a prescribed time period. Both the old and new residences must qualify as the taxpayer's principal residence. A houseboat or house trailer qualifies if used by the taxpayer as his or her principal residence.[25]

The reason for not recognizing gain when a residence is replaced by a new residence within the prescribed time period (discussed below) is that the

Cunt adj basis of NEW HOUSE

---

23. Rev.Rul. 83–39, 1983–1 C.B. 190.
24. Reg. § 1.1033(a)–2(c)(2).

25. Reg. § 1.1034–1(c)(3)(i).

new residence is viewed as a continuation of the investment. Also, if the proceeds from the sale are reinvested, the taxpayer does not have the where-withal to pay tax on the gain. Beyond these fundamental concepts, Congress, in enacting § 1034, was concerned with the hardship of involuntary moves and the socially desirable objective of encouraging the mobility of labor.

Replacement Period

For the nonrecognition treatment to apply, the old residence must be replaced by a new residence within a period *beginning two years before* the sale of the old residence and *ending two years after* such sale. This four-year period applies regardless of whether the new residence is purchased or constructed. In addition to acquiring the residence during this period, the taxpayer must *occupy* and use the new residence as the principal residence during this same time period. The occupancy requirement has been strictly construed by both the IRS and the courts, and even circumstances beyond a taxpayer's control do not excuse noncompliance.[26]

EXAMPLE 18

T sells her personal residence from which she realizes a gain of $50,000. The construction of a new residence begins immediately after the sale. However, unstable soil conditions and a trade union strike cause unforeseen delays in construction. The new residence ultimately is completed and occupied by T 25 months after the sale of the old residence. Since the occupancy requirement has not been satisfied, § 1034 is inapplicable, and T must recognize a gain of $50,000 on the sale of the old residence. □

Taxpayers might be inclined to make liberal use of § 1034 as a means of speculating when the price of residential housing is rising. Without any time restriction on its use, § 1034 would permit deferral of gain on multiple sales of principal residences, each one of which would result in an economic profit. The Code curbs this approach by precluding the application of § 1034 to any sales occurring within two years of its last use.

EXAMPLE 19

After T sells his principal residence (subsequently designated as the first residence) in March of 1988 for $150,000 (realized gain of $60,000), he buys and sells the following (all of which qualify as principal residences):

	Date of Purchase	Date of Sale	Amount Involved
Second residence	April 1988		$160,000
Second residence		May 1989	180,000
Third residence	June 1989		200,000

26. *Joseph T. Galinas*, 35 TCM 448, T.C.Memo. 1976–103; *Helen M. Welch*, 38 TCM 26, T.C. Memo. 1979–9; *James A. Henry*, 44 TCM 844, T.C.Memo. 1982–469; and *William F. Peck*, 44 TCM 1030, T.C.Memo. 1982–506.

Because multiple sales have occurred within a period of two years, § 1034 does not apply to the sale of the second residence. Thus, the realized gain of $20,000 [$180,000 (selling price) − $160,000 (purchase price)] must be recognized. □

The two-year rule precluding multiple use of § 1034 could work a hardship where a taxpayer has been transferred by his or her employer and therefore has little choice in the matter. For this reason, § 1034 was amended to provide an exception to the two-year rule when the sale results from a change in the location of employment. To qualify for the exception, a taxpayer must meet the distance and length-of-employment requirements specified for the deduction of moving expenses under § 217.[27]

EXAMPLE 20

Assume the same facts as in the previous example, except that in February of 1989, T's employer transfers T to a job in another state. Consequently, the sale of the second residence and the purchase of the third residence were due to the relocation of employment. If T satisfies the distance and length-of-employment requirements of § 217, no gain will be recognized on the sale of the first and second residences. □

Principal Residence

As indicated, both the old and new residences must qualify as the taxpayer's principal residence. Whether property is the taxpayer's principal residence is dependent ". . . upon all the facts and circumstances in each case."[28]

EXAMPLE 21

T sells his principal residence and moves to Norfolk, Virginia, where he is employed. He decides to rent an apartment in Norfolk because of its proximity to his place of employment. He purchases a beach house at Virginia Beach that he occupies most weekends. T does not intend to live in the beach house other than on weekends. The apartment in Norfolk is his principal place of residence. Therefore, the purchase of the beach house does not qualify as an appropriate replacement. □

If the old residence ceases to be the taxpayer's principal residence before its sale, the nonrecognition provision does not apply. For example, if the taxpayer abandons the old residence before its sale, the residence no longer qualifies as a principal residence.[29] If the old residence is converted to other than personal use (e.g., rental) before its sale, the nonrecognition provision does not apply. If only partially converted to business use, gain from the sale of the personal use portion still qualifies for nonrecognition. It is possible to convert part of a principal residence to business use and later to convert that part back to being part of the principal residence (e.g., a home office).[30]

27. Refer to chapter 10 for the discussion of the rules governing the deduction for moving expenses.
28. Reg. § 1.1034–1(c)(3).
29. *Richard T. Houlette*, 48 T.C. 350 (1967), and *Stolk v. Comm.*, 64–1 USTC ¶9228, 13 AFTR2d 535, 326 F.2d 760 (CA-2, 1964).
30. Rev.Rul. 82–26, 1982–1 C.B. 114.

Temporarily renting out the old residence before sale does not necessarily terminate its status as the taxpayer's principal residence,[31] nor does temporarily renting out the new residence before it is occupied by the taxpayer. An issue associated with temporarily renting out the old residence while attempting to sell it is whether a taxpayer is entitled to deduct expenses in excess of income relating to the rental of a residence before its sale. That is, is the old residence subject to the loss deduction rules for hobby loss activities? If it is, the deductions associated with the rental activity are limited to the rental income generated. The Tax Court concluded that since the property was considered to be the taxpayer's principal residence and as a result qualifies for § 1034 postponement of gain, the property was subject to the hobby loss limitations. The Court of Appeals reversed the Tax Court and held that the hobby loss provisions did not apply.[32.]

Nonrecognition of Gain Requirements

Realized gain from the sale of the old residence is not recognized if the taxpayer reinvests an amount *at least equal* to the adjusted sales price of the old residence. Realized gain is recognized to the extent the taxpayer does not reinvest the adjusted sales price in a new residence. Therefore, the amount not reinvested is treated similarly to boot received in a like-kind exchange.

The *adjusted sales price* is the amount realized from the sale of the old residence less fixing-up expenses. The *amount realized* is calculated by reducing the selling price by the selling expenses. *Selling expenses* include items such as advertising the property for sale, real estate broker commissions, legal fees in connection with the sale, and loan placement fees paid by the taxpayer as a condition of the arrangement of financing for the buyer. To the extent that the selling expenses are deducted as moving expenses, they are not allowed as deductions in the computation of the amount realized (refer to chapter 10).

Fixing-up expenses are personal in nature and are incurred by the taxpayer to assist in the sale of the old residence. Fixing-up expenses include such items as ordinary repairs, painting, and wallpapering. To qualify as a fixing-up expense, the expense must (1) be incurred for work performed during the 90-day period ending on the date of the contract of sale, (2) be paid within 30 days after the date of the sale, and (3) not be a capital expenditure.

Although selling expenses are deductible in calculating the amount realized, fixing-up expenses are not. Therefore, fixing-up expenses do not have an impact on the calculation of realized gain or loss. However, since fixing-up expenses are deductible in calculating the adjusted sales price, they do have the potential for producing tax benefit in that they reduce the amount of the reinvestment required to qualify for nonrecognition treatment. Conversely, if a replacement residence is not acquired, the fixing-up expenses produce no tax benefit.

Reducing the amount of the required reinvestment by the amount of fixing-up expenses is another application of the wherewithal to pay concept. To the extent that the taxpayer has expended part of the funds received on the sale in preparing the old residence for sale, he or she does not have the funds available to reinvest in the new residence.

31. *Robert W. Aagaard*, 56 T.C. 191 (1971), *acq.* 1971–2 C.B. 1; *Robert G. Clapham*, 63 T.C. 505 (1975); Rev.Rul. 59–72, 1959–1 C.B. 203; and Rev.Rul. 78–146, 1978–1 C.B. 260.

32. *Bolaris v. Comm.*, 85–2 USTC ¶9822, 56 AFTR2d 85–6472, 776 F.2d 1428 (CA–9, 1985).

As previously mentioned, fixing-up expenses are not considered in determining realized gain. They are considered only in determining how much realized gain is to be postponed. In addition, fixing-up expenses have no direct effect on the basis of the new residence. Indirectly, through their effect on postponed gain, they can bring about a lesser basis for the new residence. The effects of fixing-up expenses on the computation of gain realized and recognized and on the basis of the new residence are illustrated in Concept Summary 15–2 and in Example 22.

Capital Improvements

Capital improvements are added to the adjusted basis of a personal residence. The adjusted basis is used in computing gain or loss on a subsequent sale or other disposition of the property. However, in calculating the cost of a replacement residence (for determining the nonrecognition of gain under § 1034), only capital improvements made during a certain time period are counted. The time period begins two years before the date of sale of the old residence and ends two years after such date (the time period during which the old residence can be replaced).[33]

CONCEPT SUMMARY 15–2

Sale of Residence Model

Step 1 Sales price - Selling expenses = Amount realized

Step 2 Amount realized - Adjusted basis of old residence = Realized gain

Step 3 Amount realized - Fixing-up expenses = Adjusted sales price (amount which must be reinvested to avoid any recognized gain)

Step 4 Adjusted sales price - Cost of new residence = Excess of adjusted sales price, if any, over cost

Step 5 Recognized gain = Lesser of realized gain or excess determined in Step 4

Step 6 Gain not recognized (postponed) = Realized gain - Recognized gain

Step 7 Basis of new residence = Cost of new residence - Gain not recognized

---

33. *Charles M. Shaw*, 69 T.C. 1034 (1978); Reg. § 1.1034–1(c)(4)(ii); and Rev.Rul. 78–147, 1978–1 C.B. 261.

If the taxpayer receives a residence by gift or inheritance, such residence will not qualify as a replacement residence. However, if the taxpayer makes substantial capital expenditures (e.g., reconstruction or additions) to such property within the replacement time period, these expenditures do qualify.[34]

Basis of the New Residence

The *basis* of the new residence is the cost of the new residence less the realized gain not recognized (postponed gain). If there is any postponed gain, the *holding period* of the new residence includes the holding period of the old residence.

Concept Summary 15–2 summarizes the sale-of-residence concepts. Example 22 illustrates these concepts and the application of the nonrecognition provision.

EXAMPLE 22

T sells her personal residence (adjusted basis of $36,000) for $44,000. She receives only $41,400 after payment of a brokerage fee of $2,600. Ten days before the sale, T incurred and paid for qualified fixing-up expenses of $1,400. Two months later, T acquires a new residence. Determine the gain, if any, T must recognize and the basis of the new residence under each of the following circumstances:

- The new residence cost $60,000. The cost of the new residence has no effect on determining the realized gain from the sale of the old residence. The realized gain is $5,400 ($41,400 amount realized less $36,000 adjusted basis of old residence). None of the gain is recognized because T reinvested at least $40,000 ($41,400 amount realized − $1,400 fixing-up expenses = $40,000 adjusted sales price) in the new residence. The $5,400 realized gain is postponed, and the basis of the new residence is $54,600 ($60,000 cost less $5,400 postponed gain).

- The new residence cost $38,000. Of the realized gain of $5,400, $2,000 is recognized because T reinvested $2,000 less than the adjusted sales price of $40,000. The remaining gain of $3,400 is not recognized and is postponed. The basis of the new residence is $34,600 ($38,000 cost less $3,400 postponed gain).

- The new residence cost $32,000. All of the realized gain of $5,400 is recognized because T reinvested $8,000 less than the adjusted sales price of $40,000. Since the amount not reinvested exceeds the realized gain, the entire gain is recognized and § 1034 does not apply. The basis of the new residence is simply the residence's cost of $32,000 because there is no postponed gain. □

Reporting Procedures

The taxpayer is required to report the details of the sale of the residence on the tax return for the taxable year in which gain is realized, even if all of the

34. Reg. §§ 1.1034–1(b)(7) and (9) and 1.1034–1(c)(4)(i).

gain is postponed. If a new residence is acquired and occupied before filing, a statement should be attached to the return showing the purchase date, the cost, and date of occupancy. Form 2119, Sale or Exchange of Principal Residence, is used to show the details of the sale and replacement, and a copy should be retained permanently by the taxpayer as support for the basis of the new residence. If a replacement residence has not been purchased when the return is filed, the taxpayer should submit the details of the purchase on the return of the taxable year during which it occurs. If the old residence is not replaced within the prescribed time period, or if some recognized gain results, the taxpayer must file an amended return for the year in which the sale took place.

SALE OF A RESIDENCE—§ 121

Taxpayers age 55 or older who sell or exchange their principal residence may *elect to exclude* up to $125,000 ($62,500 for married individuals filing separate returns) of realized gain from the sale or exchange.[35] The election can be made *only once*.[36] This provision is contrasted with § 1034 where nonrecognition is mandatory and may occur many times during a taxpayer's lifetime. Section 121 also differs from § 1034 in that it does not require the taxpayer to purchase a new residence. The excluded gain is never recognized, whereas the realized gain not recognized under § 1034 is postponed by subtracting it from the cost of the new residence in calculating the adjusted basis.

This provision is the only case in the tax law where a realized gain from the disposition of property that is not recognized is excluded rather than merely postponed. In other words, the provision allows the taxpayer a permanent recovery of more than the cost or other basis of the residence tax-free.

The reason for § 121 is simply the desire of Congress to relieve older citizens of the large tax they might incur from the sale of a personal residence. The dollar and age limitations restrict the benefit of § 121 to taxpayers who presumably have a greater need for increased tax-free dollars.

Requirements

The taxpayer must be at least age 55 before the date of the sale and have *owned* and *used* the residence as a principal residence for at least *three years* during the *five-year* period ending on the date of sale. The ownership and use periods do not have to be the same period of time. Short temporary absences (e.g., vacations) count as periods of use. If the residence is owned jointly by husband and wife, only one of the spouses is required to meet these requirements if a joint return is filed for the taxable year in which the sale took place.

In determining whether the ownership and use period requirements are satisfied, transactions affecting prior residences may be relevant. If a former residence is involuntarily converted and any gain is postponed under § 1033, the holding period of the former residence is added to the holding period of the replacement residence for § 121 purposes. However, if the realized gain is postponed under § 1034 (sale of residence provision), the holding period of the former residence is not added to the holding period of the replacement

---

35. §§ 121(a), (b), and (c). For married taxpayers, each spouse must consent.

36. § 121(b)(2) and Reg. § 1.121–2(b). Only one election may be made by married individuals.

residence for § 121 purposes. In this instance, the holding period of the replacement residence begins with the acquisition date of the replacement residence.

EXAMPLE 23

T has lived in his residence since 1983. The residence is involuntarily converted in July 1989. T purchases a replacement residence in August 1989. In determining whether T can satisfy the ownership and use requirements at the time of the subsequent sale of the replacement residence purchased in 1989, he includes the holding period of the involuntarily converted residence. □

EXAMPLE 24

Assume the same facts as in the previous example, except that T's residence was not involuntarily converted. Instead, T sold it so that he could move into a larger house. In determining whether T can satisfy the ownership and use requirements at the time of the subsequent sale of the replacement residence purchased in 1989, T is not permitted to include the holding period of the old residence. □

Relationship to Other Provisions

The taxpayer can treat an involuntary conversion of a principal residence as a sale for purposes of § 121(a). Any gain not excluded under § 121 is then subject to postponement under § 1033 or § 1034 (condemnation only), assuming the requirements of those provisions are met.

Any gain not excluded under § 121 from the sale of a residence is subject to postponement under § 1034, assuming the requirements of that provision are met. This relationship is illustrated in Examples 25 and 26.

Making and Revoking the Election

The election not to recognize gain under § 121 may be made or revoked at any time before the statute of limitations expires. Therefore, the taxpayer generally has until the *later* of (1) three years from the due date of the return for the year the gain is realized or (2) two years from the date the tax is paid to make or revoke the election. Making the election is accomplished by attaching a signed statement (showing all the details of the sale) to the return for the taxable year in which the sale took place. Form 2119 is used for this purpose. Revocation is accomplished by filing a signed statement (showing the taxpayer's name, Social Security number, and taxable year for which the election was made) indicating such revocation.[37]

Computation Procedure

The following examples illustrate the application of both the § 121 and § 1034 provisions.

---

37. Reg. §§ 1.121–4(b) and (c).

EXAMPLE 25

T sells his personal residence (adjusted basis of $32,000) for $205,000, of which he receives only $195,400 after the payment of selling expenses. Ten days before the sale, T incurred and paid for qualified fixing-up expenses of $6,400. T is age 55 and elects the exclusion of gain under § 121. He does not acquire a replacement residence. ☐

EXAMPLE 26

Assume the same facts as in the previous example, except that T acquires a new residence for $40,000 within the prescribed time period.
The solutions to Examples 25 and 26 are as follows:

	Example 25	Example 26
Amount realized ($205,000 − $9,600)	$195,400	$195,400
Adjusted basis	32,000	32,000
Realized gain	$163,400	$163,400
§ 121 exclusion	125,000	125,000
Realized gain after exclusion	$ 38,400	$ 38,400
Amount realized	$195,400	$195,400
Fixing-up expenses	6,400	6,400
Adjusted sales price	$189,000	$189,000
§ 121 exclusion	125,000	125,000
Adjusted sales price after exclusion	$ 64,000	$ 64,000
Cost of new residence	-0-	40,000
Excess of adjusted sales price after the exclusion over reinvestment	$ 64,000	$ 24,000
Recognized gain (lower of realized gain after exclusion or above excess)	$ 38,400	$ 24,000
Realized gain after exclusion	$ 38,400	$ 38,400
Recognized gain	38,400	24,000
Postponed gain	$ -0-	$ 14,400
Cost of new residence	$ -0-	$ 40,000
Postponed gain	-0-	14,400
Basis of new residence	$ -0-	$ 25,600

☐

Comparing the results of Examples 25 and 26 provides insight into the relationship between § 1034 and § 121. If T had not made the election to postpone gain under § 121 in Example 25, his recognized gain would have been $163,400 (the realized gain). Thus, the election resulted in the permanent exclusion of the $125,000 of realized gain by reducing the recognized gain to $38,400. Further documentation of the permanent nature of the § 121 exclusion is provided in the calculation of the basis of the new residence in Example 26. The $40,000 cost of the residence is reduced only by the postponed gain of $14,400. That is, it is not reduced by the amount of the § 121 exclusion. To postpone all of the $38,400 realized gain after the exclusion, T would have needed to reinvest $64,000 (the adjusted sales price after the exclusion). Also, note that the Example 25 results demonstrate that the realized gain after the exclusion is the ceiling on recognition.

OTHER NONRECOGNITION PROVISIONS

In terms of impacting on the typical taxpayer, sales of residences and involuntary conversions occur more frequently than the other types of nontaxable exchanges. Several additional nonrecognition provisions that are not as common are treated briefly in the remainder of this chapter.

Exchange of Stock for Property—§ 1032

No real loss

Under this Section, no gain or loss is recognized to a corporation on the receipt of money or other property in exchange for its stock (including treasury stock). In other words, no gain or loss is recognized by a corporation when it deals in its own stock. This provision is consistent with the accounting treatment of such transactions.

Certain Exchanges of Insurance Policies—§ 1035

Under this provision, no gain or loss is recognized from the exchange of certain insurance contracts or policies. The rules relating to exchanges not solely in kind and the basis of the property acquired are the same as under § 1031. Exchanges qualifying for nonrecognition include the following:

- The exchange of life insurance contracts.
- The exchange of a life insurance contract for an endowment or annuity contract.
- The exchange of an endowment contract for another endowment contract that provides for regular payments beginning at a date not later than the date payments would have begun under the contract exchanged.
- The exchange of an endowment contract for an annuity contract.
- The exchange of annuity contracts.

Exchange of Stock for Stock of the Same Corporation—§ 1036

No gain or loss is recognized by a shareholder on the exchange of common stock solely for common stock in the same corporation or from the exchange of preferred stock for preferred stock in the same corporation. Exchanges between individual shareholders as well as between a shareholder and the corporation are included. The rules relating to exchanges not solely in kind and the basis of the property acquired are the same as under § 1031. For example, a nonrecognition exchange occurs when common stock with different rights, such as voting for nonvoting, is exchanged. Gain or loss from the exchange of common for preferred or preferred for common usually is recognized even though the stock exchanged is in the same corporation.

Certain Reacquisitions of Real Property—§ 1038

Under this provision, no loss is recognized from the repossession of real property sold on an installment basis. Gain is recognized to a limited extent.

Transfers of Property between Spouses or Incident to Divorce—§ 1041

Section 1041 provides that transfers of property *between spouses or former spouses incident to divorce* are nontaxable transactions. Therefore, the basis to the recipient is a carryover basis. To be treated as incident to the divorce, the transfer must be related to the cessation of marriage or occur within one year after the date on which the marriage ceases.

Section 1041 also provides for nontaxable exchange treatment on property transfers *between spouses during marriage*. The basis to the recipient spouse is a carryover basis.

Sale of Stock to Stock Ownership Plans or Certain Cooperatives—§ 1042

Section 1042 provides that the realized gain will be postponed if the taxpayer (or his or her executor) sells qualified securities to a qualified entity and, within a specified time period, such seller purchases qualified replacement property. Qualified entities include an employee stock ownership plan (ESOP) and an eligible worker-owned cooperative. To qualify for this treatment, several statutory requirements must be satisfied.

Chapter 15 has covered certain situations in which realized gains or losses are not recognized (nontaxable exchanges). Chapters 16 and 17 are concerned with the *classification* of recognized gains and losses. That is, if a gain or loss is recognized, is it an ordinary or capital gain or loss? Chapter 16 discusses the tax consequences of capital gains and losses.

TAX PLANNING CONSIDERATIONS

Like-Kind Exchanges

Since application of the like-kind provisions is mandatory rather than elective, in certain instances it may be preferable to avoid qualifying for § 1031 nonrecognition. If the like-kind provisions do not apply, the end result may be the recognition of capital gain in exchange for a higher basis in the newly acquired asset. Also, the immediate recognition of gain may be preferable in certain situations. Examples of immediate recognition being beneficial include the following:

- Taxpayer has unused net operating loss carryovers.
- Taxpayer has unused investment tax credit carryovers.

- Taxpayer has suspended or current passive activity losses.
- Taxpayer expects his or her effective tax rate to increase in the future.

EXAMPLE 27

T disposes of a machine (used in his business) with an adjusted basis of $3,000 for $4,000. T also acquires a new business machine for $9,000. If § 1031 applies, the $1,000 realized gain is not recognized, and the basis of the new machine is reduced by $1,000. If § 1031 does not apply, a $1,000 gain is recognized and may receive capital gain treatment to the extent that the gain is not recognized as ordinary income due to the depreciation recapture provisions (see chapter 17). In addition, the basis for depreciation on the new machine is $9,000 rather than $8,000, since there is no unrecognized gain. □

Another time for avoiding the application of § 1031 nonrecognition treatment is when the adjusted basis of the property being disposed of exceeds the fair market value.

EXAMPLE 28

Assume the same facts as in the previous example, except the fair market value of the machine is $2,500. If § 1031 applies, the $500 realized loss is not recognized. Therefore, to recognize the loss, T should sell the old machine and purchase the new one. The purchase and sale transactions should be with different taxpayers. □

On the other hand, the like-kind exchange procedure can be utilized to control the amount of recognized gain.

EXAMPLE 29

S has property with an adjusted basis of $40,000 and a fair market value of $100,000. P wants to buy S's property, but S wants to limit the amount of recognized gain on the proposed transaction. P acquires other like-kind property (from an outside party) for $80,000. P then exchanges this property and $20,000 cash for S's property. S has a realized gain of $60,000 ($100,000 amount realized − $40,000 adjusted basis). S's recognized gain is only $20,000, the lower of the boot received of $20,000 or the realized gain of $60,000. S's basis for the like-kind property is $40,000 ($40,000 adjusted basis + $20,000 gain recognized − $20,000 boot received). If S had sold the property to P for its fair market value of $100,000, the result would have been a $60,000 recognized gain ($100,000 amount realized − $40,000 adjusted basis) to S. It is permissible for S to identify the like-kind property that he wants P to purchase.[38] □

38. *Franklin B. Biggs,* 69 T.C. 905 (1978); Rev.Rul. 57–244, 1957–1 C.B. 247; Rev.Rul. 73–476, 1973–2 C.B. 300; *Starker vs. U.S.,* 79–2 USTC ¶9541, 44 AFTR2d 79–5525, 602 F.2d 1341 (CA–9, 1979); and *Baird Publishing Co.,* 39 T.C. 608 (1962).

Involuntary Conversions

In certain cases, a taxpayer may prefer to recognize gain from an involuntary conversion. Keep in mind that § 1033, unlike § 1031 (dealing with like-kind exchanges), generally is an elective provision.

EXAMPLE 30

T has a $40,000 realized gain from the involuntary conversion of an office building. The entire proceeds of $450,000 are reinvested in a new office building. T, however, does not elect to postpone gain under § 1033 because of an expiring net operating loss carryover that is offset against the gain. Therefore, none of the realized gain of $40,000 is postponed. By not electing § 1033 postponement, T's basis in the replacement property will be the property's cost of $450,000 rather than $410,000 ($450,000 reduced by the $40,000 realized gain). ☐

Sale of a Personal Residence

Replacement Period Requirements. Several problems arise in avoiding the recognition of gain on the sale of a principal residence. Most of these problems can be resolved favorably through appropriate planning procedures. However, a few represent situations where the taxpayer has to accept the adverse tax consequences and possesses little, if any, planning flexibility. One pitfall concerns the failure to reinvest *all* of the proceeds from the sale of the residence into a new principal residence.

EXAMPLE 31

R sells her principal residence in January 1987 for $150,000 (adjusted basis of $40,000). Shortly thereafter, R purchases for $100,000 a 50-year-old house in a historical part of the community that she uses as her principal residence. It was R's intention to significantly renovate the property over a period of time and thereby make it more suitable to her living needs. In December 1989, R enters into a contract with a home improvement company to carry out the renovation at a cost of $60,000. It is clear that only $100,000 of the proceeds from the sale of the old residence has been reinvested in a new principal residence on a *timely* basis. Of the realized gain of $110,000, therefore, $50,000 ($150,000 adjusted sales price − $100,000 reinvested) must be recognized.[39] ☐

One problem that a taxpayer may not be in a position to do anything about concerns the acquisition of property *before* the beginning of the replacement period. In this regard, recall that the replacement period begins two years before the sale and ends two years after such sale.

EXAMPLE 32

T's employer transfers T to a different city in July 1987, at which time T lists his house for sale with a realtor. T purchases a principal residence in the city to which he is transferred in September 1987. Because of market

39. It has been assumed that § 121 did not apply.

conditions, T is unable to sell his original residence until December 1989. Since this is not within the two-year time period of the purchase, T's purchase of the residence in September 1987 will not be a qualifying replacement residence. ☐

Principal Residence Requirement.   Section 1034 will not apply unless the property involved is the taxpayer's principal residence. In this connection, one potential hurdle can arise in cases where the residence has been rented and therefore has not been occupied by the taxpayer for an extended period of time. Depending on the circumstances, the IRS might contend that the taxpayer has abandoned the property as his or her principal residence. The *key* to the abandonment issue is whether or not the taxpayer intended to reoccupy the property and use it as a principal residence upon his or her return to the locale. If the residence is, in fact, not reoccupied, the taxpayer should have a good reason to explain why it is not.

EXAMPLE 33

T is transferred by her employer to another office out of the state on a three-year assignment. It is the understanding of the parties that the assignment is temporary, and upon its completion, T will return to the original job site. During her absence, T rents her principal residence and lives in an apartment at the new location. T has every intention of reoccupying her residence. However, when she returns from the temporary assignment, she finds that the residence no longer suits her needs. Specifically, the public school located nearby where she had planned to send her children has been closed. As a consequence, T sells the residence and replaces it with one more conveniently located to a public school. Under these circumstances, it would appear that T is in an excellent position to show that she has not abandoned the property as her principal residence. She can satisfactorily explain why she did not reoccupy the residence before its sale.[40] ☐

The principal residence requirement could cause difficulty where a taxpayer works in two places and maintains more than one household. In such cases, the principal residence will be the location where the taxpayer lives most of the time.[41]

EXAMPLE 34

E is a vice president of Z Corporation and in this capacity spends about an equal amount of time in the company's New York City and Miami offices. E owns a house in each location and expects to retire in about five years. At that time, he plans to sell his New York home and use some of the proceeds to make improvements on the Miami property. Both homes have appreciated in value since their acquisition, and such appreciation can be expected to continue. From a tax planning standpoint, E should be looking toward the use of §§ 121 and 1034 to shelter some or all of the

---

40. Rev.Rul. 78–146, 1978–1 C.B. 260. Compare *Rudolph M. Stucchi*, 35 TCM 1052, T.C.Memo. 1976–242.

41. Rev.Rul. 77–298, 1977–2 C.B. 308.

gain he will realize on the future sale of the New York City home.[42] To do this, he should arrange his affairs so as to spend more than six months each year at that location. Upon its sale, therefore, the New York home will be his principal residence. □

Section 121 Considerations.   Older individuals who may be contemplating a move from their home to an apartment should consider the following possibilities for minimizing or deferring taxes:

- Wait until age 55 to sell the residence and elect under § 121 to exclude up to $125,000 of the realized gain.
- Sell the personal residence under an installment contract to spread the gain over several years.[43]
- Sell the personal residence and purchase a condominium instead of renting an apartment, thereby permitting further deferral of the unrecognized gain.

The use of § 121 should be carefully considered. Although such use avoids the immediate recognition of gain, the election expends the full $125,000 allowed.

EXAMPLE 35

In 1989 T, age 55, sells his personal residence for an amount that yields a realized gain of $5,000. Presuming T does not plan to reinvest the sales proceeds in a new principal residence (take advantage of the deferral possibility of § 1034), should he avoid the recognition of this gain by utilizing § 121? Electing § 121 would mean that T would waste $120,000 of his lifetime exclusion. □

In this connection, the use of § 121 by one spouse precludes the other spouse from later taking advantage of the exclusion.

EXAMPLE 36

Assume the same facts as in the previous example, except that T was married to W at the time of the sale. Later, T and W are divorced and W marries R. If T has used the § 121 exclusion, it is unavailable to W and R even though either one of them may otherwise qualify. This result occurs because for T to make the election for the 1989 sale, it was necessary for W to join with him in making the election even if the residence was owned separately by T. For W and R to be able to make the § 121 election, it would be necessary for W and T to revoke their prior election. Another planning approach would be for R to sell his residence before the marriage to W and to elect the exclusion on that sale. □

---

42. If E qualifies, § 121 would allow the first $125,000 of gain to be nontaxable. Further gain might be avoided under § 1034 to the extent the sale proceeds are applied toward improvements on the Miami home.

43. § 453(a). See the discussion of the installment method in chapter 18.

A taxpayer who is eligible to elect § 121 exclusion treatment may choose not to do so in order to remain eligible to elect it in the future. In arriving at this decision, consideration must be given to the probability that the taxpayer will satisfy the three-out-of-five year ownership and use period requirements associated with a residence sale in the future. As previously mentioned, the holding period for the occupancy and use requirements does carry over for a § 1033 involuntary conversion but does not carry over for a § 1034 sale.

Taxpayers should maintain records of both the purchase and sale of personal residences, since the sale of one residence results in an adjustment of the basis of the new residence if the deferral provisions of § 1034 apply. Form 2119 should be filed with the tax return and a copy retained as support for the basis of the new residence. Detailed cost records should be retained for an indefinite period.

PROBLEM MATERIALS

Discussion Questions

1. In general, what is a nontaxable exchange? Are nontaxable exchanges ever taxed? If so, how?

2. Distinguish between the following:
   a. A nontaxable exchange and a tax-free transaction.
   b. A nontaxable exchange and a taxable transaction.

3. What is the justification for nontaxable exchange treatment?

4. Can the exchange of property held for productive use in a trade or business for investment property qualify for like-kind exchange treatment?

5. Which of the following qualify as like-kind exchanges under § 1031?
   a. Improved for unimproved real estate.
   b. Crane (used in business) for inventory.
   c. Rental house for truck (used in business).
   d. Business equipment for securities.
   e. Delicatessen for bakery (both used for business).
   f. Personal residence for apartment building (held for investment).
   g. Rental house for land (both held for investment).
   h. Ten shares of stock in X Corporation for 10 shares of stock in Y Corporation.

6. Under what circumstances can the exchange of partnership interests qualify for like-kind exchange treatment?

7. Is it possible for transactions to receive nontaxable exchange treatment under § 1031 even though an exchange does not occur?

8. T is planning on selling a machine used in his business so that he can recognize the realized loss. He will use the sales proceeds to purchase

a replacement machine. Are there any circumstances under which T will not be able to recognize the realized loss?

9. What is boot, and how does it affect the recognition of gain or loss on a like-kind exchange when received by the taxpayer? How is the recognition of gain or loss affected when boot is given?

10. The receipt of boot in a § 1031 exchange triggers the recognition of realized gain. Such gain recognition will affect the basis of the property received by the taxpayer.

    a. Discuss the relationship between the realized gain and the boot received if the boot received is greater than the realized gain.

    b. Discuss the relationship between the realized gain and the boot received if the boot received is less than the realized gain.

    c. What effect does the recognition of gain have on the basis of the like-kind property received? Of the boot received?

11. Like-kind property received in a § 1031 exchange is assigned a carryover basis. Boot received in such an exchange is assigned a basis equal to fair market value.

    a. Discuss the equity of these different basis rules.

    b. Under what circumstances is the carryover basis for the like-kind property received equal to the fair market value of such property?

12. Two different formulas can be used to calculate the basis of like-kind property received. Discuss each formula and the relationship between them.

13. What is the holding period of like-kind property received in a like-kind exchange? For boot received? Why?

14. Mortgaged real estate may be received in a like-kind exchange. If the taxpayer assumes the mortgage, what effect does the mortgage have on the recognition of realized gain? On the basis of the real estate received?

15. What are the differences in the replacement requirement rules for involuntary conversions under the functional use test and the taxpayer use test?

16. Taxpayer's warehouse is destroyed by fire. What are the different tax options available to the taxpayer (a) if he has a realized gain and (b) if he has a realized loss?

17. How long does a taxpayer have to replace involuntarily converted property and still qualify for nonrecognition of gain under § 1033?

18. What is the earliest date that a taxpayer can replace involuntarily converted property?

19. Discuss the tax options available to the taxpayer when the form of the transaction is (a) a direct involuntary conversion and (b) an indirect involuntary conversion.

20. When does the holding period begin in an involuntary conversion for which the similar property rule is applicable? The like-kind property rule?

21. Z is notified by the city public housing authority on April 5, 1989, that his apartment building is going to be condemned as part of an urban renewal project. On April 12, 1989, S offers to buy the building from Z. Z sells the building to S on April 30, 1989. Condemnation occurs on June 1, 1989, and S receives the condemnation proceeds from the city. Assume both Z and S are calendar year taxpayers.

    a. What is the earliest date that Z can dispose of the building and qualify for § 1033 postponement treatment?

    b. Does the sale to S qualify as a § 1033 involuntary conversion?

    c. What is the latest date that S can acquire qualifying replacement property and qualify for postponement of the realized gain?

    d. What type of property will be qualifying replacement property?

22. How are corrections made for an involuntary conversion when a taxpayer elects to postpone gain and then does not reinvest within the time limits or does not reinvest a sufficient amount? How is postponement accomplished if reinvestment is made but postponement was not elected on the return for the taxable year in which gain was realized?

23. Discuss the justification for nonrecognition of gain on the sale or exchange of a principal residence. Discuss the justification for disallowance of loss.

24. Discuss all of the requirements for the replacement period of both purchased and constructed residences. Are there any exceptions?

25. What is a principal residence? Can a taxpayer have more than one principal residence at one point in time?

26. What effect does the renting of a house that has been the taxpayer's principal residence have on the qualification of the house as a principal residence?

27. Discuss fixing-up expenses in relation to the following:

    a. Postponed gain.

    b. Realized gain.

    c. Basis of new residence.

    d. Date of contract to sell.

    e. Date of sale.

28. Explain how the following are determined on the sale or exchange of a residence:

    a. Realized gain.

    b. Recognized gain.

    c. Postponed gain.

    d. Basis of new residence.

29. Discuss the basis calculation formula as it applies to a new residence if:

   a.   Realized gain is postponed.

   b.   Realized loss is disallowed.

   c.   Realized gain is recognized because the new residence is not acquired within the two-year time period from the sale of the old residence.

30. What does the § 121 exclusion cover? Is it elective? Does the old residence have to be replaced?

31. How many times can § 121 exclusion treatment be elected by a taxpayer? If the taxpayer is filing a joint return with his or her spouse, do both taxpayers have to meet the ownership and use requirements?

32. The personal residence of C is destroyed by fire. C receives insurance proceeds. His realized gain exceeds the amount of the § 121 exclusion of $125,000. C satisfies the age, ownership, and occupancy requirements associated with the § 121 exclusion.

   a.   Can an involuntary conversion qualify for the § 121 exclusion?

   b.   If C is not going to acquire a replacement residence, should he elect the § 121 exclusion? What factors should he consider in making this decision?

   c.   If C is going to acquire a replacement residence, should he elect the § 121 exclusion? What factors should he consider in making this decision?

   d.   Assume all the facts are the same, except that C sells his personal residence. Respond to (b) and (c).

33. A and B, both age 60, are sisters who live in the house they inherited from their parents 20 years ago. H and W, age 60, are married. They purchased their principal residence 7 years ago. Comment on any differences in the application of the § 121 exclusion to the sisters and the married couple.

34. Can any other provision or provisions be applied to any remaining gain that is not excluded under § 121?

35. Distinguish between the effect of the § 121 exclusion and the § 1034 postponement on the basis of a replacement residence.

Problems

36. Q owns undeveloped land with an adjusted basis of $70,000. He exchanges it for other undeveloped land worth $65,000.

   a.   What is Q's realized and recognized gain or loss?

   b.   What is Q's basis in the undeveloped land he receives?

37. T owns an automobile that she uses exclusively in her business. The adjusted basis is $14,000, and the fair market value is $18,000. T exchanges the car for a light-duty truck that she will use exclusively in her business.

a. What is T's realized and recognized gain or loss?

b. What is her basis in the truck?

38. T owns a car that she uses exclusively for personal purposes. Its original cost was $15,000, and the fair market value is $7,000. She exchanges the car and $18,000 cash for a new car.

a. Calculate T's recognized gain or loss.

b. Calculate T's basis for the new car.

39. T owns land and building with an adjusted basis of $125,000 and a fair market value of $200,000. T exchanges the land and building for land with a fair market value of $110,000 that T will use as a parking lot. In addition, T receives stock worth $90,000.

a. What is T's realized gain or loss?

b. His recognized gain or loss?

c. The basis of the land and the stock received?

40. T owns investment land with an adjusted basis of $35,000. P has offered to purchase the land from T for $175,000 for use in a real estate development. The amount offered by P is $10,000 in excess of what T perceives as the fair market value of the land. T would like to dispose of the land to P but does not want to incur the tax liability that would result. T identifies an office building with a fair market value of $175,000 that he would like to acquire. P purchases the office building and then exchanges the office building for T's land.

a. Calculate T's realized and recognized gain on the exchange and T's basis for the office building.

b. Calculate P's realized and recognized gain on the exchange and P's basis in the land.

41. What is the basis of the new property in each of the following exchanges?

a. Apartment building held for investment (adjusted basis $160,000) for lakefront property held for investment (fair market value $180,000).

b. Barber shop (adjusted basis $30,000) for grocery store (fair market value $27,000), both held for business use.

c. Drug store (adjusted basis $30,000) for bulldozer (fair market value $35,000), both held for business use.

d. IBM common stock (adjusted basis $4,000) for shoe shine stand used in business (fair market value $5,000).

e. Rental house (adjusted basis $20,000) for land held for investment (fair market value $32,000).

42. G owns Machine A, which he uses in his business. The adjusted basis of Machine A is $12,000, and the fair market value is $15,000. G sells Machine A for $15,000 to Q, who is a dealer. G then purchases Machine B, which would qualify as like-kind property, for $15,000 from J, who also is a dealer.

a. What is G's realized and recognized gain on the sale of Machine A?

b. What is G's basis for Machine B, which was acquired from J?

c. What factors would motivate G to sell Machine A and purchase the replacement Machine B rather than exchange one machine for the other?

d. Assume that the adjusted basis of Machine A is $15,000 and the fair market value of each machine is $12,000. Respond to (a) through (c).

43. G exchanges real estate held for investment plus stock for real estate to be held for investment. The stock transferred has an adjusted basis of $5,000 and a fair market value of $2,500. The real estate transferred has an adjusted basis of $12,500 and a fair market value of $13,750. The real estate acquired has a fair market value of $16,250.

a. What is G's realized gain or loss?

b. His recognized gain or loss?

c. The basis of the newly acquired real estate?

44. H exchanges a machine (adjusted basis of $25,000 and fair market value of $45,000) and undeveloped land held for investment (adjusted basis of $50,000 and fair market value of $300,000) for land worth $290,000 to be used in her business. The undeveloped land has a mortgage of $55,000 that the other party to the exchange assumes.

a. What is H's realized gain or loss?

b. Her recognized gain or loss?

c. The basis of the newly acquired real estate?

45. Determine the realized, recognized, and postponed gain or loss and the new basis for each of the following like-kind exchanges:

	Adjusted Basis of Old Asset	Boot Given	Fair Market Value of New Asset	Boot Received
a.	$ 7,000	$ –0–	$ 4,000	$4,000
b.	4,000	2,000	5,000	–0–
c.	3,000	7,000	8,000	500
d.	8,000	–0–	10,000	–0–
e.	10,000	–0–	11,000	1,000
f.	10,000	–0–	9,000	–0–

46. K owns an apartment house that has an adjusted basis of $700,000 but is subject to a mortgage of $250,000. On September 1, 1989, she transfers the apartment house to D. K receives from D $70,000 in cash and an office building with a fair market value at the time of the exchange of $925,000. D assumes the $250,000 mortgage on the apartment house.

a. What is K's realized gain or loss?

b. Her recognized gain or loss?

c. The basis of the newly acquired office building?

47. E converted her personal residence to rental property on January 1, 1988. At that time, the adjusted basis was $80,000 and the fair market value was $100,000. During the interim rental period, E deducted depreciation of $5,576. The rental property is condemned on December 31, 1989, in connection with an urban renewal project, and E receives condemnation proceeds of $60,000.

    a. What is the adjusted basis at the condemnation date?

    b. What is the recognized gain or loss on the condemnation?

48. Do the following qualify for involuntary conversion treatment?

    a. Purchase of a sporting goods store as a replacement for a bookstore (used in a business) that was destroyed by fire.

    b. Sale of a home because a neighbor converted his residence into a nightclub.

    c. Purchase of an airplane to replace a shrimp boat (used in a business) that was wrecked by a hurricane.

    d. Taxpayer's residence destroyed by a tornado and replaced with another residence.

    e. Purchase of an apartment building to replace a rental house by an investor. The rental house was destroyed by a flood.

49. For each of the following, indicate the earliest and latest dates that qualifying replacement property can be acquired under § 1033:

    a. Business property that is stolen or destroyed.

    b. Personal use property that is stolen or destroyed.

    c. Business property that is condemned.

    d. Personal use property that is condemned.

50. R's office building, which is used in his business, is destroyed by a hurricane in September 1989. The adjusted basis is $350,000. R receives insurance proceeds of $400,000 in October 1989.

    a. Calculate R's realized gain or loss, recognized gain or loss, and basis for the replacement property if R acquires an office building for $390,000 in October 1989.

    b. Calculate R's realized gain or loss, recognized gain or loss, and basis for the replacement property if R acquires a warehouse for $410,000 in October 1989.

    c. Calculate R's realized gain or loss and recognized gain or loss if R does not acquire replacement property.

51. Rental property owned by F, a calendar year taxpayer, is destroyed by a tornado on January 1, 1989. F originally had paid $150,000 for the property, of which amount $125,000 was allocated to the building and $25,000 was allocated to the land. During the time F owned the property, ACRS deductions of $46,250 were taken. ACRS deductions of $57,500 would have been taken, except that F chose to forgo deductions of $11,250 one year when his tax return showed a net operating loss. F receives insurance proceeds of $60,000 in November 1989. As a result of continuing negotiations with the insurance company, F receives additional proceeds of $35,000 in August 1990.

a.   What is F's adjusted basis in the property?

b.   What is F's realized gain or loss on the involuntary conversion in 1989? In 1990?

c.   What is the latest date that F can replace the involuntarily converted property to qualify for § 1033 postponement?

d.   What is the latest date that F can replace the involuntarily converted property to qualify for § 1033 postponement if the form of the involuntary conversion is a condemnation?

52.   What is the *maximum* postponed gain or loss and the basis for the replacement property for the following involuntary conversions?

	Property	Type of Conversion	Amount Realized	Adjusted Basis	Amount Reinvested
a.	Drugstore (business)	Condemned	$160,000	$120,000	$100,000
b.	Apartments (investment)	Casualty	100,000	120,000	200,000
c.	Grocery store (business)	Casualty	400,000	300,000	350,000
d.	Residence (personal)	Casualty	16,000	18,000	17,000
e.	Vacant lot (investment)	Condemned	240,000	160,000	240,000
f.	Residence (personal)	Casualty	20,000	18,000	19,000
g.	Residence (personal)	Condemned	18,000	20,000	26,000
h.	Apartments (investment)	Condemned	150,000	100,000	200,000

53.   A taxpayer realizes $50,000 from the involuntary conversion of a factory. The adjusted basis of the factory was $75,000, and in the same year taxpayer spends $40,000 for a new factory.

a.   What is the realized gain or loss?

b.   What is the recognized gain or loss?

c.   What is the basis of the new factory?

54.   Which of the following are selling expenses, fixing-up expenses, or neither?

a.   New swimming pool.

b.   Legal fees to clear title to residence.

c.   Painting exterior of residence.

d.   Repair of leaky plumbing.

e.   New roof.

f.   Advertising residence for sale.

g.   Painting living and dining rooms.

h.   Broker commissions.

55.   T, age 42, has lived in her residence for three years. Her adjusted basis is $130,000. Knowing that she is going to move to another city, she lists her residence for sale in February 1987. When she moves in May 1987, she purchases another residence for $190,000. Due to market conditions, she does not sell her original residence until July 1989. The

selling price is $225,000, selling expenses are $13,000, and fixing-up expenses are $4,000.

    a.   What is T's realized gain or loss?

    b.   The recognized gain or loss?

    c.   The basis of the new residence?

56. What are the realized, recognized, and postponed gain or loss, the new basis, and the adjusted sales price for each of the following? Assume that none of the taxpayers is 55 years of age or older.

    a.   R sells her residence for $90,000. The adjusted basis was $55,000. The selling expenses were $5,000. The fixing-up expenses were $3,000. She did not reinvest in a new residence.

    b.   D sells his residence for $170,000. The adjusted basis was $120,000. The selling expenses were $4,000. The fixing-up expenses were $6,000. D reinvested $160,000 in a new residence.

    c.   M sells her residence for $65,000. The adjusted basis was $35,000. The selling expenses were $1,000. The fixing-up expenses were $2,000. She reinvested $40,000.

    d.   B sells his residence for $70,000. The adjusted basis was $65,000. The selling expenses were $6,000. He reinvested $80,000.

    e.   C sells his residence for $100,000, and his mortgage is assumed by the buyer. The adjusted basis was $80,000; the mortgage, $50,000. The selling expenses were $4,000. The fixing-up expenses were $2,000. He reinvested $120,000.

57. J, age 40, sold his residence, which he had owned and occupied for 12 years. His original cost was $200,000. Ten percent of the house has been used during the past four years as a qualifying home office under § 280A (refer to chapter 10). J deducted $4,000 of depreciation associated with the portion of the house used as a home office. The selling price was $300,000, and the selling expenses were $18,000. J purchases a new residence costing $325,000 during the statutory two-year period.

    a.   What is J's realized gain or loss?

    b.   His recognized gain or loss?

    c.   The basis of the new residence?

58. T, age 47, sells his residence in Richmond on May 5, 1989, for $115,000. He incurs realtor's commissions of $6,900 and qualified fixing-up expenses of $2,000. His adjusted basis is $70,000. T sells the house because his employer assigns him to a temporary job in another state. T moves back to Richmond in December 1990. However, he has decided that he enjoys being relieved of the responsibilities of home ownership. Therefore, he rents an apartment and does not purchase another residence by May 5, 1991.

    a.   What should T have reported on his 1989 return with respect to the sale of his residence?

    b.   What should T do in 1991 when he has not replaced the residence within the required two-year period?

59. H, age 60, and W, age 45, have been married for two years. H sells the personal residence in which H and W reside for $175,000. W has no ownership interest in the house. Legal fees and realtor's commissions are $15,000. Fixing-up expenses are $3,000. H's adjusted basis is $20,000. H has owned and occupied the house for the past 22 years and plans to elect the § 121 exclusion. H purchases a replacement residence 14 months after the sale for $102,000. Before her marriage to H, W was married to P. While married to W, P had sold his personal residence and elected § 121 treatment to exclude the realized gain. W joined P in making the election, even though she had no ownership interest in the house. P and W were divorced three years ago.

    a. Calculate H's realized gain, recognized gain, and basis for the replacement residence if H and W file a joint return.

    b. Calculate H's realized gain, recognized gain, and basis for the replacement residence if H and W file separate returns.

    c. Calculate H's realized gain, recognized gain, and basis for the replacement residence in (a) and (b) if P and W had filed separate returns during the taxable year that P elected § 121 treatment.

    d. Advise H on what action is necessary to maximize the § 121 exclusion.

60. Mr. T, age 57, is the sole owner of his principal residence. He has owned and occupied it for 10 years. Mrs. T, his spouse, refuses to join him in making the § 121 election.

    a. Can Mr. T elect the § 121 exclusion if he and Mrs. T file a joint return? If so, what is the available amount of the exclusion?

    b. Can Mr. T elect the § 121 exclusion if he files a separate return? If so, what is the available amount of the exclusion?

    c. If Mrs. T joins Mr. T in making the election, what is the available amount of the exclusion on a joint return? On a separate return?

61. L sold his residence, which he had owned and occupied for 20 years. The adjusted basis was $36,000, and the selling price was $250,000. The selling expenses were $4,000, and the fixing-up expenses were $8,000. He reinvested $60,000 in a new residence. L is 57 years old. What are the realized, recognized, and postponed gain or loss, the new basis, and the adjusted sales price if his objective is to minimize the recognized gain?

62. S, P, and K, who are sisters, sell their principal residence in which they have lived for the past 20 years. The youngest of the sisters is age 58. The selling price is $555,000, selling expenses and legal fees are $15,000, and the adjusted basis is $60,000 (the fair market value of the residence when inherited from their parents 20 years ago). Since the sisters are going to live in rental housing, they do not plan to acquire another residence.

    a. Can S, P, and K elect § 121 exclusion treatment?

    b. What is the realized and recognized gain?

63. Mr. T and Mrs. T are divorced on August 1, 1989. According to the terms of the divorce decree, Mr. T's ownership interest in the house is

to be transferred to Mrs. T in exchange for the release from marital rights. Before the divorce, the house was jointly owned by Mr. T and Mrs. T. The adjusted basis and the fair market value at the date of the transfer are $130,000 and $200,000, respectively. Does the transfer of the house produce recognized gain to either Mr. T or Mrs. T? What is the basis of the house to Mrs. T? If the same transfer was made by Mr. T to Mrs. T for $100,000 and was not associated with a divorce, would either Mr. T or Mrs. T have recognized gain?

Cumulative Problems

64. Tammy Walker, age 37, is a self-employed accountant. Tammy's Social Security number is 333–40–1111. Her address is 101 Glass Road, Richmond, VA 23236. Her income and expenses associated with her accounting practice for 1989 are as follows:

Revenues (cash receipts during 1989)	$85,000
Expenses	
Salaries	$18,000
Office supplies	1,100
Postage	500
Depreciation of equipment	12,000
Telephone	650
	$32,250

Since Tammy is a cash method taxpayer, she does not record her receivables as revenue until she receives cash payment. At the beginning of 1989, her accounts receivable were $12,000, and the balance had decreased to $9,000 by the end of the year. The balance at December 31, 1989, would have been $11,500, except that an account for $2,500 had become uncollectible in November.

Tammy used one room in her eight-room house as an office (400 square feet out of a total square footage of 4,000). She paid the following expenses related to the house during 1989:

Utilities	$3,000
Insurance	400
Property taxes	2,500
Repairs	1,400

Tammy had purchased the house on September 1, 1988, for $200,000. She sold her previous house on November 15, 1988, for $105,000. Her selling expenses had been $9,000, and qualified fixing-up expenses were $1,100. Tammy and her former husband, Lou, had purchased the house in 1987 for $80,000. Tammy had received Lou's 50% ownership interest as part of their divorce settlement in August 1987. Tammy had not used any part of the former residence as a home office.

Tammy has one child, Thomas, age 17. Thomas lives with his father during the summer and with Tammy for the rest of the year. Tammy can document that she spent $4,800 during 1989 for the child's support. The father normally provides about $1,000 per year, but this year he gave the child a new car for Christmas. The cost of the car was $15,000. The divorce decree is silent regarding the dependency exemption for the child.

Under the terms of the divorce decree, Tammy is to receive alimony of $800 per month. The payments will terminate at Tammy's death or if Tammy should remarry.

Tammy provides part of the support of her mother, age 67. The total support for 1989 for her mother was as follows:

Social Security benefits	$4,800
From Tammy	1,900
From Bob, Tammy's brother	1,300
From Susan, Tammy's sister	2,000

Bob and Susan have both indicated their willingness to sign a multiple support waiver form if it will benefit Tammy.

Tammy's deductible itemized deductions during 1989, excluding any itemized deductions related to the house, were $6,000. She made estimated tax payments of $18,500.

Part 1—Tax Computation

Compute Tammy's lowest net tax payable or refund due for 1989. Suggested software (if available): *WEST–TAX Planner* or *BNA Individual Income Tax Spreadsheet*.

Part 2—Tax Planning

Tammy and her former husband have had discussions regarding the $800 alimony he pays her each month. Due to a health problem of his new wife, he does not feel that he can afford to continue to pay the $800 each month. He is in the 15% tax bracket. If Tammy will agree to decrease the amount by 25%, he will agree that the amount paid is not alimony for tax purposes. Assume that the other data used in calculating Tammy's taxable income for 1989 will apply for her 1990 tax return. Advise Tammy as to whether she should agree to her former husband's proposal. Suggested software (if available): *WEST–TAX Planner* or *BNA Individual Income Tax Spreadsheet*.

65. Mary Gordon, age 41, is single and has no dependents. Mary's Social Security number is 999–00–1000. Mary resides at 9700 Linkmeadow, Sarasota, FL 33500. She is a self-employed operator of a sole proprietorship. During 1988, gross income from her business was $120,000 and business expenses were $65,000. In addition, she had the following property transactions related to her business (not reflected in the preceding income and expense figures):

   a. Cash received on February 26, 1988, on trade of a parcel of land on the outskirts of town (held for two years as a site for a new warehouse) for a lot near Mary's store. Mary intends to build a new warehouse on the lot. The old parcel had a fair market value of $28,000 and adjusted basis of $25,000. The fair market value of the new lot was $24,000. $ 4,000

b.	Condemnation award received on July 11, 1988, from the state for an acre of unimproved land (used for parking delivery vans) adjacent to the store (adjusted basis of the land was $12,000). The land had been purchased on October 3, 1986.	30,000
c.	Cost of an acre of unimproved land (purchased on September 18, 1988) across the street from the store (the land is to be used for parking delivery vans).	25,000

Mary's personal transactions for 1988 were as follows:

d.	Cash received on January 16, 1988, on exchange of 50 shares of X Corporation stock (adjusted basis of $20 a share, fair market value of $50 a share) for 50 shares of Y Corporation stock (fair market value of $40 a share). X Corporation and Y Corporation are not related, and Mary had held the X Corporation stock for two years.	500
e.	Amount realized on November 14, 1988, on the sale of a condominium Mary used as her personal residence. The condominium, which was built in 1975, was acquired in 1983 as a replacement for the house in which she formerly resided. She paid $60,000 for the condominium, and the amount realized for the house she sold was $80,000 (no fixing-up expenses, and adjusted basis was $50,000). Mary is moving into an apartment and does not intend to replace the condominium.	65,000
f.	Loss of amount Mary loaned to a friend in 1985 (the friend declared bankruptcy in 1988).	3,000
g.	Mary's interest income on personal savings accounts.	500
h.	Itemized deductions in 1988.	3,900
i.	Estimated Federal income tax payments.	21,000

Compute Mary's lowest net tax payable or refund due for 1988, assuming Mary makes any available elections that will reduce the tax. If you use tax forms for your computations, you will need Forms 1040, 2119, and 4797 and Schedules A, B, C, D, and SE. [Any gain recognized from item (a), (b), or (c) is § 1231 gain, (discussed in chapter 17), is reported on Form 4797 and Schedule D, and is to be treated as long-term capital gain.] Suggested software (if available): *WEST–TAX Preparer* for tax return solutions, *WEST–TAX Planner* or *BNA Individual Income Tax Spreadsheet* if tax return solutions are not desired.

Research Problems

Research Problem 1   Ms. G had owned and used her house as her principal residence since 1946. However, 20% of the house had been used for business purposes as an office. On January 1, 1989, when Ms. G was over 55, she retired and moved to North Carolina. Ms. G rented her former residence for six months before its sale, since no qualified buyer could be found. She purchased a new residence in North Carolina at a price that exceeded the adjusted sales price of the former residence.

a. What treatment should be given to the portion of the former residence used for business? Rental property?

b. May Ms. G make an election under § 121?

c. Are the nonrecognition of gain provisions of § 1034 available to Ms. G?

Research Problem 2 S owned 3,000 acres of timberland in Oregon. CZ Corporation offered to purchase the property for $4.5 million. Since the adjusted basis for the land was only $400,000, S did not want to have the large recognized gain that would result. CZ Corporation offered to purchase the land on the installment method and thereby spread the recognized gain over the period of the installment payments. S rejected the proposal and countered with the following proposal.

- The land (fair market value of $4.5 million) would be transferred from S to CZ Corporation in exchange for a five-year contract under which S would have the right to identify real property that CZ Corporation would purchase and transfer to S.

- At the end of the five-year period, the remainder of the $4.5 million that had not been so expended would be transferred to S in cash.

- During the five-year period, the amount of the $4.5 million not expended by the end of each year was to be increased by a growth factor of 12% per year.

a. Does the exchange qualify as a like-kind exchange under § 1031?

b. What is the appropriate treatment of the growth factor?

Partial list of research aids:
Starker v. U.S., 75–1 USTC ¶9443, 35 AFTR2d 75–1550 (D.Ct. Ore., 1975).

Research Problem 3 T owned property that had an adjusted basis of $125,000, of which $100,000 was allocated to the land and $25,000 to the building. The property was condemned by the state, and T received a $275,000 condemnation award. T spent $400,000 for new property, of which $100,000 was allocable to the land and $300,000 to the building. What is the basis of the replacement property, and how is it allocated to the land and the building?

Partial list of research aids:
Reg. § 1.1033(c)–1(a).
Rev.Rul. 73–18, 1973–1 C.B. 368.

16

Property Transactions: Capital Gains and Losses

Objectives

Define a capital asset and apply the definition.

Examine statutory expansions of the capital asset definition.

Discuss the rules relating to retirement of corporate obligations.

Discuss special rules for capital gain treatment: options, patents, franchises, and lease cancellation payments.

Discuss and apply the holding period rules for determining whether capital gain or loss is long term or short term.

Explain the tax treatment of capital gains and losses of noncorporate taxpayers.

·Explain the differences in the tax treatment of capital gains and losses of corporate versus noncorporate taxpayers.

GENERAL CONSIDERATIONS

Rationale for Separate Reporting of Capital Gains and Losses

Currently, capital gains are not taxed at a lower rate than ordinary gains. Therefore, the tax on a net capital gain and the tax on the same amount of net ordinary income are identical. Despite this result, however, the tax law requires that capital gains and losses be very carefully separated from other types of gains and losses. Most of this chapter and the next chapter describe the intricate capital gain and loss rules and how to distinguish capital gains and losses from other types of gains and losses.

Why does the Code still require separate reporting of gains and losses and a determination of their tax character although this appears to have no effect on the tax liability? The reason is that significant differences in taxable income may occur when ordinary gains and losses are present versus when capital gains and losses are present. Capital losses must initially be offset against capital gains. After this offset, any remaining capital loss is deductible only to the extent of $3,000 per tax year. Net capital loss exceeding this limit is carried over and may be deductible in future tax years. Since capital losses are offset against capital gains to determine whether a net capital loss exists, a separate netting of capital gains and losses is required. The netting procedure is discussed in the Tax Treatment of Capital Gains and Losses of Noncorporate Taxpayers portion of this chapter.

Historically, capital gains were taxed at a significantly lower rate than ordinary gains. This preferential treatment of capital gains is very likely to return if Congress raises ordinary income tax rates.[1] If the capital gain and loss provisions of the current tax law did not require separate reporting, it would probably be very difficult for Congress to reenact preferential treatment for capital gains. Thus, Congress deliberately retained the separate reporting of capital gains and losses even though it felt current tax rates do not justify preferential treatment of net capital gains.

As a result of the factors discussed above, the individual income tax forms include very extensive reporting requirements for capital gains and losses. The material in this chapter will help you understand the tax principles underlying those forms. The forms themselves are illustrated with examples at the end of the chapter.

General Scheme of Taxation

Recognized gains and losses must be properly classified. Proper classification depends upon three characteristics:

- The tax status of the property.
- The manner of the property's disposition.
- The holding period of the property.

---

1. The national budget deficit, low tax rates for wealthy taxpayers, and Congressional support for preferential capital gain rates will probably combine to raise tax rates on ordinary income. Since the current law contains an alternative tax on long-term capital gains (although it currently does not yield a lower tax), raising ordinary tax rates will probably make a lower tax on long-term capital gains a reality.

The three possible tax statuses are capital asset, § 1231 asset, or ordinary asset. Property disposition may be by sale, exchange, casualty, theft, or condemnation. The two holding periods are one year or less (short term) and more than one year (long term).[2]

The major focus of this chapter is capital gains and losses. Capital gains and losses usually result from the disposition of a capital asset. The most common disposition is a sale of the asset. Capital gains and losses can also result from the disposition of § 1231 assets, which is discussed in chapter 17. Except in very limited circumstances, capital gains and losses cannot result from the disposition of ordinary assets.

CAPITAL ASSETS

Definition of a Capital Asset

Personal use assets and investment assets are the most common capital assets owned by individual taxpayers. Personal use assets usually include items such as clothing, recreation equipment, a residence, and automobiles. Investment assets usually include corporate stocks and bonds, government bonds, and vacant land. Remember, however, that losses from the sale or exchange of personal use assets are not recognized. Therefore, the classification of such losses as capital losses can be ignored.

Due to the historical preferential treatment of capital gains, taxpayers have preferred that gains be capital gains rather than ordinary gains. As a result, a great many statutes, cases, and rulings have accumulated in the attempt to define what is and what is not a capital asset. Unfortunately, capital assets are not directly defined in the Code. Instead, § 1221 defines what is *not* a capital asset. A capital asset is property held by the taxpayer (whether or not it is connected with the taxpayer's business) that is *not* any of the following:

- Inventory or property held primarily for sale to customers in the ordinary course of a business. The Supreme Court, in *Malat v. Riddell,* defined *primarily* as meaning *of first importance* or *principally.*[3]

- Accounts and notes receivable acquired from the sale of inventory or acquired for services rendered in the ordinary course of business.

- Depreciable property or real estate used in a business.

- Certain copyrights; literary, musical, or artistic compositions; or letters, memoranda, or similar property held by (1) a taxpayer whose efforts created the property; (2) in the case of a letter, memorandum, or similar property, a taxpayer for whom it was produced; or (3) a taxpayer in whose hands the basis of such property is determined, for purposes of determining gain from a sale or exchange, in whole or part by reference to the basis of such property in the hands of a taxpayer described in (1) or (2).

---

2. However, for assets acquired prior to January 1, 1988, the short-term holding period is six months or less, and the long-term holding period is more than six months. See the discussion under Holding Period later in this chapter.

3. 66–1 USTC ¶9317, 17 AFTR2d 604, 86 S.Ct. 1030 (USSC, 1966).

- U.S. government publications that are (1) received by a taxpayer from the U.S. government other than by purchase at the price at which they are offered for sale to the public or (2) held by a taxpayer whose basis, for purposes of determining gain from a sale or exchange, is determined by reference to a taxpayer described in (1).

The Code defines what is not a capital asset. From the preceding list, it is apparent that inventory, accounts and notes receivable, and most fixed assets of a business are not capital assets. The following discussion provides further detail on each part of the capital asset definition.

Inventory.   What constitutes inventory is determined by the taxpayer's business.

EXAMPLE 1   T Company buys and sells used cars. Its cars would be inventory. Its gains from sale of the cars would be ordinary income. ☐

Accounts and Notes Receivable.   Usually no gain or loss results from the collection of a business receivable of an accrual basis taxpayer, because the basis of the receivable is equal to the amount collected. However, if such a taxpayer sells his or her receivables, an ordinary gain or loss may result. A cash basis taxpayer usually does not have a basis for his or her receivables. Thus, a gain will result from the sale of the receivables.

EXAMPLE 2   T Company has accounts receivable of $100,000. Because it needs working capital, it sells the receivables for $83,000 to a financial institution. T Company would have a $17,000 ordinary loss if it were an accrual basis taxpayer (it would have earlier recorded $100,000 of revenue when the receivable was established). T Company would have $83,000 of ordinary income if it were a cash basis taxpayer, because it would not have recorded any revenue earlier and because the receivable has no tax basis. ☐

Business Fixed Assets.   Depreciable property and real estate (both depreciable and nondepreciable) used by a business are not capital assets. The Code has a very complex set of rules pertaining to such property. One of these rules is discussed under Real Property Subdivided for Sale in this chapter. Chapter 17 discusses the potential capital gain treatment under § 1231 for business fixed assets.

Copyrights and Creative Works.   Generally, the person whose efforts led to the copyright or creative work has an ordinary asset, not a capital asset. *Creative works* include the works of authors, composers, and artists. Also, the person for whom a letter, memorandum, or other similar property was created has an ordinary asset. Finally, a person receiving a copyright or a creative work by gift has an ordinary asset.

EXAMPLE 3	T is a part-time music composer. One of her songs was purchased by a music publisher for $5,000. T would have a $5,000 ordinary gain from the sale of an ordinary asset. ☐

EXAMPLE 4	T received a letter from the President of the United States in 1944. In the current year, T sells the letter to a collector for $300. T has a $300 ordinary gain from the sale of an ordinary asset (because the letter was created for T). ☐

EXAMPLE 5	T gives a song she composed to her son. The son sells the song to a music publisher for $5,000. The son has a $5,000 ordinary gain from the sale of an ordinary asset. ☐

(Patents are subject to special statutory rules discussed later in the chapter.)

U.S. Government Publications.   U.S. government publications received from the U.S. government (or its agencies) for a reduced price are not capital assets. This prevents a taxpayer from later donating the publications to charity and claiming a charitable contribution equal to the fair market value of the publications. A charitable contribution of a capital asset generally yields a deduction equal to the fair market value. A charitable contribution of an ordinary asset generally yields a deduction equal to less than the fair market value. If such property is received by gift from the original purchaser, the property is not a capital asset to the donee. (For a more comprehensive explanation of charitable contributions of property, refer to chapter 11.)

Effect of Judicial Action

Court decisions play an important role in the definition of capital assets. Because the Code only lists categories of what are *not* capital assets, judicial interpretation is sometimes required to determine whether a specific item fits into one of those categories. The Supreme Court follows a literal interpretation of the categories.[4] For instance, corporate stock is not mentioned in § 1221. Is corporate stock always a capital asset? Usually it is, but not always. For a taxpayer who acquires stock and sells it to customers, the stock is inventory and would not be a capital asset. (See the discussion under Dealers in Securities below.) But what if a taxpayer who does not normally sell stock to customers acquires stock with the intention of resale? A court may have to decide whether the stock is or is not acquired primarily for sale to customers.

Often the crux of the capital asset determination hinges on whether the asset is held for investment purposes (capital asset) or business purposes (ordinary asset). The taxpayer's *use* of the property often provides objective evidence.

---

4. *Arkansas Best v. Comm.*, 88–1 USTC ¶ 9210, 61 AFTR2d 88–655, 108 S.Ct. 971 (USSC, 1988).

EXAMPLE 6   T buys an expensive painting for his business. If T depreciates the painting, the painting is depreciable property and, therefore, not a capital asset. If T is in the business of buying and selling paintings, the painting is inventory and, therefore, an ordinary asset. If T simply uses the painting to decorate his business and does not depreciate it, it is a capital asset. □

Because of the uncertainty associated with the capital asset definition, Congress has enacted several Code Sections to clarify the definition. These statutory expansions of the capital asset definition are discussed in the following section.

Statutory Expansions

Congress has often expanded the § 1221 general definition of a capital asset.

Dealers in Securities.   As a general rule, securities (stocks, bonds, and other financial instruments) held by a dealer are considered to be inventory and are not, therefore, subject to capital gain or loss treatment. A *dealer in securities* is a merchant (e.g., a brokerage firm) that regularly engages in the purchase and resale of securities to customers. The dealer must identify any securities being held for investment. Generally, if a dealer clearly identifies certain securities as held for investment purposes by the close of business on the date of acquisition, gain from the sale of such securities will be capital gain. Losses are capital losses if at any time the securities have been clearly identified by the dealer as held for investment.[5]

EXAMPLE 7   T is a securities dealer. She purchases 100 shares of XYZ stock. If T takes no further action, the stock is inventory and an ordinary asset. If she designates in her records that the stock is held for investment, the stock is a capital asset. T must designate the investment purpose by the close of business on the date of acquisition. If T later sold the stock, the gain or loss would be capital gain or loss. If T redesignated the stock as held for resale and then later sold it, any gain would be ordinary, but any loss would be capital loss. Stock designated as held for investment and then sold at a loss always yields a capital loss. □

Real Property Subdivided for Sale.   Substantial development activities relative to real property may result in the owner being considered a dealer for tax purposes. Income from the sale of real estate property lots is treated as the sale of inventory (ordinary income) if the owner is considered to be a dealer. Section 1237 provides relief for investors in real estate who engage in limited development activities by allowing capital gain treatment if the following requirements are met:

---

5. §§ 1236(a) and (b) and Reg. § 1.1236–1(a). Section 107(b)(1) of the Deficit Reduction Act of 1984 authorizes the Treasury to impose earlier identification deadlines than the close of the business day. The Treasury could also provide by Regulation for a method of identification other than on the taxpayer's records. At this writing, such Regulations have not been issued.

- The taxpayer may not be a corporation.

- The taxpayer may not be a real estate dealer.

- No substantial improvements may be made to the lots sold. *Substantial* generally means more than a 10 percent increase in the value of a lot. Shopping centers and other commercial or residential buildings are considered substantial, while filling, draining, leveling, and clearing operations are not.

- The taxpayer must hold the lots sold for at least five years, except for inherited property. The substantial improvements test is less stringent if the property is held at least 10 years.

If the preceding requirements are met, all gain is capital gain until the tax year in which the taxpayer sells the sixth lot. Starting in the tax year that the sixth lot is sold, the taxpayer's gains will be ordinary income to the extent of 5 percent of the selling price. All selling expenses offset the 5 percent of selling price ordinary income portion of the gain. Since many real estate commissions are at least 5 percent of the selling price, often the result is that none of the gain is ordinary income. Also, in counting the number of lots sold, sales of contiguous lots to a single buyer in a single sale count as the sale of one lot.

A loss from the sale of subdivided real property is an ordinary loss unless the property qualifies as a capital asset under § 1221. A gain that does not qualify under § 1237 may qualify as a capital gain under § 1221 or § 1231 if the requirements of either Section are satisfied. The following example illustrates the application of § 1237.

EXAMPLE 8

T owns a large tract of land and subdivides it for sale. Assume T meets all the requirements of § 1237 and during the tax year sells the first 10 lots to 10 different buyers for $10,000 each. T's basis in each lot sold is $3,000, and T incurs total selling expenses of $4,000 on the sales. T's gain is computed as follows:

Selling price (10 × $10,000)		$100,000
Basis (10 × $3,000)		30,000
Excess over basis		$ 70,000
Five percent of selling price	$5,000	
Selling expenses	(4,000)	
Amount of ordinary income		$ 1,000
Five percent of selling price	$5,000	
Excess of expenses over five percent of selling price	-0-	(5,000)
Capital gain		65,000
Total gain ($70,000 − $4,000 selling expenses)		$66,000

Lump–Sum Distributions.   A *lump-sum distribution* is generally a distribution of an employee's entire qualified pension or profit sharing plan balance within one tax year. The distribution must result from the employee's (1) death or disability, (2) reaching age 59½, or (3) separation from service with an employer. The TRA of 1986 repealed a provision that allowed a portion of a lump-sum distribution to be treated as a capital gain. However, partial capital gain treatment may still be available because this repeal is not yet fully effective and because transition rules allow certain taxpayers to continue using prior law. See chapter 19 for a further discussion of lump-sum distributions.

Nonbusiness Bad Debts.   A loan not made in the ordinary course of business is classified as a nonbusiness receivable. In the year the receivable becomes completely worthless, it is a *nonbusiness bad debt,* and the bad debt is treated as a short-term capital loss. Even if the receivable was outstanding for more than one year, the loss is still a short-term capital loss. This is an excellent example of the statutory expansion of capital gain and loss. It is not necessary to determine whether the asset was a capital asset or what the holding period was. The Code automatically provides that nonbusiness bad debts are short-term capital losses. Chapter 8 discusses nonbusiness bad debts more thoroughly.

SALE OR EXCHANGE

Recognition of capital gain or loss requires a sale or exchange of a capital asset. The Code uses the term *sale or exchange,* but does not define it. Generally, a sale involves the receipt of money or the assumption by the purchaser of liabilities for property, and an exchange involves the transfer of property for other property. Thus, an involuntary conversion (casualty, theft, or condemnation) is not a sale or exchange. In several situations, the determination of whether a sale or exchange has taken place has been clarified by the enactment of Code Sections that specifically provide for sale or exchange treatment.

Recognized gains or losses from the cancellation, lapse, expiration, or any other termination of a right or obligation with respect to personal property (other than stock) that is or would be a capital asset in the hands of the taxpayer are capital gains or losses.[6] See the discussion under Options later in the chapter for more details.

Worthless Securities

Occasionally, securities such as stock and, especially, bonds may become worthless due to the insolvency of their issuer. If such a security is a capital asset, the loss is deemed to have occurred as the result of a sale or exchange on the *last day* of the tax year.[7] This last-day rule may have the effect of converting what otherwise would have been a short-term capital loss into a long-term capital loss. See Treatment of Capital Losses later in this chapter.

Section 1244 allows an ordinary deduction on disposition of stock at a loss. The stock must be that of a small business company, and the ordinary

---

6. § 1234A.   7. § 165(g)(1).

deduction is limited to $50,000 ($100,000 for married individuals filing jointly) per year. For a more detailed discussion, refer to chapter 8.

Special Rule—Retirement of Corporate Obligations

A debt obligation (e.g., a bond or note payable) may have a tax basis in excess of or less than its redemption value because it may have been acquired at a premium or discount. Consequently, the collection of the redemption value may result in a loss or gain. Generally, the collection of a debt obligation is not a sale or exchange. Therefore, any loss or gain cannot be a capital loss or gain because no sale or exchange has taken place. However, if the debt obligation was issued by a corporation or certain government agencies, the collection of the redemption value is treated as a sale or exchange.[8]

EXAMPLE 9   T acquires $1,000 of XYZ Corporation bonds for $980 in the open market. If the bonds are held to maturity, the $20 difference between T's collection of the $1,000 maturity value and T's cost of $980 is treated as capital gain. If the obligation were issued to T by an individual instead of by a corporation, T's $20 gain would be ordinary, since there is no sale or exchange of the debt by T. □

Original Issue Discount.   The benefit of the sale or exchange exception that allows a capital gain from the collection of certain obligations is reduced when the obligation has original issue discount. *Original issue discount (OID)* arises when the issue price of a debt obligation is less than the maturity value of the obligation. OID must generally be amortized over the life of the debt obligation. Most new publicly traded bond issues do not carry OID, since the stated interest rate is set to make the market price on issue the same as the bond's face amount. In addition, even if the issue price is less than the face amount, the difference is not considered to be OID if the difference is less than one-fourth of 1 percent of the redemption price at maturity multiplied by the number of years to maturity.[9]

In the case where OID does exist, it may or may not have to be amortized, depending upon the date the obligation was issued. When OID is amortized, the amount of gain upon collection, sale, or exchange of the obligation is correspondingly reduced. The obligations covered by the OID amortization rules and the method of amortization are presented in §§ 1272–1275. Similar rules for other obligations can be found in §§ 1276–1288.

EXAMPLE 10   T purchases $10,000 of newly issued Y Corporation bonds for $6,000. The bonds have original issue discount of $4,000. T must amortize the discount over the life of the bonds. The OID amortization *increases* T's interest income. (The bonds were selling at a discount because the market rate of interest was greater than the bonds' interest rate.) After T has amortized $1,800 of OID, he sells the bonds for $8,000. T has a capital gain of $200 [$8,000 − ($6,000 cost + $1,800 OID amortization)]. The OID amor-

---

8. § 1271.   9. § 1273(a)(3).

tization rules prevent T from converting ordinary interest income into capital gain. Without the OID amortization, T would have had capital gain of $2,000 ($8,000 − $6,000 cost). □

Options

Generally, the sale or exchange of an option to buy or sell property results in capital gain or loss if the subject property is (or would be) a capital asset to the option holder.[10]

EXAMPLE 11

T wants to buy some vacant land for investment purposes. She cannot afford the full purchase price. Instead, she convinces the landowner to sell her the right to purchase the land for $100,000 anytime in the next two years. T pays $3,000 to obtain this option to buy the land. The option is a capital asset for T because if she actually purchased the land, the land would be a capital asset. Three months after purchasing the option, T sells it for $7,000. T would have a $4,000 short-term capital gain on this sale since she held the option for one year or less. □

Failure to Exercise Options.   If an option holder (grantee) fails to exercise the option, the lapse of the option is considered a sale or exchange on the option expiration date. Thus, the loss is a capital loss if the property subject to the option is (or would be) a capital asset in the hands of the grantee.

The grantor of an option on stocks, securities, commodities, or commodity futures receives short-term capital gain treatment upon the expiration of the option. Options on property other than stocks, securities, commodities, or commodity futures result in ordinary income to the grantor when the option expires. For example, an individual investor who owns certain stock (a capital asset) may sell a call option, entitling the buyer of the option to acquire the stock at a specified price higher than the value at the date the option is granted. The writer of the call receives a premium (e.g., 10 percent) for writing the option. If the price of the stock does not increase during the option period, the option will expire unexercised. Upon the expiration of the option, the grantor must recognize short-term capital gain. These provisions do not apply to options held for sale to customers (the inventory of a securities dealer).

Exercise of Options by Grantee.   If the option is exercised, the amount paid for the option is added to the selling price of the property subject to the option. This increases the gain to the grantor upon the sale of the property. The gain is capital or ordinary depending on the nature of the property sold. The grantee, of course, adds the cost of the option to the basis of the property.

---

10. § 1234(a) and Reg. § 1.1234–1(a)(1). See the Glossary of Tax Terms in Appendix C for a defi- nition of stock options. Stock options are discussed in chapter 19.

CONCEPT SUMMARY 16–1

Options

Event	Effect on Grantor	Effect on Grantee
Option is granted.	Receives value and has a contract obligation (a liability).	Pays value and has a contract right (an asset).
Option expires.	Has a short-term capital gain if the option property is stocks, securities, commodities, or commodity futures. Otherwise, gain is ordinary income.	Has a loss (capital loss if option property had been a capital asset for the grantee).
Option is exercised.	Amount received for option increases proceeds from sale of the option property.	Amount paid for option becomes part of basis of the option property purchased.
Option is sold or exchanged.	Result depends upon whether option later expires or is exercised (see above).	Could have gain or loss (capital gain or loss if option property had been a capital asset for the grantee).

EXAMPLE 12

On September 1, 1978, X purchases 100 shares of Y Company stock for $5,000. On April 1, 1989, he writes a call option on the stock, giving the option holder the right to buy the stock for $6,000 during the following six-month period. X receives a call premium of $500 for writing the call.

- If the call is exercised by the option holder on August 1, 1989, X has $1,500 ($6,000 + $500 − $5,000) of long-term capital gain from the sale of the stock.

- Assume that X decides to sell his stock prior to exercise for $6,000 and enters into a closing transaction by purchasing a call on 100 shares of Y Company stock for $5,000. Since the Y stock is selling for $6,000, X must pay a call premium of $1,000. He recognizes a $500 short-term capital loss [$1,000 (call premium paid) − $500 (call premium received)] on the closing transaction. On the actual sale of the Y Company stock, X has a long-term capital gain of $1,000 [$6,000 (selling price) − $5,000 (cost)].

- Assume that the original option expired unexercised. X has a $500 short-term capital gain equal to the call premium received for writing the option. This gain is not recognized until the option expires. □

Patents

Rationale for Capital Gain Treatment.   The sale of a patent may result in long-term capital gain treatment whether or not the patent is a capital asset.[11] The encouragement of technological progress is the primary reason for this provision. Ironically, authors, composers, and artists are not eligible for capital gain treatment on their creations because such works are not capital assets and the Code allows special treatment for patents, but not copyrights or trademarks. Presumably, Congress chose not to use the tax law to encourage cultural endeavors. The following example illustrates the special treatment for patents.

EXAMPLE 13   T, a druggist, invents a pill-counting machine, which he patents. In consideration of a lump-sum payment of $200,000 plus $10 per machine sold, T assigns the patent to Drug Products, Inc. Assuming T has transferred all substantial rights, the question of whether the transfer is a sale or exchange of a capital asset is not relevant. T automatically has a long-term capital gain from both the lump-sum payment and the $10 per machine royalty to the extent these proceeds exceed his basis for the patent. □

Statutory Requirements.   The key issues relating to the transfer of patent rights are (1) whether or not the patent is a capital asset, (2) whether the transfer is a sale or exchange, and (3) whether or not all substantial rights to the patent (or an undivided interest therein) are transferred. Section 1235 was enacted primarily to resolve the issue of whether the transfer is a sale or exchange of a capital asset. It provides that

> a transfer . . . of property consisting of all substantial rights to a patent, or an undivided interest therein which includes a part of all such rights, by any holder shall be considered the sale or exchange of a capital asset held for [the long-term holding period], regardless of whether or not payments in consideration of such transfer are (1) payable periodically over a period generally coterminous with the transferee's use of the patent, or (2) contingent on the productivity, use, or disposition of the property transferred.[12]

If the transfer meets the requirements, any gain or loss is automatically a long-term capital gain or loss regardless of whether the patent is a capital asset, whether the transfer is a sale or exchange, and how long the patent was held by the transferor.

Substantial Rights.   To receive favorable capital gain treatment, all *substantial rights* to the patent must be transferred. The transfer of patent rights that are limited geographically within the country of issuance or of rights that are limited in duration to a period less than the remaining life of the patent does not constitute the transfer of all substantial rights.[13]

---

11. § 1235.

12. § 1235(a) and Reg. § 1.1235–1(a).

13. Reg. § 1.1235–2(b)(1).

EXAMPLE 14   Assume T, the druggist in Example 13, only licensed Drug Products, Inc., to manufacture and sell the invention as a pill-counting machine. He retained the right to license the machine for counting chicken feed pellets. T has retained a substantial right and would not be eligible for automatic long-term capital treatment on the sale to Drug Products, Inc. ☐

Holder Defined.   The *holder* of a patent is usually the creator of the invention. A holder may also be a person who purchases the patent rights from the creator before the patented invention is reduced to practice. However, the creator's employer and certain parties related to the creator do not qualify as holders. Thus, in the common situation where an employer has all rights to an employee's inventions, the employer would not be eligible for special long-term capital gain treatment. More than likely, the employer would have an ordinary asset because the patent was developed as part of its business.

Franchises

A *franchise* is defined as an agreement that gives the transferee the right to distribute, sell, or provide goods, services, or facilities within a specified area.[14] A franchise transfer includes the granting of a franchise, the transfer of a franchise by a grantee to a third party, or the renewal of a franchise.

The key issue is whether the transfer is a sale or exchange rather than a license. Section 1253 generally solves this problem by providing that "a transfer of a franchise, trademark, or trade name shall not be treated as a sale or exchange of a capital asset if the transferor retains any significant power, right, or continuing interest with respect to the subject matter of the franchise, trademark, or trade name." Payments contingent on productivity, use, or disposition of the franchise, trademark, or trade name are not treated as a sale or exchange of a capital asset.

Significant Power, Right, or Continuing Interest.   *Significant powers, rights, or continuing interests* include control over assignment, quality of products and services, sale or advertising of other products or services, and the right to require that substantially all supplies and equipment be purchased from the transferor. Also included are the right to terminate the franchise at will and the right to substantial contingent payments. It is apparent that most modern franchising operations involve some or all of these powers, rights, or continuing interests.

Transferee Deduction.   Section 1253 is unique in that it covers the tax consequences to both the transferor and the transferee. Contingent payments are deductible as business expenses. Other payments are deductible either currently or over a longer period of time depending on the nature of the payment and the tax treatment afforded the transferor on the payments. The transferee's tax treatment is consistent with the transferor's (e.g., if the payment is ordinary income to the transferor of the franchise, it is an ordinary deduction to the transferee).

---

14. § 1253(b)(1). See the Glossary of Tax Terms in Appendix C for a definition of the term "franchise."

EXAMPLE 15   T grants a franchise to U to sell fast foods. Payments to T are contingent on the profitability of the franchise outlet. The payments are ordinary income to T and deductible as a business expense by U. □

EXAMPLE 16   T, a grantee of a franchise, sells the franchise to a third party. Payments to T are not contingent, and all significant powers, rights, and continuing interests are transferred. The payments are capital gain to T. □

Sports Franchises.   Section 1253 does not apply to professional sports franchises.[15] However, § 1056 imposes certain restrictions upon the allocation of the costs of acquiring a sports franchise to the cost basis of player contracts. In addition, if a sports franchise is sold, gain from the sale of the player contracts is subject to depreciation recapture as ordinary income under § 1245.[16]

Lease Cancellation Payments

1) Bargain purchase price
2) NPV may lease Payments > 90%
3) Economic life
3/4 of economic life owned

The tax treatment of payments received for cancelling a lease depends on whether the recipient is the lessor or the lessee and whether the lease is a capital asset or not.[17]

Lessee Treatment.   Payments received by a lessee for a lease cancellation are capital gains if the lease is a capital asset or § 1231 asset.[18] Generally, a lessee's lease would be a capital asset if the property (either personalty or realty) is used for the lessee's personal use (e.g., his or her residence). A lessee's lease would be an ordinary asset if the property is used in the lessee's trade or business.[19]

Lessor Treatment.   Payments received by a lessor for a lease cancellation are always ordinary income because they are considered to be in lieu of rental payments.[20]

EXAMPLE 17   T owns an apartment building that he is going to convert into an office building. S is one of the apartment tenants and receives $1,000 from T to cancel the lease. S would have a capital gain of $1,000 (which would be long term or short term depending upon how long S had held the lease). T would have an ordinary deduction of $1,000. □

EXAMPLE 18   M owns an apartment building near a university campus. P is one of the tenants. P is graduating early and offers M $800 to cancel P's lease. M

---

15. § 1253(e).

16. See chapter 17 for a discussion of the recapture provisions.

17. See the Glossary of Tax Terms in Appendix C for definitions of the terms "lessor" and "lessee."

18. § 1241 and Reg. § 1.1241–1(a).

19. Reg. § 1.1221–1(a).

20. *Hort v. Comm.*, 41–1 USTC ¶9354, 25 AFTR 1207, 61 S.Ct. 757 (USSC, 1941).

accepts the offer. M has ordinary income of $800. P has a nondeductible payment, since the apartment was personal use property. □

HOLDING PERIOD

Property acquired after December 31, 1987, must be held more than one year to qualify for long-term capital gain or loss treatment.[21] Property not held for the required long-term period will result in short-term capital gain or loss. To compute the holding period, start counting on the day after the property was acquired. In subsequent months, this same day is the start of a new month.[22] The following examples illustrate the computation of the holding period:

EXAMPLE 19

T purchases a capital asset on January 15, 1989, and sells it on January 16, 1990. T's holding period is more than one year. If T had sold the asset on January 15, 1990, the holding period would have been exactly one year, and the gain or loss would have been short term. □

A capital asset acquired on the last day of any month must not be disposed of until on or after the first day of the thirteenth succeeding month to be held for more than one year.[23]

EXAMPLE 20

T purchases a capital asset on February 28, 1989. If T sells the asset on February 28, 1990, the holding period is one year, and T will have a short-term capital gain or loss. If T sells the asset on March 1, 1990, the holding period is more than one year, and T will have a long-term capital gain or loss. □

Review of Special Holding Period Rules

[handwritten: More than 1yr. } or less long-term) short term]

There are several special holding period rules.[24] The application of these rules depends on the type of asset and how it was acquired.

Tax-free Exchanges. The holding period of property received in a nontaxable exchange includes the holding period of the former asset if the property that has been exchanged is a capital asset or a § 1231 asset. In certain nontaxable transactions involving a substituted basis, the holding period of the former property is *tacked on* to the holding period of the newly acquired property.

---

21. § 1222. Property acquired before January 1, 1988, had to be held more than six months to qualify for long-term capital gain or loss treatment. If such property was not held more than six months, it received short-term capital gain or loss treatment.

22. *Caspe v. U.S.*, 82–2 USTC ¶ 9714, 51 AFTR2d 83–353, 694 F.2d 1116 (CA–8, 1982).

23. Rev.Rul. 66–7, 1966–1 C.B. 188.

24. § 1223.

EXAMPLE 21   X exchanges a business truck for another truck in a like-kind exchange. The holding period of the truck exchanged tacks on to the holding period of the new truck. □

EXAMPLE 22   T sells his former personal residence and acquires a new residence. If the transaction qualifies for nonrecognition of gain on the sale of a residence, the holding period of the new residence includes the holding period of the former residence. □

Certain Nontaxable Transactions Involving a Carryover of Another Taxpayer's Basis.   The holding period of a former owner of property is tacked on to the present owner's holding period if the transaction is nontaxable and the basis of the property to the former owner carries over to the new owner.

EXAMPLE 23   T acquires 100 shares of A Corporation stock for $1,000 on December 31, 1983. The shares are transferred by gift to S on December 31, 1988, when the stock is worth $2,000. S's holding period begins with the date the stock was acquired by T, since the donor's basis of $1,000 becomes the basis for determining gain or loss on a subsequent sale by S. □

EXAMPLE 24   Assume the same facts as in Example 23, except that the fair market value of the shares is only $800 on the date of the gift. The holding period begins on the date of the gift if S sells the stock for a loss, since the value of the shares at the date of the gift is used in the determination of basis. If the shares are sold for $500 on April 1, 1989, S has a $300 recognized capital loss and the holding period is from December 31, 1988, to April 1, 1989 (thus, the loss is short term). □

Certain Disallowed Loss Transactions.   Under several Code provisions, realized losses are disallowed. When a loss is disallowed, there is no carryover of holding period. Losses can be disallowed under § 267 (sale or exchange between related taxpayers), § 707(b)(1) (sale or exchange involving controlled partnerships), and § 262 (sale or exchange of personal use assets) as well as other Code Sections. Taxpayers who acquire property in a disallowed loss transaction will have a new holding period begin and will have a basis equal to the purchase price.

EXAMPLE 25   J sold her principal residence at a loss. J may not deduct the loss, because it arises from the sale of personal use property. J purchases a replacement residence for more than the selling price of her former residence. J will have a basis equal to the cost of the replacement residence, and her holding period will begin when she acquires the replacement residence. □

Inherited Property. The holding period for inherited property is treated as long term no matter how long the property is actually held by the heir.

EXAMPLE 26

S inherits XYZ stock from her father. She receives the stock on April 1, 1989, and sells it on November 1, 1989. Even though the stock was not held more than one year, S receives long-term capital gain or loss treatment on the sale. □

Special Rules for Short Sales

The holding period of property sold short is determined under special rules provided in § 1233. A *short sale* occurs when a taxpayer sells borrowed property and repays the lender with substantially identical property either held on the date of the sale or purchased after the sale. Short sales usually involve corporate stock. The seller's objective is to make a profit in anticipation of a decline in the price of the stock. If the price declines, the seller in a short sale recognizes a profit equal to the difference between the sales price of the borrowed stock and the price paid for the replacement stock.

EXAMPLE 27

C does not own any shares of Z Corporation. However, C sells 30 shares of Z. The shares are borrowed from C's broker, and the borrowed shares must be replaced within 45 days. C has a short sale, because he was short the shares he sold. C will *close* the short sale by purchasing Z shares and delivering them to his broker. If the original 30 shares were sold for $10,000 and C later purchases 30 shares for $8,000, C would have a gain of $2,000. C's hunch that the price of Z stock would decline was correct. C was able to profit from selling high and buying low. If C had to purchase Z shares for $13,000 to close the short sale, he would have a loss of $3,000. In this case, C has sold low and bought high—not the result he wanted! C also would be making a short sale (a *short sale against the box*) if he borrowed shares from his broker to sell and then closed the short sale by delivering other Z shares he owned at the time of making the short sale. □

A short sale gain or loss is a capital gain or loss to the extent that the short sale property constitutes a capital asset of the taxpayer. The gain or loss is not recognized until the short sale is closed. Generally, the holding period of the short sale property is determined by how long the property used to close the short sale was held. However, if *substantially identical property* (e.g., other shares of the same stock) is held by the taxpayer, the short-term or long-term character of the short sale gain or loss may be affected:

- If substantially identical property has *not* been held for the long-term holding period on the short sale date, the short sale *gain or loss* is short term.

- If substantially identical property has *been* held for the long-term holding period on the short sale date, the short sale *gain* is long term if the substantially identical property is used to close the short sale and short term if it is not used to close the short sale.

- If substantially identical property has *been* held for the long-term holding period on the short sale date, the short sale *loss* is long term whether or not the substantially identical property is used to close the short sale.

- If substantially identical property is acquired *after* the short sale date and on or before the closing date, the short sale *gain or loss* is short term.

Concept Summary 16–2 summarizes the short sale rules.

The short sale rules are intended to prevent the conversion of short-term capital gains into long-term capital gains and long-term capital losses into short-term capital losses. The following examples illustrate the application of the short sale rules.

CONCEPT SUMMARY 16–2

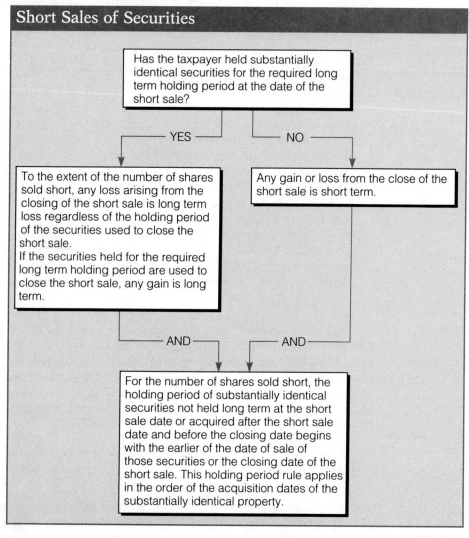

Short Sales of Securities

Has the taxpayer held substantially identical securities for the required long term holding period at the date of the short sale?

YES — NO

To the extent of the number of shares sold short, any loss arising from the closing of the short sale is long term loss regardless of the holding period of the securities used to close the short sale.
If the securities held for the required long term holding period are used to close the short sale, any gain is long term.

Any gain or loss from the close of the short sale is short term.

AND — AND

For the number of shares sold short, the holding period of substantially identical securities not held long term at the short sale date or acquired after the short sale date and before the closing date begins with the earlier of the date of sale of those securities or the closing date of the short sale. This holding period rule applies in the order of the acquisition dates of the substantially identical property.

EXAMPLE 28

On January 2, 1989, T purchases five shares of Y Corporation common stock for $100. On April 14, 1989, she engages in a short sale of five shares of the same stock for $150. On August 15, T closes the short sale by repaying the borrowed stock with the five shares purchased on January 2. T has a $50 short-term capital gain from the short sale, because she had not held substantially identical shares for the long-term holding period on the short sale date. □

EXAMPLE 29

Assume the same facts as in the previous example, except that T closes the short sale on January 30, 1990, by repaying the borrowed stock with five shares purchased on January 29, 1990, for $200. The stock used to close the short sale was not the property purchased on January 2, 1989, but since T held short-term property at the April 14, 1989, short sale date, the gain or loss from closing the short sale is short term. T has a $50 short-term loss ($200 cost of stock purchased January 29, 1990, and a short sale selling price of $150). □

EXAMPLE 30

Assume the same facts as in Example 29. On January 31, 1990, T sells for $200 the stock purchased January 2, 1989. T's holding period for that stock begins January 30, 1990, because the holding-period portion of the short sale rules applies to the substantially identical property in order of acquisition. T has a short-term gain of $100 ($100 cost of stock purchased January 2, 1989, and a selling price of $200). □

EXAMPLE 31

On January 2, 1989, T purchases five shares of X Corporation common stock for $100. She purchases five more shares of the same stock on April 14, 1989, for $200. On January 17, 1990, she sells short five shares of the same stock for $150. On September 30, 1990, she repays the borrowed stock with the five shares purchased on April 14, 1989, and sells the five shares purchased on January 2, 1989, for $200. T has a $50 long-term capital loss from the short sale, because she held substantially identical shares for more than one year on the date of the short sale. T has a $100 long-term capital gain from the sale of the shares purchased on January 2, 1989. □

TAX TREATMENT OF CAPITAL GAINS AND LOSSES OF NONCORPORATE TAXPAYERS

All taxpayers net their capital gains and losses. Short-term gains and losses (if any) are netted against one another, and long-term gains and losses (if any) are netted against one another. The results will be net short-term gain or loss and net long-term gain or loss. If these two net positions are of opposite sign (one is a gain and one is a loss), they are netted against one another.

Six possibilities exist for the result after all possible netting has been completed. Three of these final results are gains, and three are losses. One possible result is a net long-term capital gain (NLTCG). Net long-term capital gains of noncorporate taxpayers historically were subject to beneficial treatment.[25] A second possibility is a net short-term capital gain (NSTCG). Third, the netting may result in both NLTCG and NSTCG. For each of these possibilities, the gain is treated the same as ordinary income and is taxable in full.

The last three results of the capital gain and loss netting process are losses. Thus, a fourth possibility is a net long-term capital loss (NLTCL). A fifth result is a net short-term capital loss (NSTCL). Finally, a sixth possibility includes both an NLTCL and an NSTCL. Neither NLTCLs nor NSTCLs are treated as ordinary losses. Treatment as an ordinary loss generally is preferable to capital loss treatment, since ordinary losses are deductible in full while the deductibility of capital losses is subject to certain limitations. An individual taxpayer may deduct a maximum of $3,000 of net capital losses for a taxable year.[26]

Treatment of Capital Gains

Computation of Net Capital Gain.   As just discussed, the first step in the computation is to net all long-term capital gains and losses and all short-term capital gains and losses. The result is the taxpayer's net long-term capital gain (NLTCG) or loss (NLTCL) and net short-term capital gain (NSTCG) or loss (NSTCL).

EXAMPLE 32

Some possible results of the first step in netting capital gains and losses are shown below. Assume that each case is independent (assume the taxpayer's only capital gains and losses are those shown in the given case).

Case	STCG	STCL	LTCG	LTCL	Result of Netting	Description of Result
A	$8,000	($5,000)			$3,000	NSTCG
B	2,000	(7,000)			(5,000)	NSTCL
C			$9,000	($1,000)	8,000	NLTCG
D			8,800	(9,800)	(1,000)	NLTCL

□

The second step in netting capital gains and losses requires offsetting any positive and negative amounts that remain after the first netting step. This procedure is illustrated in the following examples.

---

25. The historical beneficial treatment for 1987 is presented later in this chapter.   26. § 1211(b).

EXAMPLE 33	Assume that T had all the capital gains and losses specified in Cases B and C in Example 32:	

Case C ($9,000 LTCG − $1,000 LTCL)	$8,000	NLTCG
Case B ($2,000 STCG − $7,000 STCL)	(5,000)	NSTCL
Excess of NLTCG over NSTCL	$3,000	

□

The excess of NLTCG over NSTCL is defined as *net capital gain (NCG)*. There is a $3,000 NCG in Example 33. The maximum tax rate on NCG is 28 percent, but since the maximum regular tax rate is also 28 percent, the tax on NCG does not differ from the tax on ordinary income. The current law does contain a special NCG alternative tax. The NCG alternative tax was last beneficial to taxpayers in 1987.[27] If Congress reduces the maximum tax on NCG or increases the ordinary income tax rate, this alternative tax computation will probably be beneficial again. In the meantime, the alternative tax can be ignored, and all capital gains are taxed the same as ordinary income.

The *NCG alternative tax* is the summation of the following computations. It is illustrated in Example 34.

1. The tax computed using the regular rates on the greater of:

   a. Taxable income less the net capital gain, or

   b. The amount of taxable income taxed at a rate below 28 percent.

2. Twenty-eight percent of taxable income in excess of income computed in (1).

3. Any additional tax resulting from the phase-out of the 15 percent bracket.

4. Any additional tax resulting from the phase-out of personal and dependency exemptions.

EXAMPLE 34	T, an unmarried taxpayer, has taxable income (TI) of $75,000 for 1987 and 1989. The taxable income includes NCG of $50,000. T's regular tax liability for 1987 is $22,839 [$14,754 + 38.5% ($21,000)]. T's regular tax liability for 1989 is $20,094 [($18,550 × 15%) + ($75,000 − $18,550) 28% + ($75,000 − $44,900) 5%]. His alternative tax on NCG is calculated as follows:

---

27. § 1(j). In 1987, the maximum regular rate was 38.5 percent whereas the NCG alternative tax rate was 28 percent.

	1987	1989
1. Tax on greater of:		
a. TI less NCG ($75,000 − $50,000)	$ 4,744	$ 4,589
b. TI taxed below 28% ($16,800; $18,550)		
2. 28% of TI exceeding TI used in (1) [28% × ($75,000 − $25,000)]	14,000	14,000
3. Tax from phase-out of 15% bracket (not applicable before 1988)	-0-	1,505
4. Tax from phase-out of personal and dependency exemptions (not applicable before 1988; insufficient taxable income in 1989)	-0-	-0-
Alternative tax on TI including NCG	$18,744	$20,094

The NCG alternative tax saves T $4,095 [$22,839 (regular tax) − $18,744 (NCG alternative tax)] in 1987 and zero in 1989. □

EXAMPLE 35

Assume that U had all the capital gains and losses specified in Cases A and D in Example 32:

Case A ($8,000 STCG − $5,000 STCL)	$3,000	NSTCG
Case D ($8,800 LTCG − $9,800 LTCL)	(1,000)	NLTCL
Excess of NSTCG over NLTCL	$2,000	

□

There is no special name for the excess of NSTCG over NLTCL, nor is there any special tax treatment. The nature of the gain is short term, and the gain is treated the same as ordinary gain and is included in U's gross income.

Tax Preference Item.   The 28 percent NCG alternative tax does not create an item of tax preference for purposes of the alternative minimum tax. Refer to the discussion of the alternative minimum tax in chapter 12.

Treatment of Capital Losses

Computation of Net Capital Loss.   A *net capital loss* results if capital losses exceed capital gains for the year. A net capital loss may be all long term, all short term, or part long and part short term.[28] The characterization of a net

---

28.   § 1222(10) defines a net capital loss as the net loss after the capital loss deduction. However, that definition confuses the discussion of net capital loss. Therefore, net capital loss is used here to mean the result after netting capital gains and losses and before considering the capital loss deduction. The capital loss deduction is discussed under Treatment of Net Capital Loss in this chapter.

CONCEPT SUMMARY 16–3

Noncorporate Taxpayer's Treatment of Net Capital Gain or Loss

Net Capital Gain Treatment Summarized

1. All long-term capital gain — Taxable in full as ordinary income. 28% alternative tax is available, but is not beneficial.

2. All short-term capital gain — Taxable in full as ordinary income.

3. Part long-term and part short-term capital gain — Taxable in full as ordinary income. 28% alternative tax is available for long-term capital gain portion, but is not beneficial.

Net Capital Loss Treatment Summarized

4. All long-term capital loss — $1 of loss used to make $1 of deduction. Deduction is *for* AGI and limited to $3,000 per year. Portion of loss not used to make deduction carries forward indefinitely.

5. All short-term capital loss — $1 of loss used to make $1 of deduction. Deduction is *for* AGI and limited to $3,000 per year. Portion of loss not used to make deduction carries forward indefinitely.

6. Part long-term and part short-term capital loss — Short-term losses used first to make $3,000 deduction.

capital loss as long or short term is important in determining the capital loss deduction (discussed later in this chapter).

EXAMPLE 36   Three different individual taxpayers have the following capital gains and losses during the year:

Taxpayer	LTCG	LTCL	STCG	STCL	Result of Netting	Description of Result
R	$1,000	($2,800)	$1,000	($ 500)	($1,300)	NLTCL
S	1,000	(500)	1,000	(2,800)	(1,300)	NSTCL
T	400	(1,200)	500	(1,200)	(1,500)	NLTCL ($800)
						NSTCL ($700)

R's net capital loss of $1,300 is all long term. S's net capital loss of $1,300 is all short term. T's net capital loss is $1,500, $800 of which is long term and $700 of which is short term. □

Treatment of Net Capital Loss.   A net capital loss (NCL) is deductible from gross income to the extent of $3,000 per tax year.[29] Capital losses exceeding the loss deduction limits carry forward indefinitely.[30] Notice that net capital gain is taxed the same as ordinary income, but net capital loss is deductible only to the extent of $3,000. Thus, although there is no beneficial treatment for capital gains, there is unfavorable treatment for capital losses in terms of the $3,000 annual limitation on deducting NCL against ordinary income. If the net capital loss includes both long-term and short-term capital loss, the short-term capital loss is counted first toward the $3,000 annual limitation.

EXAMPLE 37   T has an NCL of $5,000, of which $2,000 is STCL and $3,000 is LTCL. T has a capital loss deduction of $3,000 ($2,000 of STCL and $1,000 of LTCL) with an LTCL carryforward of $2,000. □

Carryovers.   Taxpayers are allowed to carry over unused capital losses indefinitely. The STCL and LTCL carried over retain their character as STCL or LTCL.

EXAMPLE 38   In 1988, T incurred $1,000 of STCL and $11,000 of LTCL. In 1989, T has a $400 LTCG.

- T's net capital loss for 1988 is $12,000. T deducts $3,000 [$1,000 STCL and $2,000 LTCL]. T has $9,000 of LTCL carried forward to 1989.

- T combines the $9,000 LTCL carryforward with the $400 LTCG for 1989. T has an $8,600 NLTCL for 1989. T deducts $3,000 of LTCL in 1989 and carries forward $5,600 of LTCL to 1990. □

Reporting Procedures

The reporting of capital gains and losses in 1989 will differ slightly from reporting procedures for 1988. Since the holding period for long-term treatment became more than one year for property acquired after December 31, 1987, the 1989 tax form will no longer reflect both the more-than-six-months and the more-than-one-year holding periods. The following discusses only 1988 tax forms because the 1989 tax forms were not available at the time of this writing.

---

29. § 1211(b)(1). Married persons filing separate returns are limited to a $1,500 deduction per taxable year.

30. § 1212(b). The potential capital loss carryforward normally is reduced by the capital loss deduction (the amount of the capital loss that is offset against ordinary income). However, the Technical and Miscellaneous Revenue Act of 1988 provides that this reduction be limited to the summation of the (1) taxable income, (2) capital loss deduction, and (3) deduction for personal and dependency exemptions. This limit will have an effect only if taxable income is negative.

Capital gains and losses are reported on Schedule D of the 1988 Form 1040. Part I of Schedule D is used to report short-term capital gains and losses. Part II of Schedule D is used to report long-term capital gains and losses. On Page 2 of Schedule D, Part III summarizes the results of Parts I and II. Part IV is used to compute the capital loss carryovers to 1989. Part V is used to elect out of the installment method and to report a note at less than face value. Line 1 of Schedule D and Part VI are used to reconcile Form 1099–B information with the Schedule D information. (Parts IV through VI are not reproduced here.)

SCHEDULE D
(Form 1040)

Department of the Treasury
Internal Revenue Service

Capital Gains and Losses
(And Reconciliation of Forms 1099-B)

▶ Attach to Form 1040.   ▶ See Instructions for Schedule D (Form 1040).
For Paperwork Reduction Act Notice, see Form 1040 Instructions.

OMB No. 1545-0074

1988
Attachment
Sequence No. **12**

Name(s) as shown on Form 1040: Erlyne Smith

Your social security number: 466 : 36 : 4596

1   Report here the total sales of stocks, bonds, etc., reported for 1988 to you on Form(s) 1099-B or on equivalent substitute statement(s). If this amount differs from the total of lines 2b and 9b, column (d), attach a statement explaining the difference. See the Instructions for line 1 for examples . . . . . | **1** | 40,000

Part I   Short-Term Capital Gains and Losses—Assets Held One Year or Less (6 months or less if acquired before 1/1/88)

(a) Description of property (Example, 100 shares 7% preferred of "Z" Co.)	(b) Date acquired (Mo., day, yr.)	(c) Date sold (Mo., day, yr.)	(d) Sales price (see Instructions)	(e) Cost or other basis (see Instructions)	(f) LOSS If (e) is more than (d), subtract (d) from (e)	(g) GAIN If (d) is more than (e), subtract (e) from (d)
2a Stocks, Bonds, and Other Securities (Include all Form 1099-B transactions. See Instructions.)						
100 Shares W Corp. common stock	10/21/88	12/3/88	11,000	10,000		1,000
300 Shares X Corp. preferred stock	7/29/88	11/25/88	5,000	5,500	500	
2b Total (add column (d)) . . . . . . **2b▶**			16,000			
2c Other Transactions (Include Real Estate Transactions From Forms 1099-S)						

3 Short-term gain from sale or exchange of your home from Form 2119, line 8a or 14 .	**3**		
4 Short-term gain from installment sales from Form 6252, line 22 or 30	**4**		
5 Net short-term gain or (loss) from partnerships, S corporations, and fiduciaries .	**5**		
6 Short-term capital loss carryover	**6**		
7 Add all of the transactions on lines 2a and 2c and lines 3 through 6 in columns (f) and (g) .	**7** (500)	1,000	
8 Net short-term gain or (loss), combine columns (f) and (g) of line 7	**8**	500	

Part II   Long-Term Capital Gains and Losses—Assets Held More Than One Year (more than 6 months if acquired before 1/1/88)

(a)	(b)	(c)	(d)	(e)	(f)	(g)
9a Stocks, Bonds, and Other Securities (Include all Form 1099-B transactions. See Instructions.)						
2,000 Shares Y Corp. common stock	1/31/81	2/12/88	8,000	7,000		1,000
40 Shares Z Corp. common stock	6/11/81	9/5/88	16,000	18,800	2,800	
9b Total (add column (d)) . . . . . . **9b▶**			24,000			
9c Other Transactions (Include Real Estate Transactions From Forms 1099-S)						

10 Long-term gain from sale or exchange of your home from Form 2119, line 8a, 10, or 14 .	**10**		
11 Long-term gain from installment sales from Form 6252, line 22 or 30	**11**		
12 Net long-term gain or (loss) from partnerships, S corporations, and fiduciaries . .	**12**		
13 Capital gain distributions.	**13**		
14 Enter gain from Form 4797, line 7 or 9	**14**		
15 Long-term capital loss carryover	**15**		
16 Add all of the transactions on lines 9a and 9c and lines 10 through 15 in columns (f) and (g) . .	**16** (2,800)	1,000	
17 Net long-term gain or (loss), combine columns (f) and (g) of line 16	**17**	(1,800)	

Schedule D (Form 1040) 1988

Schedule D (Form 1040) 1988		Attachment Sequence No. 12	Page 2
Name(s) as shown on Form 1040. (Do not enter name and social security number if shown on other side.)		Your social security number	

Part III   Summary of Parts I and II

18	Combine lines 8 and 17, and enter the net gain or (loss) here. If result is a gain, also enter the gain on Form 1040, line 13	**18**	(1,300)
19	If line 18 is a (loss), enter here and as a (loss) on Form 1040, line 13, the **smaller** of:		
a	The (loss) on line 18; or		
b	($3,000) or, if married filing a separate return, ($1,500)	**19**	(1,300)
	Note: When figuring which amount is **smaller**, treat them as if they were positive numbers.		

EXAMPLE 39

During 1988, Erlyne Smith (Social Security number, 466–36–4596) had the following sales of capital assets (a 1988 example has been used, since a 1989 form was unavailable):

Retern of principla - adjust your basis .

Description	Date Acquired	Date Sold	Selling Price	Cost Basis *
100 shares of W Corp. common stock	10/21/88	12/3/88	$11,000	$10,000
300 shares of X Corp. preferred stock	7/29/88	11/25/88	5,000	5,500
2,000 shares of Y Corp. common stock	1/31/81	2/12/88	8,000	7,000
40 shares of Z Corp. common stock	6/11/81	9/5/88	16,000	18,800

* Includes selling expenses (e.g., brokerage commissions).

Please note that Erlyne's tax position is the same as that of R in Example 36. Thus, Erlyne has a net LTCL of $1,800 (Part II of Schedule D) and a net STCG of $500 (Part I of Schedule D). These amounts are combined (see Part III on page 2 of Schedule D) for a net long-term capital loss of $1,300. All of the $1,300 is deductible *for* adjusted gross income as a capital loss deduction. There is no remaining capital loss to carry over to 1989. In completing a Schedule D for Erlyne Smith, it was assumed that she had no capital loss carryovers from prior years. Her total stock sales of $40,000 ($11,000 + $5,000 + $8,000 + $16,000) were reported to her by her broker on a Form 1099–B. □

TAX TREATMENT OF CAPITAL GAINS AND LOSSES OF CORPORATE TAXPAYERS

The treatment of a corporation's net capital gain or loss differs from the rules for individuals. Briefly, the differences are as follows:

- There is a NCG alternative tax rate of 34 percent. However, since the maximum corporate tax rate is 34 percent, the alternative tax is not beneficial unless Congress raises regular tax rates.

Capital losses offset only capital gains. No deduction is permitted against ordinary taxable income (whereas a $3,000 deduction is allowed to individuals).[31]

• There is a three-year carryback and a five-year carryover period for net capital losses.[32] Corporate carryovers and carrybacks are always treated as short term, regardless of their original nature.

EXAMPLE 40   X Corporation has a $15,000 NLTCL for the current year and $57,000 of ordinary taxable income. X Corporation may not offset the $15,000 NLTCL against its ordinary income by taking a capital loss deduction. The $15,000 NLTCL becomes a $15,000 STCL for carryback and carryover purposes. This amount may be offset by capital gains in the three-year carryback period or, if not absorbed there, offset by capital gains in the five-year carryforward period. ☐

The rules applicable to corporations are discussed in greater detail in chapter 20.

TAX PLANNING CONSIDERATIONS

Importance of Capital Asset Status

Why is capital asset status still important if long-term capital gains are no longer eligible for special tax treatment? Nearly all tax experts agree that the current taxation of long-term capital gains at ordinary tax rates is a temporary situation. Regular tax rates are probably going to rise, and the historical lower taxation of long-term capital gains will again be in place.

In the meantime, capital asset status is still important because capital gains must be offset by capital losses. If a net capital loss results, the maximum deduction is $3,000 per year. Also, because the capital asset structure remains in the Code, capital gains and losses must still be reported separately on Schedule D of Form 1040. Consequently, capital gains and losses must be segregated from other types of gains and losses.

Planning for Capital Asset Status

It is important to keep in mind that capital asset status often is a question of objective evidence. Thus, property that is not a capital asset to one party may qualify as a capital asset to another party.

EXAMPLE 41   T, a real estate dealer, transfers by gift a tract of land to S, her son. The land was recorded as part of T's inventory (it was held for resale) and was therefore not a capital asset to T. S, however, treats the land as an investment. The land is a capital asset in S's hands, and any later taxable disposition of the property by S will yield a capital gain or loss. ☐

---

31. § 1211(a).   32. § 1212(a)(1).

If proper planning is carried out, even a dealer may obtain long-term capital gain treatment on the sale of the type of property normally held for resale.

EXAMPLE 42

T, a real estate dealer, segregates tract A from the real estate he regularly holds for resale and designates such property as being held for investment purposes. The property is not advertised for sale and is disposed of several years later. The negotiations for the subsequent sale were initiated by the purchaser and not by T. Under these circumstances, it would appear that any gain or loss from the sale of tract A should be a capital gain or loss.[33]

□

When a business is being sold, one of the major decisions usually concerns whether a portion of the sales price is goodwill. For the seller, goodwill generally represents the disposition of a capital asset. Goodwill has no basis and represents a residual portion of the selling price that cannot be allocated reasonably to the known assets. The amount of goodwill thus represents capital gain. The buyer purchasing goodwill has a capitalizable, nonamortizable asset—a very disadvantageous situation.

The buyer would prefer that the residual portion of the purchase price be allocated to a covenant not to compete (a promise that the seller will not compete against the buyer by conducting a business similar to the one that the buyer has purchased). Payments for a covenant not to compete are ordinary income to the seller, but are ordinary deductions for the buyer over the life of the covenant.

The case law requires a covenant not to compete to be clearly specified in the sales contract.[34] Otherwise, unallocated payments will be regarded as payments for goodwill.[35] The parties should therefore bargain for the nature of this portion of the sales price and clearly specify its nature in the sales contract.

EXAMPLE 43

M is buying J's dry cleaning proprietorship. An appraisal of the assets indicates that a reasonable purchase price would exceed the value of the known assets by $30,000. If the purchase contract does not specify the nature of the $30,000, the amount will be goodwill, and J will have a long-term capital gain of $30,000. M will have a nonamortizable $30,000 asset. If M is paying the extra $30,000 to prevent J from conducting another dry cleaning business in the area, J will have $30,000 of ordinary income, and M will have a $30,000 deduction over the life of the covenant if the contract specifies the purpose for the payment. □

---

33. *Toledo, Peoria & Western Railroad Co.*, 35 TCM 1663, T.C.Memo. 1976–366.

34. See, for example, *James A. Patterson*, 49 TCM 670, T.C.Memo. 1985–53.

35. § 1060(a)(2).

Effect of Capital Asset Status in Other Than Sale Transactions

The nature of an asset (capital or ordinary) is important in determining the tax consequences that result when a sale or exchange occurs. It may, however, be just as significant absent a taxable sale or exchange. When a capital asset is disposed of, the result is not always a capital gain or loss. Rather, in general, the disposition must be a sale or exchange. Collection of a debt instrument having a basis less than the face value would result in an ordinary gain rather than a capital gain even though the debt instrument is a capital asset. The collection is not a sale or exchange. Sale of the debt shortly before the due date for collection will not produce a capital gain.[36] If selling the debt in such circumstances could produce a capital gain but collecting could not, the narrow interpretation of what constitutes a capital gain or loss would be frustrated. Another illustration of the sale or exchange principle could involve a donation of certain appreciated property to a qualified charity. Recall that in certain circumstances, the measure of the charitable contribution is fair market value when the property, if sold, would have yielded a long-term capital gain [refer to chapter 11 and the discussion of § 170(e)].

EXAMPLE 44	T wants to donate a tract of unimproved land (basis of $40,000 and fair market value of $200,000) held for the required long-term holding period to State University (a qualified charitable organization). However, T currently is under audit by the IRS for capital gains she reported on certain real estate transactions during an earlier tax year. Although T is not a licensed real estate broker, the IRS agent conducting the audit is contending that she has achieved dealer status by virtue of the number and frequency of the real estate transactions she has conducted. Under these circumstances, T would be well-advised to postpone the donation to State University until such time as her status is clarified. If she has achieved dealer status, the unimproved land may be inventory (refer to Example 42 for another possible result), and T's charitable contribution deduction would be limited to $40,000. If not, and if the land is held as an investment, T's deduction becomes $200,000 (the fair market value of the property). □

Stock Sales

The following rules apply in determining the date of a stock sale:

- The date the sale is executed is the date of the sale. The execution date is the date the broker completes the transaction on the stock exchange.

- The settlement date is the date the cash or other property is paid to the seller of the stock. This date is *not* relevant in determining the date of sale.

---

36. *Comm. v. Percy W. Phillips*, 60–1 USTC ¶9294, 5 AFTR2d 855, 275 F.2d 33 (CA–4, 1960).

EXAMPLE 45

T, a cash basis taxpayer, sells stock that results in a gain. The sale was executed on December 29, 1988. The settlement date is January 5, 1989. The date of sale is December 29, 1988 (the execution date). The holding period for the stock sold ends with the execution date. □

Maximizing Benefits

Ordinary losses generally are preferable to capital losses because of the limitations imposed on the deductibility of net capital losses and the requirement that capital losses be used to offset capital gains. The taxpayer may be able to convert what would otherwise have been capital loss to ordinary loss. For example, business (but not nonbusiness) bad debts, losses from the sale or exchange of small business investment company stock, and losses from the sale or exchange of small business company stock all result in ordinary losses.[37]

Although capital losses can be carried over indefinitely, *indefinite* becomes definite when a taxpayer dies. Any loss carryovers not used by such taxpayer are permanently lost. That is, no tax benefit can be derived from the carryovers subsequent to death.[38] Therefore, the potential benefit of carrying over capital losses diminishes when dealing with older taxpayers.

It is usually beneficial to spread gains over more than one taxable year. In some cases, this can be accomplished through the installment sales method of accounting.

Year-End Planning

The following general rules can be applied for timing the recognition of capital gains and losses near the end of a taxable year:

- If the taxpayer already has recognized over $3,000 of capital loss, sell assets to generate capital gain equal to the excess of the capital loss over $3,000.

EXAMPLE 46

T has already incurred a $6,000 LTCL. T should generate $3,000 of capital gain. The gain will offset $3,000 of the loss. Thus, the remaining loss of $3,000 can be deducted against ordinary income. □

- If the taxpayer already has recognized capital gain, sell assets to generate capital loss equal to the capital gain. The gain will not be taxed, and the loss will be fully *deductible* against the gain.

---

37. §§ 166(d), 1242, and 1244. Refer to the discussion in chapter 8.

38. Rev.Rul. 74–175, 1974–1 C.B. 52.

PROBLEM MATERIALS

Discussion Questions

1. Why did Congress leave the structure of the capital asset Code Sections in place even though there is no beneficial tax rate for long-term capital gains?

2. Can the sale of personal use assets result in capital losses?

3. Does the tax law define "capital asset"?

4. Compare what would be a capital asset for tax purposes with the assets that would be the subject of a capital asset budgeting decision in a managerial accounting class. Does capital asset mean the same thing in both contexts?

5. T owns the following assets. Which of them are capital assets?
   a. Ten shares of Standard Motors common stock.
   b. A copyright on a song T wrote.
   c. A U.S. government savings bond.
   d. A note T received when he loaned $100 to a friend.
   e. A very rare copy of "Your Federal Income Tax" (a U.S. government publication that T purchased many years ago from the U.S. Government Printing Office).
   f. T's personal use automobile.
   g. A letter T received from a former U.S. President. T received the letter because he had complained to the President about the President's foreign policy.

6. Under what circumstances are copyrights capital assets?

7. How does the Supreme Court interpret the statutory definition of what is not a capital asset?

8. Can a dealer in securities have investments (as opposed to inventory) in securities? Explain.

9. In what circumstances may real estate held for resale receive capital gain treatment?

10. What is a lump-sum distribution? May it receive capital gain treatment?

11. P has a $2,000 nonbusiness bad debt. How is it treated?

12. What are the two general requirements for the recognition of a capital gain or loss?

13. Why does the Code require amortization of original issue discount? What is the effect of this amortization on the interest income of the taxpayer owning the bond?

14. M, a real estate dealer, purchased for $25,000 a one-year option on 40 acres of farm land. If M is able to get the property rezoned for single-family residential development, she will exercise the option and purchase the land for $800,000. The rezoning effort is unsuccessful, and the option expires. How should the $25,000 be treated?

15. If an individual pays a $100 premium to acquire an option to buy stock, how does the call premium affect the basis of the stock if the option is exercised?

16. If a grantee of an option exercises the option, do the grantor's proceeds from the sale of the option property increase? Why?

17. When does the transfer of a patent result in long-term capital gain? Short-term capital gain? Ordinary income?

18. Is it beneficial for tax purposes to transfer all substantial rights to a patent?

19. If an inventor's employer automatically has sole patent rights to the inventor's inventions, is the employer a holder of the patent?

20. What is a franchise? In practice, does the transfer of a franchise usually result in capital gain or loss treatment? Why or why not?

21. Why do you think § 1056 limits the amount of the cost of a sports franchise that can be allocated to player contracts? (*Hint:* Where would the player contracts appear on the books of the owner of the franchise?)

22. When are lease cancellation payments received by a lessee capital in nature? When are lease cancellation payments received by a lessor capital in nature?

23. How does one determine if a capital asset has been held long enough to be eligible for long-term capital gain or loss treatment?

24. W owns A Corporation stock purchased on April 15, 1988, for $8,000 and B Corporation stock purchased on August 3, 1989, for $20,000. Both stocks are sold on December 5, 1989, for $30,000 each. What are the amount and character of the income recognized from these transactions?

25. X owns A Corporation stock purchased on June 10, 1988, for $8,000 and B Corporation stock purchased on October 23, 1988, for $20,000. Both stocks are sold on April 23, 1989, for $30,000 each. What is X's adjusted gross income for 1989 if she also had wages of $80,000?

26. S receives $10,000 of stock from her father by gift on January 18, 1989. Her father had acquired the stock 13 months earlier for $5,500. When does S's holding period for the stock begin?

27. Define a short sale. Why does a seller enter into a short sale?

28. What is the general rule used to determine the holding period of property sold short? What is an exception to this rule, and why was the exception enacted?

29. Is there any reason a taxpayer would prefer to recognize a loss as a capital loss rather than as an ordinary loss?

30. Which type of gain would a taxpayer prefer to recognize in 1989: long-term capital gain, short-term capital gain, or ordinary income?

31. Which type of loss would a taxpayer prefer to incur in 1989: long-term capital loss, short-term capital loss, or ordinary loss?

32. Differentiate between the capital loss carryover rules for unused capital losses of individuals and corporations.

Problems

33. N had three property transactions during the year. She sold a vacation home used for personal purposes at a $35,000 gain. The home had been held for five years and had never been rented. N also sold an antique clock for $3,500 that she had inherited from her grandmother. The clock was valued in N's grandmother's estate at $2,000. N owned the clock for only four months. N sold these assets to finance her full-time occupation as a songwriter. Near the end of the year, N sold one of the songs she had written two years earlier. She received cash of $15,000 and a royalty interest in revenues derived from the merchandising of the song. N had no tax basis for the song. N had no other income and $18,000 in deductible songwriting expenses. Assume the maximum tax rate applies to N.

    a. Assuming the year is 1989, what is N's adjusted gross income?

    b. What is N's tax on capital gains in 1989?

34. F, a college art student, made a humorous drawing of his school's mascot. He silk screened the drawing on 1,000 T-shirts he purchased for $3 each. The silk screening cost $1 per T-shirt. F sold the T-shirts for $8 each at a booth on his lawn near the college football stadium. All the T-shirts were sold during the fall. F incurs $150 of marketing costs. What is F's adjusted gross income? What is the character of his gain from selling the T-shirts?

35. L, an accrual basis taxpayer, is a component parts manufacturer. L's major customer is very slow to pay L's invoices. To generate cash, L sells $250,000 of accounts receivable to O, an unrelated individual, for $210,000. O then collects the full amount of the receivables from the customer. What are the tax consequences of these events for L and O?

36. A sells real estate lots, but meets all the conditions of § 1237. In 1989, she sells four lots to B, C, D, and E and two adjacent lots to F. The sales price of each lot is $20,000. A's basis is $15,000 for each lot. Sales expenses are $500 per lot.

    a. What is the realized and recognized gain?

    b. Explain the nature of the gain (ordinary income or capital gain).

    c. Would your answers change if, instead, the two lots sold to F were not adjacent? If so, how?

37. S purchases V common stock on December 7, 1988, for $3,678. She is notified in May 1989 that the stock is wholly worthless. What are the amount and nature of S's loss?

38. T is looking for vacant land to buy. She would hold the land as an investment. For $1,000, she is granted an 11-month option on January 1, 1989, to buy 10 acres of vacant land for $25,000. The owner (who is holding the land for investment) paid $10,000 for the land several years ago.

   a. Does the land owner have gross income when $1,000 is received for granting the option?

   b. Does T have an asset when the option is granted?

   c. If the option lapses, does the land owner have a recognized gain? If so, what type of gain? Does T have a recognized loss? If so, what type of loss?

   d. If the option is exercised and an additional $25,000 is paid for the land, how much recognized gain does the seller have? What type of gain? What is T's tax basis for the property?

39. In 1989, A sells to Z an option to buy 1,000 shares of X Corporation stock for $10,000 for the following three-month period. The option cost $1,000. A originally purchased the stock in 1980 for $8,000.

   a. What are the tax consequences to A if Z exercises the option?

   b. If Z allows the option to lapse?

40. In each of the following independent situations, determine whether the sale at a gain of all substantial rights in a patent qualifies for capital gain treatment:

   a. The creator sells the patent to a manufacturing company. The creator is not an employee of the manufacturing company.

   b. A manufacturing company owns a patent developed by one of its employees. It has been using the patent in its manufacturing process. The company sells the patent along with the assets of the manufacturing process.

   c. An investor buys a patent that has not been reduced to practice from the creator. After holding it for three months, she sells it to a retail company.

41. F, Inc., sells a franchise to R. The franchise contains many restrictions on how R may operate his store. For instance, R cannot use less than Grade 10 Idaho potatoes, must fry the potatoes at a constant 410 degrees, dress store personnel in F-approved uniforms, and have an F sign that meets detailed specifications on size, color, and construction. F receives a $40,000 franchise fee from R during the current year. What is the nature of this payment?

42. D is a student at State University. He is graduating in June but has an apartment lease that expires at the end of August. He cannot find someone to lease the apartment for the summer. D's landlord offers to cancel D's lease for $900 (one-half of the July and August rent). D accepts the offer. What are the tax consequences for D and his landlord?

43. F exchanges a business copying machine for another copier in a § 1031 like-kind exchange. F acquired the machine on March 12, 1986, and the exchange occurred on July 3, 1989.

    a. When does the holding period of the new machine begin?

    b. How would the answer to (a) change if the transaction were the replacement of a personal residence and the taxpayer qualified under § 1034?

44. T sells short 100 shares of A stock at $20 per share on January 15, 1989. He buys 200 shares of A stock on April 1, 1989, at $25 per share. On May 2, 1989, he closes the short sale by delivering 100 of the shares purchased April 1.

    a. What are the amount and nature of T's loss upon closing the short sale?

    b. When does the holding period for the remaining 100 shares begin?

    c. If T sells (at $27 per share) the remaining 100 shares on January 20, 1990, what will be the nature of his gain or loss?

45. U (single with no dependents) has the following transactions in 1989:

Adjusted gross income (exclusive of capital gains and losses)	$200,000
Long-term capital gain	5,000
Long-term capital loss	(900)
Short-term capital gain	1,000
Short-term capital loss	(1,900)

    What is U's net capital gain or loss? What is U's tax on net capital gain?

46. In 1989, B (single with no dependents) had a recognized $18,000 LTCG from an installment sale of a personal residence that was sold in 1982. She also purchased from an inventor for $8,000 (and resold in two months for $7,000) a patent on a rubber bonding process. The patent was purchased as an investment. Additionally, she had the following capital gains and losses from stock transactions:

Long-term capital loss	($ 3,000)
Long-term capital loss carryover from 1988	(12,000)
Short-term capital gain	11,000
Short-term capital loss	(6,000)

    What is B's net capital gain or loss?

47. In 1989, W (single with no dependents) engaged in various stock transactions. W purchased R, Inc., common stock on January 10, for $8,000. The price began to plummet almost immediately. W sold the stock short on March 31, 1989, for $3,000. On June 11, 1989, W closed the short sale by delivering identical stock that she had purchased on June 10, 1989, for $10,000. On June 11, 1989, the price of the R stock was $12,000. A very favorable first-quarter earnings report (contrary to rumored large losses) accounted for the swings in the stock price. W also had the following stock transaction results: $500 STCG, $6,300 STCL, $700 LTCL, $43,500 LTCG. W has $110,000 of taxable income

from sources other than those previously mentioned. What is W's net capital gain or loss? What is W's total tax liability?

48. For several years, K had rented a $3,000 per month apartment. In 1989, a fire destroyed the apartment building. Under local law, the landlord was required to find comparable housing for K within five days. The landlord offered K $10,000 in lieu of suitable housing and in cancellation of the remaining two years of K's lease. K accepted. K's belongings were destroyed in the fire. All the belongings had been owned more than one year. K's insurance covered everything for re-placement value. K received a check for $76,000. She prepared the following schedule to aid in your analysis:

Item	Adjusted Basis	FMV	Insurance Award	Action Taken	Amount Spent
Clothing	$25,000	$ 3,000	$25,000	Replaced	$40,000
Piano	8,000	12,000	10,000	Not replaced	—
Furniture	45,000	33,000	41,000	Replaced	38,000

K wishes to defer gains if possible. K's salary is $120,000. What is K's net capital gain or loss? K's adjusted gross income? K's basis for the re-placement assets?

49. S, a married individual filing a separate return, sold land for $6,000 during 1989. The land had been acquired by gift from S's aunt four months before S sold it. S's aunt had purchased the land in 1976 for $9,000, and the land was appraised at $6,700 when it was given to S. S is divorcing her husband. She had wages of $19,000 during 1989. She will make a deductible 1989 IRA contribution of $2,000. She has been working since 1981 and has her own IRA. S has the following gains and losses from stock transactions:

Long-term capital loss	($3,000)
Short-term capital gain	2,000
Short-term capital loss carryover	(3,000)

What is S's net capital gain or loss? What is S's adjusted gross income?

50. For 1989, B completes the following stock transactions:

	Date Acquired	Cost	Date Sold	Selling Price
1,000 shares ABC	1/6/89	$4,000	8/2/89	$3,000
200 shares DEF	7/1/82	8,800	9/18/89	9,400
3,500 shares GHI	5/2/89	7,000	11/2/89	8,900
5,000 shares JKL	8/5/89	9,700	12/15/89	5,000

What is B's includible gain or deductible loss resulting from these stock sales?

51. X, an unmarried individual with no dependents, has the following 1989 transactions:

Adjusted gross income (exclusive of capital gains and losses)	$15,000
Long-term capital loss	(5,000)
Long-term capital gain	2,000
Short-term capital loss carryover	(2,000)

What is X's net capital gain or loss? What is X's adjusted gross income?

52. During 1989, T has short-term capital gains of $2,500, long-term capital gains of $1,600, short-term capital losses of $2,800, and long-term capital losses of $9,800. Additionally, T has a $2,000 long-term capital loss carryover.

    a. What is T's capital loss deduction for 1989?

    b. What are the amount and character of T's capital loss carryover to 1990?

53. R Corporation has $15,000 of long-term capital loss for 1989 and $110,000 of other taxable income. What is its 1989 taxable income and the amount (if any) of its capital loss carryover?

Cumulative Problems

54. Marvin and Sylvia Fryer (both 53) are married and file a joint return. Their address is 767 Clinton Street, Regon, Ohio 43763. Their Social Security numbers are 686–37–8757 and 687–45–2378, respectively. Marvin had a $32,000 salary as a copy machine repairman, and Sylvia had a $37,000 salary as a nurse. Sylvia inherited and then sold in two months 3,000 Exxon shares. The stock was valued in her mother's estate at $150,000 and was sold by Sylvia for $128,000. The Fryers had other stock sales resulting in a $5,000 short-term capital loss for the year. Marvin sold his baseball card collection for $5,500. He had owned the cards since he was eight years old. The cards were included in bubble gum packages he bought for $.05 each and he sold 3,000 cards. Each package included three cards. The Fryers received $3,200 for a ramshackle cabin and 10 acres of land they had owned 11 years. The Fryers used the property for hunting and had paid $700 for it. The Fryers have $8,000 of itemized deductions and no dependents. Marvin's employer withheld Federal income tax of $4,500, and Sylvia's employer withheld $4,900. They made no estimated tax payments. What is their 1989 taxable income and their net tax payable?

55. Tom Tenor, age 28, is an automobile mechanic. Tom lives at 518 Marigold Lane, Okemos, MI 48864. His Social Security number is 393–86–4502. He is single and has no dependents. In April 1989, while tinkering with his automobile, Tom devised a carburetor modification kit that increases gas mileage by 20%. He patented the invention and in June 1989 sold it to X Corporation for a lump-sum payment of $250,000 plus $5 per kit sold. Other information of potential tax consequence is as follows:

    a. Cash received from X Corporation, which sold 20,000 kits in 1989, $100,000.

b. Wages earned as a mechanic from January 1 through June 17, $4,300.

c. Points paid on a $200,000 mortgage Tom incurred to buy a luxurious new home (he had previously lived in an apartment), $6,000.

d. State sales taxes paid on four new automobiles Tom acquired in 1989, $2,200.

e. Costs Tom incurred (including rent paid for a garage, materials, supplies, etc.) during the time he has continued his experimental activities and has worked on several potentially patentable automotive devices, $14,000.

f. Interest on home mortgage, $7,500.

g. Various miscellaneous itemized deductions (not including any potential deductions above), $9,400.

h. Interest income on savings account, $6,200.

Compute Tom's lowest legal tax liability, before prepayments or credits, for 1989. Suggested software (if available): *WEST–TAX Planner* or *BNA Individual Income Tax Spreadsheet.*

56. Margaret Gill, age 33, is single with no dependents. Margaret is an insurance adjuster. She resides at 2510 Grace Avenue, Richmond, VA 23100. Her Social Security number is 666–88–1000. The following information is for Margaret's 1988 tax year. She earned a $40,000 salary. On March 1, 1982, she purchased 500 shares of People's Power Company for $10,000. She sold those shares on October 14, 1988, for $8,500 after receiving nontaxable dividends totaling $2,600 (including $700 in 1988). She also received $300 in taxable dividends in 1988 from People's Power Company. On November 7, 1983, Margaret purchased 1,000 shares of XYZ Corporation for $22,000. On February 12, 1988, she received an additional 100 shares in a nontaxable 10% stock dividend. On February 13, 1988, she sold those 100 shares for $2,500. During 1988, she paid $6,000 in deductible home mortgage interest, $1,200 in property taxes, $2,000 in state income taxes, $600 in sales tax, and $1,500 in professional dues and subscriptions. Her employer withheld Federal income tax of $6,200. Compute Margaret's net tax payable or refund due for 1988. If you use tax forms for your computations, you will need Form 1040 and Schedules A, B, and D. Suggested software (if available): *WEST–TAX Preparer* for tax return solutions, *WEST–TAX Planner* or *BNA Individual Income Tax Spreadsheet* if tax return solutions are not desired.

Research Problems

Research Problem 1   Sam Jones has a Ph.D. in biotechnology and is a professor at State University. For the past three years, he has been very successful at acquiring a wide variety of biotechnology patents. He purchased the patents with the intention of reselling them. In 1989, he sells several patents for a $6 million gain. Is Sam a holder of the patents he sold, and does he qualify for long-term capital gain treatment under § 1235?

Research Problem 2   X Corporation has plants in a number of U.S. cities. It frequently transfers executives between those cities. If the executive cannot sell his or her home, the realty division of X Corporation will buy the home at its appraised value after 90 days. The realty division will then immediately attempt to resell the home. What is the nature of the gains and losses the realty division realizes when it sells the homes?

17

PROPERTY TRANSACTIONS: SECTION 1231 AND RECAPTURE PROVISIONS

OBJECTIVES

Explain the nature of § 1231 treatment of certain gains and losses.

Discuss the rationale for § 1231 treatment.

Define § 1231 assets.

Apply the special rules for certain § 1231 assets, including timber, coal, domestic iron ore, livestock, and unharvested crops.

Describe the procedure for computation of § 1231 gains and losses.

Explain the rationale and procedures for §§ 1245 and 1250 recapture.

Discuss certain special recapture provisions.

Explain the treatment of gains and losses from dispositions of passive activity property.

Develop tax planning ideas related to §§ 1231, 1245, and 1250.

A long-term capital gain was defined in chapter 16 as the recognized gain from the sale or exchange of a capital asset held for the required long-term holding period.[1] This chapter is concerned with § 1231, which applies to the sale or exchange of business properties and to certain involuntary conversions. This chapter also covers the recapture provisions that tax as ordinary income certain gains that might otherwise qualify for long-term capital gain treatment. The impact of the passive loss provisions (refer to chapter 7) on the taxation of property gains and losses is also discussed briefly in this chapter.

SECTION 1231 ASSETS

Relationship to Capital Assets

Depreciable property and real property used in business are not capital assets.[2] Thus, the recognized gains from the disposition of such property (principally machinery, equipment, buildings, and land) would appear to be ordinary income rather than capital gain. Due to § 1231, however, *net gain* from the disposition of such property is sometimes *treated* as *long-term capital gain*. A long-term holding period requirement must be met; the disposition must generally be from a sale, exchange, or involuntary conversion; and certain recapture provisions must be satisfied for this result to occur. Section 1231 may also apply to involuntary conversions of capital assets. Since an involuntary conversion is not a sale or exchange, such a disposition would not normally result in a capital gain.

If the disposition of depreciable property and real property used in business results in a *net loss*, § 1231 *treats* the *loss* as an *ordinary loss* rather than as a capital loss. Ordinary losses are fully deductible *for* adjusted gross income. Capital losses are offset by capital gains, and, if any loss remains, the loss is deductible to the extent of $3,000 per year for individuals and is not deductible currently at all by regular corporations. It seems, therefore, that § 1231 provides the *best* of both potential results: net gain is treated as long-term capital gain and net loss is treated as ordinary loss.

EXAMPLE 1   R sells business land and building at a $5,000 gain and business equipment at a $3,000 loss. Both properties were held for the long-term holding period. R's net gain is $2,000, and that net gain may (depending on various recapture rules discussed later in this chapter) be treated as a long-term capital gain under § 1231. □

EXAMPLE 2   S sells business equipment at a $10,000 loss and business land at a $2,000 gain. Both properties were held for the long-term holding period. S's net loss is $8,000, and that net loss is an ordinary loss. □

---

1. For assets acquired after December 31, 1987, the long-term holding period is more than one year. For assets acquired before January 1, 1988, the long-term holding period is more than six months.

2. § 1221(2).

Justification for Favorable Tax Treatment

The favorable capital gain/ordinary loss treatment sanctioned by § 1231 can be explained by examining several historical developments. Before 1938, business property had been included in the definition of capital assets. Thus, if such property was sold for a loss (not an unlikely possibility during the depression years), a capital loss resulted. If, however, such property was depreciable and could be retained for its estimated useful life, much (if not all) of its costs could be recovered in the form of depreciation. Because the allowance for depreciation was fully deductible whereas capital losses were not, the tax law favored those who did not dispose of an asset. Congress recognized this inequity when it removed business property from the capital asset classification. During the period 1938–1942, therefore, all such gains and losses were ordinary gains and losses.

With the advent of World War II, two principal conditions forced Congress to reexamine the situation regarding business assets. First, the sale of business assets at a gain was discouraged because the gain would be ordinary income. Gains were common because the war effort had inflated prices. Second, taxpayers who did not want to sell their assets often were required to because of government acquisitions through condemnation. Often the condemnation awards resulted in large gains to those taxpayers who were forced to part with their property and deprived them of the benefits of future depreciation deductions. Of course, the condemnations constituted involuntary conversions, the gain from which could be deferred through timely reinvestment in property that was "similar or related in service or use." But where was such property to be found in view of wartime restrictions and other governmental condemnations? The end product did not seem equitable: a large ordinary gain due to government action and no deferral possibility due to government restrictions.

In recognition of these two conditions, in 1942, Congress eased the tax bite on the disposition of some business property by allowing preferential capital gain treatment. Thus, the present scheme of § 1231 and the dichotomy of capital gain/ordinary loss treatment evolved from a combination of economic considerations existing in 1938 and in 1942.

The rules regarding § 1231 treatment do not apply to *all* business property. Important in this regard are the holding period requirements and the fact that the property must be either depreciable property or real estate used in business. Nor is § 1231 necessarily limited to business property. Transactions involving certain capital assets may fall into the § 1231 category. Thus, § 1231 singles out only some types of business property.

As discussed in chapter 16, for 1988 and later years, there is no beneficial tax rate for long-term capital gains. Why, then, is § 1231 still beneficial? As we will see, § 1231 requires netting of § 1231 gains and losses. If the result is a gain, the gain is treated as a long-term capital gain. The gain will therefore be available to absorb capital losses and help prevent the unfavorable net capital loss result. Also, if a special tax rate for long-term capital gains is reenacted, the § 1231 procedure would still be available and would allow net § 1231 gains to be taxed at the favorable long-term capital gain rate. Finally, § 1231 assets can create an ordinary loss and yet be treated the same as capital assets for purposes of the appreciated property charitable contribution provisions (refer to chapter 11).

Property Included

Section 1231 property includes the following:

- Depreciable or real property used in business (principally machinery and equipment, buildings, and land).

- Timber, coal, or domestic iron ore to which § 631 applies.

- Livestock held for draft, breeding, dairy, or sporting purposes.

- Unharvested crops on land used in business.

- Certain nonpersonal use capital assets.

Property Excluded

Section 1231 property does *not* include the following:

- Property not held for the long-term holding period. Since the benefit of § 1231 is long-term capital gain treatment, the holding period must correspond to the more-than-one-year holding period that applies to capital assets. Livestock must be held at least 12 months (24 months in some cases). Unharvested crops do not have to be held for the required long-term holding period, but the land must be held for the long-term holding period.

- Property where casualty losses exceed casualty gains for the taxable year. If a taxpayer has a net casualty loss, the individual casualty gains and losses are treated as ordinary gains and losses.

- Inventory and property held primarily for sale to customers.

- Copyrights; literary, musical, or artistic compositions, etc.; and certain U.S. government publications.

Notice that the last two items (inventory and copyrights, etc.) are also not capital assets (see the discussion in chapter 16).

Special Rules for Certain Section 1231 Assets

A rather diverse group of assets is included under § 1231. The following discussion summarizes the special rules for some of those assets.

Timber.   A taxpayer can *elect* to treat the cutting of timber held for sale or for use in business as a sale or exchange.[3] If the taxpayer makes this election, the transaction qualifies under § 1231. The taxpayer must have owned the timber or a contract to cut it on the first day of the year and for the long-term holding period before the date the cutting takes place. The recognized § 1231 gain or loss is determined at the time the timber is cut and is equal to the difference between the timber's fair market value as of the first day of the taxable year and the adjusted basis for depletion. If a taxpayer sells the timber for more or less than the fair market value as of the first day of the taxable year in which it is cut, the difference is ordinary income or loss.

---

3. § 631(a) and Reg. § 1.631–1.

This provision was enacted to provide preferential treatment relative to the natural growth value of timber, which has a relatively long-term maturation process. Congress believed this favorable treatment would encourage reforestation of timber lands. If a taxpayer disposes of timber held for the long-term holding period, either by sale or under a royalty contract (where the taxpayer retains an economic interest in the property), the disposal is treated as a sale of the timber. Therefore, any gain or loss qualifies under § 1231.

EXAMPLE 3

Several years ago, T purchased a tract of land with a substantial stand of trees on it. The land cost $40,000, and the timber cost $100,000. On the first day of 1989, the timber was appraised at $250,000. In August 1989, T cut the timber and sold it for $265,000. T elects to treat the cutting as a sale or exchange under § 1231. T has a $150,000 § 1231 gain ($250,000 − $100,000) and a $15,000 ordinary gain ($265,000 − $250,000). □

Coal or Domestic Iron Ore. If a taxpayer disposes of coal or domestic iron ore held for the long-term holding period, either by sale or under a royalty contract (where the taxpayer retains an economic interest in the property), the disposal is treated as a sale of the coal or domestic iron ore.[4] Therefore, any gain or loss qualifies under § 1231.

The provisions including coal and domestic iron ore royalties under § 1231 were enacted primarily to encourage the development and preservation of U.S. natural resources and to enable domestic producers to compete more favorably with foreign producers.

Livestock. Cattle and horses must be held 24 months or more and other livestock must be held 12 months or more to qualify under § 1231.[5] The primary reason for enacting this provision was the considerable amount of litigation over the character of livestock [whether livestock was held primarily for sale to customers (ordinary income) or for use in a trade or business (§ 1231 property)]. Poultry is not livestock for purposes of § 1231.

Unharvested Crops. An unharvested crop on land used in business and held for the long-term holding period qualifies under § 1231 if the crop and land are disposed of at the same time to the same person. The cost of producing the crop must be capitalized (not expensed) for § 1231 to apply. This provision was enacted because taxpayers previously were able to recover the costs of producing crops through current deductions and were usually allowed long-term capital gain treatment on the disposition of the crop.

Certain Nonpersonal Use Capital Assets. *Nonpersonal use* property disposed of by casualty or theft may receive § 1231 treatment. Nonpersonal use property includes capital assets held for the production of income, such as an investment painting or investment land. Nonpersonal use property also includes business property. The casualty or theft *long-term* gains and losses from nonpersonal use property are combined (see Concept Summary 17–1). If the result is a gain, the gains and losses are treated as § 1231 transactions. If

---

4. § 631(c) and Reg. § 1.631–3.
5. Note that the holding period is "12 months or more" and not "more than 12 months."

CONCEPT SUMMARY 17–1

Section 1231 Netting Procedure

the result is a loss, § 1231 does not apply. Instead, the gains and losses are treated as ordinary gains and losses. Thus, a nonpersonal use capital asset that is disposed of by casualty or theft may or may not be a § 1231 asset, depending on the result of the netting process. For simplicity, the rest of this chapter will use the term *casualty* to mean casualty *or* theft.

Personal use property casualty gains and losses are not subject to the § 1231 rules. If the result of netting these gains and losses is a gain, the net gain is a capital gain. If the netting results in a loss, the net loss is a deduction *from* adjusted gross income to the extent it exceeds 10 percent of AGI.

Casualties, thefts, and condemnations are *involuntary conversions.* Notice that condemnation gains and losses are not included in the netting processes discussed above. Long-term *recognized* condemnation gains and losses from the disposition of property held for business use and for the production of income are treated as § 1231 gains and losses. Involuntary conversion gains may be deferred if conversion proceeds are reinvested, but involuntary conversion losses are recognized (refer to chapter 15) regardless of whether the conversion proceeds are reinvested.

This variation in treatment between casualty and condemnation gains and losses sheds considerable light on what § 1231 is all about. Section 1231 has no effect on whether or not realized gain or loss is recognized. Instead, it merely dictates how such gain or loss might be *classified* (ordinary or capital) under certain conditions.

Personal use property condemnation gains and losses are not subject to the § 1231 rules. The gains are capital gains, and the losses are nondeductible, because they arise from the disposition of personal use property.

General Procedure for Section 1231 Computation

The tax treatment of § 1231 gains and losses depends on the results of a rather complex *netting* procedure. The steps in this netting procedure are as follows.

Step 1: Casualty Netting.   Net all long-term gains and losses from casualties of nonpersonal use property. Casualty gains result when insurance proceeds exceed the adjusted basis of the property.

    a.   If the casualty gains exceed the casualty losses, add the excess to the other § 1231 gains for the taxable year.

    b.   If the casualty losses exceed the casualty gains, exclude all losses and gains from further § 1231 computation. If this is the case, all casualty gains are ordinary income. Business casualty losses are deductible *for* adjusted gross income. Other casualty losses are deductible *from* adjusted gross income.

Step 2: § 1231 Netting.   After adding any net casualty gain from Step 1a to the other § 1231 gains and losses (including recognized condemnation gains and losses), net all § 1231 gains and losses.

    a.   If the gains exceed the losses, the net gain is offset against the nonrecaptured § 1231 losses (see below) from prior tax years. To the extent of this offset, the net § 1231 gain is classified as ordinary gain. Any remaining gain is long-term capital gain.

    b.   If the losses exceed the gains, all gains are ordinary income. Business losses are deductible *for* adjusted gross income. Other casualty losses are deductible *from* adjusted gross income.

Step 3: § 1231 Lookback.   The net § 1231 gain from Step 2a is offset by the nonrecaptured net § 1231 losses for the five preceding taxable years. For 1989, the lookback years are 1984, 1985, 1986, 1987, and 1988. To the extent of the nonrecaptured net § 1231 loss, the current year net § 1231 gain is ordinary income. The *nonrecaptured* net § 1231 losses are those that have not already been used to offset net § 1231 gains. Only the net § 1231 gain exceeding this net § 1231 loss carryforward is given long-term capital gain treatment. Concept Summary 17-1 summarizes the § 1231 computational procedure. Examples 6 and 7 illustrate the lookback procedure.

Examples 4 through 7 illustrate the application of the § 1231 computation procedure.

EXAMPLE 4

During 1989, T had $125,000 of AGI before considering the following recognized gains and losses:

Capital Gains and Losses	
Long-term capital gain	$3,000
Long-term capital loss	(400)
Short-term capital gain	1,000
Short-term capital loss	(200)
Casualties	
Theft of diamond ring (owned four months)	$ (800)*
Fire damage to personal residence (owned 10 years)	(400)*
Gain from insurance recovery on accidental destruction of business truck (owned two years)	200
§ 1231 Gains and Losses from Depreciable Business Assets Held Long Term	
Asset A	$ 300
Asset B	1,100
Asset C	(500)
Gains and Losses from Sale of Depreciable Business Assets Held Short Term	
Asset D	$ 200
Asset E	(300)

* As adjusted for the $100 floor on personal casualty losses.

T had no net § 1231 losses in tax years before 1989.

Disregarding the recapture of depreciation and passive loss offset possibilities (discussed later in the chapter), the tax treatment of the above gains and losses is as follows:

● The diamond ring and the residence are personal use assets. Therefore, these casualties are not § 1231 transactions. The $800 (ring) plus $400 (residence) losses are potentially deductible *from* adjusted gross income. However, the total loss of $1,200 does not exceed 10 percent of AGI. Thus, only the business casualty remains. The $200 gain is added to the § 1231 gains.

● The gains from § 1231 transactions (Assets A, B, and C and the business casualty gain) exceed the losses by $1,100 ($1,600 less $500). This excess is a long-term capital gain and is added to T's other long-term capital gains.

- T's net long-term capital gain is $3,700 ($3,000 plus $1,100 from
§ 1231 transactions less the long-term capital loss of $400). T's net
short-term capital gain is $800 ($1,000 less $200). The result is capi-
tal gain net income of $4,500 that is subject to tax as ordinary in-
come.[6]

- The gain and loss from Assets D and E (depreciable business assets
held for less than the long-term holding period) are treated as ordinary gain and loss by T.

**Results of the Gains
and Losses on T's Tax Computation**

NLTCG	$ 3,700
STCG	800
Ordinary gain from sale of Asset D	200
Ordinary loss from sale of Asset E	(300)
AGI from other sources	125,000
AGI	$129,400

- T would have personal casualty losses of $800 (diamond ring) +
$400 (personal residence). A personal casualty loss is deductible on-
ly to the extent it exceeds 10% of AGI. Thus, none of the $1,200 is
deductible ($129,400 × 10% = $12,940). □

EXAMPLE 5

Assume the same facts as in Example 4, except the loss from Asset C was
$1,700 instead of $500.

- The treatment of the casualty losses is the same as in Example 4.

- The losses from § 1231 transactions now exceed the gains by $100
($1,700 less $1,600). The result is that the gains from Assets A and B
and the business casualty gain are ordinary income and the loss
from Asset C is a deduction *for* adjusted gross income (a business
loss). The same result can be achieved by simply treating the $100
net loss as a deduction *for* AGI.

- Capital gain net income is $3,400 ($2,600 long-term plus $800 short-
term) and is subject to tax as ordinary income.

---

6. The $3,700 qualifies for the *alternative tax* on
long-term capital gains (see chapter 16). However, for 1989 this alternative tax rate is the
same as the maximum ordinary tax rate, so no
benefit results. The long-term capital gain in
Examples 5, 6, and 7 also qualifies for the alternative tax, but there would be no benefit from
using this tax.

Results of the Gains and Losses on T's Tax Computation	
NLTCG	$ 2,600
STCG	800
Net ordinary loss on Assets A, B, and C and business casualty gain	(100)
Ordinary gain from sale of Asset D	200
Ordinary loss from sale of Asset E	(300)
AGI from other sources	125,000
AGI	$128,200

- None of the personal casualty losses would be deductible, since $1,200 does not exceed 10% of $128,200. □

EXAMPLE 6

Assume the same facts as in Example 4, except that T has a $700 nonrecaptured net § 1231 loss from 1988.

- The treatment of the casualty losses is the same as in Example 4.

- The 1989 net § 1231 gain of $1,100 is treated as ordinary income to the extent of the 1988 nonrecaptured § 1231 loss of $700. The remaining $400 net § 1231 gain is a long-term capital gain and is added to T's other long-term capital gains.

- T's net long-term capital gain is $3,000 ($3,000 plus $400 from § 1231 transactions less the long-term capital loss of $400). T's short-term capital gain is still $800 ($1,000 less $200). The result is capital gain net income of $3,800 and is subject to tax as ordinary income.

Results of the Gains and Losses on T's Tax Computation	
NLTCG	$ 3,000
STCG	800
Ordinary gain from recapture of § 1231 losses	700
Ordinary gain from sale of Asset D	200
Ordinary loss from sale of Asset E	(300)
AGI from other sources	125,000
AGI	$129,400

- None of the personal casualty losses would be deductible, since $1,200 does not exceed 10% of $129,400. □

EXAMPLE 7

Assume the same facts as in Example 4, except that in 1987 T had a net § 1231 loss of $2,700 and in 1988 a net § 1231 gain of $300.

- The treatment of the casualty losses is the same as in Example 4.

- The 1987 net § 1231 loss of $2,700 would have been carried over to 1988 and offset against the 1988 net § 1231 gain of $300. Thus, the $300 gain would have been ordinary income and $2,400 of nonrecaptured 1987 net § 1231 loss would carry over to 1989. The 1989 net § 1231 gain of $1,100 would be offset against this loss, resulting in $1,100 of ordinary income. The nonrecaptured net § 1231 loss of $1,300 ($2,400 − $1,100) would carry over to 1990.

- Capital gain net income is $3,400 ($2,600 net long-term capital gain plus $800 net short-term capital gain) and is subject to tax as ordinary income.

Results of the Gains and Losses on T's Tax Computation

NLTCG	$ 2,600
STCG	800
Ordinary gain from recapture of § 1231 losses	1,100
Ordinary gain from sale of Asset D	200
Ordinary loss from sale of Asset E	(300)
AGI from other sources	125,000
AGI	$129,400

- None of the personal casualty losses would be deductible, since $1,200 does not exceed 10% of $129,400. ☐

SECTION 1245 RECAPTURE

Section 1245 prevents taxpayers from receiving the dual benefits of depreciation deductions that offset ordinary income plus § 1231 long-term capital gain treatment on the disposition of the depreciated property. Section 1245 applies primarily to non-real estate property and requires that gain recognized be treated as ordinary income to the extent of depreciation taken on the property disposed of. Section 1245 does not apply if property is disposed of at a loss. Generally, the loss will be a § 1231 loss unless the disposition is a casualty.

EXAMPLE 8

T purchased a $100,000 business machine and deducted $70,000 depreciation before selling it for $80,000. If it were not for § 1245, the $50,000 § 1231 gain ($80,000 less $30,000 adjusted basis) would be treated as a long-term capital gain. Section 1245 prevents this potentially favorable result by recapturing as ordinary income (not as § 1231 gain) any gain to the extent of depreciation taken. In this example, the entire $50,000 gain would be ordinary income. □

Section 1245 provides, in general, that the portion of recognized gain from the sale or other disposition of § 1245 property that represents depreciation (including § 167 depreciation, § 168 cost recovery, § 179 immediate expensing, and the investment tax credit 50 percent basis reduction) is recaptured as ordinary income. The method of depreciation (e.g., accelerated or straight-line) does not matter. All depreciation taken is potentially subject to recapture. Thus, § 1245 recapture is often referred to as *full recapture*. Any remaining gain after subtracting the amount recaptured as ordinary income will usually be § 1231 gain. The remaining gain would be casualty gain if it were disposed of in a casualty event.

Although § 1245 applies primarily to non-real estate property, it does apply to certain real estate. Nonresidential real estate acquired after 1980 and before 1987 and for which accelerated depreciation (the statutory percentage method of the accelerated cost recovery system) is used is subject to the § 1245 recapture rules. Such property includes 15-year, 18-year, and 19-year nonresidential real estate.

The following examples illustrate the general application of § 1245.

EXAMPLE 9

On January 1, 1989, T sold for $13,000 a machine acquired several years ago for $12,000. He had taken $10,000 of depreciation on the machine.

- The recognized gain from the sale is $11,000. This is the amount realized of $13,000 less the adjusted basis of $2,000 ($12,000 cost less $10,000 depreciation taken).

- Depreciation taken is $10,000. Therefore, $10,000 of the $11,000 recognized gain is ordinary income, and the remaining $1,000 gain is § 1231 gain.

- The § 1231 gain is also equal to the excess of the sales price over the original cost of the property ($13,000 − $12,000 = $1,000 § 1231 gain). □

EXAMPLE 10

Assume the same facts as in the previous example, except the asset is sold for $9,000 instead of $13,000.

- The recognized gain from the sale is $7,000. This is the amount realized of $9,000 less the adjusted basis of $2,000.

- Depreciation taken is $10,000. Therefore, since the $10,000 depreciation taken exceeds the recognized gain of $7,000, the entire $7,000 recognized gain is ordinary income. □

EXAMPLE 11   Assume the same facts as in Example 9, except the asset is sold for $1,500 instead of $13,000.

- The recognized loss from the sale is $500. This is the amount realized of $1,500 less the adjusted basis of $2,000.

- Since there is a loss, there is no depreciation recapture. All of the loss is § 1231 loss. □

The application of § 1245 recapture rules does not mean the depreciation deductions are lost. It means only that to the extent of depreciation taken, the gain does not qualify for potential long-term capital gain treatment under § 1231.

If § 1245 property is disposed of in a transaction other than a sale, exchange, or involuntary conversion, the maximum amount recaptured is the excess of the property's fair market value over its adjusted basis. See the discussion under Considerations Common to Sections 1245 and 1250 later in the chapter.

Section 1245 Property

Generally, § 1245 property includes all depreciable personal property (e.g., machinery and equipment), including livestock. Buildings and their structural components generally are not § 1245 property. The following property is also subject to § 1245 treatment:

- Amortizable personal property such as patents, copyrights, and leaseholds of § 1245 property. Professional baseball and football player contracts are § 1245 property.

- Amortization of reforestation expenditures and expensing of costs to remove architectural and transportation barriers to the handicapped and elderly.

- Immediate expensing of costs of depreciable tangible personal property under § 179.

- Elevators and escalators acquired before January 1, 1987.

- Certain depreciable tangible real property (other than buildings and their structural components) employed as an integral part of certain activities such as manufacturing and production. For example, a natural gas storage tank where the gas is used in the manufacturing process is § 1245 property.

- Pollution control facilities, railroad grading and tunnel bores, on-the-job training, and child care facilities on which amortization is taken.

- Single-purpose agricultural and horticultural structures and petroleum storage facilities (e.g., a greenhouse or silo).

- As noted above, 15-year, 18-year, and 19-year nonresidential real estate for which accelerated cost recovery is used is subject to the § 1245 recapture rules, although it is technically not § 1245 property. Such property would have been placed in service after 1980 and before 1987.

EXAMPLE 12

T acquired nonresidential real property on January 1, 1986, for $100,000. She used the statutory percentage method to compute the ACRS depreciation. She sells the asset on January 15, 1989, for $120,000. The amount and nature of T's gain are computed as follows:

Amount realized		$120,000
Adjusted basis		
Cost	$100,000	
Less cost recovery: 1986	(8,800)	
1987	(8,400)	
1988	(7,600)	
1989	(288)	
January 15, 1989, adjusted basis		(74,912)
Gain realized and recognized		$ 45,088

The gain of $45,088 is treated as ordinary income to the extent of *all* depreciation taken because the property is 19-year nonresidential real estate for which accelerated depreciation was used. Thus, T reports ordinary income of $25,088 ($8,800 + $8,400 + $7,600 + $288) and § 1231 gain of $20,000 ($45,088 − $25,088). □

Observations on Section 1245

- In most instances, the total depreciation taken will exceed the recognized gain. Therefore, the disposition of § 1245 property usually results in ordinary income rather than § 1231 gain. Thus, generally, no § 1231 gain will occur unless the § 1245 property is disposed of for more than its original cost. Refer to Example 9.

- Recapture applies to the total amount of depreciation allowed or allowable regardless of the depreciation method used.

- Recapture applies regardless of the holding period of the property. Of course, the entire recognized gain would be ordinary income if the property were held for less than the long-term holding period, because § 1231 would not apply.

- Section 1245 does not apply to losses, which receive § 1231 treatment.

- As discussed later in the chapter, gains from the disposition of § 1245 assets may also be treated as passive gains.

SECTION 1250 RECAPTURE

Section 1250 was enacted in 1964 for depreciable real property and has been revised many times. The provision prevents taxpayers from receiving the benefits of both *accelerated* depreciation (or cost recovery) deductions and subsequent long-term capital gain treatment upon the sale of real property. If straight-line depreciation is taken on the property, § 1250 does not apply. Nor does § 1250 apply if the real property is sold at a loss. The loss would generally be a § 1231 loss unless the property was disposed of by casualty.

Section 1250 as originally enacted required recapture of a percentage of the additional depreciation deducted by the taxpayer. *Additional depreciation* is the excess of accelerated depreciation actually deducted over depreciation that would have been deductible if the straight-line method had been used. Since only the additional depreciation is subject to recapture, § 1250 recapture is often referred to as *partial recapture.*

Post-1969 additional depreciation on nonresidential real property is subject to 100 percent recapture (see Example 13). Post-1969 additional depreciation on residential property may be subject to less than 100 percent recapture (see Example 14).

The following discussion describes the computational steps prescribed in § 1250 and reflected on Form 4797 (Gains and Losses from Sales or Exchanges of Assets Used in a Trade or Business and Involuntary Conversions).

If § 1250 property is disposed of in a transaction other than a sale, exchange, or involuntary conversion, the maximum amount recaptured is the excess of the property's fair market value over the adjusted basis. For example, if a corporation distributed property to its shareholders as a dividend, the property would be disposed of by the corporation at a gain if the fair market value is greater than the adjusted basis. The maximum amount of § 1250 recapture would be the amount of the gain.

Generally, *§ 1250 property* is depreciable real property (principally buildings and their structural components) that is not subject to § 1245.[7] Intangible real property, such as leaseholds of § 1250 property, is also included.

The recapture rules under § 1250 are substantially less punitive than the § 1245 recapture rules, since only the amount of additional depreciation is subject to recapture. Straight-line depreciation (except for property held one year or less) is not recaptured.

Computing Recapture on Nonresidential Real Property

For § 1250 property other than residential rental property, the potential recapture is equal to the amount of additional depreciation taken since December 31, 1969. This nonresidential real property includes buildings such as offices, warehouses, factories, and stores. (The rules for residential rental housing are discussed later in the chapter.) The lower of the potential § 1250 recapture amount or the gain is ordinary income. The following general rules apply:

- Post–1969 additional depreciation is depreciation taken in excess of straight-line after December 31, 1969.

- If the property is held for one year or less (usually not the case), all depreciation taken, even under the straight-line method, is additional depreciation.

7. As previously discussed, in one limited circumstance, § 1245 does apply to depreciable realty. If nonresidential realty is placed in service after 1980 and before 1987 and the statutory percent-age method of cost recovery is used, § 1245 recapture rules apply rather than § 1250 recapture rules.

- Special rules apply to dispositions of substantially improved § 1250 property. These rules are rather technical, and the reader should consult the examples in the Regulations for illustrations of their application.[8]

The following procedure is used to compute recapture on nonresidential real property under § 1250:

- Determine the gain from the sale or other disposition of the property.
- Determine post-1969 additional depreciation.
- The lower of the gain or the post-1969 additional depreciation is ordinary income.
- If any gain remains (total gain less recapture), it is § 1231 gain. However, it would be casualty gain if the disposition was by casualty or theft.

The following example shows the application of the § 1250 computational procedure.

EXAMPLE 13

On January 3, 1980, T, an individual, acquired a new building at a cost of $200,000 for use in his business. The building had an estimated useful life of 50 years and no estimated salvage value. Depreciation has been taken under the double-declining balance method through December 31, 1988. Pertinent information with respect to depreciation taken follows:

Year	Undepreciated Balance (Beginning of the Year)	Current Depreciation Provision	Straight-line Depreciation	Additional Depreciation
1980	$200,000	$ 8,000	$ 4,000	$ 4,000
1981	192,000	7,680	4,000	3,680
1982	184,320	7,373	4,000	3,373
1983	176,947	7,079	4,000	3,079
1984	169,868	6,795	4,000	2,795
1985	163,073	6,523	4,000	2,523
1986	156,550	6,262	4,000	2,262
1987	150,288	6,012	4,000	2,012
1988	144,276	5,771	4,000	1,771
Total 1980–1988		$61,495	$36,000	$25,495

On January 2, 1989, the building was sold for $180,000. Compute the amount of § 1250 ordinary income and § 1231 gain.

---

8.   § 1250(f) and Reg. § 1.1250–5.

- The recognized gain from the sale is $41,495. This is the difference between the $180,000 amount realized and the $138,505 adjusted basis ($200,000 cost less $61,495 depreciation taken).

- Post-1969 additional depreciation is $25,495.

- The amount of post-1969 ordinary income is $25,495. Since the post-1969 additional depreciation of $25,495 is less than the recognized gain of $41,495, the entire gain is not recaptured.

- The remaining $16,000 ($41,495 − $25,495) gain is § 1231 gain. □

Computing Recapture on Residential Rental Housing

Section 1250 recapture applies to the sale or other disposition of residential rental housing. Property qualifies as *residential rental housing* only if at least 80 percent of gross rental income is rental income from dwelling units.[9] The rules are the same as for other § 1250 property, except that only the post-1975 additional depreciation is recaptured in full. The post-1969 through 1975 recapture percentage is 100 percent less one percentage point for each full month the property is held over 100 months.[10] Therefore, the additional depreciation for periods after 1975 is initially applied against the recognized gain, and such amounts are recaptured in full as ordinary income. Any remaining recognized gain is then tested under the percentage rules applicable to the post-1969 through 1975 period. If any of the recognized gain is not absorbed by the recapture rules pertaining to the post-1969 period, the remaining gain is § 1231 gain.

EXAMPLE 14   Assume the same facts as in the previous example, except the building is residential rental housing.

- Post-1975 ordinary income is $25,495 (post-1975 additional depreciation of $25,495).

- Since the building was acquired in 1980, the post-1969 through 1975 recapture rules do not apply.[11]

- The remaining $16,000 ($41,495 − $25,495) gain is § 1231 gain. □

Under § 1250, when straight-line depreciation is used, there is no § 1250 recapture potential unless the property is disposed of in the first year of use. Before 1987, accelerated depreciation on real estate generally was available. For real property placed in service after 1986, however, only straight-line depreciation is allowed. Therefore, the § 1250 recapture rules will have no application to such property unless the property is disposed of in the first year of use.

---

9. § 167(j)(2)(B) and Reg. § 1.167(j)–3(b)(1)(i).

10. §§ 1250(a)(1) and (2) and Reg. § 1.1250–1(d)(1)(i)(c).

11. If the building had been acquired on January 3, 1975, and sold on January 2, 1989, it would have been held 168 months. The recapture percentage for the 1975 additional depreciation would be 32% [100% less (168% less 100%)].

EXAMPLE 15   T acquires a residential rental building on January 1, 1988, for $300,000. He receives an offer of $450,000 for the building in 1989 and sells it on December 23, 1989.

- T would take $20,909 [($300,000 × .03485) + ($300,000 × .03636 × 11.5/12) = $20,909] of total depreciation for 1988 and 1989, and the adjusted basis of the property would be $279,091 ($300,000 − $20,909).

- T's gain would be $170,909 ($450,000 − $279,091).

- All of the gain would be § 1231 gain. □

The § 1250 recapture rules apply to the following property for which accelerated depreciation was used:

- Residential real estate acquired before 1987.

- Nonresidential real estate acquired before 1981.

- Real property used predominantly outside the United States.

- Certain government-financed or low-income housing described in § 1250(a)(1)(B).

CONSIDERATIONS COMMON TO SECTIONS 1245 AND 1250

Exceptions

Recapture under §§ 1245 and 1250 does not apply to the following transactions.

Gifts.   The recapture potential does carry over to the donee.[12]

EXAMPLE 16   T gives his daughter, D, § 1245 property with an adjusted basis of $1,000. The amount of recapture potential is $700. D uses the property in her business and claims further depreciation of $100 before selling it for $1,900. D's recognized gain is $1,000 (amount realized of $1,900 less $900 adjusted basis), of which $800 is recaptured as ordinary income ($100 depreciation taken by D plus $700 recapture potential carried over from T). The remaining gain of $200 is § 1231 gain. Even if D used the property for personal purposes, the $700 recapture potential would still be carried over. □

Death.   Although not a very attractive tax planning approach, death eliminates all recapture potential.[13] In other words, any recapture potential does not carry over from a decedent to an estate or heir.

---

12. §§ 1245(b)(1) and 1250(d)(1) and Reg. §§ 1.1245–4(a)(1) and 1.1250–3(a)(1).

13. §§ 1245(b)(2) and 1250(d)(2).

EXAMPLE 17
Assume the same facts as in Example 16, except T's daughter receives the property as a result of T's death. The $700 recapture potential from T is extinguished. D would have a basis for the property equal to the property's fair market value (assume $1,800) at T's death. D would have a $200 gain when the property is sold, because the selling price ($1,900) exceeds the property's adjusted basis ($1,800 original basis to D less $100 depreciation) by $200. Because of § 1245, $100 would be ordinary income. The remaining gain of $100 would be § 1231 gain. □

Charitable Transfers. The recapture potential reduces the amount of the charitable contribution deduction under § 170.[14]

EXAMPLE 18
T donates to his church § 1245 property with a fair market value of $10,000 and an adjusted basis of $7,000. Assume that the amount of recapture potential is $2,000 (the amount of recapture that would occur if the property were sold). T's charitable contribution deduction (subject to the limitations discussed in chapter 11) is $8,000 ($10,000 fair market value less $2,000 recapture potential). □

Certain Tax-free Transactions. These are transactions in which the transferor's adjusted basis of property carries over to the transferee.[15] The recapture potential also carries over to the transferee.[16] Included in this category are transfers of property pursuant to (1) tax-free incorporations under § 351, (2) certain liquidations of subsidiary companies under § 332, (3) tax-free contributions to a partnership under § 721, and (4) tax-free reorganizations. Gain may be recognized in these transactions if boot is received. If gain is recognized, it is treated as ordinary income to the extent of the recapture potential or recognized gain, whichever is lower.[17]

Like-kind Exchanges (§ 1031) and Involuntary Conversions (§ 1033). Gain may be recognized to the extent of boot received under § 1031. Gain also may be recognized to the extent the proceeds from an involuntary conversion are not reinvested in similar property under § 1033. Such recognized gain is subject to recapture as ordinary income under §§ 1245 and 1250. The remaining recapture potential, if any, carries over to the property received in the exchange.

EXAMPLE 19
T exchanges § 1245 property with an adjusted basis of $300 for § 1245 property with a fair market value of $6,000. The exchange qualifies as a like-kind exchange under § 1031. T also gives $5,000 cash (boot). T's realized gain is $700 [amount realized of $6,000 less $5,300 (adjusted basis of property plus boot given)]. Assuming the recapture potential is $4,500,

14. § 170(e)(1)(A) and Reg. § 1.170A–4(b)(1). In certain circumstances, § 1231 gain also reduces the amount of the charitable contribution. See § 170(e)(1)(B).

15. §§ 1245(b)(3) and 1250(d)(3) and Reg. §§ 1.1245–4(c) and 1.1250–3(c).

16. Reg. §§ 1.1245–2(a)(4) and –2(c)(2) and 1.1250–2(d)(1) and (3) and –3(c)(3).

17. §§ 1245(b)(3) and 1250(d)(3) and Reg. §§ 1.1245–4(c) and 1.1250–3(c). Some of these special corporate problems are discussed in chapter 20.

gain is not recognized because no boot is received. The entire recapture potential of $4,500 carries over to the like-kind property received. □

Other Applications

Sections 1245 and 1250 apply notwithstanding any other provisions in the Code.[18] That is, the recapture rules under these Sections *override* all other Sections. Special applications include the following:

Installment Sales.   Recapture gain is recognized in the year of the sale.[19] All gain is ordinary income until the recapture potential is fully absorbed. Nonrecapture gain is recognized under the installment method as cash is received.

EXAMPLE 20   T sells § 1245 property for $20,000, to be paid in 10 annual installments of $2,000 each plus interest at 10%. T realizes a $6,000 gain from the sale, of which $4,000 is attributable to depreciation taken. If T uses the installment method, the entire $4,000 of recapture gain is recognized in the year of the sale. The $2,000 of nonrecapture (§ 1231) gain will be recognized at the rate of $200 per year for 10 years. □

Gain is also recognized on installment sales in the year of sale in an amount equal to the § 179 (immediate expensing) deductions taken with respect to the property sold.

Property Dividends.   A corporation generally recognizes gain if it distributes appreciated property as a dividend. Recapture under §§ 1245 and 1250 applies to the extent of the lower of the recapture potential or the excess of the property's fair market value over the adjusted basis.[20]

EXAMPLE 21   X Corporation distributes § 1245 property as a dividend to its shareholders. The amount of recapture potential is $300, and the excess of the property's fair market value over the adjusted basis is $800. X Corporation recognizes $300 of recapture income and $500 of § 1231 gain. □

Concept Summary 17–2 integrates the depreciation recapture rules with the § 1231 netting process. It is an expanded version of Concept Summary 17–1.

SPECIAL RECAPTURE PROVISIONS

Special Recapture for Corporations

Corporations (other than S corporations) selling depreciable real estate may have ordinary income in addition to that required by § 1250. The *ordinary gain adjustment* is 20 percent of the excess of the § 1245 potential recapture

---

18. §§ 1245(d) and 1250(i).

19. § 453(i). The installment method of reporting gains on the sale of property is discussed in chapter 18.

20. § 311(b) and Reg. §§ 1.1245–1(c) and –6(b) and 1.1250–1(a)(4), –1(b)(4), and –1(c)(2).

CONCEPT SUMMARY 17–2

Depreciation Recapture and Section 1231 Netting Procedure

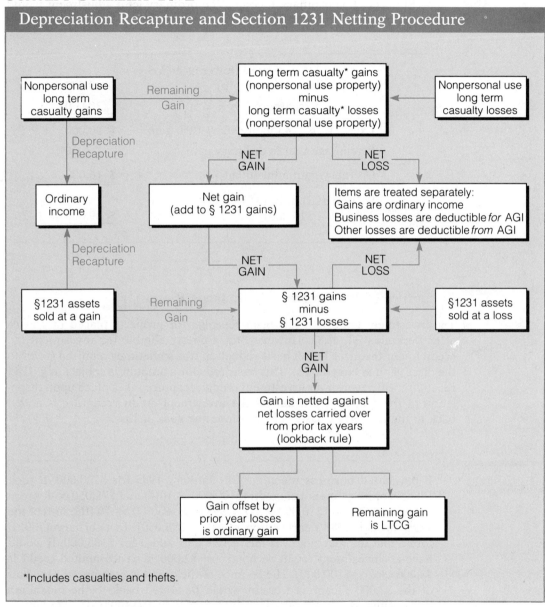

*Includes casualties and thefts.

over the § 1250 recapture.[21] The result is that the § 1231 gain is correspondingly decreased by this increase in ordinary income.

EXAMPLE 22

A corporation purchased a building in 1982 for $200,000. Accelerated depreciation of $110,000 was taken before the building was sold on January 1, 1989. The straight-line depreciation that could have been taken was $80,000. The selling price was $225,000. Section 1250 would recapture

21. § 291(a)(1).

$30,000 ($110,000 − $80,000) of the $135,000 gain [$225,000 − ($200,000 − $110,000)] as ordinary income. The ordinary gain adjustment would be computed as follows:

Section 1245 recapture (lower of depreciation taken or total gain)	$110,000
Less: Gain recaptured by § 1250	(30,000)
Excess of § 1245 gain over § 1250 gain	$ 80,000
Percentage that is ordinary gain	20%
Ordinary gain adjustment	$ 16,000
Section 1231 gain ($135,000 − $30,000 − $16,000)	$ 89,000

□

Recapture of Investment Credit Basis Reduction

The investment tax credit has been repealed for property placed in service after December 31, 1985. However, on property eligible for investment tax credit under the prior law, a basis reduction was sometimes required (refer to the discussion in chapter 13). This basis reduction amount is subject to § 1245 recapture. However, if an investment credit recapture takes place upon disposition of the property, one-half of the investment credit recapture is added back to the property's basis before computing gain or loss.

EXAMPLE 23   B purchased business machinery in January 1985 for $100,000. B took $10,000 of investment tax credit ($100,000 × 10%) and $75,050 of depreciation [$100,000 − ($10,000 × .5) = $95,000; $95,000 × .79 (the sum of the 1985 through 1988 depreciation rates) = $75,050]. In February 1989, B found that the machine was ineffective and sold it for $105,000. B would have an investment credit recapture of $2,000. B's recomputed credit is $8,000 (8% × $100,000). The balance of the credit is recaptured. One-half of the $2,000 recaptured credit would be added back to the machine's basis. Thus, the basis at sale would be $20,950 ($100,000 − $5,000 − $75,050 + $1,000). B's gain would be $84,050 ($105,000 − $20,950). Gain recaptured by § 1245 would be $79,050 (the $75,050 of depreciation plus the $4,000 of investment credit basis reduction that was not added back to basis). The remaining $5,000 gain would be § 1231 gain. □

Gain from Sale of Depreciable Property between Certain Related Parties

When the sale or exchange of property, which in the hands of the *transferee* is depreciable property (principally machinery, equipment, and buildings, but not land), is between certain related parties, any gain recognized is ordinary income.[22] This provision is applicable to both direct and indirect sales or exchanges. A *related party* is defined as an individual and his or her controlled corporation or partnership or a taxpayer and any trust in which the taxpayer (or the taxpayer's spouse) is a beneficiary.

EXAMPLE 24

T sells a personal automobile (therefore nondepreciable) to her controlled corporation. The automobile originally cost $5,000 and is sold for $7,000. The automobile is to be used in the corporation's business. If the related-party provision did not exist, T would realize a long-term capital gain (assuming the asset was held for the required long-term holding period) of $2,000. The income tax consequences would be favorable because T's controlled corporation is entitled to depreciate the automobile (assuming business use) based upon the purchase price of $7,000. Under the related-party provision, T's $2,000 gain is ordinary income. ☐

The related-party provision was enacted to prevent certain related parties from enjoying the dual benefits of long-term capital gain treatment (transferor) and a step-up in basis for depreciation (transferee). Recapture under §§ 1245 and 1250 applies first before recapture under the related-party provision.

Control means ownership of more than 50 percent in value of the corporation's outstanding stock or more than 50 percent of the capital interest or profits interest of a partnership. In determining the percentage of stock owned or partnership interest owned, the taxpayer must include that stock or partnership interest owned by related taxpayers as determined under the constructive ownership rules of § 267(c).

Section 267(a)(1) disallows a loss on the sale of property between certain related taxpayers. Therefore, a sale of property between certain related parties may result in ordinary income (if the property is depreciable in the hands of the transferee) or a nondeductible loss.

The related-party provision applies regardless of whether the transfer is from a shareholder or partner to the entity or from the entity to a shareholder or partner. Ordinary income treatment also applies to transfers between two corporations controlled by the same shareholder.

EXAMPLE 25

T, the sole shareholder of X Corporation, sells a building (adjusted basis of $40,000) to the corporation for $100,000. Since the building was depreciated by T using the straight-line method, none of the depreciation will be recaptured under § 1250. Nevertheless, the related-party provision applies to convert T's § 1231 gain of $60,000 to ordinary income. The basis of the building to X Corporation is $100,000 (the building's cost). ☐

Rehabilitation Expenditures for Low-Income Rental Housing

Section 1250 recapture applies to the sale or other disposition of federally assisted housing projects and low-income housing with respect to which rapid amortization of rehabilitation expenditures under § 167(k) has been taken.

---

22. § 1239.

The rules are generally the same as for residential rental housing except that post-1975 excess depreciation is not recaptured in full [the post-1969 percentage rules continue to apply (the recapture percentage is 100 percent less one percentage point for each full month the property is held over 100 months)].[23]

This preferential treatment afforded low-income rental housing is the result of Congressional desire to stimulate the construction and reconstruction of such residential rental property. The special rules for depreciating these properties are discussed in chapter 9.

Intangible Drilling Costs and Depletion

Taxpayers may elect to either *expense or capitalize* intangible drilling and development costs for oil, gas, or geothermal properties.[24] *Intangible drilling and development costs* (IDC) include operator (one who holds a working or operating interest in any tract or parcel of land) expenditures for wages, fuel, repairs, hauling, and supplies. These expenditures must be incident to and necessary for the drilling of wells and preparation of wells for production. In most instances, taxpayers elect to expense IDC to maximize tax deductions during drilling.

Intangible drilling costs are subject to § 1254 recapture when the property is disposed of. The gain on the disposition of the property is subject to recapture as ordinary income as follows:

- For properties acquired before 1987, the IDC expensed after 1975 in excess of what cost depletion would have been had the IDC been capitalized.

- For properties acquired after 1986, the IDC expensed.

For properties acquired after 1986, depletion on oil, gas, geothermal, and other mineral properties is subject to recapture to the extent the depletion reduced the basis of the property. The combined IDC and depletion recapture may not exceed the recognized gain from disposition of the property. If the property is disposed of at a loss, no recapture occurs.

EXAMPLE 26   X acquired a working interest in certain oil and gas properties for $50,000 during 1988. He incurred $10,000 of intangible development and drilling costs. X elected to expense these costs in 1988. In January 1989, the properties were sold for $60,000. Disregard any depreciation on tangible depreciable properties and assume that cost depletion would have amounted to $2,000 had the IDC been capitalized. The gain realized and recognized is $10,000 ($60,000 − $50,000). The gain is recaptured as ordinary income to the extent of the expensed IDC ($10,000), which is equal to the recognized gain ($10,000). Therefore, $10,000 is recaptured. □

---

23. § 1250(a)(1)(B)(iii). The Tax Reform Act of 1986 repealed the rapid amortization provision under § 167(k) effective for property acquired on or after January 1, 1987. See the Glossary of

Tax Terms in Appendix C for a discussion of rehabilitation expenditures.

24. § 263(c).

Special rules are provided for determining recapture upon the sale or other disposition of a portion or an undivided interest in oil, gas, geothermal, and other mineral properties.

PASSIVE LOSS ACTIVITIES

Passive loss activities may result in current losses that are not deductible against nonpassive activity income.[25] If there is insufficient current passive income to absorb the passive losses, the losses are *suspended* until such time as sufficient passive income is available to absorb them. (Passive loss activities are discussed in chapter 7.) When a passive loss activity is disposed of, the suspended and current year losses of that activity are fully deductible. However, they also reduce the recognized gain, if any, from disposition of the activity. Any remaining gain is then available to allow other passive activity current and suspended losses to be currently deductible. The recognized gain still receives treatment under the normal property disposition rules discussed in chapter 16 and in this chapter. If a passive activity is disposed of at a recognized loss, the loss is treated under the normal property disposition provisions. Thus, recognized *gains* from passive activity dispositions have a dual purpose: to allow deductibility of passive losses to the extent of the gain and to be treated under the normal property disposition rules. Recognized *losses* from passive activity dispositions do not have a dual purpose.

EXAMPLE 27

S disposes of a passive activity during 1989 at a $36,000 gain. The passive activity asset was a § 1231 asset, and the gain is a § 1231 gain. However, S has a current passive loss of $6,000 from this activity, no suspended losses from the activity, and $21,000 of current losses from another passive activity. The $36,000 gain allows the $6,000 and $21,000 passive losses to be fully deductible in 1989 as *for* AGI deductions. For purposes of computing S's net § 1231 gain, the full $36,000 of § 1231 gain is used. □

EXAMPLE 28

Assume the same facts as in the previous example, except that S has a $36,000 § 1231 loss rather than a gain. The § 1231 loss would be included in S's net § 1231 computation. The $6,000 current loss from the passive activity disposed of would be deductible in full as a deduction *for* AGI. The $21,000 loss from the other passive activity would not be deductible unless the phase-in of nondeductibility rules apply to it. □

REPORTING PROCEDURES

Noncapital gains and losses are reported on Form 4797, Gains and Losses from Sales or Exchanges of Assets Used in a Trade or Business and Involuntary Conversions. Before filling out Form 4797, however, Form 4684, Casualties and Thefts, must be completed to determine whether or not such transactions

---

25. § 469.

will enter into the § 1231 computation procedure. Recall that this will occur only if a net gain results from casualties and thefts of nonpersonal use property held for the long-term holding period.

The 1989 tax forms include a passive loss form (8582) for reporting the gains and losses from disposition of passive loss activities. Because the 1989 tax forms were unavailable at this writing, 1988 tax forms are used in the remainder of the discussion.

Form 4797 is divided into five parts, summarized as follows:

Part	Function
I	To report regular § 1231 gains and losses [including recognized gains and losses from certain involuntary conversions (condemnations)].
II	To report ordinary gains and losses.
III	To determine which portion of the gain is subject to recapture (e.g., §§ 1245 and 1250 gain).
IV	To elect out of the installment method when reporting a note or other installment obligation at less than full face value.
V	Computation of recapture amounts under §§ 179 and 280F when business use of depreciable property drops to 50% or less.

Generally, the best approach to completing Form 4797 is to start with Part III. Once the recapture amount has been determined, it is transferred to Part II. The balance of any gain remaining after the recapture has been accounted for is transferred from Part III to Part I. Also transferred to Part I is any net gain from certain casualties and thefts as reported on Form 4684 (refer to above and chapter 15). If the netting process in Part I results in a gain, such gain is reduced by the nonrecaptured net § 1231 losses from prior years (line 8 of Part I). Any remaining gain is shifted to Schedule D, Capital Gains and Losses, of Form 1040. If a loss results, it goes to Part II to be treated as an ordinary loss.

EXAMPLE 29

For 1988, Troy Williams (Social Security number 467–85–3036) had the following recognized gains and losses (a 1988 example has been used, since 1989 forms were unavailable):

Sale of Depreciable Business Assets Held Long-Term	
Asset A (Note 1)	$15,500
Asset B (Note 2)	20,276
Asset C (Note 3)	(1,600)

Sale of Depreciable Business Assets Held Short-Term	
Asset D (Note 4)	$ (600)

Capital Assets

Long-term gain (Note 5)	$ 3,000
Short-term loss (Note 6)	(200)

Note 1. Asset A was acquired on June 23, 1986, for $50,000. It was five-year ACRS property, and two years' cost recovery allowances totaled $18,500. The property was sold for $47,000 on August 31, 1988.

Note 2. Asset B was purchased on March 10, 1984, for $37,000. It was 15-year ACRS property. Using the statutory percentage method, cost recovery totaled $14,276. The property was sold for $43,000 on January 10, 1988. The building was residential rental property, and straight-line cost recovery for the period of ownership would have totaled $9,456.

Note 3. Asset C was purchased on December 9, 1986, for $16,000. It was five-year ACRS property, and two years' cost recovery totaled $5,920. The property was sold for $8,480 on December 30, 1988.

Note 4. Asset D was purchased for $7,000 on July 27, 1988. It was five-year ACRS property but proved unsuitable to Troy's business. Troy sold it for $6,400 on November 3, 1988.

Note 5. The LTCG resulted from the sale of 100 shares of X Corporation stock purchased for $10,000 on April 5, 1976. The shares were sold on October 21, 1988, for $13,223. Expenses of sale were $223.

Note 6. The STCL resulted from the sale of 50 shares of Y Corporation stock purchased for $350 on March 14, 1988. The shares were sold for $170 on August 20, 1988. Expenses of sale were $20.

The sale of assets A and B at a gain results in the recapture of cost recovery deductions. That recapture is shown in Part III of Form 4797. Some of the gain from the sale of asset B exceeds the recapture amount and is carried from line 32 to Part I, line 5, of Form 4797. On line 2, the loss from asset C appears. Part I is where the § 1231 netting process takes place. The net gain on line 7 or 9 is transferred to Schedule D, line 14. In Part II of Form 4797, the ordinary gains are accumulated. On line 13, the recapture from line 31 (Part III) is shown. On line 10, the loss from asset D is shown. The net gain on line 18 is ordinary income and is transferred to Form 1040, line 15.

Schedule D, Part I, line 2a, reports the short-term capital loss from the Y Corporation stock. Part II of Schedule D has the net § 1231 gain transferred from the Form 4797 on line 14 and the X Corporation gain on line 9a. The net capital gain is determined on line 18, Part III. The capital gain is then carried to line 13 of Form 1040.

The $13,393 total receipts ($13,223 + $170) from the sale of Corporations X and Y stock would be reported to Williams by his broker on a Form 1099–B. The $13,393 is entered on line 1 of Schedule D.

Form 4797 and Schedule D (Parts I–III) for Troy Williams are reproduced on the following pages. □

Form **4797**	**Sales of Business Property**	OMB No. 1545-0184
Department of the Treasury Internal Revenue Service	**(Also, Involuntary Conversions and Recapture Amounts Under Sections 179 and 280F)** ▶ Attach to your tax return. See separate Instructions.	**1988** Attachment Sequence No. **27**

Name(s) as shown on return TROY WILLIAMS	Identifying number 467-85-3036

Part I — **Sales or Exchanges of Property Used in a Trade or Business and Involuntary Conversions From Other Than Casualty and Theft—Property Held More Than 1 Year (More Than 6 Months If Acquired Before 1/1/88)**

1 Enter here the gross proceeds from the sale or exchange of real estate reported to you for 1988 on Form(s) 1099-S (or an equivalent statement) that you will be including on lines 2 or 10 (column d), or on line 20. (Form 1099-S is a Statement for Recipients of Proceeds From Real Estate Transactions.) . . . . | **1** | |

(a) Description of property	(b) Date acquired (mo., day, yr.)	(c) Date sold (mo., day, yr.)	(d) Gross sales price	(e) Depreciation allowed (or allowable) since acquisition	(f) Cost or other basis, plus improvements and expense of sale	(g) LOSS ((f) minus the sum of (d) and (e))	(h) GAIN ((d) plus (e) minus (f))
2							
Asset C	12/9/86	12/30/88	8,480	5,920	16,000	(1,600)	

		(g)	(h)
3 Gain, if any, from Form 4684, Section B, line 21		▨	
4 Section 1231 gain from installment sales from Form 6252, line 22 or 30		▨	
5 Gain, if any, from Part III, line 32, from other than casualty and theft.			15,456
6 Add lines 2 through 5 in columns (g) and (h).		(1,600)	15,456
7 Combine columns (g) and (h) of line 6. Enter gain or (loss) here, and on the appropriate line as follows (partnerships see the Instructions for line references):			13,856

If line 7 is zero or a loss, enter the amount on line 11 below and skip lines 8 and 9. (S corporations enter the loss on Schedule K (Form 1120S), line 5.) If line 7 is a gain and you did not have any prior year section 1231 losses, or they were recaptured in an earlier year, enter the gain as a long-term capital gain on Schedule D and skip lines 8, 9, and 12 below.

8 Nonrecaptured net section 1231 losses from prior years (see Instructions)		
9 Subtract line 8 from line 7. If zero or less, enter zero		

If line 9 is zero, enter the amount from line 7 on line 12 below. If line 9 is more than zero, enter the amount from line 8 on line 12 below, and enter the amount from line 9 as a long-term capital gain on Schedule D. See Specific Instructions for line 9.

Part II — **Ordinary Gains and Losses**

(a) Description of property	(b) Date acquired (mo., day, yr.)	(c) Date sold (mo., day, yr.)	(d) Gross sales price	(e) Depreciation allowed (or allowable) since acquisition	(f) Cost or other basis, plus improvements and expense of sale	(g) LOSS ((f) minus the sum of (d) and (e))	(h) GAIN ((d) plus (e) minus (f))
10 Ordinary gains and losses not included on lines 11 through 16 (include property held 1 year or less) (6 months or less if acquired before 1/1/88):							
Asset D	7/27/88	11/3/88	6,400		7,000	(600)	

		(g)	(h)
11 Loss, if any, from line 7			▨
12 Gain, if any, from line 7, or amount from line 8 if applicable		▨	
13 Gain, if any, from line 31, Part III		▨	20,320
14 Net gain or (loss) from Form 4684, Section B, lines 13 and 20a			
15 Ordinary gain from installment sales from Form 6252, line(s) 21 and/or 29		▨	
16 Recapture of section 179 deduction for partners and S corporation shareholders from property dispositions by partnerships and S corporations (see Instructions)		▨	
17 Add lines 10 through 16 in columns (g) and (h)		(600)	20,320
18 Combine columns (g) and (h) of line 17. Enter gain or (loss) here, and on the appropriate line as follows:			19,720

   a For all except individual returns: Enter the gain or (loss) from line 18, on the return being filed.
   b For individual returns:
      (1) If the loss on line 11 includes a loss from Form 4684, Section B, Part II, column (b)(ii), enter that part of the loss here and on line 21 of Schedule A (Form 1040). Identify as from "Form 4797, line 18b(1)" . . . . | ▨ |
      (2) Redetermine the gain or (loss) on line 18, excluding the loss (if any) on line 18b(1). Enter here and on Form 1040, line 15 | 19,720 |

For Paperwork Reduction Act Notice, see page 1 of separate Instructions.   Form **4797** (1988)

Form 4797 (1988) Page **2**

Part III Gain From Disposition of Property Under Sections 1245, 1250, 1252, 1254, and 1255
Skip section 1252 on line 27 and in the Instructions if you did not dispose of farmland or if you are a partnership.

19	Description of sections 1245, 1250, 1252, 1254, and 1255 property:	Date acquired (mo., day, yr.)	Date sold (mo., day, yr.)
A	Asset A	6/23/86	8/31/88
B	Asset B	3/10/84	1/10/88
C			
D			

	Relate lines 19A through 19D to these columns ▶	Property A	Property B	Property C	Property D
20	Gross sales price	47,000	43,000		
21	Cost or other basis plus expense of sale	50,000	37,000		
22	Depreciation (or depletion) allowed (or allowable)	18,500	14,276		
23	Adjusted basis, subtract line 22 from line 21	31,500	22,724		
24	Total gain, subtract line 23 from line 20	15,500	20,276		
25	**If section 1245 property:**				
	a Depreciation allowed (or allowable) (see Instructions)	18,500			
	b Enter the **smaller** of line 24 or 25a	15,500			
26	**If section 1250 property:** If straight line depreciation was used, enter zero on line 26g unless you are a corporation subject to section 291.				
	a Additional depreciation after 12/31/75		4,820		
	b Applicable percentage times the **smaller** of line 24 or line 26a (see Instructions).		4,820		
	c Subtract line 26a from line 24. If line 24 is not more than line 26a, skip lines 26d and 26e.		15,456		
	d Additional depreciation after 12/31/69 and before 1/1/76		0		
	e Applicable percentage times the **smaller** of line 26c or 26d (see Instructions).				
	f Section 291 amount (for corporations only)				
	g Add lines 26b, 26e, and 26f		4,820		
27	**If section 1252 property:**				
	a Soil, water, and land clearing expenses				
	b Line 27a times applicable percentage (see Instructions)				
	c Enter the **smaller** of line 24 or 27b				
28	**If section 1254 property:**				
	a Intangible drilling and development costs, expenditures for development of mines and other natural deposits, and mining exploration costs (see Instructions)				
	b Enter the **smaller** of line 24 or 28a				
29	**If section 1255 property:**				
	a Applicable percentage of payments excluded from income under section 126 (see Instructions).				
	b Enter the **smaller** of line 24 or 29a				

Summary of Part III Gains (Complete property columns A through D through line 29b before going to line 30.)

30	Total gains for all properties (add columns A through D, line 24)	35,776
31	Add columns A through D, lines 25b, 26g, 27c, 28b, and 29b. Enter here and in Part II, line 13. (see the Instructions for Part IV if this is an installment sale)	20,320
32	Subtract line 31 from line 30. Enter the portion from casualty and theft on Form 4684, Section B, line 15. Enter the portion from other than casualty and theft on Form 4797, Part I, line 5	15,456

Part IV Complete This Part Only If You Elect Out of the Installment Method and Report a Note or Other Obligation at Less Than Full Face Value

33	Check here if you elect out of the installment method	▶ ☐
34	Enter the face amount of the note or other obligation	▶
35	Enter the percentage of valuation of the note or other obligation	▶

Part V Computation of Recapture Amounts Under Sections 179 and 280F When Business Use Drops to 50% or Less (See Instructions for Part V.)

		(a) Section 179	(b) Section 280F
1	Section 179 expense deduction or section 280F recovery deductions		
2	Depreciation or recovery deductions (see Instructions)		
3	Recapture amount (subtract line 2 from line 1) (see Instructions for where to report)		

SCHEDULE D
(Form 1040)

Department of the Treasury
Internal Revenue Service

Capital Gains and Losses
(And Reconciliation of Forms 1099-B)

▶ Attach to Form 1040.   ▶ See Instructions for Schedule D (Form 1040).
For Paperwork Reduction Act Notice, see Form 1040 Instructions.

OMB No. 1545-0074

1988

Attachment
Sequence No. **12**

Name(s) as shown on Form 1040

TROY WILLIAMS

Your social security number

467 : 85 : 3036

1	Report here the total sales of stocks, bonds, etc., reported for 1988 to you on Form(s) 1099-B or on equivalent substitute statement(s). If this amount differs from the total of lines 2b and 9b, column (d), attach a statement explaining the difference. See the Instructions for line 1 for examples	1	13,393

Part I   Short-Term Capital Gains and Losses—Assets Held One Year or Less (6 months or less if acquired before 1/1/88)

(a) Description of property (Example, 100 shares 7% preferred of "Z" Co.)	(b) Date acquired (Mo., day, yr.)	(c) Date sold (Mo., day, yr.)	(d) Sales price (see Instructions)	(e) Cost or other basis (see Instructions)	(f) LOSS If (e) is more than (d), subtract (d) from (e)	(g) GAIN If (d) is more than (e), subtract (e) from (d)
2a Stocks, Bonds, and Other Securities (Include all Form 1099-B transactions. See Instructions.)						
Y Corp.						
50 shares	3/14/88	8/20/88	170	370	(200)	
2b Total (add column (d)) . . . . **2b▶**			170			

2c Other Transactions (Include Real Estate Transactions From Forms 1099-S)						

3	Short-term gain from sale or exchange of your home from Form 2119, line 8a or 14 .	3		
4	Short-term gain from installment sales from Form 6252, line 22 or 30	4		
5	Net short-term gain or (loss) from partnerships, S corporations, and fiduciaries . .	5		
6	Short-term capital loss carryover	6		
7	Add all of the transactions on lines 2a and 2c and lines 3 through 6 in columns (f) and (g) .	7	(200)	
8	Net short-term gain or (loss), combine columns (f) and (g) of line 7	8		(200)

Part II   Long-Term Capital Gains and Losses—Assets Held More Than One Year (more than 6 months if acquired before 1/1/88)

9a Stocks, Bonds, and Other Securities (Include all Form 1099-B transactions. See Instructions.)						
X Corp.						
100 shares	4/5/76	10/21/88	13,223	10,223		3,000
9b Total (add column (d)) . . . . **9b▶**			13,223			

9c Other Transactions (Include Real Estate Transactions From Forms 1099-S)						

10	Long-term gain from sale or exchange of your home from Form 2119, line 8a, 10, or 14 .	10		
11	Long-term gain from installment sales from Form 6252, line 22 or 30	11		
12	Net long-term gain or (loss) from partnerships, S corporations, and fiduciaries . .	12		
13	Capital gain distributions.	13		
14	Enter gain from Form 4797, line 7 or 9	14		13,856
15	Long-term capital loss carryover	15		
16	Add all of the transactions on lines 9a and 9c and lines 10 through 15 in columns (f) and (g) .	16	( )	16,856
17	Net long-term gain or (loss), combine columns (f) and (g) of line 16	17		16,856

Schedule D (Form 1040) 1988

Schedule D (Form 1040) 1988   Attachment Sequence No. **12**   Page **2**

Name(s) as shown on Form 1040. (Do not enter name and social security number if shown on other side.)

Your social security number
: :

Part III   Summary of Parts I and II

18	Combine lines 8 and 17, and enter the net gain or (loss) here. If result is a gain, also enter the gain on Form 1040, line 13	18	16,656
19	If line 18 is a (loss), enter here and as a (loss) on Form 1040, line 13, the **smaller** of:		
a	The (loss) on line 18; **or**		
b	($3,000) or, if married filing a separate return, ($1,500)	19	( )
	Note: When figuring which amount is **smaller**, treat them as if they were positive numbers.		

TAX PLANNING CONSIDERATIONS

Timing of Section 1231 Gain

Although §§ 1245 and 1250 recapture much of the gain from the disposition of business property, sometimes § 1231 gain is still substantial. For instance, land held as a business asset will generate either § 1231 gain or § 1231 loss. If the taxpayer already has a capital loss for the year, the sale of land at a gain should be postponed so that the net § 1231 gain is not netted against the capital loss. The capital loss deduction will therefore be maximized for the current tax year, and the capital loss carryforward (if any) may be offset against the gain when the land is sold. If the taxpayer already has a § 1231 loss, § 1231 gains might be postponed to maximize the ordinary loss deduction this year. However, the carryforward of nonrecaptured § 1231 losses will make the § 1231 gain next year an ordinary gain.

EXAMPLE 30

T has a $2,000 net STCL for 1989. He could sell business land for a $3,000 § 1231 gain. He will have no other capital gains and losses or § 1231 gains and losses in 1989 or 1990. He has no nonrecaptured § 1231 losses from prior years. T is in the 28% tax bracket in 1989 and 1990. If he sells the land in 1989, he will have a $1,000 net LTCG ($3,000 § 1231 gain − $2,000 STCL) and will pay a tax of $280 ($1,000 × 28%). If T sells the land in 1990, he will have a 1989 tax savings of $560 ($2,000 capital loss deduction × 28% tax rate on ordinary income). In 1990, he will pay tax of $840 ($3,000 gain × 28%). By postponing the sale for a year, T will have the use of $840 ($560 + $280). □

EXAMPLE 31

S has a $15,000 § 1231 loss in 1989. He could sell business equipment for a $20,000 § 1231 gain and a $12,000 § 1245 gain. S is in the 28% tax bracket in 1989 and 1990. He has no nonrecaptured § 1231 losses from prior years. If he sells the equipment in 1989, he will have a $5,000 net § 1231 gain and $12,000 of ordinary gain. His tax would be $4,760 [($5,000 § 1231 gain × 28%) + ($12,000 ordinary gain × 28%)].

   If S postpones the equipment sale until 1990, he would have a 1989 ordinary loss of $15,000 and tax savings of $4,200 ($15,000 × 28%). In 1990, he would have $5,000 of § 1231 gain (the 1989 § 1231 loss carries over and recaptures $15,000 of the 1990 § 1231 gain as ordinary income) and $27,000 of ordinary gain. His tax would be $8,960 [($5,000 § 1231 gain × 28%) + ($27,000 ordinary gain × 28%)]. By postponing the equipment sale, S has the use of $8,960 ($4,200 + $4,760). □

Timing of Recapture

Since recapture is usually not triggered until the property is sold or disposed of, it may be possible to plan for recapture in low bracket or in loss years. If a taxpayer has net operating loss carryovers that are about to expire, the recognition of ordinary income from recapture may be advisable to absorb the loss carryovers.

EXAMPLE 32   T has a $15,000 net operating loss carryover that will expire this year. He owns a machine that he plans to sell in the early part of next year. The expected gain of $17,000 from the sale of the machine will be recaptured as ordinary income under § 1245. T sells the machine before the end of this year and offsets $15,000 of the ordinary income against the net operating loss carryover. ☐

Postponing and Shifting Recapture

It is also possible to postpone recapture or to shift the burden of recapture to others. For example, recapture is avoided upon the disposition of a § 1231 asset if the taxpayer replaces the property by entering into a like-kind exchange. In this instance, recapture potential is merely carried over to the newly acquired property (refer to Example 19).

Recapture can be shifted to others through the gratuitous transfer of § 1245 or § 1250 property to family members. A subsequent sale of such property by the donee will trigger recapture to the donee rather than the donor (refer to Example 16). Such procedure would be advisable only if the donee is in a lower income tax bracket than the donor.

Avoiding Recapture

The immediate expensing election (§ 179) is subject to § 1245 recapture. If the election is not made, the § 1245 recapture potential will accumulate more slowly (refer to chapter 9). Since using the immediate expense deduction complicates depreciation and book accounting for the affected asset, not taking the deduction may make sense even though the time value of money might indicate it should be taken.

Disposing of Passive Activities

Taxpayers with suspended or current passive losses may wish to dispose of passive activities. The current and suspended losses of the activity disposed of will be fully deductible. If there is a recognized loss on the disposition, the loss will not be subject to the passive activity loss limitations. Rather, it will be classified and treated as a normal property disposition loss (refer to Example 28). If there is a recognized gain on the disposition, the gain will first absorb the current and suspended losses of the activity disposed of and any remaining gain will absorb losses from other passive activities. The gain will also be treated under the normal property disposition rules (refer to Example 27).

PROBLEM MATERIALS

Discussion Questions

1. What type of transactions involving capital assets are included under § 1231? Why wouldn't they qualify for long-term capital gain treatment without § 1231?

2. Does § 1231 treatment apply to all business property?

3. Is livestock held for breeding eligible for § 1231 treatment?

4. What property is excluded from § 1231?

5. Is it possible to recognize both a gain and a loss on the sale of timber in one taxable year? How?

6. What circumstances must be met for an unharvested crop to receive preferential treatment under § 1231?

7. Do casualty gains from disposition of personal use assets receive § 1231 treatment?

8. Under what circumstances is a nonpersonal use casualty gain treated as ordinary income? Why?

9. Describe the treatment that results if a taxpayer has net § 1231 losses.

10. Fully depreciated business equipment purchased for $75,000 was stolen from V. It was not recovered, and the insurance reimbursement was $10,000. Is this $10,000 gain subject to depreciation recapture? Why?

11. What is recapture potential under § 1245? What factors limit it?

12. If a farmer buys a pig and uses ACRS, are the cost recovery deductions subject to § 1245 recapture if the pig is sold at a gain?

13. Differentiate between the types of property covered by §§ 1245 and 1250.

14. How does depreciation recapture under § 1245 differ from depreciation recapture under § 1250?

15. What is additional depreciation?

16. Why does § 1250 generally not apply to real estate acquired after 1986?

17. What is the definition of residential rental housing?

18. S bought a building in 1984 for $100,000 and insisted on using accelerated depreciation because she did not intend to sell it for 30 years. In 1989, she sold the building for $200,000 and moved to a different state. Assume the depreciation taken was $37,000 and straight-line depreciation for the same time period would have been $26,000. What would be the amount of depreciation recapture if the building were a retail store? An apartment building?

19. Was it ever beneficial to use the ACRS statutory percentage method on commercial real estate placed in service before 1987?

20. What happens to recapture potential when a gift is made? What effect does the donee's use have on the recapture potential?

21. What happens to depreciation recapture potential under either § 1245 or § 1250 when a taxpayer dies?

22. List the tax-free transactions that do not cause recapture to be recognized immediately but require it to be carried over to the transferee.

23. What provisions do the recapture rules override?

24. What special recapture provision applies only to regular corporations?

25. If the basis of ACRS property was reduced by one-half of the investment tax credit in the year the property was acquired, what impact does such a reduction have when the property is later sold?

26. S bought an apartment building in 1985 for $100,000 and sold it in 1989 for $200,000 to her husband, who is going to use the building as a retail store (after suitable remodeling). S's adjusted basis was $63,000 after taking $37,000 of accelerated depreciation on the building. Straight-line depreciation for the same time period would be $26,000. What is the nature of the gain that S must recognize?

27. In general, how does the related-party ordinary income provision differ from §§ 1245 and 1250?

28. X acquired a working interest in certain oil and gas properties for $100,000 in 1988. He incurred and paid $25,000 of intangible development and drilling costs that were expensed in 1988. In January 1989, he sold the properties for $110,000. Disregard any depreciation on tangible depreciable properties and assume that cost depletion would have amounted to $6,000. What is the nature and amount of the gain recognized?

29. If a taxpayer has expensed intangible drilling and development costs, what are the possible future ramifications?

30. If a taxpayer has a § 1231 gain from disposition of a passive loss activity, what may happen to the gain before it is treated under the normal § 1231 gain and loss netting process?

Problems

31. Ms. S purchased a contract to cut timber on a 100-acre tract of land in South Dakota in March 1987 for $20,000. On January 1, 1988, the timber had a fair market value of $50,000. Because of careless cutting in November 1988, when the fair market value was $55,000, the wood was sold on January 30, 1989, for $49,000.

    a. What gain (loss) was realized in 1987, 1988, and 1989? What gain (loss) was recognized in 1987, 1988, and 1989?

    b. What was the nature of the gains (losses) in (a)? What assumption must be made?

    c. Does the answer change if the timber was sold in December of 1988? Why?

    d. If on January 1, 1988, the timber was worth only $18,000, was cut in November when worth $21,000, and was sold in December for $19,000, how would the answers to (a) and (b) change?

32. T owns an airplane that she uses only for pleasure. T's insurance company did not cover $6,000 of damage to T's plane resulting from a tornado. T had paid $35,000 for the plane. T also had a $3,800 casualty

gain on a personal use piano as a result of the same tornado. T has $22,500 of wages, is single, and has no dependents. She has $4,000 of real estate taxes, $3,000 of qualified residence interest, and $2,000 of other personal interest for the year. Compute T's taxable income for 1989.

33. V has the following net § 1231 results for each of the years shown. What would be the nature of the net gains in 1988 and 1989?

Tax Year	Net § 1231 Loss	Net § 1231 Gain
1984	$ -0-	
1985	15,000	
1986	25,000	
1987		$10,000
1988		30,000
1989		15,000

34. T had the following transactions during 1989:

   • Damage from wreck of a sailboat held more than one year due to hurricane ($15,000 loss).

   • Sale of mechanical rake bought on April 1 and sold on September 1 ($600 gain). (Disregard recapture.)

   • Sale of farm land with unharvested crops, held four years ($12,000 gain).

   • Recovery on theft of family brooch owned for 10 years ($10,000 gain).

   • Fire in silo on December 6, purchased May 8 ($1,000 loss).

   • Sale of grist mill owned 11 years ($30 loss).

   • Sale of 15 shares of Q Corporation stock held three years ($1,800 gain).

   a. How is each transaction treated?

   b. What is T's 1989 AGI?

35. R owned a number of parking lots throughout the city. In 1989, R sold two parcels of unimproved real estate that he had used since 1978 in his parking lot business. The sale of parcel A resulted in a $6,000 recognized loss, and the sale of parcel B generated a $2,000 recognized gain. R also had a long-term capital gain of $7,000 from a sale of stock he had held for investment. R's adjusted gross income was $50,000 before taking the previous transactions into consideration. Compute R's 1989 adjusted gross income after including the described transactions.

36. S Corporation sold machines A and B during the current year. The machines had been purchased for $180,000 and $240,000, respectively. The machines were purchased eight years ago and were depreciated to zero. Machine A was sold for $40,000 and machine B for $260,000. What amount of gain is recognized by S, and what is the nature of the gain?

37. On March 1, 1986, N buys and places in service a new machine for $25,000. On April 1, 1989, N sells the machine for $5,000. Cost recovery deductions to date have been $14,500.

    a.   What is N's realized and recognized loss?

    b.   What is the nature of the loss?

38. R Manufacturing purchases a $3,000,000 propane storage tank and places it on a permanent framework outside R's plant. The propane is drawn from the tank through a hose and valve system into the burners underneath R's chemical vats. After $1,800,000 of depreciation has been taken on the tank, it is sold for $2,300,000. What is the nature and amount of R's gain or loss from the disposition of the tank?

39. On June 1, 1985, T acquired a retail store for $400,000. The store was 19-year real property, and the statutory percentage cost recovery method was used. The store was sold on June 21, 1989, for $130,000. Depreciation taken totaled $128,600. Straight-line depreciation for the same period would have been $85,800. What are the amount and nature of T's gain or loss from disposition of the store?

40. On January 1, 1979, T acquired a building used in his business for $600,000. Later depreciation expense was $150,000. On January 1, 1989, the building was sold for $800,000. At the time of the sale, additional depreciation taken amounted to $35,000.

    a.   What amount is § 1250 ordinary income?

    b.   How would the answer change if the sales price was $400,000?

41. D is the sole proprietor of a trampoline shop. During 1989, the following transactions occurred:

    • Unimproved land adjacent to the store was condemned by the city on February 1. The condemnation proceeds were $25,000. The land, acquired in 1982, had an allocable basis of $15,000. D has additional parking across the street and plans to use the condemnation proceeds to build his inventory.

    • A truck used to deliver trampolines was sold on January 2 for $3,500. The truck was purchased on January 2, 1985, for $6,000. On the date of sale, the adjusted basis was $2,667.

    • D sold an antique rowing machine at an auction. Net proceeds were $3,900. The rowing machine was purchased as used equipment 17 years ago for $5,200 and is fully depreciated.

    • D sold an apartment building for $200,000 on September 1. The rental property was purchased on September 1, three years ago, for $150,000 and was being depreciated over a 35-year life using the straight-line method. At the date of sale, the adjusted basis was $135,000. This is D's only passive loss activity, and D has no current or suspended losses from this activity.

    • D's personal yacht was stolen September 5. The yacht had been purchased in August at a cost of $25,000. The fair market value immediately preceding the theft was $20,000. D was insured for 50% of the original cost, and he received $12,500 on December 1.

- D sold a Buick on May 1 for $9,600. The vehicle had been used exclusively for personal purposes. It was purchased on September 1, 1985, for $10,800.

- An adding machine used by D's bookkeeper was sold on June 1. Net proceeds of the sale were $135. The machine was purchased on June 2, four years ago, for $350. It was being depreciated over a five-year life employing the straight-line method. The adjusted basis on the date of sale was $70.

- D's trampoline stretching machine (owned two years) was stolen on May 5, but the business's insurance company will not pay any of the machine's value, because D failed to pay the insurance premium. The machine had a fair market value of $8,000 and an adjusted basis of $6,000 at the time of theft.

- D had AGI of $4,000 from sources other than those described above.

  a. For each transaction, what is the amount and nature of recognized gain or loss?

  b. What is D's 1989 adjusted gross income?

42. R purchased a building in April 1988 for $200,000. He sold the building on December 23, 1989, for $235,000. What would be the nature and amount of R's gain assuming the following:

  a. The building is residential rental real estate, and total cost recovery of $12,121 was taken?

  b. The building is a retail store, and total cost recovery of $10,583 was taken?

43. On February 10, 1989, S sold land A ($55,000 cost; $50,000 sales price), land B ($35,000 cost; $75,000 sales price), and building B ($40,000 cost; $45,000 sales price). Land A was vacant land that S had purchased for investment in 1986. Land B had building B on it, and both assets had been purchased in January 1988. The building was used in S's business, and $1,375 of depreciation had been taken on it. S has no nonrecaptured § 1231 losses from prior years. What is the amount and nature of each gain or loss, and what is S's adjusted gross income for 1989?

44. Refer to the facts of Problem 43. Rework the problem assuming S was a corporation.

45. P owned a § 1245 asset with an adjusted basis of $10,000. The amount of depreciation deducted by P was $6,000 ($10,000 adjusted basis + $6,000 depreciation = $16,000 original cost). On May 1, 1987, P made a gift of the asset to his child, C, when the fair market value was $22,500. C used the asset for two years (deducting an additional $2,000 of depreciation) in her business. On November 7, 1989, C sold the asset for $19,200.

  a. What is C's basis for the asset on November 7, 1989?

  b. What is the amount and character of C's recognized gain?

  c. How would your answers in (a) and (b) differ if C had received the asset as a result of P's death?

46. E organizes a corporation of which she is the sole shareholder. She transfers to the corporation a business machine that cost $18,000 and has an adjusted basis of $5,000 and a fair market value of $15,500. Several years later, the corporation sells the machine for $12,000 after taking cost recovery deductions of $3,000 on it. What are the tax ramifications of this transfer?

47. T transferred forklifts used in his factory with recapture potential of $6,500 to a dealer in exchange for new forklifts worth $8,000 and $1,500 of marketable securities. The transaction qualified as a § 1031 like-kind exchange. T had an adjusted basis in the equipment of $6,000.

    a. What is T's realized and recognized gain or loss?

    b. What is the nature of the gain or loss?

    c. How would the answer to (a) or (b) change if no marketable securities were involved?

48. T sells a business machine with a $4,200 basis on the installment method in 1989. The sale price is $22,000, and T will receive $6,000 in 1989 and $4,000 in each of the following four years. The machine had cost $20,000 in 1985. The installment note bears interest at the applicable Federal rate. What is the nature and amount of the gain to be recognized in 1989–1993? (Ignore interest income implications.)

49. J sold an apartment building she had owned for three years for $35,000 in 1989. The building had an adjusted basis of $40,000 and was sold to J's brother at its FMV. The furniture in the building was sold to an unrelated party, and a $28,000 gain resulted. J sold the land to her brother for a gain of $20,000. J had other income of $78,000 and $75,000 of expenses deductible for AGI. What is J's 1989 AGI? Assume the real estate was not a passive loss activity and J had no nonrecaptured § 1231 losses.

50. T purchased business machinery on January 1, 1985, costing $80,000. A full 10% investment tax credit and a $5,000 immediate expense deduction were taken. T used the ACRS statutory percentage method. On January 2, 1989, T sold the machinery for $38,000.

    a. What are the amounts of investment tax credit, cost recovery, and end-of-year adjusted basis in the year the property is purchased?

    b. What are the amounts of investment tax credit recapture, § 1245 gain, and § 1231 gain in the year of sale?

51. In 1989, M disposes of passive loss activity A for a $15,000 § 1245 gain and a $30,000 § 1231 gain. M has no suspended losses from this activity but has a current operating loss of $3,000. M also has a current operating loss of $8,700 from passive loss activity B, but has no suspended losses from that activity. M has no other property transactions during 1989 and has no nonrecaptured § 1231 losses. What is the treatment of the gains from the disposition of activity A?

52. Refer to the facts of Problem 51. Assume that M has a $45,000 § 1231 loss rather than a gain from the disposition of the passive loss activity. What is the treatment of the loss from disposition of activity A?

Cumulative Problems

53. Glen and Diane Okumura are married, file a joint return, and live at 39 Kaloa Street, Honolulu, Hawaii 56790. Glen's Social Security number is 777–88–2000 and Diane's is 888–77–1000. The Okumuras have two dependent children, Amy (age 15) and John (age 9). Glen works for the Hawaii Public Works Department, and Diane owns a retail dress shop. The Okumuras had the following transactions during 1989:

    a. Glen earned $57,000 in wages and had Federal income tax withholding of $14,000.

    b. Diane had net income of $98,000 from the dress shop and made Federal income tax estimated payments of $24,000.

    c. The Okumuras sold a small apartment building for $265,000. The building was acquired in 1986 for $300,000, accelerated cost recovery of $74,400 was taken, and $46,800 of straight-line cost recovery would have been taken for the same time period. The apartment building was a passive activity, with a $2,000 1989 operating loss, and $4,500 of prior-year suspended passive losses.

    d. Diane sold a delivery truck used in her business. The truck cost $35,000, $21,700 of cost recovery had been taken, and it was sold for $18,000.

    e. The Okumuras received $13,000 in dividends on various domestic corporation stock that they own.

    f. The Okumuras sold stock for a $15,000 long-term capital gain and other stock at a $6,000 short-term capital loss.

    g. The Okumuras had the following itemized deductions: $1,000 unreimbursed medical expenses; $10,500 personal use property taxes; $7,000 qualified residence interest; $3,000 personal interest; $1,500 of Glen's unreimbursed employee business expenses; $535 of investment-related expenses; and $6,300 of state income taxes paid.

    Compute the Okumuras' 1989 net tax payable or refund due. (Ignore self-employment tax.)

54. Linda Franklin is an attorney. She is single and lives at 1619 Merry Lane, Cantone, TN 16703. Her Social Security number is 345–67–8900. Linda receives a salary of $45,000. During 1988, she had the following property transactions:

    a. Sales of stock held for investment

Stock	Selling Price	Basis	Date Sold	Date Acquired
Acme Corporation	$2,000	$ 1,400	6/30/1988	12/31/1987
Bareham Corporation	8,000	10,500	12/31/1988	7/15/1988
Cronin, Inc.	9,400	5,400	7/26/1988	5/2/1981
Davis Corporation	1,800	2,900	10/18/1988	10/17/1984

b.   Complete destruction of a personal use travel trailer in a wreck on August 1 (basis, $6,500; fair market value, $5,000; reimbursement for loss by insurance company, $3,000). Linda had bought the trailer on June 12, 1981.

c.   Sale of photocopying machine used in business for $2,800 on November 6. Linda had acquired the machine on April 29, 1985, for $4,000 and had taken $1,800 of depreciation on it.

d.   Sale of typewriter used in business on January 15 for $500. The typewriter was acquired on May 8, 1985, at a cost of $1,000; depreciation of $440 had been deducted.

Compute Linda Franklin's adjusted gross income from these transactions. If you use tax forms in your computations, you will need Forms 1040, 4684, and 4797 and Schedule D.

Research Problems

Research Problem 1   S owns a professional football franchise. He has received an offer of $80 million for the franchise, all the football equipment, the rights to concession receipts, the rights to a stadium lease, and the rights to all the player contracts owned by S. Most of the players have been with the team for quite a long time and have contracts that were signed several years ago. The contracts have been substantially depreciated. S is concerned about potential § 1245 recapture when the contracts are sold. He has heard about "previously unrecaptured depreciation with respect to initial contracts" and would like to know more about it. Find a definition for that phrase and write an explanation of it.

Partial list of research aids:

§ 1245(a)(4).

Research Problem 2   On May 10, 1984, D purchased a $160,000 building (but not the land) that was 60 feet wide, 80 feet deep, and two stories high. The front 60 feet of the 80-foot first-floor depth was rented as a retail store. The remaining 20 feet of the first floor and all of the second floor were rented for residential use. D used the ACRS statutory percentages and sold the building for $140,000 in 1989. D is unsure whether all the depreciation is subject to recapture by § 1245, some of it is subject to recapture by § 1250, or none of it is subject to recapture.

Does § 1245 or § 1250 recapture apply in this situation?

Research Problem 3   In 1989, S recognized an installment gain from a sale that occurred in 1986. The property sold in 1986 would have been passive activity property if it had been sold in 1989. Is the 1989 installment gain recognized as a passive activity gain?

Research Problem 4   During 1989, Honest John's Auto Sales, a dealer in new and used cars, sold some new cars, some used cars, some company cars (used in the business to run errands, etc.), and some demonstrators. Since Honest John's is a dealer, can any of these sales be considered as sales of § 1231 assets?

Partial list of research aids:

§ 1231(b).

Latimer-Looney Chevrolet, Inc., 19 T.C. 120 (1953), *acq.*

6

ACCOUNTING PERIODS, ACCOUNTING METHODS, AND DEFERRED COMPENSATION

Part 6 provides a more comprehensive examination of the accounting periods and accounting methods that were introduced in Part 2. A discussion of special accounting methods is also included. Part 6 concludes with an analysis of the tax consequences of deferred compensation transactions.

CHAPTER
18
Accounting Periods and Methods

CHAPTER
19
Deferred Compensation

18

ACCOUNTING PERIODS AND METHODS

OBJECTIVES
Review the requirements for adoption and change of the tax year.
Describe the rules of income and expense recognition for the cash and accrual methods of tax accounting.
Analyze the procedures for changing accounting methods.
Explain and illustrate the installment method of accounting.
Analyze the imputed interest rules applicable to installment sales.
Explain the alternative methods of accounting for long-term contracts.
Summarize inventory accounting requirements and explain LIFO procedures.

Earlier chapters discussed the types of income subject to tax (gross income and exclusions) and allowable deductions.[1] This chapter focuses on the related issue of determining the periods in which income and deductions are reported. Generally, a taxpayer's income and deductions must be assigned to particular 12–month periods—calendar years or fiscal years.

Income and deductions are placed within particular years through the use of tax accounting methods. The basic accounting methods are the cash method, accrual method, and the hybrid method. Other special purpose methods are available for specific circumstances or types of transactions such as the installment method and the methods used for long-term construction contracts.

An entire subchapter of the Code, Subchapter E, is devoted to accounting periods and accounting methods. Over the long run, the accounting period used by a taxpayer will not affect the aggregate amount of reported taxable income. However, taxable income for any particular year may vary significantly due to the use of a particular reporting period. Also, through the choice of accounting methods or periods, it is possible to postpone the recognition of taxable income and to enjoy the benefits from such deferral of the related tax. This chapter discusses the taxpayer's alternatives for accounting periods and accounting methods.

ACCOUNTING PERIODS

➢ In General

A taxpayer who keeps adequate books and records can elect to use a *fiscal year*, a 12–month period ending on the last day of a month other than December. Otherwise, a *calendar year* must be used.[2] Frequently, corporations can satisfy the recordkeeping requirements and elect to use a fiscal year.[3] Often the fiscal year conforms to a natural business year (e.g., a summer resort's fiscal year may end on September 30, after the close of the season). Individuals seldom use a fiscal year because they do not maintain the necessary books.

Generally, a taxable year may not exceed 12 calendar months. However, if certain requirements are met, a taxpayer may elect to use an annual period that varies from 52 to 53 weeks.[4] In such case, the year-end must be on the same day of the week (e.g., the Tuesday falling closest to October 31 or the last Tuesday in October). The day of the week selected for ending the year would depend upon business considerations. For example, a retail business that is not open on Sundays may end its tax year on a Sunday so that an inventory can be taken without interrupting business operations.

EXAMPLE 1   T is in the business of selling farm supplies. His natural business year terminates at the end of October with the completion of harvesting. At the end of the fiscal year it is necessary to take an inventory, and it is most easily accomplished on a Tuesday. Therefore, T could adopt a 52–53 week tax year ending on the Tuesday closest to October 31. If this method is

---

1. See chapters 4, 5, and 6.
2. § 441(c) and Reg. § 1.441–1(b)(1)(ii).
3. Reg. § 1.441–1(e)(2).
4. § 441(f).

selected, the year-end date may fall in the following month if that Tuesday is closer to October 31. The tax year ending in 1989 will contain 52 weeks beginning on Wednesday, November 2, 1988, and ending on Tuesday, October 31, 1989. The tax year ending in 1990 will have 52 weeks beginning on Wednesday, November 1, 1989, and ending on Tuesday, October 30, 1990. □

Partnerships and S Corporations. Partnerships are subject to additional restrictions to prevent partners from deferring partnership income by selecting a different year-end for the partnership (e.g., if the tax year for the partnership ended on January 31 and the partners used a calendar year, partnership profits for the first 11 months would not be reported by the partners until the following year).[5] In general, the partnership tax year must be the same as the tax year of the majority interest partners. The *majority interest partners* are the partners who own a greater than 50 percent interest in the partnership capital and profits. If the majority owners do not have the same tax year, the partnership must adopt the same tax year as its principal partners. A *principal partner* is a partner with a 5 percent or more interest in the partnership capital or profits.[6] If the principal partners do not have the same tax year and no majority of partners have the same tax year, the partnership must use a calendar year for tax reporting.

EXAMPLE 2

The XYZ Partnership is owned equally by X Corporation, Y Corporation, and individual Z. The partners have the following tax years.

	Partner's Tax Year Ending
X	June 30
Y	June 30
Z	December 31

The partnership's tax year must end on June 30. If Y as well as Z's year ended on December 31, the partnership would be required to adopt a calendar year. □

Similarly, S corporations must adopt a calendar year.[7] However, partnerships and S corporations may *elect* an otherwise *impermissible year* under any of the following conditions:

- A business purpose for the year can be demonstrated.[8]
- The partnership's or S corporation's year results in a deferral of not more than three months' income, and the entity agrees to make required tax payments.[9]

---

5. See chapter 4 for a discussion of when the partner reports his or her share of the partnership income.

6. §§ 706(b)(1)(B) and 706(b)(3).

7. §§ 1378(a) and (b).

8. §§ 706(b)(1)(C) and 1378(b)(2).

9. § 444.

- The entity retains the same year as was used for the fiscal year ending in 1987, provided the entity agrees to make required tax payments.

Business Purpose.   The only business purpose for a fiscal year that the IRS has acknowledged is the need to conform the tax year to the natural business year of a business.[10] Generally, only seasonal businesses have a natural business year. For example, the natural business year for a department store may end on January 31, after Christmas returns have been processed and clearance sales have been completed.

Required Tax Payments.   Under this system, the partnership or S corporation has required tax payments due by April 15 of each tax year.[11] The amount due is computed by applying the highest individual tax rate plus 1 percent to an estimate of the deferral period income. The deferral period runs from the close of the fiscal year to the end of the calendar year. Estimated income for this period is based on the average monthly earnings for the previous fiscal year. The amount due is reduced by the amount of required tax payments for the previous year.[12]

EXAMPLE 3   S Inc., an S corporation, elected a fiscal year ending September 30. R is the only shareholder. For the fiscal year ending September 30, 1991, S Inc., earned $100,000. The required payment for the previous year was $5,000. The corporation must pay $2,250 by April 15, 1992, calculated as follows:

$$(\$100,000 \times {}^{3}\!/_{12} \times 29\% \text{ *}) - \$5,000 = \$2,250$$

    *   Maximum § 1 rate of 28% + 1%.

□

Personal Service Corporations   A PSC is a corporation whose shareholder-employees provide personal services (e.g., medical, dental, legal, accounting, actuarial, consulting, or performing arts). Generally, a PSC must use a calendar year.[13] However, a fiscal year can be *elected* by a PSC under any of the following conditions:

- A business purpose for the year can be demonstrated.
- The PSC year results in a deferral of not more than three months' income, the corporation pays the shareholder-employee's salary during the portion of the calendar year after the close of the fiscal year, and the salary for that period is at least proportionate to the shareholder-employee's salary received for such fiscal year.[14]

---

10. Rev.Rul. 87–57, 1987–2 C.B. 117.
11. §§ 444(c) and 7519.
12. § 7519(b).

13. § 441(i).

14. §§ 444 and 280H.

- The PSC retains the same year as was used for the fiscal year ending in 1987, provided the latter two requirements contained in the preceding option are satisfied.

EXAMPLE 4

Y's corporation paid Y $120,000 of salary during its fiscal year ending September 30, 1989. The corporation cannot satisfy the business purpose test for a fiscal year. The corporation can continue to use its fiscal year without any negative tax effects, provided Y receives as salary during the period October 1 through December 31, 1989, at least $30,000 (3 months/ 12 months $\times$ $120,000). □

If the salary test is not satisfied, the PSC can retain the fiscal year, but the corporation's deduction for salary for the fiscal year is limited to the following:

$$A + A(F/N)$$

Where A = Amount paid after the close of the fiscal year

F = Number of months in fiscal year minus number of months from the end of the fiscal year to the end of the ongoing calendar year

N = Number of months from the end of the fiscal year to the end of the ongoing calendar year.

EXAMPLE 5

Assume the corporation in the previous example paid Y $10,000 of salary during the period October 1 through December 31, 1989. The deduction for Y's salary for the corporation's fiscal year ending September 30, 1990 is thus limited to $40,000 calculated as follows:

$$\$10,000 + \left[\$10,000 \left(\frac{12-3}{3}\right)\right] =$$
$$\$10,000 + \$30,000 = \$40,000$$

□

Making the Election

A taxpayer elects to use a calendar or fiscal year by the timely filing of his or her initial tax return. For all subsequent years, this same period must be used unless approval for change is obtained from the IRS.[15]

15. Reg. §§ 1.441–1(b)(3) and 1.441–1(b)(4).

Changes in the Accounting Period

A taxpayer must obtain consent from the IRS before changing the tax year.[16] This power to approve or not to approve a change is significant in that it permits the IRS to issue authoritative administrative guidelines that must be met by taxpayers who wish to change their accounting period. An application for permission to change tax years must be made on Form 1128, Application for Change in Accounting Period, and must be filed on or before the fifteenth day of the second calendar month following the close of the short period that results from the change in accounting period.[17]

EXAMPLE 6   Beginning in 1989, T Corporation, a calendar year taxpayer, would like to switch to a fiscal year ending March 31. The corporation must file Form 1128 by May 15, 1989. □

IRS Requirements.   The IRS will not grant permission for the change unless the taxpayer can establish a substantial business purpose for the change. One substantial business purpose is a request to change to a tax year that coincides with the *natural business year* (the completion of an annual business cycle). The IRS applies an objective gross receipts test to determine if the entity has a natural business year. Twenty-five percent of the entity's gross receipts for the 12-month period must be realized in the final two months of the 12-month period for three consecutive years.[18]

EXAMPLE 7   A Virginia Beach motel had gross receipts as follows:

	1987	1988	1989
July–August receipts	$ 300,000	$250,000	$ 325,000
September 1–August 31 receipts	1,000,000	900,000	1,250,000
Receipts for 2 months divided by receipts for 12 months	30.0%	27.8%	26.0%

Since the natural business year test is satisfied, the entity will be allowed to use a fiscal year ending August 31. □

---

16. § 442. Under certain conditions, corporations are allowed to change tax years without obtaining IRS approval. See Reg. § 1.442–1(c)(1).
17. Reg. § 1.442–1(b)(1). In Example 6, the first period after the change in accounting period (January 1, 1989, through March 31, 1989) is less than a 12-month period and is referred to as a short period.
18. Rev.Proc. 87–32, 1987–1 C.B. 131, and Rev.Rul. 87–57, 1987–2 C.B. 117.

The IRS usually will establish certain conditions that the taxpayer must accept if the approval for change is to be granted. In particular, if the taxpayer has a net operating loss for the short period, the IRS may require that the loss be carried forward and allocated equally over the six following years.[19] As you may recall (refer to chapter 8), net operating losses are ordinarily carried back for three years and forward for 15 years.

EXAMPLE 8

X Corporation changed from a calendar year to a fiscal year ending September 30. The short period return for the nine months ending September 30, 1989, reflected a $60,000 net operating loss. The corporation had taxable income for 1986, 1987, and 1988. As a condition for granting approval, the IRS will require X Corporation to allocate the $60,000 loss over the next six years. Thus, X Corporation will reduce its taxable income by $10,000 each year ending September 30, 1990, through September 30, 1995. □

Taxable Periods of Less Than One Year

A *short year* is a period of less than 12 calendar months. A taxpayer may have a short year for (1) the first tax reporting period, (2) the final income tax return, or (3) a change in the tax year. If the short period results from a change in the taxpayer's annual accounting period, the taxable income for such period must be annualized. Due to the progressive tax rate structure, taxpayers could reap benefits from a short-period return if some adjustments were not required. Thus, the taxpayer is required to do the following:

1. Annualize the short-period income.

$$\text{Annualized income} = \text{Short-period income} \times \frac{12}{\substack{\text{Number of months} \\ \text{in the short period}}}$$

2. Compute the tax on the annualized income.

3. Convert the tax on the annualized income to a short-period tax.

$$\text{Short-period tax} = \text{Tax on annualized income} \times \frac{\substack{\text{Number of months} \\ \text{in the short period}}}{12}$$

EXAMPLE 9

B Corporation obtained permission to change from a calendar year to a fiscal year ending September 30, beginning in 1989. For the short period January 1 through September 30, 1989, the corporation's taxable income was $48,000. The relevant tax rates and the resultant short-period tax are as follows:

---

19. Rev.Proc. 85–16, 1985–1 C.B. 517.

Amount of Taxable Income	Tax Calculation
$1–$50,000	15% of taxable income
$50,001–$75,000	$7,500 plus 25% of taxable income in excess of $50,000

Annualized income

   ($48,000 × 12/9) = <u>$64,000</u>

Tax on annualized income

   $7,500 + .25 ($64,000 − $50,000) =
   $7,500 + $3,500 = <u>$11,000</u>

Short-period tax = ($11,000 × 9/12) = <u>$8,250</u>

Annualizing the income increased the tax by
   $1,050:

Tax with annualizing	$8,250
Tax without annualizing (.15 × $48,000)	<u>7,200</u>
	<u>$1,050</u>

☐

Rather than annualize the short-period income, the taxpayer can elect to (1) calculate the tax for a 12-month period beginning on the first day of the short period and (2) convert the tax in (1) to a short-period tax as follows: [20]

$$\frac{\text{Taxable income for short period}}{\text{Taxable income for the 12-month period}} \times \begin{array}{c}\text{Tax on the 12 months of}\\ \text{income}\end{array}$$

EXAMPLE 10   Assume B Corporation's taxable income for the calendar year 1989 was $60,000. The tax on the full 12 months of income would have been $10,000 [$7,500 + .25 ($60,000 − $50,000)]. The short-period tax would be $8,000 ($48,000/$60,000 × $10,000). Thus, if the corporation utilized this option, the tax for the short period would be $8,000 (rather than $8,250, as calculated in Example 9). ☐

For individuals, annualizing requires some special adjustments: [21]

- Deductions must be itemized for the short period (the standard deduction is not allowed).

- Personal and dependency exemptions must be prorated.

Fortunately, individuals rarely change tax years.

---

20. § 443(b)(1).   21. § 443(b)(2) and Reg. § 1.443–1(a)(2).

Mitigation of the Annual Accounting Period Concept

Several provisions in the Code are designed to give the taxpayer relief from the seemingly harsh results that may be produced by the combined effects of an arbitrary accounting period and a progressive rate structure. For example, under the net operating loss carryback and carryover rules, a loss in one year can be carried back and offset against taxable income for the preceding three years. Unused net operating losses are then carried over for 15 years.[22] In addition, the Code provides special relief provisions for casualty losses pursuant to a disaster and for the reporting of insurance proceeds from destruction of crops.[23]

Restoration of Amounts Received under a Claim of Right. The court-made *claim of right doctrine* applies when the taxpayer has received as income property that he or she treats as his or her own but the taxpayer's rights to the income are disputed.[24] According to the doctrine, the taxpayer must include the amount as income in the year of receipt. The rationale for the doctrine is that the Federal government cannot await the resolution of all disputes before exacting a tax. As a corollary to the doctrine, if the taxpayer is later required to repay the funds, generally a deduction is allowed in the year of repayment.[25]

EXAMPLE 11

In 1989, T received a $5,000 bonus computed as a percentage of profits. In 1990, it was determined that the 1989 profits had been incorrectly computed, and T had to refund the $5,000 to his employer in 1990. T was required to include the $5,000 in his 1989 income, but he can claim a $5,000 deduction in 1990. □

In Example 11 the transactions were a wash; that is, the income and deduction were the same ($5,000). Suppose, however, T was in the 28 percent tax bracket in 1989 but in the 15 percent bracket in 1990. Without some relief provision, the mistake would be costly to T. T paid $1,400 tax in 1989 (.28 × $5,000), but the deduction reduced his tax liability in 1990 by only $750 (.15 × $5,000). The Code does provide the needed relief in such cases. Under § 1341, when income has been taxed under the claim of right doctrine but must later be repaid, in effect, the taxpayer gets the deduction in the year he or she can receive the greater tax benefit. Thus, in Example 11, the repayment in 1990 would reduce T's 1990 tax liability by the greater 1989 rate (.28) applied to the $5,000. However, relief is provided only for cases in which there is a significant difference in the tax: when the deduction for the amount previously included in income exceeds $3,000.

22. § 172. Refer to chapter 8.
23. §§ 165(i) and 451(d). Refer to chapter 8.
24. *North American Consolidated Oil Co. v. Burnet*, 49 USTC ¶943, 11 AFTR 16, 52 S.Ct. 613 (USSC, 1932). See the Glossary of Tax Terms in Appendix C for a discussion of the term "claim of right doctrine."
25. *U.S. v. Lewis*, 51–1 USTC ¶9211, 40 AFTR 258, 71 S.Ct. 522 (USSC, 1951).

ACCOUNTING METHODS

Permissible Methods

Section 446 requires that taxable income be computed under the method of accounting regularly employed by the taxpayer in keeping his or her books, provided the method clearly reflects income. The Code recognizes the following as generally permissible methods:

- The cash receipts and disbursements method.
- The accrual method.
- A hybrid method (a combination of cash and accrual).

The Regulations refer to these alternatives as *overall methods* and add that the term *method of accounting* includes not only the overall method of accounting of the taxpayer but also the accounting treatment of any item.[26]

Generally, any of the three methods of accounting may be used if the method is consistently employed and clearly reflects income. However, the taxpayer is required to use the accrual method for sales and costs of goods sold if inventories are an income-producing factor to the business.[27] Other situations in which the accrual method is required are discussed later. Special methods are also permitted for installment sales, for long-term construction contracts, and for farmers.

A taxpayer who has more than one trade or business may use a different method of accounting for each trade or business activity.[28] Furthermore, a different method of accounting may be used to determine income from a trade or business than is used to compute nonbusiness items of income and deductions.[29]

EXAMPLE 12   T operates a grocery store and owns stock and bonds. The income from the grocery store must be computed by the accrual basis because inventories are material. However, T can report his dividends and interest under the cash method. □

The Code grants the IRS broad powers to determine whether the taxpayer's accounting method *clearly reflects income*. Thus, if the method employed does not clearly reflect income, the IRS has the power to prescribe the method to be used by the taxpayer.[30]

Cash Receipts and Disbursements Method—Cash Basis

Most individuals and many businesses use the cash basis to report income and deductions. The popularity of this method can largely be attributed to its simplicity and flexibility.

---

26. Reg. § 1.446–1(a)(1).
27. Reg. § 1.446–1(a)(4)(i).
28. § 446(d).

29. Reg. § 1.446–1(c)(1)(iv)(b).

30. § 446(b).

Under the cash method, income is not recognized until the taxpayer actually receives, or constructively receives, cash or its equivalent. Cash is constructively received if it is available to the taxpayer.[31] Deductions are generally permitted in the year of payment. Thus, year-end accounts receivable, accounts payable, and accrued income and deductions are not included in the determination of taxable income.

The cash method permits a taxpayer in many cases to choose the year in which he or she claims the deduction by simply postponing or accelerating the payment of expenses. However, for fixed assets, the cash basis taxpayer claims deductions through depreciation or amortization, the same as an accrual basis taxpayer does. In addition, prepaid expenses must be capitalized and amortized if the life of the asset extends substantially beyond the end of the tax year.[32] Most courts have applied the one-year rule to determine whether capitalization and amortization are required. According to this rule, capitalization is required only if the asset has a life that extends beyond the tax year following the year of payment.[33]

Restrictions on Use of the Cash Method. The use of the cash method to measure income from a merchandising or manufacturing operation would often yield a distorted picture of the results of operations. Income for the period would largely be a function of when payments were made for goods or materials. Thus, the Regulations prohibit the use of the cash method (and require the accrual method) to measure sales and cost of goods sold if inventories are material to the business.[34]

The prohibition on the use of the cash method if inventories are material and the rules regarding prepaid expenses (discussed above) are intended to assure that annual income is clearly reflected. However, certain taxpayers may not use the cash method of accounting for Federal income tax purposes regardless of whether inventories are material. The accrual basis must be used to report the income earned by (1) a corporation (other than an S corporation), (2) a partnership with a corporate partner, and (3) a tax shelter.[35] This accrual basis requirement has three exceptions:

- A farming business.
- A qualified personal service corporation (e.g., a corporation performing services in health, law, engineering, architecture, accounting, actuarial science, performing arts, or consulting).
- An entity that is not a tax shelter whose average annual gross receipts for the most recent three-year period are $5,000,000 or less.[36]

Farming. Although inventories are material to farming operations, the IRS long ago created an exception to the general rule and has allowed farmers to use the cash method of accounting.[37] The purpose of the exception is to relieve the small farmer from the bookkeeping burden of accrual accounting.

31. Reg. § 1.451–1(a). Refer to chapter 4 for a discussion of constructive receipt.
32. Reg. § 1.461–1(a)(1).
33. *Martin J. Zaninovich v. Comm.*, 80–1 USTC ¶9342, 45 AFTR2d 80–1442, 616 F.2d 429 (CA–9 1980), *rev'g* 69 T.C. 605 (1978). Refer to chapter 6 for further discussion of the one-year rule.
34. Reg. § 1.446–1(a)(4)(i).
35. § 448(a). For this purpose, the hybrid method of accounting is considered the same as the use of the cash method.
36. Refer to Limitations on Who Can Use the Cash Method in chapter 6.
37. Reg. § 1.471–6(a).

However, tax shelter promoters recognized, for example, that by deducting the costs of a crop in one tax year and harvesting the crop in a later year, income could be deferred from tax. Thus, §§ 447 and 464 were enacted to prevent the use of the cash method by certain farming corporations and limited partnerships (farming syndicates).[38]

Farmers who are allowed to use the cash method of accounting must nevertheless capitalize their costs of raising trees when the preproduction period is greater than two years.[39] Thus, a cash basis apple farmer must capitalize the cost of raising trees until the trees produce in merchantable quantities. Cash basis farmers can elect not to capitalize these costs, but if the election is made, the alternative depreciation system (refer to chapter 9) must be used for all farming property.

Generally, the cost of purchasing an animal must be capitalized. However, the cash basis farmer's cost of raising the animal can be expensed.[40]

Accrual Method

All Events Test.   The Regulations provide that "under the accrual method of accounting, income is includible in gross income when (1) all the events have occurred that fix the right to receive such income and (2) the amount thereof can be determined with reasonable accuracy."[41]

EXAMPLE 13   A, a calendar year taxpayer who uses the accrual basis of accounting, was to receive a bonus equal to 6% of B Corporation's net income for its fiscal year ending each June 30. For the fiscal year ending June 30, 1989, B Corporation had net income of $240,000, and for the six months ending December 31, 1989, the corporation's net income was $150,000. A will report $14,400 (.06 × $240,000) for 1989, because her rights to the amount became fixed when B Corporation's year closed. However, A would not accrue income based on the corporation's profits for the last six months of 1989, since her right to the income does not accrue until the close of the corporation's tax year. □

In a situation where the accrual basis taxpayer's right to income is being contested and the income has not yet been collected, generally no income is recognized until the dispute has been settled.[42] Before the settlement, "all of the events have not occurred that fix the right to receive the income."

Deductions.   An all events test also applies to deductions. According to the all events test, a deduction cannot be claimed until "all the events have occurred which determine the fact of liability and the amount of such liability can be determined with reasonable accuracy."[43] In addition, the all events test will not be deemed satisfied until economic performance has occurred.[44]

---

38. Section 447(c) contains counter-exceptions that allow certain closely held corporations to use the cash method. See also § 464(c).

39. § 263A(d).

40. Reg. § 1.162–12(a).

41. Reg. § 1.451–1(a). Refer to chapter 4 for fur-

ther discussion of the accrual basis.

42. *Burnet v. Sanford & Brooks Co.*, 2 USTC ¶636, 9 AFTR 603, 51 S.Ct. 150 (USSC, 1931).

43. § 461(h)(4).

44. § 461(h).

The economic performance test addresses situations in which the taxpayer's obligation is either of the following:

1. To pay for services or property to be provided in the future.
2. To provide services or property (other than money) in the future.

Regarding services or property to be provided to the taxpayer in the future (situation 1), economic performance occurs when the property or services are actually provided by the other party.

EXAMPLE 14   An accrual basis calendar year taxpayer, PS, Inc., promoted a boxing match held in the company's arena on December 31, 1989. AM, Inc., had contracted to clean the arena for $5,000, but the work was not actually performed until January 1, 1990. PS, Inc., did not pay the $5,000 until 1991. Although financial accounting would require PS, Inc., to accrue the $5,000 cleaning expense to match the revenues from the fight in 1989, the economic performance test has not been satisfied until 1990, when AM, Inc., performed the service. Thus, the expense must be deducted by PS, Inc., in 1990. □

If the taxpayer is obligated to provide property or services, economic performance occurs (and thus the deduction is allowed) in the year the taxpayer provides the property or services.

EXAMPLE 15   T Corporation, an accrual basis taxpayer, is in the strip mining business. According to the contract with the landowner, the company must reclaim the land. The estimated cost of reclaiming land mined in 1989 was $500,000, but the land was not actually reclaimed until 1991. The all events test was satisfied in 1989. The obligation existed, and the amount of the liability could be determined with reasonable accuracy. However, the economic performance test was not satisfied until 1991. Therefore, the deduction is not allowed until 1991. □

The economic performance test is waived, and thus year-end accruals can be deducted, if all the following conditions are met:

- The obligation exists and the amount of the liability can be reasonably estimated.
- Economic performance occurs within a reasonable period (but not later than 8½ months after the close of the taxable year).
- The item is recurring in nature.
- Either the accrued item is not material, or accruing it results in a better matching of revenues and expenses.

EXAMPLE 16   M Corporation often sells goods that are on hand but cannot be shipped for another week. Thus, the sales account usually includes revenues for some items that have not been shipped at year-end. M Corporation is obligated to pay shipping costs. Although the company's obligation for shipping costs can be determined with reasonable accuracy, economic performance will not be satisfied until M Corporation (or its agent) actually delivers the goods. However, accruing shipping costs on sold items will better match expenses with revenues for the period. Therefore, the company should be allowed to accrue the shipping costs on items sold but not shipped at year-end. □

It should be noted that the economic performance test does not address all possible accrued expenses. For example, an accrual for state income taxes or payroll taxes is not a liability for property or services received. In such cases, the taxpayer must apply the all events test without considering economic performance.

Reserves.   Generally, the all events and economic performance tests will prevent the use of reserves (e.g., for product warranty expense) frequently used in financial accounting to match expenses with revenues. However, small banks are allowed to use a bad debt reserve.[45] Furthermore, an accrual basis taxpayer in a service business is permitted to not accrue revenue that appears uncollectible based on experience. In effect, this is an indirect approach to allowing a reserve.[46]

Hybrid Method

A *hybrid method* of accounting involves the use of more than one method. For example, a taxpayer who uses the accrual basis to report sales and cost of goods sold but uses the cash basis to report other items of income and expense is employing a hybrid method. The Code permits the use of a hybrid method provided the taxpayer's income is clearly reflected.[47] A taxpayer who uses the accrual method for business expenses must also use the accrual method for business income (a cash method for income items may not be used if the taxpayer's expenses are accounted for under the accrual basis.)

It may be preferable for a business that is required to report sales and cost of sales on the accrual method to report other items of income and expense under the cash method. The cash method permits greater flexibility in the timing of income and expense recognition.

Change of Method

The taxpayer, in effect, makes an election to use a particular accounting method when an initial tax return is filed using a particular method. If a subsequent change in method is desired, the taxpayer must obtain the permission of the IRS. The request for change is made on Form 3115, Application for Change in Accounting Method. Generally, the form must be filed within the first 180 days of the taxable year of the desired change.[48]

---

45. § 585.
46. § 448(d)(5).
47. § 446(c).
48. Reg. § 1.446–1(e)(3). The deadline may be ex-

tended to within the first nine months of the year of the change if the taxpayer can show good cause for the delay in filing the request.

As previously mentioned, the term *accounting method* encompasses not only the overall accounting method used by the taxpayer (the cash or accrual method) but also the treatment of any material item of income or deduction.[49] Thus, a change in the method of deducting property taxes from a cash basis to an accrual basis that results in a deduction for taxes in a different year would constitute a change in an accounting method. Another example of accounting method change is a change involving the method or basis used in the valuation of inventories. However, a change in treatment resulting from a change in underlying facts does not constitute a change in the taxpayer's method of accounting.[50] For example, a change in employment contracts so that an employee accrues one day of vacation pay for each month of service rather than 12 days of vacation pay for a full year of service is a change in the underlying facts and is not, therefore, an accounting method change.

Correction of an Error.   A change in accounting method should be distinguished from the *correction of an error.* An error can be corrected (by filing amended returns) by the taxpayer without special permission, and the IRS can simply adjust the taxpayer's liability if an error is discovered on audit of the return. Some examples of errors are incorrect postings, errors in the calculation of tax liability or tax credits, deductions of business expense items that are actually personal, and omissions of income and deductions.[51] Unless the taxpayer or the IRS corrects the error within the statute of limitations, the taxpayer's total lifetime taxable income will be overstated or understated by the amount of the error.

Change from an Incorrect Method.   An *incorrect accounting method* is the consistent (year-after-year) use of an incorrect rule to report an item of income or expense. The incorrect accounting method generally will not affect the taxpayer's total lifetime income (unlike the error). That is, an incorrect method has a self-balancing mechanism. For example, deducting freight on inventory in the year the goods are purchased, rather than when the inventory is sold, is an incorrect accounting method. The total cost of goods sold over the life of the business is not affected, but the year-to-year income is incorrect.[52]

If a taxpayer is employing an erroneous method of accounting, permission must be obtained from the IRS to change to a correct method. An erroneous method is not treated as a mechanical error that can be corrected by merely filing an amended tax return.

It should be noted that the tax return preparer as well as the taxpayer will be subject to penalties if the tax return is prepared using an incorrect method of accounting and permission for a change to a correct method has not been requested.[53]

Net Adjustments Due to Change in Accounting Method.   In the year of change in accounting method, certain adjustments may be required to items of income and expense to prevent a distortion of taxable income resulting from the change.

49. Reg. § 1.446–1(a)(1). See the Glossary of Tax Terms in Appendix C for a discussion of the term "accounting method."

50. Reg. § 1.446–1(e)(2)(ii)(b).

51. Reg. § 1.446–1(e)(2)(ii)(b).

52. But see *Korn Industries v. U.S.,* 76–1 USTC ¶9354, 37 AFTR2d 76–1228, 532 F.2d 1352 (Ct. Cls., 1976).

53. § 446(f). See *West's Federal Taxation: Corporations, Partnerships, Estates, and Trusts,* chapter 13.

EXAMPLE 17

In 1989, Z Corporation, with consent from the IRS, switched from the cash to the accrual basis for reporting sales and cost of goods sold. The corporation's accrual basis gross profit for the year was computed as follows:

Sales		$100,000
Beginning inventory	$15,000	
Purchases	60,000	
Less: Ending inventory	(10,000)	
Cost of goods sold		(65,000)
Gross profit		$ 35,000

At the end of the previous year, Z Corporation had accounts receivable of $25,000 and accounts payable for merchandise of $34,000. The accounts receivable from the previous year in the amount of $25,000 were never included in gross income, since the taxpayer was on the cash basis and did not recognize the uncollected receivables. In the current year, the $25,000 was not included in the accrual basis sales, since the sales were made in a prior year. Therefore, a $25,000 adjustment to income would be required to prevent the omission of the receivables from income.

The corollary of failure to recognize a prior year's receivables is the failure to recognize a prior year's accounts payable. The beginning of the year's accounts payable were not included in the current or prior year's purchases. Thus, a deduction for the $34,000 was not taken in either year and is therefore included as an adjustment to income for the period of change.

An adjustment is also required to reflect the $15,000 beginning inventory that was deducted (due to the use of a cash method of accounting) by the taxpayer in the previous year. In this instance, the cost of goods sold during the year of change was increased by the beginning inventory and resulted in a double deduction.

The net adjustment due to the change in accounting method would be computed as follows:

Beginning inventory (deducted in prior and current year)	$15,000
Beginning accounts receivable (omitted from income)	25,000
Beginning accounts payable (omitted from deductions)	(34,000)
Net increase in taxable income	$ 6,000

□

Disposition of the Net Adjustment.   Generally, if the IRS *requires* the taxpayer to change an accounting method, the net adjustment is added to or subtracted from the income for the year of the change. In cases of positive (an increase in income) adjustments in excess of $3,000, the taxpayer is allowed to calculate the tax by spreading the adjustment over one or more previous years.[54]

To encourage taxpayers to *voluntarily* change from incorrect methods and to facilitate changes from one correct method to another, the IRS generally allows the taxpayer to spread the adjustment into future years. Assuming the taxpayer files a timely request for change (Form 3115), the allocation periods that generally apply appear in Concept Summary 18–1.[55]

Concept Summary 18–1

Adjustment Periods

Change	Type of Adjustment	Allocation Period
Incorrect to correct method	Positive	Three years—year of change and the two succeeding years
Incorrect to correct method	Negative	Year of change
Correct to correct	Positive	Six years—year of change and the five succeeding years
Correct to correct	Negative	Six years—year of change and the five succeeding years

EXAMPLE 18   Z Corporation in Example 17 voluntarily changed from an incorrect method (the cash basis was incorrect because inventories were material to the business) to a correct method. The company must add $2,000 (1/3 × $6,000 positive adjustment) to its 1989, 1990, and 1991 income. □

Special Accounting Methods

Generally, accrual basis taxpayers recognize income when goods are sold and shipped to the customer. Cash basis taxpayers generally recognize income from a sale on the collection of cash from the customer. The tax law provides special accounting methods for certain installment sales and long-term contracts. These special methods were enacted, in part, to assure that the tax will be due when the taxpayer is best able to pay the tax.

Installment Method

Under the general rule for computing the gain or loss from the sale of property, the entire amount of gain or loss is recognized upon the sale or other disposition of the property.

---

54. § 481(b).
55. Rev.Proc. 84–74, 1984–2 C.B. 736, modifying

Rev.Proc. 80–51, 1980–2 C.B. 818.

EXAMPLE 19 A sold property to B for $10,000 cash plus B's note (fair market value and face amount of $90,000). A's basis in the property was $40,000. Gain or loss computed under the cash or accrual basis would be as follows:

Amount realized		
	Cash down payment	$ 10,000
	Note receivable	90,000
		$100,000
	Basis in the property	(40,000)
	Realized gain	$ 60,000

☐

In Example 19, the general rule for recognizing gain or loss requires A to pay a substantial amount of tax on the gain in the year of sale even though only $10,000 cash was received. Congress enacted the installment sales provisions to prevent this sort of hardship by allowing the taxpayer to spread the gain from installment sales over the collection period.

The installment method is a very important planning tool because of the tax deferral possibilities, as Example 20 illustrates.

EXAMPLE 20 P would like to purchase property from S for either (1) $100,000 on the date of the sale or (2) $100,000 due in two years and 10% interest to be paid each year. S's basis in the asset is $0, and her effective tax rate is 28%. If S sells for cash, she will invest the after-tax proceeds in assets yielding 10% with risk comparable to P's note.

	Sell for Cash	Installment Sale
Sales proceeds, 1989	$100,000	
Less tax	(28,000)	
	$ 72,000	
Interest income		
1989 (.10 × $72,000)	7,200	
(.10 × $100,000)		$ 10,000
Less, tax (.28)	(2,016)	(2,800)
1990	7,200	10,000
	(2,016)	(2,800)
Sales proceeds, 1990		100,000
Less tax (.28)		(28,000)
After-tax proceeds and interest	$ 82,368	$ 86,400

☐

With the installment sale, S earns interest on the $28,000 deferred taxes.

Overview of the Installment Sales Provisions.   The relevant Code provisions are summarized as follows:

Section	Subject
453	General rules governing the installment method (e.g., when applicable), related-party transfers, and special situations (e.g., certain corporate liquidations).
453A	Special rules for nondealers of real property.
453B	Gain or loss recognition upon the disposition of installment obligations.
1038	Rules governing the repossession of real estate sold under the installment method.
483 1272 1274	Calculation and amortization of imputed interest.

Eligibility and Calculations.   The installment method applies to *gains* (but not losses) from the sale of property where the seller will receive at least one payment after the year of sale. For many years, practically all gains from the sale of property were eligible for the installment method. However, in recent years, the Code has been amended to deny the use of the installment method for the following:[56]

- Gains on property held for sale in the ordinary course of business.
- Depreciation recapture under § 1245 or § 1250.
- Gains on stocks or securities traded on an established market.

As an exception to the first item, the installment method may be used to report gains from sales of the following:[57]

- Timeshares units (e.g., the right to use real property for two weeks each year).
- Residential lots (if the seller is not to make any improvements).
- Any property used or produced in the trade or business of farming.

The Nonelective Aspect.   Regardless of the taxpayer's method of accounting, as a general rule, eligible sales *must* be reported by the installment method.[58] A special election is required to report the gain by any other method of accounting (see further discussion in a subsequent section of this chapter).

---

56. §§ 453(b), (i), and (*l*).

57. § 453(*l*)(2).

58. § 453(a).

EXAMPLE 21

In December 1989, S sold investment land to B. S is an accrual basis taxpayer, but he did not report the sale on his 1989 return because he was mistaken as to when the sales transaction was completed. B paid some of S's expenses of the sale in 1989, and these payments were considered collections by S for installment method purposes.

In the process of completing S's 1990 return, the accountant discovered the installment sale should have been reported on the 1989 return. Because the installment method is not elective, S must amend his 1989 return and report the gain attributable to the payments in 1989. S will not be required to report the entire gain in 1989 even though it would have been taxable in that year under his overall method of accounting. □

Computing the Gain for the Period.   The gain reported on each sale is computed by the following formula:

$$\frac{\text{Total gain}}{\text{Contract price}} \times \text{Payments received} = \text{Recognized gain}$$

The taxpayer must compute each variable as follows:

1. *Total gain* is the selling price reduced by selling expenses and the adjusted basis of the property. The selling price is the total consideration received by the seller, including notes receivable from the buyer and the seller's liabilities assumed by the buyer.

2. *Contract price* is the selling price less the seller's liabilities that are assumed by the buyer. Generally, the contract price is the amount, other than interest, the seller will receive from the purchaser.

3. *Payments received* are the collections on the contract price received in the tax year. This generally is equal to the cash received less the interest income collected for the period. If the buyer pays any of the seller's expenses, the amount paid is considered as received by the seller.

EXAMPLE 22

The seller is not a dealer, and the facts are as follows:

Sales price		
Cash down payment	$ 1,000	
Seller's mortgage assumed	3,000	
Notes payable to the seller	13,000	$17,000
Selling expenses		(500)
Seller's basis		(10,000)
Total gain		$ 6,500

The contract price is $14,000 ($17,000 − $3,000). Assuming the $1,000 is the only payment in the year of sale, the gain in that year is computed as follows:

$$\frac{\$6,500 \text{ (total gain)}}{\$14,000 \text{ (contract price)}} \times \$1,000 = \$464 \text{ (gain recognized in year of sale)}$$

□

If the sum of the seller's basis and selling expenses is less than the liabilities assumed by the buyer, the difference must be added to the contract price and to the payments (treated as *deemed payments*) received in the year of sale.[59] This adjustment to the contract price is required so that the ratio of total gain divided by contract price will not be greater than one.

EXAMPLE 23

Assume the same facts as in Example 22, except that the seller's basis in the property is only $2,000. The total gain, therefore, is $14,500 [$17,000 − ($2,000 + $500)]. Payments in the year of sale are $1,500 and are calculated as follows:

Down payment	$1,000
Excess of mortgage assumed over seller's basis and expenses ($3,000 − $2,000 − $500)	500
	$1,500

The contract price is $14,500 [$17,000 (selling price) − $3,000 (seller's mortgage assumed) + $500 (excess of mortgage assumed over seller's basis and seller's expenses)]. The gain in the year of sale is computed as follows:

$$\frac{\$14,500 \text{ (total gain)}}{\$14,500 \text{ (contract price)}} \times \$1,500 = \$1,500$$

In subsequent years, all amounts the seller collects on note principal ($13,000) will be recognized gain. □

As previously discussed, gain attributable to ordinary income recapture under §§ 1245 and 1250 is *ineligible* for installment reporting. Therefore, the § 1245 or § 1250 gain realized must be recognized in the year of sale, and the installment sale gain is the remaining gain.

EXAMPLE 24

T sold an apartment building for $50,000 cash and a $75,000 note due in two years. T's basis in the property was $25,000, and there was $40,000 ordinary income recapture under § 1250.

The realized gain is $100,000 ($125,000 − $25,000), and the $40,000 recapture must be recognized in the year of sale. Of the $60,000 remaining § 1231 gain, $24,000 must be recognized in the year of sale:

---

59. Temp.Reg. § 15a.453–1(b)(2)(iii).

$$\frac{\S\ 1231\ \text{gain}}{\text{Contract price}} \times \text{Payments received}$$

$$= \frac{\$125,000 - \$25,000 - \$40,000}{\$125,000} \times \$50,000$$

$$= \frac{\$60,000}{\$125,000} \times \$50,000 = \$24,000$$

The remaining realized gain of \$36,000 (\$60,000 − \$24,000) will be recognized as the \$75,000 note is collected. □

Other Amounts Considered Payments Received.   Congress and the IRS have added the following items to be considered as payments received in the year of sale: [60]

- Purchaser's evidence of indebtedness payable on demand and certain other readily tradable obligations (e.g., bonds traded on a stock exchange).

- Purchaser's evidence of indebtedness secured by cash or its equivalent.

In the absence of the first adjustment, the seller would have almost complete control over the year he or she reported the gain—whenever he or she demands payment or sells the tradable obligations. Also, the seller receiving the obligations secured by cash can often post them as collateral for a loan and have the cash from the sale. Thus, there would be no justification for deferring the tax.

Imputed Interest.   Sections 483 and 1274 provide that if a deferred payment contract for the sale of property with a selling price greater than \$3,000 does not contain a reasonable interest rate, a reasonable rate is imputed. The imputing of interest effectively restates the selling price of the property to equal the sum of the payments at the date of the sale and the discounted present value of the future payments. The difference between the present value of a future payment and the payment's face amount is taxed as interest income, as discussed in the following paragraphs. Thus, the imputed interest rules prevent sellers of capital assets from increasing the selling price to reflect the equivalent of unstated interest on deferred payments and thereby converting ordinary (interest) income into long-term capital gains. Although the capital gain versus ordinary income distinction has lost much of its significance as a result of changes in the Code made by TRA of 1986, the imputed interest rules are important because of their effect on the timing of income recognition.

Generally, if the contract does not charge at least the Federal rate, interest will be imputed at the Federal rate. The Federal rate is the interest rate the Federal government pays on new borrowing and is published monthly by the IRS.[61]

As a general rule, the buyer and seller must account for interest on the accrual basis with semiannual compounding.[62] The purpose of the accrual basis requirement is to assure that the seller's interest income and

---

60. § 453(f)(4) and Temp.Reg. § 15a.453–1(e).
61. § 1274(d)(1). There are three Federal rates: short-term (not over three years), mid-term (over three years but not over nine years), and long-term (over nine years).
62. §§ 1274(a), 1273(a), and 1272(a).

the buyer's interest expense are reported in the same tax year. Under pre-1984 law, the cash basis seller would not report interest income until it was actually collected, but an accrual basis buyer could deduct the interest as it accrued. The calculation and amortization of imputed interest are illustrated as follows:

EXAMPLE 25

T, a cash basis taxpayer, sold land on January 1, 1989, for $100,000 cash and $3,000,000 due on December 31, 1990, with 5% interest payable December 31, 1989, and December 31, 1990. At the time of the sale, the Federal rate was 12% (compounded semiannually). Because T did not charge at least the Federal rate, interest will be imputed at 12% (compounded semiannually).

Date	Payment	Present Value (at 12%) on 1/1/1989	Imputed Interest
12/31/1989	$ 150,000	$ 133,500	$ 16,500
12/31/1990	3,150,000	2,495,095	654,905
	$3,300,000	$2,628,595	$671,405

Thus, the selling price will be restated to $2,728,595 ($100,000 + $2,628,595) rather than $3,100,000 ($100,000 + $3,000,000), and T will recognize interest income in accordance with the following amortization schedule:

	Beginning Balance	Interest Income (at 12%)*	Received	Ending Balance
1989	$2,628,595	$324,895	$ 150,000	$2,803,490
1990	2,803,490	346,510	3,150,000	–0–

* Compounded semiannually.

☐

Congress has created several exceptions regarding the rate at which interest is imputed and the method of accounting for the interest income and expense. The general rules and exceptions are summarized in Concept Summary 18–2.

EXAMPLE 26

T is a cash basis taxpayer who made installment sales of property to accrual basis purchasers. No interest was charged on the contracts, and the Federal rate exceeded 9%. Imputed interest rates and methods of accounting for the interest are summarized as follows:

Transaction	Imputed Interest Rate	Method of Accounting for Interest	
		Seller (T)	Purchaser
Sale of land for $4 million.	Federal rate	Accrual	Accrual
Sale of used equipment for $1 million.	9%	Accrual	Accrual
Sale of used equipment for $1 million, the property was not inventory, and the buyer agreed to report interest by the cash method.	9%	Cash	Cash

□

Related-Party Sales of Nondepreciable Property.   Because of favorable judicial authority, it was possible (with proper planning) to use the installment sales approach in sales between related parties.

EXAMPLE 27

F and D (father and daughter) each own substantial investment properties. F would like to sell a capital asset that has a basis of $20,000 and a value of $100,000. He could easily sell the property for cash, but that would result in a taxable gain for the year. To defer the tax while enjoying the proceeds of the sale, F and D could structure transactions as follows:

First Disposition. F sells the asset to D for $100,000 and receives $10,000 cash and a $90,000 interest-bearing long-term note. In the year of the sale, he reports a gain of $8,000, computed as follows:

$$\frac{\$100,000 - \$20,000}{\$100,000} \times \$10,000 = \$8,000$$

F has a $72,000 deferred gain.

Second Disposition. D has a basis in the asset of $100,000 (cost). Soon after purchasing the asset from F, D sells it on the open market for $100,000. The net result of the two transactions is that the family unit (F and D) has $100,000 cash and a deferred tax liability that will not come due until the future, when D pays F the principal on the note. The interest payments will be a wash within the family—F's income will be offset by D's deduction. □

Although transactions as depicted in Example 27 had to be carefully planned, before 1980 they could succeed.[63] Obviously, this scheme was too good to be true. Thus, Congress added a provision to the Code to close this loophole.[64] The basic approach of the related-party installment sales rules is to assume that the proceeds of the second sale are used to pay the

63. For a taxpayer success in this area, see *Rushing v. Comm.*, 1971–1 USTC ¶9339, 27 AFTR2d 71–1139, 441 F.2d 593 (CA–5, 1971), *aff'g* 52 T.C. 888 (1969). For examples of where the plan was unsuccessful, see *Paul G. Lustgarten*, 71 T.C. 303 (1978), and *Phillip W. Wrenn*, 67 T.C. 576 (1976).

64. § 453(e).

CONCEPT SUMMARY 18–2

Interest on Installment Sales

	Imputed Interest Rate
General rule	Federal rate
Exceptions	
• Principal amount not over $2.8 million.*	Lesser of Federal rate or 9%
• Sale of land (with a calendar year ceiling of $500,000) between family members (the seller's spouse, brothers, sisters, ancestors, or lineal descendants).**	Lesser of Federal rate or 6%

	Method of Accounting for Interest	
	Seller's Interest Income	Buyer's Interest Expense
General rule ***	Accrual	Accrual
Exceptions		
• Total payments under the contract are $250,000 or less.†	Taxpayer's overall method	Taxpayer's overall method
• Sale of a farm (sales price of $1 million or less).††	Taxpayer's overall method	Taxpayer's overall method
• Sale of a principal residence.†††	Taxpayer's overall method	Taxpayer's overall method
• Sale for a note with a principal amount of not over $2 million, the seller is on the cash basis, the property sold is not inventory, and the buyer agrees to report expense by the cash method.‡	Cash	Cash

*	§ 1274A.
**	§§ 1274(c)(3)(F) and 483(e).
***	§§ 1274(a) and 1272(a)(3).
†	§§ 1274(c)(3)(C) and 483.
††	§§ 1274(c)(3)(A) and 483.
†††	§§ 1274(c)(3)(B) and 483.
‡	§ 1274A(c).

note owed to the first seller. Thus, the deferred gain from the first disposition is accelerated to the date of the second disposition.

EXAMPLE 28   Assume the same facts as in Example 27, except D sold the asset for $110,000. D realized and must recognize a $10,000 gain, and F must recognize his previously deferred $72,000 gain, even though D did not retire the note payable to F. ☐

A realized loss from the second sale complicates the analysis. The first seller is deemed to have received in the year of the second sale the *lesser* of the following:

- The total amount realized from the second disposition.
- The total contract price reduced by the total amount already received.

EXAMPLE 29

Assume D in Example 27 realized only $70,000 from the second disposition when the balance on the contract price was $90,000 ($100,000 selling price − $10,000 down payment). D recognizes a $30,000 loss, and F must recognize a $56,000 gain, computed as follows:

$$\frac{\$80,000}{\$100,000} \times \$70,000 = \$56,000$$

The $16,000 balance of F's gain ($80,000 − $8,000 − $56,000 = $16,000) will be reported as F collects from D on the installment contract. ☐

However, even with this modification of the rules, Congress did not eliminate the benefits of all related-party installment sales:

- Related parties include the first seller's brothers, sisters, ancestors, lineal descendants, controlled corporations, and partnerships, trusts, and estates in which the seller has an interest.[65]
- There is no acceleration if the second disposition occurs more than two years after the first sale.[66]

Thus, if the taxpayer can sell the property to an unrelated party (not a related party) or patient family member, the intrafamily installment sale is still a powerful tax planning tool.

There are other exceptions that can be applied in some circumstances. Gain is not accelerated if the second disposition is an involuntary conversion or a stock redemption or if it occurs after the death of either of the related parties. Nor is gain accelerated where tax avoidance was not a principal purpose of either the first or second disposition.[67] Obviously, the availability of these exceptions invites the structuring of transactions to come within the exceptions.

Related-Party Sales of Depreciable Property. The installment method cannot be used to report a gain on the sale of depreciable property to a controlled entity. The purpose of this rule is to prevent the seller from deferring gain (until collections are received) while the related purchaser is enjoying a stepped-up basis for depreciation purposes.[68]

---

65. § 453(f)(1), cross-referencing §§ 267(b) and 318(a). Although spouses are related parties, the exemption of gain between spouses (§ 1041) makes the second disposition rules inapplicable when the first sale was between spouses.

66. § 453(e)(2). But see § 453(e)(2)(B) for extensions of the two-year period.

67. §§ 453(e)(6) and (7).

68. § 453(g).

The prohibition on the use of the installment method applies to sales between the taxpayer and a partnership or corporation in which the taxpayer holds a more-than-50 percent interest. Constructive ownership rules apply in applying the ownership test (e.g., the taxpayer is considered to own stock owned by a spouse and certain other family members).[69] However, if the taxpayer can establish that tax avoidance was not a principal purpose of the transaction, the installment method can be used to report the gain.

EXAMPLE 30

P purchased an apartment building from his controlled corporation, S Corporation. P was short of cash at the time of the purchase (December 1989) but was to collect a large cash payment in January 1990. The agreement required P to pay the entire arm's length price in January 1990. There were good business reasons for P's acquiring the building. Because S Corporation will report all of the gain in the year following the year of sale if the installment method is allowed and the building must be expensed over 27.5 years (ACRS recovery period), S Corporation should be able to convince the IRS that tax avoidance was not a principal purpose for the installment sale. □

Disposition of Installment Obligations

The law prevents taxpayers from avoiding the recognition of deferred gross profit on installment obligations through various means (e.g., the sale of installment notes or the distribution of such notes to shareholders). The taxpayer must pay the tax on the portion of gross profits that was previously deferred as follows: [70]

If an installment obligation is satisfied at other than its face value or distributed, transmitted, sold, or otherwise disposed of, gain or loss shall result to the extent of the difference between the basis of the obligation and either of the following:

- The amount realized, in the case of satisfaction at other than face value or in a sale or exchange.

- The fair market value of the obligation at the time of distribution, transmission, or disposition, in the case of the distribution, transmission, or disposition other than by sale or exchange.

The gift of an installment note will be treated as a taxable disposition by the donor. Also, the amount realized from the cancellation is the face amount of the note if the parties (obligor and obligee) are related to each other.[71]

EXAMPLE 31

F cancels a note issued by D (F's daughter) that arose in connection with the sale of property. At the time of the cancellation, the note had a basis to F of $10,000, a face amount of $25,000, and a fair market value of $20,000. Presuming the sale fell under § 453, the cancellation would result in gain of $15,000 ($25,000 − $10,000) to F. □

---

69. §§ 1239(b) and (c).
70. § 453B(a).

71. § 453B(f)(2).

Certain exceptions to the recognition of gain provisions are provided for transfers of installment obligations pursuant to tax-free incorporations under § 351, contributions of capital to a partnership, certain corporate liquidations, transfers due to the taxpayer's death, and transfers between spouses or incident to divorce.[72] In such instances, the deferred profit is merely shifted to the transferee, who is responsible for the payment of tax on the subsequent collections of the installment obligations.

Pledging Installment Obligations

Borrowing and using installment obligations as security for the loan may be a means of receiving the cash from installment obligations without recognizing income. However, the Code specifically requires that a seller of property (other than farming property) must treat amounts borrowed as collections on the contract, where the installment obligations serve as security for the debt.[73] This acceleration of gain applies to an amount borrowed when the indebtedness is secured by an installment obligation arising from the sale of property (realty and personalty) for more than $150,000 and the property was either used in the taxpayer's trade or business or held for the production of rental income.

EXAMPLE 32

In 1989, T sold land used in his business for $500,000 (basis of $150,000). T received $200,000 cash and an interest-bearing note for $300,000 due in 1992. In 1990, T borrowed $250,000 using the note as security. The receipt of the loan proceeds will cause T to recognize gain of $175,000 [($500,000 − $150,000)/$500,000 × $250,000]. When T collects the note in 1992, he must recognize the balance of the realized gain of $35,000 (.70 × $50,000). □

Interest on Deferred Taxes

As illustrated in Example 20, the installment method, unlike a cash sale, enables the seller to earn interest on the deferred taxes. Some commentators reason that the government is, in effect, making interest-free loans to taxpayers who report gains by the installment method. Following the line of reasoning that the amount of the deferred taxes is a loan, in some situations, the taxpayer is required to pay interest on the deferred taxes.[74]

The taxpayer is required to pay interest on the deferred taxes only if both of the following requirements are met:

- The installment obligation arises from the sale of property (other than farming property) for more than $150,000.

- Such installment obligations outstanding at the close of the tax year exceed $5 million.

---

72. §§ 453B(c), (d), and (g). See chapter 20 for a discussion of some of these subjects.

73. §§ 453A(b) and (d).

74. § 453A.

Interest on the deferred taxes is payable only for the portion of such deferred taxes that relates to the installment obligations in *excess* of $5 million. The interest is calculated using the underpayment rate in § 6621.

Repossessions of Property

Generally, the repossession of property is a taxable event. Thus, gain or loss equal to the fair market value of the property received (reduced by repossession expenses) less the unrecovered basis must be recognized.[75]

EXAMPLE 33

T sold the stock in his closely held corporation to B for $125,000 (a down payment of $30,000 and an installment note for $95,000). T's basis for the stock was $50,000. B defaulted on the note after paying $10,000 on the principal. T foreclosed and received the stock when it had a fair market value of $60,000.

T had recognized gain of $24,000 under the installment method as follows:

$$\frac{\$125,000 - \$50,000}{\$125,000} \times (\$30,000 + \$10,000) = \$24,000$$

Therefore, at the time of repossession, T's unrecovered basis in the note is $34,000 ($50,000 original basis − $16,000 amount of collections treated as a recovery of capital). T must recognize a $26,000 ($60,000 − $34,000) gain from the repossession. □

Repossession of Real Property. A special provision prohibits the recognition of loss and limits the gain recognized from a repossession of real property.[76] Generally, the gain recognized from the repossession cannot exceed the total cash collected (other than interest) by the seller less the gain previously recognized from collections.[77] In other words, the total gain from the repossessed property cannot exceed the net cash receipts.

EXAMPLE 34

S sold land for $100,000, but collected only $30,000 before the purchaser defaulted. S's basis in the land was $20,000, repossession expenses are $5,000, and the fair market value of the land at the time of repossession is $110,000. The recognized gain from repossession of $6,000 is calculated as follows:

75. Reg. § 1.453–2(d).

76. § 1038.

77. If property other than the repossessed property is received by the seller, its fair market value is added to the cash proceeds.

Cash collected	$30,000
Less: Gain previously recognized (80% × $30,000)	(24,000)
Gain on repossession	$ 6,000

As a further limitation, the gain from repossession cannot exceed the seller's original gain less the summation of the previously recognized gain and the expenses of repossession [in Example 34, $80,000 − ($24,000 + $5,000) = $51,000].[78] Thus, the seller is not taxed on appreciation in the value of the property from the date of sale to the date of repossession.

The seller's basis for the repossessed property is calculated as follows: [79]

Seller's unrecovered basis for the note

+Recognized gain on the repossession

+Repossession expenses

In Example 34, S's basis for the repossessed land would be $25,000 [($70,000 × 20%) + $6,000 + $5,000].

Electing Out of the Installment Method

A taxpayer can *elect not to use* the installment method. The election is made by reporting on a timely filed return the gain computed by the taxpayer's usual method of accounting (cash or accrual).[80] However, the Regulations provide that the amount realized by a cash basis taxpayer cannot be less than the value of the property sold reduced by the cash down payment. This rule differs from the usual cash basis accounting rules (discussed earlier),[81] which measure the amount realized in terms of the fair market value of the property received. The net effect of the Regulations is to allow the cash basis taxpayer to report his or her gain as an accrual basis taxpayer. The election has frequent application to year-end sales by taxpayers who expect to be in a higher tax bracket in the following year.

EXAMPLE 35

On December 31, 1989, T sold land to B for $20,000 (fair market value). The cash was to be paid on January 4, 1990. T is a cash basis taxpayer, and his basis in the land is $8,000. He expects to have substantially greater taxable income in 1990 than he did in 1989.

The transaction constitutes an installment sale because a payment will be received in a tax year after the tax year of disposition. B's promise to pay T is an installment obligation, and under the Regulations, the value of the installment obligation is equal to the value of the property sold

78.   Reg. §§ 1.1038–1(c) and (h).

79.   Reg. § 1.1038–1(g)(1).

80.   § 453(d) and Temp.Reg. § 15a.453–1(d). See

also Rev.Rul. 82–227, 1982–2 C.B. 89.

81.   Refer to chapter 4, Example 8.

($20,000). If T were to elect out of the installment method, he would report a $12,000 gain ($20,000 − $8,000) in 1989 rather than in 1990. □

Contingent Payments. Under the Regulations, the lower limit on the valuation of rights to contingent payments is the fair market value of the property sold less the sum of the cash and the value of fixed obligations received.[82] As a result, whether the sales price is contingent or fixed, generally the cash basis taxpayer who does not use the installment method must recognize the same amount of gain in the year of sale—the excess of the value of the property sold over the seller's basis.

In the rare situation where the seller receives a contingent obligation and the property sold does not have a fair market value, the taxpayer may treat the transaction as *open* and thus report no income until the basis has been recovered.

EXAMPLE 36

T sold a mineral interest in land to X Oil Company for 30% of the gross income from the property for the first three years of production. She paid $10,000 for the interest 20 years ago. All mineral interests in the area are sold on similar contingent terms. Thus, a cash price cannot be determined. Because the venture was so speculative, the contingent payment obligation did not have a fair market value. Over the three years, T received $35,000 ($5,000, $20,000, and $10,000). The Federal rate was 10%. T must report gain as follows:

Year	Amount Received	Imputed Interest	Recovery of Capital	Gain
1	$ 5,000	$ 455	$ 4,545	$ –0–
2	20,000	3,471	5,455	11,074
3	10,000	2,487	–0–	7,513
	$35,000	$6,413	$10,000	$18,587

□

Revocation of the Election. Permission of the IRS is required to revoke an election not to use the installment method.[83] The stickiness of the election is an added peril.

EXAMPLE 37

The taxpayer in Example 36 elected to report the transaction as open in the year of sale. Subsequently the IRS brought forth unimpeachable evidence that the mineral interest had a fair market value of $30,000 at the time of the sale. The taxpayer would be required to report a $20,000 gain in the year of sale ($30,000 − $10,000 basis). Moreover, the $5,000 gain

---

82. Temp.Reg. § 15a.453–1(d)(2)(iii).

83. § 453(d)(3) and Temp.Reg. § 15a.453–1(d)(4).

from collections ($35,000 − $30,000) would be ordinary income (because collection of a receivable is not a sale or exchange of a capital asset).

Under the installment method, no gain would have been recognized until the first collection was received, at which time $3,333 would be recognized:

$$\frac{\$20,000}{\$30,000} \times \$5,000 = \underline{\$3,333}$$

Also, except for imputed interest, the entire gain would be capital gain.

□

In conclusion, before a taxpayer elects out of the installment method, he or she should be confident that his or her valuations will withstand close scrutiny. Also, the taxpayer must consider the effects of converting the capital gain from an installment sale into ordinary income under the alternative methods.

Long-Term Contracts

A *long-term contract* is a building, installation, construction, or manufacturing contract that is entered into but not completed within the same tax year. Furthermore, a manufacturing contract is long term only if the contract is to manufacture (1) a unique item not normally carried in finished goods inventory or (2) items that normally require more than 12 calendar months to complete.[84]

EXAMPLE 38

T, a calendar year taxpayer, entered into two contracts during the year. One contract was to construct a building foundation. Work was to begin in October 1989 and was to be completed by June 1990. The contract is long term because it will not be entered into and completed in the same tax year. The fact that the contract requires less than 12 calendar months to complete is not relevant because the contract is not for manufacturing. The second contract was for architectural services to be performed over two years. These services will not qualify for long-term contract treatment because the taxpayer will not build, install, construct, or manufacture a product. □

Generally, the taxpayer must accumulate all of the direct and indirect costs incurred under a contract. This will require the accumulation of production costs and the allocation of these costs to individual contracts. Furthermore, mixed services costs, costs that benefit contracts as well as the general administrative operations of the business, must be allocated to production. Concept Summary 18–3 contains a list of the types of costs that must be accumulated and allocated to contracts. Reasonable bases for cost allocations must be developed by the taxpayer.[85]

---

84. § 460(f) and Reg. § 1.451–3(b).   85. Temp.Reg. § 1.263A–1T(b)(3)(iii)(A)(1).

CONCEPT SUMMARY 18–3

Contract Costs, Mixed Services Costs, and Current Expense Items for Contracts

	Contracts Eligible for the Completed Contract Method	Other Contracts
Contract Costs		
Direct materials (a part of the finished product).	Capital	Capital
Indirect materials (consumed in production but not in the finished product, e.g., grease and oil for equipment).	Capital	Capital
Storage, handling, and insurance on materials.	Expense	Capital
Direct labor (worked on the product).	Capital	Capital
Indirect labor (worked in the production process but not directly on the product, e.g., a construction supervisor).	Capital	Capital
Fringe benefits for direct and indirect labor (e.g., vacation, sick pay, unemployment, and other insurance).	Capital	Capital
Pension costs for direct and indirect labor:		
• Current cost.	Expense	Capital
• Past service costs.	Expense	Capital
Depreciation on production facilities:		
• For financial statements.	Capital	Capital
• Tax depreciation in excess of financial statements.	Expense	Capital
Depreciation on idle facilities.	Expense	Expense
Property taxes, insurance, rent, and maintenance on production facilities.	Capital	Capital
Bidding expenses—successful.	Capital	Capital
Bidding expenses—unsuccessful.	Expense	Capital
Interest to finance real estate construction.	Capital	Capital
Interest to finance personal property:		
• Construction period of one year or less.	Not applicable	Expense
• Construction period exceeds one year and costs exceed $1,000,000.	Not applicable	Capital
• Construction period exceeds two years.	Not applicable	Capital
Mixed services costs		
Personnel operations.	Expense	Allocate
Data processing.	Expense	Allocate
Purchasing.	Expense	Allocate
Selling, general, and administrative expenses (including an allocated share of mixed services)	Expense	Expense
Losses	Expense	Expense

EXAMPLE 39   C, Inc., uses detailed cost accumulation records to assign labor and materials to its contracts in progress. The total cost of fringe benefits is allocated to a contract on the following basis:

$$\frac{\text{Labor on the contract}}{\text{Total salaries and labor}} \times \text{Total cost of fringe benefits}$$

Similarly, storage and handling costs for materials are allocated to contracts on the following basis:

$$\frac{\text{Contract materials}}{\text{Materials purchases}} \times \text{Storage and handling cost}$$

The cost of the personnel operations, a mixed services cost, is allocated between production and general administration based on the number of employees in each function. The personnel cost allocated to production is allocated to individual contracts on the basis of the formula used to allocate fringe benefits. □

The accumulated costs are deducted when the revenue from the contract is recognized. Generally, three methods of accounting are used in varying circumstances to determine when the revenue from a contract is recognized. These are as follows: [86]

1.   The completed contract method. *Changing*

2.   The percentage of completion method. *Changing*

3.   The percentage of completion–capitalized cost method.

The completed contract method may be used for (1) home construction contracts (contracts in which at least 80 percent of the estimated costs are for dwelling units in buildings with four or fewer units) and (2) certain other real estate construction contracts. Other real estate contracts can qualify for the completed contract method if the following requirements are satisfied:

- The contract is expected to be completed within the two-year period beginning on the commencement date of the contract.

- The contract is performed by a taxpayer whose average annual gross receipts for the three taxable years preceding the taxable year in which the contract is entered into do not exceed $10 million.

All other contractors must use either the percentage of completion method or the percentage of completion–capitalized cost method.

Completed Contract Method.   Under the *completed contract method,* no revenue from the contract is recognized until the contract is completed and accepted. However, a taxpayer may not delay completion of a contract for the principal purpose of deferring tax.[87]

In some instances, the original contract price may be disputed or the buyer may want additional work to be done on a long-term contract. If the disputed amount is substantial (it is not possible to determine whether a profit or loss will ultimately be realized on the contract), the Regulations

---

86. § 460.   87. Reg. § 1.451–3(b)(2).

provide that no amount of income or loss is recognized until the dispute is resolved. In all other cases, the profit or loss (reduced by the amount in dispute) is recognized in the current period on completion of the contract. However, additional work may need to be performed with respect to the disputed contract. In this case, the difference between the amount in dispute and the actual cost of the additional work will be recognized in the year such work is completed rather than in the year in which the dispute is resolved.[88]

EXAMPLE 40

B, a calendar year taxpayer utilizing the completed contract method of accounting, constructed a building for C pursuant to a long-term contract. The gross contract price was $500,000. B finished construction in 1989 at a cost of $475,000. When C examined the building, he insisted that the building be repainted or the contract price be reduced. The estimated cost of repainting is $10,000. Since under the terms of the contract, B would be assured of a profit of at least $15,000 ($500,000 − $475,000 − $10,000) even if the dispute was ultimately resolved in favor of C, B must include $490,000 ($500,000 − $10,000) in gross income and is allowed deductions of $475,000 for 1989.

In 1990, B and C resolved the dispute, and B repainted certain portions of the building at a cost of $6,000. B must include $10,000 in 1990 gross income and may deduct the $6,000 expense in that year. ☐

EXAMPLE 41

Assume the same facts as in the previous example, except the estimated cost of repainting the building is $50,000. Since the resolution of the dispute completely in C's favor would mean that there would be a net loss on the contract ($500,000 − $475,000 − $50,000 = $25,000 loss), no income or loss would be recognized until the year in which the dispute is resolved. ☐

Frequently the contractor will receive payment at various stages of completion. For example, when the contract is 50 percent complete, the contractor may receive 50 percent of the contract price less a retainage. The taxation of these payments is generally governed by Regulation § 1.451–5 "advance payments for goods and long-term contracts" (discussed in chapter 4). Generally, contractors are permitted to defer the advance payments until such payments are recognized as income under the taxpayer's method of accounting.

Percentage of Completion–Capitalized Cost Method.   In 1986, Congress decided that the completed contract method of accounting was too much of a good thing. Therefore, the law was changed so that now contractors, subject to the exceptions discussed earlier, must use the percentage of completion method to account for 90 percent of the items produced under a contract. The remaining 10 percent of the items may be accounted for by the completed contract method. This 90 percent–10 percent scheme is referred to as the *percentage of completion–capitalized cost method.*

---

88. Reg. § 1.451–3(d)(2)(ii)–(vii), Example (2).

Percentage of Completion Method.   Under the *percentage of completion method,* a portion of the gross contract price is included in income during each period. The revenue accrued each period is computed as follows:[89]

$$\frac{C}{T} \times P$$

Where C = Contract costs incurred during the period

T = Estimated total cost of the contract

P = Contract price

All of the costs allocated to the contract during the period are deductible from the accrued revenue.[90] Because T in the above formula is an estimate that frequently differs from total actual costs, which are not known until the contract has been completed, the profit on a contract for a particular period may be overstated or understated.

EXAMPLE 42

B, Inc., entered into a contract that was to take two years to complete, with estimated total costs of $225,000. The contract price was $300,000. Costs of the contract for 1989, the first year, totaled $135,000. The gross profit reported by the percentage of completion method for 1989 was $45,000 [($135,000/$225,000 × $300,000) − $135,000]. The contract was completed at the end of 1990 at a total cost of $270,000. In retrospect, 1989 profit should have been $15,000 [($135,000/$270,000 × $300,000) − $135,000]. Thus, taxes were overpaid in 1989. ☐

Lookback Provisions.   In the year a contract is completed, a *lookback* provision requires the recalculation of annual profits reported on the contract accounted for by the percentage of completion method. Interest is paid to the taxpayer if there was an overpayment of taxes, and interest is payable by the taxpayer if there was an underpayment.[91]

EXAMPLE 43

Assume B, Inc., in Example 42, was in the 34% tax bracket in both years and the relevant interest rate was 10%. For 1989, the company paid excess taxes of $10,200 [($45,000 − $15,000) × .34]. When the contract is completed at the end of 1990, B, Inc., should receive interest of $1,020 for one year on the tax overpayment ($10,200 × .10). ☐

If the taxpayer reports income by the percentage of completion–capitalized cost method, the lookback method is applied to 90 percent of the items with respect to the contract.

---

89. § 460(b)(2)(A).
90. Reg. § 1.451–3(c)(3).
91. §§ 460(a)(2) and (b)(3).

Comparison of the Completed Contract and Percentage of Completion Methods.   To illustrate the two methods, assume a contractor agrees to construct a building for $125,000. The contractor's average annual gross receipts for the three preceding taxable years are $7 million. In the initial year of construction, costs of $80,000 are incurred, and the architect estimates total cost will be $100,000. In the second year, the contract is completed at an additional cost of $20,000.

Percentage of Completion Method

	Year 1	Year 2
Revenue (80% × $125,000 in Year 1)	$100,000	$ 25,000
Costs incurred on the contract	(80,000)	(20,000)
Gross profit	$ 20,000	$ 5,000

Completed Contract Method

	Year 1	Year 2
Revenue	$ –0–	$125,000
Costs incurred on the contract	–0–	(100,000)
Gross profit	$ –0–	$ 25,000

As illustrated above, an advantage of the completed contract method is the deferral of income. This means that the contractor has the use of funds that would otherwise be paid to the government as income taxes during periods before completion. Of course, the completed contract method can result in a bunching of income in one year. However, if the contractor is incorporated and regularly reports taxable income of more than $75,000, the 34 percent rate always will apply. Therefore, the deferral can be accomplished with no increase in total tax. In addition, the completed contract method may minimize disputes with the IRS, since there is no need to make yearly estimates of the percentage of completion.

INVENTORIES

Generally, tax accounting and financial accounting for inventories are much the same:

- The use of inventories is necessary to clearly reflect the income of any business engaged in the production and sale or purchase and sale of goods.[92]

- The inventories should include all finished goods, goods in process, and raw materials and supplies that will become part of the product (including containers).

---

92. § 471(a) and Reg. §§ 1.471–1 and –2.

- Inventory rules must give effect to the *best* accounting practice of a particular trade or business, and the taxpayer's method should be consistently followed from year to year.

 • All items included in inventory should be valued at either (1) cost or (2) the lower of cost or market value.

The following are not acceptable methods or practices in valuing inventories:

- A deduction for a reserve for anticipated price changes.

- The use of a constant price or nominal value for a so-called normal quantity of materials or goods in stock (e.g., the base stock method).

- The inclusion of stock in transit in inventory to which title is not vested in the taxpayer.

- The direct costing approach (excluding fixed indirect production costs from inventory).

- The prime costing approach (excluding all indirect production costs from inventory).

The reason for the similarities between tax and financial accounting for inventories is that § 471 sets forth what appears to be a two-prong test. Under this provision "inventories shall be taken . . . on such basis . . . as conforming as nearly as may be to the *best accounting practice* in the trade or business and as most *clearly reflecting the income.*" The best accounting practice is synonymous with generally accepted accounting principles (hereafter referred to as GAAP). However, the IRS determines whether an inventory method clearly reflects income.

In *Thor Power Tool Co. v. Comm.*, there was a conflict between the two tests.[93] The taxpayer's method of valuing obsolete parts was in conformity with GAAP. The IRS, however, successfully argued that the clear reflection of income test was not satisfied because the taxpayer's procedures for valuing its inventories were contrary to the Regulations. Under the taxpayer's method, inventories for parts in excess of estimated future sales were written off (expensed), although the parts were kept on hand and their asking prices were not reduced. (Under Reg. § 1.471–4(b), inventories cannot be written down unless the selling prices also are reduced.) The taxpayer contended that conformity to GAAP creates a presumption that the method clearly reflects income. The Supreme Court disagreed, concluding that the clear reflection of income test was *paramount.* Moreover, it is the opinion of the IRS that controls in determining whether the method of inventory clearly reflects income. Thus, the best accounting practice test was rendered practically meaningless. It follows that the taxpayer's method of inventory must strictly conform to the Regulations regardless of what GAAP might require.

GAAP is
CRAP

---

93. 79–1 USTC ¶9139, 43 AFTR2d 79–362, 99 S.Ct. 773 (USSC, 1979).

Determining Inventory Cost

For merchandise purchased, cost is the invoice price less trade discounts plus freight and other handling charges.[94] Cash discounts approximating a fair interest rate can be deducted or capitalized at the taxpayer's option, providing the method used is consistently applied.

Uniform Capitalization.   In 1986, Congress added § 263A, which significantly affects the inventory rules, to the Code. Section 263A provides that for inventory and property produced by the taxpayer, ". . . (A) the direct cost of such property, and (B) such property's share of those indirect costs (including taxes) part or all of which are allocable to such property" must be capitalized. The Committee Reports express the concept that Congress is attempting to achieve a set of capitalization rules that will apply to all types of businesses: contractors, manufacturers, farmers, wholesalers, and retailers.[95] Congress has labeled the system as *uniform capitalization rules,* and practitioners refer to the rules as a *super-full absorption costing system.*

According to the Committee Reports, the cost of goods produced or manufactured by the taxpayer must be determined by using the rules developed for long-term contracts as outlined in Concept Summary 18–3 (see the "Other Contracts" column). In general, these rules result in capitalization (as inventory) of all costs except selling and general and administrative expenses that are not related to production (e.g., general accounting).

Wholesalers and retailers are required to capitalize the costs of acquiring and storing goods as well as the purchase price of the goods and any related taxes. The Conference Committee Report lists the following indirect costs that must be capitalized: [96]

- All storage costs for wholesalers.
- Offsite storage costs for retailers.
- Purchasing costs (e.g., buyers' wages or salaries).
- Handling, processing, assembly, and repackaging.
- The portion of general and administrative costs allocable to these functions.

Mixed services costs must be allocated to offsite storage, purchasing, and packaging on the basis of direct labor costs of these departments as a percentage of total payroll. Thus, the storage, purchasing, and packaging costs allocated to ending inventory include some general and administrative expense.

It should be noted that the uniform capitalization rules may result in some costs being capitalized for tax purposes but not for financial accounting purposes. For example, a wholesaler's or a manufacturer's storage costs are generally expensed for financial reporting purposes, but are capitalized for tax purposes. Also, the taxpayer may capitalize straight-line depreciation of production equipment for financial accounting purposes, but the total tax depreciation must be capitalized under uniform capitalization.

94. Reg. § 1.471–3(b).
95. H. Rep. 99–841, 99th Cong., 2nd Sess., 1986, pp. 302–309. See also Temp Reg. § 1.263A–1T.
96. Ibid., p. 305.

Lower of Cost or Market.   Except for those taxpayers who use the LIFO method, inventories may be valued at the lower of cost or replacement cost (*market*).[97] Those taxpayers using LIFO must value inventory at cost. However, the write-down of damaged or shopworn merchandise and goods that are otherwise unsaleable at normal prices is not considered to be an application of the lower of cost or market method. Such items should be valued at bona fide selling price less direct cost of disposal.[98]

In the case of excess inventories (as in *Thor Power Tool Co.*, previously discussed), the goods can be written down only to the taxpayer's offering price. If the offering price on the goods is not reduced, the goods must be valued at cost.

EXAMPLE 44

The Z Publishing Company invested $50,000 in printing 10,000 copies of a book. Although only 7,000 copies were sold in the first three years and none in the next five years, management is convinced that the book will become a classic in 20 years. Z Company leaves the price the same as it was when first distributed ($15 per copy). The remaining 3,000 books must be valued at cost ($15,000). It should be noted that the tax law provides an incentive for the taxpayer to destroy or abandon its excess inventory and obtain an immediate deduction rather than wait for the event of future sales. □

In applying the lower of cost or market method, *each* item included in the inventory must be valued at the lower of its cost or market value.[99]

EXAMPLE 45

The taxpayer's ending inventory is valued as follows:

Item	Cost	Market	Lower of Cost or Market
A	$5,000	$ 4,000	$4,000
B	3,000	2,000	2,000
C	1,500	6,000	1,500
	$9,500	$12,000	$7,500

Under the lower of cost or market method, the taxpayer's inventory would be valued at $7,500 rather than $9,500. □

Determining Cost—Specific Identification, FIFO, and LIFO.   In some cases it is feasible to determine the cost of the particular item sold. For example, an automobile dealer can easily determine the specific cost of each automobile that has been sold. However, in most businesses it is necessary to resort to a flow of goods assumption such as *first in, first out* (FIFO), *last in, first out* (LIFO), or an *average cost* method. A taxpayer may use any of these

---

97. Reg. § 1.472–4.
98. Reg. § 1.471–2(c).

99. Reg. § 1.471–4(c).

methods, provided the method selected is consistently applied from year to year.

During a period of rising prices, LIFO will generally produce a lower ending inventory valuation and will result in a greater cost of goods sold than would be obtained under the FIFO method. The effects on computing cost of goods sold using LIFO and FIFO are illustrated in the following example.

EXAMPLE 46

On January 1, 1989, the taxpayer opened a retail store to sell refrigerators. At least 10 refrigerators must be carried in inventory to satisfy customer demands. The initial investment in the 10 refrigerators is $5,000. During the year, 10 refrigerators were sold at $750 each and were replaced at a cost of $6,000 ($600 each). Gross profit under the LIFO and FIFO methods is computed below:

		FIFO		LIFO
Sales (10 × $750)		$7,500		$7,500
Beginning inventory	$ 5,000		$ 5,000	
Purchases	6,000		6,000	
	$11,000		$11,000	
Ending inventory				
10 × $600	(6,000)			
10 × $500	_____		(5,000)	
Cost of goods sold		(5,000)		(6,000)
Gross profit		$2,500		$1,500

□

The LIFO Election

A taxpayer may adopt LIFO by merely using the method in the tax return for the year of the change and by attaching Form 970 to the tax return. Thus, a taxpayer does not have to request approval for changes within the first 180 days of the tax year. Once the election is made, it cannot be revoked. However, a prospective change from LIFO to any other inventory method can be made if the consent of the IRS is obtained.[100]

The beginning inventory valuation for the first year LIFO is used is computed by the costing method employed in the preceding year. Thus, the beginning LIFO inventory is generally the same as the closing inventory for the preceding year. However, since lower of cost or market cannot be used in conjunction with LIFO, previous write-downs to market for items included in the beginning inventory must be restored to income. The amount the inventories are written up is an adjustment due to a change in accounting method.[101]

100. Reg. §§ 1.472–3(a) and 1.472–5 and Rev.Proc. 84–74, 1984–2 C.B. 736 at 742.

101. Reg. § 1.472–2(c). In Rev.Rul. 76–282, 1976–2 C.B. 137, the IRS required the restoration of write-downs for damaged and shopworn goods when the taxpayer switched to LIFO.

However, the usual rules for disposition of the adjustments under Rev.Proc. 84–74 are not applicable.[102] The taxpayer is allowed to spread the adjustment ratably over the year of the change and the two succeeding years.

EXAMPLE 47

In 1988, T used the lower of cost or market FIFO inventory method. The FIFO cost of its ending inventory was $30,000, and the market value of the inventory was $24,000. Therefore, the ending inventory for 1988 was $24,000. T switched to LIFO in 1989 and was required to write up the beginning inventory to $30,000. T must add $2,000 ($6,000 ÷ 3) to his income for each of the years 1989, 1990, and 1991. □

Congress added this provision to the Code to overrule the previous IRS policy of requiring that the entire adjustment be included in income for the year preceding the change to LIFO.[103]

Once the LIFO election is made for tax purposes, the taxpayer's financial reports to owners and creditors must also be prepared on the basis of LIFO.[104] The *conformity* of financial reports to tax reporting is specifically required by the Code and is strictly enforced by the IRS. However, under Regulations, the taxpayer is allowed to make a footnote disclosure of the net income computed by another method of inventory valuation (e.g., FIFO).[105]

TAX PLANNING CONSIDERATIONS

Taxable Year

Under the general rules for tax years, partnerships and S corporations frequently will be required to use a calendar year. However, if the partnership or S corporation can demonstrate a business purpose for a fiscal year, the IRS will allow the entity to use the requested year. The advantage to the fiscal year is that the calendar year partners and S corporation shareholders may be able to defer from tax the income earned from the close of the fiscal year until the end of the calendar year. Tax advisers for these entities should apply the IRS's gross receipts test described in Rev.Proc. 87–32 to determine if permission for the fiscal year will be granted.

Cash Method of Accounting

The cash method of accounting gives the taxpayer considerable control over the recognition of expenses and some control over the recognition of income. This method can be used by proprietorships, partnerships, and small corporations (gross receipts of $5 million or less) that provide services (inventories are not material to the service business). Farmers (except certain farming corporations) can also use the cash method.

---

102. 1984–2 C.B. 736.

103. § 472(d), overruling the IRS position cited in Footnote 101.

104. § 472(c).

105. Reg. § 1.472–2(e).

Installment Method

Unlike the accrual and cash methods, the installment method results in an interest-free loan (of deferred taxes) from the government. Thus, the installment method is a powerful tax planning tool and should be considered when a sale of eligible property is being planned. Note, however, that the provision that requires interest to be paid on the deferred taxes on certain installment obligations reduces this benefit.

Related Parties. Intrafamily installment sales can still be a useful family tax planning tool. If the related party holds the property more than two years, a subsequent sale will not accelerate the gain from the first disposition. Patience and forethought are rewarded.

The 6 percent limitation on imputed interest on sales of land between family members enables the seller to convert ordinary income into capital gain, or make what is, in effect, a nontaxable gift. If the selling price is raised to adjust for the low interest rate charges on an installment sale, the seller has more capital gain but less ordinary income than would be realized from a sale to an unrelated party. If the selling price is not raised and the specified interest of 6 percent is charged, the seller enables the relative to have the use of the property without having to pay for its full market value. Moreover, this bargain sale is not a taxable gift.

Disposition of Installment Obligations. A disposition of an installment obligation is also a serious matter. Gifts of the obligations will accelerate income to the seller. The list of taxable and nontaxable dispositions of installment obligations should not be trusted to memory. In each instance where transfers of installment obligations are contemplated, the practitioner should conduct research to be sure he or she knows the consequences.

LIFO

During periods of inflation, LIFO results in the deferral of tax. The only major disadvantage to LIFO is the financial-tax conformity requirement. However, this disadvantage can be overcome through footnote disclosure of earnings as computed under FIFO.

PROBLEM MATERIALS

Discussion Questions

1. X recently began conducting an office supply business as a corporation. Z began conducting his law practice through a corporation. Neither corporation has made an S election. What tax year alternatives are available to the X business that are not available to the Z business?

2. When should a business be on a 52–53 week basis?

3. Why are partnerships generally required to adopt the same tax year as their partners and S corporations generally required to adopt a calendar year?

4. How does a partnership establish a business purpose for a tax year that differs from its partners' tax years?

5. What is the procedure for changing a tax year?

6. T Corporation began business on October 29, 1989. The end of July would be a convenient time for the company to close its tax year. In July 1990, the president of the company informs you of his desired tax year. Can T adopt a July 31 year-end and, if so, is annualization required?

7. In which of the following situations must a taxpayer annualize income?

   a. The first tax year.

   b. The year an individual marries.

   c. The final return.

   d. A year of a change in the tax year.

8. In 1989 R, a cash basis taxpayer, received a $15,000 cash bonus. The bonus was a percentage of the sales he made that year. An error in 1989 sales was discovered in 1990, and R was required to repay $4,000 of his 1989 bonus. R was in the 28% tax bracket in 1989 but is in the 15% bracket in 1990. What are the tax consequences of R's paying the employer $4,000 in 1990?

9. X owns bonds and stocks that pay interest and dividends. He is also a partner in a partnership in the rental business and is the sole shareholder of a grocery store that is operated as an S corporation. If the S corporation uses the accrual method, does this mean that X's interest, dividends, and partnership income must be determined by the accrual method?

10. B, a certified public accountant, recently obtained a new client. The client is a retail grocery store that has used the cash method to report its income since it began doing business. Will B incur any liability if he prepares the tax return in accordance with the cash method and does not advise the client of the necessity of seeking the IRS's permission to change to the accrual method?

11. In December 1989, a cash basis taxpayer paid January through June 1990 management fees in connection with his rental properties. The fees were $4,000 per month. Compute the 1989 expense under the following assumptions:

   a. The fees were paid by an individual who derived substantially all of his income from the properties.

   b. The fees were paid by a tax-shelter partnership.

12. Why is the accrual method required for sales and cost of goods sold when inventories are material to the business?

13. What is the general rule as to when a deduction will be recognized under the accrual basis of accounting?

14. P, an accrual basis taxpayer, did not pay his 1989 state income taxes until March 15, 1990. In what year can P deduct the state income tax on his Federal return?

15. Compare the cash basis and accrual basis of accounting as applied to the following:

    a. Fixed assets.

    b. Prepaid rental income.

    c. Prepaid interest expense.

    d. A note received for services performed if the market value and face amount of the note differ.

16. When are reserves for estimated expenses allowed for tax purposes? What is the role of the matching concept in tax accounting?

17. What difference does it make whether the taxpayer or the IRS initiates the change in accounting method?

18. What is the procedure for obtaining consent to change a method of accounting?

19. Which of the following require the permission of the IRS?

    a. A change from the cash to the accrual basis for deducting property tax expenses.

    b. The correction of a prior year's return when the double-declining balance method was incorrectly used to compute the amortization of a patent.

    c. A change from direct costing to the full absorption method of valuing inventories.

    d. A change from the FIFO to the LIFO inventory method.

    e. A change from cost to the lower of cost or market method of valuing inventories.

    f. A write-down of damaged merchandise to net realizable value when the taxpayer has consistently used cost to value the inventories.

    g. The use of the lower of cost or market method in conjunction with the LIFO inventory method.

    h. A change from the LIFO to the FIFO inventory method.

20. X has made Y an offer on the purchase of a capital asset. X will pay (1) $200,000 cash or (2) $50,000 cash and a 12% installment note for $150,000 guaranteed by City Bank of New York. If Y sells for $200,000 cash, he will invest the after-tax proceeds in certificates of deposit yielding 12% interest. Y's cost of the asset is $25,000. Why would Y prefer the installment sale?

21. Which of the following are eligible for installment reporting? Assume some payments are received after the year of sale and the sales are for gains.

    a. Fully depreciated equipment sold for $50,000. The original cost of the equipment was $75,000.

    b.   Sale of a tractor by a farm equipment dealer.

    c.   Sale of stock in a family controlled corporation.

    d.   Sale of residential lots.

22. In 1989, the taxpayer sold some real estate and received an installment note. The sale met all of the requirements for using the installment method, but the taxpayer did not know that the installment method could be used. Thus, the entire gain was reported in the year of sale. In 1990, the taxpayer learns that he could have used the installment method. Is there anything he can do? Explain.

23. T, a cash basis taxpayer, sold land in December 1989. At the time of the sale, T received $10,000 cash and a note for $90,000 due in 90 days. T expects to be in a much higher tax bracket in 1990. Can T report the entire gain in 1989?

24. How does the buyer's assumption of the seller's liabilities in an installment sale affect the following:

    a.   Selling price.

    b.   Contract price.

    c.   Buyer's payments in the year of sale.

25. In 1989 S, a cash basis taxpayer, sold land to P, an accrual basis taxpayer. The principal and interest were due in two years, and the interest was equal to the Federal rate. Neither the buyer nor the seller is a dealer in real estate. Indicate when the buyer and seller will report their interest expense and income in each of the following cases:

    a.   The selling price is $2.5 million.

    b.   The selling price is $200,000.

    c.   The selling price is $600,000.

26. On June 1, 1987, Father sold land to Son for $100,000. Father reported the gain by the installment method, with the gain to be spread over five years. In May 1989, Son received an offer of $150,000 for the land, to be paid over three years. What would be the tax consequences of Son's sale?

27. In 1988, T sold a building to his 100% controlled corporation. The entire purchase price is to be paid in 1989. When should T report the gain on the sale of the building?

28. What is the tax effect of a gift of an installment obligation?

29. T is considering selling his stock in a family-owned corporation for $6 million. The buyer would prefer to pay the price in installments. What is the minimum amount T should receive in the year of sale?

30. The taxpayer began work on a contract in June 1989 and completed the contract in April 1990.

    a.   Can the percentage of completion method be used to report the income from the contract?

b.   If the taxpayer in (a) uses the accrual basis to report income, assuming no advance payments are received, when will the income be recognized?

31.   How does the tax accounting for an accrual basis taxpayer's inventories differ from that for supplies?

32.   Explain how inventory Regulations provide an incentive for a corporation to dispose of its obsolete excess inventories.

33.   Contrast the procedures for changing to the LIFO inventory method with the general requirements for making a change in an accounting method.

34.   Discuss the problems that could result from footnote disclosures of net income computed by the FIFO method when the taxpayer uses the LIFO method to report its taxable income.

Problems

35.   L, M, and N are unrelated corporations engaged in real estate development. The three corporations formed a joint venture (treated as a partnership) to develop a tract of land. Assuming the venture does not have a natural business year, what tax year must the joint venture adopt under the following circumstances?

		Tax Year Ending	Interest in Joint Venture
a.	L	Sept. 30	33%
	M	June 30	33%
	N	March 31	34%
b.	L	Sept. 30	20%
	M	June 30	60%
	N	March 31	20%
c.	L	Jan. 31	30%
	M	Jan. 31	25%
	N	Dec. 31	45%

36.   What tax years should be used in the following cases?

a.   A department store operated by an S corporation.

b.   A public accounting practice operated by a professional corporation.

c.   A farm operated by a partnership whose partners are calendar year individuals.

37.   Z conducted his professional practice through Z, Inc. The corporation uses a fiscal year ending September 30 even though the business purpose test for a fiscal year cannot be satisfied. For the year ending September 30, 1989, the corporation paid Z a salary of $150,000, and during the period January through September 1989, the corporation paid Z a salary of $120,000.

    a.   How much salary should Z receive during the period October 1 through December 31, 1989?

    b.   Assume Z received only $30,000 salary during the period October 1 through December 31, 1989. What would be the consequences to Z, Inc.?

38.   P Corporation is in the business of sales and home deliveries of fuel oil and currently uses a calendar year for reporting its taxable income. However, P's natural business year ends April 30. For the short period, January 1, 1989, through April 30, 1989, the corporation earned $26,000. Assume the corporate tax rates are as follows: 15% on taxable income of $50,000 or less, 25% on taxable income over $50,000 but not over $75,000, and 34% on taxable income over $75,000.

    a.   What must P Corporation do to change its taxable year?

    b.   Compute P Corporation's tax for the short period.

39.   L owned a building that he had leased to T. In 1989, T prepaid the 1990 rent. During 1990, the building was destroyed by fire. Under the lease agreement, L was required to refund $8,000 in 1990 rent to T. L, a cash basis taxpayer, was in the 28% tax bracket in 1989 but was in the 15% bracket in 1990. What are the effects of the repayment on L's and T's 1990 tax liabilities?

40.   Compute the taxpayer's income or deductions for 1989 using (1) the cash basis and (2) the accrual basis for each of the following:

    a.   In 1989, the taxpayer purchased new equipment for $100,000. The taxpayer paid $25,000 in cash and gave a $75,000 interest-bearing note for the balance. The equipment has an ACRS life of five years, the mid-year convention applies, and the § 179 election was not made.

    b.   In December 1989, the taxpayer collected $10,000 for January rents. In January 1990, the taxpayer collected $2,000 for December 1989 rents.

    c.   In December 1989, the taxpayer paid office equipment insurance premiums for January–June 1990 of $30,000.

41.   Which of the following businesses must use the accrual method of accounting?

    a.   A corporation with annual gross receipts of $12 million from equipment rentals.

    b.   A partnership (not a tax shelter) engaged in farming and with annual gross receipts of $8 million.

    c.   A corporation that acts as an insurance agent, with annual gross receipts of $1 million.

    d.   A manufacturer with annual gross receipts of $600,000.

    e.   A retailer with annual gross receipts of $250,000.

42.   Z Company calculated its accrual basis income for its first year of operations. Net income before tax was $30,000. For tax purposes, the company would like to elect the method that will minimize its taxable

income for the year. Compute Z's minimum taxable income, given the following information at the end of the first year:

Inventory	$12,000
Accounts receivable	25,000
Office supplies	1,800
Prepaid insurance (6 months)	1,200
Accounts payable (merchandise)	3,000

43. T, a cash basis taxpayer, has substantial income from trust funds established for him. He has recently purchased some unincorporated businesses. For each of the following businesses, explain which accounting method should be used and why that method should be used:

    a. *Cattle raising.* In October, T will purchase cattle that will be shipped to a feed lot operated by an independent party. The feed lot charges will be paid in December, and the cattle will be sold in January. A bank loan (with recourse) will finance the feed lot charges. The loan will be retired out of the proceeds from the sale of the cattle.

    b. *Vegetable growing.* Vegetables will be raised under a contract with a large canner. At the time of delivery, the canner will issue a note to T. The note is due in the year following the year of delivery and has a market value equal to its face amount.

    c. *Land development.* Lots are sold for cash and are fully developed, except for sewerage. For each lot sold, T must pay the city $800 for sewerage lines. However, the payment is deferred until the year after the lot is sold.

44. T receives appliances from the manufacturer on consignment and collects a 5% commission on any sales made during the year. T is an accrual basis taxpayer and made total sales during the year of $750,000. However, the manufacturer is usually a few weeks behind in recording T's sales and at the end of the year recorded only $600,000 in sales. T argues that he should report income for the year of only $30,000 (5% × $600,000), since that was all he had a right to receive for the year. T had no right to the commissions on the other $150,000 sales until the manufacturer reported them in the following year. What is T's correct taxable income for the year? Explain.

45. When is the economic performance test satisfied in the following cases?

    a. R Corporation sponsored a contest to promote the company's products. In 1989, the winner was announced. The winner is to receive $10,000 each year for 10 years.

    b. S Corporation is a strip miner and is liable for reclaiming the land. The estimated reclamation cost for land mined in 1989 was $200,000. The company hired Z Corporation to perform the work. Z reclaimed the land in 1990, and S Corporation paid Z in 1991.

    c. T Corporation guarantees its products against all defects for 12 months. At the end of 1989, several customers had returned products for corrections of defects. The estimated cost of servicing the goods was $150,000. All claims were valid, and the claims were satisfied in 1990.

d.   P Corporation had state taxable income of $100,000 for 1989. However, the taxes on the income were not actually paid until the company filed its tax return in March 1990.

46.   In 1989, the taxpayer was required to switch from the cash to the accrual basis of accounting for sales and cost of goods sold. Taxable income for 1989 computed under the cash basis was $40,000.

	Beginning of the Year	End of the Year
Accounts receivable	$28,000	$30,000
Accounts payable	10,000	9,000
Inventory	4,900	4,000

Compute the following:

a.   The adjustment due to the change in accounting method.

b.   The accrual basis taxable income for 1989.

47.   Z Corporation has incorrectly used a reserve for liability under warranties for the three preceding years.

	(1) Taxable Income before Warranty	(2) Net Addition to Reserve	(3) Cost of Warranty Services Rendered	(1) – (2) Taxable Income Reported	(1) – (3) Correct Taxable Income
1987	$18,000	$ 5,000	$1,000	$13,000	$17,000
1988	22,000	3,000	4,000	19,000	18,000
1989	36,000	6,000	2,000	30,000	34,000
	$76,000	$14,000	$7,000	$62,000	$69,000

a.   Compute the adjustment due to change in accounting method as of January 1, 1990.

b.   Assume the IRS requires Z Corporation to change its method of accounting. What would you recommend with respect to the disposition of the adjustment?

48.   In 1989, the taxpayer changed from the cash to the accrual basis of accounting for sales, cost of goods sold, and accrued expenses. Taxable income for 1989 computed under the cash method was $45,000. Relevant account balances are as follows:

	Beginning of the Year	End of the Year
Accounts receivable	$ 4,000	$ 9,000
Accounts payable	–0–	–0–
Accrued expenses	2,000	1,000
Inventory	10,000	15,000

a.   Compute the accrual basis taxable income for 1989 and the adjustment due to the change in accounting method.

b.   Assuming the changes were voluntary, how will the adjustment due to change be treated?

49. T, a cash basis taxpayer, has agreed to sell land to Z, Inc., a well-established and highly profitable company. Z is willing to (1) pay $100,000 cash or (2) pay $25,000 cash and the balance ($75,000) plus interest at 10% (the Federal rate) in two years. T is in the 35% marginal tax bracket (combined Federal and state) for all years, and he believes he can reinvest the sales proceeds and earn a 14% before-tax rate of return.

    a. Should T accept the deferred payments option if his basis in the land is $10,000?

    b. Do you think your results would change if T's basis in the land is $90,000?

50. S, who is not a dealer, sold an apartment house to P during the current year (1990). The closing statement for the sale is as follows:

Total selling price		$100,000
Add: P's share of property taxes (6 months) paid by S		2,500
Less: S's 11% mortgage assumed by P	$55,000	
P's refundable binder ("earnest money") paid in 1989	1,000	
P's 11% installment note given to S	30,000	
S's real estate commissions and attorney's fees	7,500	(93,500)
Cash paid to S at closing		$ 9,000
Cash due from P = $9,000 + $7,500 expenses		$ 16,500

    During 1990, S collected $4,000 in principal on the installment note and $2,000 interest. S's basis in the property was $70,000 [$85,000 − $15,000 (depreciation)], and there was $9,000 in potential depreciation recapture under § 1250. The Federal rate is 9%.

    a. Compute the following:

        1. Total gain.

        2. Contract price.

        3. Payments received in the year of sale.

        4. Recognized gain in the year of sale and the character of such gain.

    (*Hint:* Think carefully about the manner in which the property taxes are handled before you begin your computations.)

    b. Same as (a)(2) and (3), except S's basis in the property was $45,000.

    c. Assume that S was considering selling the apartment house but there was no mortgage on the property. Would there be any tax benefits if S borrowed on the property before the sale?

51. On June 30, 1989, T sold property for $250,000 cash on the date of sale and a $750,000 note due on September 30, 1990. No interest was stated in the contract. The present value of the note (using 13.2%, which was the Federal rate) was $640,000. T's basis in the property was $400,000, and $40,000 of the gain was depreciation recapture under § 1245. Expenses of the sale totaled $10,000, and T was not a dealer in the property sold.

    a.   Compute T's gain to be reported in 1989.

    b.   Compute T's interest income for 1990.

52.   On July 1, 1988, a cash basis taxpayer sold land for $400,000 due on the date of the sale and $3,000,000 principal and $763,200 interest (12%) due on June 30, 1990. The seller's basis in the land was $500,000. The Federal short-term rate was 13%, compounded semiannually.

    a.   Compute the seller's interest income and gain in 1988, 1989, and 1990.

    b.   Same as (a), except that the amount due in two years was $1,000,000 principal and $254,400 interest and the purchaser will use the cash method to account for interest.

53.   M made an installment sale of land and a building to N. There was no ordinary income recapture on the building. At the time of the sale, the Federal rate was 12% and the market rate on similar contracts was 15%. Under the contract, N would make payments as follows:

Cash at closing, July 1, 1989	$ 50,000
Interest at 10%, due June 30, 1990*	30,750
Interest at 10%, due June 30, 1991*	30,750
Principal due June 30, 1991	300,000

    * Interest is compounded semiannually.

    a.   Will interest be imputed on the contract?

    b.   Assuming M is a cash basis taxpayer, what is her interest income for 1989 under the contract?

    c.   Assuming N is an accrual basis taxpayer, what is her interest expense for 1989 under the contract?

54.   On December 30, 1989, Father sold land to Son for $10,000 cash and a 7% installment note with a face amount of $190,000. In 1990, after paying $30,000 on the principal of the note, Son sold the land. In 1991, Son paid Father $25,000 on the note principal. Father's basis in the land was $50,000.

    a.   Assuming Son sold the land for $250,000, compute Father's taxable gain in 1990.

    b.   Assuming Son sold the land for $150,000, compute Father's taxable gain in 1990.

55.   X sold land to an unrelated party in 1988. X's basis in the land was $40,000, and the selling price was $100,000—$25,000 payable at closing and $25,000 (plus 10% interest) due January 1, 1989, 1990, and 1991. What would be the tax consequences of the following? [Treat each part independently and assume (1) X did not elect out of the installment method and (2) the installment obligations have values equal to their face amounts.]

    a.   In 1989, X gave to his daughter the right to collect all future payments on the installment obligations.

b. In 1989, after collecting the payment due on January 1, X transferred the installment obligation to his 100% controlled corporation in exchange for additional shares of stock.

c. X received on December 31, 1989, the payment due on January 1, 1990. On December 15, 1990, X died, and the remaining installment obligation was transferred to X's estate. The estate collected the amount due on January 1, 1991.

56. T, a cash basis taxpayer, sold stock in 1989 for $40,000 plus 12% notes with a face amount of $60,000 and a fair market value of only $40,000. T's basis in the stock was $25,000, and the fair market value was $85,000. In 1990, T collected the face amounts of the notes. What is T's income in 1989 and 1990 from the sale and collections, presuming she elects out of the installment method?

57. T, who is not a dealer in real estate, sold rental real estate for $75,000 cash and $225,000 due in three years, plus interest equal to the Federal rate. T's cost of the real estate was $90,000, and there was no depreciation recapture. T did not elect out of the installment method. Determine the tax consequences of the following:

a. When the $225,000 note came due, the purchaser defaulted and T repossessed the property. The property's value was $300,000.

b. One year before maturity, T borrowed $100,000 and used the installment obligation as collateral for the loan.

58. The R Construction Company reports its income by the completed contract method. At the end of 1989, the company completed a contract to construct a building at a total cost of $980,000. The contract price was $1,200,000. However, the customer refused to accept the work and would not pay anything on the contract because he claimed the roof did not meet specifications. R's engineers estimated it would cost $140,000 to bring the roof up to the customer's standards. In 1990, the dispute was settled in the customer's favor; the roof was improved at a cost of $170,000, and the customer accepted the building and paid the $1,200,000.

a. What would be the effects of the above on R's taxable income for 1989 and 1990?

b. Same as (a), except R had $1,100,000 accumulated cost under the contract at the end of 1989.

59. X Company is a construction company with average annual gross receipts of $3 million. Y Company is also in the construction business but has average annual gross receipts of $15 million. Both companies use the completed contract method, and the contracts require 18 months to complete. Which of the following costs would be allocated to construction in progress by X and Y?

a. The payroll taxes on direct labor.

b. The current services pension costs for employees whose wages are included in direct labor.

c. Accelerated depreciation on equipment used on contracts.

d. Sales tax on materials assigned to contracts.

e.   The past service costs in employees whose wages are included in direct labor.

f.   Bidding expenses for contracts awarded.

60. Indicate the accounting method that should be used to compute the income from the following contracts:

a.   A contract to build six jet aircraft.

b.   A contract to build a new home. The contractor's average annual gross receipts are $15 million.

c.   A contract to manufacture 3,000 pairs of boots for a large retail chain. The manufacturer has several contracts to produce the same boot for other retailers.

d.   A contract to pave a parking lot. The contractor's average annual gross receipts are $2 million.

61. Determine whether the following costs must be added to inventory:

a.   The taxpayer bottles wine as part of his wholesale business and must incur $150,000 in warehousing to store the wine for six months before the wine is offered for sale. The taxpayer owns the warehouse.

b.   Interest allocable to the wine in storage [in (a)] is $30,000.

c.   A real estate developer incurred $50,000 interest during construction.

d.   A chain of retail stores operates a warehouse. The total cost of operating the warehouse (e.g., depreciation, wages) for the year was $2 million, of which $500,000 is attributable to (allocated on the basis of costs) storing goods still on hand at year-end.

62. H Company is a manufacturer. Indicate how the costs of the following affect H Company's inventory valuation for tax purposes, assuming the company uses the FIFO inventory method.

a.   Depreciation on computers used by the data processing department. The company uses the straight-line method for financial reporting and the double-declining balance method for tax purposes.

b.   Salaries for the personnel department.

c.   Costs of the shipping and receiving department.

d.   Depreciation on the factory for one week when the plant was closed because of a supplier's strike.

63. In 1989, T changed from the use of the lower of cost or market FIFO method to the LIFO method. The ending inventory for 1988 was computed as follows:

Item	FIFO Cost	Replacement Cost	Lower of Cost or Market
A	$10,000	$18,000	$10,000
B	25,000	20,000	20,000
			$30,000

a. What is the correct beginning inventory in 1989 under the LIFO method?

b. What immediate tax consequences (if any) would result from the switch to LIFO?

Research Problems

Research Problem 1   R Company is a wholesaler with a fiscal year ending October 31, after it has shipped all of its Christmas goods. Management of R is considering changing its terms of sale for some of its goods so that the goods are on consignment until November 30, and title does not pass to the retailer until that date. Under present terms, title to the goods passes at the time of shipment. Management would like to know the tax consequences of the change in terms.

Research Problem 2   C (not a dealer in real estate) sold land to a developer who built condominiums on the property. The sales price was $400,000. After C had collected $200,000 on the contract, the developer defaulted. C exercised his right of foreclosure and received the land and condominiums in full settlement of the debt. The value of the property C received was $300,000 ($200,000 plus $100,000 improvements), and C's original basis in the land was $75,000. Is C required to recognize gain from the foreclosure?

Research Problem 3   In November 1989, A agreed to purchase stock from B for $1,000,000. The transaction was to be closed on December 28, 1989. In early December 1989, B became concerned about the taxes due on the sale in 1989. B suggested that the transaction be deferred until January 1990, but A insisted that the stock be transferred on December 28, 1989. A and B agreed that the cash paid by A on December 28, 1989, would be held by the First Bank as A's escrow agent, and the funds would be dispersed to B on January 4, 1990. The IRS agent insists that the escrow amount was constructively received by B in 1989 and that B therefore cannot defer his gain until 1990 under the installment sales rules. Is the agent correct?

Partial list of research aids:

Reed v. Comm., 83–2 USTC ¶9728, 53 AFTR2d 84–335 (CA–1, 1983).

Research Problem 4   In November 1989, M Corporation's accountant discovered that one of the company's warehouses was empty. The perpetual inventory records indicated that $200,000 of merchandise should have been in the warehouse. For 1989, the missing inventory was not included in the company's ending inventory. The stolen merchandise thus became a part of cost of goods sold for the year. The IRS claims the missing merchandise should have been deducted as a theft loss and under Reg. §§ 1.165–1(d)(2)(i) and 1.165–8(a)(2) is not deductible if there is a reasonable prospect for recovery. Moreover, the company had good prospects of recovery of the loss from the employees, insurance company, or auditors. Assuming the IRS is correct—that there is a reasonable prospect for recovery as of the end of the year—is the taxpayer foreclosed from deducting the $200,000 in 1989?

Partial list of research aids:

National Home Products, Inc., 71 T.C. 501 (1979).

Research Problem 5   You recently contracted to perform tax services for a new funeral home. In preparing the initial tax return, you must decide whether the funeral home can use the cash method of accounting. When discussing this issue with the manager, the manager points out that the company is actually a service business and that the only materials involved are caskets, which average only 15% of the price of a funeral. Is the funeral home required to use the accrual method of accounting?

19

DEFERRED COMPENSATION

This chapter discusses the various types of deferred compensation arrangements available to employees and self-employed individuals. *Deferred compensation* refers to an arrangement under which an employee receives compensation after the period when the services for which the compensation is paid were performed.[1] The tax law encourages employers to offer deferred compensation plans to their employees to supplement the Federal Social Security retirement system. Contributions to a qualified pension, profit sharing, or stock bonus plan are immediately deductible by the employer. Employees are generally not taxed until the funds are made available to them. In addition, the income earned on the contributions to the plan is not subject to tax until such amounts are made available to the employees.

The following is a sample of various deferred compensation arrangements being offered to employees:

- Qualified profit sharing plans.

- Qualified pension plans.

- Employee stock ownership plans.

- Cash or deferred arrangement plans.

- Tax-deferred annuities.

- Incentive stock option plans.

- Nonqualified deferred compensation plans.

- Restricted property plans.

- Cafeteria benefit plans.

In addition to the various types of deferred compensation, employees may receive other valuable fringe benefits. Examples of such benefits include group term life insurance, medical reimbursement plans, company-supplied automobiles, education expense reimbursement plans, and group legal services.[2]

The Code, in certain circumstances, prohibits a deduction for particular types of fringe benefits such as a golden parachute payment. Refer to the subsequent discussion under Nonqualified Deferred Compensation Plans.

QUALIFIED PENSION, PROFIT SHARING, AND STOCK BONUS PLANS

The Federal government has encouraged private pension and profit sharing plans to keep retired people from becoming dependent on the government. Therefore, the Federal tax law provides substantial tax benefits for plans that meet certain requirements. The major requirement for qualification is that a plan not discriminate in favor of highly compensated employees.

Types of Plans

There are three types of qualified plans: pension, profit sharing, and stock bonus plans.

---

1. For a more comprehensive definition of deferred compensation, see the Glossary of Tax Terms in Appendix C.

2. Refer to the discussions in chapters 4 and 5.

Pension Plans.   A *pension plan* is a deferred compensation arrangement that provides for systematic payments of definitely determinable retirement benefits to employees who meet the requirements set forth in the plan. Benefits are generally measured by and based on such factors as years of service and employee compensation. Employer contributions under a qualified pension plan must *not* depend on profits. In addition, they must be sufficient to provide definitely determinable benefits on some actuarial basis (except for a defined contribution pension plan).

There are basically two types of qualified pension plans: a defined contribution plan and a defined benefit plan.

A *defined contribution pension plan* (or money purchase plan) requires a separate account for each participant, with benefits based solely on (1) the amount contributed and (2) income from the fund that accrues to the participant's account.[3] In essence, the plan defines the amount the employer is required to contribute (e.g., a flat dollar amount, an amount based on a special formula, or an amount equal to a certain percentage of compensation). Consequently, actuarial calculations are not required to determine the employer's annual contribution. Upon retirement, the employee's pension depends on the value of the employee's account. It is possible, although not required, for a plan to require or permit employee contributions to the pension fund.

A *defined benefit plan* includes a formula that defines the benefits employees are to receive.[4] Under such a plan, an employer must make annual contributions based upon actuarial computations that will be sufficient to pay the vested retirement benefits. If a plan document so permits, employee contributions may be made to the pension fund. Separate accounts are not maintained for each participant. A defined benefit plan provides some sense of security for employees, since the benefits may be expressed in fixed dollar amounts.

EXAMPLE 1   The qualified pension plan of X Company calls for both the employer and employee to contribute annually to the pension trust an amount equal to 5% of the employee's compensation. Since the rate of contribution of the employer is fixed, this pension plan is a defined contribution plan. If the plan called for contributions sufficient to provide retirement benefits equal to 30% of the employee's average salary for the last five years, it would be a defined benefit plan. □

Concept Summary 19–1 compares and contrasts a defined benefit plan and a defined contribution plan.

Profit Sharing Plans.   A *profit sharing plan* is a deferred compensation arrangement established and maintained by an employer to provide for employee participation in the company's profits. Contributions are paid from the current or accumulated profits of the employer to a trustee and are commingled in a single trust fund. Thus, an employer does not need a profit for the current year to make a contribution (the contribution can be from accumulated profits).

---

3. § 414(i).   4. § 414(j).

CONCEPT SUMMARY 19–1

Defined Benefit Plan and Defined Contribution Plan Compared

Defined Benefit Plan	Defined Contribution Plan
Includes a pension plan.	Includes profit sharing, stock bonus, money purchase, target benefit, qualified cash or deferred compensation, and employee stock ownership plans.
Determinable benefits based upon years of service and average compensation. Benefits calculated by a formula.	An account for each participant. Ultimate benefits depend upon investment performance.
Maximum annual *benefits* payable may not exceed the smaller of (a) $94,023 (in 1988 [5]) or (b) 100% of the participant's average earnings in the three highest years of employment.	Maximum annual *contribution* to an account may not exceed the smaller of (a) $30,000 [6] or (b) 25% of participant's compensation.
Forfeitures must reduce subsequent funding costs and cannot increase the benefits any participant can receive under the plan.	Forfeitures may be allocated to the accounts of remaining participants.
Subject to minimum funding requirement in order to avoid penalties.	Exempt from funding requirements.
Greater administrative and actuarial costs and greater reporting requirements.	Costs and reporting requirements less burdensome.
Subject to plan termination insurance.	Not subject to plan termination insurance.
More favorable to employees who are older when plan is adopted, since it is possible to fund higher benefits over a shorter period.	More favorable to younger employees, since over a longer period, higher benefits may result.

In a profit sharing plan, separate accounts are maintained for each participant. The plan must provide a definite, predetermined formula for allocating the contributions (made to the trustee) among the participants and for distributing the accumulated funds after a fixed number of years or the attainment of a stated age or on the occurrence of certain events such as illness, layoff, or retirement. A company is not required to contribute a definite, predetermined amount to the plan, although substantial and recurring

---

5. This amount is indexed annually. The indexed amount for 1989 was not available at the time of this writing.

6. The $30,000 amount becomes subject to indexing when the dollar limitation for a defined benefit plan exceeds $120,000.

contributions must be made to meet the permanency requirement. Forfeitures arising under this plan do not have to be used to reduce the employer's contribution. Instead, forfeitures may be used to increase the individual accounts of the remaining participants as long as such increases do not result in prohibited discrimination.[7] Since the primary emphasis of a profit sharing plan is not necessarily on retirement income, lump-sum payouts may be the normal method of distributing benefits to employees.

An employer may allow an employee to choose between receiving a specified amount of cash as current compensation and having this amount contributed to a qualified profit sharing plan. Such a cash or deferred profit sharing plan must satisfy the pension plan qualification rules. The plan must also prohibit the distribution of amounts attributable to employer contributions merely because of the completion of a stated period of plan participation or the passage of a fixed period of time. Also, nondiscrimination rules require a minimum number of lower-paid individuals to elect deferral.[8]

Stock Bonus Plans. A *stock bonus plan* is a form of deferred compensation, established and maintained by an employer to provide contributions of the employer's stock to the plan. There is no requirement that such contributions be dependent on profits. This plan is subject to the same requirements as a profit sharing plan for purposes of allocating and distributing the stock among the employees.[9] Any benefits of the plan are distributable in the form of stock of the employer company, except that distributable fractional shares may be paid in cash.

Employee Stock Ownership Plans. An *employee stock ownership plan* (ESOP) is a stock bonus trust that qualifies as a tax-exempt employee trust under § 401(a). Technically, an ESOP is a defined contribution plan that is either a qualified stock bonus plan or a stock bonus and a money purchase plan, each of which is qualified under § 401(a). An ESOP must be designed to invest primarily in qualifying employer securities.[10]

Since the corporation can contribute stock rather than cash, there is no cash flow drain. If stock is contributed, there is no cash outlay, and the corporation receives a tax deduction equal to the fair market value of the stock, with no gain or loss recognized by the employer under § 1032. The employer-corporation may deduct dividends paid in cash (or dividends used to repay ESOP loans) on shares held by an ESOP. One-half of the interest earned by an institutional lender or mutual fund on a loan to an ESOP may be excluded from gross income where the proceeds are used to buy employer securities. In addition, the tax savings accruing under the plan may have a favorable impact on working capital for the company. This plan provides flexibility, since contributions may vary from year to year and, in fact, may be omitted in any one year.[11]

A company can fund the ESOP by acquiring outstanding shares of stock from its shareholders, who receive capital gain treatment upon the sale of their stock. Owners of small closely held corporations may elect nonrecognition treatment for any gain realized on the sale of securities to an ESOP where qualified replacement property [defined in § 1042(c)(4)] is purchased during

---

7. Reg. §§ 1.401–1(b) and 1.401–4(a)(1)(iii).
8. §§ 401(k) and 402(a)(8).
9. Reg. § 1.401–1(b)(1)(iii).

10. § 4975(e)(7).

11. Reg. § 1.401–1(b)(2).

a 15-month period (beginning 3 months before the date of the sale and ending 12 months after such date).[12]

Employees are not subject to tax until they receive a distribution of stock from the trust. Any distribution of employer securities treated as a lump-sum distribution qualifies for postponement of recognition of the net unrealized appreciation in such securities in the year of distribution. Unless a taxpayer elects, such net unrealized appreciation is not included in the basis of the securities, and the appreciation is recognized in a subsequent taxable transaction.[13] Distributions to employees may be made entirely in cash or partly in cash and partly in employer securities. A participant must have the right to demand the entire distribution in the form of employer securities.[14]

EXAMPLE 2   The ESOP of T Company borrows $100,000 from City Bank. The loan is secured by the stock interest and is guaranteed by the company. The ESOP buys stock for the trust from a shareholder of T Company for $100,000. The shares are then allocated among the employees' retirement accounts. The shareholder obtains capital gain treatment on the sale or can elect nonrecognition treatment if qualified replacement securities are purchased during a 15-month period. T Company makes deductible contributions to the ESOP, which, in turn, pays off the loan. The bank can exclude from gross income 50% of any interest earned on the loan to T Company. □

Qualification Requirements

A number of qualification requirements must be satisfied in order for a plan to receive favorable tax treatment. To be *qualified,* a plan must meet the following requirements:

- Exclusive benefit requirement.
- Nondiscrimination rules.
- Participation and coverage requirements.
- Vesting rules.
- Distribution requirements.

These qualification rules are highly technical and numerous. Thus, an employer should submit a retirement plan to the IRS for a determination letter regarding the qualified status of the plan and trust. A favorable determination letter may be expected within six to twelve months, indicating that the plan meets the qualification requirements and that the trust is tax exempt. However, the continued qualification of the plan depends upon its actual operations. Therefore, the operations of the plan should be reviewed periodically.

Exclusive Benefit Requirement.   A pension, profit sharing, or stock bonus trust must be created by an employer for the exclusive benefit of employees or

---

12. Refer to the discussion in chapter 15.   14. § 409(h)(1).
13. §§ 402(e)(4)(D)(ii) and (J).

their beneficiaries. Under a prudent man concept, the IRS specifies four investment conditions for meeting the *exclusive benefit* requirement: [15]

- The cost of the investment must not exceed the fair market value at the time of purchase.

- A fair return commensurate with prevailing rates must be provided.

- Sufficient liquidity must be maintained to permit distributions in accordance with the terms of the qualified plan.

- The safeguards and diversity that a prudent investor would adhere to must be present.

Nondiscrimination Rules. The contributions and benefits under a plan must *not discriminate* in favor of highly compensated employees. A plan is not considered discriminatory merely because the contributions and benefits on behalf of the employees bear a uniform relationship to their compensation.[16] Thus, a pension plan that provides for the allocation of employer contributions based upon a flat three percent of each employee's compensation would not be discriminatory despite the fact that highly paid employees receive greater benefits.

Qualified plans may be integrated with Social Security (employer FICA contributions for covered employees may be taken into account) in order to avoid giving lower-level employees proportionately greater benefits or contributions. Beginning in 1989, integrated plans may no longer reduce a participant's benefits or contributions to less than one-half of what they would have been without integration.

Participation and Coverage Requirements. A qualified plan must provide, at a minimum, that all employees in the covered group who are 21 years of age are eligible to participate after completing one year of service. A year of service is generally defined as the completion of 1,000 hours of service within a measuring period of twelve consecutive months. As an alternative, where the plan provides for 100 percent vesting of an employee's accrued benefits upon commencing participation, such participation may be postponed until the later of two years from the date of employment or age 21.[17] Once the age and service requirements are met, an employee must begin participating no later than the earlier of the following:

- The first day of the first plan year beginning after the date upon which the requirements were satisfied.

- Six months after the date on which the requirements were satisfied.[18]

EXAMPLE 3

X Corporation has a calendar year retirement plan covering its employees. The corporation adopts the most restrictive eligibility rules permitted. Employee A, age 21, is hired on January 31, 1989, and meets the service requirement over the next twelve months (completes at least 1,000 hours by January 31, 1990). A must be included in this plan no later than July

---

15. § 401(a); Rev.Rul. 65–178, 1965–2 C.B. 94, and Rev.Rul. 73–380, 1973–2 C.B. 124.

16. §§ 401(a)(4) and (5).

17. §§ 410(a)(1)(A) and (B).

18. § 410(a)(4).

31, 1990, because the six-month limitation would be applicable. If the company had adopted the two-year participation rule, A must be included in the plan no later than July 31, 1991. ☐

Since a qualified plan must be primarily for the benefit of employees and be nondiscriminatory, the plan has to cover a reasonable percentage of the company employees. A plan will be qualified only if it satisfies one of the following tests: [19]

- The plan benefits at least 70 percent of all non-highly compensated employees (the percentage test).

- The plan benefits a percentage of non-highly compensated employees that is at least 70 percent of the percentage of highly compensated employees benefiting under the plan (the ratio test).

- The plan meets the average benefits test.

If a company has no highly compensated employees, the retirement plan would automatically satisfy these coverage rules.

To satisfy the *average benefits test,* the plan must benefit such employees as qualify under a classification set up by the employer and found by the Secretary of the Treasury not to be discriminatory in favor of highly compensated employees (the classification test). In addition, the average benefit percentage for non-highly compensated employees must be at least 70 percent of the average benefit percentage for highly compensated employees. The *average benefit percentage* means, with respect to any group of employees, the average of the benefit percentages calculated separately with respect to each employee in such group. The term *benefit percentage* means the employer-provided contributions (including forfeitures) or benefits of an employee under all qualified plans of the employer, expressed as a percentage of such employee's compensation.

An employee is *highly compensated* if, at any time during the year or the preceding year, the employee satisfies any of the following: [20]

- Was a 5 percent owner of the company.

- Received more than $78,353 (in 1988) in annual compensation from the employer.

- Received more than $52,235 (in 1988) in annual compensation from the employer *and* was a member of the top-paid group of the employer.

- Was an officer of the company and received compensation greater than 150 percent of the maximum statutory dollar amount of the annual addition to a defined contribution plan ($30,000 $\times$ 150% = $45,000).

An employee who is in the group that consists of the top 20 percent of the employees on the basis of compensation paid during the year is a member of the top-paid group. The $52,235 and $78,353 amounts are indexed annually.[21]

An additional minimum participation test must also be met. A plan must cover at least 40 percent of all employees or, if fewer, at least 50 employees. In determining all employees, nonresident aliens, certain union members, and

---

19. § 410(b).

20. §§ 401(a)(4) and 414(q).

21. The indexed amounts for 1989 were not available at the time of this writing.

employees not fulfilling the minimum age or years-of-service requirement of the plan may be excluded.[22]

EXAMPLE 4

M Corporation's retirement plan meets the 70% test (the percentage test) because 70% of all non-highly compensated employees are benefited. The company has 100 employees, but only 38 of these employees are covered by the plan. Therefore, this retirement plan does not meet the minimum participation requirement. □

Vesting Requirements. An employee's right to accrued benefits derived from his or her own contributions must be nonforfeitable from the date of contribution. The accrued benefits derived from employer contributions must be nonforfeitable in accordance with one of two alternative minimum vesting schedules. The purpose of the *vesting requirements* is to protect an employee who has worked a reasonable period of time for an employer from losing employer contributions because of being fired or changing jobs.

A plan will not be a qualified plan unless a participant's employer-provided benefits vest at least as rapidly as under one of *two alternative minimum vesting schedules.* A plan satisfies the *first alternative* if a participant has a nonforfeitable right to 100 percent of the participant's accrued benefits derived from employer contributions upon completion of five years of service (five-year or cliff vesting). The *second alternative* is satisfied if a participant has a nonforfeitable right at least equal to a percentage of the accrued benefits derived from employer contributions determined as depicted in Figure 19–1 (graded vesting). The two alternative vesting schedules do not apply to top-heavy plans.

Participants with at least three years of service may elect to remain under the less liberal vesting schedules in effect before 1989.[23]

FIGURE 19–1   Three-to-Seven Year Vesting

Years of Service	Nonforfeitable Percentage
3	20%
4	40%
5	60%
6	80%
7 or more	100%

EXAMPLE 5

M has six years of service completed as of February 2, 1989, his employment anniversary date. If his defined benefit plan has a five-year (cliff) vesting schedule, M is vested in 100% of his accrued benefits. If, however, the plan uses the graded vesting rule, M's nonforfeitable percentage is 80%. The cliff vesting rule minimizes administration expenses for a company and provides the most vesting for a long-term employee. □

22. §§ 401(a)(26) and 410(b)(3) and (4).
23. §§ 411(a)(2) and (10)(B). Prior to 1989, three alternative minimum vesting schedules were in effect (the 10-year rule, the 5-to-15 year rule, and the Rule of 45).

Distribution Requirements.   Uniform *minimum distribution rules* exist for all qualified defined benefit and defined contribution plans, Individual Retirement Accounts (IRAs) and annuities, unfunded deferred compensation plans of state and local governments and tax-exempt employers, and tax-sheltered custodial accounts and annuities. Distributions must begin no later than April 1 of the calendar year following the calendar year in which the participant attains age 70½. This commencement date is not affected by the actual date of retirement or termination.[24]

Once age 70½ is reached, minimum annual distributions must be made over the life of the participant or the lives of the participant and a designated individual beneficiary. The amount of the required minimum distribution for a particular year is determined by dividing the account balance as of December 31 of the prior year by the applicable life expectancy. Life expectancy of the owner and his or her beneficiary is based upon the expected return multiples in the Regulations, using ages attained within the calendar year the participant reaches age 70½.[25]

EXAMPLE 6

B reaches age 70½ in 1989, and he will also be 71 in 1989. His retirement account (an IRA) has a balance of $120,000 on December 31, 1988. B must withdraw $7,843 for the 1989 calendar year, assuming his multiple is 15.3 ($120,000 ÷ 15.3). This distribution need not be made until April 1, 1990, but a second distribution must be made by December 31, 1990. □

Failure to make a minimum required distribution to a particular participant results in a 50 percent nondeductible excise tax on the excess in any taxable year of the amount that should have been distributed over the amount that actually was distributed. The tax is imposed on the individual required to take the distribution (the payee).[26] The Secretary of the Treasury is authorized to waive the tax for a given taxpayer year if the taxpayer is able to establish that the shortfall is due to reasonable error and that reasonable steps are being taken to remedy the shortfall.

If a taxpayer receives an *early distribution* from a qualified retirement plan, a 10 percent additional tax is levied on the full amount of any distribution includible in gross income.[27] For this purpose, the term qualified retirement plan includes a qualified defined benefit plan or defined contribution plan, a tax-sheltered annuity or custodial account, or an IRA. Certain distributions, however, are *not* treated as early distributions:

- Made on or after the date the employee attains age 59½.
- Made to a beneficiary (or the estate of an employee) on or after the death of the employee.
- Attributable to the employee's being disabled.
- Made as part of a scheduled series of substantially equal periodic payments (made not less frequently than annually) for the life of the participant (or the joint lives of the participant and the participant's beneficiary).

24. § 401(a)(9).
25. Reg. § 1.72–9. Refer to chapter 4.

26. § 4974(a).
27. § 72(t). See Lt.Rul. 8837071.

- Made to an employee after separation from service because of early retirement under the plan after attaining age 55. This exception to early distribution treatment does not apply to an IRA.

- Used to pay medical expenses to the extent that the expenses are deductible under § 213 (determined regardless of whether or not the taxpayer itemizes deductions). This exception to early distribution treatment does not apply to an IRA.

A 15 percent excise tax is imposed on *excess distributions* from qualified plans.[28] The tax is levied on the individual with respect to whom the excess distribution is made and is reduced by the amount of the tax imposed on early distributions (to the extent attributable to the excess distribution). An excess distribution is the aggregate amount of the retirement distributions during the taxable year for an individual to the extent such amount exceeds the greater of $150,000 or $112,500 (1988 indexed amount is $117,529). Thus, for 1989 the annual limitation is $150,000. Once the indexed $112,500 amount exceeds the $150,000, the indexed amount will become the annual limit. The following distributions are *not* subject to this limitation:

- Any retirement distribution made after the death of the individual.

- Any retirement distribution payable to an alternate payee in conformance with a qualified domestic relations order.

- Any retirement distribution attributable to the employee's investment in the contract (after-tax contributions).

- Any retirement distribution not included in gross income by reason of a rollover contribution.

If the taxpayer elects lump-sum distribution treatment,[29] the $150,000 limit is applied separately to such lump-sum distribution, and the limit is increased to five times the generally applicable limit with respect to the lump-sum distribution ($750,000).

EXAMPLE 7	E, age 65, has accumulated $960,000 in a defined contribution plan, $105,000 of which represents her own after-tax contributions. Receiving a lump-sum distribution would result in an excise tax of $15,750.

Account balance	$960,000
Less after-tax contributions	(105,000)
Less lump-sum limitation	(750,000)
Amount subject to tax	$105,000
15% excise tax	× .15
Excise tax due	$ 15,750

---

28. § 4981A.
29. Refer to chapter 16 for the definition of a lump-sum distribution.

If E receives the distribution in the form of an annuity over her expected lifetime of 20 years, her yearly distributions of $48,000 plus related interest would probably be less than the $150,000 annual distribution limit.

$\square$

A grandfather provision exists with respect to accrued benefits as of August 1, 1986.[30]

Tax Consequences to the Employee and Employer

In General.   Although employer contributions to qualified plans are generally deductible immediately (subject to contribution and deductibility rules), these amounts are not subject to taxation until distributed to employees.[31] If benefits are paid with respect to an employee (to a creditor of the employee, a child of the employee, etc.), the benefits paid would be treated as if paid to the employee. When benefits are distributed to employees, or paid with respect to an employee, the employer does not receive another deduction.

The tax benefit to the employee amounts to a substantial tax deferral and may be viewed as an interest-free loan from the government to the trust fund. Another advantage of a qualified plan is that any income earned by the trust is not taxable to the trust.[32] Employees, in effect, are taxed on such earnings when they receive the retirement benefits.

The taxation of amounts received by employees in period or installment payments is generally subject to the annuity rules in § 72 (refer to chapter 4). Employee contributions have previously been subject to tax and are therefore included in the employee's "investment in the contract." There are two other alternative options for benefit distributions. A taxpayer may roll over the benefits into an IRA or another qualified employer retirement plan. Also, a taxpayer may receive the distribution in a lump-sum payment.

Lump-Sum Distributions from Qualified Plans.   The annuity rules do not apply to a lump-sum distribution. All such payments are taxed in one year. Since lump-sum payments have been accumulated over a number of years and bunching retirement benefits into one taxable year may impose a high tax burden because of progressive rates, for many years the law has provided favorable tax treatment for certain lump-sum distributions. Major changes were made in the lump-sum distribution rules by TRA of 1986. Transitional provisions allow pre-1987 rules to be elected on a limited basis by a participant who has attained age 50 before January 1, 1986 (born before 1936). Consequently, the pre-1987 rules related to this election are discussed first.

Under the pre-1987 rules, the taxable amount is allocated between a capital gain portion and an ordinary income portion (which may be subject to a special 10-year averaging treatment).[33] That portion attributable to the employee's service after 1973 is included as ordinary income when received and may be taxed under the 10-year averaging provision. An employee must be a plan participant for at least five years to take advantage of the 10-year averaging option. It is possible to defer tax on some or all of the distribution,

---

30. § 4981A(c)(5).

31. § 402(a)(1).

32. § 501(a).

33. § 402(e)(1)(C) of the IRC of 1954.

provided that the employee elects to roll over the distribution by transferring the proceeds to an IRA.[34]

An employee may elect to treat all of the distribution as ordinary income subject to the 10-year forward averaging provision.[35] In some instances, ordinary income treatment is preferable to long-term capital gain treatment because of the favorable averaging technique.

Special preferential averaging treatment of qualified lump-sum distributions can be used only once during a recipient's lifetime. In the case of a small lump-sum distribution amount, a recipient may prefer to pay ordinary income tax on the amount and save the averaging election for a larger lump-sum distribution in the future.

To determine the tax on a lump-sum distribution, it is necessary to compute the taxable portion of the distribution by subtracting employee contributions and the net unrealized appreciation in the value of any distributed securities of the employer corporation.[36] The taxable amount is then reduced by a minimum distribution allowance to arrive at the amount that is eligible for the 10-year income averaging provisions.[37] The portion of the lump-sum distribution that is treated as a long-term capital gain is equal to the following:

$$\text{Taxable amount} \times \frac{\text{Years of service before 1974}}{\text{Total years of service}}$$

(computed without being reduced by the minimum distribution allowance)

The applicable capital gain rate is 20 percent.

After 1986, subject to the transition rule for recipients born before 1936 mentioned earlier, the 10-year forward averaging rule for lump-sum distributions is replaced by a 5-year forward averaging rule.[38] Only one lump-sum distribution received after age 59½ is eligible for the averaging treatment. Furthermore, capital gain treatment for lump-sum distributions (associated with participation before 1974) is repealed. However, for a lump-sum distribution after December 31, 1986, and before January 1, 1992, an employee may elect capital gain treatment for a percentage of the amount that would have qualified for capital gain treatment before TRA of 1986 (see Figure 19–2).

FIGURE 19–2   Phase-Out of Capital Gain Percentage for Lump-Sum Distributions

Distributions during Calendar Year	Available Percentage
1987	100%
1988	95%
1989	75%
1990	50%
1991	25%
1992 and thereafter	0%

---

34. § 402(a)(5).

35. § 402(e)(4)(L).

36. § 402(e)(4)(J) provides that before any distribution a taxpayer may elect not to have this subtraction associated with employer securities apply.

37. § 402(e)(1)(D) defines the minimum distribution allowance as the smaller of $10,000 or one-half of the total taxable amount of the lump-sum distribution, reduced by 20% of the amount, if any, by which such total taxable amount exceeds $20,000. For lump-sum distributions of $70,000 or more, there will be no minimum distribution allowance.

38. § 402(e)(1).

EXAMPLE 8

T, age 65 and married, retires at the end of 1989 and receives a lump-sum distribution of $100,000 from his company's profit sharing plan. This plan includes $5,000 of his own contributions and $10,000 of unrealized appreciation on his employer's common stock. The distributee has been a participant in the plan for 20 years. Since T had attained age 50 before January 1, 1986, he is eligible to elect the pre-1987 10-year forward averaging technique (using 1986 rates and the zero bracket amount).[39] Refer to the computation model in Concept Summary 19–2.

Taxable portion of the lump-sum distribution
[$100,000 − $5,000 (employee contribution) − $10,000 (unrealized appreciation of employer securities)] $85,000

Less: Minimum distribution allowance
½ of the taxable amount up to $20,000 .... $10,000

Less: 20% of the taxable amount in excess of $20,000:
20% × ($85,000 − $20,000) .... (13,000)

Minimum distribution allowance .... -0-

Taxable amount subject to averaging $85,000

Computation of tax under 10-year averaging:
10 times the tax on $10,980
[(1/10 of $85,000) + $2,480][40] $11,900

$$\$11,900 \times \frac{16 \text{ (service after 1973)}}{20 \text{ (total service years)}} = \$9,520$$

(ordinary income tax due on ordinary income portion)

Long-term capital gain portion

$$\$85,000 \times \frac{4 \text{ (service before 1974)}}{20 \text{ (total service years)}} = \$17,000$$

Thus, T's capital gain on the distribution is $17,000 and is subject to a 20 percent capital gain rate. Here T may wish to elect to treat the entire distribution as ordinary income using the 10-year forward averaging approach. The tax liability of $11,900 would be less than if the 20 percent rate is applied to the capital gain portion [$9,520 + ($17,000 × 20%) = $12,920]. The capital gain on the unrealized appreciation in the employer's common stock is not taxable until T sells the stock. In essence, the cost basis of the securities to the trust becomes the tax basis to the employee.[41] If T keeps the securities until he dies, there may be some income tax savings on this gain to the extent the estate or the heirs obtain a step-up in basis. □

---

39. See the Glossary of Tax Terms in Appendix C for a definition of the zero bracket amount.

40. In making this tax computation, it is necessary to use the 1986 Tax Rate Schedule for single taxpayers and to add $2,480 (the zero bracket amount) to the taxable income. Thus, tax was computed on $10,980, which is $8,500 (1/10 of $85,000) plus $2,480.

41. § 402(e)(4)(J).

If T (in Example 8) uses the 5-year forward averaging provision instead, the following results are produced:

Taxable amount subject to averaging	$85,000

Computation of tax under 5-year averaging:
5 times the tax on $17,000 [42]
(1/5 of $85,000) $12,750

$$\$12,750 \times \frac{16 \text{ (service after 1973)}}{20 \text{ (total service years)}} = \$10,200$$

(ordinary income tax due on ordinary income portion)

Long-term capital gain portion

$$\$85,000 \times \frac{4 \text{ (service before 1974)}}{20 \text{ (total service years)}} = \$17,000$$

Thus, T's capital gain on the distribution is $17,000 (the same as in the 10-year averaging calculation). The capital gain is subject to a 20 percent capital gain rate.[43] Once again the taxpayer may wish to elect to treat the entire distribu-

CONCEPT SUMMARY 19–2

Model for Lump-Sum Computation

1. Start with the total lump-sum distribution and deduct any employee contributions, unrealized appreciation in employer securities, and available minimum distribution allowance.

2. Divide the result into 5 or 10 equal portions, whichever is appropriate.

3. Compute the tax on one portion using the 1986 or current rate schedules (whichever is appropriate) for single taxpayers.

4. Multiply the resulting tax by 5 or 10, whichever is appropriate.

5. Multiply the result in (4) by the ordinary income percentage (years of service after 1973 divided by total service years) to determine the tax liability on the ordinary income portion.*

6. Multiply the result in (1) by the capital gain percentage (years of service before 1974 divided by total service years) to determine the taxable amount subject to capital gain treatment.*

* In certain circumstances, none of the taxable amount of the distribution will be eligible for capital gain treatment. In other circumstances, the taxpayer may choose to treat none of the taxable amount as capital gain even though part could qualify.

42. In making this tax computation, it is necessary to use the 1989 Tax Rate Schedule for single taxpayers (including the 5% phase-out provision).

43. Note that since T qualifies under the transition rules (attained age 50 before January 1, 1986), he is eligible to elect capital gain treatment (without any percentage reduction) in conjunction with 5-year forward averaging.

tion as ordinary income using the 5-year forward averaging approach. The tax liability of $12,750 would be less than if the 20 percent rate is applied to the capital gain portion [$10,200 + ($17,000 × 20%) = $13,600]. Since the ordinary income tax under 10-year forward averaging is less than the ordinary income tax under 5-year forward averaging, it appears that T's best alternative is to use the 10-year forward averaging provision and treat the capital gain as ordinary income.

Limitations on Contributions to and Benefits from Qualified Plans

In General. The limitations on contributions to and benefits from qualified plans appearing in § 415 must be written into a qualified plan. The plan terminates if these limits are exceeded. Section 404 sets the limits on deductibility applicable to the employer. The limit on the amount deductible under § 404 may have an impact, however, on the amount the employer is willing to contribute. In fact, § 404(j) provides that no deduction is allowable by a defined benefit plan or defined contribution plan for the amount that exceeds the § 415 limitations.

Defined Contribution Plans. Under a *defined contribution plan* (money purchase pension, profit sharing, or stock bonus plan), the amount of the annual addition to an employee's account cannot exceed the smaller of $30,000 or 25 percent of the employee's compensation.[44] The $30,000 amount is to be indexed once the statutory ceiling for defined benefit plans (discussed next) reaches $120,000.

Defined Benefit Plans. Under a *defined benefit plan*, the annual benefit payable to an employee is limited to the smaller of $94,023 (in 1988)[45] or 100 percent of the employee's average compensation for the highest three years of employment. This benefit limit is subject to a $10,000 *de minimis* floor. The $94,023 limitation is reduced actuarially if the benefits begin before the Social Security normal retirement age (currently age 65). The $94,023 amount is increased actuarially if the benefits begin after the Social Security normal retirement age. The dollar limit on annual benefits (i.e., $94,023) is reduced by one-tenth for each year of *participation* under 10 years by the employee. Furthermore, the 100 percent of compensation limitation and the $10,000 *de minimis* floor are reduced proportionately for a participant who has less than 10 years of *service* with the employer.[46]

EXAMPLE 9   Employee A's average compensation for the highest three years of employment is $87,000. Although the § 415(b)(1) limitation does not limit the deduction, the defined benefit plan would not qualify if the plan provides for benefits in excess of the smaller of (1) $87,000 or (2) $94,023 for Employee A in 1988 (assuming retirement age of 65). ☐

---

44. § 415(c).

45. This amount is indexed annually. The indexed amount for 1989 was not available at the time of this writing.

46. § 415(b).

EXAMPLE 10   P has four years of participation in a defined benefit plan and has six years of service with her employer. She has average compensation for the highest three years of $50,000. Her four years of participation reduce her dollar limitation to $37,609 ($94,023 × ⁴/₁₀). Her six years of service reduce her 100% of compensation limitation to 60% ($50,000 × 60% = $30,000). Therefore, her limit on annual benefits is $30,000. □

For collectively bargained plans with at least 100 participants, the annual dollar limitation is the greater of $68,212 or one-half of the $94,023 monetary limit.

The amount of compensation that may be taken into account under any plan is limited to $200,000 (in 1988).[47] Thus, highly compensated individuals will receive less of a benefit as a percentage of pay than will non-highly compensated employees.

EXAMPLE 11   M corporation has a defined contribution plan with a 10% contribution formula. An employee earning less than $200,000 in 1988 would not be affected by this includible compensation limitation. However, an employee earning $300,000 in 1988 would have only 6.67% of compensation allocated to his or her account because of the $200,000 limit on includible compensation. □

Two methods exist for determining the maximum deduction by a corporation for contributions to pension plans. First, an aggregate cost method allows an actuarially determined deduction based on a level amount, or a level percentage, of compensation over the remaining future service of covered participants. Second, the employer is permitted to deduct the so-called normal cost plus no more than 10 percent of the past service costs.

EXAMPLE 12   During 1989, Y Corporation contributes $17,500 to its qualified pension plan. Normal cost for this year is $7,200, and the amount necessary to pay retirement benefits on behalf of employee services before 1989 is $82,000 (past service costs). The corporation's maximum deduction would be $15,400. This amount consists of the $7,200 normal cost plus 10% ($8,200) of the past service costs. The corporation would have a $2,100 [$17,500 (contribution) − $15,400 (deduction)] contribution carryover. □

EXAMPLE 13   Assume in the previous example that Y Corporation has normal cost in 1990 of $7,200 and contributes $10,000 to the pension trust. The corporation's maximum deduction would be $15,400. Y Corporation may deduct $12,100, composed of this year's contribution ($10,000) plus the $2,100 contribution carryover. □

---

47. §§ 401(a)(17) and 404(l). This amount is to be indexed annually starting in 1989. The indexed   amount for 1989 was not available at the time of this writing.

The employer's contribution is deductible in the tax year such amounts are paid to the pension trust. However, both cash and accrual basis employers may defer the payment of contributions with respect to any tax year until the date fixed for filing the taxpayer's Federal income tax return for that year (including extensions thereof).[48] In effect, the corporation is allowed a deduction to the extent it is compelled to make such contributions to satisfy the funding requirement. If an amount in excess of the allowable amount is contributed in any tax year, the excess may be carried forward and deducted in succeeding tax years (to the extent such carryover plus that year's contribution does not exceed the deductible limitation for such succeeding year).[49]

A 10 percent excise tax is imposed on nondeductible contributions. The tax is levied on the employer making the contribution. The tax applies to nondeductible contributions for the current year and any nondeductible contributions for the preceding year that have not been eliminated by the end of the current year (as a carryover or by being returned to the employer in the current year).[50]

Profit Sharing and Stock Bonus Plan Limitations.   The maximum deduction permitted to an employer each year with respect to contributions to profit sharing and stock bonus plans is 15 percent of the compensation paid or accrued with respect to plan participants. Any nondeductible excess, a so-called contribution carryover, may be carried forward indefinitely and deducted in subsequent years. The maximum deduction in any succeeding year is 15 percent of all compensation paid or accrued during such taxable year. An employer can circumvent the 15 percent limitation by establishing a money purchase pension plan as a supplement to the profit sharing or stock bonus plan. When there are two or more plans, a maximum deduction of 25 percent of the compensation paid is allowable.[51]

Top-Heavy Plans

A special set of rules is imposed upon so-called top-heavy plans to discourage retirement plans from conferring disproportionate benefits upon key employees. Top-heaviness is determined on an annual basis.

In general, a *top-heavy plan* provides more than 60 percent of the cumulative benefits to key employees, or the plan is part of a top-heavy plan. *Key employees* are defined as follows:

- Officers. However, for purposes of this definition, only the smaller of (1) 50 officers or (2) three employees or 10 percent of all employees (whichever is greater) may be considered officers.

- The 10 employees owning the largest interest in the employer (using the constructive ownership rules of § 318).

- A greater-than-5 percent owner of the employer.

- A greater-than-1 percent owner of the employer with annual compensation in excess of $150,000.[52]

---

48. §§ 404(a)(1) and (6).
49. § 404(a)(1)(D).
50. § 4972.

51. §§ 404(a)(3)(A) and (a)(7).

52. § 416(i)(1).

An employee need fall within only one of these categories to be classified as a key employee. However, a key employee does not include officers paid $45,000 or less a year. In addition, for purposes of the 10-employees provision, a key employee does not include an employee whose annual compensation from the employer is $30,000 or less. Employees receiving no compensation for five years are disregarded in testing for top-heavy status.

Top-heavy plans have the following additional requirements:

- There shall be greater portability for plan participants who are non-key employees. An employee's right to the accrued benefits derived from employer contributions must become nonforfeitable under either of two vesting schedules. Under the first schedule, an employee who has at least three years of service with the employer must have a nonforfeitable right to 100 percent of his or her accrued benefits derived from employer contributions. Under the second schedule, a six-year graded vesting schedule must be met (see Figure 19–3): [53]

- There must be minimum nonintegrated contributions or benefits for plan participants who are non-key employees. In a *defined benefit plan*, these employees must be provided with a minimum nonintegrated normal retirement benefit of 2 percent of their average compensation (for their high five years of compensation) per year of service. However, this minimum benefit does not have to provide more than 20 percent of their high five-year average compensation. In a *defined contribution plan*, non-key employees must receive a minimum nonintegrated contribution of the smaller of 3 percent of pay per year or the largest percentage at which contributions are made on behalf of a key employee for the year.[54]

- There is a reduction in the aggregate limit on contributions and benefits for certain key employees. The aggregate limit for a key employee is the smaller of 1.0 (with respect to the dollar limit) or 1.4 (as applied to the percentage limitation). However, the aggregate limit may be increased to the smaller of 1.25 or 1.4, respectively, if certain conditions are met.[55]

- A 10 percent penalty tax is imposed upon distributions before age 59½ to the extent that the amounts distributed are attributable to years in which the person was a 5 percent owner of the company (whether or

FIGURE 19–3   Top-Heavy Graded Vesting

Years of Service	Vested Percentage
2	20%
3	40%
4	60%
5	80%
6 or more	100%

---

53. § 416(b).   55. § 415(e).
54. §§ 416(c) and (e).

not the plan was top-heavy in those years). A distribution of a person's interest must begin no later than April 1 of the calendar year following the calendar year in which the person attains age $70\frac{1}{2}$. The entire interest need not be distributed, as there are several permissible payout periods.[56]

To stop an employer from avoiding the top-heavy rules by establishing a one-person corporate shell, § 269A allows the IRS to allocate any income or deductions between the personal service corporation and its employee-owner. An employee-owner is any employee who owns more than 10 percent of the outstanding stock of the personal service corporation on any day during the tax year.

Cash or Deferred Arrangement Plans

A *cash or deferred arrangement plan*, hereafter referred to as a *§ 401(k) plan*, allows participants to elect either to receive up to $7,313 (in 1988) [57] in cash or to have a contribution made on their behalf to a profit sharing or stock bonus plan. The plan may also be in the form of a salary reduction agreement between an eligible participant and an employer under which a contribution will be made only if the participant elects to reduce his or her compensation or to forgo an increase in compensation.

Any pretax amount elected by the employee as a plan contribution is not includible in gross income and is 100 percent vested. Any employer contributions are tax deferred, as are earnings on contributions in the plan.

EXAMPLE 14   X participates in a § 401(k) plan of his employer. The plan permits the participants to choose between a full salary or a reduced salary where the reduction becomes a before-tax contribution to a retirement plan. X elects to contribute 10% of his annual compensation of $30,000 to the plan. Income taxes are paid on only $27,000. No income taxes are paid on the $3,000—or on any earnings—until it is distributed from the plan to X. The main benefit of a § 401(k) plan is that X can shift a portion of his income to a later taxable year. □

The maximum employee annual elective contribution to a § 401(k) plan is $7,313 (in 1988), but such amount is reduced dollar for dollar by other salary-reduction contributions to tax-sheltered annuities and simplified employee pension plans. Elective contributions in excess of the maximum limitation are taxable in the year of deferral. These amounts may be distributed from the plan tax-free before April 15 of the following year. Excess amounts not timely distributed will be taxable in the year of distribution, even though they were included in income in the year of deferral.

There is a 10 percent excise tax on the employer for excess contributions not withdrawn from the plan within $2\frac{1}{2}$ months after the close of the plan year. The plan will lose its qualified status if these excess contributions (and

---

56. § 401(a)(9).

57. This amount is indexed annually. The indexed amount for 1989 was not available at the time of this writing.

any related income) are not withdrawn by the end of the plan year following the plan year with the excess contributions.[58]

EXAMPLE 15

T, an employee of a manufacturing corporation, defers $9,313 in a § 401(k) plan in 1988. The $2,000 excess deferral, along with the appropriate earnings, must be returned to the employee by April 15, 1989. This $2,000 excess amount plus related income is taxable to the employee in 1988 and will be taxed again upon distribution (if made after April 15, 1989). There will be a 10% tax on the employer on any excess contributions not returned within 2½ months after the close of the plan year. ☐

Complicated antidiscrimination provisions apply to § 401(k) plans.

RETIREMENT PLANS FOR SELF-EMPLOYED INDIVIDUALS

Since 1962, self-employed individuals and their employees have been eligible to receive qualified retirement benefits under what is known as *H.R. 10 (Keogh) plans*. Because of contribution limitations and other restrictions, self-employed plans previously were less attractive when compared to corporate plans. Contributions and benefits of a self-employed person now are subject to the general corporate provisions. Basically, self-employed persons are now on a parity with corporate employees. H.R. 10 plans can now provide a self-employed person with an adequate retirement base.

A variety of funding vehicles can be used for Keogh investments, such as mutual funds, annuities, real estate shares, certificates of deposit, debt instruments, commodities, securities, and personal properties. Investment in most collectibles is not allowed in a self-directed plan. When an individual decides to make all investment decisions, a self-directed retirement plan is established. Otherwise the individual may prefer to invest the funds with a particular financial institution such as a broker, a bank, or a savings and loan institution.

Coverage Requirements

Generally, the corporate coverage rules apply to H.R. 10 plans. Thus, the percentage, ratio, and average benefits tests previously discussed also apply to self-employed plans. In addition, the more restrictive top-heavy plan rules apply to H.R. 10 plans.[59]

Contribution Limitations

A self-employed individual may annually contribute the smaller of $30,000 or 25 percent of earned income to a *defined contribution* Keogh plan.[60] However, if the defined contribution plan is a profit sharing plan, a 15 percent deduction limit applies. Under a *defined benefit* Keogh plan, the annual benefit payable to an employee is limited to the smaller of $94,023 (in 1988) or 100

---

58. § 4979(a).

59. § 401(d).

60. § 415(c)(1).

percent of the employee's average compensation for the highest three years of employment.[61] An employee includes a self-employed person. More restrictive rules apply to a top-heavy plan.

Earned income refers to net earnings from self-employment as defined in § 1402(a).[62] Net earnings from self-employment means the gross income derived by an individual from any trade or business carried on by such individual, less appropriate deductions, plus the distributive share of income or loss from a partnership.[63] Earned income is reduced by contributions to qualified plans on such an individual's behalf.[64]

EXAMPLE 16   P, a partner, has earned income in 1989 (before any Keogh contribution) of $130,000. The maximum contribution to a defined contribution plan is $26,000, calculated from the following formula: $130,000 − .25X = X$, where X is earned income reduced by P's Keogh contribution. Solving this equation, X = $104,000; thus, the contribution limit is .25 × $104,000 = $26,000. To achieve the maximum contribution of $30,000, P would have to earn at least $150,000. In essence, a self-employed individual can contribute 20% of *gross* earned income. (The partner could contribute only 13.043% of self-employment gross earned income if this were a profit sharing plan.) □

Many Keogh plans will be top-heavy plans (refer to previous discussion). For nondiscrimination purposes, the 25 percent limitation on the employee contribution is computed on the first $200,000 of earned income.

EXAMPLE 17   T, a self-employed accountant, has a money purchase plan with a contribution rate of 5% of compensation. T's earned income before the retirement contribution is $220,000. T's contribution would be limited to $9,523.81 ($200,000 − .05X = X$), since X = $190,476.19 and .05 × $190,476.19 = $9,523.81. □

Although an H.R. 10 plan must be established before the end of the year in question, contributions may be made up to the normal filing date for such year. Also, an employee who is covered under a qualified corporate retirement plan may set up an H.R. 10 plan (and possibly an IRA) for earned income from self-employment sources.

INDIVIDUAL RETIREMENT ACCOUNTS (IRAS)

General Rules

Employees not covered by another qualified plan can establish their own tax-deductible IRAs subject to the smaller of $2,000 (or $2,250 for spousal IRAs)

---

61. § 415(b)(1). This amount is indexed annually. The indexed amount for 1989 was not available at the time of this writing.
62. § 401(c)(2).
63. § 1402(a).
64. § 401(c)(2)(A)(v).

or 100 percent of compensation.[65] If the taxpayer or spouse is an active participant in another qualified plan, the IRA deduction limitation is phased out *proportionately* between certain adjusted gross income (AGI) ranges.[66] Refer to Figure 19–4.

AGI is calculated taking into account any § 469 passive losses and § 86 taxable Social Security benefits and ignoring any § 911 foreign income exclusion, § 135 savings bonds interest exclusion, and the IRA deduction. There is a $200 floor on the IRA deduction limitation for individuals whose AGI is not above the phase-out range.

FIGURE 19–4　　Phase-Out of IRA Deduction

AGI Filing Status	Phase-Out Begins	Phase-Out Ends
Single and head of household	$25,000	$35,000
Married, filing joint return	40,000	50,000
Married, filing separate return	-0-	10,000

EXAMPLE 18

In 1989, Mr. and Mrs. Q had compensation income of $27,000 and $20,000, respectively. Their adjusted gross income for 1989 was $47,000. Mr. Q was an active participant in his employer's qualified retirement plan. Mr. and Mrs. Q may *each* contribute $600 to an IRA. The deductible amount for each is reduced from $2,000 by $1,400 because of the phase-out mechanism:

$$\frac{\$7,000}{\$10,000} \times \$2,000 = \$1,400 \text{ reduction}$$

□

EXAMPLE 19

An unmarried individual with AGI of $34,500 would normally have an IRA deduction limit of $100 ($2,000 − [($34,500 − $25,000)/$10,000 × $2,000]). However, because of the special provision, a $200 IRA deduction is allowable. □

To the extent that an individual is ineligible to make a deductible contribution to an IRA, *nondeductible contributions* can be made to separate accounts.[67] The nondeductible contribution will be subject to the same dollar limits for deductible contributions of $2,000 of earned income ($2,250 for a spousal IRA). Income in the account accumulates tax-free until distributed. Only the account earnings will be taxed upon distribution. A taxpayer may elect to treat deductible IRA contributions as nondeductible. If an individual has no taxable income for the year after taking into account other deductions,

---

65. §§ 219(b)(1) and (c)(2).
66. § 219(g). However, a special rule in § 219(g)(4) allows a married person filing a separate return who lives apart from the spouse at all times during the taxable year and who is not an active participant to avoid the phase-out rules even though the spouse is an active participant.
67. § 408(o).

the election would be beneficial. Such designation is to be made on the individual's tax return for the taxable year to which the designation relates.

Simplified Employee Pension Plans.   An employer may contribute to an IRA covering an employee an amount equal to the lesser of $30,000 or 15 percent of the employee's earned income.[68] For such a plan, the corporation must make contributions for *each* employee who has reached age 21, has performed service for the employer during the calendar year and at least three of the five preceding calendar years, and has received at least $313 (in 1988) in compensation from the employer for the year.[69] Known as *simplified employee pension (SEP) plans*, the plans are subject to many of the same restrictions applicable to qualified plans (e.g., age and period of service requirements, top-heavy rules, and nondiscrimination limitations). Concept Summary 19–3 compares a SEP with a Keogh plan.

Employees who participate in salary reduction SEPs may elect to have contributions made to the SEP or to receive contributions in cash.[70] If an employee elects to have contributions made on the employee's behalf to the SEP, the contribution is not treated as having been distributed or made available to the employee (i.e., no constructive receipt). The election to have amounts contributed to a SEP or received in cash is available only if at least 50 percent of the employees eligible to participate elect to have amounts contributed to the SEP. This exception to the constructive receipt principle is available only in a taxable year in which the employer maintaining the SEP has 25 or fewer employees eligible to participate at all times during the preceding year. In addition, the deferral percentage for each highly compensated employee cannot exceed 125 percent of the average deferral percentage for all other eligible employees.

The amounts contributed to a SEP by an employer on behalf of an employee and the elective deferrals under a SEP are excludible from gross income. Elective deferrals under a SEP are subject to a statutory ceiling of $7,313 (in 1988). Only $208,940 (in 1988) in compensation may be taken into account in making the SEP computation. An employer is permitted to elect to use its taxable year rather than the calendar year for purposes of determining contributions to a SEP.[71]

Spousal IRA.   If both spouses work, each can individually establish an IRA. However, when only one spouse is employed, an IRA can be established for the nonemployed spouse if the employed spouse is eligible to establish an IRA. The maximum deduction for the individual and spouse is the lesser of 100 percent of the compensation income of the working spouse or $2,250. One spouse is permitted to elect to be treated, for this purpose, as having no earned income, thus allowing the contributing spouse to make the additional $250 contribution to an IRA. The contribution may be allocated to either spouse in any amount up to $2,000, and a joint return must be filed. The spousal IRA deduction is also proportionately reduced for active participants whose AGI exceeds the above target ranges.

---

68. § 408(j).

69. § 408(k)(2). This amount is indexed annually. The indexed amount for 1989 was not available at the time of this writing.

70. § 408(k)(6).

71. § 404(h)(1)(A). The $7,313 and $208,940 amounts are indexed annually. The indexed amounts for 1989 were not available at the time of this writing.

EXAMPLE 20   X, who is married, is eligible to establish an IRA. He received $30,000 in compensation in 1989. He can contribute a total of $2,250 to a spousal IRA, to be divided in any manner between the two spouses, except that no more than $2,000 can be allocated to either spouse. □

EXAMPLE 21   Assume the same facts as in the previous example, except that X's spouse has earned income of $100. Absent the election to treat the spouse's earned income as zero, the maximum IRA contribution is $2,100 ($2,000 for X and $100 for X's spouse). With the election, $2,250 can be contributed under the spousal IRA provision. □

Alimony is considered to be earned income for purposes of IRA contributions. Thus, a person whose only income is alimony can contribute to an IRA.[72]

Timing of Contributions.   Contributions (both deductible and nondeductible) can be made to an IRA anytime before the due date of the individual's tax return.[73] For example, an individual can establish and contribute to an IRA through April 15, 1990 (the return due date), and deduct this amount on his or her tax return for 1989. IRA contributions that are made during a tax return extension period do not satisfy the requirement of being made by the return due date. An employer can make contributions up until the time of the due date for filing the return (including extensions thereof) and treat such amounts as a deduction for the prior year.[74] As noted earlier, a similar rule applies to H.R. 10 plans. However, the H.R. 10 plan must be established before the end of the tax year. Contributions to the H.R. 10 plan may then be made anytime before the due date of the individual's tax return.

Penalty Taxes for Excess Contributions

A cumulative, nondeductible 6 percent excise penalty tax is imposed on the smaller of (1) any excess contributions or (2) the market value of the plan assets determined as of the close of the tax year. *Excess contributions* are any contributions that exceed the maximum limitation and contributions made during or after the tax year in which the individual reaches age 70½.[75] A taxpayer is not allowed a deduction for excess contributions. If the excess is corrected by contributing less than the deductible amount for a later year, a deduction then is allowable in the later year as a *make-up* deduction.

An excess contribution is taxable annually until returned to the taxpayer or reduced by the underutilization of the maximum contribution limitation in a subsequent year. The 6 percent penalty tax can be avoided if the excess amounts are returned.[76]

EXAMPLE 22   T, age 55, creates an IRA in 1989 and contributes $2,300 in cash to the plan. T has earned income of $22,000. T is allowed a $2,000 deduction *for*

72. § 219(f)(1).
73. § 219(f)(3).
74. § 404(h)(1)(B).

75. §§ 4973(a)(1) and (b).

76. §§ 408(d)(4) and 4973(b)(2).

adjusted gross income for 1989. Assuming the market value of the plan assets is at least $300, there is a nondeductible 6% excise penalty tax of $18.00 ($300 × 6%). The $300 may be subject to an additional penalty tax in future years if it is not returned to T or reduced by underutilization of the $2,000 maximum contribution limitation. ☐

Taxation of Benefits

A participant has a zero basis in the deductible contributions to an IRA, since such contributions are not taxed currently.[77] Once retirement payments are received, they are ordinary income and are not subject to the 5-year or 10-year averaging allowed for lump-sum distributions. Payments made to a participant from deductible IRAs before age 59½ are subject to a nondeductible 10 percent penalty tax on such actual, or constructive, payments.[78]

All IRAs of an individual are treated as one contract, and all distributions during a taxable year are treated as one distribution. If an individual withdraws an amount from an IRA during a taxable year and the individual previously has made both deductible and nondeductible IRA contributions,

CONCEPT SUMMARY 19–3

Keogh Plan and SEP Compared

	Keogh	SEP
Form	Trust.	IRA.
Establishment	By end of year.	By extension due date of employer.
Type of plan	Qualified.	Nonqualified.
Contributions to plan	By extension due date.	By extension due date of employer.
Vesting rules	Qualified plan rules.	100% immediately.
Participants' rules	Flexible.	Stricter.
Lump-sum distributions	Yes, favorable 5-year or 10-year forward averaging.	No, ordinary income.
$5,000 death benefit exclusion	Yes.	No.
Deduction limitation	Varies.*	Smaller of $30,000 or 15% of gross income.
Self as trustee	Yes.	No.

* For a defined contribution pension plan, the limit is the smaller of $30,000 or 20% of self-employment income. A defined contribution profit sharing plan has a 13.043% deduction limit. A defined benefit Keogh plan's limit is the smaller of $94,023 (in 1988) or 100% of the employee's average compensation for the highest three years of employment.

77. § 408(d)(1).   78. § 72(t).

the excludible amount must be calculated. The amount excludible from gross income for the taxable year is calculated by multiplying the amount withdrawn by a percentage. The percentage is calculated by dividing the individual's aggregate nondeductible IRA contributions by the aggregate balance of all IRAs of the individual (including rollover IRAs and SEPs).[79]

EXAMPLE 23

P, age 59, has a $12,000 deductible IRA and a $2,000 nondeductible IRA (without any earnings). P withdraws $1,000 from the nondeductible IRA in 1989. The excludible portion is $143 ($2,000/$14,000 × $1,000), and the includible portion is $857 ($12,000/$14,000 × $1,000). P must pay a 10% penalty tax on a prorated portion considered withdrawn from the deductible IRA and earnings in either type of IRA. Thus, the 10% penalty tax is $85.70 (10% × $857). □

NONQUALIFIED DEFERRED COMPENSATION PLANS

Underlying Rationale for Tax Treatment

Nonqualified deferred compensation (NQDC) plans provide a flexible way for an executive to defer income taxes on income payments until a possible lower tax bracket year. Where the deferred compensation is credited with annual earnings until payment, the entire deferred compensation, not the after-tax amount, is generating investment income. Also, most deferred compensation plans do not have to meet the discrimination, funding, coverage, and other requirements of qualified plans. In addition to these advantages for the employee, the employer may not have a current cash outflow.

The doctrine of constructive receipt is an important concept relating to the taxability of nonqualified deferred compensation.[80] In essence, if a taxpayer irrevocably earns income but may elect to receive it now or at a later date, the income is constructively received and is immediately taxed. Income is not constructively received, however, if the taxpayer's control over the amounts earned is subject to substantial limitations or restrictions.

Still another concept is the economic benefit theory. Although a taxpayer does not have a present right to income, the income will be taxable if a right in the form of a negotiable promissory note exists. Notes and other evidences of indebtedness received in payment for services constitute income to the extent of their fair market value at the time of the transfer.[81]

EXAMPLE 24

R Corporation and B, a cash basis employee, enter into an employment agreement that provides an annual salary of $120,000 to B. Of this amount, $100,000 is to be paid in current monthly installments and $20,000 is to be paid in 10 annual installments beginning at B's retirement or death. Although R Corporation maintains a separate account for B, such account is not funded (the employee is merely an unsecured creditor

---

79. § 408(d)(2).
80. § 451(a) and Reg. § 1.451–2.

81. Reg. § 1.61–2(d)(4).

of the corporation). The $20,000 is not considered constructively received and is deferred. Compensation of $100,000 is currently taxable to B and deductible to R Corporation. The other $20,000 will be taxable and deductible when paid in future years. □

Tax Treatment to the Employer and Employee

The tax treatment of an NQDC plan depends on whether it is *funded* or *nonfunded* and whether it is *forfeitable* or *nonforfeitable*. In an unfunded NQDC plan, the employee relies upon the company's mere promise to make the compensation payment in the future. An unfunded, unsecured promise to pay, not represented by a negotiable note, is effective to defer the recognition of income. Thus, the employee is taxed later when the compensation is actually paid or made available.[82] Similarly, the employer is allowed a deduction when the employee recognizes income.[83]

An escrow account can be set up by the employer to accumulate deferred payments on behalf of the employee. These funds may be invested by the escrow agent for the benefit of the employee.[84] By avoiding income recognition until the employee receives the benefits from the escrow custodial account, there is a postponement of tax to the employee. It is usually desirable not to transfer securities to the escrow agent because the IRS might attempt to treat such transfers as property transferred in connection with the performance of services under § 83. Such a treatment would force the transaction to have a substantial risk of forfeiture and nontransferability (or else the compensation income would be taxable immediately). An escrow arrangement can be well suited for a professional athlete or entertainer whose income is earned in a few peak years.

EXAMPLE 25

H, a professional athlete, is to receive a bonus for signing an employment contract. An NQDC plan is established to defer the income beyond H's peak income years. The bonus is transferred by the employer to an escrow agent who invests the funds in securities, etc., which may act as a hedge against inflation. The bonus is deferred for 10 years and becomes payable gradually from years 11 through 15. The bonus is taxable when H begins to receive the payments. □

It is also possible to provide for NQDC through an internally funded revocable trust or through an externally funded nonexempt trust.[85] The detailed requirements relative to such arrangements are beyond the scope of this text. Generally, however, funded nonqualified deferred compensation plans must be forfeitable to keep the compensation payments from being taxable immediately. In most instances, employees prefer to have some assurance that they will ultimately receive benefits from the nonqualified deferred compensation (that the plan provides for nonforfeitable benefits). In such instances, the plan will have to be unfunded to prevent immediate taxation to

---

82. Rev.Rul. 60–31, 1960–1 C.B. 174; Reg. § 1.451–2(a); *U.S. v. Basye,* 73–1 USTC ¶9250, 31 AFTR2d 73–802, 93 S.Ct. 1080 (USSC, 1973).

83. §§ 404(a) and (d).

84. Rev.Rul. 55–525, 1955–2 C.B. 543.

85. Rev.Rul. 67–289, 1967–2 C.B. 163; Reg. § 1.83–1(a).

the employee. Note that most funded NQDC plans are subject to many of the provisions that apply to qualified plans.

When to Use an NQDC Arrangement.   As a general rule, nonqualified deferred compensation (NQDC) plans are more appropriate for executives in a financially secure company. Because of the need for currently disposable income, such plans are usually not appropriate for young employees.

An NQDC plan can reduce an employee's overall tax payments by deferring the taxation of income to later years (possibly when the employee is in a lower tax bracket). In effect, these plans may produce a form of income averaging. Further, NQDC plans may discriminate in favor of shareholders, officers, specific highly compensated key employees, or a single individual.

Certain disadvantages should be noted. Nonqualified plans are usually required to be unfunded, which means that an employee is not assured that funds ultimately will be available to pay the benefits. Also, the employer's tax deduction is postponed until the employee is taxed on such amounts.

Golden Parachute Arrangements.   Certain excessive severance payments to employees may be penalized. The Code denies a deduction to an employer if there is a payment of cash or property to an employee or independent contractor (1) that is contingent on a change of ownership of a corporation through a stock or asset acquisition and (2) the aggregate present value of which equals or exceeds three times the employee's (or independent contractor's) average annual compensation.[86] The law recognizes that a corporation may provide monetary benefits to key employees if such employees lose their jobs as a result of a change in ownership of the corporation. These payments may be unreasonable or not really for services rendered. Such payments are referred to in the Code as *golden parachute payments*, a term that, in essence, means *excess severance pay*. The disallowed amount is the excess of the payment over a statutory base amount (a five-year average of compensation if the taxpayer was an employee for the entire five-year period). Further, a 20 percent excise tax is imposed on the receipt of these parachute payments, to be withheld at the time of payment.[87]

Golden parachute payments do not include payments to or from qualified pension, profit sharing, stock bonus, annuity, or simplified employee pension plans. Also excluded is the amount of the payment that, in fact, represents reasonable compensation for personal services actually rendered or to be rendered. Finally, not subject to the golden parachute rules are S corporations and, generally, corporations that have no stock that is readily tradable on an established securities market or elsewhere. Such excluded payments are not taken into account when determining whether the threshold (the aggregate present value calculation) is exceeded.

RESTRICTED PROPERTY PLANS

General Provisions

A *restricted property plan* is an arrangement whereby an employer transfers property (e.g., stock of the employer corporation) to a provider of services at no cost or at a bargain price. The purpose of a restricted stock plan is to retain

---

86. § 280G.   87. § 4999.

the services of key employees who might otherwise leave. The employer hopes that such compensation arrangements will encourage company growth and attainment of performance objectives. Section 83 was enacted in 1969 to provide rules for the taxation of such incentive compensation arrangements that previously were governed by judicial and administrative interpretations. Although the following discussion refers to an employee as the provider of the services, the services are not required to be performed by an employee (§ 83 also applies to independent contractors).

As a general rule, if an employee performs services and receives property (e.g., stock), the fair market value of such property in excess of any amount paid by the employee is includible in the gross income of the employee. The time for inclusion is the earlier of (1) the time the property is no longer subject to a substantial risk of forfeiture or (2) the moment the employee has the right to transfer the property free of the substantial risk of forfeiture. The fair market value of the property is determined without regard to any restriction, except a restriction that by its terms will never lapse.[88] Since the amount of the compensation is determined at the date that the restrictions lapse or when the property is transferable, the opportunity to generate capital gain treatment on the property is denied during a period when the ordinary income element is being deferred.

| EXAMPLE 26 | On October 1, 1985, W Corporation sold to J, an employee, 100 shares of W Corporation stock for $10 per share. At the time of the sale, the fair market value of the stock was $100 per share. Under the terms of the sale, each share of stock was nontransferable and subject to a substantial risk of forfeiture (which was not to lapse until October 1, 1989). Evidence of these restrictions was stamped on the face of the stock certificates. On October 1, 1989, the fair market value of the stock was $250 per share. Since the stock was nontransferable and was subject to a substantial risk of forfeiture, J did not include any compensation in gross income during 1985 (assuming no special election was made). Instead, J was required to include $24,000 of compensation in gross income [100 shares × ($250 less $10 per share)] during 1989. If for some reason the substantial risk of forfeiture had occurred (e.g., the plan required J to surrender the stock to the corporation if he voluntarily terminated his employment with the company before October 1, 1989) and J never received the stock certificates, he would have been allowed a capital loss of $1,000 (the extent of his investment). ☐ |

Substantial Risk of Forfeiture

A *substantial risk of forfeiture* exists if a person's rights to full enjoyment of such property are conditioned upon the future performance, or the refraining from the performance, of substantial services by an individual.[89] For example, if an employee must return the property (receiving only his or her original cost, if any) should there be a failure to complete a substantial period of service (for any reason), the property is subject to a substantial risk of forfei-

---

88. § 83(a)(1); *Miriam Sakol*, 67 T.C. 986 (1977); *T. M. Horwith*, 71 T.C. 932 (1979).

89. § 83(c); Regulation § 1.83–3(c)(2) includes several examples of restricted property arrangements.

ture. Another such situation exists in which an employer can compel an employee to return the property due to a breach of a substantial covenant not to compete. Any substantial risk of forfeiture should be stated on the face of the stock certificates. Assuming that a substantial risk of forfeiture does not exist, the property received is valued at its fair market value, ignoring any restrictions, except for one instance dealing with closely held stock.

Special Election Available. An employee may elect within 30 days after the receipt of restricted property to recognize immediately as ordinary income the fair market value in excess of the amount paid for the property. Any appreciation in the value of the property after receipt is classified as capital gain instead of ordinary income. No deduction is allowed to the employee for taxes paid on the original amount included in income if the property is subsequently forfeited.[90] The employee is permitted to take a capital loss for any amounts that were actually paid for the property. Furthermore, in such a case, the employer must repay taxes saved by any compensation deduction taken in the earlier year.[91]

Any increase in value between the time the property is received and the time it becomes either nonforfeitable or transferable is taxed as ordinary income (if no special election is made by the employee). However, if the employee elects to be taxed immediately on the difference between the cost and fair market value on the date of issue, any future appreciation is treated as capital gain. In determining whether the gain is long term or short term, the holding period starts when the employee is taxed on the ordinary income.[92]

EXAMPLE 27

On July 1, 1979, F Company sold 100 shares of its preferred stock, worth $15 per share, to D (an employee) for $5 per share. The sale was subject to D's agreement to resell the preferred shares to the company for $5 per share if D terminated employment during the following 10 years. Assume that the stock had a value of $25 per share on July 1, 1989, and D sold the stock for $30 per share on October 10, 1989. D made the special election to include the original spread (between the value in 1979 of $15 and the amount paid of $5) in income for 1979. D was required to recognize $1,000 of compensation income in 1979 ($15 − $5 = $10 × 100 shares), at which time his holding period in his stock began. D's tax basis in the stock was $1,500 ($1,000 + $500). When the preferred stock was sold in 1989, D recognized a $1,500 long-term capital gain ($30 × 100 shares − $1,500). □

EXAMPLE 28

Assume the same facts as in Example 27, except that D sells the stock in 1990 (rather than 1989). There would be no gain recognized by D in 1989 when the substantial risk of forfeiture lapses. Instead, D would recognize the $1,500 long-term capital gain in 1990. □

This special provision is usually not elected, since it results in an immediate recognition of income and adverse tax consequences result from a subse-

---

90. § 83(b).
91. Reg. §§ 1.83–6(c) and 2(a).

92. § 1223(6).

quent forfeiture. However, the special election may be attractive in the following situations:

- The bargain element is relatively small.
- Substantial appreciation is expected in the future.
- A high probability exists that the restrictions will be met.

Employer Deductions

At the time the employee is required to include the compensation in income, the employer is allowed a tax deduction for the same amount. The employer must withhold on this amount in accordance with § 3402. In the no-election situation, the deduction is limited to the fair market value of the restricted property (without regard to the restrictions) at the time the restrictions lapse, reduced by the amount originally paid for the property by the employee.[93] When the employee elects to be taxed immediately, the corporate deduction also is accelerated and deductible in like amount. In those cases of deferred income recognition, the employer can receive a very sizable deduction if the property has appreciated.

EXAMPLE 29

On March 14, 1987, F Corporation sold to G, an employee, 10 shares of F common stock for $100 per share. The employer corporation and the employee were calendar year taxpayers. The common stock was subject to a substantial risk of forfeiture and was nontransferable; both conditions were to lapse on March 14, 1989. At the time of the sale, the fair market value of the common stock (without considering the restrictions) was $1,000 per share. On March 14, 1989, the restrictions lapsed when the fair market value of the stock was $2,000 per share. No special election was made by the employee. In 1989, G realized ordinary income of $19,000 (10 shares at $2,000 per share less the $100 per share paid by G). Likewise, F Corporation was allowed a $19,000 compensation deduction in 1989. ☐

EXAMPLE 30

In the previous example, assume that the employee had made the election. Since the employee was taxed on $9,000 in 1987, the corporation was allowed to deduct a like amount in 1987. No deduction would be available in 1989. ☐

STOCK OPTIONS

In General

Various equity types of stock option programs are available for an employer's compensation package. Some authorities believe that there is a need for some

---

93. Reg. § 1.83–6(a).

form of *equity kicker* to attract new management, to convert key officers into *partners* by giving them a share of the business, and to retain the services of executives who might otherwise leave. An option gives an individual the right to purchase a stated number of shares of stock from a corporation at a certain price within a specified period of time. The optionee must be under no obligation to purchase the stock, and the option may be revocable by the corporation. The option must be in writing, and its terms must be clearly expressed.[94]

Incentive Stock Options

An equity type of stock option called incentive stock options (ISOs) is available for options granted after 1975 and exercised after 1980.[95] The congressional motivation underlying a stock option program is to furnish an important incentive device for corporations to attract new management and to retain the services of those already employed. Encouraging the management of a business to have a proprietary interest in its successful operation should provide a key motive to expand and improve the profit position of the companies involved.

An incentive stock option arrangement follows much the same tax treatment previously accorded to restricted and qualified stock option plans. There are no tax consequences when the option is granted, but the spread (the excess of fair market value of the share at the date of exercise over the option price[96]) is a tax preference item for purposes of the alternative minimum tax. The determination of fair market value is made without regard to any lapse restrictions (a restriction that will expire after a period of time). After the option is exercised and when the stock is sold, any gain therefrom is taxed as a long-term capital gain if certain holding period requirements are met. To qualify as a long-term capital gain, the employee must not dispose of the stock within two years after the option is granted or within one year after acquiring the stock.[97] If the employee meets the holding period requirements, none of these transactions generate any business deduction for the employer.[98]

Since the beneficial treatment for long-term capital gains for the individual expired after 1987, ISOs have lost much of their tax appeal. However, an employee who has capital losses would prefer capital gain treatment.

EXAMPLE 31

E Corporation granted an incentive stock option for 100 shares of its stock to R, an employee, on March 18, 1986. The option price was $100 and the fair market value was $100 on the date of grant. R exercised the option on April 1, 1988, when the market value of the stock was $200 per share. He sold the stock on April 6, 1989, for $300 per share. No ordinary income was recognized by R on the date of the grant or the exercise date, since the option qualified as an ISO. E corporation received no compensation deduction. R would have a $10,000 tax preference item on the exercise date. R would have a long-term capital gain upon the sale of the stock in 1989

---

94. Reg. §§ 1.421–1(a)(1) and –7(a)(1).

95. Qualified stock options were available under § 422 for certain qualified options granted before May 21, 1976. These qualified stock options had many of the statutory requirements of ISOs, but ISOs have a more favorable tax treatment.

96. §§ 422A(a), 421(a)(1), and 57(a)(3).

97. § 422A(a)(1).

98. § 421(a)(2).

of $20,000 [($300 − $100) × 100], since the one-year and two-year hold-ing periods and other requirements would have been met. □

As a further requirement for incentive stock option treatment, the option holder must be an employee of the issuing corporation from the date the option is granted until three months (12 months if disabled) before the date of exercise. Exceptions are made for parent and subsidiary situations, corporate reorganizations, and liquidations. The holding period and the employee-status rules just described (the one-year, two-year, and three-month requirements) are waived in the case of the death of an employee. Also, in certain situations involving an insolvent employee, the holding period rules are modified.[99]

EXAMPLE 32	Assume the same facts as in the previous example, except that R was not employed by E Corporation for six months before the date he exercised the options. R must recognize ordinary income to the extent of the spread, assuming there was no substantial risk of forfeiture. Thus, R would recog-nize $10,000 [($200 − $100) × 100] of ordinary income on the exercise date, since R was not an employee of E Corporation at all times during the period beginning on the grant date and ending three months before the exercise date. □

If the holding period requirements are not satisfied but all other condi-tions are met, the tax is still deferred to the point of the sale. However, the difference between the option price and the value of the stock at the date the option was exercised will be treated as ordinary income. The difference be-tween the amount realized for the stock and the value of the stock at the date of exercise will be short-term or long-term capital gain, depending on the holding period of the stock itself. The employer will be allowed a deduction equal to the amount recognized by the employee as ordinary income.

EXAMPLE 33	Assume the same facts as in Example 31, except that R sold the stock on March 22, 1989, for $290 per share. Since R did not hold the stock itself for at least one year, $10,000 of the gain would be treated as ordinary income in 1989, and E Corporation would be allowed a $10,000 compen-sation deduction in 1989. The remaining $9,000 would be a short-term capital gain ($29,000 − $20,000). □

Qualification Requirements for Incentive Stock Option Plans.   The term *incentive stock option* means an option granted to an individual, for any reason connected with his or her employment, by the employer corporation or by a parent or subsidiary corporation of the employer corporation to purchase stock of any such corporations.[100] An employee can use company stock to pay for the stock when exercising an option without disqualifying the incentive stock option plan.

For an option to qualify as an incentive stock option, the terms of the option itself must meet the following conditions:

---

99. §§ 422A(a)(2) and (c)(3).   100. § 422A(b).

- The option must be granted under a plan specifying the number of shares of stock to be issued and the employees or class of employees eligible to receive the options. The plan must be approved by the shareholders of the corporation within 12 months before or after the plan is adopted.

- The option must be granted within 10 years of the date the plan is adopted or of the date the plan is approved by the shareholders, whichever date is earlier.

- The option must by its terms be exercisable only within 10 years of the date it is granted.

- The option price must equal or exceed the fair market value of the stock at the time the option is granted. This requirement is deemed satisfied if there has been a good faith attempt to value the stock accurately, even if the option price is less than the stock value.

- The option by its terms must be nontransferable other than at death and must be exercisable during the employee's lifetime only by the employee.

- The employee must not, immediately before the option is granted, own stock representing more than 10 percent of the voting power or value of all classes of stock in the employer corporation or its parent or subsidiary. (Here, the attribution rules of § 267 are applied in modified form.) However, the stock ownership limitation will be waived if the option price is at least 110 percent of the fair market value (at the time the option is granted) of the stock subject to the option and the option by its terms is not exercisable more than five years from the date it is granted.[101]

An overall limitation is imposed on the amount of incentive stock options that can be exercised in one year. This limit is set at $100,000 per year (based on the value of the stock determined at the time the option is granted) per employee.

Nonqualified Stock Options

The IRS has prescribed rules for the treatment of nonqualified stock options.[102] A *nonqualified stock option* does not satisfy the statutory requirements for incentive stock options. In addition, a stock option that otherwise would qualify as an incentive stock option will be treated as a nonqualified stock option if the terms of the stock option provide that it is not an incentive stock option. If the nonqualified stock option has a readily ascertainable fair market value (e.g., the option is traded on an established exchange), the value of the option must be included in the employee's income at the date of grant. Thereafter, capital gain or loss is recognized only upon the disposal of the optioned stock. The employee's basis is the amount paid for the stock plus any amount reported as ordinary income. The employer obtains a corresponding tax deduction at the same time and to the extent that income is recognized by the employee.[103]

---

101. § 422A(c)(6).
102. Reg. §§ 1.421–6(c), (d), and (e); Reg. § 1.83–7.
103. Reg. § 1.421–6(f).

EXAMPLE 34

On February 1, 1988, J is granted a nonqualified stock option to purchase 100 shares of stock from the employer at $10 per share. On this date, the option is selling for $2 on an established exchange. J exercised the option on March 30, 1989, when the stock was worth $20 per share. On June 5, 1989, J sold the optioned stock for $22 per share.

- J must report ordinary income of $200 ($2 × 100 shares) on the date of grant (February 1, 1988), since the option has a readily ascertainable fair market value.

- Upon the sale of the stock, J must report a long-term capital gain of $1,000 [($22 − $12) × 100 shares].

- At the date of grant (February 1, 1988), the employer will receive a tax deduction of $200, the amount of income reported by J. ☐

If a nonqualified stock option does not have a readily ascertainable fair market value, an employee does not recognize income at the grant date. However, as a general rule, ordinary income must be reported in the year of exercise (the difference between the fair market value of the stock at the exercise date and option price).[104] The amount paid by the employee for the stock plus the amount reported as ordinary income becomes the basis. Any appreciation above such basis is taxed as a long-term capital gain upon disposition (assuming the stock is held for the required long-term holding period after exercise). The corporation receives a corresponding tax deduction at the same time and to the extent that income is recognized by the employee.

EXAMPLE 35

On February 3, 1988, S was granted a nonqualified stock option for 100 shares of common stock at $10 per share. On the date of the grant, there was no readily ascertainable fair market value for the option. S exercised the options on January 3, 1989, when the stock was selling for $15 per share. S sold one-half of the shares on April 15, 1989, and the other half on September 17, 1990. The sale price on both dates was $21 per share. S would recognize no income on the grant date (February 3, 1988) but would recognize $500 ($1,500 − $1,000) of ordinary income on the exercise date (January 3, 1989). S would recognize a short-term capital gain of $300 on the sale of the first half and a $300 long-term capital gain on the sale of the second batch of stock [½ ($2,100 − $1,500)]. ☐

The major *advantages* of nonqualified stock options are summarized as follows:

- A tax deduction is available to the corporation without a cash outlay.

- The employee receives capital gain treatment on any appreciation in the stock starting either at the exercise date or at the date of grant if the option has a readily ascertainable fair market value.

- Options can be issued at more flexible terms than under incentive stock option plans (e.g., longer exercise period and discount on exercise price).

---

104. Reg. § 1.83–7(a); Reg. § 1.421–6(d).

A major *disadvantage is* that the employee must recognize ordinary income on exercise of the option or at the date of grant if the option has a readily ascertainable market value, without receiving cash to pay the tax.

TAX PLANNING CONSIDERATIONS

Deferred Compensation

The dramatic lowering of individual tax rates to 28 percent (33 percent for certain individuals due to the phase-out of the 15 percent rate and personal exemptions) and the elimination of favorable capital gain treatment have had an impact on the attractiveness of deferral techniques. Further, with individual rates generally lower than corporate tax rates, current deductibility to the employer is more advantageous. The tightening of the antidiscrimination rules may result in increases in costs to the employer of providing deferred compensation. Finally, restrictions upon interest expense deductibility make borrowing money by an employee as part of a compensation program more costly. Payment of compensation in cash in 1989 may be quite beneficial, especially if tax rates increase in future years.

Qualified Plans

Qualified plans provide maximum tax benefits for employers, since the employer receives an immediate tax deduction for contributions to such plans and the income that is earned on the contributions is not taxable to the employer. The employer contributions and the trust earnings are not taxed to the employees until such amounts are made available to them.

Qualified plans are most appropriate where it is desirable to provide benefits for a cross section of employees. In some closely held corporations, the primary objective is to provide benefits for the officer-shareholder group and other highly paid personnel. The nondiscrimination requirements that must be met in a qualified plan may prevent such companies from attaining these objectives. Thus, a nonqualified arrangement may be needed as a supplement to, or used in lieu of, the qualified plan.

Self-Employed Retirement Plans

A Keogh or IRA participant may make a deductible contribution for a tax year up to the time prescribed for filing the individual's tax return. A Keogh plan must have been established by the end of the tax year (December 31) to obtain a current deduction for the contribution made in the subsequent year. An individual can establish an IRA after the end of the tax year and still receive a current deduction for the contribution made in the subsequent year. However, with the new restrictions on deducting contributions to IRAs for many middle-income and upper-income taxpayers, Keogh plans should become more important.

Individual Retirement Accounts

Fewer taxpayers are allowed to make deductible contributions to IRAs after 1986. A working taxpayer not covered by another qualified plan may still deduct IRA contributions up to the smaller of $2,000 or 100 percent of earned income. If both spouses work, each may individually establish an IRA. Where only one spouse has earned income, an IRA may be established for the non-working spouse. A total of $2,250 may then be contributed to the two IRAs. If the nonworking spouse has a small amount of income (e.g., jury duty), an election may be made to ignore such income for spousal IRA purposes.

A married couple may put $4,000 into an IRA when one spouse works for the other spouse. This requires paying the *employee spouse* $2,000 in salary and having him or her make an independent contribution to an IRA. This extra $2,000, however, is subject to FICA.

A single working taxpayer covered by another retirement plan may deduct a $2,000 IRA contribution only if adjusted gross income (AGI) is less than $25,000 a year. For married couples filing jointly, the ceiling is $40,000. The IRA deduction is reduced proportionately as AGI increases within a $10,000 phase-out range above the $25,000 and $40,000 ceilings.

A tax-free rollover for distributions from qualified plans (as well as from another IRA) is an alternative to 5-year or 10-year forward averaging.[105] A partial rollover (at least 50 percent of the balance) from an IRA is also subject to tax-free treatment. A distribution is not included in gross income if transferred within 60 days of distribution to an IRA or another qualified plan. Further, any rollover amount in an IRA can later be rolled over into another qualified plan if the IRA consists of only the amounts from the original qualified plan.

IRA and Keogh participants can self-direct their investments into a wide variety of assets. The participant self-directs the investments into various assets even though the assets are under the control of a trustee or custodian. The acquisition by an IRA or self-directed Keogh or corporate plan of collectibles (e.g., art, gems, metals) is treated as a distribution (taxed). For an IRA or Keogh participant under age 59½, there would also be a 10 percent premature distribution penalty. However, state-issued coins and gold and silver eagle coins issued by the United States may be placed in IRAs.

Comparison of § 401(k) Plan with IRA

Most employees will find a § 401(k) plan more attractive than an IRA. Probably the biggest limitation of an IRA is the $2,000 maximum shelter. Under § 401(k), the law permits the employees to shelter compensation up to $7,313 (in 1988).[106]

Another difference between § 401(k) and IRAs is the manner in which the money is treated. Money placed in an IRA may be tax deductible, whereas dollars placed in a § 401(k) plan are considered to be deferred compensation. Thus, a § 401(k) reduction may reduce profit sharing payments, group life insurance, and Social Security benefits. The new restrictions on deducting contributions to IRAs for many middle-income and upper-income taxpayers may cause many employees to utilize § 401(k) plans more frequently. Concept Summary 19–4 compares a § 401(k) plan with an IRA.

---

105. §§ 402(a)(5) and 408(d)(3).

106. This amount is indexed annually. The indexed amount for 1989 was not available at the time of this writing.

CONCEPT SUMMARY 19–4

Section 401(k) Plan and IRA Compared

	§ 401(k) Plan	IRA
Deduction limitation	Smaller of $7,313 (in 1988) or approximately 25% of total earnings. Limited by antidiscrimination requirements of § 401(k)(3).	$2,000 or 100% of compensation.
Distributions	Early withdrawal possible if for early retirement (55 or over) or to pay medical expenses.	10% penalty for early withdrawals.
Effect on gross earnings	Gross salary reduction, which may reduce profit sharing contributions, Social Security benefits, and group life insurance.	No effect.
Employer involvement	Must keep records; monitor for compliance with antidiscrimination test.	Minimal.
Lump-sum distributions	Favorable 5-year or 10-year forward averaging.	Ordinary income.
Timing of contribution	Within 30 days of plan year-end or due date of employer's return.*	Grace period up to due date of tax return.
Loans from plan	Yes.	No.

* Elective contributions must be made to the plan no later than 30 days after the end of the plan year, and non-elective contributions no later than the due date of the tax return (including extensions). Prop.Reg. § 1.401(a)–1(b)(7).

Nonqualified Deferred Compensation (NQDC) Plans

Nonqualified deferred compensation arrangements such as restricted property plans can be useful to attract executive talent or to provide substantial retirement benefits for executives. A restricted property plan may be used to retain a key employee of a closely held company when management continuity problems are anticipated. Without such employees, the untimely death or disability of one of the owners might cause a disruption of the business with an attendant loss in value for his or her heirs. Such plans may discriminate in favor of officers and other highly paid employees. The employer, however, does not receive a tax deduction until the employee is required to include the deferred compensation in income (upon the lapse of the restrictions).

The principal advantage of NQDC plans is that the employee can defer the recognition of income to future periods when his or her income tax bracket may be lower (e.g., during retirement years). The time value benefits from the deferral of income should also be considered. However, with such low individual tax rates in 1988 and 1989, an executive with a deferred compensation arrangement entered into in a prior year may wish to accelerate the income into 1989, since individual tax rates in future years may be higher.

The principal disadvantage of NQDC plans could be the bunching effect that takes place on the expiration of the period of deferral. In some cases, planning can alleviate this result.

EXAMPLE 36   During 1989, executive A enters into an agreement to postpone a portion of the payment for current services until retirement. The deferred amount is not segregated from the company's general assets and is subject to normal business risk. The entire payment, not the after-tax amount, is invested in securities and variable annuity contracts. A is not taxed on the payment in 1989, and the company receives no deduction in 1989. If A receives the deferred payment in a lump-sum when he retires, the tax rates may be higher and more progressive than in 1989. Thus, A may wish to arrange for a number of payments over a number of years to be made to him or a designated beneficiary. □

Stock Options

Rather than paying compensation in the form of corporate stock, an alternative approach is to issue options to an employee to purchase stock at a specific price. Stock option plans are used more frequently by publicly traded companies than by closely held companies. This difference is due to the problems of determining the stock value of a company that is not publicly held.

Nonqualified stock options (NQSOs) are more flexible and less restrictive than incentive stock options (ISOs). For example, the holding period for a nonqualified stock option is not as long as that for an ISO. Further, the option price of a nonqualified stock option may be less than the fair market value of the stock at the time the option is granted. A nonqualified stock option creates an employer deduction that lowers the cost of the nonqualified stock option to the employer. The employer may pass along this tax savings to the employee in the form of a cash payment. Both the employer and the employee may be better off by combining nonqualified stock options with additional cash payments rather than using ISOs. See Concept Summary 19–5.

Flexible Benefit Plans

Employees may be permitted to choose from a package of employer-provided fringe benefits.[107] In these so-called cafeteria benefit plans, some of the benefits chosen by an employee may be taxable, and some may be statutory nontaxable benefits (e.g., health and accident insurance and group term life insurance).

Employer contributions made to a flexible plan are included in an employee's gross income only to the extent that the employee actually elects the taxable benefits. Certain nondiscrimination standards with respect to coverage, eligibility for participation, contributions, and benefits must be met. Thus, such a plan must cover a fair cross section of employees. Also, a flexible plan cannot include an election to defer compensation, and a key employee is not exempt

---

107. § 125.

CONCEPT SUMMARY 19–5

Incentive Stock Options and Nonqualified Stock Options Compared

	ISO	NQSO
Granted at any price	No	Yes
May have any duration	No	Yes
Governing Code Section	§ 422A	§ 83
Spread subject to alternative minimum tax	Yes	No
Deduction to employer for spread	No	Yes
Type of gain/loss on disposal	Capital	Capital
Statutory amount ($100,000) limitation	Yes	No

from taxation on the taxable benefits made available where more than 25 percent of the statutory nontaxable benefits are provided to key employees.

PROBLEM MATERIALS

Discussion Questions

1. Compare and contrast defined contribution and defined benefit pension plans.

2. Compare and contrast qualified pension and profit sharing plans.

3. Determine whether each of the following independent statements best applies to a defined contribution plan (DCP), defined benefit plan (DBP), both (B), or neither (N):

    a. Includes an employee stock ownership plan (ESOP).

    b. Forfeitures can be allocated to the remaining participants' accounts.

    c. Requires greater reporting requirements and more actuarial and administrative costs.

    d. Forfeitures can revert to the employer.

    e. More favorable to employees who are older at the time of the adoption of the plan.

    f. Employee forfeitures can be used to reduce future contributions by the employer.

    g. May exclude employees who begin employment within five years of normal retirement age.

    h. Annual addition to each employee's account may not exceed the smaller of $30,000 or 25% of the employee's salary.

    i. The final benefit to a participant depends upon investment performance.

      j.   To avoid penalties, amount of annual contributions must meet minimum funding requirements.

4. Indicate whether the following statements apply to a pension plan (P), a profit sharing plan (PS), both (B), or neither (N):

      a.   Forfeited amounts can be used to reduce future contributions by the employer.

      b.   Allocation of forfeitures may discriminate in favor of the prohibited group (highly compensated employees).

      c.   Forfeitures can revert to the employer.

      d.   Forfeitures can increase plan benefits by allocating the forfeitures to participants.

      e.   An annual benefit of $60,000 could be payable on behalf of a participant.

      f.   More favorable to employees who are older at the time of the adoption of the qualified plan.

5. When will the $30,000 maximum annual contribution to a defined contribution plan be indexed?

6. What are the tax and financial advantages accruing to a company that adopts an employee stock ownership plan (ESOP) for employees?

7. List the qualification requirements that must be satisfied in order for a qualified plan to receive favorable tax treatment.

8. Is it possible to provide greater vested benefits for highly paid employees and still meet the nondiscrimination requirements under a qualified pension plan? Explain.

9. With respect to the participation requirement, what is a year of service?

10. What is vesting, and how will vesting requirements help employees who do not remain with one employer during their working years?

11. What are the minimum coverage requirements for qualified pension or profit sharing plans beginning in 1989?

12. Discuss the tax consequences to employee, employer, and the trust of a qualified pension or profit sharing plan.

13. What three alternative options are available for distributions of benefits from a qualified retirement plan?

14. How are lump-sum distributions from qualified plans taxed to the recipients (capital gain or ordinary income)? Is income averaging available to an employee who receives a lump-sum distribution?

15. Which of the following would be considered a tax benefit or advantage of a qualified retirement plan:

      a.   Certain lump-sum distributions may be subject to capital gain rates.

      b.   Employer contributions are currently deductible.

      c.   Employee contributions are currently deductible.

     d.   The qualified trust is tax-exempt as to all income (other than unrelated business income).

     e.   In a lump-sum distribution, any capital gain tax on the portion attributable to any unrealized appreciation in the stock of the employer at the time of distribution is deferred until the time the employee disposes of such stock in a taxable transaction.

     f.   Election may be made to allow a lump-sum distribution to be subject to a 5-year or 10-year forward averaging technique.

16. What ceiling limitations have been placed on employer contributions (relative to individual employees) to defined contribution and defined benefit plans?

17. List the additional qualification requirements for top-heavy retirement plans.

18. Define key employee for purposes of a top-heavy plan.

19. Discuss the differences between a Keogh plan and an Individual Retirement Account (IRA).

20. What individuals may make a deductible contribution to an IRA?

21. Discuss the dilemma of an employee with respect to a nonqualified deferred compensation (NQDC) plan and the following items: funded and nonfunded, forfeitable and nonforfeitable.

22. A nonqualified deferred compensation contract is taxable under the constructive receipt doctrine for which of the following situations:

     a.   The contract is funded and there is no substantial risk of forfeiture.

     b.   Same as (a), except the employee must work for three years.

     c.   An agreement to defer payment is entered into after compensation is earned.

     d.   The agreement is entered into before rendering of services.

     e.   In (a), the contract is not funded.

23. What is the purpose of the golden parachute provision?

24. Explain the differences in tax treatment of an employer and employee (or other provider of services) with respect to the general rule (no election) and the special election under § 83(b) when dealing with a restricted property plan. Explain the risk aspect of this tax provision.

25. What is a substantial risk of forfeiture? Why is it necessary to impose this restriction on the transfer of restricted property?

26. Determine which of the following conditions would cause options to fall *outside* of § 422A(b) (incentive stock options):

     a.   The employee disposes of his stock within 15 months from the date of the granting of the options.

     b.   The employee is allowed to exercise the options up to 12 years from the date the options are granted.

    c.   The employee is transferred to the parent of the corporation six months before he exercises the options.

    d.   The option price is 112% of the fair market value of the stock on the grant date, and the shareholder owns 15% of the stock.

    e.   The option may be exercised by the employee's spouse in case of the employee's death.

27. Discuss the advantages of a nonqualified stock option plan versus an incentive stock option plan.

28. Would a 30-year-old executive of T Corporation earning $100,000 prefer an extra $20,000 bonus or the option to purchase $20,000 worth of securities for $5,000 from the employer under a nonqualified stock option plan in 1989?

29. Compare and contrast an IRA and a § 401(k) plan.

30. Explain what is meant by a cafeteria benefit plan.

31. Indicate whether each of the following items is considered a nonqualified compensation plan (N), a qualified compensation plan (Q), or both (B):

    a.   Individual Retirement Account.

    b.   Incentive stock option.

    c.   Group term life insurance.

    d.   Cafeteria plan.

    e.   Pension plan.

    f.   Employee stock ownership plan.

    g.   Nonqualified stock option.

    h.   Restricted stock option.

    i.   Keogh plan.

    j.   Simplified employee pension plan.

Problems

32. N Corporation has a total of 1,000 employees, of whom 700 are non-highly compensated. The retirement plan covers 300 non-highly compensated employees and 200 highly compensated employees. Does this plan satisfy the minimum coverage test for 1989?

33. R Corporation's pension plan benefits 60 of its 100 highly compensated employees during 1989. How many of its 60 non-highly compensated employees must benefit to meet the ratio test for the minimum coverage requirement?

34. A retirement plan covers 72% of the non-highly compensated individuals. The plan benefits 49 of the 131 employees. Determine if the participation requirement is met for 1989.

35. An employee of P, Inc., has completed five years of employment and is 50% vested in her retirement plan. Does this plan meet the new minimum vesting standards required for 1989?

36. P, age 46, is the sole remaining participant of a money purchase pension plan. The plan is terminated, and a $140,000 taxable distribution is made to P. Calculate the amount of any early distribution penalty tax.

37. In 1989, T receives a $170,000 distribution from his qualified retirement plan. If this amount is not a lump-sum distribution, calculate the amount of any excess distribution penalty tax. No after-tax contributions were made by T to the plan.

38. Participant T received a distribution from a qualified plan that was entitled to capital gain treatment under § 402(a)(2). The 100 shares of the employer company stock received have a tax basis of $20 per share and a fair market value of $85 per share. T sold this stock five months after the distribution for $110 per share. Calculate the amount and character of any gain to T.

39. When K retires in 1989, he receives a lump-sum distribution of $50,000 from a noncontributory qualified pension plan. His active period of participation was from January 1, 1971, through December 31, 1978. If K files a joint return with his wife in 1989 and elects to use the 10-year forward averaging provision, calculate (a) his separate tax on this distribution and (b) the capital gain portion.

40. E receives a $150,000 lump-sum distribution in 1989 from a contributory pension plan, which includes employer common stock with net unrealized appreciation of $20,000. E contributed $20,000 to the qualified plan while he was an active participant from February 10, 1973, to February 10, 1978.
    a. Calculate the total taxable amount.
    b. Calculate the separate tax assuming E elects to use the 5-year or 10-year forward averaging provision.
    c. Calculate the capital gain portion. (Treat part of a calendar month as one month.)

41. R has been an active participant in a defined benefit plan for 17 years. During her last five years of employment, R earned $20,000, $30,000, $45,000, $50,000, and $60,000, respectively (representing R's highest income years).
    a. Calculate R's maximum allowable benefits from this qualified plan (assume there are fewer than 100 participants).
    b. Assume that R's average compensation for her high three years is $80,000. Calculate R's maximum allowable benefits.

42. The compensation paid by M Corporation to the plan participants of a profit sharing plan in 1989 was $33,300. During 1989, M Corporation contributed $10,000 to the plan.
    a. Calculate M Corporation's deductible amount for 1989.
    b. Calculate the amount of the contribution carryover from 1989.

43. Determine the maximum contributions to a qualified plan in the following independent situations:

    a. M is covered by a money purchase pension plan and has an annual salary of $160,000 in 1989.

    b. N is a participant in a profit sharing plan and has an annual salary of $110,000 in 1989.

    c. P is a participant in a money purchase pension plan and has an annual salary of $220,000 in 1989. The plan has a 10% contribution formula.

44. During 1989, P is a key employee of a top-heavy pension plan. His salary is $240,000. Calculate P's maximum contribution to such a defined benefit plan.

45. Determine the maximum annual benefits payable to an employee from a defined benefit plan in the following independent situations:

    a. Q, age 65, has been a participant for 12 years, and his highest average compensation for three years is $85,000.

    b. M, age 66, has been a participant for 8 years (11 years of service) and his highest average compensation for three years is $86,000.

    c. P, age 67, has been a participant for 11 years in a collectively bargained plan with 238 participants. His highest average compensation for three years is $70,300.

46. Determine the minimum nonintegrated contributions or benefits for a plan participant who is a non-key employee in a top-heavy plan for the following independent situations:

    a. X is a participant in P Company's defined contribution plan. His high five-year average compensation is $26,000, and his current year compensation is $32,000.

    b. Assume the same data as in (a), except that the largest percentage contribution on behalf of a key employee is 2%.

    c. Y is an 11-year participant in D Company's defined benefit plan. His high five-year average compensation is $30,000, and his current year compensation is $34,000. His company has contributed $5,600 to his plan during the past 10 years.

47. N has five years of service completed as of March 2, 1989, his employment anniversary date. His plan uses the graded vesting rule.

    a. How much is N's nonforfeitable percentage if the plan is not top-heavy?

    b. Assume the plan is top-heavy in 1989. How much is N's nonforfeitable percentage?

    c. Assume the plan is top-heavy in 1989 and the company uses cliff vesting. How much is N's nonforfeitable percentage?

48. F earns $220,000 of self-employment net income in 1989 in a sole proprietorship.

    a. Calculate the maximum amount that F can deduct for contributions to a Keogh plan.

b. Suppose F contributes more than the allowable amount to the Keogh plan? What are the consequences to F?

c. Can F retire and begin receiving Keogh payments at age 55?

49. B, a married individual, decides in 1989 to start an IRA even though he is a member of a corporate pension plan. B's total income for 1989 is as follows:

Salary	$19,000
Dividends	1,500
Interest	700
Veteran's education benefits	2,200
Adjusted gross income	21,200

If B contributes $1,600 to his IRA on December 20, 1989, what is his allowable IRA deduction, if any, for 1989.

50. Answer the following independent statements with respect to IRA contributions:

a. During 1989, A earns a salary of $22,000 and is not an active participant in any other qualified plan. His wife has no earned income. What is the maximum total deductible contribution to their IRAs? A wishes to contribute as much as possible to his own IRA.

b. B has earned income during 1989 of $21,000, and her husband has earned income of $1,700. They are not active participants in any other qualified plan. What is the maximum contribution to their IRAs?

c. X's employer makes a contribution of $3,500 to X's simplified employee pension plan. If X's earned income is $27,000 and AGI is $24,000 during 1989, what amount, if any, can X also contribute to an IRA?

51. G Company pays bonuses each year to its key executives. The specific employees to receive bonuses and the amount of bonus for each recipient are determined on December 1 of each year. Each employee eligible for a bonus may decide on or before November 15 of each year to postpone the receipt of the bonus until retirement or death. An employee electing to postpone receipt of a bonus is allowed to designate, at any time before retirement, the time and manner of the post-retirement payments and to designate the persons to receive any amount payable after death. Since most employees elect to defer their bonuses, separate accounts are not maintained for each employee. When would these bonuses be taxed to the executive and be deductible by G Company?

52. N is a disqualifying individual, as defined under § 280G, who receives a possible golden parachute payment of $500,000 from her employer. Her base amount (average annual compensation for the most recent five tax years) is $200,000.

a. Calculate the amount deductible by N's employer and any excise tax payable by N.

b. Assume that N's base amount is $100,000 and N receives $310,000. Calculate the employer's deduction and N's excise tax.

53. Executive R receives a $600,000 payment under a golden parachute agreement entered into on January 14, 1989. R's base amount from C Corporation is $140,000.

    a. What amount is not deductible to C Corporation under § 280G?

    b. What total tax must R pay, assuming a 28% tax rate?

    c. Answer (a) and (b) assuming the payment is $400,000.

54. On February 20, 1989, G (an executive of R Corporation) purchased 100 shares of R stock (selling at $20 a share) for $10. A condition of the transaction was that G must resell the stock to R at cost if he leaves his employer voluntarily within five years of receiving the stock (assume this represents a substantial risk of forfeiture).

    a. Assuming that no special election is made under § 83(b), what amount, if any, is taxable to G in 1989?

    b. Five years later when the stock is selling for $40 a share, G is still employed by the same firm. What amount of ordinary income, if any, is taxable to G?

    c. What amount, if any, is deductible by R as compensation expense five years later?

    d. Assuming G made the § 83(b) special election in 1989, what amount would be taxable in 1989?

    e. In (d), what amount would be deductible by R Corporation five years later?

    f. Under (d), assume G sold all the stock six years later for $65 per share. How much capital gain is included in G's gross income?

    g. In (d), what loss is available to G if he voluntarily resigns before the five-year period and does not sell the stock back to the corporation?

    h. In (g), in the year G resigns, what amount, if any, would be taxable to R Corporation?

55. On July 2, 1985, P Corporation sold 1,000 of its common shares (worth $14 per share) to its employee C for $5 per share. The sale was subject to C's agreement to resell the shares to the corporation for $5 per share if his employment is terminated within the following four years. The shares had a value of $24 per share on July 2, 1989. C sold the shares for $31 per share on September 16, 1989. No special election under § 83(b) is made.

    a. What amount, if any, will be taxed to C on July 2, 1985?

    b. On July 2, 1989?

    c. On September 16, 1989?

    d. What deduction, if any, will P Corporation obtain?

    e. Assume the same facts but that C makes the election under § 83(b). What amount, if any, will be taxed to C on July 2, 1985?

    f. Will the assumption made in (e) have any effect on any deduction P Corporation will receive? Explain.

56. R exercises 100 incentive stock options of X Corporation on May 21, 1989, at the option price of $100 per share when the fair market value is $120 per share. He sells the 100 shares of common stock three and one-half years later for $140.

    a. Calculate the total long-term capital gain on this sale.

    b. Assume R holds the stock seven months and sells the shares for $140 per share. Calculate any ordinary income on the sale.

    c. In (b), what amount can X Corporation deduct?

    d. Suppose R holds the stock for two years and sells the shares for $115 per share. Calculate any capital gain on this transaction.

    e. In (a), assume the options are nonqualified options with a nonascertainable fair market value on the date of the grant. Calculate total long-term capital gain, if any, in the year of sale.

    f. In (e), assume that each option has an ascertainable fair market value of $10 on the date of the grant and no substantial risk of forfeiture exists. Calculate total long-term capital gain, if any, on the date of the sale.

57. On November 19, 1988, J is granted a nonqualified stock option to purchase 100 shares of S Company (on such date the stock is selling for $8 per share and the option price is $9 per share). J exercises the option on August 21, 1989, when the stock is selling for $10 per share. Five months later, J sells the shares for $11.50 per share.

    a. What amount is taxable to J in 1988?

    b. What amount is taxable to J in 1989?

    c. What amount and type of gain is taxable to J in 1990?

    d. What amount, if any, is deductible by S Company in 1989?

    e. What amount, if any, is recognized in 1990 if the stock is sold for $9.50 per share?

Research Problems

Research Problem 1   Several years ago, executive L received restricted stock containing a buy-sell restriction that, by its terms, would never lapse. A § 83(b) election was not made. During 1989, this nonlapsing restriction is cancelled in connection with a public offering of the stock. What are the tax consequences to L?

Research Problem 2   F had been a participant in the pension plan of Post, Inc., since 1974. In 1987, he terminated employment with Post, Inc., and became an employee of Daily, Inc. In 1973, the IRS issued a letter that the pension plan was qualified under § 401(a) and that the pension trust was therefore exempt from tax under § 501(a). In 1988, the Commissioner examined the pension plan and determined that the plan discriminated among salaried employees. The Commissioner revoked the plan's qualified status and the trust's exempt status retroactively to January 1, 1985. When F changed jobs in 1987, he rolled over his distribution from the pension plan to an IRA under § 402(a)(5). Discuss F's tax situation.

Research Problem 3   H and W were married, but H died on February 25, 1989. During 1989, H earned $5,226 in wages, but W had no earned income. Neither had contributed any money to an IRA during 1989. What amount, if any, can be contributed to H's IRA and/or W's spousal IRA?

Research Problem 4   Determine the validity of the use of a rabbi trust for a nonqualified deferred compensation plan.

Research Problem 5   What are stock appreciation rights? Determine their tax treatment.

7

CORPORATIONS AND PARTNERSHIPS

The primary orientation of this text is toward basic tax concepts and the individual taxpayer. Although many of these tax concepts also apply to corporations and partnerships, numerous tax concepts apply specifically to corporations or partnerships. An overview of these provisions is presented in Part 7. Comprehensive coverage of these topics appears in *West's Federal Taxation: Corporations, Partnerships, Estates, and Trusts.*

CHAPTER
20
Corporations and Partnerships

20

CORPORATIONS AND PARTNERSHIPS

OBJECTIVES

Compare the income tax treatment of corporations with that applicable to individuals.

Introduce the rules governing the formation, operation, and liquidation of a corporation.

Stress the utility of an S election and the tax consequences that result.

Summarize the tax rules that apply to the formation and operation of a partnership.

Evaluate the advantages and disadvantages of the various forms of conducting a business.

Illustrate how to use various entities to reduce the overall income tax burden of the family unit.

OUTLINE

Until now this text has concentrated on Federal income taxation as applicable to individual taxpayers. However, some awareness of the tax implications of other business forms is necessary in order to make even the most basic decisions.

EXAMPLE 1

U and T are contemplating entering into a new business venture that will require additional capital investment by other parties. As the venture will involve financial risk, both U and T are concerned about personal liability. Further, they would prefer to avoid any income taxes at the entity level. Both U and T would like to take advantage of any losses the venture might generate during its formative period. ☐

In choosing the form for carrying out the venture, U and T would have to consider using a corporation. The corporate form limits a shareholder's liability to the amount invested in the stock. Regular corporations, however, are subject to the corporate income tax. Furthermore, losses incurred by corporations do not pass through to the shareholders. Perhaps the ideal solution would be to use the corporate form and make a Subchapter S election. The election would avoid the corporate income tax and permit the pass-through of losses while providing limited liability for the shareholders.

Although the resolution of the problem posed by Example 1 seemed simple enough, it did not consider the possible use of a partnership. More important, the decision required *some* knowledge of corporations and the Subchapter S election. This chapter is intended to provide such knowledge by briefly reviewing the tax consequences of the various forms of business organization.

WHAT IS A CORPORATION?

Compliance with State Law

Initially, a company must comply with the specific requirements for corporate status under state law. For example, it is necessary to draft and file articles of incorporation with the state regulatory agency, be granted a charter, and issue stock to shareholders.

Compliance with state law, although important, is not the only requirement that must be met to qualify for corporate tax status. For example, a corporation qualifying under state law may be disregarded as a taxable entity if it is a mere sham lacking in economic substance. The key consideration is the degree of business activity conducted at the corporate level.

EXAMPLE 2

C and D are joint owners of a tract of unimproved real estate that they wish to protect from future creditors. C and D form R Corporation, to which they transfer the land in return for all of the corporation's stock. The corporation merely holds title to the land and conducts no other activities. In all respects, R Corporation meets the legal requirements of a corporation under applicable state law. R Corporation probably would not be recognized as a separate entity for corporate tax purposes under the facts set forth in this example.[1] ☐

EXAMPLE 3

Assume the same facts as in Example 2. In addition to holding title to the land, R Corporation leases the property, collects rents, and pays the property taxes thereon. R Corporation probably would be treated as a corporation for Federal income tax purposes because of the scope of its activities. ☐

In some instances, the IRS has attempted to disregard (or collapse) a corporation in order to make its income taxable directly to the shareholders.[2] In other cases, the IRS has asserted that the corporation is a separate taxable entity so as to assess tax at the corporate level and to tax corporate distributions to shareholders as dividend income (double taxation).[3]

The Association Approach

An organization not qualifying as a regular corporation under state law may nevertheless be taxed as a corporation under the association approach. The designation given to an entity under the state law is not controlling. For example, a partnership of physicians has been treated as an association even though state law prohibited the practice of medicine in the corporate form. The partnership thus was subject to the Federal income tax rules applicable to corporations.[4] Another sensitive area involves limited partnerships where the only general partner is a corporation. Unless certain prescribed guidelines are carefully followed, the IRS will treat the partnership as an association.[5]

Whether or not an entity will be considered an association for Federal income tax purposes depends upon the number of corporate characteristics it possesses. According to court decisions and the Regulations, corporate characteristics include the following:[6]

1. Associates.

2. An objective to carry on a business and divide the gains therefrom.

3. Continuity of life.

4. Centralized management.

5. Limited liability.

6. Free transferability of interests.

The Regulations state that an unincorporated organization shall not be classified as an association unless it possesses *more* corporate than noncorpo-

---

1. See *Paymer v. Comm.*, 45–2 USTC ¶9353, 33 AFTR 1536, 150 F.2d 334 (CA–2, 1945).
2. *Floyd Patterson*, 25 TCM 1230, T.C.Memo. 1966–239, *aff'd.* in 68–2 USTC ¶9471, 22 AFTR2d 5810 (CA–2, 1968).
3. *Raffety Farms Inc. v. U.S.*, 75–1 USTC ¶9271, 35 AFTR2d 75–811, 511 F.2d 1234 (CA–8, 1975).
4. *U.S. v. Kintner*, 54–2 USTC ¶9626, 47 AFTR 995, 216 F.2d 418 (CA–5, 1954).
5. Rev.Proc. 72–13, 1972–1 C.B. 735.
6. Reg. § 301.7701–2(a).

rate characteristics. In making this determination, the characteristics common to both corporate and noncorporate business organizations are to be disregarded. Both corporations and partnerships generally have associates (shareholders and partners) and an objective to carry on a business and divide the gains. Therefore, only if a partnership has at least three of attributes 3 through 6 will it be treated as an association (taxable as a corporation).

EXAMPLE 4   The XYZ Partnership agreement provides for the following: the partnership terminates with the withdrawal of a partner; all of the partners have authority to participate in the management of the partnership; all of the partners are individually liable for the debts of the partnership; and a partner may not freely transfer his or her interest in the partnership to another. None of the corporate attributes 3 through 6 are present. Since the majority requirement contained in the Regulations is not satisfied, XYZ is not taxable as an association. □

INCOME TAX CONSIDERATIONS

Individuals and Corporations Compared—An Overview

Business operations may be conducted as a sole proprietorship, as a partnership, or in corporate form.

- Sole proprietorships are not separate taxable entities. Therefore, the owner of the business will report all business transactions on his or her individual income tax return.

- Partnerships are not subject to the income tax. Under the *conduit* concept, the various tax attributes of the partnership's operations flow through to the individual partners to be reported on their personal income tax returns.

- The regular corporate form of doing business carries with it the imposition of the corporate income tax. The corporation is recognized as a separate taxpaying entity. Thus, income is taxed to the corporation as earned and taxed again to the shareholders as dividends when distributed.

- A regular corporation may elect to be taxed as an S corporation. Such special treatment is similar (although not identical) to the partnership rules. Income tax is generally avoided at the corporate level, and shareholders are taxed currently on the taxable income of the S corporation.

Similarities between Corporate and Individual Tax Rules.   The gross income of a corporation is determined in much the same manner as for individuals. Both individuals and corporations are entitled to exclusions from gross income, such as interest on municipal bonds. The tax rules for gains and losses from property transactions are also treated similarly. For example, whether a gain or loss is capital or ordinary depends on the nature and use of the asset rather than the type of taxpayer. Upon the sale or other taxable disposition of depreciable personalty, the recapture rules of § 1245 make no distinction between corporate and noncorporate taxpayers. In the case of the recapture of depreciation on real property (§ 1250), however, corporate tax-payers are treated more severely in terms of tax consequences. Under § 291, corporations must recognize as additional ordinary income 20 percent of the excess of the amount that would be recaptured under § 1245 over the amount recaptured under § 1250 (refer to Example 22, chapter 17).

The business deductions of corporations also parallel those available to individuals. Therefore, corporate deductions are allowed for all ordinary and necessary expenses paid or incurred in carrying on a trade or business under the general rule of § 162(a). Corporations may also deduct interest (§ 163), certain taxes (§ 164), losses (§ 165), bad debts (§ 166), depreciation (§ 167), cost recovery (§ 168), charitable contributions subject to corporate limitation rules (§ 170), net operating losses (§ 172), research and experimental expend-itures (§ 174), and other less common deductions.

Many of the tax credits available to individuals, such as the foreign tax credit (§ 27), can be claimed by corporations. Not available to corporations are certain credits that are personal in nature, such as the child and depen-dent care credit (§ 21), the credit for the elderly or disabled (§ 22), and the earned income credit (§ 32).

Corporations generally have the same choices of accounting periods as do individuals. Like an individual, a corporation may choose a calendar year or a fiscal year for reporting purposes. Corporations do enjoy greater flexibility in the election of a tax year. For example, corporations usually can have differ-ent tax years from those of their shareholders. Also, a newly formed corpora-tion (as a new taxpayer) generally has a free choice of any approved account-ing period without having to obtain the consent of the IRS. As noted in chapter 18, however, personal service corporations are subject to severe re-strictions on the use of a fiscal year.

In terms of accounting methods, the use of the cash method is denied to large corporations (those with average annual gross receipts in excess of $5 million). Smaller corporations as well as qualified personal service corpora-tions and other corporations engaged in the trade or business of farming have a choice between the cash or accrual method of accounting for tax purposes. Both individuals and corporations that maintain inventory for sale to custom-ers are required to use the accrual method of accounting for determining sales and cost of goods sold.

Dissimilarities. In terms of income tax rates, noncorporate taxpayers are subject to two rates (15 and 28 percent). Corporations, however, are subject to three rates (15, 25, and 34 percent). Both noncorporate and corporate taxpay-ers suffer a phase-out of the benefits of the lower brackets once taxable income reaches a certain level.

Both corporate and noncorporate taxpayers are subject to the alternative minimum tax (AMT). For AMT purposes, many adjustments and tax prefer-ence items are the same for both, but other adjustments and tax preferences exist that apply only to corporations or only to individuals. Corporate tax rates are discussed later in the chapter. The AMT applicable to corporations is discussed at length in chapter 12.

All allowable corporate deductions are treated as business expenses. Thus, the determination of adjusted gross income, so essential for individuals, has no relevance to corporations. Corporations need not be concerned with classifying deductions into *deduction for* and *deduction from* categories. The standard deduction, itemized deductions, and personal and dependency ex-emptions are not available to corporations.

Specific Provisions Compared

Corporate and individual tax rules differ in the following additional areas:

- Capital gains and losses.
- Charitable contributions.
- Net operating losses.
- Special deductions for corporations.

Capital Gains and Losses.   Both corporate and noncorporate taxpayers are still required to aggregate gains and losses from the taxable sale or exchange of capital assets. (Refer to chapter 16 for a description of the netting process that takes place after the aggregation has been completed.) The favored tax treatment of a net capital gain has been eliminated. For both corporate and noncorporate taxpayers, therefore, net capital gains are taxed at ordinary income rates.

Significant differences still exist in the treatment of capital losses for income tax purposes. Individuals, for example, can annually deduct up to $3,000 of net capital losses against ordinary income. Corporations are not permitted to use net capital losses to offset ordinary income. Net capital losses can be used only to offset past or future capital gains.[7] Also, unlike individuals, corporations are not allowed an unlimited carryover period for capital losses. Instead, they may carry back excess capital losses to the three preceding years, applying them initially to the earliest year. If not exhausted by the carryback, remaining unused capital losses may be carried over for a period of five years from the year of the loss.[8] When carried back or over, a long-term capital loss is treated as a short-term capital loss. For noncorporate taxpayers, a capital loss does not lose its identity. Thus, long-term capital losses of noncorporate taxpayers are carried forward as long-term capital losses.

EXAMPLE 5   T Corporation, a calendar year taxpayer, incurs a long-term net capital loss of $5,000 for 1989. None of the capital loss may be deducted in 1989. T Corporation may, however, carry the loss back to years 1986, 1987, and 1988 (in this order) and offset any capital gains recognized in these years. If the carryback does not exhaust the loss, the loss may be carried over to 1990, 1991, 1992, 1993, and 1994 (in this order). Such capital loss carrybacks or carryovers are treated as short-term capital losses. □

Charitable Contributions.   Generally, a charitable contribution deduction is allowed only for the tax year in which the payment is made. However, an important exception is made for accrual basis corporations. The deduction may be claimed in the tax year preceding payment if the contribution has been authorized by the board of directors by the end of that tax year and is, in fact, paid on or before the fifteenth day of the third month of the next tax year.[9]

---

7. §§ 1211(a) and (b).
8. § 1212(a).

9. § 170(a)(2).

EXAMPLE 6

On December 28, 1989, the board of directors of the XYZ Company, a calendar year accrual basis taxpayer, authorizes a $5,000 donation to a qualified charity. The donation is paid on March 14, 1990. XYZ Corporation may claim the $5,000 donation as a deduction for 1989. As an alternative, XYZ Corporation may claim the deduction in 1990 (the year of payment). □

Like individuals, corporations are not permitted an unlimited charitable contribution deduction. For any one year, a corporate taxpayer is limited to 10 percent of taxable income computed without regard to the charitable contribution deduction, any net operating loss carryback or capital loss carryback, or the dividends received deduction.[10] Any contributions in excess of the 10 percent limitation may be carried over to the five succeeding tax years. Any carryover must be added to subsequent contributions and will be subject to the 10 percent limitation. In applying this limitation, however, the most recent contributions must be deducted first.[11]

EXAMPLE 7

During 1989, T Corporation (a calendar year taxpayer) had the following income and expenses:

Income from operations	$140,000
Expenses from operations	110,000
Dividends received	10,000
Charitable contributions made in 1989	5,000

For the purposes of the 10% limitation only, T Corporation's taxable income is $40,000 ($140,000 − $110,000 + $10,000). Consequently, the allowable charitable contribution deduction for 1989 is $4,000 (10% × $40,000). The $1,000 unused portion of the contribution may bc carried over to 1990, 1991, 1992, 1993, and 1994 (in that order) until exhausted.

□

EXAMPLE 8

Assume the same facts as in Example 7. In 1990, T Corporation has taxable income (after adjustments) of $50,000 and makes a charitable contribution of $4,800. The maximum deduction allowed for 1990 is $5,000 (10% × $50,000). The first $4,800 of the allowed deduction must be allocated to the 1990 contributions, and the $200 excess is carried over from 1989. The remaining $800 of the 1989 contribution may be carried over to 1991, etc. □

As noted in chapter 11, the deduction for charitable contributions of ordinary income property is limited to the lesser of the fair market value or the adjusted basis of the property. A special rule permits a corporation

---

10. § 170(b)(2).

11. § 170(d)(2).

to contribute inventory (ordinary income property) to certain charitable organizations and receive a deduction equal to the adjusted basis plus one-half of the difference between the fair market value and the adjusted basis of the property.[12] In no event, however, may the deduction exceed twice the adjusted basis of the property. To qualify for this exception, the inventory must be used by the charity in its exempt purpose for the care of children, the ill, or the needy.

Net Operating Losses.   The computation of a net operating loss for individuals was discussed in chapter 8. Corporations are not subject to the complex adjustments required for individuals (e.g., a corporation has no adjustments for nonbusiness deductions or capital gains and losses). The reason corporations are subject to fewer adjustments than are individuals is that their loss more clearly approximates a true economic loss. Artificial deductions (e.g., personal and dependency exemptions) that merely generate paper losses are not a problem with corporations.

In computing the net operating loss of a corporation, the dividends received deduction (discussed below) can be claimed in determining the amount of the loss.[13] Corporate net operating losses may be carried back three years and over fifteen years (or taxpayers may elect to forgo the carryback period) to offset taxable income for those years.

EXAMPLE 9

In 1989, XYZ Corporation has gross income of $200,000 and deductions of $300,000, excluding the dividends received deduction. XYZ Corporation received taxable dividends of $100,000 from Exxon stock. XYZ Corporation has a net operating loss of $170,000, computed as follows:

Gross income (including Exxon dividends)		$200,000
Less: Business deductions	$300,000	
Dividends received deduction (70% × $100,000)	70,000	370,000
Taxable income (loss)		($170,000)

□

EXAMPLE 10

Assume the same facts as in Example 9 and that XYZ Corporation had taxable income of $40,000 in 1986. The net operating loss of $170,000 is carried back to 1986 (unless XYZ elects not to carry back the loss to such year). The carryover to 1987 is $130,000, computed as follows:

---

12. § 170(e)(3).   13. § 172(d).

Taxable income for 1986	$ 40,000
Less: Net operating loss carryback from 1989	170,000
Carryover of unabsorbed 1989 loss	($130,000)

☐

In Example 10, the carryback to 1986 might have been ill-advised had XYZ Corporation little, if any, taxable income in 1987 and 1988 and had it anticipated large amounts of taxable income in the immediate future. If such were the case, the election to forgo the carryback might generate greater tax savings. In this regard, three considerations should be taken into account. First, the time value of the tax refund that is lost by not using the carryback procedure must be considered. Second, the election to forgo a net operating loss carryback is irrevocable. Thus, it cannot be changed later if the future high profits do not materialize. Third, future increases or decreases in corporate income tax rates that can reasonably be anticipated should be considered.

Deductions Available Only to Corporations

Dividends Received Deduction.   The purpose of the dividends received deduction is to prevent triple taxation. Absent the deduction, income paid to a corporation in the form of a dividend would be subject to taxation for a second time (once to the distributing corporation) with no corresponding deduction to the distributing corporation. A third level of tax would be assessed when the recipient corporation paid the income to its shareholders. Since the dividends received deduction may be less than 100 percent, only partial relief is provided under the law.

The amount of the dividends received deduction depends upon the percentage of ownership the recipient corporate shareholder holds in the corporation making the dividend distribution.[14] For dividends received or accrued, the deduction percentage is summarized as follows:

Percentage of Ownership by Corporate Shareholder	Deduction Percentage
Less than 20%	70%
20% or more (but less than 80%)	80%
80% or more	100%

The dividends received deduction may be limited to a percentage of the taxable income of a corporation computed without regard to the net operating loss deduction, the dividends received deduction, or any capital loss carryback to the current tax year. The percentage of taxable income limitation corresponds to the deduction percentage. Thus, if a corporate shareholder owns less than 20 percent of the stock in the distributing corporation, the dividends received deduction is limited to 70 percent of taxable income (as

---

14. § 243(a).

previously defined). However, this limitation does not apply if the corporation has a net operating loss for the current taxable year.[15]

In working with these myriad rules, the following steps need to be taken:

1. Multiply the dividends received by the deduction percentage.

2. Multiply the taxable income (as previously defined) by the deduction percentage.

3. The deduction is limited to the lesser of Step 1 or Step 2, unless subtracting the amount derived from Step 1 from taxable income (as previously defined) generates a negative number. If so, the amount derived in Step 1 should be used.

EXAMPLE 11

P, R, and T Corporations are three unrelated calendar year corporations and for 1989 have the following transactions:

	P Corporation	R Corporation	T Corporation
Gross income from operations	$400,000	$320,000	$260,000
Expenses from operations	(340,000)	(340,000)	(340,000)
Dividends received from domestic corporations (less than 20% ownership)	200,000	200,000	200,000
Taxable income before the dividends received deduction	$260,000	$180,000	$120,000

In determining the dividends received deduction, use the step procedure just described:

	P	R	T
Step 1 (70% × $200,000)	$140,000	$140,000	$140,000
Step 2			
70% × $260,000 (taxable income)	$182,000		
70% × $180,000 (taxable income)		$126,000	
70% × $120,000 (taxable income)			$84,000
Step 3			
Lesser of Step 1 or Step 2	$140,000	$126,000	
Generates a net operating loss			$140,000

□

---

15. § 246(b).

R Corporation is subject to the 70 percent of taxable income limitation. It does not qualify for the loss rule treatment, since subtracting $140,000 (Step 1) from $180,000 does not yield a negative figure. T Corporation does qualify for the loss rule treatment because subtracting $140,000 (Step 1) from $120,000 does yield a negative figure. In summary, the dividends received deduction for each corporation for 1989 is as follows: $140,000 for P Corporation, $126,000 for R Corporation, and $140,000 for T Corporation. If a corporation already has a net operating loss before any dividends received deduction is claimed, the taxable income limitation does not apply. Consequently, the full dividends received deduction (as calculated in Step 1) is allowed.

Deduction of Organizational Expenditures.   Under § 248, a corporation may elect to amortize organizational expenses over a period of 60 months or more. If the election is not made on a timely basis, such expenditures cannot be deducted until the corporation ceases to conduct business and liquidates. The election is made in a statement attached to the corporation's return for its first taxable year.

Organizational expenditures include the following:

- Legal services incident to organization (e.g., drafting the corporate charter, bylaws, minutes of organizational meetings, terms of original stock certificates).
- Necessary accounting services.
- Expenses of temporary directors and of organizational meetings of directors and shareholders.
- Fees paid to the state of incorporation.

Expenditures that do not qualify include those connected with issuing or selling shares of stock or other securities (e.g., commissions, professional fees, and printing costs) or with the transfer of assets to a corporation. Such expenditures are generally added to the capital account and are not subject to amortization.

Determination of Tax Liability

Income Tax Rates.   Current rates applicable to corporations are as follows:

Taxable Income	Tax Rate
$50,000 or less	15%
Over $50,000 but not over $75,000	25
Over $75,000	34

For a corporation that has taxable income in excess of $100,000 for any taxable year, the amount of the tax shall be increased by the lesser of (1) 5 percent of such excess or (2) $11,750. In effect, the additional tax means a 39 percent rate for every dollar of taxable income from $100,000 to $335,000.[16] Thus, the benefits of the lower rates on the first $75,000 of taxable income completely phase out at $335,000.

EXAMPLE 12   X Corporation, a calendar year taxpayer, has taxable income of $90,000 for 1989. Its income tax liability will be $18,850 determined as follows: $7,500 (15% × $50,000) + $6,250 (25% × $25,000) + $5,100 (34% × $15,000). □

EXAMPLE 13   Y Corporation, a calendar year taxpayer, has taxable income of $335,000 for 1989. Its income tax liability will be $113,900 determined as follows: $7,500 (15% × $50,000) + $6,250 (25% × $25,000) + $88,400 (34% × $260,000) + $11,750 (5% × $235,000). Note that the tax liability of $113,900 is 34% of $335,000. □

Qualified personal service corporations are taxed at a flat 34 percent rate on all taxable income. Thus, they do not enjoy the tax savings of the 15 percent (on the first $50,000) and 25 percent (on the next $25,000) lower brackets. For this purpose, a *qualified personal service corporation* is one that is substantially employee owned and engages in one of the following activities: health, law, engineering, architecture, accounting, actuarial science, performing arts, or consulting.

Alternative Minimum Tax.   Corporations are subject to an alternative minimum tax (AMT) that is structured in the same manner as that applicable to individuals. The AMT for corporations, as for individuals, defines a more expansive tax base than for the regular tax. Like individuals, corporations are required to apply a minimum tax rate to the expanded base and pay the difference between the tentative AMT liability and the regular tax. Many of the adjustments and tax preference items necessary to arrive at alternative minimum taxable income (AMTI) are the same for individuals and corporations. Although the objective of the AMT is the same for individuals and for corporations, the rate and the exemptions are different. Computation of the AMT for corporations is discussed in chapter 12.

Filing Requirements

A corporation must file a return whether or not it has taxable income.[17] A corporation that was not in existence throughout an entire annual accounting period is required to file a return for the fraction of the year during which it was in existence. In addition, the corporation must file a return even though it has ceased to do business if it has valuable claims for which it will bring suit. It is relieved of filing returns once it ceases business and dissolves.

The corporate return is filed on Form 1120 unless the corporation is a small corporation entitled to file the shorter Form 1120–A. Corporations whose gross receipts or sales, total income (gross profits plus other income including gains on sales of property), and total assets not exceeding $250,000 each may file Form 1120–A if additional requirements are met. The corpora-

---

16. § 11(b).   17. § 6012(a)(2).

tion may not be involved in a dissolution or liquidation, be a member of a controlled group under §§ 1561 and 1563, file a consolidated return, have ownership in a foreign corporation, or have foreign shareholders who directly or indirectly own 50 percent or more of its stock. Corporations electing under Subchapter S (discussed later in the chapter) file on Form 1120S.

The return must be filed on or before the fifteenth day of the third month following the close of a corporation's tax year.

Corporations can receive an automatic extension of six months for filing the corporate return by filing Form 7004 by the due date of the return. However, the IRS may terminate an extension by mailing a 10-day notice to the taxpayer corporation.[18]

A corporation must make payments of estimated tax unless its tax liability can reasonably be expected to be less than $500.[19] The payments must be at least 90 percent of the corporation's final tax. These payments may be made in four installments due on or before the fifteenth day of the fourth, sixth, ninth, and twelfth months of the corporate taxable year. The full amount of the unpaid tax is due on the date of the return. Failure to make the required estimated tax prepayments will result in a nondeductible penalty being imposed on the corporation. The penalty can be avoided, however, if any of the various exceptions apply.[20]

Reconciliation of Taxable Income and Accounting Income

Taxable income and financial net income are seldom the same amount. For example, a difference may arise if the corporation uses accelerated depreciation for tax purposes and straight-line depreciation for financial purposes.

Many items of income for accounting purposes, such as proceeds from a life insurance policy on the death of a corporate officer and interest on municipal bonds, may not be includible in calculating taxable income. Some expense items for financial accounting purposes, such as expenses to produce tax-exempt income, estimated warranty reserves, a net capital loss, and Federal income taxes, may not be deductible for tax purposes.

Schedule M–1 on the last page of Form 1120 is used to reconcile financial net income (net income after Federal income taxes) with taxable income (as computed on the corporate tax return before the deduction for a net operating loss and for the dividends received deduction). In the left-hand column of Schedule M–1, net income per books is added to the following: the Federal income tax liability for the year, the excess of capital losses over capital gains (which cannot be deducted in the current year), income for tax purposes that is not income in the current year for financial accounting purposes, and expenses recorded on the books that are not deductible on the tax return. In the right-hand column, income recorded on the books that is not currently taxable or is tax-exempt and deductions for tax purposes that are not expenses for financial accounting purposes are totaled and subtracted from the left-hand column total to arrive at taxable income (before the net operating loss or dividends received deductions).

EXAMPLE 14   During 1989, T Corporation had the following transactions:

---

18. § 6081.
19. § 6655(f).

20. See § 6655 for the penalty involved and the various exceptions thereto.

Net income per books (after tax)	$92,400
Taxable income	50,000
Federal income tax liability (15% × $50,000)	7,500
Interest income from tax-exempt bonds	5,000
Interest paid on loan, the proceeds of which were used to purchase the tax-exempt bonds	500
Life insurance proceeds received as a result of the death of a key employee	50,000
Premiums paid on keyman life insurance policy	2,600
Excess of capital losses over capital gains	2,000

For book and tax purposes, T Corporation determines depreciation under the straight-line method. T Corporation's Schedule M–1 for the current year follows.

Schedule M-1 | **Reconciliation of Income per Books With Income per Return** (You are not required to complete this schedule if the total assets on line 14, column (d), of Schedule L are less than $25,000.)

1 Net income per books	92,400	7 Income recorded on books this year not included in this return (itemize):		
2 Federal income tax	7,500			
3 Excess of capital losses over capital gains . .	2,000	a Tax-exempt interest $ _5,000_		
4 Income subject to tax not recorded on books this year (itemize): _____		Life insurance proceeds on keyman $50,000		55,000
_____		8 Deductions in this tax return not charged against book income this year (itemize):		
5 Expenses recorded on books this year not deducted in this return (itemize):		a Depreciation . . . $_____		
a Depreciation . . . $_____		b Contributions carryover $_____		
b Contributions carryover $_____		_____		
c Travel and entertainment . $_____		_____		
_____		_____		
6 Total of lines 1 through 5	3,100* / 105,000	9 Total of lines 7 and 8		55,000
		10 Income (line 28, page 1)—line 6 less line 9		50,000

* Int. on tax exempt bonds $ 500
Prem. on keyman insurance $2,600

Schedule M–2 reconciles unappropriated retained earnings at the beginning of the year with unappropriated retained earnings at year-end. Beginning balance plus net income per books, as entered on line 1 of Schedule M–1, less dividend distributions during the year equals ending retained earnings. Other sources of increases or decreases in retained earnings are also listed on Schedule M–2.

EXAMPLE 15

Assume the same facts as in Example 14. T Corporation's beginning balance in unappropriated retained earnings is $125,000, and during the year T Corporation distributed a cash dividend of $30,000 to its shareholders. Based on these further assumptions, T Corporation's Schedule M–2 for the current year follows.

Schedule M-2 | **Analysis of Unappropriated Retained Earnings per Books (line 24, Schedule L)** (You are not required to complete this schedule if the total assets on line 14, column (d), of Schedule L are less than $25,000.)

1 Balance at beginning of year	125,000	5 Distributions: a Cash		30,000
2 Net income per books	92,400	b Stock		
3 Other increases (itemize): _____		c Property . . .		
_____		6 Other decreases (itemize): _____		
_____		_____		
4 Total of lines 1, 2, and 3	217,400	7 Total of lines 5 and 6		30,000
		8 Balance at end of year (line 4 less line 7)		187,400

Concept Summary 20-1

Summary of Income Tax Consequences

	Individuals	Corporations
Computation of gross income	§ 61.	§ 61.
Computation of taxable income	§§ 62, 63(b) through (h).	§ 63(a). Concept of AGI has no relevance.
Deductions	Trade or business (§ 162); nonbusiness (§ 212); some personal and employee expenses (generally deductible as itemized deductions).	Trade or business (§ 162).
Charitable contributions	Limited in any tax year to 50% of AGI; 30% for long-term capital gain property unless election is made to reduce fair market value of gift; 20% for long-term capital gain property contributed to private nonoperating foundations. Time of deduction—year in which payment is made.	Limited in any tax year to 10% of taxable income computed without regard to the charitable contribution deduction, net operating loss or capital loss carryback, and dividends received deduction. Time of deduction—year in which payment is made unless accrual basis taxpayer. Accrual basis corporation may take deduction in year preceding payment if contribution was authorized by board of directors by end of that year and contribution is paid by fifteenth day of third month of following year.
Casualty losses	$100 floor on nonbusiness casualty and theft losses; nonbusiness casualty and theft losses deductible only to extent losses exceed 10% of AGI.	Deductible in full.
Depreciation recapture under § 1250	Recaptured to extent accelerated depreciation exceeds straight-line.	20% of excess of amount that would be recaptured under § 1245 over amount recaptured under § 1250 is additional ordinary income.
Net operating loss	Adjusted for nonbusiness deductions over nonbusiness income and for personal and dependency exemptions.	Generally no adjustments.
Dividend exclusion or deduction	None.	Generally 70% of dividends received.

	Individuals	Corporations
Long-term capital gains	Taxed in full.	Taxed in full.
Capital losses	Only $3,000 of capital loss can offset ordinary income; loss is carried forward indefinitely to offset capital gains or ordinary income up to $3,000; carryovers remain long term or short term (as the case may be).	Can offset only capital gains; carried back three years and forward five; carrybacks and carryovers are treated as short-term losses.
Passive activity losses	Generally, deductible only against income from passive activities.	For regular corporations, no limitation on deductibility. Personal service corporations and certain closely held corporations, however, are subject to same limitations as imposed on individuals. A closely held corporation is one where 5 or fewer individuals own more than 50% of the stock either directly or indirectly.
Tax rates	Mildly progressive with two rates (15% and 28%); phase-out of 15% bracket begins as taxpayers (depending on filing status) reach a certain level of taxable income.	Mildly progressive with three rates (15%, 25%, and 34%); lower brackets phased out between $100,000 and $335,000 of taxable income.
Alternative minimum tax	Applied at a 21% rate to AMTB (taxable income as modified by certain adjustments plus preference items minus exemption amount); exemption allowed depending on filing status (e.g., $40,000 for married filing jointly); exemption phase-out begins when AMTI reaches a certain amount (e.g., $150,000 for married filing jointly).	Applied at a 20% rate to AMTB (taxable income as modified by certain adjustments plus preference items minus exemption amount); $40,000 exemption allowed but phase-out begins once AMTI reaches $150,000; adjustments and tax preference items similar to those applicable to individuals but also includes one-half of pretax book profits over AMTI.

FORMING THE CORPORATION

Capital Contributions

The receipt of money or property in exchange for capital stock produces neither gain nor loss to the recipient corporation.[21] Gross income of a corpo-

---

21. § 1032.

ration does not include shareholders' contributions of money or property to the capital of the corporation.[22] Contributions by nonshareholders, such as land contributed to a corporation by a civic group or a contribution by a municipality to induce the corporation to locate in a particular community, are also excluded from the gross income of a corporation.[23] The basis of such property (capital transfers by nonshareholders) to the corporation is zero.

EXAMPLE 16

A city donates land worth $200,000 to X Corporation as an inducement for X to locate in the city. The receipt of the land does not represent taxable income. However, the land's basis to the corporation is zero. □

Thin Capitalization. The advantages of capitalizing a corporation with debt may be substantial. Interest on debt is deductible by the corporation, whereas dividend payments are not. Further, the shareholders are not taxed on loan repayments unless such payments exceed basis. If a company is capitalized solely with common stock, subsequent repayments of such capital contributions are likely to be treated as dividends to the shareholders.

In certain instances, the IRS will contend that debt is really an equity interest and will deny the shareholders the tax advantages of debt financing. If the debt instrument has too many features of stock, it may be treated as a form of stock, and principal and interest payments will be considered dividends.[24]

Though the form of the instrument will not assure debt treatment, the failure to observe certain formalities in the creation of the debt may lead to an assumption that the purported debt is, in fact, a form of stock. The debt should be in proper legal form, bear a legitimate rate of interest, have a definite maturity date, and be repaid on a timely basis. Payments should not be contingent upon earnings. Further, the debt should not be subordinated to other liabilities, and proportionate holdings of stock and debt should be avoided.

Transfers to Controlled Corporations

Absent special provisions in the Code, a transfer of property to a corporation in exchange for its stock would be a sale or exchange of property and would constitute a taxable transaction to the transferor shareholder. Section 351 provides for the nonrecognition of gain or loss upon such transfers of property if the transferors are in control of the corporation immediately after the transfer. Gain or loss is merely postponed in a manner similar to a like-kind exchange.[25] The following requirements must be met to qualify under § 351:

- The transferors must be in control of the corporation immediately after the exchange. *Control* is defined as ownership of at least 80 percent of the total combined voting power of all classes of stock entitled to vote and at least 80 percent of the total number of shares of all other classes of stock.[26]

---

22. § 118.
23. *Edwards v. Cuba Railroad Co.*, 1 USTC ¶139, 5 AFTR 5398, 45 S.Ct. 614 (USSC, 1925).
24. Section 385 lists several factors that might be used to determine whether a debtor-creditor relationship or a shareholder-corporation relationship exists.
25. Refer to the discussion in chapter 15.
26. § 368(c).

- Gain (but not loss) is recognized to the extent that the transferors receive property other than stock and securities (e.g., cash or short-term notes).[27] Such nonqualifying property is known as boot under the tax law.

If the requirements of § 351 are satisfied and no boot is involved, nonrecognition of gain or loss is *mandatory.*

Basis Considerations and Computation of Gain.   The nonrecognition of gain or loss is accompanied by a carryover of basis. The Code provides that the basis of stock or securities received in a § 351 transfer is the same as the basis the shareholder had in the property transferred, increased by any gain recognized by the shareholder on the exchange and decreased by the fair market value of boot received.[28] The Code further provides that the basis of properties received by the corporation is the basis in the hands of the transferor increased by the amount of any gain recognized to the transferor shareholder.[29]

EXAMPLE 17

A and B, individuals, form X Corporation. A transfers property with an adjusted basis of $30,000, fair market value of $60,000, for 50% of the stock. B transfers property with an adjusted basis of $40,000, fair market value of $60,000, for the remaining 50% of the stock. Gain is not recognized on the transfer because the transfer qualifies under § 351. The basis of the stock to A is $30,000, and the basis of the stock to B is $40,000. X Corporation has a basis of $30,000 in the property transferred by A and a basis of $40,000 in the property transferred by B. □

EXAMPLE 18

C and D form Y Corporation with the following investment: C transfers property (basis of $30,000 and fair market value of $70,000), and D transfers cash of $60,000. Each receives 50 shares of the Y Corporation stock, but C also receives $10,000 in cash. Assume each share of the Y Corporation stock is worth $1,200. C's realized gain is $40,000, determined as follows:

Value of the Y Corporation stock received [50 (shares) × $1,200 (value per share)]	$60,000
Cash received	10,000
Total value received	$70,000
Less basis of property transferred	(30,000)
Realized gain	$40,000

---

27. The courts have required that the definition of a security be limited to long-term obligations and exclude short-term notes. See *Turner v. Comm.*, 62–1 USTC ¶9488, 9 AFTR2d 1528, 303 F.2d 94 (CA–4, 1962). The required length of maturity to qualify as a security is questiona-

ble. Some cases draw the line at five years; others at ten years.

28. § 358(a).

29. § 362(a).

C's recognized gain is $10,000, the lesser of the realized gain ($40,000) or the fair market value of the boot received ($10,000). C's basis in the Y Corporation stock is $30,000, computed as follows:

Basis in the property transferred	$30,000
Plus recognized gain	10,000
	$40,000
Less boot received	(10,000)
Basis to C of the Y Corporation stock	$30,000

Y Corporation's basis in the property transferred by C is $40,000 [$30,000 (basis of the property to C) + $10,000 (gain recognized to C)]. D neither realizes nor recognizes gain or loss and will have a basis in the Y Corporation stock of $60,000. □

Shareholders who receive noncash boot will have a basis in the property equal to the fair market value. The receipt of stock for the performance of *services* always results in ordinary income to the transferor shareholder. Such might be the case if an attorney does not charge a fee for incorporating a business but instead receives the value equivalent in stock of the newly formed corporation.

OPERATING THE CORPORATION

Dividend Distributions

Corporate distributions of cash or property to shareholders are treated as ordinary dividend income to the extent the corporation has accumulated *or* current earnings and profits (E & P).[30] In determining the source of the distribution, a dividend is deemed to have been made initially from current E & P.

EXAMPLE 19 | As of January 1, 1989, Y Corporation has a deficit in accumulated E & P of $30,000. For tax year 1989, it has current E & P of $10,000. In 1989, the corporation distributes $5,000 to its shareholders. The $5,000 distribution will be treated as a taxable dividend, since it is deemed to have been made from current E & P. This will be the case even though Y Corporation will still have a deficit in its accumulated E & P at the end of 1989. □

If a corporate distribution is not covered by earnings and profits (either current or past), it is treated as a return of capital (refer to the discussion of the recovery of capital doctrine in chapter 4). This treatment allows the shareholder to apply the amount of the distribution against the basis of the stock investment and therefore represents a nontaxable return of capital. Any

30.   § 316.

amount received in excess of the stock basis is classified as a capital gain (if the stock is a capital asset in the hands of the shareholder).

EXAMPLE 20

At a time when X Corporation has no earnings and profits (either current or accumulated), it distributes cash of $30,000 to its sole shareholder, Ms. T. The basis of Ms. T's stock investment is $20,000. Based on these facts, the $30,000 distribution Ms. T receives is accounted for as follows:

Return of capital (nontaxable)	$20,000
Capital gain	10,000
Total amount of distribution	$30,000

After the distribution, Ms. T will have a basis of zero in her stock investment. □

Concept of Earnings and Profits.   The term *earnings and profits* is not defined in the Code, although § 312 does include certain transactions that affect E & P. Although E & P possesses certain similarities to the financial accounting concept of retained earnings, numerous differences may arise. For example, although a nontaxable stock dividend is treated for financial accounting purposes as a capitalization of retained earnings, it does not decrease E & P for tax purposes. Taxable dividends, however, do reduce E & P but cannot yield a deficit. Referring to Example 20, after the distribution, X Corporation's E & P remains zero rather than being a negative $30,000.

Generally, *current E & P* for a taxable year is taxable income plus or minus certain adjustments (e.g., an addition is made for tax-exempt income). Federal income taxes are subtracted from taxable income in arriving at the current E & P. *Accumulated E & P* is the sum of the corporation's past current E & P. A detailed discussion of the concept of E & P is beyond the scope of this chapter.

Property Dividends.   A distribution of property to a shareholder is measured by the fair market value of the property on the date of distribution. The shareholder's basis in the property received is also the fair market value.[31]

EXAMPLE 21

P Corporation has E & P of $60,000. It distributes land with a fair market value of $50,000 (adjusted basis of $30,000) to its sole shareholder, T (an individual). T has a taxable dividend of $50,000 and a basis in the land of $50,000. □

A corporation that distributes appreciated property to its shareholders as a dividend must recognize a gain as to the appreciation.

---

31. § 301.

EXAMPLE 22
Assume the same facts as in Example 21. P Corporation must recognize a gain of $20,000 on the distribution it made to T. □

However, if the property distributed has a basis in excess of its fair market value, any loss cannot be recognized by the distributing corporation.

Constructive Dividends. Many taxpayers mistakenly assume that dividend consequences do not take place unless the distribution carries the formalities of a dividend (declaration date, record date, payment day) and is paid out to all shareholders on a pro rata basis. This may not be the case when closely held corporations are involved. Here, the key to dividend treatment depends upon whether the shareholders derive a benefit from the corporation that cannot be otherwise classified (e.g., reasonable salary, interest on bona fide debt, arm's length rents). The following are examples of *constructive dividends*:

- Salaries paid to shareholder-employees that are not reasonable (refer to Example 6 in chapter 6).

- Interest on debt owed by the corporation to shareholders that is reclassified as equity because the corporation is thinly capitalized (refer to the earlier discussion in this chapter).

- Excessive rent paid by a corporation for the use of shareholder property. Whether the rent is excessive is to be tested by use of the arm's length standard (refer to Example 23 in chapter 1).

- Advances to shareholders that are not bona fide loans.

- Interest-free (or below-market) loans to shareholders. In this situation, the dividend component would be the difference between the interest provided for, if any, and the market rate.

- Shareholder use of corporate property for less than an arm's length rate.

- Absorption by the corporation of a shareholder's personal expenses.

- Bargain purchase by shareholders of corporate property.

Like regular dividends, constructive dividends must be covered by E & P to carry dividend income consequences to the shareholders. As noted above, however, constructive dividends need not be available to all shareholders on a pro rata basis.

Although dividends reduce the earnings and profits of a corporation, they are not deductible for income tax purposes. In this regard, certain constructive dividends could have subtle tax consequences for all parties concerned.

EXAMPLE 23
Z Corporation makes a loan to one of its shareholders, T. No interest is provided for, but application of the market rate would produce $20,000 of interest for the term of the loan. Presuming the loan is bona fide, the following results occur:

- T has dividend income of $20,000.

- Z Corporation has interest income of $20,000.

- T might obtain an interest deduction of $20,000.

Not only does Z Corporation have to recognize income of $20,000, but it also obtains no income tax deduction for the $20,000 constructive dividend. □

EXAMPLE 24   Assume the same facts as in Example 23, except that the loan to T was not bona fide. In this event, the full amount of the loan will be regarded as a dividend to T. Therefore, the interest element is not a factor, as no bona fide loan ever existed. □

Stock Redemptions

If a shareholder's stock is redeemed by the corporation, one of two possible outcomes will occur:

- The redemption may qualify as a sale or exchange under § 302 or § 303. In such case, capital gain or loss treatment usually applies to the qualifying shareholders.

- The redemption will be treated as a dividend under § 301, providing the distributing corporation has earnings and profits.

EXAMPLE 25   T owns 300 shares of X Corporation stock as an investment. The shares have a basis to T of $100 each, for a total of $30,000. When the fair market value of a share is $200, X Corporation redeems 200 of T's shares. If the redemption qualifies for sale or exchange treatment, the result is a capital gain to T of $20,000 [$40,000 (redemption price) − $20,000 (basis in 200 shares)]. T's basis in the remaining 100 shares is $10,000 [$30,000 (basis in the original shares) − $20,000 (basis in the shares redeemed)]. □

EXAMPLE 26   Assume the same facts as in Example 25, except that the redemption does not qualify for sale or exchange treatment. Presuming adequate E & P, the redemption results in $40,000 dividend income. T's basis in the remaining 100 shares now becomes $30,000, or $300 per share. □

A stock redemption qualifies as a sale or exchange if it meets any of the safe harbors of § 302 or § 303. For a discussion of these provisions, see *West's Federal Taxation: Corporations, Partnerships, Estates, and Trusts.*

LIQUIDATING THE CORPORATION

Unlike dividend distributions or stock redemptions, wherein the distributing corporation continues its operations, *liquidating distributions* are directed toward the termination of the business. All debts are paid, and any remaining corporate assets are distributed pro rata to the shareholders in exchange for their stock. Once these distributions are completed, the corporation undergoing liquidation will cease to be a separate tax entity.

General Rule of Section 331

Under the general rule, gain or loss is recognized by the shareholders in a corporate liquidation. The amount of recognized gain or loss is measured by the difference between the fair market value of the assets received from the corporation and the adjusted basis of the stock surrendered. Capital gain or loss is recognized by the shareholders if the stock is a capital asset.[32]

EXAMPLE 27

Pursuant to a complete liquidation, X Corporation distributes $100,000 in cash to T, one of its shareholders. If T's basis in the stock surrendered is $40,000, T must recognize a gain of $60,000. If the stock is held by T as an investment, the $60,000 gain will be capital gain—either short term or long term (depending on the holding period). ☐

Exception to the General Rule

Section 332 is an exception to the general rule that the shareholder recognizes gain or loss on a corporate liquidation. If a parent corporation liquidates a subsidiary corporation in which it owns at least 80 percent of the voting power and value of the stock, no gain or loss is recognized by the parent company. The subsidiary must distribute all of its property in complete liquidation of all of its stock within the taxable year or within three years from the close of the tax year in which the first distribution occurred.

Basis Determination—Section 334

General Rule.   Where gain or loss is recognized upon the complete liquidation of a corporation, the basis of the property received by the shareholders is the property's fair market value.[33]

Subsidiary Liquidation Basis Rules.   The general rule is that the property received by the parent corporation in a complete liquidation of its subsidiary under § 332 has the same basis it had in the hands of the subsidiary (a carryover basis).[34] The parent's basis in stock of the liquidated subsidiary disappears.

EXAMPLE 28

P, the parent corporation, has a basis of $20,000 in stock of S Corporation, a subsidiary in which it owns 85% of all classes of stock. P Corporation purchased the stock of S Corporation 10 years ago. In the current year, P Corporation liquidates S Corporation and receives assets worth $50,000 with a tax basis to S Corporation of $40,000. P Corporation would have a basis of $40,000 in the assets, with a potential gain upon sale of $10,000. P

---

32. If the stock is held as an investment, which is usually the case, gain or loss will be capital. Stock owned by a broker probably would be inventory and would therefore not constitute a capital asset. Thus, the gain or loss on this type of stock would be ordinary and not capital.

33. § 334(a).

34. § 334(b)(1).

Corporation's original $20,000 basis in the S Corporation stock disappears. □

An exception to the carryover of basis rule is provided in § 338. Under this exception, the parent company may elect to receive a change in basis for the assets equal to the adjusted basis of the stock of the subsidiary. In effect, the initial acquisition of the subsidiary is treated as if the parent company had acquired the assets (rather than the stock) of the subsidiary.

The following requirements must be met:

- The parent must *purchase* at least 80 percent of the total combined voting power of all classes of stock and at least 80 percent of all other classes of stock (except nonvoting preferred) within a 12-month period.

- By the fifteenth day of the ninth month beginning after the month in which the 80 percent control requirement noted above is met, the parent corporation elects to have § 338 apply.

EXAMPLE 29

P Corporation acquires 100% of the stock of S Corporation for $1,000,000 cash in a taxable purchase transaction on January 1, 1989. On February 1, 1989, S Corporation is liquidated into P under § 338. The adjusted basis of S Corporation's net assets is $800,000. Since P acquired at least 80% of the stock in a taxable purchase transaction and made a timely election under § 338, P Corporation's basis in the net assets of S is $1,000,000 (the amount paid for the S stock). The transaction is treated as if P acquired the S Corporation assets for $1,000,000 instead of acquiring S's stock for $1,000,000. □

Effect of the Liquidation on the Corporation

Having examined what happens to the shareholder upon the liquidation of a corporation, what happens at the corporate level? Here, § 336 will apply to dictate the tax consequences to the corporation being liquidated.

Under § 336, gain and loss will be recognized to the distributing corporation upon complete liquidation. In this regard, it does not matter whether the corporation distributes the property in-kind (*as is*) to the shareholders or first sells the property and then distributes the proceeds.

EXAMPLE 30

Pursuant to a complete liquidation, R Corporation distributes the following assets to its shareholders: undeveloped land held as an investment (basis of $150,000 and fair market value of $140,000) and marketable securities (basis of $160,000 and fair market value of $200,000). Since R Corporation will be treated as if it had sold the property, a gain of $40,000 results from the securities, and a loss of $10,000 results from the land. □

The deductibility of losses, however, may be restricted by the related-party rules of § 267 (refer to chapter 6) if certain conditions exist (e.g., the distributions are not pro rata).[35]

Gain or loss will not be recognized by a wholly owned subsidiary corporation when the parent corporation uses the basis option of § 334(b)(1). The reason for this special treatment is that under § 334(b)(1), the subsidiary's basis (and all other tax attributes) in the assets carries over to the parent corporation.

THE S ELECTION

Justification for the Election

Since there may be numerous nontax reasons for operating a business in the corporate form, the existence of income tax disadvantages (e.g., double taxation of corporate income and shareholder dividends) should not deter business people from using the corporate form. In the interest of preventing tax considerations from interfering with the exercise of sound business judgment, Congress enacted Subchapter S of the Code.

To qualify for S status, the corporation must be a *small business corporation*.[36] This includes any corporation that has the following characteristics:

- Is a domestic corporation.
- Is not a member of an affiliated group.
- Has no more than 35 shareholders.
- Has as its shareholders only individuals, estates, and certain trusts.
- Does not have a nonresident alien as a shareholder.
- Issues only one class of stock.

These characteristics must continue to exist if an electing S corporation is to maintain S status.

Making the Election.   The election is made by filing Form 2553, and *all* shareholders must consent. Special rules apply to husbands and wives where stock is jointly held and to minors.

For the election to be effective for the current year, the election must be filed anytime during the preceding taxable year or on or before the fifteenth day of the third month of the current year.[37]

EXAMPLE 31   T, a calendar year taxpayer, is a regular corporation that wishes to elect S status for 1989. If the election is filed anytime from January 1, 1988, through March 15, 1989, it will be effective for 1989. □

---

35. § 336(d).   37. § 1362.
36. § 1361(b).

Loss of the Election.   Revocation of the S election may occur voluntarily (a majority of the shareholders file to revoke the election) or involuntarily, in any of the following ways:

- The corporation ceases to qualify as a small business corporation (e.g., the number of shareholders exceeds 35, or a partnership becomes a shareholder).

- When the corporation has passive investment income (e.g., interest, dividends) in excess of 25 percent of gross receipts for a period of three consecutive years. This possibility only applies if the corporation was previously a regular corporation and has earnings and profits from that period.

If the holders of a *majority* of the shares consent to a voluntary revocation of S status, the election to revoke must be made on or before the fifteenth day of the third month of the tax year to be effective for that year.

EXAMPLE 32   The shareholders of T Corporation, a calendar year S corporation, elect to revoke the election on January 5, 1989. Assuming the election is duly executed and timely filed, T Corporation will become a regular corporation for calendar year 1989. If, on the other hand, the election to revoke is not made until June 1989, T Corporation will not become a regular corporation until calendar year 1990. □

Suppose the shareholders in Example 32 file the election to revoke on January 5, 1989, but do not want the revocation to take place until 1990. If the election so specifies, T Corporation will cease to have S status as of January 1, 1990.

In the case where S status is lost because of a disqualifying act (involuntarily), the loss of the election takes effect as of the date on which the event occurs.

EXAMPLE 33   T Corporation has been a calendar year S corporation for several years. On August 13, 1989, one of its shareholders sells her stock to Y Corporation. Since T Corporation no longer satisfies the definition of a small business corporation (it has another corporation as a shareholder), the election has been involuntarily terminated. For calendar year 1989, therefore, T Corporation will be an S corporation through August 12 and a regular corporation from August 13 through December 31, 1989. □

In the event the election is lost through a violation of the passive investment income limitation, the loss of S status starts at the beginning of the next tax year.

Barring certain exceptions, the loss of the election places the corporation in a five-year holding period before S status can be reelected.

Operational Rules

The S corporation is primarily a tax-reporting rather than a tax-paying entity. In this respect, the entity is taxed much like a partnership.[38] Under the conduit concept, the taxable income and losses of an S corporation flow through to the shareholders who report them on their personal income tax returns.

To ascertain the annual tax consequences to each shareholder, it is necessary to carry out two steps at the S corporation level. First, all corporate transactions that will flow through to the shareholders on an *as is* basis under the conduit approach must be set aside. Second, what remains is aggregated as the taxable income of the S corporation and is allocated to each shareholder on a per-share and per-day of stock ownership basis.[39]

Separately Stated Items.   The following are some of the items that do not lose their identity as they pass through the S corporation and are therefore picked up by each shareholder on an *as is* basis:

- Tax-exempt income.
- Long-term and short-term capital gains and losses.
- Section 1231 gains and losses.
- Charitable contributions.
- Foreign tax credits.
- Depletion.
- Nonbusiness income or loss under § 212.
- Intangible drilling costs.
- Investment interest, income, and expenses covered under § 163(d).
- Certain portfolio income.
- Passive gains, losses, and credits under § 469.
- Tax preference items.

The reason these items are separately stated is that each may lead to a different tax result when combined with a particular shareholder's other transactions.

EXAMPLE 34   X and Y are equal shareholders in P Corporation (an S corporation). For calendar year 1989, each must account for one-half of a corporate short-term capital gain of $6,000. X has no other capital asset transactions, and Y has a short-term capital loss of $3,000 from the sale of stock in ABC Corporation. In terms of overall effect, the difference between the two taxpayers should be clear. Although both must report the short-term capital gain pass-through, Y will neutralize its inclusion in gross income through an offset with the $3,000 short-term capital loss from the sale of

---

38. This is not to imply that an S corporation is always free from the income tax. For example, a tax may be imposed on certain built-in gains or

certain excessive passive investment income.

39. § 1366.

the stock in ABC Corporation. To X, the short-term capital gain pass-through results in additional ordinary income of $3,000. □

Taxable Income.   After the separately stated items have been removed, the balance represents the taxable income of the S corporation. In arriving at taxable income, the dividends received deduction (§ 243) and the net operating loss deduction (§ 172) are not allowed. An S corporation does come under the regular corporate rules, however, for purposes of amortization of organizational expenditures (§ 248).

Once taxable income has been determined, it passes through to each shareholder as of the last day of the S corporation's tax year.

EXAMPLE 35

X Corporation, a calendar year S corporation, had the following transactions during the current year:

Sales		$40,000
Cost of goods sold		(23,000)
Other income		
*Tax-exempt interest	$ 300	
*Long-term capital gain	500	800
Other expenses		
*Charitable contributions	$ 400	
Advertising expense	1,500	
Other operating expenses	2,000	
*Short-term capital loss	150	(4,050)
Net income per books		$13,750

When the items that are to be separately stated [those preceded by an asterisk (*)] and shown *as is* by each shareholder are withdrawn, the taxable income of X Corporation becomes as follows:

Sales		$40,000
Cost of goods sold		(23,000)
Other expenses		
Advertising expense	$1,500	
Other operating expenses	2,000	(3,500)
Taxable income		$13,500

□

EXAMPLE 36   If T owned 10% of the stock in X Corporation (refer to Example 35) during all of the current year, he must account for the following:

Separately stated items	
Tax-exempt interest	$ 30
Long-term capital gain	50
Charitable contributions	40
Short-term capital loss	15
Taxable income (10% of $13,500)	1,350

Some of the separately stated items need not be reported on T's individual income tax return (e.g., the tax-exempt interest), although others must be reported but may not lead to tax consequences. T's share of X Corporation's taxable income ($1,350) must be picked up by T as ordinary income.   □

Treatment of Losses.   Separately stated loss items (e.g., capital losses, § 1231 losses) will, as previously noted, flow through to the shareholders on an *as is* basis. Thus, their treatment by a shareholder will depend on the shareholder's individual income tax position. If, moreover, the S corporation's taxable income determination results in an operating loss, it also will pass through to the shareholders. As is the case with separately stated items, the amount of the loss each shareholder receives depends on the stock ownership during the year.

EXAMPLE 37   In 1989, Y Corporation (a calendar year S corporation) incurred an operating loss of $36,500. During 1989, T's ownership in Y Corporation was as follows: 20% for 200 days and 30% for 165 days. T's share of the loss is determined as follows:

$$(\$36{,}500 \times 200/365) \times 20\% = \$4{,}000$$
$$(\$36{,}500 \times 165/365) \times 30\% = \underline{4{,}950}$$

Total loss $\underline{\$8{,}950}$

Presuming the basis limitation does not come into play (see the following discussion), T may deduct $8,950 in arriving at adjusted gross income.   □

Basis Determination.   A shareholder's *basis* in the stock of an S corporation, like that of a regular corporation, will be the original investment plus additional capital contributions less return of capital distributions. At this point, however, the symmetry disappears. Generally, basis will be increased by the pass-through of income items (including those separately stated) and decreased by the loss items (including those separately stated).[40]

EXAMPLE 38

In 1989, M Corporation is formed with an investment of $100,000, of which T contributed $20,000 for a 20% stock interest. A timely S election is made, and for 1989, M Corporation earns taxable income of $15,000. T's basis in her stock investment now becomes $23,000 [$20,000 (original capital contribution) + $3,000 (the 20% share of the corporation's taxable income assigned to T)]. □

Distributions by an S corporation reduce the basis of a shareholder's stock investment. However, if the amount of the distribution exceeds basis, such excess normally will be accorded capital gain treatment.

As previously noted, operating losses of an S corporation pass through to the shareholders and reduce the basis in their stock investment. Because the basis of the stock cannot fall below zero, an excess loss is then applied against the basis of any loans the shareholder may have made to the corporation.

EXAMPLE 39

Z Corporation, a calendar year S corporation, has an operating loss of $60,000 for 1989. T, a 50% shareholder, has an adjusted basis in his stock investment of $25,000 and has made loans to the corporation of $5,000. Based on these facts, T may take full advantage of the $30,000 loss (i.e., 50% of $60,000) on his 1989 individual income tax return. T's basis in the stock and the loans must be reduced accordingly, and both will be zero after the pass-through. □

In the event the basis limitation precludes an operating loss from being absorbed, the loss can be carried forward and deducted when and if it is covered by basis.

EXAMPLE 40

Assume the same facts as in Example 39, except that T had not made any loans to Z Corporation. Further assume that Z Corporation has taxable income of $15,000 in the following year (1990). T's tax situation for 1989 and 1990 is summarized as follows:

Ordinary loss for 1989	$25,000
Restoration of stock basis in 1990 (50% of $15,000)	7,500
Income to be reported in 1990	7,500
Loss allowed for 1990 ($30,000 − $25,000)	5,000
Basis in stock account after 1990 ($7,500 − $5,000)	2,500

---

40. § 1367.

Thus, T's unabsorbed loss of $5,000 from 1989 carries over to 1990 and is applied against the $7,500 of ordinary income for that year. □

PARTNERSHIPS

Nature of Partnership Taxation

Unlike corporations, partnerships are not considered separate taxable entities. Instead, each member of a partnership is subject to income tax on his or her distributive share of the partnership's income, even if an actual distribution is not made. Thus, the tax return (Form 1065) required of a partnership serves only to provide information necessary in determining the character and amount of each partner's distributive share of the partnership's income and expense. Because partnerships act as a conduit, items that pass through to the partners do not lose their identity. For example, tax-exempt income earned by a partnership will be picked up by the partners as tax-exempt income. In this regard, partnerships function in much the same fashion as S corporations, which also serve as conduits.

Although a partnership is not considered a separate taxable entity for purposes of determining and paying Federal income taxes, it is treated as such for purposes of making various elections and selecting its taxable year, method of depreciation, and accounting method. Also, a partnership is treated as a separate legal entity under civil law with the right to own property in its own name and to transact business free from the personal debts of its partners.

Partnership Formation

Recognition of Gain or Loss.   Section 721 contains the general rule that no gain or loss is recognized by a partnership or any of its partners on the contribution of property in exchange for a capital interest in the partnership. This general rule also applies to all subsequent contributions of property.

Certain exceptions to the nonrecognition of gain or loss rule include the following:

- If the transfer of property by a partner to the partnership results in the receipt of money or other consideration by the partner, the transaction will be treated as a sale or exchange rather than as a contribution of capital under § 721.

- If a partnership interest is received in exchange for services rendered or to be rendered by the partner to the partnership, the fair market value of the transferred capital interest is considered as compensation for services rendered. In such cases, the recipient of the capital interest must recognize the amount as ordinary income in the year actually or constructively received.

- If property that is subject to a liability in excess of its basis is contributed to a partnership, gain may be recognized by the contributing partner.

Basis of a Partnership Interest.   The contributing *partner's basis* in the partnership interest received is the sum of money contributed plus the adjusted basis of any other property transferred to the partnership.

EXAMPLE 41

In return for the contribution of property (with a basis of $50,000 and a fair market value of $80,000) and cash of $10,000 to the KLM Partnership, T receives a 10% capital interest worth $90,000. Although T has a realized gain of $30,000 ($90,000 − $60,000) on the transfer, none of the gain is recognized. The basis of T's interest in the KLM Partnership is $60,000 [$50,000 (basis of property contributed) + $10,000 (cash contribution)].
□

A partner's basis in the partnership interest is determined without regard to any amount reflected on the partnership's books as capital, equity, or a similar account.

EXAMPLE 42

U and V form an equal partnership with a cash contribution of $30,000 from U and a property contribution (adjusted basis of $18,000 and fair market value of $30,000) from V. Although the books of the UV Partnership may reflect a credit of $30,000 to each partner's capital account, only U will have a tax basis of $30,000 in his partnership interest. V's tax basis in his partnership interest will be $18,000, the amount of his tax basis in the property contributed to the partnership. □

After its initial determination, the basis of a partnership interest is subject to continuous fluctuations. A partner's basis will be increased by additional contributions and the sum of his or her current and prior years' distributive share of the following:

- Taxable income of the partnership, including capital gains.

- Tax-exempt income of the partnership.

- The excess of the deductions for depletion over the basis of the partnership's property subject to depletion.[41]

Similarly, the basis of a partner's interest will be decreased, but not below zero, by distributions of partnership property and by the sum of the current and prior years' distributive share of the following:

- Partnership losses, including capital losses.

- Partnership expenditures that are not deductible in computing taxable income or loss and that are not capital expenditures.

Changes in the liabilities (including trade accounts payable, bank loans, etc.) of a partnership will also affect the basis of a partnership interest. For instance, a partner's basis is increased by his or her assumption of partnership liabilities and by his or her pro rata share of liabilities incurred by the

---

41. § 705(a).

partnership. Likewise, the partner's basis is decreased by the amount of any of the partner's personal liabilities assumed by the partnership and by the pro rata share of any decreases in the liabilities of the partnership.

EXAMPLE 43

X, Y, and Z form the XYZ Partnership with the following contributions: cash of $50,000 from X for a 50% interest in capital and profits, cash of $25,000 from Y for a 25% interest, and property valued at $33,000 from Z for a 25% interest. The property contributed by Z has an adjusted basis of $15,000 and is subject to a mortgage of $8,000, which is assumed by the partnership. Z's basis in his interest in the XYZ Partnership is $9,000, determined as follows:

Adjusted basis of Z's contributed property	$15,000
Less portion of mortgage assumed by X and Y and treated as a distribution of money to Z (75% of $8,000)	(6,000)
Basis of Z's interest in XYZ Partnership	$ 9,000

☐

EXAMPLE 44

Assuming the same facts as in Example 43, X and Y will have a basis in their partnership interest of $54,000 and $27,000, respectively.

	X	Y
Cash contribution	$50,000	$25,000
Plus portion of mortgage assumed and treated as an additional cash contribution:		
(50% of $8,000)	4,000	
(25% of $8,000)		2,000
Basis of interest in XYZ Partnership	$54,000	$27,000

☐

Partnership's Basis in Contributed Property.   Section 723 states that the *basis of property* contributed to a partnership by a partner shall be the adjusted basis of such property to the contributing partner at the time of the contribution. Additionally, the holding period of such property for the partnership includes the period during which the property was held by the contributing partner. This is true, since the partnership's basis in the property is the same basis the property had in the hands of the partner.[42]

EXAMPLE 45

In 1989, R contributed equipment with an adjusted basis of $10,000 and fair market value of $30,000 to the RST Partnership in exchange for a one-third interest in the partnership. No gain or loss is recognized by R. The basis in the equipment is $10,000 to the RST Partnership. If R had acquired the equipment in 1984, the holding period for the RST Partnership would include the period from 1984 through 1989. □

Partnership Operation

Measuring and Reporting Partnership Income.   Although a partnership is not subject to Federal income taxation, it is required to determine its taxable income and file an income tax return for information purposes.[43] The tax return, Form 1065, is due on the fifteenth day of the fourth month following the close of the taxable year of the partnership.

The measurement and reporting of partnership income require that certain transactions be segregated and reported separately on the partnership return. Items such as charitable contributions, capital gains and losses, and foreign taxes are excluded from partnership taxable income and are allocated separately to the partners.[44] The required segregation and direct allocation of the preceding items are necessary because such items affect the computation of various exclusions, deductions, and credits at the individual partner level. For example, one of the partners may have made personal charitable contributions in excess of the ceiling limitations on his or her individual tax return. Therefore, partnership charitable contributions are excluded from partnership taxable income and are reported separately on the partnership return.

A second step in the measurement and reporting process is the computation of the partnership's ordinary income or loss. In this process, the taxable income of a partnership is computed in the same manner as is the taxable income of an individual taxpayer, except that a partnership is not allowed the following deductions:[45]

- The deduction for personal and dependency exemptions.
- The deduction for taxes paid to foreign countries or possessions of the United States.
- The deduction for charitable contributions.
- The deduction for net operating losses.
- The additional itemized deductions allowed individuals in §§ 211 through 219.

The partnership's ordinary income or loss and each of the items requiring separate treatment are reported in the partnership's information return and allocated to the partners in accordance with the distributive share of each.

---

42. § 1223(2).
43. § 6031.

44. § 702(a).
45. § 703(a).

Limitation on Partner's Share of Losses.   A partner's deduction of the distributive share of partnership losses (including capital losses) is limited to the adjusted basis of the partnership interest at the end of the partnership year in which the losses were incurred.

The limitation for partnership loss deductions is similar to the limitation on losses for S corporations. Like S corporation losses, partnership losses may be carried forward by the partner and utilized against future increases in the basis of the partnership interest. Such increases might result from additional capital contributions to the partnership, from additional partnership liabilities, or from future partnership income.

EXAMPLE 46

C and D do business as the CD Partnership, sharing profits and losses equally. All parties use the calendar year for tax purposes. As of January 1, 1989, C's basis in his partnership interest is $25,000. The partnership sustained an operating loss of $80,000 in 1989 and earned a profit of $70,000 in 1990. For the calendar year 1989, C may claim only $25,000 of his $40,000 distributive share of the partnership loss (one-half of the $80,000 loss). As a result, the basis in his partnership interest will be reduced to zero as of January 1, 1990, and he must carry forward the remaining $15,000 of partnership losses. □

EXAMPLE 47

Assuming the same facts as in Example 46, what will be the income tax consequences for C in 1990? Since the partnership earned a profit of $70,000 for the calendar year 1990, C will report income from the partnership of $20,000 ($35,000 distributive share of income for 1990 less the $15,000 loss not allowed for 1989). The adjusted basis of his partnership interest now becomes $20,000. □

Transactions between Partner and Partnership.   A partner engaging in a transaction with the partnership is generally regarded as a nonpartner or outsider. However, certain exceptions have been provided to prevent unwarranted tax avoidance. For instance, under § 707(b)(1), losses from the sale or exchange of property will be disallowed if they arise in either of the following cases:

- Between a partnership and a person whose direct or indirect interest in the capital or profits of the partnership is more than 50 percent.

- Between two partnerships in which the same persons own more than 50 percent interest in the capital or profits.

If one of the purchasers later sells the property, any gain realized will be recognized only to the extent that it exceeds the loss previously disallowed.

EXAMPLE 48

R owns a 60% interest in the capital and profits of the RST Partnership. In the current year, R sells property with an adjusted basis of $50,000 to the partnership for its fair market value of $35,000. The $15,000 loss is not deductible, since R's ownership interest is more than 50%. If the RST

Partnership later sells the property for $40,000, none of the $5,000 (sale price of $40,000 less adjusted basis to partnership of $35,000) gain will be recognized, since it is offset by $5,000 of the previously disallowed loss of $15,000. The unused loss of $10,000, however, is of no tax benefit either to the partnership or to R. □

Payments made by a partnership to one of its partners for services rendered or for the use of capital, to the extent they are determined without regard to the income of the partnership, are treated by the partnership in the same manner as payments made to a person who is not a partner. Referred to as *guaranteed payments* under § 707(c), such payments are generally deductible by the partnership as a business expense and must be reported as ordinary income by the receiving partner. Their deductibility distinguishes guaranteed payments from a partner's distributive share of income that is not deductible by the partnership.

EXAMPLE 49   Under the terms of the LMN Partnership agreement, N is entitled to a fixed annual salary of $18,000 without regard to the income of the partnership. He is also to share in the profits and losses of the partnership as an equal partner. After deducting the guaranteed payment, the partnership has $36,000 of ordinary income. N must include $30,000 as ordinary income on his income tax return for his tax year with or within which the partnership tax year ends ($18,000 guaranteed payment plus his one-third distributive share of partnership income of $12,000). □

Other Partnership Considerations.   Complex tax provisions involving liquidating and nonliquidating distributions and the sale of a partnership interest are beyond the scope of this text and are discussed in depth in *West's Federal Taxation: Corporations, Partnerships, Estates, and Trusts.*

TAX PLANNING CONSIDERATIONS

Corporate versus Noncorporate Forms of Business Organization

The decision to use the corporate form in conducting a trade or business must be weighed carefully. Besides the nontax considerations attendant to the corporate form (limited liability, continuity of life, free transferability of interest, centralized management), tax ramifications will play an important role in any such decision. Close attention should be paid to the following:

1. The corporate form means the imposition of the corporate income tax. Corporate-source income will be taxed twice—once as earned by the corporation and again when distributed to the shareholders. Since dividends are not deductible, a strong incentive exists in a closely held corporation to structure corporate distributions in a deductible form. Thus, profits may be bailed out by the shareholders in the form of salaries, interest, or rents. Such procedures lead to a multitude of problems, one of which, the reclassification of debt as equity, has been discussed. The

problems of unreasonable salaries and rents were discussed in chapter 6.

2. Assuming the current tax rates remain in effect, the top rates definitely favor the noncorporate taxpayer over the corporate taxpayer. For example, the top rate for individuals is 28 percent for 1989. For corporations, the top rate is 34 percent. The differential is not so pronounced, however, if one presumes a shareholder with a top rate of 28 percent and a corporation that limits its taxable income to $100,000 to avoid the phase-out of the 15 percent and 25 percent lower brackets. Here, the time value of the taxes saved (by not distributing dividends and postponing the effect of the double tax that otherwise results) could make operating a business in the corporate form advantageous.

3. Corporate-source income loses its identity as it passes through the corporation to the shareholders. Thus, items possessing preferential tax treatment (e.g., interest on municipal bonds) are not taxed as such to the shareholders.

4. As noted earlier, it may be difficult for shareholders to recover some or all of their investment in the corporation without an ordinary income result, since most corporate distributions are treated as dividends to the extent of the corporation's earnings and profits. Structuring the capital of the corporation to include debt is a partial solution to this problem. Thus, the shareholder-creditor could recoup part of his or her investment through the tax-free payment of principal. Too much debt, however, may lead to such debt being reclassified as equity.

5. Corporate losses cannot be passed through to the shareholders.

6. The liquidation of a corporation may generate tax consequences to both the corporation and its shareholders.

7. The corporate form provides the shareholders with the opportunity to be treated as employees for tax purposes if they, in fact, render services to the corporation. Such status makes a number of attractive tax-sheltered fringe benefits available (e.g., group term life insurance). These benefits are not available to partners and sole proprietors.

Regular Corporation versus S Status

Because of the pass-through concept, the use of S status generally avoids the income tax at the corporate level, bringing the individual income tax into play. As noted in item 2 in the previous section, the differential between the maximum rates applicable to noncorporate and corporate taxpayers generally is such that the former is more advantageous from a tax standpoint. Thus, the S election enables a business to operate in the corporate form, avoid the corporate income tax, and take advantage of the lower rates usually applicable to individuals. Also, losses incurred at the corporate level will pass through to the shareholders, who will utilize them on their individual returns (compare item 5).

Several problems exist with corporations electing S status. First, the election is available only to small business corporations. Consequently, many corporations will not qualify for the election. Second, S corporations are subject to the rules governing regular corporations unless otherwise specified in the Code. For example, if an S corporation carries out a stock redemption or is liquidated, the rules covering regular corporations will apply. Third, many states do not recognize S status for purposes of state and local taxation. In some cases, therefore, an S corporation might be subject to a state franchise tax (refer to chapter 1) or a state or local income tax.

Use of an Entity to Reduce the Family Income Tax Burden

One objective of tax planning is to keep the income from a business within the family unit but to arrange its dispersion in such a manner as to minimize the overall income tax burden. To the extent feasible, therefore, income should be shifted from higher bracket to lower bracket family members.

Unfortunately, the income from property (a business) cannot be shifted to another without also transferring an interest in the property. If, for example, a father wants to assign income from his sole proprietorship to his children, he must form a partnership or incorporate the business.[46] In either case, the transfer of the interest may be subject to the Federal gift tax. But any such potential gift tax can be eliminated or controlled through judicious use of the annual exclusion, the election to split gifts (for married donors), and the unified tax credit (refer to the discussion of the Federal gift tax in chapter 1).

Consequently, the first problem to be resolved becomes which form of business organization will best fit the objective of income shifting. For the partnership form, one major obstacle arises. The family partnership rules of § 704(e) preclude the assignment of income to a family member unless capital is a material income-producing factor or, if not, the family member contributes substantial or vital services. Ordinarily, capital is not a material income-producing factor if the income of the business consists principally of fees, commissions, or other compensation for personal services performed by members or employees of the partnership. Conversely, capital will be a material income-producing factor if the operation of the business entails a substantial investment in physical assets (e.g., inventory, plant, machinery, or equipment).

Income shifting through the use of a partnership, therefore, may be ineffectual if a personal service business is involved. In fact, it could be hopeless if the assignees are minors. With the use of the corporate form, usually no such impediment exists. Regardless of the nature of the business, a gift of stock will carry with it the emoluments of ownership. Thus, dividends paid on stock will be taxed to the owner of the stock.

But what if the corporate form is utilized and the S election is made? A new hurdle arises under the Code. Section 1366(e) authorizes the IRS to make adjustments in situations where shareholders are not being adequately compensated for the value of their services or capital provided to an S corporation in a family setting.

EXAMPLE 50 | The stock of an S corporation is held equally by T and his three minor children (ages 14, 15, and 16). Without help from his children, T runs the business for which he pays himself an annual salary of $20,000. If $50,000 is a reasonable amount for the value of these services, the IRS may

---

46. Income shifting will not work, however, if the minor is under 14 years of age. In such cases, net unearned income (refer to the discussion in chapter 3) of the child will be taxed at the parents' tax rate. § 1(i).

allocate $30,000 of the corporation's taxable income from the children to T. ☐

Thus, an S corporation suffers from the same vulnerability that exists with family partnerships.

A further factor that would favor the corporate form (either a regular or an S corporation) as a device for income splitting is the ease with which it can be carried out. Presuming the entity already exists, the transfer of stock merely requires an entry in the corporation's stock ledger account. In contrast, a gift of a partnership interest probably will necessitate an amendment to the articles of copartnership. If minors are to be the assignees (donees), a state's Uniform Gifts to Minors Act provides a useful and flexible means of holding a stock interest until such assignees become adults.[47] In the case of a partnership interest, however, a guardianship may have to be set up to achieve the same flexibility. In summary, the transfer of stock is more convenient and, because it usually avoids legal problems, can be less expensive.

Regardless of what form of organization is used for the business, income shifting will not take place unless the transfer is complete.[48] If the donor continues to exercise control over the interest transferred and does not recognize and protect the ownership rights of the donee, the IRS may argue that the transfer was ineffective for tax purposes. If such be the case, the income from the transferred interest will continue to be taxed to the donor.

PROBLEM MATERIALS

Discussion Questions

1. Will a business be treated as a corporation for Federal income tax purposes if the state legal requirements for a corporation are met, even if the business does not possess corporate characteristics?

2. Why would the IRS in some instances assert that an entity be taxed as a corporation rather than be taxed as a noncorporate entity?

3. Section 1250 may compel the recapture of depreciation as ordinary income upon the sale or other taxable disposition of depreciable real estate. In the application of § 1250, are corporate and noncorporate taxpayers treated the same way? Explain.

4. Contrast the corporate tax rules for deducting net capital losses with the rules for individuals. Are the corporate capital loss rules *more* or *less* favorable than the capital loss provisions for individuals? Why?

5. What requirements must be met to properly accrue a charitable contribution, the payment of which is made in the year following the year of the deduction?

6. How are corporate charitable contributions treated if such amounts are in excess of the maximum limitations?

---

47. The Uniform Gifts to Minors Act is explained in the discussion following Example 57 in chapter 4.

48. *Ginsberg v. Comm.*, 74–2 USTC ¶9660, 34 AFTR2d 74–5760, 502 F.2d 965 (CA–6, 1974), and *Michael F. Beirne*, 61 T.C. 268 (1973).

7. When would a corporate taxpayer use the fair market value of inventory as the measure of a charitable contribution to a qualified charity?

8. Why are the corporate net operating loss adjustments substantially different from the NOL adjustments for individual taxpayers?

9. Why would a corporation elect not to carry back an NOL to a particular year?

10. What is the rationale for the dividends received deduction for corporate shareholders?

11. The amount of the dividends received deduction may depend on the percentage of ownership held by the corporate shareholder. Explain.

12. Distinguish between expenditures that qualify as organizational expenditures and those that do not qualify.

13. The corporate income tax can be expressed by use of the following formula: $13,750 + (34% of taxable income in excess of $75,000).

    a. Do you agree? Explain.

    b. When would the formula work?

14. Qualified personal service corporations need not be concerned about keeping taxable income at $100,000 or less. Please comment.

15. What purpose does the Schedule M–1 reconciliation of Form 1120 serve for the taxpayer? For the IRS?

16. Are corporations subject to the limitations on the deductibility of passive activity losses? Explain.

17. In order to convince a corporation to open a manufacturing facility in its community, a city donates land to the corporation. Does the donation generate income to the corporation? What basis will the corporation have in the land?

18. Why is it usually advantageous to capitalize a corporation by using debt? Is it possible that the debt will be reclassified as equity? Why?

19. What is the rationale for § 351? What is "boot"? Why is realized gain recognized to the extent of boot received?

20. If appreciated property is transferred to a corporation in a nontaxable exchange under § 351, is gain recognized by the corporation if the property is immediately sold by the corporation at its fair market value? Why?

21. How do the following transactions affect the earnings and profits of a corporation?

    a. A nontaxable stock dividend issued to the shareholders.

    b. Receipt of interest on municipal bonds.

    c. Federal corporate income tax liability.

22. When is a distribution by a corporation to its shareholders treated by the shareholders as a return of capital? When can a shareholder have a capital gain on a distribution received from a corporation?

23. How is the basis of the assets of a subsidiary determined on the transfer of such assets to the parent in a § 332 liquidation? How is it possible for the parent company to receive a step-up in basis for the subsidiary assets if certain requirements are met?

24. What are the requirements to be a small business corporation under Subchapter S?

25. On March 17, 1989, the holders of 80% of the shares of X Corporation, a calendar year taxpayer, elect to terminate S status. For what year will X Corporation first become a regular corporation?

26. What are some examples of separately stated items that pass through "as is" to an S corporation's shareholders? Why is this procedure required?

27. If an S corporation incurs an operating loss, how is such a loss apportioned to the shareholders?

28. Are net operating losses of an S corporation deductible by the shareholders without limit? Why?

29. Why is a partnership required to file an information return (Form 1065)?

30. Compare the nonrecognition of gain or loss on contributions to a partnership with the similar provision found in corporate formation (§ 351). What are the major differences and similarities?

31. Under what circumstances does the receipt of a partnership interest result in the recognition of ordinary income? What is the effect of this on the partnership and the other partners?

32. How is a contributing partner's basis in a partnership interest determined?

33. What transactions or events will cause a partner's basis in his or her partnership interest to fluctuate continuously?

34. Describe the two-step approach used in determining partnership income. Why is the computation necessary?

35. To what extent can a partner deduct his or her distributive share of partnership losses? What happens to any unused losses?

36. What are guaranteed payments? When might such payments be used?

Problems

37. XYZ Corporation incurred net short-term capital gains of $30,000 and net long-term capital losses of $80,000 during 1989. Taxable income from other sources was $400,000. Prior years' transactions included the following:

1985	Net long-term capital gains	$80,000
1986	Net short-term capital gains	20,000
1987	Net long-term capital gains	10,000
1988	Net long-term capital gains	10,000

a.   How are the capital gains and losses treated on the 1989 tax return?

b.   Compute the capital loss carryback to the carryback years.

c.   Compute the amount of capital loss carryover, if any, and designate the years to which the loss may be carried.

38. During 1989, T Corporation, a calendar year taxpayer, had the following income and expenses:

Income from operations	$225,000
Expenses from operations	165,000
Dividends from domestic corporations	15,000
NOL carryover from 1988	4,500

On May 1, 1989, T Corporation made a contribution to a qualified charitable organization of $10,500 in cash (not included in any of the items listed above).

a.   Determine T Corporation's deduction for charitable contributions for 1989.

b.   What happens to any portion of the contribution not deductible in 1989?

39. In each of the following independent situations, determine the dividends received deduction. Assume that none of the corporate shareholders owns 20% or more of the stock in the corporations paying the dividends.

	E Corporation	F Corporation	G Corporation
Income from operations	$ 700,000	$ 800,000	$ 700,000
Expenses from operations	(600,000)	(900,000)	(740,000)
Qualifying dividends	100,000	200,000	200,000

40. T Corporation, an accrual basis taxpayer, was formed and began operations on July 1, 1989. The following expenses were incurred during its first year of operations (July 1 to December 31, 1989):

Expenses of temporary directors and of organizational meetings	$2,500
Fee paid to the state for incorporation	300
Accounting services incident to organization	600
Legal services for drafting the corporate charter and bylaws	1,400
Expenses incident to the printing and sale of stock certificates	500
	$5,300

Assume T Corporation makes an appropriate and timely election under § 248 and the Regulations.

a. What is the maximum organizational expense T may write off for the calendar year 1989?

b. What would be the result if a proper election had not been made?

41. In each of the following independent situations, determine the corporation's income tax liability. Assume that all corporations use a calendar year for tax purposes and that the tax year involved is 1989.

	Taxable Income
J Corporation	$ 30,000
K Corporation	120,000
L Corporation	390,000
M Corporation	80,000

42. Using the following legend, classify each statement accordingly:

Legend

I =	Applies to the income taxation of individuals.
C =	Applies to the income taxation of regular corporations.
B =	Applies to the income taxation of both individuals and regular corporations.
N =	Applies to the income taxation of neither individuals nor regular corporations.

a. Net capital losses cannot be carried back.

b. Net capital losses can be carried over indefinitely.

c. Net capital losses cannot offset other income.

d. An accrual basis taxpayer cannot deduct charitable contributions until the year of payment.

e. A dividends received deduction may be available.

f. The application of § 1250 (the recapture of depreciation claimed on certain real property) may yield more ordinary income.

g. The concept of adjusted gross income (AGI) has no relevance.

h. Percentage limitations may restrict the amount of charitable deductions that can be claimed in any one tax year.

i. Casualty losses are deductible in full.

j. Tax rates are only mildly progressive.

k. More adjustments are necessary to arrive at a net operating loss deduction.

43. X and Y formed XY Corporation with the following investments: X transferred property with a fair market value of $50,000 and basis of $30,000, and Y transferred property with a fair market value of $50,000 and adjusted basis of $75,000. X received $50,000 of XY voting stock, and Y received $40,000 of XY voting stock and a demand note for $10,000.

a. Do the transfers qualify under § 351?

b. How much gain or loss is recognized by X? By Y?

c. If Y received $10,000 cash instead of the note, would your answer be different?

d. Would either X or Y prefer that the transaction be completely taxable? Why?

44. T, the sole shareholder of X Corporation, has a basis in her stock investment of $15,000. At a time when X Corporation has earnings and profits of $20,000, it distributes cash of $80,000 to T. What are the tax consequences to T of the $80,000 distribution?

45. The stock of R Corporation is held equally by V (an individual) and T Corporation. At a time when R Corporation has earnings and profits of $200,000, it distributes the following property dividends to V and to T Corporation:

	Asset Distributed	Adjusted Basis to R Corporation	Fair Market Value
To V	Land (Pa᛫ ᛫ A)	$10,000	$50,000
To T Corp.	Land (Parcel B)	60,000	50,000

a. What are the income tax consequences to V?

b. What are the income tax consequences to T Corporation?

c. What are the income tax consequences to R Corporation?

46. Q Corporation makes a loan to one of its shareholders, R. No interest is provided for, but the application of the market rate would produce $30,000 of interest for the term of the loan.

a. Presuming the loan is bona fide, what tax consequence results to Q Corporation? To R?

b. Presuming the loan is not bona fide, what tax consequence results to Q Corporation? To R?

47. At a time when O Corporation has ample earnings and profits, it redeems 500 of T's 1,500 shares for their fair market value of $500,000 ($1,000 for each share). All of T's shares were acquired 10 years ago as an investment and have an adjusted basis of $150,000 ($100 for each share).

a. Describe the tax effect of the redemption if it qualifies for sale or exchange treatment.

b. Describe the tax effect of the redemption if it does not qualify for sale or exchange treatment.

48. In 1989, X Corporation is liquidated under the general rules of § 331. The company distributes its only asset (land with a fair market value of $100,000 and adjusted cost basis of $20,000) to T, an individual who held all of the X Corporation stock as an investment. T's basis in the stock of X Corporation was $60,000. X Corporation had earnings and profits of $10,000.

a. What is the amount and character of gain or loss recognized by T upon the receipt of the land in exchange for T's stock?

b. What is T's basis in the land?

c. Is there any tax effect to X Corporation? Explain.

d. If T is a corporate shareholder and X Corporation is liquidated into T, what liquidation section would apply? How much gain or loss would T recognize, and what would be T's basis in the land?

49. T Corporation has been a calendar year S corporation for several years. On June 1, 1989, one of its shareholders sells her stock to Y Corporation. Does this sale cause any tax consequences to T Corporation? Explain.

50. During 1989, X Corporation (a calendar year accrual basis S corporation) had the following transactions:

Sales	$300,000
Cost of goods sold	210,000
Interest on municipal bonds	1,000
Long-term capital gain	2,000
Short-term capital loss	3,000
Advertising expense	4,000
Cash dividends on Exxon stock	2,500
Charitable contributions	500
Salaries and wages	45,000
Amortization of organizational expenditures	400

a. Determine X Corporation's separately stated items for 1989.

b. Determine X Corporation's taxable income for 1989.

51. XYZ Corporation, a calendar year taxpayer, was formed in January 1988. For tax year 1988, it had taxable income of $25,000. For tax year 1989, a net operating loss of $25,000 resulted. XYZ anticipates taxable income of $100,000 for tax year 1990. Discuss the disposition of the 1989 net operating loss under each of the following assumptions:

a. XYZ Corporation is an S corporation.

b. XYZ Corporation is not an S corporation.

52. In 1989, Y Corporation (a calendar year S corporation) had a net operating loss of $109,500. T, a calendar year individual, held stock in Y Corporation as follows: 40% for 300 days and 60% for 65 days. Based on these facts, what is T's loss pass-through for 1989?

53. B owns 50% of the stock in an S corporation. The corporation sustains a $24,000 operating loss during the current year. B's adjusted basis in the stock is $2,000, but B has a loan outstanding to the corporation in the amount of $2,000. What amount, if any, is B entitled to deduct with respect to these losses on her Form 1040 for the current year?

54. A, B, and C form the ABC Partnership on January 1, 1989. In exchange for a 30% capital interest, A transfers property (basis of $14,000, fair market value of $25,000) subject to a liability of $10,000. The liability is assumed by the partnership. B transfers property (basis of $24,000, fair market value of $15,000) for a 30% capital interest, and C transfers cash of $20,000 for the remaining 40% interest.

a. How much gain must A recognize on the transfer?

b. What is A's basis in her partnership interest?

    c.   How much loss may B recognize on the transfer?

    d.   What is B's basis in her partnership interest?

    e.   What is C's basis in her partnership interest?

    f.   What basis will the ABC Partnership have in the property transferred by A? The property transferred by B?

    g.   What would be the tax consequences to A if the basis of the property she contributed is only $9,000?

55.   As of January 1, 1988, D had a basis of $26,000 in his 25% capital interest in the DEF Partnership. He and the partnership use the calendar year for tax purposes. The partnership incurred an operating loss of $120,000 for 1988 and a profit of $80,000 for 1989.

    a.   How much, if any, loss may D recognize for 1988?

    b.   How much income must D recognize for 1989?

    c.   What basis will D have in his partnership interest as of January 1, 1989?

    d.   What basis will D have in his partnership interest as of January 1, 1990?

    e.   What year-end tax planning would you suggest to ensure that a partner could deduct all of his or her share of any partnership losses?

56.   T owns a 51% interest in the capital and profits of the TUV Partnership. In 1988, T sells property (adjusted basis of $120,000) to the partnership for the property's fair market value of $109,000. In 1989, TUV Partnership sells the same property to an outsider for $112,000.

    a.   What are T's tax consequences on the 1988 sale?

    b.   What are TUV Partnership's tax consequences on the 1989 sale?

Research Problems

Research Problem 1   T incorporates her retail clothing business. She transfers all her business assets (total basis of $100,000 and fair market value of $95,000) along with business liabilities of $10,000 and a personal note in the amount of $15,000 to the corporation for 100% of its stock. The note is for money borrowed from the bank six months before incorporation to finance improvements on her home. What are the tax consequences of the transfer?

Research Problem 2   The stock of Y Corporation was owned equally by 20 individuals. It became necessary for Y to borrow money to purchase inventory and to pay its operating expenses. Y Corporation was able to obtain loans for three years but only on the condition that individuals with substantial net worth guarantee the loans. Three of Y's shareholders agreed to guarantee the loans. They were paid a fee for the guaranty in the amount of 5% of the average outstanding indebtedness, prorated among the guarantors in proportion to the sum each personally guaranteed. Y Corporation deducted these fees as follows: $30,000 in 1986 and $35,000 in 1987. Upon audit of Y's return in 1989, the IRS disallowed the deductions, reclassifying them as dividends. What is the result if Y challenges the tax deficiency?

Research Problem 3   On February 10, 1989, a calendar year S corporation mistakenly issues a second class of stock, thereby terminating the S election. During 1989, the corporation had nonseparately computed income of $200,000, nonseparately computed deductions of $60,000, tax-exempt income of $20,000, and tax credits of $30,000. The corporate records indicate that through February 9, 1989, the S corporation earned $20,000 of non-separately computed income, incurred $5,000 of nonseparately computed deductions, and had no tax-exempt income or tax credits. Discuss the annualization procedure for this corporation, including the special election provided for in § 1362(e)(3).

Research Problem 4   T and a number of her friends want to diversify their investment portfolios. With this in mind, they form a partnership to which they transfer appreciated securities. Each transferor receives an interest in the new partnership proportionate to the value of the securities transferred. Will the creation of the partnership be tax-free? Why or why not?

APPENDIX A

Tax Rate Schedules and Tables

1988 Tax Rate Schedules

Caution: *Use ONLY if your taxable income (Form 1040, line 37) is $50,000 or more. If less, use the* **Tax Table.**

Schedule X—Use if your filing status is **Single**

If the amount on Form 1040, line 37, is: Over—	But not over—	Enter on Form 1040, line 38	of the amount over—
$0	$17,850	........15%	$0
17,850	43,150	**$2,677.50 + 28%**	17,850
43,150	89,560	**9,761.50 + 33%**	43,150
89,560	....	Use **Worksheet** below to figure your tax.	

Schedule Z—Use if your filing status is **Head of household**

If the amount on Form 1040, line 37, is: Over—	But not over—	Enter on Form 1040, line 38	of the amount over—
$0	$23,900	........15%	$0
23,900	61,650	**$3,585 + 28%**	23,900
61,650	123,790	**14,155 + 33%**	61,650
123,790	....	Use **Worksheet** below to figure your tax.	

Schedule Y-1—Use if your filing status is **Married filing jointly or Qualifying widow(er)**

If the amount on Form 1040, line 37, is: Over—	But not over—	Enter on Form 1040, line 38	of the amount over—
$0	$29,750	........15%	$0
29,750	71,900	**$4,462.50 + 28%**	29,750
71,900	149,250	**16,264.50 + 33%**	71,900
149,250	....	Use **Worksheet** below to figure your tax.	

Schedule Y-2—Use if your filing status is **Married filing separately**

If the amount on Form 1040, line 37, is: Over—	But not over—	Enter on Form 1040, line 38	of the amount over—
$0	$14,875	........15%	$0
14,875	35,950	**$2,231.25 + 28%**	14,875
35,950	113,300	**8,132.25 + 33%**	35,950
113,300	....	Use **Worksheet** below to figure your tax.	

Worksheet (Keep for your records)

1. If your filing status is:
   - Single, enter $25,076.80
   - Head of household, enter $34,661.20
   - Married filing jointly or Qualifying widow(er), enter $41,790.00
   - Married filing separately, enter $33,657.75   . . . .   **1.** _____

2. Enter your taxable income . . . . **2.** _____

3. If your filing status is:
   - Single, enter $89,560
   - Head of household, enter $123,790
   - Married filing jointly or Qualifying widow(er), enter $149,250
   - Married filing separately, enter $113,300   . . . . .   **3.** _____

4. Subtract line 3 from line 2. Enter the result. (If the result is zero or less, use the schedule above for your filing status to figure your tax. DO NOT use this worksheet.)   **4.** _____

5. Multiply the amount on line 4 by 28% (.28). Enter the result . . . .   **5.** _____

6. Multiply the amount on line 4 by 5% (.05). Enter the result . . . .   **6.** _____

7. Multiply $546 by the number of exemptions claimed on Form 1040, line 6e. (If married filing separately, see the **Note** below.) Enter the result . . . .   **7.** _____

8. Compare the amounts on lines 6 and 7. Enter the **smaller** of the two amounts . . . .   **8.** _____

9. Tax. Add lines 1, 5, and 8. . . . .   **9.** _____

Note: *If married filing separately and you did **not** claim an exemption for your spouse, multiply $546 by the number of exemptions claimed. Add $546 to the result and enter the total on line 7 above.*

1988 Tax Table

Use if your taxable income is less than $50,000. If $50,000 or more, use the Tax Rate Schedules.

Example: Mr. and Mrs. Brown are filing a joint return. Their taxable income on line 37 of Form 1040 is $25,300. First, they find the $25,300–25,350 income line. Next, they find the column for married filing jointly and read down the column. The amount shown where the income line and filing status column meet is $3,799. This is the tax amount they must write on line 38 of their return.

At least	But less than	Single	Married filing jointly *	Married filing sepa-rately	Head of a house-hold
				Your tax is—	
25,200	25,250	4,743	3,784	5,129	3,956
25,250	25,300	4,757	3,791	5,143	3,970
25,300	25,350	4,771	(3,799)	5,157	3,984
25,350	25,400	4,785	3,806	5,171	3,998

At least	But less than	Single	Married filing jointly *	Married filing sepa-rately	Head of a house-hold	At least	But less than	Single	Married filing jointly *	Married filing sepa-rately	Head of a house-hold	At least	But less than	Single	Married filing jointly *	Married filing sepa-rately	Head of a house-hold
				Your tax is—						Your tax is—						Your tax is—	
$0	$5	$0	$0	$0	$0	1,400	1,425	212	212	212	212	2,700	2,725	407	407	407	407
5	15	2	2	2	2	1,425	1,450	216	216	216	216	2,725	2,750	411	411	411	411
15	25	3	3	3	3	1,450	1,475	219	219	219	219	2,750	2,775	414	414	414	414
25	50	6	6	6	6	1,475	1,500	223	223	223	223	2,775	2,800	418	418	418	418
50	75	9	9	9	9	1,500	1,525	227	227	227	227	2,800	2,825	422	422	422	422
75	100	13	13	13	13	1,525	1,550	231	231	231	231	2,825	2,850	426	426	426	426
100	125	17	17	17	17	1,550	1,575	234	234	234	234	2,850	2,875	429	429	429	429
125	150	21	21	21	21	1,575	1,600	238	238	238	238	2,875	2,900	433	433	433	433
150	175	24	24	24	24	1,600	1,625	242	242	242	242	2,900	2,925	437	437	437	437
175	200	28	28	28	28	1,625	1,650	246	246	246	246	2,925	2,950	441	441	441	441
200	225	32	32	32	32	1,650	1,675	249	249	249	249	2,950	2,975	444	444	444	444
225	250	36	36	36	36	1,675	1,700	253	253	253	253	2,975	3,000	448	448	448	448
250	275	39	39	39	39	1,700	1,725	257	257	257	257	**3,000**					
275	300	43	43	43	43	1,725	1,750	261	261	261	261	3,000	3,050	454	454	454	454
300	325	47	47	47	47	1,750	1,775	264	264	264	264	3,050	3,100	461	461	461	461
325	350	51	51	51	51	1,775	1,800	268	268	268	268	3,100	3,150	469	469	469	469
350	375	54	54	54	54	1,800	1,825	272	272	272	272	3,150	3,200	476	476	476	476
375	400	58	58	58	58	1,825	1,850	276	276	276	276	3,200	3,250	484	484	484	484
400	425	62	62	62	62	1,850	1,875	279	279	279	279	3,250	3,300	491	491	491	491
425	450	66	66	66	66	1,875	1,900	283	283	283	283	3,300	3,350	499	499	499	499
450	475	69	69	69	69	1,900	1,925	287	287	287	287	3,350	3,400	506	506	506	506
475	500	73	73	73	73	1,925	1,950	291	291	291	291	3,400	3,450	514	514	514	514
500	525	77	77	77	77	1,950	1,975	294	294	294	294	3,450	3,500	521	521	521	521
525	550	81	81	81	81	1,975	2,000	298	298	298	298	3,500	3,550	529	529	529	529
550	575	84	84	84	84	**2,000**						3,550	3,600	536	536	536	536
575	600	88	88	88	88	2,000	2,025	302	302	302	302	3,600	3,650	544	544	544	544
600	625	92	92	92	92	2,025	2,050	306	306	306	306	3,650	3,700	551	551	551	551
625	650	96	96	96	96	2,050	2,075	309	309	309	309	3,700	3,750	559	559	559	559
650	675	99	99	99	99	2,075	2,100	313	313	313	313	3,750	3,800	566	566	566	566
675	700	103	103	103	103	2,100	2,125	317	317	317	317	3,800	3,850	574	574	574	574
700	725	107	107	107	107	2,125	2,150	321	321	321	321	3,850	3,900	581	581	581	581
725	750	111	111	111	111	2,150	2,175	324	324	324	324	3,900	3,950	589	589	589	589
750	775	114	114	114	114	2,175	2,200	328	328	328	328	3,950	4,000	596	596	596	596
775	800	118	118	118	118	2,200	2,225	332	332	332	332	**4,000**					
800	825	122	122	122	122	2,225	2,250	336	336	336	336	4,000	4,050	604	604	604	604
825	850	126	126	126	126	2,250	2,275	339	339	339	339	4,050	4,100	611	611	611	611
850	875	129	129	129	129	2,275	2,300	343	343	343	343	4,100	4,150	619	619	619	619
875	900	133	133	133	133	2,300	2,325	347	347	347	347	4,150	4,200	626	626	626	626
900	925	137	137	137	137	2,325	2,350	351	351	351	351	4,200	4,250	634	634	634	634
925	950	141	141	141	141	2,350	2,375	354	354	354	354	4,250	4,300	641	641	641	641
950	975	144	144	144	144	2,375	2,400	358	358	358	358	4,300	4,350	649	649	649	649
975	1,000	148	148	148	148	2,400	2,425	362	362	362	362	4,350	4,400	656	656	656	656
1,000						2,425	2,450	366	366	366	366	4,400	4,450	664	664	664	664
1,000	1,025	152	152	152	152	2,450	2,475	369	369	369	369	4,450	4,500	671	671	671	671
1,025	1,050	156	156	156	156	2,475	2,500	373	373	373	373	4,500	4,550	679	679	679	679
1,050	1,075	159	159	159	159	2,500	2,525	377	377	377	377	4,550	4,600	686	686	686	686
1,075	1,100	163	163	163	163	2,525	2,550	381	381	381	381	4,600	4,650	694	694	694	694
1,100	1,125	167	167	167	167	2,550	2,575	384	384	384	384	4,650	4,700	701	701	701	701
1,125	1,150	171	171	171	171	2,575	2,600	388	388	388	388	4,700	4,750	709	709	709	709
1,150	1,175	174	174	174	174	2,600	2,625	392	392	392	392	4,750	4,800	716	716	716	716
1,175	1,200	178	178	178	178	2,625	2,650	396	396	396	396	4,800	4,850	724	724	724	724
1,200	1,225	182	182	182	182	2,650	2,675	399	399	399	399	4,850	4,900	731	731	731	731
1,225	1,250	186	186	186	186	2,675	2,700	403	403	403	403	4,900	4,950	739	739	739	739
1,250	1,275	189	189	189	189							4,950	5,000	746	746	746	746
1,275	1,300	193	193	193	193												
1,300	1,325	197	197	197	197												
1,325	1,350	201	201	201	201												
1,350	1,375	204	204	204	204												
1,375	1,400	208	208	208	208												

* This column must also be used by a qualifying widow(er).

Continued on next page

1988 Tax Table—Continued

If line 37 (taxable income) is— At least	But less than	And you are— Single	Married filing jointly *	Married filing separately	Head of a household
5,000					
5,000	5,050	754	754	754	754
5,050	5,100	761	761	761	761
5,100	5,150	769	769	769	769
5,150	5,200	776	776	776	776
5,200	5,250	784	784	784	784
5,250	5,300	791	791	791	791
5,300	5,350	799	799	799	799
5,350	5,400	806	806	806	806
5,400	5,450	814	814	814	814
5,450	5,500	821	821	821	821
5,500	5,550	829	829	829	829
5,550	5,600	836	836	836	836
5,600	5,650	844	844	844	844
5,650	5,700	851	851	851	851
5,700	5,750	859	859	859	859
5,750	5,800	866	866	866	866
5,800	5,850	874	874	874	874
5,850	5,900	881	881	881	881
5,900	5,950	889	889	889	889
5,950	6,000	896	896	896	896
6,000					
6,000	6,050	904	904	904	904
6,050	6,100	911	911	911	911
6,100	6,150	919	919	919	919
6,150	6,200	926	926	926	926
6,200	6,250	934	934	934	934
6,250	6,300	941	941	941	941
6,300	6,350	949	949	949	949
6,350	6,400	956	956	956	956
6,400	6,450	964	964	964	964
6,450	6,500	971	971	971	971
6,500	6,550	979	979	979	979
6,550	6,600	986	986	986	986
6,600	6,650	994	994	994	994
6,650	6,700	1,001	1,001	1,001	1,001
6,700	6,750	1,009	1,009	1,009	1,009
6,750	6,800	1,016	1,016	1,016	1,016
6,800	6,850	1,024	1,024	1,024	1,024
6,850	6,900	1,031	1,031	1,031	1,031
6,900	6,950	1,039	1,039	1,039	1,039
6,950	7,000	1,046	1,046	1,046	1,046
7,000					
7,000	7,050	1,054	1,054	1,054	1,054
7,050	7,100	1,061	1,061	1,061	1,061
7,100	7,150	1,069	1,069	1,069	1,069
7,150	7,200	1,076	1,076	1,076	1,076
7,200	7,250	1,084	1,084	1,084	1,084
7,250	7,300	1,091	1,091	1,091	1,091
7,300	7,350	1,099	1,099	1,099	1,099
7,350	7,400	1,106	1,106	1,106	1,106
7,400	7,450	1,114	1,114	1,114	1,114
7,450	7,500	1,121	1,121	1,121	1,121
7,500	7,550	1,129	1,129	1,129	1,129
7,550	7,600	1,136	1,136	1,136	1,136
7,600	7,650	1,144	1,144	1,144	1,144
7,650	7,700	1,151	1,151	1,151	1,151
7,700	7,750	1,159	1,159	1,159	1,159
7,750	7,800	1,166	1,166	1,166	1,166
7,800	7,850	1,174	1,174	1,174	1,174
7,850	7,900	1,181	1,181	1,181	1,181
7,900	7,950	1,189	1,189	1,189	1,189
7,950	8,000	1,196	1,196	1,196	1,196

If line 37 (taxable income) is— At least	But less than	And you are— Single	Married filing jointly *	Married filing separately	Head of a household
8,000					
8,000	8,050	1,204	1,204	1,204	1,204
8,050	8,100	1,211	1,211	1,211	1,211
8,100	8,150	1,219	1,219	1,219	1,219
8,150	8,200	1,226	1,226	1,226	1,226
8,200	8,250	1,234	1,234	1,234	1,234
8,250	8,300	1,241	1,241	1,241	1,241
8,300	8,350	1,249	1,249	1,249	1,249
8,350	8,400	1,256	1,256	1,256	1,256
8,400	8,450	1,264	1,264	1,264	1,264
8,450	8,500	1,271	1,271	1,271	1,271
8,500	8,550	1,279	1,279	1,279	1,279
8,550	8,600	1,286	1,286	1,286	1,286
8,600	8,650	1,294	1,294	1,294	1,294
8,650	8,700	1,301	1,301	1,301	1,301
8,700	8,750	1,309	1,309	1,309	1,309
8,750	8,800	1,316	1,316	1,316	1,316
8,800	8,850	1,324	1,324	1,324	1,324
8,850	8,900	1,331	1,331	1,331	1,331
8,900	8,950	1,339	1,339	1,339	1,339
8,950	9,000	1,346	1,346	1,346	1,346
9,000					
9,000	9,050	1,354	1,354	1,354	1,354
9,050	9,100	1,361	1,361	1,361	1,361
9,100	9,150	1,369	1,369	1,369	1,369
9,150	9,200	1,376	1,376	1,376	1,376
9,200	9,250	1,384	1,384	1,384	1,384
9,250	9,300	1,391	1,391	1,391	1,391
9,300	9,350	1,399	1,399	1,399	1,399
9,350	9,400	1,406	1,406	1,406	1,406
9,400	9,450	1,414	1,414	1,414	1,414
9,450	9,500	1,421	1,421	1,421	1,421
9,500	9,550	1,429	1,429	1,429	1,429
9,550	9,600	1,436	1,436	1,436	1,436
9,600	9,650	1,444	1,444	1,444	1,444
9,650	9,700	1,451	1,451	1,451	1,451
9,700	9,750	1,459	1,459	1,459	1,459
9,750	9,800	1,466	1,466	1,466	1,466
9,800	9,850	1,474	1,474	1,474	1,474
9,850	9,900	1,481	1,481	1,481	1,481
9,900	9,950	1,489	1,489	1,489	1,489
9,950	10,000	1,496	1,496	1,496	1,496
10,000					
10,000	10,050	1,504	1,504	1,504	1,504
10,050	10,100	1,511	1,511	1,511	1,511
10,100	10,150	1,519	1,519	1,519	1,519
10,150	10,200	1,526	1,526	1,526	1,526
10,200	10,250	1,534	1,534	1,534	1,534
10,250	10,300	1,541	1,541	1,541	1,541
10,300	10,350	1,549	1,549	1,549	1,549
10,350	10,400	1,556	1,556	1,556	1,556
10,400	10,450	1,564	1,564	1,564	1,564
10,450	10,500	1,571	1,571	1,571	1,571
10,500	10,550	1,579	1,579	1,579	1,579
10,550	10,600	1,586	1,586	1,586	1,586
10,600	10,650	1,594	1,594	1,594	1,594
10,650	10,700	1,601	1,601	1,601	1,601
10,700	10,750	1,609	1,609	1,609	1,609
10,750	10,800	1,616	1,616	1,616	1,616
10,800	10,850	1,624	1,624	1,624	1,624
10,850	10,900	1,631	1,631	1,631	1,631
10,900	10,950	1,639	1,639	1,639	1,639
10,950	11,000	1,646	1,646	1,646	1,646

If line 37 (taxable income) is— At least	But less than	And you are— Single	Married filing jointly *	Married filing separately	Head of a household
11,000					
11,000	11,050	1,654	1,654	1,654	1,654
11,050	11,100	1,661	1,661	1,661	1,661
11,100	11,150	1,669	1,669	1,669	1,669
11,150	11,200	1,676	1,676	1,676	1,676
11,200	11,250	1,684	1,684	1,684	1,684
11,250	11,300	1,691	1,691	1,691	1,691
11,300	11,350	1,699	1,699	1,699	1,699
11,350	11,400	1,706	1,706	1,706	1,706
11,400	11,450	1,714	1,714	1,714	1,714
11,450	11,500	1,721	1,721	1,721	1,721
11,500	11,550	1,729	1,729	1,729	1,729
11,550	11,600	1,736	1,736	1,736	1,736
11,600	11,650	1,744	1,744	1,744	1,744
11,650	11,700	1,751	1,751	1,751	1,751
11,700	11,750	1,759	1,759	1,759	1,759
11,750	11,800	1,766	1,766	1,766	1,766
11,800	11,850	1,774	1,774	1,774	1,774
11,850	11,900	1,781	1,781	1,781	1,781
11,900	11,950	1,789	1,789	1,789	1,789
11,950	12,000	1,796	1,796	1,796	1,796
12,000					
12,000	12,050	1,804	1,804	1,804	1,804
12,050	12,100	1,811	1,811	1,811	1,811
12,100	12,150	1,819	1,819	1,819	1,819
12,150	12,200	1,826	1,826	1,826	1,826
12,200	12,250	1,834	1,834	1,834	1,834
12,250	12,300	1,841	1,841	1,841	1,841
12,300	12,350	1,849	1,849	1,849	1,849
12,350	12,400	1,856	1,856	1,856	1,856
12,400	12,450	1,864	1,864	1,864	1,864
12,450	12,500	1,871	1,871	1,871	1,871
12,500	12,550	1,879	1,879	1,879	1,879
12,550	12,600	1,886	1,886	1,886	1,886
12,600	12,650	1,894	1,894	1,894	1,894
12,650	12,700	1,901	1,901	1,901	1,901
12,700	12,750	1,909	1,909	1,909	1,909
12,750	12,800	1,916	1,916	1,916	1,916
12,800	12,850	1,924	1,924	1,924	1,924
12,850	12,900	1,931	1,931	1,931	1,931
12,900	12,950	1,939	1,939	1,939	1,939
12,950	13,000	1,946	1,946	1,946	1,946
13,000					
13,000	13,050	1,954	1,954	1,954	1,954
13,050	13,100	1,961	1,961	1,961	1,961
13,100	13,150	1,969	1,969	1,969	1,969
13,150	13,200	1,976	1,976	1,976	1,976
13,200	13,250	1,984	1,984	1,984	1,984
13,250	13,300	1,991	1,991	1,991	1,991
13,300	13,350	1,999	1,999	1,999	1,999
13,350	13,400	2,006	2,006	2,006	2,006
13,400	13,450	2,014	2,014	2,014	2,014
13,450	13,500	2,021	2,021	2,021	2,021
13,500	13,550	2,029	2,029	2,029	2,029
13,550	13,600	2,036	2,036	2,036	2,036
13,600	13,650	2,044	2,044	2,044	2,044
13,650	13,700	2,051	2,051	2,051	2,051
13,700	13,750	2,059	2,059	2,059	2,059
13,750	13,800	2,066	2,066	2,066	2,066
13,800	13,850	2,074	2,074	2,074	2,074
13,850	13,900	2,081	2,081	2,081	2,081
13,900	13,950	2,089	2,089	2,089	2,089
13,950	14,000	2,096	2,096	2,096	2,096

* This column must also be used by a qualifying widow(er).

Continued on next page

1988 Tax Table—*Continued*

If line 37 (taxable income) is— / And you are—

At least	But less than	Single	Married filing jointly *	Married filing separately	Head of a household

14,000

At least	But less than	Single	Married filing jointly	Married filing separately	Head of household
14,000	14,050	2,104	2,104	2,104	2,104
14,050	14,100	2,111	2,111	2,111	2,111
14,100	14,150	2,119	2,119	2,119	2,119
14,150	14,200	2,126	2,126	2,126	2,126
14,200	14,250	2,134	2,134	2,134	2,134
14,250	14,300	2,141	2,141	2,141	2,141
14,300	14,350	2,149	2,149	2,149	2,149
14,350	14,400	2,156	2,156	2,156	2,156
14,400	14,450	2,164	2,164	2,164	2,164
14,450	14,500	2,171	2,171	2,171	2,171
14,500	14,550	2,179	2,179	2,179	2,179
14,550	14,600	2,186	2,186	2,186	2,186
14,600	14,650	2,194	2,194	2,194	2,194
14,650	14,700	2,201	2,201	2,201	2,201
14,700	14,750	2,209	2,209	2,209	2,209
14,750	14,800	2,216	2,216	2,216	2,216
14,800	14,850	2,224	2,224	2,224	2,224
14,850	14,900	2,231	2,231	2,231	2,231
14,900	14,950	2,239	2,239	2,245	2,239
14,950	15,000	2,246	2,246	2,259	2,246

15,000

At least	But less than	Single	Married filing jointly	Married filing separately	Head of household
15,000	15,050	2,254	2,254	2,273	2,254
15,050	15,100	2,261	2,261	2,287	2,261
15,100	15,150	2,269	2,269	2,301	2,269
15,150	15,200	2,276	2,276	2,315	2,276
15,200	15,250	2,284	2,284	2,329	2,284
15,250	15,300	2,291	2,291	2,343	2,291
15,300	15,350	2,299	2,299	2,357	2,299
15,350	15,400	2,306	2,306	2,371	2,306
15,400	15,450	2,314	2,314	2,385	2,314
15,450	15,500	2,321	2,321	2,399	2,321
15,500	15,550	2,329	2,329	2,413	2,329
15,550	15,600	2,336	2,336	2,427	2,336
15,600	15,650	2,344	2,344	2,441	2,344
15,650	15,700	2,351	2,351	2,455	2,351
15,700	15,750	2,359	2,359	2,469	2,359
15,750	15,800	2,366	2,366	2,483	2,366
15,800	15,850	2,374	2,374	2,497	2,374
15,850	15,900	2,381	2,381	2,511	2,381
15,900	15,950	2,389	2,389	2,525	2,389
15,950	16,000	2,396	2,396	2,539	2,396

16,000

At least	But less than	Single	Married filing jointly	Married filing separately	Head of household
16,000	16,050	2,404	2,404	2,553	2,404
16,050	16,100	2,411	2,411	2,567	2,411
16,100	16,150	2,419	2,419	2,581	2,419
16,150	16,200	2,426	2,426	2,595	2,426
16,200	16,250	2,434	2,434	2,609	2,434
16,250	16,300	2,441	2,441	2,623	2,441
16,300	16,350	2,449	2,449	2,637	2,449
16,350	16,400	2,456	2,456	2,651	2,456
16,400	16,450	2,464	2,464	2,665	2,464
16,450	16,500	2,471	2,471	2,679	2,471
16,500	16,550	2,479	2,479	2,693	2,479
16,550	16,600	2,486	2,486	2,707	2,486
16,600	16,650	2,494	2,494	2,721	2,494
16,650	16,700	2,501	2,501	2,735	2,501
16,700	16,750	2,509	2,509	2,749	2,509
16,750	16,800	2,516	2,516	2,763	2,516
16,800	16,850	2,524	2,524	2,777	2,524
16,850	16,900	2,531	2,531	2,791	2,531
16,900	16,950	2,539	2,539	2,805	2,539
16,950	17,000	2,546	2,546	2,819	2,546

17,000

At least	But less than	Single	Married filing jointly	Married filing separately	Head of household
17,000	17,050	2,554	2,554	2,833	2,554
17,050	17,100	2,561	2,561	2,847	2,561
17,100	17,150	2,569	2,569	2,861	2,569
17,150	17,200	2,576	2,576	2,875	2,576
17,200	17,250	2,584	2,584	2,889	2,584
17,250	17,300	2,591	2,591	2,903	2,591
17,300	17,350	2,599	2,599	2,917	2,599
17,350	17,400	2,606	2,606	2,931	2,606
17,400	17,450	2,614	2,614	2,945	2,614
17,450	17,500	2,621	2,621	2,959	2,621
17,500	17,550	2,629	2,629	2,973	2,629
17,550	17,600	2,636	2,636	2,987	2,636
17,600	17,650	2,644	2,644	3,001	2,644
17,650	17,700	2,651	2,651	3,015	2,651
17,700	17,750	2,659	2,659	3,029	2,659
17,750	17,800	2,666	2,666	3,043	2,666
17,800	17,850	2,674	2,674	3,057	2,674
17,850	17,900	2,685	2,681	3,071	2,681
17,900	17,950	2,699	2,689	3,085	2,689
17,950	18,000	2,713	2,696	3,099	2,696

18,000

At least	But less than	Single	Married filing jointly	Married filing separately	Head of household
18,000	18,050	2,727	2,704	3,113	2,704
18,050	18,100	2,741	2,711	3,127	2,711
18,100	18,150	2,755	2,719	3,141	2,719
18,150	18,200	2,769	2,726	3,155	2,726
18,200	18,250	2,783	2,734	3,169	2,734
18,250	18,300	2,797	2,741	3,183	2,741
18,300	18,350	2,811	2,749	3,197	2,749
18,350	18,400	2,825	2,756	3,211	2,756
18,400	18,450	2,839	2,764	3,225	2,764
18,450	18,500	2,853	2,771	3,239	2,771
18,500	18,550	2,867	2,779	3,253	2,779
18,550	18,600	2,881	2,786	3,267	2,786
18,600	18,650	2,895	2,794	3,281	2,794
18,650	18,700	2,909	2,801	3,295	2,801
18,700	18,750	2,923	2,809	3,309	2,809
18,750	18,800	2,937	2,816	3,323	2,816
18,800	18,850	2,951	2,824	3,337	2,824
18,850	18,900	2,965	2,831	3,351	2,831
18,900	18,950	2,979	2,839	3,365	2,839
18,950	19,000	2,993	2,846	3,379	2,846

19,000

At least	But less than	Single	Married filing jointly	Married filing separately	Head of household
19,000	19,050	3,007	2,854	3,393	2,854
19,050	19,100	3,021	2,861	3,407	2,861
19,100	19,150	3,035	2,869	3,421	2,869
19,150	19,200	3,049	2,876	3,435	2,876
19,200	19,250	3,063	2,884	3,449	2,884
19,250	19,300	3,077	2,891	3,463	2,891
19,300	19,350	3,091	2,899	3,477	2,899
19,350	19,400	3,105	2,906	3,491	2,906
19,400	19,450	3,119	2,914	3,505	2,914
19,450	19,500	3,133	2,921	3,519	2,921
19,500	19,550	3,147	2,929	3,533	2,929
19,550	19,600	3,161	2,936	3,547	2,936
19,600	19,650	3,175	2,944	3,561	2,944
19,650	19,700	3,189	2,951	3,575	2,951
19,700	19,750	3,203	2,959	3,589	2,959
19,750	19,800	3,217	2,966	3,603	2,966
19,800	19,850	3,231	2,974	3,617	2,974
19,850	19,900	3,245	2,981	3,631	2,981
19,900	19,950	3,259	2,989	3,645	2,989
19,950	20,000	3,273	2,996	3,659	2,996

20,000

At least	But less than	Single	Married filing jointly	Married filing separately	Head of household
20,000	20,050	3,287	3,004	3,673	3,004
20,050	20,100	3,301	3,011	3,687	3,011
20,100	20,150	3,315	3,019	3,701	3,019
20,150	20,200	3,329	3,026	3,715	3,026
20,200	20,250	3,343	3,034	3,729	3,034
20,250	20,300	3,357	3,041	3,743	3,041
20,300	20,350	3,371	3,049	3,757	3,049
20,350	20,400	3,385	3,056	3,771	3,056
20,400	20,450	3,399	3,064	3,785	3,064
20,450	20,500	3,413	3,071	3,799	3,071
20,500	20,550	3,427	3,079	3,813	3,079
20,550	20,600	3,441	3,086	3,827	3,086
20,600	20,650	3,455	3,094	3,841	3,094
20,650	20,700	3,469	3,101	3,855	3,101
20,700	20,750	3,483	3,109	3,869	3,109
20,750	20,800	3,497	3,116	3,883	3,116
20,800	20,850	3,511	3,124	3,897	3,124
20,850	20,900	3,525	3,131	3,911	3,131
20,900	20,950	3,539	3,139	3,925	3,139
20,950	21,000	3,553	3,146	3,939	3,146

21,000

At least	But less than	Single	Married filing jointly	Married filing separately	Head of household
21,000	21,050	3,567	3,154	3,953	3,154
21,050	21,100	3,581	3,161	3,967	3,161
21,100	21,150	3,595	3,169	3,981	3,169
21,150	21,200	3,609	3,176	3,995	3,176
21,200	21,250	3,623	3,184	4,009	3,184
21,250	21,300	3,637	3,191	4,023	3,191
21,300	21,350	3,651	3,199	4,037	3,199
21,350	21,400	3,665	3,206	4,051	3,206
21,400	21,450	3,679	3,214	4,065	3,214
21,450	21,500	3,693	3,221	4,079	3,221
21,500	21,550	3,707	3,229	4,093	3,229
21,550	21,600	3,721	3,236	4,107	3,236
21,600	21,650	3,735	3,244	4,121	3,244
21,650	21,700	3,749	3,251	4,135	3,251
21,700	21,750	3,763	3,259	4,149	3,259
21,750	21,800	3,777	3,266	4,163	3,266
21,800	21,850	3,791	3,274	4,177	3,274
21,850	21,900	3,805	3,281	4,191	3,281
21,900	21,950	3,819	3,289	4,205	3,289
21,950	22,000	3,833	3,296	4,219	3,296

22,000

At least	But less than	Single	Married filing jointly	Married filing separately	Head of household
22,000	22,050	3,847	3,304	4,233	3,304
22,050	22,100	3,861	3,311	4,247	3,311
22,100	22,150	3,875	3,319	4,261	3,319
22,150	22,200	3,889	3,326	4,275	3,326
22,200	22,250	3,903	3,334	4,289	3,334
22,250	22,300	3,917	3,341	4,303	3,341
22,300	22,350	3,931	3,349	4,317	3,349
22,350	22,400	3,945	3,356	4,331	3,356
22,400	22,450	3,959	3,364	4,345	3,364
22,450	22,500	3,973	3,371	4,359	3,371
22,500	22,550	3,987	3,379	4,373	3,379
22,550	22,600	4,001	3,386	4,387	3,386
22,600	22,650	4,015	3,394	4,401	3,394
22,650	22,700	4,029	3,401	4,415	3,401
22,700	22,750	4,043	3,409	4,429	3,409
22,750	22,800	4,057	3,416	4,443	3,416
22,800	22,850	4,071	3,424	4,457	3,424
22,850	22,900	4,085	3,431	4,471	3,431
22,900	22,950	4,099	3,439	4,485	3,439
22,950	23,000	4,113	3,446	4,499	3,446

* This column must also be used by a qualifying widow(er).

Continued on next page

1988 Tax Table—*Continued*

If line 37 (taxable income) is— At least	But less than	Single	Married filing jointly *	Married filing separately	Head of a household
23,000					
23,000	23,050	4,127	3,454	4,513	3,454
23,050	23,100	4,141	3,461	4,527	3,461
23,100	23,150	4,155	3,469	4,541	3,469
23,150	23,200	4,169	3,476	4,555	3,476
23,200	23,250	4,183	3,484	4,569	3,484
23,250	23,300	4,197	3,491	4,583	3,491
23,300	23,350	4,211	3,499	4,597	3,499
23,350	23,400	4,225	3,506	4,611	3,506
23,400	23,450	4,239	3,514	4,625	3,514
23,450	23,500	4,253	3,521	4,639	3,521
23,500	23,550	4,267	3,529	4,653	3,529
23,550	23,600	4,281	3,536	4,667	3,536
23,600	23,650	4,295	3,544	4,681	3,544
23,650	23,700	4,309	3,551	4,695	3,551
23,700	23,750	4,323	3,559	4,709	3,559
23,750	23,800	4,337	3,566	4,723	3,566
23,800	23,850	4,351	3,574	4,737	3,574
23,850	23,900	4,365	3,581	4,751	3,581
23,900	23,950	4,379	3,589	4,765	3,592
23,950	24,000	4,393	3,596	4,779	3,606
24,000					
24,000	24,050	4,407	3,604	4,793	3,620
24,050	24,100	4,421	3,611	4,807	3,634
24,100	24,150	4,435	3,619	4,821	3,648
24,150	24,200	4,449	3,626	4,835	3,662
24,200	24,250	4,463	3,634	4,849	3,676
24,250	24,300	4,477	3,641	4,863	3,690
24,300	24,350	4,491	3,649	4,877	3,704
24,350	24,400	4,505	3,656	4,891	3,718
24,400	24,450	4,519	3,664	4,905	3,732
24,450	24,500	4,533	3,671	4,919	3,746
24,500	24,550	4,547	3,679	4,933	3,760
24,550	24,600	4,561	3,686	4,947	3,774
24,600	24,650	4,575	3,694	4,961	3,788
24,650	24,700	4,589	3,701	4,975	3,802
24,700	24,750	4,603	3,709	4,989	3,816
24,750	24,800	4,617	3,716	5,003	3,830
24,800	24,850	4,631	3,724	5,017	3,844
24,850	24,900	4,645	3,731	5,031	3,858
24,900	24,950	4,659	3,739	5,045	3,872
24,950	25,000	4,673	3,746	5,059	3,886
25,000					
25,000	25,050	4,687	3,754	5,073	3,900
25,050	25,100	4,701	3,761	5,087	3,914
25,100	25,150	4,715	3,769	5,101	3,928
25,150	25,200	4,729	3,776	5,115	3,942
25,200	25,250	4,743	3,784	5,129	3,956
25,250	25,300	4,757	3,791	5,143	3,970
25,300	25,350	4,771	3,799	5,157	3,984
25,350	25,400	4,785	3,806	5,171	3,998
25,400	25,450	4,799	3,814	5,185	4,012
25,450	25,500	4,813	3,821	5,199	4,026
25,500	25,550	4,827	3,829	5,213	4,040
25,550	25,600	4,841	3,836	5,227	4,054
25,600	25,650	4,855	3,844	5,241	4,068
25,650	25,700	4,869	3,851	5,255	4,082
25,700	25,750	4,883	3,859	5,269	4,096
25,750	25,800	4,897	3,866	5,283	4,110
25,800	25,850	4,911	3,874	5,297	4,124
25,850	25,900	4,925	3,881	5,311	4,138
25,900	25,950	4,939	3,889	5,325	4,152
25,950	26,000	4,953	3,896	5,339	4,166

If line 37 (taxable income) is— At least	But less than	Single	Married filing jointly *	Married filing separately	Head of a household
26,000					
26,000	26,050	4,967	3,904	5,353	4,180
26,050	26,100	4,981	3,911	5,367	4,194
26,100	26,150	4,995	3,919	5,381	4,208
26,150	26,200	5,009	3,926	5,395	4,222
26,200	26,250	5,023	3,934	5,409	4,236
26,250	26,300	5,037	3,941	5,423	4,250
26,300	26,350	5,051	3,949	5,437	4,264
26,350	26,400	5,065	3,956	5,451	4,278
26,400	26,450	5,079	3,964	5,465	4,292
26,450	26,500	5,093	3,971	5,479	4,306
26,500	26,550	5,107	3,979	5,493	4,320
26,550	26,600	5,121	3,986	5,507	4,334
26,600	26,650	5,135	3,994	5,521	4,348
26,650	26,700	5,149	4,001	5,535	4,362
26,700	26,750	5,163	4,009	5,549	4,376
26,750	26,800	5,177	4,016	5,563	4,390
26,800	26,850	5,191	4,024	5,577	4,404
26,850	26,900	5,205	4,031	5,591	4,418
26,900	26,950	5,219	4,039	5,605	4,432
26,950	27,000	5,233	4,046	5,619	4,446
27,000					
27,000	27,050	5,247	4,054	5,633	4,460
27,050	27,100	5,261	4,061	5,647	4,474
27,100	27,150	5,275	4,069	5,661	4,488
27,150	27,200	5,289	4,076	5,675	4,502
27,200	27,250	5,303	4,084	5,689	4,516
27,250	27,300	5,317	4,091	5,703	4,530
27,300	27,350	5,331	4,099	5,717	4,544
27,350	27,400	5,345	4,106	5,731	4,558
27,400	27,450	5,359	4,114	5,745	4,572
27,450	27,500	5,373	4,121	5,759	4,586
27,500	27,550	5,387	4,129	5,773	4,600
27,550	27,600	5,401	4,136	5,787	4,614
27,600	27,650	5,415	4,144	5,801	4,628
27,650	27,700	5,429	4,151	5,815	4,642
27,700	27,750	5,443	4,159	5,829	4,656
27,750	27,800	5,457	4,166	5,843	4,670
27,800	27,850	5,471	4,174	5,857	4,684
27,850	27,900	5,485	4,181	5,871	4,698
27,900	27,950	5,499	4,189	5,885	4,712
27,950	28,000	5,513	4,196	5,899	4,726
28,000					
28,000	28,050	5,527	4,204	5,913	4,740
28,050	28,100	5,541	4,211	5,927	4,754
28,100	28,150	5,555	4,219	5,941	4,768
28,150	28,200	5,569	4,226	5,955	4,782
28,200	28,250	5,583	4,234	5,969	4,796
28,250	28,300	5,597	4,241	5,983	4,810
28,300	28,350	5,611	4,249	5,997	4,824
28,350	28,400	5,625	4,256	6,011	4,838
28,400	28,450	5,639	4,264	6,025	4,852
28,450	28,500	5,653	4,271	6,039	4,866
28,500	28,550	5,667	4,279	6,053	4,880
28,550	28,600	5,681	4,286	6,067	4,894
28,600	28,650	5,695	4,294	6,081	4,908
28,650	28,700	5,709	4,301	6,095	4,922
28,700	28,750	5,723	4,309	6,109	4,936
28,750	28,800	5,737	4,316	6,123	4,950
28,800	28,850	5,751	4,324	6,137	4,964
28,850	28,900	5,765	4,331	6,151	4,978
28,900	28,950	5,779	4,339	6,165	4,992
28,950	29,000	5,793	4,346	6,179	5,006

If line 37 (taxable income) is— At least	But less than	Single	Married filing jointly *	Married filing separately	Head of a household
29,000					
29,000	29,050	5,807	4,354	6,193	5,020
29,050	29,100	5,821	4,361	6,207	5,034
29,100	29,150	5,835	4,369	6,221	5,048
29,150	29,200	5,849	4,376	6,235	5,062
29,200	29,250	5,863	4,384	6,249	5,076
29,250	29,300	5,877	4,391	6,263	5,090
29,300	29,350	5,891	4,399	6,277	5,104
29,350	29,400	5,905	4,406	6,291	5,118
29,400	29,450	5,919	4,414	6,305	5,132
29,450	29,500	5,933	4,421	6,319	5,146
29,500	29,550	5,947	4,429	6,333	5,160
29,550	29,600	5,961	4,436	6,347	5,174
29,600	29,650	5,975	4,444	6,361	5,188
29,650	29,700	5,989	4,451	6,375	5,202
29,700	29,750	6,003	4,459	6,389	5,216
29,750	29,800	6,017	4,470	6,403	5,230
29,800	29,850	6,031	4,484	6,417	5,244
29,850	29,900	6,045	4,498	6,431	5,258
29,900	29,950	6,059	4,512	6,445	5,272
29,950	30,000	6,073	4,526	6,459	5,286
30,000					
30,000	30,050	6,087	4,540	6,473	5,300
30,050	30,100	6,101	4,554	6,487	5,314
30,100	30,150	6,115	4,568	6,501	5,328
30,150	30,200	6,129	4,582	6,515	5,342
30,200	30,250	6,143	4,596	6,529	5,356
30,250	30,300	6,157	4,610	6,543	5,370
30,300	30,350	6,171	4,624	6,557	5,384
30,350	30,400	6,185	4,638	6,571	5,398
30,400	30,450	6,199	4,652	6,585	5,412
30,450	30,500	6,213	4,666	6,599	5,426
30,500	30,550	6,227	4,680	6,613	5,440
30,550	30,600	6,241	4,694	6,627	5,454
30,600	30,650	6,255	4,708	6,641	5,468
30,650	30,700	6,269	4,722	6,655	5,482
30,700	30,750	6,283	4,736	6,669	5,496
30,750	30,800	6,297	4,750	6,683	5,510
30,800	30,850	6,311	4,764	6,697	5,524
30,850	30,900	6,325	4,778	6,711	5,538
30,900	30,950	6,339	4,792	6,725	5,552
30,950	31,000	6,353	4,806	6,739	5,566
31,000					
31,000	31,050	6,367	4,820	6,753	5,580
31,050	31,100	6,381	4,834	6,767	5,594
31,100	31,150	6,395	4,848	6,781	5,608
31,150	31,200	6,409	4,862	6,795	5,622
31,200	31,250	6,423	4,876	6,809	5,636
31,250	31,300	6,437	4,890	6,823	5,650
31,300	31,350	6,451	4,904	6,837	5,664
31,350	31,400	6,465	4,918	6,851	5,678
31,400	31,450	6,479	4,932	6,865	5,692
31,450	31,500	6,493	4,946	6,879	5,706
31,500	31,550	6,507	4,960	6,893	5,720
31,550	31,600	6,521	4,974	6,907	5,734
31,600	31,650	6,535	4,988	6,921	5,748
31,650	31,700	6,549	5,002	6,935	5,762
31,700	31,750	6,563	5,016	6,949	5,776
31,750	31,800	6,577	5,030	6,963	5,790
31,800	31,850	6,591	5,044	6,977	5,804
31,850	31,900	6,605	5,058	6,991	5,818
31,900	31,950	6,619	5,072	7,005	5,832
31,950	32,000	6,633	5,086	7,019	5,846

* This column must also be used by a qualifying widow(er).

Continued on next page

1988 Tax Table—*Continued*

If line 37 (taxable income) is— At least	But less than	Single	Married filing jointly *	Married filing separately	Head of a household
32,000					
32,000	32,050	6,647	5,100	7,033	5,860
32,050	32,100	6,661	5,114	7,047	5,874
32,100	32,150	6,675	5,128	7,061	5,888
32,150	32,200	6,689	5,142	7,075	5,902
32,200	32,250	6,703	5,156	7,089	5,916
32,250	32,300	6,717	5,170	7,103	5,930
32,300	32,350	6,731	5,184	7,117	5,944
32,350	32,400	6,745	5,198	7,131	5,958
32,400	32,450	6,759	5,212	7,145	5,972
32,450	32,500	6,773	5,226	7,159	5,986
32,500	32,550	6,787	5,240	7,173	6,000
32,550	32,600	6,801	5,254	7,187	6,014
32,600	32,650	6,815	5,268	7,201	6,028
32,650	32,700	6,829	5,282	7,215	6,042
32,700	32,750	6,843	5,296	7,229	6,056
32,750	32,800	6,857	5,310	7,243	6,070
32,800	32,850	6,871	5,324	7,257	6,084
32,850	32,900	6,885	5,338	7,271	6,098
32,900	32,950	6,899	5,352	7,285	6,112
32,950	33,000	6,913	5,366	7,299	6,126
33,000					
33,000	33,050	6,927	5,380	7,313	6,140
33,050	33,100	6,941	5,394	7,327	6,154
33,100	33,150	6,955	5,408	7,341	6,168
33,150	33,200	6,969	5,422	7,355	6,182
33,200	33,250	6,983	5,436	7,369	6,196
33,250	33,300	6,997	5,450	7,383	6,210
33,300	33,350	7,011	5,464	7,397	6,224
33,350	33,400	7,025	5,478	7,411	6,238
33,400	33,450	7,039	5,492	7,425	6,252
33,450	33,500	7,053	5,506	7,439	6,266
33,500	33,550	7,067	5,520	7,453	6,280
33,550	33,600	7,081	5,534	7,467	6,294
33,600	33,650	7,095	5,548	7,481	6,308
33,650	33,700	7,109	5,562	7,495	6,322
33,700	33,750	7,123	5,576	7,509	6,336
33,750	33,800	7,137	5,590	7,523	6,350
33,800	33,850	7,151	5,604	7,537	6,364
33,850	33,900	7,165	5,618	7,551	6,378
33,900	33,950	7,179	5,632	7,565	6,392
33,950	34,000	7,193	5,646	7,579	6,406
34,000					
34,000	34,050	7,207	5,660	7,593	6,420
34,050	34,100	7,221	5,674	7,607	6,434
34,100	34,150	7,235	5,688	7,621	6,448
34,150	34,200	7,249	5,702	7,635	6,462
34,200	34,250	7,263	5,716	7,649	6,476
34,250	34,300	7,277	5,730	7,663	6,490
34,300	34,350	7,291	5,744	7,677	6,504
34,350	34,400	7,305	5,758	7,691	6,518
34,400	34,450	7,319	5,772	7,705	6,532
34,450	34,500	7,333	5,786	7,719	6,546
34,500	34,550	7,347	5,800	7,733	6,560
34,550	34,600	7,361	5,814	7,747	6,574
34,600	34,650	7,375	5,828	7,761	6,588
34,650	34,700	7,389	5,842	7,775	6,602
34,700	34,750	7,403	5,856	7,789	6,616
34,750	34,800	7,417	5,870	7,803	6,630
34,800	34,850	7,431	5,884	7,817	6,644
34,850	34,900	7,445	5,898	7,831	6,658
34,900	34,950	7,459	5,912	7,845	6,672
34,950	35,000	7,473	5,926	7,859	6,686

If line 37 (taxable income) is— At least	But less than	Single	Married filing jointly *	Married filing separately	Head of a household
35,000					
35,000	35,050	7,487	5,940	7,873	6,700
35,050	35,100	7,501	5,954	7,887	6,714
35,100	35,150	7,515	5,968	7,901	6,728
35,150	35,200	7,529	5,982	7,915	6,742
35,200	35,250	7,543	5,996	7,929	6,756
35,250	35,300	7,557	6,010	7,943	6,770
35,300	35,350	7,571	6,024	7,957	6,784
35,350	35,400	7,585	6,038	7,971	6,798
35,400	35,450	7,599	6,052	7,985	6,812
35,450	35,500	7,613	6,066	7,999	6,826
35,500	35,550	7,627	6,080	8,013	6,840
35,550	35,600	7,641	6,094	8,027	6,854
35,600	35,650	7,655	6,108	8,041	6,868
35,650	35,700	7,669	6,122	8,055	6,882
35,700	35,750	7,683	6,136	8,069	6,896
35,750	35,800	7,697	6,150	8,083	6,910
35,800	35,850	7,711	6,164	8,097	6,924
35,850	35,900	7,725	6,178	8,111	6,938
35,900	35,950	7,739	6,192	8,125	6,952
35,950	36,000	7,753	6,206	8,141	6,966
36,000					
36,000	36,050	7,767	6,220	8,157	6,980
36,050	36,100	7,781	6,234	8,174	6,994
36,100	36,150	7,795	6,248	8,190	7,008
36,150	36,200	7,809	6,262	8,207	7,022
36,200	36,250	7,823	6,276	8,223	7,036
36,250	36,300	7,837	6,290	8,240	7,050
36,300	36,350	7,851	6,304	8,256	7,064
36,350	36,400	7,865	6,318	8,273	7,078
36,400	36,450	7,879	6,332	8,289	7,092
36,450	36,500	7,893	6,346	8,306	7,106
36,500	36,550	7,907	6,360	8,322	7,120
36,550	36,600	7,921	6,374	8,339	7,134
36,600	36,650	7,935	6,388	8,355	7,148
36,650	36,700	7,949	6,402	8,372	7,162
36,700	36,750	7,963	6,416	8,388	7,176
36,750	36,800	7,977	6,430	8,405	7,190
36,800	36,850	7,991	6,444	8,421	7,204
36,850	36,900	8,005	6,458	8,438	7,218
36,900	36,950	8,019	6,472	8,454	7,232
36,950	37,000	8,033	6,486	8,471	7,246
37,000					
37,000	37,050	8,047	6,500	8,487	7,260
37,050	37,100	8,061	6,514	8,504	7,274
37,100	37,150	8,075	6,528	8,520	7,288
37,150	37,200	8,089	6,542	8,537	7,302
37,200	37,250	8,103	6,556	8,553	7,316
37,250	37,300	8,117	6,570	8,570	7,330
37,300	37,350	8,131	6,584	8,586	7,344
37,350	37,400	8,145	6,598	8,603	7,358
37,400	37,450	8,159	6,612	8,619	7,372
37,450	37,500	8,173	6,626	8,636	7,386
37,500	37,550	8,187	6,640	8,652	7,400
37,550	37,600	8,201	6,654	8,669	7,414
37,600	37,650	8,215	6,668	8,685	7,428
37,650	37,700	8,229	6,682	8,702	7,442
37,700	37,750	8,243	6,696	8,718	7,456
37,750	37,800	8,257	6,710	8,735	7,470
37,800	37,850	8,271	6,724	8,751	7,484
37,850	37,900	8,285	6,738	8,768	7,498
37,900	37,950	8,299	6,752	8,784	7,512
37,950	38,000	8,313	6,766	8,801	7,526

If line 37 (taxable income) is— At least	But less than	Single	Married filing jointly *	Married filing separately	Head of a household
38,000					
38,000	38,050	8,327	6,780	8,817	7,540
38,050	38,100	8,341	6,794	8,834	7,554
38,100	38,150	8,355	6,808	8,850	7,568
38,150	38,200	8,369	6,822	8,867	7,582
38,200	38,250	8,383	6,836	8,883	7,596
38,250	38,300	8,397	6,850	8,900	7,610
38,300	38,350	8,411	6,864	8,916	7,624
38,350	38,400	8,425	6,878	8,933	7,638
38,400	38,450	8,439	6,892	8,949	7,652
38,450	38,500	8,453	6,906	8,966	7,666
38,500	38,550	8,467	6,920	8,982	7,680
38,550	38,600	8,481	6,934	8,999	7,694
38,600	38,650	8,495	6,948	9,015	7,708
38,650	38,700	8,509	6,962	9,032	7,722
38,700	38,750	8,523	6,976	9,048	7,736
38,750	38,800	8,537	6,990	9,065	7,750
38,800	38,850	8,551	7,004	9,081	7,764
38,850	38,900	8,565	7,018	9,098	7,778
38,900	38,950	8,579	7,032	9,114	7,792
38,950	39,000	8,593	7,046	9,131	7,806
39,000					
39,000	39,050	8,607	7,060	9,147	7,820
39,050	39,100	8,621	7,074	9,164	7,834
39,100	39,150	8,635	7,088	9,180	7,848
39,150	39,200	8,649	7,102	9,197	7,862
39,200	39,250	8,663	7,116	9,213	7,876
39,250	39,300	8,677	7,130	9,230	7,890
39,300	39,350	8,691	7,144	9,246	7,904
39,350	39,400	8,705	7,158	9,263	7,918
39,400	39,450	8,719	7,172	9,279	7,932
39,450	39,500	8,733	7,186	9,296	7,946
39,500	39,550	8,747	7,200	9,312	7,960
39,550	39,600	8,761	7,214	9,329	7,974
39,600	39,650	8,775	7,228	9,345	7,988
39,650	39,700	8,789	7,242	9,362	8,002
39,700	39,750	8,803	7,256	9,378	8,016
39,750	39,800	8,817	7,270	9,395	8,030
39,800	39,850	8,831	7,284	9,411	8,044
39,850	39,900	8,845	7,298	9,428	8,058
39,900	39,950	8,859	7,312	9,444	8,072
39,950	40,000	8,873	7,326	9,461	8,086
40,000					
40,000	40,050	8,887	7,340	9,477	8,100
40,050	40,100	8,901	7,354	9,494	8,114
40,100	40,150	8,915	7,368	9,510	8,128
40,150	40,200	8,929	7,382	9,527	8,142
40,200	40,250	8,943	7,396	9,543	8,156
40,250	40,300	8,957	7,410	9,560	8,170
40,300	40,350	8,971	7,424	9,576	8,184
40,350	40,400	8,985	7,438	9,593	8,198
40,400	40,450	8,999	7,452	9,609	8,212
40,450	40,500	9,013	7,466	9,626	8,226
40,500	40,550	9,027	7,480	9,642	8,240
40,550	40,600	9,041	7,494	9,659	8,254
40,600	40,650	9,055	7,508	9,675	8,268
40,650	40,700	9,069	7,522	9,692	8,282
40,700	40,750	9,083	7,536	9,708	8,296
40,750	40,800	9,097	7,550	9,725	8,310
40,800	40,850	9,111	7,564	9,741	8,324
40,850	40,900	9,125	7,578	9,758	8,338
40,900	40,950	9,139	7,592	9,774	8,352
40,950	41,000	9,153	7,606	9,791	8,366

* This column must also be used by a qualifying widow(er).

Continued on next page

1988 Tax Table—*Continued*

41,000

At least	But less than	Single	Married filing jointly *	Married filing separately	Head of a household
41,000	41,050	9,167	7,620	9,807	8,380
41,050	41,100	9,181	7,634	9,824	8,394
41,100	41,150	9,195	7,648	9,840	8,408
41,150	41,200	9,209	7,662	9,857	8,422
41,200	41,250	9,223	7,676	9,873	8,436
41,250	41,300	9,237	7,690	9,890	8,450
41,300	41,350	9,251	7,704	9,906	8,464
41,350	41,400	9,265	7,718	9,923	8,478
41,400	41,450	9,279	7,732	9,939	8,492
41,450	41,500	9,293	7,746	9,956	8,506
41,500	41,550	9,307	7,760	9,972	8,520
41,550	41,600	9,321	7,774	9,989	8,534
41,600	41,650	9,335	7,788	10,005	8,548
41,650	41,700	9,349	7,802	10,022	8,562
41,700	41,750	9,363	7,816	10,038	8,576
41,750	41,800	9,377	7,830	10,055	8,590
41,800	41,850	9,391	7,844	10,071	8,604
41,850	41,900	9,405	7,858	10,088	8,618
41,900	41,950	9,419	7,872	10,104	8,632
41,950	42,000	9,433	7,886	10,121	8,646

42,000

At least	But less than	Single	Married filing jointly *	Married filing separately	Head of a household
42,000	42,050	9,447	7,900	10,137	8,660
42,050	42,100	9,461	7,914	10,154	8,674
42,100	42,150	9,475	7,928	10,170	8,688
42,150	42,200	9,489	7,942	10,187	8,702
42,200	42,250	9,503	7,956	10,203	8,716
42,250	42,300	9,517	7,970	10,220	8,730
42,300	42,350	9,531	7,984	10,236	8,744
42,350	42,400	9,545	7,998	10,253	8,758
42,400	42,450	9,559	8,012	10,269	8,772
42,450	42,500	9,573	8,026	10,286	8,786
42,500	42,550	9,587	8,040	10,302	8,800
42,550	42,600	9,601	8,054	10,319	8,814
42,600	42,650	9,615	8,068	10,335	8,828
42,650	42,700	9,629	8,082	10,352	8,842
42,700	42,750	9,643	8,096	10,368	8,856
42,750	42,800	9,657	8,110	10,385	8,870
42,800	42,850	9,671	8,124	10,401	8,884
42,850	42,900	9,685	8,138	10,418	8,898
42,900	42,950	9,699	8,152	10,434	8,912
42,950	43,000	9,713	8,166	10,451	8,926

43,000

At least	But less than	Single	Married filing jointly *	Married filing separately	Head of a household
43,000	43,050	9,727	8,180	10,467	8,940
43,050	43,100	9,741	8,194	10,484	8,954
43,100	43,150	9,755	8,208	10,500	8,968
43,150	43,200	9,770	8,222	10,517	8,982
43,200	43,250	9,786	8,236	10,533	8,996
43,250	43,300	9,803	8,250	10,550	9,010
43,300	43,350	9,819	8,264	10,566	9,024
43,350	43,400	9,836	8,278	10,583	9,038
43,400	43,450	9,852	8,292	10,599	9,052
43,450	43,500	9,869	8,306	10,616	9,066
43,500	43,550	9,885	8,320	10,632	9,080
43,550	43,600	9,902	8,334	10,649	9,094
43,600	43,650	9,918	8,348	10,665	9,108
43,650	43,700	9,935	8,362	10,682	9,122
43,700	43,750	9,951	8,376	10,698	9,136
43,750	43,800	9,968	8,390	10,715	9,150
43,800	43,850	9,984	8,404	10,731	9,164
43,850	43,900	10,001	8,418	10,748	9,178
43,900	43,950	10,017	8,432	10,764	9,192
43,950	44,000	10,034	8,446	10,781	9,206

44,000

At least	But less than	Single	Married filing jointly *	Married filing separately	Head of a household
44,000	44,050	10,050	8,460	10,797	9,220
44,050	44,100	10,067	8,474	10,814	9,234
44,100	44,150	10,083	8,488	10,830	9,248
44,150	44,200	10,100	8,502	10,847	9,262
44,200	44,250	10,116	8,516	10,863	9,276
44,250	44,300	10,133	8,530	10,880	9,290
44,300	44,350	10,149	8,544	10,896	9,304
44,350	44,400	10,166	8,558	10,913	9,318
44,400	44,450	10,182	8,572	10,929	9,332
44,450	44,500	10,199	8,586	10,946	9,346
44,500	44,550	10,215	8,600	10,962	9,360
44,550	44,600	10,232	8,614	10,979	9,374
44,600	44,650	10,248	8,628	10,995	9,388
44,650	44,700	10,265	8,642	11,012	9,402
44,700	44,750	10,281	8,656	11,028	9,416
44,750	44,800	10,298	8,670	11,045	9,430
44,800	44,850	10,314	8,684	11,061	9,444
44,850	44,900	10,331	8,698	11,078	9,458
44,900	44,950	10,347	8,712	11,094	9,472
44,950	45,000	10,364	8,726	11,111	9,486

45,000

At least	But less than	Single	Married filing jointly *	Married filing separately	Head of a household
45,000	45,050	10,380	8,740	11,127	9,500
45,050	45,100	10,397	8,754	11,144	9,514
45,100	45,150	10,413	8,768	11,160	9,528
45,150	45,200	10,430	8,782	11,177	9,542
45,200	45,250	10,446	8,796	11,193	9,556
45,250	45,300	10,463	8,810	11,210	9,570
45,300	45,350	10,479	8,824	11,226	9,584
45,350	45,400	10,496	8,838	11,243	9,598
45,400	45,450	10,512	8,852	11,259	9,612
45,450	45,500	10,529	8,866	11,276	9,626
45,500	45,550	10,545	8,880	11,292	9,640
45,550	45,600	10,562	8,894	11,309	9,654
45,600	45,650	10,578	8,908	11,325	9,668
45,650	45,700	10,595	8,922	11,342	9,682
45,700	45,750	10,611	8,936	11,358	9,696
45,750	45,800	10,628	8,950	11,375	9,710
45,800	45,850	10,644	8,964	11,391	9,724
45,850	45,900	10,661	8,978	11,408	9,738
45,900	45,950	10,677	8,992	11,424	9,752
45,950	46,000	10,694	9,006	11,441	9,766

46,000

At least	But less than	Single	Married filing jointly *	Married filing separately	Head of a household
46,000	46,050	10,710	9,020	11,457	9,780
46,050	46,100	10,727	9,034	11,474	9,794
46,100	46,150	10,743	9,048	11,490	9,808
46,150	46,200	10,760	9,062	11,507	9,822
46,200	46,250	10,776	9,076	11,523	9,836
46,250	46,300	10,793	9,090	11,540	9,850
46,300	46,350	10,809	9,104	11,556	9,864
46,350	46,400	10,826	9,118	11,573	9,878
46,400	46,450	10,842	9,132	11,589	9,892
46,450	46,500	10,859	9,146	11,606	9,906
46,500	46,550	10,875	9,160	11,622	9,920
46,550	46,600	10,892	9,174	11,639	9,934
46,600	46,650	10,908	9,188	11,655	9,948
46,650	46,700	10,925	9,202	11,672	9,962
46,700	46,750	10,941	9,216	11,688	9,976
46,750	46,800	10,958	9,230	11,705	9,990
46,800	46,850	10,974	9,244	11,721	10,004
46,850	46,900	10,991	9,258	11,738	10,018
46,900	46,950	11,007	9,272	11,754	10,032
46,950	47,000	11,024	9,286	11,771	10,046

47,000

At least	But less than	Single	Married filing jointly *	Married filing separately	Head of a household
47,000	47,050	11,040	9,300	11,787	10,060
47,050	47,100	11,057	9,314	11,804	10,074
47,100	47,150	11,073	9,328	11,820	10,088
47,150	47,200	11,090	9,342	11,837	10,102
47,200	47,250	11,106	9,356	11,853	10,116
47,250	47,300	11,123	9,370	11,870	10,130
47,300	47,350	11,139	9,384	11,886	10,144
47,350	47,400	11,156	9,398	11,903	10,158
47,400	47,450	11,172	9,412	11,919	10,172
47,450	47,500	11,189	9,426	11,936	10,186
47,500	47,550	11,205	9,440	11,952	10,200
47,550	47,600	11,222	9,454	11,969	10,214
47,600	47,650	11,238	9,468	11,985	10,228
47,650	47,700	11,255	9,482	12,002	10,242
47,700	47,750	11,271	9,496	12,018	10,256
47,750	47,800	11,288	9,510	12,035	10,270
47,800	47,850	11,304	9,524	12,051	10,284
47,850	47,900	11,321	9,538	12,068	10,298
47,900	47,950	11,337	9,552	12,084	10,312
47,950	48,000	11,354	9,566	12,101	10,326

48,000

At least	But less than	Single	Married filing jointly *	Married filing separately	Head of a household
48,000	48,050	11,370	9,580	12,117	10,340
48,050	48,100	11,387	9,594	12,134	10,354
48,100	48,150	11,403	9,608	12,150	10,368
48,150	48,200	11,420	9,622	12,167	10,382
48,200	48,250	11,436	9,636	12,183	10,396
48,250	48,300	11,453	9,650	12,200	10,410
48,300	48,350	11,469	9,664	12,216	10,424
48,350	48,400	11,486	9,678	12,233	10,438
48,400	48,450	11,502	9,692	12,249	10,452
48,450	48,500	11,519	9,706	12,266	10,466
48,500	48,550	11,535	9,720	12,282	10,480
48,550	48,600	11,552	9,734	12,299	10,494
48,600	48,650	11,568	9,748	12,315	10,508
48,650	48,700	11,585	9,762	12,332	10,522
48,700	48,750	11,601	9,776	12,348	10,536
48,750	48,800	11,618	9,790	12,365	10,550
48,800	48,850	11,634	9,804	12,381	10,564
48,850	48,900	11,651	9,818	12,398	10,578
48,900	48,950	11,667	9,832	12,414	10,592
48,950	49,000	11,684	9,846	12,431	10,606

49,000

At least	But less than	Single	Married filing jointly *	Married filing separately	Head of a household
49,000	49,050	11,700	9,860	12,447	10,620
49,050	49,100	11,717	9,874	12,464	10,634
49,100	49,150	11,733	9,888	12,480	10,648
49,150	49,200	11,750	9,902	12,497	10,662
49,200	49,250	11,766	9,916	12,513	10,676
49,250	49,300	11,783	9,930	12,530	10,690
49,300	49,350	11,799	9,944	12,546	10,704
49,350	49,400	11,816	9,958	12,563	10,718
49,400	49,450	11,832	9,972	12,579	10,732
49,450	49,500	11,849	9,986	12,596	10,746
49,500	49,550	11,865	10,000	12,612	10,760
49,550	49,600	11,882	10,014	12,629	10,774
49,600	49,650	11,898	10,028	12,645	10,788
49,650	49,700	11,915	10,042	12,662	10,802
49,700	49,750	11,931	10,056	12,678	10,816
49,750	49,800	11,948	10,070	12,695	10,830
49,800	49,850	11,964	10,084	12,711	10,844
49,850	49,900	11,981	10,098	12,728	10,858
49,900	49,950	11,997	10,112	12,744	10,872
49,950	50,000	12,014	10,126	12,761	10,886

* This column must also be used by a qualifying widow(er).

50,000 or over—use tax rate schedules

1989 Tax Rate Schedules

Schedule X—Single

If taxable income is:		The tax is:	of the amount over—
Over—	But not over—		
$0	$18,550	........15%	$0
18,550	44,900	**$2,782.50 + 28%**	**18,550**
44,900	93,130	**10,160.50 + 33%**	**44,900**
93,130	....	Use **Worksheet** below to figure your tax.	

Schedule Z— Head of household

If taxable income is:		The tax is:	of the amount over—
Over—	But not over—		
$0	$24,850	........15%	$0
24,850	64,200	**$3,727.50+ 28%**	**24,850**
64,200	128,810	**14,745.50 + 33%**	**64,200**
128,810	....	Use **Worksheet** below to figure your tax.	

Schedule Y-1—Married filing jointly or Qualifying widow(er)

If taxable income is:		The tax is:	of the amount over—
Over—	But not over—		
$0	$30,950	........15%	$0
30,950	74,850	**$4,642.50 + 28%**	**30,950**
74,850	155,320	**16,934.50 + 33%**	**74,850**
155,320	....	Use **Worksheet** below to figure your tax.	

Schedule Y-2— Married filing separately

If taxable income is:		The tax is:	of the amount over—
Over—	But not over—		
$0	$15,475	........15%	$0
15,475	37,425	**$2,321.25 + 28%**	**15,475**
37,425	117,895	**8,467.25 + 33%**	**37,425**
117,895	....	Use **Worksheet** below to figure your tax.	

Worksheet (Keep for your records)

1. If your filing status is:
   - Single, enter $26,076.40
   - Head of household, enter $36,066.80
   - Married filing jointly or Qualifying widow(er), enter $43,489.60
   - Married filing separately, enter $35,022.35   ....   **1.** _____

2. Enter your taxable income   .   .   .   .   **2.** _____

3. If your filing status is:
   - Single, enter $93,130
   - Head of household, enter $128,810
   - Married filing jointly or Qualifying widow(er), enter $155,320
   - Married filing separately, enter $117,895   .   .   .   .   **3.** _____

4. Subtract line 3 from line 2. Enter the result. (If the result is zero or less, use the schedule above for your filing status to figure your tax. DON'T use this worksheet.)   .   .   .   .   .   .   **4.** _____

5. Multiply the amount on line 4 by 28% (.28). Enter the result   .   .   .   .   **5.** _____

6. Multiply the amount on line 4 by 5% (.05). Enter the result   .   .   .   .   **6.** _____

7. Multiply $560 by the number of exemptions claimed. (If married filing separately, see Note below.) Enter the result   .   .   .   .   **7.** _____

8. Compare the amounts on lines 6 and 7. Enter the **smaller** of the two amounts   .   .   .   .   .   .   **8.** _____

9. **Tax.** Add lines 1, 5, and 8.   .   .   .   .   **9.** _____

Note: *If married filing separately and you did **not** claim an exemption for your spouse, multiply $560 by the number of exemptions claimed. Add $560 to the result and enter the total on line 7 above.*

APPENDIX B

Tax Forms

Department of the Treasury - Internal Revenue Service

Form 1040EZ

Income Tax Return for Single filers with no dependents **1988**

OMB No. 1545-0675

Name & address

Use the IRS mailing label. If you don't have one, please print.

L A B E L   Print your name above (first, initial, last)

H E R E   Present home address (number, street, and apt. no.). (If you have a P.O. box, see back.)

City, town, or post office, state, and ZIP code

Please print your numbers like this:

0 1 2 3 4 5 6 7 8 9

Your social security number

Please read the instructions on the back of this form. Also, see page 13 of the booklet for a helpful checklist.

Presidential Election Campaign Fund
Do you want $1 to go to this fund?

Note: Checking "Yes" will not change your tax or reduce your refund.

Yes No

Dollars   Cents

Report your income

Attach Copy B of Form(s) W-2 here

Note: You **must** check Yes or No.

1 Total wages, salaries, and tips. This should be shown in Box 10 of your W-2 form(s). (Attach your W-2 form(s).) **1**

2 Taxable interest income of $400 or less. If the total is more than $400, you cannot use Form 1040EZ. **2**

3 Add line 1 and line 2. This is your **adjusted gross income.** **3**

4 Can your parents or someone else claim you on their return?
☐ **Yes.** Do worksheet on back; enter amount from line E here.
☐ **No.** Enter 3,000 as your standard deduction. **4**

5 Subtract line 4 from line 3. If line 4 is larger than line 3, enter 0. **5**

6 If you checked the "Yes" box on line 4, enter **0.**
If you checked the "No" box on line 4, enter **1,950.**
This is your **personal exemption.** **6**

7 Subtract line 6 from line 5. If line 6 is larger than line 5, enter 0. This is your **taxable income.** **7**

Figure your tax

8 Enter your Federal income tax withheld from Box 9 of your W-2 form(s). **8**

9 Use the **single** column in the tax table on pages 37–42 of the Form 1040A/1040EZ booklet to find the **tax** on the amount shown on **line 7** above. Enter the amount of tax. **9**

Refund or amount you owe

Attach tax payment here

10 If line 8 is larger than line 9, subtract line 9 from line 8. Enter the **amount of your refund.** **10**

11 If line 9 is larger than line 8, subtract line 8 from line 9. Enter the **amount you owe.** Attach check or money order for the full amount, payable to "Internal Revenue Service." **11**

Sign your return

I have read this return. Under penalties of perjury, I declare that to the best of my knowledge and belief, the return is true, correct, and complete.

Your signature   Date

For IRS Use Only—Please do not write in boxes below.

1988   Instructions for Form 1040EZ

Use this form if:	• Your filing status is **single.** • You are under 65 and not blind. • You do not claim any dependents. • Your taxable income (line 7) is less than $50,000. • You had **only** wages, salaries, tips, and taxable scholarships or fellowships, and your taxable interest income was $400 or less. *Caution: If you earned tips (including allocated tips) that are not included in Box 14 of your W-2, you may not be able to use Form 1040EZ. See page 22 in the 1040A and 1040EZ instruction booklet.* If you can't use this form, use Form 1040A or Form 1040. See pages 10 through 12 in the booklet.
Completing your return	Please print your numbers inside the boxes. Do not type your numbers. Do not use dollar signs. You may round off cents to whole dollars. To do so, drop amounts under 50 cents and increase amounts that are 50 cents or more. For example, $129.49 becomes $129 and $129.50 becomes $130. If you round off, do so for all amounts. But if you have to add two or more amounts to figure the amount to enter on a line, include cents when adding and round off only the total.
Name & address	Please use the mailing label we sent you. It can help speed your refund. After you complete your return, put the label in the name and address area. Cross out any errors. Print the right information on the label (including apartment number). If you don't have a label, print your name, address, and social security number. If your post office does not deliver mail to your home and you have a P.O. box, show your P.O. box number instead of your home address.
Presidential campaign fund	Congress set up this fund to help pay for Presidential election costs. If you want $1 of your tax to go to this fund, check the "Yes" box. If you check "Yes," your tax or refund will not change.
Report your income	**Line 1.** If you don't get your W-2 by February 15, contact your local IRS office. You must still report your wages, salaries, and tips even if you don't get a W-2 from your employer. Students, if you received a scholarship or fellowship, see page 22 in the booklet.

Line 2. Banks, savings and loans, credit unions, etc., should send you a Form 1099-INT showing the amount of taxable interest paid to you. You must report all your taxable interest even if you don't get a Form 1099-INT. If you had tax-exempt interest, such as on municipal bonds, write "TEI" in the space to the left of line 2. After "TEI," show the amount of your tax-exempt interest. **Do not** add tax-exempt interest in the total on line 2.

Line 4. If you checked the "Yes" box because your parents or someone else can claim you as a dependent on their tax return, fill in this worksheet. If you don't know if someone can claim you as a dependent, see page 17 in the booklet.

Standard deduction worksheet for dependents who checked "Yes" on line 4

A. Enter the amount from line 1 on front.   A. _____
B. Minimum amount.   B. _____ 500.00
C. **Compare** the amounts on lines A and B above. Enter the LARGER of the two amounts here.   C. _____
D. Maximum amount.   D. _____ 3,000.00
E. **Compare** the amounts on lines C and D above. Enter the SMALLER of the two amounts here and on line 4 on front.   E. _____

Figure your tax	**Line 8.** If you received a Form 1099-INT showing income tax withheld (backup withholding), include the amount in the total on line 8. To the left of line 8, write "Form 1099." If you had two or more employers and had total wages of over $45,000, see page 33. If you want IRS to figure your tax, skip lines 9 through 11. Then sign and date your return. If you paid too much tax, we will send you a refund. If you didn't pay enough tax, we will send you a bill. We won't charge you interest or a late payment penalty if you pay within 30 days of the notice date or by April 17, 1989, whichever is later. If you want to figure your own tax, complete the rest of your return.
Amount you owe	**Line 11.** If you owe tax, attach your check or money order for the full amount. Write your social security number, daytime phone number, and "1988 Form 1040EZ" on your payment.
Sign your return	You must sign and date your return. If you pay someone to prepare your return, that person must sign it and show other information. See page 36 in the booklet.
Mailing your return	Mail your return by **April 17, 1989.** Use the envelope that came with your booklet. If you don't have that envelope, see page 45 for the address.

Form **1040A**	Department of the Treasury—Internal Revenue Service **U.S. Individual Income Tax Return**	**1988**

OMB No. 1545-0085

Step 1
Label

Use IRS label. Otherwise, please print or type.

L A B E L H E R E	Your first name and initial (if joint return, also give spouse's name and initial) Last name	**Your social security no.**
	Present home address (number, street, and apt. no.). (If you have a P.O. Box, see page 13 of the instructions.)	**Spouse's social security no.**
	City, town or post office, state, and ZIP code	For **Privacy Act and Paperwork Reduction Act Notice**, see page 3.

Presidential Election Campaign Fund

Do you want $1 to go to this fund?. . . . . ☐ Yes ☐ No
If joint return, does your spouse want $1 to go to this fund? ☐ Yes ☐ No

Note: *Checking "Yes" will not change your tax or reduce your refund.*

Step 2
Check your filing status
(Check only one)

1 ☐ Single (See if you can use Form 1040EZ.)
2 ☐ Married filing joint return (even if only one had income)
3 ☐ Married filing separate return. Enter spouse's social security number above and spouse's full name here. _____
4 ☐ Head of household (with qualifying person). (See page 15.) If the qualifying person is your child but not your dependent, enter this child's name here. _____
5 ☐ Qualifying widow(er) with dependent child (year spouse died ▶ 19____). (See page 16.)

Step 3
Figure your exemptions
(See page 16 of instructions.)

If more than 7 dependents, see page 19.

6a ☐ Yourself   If someone (such as your parent) can claim you as a dependent on his or her tax return, do not check box 6a. But be sure to check the box on line 15b on page 2.
6b ☐ Spouse

c Dependents: 1. Name (first, initial, and last name)	2. Check if under age 5	3. If age 5 or older, dependent's social security number	4. Relationship	5. No. of months lived in your home in 1988
		:		
		:		
		:		
		:		
		:		

No. of boxes checked on 6a and 6b _____

No. of your children on 6c who:
● lived with you _____
● didn't live with you due to divorce or separation (see page 19) _____

No. of **other** dependents listed on 6c _____

Attach Copy B of Form(s) W-2 here.

d If your child didn't live with you but is claimed as your dependent under a pre-1985 agreement, check here . . . . ▶ ☐
e Total number of exemptions claimed.

Add numbers entered on lines above ☐

Step 4
Figure your total income

Attach check or money order here.

7 Wages, salaries, tips, etc. This should be shown in Box 10 of your W-2 form(s). (Attach Form(s) W-2.)   7
8a **Taxable** interest income (see page 22). (If over $400, also complete and attach Schedule 1, Part II.)   8a
b **Tax-exempt** interest income (see page 23). (DO NOT include on line 8a.)   8b
9 Dividends. (If over $400, also complete and attach Schedule 1, Part III.)   9
10 Unemployment compensation (insurance) from Form(s) 1099-G.   10
11 Add lines 7, 8a, 9, and 10. Enter the total. This is your **total income.** ▶ 11

Step 5
Figure your adjusted gross income

12a Your IRA deduction from applicable worksheet. Rules for IRAs begin on page 24.   12a
b Spouse's IRA deduction from applicable worksheet. Rules for IRAs begin on page 24.   12b
c Add lines 12a and 12b. Enter the total. These are your **total adjustments.**   12c
13 Subtract line 12c from line 11. Enter the result. This is your **adjusted gross income.** (If this line is less than $18,576 and a child lived with you, see "Earned Income Credit" (line 23b) on page 34 of instructions.) ▶ 13

Form **1040A** (1988)

1988   **Form 1040A**   Page 2

Step 6 **Figure your standard deduction,**	**14** Enter the amount from line 13. 14

15a Check if: { ☐ **You** were 65 or older   ☐ Blind } **Enter number of**
                { ☐ **Spouse** was 65 or older ☐ Blind } **boxes checked** ▶ 15a ☐

    b If someone (such as your parent) can claim you as a dependent,
    check here . . . . ▶ 15b ☐

    c If you are married filing separately and your spouse files Form
    1040 and itemizes deductions, see page 28 and check here. . . . ▶ 15c ☐

16 **Standard deduction.** See pages 28–29 for the amount to enter.   16

17 Subtract line 16 from line 14. Enter the result. (If line 16 is more
than line 14, enter -0-.)   17

exemption amount, and

18 Multiply $1,950 by the total number of exemptions claimed on line 6e.   18

taxable income

19 Subtract line 18 from line 17. Enter the result. (If line 18 is more than line 17,
enter -0-.) This is your **taxable income.**   ▶ 19

Step 7 **Figure your tax, credits, and payments** (including advance EIC payments)	**If You Want IRS To Figure Your Tax, See Page 29 of the Instructions.**

    Caution: If you are under age 14 and have more than $1,000 of investment
       income, check here . . . . ▶ ☐
       Also see page 30 to see if you have to use Form 8615 to figure your tax.

20 Find the tax on the amount on line 19. Check if from:
    ☐ Tax Table (pages 37–42) or ☐ Form 8615   20

21 Credit for child and dependent care expenses. Complete and
attach Schedule 1, Part I.   21

22 Subtract line 21 from line 20. Enter the result. (If line 21 is more than
line 20, enter -0-.) This is your **total tax.**   ▶ 22

23a Total Federal income tax withheld—from Box
9 of your W-2 form(s). (If any is from Form(s)
1099, check here ▶ ☐ .)   23a

    b Earned income credit, from the worksheet on
    page 35 of the instructions. Also see page 34.   23b

24 Add lines 23a and 23b. Enter the total. These are your **total payments.** ▶ 24

Step 8 **Figure your refund or amount you owe**	**25** If line 24 is more than line 22, subtract line 22 from line 24. Enter the result. This is the **amount of your refund.** 25

26 If line 22 is more than line 24, subtract line 24 from line 22. Enter the result.
This is the **amount you owe.** Attach check or money order for full amount
payable to "Internal Revenue Service." Write your social security number,
daytime phone number, and "1988 Form 1040A" on it.   26

Step 9 **Sign your return**	Under penalties of perjury, I declare that I have examined this return and accompanying schedules and statements, and to the best of my knowledge and belief, they are true, correct, and complete. Declaration of preparer (other than the taxpayer) is based on all information of which the preparer has any knowledge.

Your signature	Date	Your occupation
X		

Spouse's signature (if joint return, both must sign)	Date	Spouse's occupation
X		

Paid preparer's use only	

Preparer's signature	Date	Preparer's social security no.
X		

Firm's name (or yours if self-employed)	Employer identification no.

Address and ZIP code	Check if self-employed ☐

1988   **Schedule 1 (Form 1040A)**   OMB No. 1545-0085

Name(s) as shown on Form 1040A	Your social security number
	: :

You MUST complete and attach Schedule 1 to Form 1040A only if you:

- Claim the credit for child and dependent care expenses (complete **Part I**)
- Have over $400 of taxable interest income (complete **Part II**)
- Have over $400 of dividend income (complete **Part III**)

Part I   **Credit for child and dependent care expenses** (see page 30 of the instructions)

Complete this part to figure the amount of credit you can take on Form 1040A, line 21. Attach Schedule 1 to Form 1040A.

Note: *If you paid cash wages of $50 or more in a calendar quarter to an individual for services performed in your home, you must file an employment tax return. Get **Form 942** for details.*

1 Enter the number of qualifying persons who were cared for in 1988. You must have shared the same home with any person you claim. (See the instructions for the definition of a qualifying person.)   **1**

2 Enter the amount of **qualified** expenses you incurred and actually paid in 1988 for the care of the qualifying person. (See the instructions to find out which expenses qualify.) DO NOT enter more than $2,400 ($4,800 if you paid for the care of two or more qualifying persons).   **2**

3 a You **must** enter your earned income on line 3a (see page 32).   **3a**

   b If you are married, filing a joint return for 1988, you must enter your spouse's earned income on line 3b. (If spouse is a full-time student or is disabled, see the instructions for the amount to enter on this line.)   **3b**

   c If you are married, compare the amounts on lines 3a and 3b, and enter the **smaller** of the two amounts on line 3c.   **3c**

4 • If you were unmarried at the end of 1988, compare the amounts on lines 2 and 3a, and enter the **smaller** of the two amounts on line 4.

   • If you are married, filing a joint return for 1988, compare the amounts on lines 2 and 3c, and enter the **smaller** of the two amounts on line 4.   **4**

5 Enter the decimal amount from the table below that applies to the amount on Form 1040A, line 14.

If line 14 is:		Decimal amount is:	If line 14 is:		Decimal amount is:
Over—	**But not over—**		**Over—**	**But not over—**	
$0	—10,000	.30	$20,000	—22,000	.24
10,000	—12,000	.29	22,000	—24,000	.23
12,000	—14,000	.28	24,000	—26,000	.22
14,000	—16,000	.27	26,000	—28,000	.21
16,000	—18,000	.26	28,000		.20
18,000	—20,000	.25			

5   × .

6 Multiply the amount on line 4 by the decimal amount on line 5. Enter the result here and on Form 1040A, line 21.   **6 =**

1988	**Schedule 1 (Form 1040A)**	OMB No. 1545-0085

Name(s) as shown on Form 1040A. (Do not complete if shown on other side.) | Your social security number

---

Part II   **Interest income** (see page 22 of the instructions)

Complete this part and attach Schedule 1 to Form 1040A if you received over $400 in taxable interest.
Even if you are not required to complete this part, you must report all interest on Form 1040A.

Note: *If you received a Form 1099–INT or Form 1099–OID from a brokerage firm, enter the firm's name and the total interest shown on that form.*

1 List name of payer   Amount

	Amount
	$
	$
	$
	$
	$
	$
	$
	$
	$
	$
	$
	$
	$
	$
	$
	$
	$
	$
	$

2 Add amounts on line 1. Enter the total here and on Form 1040A, line 8a.   2

Part III   **Dividend income** (see page 23 of the instructions)

Complete this part and attach Schedule 1 to Form 1040A if you received over $400 in dividends.
Even if you are not required to complete this part, you must report all taxable dividends on Form 1040A.

Note: *If you received a Form 1099–DIV from a brokerage firm, enter the firm's name and the total dividends shown on that form.*

1 List name of payer   Amount

	Amount
	$
	$
	$
	$
	$
	$
	$
	$
	$
	$
	$
	$
	$
	$
	$
	$
	$
	$
	$

2 Add amounts on line 1. Enter the total here and on Form 1040A, line 9.   2

Form **1040** Department of the Treasury—Internal Revenue Service
U.S. Individual Income Tax Return 1988

For the year Jan.–Dec. 31, 1988, or other tax year beginning   , 1988, ending   , 19 | OMB No. 1545-0074

Label

Use IRS label.
Otherwise,
please print or
type.

L A B E L H E R E	Your first name and initial (if joint return, also give spouse's name and initial) Last name
	Present home address (number, street, and apt. no. or rural route). (If a P.O. Box, see page 6 of Instructions.)
	City, town or post office, state, and ZIP code

Your social security number

Spouse's social security number

For Privacy Act and Paperwork
Reduction Act Notice, see Instructions.

**Presidential
Election Campaign** ▶

Do you want $1 to go to this fund? . . . .   Yes ▨ No
If joint return, does your spouse want $1 to go to this fund?. .   Yes ▨ No

Note: *Checking "Yes" will
not change your tax or
reduce your refund.*

Filing Status

Check only
one box.

1 ☐ Single
2 ☐ Married filing joint return (even if only one had income)
3 ☐ Married filing separate return. Enter spouse's social security no. above and full name here. _____
4 ☐ Head of household (with qualifying person). (See page 7 of Instructions.) If the qualifying person is your child but not your dependent, enter child's name here. _____
5 ☐ Qualifying widow(er) with dependent child (year spouse died ▶ 19   ). (See page 7 of Instructions.)

Exemptions

(See
Instructions
on page 8.)

If more than 6
dependents, see
Instructions on
page 8.

6a ☐ Yourself If someone (such as your parent) can claim you as a dependent, do not check box 6a.
But be sure to check the box on line 33b on page 2. . . . .
b ☐ Spouse . . . .

No. of boxes
checked on 6a
and 6b ____

c **Dependents:**

(1) Name (first, initial, and last name)	(2) Check if under age 5	(3) If age 5 or older, dependent's social security number	(4) Relationship	(5) No. of months lived in your home in 1988
		: :		
		: :		
		: :		
		: :		
		: :		
		: :		

No. of your
children on 6c
who:
● lived with you ____
● didn't live with
you due to divorce
or separation ____
No. of other
dependents listed
on 6c ____

d If your child didn't live with you but is claimed as your dependent under a pre-1985 agreement, check here . ▶ ☐
e Total number of exemptions claimed . . . .

Add numbers
entered on
lines above ▶ ☐

Income

Please attach
Copy B of your
Forms W-2, W-2G,
and W-2P here.

If you do not have
a W-2, see
page 6 of
Instructions.

Please
attach check
or money
order here.

7	Wages, salaries, tips, etc. *(attach Form(s) W-2)*	**7**	
8a	**Taxable** interest income *(also attach Schedule B if over $400)*	**8a**	
b	**Tax-exempt** interest income (see page 11). DON'T include on line 8a **8b**		▨
9	Dividend income *(also attach Schedule B if over $400)*	**9**	
10	Taxable refunds of state and local income taxes, if any, from worksheet on page 11 of Instructions . .	**10**	
11	Alimony received	**11**	
12	Business income or (loss) *(attach Schedule C)*.	**12**	
13	Capital gain or (loss) *(attach Schedule D)*	**13**	
14	Capital gain distributions not reported on line 13 (see page 11)	**14**	
15	Other gains or (losses) *(attach Form 4797)*	**15**	
16a	Total IRA distributions . **16a**	16b Taxable amount (see page 11)	**16b**	
17a	Total pensions and annuities **17a**	17b Taxable amount (see page 12)	**17b**	
18	Rents, royalties, partnerships, estates, trusts, etc. *(attach Schedule E)*	**18**	
19	Farm income or (loss) *(attach Schedule F)*	**19**	
20	Unemployment compensation (insurance) (see page 13)	**20**	
21a	Social security benefits (see page 13) **21a**		▨
b	Taxable amount, if any, from the worksheet on page 13	**21b**	
22	Other income (list type and amount—see page 13) _____	**22**	
23	Add the amounts shown in the far right column for lines 7 through 22. This is your **total income** . ▶	**23**	

**Adjustments
to Income**

(See
Instructions
on page 13.)

24	Reimbursed employee business expenses from Form 2106, line 13 .	**24**	▨
25a	Your IRA deduction, from applicable worksheet on page 14 or 15	**25a**	▨
b	Spouse's IRA deduction, from applicable worksheet on page 14 or 15	**25b**	▨
26	Self-employed health insurance deduction, from worksheet on page 15 .	**26**	▨
27	Keogh retirement plan and self-employed SEP deduction . .	**27**	▨
28	Penalty on early withdrawal of savings	**28**	▨
29	Alimony paid (recipient's last name _____ and social security no. _____) .	**29**	▨
30	Add lines 24 through 29. These are your **total adjustments** . . . . ▶	**30**	

**Adjusted
Gross Income**

31 Subtract line 30 from line 23. This is your **adjusted gross income.** *If this line is less than
$18,576 and a child lived with you, see "Earned Income Credit" (line 56) on page 19 of
the Instructions. If you want IRS to figure your tax, see page 16 of the Instructions* . . . ▶ | **31** |

Form 1040 (1988)   Page **2**

Tax Compu- tation	**32**	Amount from line 31 (adjusted gross income)	**32**
	33a	Check if: ☐ **You** were 65 or older ☐ Blind; ☐ **Spouse** was 65 or older ☐ Blind. Add the number of boxes checked and enter the total here . . . . ▶	**33a**
	b	If someone (such as your parent) can claim you as a dependent, check here . . ▶	**33b** ☐
	c	If you are married filing a separate return and your spouse itemizes deductions, or you are a dual-status alien, see page 16 and check here . . . . ▶	**33c** ☐
	34	Enter the larger of: { • Your **standard deduction** (from page 17 of the Instructions), **OR** • Your **itemized deductions** (from Schedule A, line 26). If you itemize, attach Schedule A and check here ▶ ☐ }	**34**
	35	Subtract line 34 from line 32. Enter the result here	**35**
	36	Multiply $1,950 by the total number of exemptions claimed on line 6e	**36**
	37	**Taxable income.** Subtract line 36 from line 35. Enter the result (if less than zero, enter zero) . .	**37**
		Caution: If under age 14 and you have more than $1,000 of investment income, check here ▶ ☐ and see page 17 to see if you have to use Form 8615 to figure your tax.	
	38	Enter tax. Check if from: ☐ Tax Table, ☐ Tax Rate Schedules, or ☐ Form 8615	**38**
	39	Additional taxes (see page 17). Check if from: ☐ Form 4970 ☐ Form 4972	**39**
	40	Add lines 38 and 39. Enter the total . . . . ▶	**40**

Credits (See Instructions on page 18.)	**41**	Credit for child and dependent care expenses *(attach Form 2441)*	**41**	
	42	Credit for the elderly or the disabled *(attach Schedule R)* . . .	**42**	
	43	Foreign tax credit *(attach Form 1116)*	**43**	
	44	General business credit. Check if from: ☐ Form 3800 or ☐ Form (specify) _____ . . .	**44**	
	45	Credit for prior year minimum tax *(attach Form 8801)* . . .	**45**	
	46	Add lines 41 through 45. Enter the total		**46**
	47	Subtract line 46 from line 40. Enter the result (if less than zero, enter zero) . . . . ▶		**47**

Other Taxes (Including Advance EIC Payments)	**48**	Self-employment tax *(attach Schedule SE)*	**48**
	49	Alternative minimum tax *(attach Form 6251)*	**49**
	50	Recapture taxes (see page 18). Check if from: ☐ Form 4255 ☐ Form 8611	**50**
	51	Social security tax on tip income not reported to employer *(attach Form 4137)*	**51**
	52	Tax on an IRA or a qualified retirement plan *(attach Form 5329)*	**52**
	53	Add lines 47 through 52. This is your **total tax** . . . . ▶	**53**

Payments Attach Forms W-2, W-2G, and W-2P to front.	**54**	Federal income tax withheld (If any is from Form(s) 1099, check ▶ ☐)	**54**	
	55	1988 estimated tax payments and amount applied from 1987 return	**55**	
	56	Earned income credit (see page 19)	**56**	
	57	Amount paid with Form 4868 (extension request).	**57**	
	58	Excess social security tax and RRTA tax withheld (see page 20) . .	**58**	
	59	Credit for Federal tax on fuels *(attach Form 4136)*.	**59**	
	60	Regulated investment company credit *(attach Form 2439)* . . .	**60**	
	61	Add lines 54 through 60. These are your **total payments** . . . . ▶		**61**

Refund or Amount You Owe	**62**	If line 61 is larger than line 53, enter amount **OVERPAID** . . . . ▶	**62**
	63	Amount of line 62 to be **REFUNDED TO YOU** . . . . ▶	**63**
	64	Amount of line 62 to be applied to your 1989 estimated tax . . ▶	**64**	
	65	If line 53 is larger than line 61, enter **AMOUNT YOU OWE.** Attach check or money order for full amount payable to "Internal Revenue Service." Write your social security number, daytime phone number, and "1988 Form 1040" on it	**65**
		Check ▶ ☐ if Form 2210 (2210F) is attached. See page 21. **Penalty: $**	

Please Sign Here	Under penalties of perjury, I declare that I have examined this return and accompanying schedules and statements, and to the best of my knowledge and belief, they are true, correct, and complete. Declaration of preparer (other than taxpayer) is based on all information of which preparer has any knowledge.

	Date	
Your signature ▶		Your occupation
Spouse's signature (if joint return, BOTH must sign) ▶	Date	Spouse's occupation

Paid Preparer's Use Only	Preparer's signature ▶	Date	Check if self-employed ☐	Preparer's social security no.
	Firm's name (or yours if self-employed) and address ▶		E.I. No. / ZIP code

SCHEDULES A&B	**Schedule A—Itemized Deductions**	OMB No. 1545-0074

SCHEDULES A&B
(Form 1040)
Department of the Treasury
Internal Revenue Service

Schedule A—Itemized Deductions
(Schedule B is on back)
▶ Attach to Form 1040. ▶ See Instructions for Schedules A and B (Form 1040).

OMB No. 1545-0074
19**88**
Attachment
Sequence No. **07**

Name(s) as shown on Form 1040   Your social security number

Medical and Dental Expenses
(Do not include expenses reimbursed or paid by others.)
(See Instructions on page 23.)

1a Prescription medicines and drugs, insulin, doctors, dentists, nurses, hospitals, medical insurance premiums you paid, etc . . | **1a**
b Other (list—include hearing aids, dentures, eyeglasses, transportation and lodging, etc.) ▶ _____
_____ | **1b**
2 Add lines 1a and 1b, and enter the total here . . . . . . | **2**
3 Multiply the amount on Form 1040, line 32, by 7.5% (.075) . . | **3**
4 Subtract line 3 from line 2. If zero or less, enter -0-. **Total** medical and dental . . ▶ | **4**

Taxes You Paid
(See Instructions on page 23.)

5 State and local income taxes . . . . | **5**
6 Real estate taxes . . . . | **6**
7 Other taxes (list—include personal property taxes) ▶ _____ | **7**
8 Add the amounts on lines 5 through 7. Enter the total here. **Total** taxes . . ▶ | **8**

Interest You Paid
(See Instructions on page 24.)

Note: New rules apply to the home mortgage interest deduction. See Instructions.
9a Deductible home mortgage interest you paid to financial institutions (report deductible points on line 10) . . . . | **9a**
b Deductible home mortgage interest you paid to individuals (show that person's name and address) ▶ _____ | **9b**
10 Deductible points. (See Instructions for special rules.) . . . | **10**
11 Deductible investment interest (see page 24) . . . . . . | **11**
12a Personal interest you paid (see page 24) . **12a**
b Multiply the amount on line 12a by 40% (.40). Enter the result . | **12b**
13 Add the amounts on lines 9a through 11, and 12b. Enter the total here. **Total** interest ▶ | **13**

Gifts to Charity
(See Instructions on page 25.)

14 Contributions by cash or check. (If you gave $3,000 or more to any one organization, show to whom you gave and how much you gave.) ▶ _____ | **14**
15 Other than cash or check. (You must attach Form 8283 if over $500.) | **15**
16 Carryover from prior year . . . . | **16**
17 Add the amounts on lines 14 through 16. Enter the total here. **Total** contributions . . ▶ | **17**

Casualty and Theft Losses
18 Casualty or theft loss(es) (attach Form 4684). (See page 25 of the Instructions.) . ▶ | **18**

Moving Expenses
19 Moving expenses (attach Form 3903 or 3903F). (See page 26 of the Instructions.) ▶ | **19**

Job Expenses and Most Other Miscellaneous Deductions
(See page 26 for expenses to deduct here.)

20 Unreimbursed employee expenses—job travel, union dues, job education, etc. (You MUST attach Form 2106 in some cases. See Instructions.) ▶ _____ | **20**
21 Other expenses (investment, tax preparation, safe deposit box, etc.). List type and amount ▶ _____
_____ | **21**
22 Add the amounts on lines 20 and 21. Enter the total. . . . | **22**
23 Multiply the amount on Form 1040, line 32, by 2% (.02). Enter the result here . . . . | **23**
24 Subtract line 23 from line 22. Enter the result (if zero or less, enter zero) . . . . ▶ | **24**

Other Miscellaneous Deductions
25 Other (from list on page 26 of Instructions). Enter type and amount ▶ _____
▶ | **25**

Total Itemized Deductions
26 Add the amounts on lines 4, 8, 13, 17, 18, 19, 24, and 25. Enter the total here. Then enter on Form 1040, line 34, the LARGER of this total or your standard deduction from page 17 of the Instructions . . . . ▶ | **26**

For Paperwork Reduction Act Notice, see Form 1040 Instructions.   Schedule A (Form 1040) 1988

Schedules A&B (Form 1040) 1988   OMB No. 1545-0074   Page **2**

Name(s) as shown on Form 1040. (Do not enter name and social security number if shown on other side.)	Your social security number

Schedule B—Interest and Dividend Income   Attachment Sequence No. **08**

Part I Interest Income

(See Instructions on pages 10 and 26.)

If you received more than $400 in taxable interest income, you must complete Part I and Part III and list ALL interest received. You must report all interest on Form 1040, even if you are not required to complete Part I and Part III. If you received, as a nominee, interest that actually belongs to another person, or you received or paid accrued interest on securities transferred between interest payment dates, see page 27.

Interest Income		Amount	
1 Interest income from seller-financed mortgages. (See Instructions and list name of payer.) ▶ -------------------------------	**1**		
2 Other interest income (list name of payer) ▶-----------------------------			

---	**2**		

---			
3 Add the amounts on lines 1 and 2. Enter the total here and on Form 1040, line 8a. ▶	**3**		

Note: If you received a Form 1099–INT or Form 1099–OID from a brokerage firm, list the firm's name as the payer and enter the total interest shown on that form.

Part II Dividend Income

(See Instructions on pages 11 and 27.)

If you received more than $400 in gross dividends and/or other distributions on stock, complete Part II and Part III. You must report all taxable dividends on Form 1040, even if you are not required to complete Part II and Part III. If you received, as a nominee, dividends that actually belong to another person, see page 27.

Dividend Income		Amount	
4 Dividend income (list name of payer—include on this line capital gain distributions, nontaxable distributions, etc.) ▶ ---------------------------------			

---	**4**		

Note: If you received a Form 1099-DIV from a brokerage firm, list the firm's name as the payer and enter the total dividends shown on that form.

5 Add the amounts on line 4. Enter the total here	**5**		
6 Capital gain distributions. Enter here and on line 13, Schedule D.*	**6**		
7 Nontaxable distributions. (See Schedule D Instructions for adjustment to basis.)	**7**		
8 Add the amounts on lines 6 and 7. Enter the total here	**8**		
9 Subtract line 8 from line 5. Enter the result here and on Form 1040, line 9 . . . ▶	**9**		

*If you received capital gain distributions but do not need Schedule D to report any other gains or losses, enter your capital gain distributions on Form 1040, line 14.

Part III Foreign Accounts and Foreign Trusts

(See Instructions on page 27.)

If you received more than $400 of interest or dividends, OR if you had a foreign account or were a grantor of, or a transferor to, a foreign trust, you must answer both questions in Part III.	Yes	No
10 At any time during the tax year, did you have an interest in or a signature or other authority over a financial account in a foreign country (such as a bank account, securities account, or other financial account)? (See page 27 of the Instructions for exceptions and filing requirements for Form TD F 90-22.1.)		
If "Yes," enter the name of the foreign country ▶ ---		
11 Were you the grantor of, or transferor to, a foreign trust which existed during the current tax year, whether or not you have any beneficial interest in it? If "Yes," you may have to file Form 3520, 3520-A, or 926		

For Paperwork Reduction Act Notice, see Form 1040 Instructions.   **Schedule B (Form 1040) 1988**

SCHEDULE C (Form 1040) Department of the Treasury Internal Revenue Service	**Profit or Loss From Business** (Sole Proprietorship) Partnerships, Joint Ventures, Etc., Must File Form 1065. ▶ Attach to Form 1040, Form 1041, or Form 1041S. ▶ See Instructions for Schedule C (Form 1040).	OMB No. 1545-0074 **1988** Attachment Sequence No. 09

Name of proprietor — Social security number (SSN)

A Principal business or profession, including product or service (see Instructions)

B Principal business code (from Part IV) ▶

C Business name and address ▶

D Employer ID number (Not SSN)

E Method(s) used to value closing inventory:
(1) ☐ Cost (2) ☐ Lower of cost or market (3) ☐ Other (attach explanation)

F Accounting method: (1) ☐ Cash (2) ☐ Accrual (3) ☐ Other (specify) ▶

Yes No

G Was there any change in determining quantities, costs, or valuations between opening and closing inventory? (If "Yes," attach explanation.)

H Are you deducting expenses for business use of your home? (If "Yes," see Instructions for limitations.)

I Did you "materially participate" in the operation of this business during 1988? (If "No," see Instructions for limitations on losses.)

J If this schedule includes a loss, credit, deduction, income, or other tax benefit relating to a tax shelter required to be registered, check here. ▶ ☐
If you check this box, you MUST attach **Form 8271**.

Part I Income

1a Gross receipts or sales	1a	
b Less: Returns and allowances	1b	
c Subtract line 1b from line 1a. Enter the result here	1c	
2 Cost of goods sold and/or operations (from Part III, line 8)	2	
3 Subtract line 2 from line 1c and enter the **gross profit** here	3	
4 Other income (including windfall profit tax credit or refund received in 1988)	4	
5 Add lines 3 and 4. This is the **gross income** ▶	5	

Part II Deductions

6 Advertising	6		**23** Repairs	23	
7 Bad debts from sales or services (see Instructions)	7		**24** Supplies (not included in Part III)	24	
8 Bank service charges	8		**25** Taxes	25	
9 Car and truck expenses	9		**26** Travel, meals, and entertainment:		
10 Commissions	10		**a** Travel	26a	
11 Depletion	11		**b** Meals and entertainment		
12 Depreciation and section 179 deduction from Form 4562 (not included in Part III)	12		**c** Enter 20% of line 26b subject to limitations (see Instructions)		
13 Dues and publications	13		**d** Subtract line 26c from 26b	26d	
14 Employee benefit programs	14		**27** Utilities and telephone	27	
15 Freight (not included in Part III)	15		**28a** Wages		
16 Insurance	16		**b** Jobs credit		
17 Interest:			**c** Subtract line 28b from 28a	28c	
a Mortgage (paid to banks, etc.)	17a		**29** Other expenses (list type and amount):		
b Other	17b				
18 Laundry and cleaning	18				
19 Legal and professional services	19				
20 Office expense	20				
21 Pension and profit-sharing plans	21				
22 Rent on business property	22			29	

30 Add amounts in columns for lines 6 through 29. These are the **total deductions** ▶ | 30 |

31 **Net profit or (loss).** Subtract line 30 from line 5. If a profit, enter here and on Form 1040, line 12, and on Schedule SE, line 2. If a loss, you MUST go on to line 32. (Fiduciaries, see instructions.) | 31 |

32 If you have a loss, you MUST check the box that describes your investment in this activity (see Instructions)
32a ☐ All investment is at risk.
32b ☐ Some investment is not at risk.

If you checked 32a, enter the loss on Form 1040, line 12, and Schedule SE, line 2. If you checked 32b, you MUST attach **Form 6198**.

For Paperwork Reduction Act Notice, see Form 1040 Instructions.   Schedule C (Form 1040) 1988

Schedule C (Form 1040) 1988   Page **2**

Part III   Cost of Goods Sold and/or Operations (See Schedule C Instructions for Part III)

1	Inventory at beginning of year. (If different from last year's closing inventory, attach explanation.)	1
2	Purchases less cost of items withdrawn for personal use	2
3	Cost of labor. (Do not include salary paid to yourself.)	3
4	Materials and supplies	4
5	Other costs	5
6	Add lines 1 through 5	6
7	Less: Inventory at end of year	7
8	**Cost of goods sold and/or operations.** Subtract line 7 from line 6. Enter the result here and in Part I, line 2.	8

Part IV   Codes for Principal Business or Professional Activity

Locate the major business category that best describes your activity (for example, Retail Trade, Services, etc.). Within the major category, select the activity code that identifies (or most closely identifies) the business or profession that is the principal source of your sales or receipts. **Enter this 4-digit code on line B on page 1 of Schedule C.** (Note: *If your principal source of income is from farming activities, you should file **Schedule F** (Form 1040), Farm Income and Expenses.*)

Construction

Code

0018 Operative builders (building for own account)

General contractors

0034 Residential building
0059 Nonresidential building
0075 Highway and street construction
3889 Other heavy construction (pipe laying, bridge construction, etc.)

Building trade contractors, including repairs

0232 Plumbing, heating, air conditioning
0257 Painting and paper hanging
0273 Electrical work
0299 Masonry, dry wall, stone, tile
0414 Carpentering and flooring
0430 Roofing, siding, and sheet metal
0455 Concrete work
0471 Water well drilling
0885 Other building trade contractors (excavation, glazing, etc.)

Manufacturing, Including Printing and Publishing

0612 Bakeries selling at retail
0638 Other food products and beverages
0653 Textile mill products
0679 Apparel and other textile products
0695 Leather, footware, handbags, etc.
0810 Furniture and fixtures
0836 Lumber and other wood products
0851 Printing and publishing
0877 Paper and allied products
0893 Chemicals and allied products
1016 Rubber and plastics products
1032 Stone, clay, and glass products
1057 Primary metal industries
1073 Fabricated metal products
1099 Machinery and machine shops
1115 Electric and electronic equipment
1313 Transportation equipment
1339 Instruments and related products
1883 Other manufacturing industries

Mining and Mineral Extraction

1511 Metal mining
1537 Coal mining
1552 Oil and gas
1719 Quarrying and nonmetallic mining

Agricultural Services, Forestry, and Fishing

1917 Soil preparation services
1933 Crop services
1958 Veterinary services, including pets
1974 Livestock breeding
1990 Other animal services
2113 Farm labor and management services
2212 Horticulture and landscaping
2238 Forestry, except logging
0836 Logging
2279 Fishing, hunting, and trapping

Wholesale Trade—Selling Goods to Other Businesses, Government, or Institutions, Etc.

Durable goods, including machinery, equipment, wood, metals, etc.

2618 Selling for your own account

Code

2634 Agent or broker for other firms— more than 50% of gross sales on commission

Nondurable goods, including food, fiber, chemicals, etc.

2659 Selling for your own account
2675 Agent or broker for other firms— more than 50% of gross sales on commission

Retail Trade—Selling Goods to Individuals and Households

3012 Selling door-to-door, by telephone or party plan, or from mobile unit
3038 Catalog or mail order
3053 Vending machine selling

Selling From Store, Showroom, or Other Fixed Location

Food, beverages, and drugs

3079 Eating places (meals or snacks)
3095 Drinking places (alcoholic beverages)
3210 Grocery stores (general line)
0612 Bakeries selling at retail
3236 Other food stores (meat, produce, candy, etc.)
3251 Liquor stores
3277 Drug stores

Automotive and service stations

3319 New car dealers (franchised)
3335 Used car dealers
3517 Other automotive dealers (motorcycles, recreational vehicles, etc.)
3533 Tires, accessories, and parts
3558 Gasoline service stations

General merchandise, apparel, and furniture

3715 Variety stores
3731 Other general merchandise stores
3756 Shoe stores
3772 Men's and boys' clothing stores
3913 Women's ready-to-wear stores
3921 Women's accessory and specialty stores and furriers
3939 Family clothing stores
3954 Other apparel and accessory stores
3970 Furniture stores
3996 TV, audio, and electronics
3988 Computer and software stores
4119 Household appliance stores
4317 Other home furnishing stores (china, floor coverings, drapes, etc.)
4333 Music and record stores

Building, hardware, and garden supply

4416 Building materials dealers
4432 Paint, glass, and wallpaper stores
4457 Hardware stores
4473 Nurseries and garden supply stores

Other retail stores

4614 Used merchandise and antique stores (except used motor vehicle parts)
4630 Gift, novelty, and souvenir shops
4655 Florists
4671 Jewelry stores

Code

4697 Sporting goods and bicycle shops
4812 Boat dealers
4838 Hobby, toy, and game shops
4853 Camera and photo supply stores
4879 Optical goods stores
4895 Luggage and leather goods stores
5017 Book stores, excluding newsstands
5033 Stationery stores
5058 Fabric and needlework stores
5074 Mobile home dealers
5090 Fuel dealers (except gasoline)
5884 Other retail stores

Real Estate, Insurance, Finance, and Related Services

5512 Real estate agents and managers
5538 Operators and lessors of buildings (except developers)
5553 Operators and lessors of other real property (except developers)
5710 Subdividers and developers, except cemeteries
5736 Insurance agents and services
5751 Security and commodity brokers, dealers, and investment services
5777 Other real estate, insurance, and financial activities

Transportation, Communications, Public Utilities, and Related Services

6114 Taxicabs
6312 Bus and limousine transportation
6338 Trucking (except trash collection)
6510 Trash collection without own dump
6536 Public warehousing
6551 Water transportation
6619 Air transportation
6635 Travel agents and tour operators
6650 Other transportation and related services
6676 Communication services
6692 Utilities, including dumps, snowplowing, road cleaning, etc.

Services (Providing Personal, Professional, and Business Services)

Hotels and other lodging places

7096 Hotels, motels, and tourist homes
7211 Rooming and boarding houses
7237 Camps and camping parks

Laundry and cleaning services

7419 Coin-operated laundries and dry cleaning
7435 Other laundry, dry cleaning, and garment services
7450 Carpet and upholstery cleaning
7476 Janitorial and related services (building, house, and window cleaning)

Business and/or personal services

7617 Legal services (or lawyer)
7633 Income tax preparation
7658 Accounting and bookkeeping
7674 Engineering, surveying, and architectural

Code

7690 Management, consulting, and public relations
7716 Advertising, except direct mail
7732 Employment agencies and personnel supply
7757 Computer and data processing, including repair and leasing
7773 Equipment rental and leasing (except computer or automotive)
7914 Investigative and protective services
7880 Other business services

Personal services

8110 Beauty shops (or beautician)
8318 Barber shop (or barber)
8334 Photographic portrait studios
8516 Shoe repair and shine services
8532 Funeral services and crematories
8714 Child day care
8730 Teaching or tutoring
8755 Counseling (except health practitioners)
8771 Ministers and chaplains
6882 Other personal services

Automotive services

8813 Automotive rental or leasing, without driver
8839 Parking, except valet
8854 General automotive repairs
8870 Specialized automotive repairs (brake, body repairs, paint, etc.)
8896 Other automotive services (wash, towing, etc.)

Miscellaneous repair, except computers

9019 TV and audio equipment repair
9035 Other electrical equipment repair
9050 Reupholstery and furniture repair
2881 Other equipment repair

Medical and health services

9217 Offices and clinics of medical doctors (MDs)
9233 Offices and clinics of dentists
9258 Osteopathic physicians and surgeons
9274 Chiropractors
9290 Optometrists
9415 Registered and practical nurses
9431 Other licensed health practitioners
9456 Dental laboratories
9472 Nursing and personal care facilities
9886 Other health services

Amusement and recreational services

8557 Physical fitness facilities
9613 Videotape rental stores
9639 Motion picture theaters
9654 Other motion picture and TV film and tape activities
9670 Bowling alleys
9696 Professional sports and racing, including promoters and managers
9811 Theatrical performers, musicians, agents, producers, and related services
9837 Other amusement and recreational services

8888 Unable to classify

SCHEDULE D
(Form 1040)

Department of the Treasury
Internal Revenue Service

Capital Gains and Losses
(And Reconciliation of Forms 1099-B)

▶ Attach to Form 1040.   ▶ See Instructions for Schedule D (Form 1040).
For Paperwork Reduction Act Notice, see Form 1040 Instructions.

OMB No. 1545-0074

19**88**

Attachment
Sequence No. **12**

Name(s) as shown on Form 1040

Your social security number

1 Report here the total sales of stocks, bonds, etc., reported for 1988 to you on Form(s) 1099-B or on equivalent substitute statement(s). If this amount differs from the total of lines 2b and 9b, column (d), attach a statement explaining the difference. See the Instructions for line 1 for examples **1**

Part I   Short-Term Capital Gains and Losses—Assets Held One Year or Less (6 months or less if acquired before 1/1/88)

(a) Description of property (Example, 100 shares 7% preferred of "Z" Co.)	(b) Date acquired (Mo., day, yr.)	(c) Date sold (Mo., day, yr.)	(d) Sales price (see Instructions)	(e) Cost or other basis (see Instructions)	(f) LOSS If (e) is more than (d), subtract (d) from (e)	(g) GAIN If (d) is more than (e), subtract (e) from (d)
2a Stocks, Bonds, and Other Securities (Include all Form 1099-B transactions. See Instructions.)						

2b **Total** (add column (d)) . . . . . . 2b▶

2c Other Transactions (Include Real Estate Transactions From Forms 1099-S)

3 Short-term gain from sale or exchange of your home from Form 2119, line 8a or 14 . **3**
4 Short-term gain from installment sales from Form 6252, line 22 or 30 . . . . . **4**
5 Net short-term gain or (loss) from partnerships, S corporations, and fiduciaries . **5**
6 Short-term capital loss carryover **6**
7 Add all of the transactions on lines 2a and 2c and lines 3 through 6 in columns (f) and (g) . **7** ( )
8 Net short-term gain or (loss), combine columns (f) and (g) of line 7 . . . . **8**

Part II   Long-Term Capital Gains and Losses—Assets Held More Than One Year (more than 6 months if acquired before 1/1/88)

9a Stocks, Bonds, and Other Securities (Include all Form 1099-B transactions. See Instructions.)						

9b **Total** (add column (d)) . . . . . . 9b▶

9c Other Transactions (Include Real Estate Transactions From Forms 1099-S)

10 Long-term gain from sale or exchange of your home from Form 2119, line 8a, 10, or 14 . **10**
11 Long-term gain from installment sales from Form 6252, line 22 or 30 . . . . **11**
12 Net long-term gain or (loss) from partnerships, S corporations, and fiduciaries . **12**
13 Capital gain distributions. **13**
14 Enter gain from Form 4797, line 7 or 9 . . . . **14**
15 Long-term capital loss carryover **15**
16 Add all of the transactions on lines 9a and 9c and lines 10 through 15 in columns (f) and (g) . . **16** ( )
17 Net long-term gain or (loss), combine columns (f) and (g) of line 16 . . . . **17**

Schedule D (Form 1040) 1988

Schedule D (Form 1040) 1988   Attachment Sequence No. **12**   Page **2**

Name(s) as shown on Form 1040. (Do not enter name and social security number if shown on other side.)	Your social security number
	: :

Part III   Summary of Parts I and II

18 Combine lines 8 and 17, and enter the net gain or (loss) here. If result is a gain, also enter the gain on Form 1040, line 13	**18**	
19 If line 18 is a (loss), enter here and as a (loss) on Form 1040, line 13, the **smaller** of:		
a The (loss) on line 18; **or**		
b ($3,000) or, if married filing a separate return, ($1,500)	**19** (	)
Note: When figuring which amount is **smaller,** treat them as if they were positive numbers.		

Part IV   Computation of Capital Loss Carryovers From 1988 to 1989
            (Complete this part if the loss on line 18 is more than the loss on line 19.)

20 Enter the loss shown on line 8; if none, enter zero and skip lines 21 through 24.	**20**	
21 Enter gain shown on line 17. If that line is blank or shows a loss, enter zero	**21**	
22 Subtract line 21 from line 20	**22**	
23 Enter the **smaller** of line 19 or 22	**23**	
24 Subtract line 23 from line 22. This is your **short-term capital loss carryover from 1988 to 1989** . .	**24**	
25 Enter loss from line 17; if none, enter zero and skip lines 26 through 29	**25**	
26 Enter gain shown on line 8. If that line is blank or shows a loss, enter zero	**26**	
27 Subtract line 26 from line 25	**27**	
28 Subtract line 23 from line 19. (**Note:** *If you skipped lines 21 through 24, enter the amount from line 19.*)	**28**	
29 Subtract line 28 from line 27. This is your **long-term capital loss carryover from 1988 to 1989** . . .	**29**	

Part V   Complete This Part Only If You Elect Out of the Installment Method and Report a Note or Other Obligation at Less Than Full Face Value

30 Check here if you elect out of the installment method . . . . ▶ ☐
31 Enter the face amount of the note or other obligation . . . . ▶
32 Enter the percentage of valuation of the note or other obligation . . . . ▶

Part VI   Reconciliation of Forms 1099-B for Bartering Transactions

(Complete this part if you received one or more Form(s) 1099-B or an equivalent substitute statement(s) reporting bartering income.)	Amount of bartering income from Form 1099-B or equivalent statement reported on form or schedule
33 Form 1040, line 22 . . . . **33**	
34 Schedule C (Form 1040) **34**	
35 Schedule D (Form 1040) **35**	
36 Schedule E (Form 1040) **36**	
37 Schedule F (Form 1040) **37**	
38 Other (identify) (if not taxable, indicate reason—attach additional sheets if necessary) ▶	
--	
-- **38**	
39 Total (add lines 33 through 38) **39**	
Note: *The amount on line 39 should be the same as the total bartering income on all Forms 1099-B and equivalent statements received.*	

SCHEDULE E (Form 1040) Department of the Treasury Internal Revenue Service	**Supplemental Income Schedule** (From rents, royalties, partnerships, estates, trusts, REMICs, etc.) ▶ Attach to Form 1040, Form 1041, or Form 1041S. ▶ See Instructions for Schedule E (Form 1040).	OMB No. 1545-0074 19**88** Attachment Sequence No. **13**

Name(s) as shown on return	Your social security number

Part I Rental and Royalty Income or Loss   Caution: *Your rental loss may be limited. See Instructions.*

1 In the space provided below, show the kind and location of each rental property.	2 For each rental property listed, did you or a member of your family use it for personal purposes for more than the greater of 14 days or 10% of the total days rented at fair rental value during the tax year?			3 For each rental real estate property listed in item 1, did you actively participate in its operation during the tax year? (See Instructions.)		
		Yes	**No**		**Yes**	**No**
Property A .... ▶				Property A . . . . ▶		
Property B .... ▶				Property B . . . . ▶		
Property C .... ▶				Property C . . . . ▶		

Rental and Royalty Income

		Properties			Totals (Add columns A, B, and C)
		A	**B**	**C**	
4 Rents received					**4**
5 Royalties received					**5**

Rental and Royalty Expenses

		A	B	C	Totals
6 Advertising	**6**				
7 Auto and travel	**7**				
8 Cleaning and maintenance . . .	**8**				
9 Commissions	**9**				
10 Insurance	**10**				
11 Legal and other professional fees .	**11**				
12 Mortgage interest paid to banks, etc. (see Instructions)	**12**				**12**
13 Other interest.	**13**				
14 Repairs	**14**				
15 Supplies	**15**				
16 Taxes (Do **not** include windfall profit tax here. See Part V, line 40.).	**16**				
17 Utilities	**17**				
18 Wages and salaries	**18**				
19 Other (list) ▶	**19**				
20 Total expenses other than depreciation and depletion. Add lines 6 through 19.	**20**				**20**
21 Depreciation expense (see Instructions), or depletion (see Pub. 535)	**21**				**21**
22 Total. Add lines 20 and 21 . .	**22**				
23 Income or (loss) from rental or royalty properties. Subtract line 22 from line 4 (rents) or 5 (royalties) .	**23**				
24 Deductible rental loss. **Caution:** *Your rental loss on line 23 may be limited. See Instructions to determine if you must file* **Form 8582**, *Passive Activity Loss Limitations*	**24**				

25 **Profits.** Add rental and royalty profits from line 23. Enter the total profits here	**25**	
26 **Losses.** Add royalty losses from line 23 and rental losses from line 24. Enter the total (losses) here . . .	**26**	( )
27 Combine amounts on lines 25 and 26. Enter the net profit or (loss) here	**27**	
28 Net farm rental profit or loss from Form 4835. (Also complete Part VI, line 43.)	**28**	
29 Total rental or royalty income or (loss). Combine amounts on lines 27 and 28. Enter the total here. If Parts II, III, IV, and V on page 2 do not apply to you, enter the amount from line 29 on Form 1040, line 18. Otherwise, include the amount from line 29 in line 42 on page 2 of Schedule E	**29**	

For Paperwork Reduction Act Notice, see Form 1040 Instructions.   Schedule E (Form 1040) 1988

Schedule E (Form 1040) 1988   Attachment Sequence No. **13**   Page **2**

Name(s) as shown on return. (Do not enter name and social security number if shown on other side.)	Your social security number

Part II Income or Loss From Partnerships and S Corporations

If you report a loss from an at-risk activity, you MUST check either column (e) or (f) to describe your investment in the activity. See Instructions. If you check column (f), you must attach **Form 6198.**

	(a) Name	(b) Enter **P** for partnership; **S** for S corporation	(c) Check if foreign partnership	(d) Employer identification number	Investment At Risk? (e) All is at risk	(f) Some is not at risk
A						
B						
C						
D						
E						

	Passive Income and Loss		Nonpassive Income and Loss		
	(g) Passive loss allowed from Form 8582	(h) Passive income from Schedule K-1	(i) Nonpassive loss from Schedule K-1	(j) Section 179 deduction (see Instructions for limits)	(k) Nonpassive income from Schedule K-1
A					
B					
C					
D					
E					
30a Totals					
b Totals					

31 Add amounts in columns (h) and (k), line 30a. Enter total income here . . . . | **31** |

32 Add amounts in columns (g), (i), and (j), line 30b. Enter total here . . . . | **32** (   )

33 Total partnership and S corporation income or (loss). Combine amounts on lines 31 and 32. Enter the total here and include in line 42 below . . . . | **33** |

Part III Income or Loss From Estates and Trusts

	(a) Name	(b) Employer identification number
A		
B		
C		

	Passive Income and Loss		Nonpassive Income and Loss	
	(c) Passive deduction or loss allowed from Form 8582	(d) Passive income from Schedule K-1	(e) Deduction or loss from Schedule K-1	(f) Other income from Schedule K-1
A				
B				
C				
34a Totals				
b Totals				

35 Add amounts in columns (d) and (f), line 34a. Enter total income here . . . . | **35** |

36 Add amounts in columns (c) and (e), line 34b. Enter total here . . . . | **36** (   )

37 Total estate and trust income or (loss). Combine amounts on lines 35 and 36. Enter the total here and include in line 42 below . . . . | **37** |

Part IV Income or Loss From Real Estate Mortgage Investment Conduits (REMICs)—Residual Holder

(a) Name	(b) Employer identification number	(c) Excess inclusion from Schedules Q, line 2c (see Instructions)	(d) Taxable income (net loss) from Schedules Q, line 1b	(e) Income from Schedules Q, line 3b

38 Combine amounts in columns (d) and (e) only. Enter the total here and include in line 42 below . . . | **38** |

Part V Windfall Profit Tax Summary

39 Windfall profit tax credit or refund received in 1988 (see Instructions) . . . . | **39** |

40 Windfall profit tax withheld in 1988 (see Instructions) . . . . | **40** (   )

41 Combine amounts on lines 39 and 40. Enter the total here and include in line 42 below . . . . . . | **41** |

Part VI Summary

42 TOTAL income or (loss). Combine amounts on lines 29, 33, 37, 38, and 41. Enter the total here and on Form 1040, line 18 . . . . ▶ | **42** |

43 Farmers and fishermen: Enter your share of GROSS FARMING AND FISHING INCOME applicable to Parts I, II, and III (see Instructions) . . . | **43** |

Schedule R
(Form 1040)
Department of the Treasury
Internal Revenue Service

Credit for the Elderly or the Disabled

▶ For Paperwork Reduction Act Notice, see Form 1040 Instructions.
▶ Attach to Form 1040.   ▶ See separate Instructions for Schedule R.

OMB No. 1545-0074

1988

Attachment
Sequence No. **17**

Name(s) as shown on Form 1040	Your social security number
	⋮ ⋮

You may be able to use Schedule R to reduce your tax if by the end of 1988:

● You were 65 or older, **OR**

● You were under 65, you retired on **permanent and total** disability, and you received taxable disability income.

Even if one of the situations described above applies to you, you must meet other tests to be able to take the credit on Schedule R. See the separate Schedule R Instructions for details.

Note: *In most cases IRS can figure this credit for you. See page 16 of the Form 1040 Instructions.*

Part I   **Check the Box That Applies to Your Filing Status and Age** (Check only one box)

If your filing status is:	And by the end of 1988:	Check box:
Single*	1 You were 65 or older.	1 ☐
	2 You were under 65 and you retired on permanent and total disability .	2 ☐

* Includes Head of household and Qualifying widow(er) with dependent child

	3 Both spouses were 65 or older .	3 ☐
Married filing a joint return	4 Both spouses were under 65, but only one spouse retired on permanent and total disability .	4 ☐
	5 Both spouses were under 65, and both retired on permanent and total disability .	5 ☐
	6 One spouse was 65 or older, and the other spouse was under 65 and retired on permanent and total disability	6 ☐
	7 One spouse was 65 or older, and the other spouse was under 65 and **NOT** retired on permanent and total disability .	7 ☐
Married filing a separate return	8 You were 65 or older, and you did not live with your spouse at any time in 1988.	8 ☐
	9 You were under 65, you retired on permanent and total disability, and you did not live with your spouse at any time in 1988 .	9 ☐

Note: *If you checked the box on line 1, 3, 7, or 8, skip Part II and complete Part III. If you checked the box on line 2, 4, 5, 6, or 9, complete Parts II and III.*

Part II   **Statement of Permanent and Total Disability** (Complete **only** if you checked the box on line 2, 4, 5, 6, or 9 above)

IF: 1 You filed a physician's statement for this disability for 1983 or an earlier year, or you filed a statement for tax years after 1983 and your physician checked Box B on the statement, **AND**

2 Due to your continued disabled condition you were unable to engage in any substantial gainful activity in 1988, check this box. ▶ ☐

If you checked this box, you do not have to file another statement for 1988. If you did not check this box, have your physician complete the following statement:

Physician's Statement

I certify that _____
Name of disabled person

was permanently and totally disabled on January 1, 1976, or January 1, 1977, **OR** was permanently and totally disabled on the date he or she retired. Date retired if retired after December 31, 1976. ▶ _____

Physician: Sign your name on **either** line A or B below and check the box to the right of your signature.

A The disability has lasted, or can be expected to last, continuously for at least a year . _____   **A** ☐
Physician's signature   Date

B There is no reasonable probability that the disabled condition will ever improve . _____   **B** ☐
Physician's signature   Date

Physician's name	Physician's address

Instructions for Statement

Taxpayer

Enter in the space provided the date you retired if you retired after December 31, 1976.

Physician

A person is permanently and totally disabled when—

● He or she cannot engage in any substantial gainful activity because of a physical or mental condition; and

● A physician determines that the disability:

1. has lasted, or can be expected to last, continuously for at least a year; or

2. can be expected to lead to death.

(Continued on back)   **Schedule R (Form 1040) 1988**

Schedule R (Form 1040) 1988   Page **2**

Part III	**Figure the Amount of Your Credit**

10 Enter: $5,000 if you checked the box on line 1, 2, 4, or 7 in Part I, **OR**
        $7,500 if you checked the box on line 3, 5, or 6 in Part I, **OR** } **10**
        $3,750 if you checked the box on line 8 or 9 in Part I.

   Caution: *If you checked the box on line 2, 4, 5, 6, or 9 in Part I, you **MUST** complete line 11 below. Otherwise, skip line 11 and enter the amount from line 10 on line 12.*

11 Enter on this line your taxable disability income (and also your spouse's if you checked the box on line 5 in Part I) that you reported on Form 1040. However, if you checked the box on line 6 in Part I, enter on this line the taxable disability income of the spouse who was under age 65 **PLUS** $5,000. (For more details on what to include, see the Instructions.) **11**

12 If you completed line 11 above, compare the amounts on lines 10 and 11, and enter the **smaller** of the two amounts on this line. Otherwise, enter the amount from line 10 on this line **12**

13 Enter the following pensions, annuities, or disability income that you (and your spouse if you file a joint return) received in 1988 (see Instructions):

   a Nontaxable part of social security benefits; and
       Nontaxable part of railroad retirement benefits treated as } **13a**
       social security.

   b Nontaxable veterans' pensions; and
       Any other pension, annuity, or disability benefit that is } **13b**
       excluded from income under any other provision of law.

   c Add lines 13a and 13b. (Even though these income items are not subject to income tax, they **must** be included to figure your credit.) If you did not receive any of the types of nontaxable income listed on line 13a or 13b, enter -0- on line 13c **13c**

14 Enter the amount from Form 1040, line 32. **14**

15 Enter: $7,500 if you checked the box on
        line 1 or 2 in Part I, **OR**
        $10,000 if you checked the box on } **15**
        line 3, 4, 5, 6, or 7 in Part I, **OR**
        $5,000 if you checked the box
        on line 8 or 9 in Part I.

16 Subtract line 15 from line 14. Enter the
        result. If line 15 is more than line 14,
        enter -0- **16**

17 Divide the amount on line 16 by 2. Enter the result **17**

18 Add lines 13c and 17. Enter the total **18**

19 Subtract line 18 from line 12. Enter the result. If the result is zero or less, stop here; you **cannot** take the credit. Otherwise, go on to line 21 . . . . **19**

20 Percentage used to figure the credit . . . . **20**   × .15

21 Multiply the amount on line 19 by the percentage (.15) on line 20 and enter the result. If you do not file Schedule C, D, E, or F (Form 1040), enter the amount from line 21 on Form 1040, line 42. Otherwise, see the instructions to determine if your credit may be further limited **21**

SCHEDULE SE (Form 1040) Department of the Treasury Internal Revenue Service	**Social Security Self-Employment Tax** ▶ See Instructions for Schedule SE (Form 1040). ▶ Attach to Form 1040.	OMB No. 1545-0074 **1988** Attachment Sequence No. **18**

Name of person with **self-employment** income (as shown on social security card)	Social security number of person with **self-employment** income ▶	⋮ . ⋮

Who Must File Schedule SE

You must file Schedule SE if:

● Your net earnings from self-employment were $400 or more (or you had wages of $100 or more from an electing church or church organization); AND

● You did not have wages (subject to social security or railroad retirement tax) of $45,000 or more.

For more information about Schedule SE, see the Instructions.

Note: *Most taxpayers can now use the new short Schedule SE on this page. But, you may have to use the longer Schedule SE that is on the back.*

Who MUST Use the Long Schedule SE (Section B)

You must use Section B if ANY of the following applies:

● You choose the "optional method" to figure your self-employment tax. See Section B, Part II;

● You are a minister, member of a religious order, or Christian Science practitioner and received IRS approval (from **Form 4361**) not to be taxed on your earnings from these sources, but you owe self-employment tax on other earnings;

● You are an employee of a church or church organization that chose by law not to pay employer social security taxes;

● You have tip income that is subject to social security tax, but you did not report those tips to your employer; OR

● You are a government employee with wages subject ONLY to the 1.45% medicare part of the social security tax.

Section A—Short Schedule SE
(Read above to see if you must use the long Schedule SE on the back (Section B).)

1	Net farm profit or (loss) from Schedule F (Form 1040), line 39, and farm partnerships, Schedule K-1 (Form 1065), line 14a	**1**	
2	Net profit or (loss) from Schedule C (Form 1040), line 31, and Schedule K-1 (Form 1065), line 14a (other than farming). See the Instructions for other income to report	**2**	
3	Add lines 1 and 2. Enter the total. If the total is less than $400, **do not** file this schedule	**3**	
4	The largest amount of combined wages and self-employment earnings subject to social security or railroad retirement tax (tier 1) for 1988 is	**4**	$45,000 | 00
5	Total social security wages and tips from Forms W-2 and railroad retirement compensation (tier 1)	**5**	
6	Subtract line 5 from line 4. Enter the result. (If the result is zero or less, **do not** file this schedule.) . . .	**6**	
7	Enter the **smaller** of line 3 or line 6	**7**	
	If line 7 is $45,000, enter $5,859 on line 8. Otherwise, multiply line 7 by .1302 and enter the result on line 8		×.1302
8	Self-employment tax. Enter this amount on Form 1040, line 48	**8**	

For Paperwork Reduction Act Notice, see Form 1040 Instructions.   Schedule SE (Form 1040) 1988

Schedule SE (Form 1040) 1988   Attachment Sequence No. **18**   Page **2**

Name of person with **self-employment** income (as shown on social security card)	Social security number of person with **self-employment** income ▶

Section B—Long Schedule SE

(Before completing, see if you can use the short Schedule SE on the other side (Section A).)

A   If your only self-employment income was from earnings as a minister, member of a religious order, or Christian Science practitioner, AND you filed **Form 4361,** then DO NOT file Schedule SE. Instead, write "Exempt-Form 4361" on Form 1040, line 48. However, if you filed Form 4361, but have $400 or more of other earnings subject to self-employment tax, continue with Part I and check here. ▶ ☐

B   If your only earnings subject to self-employment tax are wages from an electing church or church-controlled organization that is exempt from employer social security taxes and you are not a minister or a member of a religious order, skip lines 1–3b. Enter zero on line 3c and go on to line 5a.

Part I   Figure Social Security Self-Employment Tax

1	Net farm profit or (loss) from Schedule F (Form 1040), line 39, and farm partnerships, Schedule K-1 (Form 1065), line 14a	**1**	
2	Net profit or (loss) from Schedule C (Form 1040), line 31, and Schedule K-1 (Form 1065), line 14a (other than farming). (See Instructions for other income to report.) Employees of an electing church or church-controlled organization **do not** enter your Form W-2 wages on line 2. See the Instructions . . .	**2**	
3a	Enter the amount from line 1 (**or,** if you elected the farm optional method, Part II, line 10)	**3a**	
b	Enter the amount from line 2 (**or,** if you elected the nonfarm optional method, Part II, line 12)	**3b**	
c	Add lines 3a and 3b. Enter the total. If the total is less than $400, **do not** file this schedule. (**Exception:** *If you are an employee of an electing church or church-controlled organization and the total of lines 3a and 3b is less than $400, enter zero and complete the rest of this schedule.*)	**3c**	
4	The largest amount of combined wages and self-employment earnings subject to social security or railroad retirement tax (tier 1) for 1988 is	**4**	$45,000 00
5a	Total social security wages and tips from Forms W-2 and railroad retirement compensation (tier 1). **Note:** *Government employees whose wages are subject only to the 1.45% medicare tax and employees of certain church or church-controlled organizations should **not** include those wages on this line. See Instructions* **5a**		
b	Unreported tips subject to social security tax from Form 4137, line 9, or to railroad retirement tax (tier 1) **5b**		
c	Add lines 5a and 5b. Enter the total	**5c**	
6a	Subtract line 5c from line 4. Enter the result. (If the result is zero or less, enter zero.)	**6a**	
b	Enter your medicare qualified government wages if you are required to use the worksheet in the Instructions . . . **6b**		
c	Enter your Form W-2 wages of $100 or more from an electing church or church-controlled organization . . . **6c**		
d	Add lines 3c and 6c. Enter the total	**6d**	
7	Enter the **smaller** of line 6a or line 6d	**7**	
	If line 7 is $45,000, enter $5,859 on line 8. Otherwise, multiply line 7 by .1302 and enter the result on line 8		×.1302
8	Self-employment tax. Enter this amount on Form 1040, line 48	**8**	

Part II   Optional Method To Figure Net Earnings (See "Who Can File Schedule SE" in the Instructions.)

See Instructions for limitations. Generally, you may use this part **only** if:

A   Your **gross** farm income[1] was not more than $2,400; **or**

B   Your **gross** farm income[1] was more than $2,400 and your **net** farm profits[2] were **less** than $1,600; **or**

C   Your **net** nonfarm profits[3] were less than $1,600 and also **less** than two-thirds (⅔) of your **gross** nonfarm income.[4]

Note: *If line 2 above is two-thirds (⅔) or more of your gross nonfarm income,[4] or if line 2 is $1,600 or more, you may **not** use the optional method.*

[1]From Schedule F (Form 1040), line 12, and Schedule K-1 (Form 1065), line 14b.   [3]From Schedule C (Form 1040), line 31, and Schedule K-1 (Form 1065), line 14a.
[2]From Schedule F (Form 1040), line 39, and Schedule K-1 (Form 1065), line 14a.   [4]From Schedule C (Form 1040), line 5, and Schedule K-1 (Form 1065), line 14c.

9	Maximum income for optional methods	**9**	$1,600 00
10	**Farm Optional Method**—If you meet test A or B above, enter the **smaller** of: two-thirds (⅔) of gross farm income from Schedule F (Form 1040), line 12, and farm partnerships, Schedule K-1 (Form 1065), line 14b; **or** $1,600. Also enter this amount on **line 3a** above	**10**	
11	Subtract line 10 from line 9. Enter the result	**11**	
12	**Nonfarm Optional Method**—If you meet test C above, enter the **smallest** of: two-thirds (⅔) of gross nonfarm income from Schedule C (Form 1040), line 5, and Schedule K-1 (Form 1065), line 14c (other than farming); **or** $1,600; **or,** if you elected the farm optional method, the amount on line 11. Also enter this amount on line 3b above	**12**	

For Paperwork Reduction Act Notice, see Form 1040 Instructions.   **Schedule SE (Form 1040) 1988**

Form **1040-ES**	**Estimated Tax for Individuals**	OMB No. 1545-0087 Expires 8-31-91
Department of the Treasury Internal Revenue Service	▶ **This form is primarily for first-time filers of estimated tax .**	1989

Instructions

Paperwork Reduction Act Notice.— We ask for this information to carry out the Internal Revenue laws of the United States. We need it to ensure that taxpayers are complying with these laws and to allow us to figure and collect the right amount of tax. You are required to give us this information.

The time needed to complete and file this form will vary depending on individual circumstances. The estimated average time is: **Recordkeeping,** 1 hr., 25 min.; **Learning about the law or the form,** 21 min.; **Preparing the form,** 1 hr., 17 min.; **Copying, assembling, and sending the form to IRS,** 10 min.

If you have comments concerning the accuracy of these time estimates or suggestions for making this form more simple, we would be happy to hear from you. You can write to the **Internal Revenue Service,** Washington, DC 20224, Attention: IRS Reports Clearance Officer, TR:FP; or the **Office of Management and Budget,** Paperwork Reduction Project, Washington, DC 20503.

Changes To Note

Tax Indexing.—The Tax Rate Schedules have been adjusted so that inflation will not result in tax increases (see page 4).

Changes in the law for 1989 affect the personal interest deduction, the standard deduction, personal exemptions, and the earned income credit (see page 4). Also see **Pub. 553,** Highlights of 1988 Tax Changes, for other tax law changes.

Supplemental Medicare Premium.—You may owe a supplemental Medicare premium if you are eligible for Medicare Part A benefits for more than 6 months in 1989 and your 1989 income tax will be $150 or more. The supplemental premium will be used to help pay the cost of the new Medicare coverage for catastrophic expenses and prescription drugs.

You will have to add the premium to the tax on your 1989 income tax return. So that you won't have to pay too much tax with your 1989 return, you may want to increase your estimated tax payments for 1989 to cover the amount of any supplemental Medicare premium you may owe. To do so, include on line 12 of the worksheet on page 3 the amount of the premium you expect to owe for 1989. For 1989, you will not owe a penalty for any underpayment of estimated tax due to the supplemental premium.

The 1989 premium is $22.50 for each $150 of your income tax (with certain adjustments), up to a maximum premium of $800. The maximum premium is $1,600, however, if you are married filing a joint return and both you and your spouse are eligible for Medicare Part A. Special rules apply to married persons filing separate returns.

If you want more information, including a worksheet and tables for figuring the exact premium, get **Pub. 934,** Supplemental Medicare Premium.

Purpose of Form.—Use this form to figure and pay your estimated tax.

Estimated tax is the tax you expect to owe for the year after subtracting the tax you expect to have withheld and any credits you plan to take.

This form is primarily for first-time filers. After we receive your first payment-voucher, we will mail you a 1040-ES package. Your name, address, and social security number will be preprinted on the vouchers. You should use these vouchers in making the **remaining** payments of estimated tax for the year. Using the preprinted vouchers will speed processing, reduce the chance of error, and help us save processing costs.

This form can also be used if you did not receive "or if you lost" your 1040-ES package. Complete the appropriate payment-voucher and mail it with your payment.

A. Who Must Make Estimated Tax Payments

The rules are for U.S. citizens or residents and for residents of Puerto Rico, Virgin Islands, Guam, the Commonwealth of the Northern Mariana Islands, and American Samoa. (If you are a nonresident alien, use **Form 1040-ES (NR).**)

Generally, you must pay estimated tax if you expect to owe, after subtracting your withholding and credits, at least $500 in tax for 1989; and you expect your withholding and credits to be less than the smaller of:

1. 90% of the tax shown on your 1989 tax return, **OR**

2. 100% of the tax shown on your 1988 tax return (assuming the return covered all 12 months).

Exceptions.—Generally, you do not have to pay estimated tax if your 1989 income tax return will show (1) a tax refund, or (2) a tax balance due of less than $500. Also, you do not have to pay estimated tax if you were a U.S. citizen or resident and you had no tax liability for the full 12-month preceding tax year.

Note: *If you have to make estimated tax payments and receive salaries and wages, you may not have enough tax withheld during the year. To avoid making estimated tax payments, consider asking your employer to take more tax out of your earnings. To do this, file a new* **Form W-4,** *Employee's Withholding Allowance Certificate, with your employer to make sure you will not owe $500 or more in tax.*

B. How To Figure Your Estimated Tax

Use the Estimated Tax Worksheet on page 3, the 1989 Tax Rate Schedules and the instructions on page 4, and your 1988 tax return as a guide for figuring your estimated tax. See the 1988 Instructions for Form 1040 for information on figuring your income, deductions, and credits, including the taxable amount of **social security income.**

Note: *You may not make joint estimated tax payments if: (1) either you or your spouse is a nonresident alien, (2) you are separated under a decree of divorce or separate maintenance, or (3) you and your spouse have different tax years.*

Line 7—Additional taxes.—Enter on line 7 any additional taxes from:

● **Form 4970,** Tax on Accumulation Distribution of Trusts, **OR**

● **Form 4972,** Tax on Lump-Sum Distributions.

Line 9—Credits.—For details on credits you may take, see Form 1040, lines 41 through 46, and the related instructions.

Line 11—Self-employment tax.—If you and your spouse make joint estimated tax payments and both have self-employment income, figure the estimated self-employment tax separately. Enter the total amount on line 11.

Line 12—Other taxes.—Enter any other taxes such as recapture of investment credit, tax on premature distributions (Form 5329, Part II only), and alternative minimum tax. For details, see pages 18 and 19 of the 1988 Instructions for Form 1040. You do not have to include social security tax on tip income not reported to employer or uncollected employee social security and RRTA tax on tips.

C. How To Use the Payment-Voucher

Each payment-voucher has the date when the voucher is due for calendar year taxpayers. Please use the correct voucher.

(1) Enter your name, address, and social security number in the space provided on the payment-voucher. If you are filing a joint payment-voucher, your spouse's name and social security number should be included on the voucher.

(2) Enter the net amount of your payment on line 1 of the payment-voucher. If you paid too much tax on your 1988 Form 1040, you may have chosen to apply the overpayment to your estimated tax for 1989. If so, you may apply all or part of the overpayment to any voucher. **Send the payment-voucher to IRS ONLY when you are making a payment.**

(3) Enclose, but please do not staple or attach, your check or money order with the payment-voucher. Make the check or money order payable to "Internal Revenue Service" (not "IRS"). Write your social security number and **"1989 Form 1040-ES"** on your check or money order. **Do not** include any balance due on your Form 1040 with your check for estimated tax. Fill in the Record of Estimated Tax Payments on page 2 so you will have a record of your payments.

(4) Mail your payment-voucher to the address for the place where you live shown on page 2.

(Continued on page 2)

D. When To Pay Your Estimated Tax

In general, you must make your first estimated tax payment by April 17, 1989. The April 17th date applies whether or not you are outside the United States and Puerto Rico on April 17. You may either pay all of your estimated tax at that time or pay in four equal amounts that are due by April 17, 1989; June 15, 1989; September 15, 1989; and January 16, 1990. Exceptions to these rules are listed below.

(1) Other payment dates.—In some cases, such as a change in income, you may have to make your first estimated tax payment after April 17, 1989. The payment dates are as follows:

If the requirement to pay estimated tax is met after:	Payment date is:
• March 31 and before June 1	June 15, 1989
• May 31 and before Sept. 1	Sept. 15, 1989
• August 31	Jan. 16, 1990

Note: *You may use the "Amended Estimated Tax Schedule" on page 3 to figure your amended estimated tax.*

If the first payment you are required to make is due:

- June 15, 1989, enter ½;
- September 15, 1989, enter ¾;
- January 16, 1990, enter all of line 16 (less any 1988 overpayment applied to this installment) on line 17 of the worksheet and on line 1 of the payment-voucher.

If you file your 1989 Form 1040 by January 31, 1990, and pay the entire balance due, then you do not have to make the payment which would otherwise be due January 16, 1990.

(2) Farmers and fishermen.—If at least two-thirds of your gross income for 1988 or 1989 is from farming or fishing, you may do one of the following:

- Pay all of your estimated tax by January 16, 1990; OR
- File Form 1040 for 1989 by March 1, 1990, and pay the total tax due. In this case, you do not need to make estimated tax payments for 1989.

(3) Fiscal year.—If your return is on a fiscal year basis, your due dates are the 15th day of the 4th, 6th, and 9th months of your fiscal year and the 1st month of the following fiscal year. If any date falls on a Saturday, Sunday, or legal holiday, use the next regular workday.

E. Penalty for Not Paying Enough Estimated Tax

You may be charged a penalty for not paying enough estimated tax, or for not making the payments on time in the required amount (even if you have an overpayment on your tax return). The penalty does not apply if each required payment is timely and the total tax paid:

- Is at least 90% (66⅔% for farmers and fishermen) of the amount of income tax (including alternative minimum tax) and self-employment tax due as shown on your return for 1989, or 90% of the tax due if no return was filed;

- Is 100% of the tax shown on your return for 1988 (you must have filed a return for 1988 and it must have been for a full 12-month year); OR
- Is 90% of the tax figured by annualizing the taxable income, alternative minimum taxable income, and adjusted self-employment income received for the months ending before the due date of the installment.

Note: *The penalty may be waived under certain conditions. Get **Pub. 505**, Tax Withholding and Estimated Tax, for details.*
Caution: *You may be required to make payments of past due amounts to avoid further penalty. You may have to make these payments if you do not make your estimated tax payments on time, or if you did not pay the correct amount for a previous payment date.*
Example: *On June 1, 1989, you find out that you should have made an estimated tax payment for April 17. You should immediately fill out the payment-voucher due April 17, 1989, and send in the required amount (¼ × 1989 estimated tax).*

For more details about the penalty, get Pub. 505.

If you changed your name because of marriage, divorce, etc., and you made estimated tax payments using your old name, you should attach a brief statement to the front of your 1989 Form 1040. In it, explain all the estimated tax payments you and your spouse made for 1989, the address where you made the payments, and the name(s) and social security number(s) under which you made payments.

F. Where To File Your Payment-Voucher

Mail your payment-voucher to the Internal Revenue Service at the following address. *Do not mail your tax return to these addresses. Also do not mail your estimated tax payments to the address shown in the Forms 1040 or 1040A Package.*
Note: *For proper delivery of your estimated tax payment, you must include the P.O. Box number in the address.*

If you are located in: ▼	Use this address: ▼
New Jersey, New York (New York City and counties of Nassau, Rockland, Suffolk, and Westchester)	P.O. Box 162 Newark, NJ 07101-0162
New York (all other counties), Connecticut, Maine, Massachusetts, New Hampshire, Rhode Island, Vermont	P.O. Box 371999 Pittsburgh, PA 15250-7999
Delaware, District of Columbia, Maryland, Pennsylvania, Virginia	P.O. Box 8318 Philadelphia, PA 19162-0825
Florida, Georgia, South Carolina	P.O. Box 62001 Philadelphia, PA 19162-0300
Indiana, Kentucky, Michigan, Ohio, West Virginia	P.O. Box 7422 Chicago, IL 60682-7422
Alabama, Arkansas, Louisiana, Mississippi, North Carolina, Tennessee	P.O. Box 371300M Pittsburgh, PA 15250-7300
Illinois, Iowa, Minnesota, Missouri, Wisconsin	P.O. Box 6413 Chicago, IL 60680-6413
Kansas, New Mexico, Oklahoma, Texas	P.O. Box 970001 St. Louis, MO 63197-0001
Alaska, Arizona, California (counties of Alpine, Amador, Butte, Calaveras, Colusa, Contra Costa, Del Norte, El Dorado, Glenn, Humboldt, Lake, Lassen, Marin, Mendocino, Modoc, Napa, Nevada, Placer, Plumas, Sacramento, San Joaquin, Shasta, Sierra, Siskiyou, Solano, Sonoma, Sutter, Tehama, Trinity, Yolo, and Yuba), Colorado, Idaho, Montana, Nebraska, Nevada, North Dakota, Oregon, South Dakota, Utah, Washington, Wyoming	P.O. Box 450001 San Francisco, CA 94145-4501
California (all other counties), Hawaii	P.O. Box 54030 Los Angeles, CA 90054-0030
American Samoa	P.O. Box 8318 Philadelphia, PA 19162-0825
Guam	Commissioner of Revenue and Taxation 855 West Marine Drive Agana, GU 96910
The Commonwealth of the Northern Mariana Islands	P.O. Box 8318 Philadelphia, PA 19162-0825
Puerto Rico (or if excluding income under section 933) Virgin Islands: Nonpermanent residents	P.O. Box 8318 Philadelphia, PA 19162-0825
Virgin Islands: Permanent residents	V.I. Bureau of Internal Revenue Lockharts Garden No. 1A Charlotte Amalie St. Thomas, VI 00802
A.P.O. or F.P.O. address of:	Miami—Atlanta, GA 39901 New York—Holtsville, NY 00501 San Francisco—Fresno, CA 93888 Seattle—Ogden, UT 84201
Foreign country: U.S. citizens and those filing Form 2555 or Form 4563, even if you have an A.P.O. or F.P.O. address	P.O. Box 8318 Philadelphia, PA 19162-0825

Record of Estimated Tax Payments

Payment number	(a) Date	(b) Amount	(c) 1988 overpayment credit applied	(d) Total amount paid and credited (add (b) and (c))
1				
2				
3				
4				
Total . . . . ▶				

Note. If you are not required to make the estimated tax payment due April 17, 1989, at this time, you may have to make a payment by a later date. See Instruction D(1).

Amended Estimated Tax Schedule (Use if your estimated tax changes during the year.)

1 Amended estimated tax		**1**	
2a Amount of 1988 overpayment chosen for credit to 1989 estimated tax and applied to date	**2a**		
b Estimated tax payments to date	**2b**		
c Total of lines 2a and 2b		**2c**	
3 Unpaid balance (subtract line 2c from line 1)		**3**	
4 Amount to be paid (see Instructions D(1) and E)		**4**	

1989 Estimated Tax Worksheet (Keep for Your Records—Do Not Send to Internal Revenue Service)

1 Enter amount of Adjusted Gross Income you expect in 1989	**1**	
2 If you plan to itemize deductions, enter the estimated total of your deductions. If you do not plan to itemize deductions, see **Standard Deduction for 1989** on page 4. Enter the amount here	**2**	
3 Subtract line 2 from line 1. Enter the difference here	**3**	
4 Exemptions (multiply $2,000 times number of personal exemptions). If you are eligible to be claimed as a dependent on another person's return, your personal exemption is not allowed	**4**	
5 Subtract line 4 from line 3	**5**	
6 Tax. (Figure your tax on line 5 by using the Tax Rate Schedules on page 4. DO NOT use the Tax Table or the Tax Rate Schedules in the 1988 Form 1040 Instructions.)	**6**	
7 Enter any additional taxes (see line 7 Instructions)	**7**	
8 Add lines 6 and 7	**8**	
9 Credits (see line 9 Instructions)	**9**	
10 Subtract line 9 from line 8	**10**	
11 Self-employment tax. Estimate of 1989 self-employment income $_____; if $48,000 or more, enter $6,249.60; **If less, multiply the amount by .1302** (see line 11 Instructions for additional information).	**11**	
12 Other taxes (see line 12 Instructions).	**12**	
13a Total. Add lines 10 through 12	**13a**	
b Earned income credit and credit from **Form 4136**	**13b**	
c Total. Subtract line 13b from line 13a	**13c**	

14a Enter 90% (66 ⅔% for farmers and fishermen) of line 13c.	**14a**		
b Enter 100% of the tax shown on your 1988 tax return	**14b**		
c Enter the smaller of lines 14a or 14b. This is your required annual payment		**14c**	

Caution: Generally, if you do not prepay at least the amount on line 14c, you may be subject to a penalty for not paying enough estimated tax. To avoid a penalty, make sure your estimate on line 13c is as accurate as possible. If you are unsure of your estimate and line 14a is smaller than line 14b, you may want to pay up to the amount shown on line 14b. For more information, get Pub. 505.

15 Income tax withheld and estimated to be withheld (including income tax withholding on pensions, annuities, certain deferred income, etc.) during 1989	**15**	
16 Balance (subtract line 15 from line 14c). (**Note:** If line 13c less line 15 is less than $500, you are not required to make estimated tax payments.) If you are applying an overpayment from 1988 to 1989 estimated tax, see Instruction C(2), page 1	**16**	
17 If the first payment you are required to make is due April 17, 1989, enter ¼ of line 16 (less any 1988 overpayment that you are applying to this installment) here and on line 1 of your payment-voucher(s). You may round off cents to the nearest whole dollar	**17**	

Tax Law Changes Effective for 1989

Use your 1988 tax return as a guide in figuring your estimated tax, but be sure to consider the tax law changes noted in this section.

Itemized Deductions

Personal Interest.—For 1989, only 20% of personal interest (such as interest on car loans or credit card balances for personal expenditures) is deductible.

Standard Deduction for 1989

If you do not itemize your deductions, you may take the standard deduction instead.

For 1989, the standard deduction amounts are:

Filing Status	Standard Deduction
Married filing joint return and Qualifying widow(er)	$5,200*
Head of household	$4,550*
Single	$3,100*
Married filing separately	$2,600*

*To these amounts, add the additional amount below.

Additional Amount for the Elderly or Blind.—An additional standard deduction amount of $600 is allowed for a married individual (whether filing jointly or separately) or a qualifying widow(er) who is 65 or over or blind ($1,200 if the individual is both 65 or over and blind, $2,400 if both spouses are 65 or over and blind). An additional standard deduction amount of $750 is allowed for an unmarried individual (single or head of household) who is 65 or over or blind ($1,500 if both 65 or over and blind).

Limited Standard Deduction for Dependents.—If you can be claimed as a dependent on another person's return, your standard deduction is the greater of (a) $500 or (b) your earned income, up to the standard deduction amount. To this amount add any additional amount for the elderly or blind discussed on this page.

For more information about the standard deduction, see Pub. 505.

Personal Exemptions

Exemption Amount.—The personal exemption amount has increased to $2,000 for each individual, the individual's spouse, and each dependent.

You may not claim an exemption in 1989 for your child who is a full-time student and who has attained age 24 in 1989, unless the child's gross income for 1989 is less than $2,000. If you can not claim the exemption under this rule, the child may claim an exemption on his or her own return.

Credits

Earned Income Credit.—The maximum earned income credit is increased to $910 and the income limitation amount is increased to $19,340.

1989 Tax Rate Schedules

Caution: *Do not use these Tax Rate Schedules to figure your 1988 taxes. Use only to figure your 1989 estimated taxes.*

Schedule X—Single

If line 5 is: Over—	But not over—	The tax is:	of the amount over—
$0	$18,550	.......15%	$0
18,550	44,900	$2,782.50 + 28%	18,550
44,900	93,130	10,160.50 + 33%	44,900
93,130	....	Use **Worksheet** below to figure your tax.	

Schedule Z— Head of household

If line 5 is: Over—	But not over—	The tax is:	of the amount over—
$0	$24,850	.......15%	$0
24,850	64,200	$3,727.50+ 28%	24,850
64,200	128,810	14,745.50 + 33%	64,200
128,810	....	Use **Worksheet** below to figure your tax.	

Schedule Y-1—Married filing jointly or Qualifying widow(er)

If line 5 is: Over—	But not over—	The tax is:	of the amount over—
$0	$30,950	.......15%	$0
30,950	74,850	$4,642.50 + 28%	30,950
74,850	155,320	16,934.50 + 33%	74,850
155,320	....	Use **Worksheet** below to figure your tax.	

Schedule Y-2— Married filing separately

If line 5 is: Over—	But not over—	The tax is:	of the amount over—
$0	$15,475	.......15%	$0
15,475	37,425	$2,321.25 + 28%	15,475
37,425	117,895	8,467.25 + 33%	37,425
117,895	....	Use **Worksheet** below to figure your tax.	

Worksheet (Keep for your records)

1. If your filing status is: { Single, enter $26,076.40; Head of household, enter $36,066.80; Married filing jointly or Qualifying widow(er), enter $43,489.60; Married filing separately, enter $35,022.35 } . . . . **1.** _____

2. Enter your taxable income from line 5 of the Form 1040-ES worksheet . . . . . . **2.** _____

3. If your filing status is: { Single, enter $93,130; Head of household, enter $128,810; Married filing jointly or Qualifying widow(er), enter $155,320; Married filing separately, enter $117,895 } . . . **3.** _____

4. Subtract line 3 from line 2. Enter the result. (If the result is zero or less, use the schedule above for your filing status to figure your tax. DON'T use this worksheet.) . . . . . . **4.** _____

5. Multiply the amount on line 4 by 28% (.28). Enter the result . . . . **5.** _____

6. Multiply the amount on line 4 by 5% (.05). Enter the result . . . . . **6.** _____

7. Multiply $560 by the number of exemptions claimed. (If married filing separately, see Note below.) Enter the result . . . . **7.** _____

8. Compare the amounts on lines 6 and 7. Enter the **smaller** of the two amounts . . . . **8.** _____

9. **Tax.** Add lines 1, 5, and 8. Enter the total here and on line 6 of the Form 1040-ES worksheet . . . . . . **9.** _____

Note: *If married filing separately and you did **not** claim an exemption for your spouse, multiply $560 by the number of exemptions claimed. Add $560 to the result and enter the total on line 7 above.*

- **Tear off here** -

Form **1040-ES** | **1989**

Department of the Treasury
Internal Revenue Service

Payment-Voucher

Return this voucher with check or money order payable to the Internal Revenue Service. Please write your social security number and "1989 Form 1040-ES" on your check or money order. Please do not send cash. Enclose, but do not staple or attach, your payment with this voucher. File only if you are making a payment of estimated tax.	OMB No. 1545-0087 Expires 8-31-91 (Calendar year—Due Jan. 16, 1990)

		Your first name and initial	Your last name	Your social security number
1 Amount of payment $ - - - - - - - - - - - - - - - -	Please type or print	(If joint payment, complete for spouse) Spouse's first name and initial	Spouse's last name if different from yours	If joint payment, spouse's social security number
2 Fiscal year filers enter year ending - - - - - - - - - - - - - - (month and year)		Address (number and street)		
		City, state, and ZIP code		

For Paperwork Reduction Act Notice, see instructions on page 1.

Page 5

Form **1040-ES**

Department of the Treasury
Internal Revenue Service

1989
Payment-
Voucher

Return this voucher with check or money order payable to the Internal Revenue Service.
Please write your social security number and "1989 Form 1040-ES" on your check or
money order. Please do not send cash. Enclose, but do not staple or attach, your payment
with this voucher.
File only if you are making a payment of estimated tax.

OMB No. 1545-0087
Expires 8-31-91

(Calendar year—Due Sept. 15, 1989)

1 Amount of payment
$ _ _ _ _ _ _ _ _ _ _ _ _ _
2 Fiscal year filers
enter year ending

_ _ _ _ _ _ _ _ _ _ _ _ _
(month and year)

Please type or print

Your first name and initial	Your last name	Your social security number
(If joint payment, complete for spouse) Spouse's first name and initial	Spouse's last name if different from yours	If joint payment, spouse's social security number
Address (number and street)		
City, state, and ZIP code		

For Paperwork Reduction Act Notice, see instructions on page 1.

Tear off here

Form **1040-ES**

Department of the Treasury
Internal Revenue Service

1989
Payment-
Voucher

Return this voucher with check or money order payable to the Internal Revenue Service.
Please write your social security number and "1989 Form 1040-ES" on your check or
money order. Please do not send cash. Enclose, but do not staple or attach, your payment
with this voucher.
File only if you are making a payment of estimated tax.

OMB No. 1545-0087
Expires 8-31-91

(Calendar year—Due June 15, 1989)

1 Amount of payment
$ _ _ _ _ _ _ _ _ _ _ _ _ _
2 Fiscal year filers
enter year ending

_ _ _ _ _ _ _ _ _ _ _ _ _
(month and year)

Please type or print

Your first name and initial	Your last name	Your social security number
(If joint payment, complete for spouse) Spouse's first name and initial	Spouse's last name if different from yours	If joint payment, spouse's social security number
Address (number and street)		
City, state, and ZIP code		

For Paperwork Reduction Act Notice, see instructions on page 1.

Tear off here

Form **1040-ES**

Department of the Treasury
Internal Revenue Service

1989
Payment-
Voucher

Return this voucher with check or money order payable to the Internal Revenue Service.
Please write your social security number and "1989 Form 1040-ES" on your check or
money order. Please do not send cash. Enclose, but do not staple or attach, your payment
with this voucher.
File only if you are making a payment of estimated tax.

OMB No. 1545-0087
Expires 8-31-91

(Calendar year—Due April 17, 1989)

1 Amount of payment
$ _ _ _ _ _ _ _ _ _ _ _ _ _
2 Fiscal year filers
enter year ending

_ _ _ _ _ _ _ _ _ _ _ _ _
(month and year)

Please type or print

Your first name and initial	Your last name	Your social security number
(If joint payment, complete for spouse) Spouse's first name and initial	Spouse's last name if different from yours	If joint payment, spouse's social security number
Address (number and street)		
City, state, and ZIP code		

For Paperwork Reduction Act Notice, see instructions on page 1.

Form **2106** Department of the Treasury Internal Revenue Service	**Employee Business Expenses** ▶ See separate Instructions. ▶ Attach to Form 1040.	OMB No. 1545-0139 19**88** Attachment Sequence No. **54**

Your name	Social security number	Occupation in which expenses were incurred

Part I   **Employee Business Expenses**

STEP 1 Enter Your Expenses		Column A Other than Meals and Entertainment		Column B Meals and Entertainment	
1 Vehicle expense from Part II, line 15 or line 22	1				
2 Parking fees, tolls, and local transportation, including train, bus, etc. . .	2				
3 Travel expense while away from home, including lodging, airplane, car rental, etc. **Do not** include meals and entertainment	3				
4 Business expenses not included in lines 1 through 3. **Do not** include meals and entertainment	4				
5 Meals and entertainment expenses. (See Instructions.)	5				
6 Add lines 1 through 5 and enter the **total expenses** here	6				

Note: *If you were not reimbursed for any expenses in Step 1, skip lines 7–13 and enter the amount from line 6 on line 14.*

STEP 2   Figure Any Excess Reimbursements To Report in Income

7 Reimbursements for the expenses listed in Step 1 that your employer did **not** report to you on Form W-2 or Form 1099	7				
Note: *If, in **both columns**, line 6 is more than line 7, skip lines 8 and 9 and go to line 10. You do not have excess reimbursements.*					
8 Subtract line 6 from line 7. If zero or less, enter zero	8				
9 Add the amounts on line 8 of both columns and enter the total here. This is an **excess reimbursement** reportable as income. **Add this amount to any amount shown on Form 1040, line 7** . . . . . . ▶	9				

STEP 3   Figure Fully Deductible Reimbursed Expenses

10 Subtract line 7 from line 6. If zero or less, enter zero	10				
11 Reimbursements or allowances for the expenses in Step 1 that your employer identified to you, included on Form W-2 or Form 1099, and were not subject to withholding tax	11				
Note: *The amount entered on line 11 must be reported as income on Form 1040.*					
12 Enter the smaller of line 10 or line 11	12				
13 Add the amounts on line 12 of both columns and enter the total here. This is your **fully deductible reimbursed expenses. Also enter the total on Form 1040, line 24** . . . . ▶	13				

STEP 4   Figure Unreimbursed Expenses To Deduct on Schedule A (Form 1040)

14 Subtract line 12 from line 10	14				
Note: *If both columns of line 14 are zero, stop here.*					
15 Enter 20% (.20) of line 14, Column B	15				
16 Subtract line 15 from line 14	16				
17 Add the amounts on line 16 of both columns and enter the total here. **Also enter the total on Schedule A (Form 1040), line 20.** (Qualified Performing Artists and handicapped employees, see Instructions.) ▶	17				

For Paperwork Reduction Act Notice, see Instructions.   Form **2106** (1988)

Part II   Vehicle Expenses (Use either your actual expenses (Section C) or the standard mileage rate (Section B).)

Section A.—General Information

		Vehicle 1	Vehicle 2
1 Enter the date vehicle was placed in service	**1**	/ /	/ /
2 Total mileage vehicle was used during 1988	**2**	miles	miles
3 Miles included on line 2 that vehicle was used for business . . .	**3**	miles	miles
4 Percent of business use (divide line 3 by line 2)	**4**	%	%
5 Average daily round trip commuting distance	**5**	miles	miles
6 Miles included on line 2 that vehicle was used for commuting . .	**6**	miles	miles
7 Other personal mileage (subtract line 6 plus line 3 from line 2) . .	**7**	miles	miles

8 Do you (or your spouse) have another vehicle available for personal purposes? . . . . ☐ Yes   ☐ No

9 If your employer provided you with a vehicle, is personal use during off duty hours permitted? . . . ☐ Yes   ☐ No   ☐ Not applicable

10 Do you have evidence to support your deduction? ☐ Yes   ☐ No. If "Yes," is the evidence written? ☐ Yes   ☐ No

Section B.—Standard Mileage Rate (Do not use this section unless you own the vehicle.)

11 Enter the smaller of Part II, line 3, or 15,000 miles	**11**	miles
12 Subtract line 11 from Part II, line 3	**12**	miles
13 Multiply line 11 by 24¢ (.24) (see Instructions if vehicle is fully depreciated)	**13**	
14 Multiply line 12 by 11¢ (.11)	**14**	
15 Add lines 13 and 14. Enter total here and on Part I, line 1	**15**	

Section C.—Actual Expenses

		Vehicle 1		Vehicle 2	
16 Gasoline, oil, repairs, vehicle insurance, etc	**16**				
17 Vehicle rentals	**17**				
18 Value of employer-provided vehicle (applies only if included on Form W-2 at 100% fair rental value, see Instructions)	**18**				
19 Add lines 16 through 18	**19**				
20 Multiply line 19 by the percentage on Part II, line 4	**20**				
21 Depreciation from Section D, column (f) (see Instructions) . . .	**21**				
22 Add lines 20 and 21. Enter total here and on Part I, line 1 . . .	**22**				

Section D.—Depreciation of Vehicles (You can only claim depreciation for a vehicle you own. If you use a vehicle 50 percent or less in a trade or business, you cannot claim the Section 179 deduction and you must figure depreciation using the straight line method over 5 years. For other limitations, see Instructions.)

	Cost or other basis (a)	Basis for depreciation (Business use only—see Instructions) (b)	Method of figuring depreciation (c)	Depreciation deduction (d)	Section 179 expense (e)	Total column (d) + column (e) (enter in Section C, line 21) (f)
Vehicle 1						
Vehicle 2						

Form **2119**	**Sale of Your Home**	OMB No. 1545–0072
Department of the Treasury Internal Revenue Service	▶ See Separate Instructions ▶ Attach to Form 1040 for year of sale.	**1988** Attachment Sequence No. **22**

Please Type or Print	Your first name and initial (If joint, also give spouse's name and initial.)	Last name	Your social security number
	Present home address (no., street, and apt. no., or rural route) (or P.O. box no. if mail is not delivered to street address)		Spouse's social security number
	City, town, or post office, state, and ZIP code		

Part I Facts About You and Your Home

1a Date former main home was sold ▶

b Enter the face amount of any mortgage, note (for example, second trust), or other financial instrument on which you will receive periodic payments of principal or interest from this sale. (See Instructions for line 1b.) ▶ $

		Yes	**No**
2a	Have you bought or built a new main home?		
b	Are any rooms in either main home rented out or used for business for which a deduction is allowed? . . . . . (If "Yes," see Instructions.)		
3a	Were you 55 or older on date of sale?		
b	Was your spouse 55 or older on date of sale? . . . . **If you answered "No" to 3a and 3b, do not complete 3c through 3f or Part III.**		
c	Did the person who answered "Yes" to 3a or 3b own and use the property sold as a main home for a total of at least 3 years (except for short absences) of the 5-year period before the sale?		
d	**If you answered "Yes" to 3c, do you choose to take the one-time exclusion of the gain on the sale?**		
e	At time of sale, who owned the home? ☐ you ☐ your spouse ☐ both of you		
f	Social security number of spouse, at time of sale, if different from above ▶ (Enter "None" if you were not married at time of sale.)		

Part II Figure Your Gain (Do not include amounts that you deduct as moving expenses.)

4	Selling price of home. (Do not include personal property items.)	**4**	
5	Expense of sale. (Include sales commissions, advertising, legal, etc.)	**5**	
6	Subtract line 5 from line 4. This is the amount realized	**6**	
7	Basis of home sold	**7**	
8a	Subtract line 7 from line 6 (gain on sale). If zero or less, enter zero and do not complete the rest of the form. Enter the gain from this line on Schedule D, line 3 or 10,* unless you bought another main home or checked "Yes" to 3d. Then continue with this form	**8a**	
b	If you haven't replaced your home, do you plan to do so within the replacement period? . . . . ☐ Yes ☐ No (If "Yes," see Instructions under When and Where To File.)		

Part III If Age 55 or Older, Figure Your One-Time Exclusion *(Complete this part only if you checked "Yes" to 3d.)*

9	Enter the **smaller** of line 8a or $125,000 ($62,500, if married filing separate return) (see Instructions)	**9**	
10	Subtract line 9 from line 8a (gain). If zero, do not complete rest of form. Enter the gain from this line on Schedule D, line 10,* unless you bought another main home. Then continue with this form . . .	**10**	

Part IV Figure Gain To Be Postponed and Adjusted Basis of New Home *(Complete this part if you bought another main home.)*

11	Fixing-up expenses. (See Instructions for time limits.)	**11**	
12	Subtract line 11 from line 6 (adjusted sales price)	**12**	
13a	Cost of new home	**13a**	
b	Enter the date you moved into your new main home ▶ ---------------------------		
14	Subtract line 13a plus line 9 (if applicable) from line 12. If result is zero or less, enter zero. Do not enter more than line 8a or line 10 (if applicable). This is the gain taxable this year. Enter the gain from this line on Schedule D, line 3 or 10*.	**14**	
15	Subtract line 14 from line 8a. **However,** if you completed Part III, subtract line 14 from line 10. (This is the gain to be postponed.)	**15**	
16	Subtract line 15 from line 13 (adjusted basis of new main home)	**16**	

*Caution: If you completed Form 6252 for the home in 1a, do not enter your taxable gain from Form 2119 on Schedule D.

Please Sign Here	Under penalties of perjury, I declare that I have examined this form, including attachments, and to the best of my knowledge and belief, it is true, correct, and complete.	
	Your signature Date	Spouse's Signature Date
	▶	▶
	(If joint return, both must sign.) (Sign and date only **if not** attached to your tax return.)	

For Paperwork Reduction Act Notice, see separate Instructions.   Form **2119** (1988)

1988 Department of the Treasury
Internal Revenue Service

Instructions for Form 2119
Sale of Your Home
(Section references are to the Internal Revenue Code.)

Paperwork Reduction Act Notice.—We ask for this information to carry out the Internal Revenue laws of the United States. We need it to ensure that taxpayers are complying with these laws and to allow us to figure and collect the right amount of tax. You are required to give us this information.

The time needed to complete and file this form will vary depending on individual circumstances. The estimated average time is:

Recordkeeping	46 min.
Learning about the law or the form	10 min.
Preparing the form	42 min.
Copying, assembling, and sending the form to IRS	20 min.

If you have comments concerning the accuracy of these time estimates or suggestions for making this form more simple, we would be happy to hear from you. You can write to the **Internal Revenue Service,** Washington, DC 20224, Attention: IRS Reports Clearance Officer, TR:FP; or the **Office of Management and Budget,** Paperwork Reduction Project, Washington, DC 20503.

Who Must File.—You must use Form 2119 to report the sale of your main home even if you had a loss. If you had a gain, use this form to postpone paying tax on it. If you were age 55 or older on the date you sold your home and certain other conditions are met, you can choose to exclude all or part of the gain from your income. See the instructions for Part III.

If you sold your home on the installment method, complete **Form 6252,** Installment Sale Income, and Form 2119.

Get **Pub. 523,** Tax Information on Selling Your Home, for more information.

Main Home.—You file Form 2119 only for the sale of your main home. It can be a house, a houseboat, housetrailer, cooperative apartment, condominium, etc. If you have more than one home, your main home is the one you live in most of the time.

Replacement Period for Postponing Gain.—If you buy or build, and move into another main home within the replacement period, you must usually postpone paying tax on all or part of the gain. (See instructions for Part IV.) The replacement period is 48 months. It runs from 2 years before to 2 years after you sell your former home.

If at the time or after you sell your former main home, you are on active duty in the U.S. Armed Forces for more than 90 days, or if you live and work outside the U.S., you have a longer replacement period. Get Pub. 523 for details.

When and Where To File.—File Form 2119 with your tax return for the year of sale even if you did not replace your home.

If you plan to replace the home, but have not done so by the time you file your return, complete lines 1 and 2 and Part II only. Do not enter on Schedule D the gain from line 8a of Form 2119. See the following instructions for filing a second Form 2119.

If you had a gain on the sale and did not replace your home by the time you file your tax return, you may have to file a second Form 2119 at a later date. The following tells when another Form 2119 is required and how to file it.

● File a second Form 2119 if, after you file your return, you replace your home within the replacement period.

If the new home costs at least as much as the adjusted sales price of the old home (line 12), no tax is due. But, you must still file the form. Send it to the place you would file your next tax return based on the address where you live. You must enter your name, address, signature, and the date, since the form will not be attached to your return.

If the new home costs less than the adjusted sales price of the old home (line 12), part of your gain will have to be included in income for the year of sale. In this case, amend your tax return for the year of sale using **Form 1040X,** Amended U.S. Individual Income Tax Return. Fill out and attach Form 2119 to Form 1040X, along with Schedule D (Form 1040) showing the gain. Interest will be charged on any additional tax due.

● If, when you filed your return, you had planned to replace your home within the replacement period, but later you did not do so, your entire gain is taxable for the year of sale. Amend your tax return for that year using Form 1040X. Fill out and attach Form 2119 to Form 1040X, along with Schedule D (Form 1040) showing the gain.

● If, when you filed your return, you paid taxes on the gain because you had not planned to replace your residence, but you later did replace it within the replacement period, you can claim a refund for part or all of those taxes. Claim the refund by filing Form 1040X for the year of sale. Attach Form 2119.

Part III—One-Time Exclusion for People Age 55 or Older.—Generally, you can choose to exclude from your income up to $125,000 ($62,500 if married filing a separate return) of the gain from the sale of your main home. (See the instructions for line 9.) You make this choice by answering "Yes" to question 3d in Part I, and by filling in Part III. But, you must meet all of the following tests:

1. You or your spouse were age 55 or older on the date of sale.

2. Neither you nor your spouse has made this choice before.

3. The person who was age 55 or older owned and lived in your home for periods adding up to at least 3 years within the 5 years ending on the date of sale.

As long as you meet the above tests, you can choose the exclusion for the sale of any main home you wish. However, you can make the choice only once in your lifetime.

The gain you exclude is never taxed. But, if the gain is more than the amount you are allowed to exclude, the excess is either included in your income in the year of sale, or it is postponed as explained in Part IV. Generally, you can make or revoke the choice within 3 years from the due date (including extensions) of your tax return for the year of sale. Use Form 1040X with Form 2119 attached to amend your return.

Married Taxpayers. If you and your spouse own the property jointly and file a joint return, only one of you must meet the age, ownership, and use tests to be able to make the choice. If you do not own the property jointly, the spouse who owns the property must meet these tests.

If you are married at the time of sale, both you and your spouse must agree to exclude the gain. If you do not file a joint return with that spouse, your spouse must agree to exclude the gain by signing a statement saying, "I agree to the Part III election." The statement and signature may be made on a separate piece of paper or in the bottom margin of Form 2119.

If you sell a home while you are married, and one spouse already made an election prior to the marriage, neither of you can exclude gain on the sale.

The choice to exclude gain does not apply separately to you and your spouse. If you choose to exclude gain during marriage and later divorce, neither of you can make the choice again.

Part IV—Postponing Gain.—If you buy or build, and move into another main home within the replacement period, you must usually postpone paying tax on all or part of the gain. If your new home costs at least as much as the adjusted sales price (line 12) of your old home, you must postpone paying tax on the entire gain. If it costs less, in most cases you must postpone paying tax on part of the gain.

If you sell your new home in a later year and do not replace it, the gain on which you postponed the tax will be taxed then. If you do replace it, you must continue to postpone paying tax on the gain. If you bought more than one home during the replacement period, only the last one you bought qualifies as your new home for postponing the tax.

During the replacement period, any sale after the first one does not qualify for postponing tax, unless you sold the home because of a job change and you qualify for a moving expense deduction. Get **Pub. 521,** Moving Expenses, for details.

Applying Separate Gain to Basis of New Home.—If the old home was owned by only one spouse, but you and your spouse own the new home jointly, you and your spouse may elect to divide the gain and the adjusted basis. If you owned the old home jointly, and you own new homes separately, you may elect to divide the gain to be postponed. In both situations, you both must:

1. Use the old and new homes as your main homes; and

2. Sign a statement that says, "We agree to reduce the basis of the new home(s) by the gain from selling the old home(s)." This statement can be made in the bottom margin of Form 2119 or on an attached sheet. If both of you do not sign, you must figure gain to be taxed in the regular way without allocation.

Line-by-Line Instructions

Line 1b.—If you report the sale of your home on Form 6252, using the installment method, fill out Form 2119 first. Do not enter the taxable gain from line 8a of Form 2119 on Schedule D (Form 1040).

Line 2b.—If you rent out any rooms, or use part of your home for business for which you take a deduction on your tax return, check "Yes." Report the part of the gain that applies to such use on **Form 4797,** Sales of Business Property, and subtract it from line 8a or line 10 of Form 2119. You cannot postpone tax or take the exclusion on the part of the gain that is reported on Form 4797.

Line 4—Selling Price of Home.—Enter the amount of money you received, plus the amount of all notes, mortgages, or other debts that are part of the sale, and the fair market value of any other property you received.

Note: *Report interest received on a note as income for the tax year in which you received it.*

Line 5—Expense of Sale.—Enter your expense of sale, such as commissions, advertising expenses, attorney and legal fees, you paid in selling the old home. Loan charges, such as points charged the seller, are selling expenses.

Line 7—Basis of Home Sold.—Include the original cost of the home, commissions, and other expenses you paid when you bought the home, plus the cost of improvements. Subtract any depreciation, casualty losses, or energy credits you took on your tax return(s), and the postponed gain on the sale or exchange of a previous home. Get **Pub. 551,** Basis of Assets, for details.

Line 9—One-Time Exclusions.—Enter the smaller of the gain on line 8a or $125,000 ($62,500 if you are married filing a separate return). However, see Pub. 523 if either of the following is true:

● Before you and your spouse were married, either of you sold a home and was age 55 or older at the time of that sale.

● You are now single but sold a home while you were married, and at the time of sale, you or your spouse was age 55 or older.

Line 11—Fixing-Up Expenses.—These are expenses for decorating and repairing to help sell your old home. Include on line 11 only expenses for work performed within 90 days before the contract to sell was signed **and** that you paid for within 30 days after the sale. Do not include capital expenses for permanent improvements or replacements. These are added to the basis of the property sold.

Line 13—Cost of New Home.—The cost of your new home includes one or more of the following:

(a) cash payments;

(b) the amount of any mortgage or other debt on the new home;

(c) commissions and other purchase expenses you paid that were not deducted as moving expenses;

(d) construction costs made within 2 years before and 2 years after the sale of the old home (when you build your own home, do not include the value of your own labor);

(e) if you buy rather than build your new home, all capital expenses made within 2 years before and 2 years after the sale of the old home.

Name and Signature.—Enter your name and social security number. You do not need to enter your address or to sign and date Form 2119 if you attach it to your Form 1040 or Form 1040X. But, you must enter your address, sign, and date it if you send it in by itself. If this Form 2119 is for you and your spouse, you both must sign it.

Form **2120** (Rev. August 1988)	Department of the Treasury—Internal Revenue Service **Multiple Support Declaration**	OMB No. 1545-0071 Expires 6-30-91 Attachment Sequence No. **50**

During the calendar year 19 _____ , I paid more than 10% of the support of

_____
(Name of person)

I could have claimed this person as a dependent except that I did not pay more than 50% of his or her support. I understand that this person is being claimed as a dependent on the income tax return of

_____
(Name)

_____
(Address)

I agree not to claim an exemption for this person on my Federal income tax return for any tax year that began in this calendar year.

_____   _____
(Your signature)   (Your social security number)

_____   _____
(Date)   (Address)

For Paperwork Reduction Act Notice, see back of form.   Form **2120** (Rev. 8-88)

Form 2120 (Rev. 8-88)   Page **2**

Instructions

Paperwork Reduction Act Notice.—We ask for this information to carry out the Internal Revenue Laws of the United States. We need it to ensure that taxpayers are complying with these laws and to allow us to figure and collect the right amount of tax. You are required to give us this information.

The estimated average time needed to complete this form, depending on individual circumstances, is 5 minutes. If you have comments concerning the accuracy of this time estimate or suggestions for making this form more simple, we would be happy to hear from you. You can write either IRS or the Office of Management and Budget at the addresses listed in the instructions of the tax return with which this form is filed.

Purpose.—When two or more persons together pay over 50% of a dependent's support, Form 2120 is used to allow one person to claim the dependent for tax purposes.

General Information.—To claim an exemption for a dependent, you must pay over 50% of the person's living expenses (support). However, sometimes no one person pays over 50%. Instead, two or more people do as a group. If each could have claimed the dependent but for the 50% support rule, then one person in the group can still claim the dependent.

All people who paid more than 10% of the support should decide who will claim the dependent. If you are chosen, you can claim the dependent if:

● you paid over 10% of the support, AND

● all others who paid over 10% agree not to claim the dependent.

How to File.—The people who agree not to claim the dependent do so by each signing Form 2120. They give the signed forms to the person who does claim the dependent.

If you are the one who claims the dependent, attach all Forms 2120 from the others to YOUR return. You must meet all of the other rules for claiming dependents. See **Pub. 501,** Exemptions, Standard Deduction, and Filing Information.

Form **2210**	**Underpayment of**	OMB No. 1545-0140

Form **2210**
Department of the Treasury
Internal Revenue Service (X)

**Underpayment of
Estimated Tax by Individuals and Fiduciaries**
▶ **See separate instructions.**
▶ **Attach to Form 1040 or Form 1041.**

OMB No. 1545-0140
19**88**
Attachment Sequence No. **39**

Name(s) as shown on tax return | Identifying number

Note: *In most cases, IRS can figure the penalty for you and you do not have to complete this form. See the separate instructions for more information.*

Part I   Figuring Your Underpayment

1 1988 tax after credits (from Form 1040, line 47 or Form 1041, Schedule G, line 4) . . . . | **1**
2 Other taxes (see instructions). . . . . | **2**

3 Add lines 1 and 2 . . . . | **3**
4 Earned income credit . . . . | **4**
5 Credit for Federal tax on fuels . . . . | **5**

6 Add lines 4 and 5 . . . . | **6**

7 Subtract line 6 from line 3 . . . . | **7**
8 Multiply line 7 by 90% (.90) . . . . | **8**
9 Withholding taxes from 1988 Form 1040, lines 54 and 58 (or Form 1041, line 24e). (Include any credit from Form 4469.) . . . . | **9**

10 Subtract line 9 from line 7. If the result is less than $500, do not complete this form. You do not owe the penalty . . . . | **10**
11 Enter your 1987 tax. (**Caution:** *See instructions.*) . . . . | **11**
12 Enter the smaller of line 8 or line 11 . . . . | **12**
    If line 9 is equal to or more than line 12, do not complete this form. You do not owe the penalty.

		Payment Due Dates			
		(a) Apr. 15, 1988	(b) June 15, 1988	(c) Sept. 15, 1988	(d) Jan. 15, 1989
13	Divide line 12 by four (4) and enter the result in each column. However, if you use the annualized income installment method, complete the worksheet in the instructions and enter the amount from line 26 in each column of line 13. Also check this box ▶ ☐ and attach a copy of the worksheet **13**				

Complete lines 14 through 21 for one column before completing the next column.

| 14 | Estimated tax paid and tax withheld. For column (a) only, enter the amount from line 14 on line 18 (see instructions) . . . . **14** | | | | |

If line 14 is equal to or more than line 13 for all payment periods, do not complete the rest of this form. However, if you used the annualized income installment method, you must attach Form 2210 and the worksheet to your return.

15	Enter amount, if any, from line 21 of previous column **15**				
16	Add lines 14 and 15 . . . . **16**				
17	Add amounts on lines 19 and 20 of the previous column and enter the result **17**				
18	Enter line 16 minus line 17. If zero or less, enter zero. (For column (a) only, enter the amount from line 14.) . **18**				
19	Remaining underpayment from previous period. If the amount on line 18 is zero, subtract line 16 from line 17 and enter the result. Otherwise, enter zero **19**				
20	UNDERPAYMENT. If line 13 is larger than or equal to line 18, enter line 13 minus line 18. Then go to line 14 of next column. Otherwise, go to line 21 . . . . . . **20**				
21	OVERPAYMENT. If line 18 is larger than line 13, enter line 18 minus line 13. Then go to line 14 of next column . **21**				

For Paperwork Reduction Act Notice, see page 1 of separate instructions.

Form **2210** (1988)

Form 2210 (1988)   Page **2**

Part II   **Figuring the Penalty**

		Payment Due Dates			
		(a) Apr. 15, 1988	(b) June 15, 1988	(c) Sept. 15, 1988	(d) Jan. 15, 1989
22	Underpayment from line 20, page 1	**22**			
	Rate Period 1 – 10% (April 15, 1988—September 30, 1988)				
23a	Computation starting date for this period	**23a** Apr. 15, 1988	June 15, 1988	Sept. 15, 1988	
b	Number of days FROM the date on line 23a TO the date line 22 was paid or September 30, 1988, whichever is earlier	**23b** Days	Days	Days	
c	$\dfrac{\text{Number of days on line 23b}}{366} \times 10\% \times$ underpayment on line 22 (see instructions) .	**23c** $	$	$	
	Rate Period 2 – 11% (October 1, 1988—December 31, 1988)				
24a	Computation starting date for this period	**24a** Sept. 30, 1988	Sept. 30, 1988	Sept. 30, 1988	
b	Number of days FROM the date on line 24a TO the date line 22 was paid or December 31, 1988, whichever is earlier	**24b** Days	Days	Days	
c	$\dfrac{\text{Number of days on line 24b}}{366} \times 11\% \times$ underpayment on line 22 (see instructions) .	**24c** $	$	$	
	Rate Period 3 – 11% (January 1, 1989—April 15, 1989)				
25a	Computation starting date for this period	**25a** Dec. 31, 1988	Dec. 31, 1988	Dec. 31, 1988	Jan. 15, 1989
		Days	Days	Days	Days
b	Number of days FROM the date on line 25a TO the date line 22 was paid or April 15, 1989, whichever is earlier .	**25b**			
c	$\dfrac{\text{Number of days on line 25b}}{365} \times 11\% \times$ underpayment on line 22 (see instructions) .	**25c** $	$	$	$

26 PENALTY. (Add all amounts on lines 23c, 24c, and 25c in all columns and enter the total.) Form 1040 filers, enter the amount from line 26 in the space provided on Form 1040, line 65, and check the box on that line. Form 1041 filers, enter the amount from line 26 in the space provided on Form 1041, line 29 and check the box on that line . . . . **26** $

Form **2441**	**Credit for Child and Dependent Care Expenses**	OMB No. 1545-0068
Department of the Treasury Internal Revenue Service	▶ **Attach to Form 1040.** ▶ **See instructions below.**	19**88** Attachment Sequence No. **23**

Name(s) as shown on Form 1040 | Your social security number

Note: *If you paid cash wages of $50 or more in a calendar quarter to an individual for services performed in your home, you must file an employment tax return. Get **Form 942** for details.*

1 Enter number of qualifying persons who were cared for in 1988. (See instructions for definition of qualifying persons.) ▶ | **1**
Caution: *To qualify, the person(s) **must** have shared the same home with you in 1988.*

2 Enter the amount of **qualified** expenses you incurred and actually paid in 1988 for the care of the qualifying person. (See **What Are Qualified Expenses?** in the instructions.) **Do not** enter more than $2,400 ($4,800 if you paid for the care of two or more qualifying persons) . . . . | **2**

3a You **must** enter your earned income on line 3a. See line 3 instructions for definition of earned income | **3a**

b If you are married, filing a joint return for 1988, you must enter your spouse's earned income on line 3b. (If spouse is a full-time student or is disabled, see the line 3 instructions for amount to enter.) . . | **3b**

c If you are married filing a joint return, compare the amounts on lines 3a and 3b, and enter the **smaller** of the two amounts on line 3c . . . . | **3c**

4 • If you were unmarried at the end of 1988, compare the amounts on lines 2 and 3a, and enter the **smaller** of the two amounts on line 4.
• If you are married filing a joint return, compare the amounts on lines 2 and 3c, and enter the **smaller** of the two amounts on line 4. | **4**

5 Enter decimal amount from table below that applies to the adjusted gross income on Form 1040, line 31 | **5** | × .

If line 31 is:		Decimal amount is:	If line 31 is:		Decimal amount is:
Over—	But not over—		Over—	But not over—	
$0–10,000		.30	$20,000–22,000		.24
10,000–12,000		.29	22,000–24,000		.23
12,000–14,000		.28	24,000–26,000		.22
14,000–16,000		.27	26,000–28,000		.21
16,000–18,000		.26	28,000		.20
18,000–20,000		.25			

6 Multiply the amount on line 4 by the decimal amount on line 5, and enter the result . . . . . . | **6**

7 Multiply any child and dependent care expenses for 1987 that you paid in 1988 by the percentage that applies to the adjusted gross income on your 1987 Form 1040, line 31, or Form 1040A, line 13. Enter the result. (See line 7 instructions for the required statement.) . . . . | **7**

8 Add amounts on lines 6 and 7. See the worksheet in the instructions for line 8 for the amount of credit you can claim . . . . | **8**

General Instructions

Paperwork Reduction Act Notice.—We ask for this information to carry out the Internal Revenue laws of the United States. We need it to ensure that taxpayers are complying with these laws and to allow us to figure and collect the right amount of tax. You are required to give us this information.

The time needed to complete and file this form will vary depending on individual circumstances. The estimated average time is:

Recordkeeping	20 minutes
Learning about the law or the form	11 minutes
Preparing the form	16 minutes
Copying, assembling, and sending the form to IRS	17 minutes

If you have comments concerning the accuracy of these time estimates or suggestions for making this form more simple, we would be happy to hear from you. You can write to either IRS or the Office of Management and Budget at the addresses listed in the instructions of Form 1040.

What Is the Child and Dependent Care Expenses Credit?

You may be able to take this credit if you paid someone to care for your child or other qualifying person so you could work or look for work in 1988. The credit may be as much as $720 ($1,440 if two or more qualifying persons were cared for).

Additional information.—For more details, please get **Pub. 503,** Child and Dependent Care Credit.

Who Is a Qualifying Person?

A qualifying person is:
• Any person under age 15 whom you claim as a dependent (but see **Children of divorced or separated parents**).
• Your disabled spouse who is mentally or physically unable to care for himself or herself.
• Any disabled person who is mentally or physically unable to care for himself or herself and whom you claim as a dependent, or could claim as a dependent except that he or she had income of $1,950 or more.

Children of divorced or separated parents.—If you were divorced, legally separated, or lived apart from your spouse during the last 6 months of 1988, you may be able to claim the credit even if your child is not your dependent. If your child is not

your dependent, he or she is a qualifying person if **all five** of the following apply:
1. You had custody of the child for the longer period during the year; and
2. The child received over half of his or her support from one or both of the parents; and
3. The child was in the custody of one or both of the parents over half of the year; and
4. The child was under age 15, or was physically or mentally unable to care for himself or herself; and
5. The child is not your dependent because—
a. As the custodial parent, you have signed **Form 8332,** or a similar statement, agreeing not to claim the child's exemption for 1988; or
b. You were divorced or separated before 1985 and your divorce decree or written agreement states that the other parent can claim the child's exemption, and the other parent provides at least $600 in child support during the year. **Note:** *This rule does not apply if your decree or agreement was changed after 1984 to specify that the other parent cannot claim the child's exemption.*

Who May Take the Credit?

To claim the credit, **all five** of the following must apply:

(Continued on back)

Form **2441** (1988)

1. You paid for the care so you (and your spouse if you were married) could work or look for work (but see **Spouse who is a full-time student or is disabled**).

2. You and the qualifying person(s) lived in the same home.

3. You (and your spouse if you were married) paid over half the cost of keeping up your home. The cost includes: rent; mortgage interest; property taxes; utilities; home repairs; and food eaten at home.

4. The person you paid to provide the care was not your spouse or a person you could claim as a dependent.

Note: *If you paid your child to provide the care, he or she must have been 19 or older by the end of 1988.*

5. If you were married at the end of 1988, generally, you must file a joint tax return. But you will be treated as unmarried and still be eligible to take the credit if:

a. You were legally separated; or

b. You were living apart from your spouse during the last 6 months of the year, the qualifying person lived with you in your home over 6 months, and you provided over half the cost of keeping up your home.

What Are Qualified Expenses?

Qualified expenses include amounts paid for household services and care of the qualifying person while you work or look for work. Child support payments are **not** qualified expenses.

Household services.—These services must be needed to care for the qualifying person as well as to run the home. They include, for example, the services of a cook, maid, babysitter, housekeeper, or cleaning person if the services were partly for the care of the qualifying person. Do not include services of a chauffeur or gardener.

Note: *If you paid cash wages of $1,000 or more for household services in any calendar quarter in 1987 or 1988, you should file a* **Form 940** *for 1988 by January 31, 1989.*

Care of the qualifying person.—Care includes the cost of services for the qualifying person's well-being and protection. It does not include the cost of clothing or entertainment.

You may count care provided outside your home if the care was for your dependent under age 15, or any other qualifying person who regularly spends at least 8 hours a day in your home.

Generally, care does not include food or schooling expenses. However, if these items are included as part of the total care, and they are incident to, and cannot be separated from, the total cost, you may count the total payment. However, you may not count the cost of schooling for a child in the first grade or above, or the expenses for sending your child to an overnight camp.

Medical expenses.—Some dependent care expenses may qualify as medical expenses. If you itemize deductions, you may want to take all or part of these medical expenses on Schedule A (Form 1040). Get Pub. 503 for details.

Specific Instructions

Line 2. Dollar limit.—Enter the amount of qualified expenses you incurred and actually paid in 1988. But the most you may figure the credit on is $2,400 a year for one qualifying person, or $4,800 a year for two or more qualifying persons. Do not

include amounts paid or incurred by your employer to the extent they are excluded from gross income.

Note: *Do not include on line 2 qualified expenses that you incurred in 1988 but did not pay until 1989. Instead, you may be able to increase your 1989 credit when you pay the 1988 expenses in 1989.*

Line 3. Earned income limit.—The amount of your qualified expenses **may not** be more than your earned income or, if married filing a joint return, the **smaller** of your earned income or your spouse's earned income.

In general, earned income is wages, salaries, tips, and other employee compensation. It also includes net earnings from self-employment. This is usually the amount shown on Schedule SE (Form 1040), line 3 (or 3c if you file section B).

Unmarried taxpayers.—If you were unmarried at the end of 1988 or are treated as being unmarried at the end of the year, enter your earned income on line 3a.

Married taxpayers.—If you are married, filing a joint return, disregard community property laws. Enter your earned income on line 3a and your spouse's earned income on line 3b. Then, enter the smaller of the two incomes on line 3c. If your spouse died in 1988, had no earned income, and you file a joint return for 1988, see Pub. 503.

Spouse who is a full-time student or is disabled.—If your spouse was a full-time student or was mentally or physically unable to care for himself or herself, figure your spouse's earned income on a monthly basis to determine your spouse's earned income for the year. For each month that your spouse was disabled or a full-time student, your spouse is considered to have earned income of not less than $200 a month ($400 a month if more than one qualifying person was cared for in 1988).

If, in the same month, both you and your spouse were full-time students and did not work, you may not use any amount paid that month to figure the credit. The same applies to a couple who did not work because neither was capable of self-care.

A full-time student is one who was enrolled in a school for the number of hours or classes that the school considers full time. The student must have been enrolled during each of 5 months during 1988. The months need not be consecutive.

Self-employment income.—You must reduce your earned income by any loss from self-employment. If your net earnings from self-employment are less than $1,600, and you use the optional method to figure your self-employment tax, you may be able to increase your net earnings to $1,600 for this credit. Get **Pub. 533,** Self-Employment Tax, for details. If you only have a loss from self-employment, or your loss is more than your other earned income and you do not use the optional method, you may not take the credit.

Line 7.—If you had qualified expenses for 1987 that you did not pay until 1988, you may be able to increase the amount of credit you may take in 1988. To do this, multiply the 1987 expenses you paid in 1988 by the percentage from the table on line 5 that applies to the adjusted gross income shown on your 1987 Form 1040, line 31, or Form 1040A, line 13. Your 1987 expenses must be within the 1987 limits.

Attach a computation showing how you figured the increase.

Line 8.—In certain cases, the amount of credit you figured on line 8 may be limited. Some taxpayers will need to complete **Form 6251,** Alternative Minimum Tax—Individuals, because the computation of this limit uses an amount from line 15 of that form. Other taxpayers, however, will not be affected by the limit and will not need Form 6251. The following will help you determine if you need Form 6251.

First, complete line 1 of the worksheet below.

Get Form 6251 if:

• You filed Schedule C, D, E, or F (Form 1040); **OR**

• The amount you enter on line 1 of the worksheet below is more than: $112,500 for single or head of household; $150,000 for married filing jointly; or $75,000 for married filing separately.

If **either** of the above applies to you, complete Form 6251 through line 15. Skip lines 2 through 6 of the worksheet and go directly to line A of the worksheet.

If **neither** of the above applies to you, continue with line 2 of the worksheet. You may still need to get Form 6251.

1. Enter the amount from Form 1040, line 23 ... *34,100*

   (Add to line 1 any tax-exempt interest from private activity bonds issued after August 7, 1986, and any net operating loss deduction.)

2. Enter: $30,000 if single or head of household; $40,000 if married filing jointly; or $20,000 if married filing separately ... *30,000*

3. Subtract line 2 from line 1. If the result is zero or less, **STOP HERE** and enter on Form 1040, line 41, the amount of your credit shown on line 8 of Form 2441. Otherwise, go on to line 4 ... *4,100*

4. Enter the amount from Form 1040, line 40 ... *2,629*

5. Multiply line 3 by .21 ... *861*

6. Subtract line 5 from line 4 (if zero or less, enter zero) ... *1,768*

Compare line 6 of the worksheet with the amount of credit shown on Form 2441, line 8.

• **If line 6 (above) is more than your credit,** you do not have to complete Form 6251. Enter on Form 1040, line 41, the amount of your credit shown on Form 2441, line 8.

• **If your credit is more than the amount on line 6 (above),** get Form 6251 and complete it through line 15. Then figure the limit on your credit as follows:

A. Enter amount from Form 1040, line 40 ... _____

B. Enter the amount from Form 6251, line 15 ... _____

C. Maximum credit. Subtract line B from line A (if zero or less, enter zero) ... _____

Compare the credit you first figured on line 8 of Form 2441 with line C above. Enter the **smaller** of the two amounts on line 8 of Form 2441, and on Form 1040, line 41. If line C above is the smaller amount, also write "AMT" in the left margin next to line 41.

Form **3800** Department of the Treasury Internal Revenue Service	**General Business Credit** ▶ **Attach to your tax return.**	OMB No. 1545–0895 **1988** Attachment Sequence No. **24**

Name(s) as shown on return	Identifying number

Part I   **Tentative Credit**

1	Investment credit (Form 3468, line 8)	**1**	
2	Jobs credit (Form 5884, line 6)	**2**	
3	Credit for alcohol used as fuel (Form 6478, line 11)	**3**	
4	Credit for increasing research activities (Form 6765, line 25)	**4**	
5	Low-income housing credit (Form 8586, line 6)	**5**	
6	**Current year general business credit**—Add lines 1 through 5	**6**	
7	Carryforward of general business credit (investment (see instructions), WIN, jobs, alcohol fuel, research, ESOP, or low-income housing credits)	**7**	
8	Carryback of general business credit to 1988.	**8**	
9	Tentative general business credit—Add lines 6, 7, and 8	**9**	

Part II   **Tax Liability Limitations**

10a	Individuals—From Form 1040, enter amount from line 40		
b	Corporations—From Form 1120, Schedule J, enter tax from line 3 (or Form 1120-A, Part I, line 1)		
c	Other filers—Enter income tax before credits from return	**10**	
11a	Individuals—From Form 1040, enter credits from lines 41, 42, and 43, plus any orphan drug credit, mortgage interest credit, and nonconventional source fuel credit included on line 46 . .		
b	Corporations—From Form 1120, Schedule J, enter credits from lines 4a through 4d (Form 1120-A filers, enter zero)		
c	Other filers—See instructions for line 11c	**11**	
12	Income tax liability as adjusted—Subtract line 11 from line 10	**12**	
13	Tentative minimum tax—		
a	Individuals—From Form 6251, enter amount from line 17		
b	Corporations—From Form 4626, enter amount from line 13		
c	Estates and Trusts—From Form 8656, enter amount from Part III, line 10	**13**	
14	Net income tax—		
a	Individuals—Enter the sum of line 12, above, and line 19 of Form 6251		
b	Corporations—Enter the sum of line 12, above, and line 16 of Form 4626		
c	Other filers—See instructions for line 14c	**14**	
15	If line 12 is more than $25,000—Enter 25% of the excess	**15**	
16	Enter—Line 14 less whichever is greater, line 13 or line 15 (if less than zero, enter zero)	**16**	
17	General business credit—Enter the smaller of line 9, or line 16 (corporations, see instructions) here and on Form 1040, line 44; Form 1120, Schedule J, line 4e; Form 1120-A, Part I, line 2a; or the proper line on other returns	**17**	

For Paperwork Reduction Act Notice, see page 1 of the separate Instructions to this form.   Form **3800** (1988)

Form **3903**	**Moving Expenses**	OMB No. 1545-0062
Department of the Treasury Internal Revenue Service	▶ **Attach to Form 1040.** ▶ **See separate Instructions.**	19**88** Attachment Sequence No. **62**

Name(s) as shown on Form 1040	Your social security number

1 Enter the number of miles from your **old** home to your **new** workplace **1**

2 Enter the number of miles from your **old** home to your **old** workplace **2**

3 Subtract line 2 from line 1. Enter the result (but not less than zero) . . . . ▶ **3**

If line **3** is 35 or more miles, complete the rest of this form. If line 3 is less than 35 miles, you may not take a deduction for moving expenses. This rule does not apply to members of the armed forces.

Part I   Moving Expenses

Section A.—Transportation of Household Goods

4 Transportation and storage for household goods and personal effects **4**

Section B.—Expenses of Moving From Old to New Home

5 Travel and lodging **not** including meals **5**

6 Total meals . . . . | **6**

7 Multiply line 6 by 80% (.80) **7**

8 Add lines 5 and 7 . . . . **8**

Section C.—Pre-move Househunting Expenses

9 Travel and lodging **not** including meals **9**

10 Total meals . . . . | **10**

11 Multiply line 10 by 80% (.80) **11**

12 Add lines 9 and 11 . . . . **12**

Section D.—Temporary Quarters (for any 30 days in a row after getting your job)

13 Lodging expenses **not** including meals **13**

14 Total meals . . . . | **14**

15 Multiply line 14 by 80% (.80) **15**

16 Add lines 13 and 15 . . . . **16**

Section E.—Qualified Real Estate Expenses

17 Expenses of (check one): **a** ☐ selling or exchanging your old home; or
 b ☐ if renting, settling an unexpired lease **17**

18 Expenses of (check one): **a** ☐ buying your new home, or
 b ☐ if renting, getting a new lease **18**

Part II   Dollar Limitations

19 Add lines 12 and 16 . . . . | **19**

20 Enter the smaller of line 19 or $1,500 ($750 if married, filing a separate return, and at the end of the tax year you lived with your spouse who also started work during the tax year) **20**

21 Add lines 17, 18, and 20 . . . . **21**

22 Enter the smaller of line 21 or $3,000 ($1,500 if married, filing a separate return, and at the end of the tax year you lived with your spouse who also started work during the tax year) **22**

23 Add lines 4, 8, and 22. This is your moving expense deduction. **Enter here and on Schedule A (Form 1040), line 19.** (Note: *Any payments your employer made for any part of your move (including the value of any services furnished in kind) should be included on Form W-2. Report that amount on **Form 1040, line 7.** See **Reimbursements** in the Instructions.)* . . . . ▶ **23**

For Paperwork Reduction Act Notice, see separate Instructions.   Form **3903** (1988)

Form **4255**		

Form **4255**
(Rev. July 1988)
Department of the Treasury
Internal Revenue Service

Recapture of Investment Credit
(Including Energy Investment Credit)
▶ Attach to your income tax return.

OMB No. 1545-0166
Expires 6-30-91

Attachment
Sequence No. **65**

Name(s) as shown on return

Identifying number

Properties	Kind of property—State whether recovery or nonrecovery (see the Instructions for Form 3468 for definitions). If energy property, show type. Also indicate if rehabilitation expenditure property.
A	
B	
C	
D	

Original Investment Credit

Computation Steps: (see Specific Instructions)		Properties			
		A	**B**	**C**	**D**
1	Original rate of credit				
2	Date property was placed in service				
3	Cost or other basis				
4	Original estimated useful life or class of property . .				
5	Applicable percentage				
6	Original qualified investment (line 3 times line 5) .				
7	Original credit (line 1 times line 6)				
8	Date property ceased to be qualified investment credit property				
9	Number of full years between the date on line 2 and the date on line 8				

Computation of Recapture Tax

10	Recapture percentage (from instructions)				
11	Tentative recapture tax (line 7 times line 10) . . .				
12	Add line 11, columns A through D				
13	Enter tax from property ceasing to be at risk, or for which there was an increase in nonqualified nonrecourse financing (attach separate computation)				
14	Total—Add lines 12 and 13				
15	Portion of original credit (line 7) not used to offset tax in any year, **plus** any carryback and carryforward of credits you can now apply to the original credit year because you have freed up tax liability in the amount of the tax recaptured (Do not enter more than line 14—see instructions)				
16	Total increase in tax—Subtract line 15 from line 14. Enter here and on the proper line of your tax return				

General Instructions

(Section references are to the Internal Revenue Code, unless otherwise noted.)

Paperwork Reduction Act Notice.—We ask for this information to carry out the Internal Revenue laws of the United States. We need it to ensure that taxpayers are complying with these laws and to allow us to figure and collect the right amount of tax. You are required to give us this information.

Purpose of Form.—Use Form 4255 to figure the increase in tax for the recapture of investment credit for regular and energy property.

You must refigure the credit if you took it in an earlier year, but disposed of the property before the end of the recapture period or the useful life you used to figure the original credit. You must also refigure the credit if you returned leased property (on which you had taken a credit) to the lessor before the end of the recapture period or useful life.

You must refigure the credit if you changed the use of property so that it no longer qualifies as regular or energy investment credit property. For example, you must refigure the credit if you change the use of property from business use to personal use, or if there is any decrease in the percentage of business use of investment credit property. See sections 47(a)(3), 47(a)(5)(C), and 49(e)(2) for information on recapture for progress expenditure property. Also, see the

Form **4255** (Rev. 7-88)

Form 4255 (Rev. 7-88)

instructions for line 13 regarding recapture if property ceases to be at risk, or if there is an increase in nonqualified, nonrecourse financing related to certain at-risk property placed in service after July 18, 1984.

If certain "listed property" (i.e., transportation property, entertainment, recreation or amusement property, or certain home computer equipment) placed in service after June 18, 1984, ceases to be used more than 50% for business, you may have to recapture investment credit taken on the property. See section 280F for details.

An election to be treated as an S corporation does not automatically trigger recapture of investment credit taken before the election was effective. However, the S corporation is liable for any recapture of investment credit taken before the election.

If property on which you took both regular and energy investment credit ceases to be energy credit property, but still qualifies as regular investment credit property, you need only refigure the energy investment credit. However, if you took both credits, and you dispose of the property, or the property ceases to be both energy and regular investment credit property, you must refigure both credits.

If you are an S corporation, a partnership, or an estate or trust that allocated any or all of the investment credit to the beneficiaries, you must give your shareholders, partners, or beneficiaries the information they need to refigure the credit. See regulations sections 1.47-4, 1.47-5 and 1.47-6.

Partners, shareholders and beneficiaries.—If your Schedule K-1 shows that you must recapture investment credit taken in an earlier year, you will need your retained copy of the original Form 3468 to complete lines 1 through 9 of this Form 4255.

Special Rules.—If you took a credit on the following kinds of property, see the sections listed below before you complete Form 4255:

Property	Section
Motion picture films and video tapes . . .	47(a)(8)
Ships	46(g)(4)
Commuter highway vehicles	47(a)(4)

If you took any nonconventional source fuel credit, see section 29(b)(4).

If, before the end of the recapture period, you dispose of recovery property placed in service after 1982 (or the business use percentage decreases), increase the basis of this property by 50% of the recapture amount unless you originally made the section 48(q)(4) election to take a reduced credit instead of reducing the basis of the property.

Note: *Legislation pending at the time this form went to print would change these rules for transition property (as defined in section 49(e)) that was placed in service after 1985 and was eligible for the regular percentage. The proposed legislation would permit you to increase the basis of this property by 100% of the recapture amount instead of 50%.*

For more information, see **Publication 572,** General Business Credit.

Specific Instructions

Note: *Do not figure the recapture tax on lines 1 through 12 for property ceasing to be at risk, or if there is an increase in nonqualified, nonrecourse financing related to certain at-risk property placed in service after July 18, 1984. Figure the recapture tax for these properties on separate schedules and enter the recapture tax on line 13. Include any unused credit for these properties on line 15.*

Lines A through D.—Describe the property for which you must refigure the credit.

Fill in lines 1 through 11 for each property on which you are refiguring the credit. Use a separate column for each item. If you must recapture both the energy investment credit and the regular investment credit for the same item, use a separate column for each credit. If you need more columns, use additional Forms 4255, or other schedules with all the information shown on Form 4255. Enter the total from the separate sheets on line 12.

Line 1.—Enter the rate you used to figure the original credit from the tables below:

Regular Investment Property

Qualifying property acquired or constructed and placed in service 10%

If at the time the credit was taken the regular 10% credit above was subject to all or part of the 35% reduction under section 49(c), reduce the 10% accordingly.

For example, if a 10% regular credit was used in calendar year 1987 where it was reduced by 17.5% under section 49(c), enter 8.25% on line 1 (10% minus 17.5% of 10%). If parts of the credit were used in different tax years (for example, part in 1986 where the full 10% was allowed, part in 1987 where the 10% credit was reduced under 49(c) by a portion of 35%, and part in 1988 where the credit was reduced by 35%), use a weighted average based on the portion of the credit used in each year.

Be sure to include any ESOP credit, or other credits listed under the special rules above.

See section 46(b)(4) for the rates for qualified rehabilitation expenditures made after 1981.

Energy Investment Property

See the table in section 46(b)(2)(A) for a listing of the energy percentages.

Line 2.—For both recovery and nonrecovery property, enter the first day of the first month, and the year, that the property was available for service.

Line 3.—Enter the cost or other basis that you used to figure the original credit.

Line 4.—Enter the estimated useful life that you used to figure the original credit for nonrecovery property. Enter the class of property for recovery property.

Line 5.—Enter the applicable percentage that you used to figure the original qualified investment from the tables below:

Nonrecovery Property

Original estimated useful life	Applicable percentage
3 or more but less than 5 years	33⅓%
5 or more but less than 7 years	66⅔%
7 or more years	100%

Recovery Property

Class of property	Applicable percentage
3-year	60%
Other	100%

Section 48(q) Election Recovery Property
(Placed in service after 12/31/82 and before 1/1/86)

Class of property	Applicable percentage
3-year	40%
Other	80%

Line 8.—Generally, this will be the date you disposed of the property. See regulations section 1.47-1(c) for more information.

Line 9.—Do not enter partial years. If the property was held less than 12 months, enter zero.

Line 10.—Enter the recapture percentage from the following tables:

Nonrecovery Property

If number of full years on line 9 of Form 4255 is:	3 or more but less than 5 years is	5 or more but less than 7 years is	7 or more years is
	The recapture percentage for property with an original useful life of:		
0	100	100	100
1	100	100	100
2	100	100	100
3	0	50	66.6
4	0	50	66.6
5	0	0	33.3
6	0	0	33.3

Recovery Property

If number of full years on line 9 of Form 4255 is:	3-year property is	Other than 3-year property is
	The recapture percentage for:	
0	100	100
1	66	80
2	33	60
3	0	40
4	0	20

Decrease in Business Use.—If you take investment credit for property and the percentage of business use in a later year falls below the percentage for the year placed in service, you are treated as having disposed of part of the property and may have to recapture part of the investment credit.

Line 12.—If you have used more than one Form 4255, or separate sheets to list additional items on which you figured an increase in tax, write on the dotted line "Tax from attached, $ _ _ _ _ _ _ ." Include the amount in the total for line 12.

Line 13.—For certain taxpayers, the basis or cost of property placed in service after February 18, 1981, is limited to the amount the taxpayer is at risk for the property at year end. For property placed in service after July 18, 1984, the basis or cost must be reduced by the amount of any "nonqualified, nonrecourse financing" related to the property at year end. If property ceases to be at risk in a later year, or if there is an increase in nonqualified, nonrecourse financing, recapture may be required. See section 47(d) for details. Attach a separate computation schedule to figure the recapture tax and enter the total tax on line 13.

Line 15.—If you did not use all the credit you originally figured, either in the year you figured it or in a carryback or carryforward year, you do not have to recapture the amount of the credit you did not use. In refiguring the credit for the original credit year, be sure to take into account any carryforwards from previous years, plus any carrybacks arising within the 3 taxable years after the original credit year that are now allowed because the recapture and recomputation of the original credit made available some additional tax liability in that year. See regulations section 1.47-1(d), Revenue Ruling 72-221, and Publication 572 for more information.

Note: *You must also take into account any reduction in credit under section 49(c)(2) when computing the amount to enter on line 15.*

Figure the unused portion on a separate sheet and enter it on this line. Do not enter more than the recapture tax on line 14.

Reminder: Be sure to adjust your *current* unused credit to reflect any unused portion of the original credit that was recaptured on this form.

Form **4562** Department of the Treasury Internal Revenue Service	**Depreciation and Amortization** ▶ **See separate instructions.** ▶ **Attach this form to your return.**	OMB No. 1545-0172 **1988** Attachment Sequence No. **67**

Name(s) as shown on return | Identifying number

Business or activity to which this form relates

Part I **Depreciation** *(Use Part III for automobiles, certain other vehicles, computers, and property used for entertainment, recreation, or amusement.)*

Section A.—Election To Expense Depreciable Assets (Section 179)

(a) Description of property	**(b)** Date placed in service	**(c)** Cost	**(d)** Expense deduction
1			

2 Listed property—Enter total from Part III, Section A, column (h)
3 Total (add lines 1 and 2, but do not enter more than $10,000)
4 Enter the amount, if any, by which the cost of all section 179 property placed in service during this tax year is more than $200,000
5 Subtract line 4 from line 3. If less than zero, enter zero. (See instructions for other limitations.)

Section B.—Depreciation

(a) Class of property	**(b)** Date placed in service	**(c)** Basis for depreciation (Business use only—see instructions)	**(d)** Recovery period	**(e)** Method of figuring depreciation	**(f)** Deduction
6 Modified Accelerated Cost Recovery System (MACRS) (see instructions): For assets placed in service ONLY during tax year beginning in 1988					
a 3-year property					
b 5-year property					
c 7-year property					
d 10-year property					
e 15-year property					
f 20-year property					
g Residential rental property					
h Nonresidential real property					
7 Alternative Depreciation System (ADS)					

8 Listed property—Enter total from Part III, Section A, column (g)
9 MACRS deduction for assets placed in service prior to 1988 (see instructions)

Section C.—ACRS and/or Other Depreciation

10 Property subject to section 168(f)(1) election (see instructions)
11 ACRS and/or other depreciation (see instructions)

Section D.—Summary

12 Total (add deductions on lines 5 through 11). Enter here and on the Depreciation line of your return (Partnerships and S corporations—Do NOT include any amounts entered on line 5.)
13 For assets above placed in service during the current year, enter the portion of the basis attributable to section 263A costs. (see instructions).

Part II **Amortization**

(a) Description of property	**(b)** Date acquired	**(c)** Cost or other basis	**(d)** Code section	**(e)** Amortization period or percentage	**(f)** Amortization for this year
1 Amortization for property placed in service **only** during tax year beginning in 1988					

2 Amortization for property placed in service prior to 1988
3 Total. Enter here and on Other Deductions or Other Expenses line of your return

See Paperwork Reduction Act Notice on page 1 of the separate instructions. Form **4562** (1988)

Form 4562 (1988)

Page **2**

Part III **Automobiles, Certain Other Vehicles, Computers, and Property Used for Entertainment, Recreation, or Amusement (Listed Property).**

If you are using the standard mileage rate or deducting vehicle lease expense, complete columns (a) through (d) of Section A, all of Section B, and Section C if applicable.

Section A.—Depreciation (If automobiles and other listed property placed in service after June 18, 1984, are used 50% or less in a trade or business, the section 179 deduction is not allowed and depreciation must be taken using the straight line method over 5 years. For other limitations, see instructions.)

Do you have evidence to support the business use claimed? ☐ **Yes** ☐ **No** If "Yes," is the evidence written? ☐ **Yes** ☐ **No**

(a) Type of property (list vehicles first)	(b) Date placed in service	(c) Business use percentage (%)	(d) Cost or other basis (see instructions for leased property)	(e) Basis for depreciation (Business use only—see instructions)	(f) Depreciation method and recovery period	(g) Depreciation deduction	(h) Section 179 expense

Total (Enter here and on line 2, page 1.) . . . .

Total (Enter here and on line 8, page 1.) . . . .

Section B.—Information Regarding Use of Vehicles

Complete this section as follows, if you deduct expenses for vehicles:

- *Always complete this section for vehicles used by a sole proprietor, partner, or other more than 5% owner or related person.*
- *If you provided vehicles to employees, first answer the questions in Section C to see if you meet an exception to completing this section for those items.*

	Vehicle 1		Vehicle 2		Vehicle 3		Vehicle 4		Vehicle 5		Vehicle 6	
1 Total miles driven during the year . . .												
2 Total business miles driven during the year												
3 Total commuting miles driven during the year.												
4 Total other personal (noncommuting) miles driven												
	Yes	No	Yes	No	Yes	No	Yes	No	Yes	No	Yes	No
5 Was the vehicle available for personal use during off-duty hours?												
6 Was the vehicle used primarily by a more than 5% owner or related person? . . .												
7 Is another vehicle available for personal use?.												

Section C.—Questions for Employers Who Provide Vehicles for Use by Employees.

(Answer these questions to determine if you meet an exception to completing Section B. **Note:** *Section B must always be completed for vehicles used by sole proprietors, partners, or other more than 5% owners or related persons.)*

	Yes	No
8 Do you maintain a written policy statement that prohibits all personal use of vehicles, including commuting, by your employees?		
9 Do you maintain a written policy statement that prohibits personal use of vehicles, except commuting, by your employees? (See instructions for vehicles used by corporate officers, directors, or 1% or more owners.)		
10 Do you treat all use of vehicles by employees as personal use?		
11 Do you provide more than five vehicles to your employees and retain the information received from your employees concerning the use of the vehicles?.		
12 Do you meet the requirements concerning qualified automobile demonstration use (see instructions)?		

Note: *If your answer to 8, 9, 10, 11, or 12 is "Yes," you need not complete Section B for the covered vehicles.*

Form **4684**	**Casualties and Thefts**	OMB No. 1545-0177

Form **4684**

Department of the Treasury
Internal Revenue Service

Casualties and Thefts

▶ **See separate Instructions.**
▶ **To be filed with Form 1040, 1041, 1065, 1120, etc.**
Use a separate Form 4684 for each different casualty or theft.

OMB No. 1545-0177

1988

Attachment
Sequence No. **26**

Name(s) as shown on tax return | Identifying number

SECTION A.—Personal Use Property *(Casualties and thefts to property **not** used in a trade or business or for income-producing purposes.)*

1 Description of Properties (Show kind, location, and date of purchase for each)

Property A ....

Property B ....

Property C ....

Property D ....

	Properties (Use a separate column for each property lost or damaged from one casualty or theft.)			
	A	B	C	D
2 Cost or other basis of each property				
3 Insurance or other reimbursement (whether or not you submit a claim). See Instructions.				
Note: *If line 2 is **more** than line 3, skip line 4.*				
4 Gain from casualty or theft. If line 3 is **more** than line 2, enter the difference here and skip lines 5 through 13				
5 Fair market value before casualty or theft . .				
6 Fair market value after casualty or theft. . . .				
7 Subtract line 6 from line 5				
8 Enter the **smaller** of line 2 or line 7				
9 Subtract line 3 from line 8				

10 Casualty or theft loss. Add amounts from line 9 for all columns . . . .

11 Enter the amount from line 10 or $100, whichever is **smaller**. . . . .

12 Subtract line 11 from line 10 . . . .
Caution: *Use only one Form 4684 for lines 13 through 18.*

13 Add the line 12 amounts from all Forms 4684, Section A . . . .

14 Add the line 4 amounts from all Forms 4684, Section A . . . .

15 If line 14 is **more** than line 13, enter difference here and on Schedule D. Do not complete the rest of the form. (See Instructions.) Otherwise, enter zero and complete lines 16 through 18. If line 14 is **equal** to line 13, do not complete the rest of the form . . . .

16 If line 13 is **more** than line 14, enter the difference . . . .

17 Enter 10% of your adjusted gross income (Form 1040, line 31). Estates and trusts, see Instructions . . . .

18 Subtract line 17 from line 16. If zero or less, enter zero. Enter on Schedule A (Form 1040), line 18. Estates and trusts, enter on the "other deductions" line of your tax return . . . .

For Paperwork Reduction Act Notice, see page 1 of separate Instructions.   Form **4684** (1988)

Form 4684 (1988)   **26**   Page **2**

Name(s) as shown on tax return (Do not enter name and identifying number if shown on other side.) | Identifying number

SECTION B.—Business and Income-Producing Property (Note: If from a passive activity, see Instructions.)
(Casualties and thefts to property used in a trade or business or for income-producing purposes.)

Part I   Casualty or Theft Gain or Loss (Use a separate Part I for each different casualty or theft.)

1   Description of Properties (Show kind, location, and date of purchase for each)

Property A ....

Property B ....

Property C ....

Property D ....

	Properties (Use a separate column for each property lost or damaged from one casualty or theft.)			
	A	B	C	D
2 Cost or adjusted basis of each property				
3 Insurance or other reimbursement (whether or not you submit a claim). See Instructions				
Note: *If line 2 is **more** than line 3, skip line 4.*				
4 Gain from casualty or theft. If line 3 is **more** than line 2, enter difference here and on line 11 or 16, column (c). However, see Instructions for line 15. Also, skip lines 5 through 10				
5 Fair market value before casualty or theft . .				
6 Fair market value after casualty or theft . .				
7 Subtract line 6 from line 5				
8 Enter **smaller** of line 2 or line 7				
Note: *If the property was totally destroyed by casualty, or lost from theft, enter on line 8, in each column, the amount from line 2.*				
9 Subtract line 3 from line 8				

10   Casualty or theft loss. Add amounts from line 9 for all columns. Enter here and on line 11 **or** 16 . . . . . .

Part II   Summary of Gains and Losses (From separate Parts I)

(a) Identify casualty or theft	(b) Losses from casualties or thefts		(c) Gains from casualties or thefts includible in income
	(i) Trade, business, rental or royalty property	(ii) Income-producing property	

Casualty or Theft of Property Held One Year or Less (6 months or less if acquired before 1/1/88)

11			

12   Totals. Add amounts on line 11 for each column . . . .

13   Combine line 12, columns (b)(i) and (c). Enter the net gain or (loss) here and on Form 4797, Part II, line 14. (If Form 4797 is not otherwise required, see Instructions.) . . . .

14   Enter the amount from line 12, column (b)(ii) here and on Schedule A (Form 1040), line 21. Partnerships, S corporations, estates and trusts, see Instructions . . . .

Casualty or Theft of Property Held More Than One Year (more than 6 months if acquired before 1/1/88)

15   Casualty or theft gains from Form 4797, Part III, line 32 . . . .

16			

17   Total losses. Add amounts on line 16, columns (b)(i) and (b)(ii) . . . .

18   Total gains. Add lines 15 and 16, column (c) . . . .

19   Add amounts on line 17, columns (b)(i) and (b)(ii) . . . .
  Partnerships, enter the amount from line 20 or line 21 on your Schedule K-1, line 7. S corporations, enter the amount from line 20 on your Schedule K-1, line 6.

20   If the loss on line 19 is **more** than the gain on line 18:

  a   Combine line 17, column (b)(i) and line 18. Enter the net gain or (loss) here and on Form 4797, Part II, line 14. (If Form 4797 is not otherwise required, see Instructions.) . . . .

  b   Enter the amount from line 17, column (b)(ii) here and on Schedule A (Form 1040), line 21. Estates and trusts, enter on the "other deductions" line of your tax return . . . .

21   If the loss on line 19 is **equal** to or **smaller** than the gain on line 18, combine these lines and enter here and on Form 4797, Part I, line 3 . . . .

Form **4797**	**Sales of Business Property**	OMB No. 1545-0184
	(Also, Involuntary Conversions and Recapture Amounts Under Sections 179 and 280F)	19**88**
Department of the Treasury Internal Revenue Service	▶ **Attach to your tax return. See separate Instructions.**	Attachment Sequence No. **27**

Name(s) as shown on return	Identifying number

Part I   **Sales or Exchanges of Property Used in a Trade or Business and Involuntary Conversions From Other Than Casualty and Theft—Property Held More Than 1 Year (More Than 6 Months If Acquired Before 1/1/88)**

1   Enter here the gross proceeds from the sale or exchange of real estate reported to you for 1988 on Form(s) 1099-S (or an equivalent statement) that you will be including on lines 2 or 10 (column d), or on line 20. (Form 1099-S is a Statement for Recipients of Proceeds From Real Estate Transactions.) . . . . | **1**

(a) Description of property	(b) Date acquired (mo., day, yr.)	(c) Date sold (mo., day, yr.)	(d) Gross sales price	(e) Depreciation allowed (or allowable) since acquisition	(f) Cost or other basis, plus improvements and expense of sale	(g) LOSS ((f) minus the sum of (d) and (e))	(h) GAIN ((d) plus (e) minus (f))
2							

3   Gain, if any, from Form 4684, Section B, line 21   . . . .

4   Section 1231 gain from installment sales from Form 6252, line 22 or 30   . . . .

5   Gain, if any, from Part III, line 32, from other than casualty and theft. . . . .

6   Add lines 2 through 5 in columns (g) and (h) . . . .   (   )

7   Combine columns (g) and (h) of line 6. Enter gain or (loss) here, and on the appropriate line as follows (partnerships see the Instructions for line references):   . . . .

    If line 7 is zero or a loss, enter the amount on line 11 below and skip lines 8 and 9. (S corporations enter the loss on Schedule K (Form 1120S), line 5.) If line 7 is a gain and you did not have any prior year section 1231 losses, or they were recaptured in an earlier year, enter the gain as a long-term capital gain on Schedule D and skip lines 8, 9, and 12 below.

8   Nonrecaptured net section 1231 losses from prior years (see Instructions) . . . .

9   Subtract line 8 from line 7. If zero or less, enter zero . . . .

    If line 9 is zero, enter the amount from line 7 on line 12 below. If line 9 is more than zero, enter the amount from line 8 on line 12 below, and enter the amount from line 9 as a long-term capital gain on Schedule D. See Specific Instructions for line 9.

Part II   **Ordinary Gains and Losses**

(a) Description of property	(b) Date acquired (mo., day, yr.)	(c) Date sold (mo., day, yr.)	(d) Gross sales price	(e) Depreciation allowed (or allowable) since acquisition	(f) Cost or other basis, plus improvements and expense of sale	(g) LOSS ((f) minus the sum of (d) and (e))	(h) GAIN ((d) plus (e) minus (f))
10 Ordinary gains and losses not included on lines 11 through 16 (include property held 1 year or less) (6 months or less if acquired before 1/1/88):							

11   Loss, if any, from line 7 . . . .

12   Gain, if any, from line 7, or amount from line 8 if applicable   . . . .

13   Gain, if any, from line 31, Part III . . . .

14   Net gain or (loss) from Form 4684, Section B, lines 13 and 20a . . . .

15   Ordinary gain from installment sales from Form 6252, line(s) 21 and/or 29. . . . .

16   Recapture of section 179 deduction for partners and S corporation shareholders from property dispositions by partnerships and S corporations (see Instructions)   . . . .

17   Add lines 10 through 16 in columns (g) and (h) . . . .   (   )

18   Combine columns (g) and (h) of line 17. Enter gain or (loss) here, and on the appropriate line as follows: . . . .
   a   For all except individual returns: Enter the gain or (loss) from line 18, on the return being filed.
   b   For individual returns:
      (1) If the loss on line 11 includes a loss from Form 4684, Section B, Part II, column (b)(ii), enter that part of the loss here and on line 21 of Schedule A (Form 1040). Identify as from "Form 4797, line 18b(1)"   . . . .
      (2) Redetermine the gain or (loss) on line 18, excluding the loss (if any) on line 18b(1). Enter here and on Form 1040, line 15

For Paperwork Reduction Act Notice, see page 1 of separate Instructions.   Form **4797** (1988)

Form 4797 (1988)   Page **2**

Part III Gain From Disposition of Property Under Sections 1245, 1250, 1252, 1254, and 1255
Skip section 1252 on line 27 and in the Instructions if you did not dispose of farmland or if you are a partnership.

19 Description of sections 1245, 1250, 1252, 1254, and 1255 property:

	Date acquired (mo., day, yr.)	Date sold (mo., day, yr.)
A		
B		
C		
D		

Relate lines 19A through 19D to these columns ▶	Property A	Property B	Property C	Property D
20 Gross sales price				
21 Cost or other basis plus expense of sale				
22 Depreciation (or depletion) allowed (or allowable)				
23 Adjusted basis, subtract line 22 from line 21				
24 Total gain, subtract line 23 from line 20				
25 **If section 1245 property:**				
a Depreciation allowed (or allowable) (see Instructions)				
b Enter the **smaller** of line 24 or 25a				
26 **If section 1250 property:** If straight line depreciation was used, enter zero on line 26g unless you are a corporation subject to section 291.				
a Additional depreciation after 12/31/75				
b Applicable percentage times the **smaller** of line 24 or line 26a (see Instructions)				
c Subtract line 26a from line 24. If line 24 is not more than line 26a, skip lines 26d and 26e				
d Additional depreciation after 12/31/69 and before 1/1/76				
e Applicable percentage times the **smaller** of line 26c or 26d (see Instructions)				
f Section 291 amount (for corporations only)				
g Add lines 26b, 26e, and 26f				
27 **If section 1252 property:**				
a Soil, water, and land clearing expenses				
b Line 27a times applicable percentage (see Instructions)				
c Enter the **smaller** of line 24 or 27b				
28 **If section 1254 property:**				
a Intangible drilling and development costs, expenditures for development of mines and other natural deposits, and mining exploration costs (see Instructions)				
b Enter the **smaller** of line 24 or 28a				
29 **If section 1255 property:**				
a Applicable percentage of payments excluded from income under section 126 (see Instructions)				
b Enter the **smaller** of line 24 or 29a				

Summary of Part III Gains (Complete property columns A through D through line 29b before going to line 30.)

30 Total gains for all properties (add columns A through D, line 24)

31 Add columns A through D, lines 25b, 26g, 27c, 28b, and 29b. Enter here and in Part II, line 13. (see the Instructions for Part IV if this is an installment sale)

32 Subtract line 31 from line 30. Enter the portion from casualty and theft on Form 4684, Section B, line 15. Enter the portion from other than casualty and theft on Form 4797, Part I, line 5

Part IV Complete This Part Only if You Elect Out of the Installment Method and Report a Note or Other Obligation at Less Than Full Face Value

33 Check here if you elect out of the installment method ▶ ☐

34 Enter the face amount of the note or other obligation ▶

35 Enter the percentage of valuation of the note or other obligation ▶ - - - - - - - - - - - -

Part V Computation of Recapture Amounts Under Sections 179 and 280F When Business Use Drops to 50% or Less
(See Instructions for Part V.)

	(a) Section 179	(b) Section 280F
1 Section 179 expense deduction or section 280F recovery deductions		
2 Depreciation or recovery deductions (see Instructions)		
3 Recapture amount (subtract line 2 from line 1) (see Instructions for where to report)		

Form **4868**
Department of the Treasury
Internal Revenue Service

Application for Automatic Extension of Time To File U.S. Individual Income Tax Return

OMB No. 1545-0188

1988

Please Type or Print	Your first name and initial (if joint return, also give spouse's name and initial)	Last name	Your social security number
	Present home address (number, street, and apt. no. or rural route). (If you have a P.O. box, see the instructions.)		Spouse's social security no.
	City, town or post office, state, and ZIP code		

If you or your spouse expect to file a gift tax return (Form 709 or 709-A) for 1988, generally due by April 17, 1989, see the instructions and check here . . . .   Yourself . . ▶ ☐   Spouse . . ▶ ☐

Note: *File this form with the Internal Revenue Service Center where you are required to file your income tax return, and pay any amount(s) you owe.* **This is not an extension of time for payment of tax.**

I request an automatic 4-month extension of time to August 15, 1989, to file Form 1040A or Form 1040 for the calendar year 1988 (or if a fiscal year Form 1040 to _____, 19 _____, for the tax year ending _____, 19 _____).

1 Total tax liability for 1988. You **MUST** enter an amount on line 1. (You may estimate this amount.) **If you do not expect to owe tax, enter zero (–0–)** . . . . | **1** |

2 Federal income tax withheld . . . . | **2** |

3 1988 estimated tax payments (include 1987 overpayment allowed as a credit) . | **3** |

4 Other payments and credits you expect to show on Form 1040A or Form 1040 . | **4** |

5 Add lines 2, 3, and 4 . . . . | **5** |

6 **BALANCE DUE** (subtract line 5 from line 1). *In order to obtain this extension, you MUST pay in full the balance due with this form.* (If line 5 is more than line 1, enter zero (–0–) . . . . ▶ | **6** |

Note: *Complete line 7a and/or 7b if you expect to owe gift or generation-skipping transfer (GST) tax. Do not include income tax on these lines (See the instructions.)*

7 Enter the amount of gift or generation-skipping transfer (GST) tax that:
a You are paying with this form . . . . ▶ | **7a** |
b Your spouse is paying with this form. . . . . ▶ | **7b** |

Signature and Verification

Under penalties of perjury, I declare that I have examined this form, including accompanying schedules and statements, and to the best of my knowledge and belief, it is true, correct, and complete; and, if prepared by someone other than the taxpayer, that I am authorized to prepare this form.

Signature of taxpayer ▶ _____   Date ▶ _____

Signature of spouse ▶ _____   Date ▶ _____
(If filing jointly, BOTH must sign even if only one had income)

Signature of preparer
other than taxpayer ▶ _____   Date ▶

General Instructions

Paperwork Reduction Act Notice.— We ask for this information to carry out the Internal Revenue laws of the United States. We need it to ensure that taxpayers are complying with these laws and to allow us to figure and collect the right amount of tax. You are required to give us this information.

The time needed to complete and file this form will vary depending on individual circumstances. The estimated average time is: **Recordkeeping,** 26 minutes; **Learning about the law or the form,** 11 minutes; **Preparing the form,** 18 minutes; and **Copying, assembling, and sending the form to IRS,** 20 minutes.

If you have comments concerning the accuracy of these time estimates or suggestions for making this form more simple, we would be happy to hear from you. You can write to the **Internal Revenue Service,** Washington, DC 20224, Attention: IRS Reports Clearance Officer, TR:FP; or the **Office of Management and Budget,** Paperwork Reduction Project, Washington, DC 20503.

Purpose
Use Form 4868 to ask for 4 more months to file **Form 1040A** or **Form 1040.** You do not have to give a reason why you are asking for the extension.

To get the extra time you **MUST:**
1. Fill in Form 4868 correctly, **AND**
2. File it by the due date of your return, **AND**
3. Pay ALL of the tax shown on line 6.

We will contact you only if your request is denied.

If you already had 2 extra months to file because you were "out of the country" (see page 2) when your return was due, then you can only get 2 more months using this form.

Do **not** file Form 4868 if you want IRS to figure your tax, or are under a court order to file your return by the regular due date.

Note: *An extension to file your 1988 calendar year income tax return also extends time to file a gift tax return (Form 709 or 709-A) for 1988.*

If these 4 months do not give you enough time to file your return, you can later ask for more time. But you'll have to give a good reason, and it must be approved by IRS. To ask for the extra time, you must:

1. File **Form 2688,** Application for Additional Extension of Time To File U.S. Individual Income Tax Return, OR

2. Explain your reason in a letter. Mail it to the address under **Where To File.**

File Form 4868 *before* you file Form 2688 or write a letter asking for more time. Only in cases of undue hardship will we approve your request for more time without first receiving Form 4868. If you need this extra time, ask for it early so that you can still file your return on time if your request is not approved.

Form **4868** (1988)

Form 4868 (1988)   Page **2**

When To File Form 4868

File Form 4868 by April 17, 1989. If you are filing a fiscal year Form 1040, file Form 4868 by the regular due date of your return. If you had 2 extra months to file your return because you were out of the country, file this form by the end of those 2 months (June 15, 1989, for a 1988 calendar year return).

Where To File

Mail this form to the **Internal Revenue Service Center** for the place where you live.

If you are located in:	Use this address:
New Jersey, New York (New York City and counties of Nassau, Rockland, Suffolk, and Westchester)	Holtsville, NY 00501
New York (all other counties), Connecticut, Maine, Massachusetts, New Hampshire, Rhode Island, Vermont	Andover, MA 05501
Delaware, District of Columbia, Maryland, Pennsylvania, Virginia	Philadelphia, PA 19255
Florida, Georgia, South Carolina	Atlanta, GA 39901
Indiana, Kentucky, Michigan, Ohio, West Virginia	Cincinnati, OH 45999
Kansas, New Mexico, Oklahoma, Texas	Austin, TX 73301
Alaska, Arizona, California (counties of Alpine, Amador, Butte, Calaveras, Colusa, Contra Costa, Del Norte, El Dorado, Glenn, Humboldt, Lake, Lassen, Marin, Mendocino, Modoc, Napa, Nevada, Placer, Plumas, Sacramento, San Joaquin, Shasta, Sierra, Siskiyou, Solano, Sonoma, Sutter, Tehama, Trinity, Yolo, and Yuba), Colorado, Idaho, Montana, Nebraska, Nevada, North Dakota, Oregon, South Dakota, Utah, Washington, Wyoming	Ogden, UT 84201
California (all other counties), Hawaii	Fresno, CA 93888
Illinois, Iowa, Minnesota, Missouri, Wisconsin	Kansas City, MO 64999
Alabama, Arkansas, Louisiana, Mississippi, North Carolina, Tennessee	Memphis, TN 37501
American Samoa	Philadelphia, PA 19255
Guam	Commissioner of Taxes Agana, GU 96910
Puerto Rico (or if excluding income under section 933) Virgin Islands: Nonpermanent residents	Philadelphia, PA 19255
Virgin Islands: Permanent residents	V.I. Bureau of Internal Revenue Lockharts Garden No. 1 A Charlotte Amalie, St. Thomas, VI 00802
Foreign country: U.S. citizens and those filing Form 2555 or Form 4563, even if you have an A.P.O. or F.P.O. address	Philadelphia, PA 19255
A.P.O. or F.P.O. address of:	Miami—Atlanta, GA 39901 New York—Holtsville, NY 00501 San Francisco—Fresno, CA 93888 Seattle—Ogden, UT 84201

Filing Your Tax Return

You may file Form 1040A or Form 1040 any time before the 4 months are up. But remember, Form 4868 does not extend the time to pay these taxes. If you do not pay the amount due by the regular due date, you will owe interest. You may also be charged penalties.

Interest.—You will owe interest on tax not paid by the regular due date of your return. The interest runs until you pay the tax. Even if you had a good reason not to pay on time, you will still owe interest.

Late payment penalty.—Generally, the penalty is ½ of 1% of any tax (other than estimated tax) not paid by the regular due date. It is charged for each month, or part of a month, that the tax is unpaid. You might not owe this penalty if you have a good reason for not paying on time. Attach a statement to your return explaining the reason.

Late filing penalty.—A penalty is usually charged if your return is filed after the due date (including extensions). It is 5% of the tax not paid by the regular due date for each month, or part of a month, that your return is late. The most you have to pay is 25%. If your return is more than 60 days late, the penalty will not be less than $100 or the balance of tax due on your return, whichever is smaller. You might not owe the penalty if you have a good reason for filing late. Attach a full explanation to your return if you file late.

How to claim credit for payment made with this form.—When you file your return, show the amount of any income tax payment (line 6) sent with Form 4868. Form 1040A filers should enter it on line 24 and write "Form 4868" in the space to the left. Form 1040 filers should enter it on line 57.

If you and your spouse each filed a separate Form 4868, but later file a joint return for 1988, then enter the total paid with the two Forms 4868 on the correct line of your joint return.

If you and your spouse jointly filed Form 4868, but later file separate returns for 1988, you may enter the total amount paid with Form 4868 on either of your separate returns. Or, you and your spouse may divide the payment in any agreed amounts. Be sure each separate return has the social security numbers of both spouses.

Specific Instructions

Name, address, and social security numbers.—Write your name, address, social security number, and spouse's social security number if filing a joint return. If your post office does not bring mail to your street address and you have a P.O. box, write your P.O. box number instead of your street address.

Gift tax return filers.—If you or your spouse expect to file a gift tax return for 1988, check whichever box applies. However, if your spouse is filing a separate Form 4868, do not check the box for your spouse.

Fiscal year filers.—Below the check boxes, write the date that your 4-month extension will end and the date your tax year ends.

Out of the country.—If you already had 2 extra months to file because you were a U.S. citizen or resident who was out of the country on the due date of your return, write **"Taxpayer Abroad"** across the top of this form.

For this purpose, "out of the country" means you meet one of the following conditions: (1) You live outside the U.S. and Puerto Rico, AND your main place of business is outside the U.S. and Puerto Rico; or (2) You are in military or naval service outside the U.S. and Puerto Rico.

Line 1.—Enter the total amount of income tax you expect to owe for 1988. This is the amount you expect to enter on line 20 of Form 1040A, or on line 53 of Form 1040. Be as exact as you can. If you underestimate, you may be charged interest and penalties.

Line 6.—We will not give you more time to file unless:

● There is an entry on line 6, AND

● You send full payment for any amount on line 6 with this form.

Lines 7a and 7b.—If you or your spouse are also using the extra 4 months to file a 1988 gift tax return, be sure you checked the box(es) at the top of the form. Enter the amount you (or your spouse) expect to owe on line(s) 7a and/or 7b. If your spouse is filing a separate Form 4868, enter on your form only the total gift tax and GST tax you expect to owe. Pay the tax in full with this form to avoid interest and penalties. If paying gift and GST taxes on time would cause you undue hardship (not just inconvenience), attach an explanation to this form.

Your signature.—This form must be signed. If you plan to file a joint return, then both of you should sign. But if there is a good reason why one of you cannot, then the other spouse may sign for both. Attach an explanation why the other spouse cannot sign.

Others who can sign for you.—Anyone with a power of attorney can sign. But, the following can sign for you without a power of attorney:

● Attorneys, CPAs, and other persons qualified to practice before the IRS, or

● A person in close personal or business relationship to you who is signing because you cannot. There must be a good reason why you cannot sign. Attach an explanation to the form.

| Form **4952**
Department of the Treasury
Internal Revenue Service | **Investment Interest Expense Deduction**
▶ See separate instructions.
▶ Attach to your tax return. | OMB No. 1545-0191
19**88**
Attachment Sequence No. **72** |
|---|---|---|

Name(s) as shown on return | Social security number or employer identification number

Kind of return . . . . ▶ ☐ Individual   ☐ Estate   ☐ Trust

1	Interest expense on investment debts paid or accrued in 1988. See instructions	**1**	
2	Investment income minus investment expenses. See instructions **2**		
3	Phase-in adjustment from passive activities. See instructions **3**		
4	Net investment income. Subtract line 3 from line 2. If -0- or less, enter -0-.	**4**	
5	Subtract line 4 from line 1. If -0- or less, enter -0- here and on line 13, and skip lines 6 through 12	**5**	
6	Enter the amount from line 1, but see the instructions **6**		
7	Enter the amount from line 2, but see the instructions . . **7**		
8a	Individuals, enter $10,000; ($5,000 if married filing separate returns) **8a**		
b	Estates, enter $10,000; trusts, enter -0- **8b**		
9	Add lines 7 and 8 . . . . **9**		
10	Subtract line 9 from line 6. If -0- or less, enter -0- . . **10**		
11	Subtract line 10 from line 5. If -0- or less, enter -0- . .	**11**	
12	Multiply line 11 by 60% (.6)	**12**	
13	Add lines 10 and 12	**13**	
14	Enter amount from line 1 . . . . **14**		
15	Enter the smaller of line 5 or line 13 . . . . . . **15**		
16	Subtract line 15 from line 14 . . . . **16**		
17	Disallowed investment interest expense from 1987 Form 4952, line 14. If -0-, enter -0- here and on lines 21 and 22, and skip lines 18 through 20. See instructions . . **17**		
18	Enter amount from line 4. If -0- or less, enter -0- here and on line 20 . . . . **18**		
19	Enter amount from line 1 . . . . **19**		
20	Subtract line 19 from line 18. If -0- or less, enter -0-. . . **20**		
21	Enter the smaller of line 17 or line 20 . . . . . **21**		
22	Subtract line 21 from line 17 . . . . **22**		
23	**Disallowed investment interest expense.** Add lines 15 and 22	**23**	
24	**Allowed investment interest expense.** Add lines 16 and 21. See instructions	**24**	

For Paperwork Reduction Act Notice, see page 1 of separate instructions.   Form **4952** (1988)

Form **4972**

Department of the Treasury
Internal Revenue Service

Tax on Lump-Sum Distributions

(Use This Form Only for Lump-Sum Distributions From
Qualified Retirement Plans)

▶ Attach to Form 1040 or Form 1041.   ▶ See separate Instructions.

OMB No. 1545-0193

1988

Attachment
Sequence No. **28**

Name(s) as shown on return

Identifying number

Part I   Complete this part to see if you qualify to use Form 4972

			Yes	No
1	Did you rollover any part of the distribution?	1		
	If "Yes," do not complete the rest of this form.			
2	Was the participant age 50 or older on January 1, 1986?	2		
3	Was this a lump-sum distribution from a qualifying pension, profit-sharing or stock bonus plan?	3		
	If you answered "No" to 2 **or** 3, do not complete the rest of this form.			
4	Was the employee a participant in the plan for at least 5 years before the year of the distribution?	4		
5	Is this a distribution paid to a beneficiary of an employee who died?	5		
	If you answered "No" to 4 **and** 5, do not complete the rest of this form.			
6	Did you quit, retire, get laid off, or get fired from your job before receiving the distribution?	6		
7	Were you self-employed or an owner-employee and became disabled? (See Instructions under Distributions That Qualify)	7		
8	Were you 59½ or older at the time of the distribution?	8		
	If you answered "No" to **all** questions 5 through 8, do not complete the rest of this form.			

If you qualify to use this form, you may elect to use Part II, Part III, or Part IV; or elect to use Part II and Part III, or Part II and Part IV.

Part II   Complete this part to choose the 20% capital gain election (See Instructions for a different capital gain election.)

Check this box to choose the 20% capital gain election . . . . ▶ ☐

1	Capital gain part from Box 3 of Form 1099-R. If you did not check the box above, enter zero	1	
2	Multiply line 1 by 20% (.20) and enter here. If you do not elect to use Part III or Part IV, also enter the amount on Form 1040, line 39, or Form 1041, Schedule G, line 1b	2	

Part III   Complete this part to choose the 5-year averaging method

1	Ordinary income from Form 1099-R, Box 2 minus Box 3. If you did not check the box in Part II, enter the amount from Box 2 of Form 1099-R (taxable amount)	1	
2	Death benefit exclusion (see Instructions)	2	
3	Subtract line 2 from line 1 (total taxable amount)	3	
4	Current actuarial value of annuity, if applicable (from Form 1099-R, Box 8)	4	
5	Add lines 3 and 4 (adjusted total taxable income). If this amount is $70,000 or more, skip lines 6 through 9, and enter this amount on line 10	5	
6	Multiply line 5 by 50% (.50), but do not enter more than $10,000 ⟨6⟩		
7	Subtract $20,000 from line 5. Enter difference. If line 5 is $20,000 or less, enter zero ⟨7⟩		
8	Multiply line 7 by 20% (.20) ⟨8⟩		
9	Subtract line 8 from line 6 (minimum distribution allowance)	9	
10	Subtract line 9 from line 5	10	
11	Federal estate tax attributable to lump-sum distribution. Do not deduct on Form 1040 or Form 1041 the amount attributable to the ordinary income entered on line 1 (see Instructions)	11	
12	Subtract line 11 from line 10	12	
13	Multiply line 12 by 20% (.20)	13	
14	Tax on amount on line 13. Use Tax Rate Schedule X (for single taxpayers) in Form 1040 Instructions (see Instructions)	14	
15	Multiply line 14 by 5. If no entry on line 4, skip lines 16 through 21, and enter this amount on line 22	15	
16	Divide line 4 by line 5 and enter the result as a decimal (see Instructions)	16	
17	Multiply line 9 by the decimal amount on line 16	17	
18	Subtract line 17 from line 4	18	
19	Multiply line 18 by 20% (.20)	19	
20	Tax on amount on line 19. Use Tax Rate Schedule X (for single taxpayers) in Form 1040 Instructions	20	
21	Multiply line 20 by 5	21	
22	Subtract line 21 from line 15	22	
23	Tax on lump-sum distribution (add Part II, line 2, and Part III, line 22). Enter on Form 1040, line 39, or Form 1041, Schedule G, line 1b ▶	23	

For Paperwork Reduction Act Notice, see separate Instructions.

Form **4972** (1988)

Form 4972 (1988) Page **2**

Part IV Complete this part to choose the 10-year averaging method

1	Ordinary income part from Form 1099-R, Box 2 minus Box 3. If you did not check the box in Part II, enter the amount from Box 2 of Form 1099-R (taxable amount)	**1**
2	Death benefit exclusion (see Instructions)	**2**
3	Subtract line 2 from line 1 (total taxable amount)	**3**
4	Current actuarial value of annuity, if applicable (from Form 1099-R, Box 8)	**4**
5	Add lines 3 and 4 (adjusted total taxable amount). If this amount is $70,000 or more, skip lines 6 through 9, and enter this amount on line 10	**5**
6	Multiply line 5 by 50% (.50), but do not enter more than $10,000 . . . . **6**	
7	Subtract $20,000 from line 5. Enter difference. If line 5 is $20,000 or less, enter zero **7**	
8	Multiply line 7 by 20% (.20) **8**	
9	Subtract line 8 from line 6 (minimum distribution allowance)	**9**
10	Subtract line 9 from line 5	**10**
11	Federal estate tax attributable to lump-sum distribution. Do not deduct on Form 1040 or Form 1041 the amount attributable to the ordinary income entered on line 1 (see Instructions)	**11**
12	Subtract line 11 from line 10	**12**
13	Multiply line 12 by 10% (.10)	**13**
14	Tax on amount on line 13. Use Tax Rate Schedule in Form 4972 Instructions	**14**
15	Multiply line 14 by 10. If no entry on line 4, skip lines 16 through 21, and enter this amount on line 22 .	**15**
16	Divide line 4 by line 5 and enter the result as a decimal (see Instructions)	**16**
17	Multiply line 9 by the decimal amount on line 16	**17**
18	Subtract line 17 from line 4	**18**
19	Multiply line 18 by 10% (.10)	**19**
20	Tax on amount on line 19. Use Tax Rate Schedule in Form 4972 Instructions	**20**
21	Multiply line 20 by 10	**21**
22	Subtract line 21 from line 15	**22**
23	Tax on lump-sum distribution (add Part II, line 2, and Part IV, line 22). Enter on Form 1040, line 39, or Form 1041, Schedule G, line 1b . . . . ▶	**23**

Form **6251**	**Alternative Minimum Tax—Individuals**	OMB No. 1545-0227
Department of the Treasury Internal Revenue Service	▶ See separate Instructions. ▶ Attach to Form 1040 or Form 1040NR. Estates and trusts, use Form 8656.	**1988** Attachment Sequence No. **32**

Name(s) as shown on Form 1040	Your social security number

1	Taxable income from Form 1040, line 37 (can be less than zero)	**1**	17517	5
2	Net operating loss deduction. (Do not enter as a negative amount.)	**2**		
3	Add lines 1 and 2	**3**	17517	50
4	**Adjustments:** (See line-by-line instructions before completing.)			
a	Standard deduction from Form 1040, line 34	**4a** 9582 50		
b	Personal exemption amount from Form 1040, line 36 . .	**4b** 6000 00		
c	Medical and dental expense	**4c** 6492 50		
d	Miscellaneous itemized deductions from Schedule A, line 24	**4d** 0		
e	Taxes from Schedule A, line 8	**4e** 1800 00		
f	Refund of taxes	**4f** (–)		
g	Interest from Schedule A, line 12b	**4g** 1000 00		
h	Other interest adjustments	**4h** –		
i	Combine lines 4a through 4h		**4i**	24865 00
j	Depreciation of property placed in service after 1986 . .	**4j** –		
k	Circulation and research and experimental expenditures paid or incurred after 1986	**4k** ~		
l	Mining exploration and development costs paid or incurred after 1986 . . .	**4l** ~		
m	Long-term contracts entered into after 2/28/86	**4m** –		
n	Pollution control facilities placed in service after 1986 . .	**4n** ~		
o	Installment sales of certain property	**4o** ~		
p	Adjusted gain or loss	**4p** ~		
q	Certain loss limitations	**4q** ~		
r	Tax shelter farm loss	**4r** ~		
s	Passive activity loss	**4s** ~		
t	Beneficiaries of estates and trusts	**4t**		
u	Combine lines 4j through 4t		**4u**	0
5	**Tax preference items:** (See line-by-line instructions before completing.) . .			
a	Appreciated property charitable deduction	**5a**		
b	Tax-exempt interest from private activity bonds issued after August 7, 1986	**5b** ~		
c	Depletion	**5c**		
d	Add lines 5a through 5c		**5d**	~
e	Accelerated depreciation of real property placed in service before 1987 . .	**5e** ~		
f	Accelerated depreciation of leased personal property placed in service before 1987	**5f** ~		
g	Amortization of certified pollution control facilities placed in service before 1987	**5g** ~		
h	Incentive stock options. See instructions	**5h**		
i	Intangible drilling costs	**5i** ~		
j	Reserves for losses on bad debts of financial institutions .	**5j** ~		
k	Add lines 5e through 5j		**5k**	~
6	Combine lines 3, 4i, 4u, 5d, and 5k	**6**	42382	00
7	Alternative tax net operating loss deduction. (Do not enter more than 90% of line 6.) See instructions . .	**7**	–	
8	Alternative minimum taxable income (subtract line 7 from line 6). If married filing separate returns, see instructions .	**8**	42382	00
9	Enter: $40,000 ($20,000 if married filing separately; $30,000 if single or head of household)	**9**	30000	00
10	Enter: $150,000 ($75,000 if married filing separately; $112,500 if single or head of household) . . .	**10**	112500	00
11	Subtract line 10 from line 8. If -0- or less, enter -0- here and on line 12 and go to line 13. If this line is more than -0-, go to line 12	**11**	0	
12	Multiply line 11 by 25% (.25)	**12**	0	
13	Subtract line 12 from line 9. If -0- or less, enter -0-	**13**	30000	00
14	Subtract line 13 from line 8. If -0- or less, enter -0- here and on line 19. If this line is more than -0-, go to line 15	**14**	12382	00
15	Multiply line 14 by 21% (.21)	**15**	2600	22
16	Alternative minimum tax foreign tax credit. See instructions	**16**		
17	Tentative minimum tax (subtract line 16 from line 15)	**17**	2600	22
18	Regular tax before credits (Form 1040, line 38) minus foreign tax credit (Form 1040, line 43). See instructions	**18**	2600	50
19	Alternative minimum tax (subtract line 18 from line 17). Enter on Form 1040, line 49. If -0- or less, enter -0- .	**19**	0	

For Paperwork Reduction Act Notice, see separate Instructions.   Form **6251** (1988)

Form **6252**	**Installment Sale Income**	OMB No. 1545-0228
Department of the Treasury Internal Revenue Service	▶ See separate Instructions. ▶ Attach to your tax return. Use a separate form for each sale or other disposition of property on the installment method.	**1988** Attachment Sequence No. **79**

Name(s) as shown on tax return	Identifying number

A Description of the property ▶ ....

B Date acquired (month, day, and year) ▶ .... **C** Date sold (month, day, and year) ▶ ....

D Was the property sold to a related party after May 14, 1980? (See Instructions.) . . . . ☐ Yes ☐ No

E If the answer to D is "Yes," was the property a marketable security? . . . . ☐ Yes ☐ No

If you checked "Yes" to question E, complete Part III.
If you checked "No" to question E, complete Part III for the year of sale and for 2 years after the year of sale.

Part I   Figure the Gross Profit and Contract Price *(Complete this part for the year of sale only.)*

1 Selling price including mortgages and other debts. (Do not include stated or unstated interest.)		**1**	
2 Mortgages and other debts the buyer assumed or took the property subject to, but not new mortgages the buyer got from a bank or other source	**2**		
3 Subtract line 2 from line 1	**3**		
4 Cost or other basis of property sold	**4**		
5 Depreciation allowed or allowable	**5**		
6 Subtract line 5 from line 4 (adjusted basis)	**6**		
7 Commissions and other expenses of sale	**7**		
8 Income recapture from Form 4797, Part III. (See Instructions.) . . .	**8**		
9 Add lines 6, 7, and 8		**9**	
10 Subtract line 9 from line 1. If zero or less, do not complete the rest of this form		**10**	
11 If the property described in question A above was your main home, enter the total of lines 9 and 15 from Form 2119 here		**11**	
12 Subtract line 11 from line 10 (gross profit)		**12**	
13 Subtract line 9 from line 2. If zero or less, enter zero .		**13**	
14 Add line 3 and line 13 (contract price)		**14**	

Part II   Figure the Taxable Part of Installment Sale *(Complete this part for the year of sale and any year you receive a payment or have certain debts you must treat as a payment on installment obligations.)*

15 Divide line 12 by line 14 (gross profit percentage). (For years after the year of sale, see Instructions.) . .	**15**		
16 **For year of sale only**—enter amount from line 13 above; otherwise, enter zero	**16**		
17 Payments received during year. (See Instructions.) (Do not include stated or unstated interest.) . . .	**17**		
18 Add lines 16 and 17	**18**		
19 Payments received in prior years. (See Instructions.) (Do not include stated or unstated interest.) . . .	**19**		
20 Multiply line 18 by line 15 (taxable part of installment sale)	**20**		
21 Part of line 20 that is ordinary income under recapture rules. (See Instructions.)	**21**		
22 Subtract line 21 from line 20. Enter the result here and on Schedule D or Form 4797	**22**		

Part III   Figure the Taxable Part of Related Party Installment Sale *(Do not complete this part if you received the final installment payment this tax year.)*

F Name, address, and taxpayer identifying number of related party ....

G Did the related party, during this tax year, resell or dispose of the property? . . . . ☐ Yes ☐ No

H If the answer to question G is "Yes," complete lines 23 through 30 below unless one of the following conditions is met (check only the box that applies).

☐ The first disposition was a sale or exchange of stock to the issuing corporation.

☐ The second disposition was an involuntary conversion where the threat of conversion occurred after the first disposition.

☐ The second disposition occurred after the death of the original seller or buyer.

☐ It can be established to the satisfaction of the Internal Revenue Service that tax avoidance was not a principal purpose for either of the dispositions. If this box is checked, attach an explanation. (See Instructions.)

23 Selling price of property sold by related party	**23**	
24 Enter contract price from line 14 for year of first sale . . .	**24**	
25 Enter the **smaller** of line 23 or line 24	**25**	
26 Total payments received by the end of your 1988 tax year. Add lines 18 and 19 .	**26**	
27 Subtract line 26 from line 25. If line 26 is more than line 25, enter zero .	**27**	
28 Multiply line 27 by the gross profit percentage on line 15 for year of first sale .	**28**	
29 Part of line 28 that is ordinary income under recapture rules. (See Instructions.) .	**29**	
30 Subtract line 29 from line 28. Enter the result here and on Schedule D or Form 4797 .	**30**	

For Paperwork Reduction Act Notice, see separate Instructions.   Form **6252** (1988)

Form **8283**
(Rev. August 1988)

Department of the Treasury
Internal Revenue Service

Noncash Charitable Contributions

▶ Attach to your Federal income tax return if the total claimed deduction for all property contributed exceeds $500.
▶ See separate Instructions.

OMB No. 1545-0908
Expires 3-31-90

Attachment Sequence No. **55**

Name(s) as shown on your income tax return

Identification number

Note: *Compute the amount of your contribution deduction before completing Form 8283. (See your tax return instructions.)*

Section A   Include in Section A **only** items (or groups of similar items) for which you claimed a deduction of $5,000 or less per item or group, and certain publicly traded securities (see Instructions).

Part I   Information on Donated Property

1	(a) Name and address of the donee organization	(b) Description of donated property (attach a separate sheet if more space is needed)
A		
B		
C		
D		
E		

Note: *Columns (d), (e), and (f) do not have to be completed if the amount you claimed as a deduction for the item is $500 or less.*

	(c) Date of the contribution	(d) Date acquired by donor (mo., yr.)	(e) How acquired by donor	(f) Donor's cost or adjusted basis	(g) Fair market value	(h) Method used to determine the fair market value
A						
B						
C						
D						
E						

Part II   Other Information—Complete question 2 if you gave less than an entire interest in property listed in Part I.
Complete question 3 if restrictions were attached to a contribution listed in Part I.

2   If less than the entire interest in the property is contributed during the year, complete the following:

(a) Enter letter from Part I which identifies the property _____. (Attach a separate statement if Part II applies to more than one property.)

(b) Total amount claimed as a deduction for the property listed in Part I for this tax year _____;
for any prior tax year(s) _____

(c) Name and address of each organization to which any such contribution was made in a prior year (complete only if different from the donee organization above).

Charitable organization (donee) name

Number and street

City or town, state, and ZIP code

(d) The place where any tangible property is located or kept. _____

(e) Name of any person, other than the donee organization, having actual possession of the property. _____

3   If conditions were attached to any contribution listed in Part I, answer the following questions:

	Yes	No
(a) Is there a restriction either temporarily or permanently on the donee's right to use or dispose of the donated property? .		
(b) Did you give to anyone (other than the donee organization or another organization participating with the donee organization in cooperative fundraising) the right to the income from the donated property or to the possession of the property, including the right to vote donated securities, to acquire the property by purchase or otherwise, or to designate the person having such income, possession, or right to acquire?		
(c) Is there a restriction limiting the donated property for a particular use?		

For Paperwork Reduction Act Notice, see separate Instructions.

Form **8283** (Rev. 8-88)

Form 8283 (Rev. 8-88)   Page **2**

Name(s) as shown on your income tax return	Identification number

Section B **Appraisal Summary**—Include in Section B only items (or groups of similar items) for which you claimed a deduction of more than $5,000 per item or group. *(Report contributions of certain publicly traded securities only in Section A.)*

If you donated art, you may have to attach the complete appraisal. See the **Note** in Part II below.

Part I **Donee Acknowledgment** *(To be completed by the charitable organization.)*

1 This charitable organization acknowledges that it is a qualified organization under section 170(c) and that it received the donated property as described in Part II on _____ .
(Date)

Furthermore, this organization affirms that in the event it sells, exchanges, or otherwise disposes of the property (or any portion thereof) within two years after the date of receipt, it will file an information return (**Form 8282,** Donee Information Return) with the IRS and furnish the donor a copy of that return. This acknowledgment does not represent concurrence in the claimed fair market value.

Charitable organization (donee) name	Employer identification number
Number and street	City or town, state, and ZIP code
Authorized signature	Title Date

Part II **Information on Donated Property** *(To be completed by the taxpayer and/or appraiser.)*

2 Check type of property:

☐ Art* (contribution of $20,000 or more)   ☐ Real Estate   ☐ Gems/Jewelry   ☐ Stamp Collections
☐ Art* (contribution of less than $20,000)   ☐ Coin Collections   ☐ Books   ☐ Other

*Art includes paintings, sculptures, watercolors, prints, drawings, ceramics, antique furniture, decorative arts, textiles, carpets, silver, rare manuscripts, historical memorabilia, and other similar objects. **Note:** *If you donated art after December 31, 1987, and your total art contribution deduction was $20,000 or more, you must attach a complete copy of the signed appraisal and include an 8 x 10 inch color photograph (or a color transparency, no smaller than 4 x 5 inches).*

3	**(a)** Description of donated property (attach a separate sheet if more space is needed)	**(b)** If tangible property was donated, give a brief summary of the overall physical condition at the time of the gift	**(c)** Appraised fair market value
A			
B			
C			
D			

	(d) Date acquired by donor (mo., yr.)	**(e)** How acquired by donor	**(f)** Donor's cost or adjusted basis	**(g)** For bargain sales after 6/6/88, enter amount received	**(h)** Amount claimed as a deduction	**(i)** Average trading price of securities
					See instructions	
A						
B						
C						
D						

Part III **Taxpayer (Donor) Statement**—List any item(s) included in Section B, Part II, that is (are) separately identified in the appraisal as having a value of $500 or less. See instructions.

I declare that the following item(s) included in Part II above has (have) to the best of my knowledge and belief an appraised value of not more than $500 (per item). *(Enter identifying letter from Part II and describe the specific item):* _____

Signature of taxpayer (donor) ▶   Date ▶

Part IV **Certification of Appraiser** *(To be completed by the appraiser of the above donated property.)*

I declare that I am not the donor, the donee, a party to the transaction in which the donor acquired the property, employed by, married to, or related to any of the foregoing persons, or an appraiser regularly used by any of the foregoing persons and who does not perform a majority of appraisals during the taxable year for other persons.

Also, I declare that I hold myself out to the public as an appraiser or perform appraisals on a regular basis; and that because of my qualifications as described in the appraisal, I am qualified to make appraisals of the type of property being valued. I certify the appraisal fees were not based upon a percentage of the appraised property value. Furthermore, I understand that a false or fraudulent overstatement of the property value as described in the qualified appraisal or this appraisal summary may subject me to the civil penalty under section 6701(a) (aiding and abetting the understatement of tax liability). I affirm that I have not been barred from presenting evidence or testimony by the Director of Practice.

Please Sign Here	Signature ▶ Title ▶ Date of appraisal ▶
	Business address Identification number

City or town, state, and ZIP code

Form **8332** (Rev. December 1987)	**Release of Claim to Exemption for Child of Divorced or Separated Parents**	OMB No. 1545-0915 Expires 10-31-90
Department of the Treasury Internal Revenue Service	▶ **Attach to Tax Return of Parent Claiming Exemption**	Attachment Sequence No. **51**

Name(s) of parent claiming exemption as shown on tax return	Social security number

Part I   **Release of Claim to Exemption for Current Year**

I agree not to claim an exemption for _____

                                         Name(s) of child (or children)

for the calendar year 19 ____ .

Signature of parent releasing claim to exemption	Social security number	Date

    If you choose not to claim an exemption for this child (or children) for future tax years, complete Part II, as explained in the instructions below.

Part II   **Release of Claim to Exemption for Future Years**

I agree not to claim an exemption for _____

                                         Name(s) of child (or children)

for tax year(s) _____

               (Specify. See instructions.)

Signature of parent releasing claim to exemption	Social security number	Date

Paperwork Reduction Act Notice.— We ask for this information to carry out the Internal Revenue laws of the United States. We need it to ensure that taxpayers are complying with these laws and to allow us to figure and collect the right amount of tax. You are required to give us this information.

Purpose of Form.— This form may be used to release the claim to a child's exemption by a parent who has custody of his or her child and might have been entitled to claim the exemption for this child. This form is completed by the parent who has custody of the child and is given to the parent who will claim the exemption. The parent who will claim the child's exemption must attach this form, or a similar statement, to his or her tax return. See **How To File Form 8332,** below.

Exemption for Child of Divorced or Separated Parents.— In general, the parent who has custody of the child (or children) for the greater part of the year is treated as having provided over half of the child's support for purposes of the dependency exemption for the child if:

1. The child receives over half of his or her support from both of the parents; **AND**

2. The child was in the custody of one or both of his or her parents for more than half of the year.

    This general rule applies to parents who are divorced or legally separated under a decree of divorce or separate maintenance, separated under a

written separation agreement, or who lived apart at all times during the last 6 months of the calendar year.

    This general rule does not apply if **any** of the following apply:

    (a) The parent having custody signs a written statement agreeing not to claim the child's exemption and the parent not having custody attaches this statement to his or her tax return for the tax year. (See **Parent Who Releases Claim to Exemption,** below.)

    (b) The child is treated as having received over half of his or her support from a person under a multiple support agreement (**Form 2120,** Multiple Support Declaration).

    (c) A qualified divorce decree or written agreement was in effect before January 1, 1985, and provides that the noncustodial parent can claim the exemption for the child, and the noncustodial parent provides at least $600 for the support of the child during the year.

Note: *If items (b) or (c) above do not apply, the noncustodial parent must attach a completed Form 8332, or similar statement, to his or her tax return for each year in which the noncustodial parent claims the child's exemption.*

Parent Who Releases Claim to Exemption.— A parent who might be entitled to claim the child's (or children's) exemption because of having custody of the child for a greater part of the calendar year may agree to

release claim to the child's exemption for the current calendar year or for future years, or both. The release can be made by completing Form 8332 or a similar statement.

    Part I should be completed by the parent who chooses to release claim to the child's (or children's) exemption for the current calendar year.

    Part II should be completed by the parent who chooses to release claim to the child's (or children's) exemption for a specified number of future years, or for all future years. If the parent is releasing claim for all future years, "all future years" should be written in the space provided for in Part II.

How To File Form 8332.— The noncustodial parent must attach Form 8332, or a similar statement, to his or her tax return for the tax year in which the noncustodial parent claims the child's exemption. If the parent having custody of the child completes Part II of Form 8332, the noncustodial parent must attach a copy of this form to his or her tax return for each succeeding year in which the noncustodial parent claims the exemption

    The parent who receives the release of claim to the child's exemption may claim the exemption **only** if the other tests in the Form 1040 or 1040A Instructions for dependency exemptions are met.

    For more information, get **Publication 504,** Tax Information for Divorced or Separated Individuals.

Form **8332** (Rev. 12-87)

Form **8582**	**Passive Activity Loss Limitations**	OMB No. 1545-1008
Department of the Treasury Internal Revenue Service	▶ See separate instructions. ▶ Attach to Form 1040 or 1041.	**1988** Attachment Sequence No. **88**

Name(s) as shown on return	Social security or employer identification number

Part I **Computation of 1988 Passive Activity Loss**
Caution: *See the instructions for Worksheet I before completing Part I.*

Rental Real Estate Activities With Active Participation (See the definition of active participation under **Rental Activities** in the instructions.)

Activities acquired before 10-23-86 (Pre-enactment):

1a	Activities with net income, Worksheet 1, Part 1, column (a)	1a		
1b	Activities with net loss, Worksheet 1, Part 1, column (b)	1b		
1c	Combine lines 1a and 1b	1c		

Activities acquired after 10-22-86 (Post-enactment):

1d	Activities with net income, Worksheet 1, Part 2, column (a)	1d		
1e	Activities with net loss, Worksheet 1, Part 2, column (b)	1e		
1f	Combine lines 1d and 1e	1f		
1g	Net income or (loss). Combine lines 1c and 1f.		1g	
1h	Prior year unallowed losses from 1987, Worksheet 1, Parts 1 and 2, column (c) . . .		1h	
1i	Combine lines 1g and 1h		1i	

All Other Passive Activities (See the instructions for lines 2a through 2h.)

Activities acquired before 10-23-86 (Pre-enactment):

2a	Activities with net income, Worksheet 2, Part 1, column (a)	2a		
2b	Activities with net loss, Worksheet 2, Part 1, column (b)	2b		
2c	Combine lines 2a and 2b	2c		

Activities acquired after 10-22-86 (Post-enactment):

2d	Activities with net income, Worksheet 2, Part 2, column (a)	2d		
2e	Activities with net loss, Worksheet 2, Part 2, column (b)	2e		
2f	Combine lines 2d and 2e	2f		
2g	Net income or (loss). Combine lines 2c and 2f.		2g	
2h	Prior year unallowed losses from 1987, Worksheet 2, Parts 1 and 2, column (c) . . .		2h	
2i	Combine lines 2g and 2h		2i	
3	Combine lines 1i and 2i. If the result is net income or -0-, see the instructions for line 3. If this line and line 1c or line 1i are losses, go to line 4. Otherwise, enter -0- on lines 8 and 9 and go to line 10 .		3	

Part II **Computation of the Special Allowance for Rental Real Estate With Active Participation**
Note: *Before completing Parts II and III, see the instructions for how to treat numbers as if they were all positive.*

4	Enter the smaller of the loss on line 1i or the loss on line 3. If line 1i is -0- or net income, enter -0- and complete lines 5 through 9		4
5	Enter $150,000. If married filing separately, see instructions.	5	
6	Enter modified adjusted gross income, but not less than -0- (see instructions). If line 6 is equal to or greater than line 5, skip line 7, enter -0- on lines 8 and 9, and then go to line 10. Otherwise, go to line 7 . .	6	
7	Subtract line 6 from line 5	7	
8	Multiply line 7 by 50% (.5). **Do not** enter more than $25,000. If married filing separately, see instructions		8
9	Enter the smaller of line 4 or line 8		9

Part III **Computation of Passive Activity Loss Allowed**

10	Combine lines 1c and 2c and enter the result. If the result is -0- or net income, skip to line 16. (See instructions.)	10
11	If line 1c shows income, has no entry, or shows -0-, enter -0- on line 11. Otherwise, enter the smaller of line 1c or line 8	11
12	Subtract line 11 from line 10. If line 11 is equal to or greater than line 10, enter -0-.	12
13	Subtract line 9 from line 3	13
14	Enter the smaller of line 12 or line 13	14
15	Multiply line 14 by 40% (.4) and enter the result	15
16	Enter the amount from line 9	16
17	**Passive Activity Loss Allowed for 1988.** Add lines 15 and 16	17
18	Add the income, if any, on lines 1a, 1d, 2a, and 2d and enter the result	18
19	**Total losses allowed from all passive activities for 1988.** Add lines 17 and 18. See the instructions to see how to report the losses on your tax return	19

For Paperwork Reduction Act Notice, see separate instructions.

Form **8582** (1988)

B–60   *Tax Forms*

Form **8606**

Department of the Treasury
Internal Revenue Service

Nondeductible IRA Contributions, IRA Basis, and Nontaxable IRA Distributions
▶ Please see Recordkeeping Requirements on back.
▶ Attach to Form 1040, Form 1040A, or Form 1040NR.

OMB No. 1545-1007

1988

Attachment Sequence No. **86**

Name (If married, file a separate Form 8606 for each spouse. See instructions.) | Your social security number

Fill In Your Address Only If You Are Not Filing a Tax Return ▷

Present home address (number and street) (or P.O. Box number if mail is not delivered to street address)

City, town or post office, state, and ZIP code

		Value on 12/31/88
1	Enter name of trustee and value of all your IRAs (attach list if more than three)— Name of trustee (bank, credit union, mutual fund, etc.)	
a		1a
b		1b
c		1c
2	Total value of all IRAs. Add lines 1a through 1c	2
3	Enter the basis in your IRA(s) as of 12/31/87. This is the amount shown on line 13 of your **1987** Form 8606 .	3
4	Enter your nondeductible IRA contributions for 1987 that were made during 1/1/88–4/15/88. This is the amount shown on line 4 of your **1987** Form 8606	4
5	Enter your IRA contributions for 1988 that you choose to be nondeductible. (Include those made during 1/1/89–4/17/89 that were for 1988.) (See instructions.)	5
6	Add lines 3, 4, and 5 and enter the total	6
7	Enter only those contributions included on line 5 that were made during 1/1/89–4/17/89. (This amount may be the same as line 5 if all of your nondeductible contributions for 1988 were made in 1989 by 4/17/89.) (See instructions.)	7
8	Subtract line 7 from line 6 and enter the result	8
9	Adjustments. (See instructions.)	9
10	Combine lines 8 and 9 and enter the result. If you did not receive any IRA distributions (withdrawals) in 1988, skip lines 11 through 15 and enter the amount (or zero, if applicable) from line 10 on line 16 . .	10

11	Enter the value of all your IRAs as of 12/31/88 (from line 2). Include any outstanding rollovers. (See instructions.)	11	
12	Enter total IRA distributions received during 1988. Do not include amounts rolled over before 1/1/89. (See instructions.)	12	
13	Add lines 11 and 12 and enter the total	13	
14	Divide line 10 by line 13 and enter the result as a decimal (to at least two places)	14	.
15	Multiply line 12 by the decimal amount on line 14 and enter the result. This is the amount of your nontaxable distributions for 1988. (See instructions.) ▶	15
16	Subtract line 15 from line 10 and enter the result. This is the basis in your IRA(s) as of 12/31/88 . ▶	16

Sign Here Only If You Are Not Filing a Tax Return ▶

Under penalties of perjury, I declare that I have examined this form, including accompanying attachments, and to the best of my knowledge and belief, it is true, correct, and complete.

Your signature _____ Date _____

General Instructions

Note: *If you made a nondeductible contribution in 1987, do not fill out this form unless you meet one of the requirements under Who Must File.*

Paperwork Reduction Act Notice.—We ask for this information to carry out the Internal Revenue laws of the United States. We need it to ensure that taxpayers are complying with these laws and to allow us to figure and collect the right amount of tax. You are required to give us this information.

The time needed to complete and file this form will vary depending on individual circumstances. The estimated average time is:

Recordkeeping . . . . . . 26 minutes

Learning about the law or the form . . . . . . 7 minutes
Preparing the form . . . . 28 minutes
Copying, assembling, and sending the form to IRS . . 20 minutes

If you have comments concerning the accuracy of these time estimates or suggestions for making this form more simple, we would be happy to hear from you. You can write to either IRS or the Office of Management and Budget at the addresses listed in the instructions of the tax return with which this form is filed.

Purpose of Form.—You must use Form 8606 to report the amount of your IRA contributions that you choose to be nondeductible. You may wish to make nondeductible contributions, for example, if all or part of your contributions are not

deductible because of the income limitations for IRAs. First, figure the amount of your deductible contributions using the Instructions for Form 1040 or Form 1040A, whichever applies to you. Then enter on line 5 of Form 8606 the amount you choose to be nondeductible.

The part of any distributions you receive attributable to nondeductible contributions will not be taxable. If you made nondeductible contributions in 1987 or 1988, also use Form 8606 to figure the nontaxable portion of any IRA distributions you receive. If you received any distributions in 1988, line 15 will show the amount that is not taxable.

Who Must File.—You must file Form 8606 for 1988 if:

● You made nondeductible contributions to your IRA during 1988 for 1987 or 1988, or

Form **8606** (1988)

● You made nondeductible contributions to your IRA during 1989 for 1988, or

● You received IRA distributions in 1988 and you made nondeductible contributions to your IRA.

If you and your spouse each choose to make nondeductible IRA contributions, you each must file a Form 8606.

Report your deductible contributions on Form 1040, Form 1040A, or Form 1040NR but not on Form 8606.

When and Where To File.—Attach Form 8606 to your 1988 Form 1040, Form 1040A, or Form 1040NR.

If you are required to complete Form 8606, but you do not have to file an income tax return because you do not meet the requirements for filing a return, you still have to file a Form 8606 with the Internal Revenue Service at the time and place you would normally be required to file Form 1040, Form 1040A, or Form 1040NR.

Name and Social Security Number.— Enter your name and social security number on Form 8606.

Note: *If you file a joint return on Form 1040 or Form 1040A, show the name and social security number of the spouse whose IRA information is shown.*

Recordkeeping Requirements.—To be able to verify the nontaxable part of distributions from your IRA, keep a copy of this form together with copies of the following forms and records until all distributions are made from your IRA(s):

● Forms 1040 (or Forms 1040A or Forms 1040NR) filed for each year you make a nondeductible contribution;

● Forms 5498 or similar statements received each year showing contributions you made;

● Forms 5498 or similar statements you received showing the value of your IRA(s) for each year you received a distribution; and

● Forms 1099-R and W-2P received for each year you received a distribution.

Additional Information.—For more information on nondeductible contributions, get **Pub. 590,** Individual Retirement Arrangements (IRAs).

Penalty for Overstatement.—If you overstate your nondeductible contributions on this form for any tax year, you must pay a penalty of $100 for each overstatement, unless it was due to reasonable cause.

Specific Instructions

Line 1.—Separately list all of your IRAs and their values at the end of the year, regardless of whether you make deductible or nondeductible contributions to them. For married couples, each spouse must list his or her own IRA(s) on a separate Form 8606.

If you have more than three IRAs, list them on a separate attachment and follow the format of line 1. Include on line 2 the total value of all of your IRAs.

You should receive a statement by January 31, 1989, for each IRA account showing the value on December 31, 1988.

Line 5—Covered by a Retirement Plan at Work.—If you were covered by a retirement plan at work and used Worksheet 2 in the Instructions for

Form 1040 or Form 1040A, you should enter on line 5 of Form 8606 any nondeductible contributions shown on line 10 of the worksheet in the Form 1040 Instructions or line 8 of the Form 1040A Instructions . If you made any nondeductible contributions to an IRA for your nonworking spouse, you should complete a separate Form 8606 for your spouse and enter on line 5 of your spouse's Form 8606 any nondeductible contributions for your nonworking spouse from the appropriate lines of Worksheet 2.

If you were covered by a retirement plan at work but you used Worksheet 1 because your income was $25,000 or less ($40,000 or less if you are married filing a joint return or a qualifying widow(er)), follow the instructions below under "Not Covered by a Retirement Plan at Work."

You may also choose to treat any part of deductible contributions as nondeductible. To do this, include on line 5 of Form 8606 any deductible contributions that you are treating as nondeductible.

Note: *You cannot take a deduction for any part of the deductible contributions you are treating as nondeductible.*

If none of your contributions are deductible and you did not use Worksheet 1 or 2 in the Form 1040 or 1040A Instructions, you may still choose to make a nondeductible contribution up to a maximum of $2,000 (but not more than your earned income). Enter the amount of your contributions that you are treating as nondeductible on line 5 of Form 8606.

If contributions were also made to an IRA for your nonworking spouse and none of the contributions are deductible, you may still make nondeductible contributions up to a maximum of $2,250 (but not more than your earned income). Enter on line 5 of your Form 8606 the total nondeductible contributions that you are making to your IRA. Enter the balance on line 5 of your nonworking spouse's Form 8606. You cannot contribute more than $2,000 to either your or your spouse's IRA. Also, the total of the two amounts cannot be more than $2,250 and not more than your earned income.

Not Covered by a Retirement Plan at Work.—If you were not covered by a retirement plan at work or were covered, but had income of $25,000 or less ($40,000 or less if married filing a joint return or a qualifying widow(er)), complete Worksheet 1 in the Instructions for Form 1040 or Form 1040A. The amount shown on line 3 of the worksheet is the amount of your contributions that you may deduct. However, you may choose to make all or part of that amount nondeductible. Enter on line 5 of your Form 8606 the difference between the amount you are deducting and the amount shown on line 3 of Worksheet 1.

If contributions were made to an IRA for your nonworking spouse, the amount shown on line 8 of Worksheet 1 is the amount of the allowable deduction for your nonworking spouse's IRA. However, you can treat all or part of that amount as nondeductible. Enter on line 5 of your nonworking spouse's Form 8606 the difference between the amount that is

deducted for your nonworking spouse and the amount on line 8 of Worksheet 1.

Line 7.—If you made contributions both in 1988 and 1989 that are for 1988, you may choose to apply the contributions made in 1988 first to nondeductible contributions and then to deductible contributions, or vice versa. However, you may not apply to nondeductible contributions more than the amount actually made in 1988.

For example, assume you make contributions of $1,000 in 1988, and $1,000 in 1989. Assume further that $1,500 of your contributions are deductible and $500 are nondeductible. You choose $500 of your contribution in 1988 to be nondeductible. In this case, the $500 would be entered on line 5 instead of line 7 and would become part of your basis for 1988. Otherwise, the amount would be entered on line 7.

Line 8.—Although the 1988 IRA contributions you made during 1/1/89– 4/17/89 (line 7) can be treated as nondeductible (for purposes of line 5), these amounts are not included in your basis for 1988. This is the reason you subtract the amount on line 7 from the amount on line 6. The amount on line 7 will be included in basis on your 1989 Form 8606.

Line 9.—Use this line if you wish to change a nondeductible contribution made on a prior year's return to a deductible contribution, or vice versa. For example, if you were eligible to deduct your IRA contributions for 1988 but you chose to treat them as nondeductible when you filed your 1988 tax return, you can at a later date change the designation to a deductible contribution by filing an amended tax return on **Form 1040X,** Amended U.S. Individual Income Tax Return, and show the change in designation on line 9 of Form 8606.

Line 11.—Enter the total value of all your IRAs as of 12/31/88 from line 2. Include any outstanding rollovers. A **rollover** is a tax-free distribution from one IRA which is then contributed to another IRA. The rollover contribution must be made within 60 days of receiving the distribution from the first IRA. An **outstanding rollover** is any amount distributed to you from one IRA within 60 days of the end of 1988 (between November 2 and December 31) that you did not roll over to another IRA by 12/31/88, but that you roll over to another IRA in 1989 within the normal 60-day rollover period.

Line 12.—Do not include any distributions that were: (1) received in 1988 that you rolled over to another IRA by 12/31/88; (2) outstanding rollovers included on line 11; (3) contributions under Internal Revenue Code section 408(d)(4) that were returned to you before the due date of the return; or (4) excess contributions made under Internal Revenue Code section 408(d)(5).

Line 15.—The amount shown on this line is your nontaxable IRA distribution for 1988. Subtract this amount from your total distributions shown on line 12. The difference is your taxable distributions to be reported on Form 1040, line 16b.

Line 16.—This is the basis in your IRA as of 12/31/88. This amount will be used on Form 8606 in future years if you make nondeductible IRA contributions or receive distributions in those years.

Form **8615**	**Computation of Tax for Children Under Age 14 Who Have Investment Income of More Than $1,000**	OMB No. 1545-0998
Department of the Treasury Internal Revenue Service	▶ See Instructions below and on back. ▶ Attach ONLY to the Child's Form 1040, Form 1040A, or Form 1040NR.	19**88** Attachment Sequence No. **33**

General Instructions

Purpose of Form. For children under age 14, investment income (such as taxable interest and dividends) over $1,000 is taxed at the parent's rate if the parent's rate is higher than the child's rate.

Do not use this form if the child's investment income is $1,000 or less. Instead, figure the tax in the normal manner on the child's income tax return. For example, if the child had $900 of taxable interest income and $200 of income from wages, Form 8615 is not required to be completed and the child's tax should be figured on Form 1040A using the Tax Table.

If the child's investment income is more than $1,000, use this form to see if any of the child's investment income is taxed at the parent's rate and, if so, to figure the child's tax. For example, if the child had $1,100 of taxable interest income and $200 of income from wages, Form 8615 should be completed and attached to the child's Form 1040A.

Investment Income. As used on this form, "investment income" includes all taxable income other than earned income as defined on page 2. It includes income such as taxable interest, dividends, capital gains, rents, royalties, etc. It also includes pension and annuity income and income (other than

earned income) received as the beneficiary of a trust.

Who Must File. Generally, Form 8615 must be filed for any child who was under age 14 on January 1, 1989, and who had more than $1,000 of investment income. If neither parent was alive on December 31, 1988 do not use Form 8615. Instead, figure the child's tax based on his or her own rate.

Additional Information. For more information about the tax on investment income of children, please get **Pub. 929**, Tax Rules for Children and Dependents.

(Instructions continue on back.)

Child's name as shown on return

Child's social security number

Parent's name (first, initial, and last). (**Caution:** See Instructions on back before completing.)

Parent's social security number

Parent's filing status (check one): ☐ Single, ☐ Married filing jointly, ☐ Married filing separately, ☐ Head of household, or ☐ Qualifying widow(er)

Enter number of exemptions claimed on parent's return ▶   ☐

Step 1   Figure child's net investment income

1	Enter the child's investment income, such as taxable interest and dividend income (see Instructions). (If this amount is $1,000 or less, stop here; do not file this form.)	**1**
2	If the child DID NOT itemize deductions on Schedule A (Form 1040 or Form 1040NR), enter $1,000. If the child ITEMIZED deductions, see the Instructions.	**2**
3	Subtract the amount on line 2 from the amount on line 1. Enter the result. (If zero or less, stop here; do not complete the rest of this form but ATTACH it to the child's return.)	**3**
4	Enter the child's **taxable** income (from Form 1040, line 37; Form 1040A, line 19; or Form 1040NR, line 36)	**4**
5	Compare the amounts on lines 3 and 4. Enter the **smaller** of the two amounts ▶	**5**

Step 2   Figure tentative tax based on the tax rate of the parent listed above

6	Enter the parent's **taxable** income (from Form 1040, line 37; Form 1040A, line 19; Form 1040EZ, line 7; or Form 1040NR, line 36)	**6**
7	Enter the total, if any, of the net investment income from Forms 8615, line 5, of ALL OTHER children of the parent. (Do not include the amount on line 5 above.)	**7**
8	Add the amounts on lines 5, 6, and 7. Enter the total	**8**
9	Tax on the amount on line 8 based on the **parent's** filing status (see Instructions). Check if from ☐ Tax Table or ☐ Tax Rate Schedules	**9**
10	Enter the parent's tax (from Form 1040, line 38; Form 1040A, line 20; Form 1040EZ, line 9; or Form 1040NR, line 37). Check if from ☐ Tax Table or ☐ Tax Rate Schedules	**10**
11	Subtract the amount on line 10 from the amount on line 9. Enter the result. (If no amount is entered on line 7, enter the amount from line 11 on line 13; skip lines 12a and 12b.)	**11**
12a	Add the amounts on lines 5 and 7. Enter the total **12a**	
b	Divide the amount on line 5 by the amount on line 12a. Enter the result as a decimal (rounded to two places)	**12b** ✕ .
13	Multiply the amount on line 11 by the decimal amount on line 12b. Enter the result . . . . . . ▶	**13**

Step 3   Figure child's tax

Note: *If the amounts on lines 4 and 5 are the same, skip to line 16.*

14	Subtract the amount on line 5 from the amount on line 4. Enter the result . . **14**	
15	Tax on the amount on line 14 based on the **child's** filing status (see Instructions). Check if from ☐ Tax Table or ☐ Tax Rate Schedule X	**15**
16	Add the amounts on lines 13 and 15. Enter the total	**16**
17	Tax on the amount on line 4 based on the **child's** filing status. Check if from ☐ Tax Table or ☐ Tax Rate Schedule X	**17**
18	Compare the amounts on lines 16 and 17. Enter the **larger** of the two amounts here and on Form 1040, line 38; Form 1040A, line 20; or Form 1040NR, line 37. Be sure to check the box for "Form 8615" . ▶	**18**

For Paperwork Reduction Act Notice, see back of form.   Form **8615** (1988)

Paperwork Reduction Act Notice. We ask for this information to carry out the Internal Revenue laws of the United States. We need it to ensure that taxpayers are complying with these laws and to allow us to figure and collect the right amount of tax. You are required to give us this information. The time needed to complete and file this form will vary depending on individual circumstances. The estimated average time is:

Recordkeeping	7 minutes
Learning about the law or the form	4 minutes
Preparing the form . . .	34 minutes
Copying, assembling, and sending the form to IRS . . .	.17 minutes

If you have comments regarding the accuracy of these time estimates or suggestions for making this form more simple, we would be happy to hear from you. You can write to either IRS or the Office of Management and Budget at the addresses listed in the instructions of the tax return with which this form is filed.

Line-by-Line Instructions

We have provided specific instructions for most of the lines on the form. Those lines that do not appear in these instructions are self-explanatory.

Parent's Name and Social Security Number. If the child's parents were married to each other and filed a joint return, enter the name and social security number of the parent who is listed first on the joint return. For example, if the father's name is listed first on the return and his social security number is entered in the block labeled "Your social security number," enter his name and social security number in the spaces provided on Form 8615.

If the parents were married but filed separate returns, enter the name and social security number of the parent who had the **higher** taxable income. If you do not know which parent had the higher taxable income, see Pub. 929.

If the parents were unmarried, treated as unmarried for Federal income tax purposes, or separated either by a divorce or separate maintenance decree, enter the name and social security number of the parent who had custody of the child for most of the year (the custodial parent). **Exception.** If the custodial parent remarried and filed a joint return with his or her spouse, enter the name and social security number of the individual who is listed first on the joint return even if that individual is not the child's parent.

Line 1. If the child had no earned income (defined later), enter the child's adjusted gross income (from Form 1040, line 31; Form 1040A, line 13; or Form 1040NR, line 31).

If the child had earned income, use the following worksheet to figure the amount to enter on line 1. However, if any of the following applies, use the worksheet in Pub. 929 instead of the one below to figure the amount to enter on Form 8615, line 1:

● The child files **Form 2555,** Foreign Earned Income.

● The child had a net loss from self-employment.

● The child claims a net operating loss deduction.

Worksheet (keep for your records)

1. Enter the amount from the child's Form 1040, line 23; Form 1040A, line 11; or Form 1040NR, line 23, whichever applies . . _____

2. Enter the child's earned income (defined below) plus any deduction the child claims on Form 1040, line 28, or Form 1040NR, line 28, whichever applies . . _____

3. Subtract the amount on line 2 from the amount on line 1. Enter the result here and on Form 8615, line 1 . . . . _____

Earned income includes wages, tips, and other payments received for personal services performed. Generally, earned income is the total of the amount(s) reported on Form 1040, lines 7, 12, and 19; Form 1040A, line 7; or Form 1040NR, lines 8, 13, and 20.

Line 2. If the child itemized deductions on **Schedule A** (Form 1040 or Form 1040NR), enter on line 2 the **greater** of:

● $500 plus the portion of the amount on Schedule A (Form 1040), line 26 (or Schedule A (Form 1040NR), line 10), that is directly connected with the production of the investment income on Form 8615, line 1; OR

● $1,000.

Line 6. Enter the taxable income shown on the tax return of the parent identified at the top of Form 8615. If the parent's taxable income is less than zero, enter zero on line 6.

If the parent filed a joint return, enter the total taxable income shown on that return even if the parent's spouse is not the child's parent.

Line 7. If the individual identified as the parent on this Form 8615 is also identified as the parent on any other Form 8615, add the amounts, if any, from line 5 of each of the other Forms 8615 and enter the total on line 7.

Line 9. Figure the tax on the amount on line 8 using the Tax Table or Tax Rate Schedules, whichever applies.

Line 10. Enter the tax shown on the tax return of the parent identified at the top of Form 8615. If the parent filed a joint return, enter the tax shown on that return even if the parent's spouse is not the child's parent.

Line 15. Figure the tax on the amount on line 14 using the Tax Table or Tax Rate Schedule X, whichever applies.

Line 17. Figure the tax on the child's taxable income as if these rules did not apply.

Line 18. Compare the amounts on lines 16 and 17 and enter the **larger** of the two amounts on line 18. Be sure to check the box for "Form 8615" on the appropriate line of the child's tax return even if the amount on line 17 is the larger of the two amounts.

Incomplete Information for Parent. If a parent or guardian of a child cannot obtain the necessary information to complete Form 8615 before the due date of the child's return, reasonable estimates of the parent's taxable income or filing status and the net investment income of other children may be made. The appropriate line of Form 8615 must be marked "Estimated." For more information, see Pub. 929, Tax Rules for Children and Dependents.

Amended Return. If after the child's return is filed the parent's taxable income is changed or the net investment income of any of the parent's other children is changed, the child's tax must be refigured using the adjusted amounts. If the child's tax is changed as a result of the adjustment(s), file **Form 1040X,** Amended U.S. Individual Income Tax Return, to correct the child's tax.

Alternative Minimum Tax. Pending legislation would provide special rules to determine if a child whose tax is figured on Form 8615 is subject to the alternative minimum tax. Get **Pub 553,** Highlights of the 1988 Tax Changes, to find out whether this law was passed.

APPENDIX C

Glossary of Tax Terms

NOTE: The words and phrases appearing below have been defined to reflect their conventional use in the field of taxation. Such definitions may therefore be incomplete for other purposes.

A

Accelerated cost recovery system (ACRS). A method whereby the cost of tangible property is recovered over a prescribed period of time. Enacted by the Economic Recovery Tax Act (ERTA) of 1981 and modified by the Tax Reform Act (TRA) of 1986, the approach disregards salvage value, imposes a period of cost recovery that depends upon the classification of the asset into one of various recovery periods, and prescribes the applicable percentage of cost that can be deducted each year. § 168.

Accelerated depreciation. Various methods of depreciation that yield larger deductions in the earlier years of the life of an asset than the straight-line method. Examples include the double declining-balance and the sum-of-the-years' digits methods of depreciation. §§ 167(b)(2) and (3).

Accident and health benefits. Employee fringe benefits provided by employers through the payment of health and accident insurance premiums or the establishment of employer-funded medical reimbursement plans. Employers generally are entitled to a deduction for such payments, whereas employees generally exclude the fringe benefits from gross income. §§ 105 and 106.

Accounting income. The accountant's concept of income is generally based upon the realization principle. Financial accounting income may differ from taxable income (e.g., accelerated depreciation might be used for Federal income tax and straight-line depreciation for financial accounting purposes). Differences are included in a reconciliation of taxable and accounting income on Schedule M–1 of Form 1120 for corporations. Fifty percent of the excess of pretax financial accounting income over alternative minimum taxable income is an adjustment for alter-

native minimum tax purposes for a corporation in 1989. See *alternative minimum tax.*

Accounting method. The method under which income and expenses are determined for tax purposes. Major accounting methods are the cash basis and the accrual basis. Special methods are available for the reporting of gain on installment sales, recognition of income on construction projects (the completed contract, percentage of completion, and percentage of completion-capitalized cost methods), and the valuation of inventories (last-in, first-out and first-in, first-out). §§ 446–474. See also *accrual method, cash method, completed contract method, percentage of completion-capitalized cost method, percentage of completion method,* etc.

Accounting period. The period of time, usually a year, used by a taxpayer for the determination of tax liability. Unless a fiscal year is chosen, taxpayers must determine and pay their income tax liability by using the calendar year (January 1 through December 31) as the period of measurement. An example of a fiscal year is July 1 through June 30. A change in accounting periods (e.g., from a calendar year to a fiscal year) generally requires the consent of the IRS. A new taxpayer, such as a newly formed corporation or an estate created upon the death of an individual taxpayer, is free to select either a calendar or a fiscal year without the consent of the IRS. Limitations exist on the selection of an accounting period by a partnership, an S corporation, and a personal service corporation. §§ 441–444.

Accrual method. A method of accounting that reflects expenses incurred and income earned for any one tax year. In contrast to the cash basis of accounting, expenses do not have to be paid to be deductible nor does income have to be received to be taxable. Unearned income (e.g., prepaid interest and rent) generally is taxed in the year of receipt regardless of the method of accounting used by the taxpayer. § 446(c) (2). See also *accounting method, cash method,* and *unearned income.*

Accumulated earnings tax. A special tax imposed on corporations that accumulate (rather than distribute) their earnings beyond the reasonable needs of the business. The tax is imposed on accumulated taxable income and is imposed in addition to the corporate income tax. §§ 531–537.

Acquiescence. In agreement with the result reached. The IRS follows a policy of either acquiescing (*A, Acq.*) or nonacquiescing (*NA, Non-Acq.*) in the results reached in the Regular decisions of the U.S. Tax Court.

ACRS. See *accelerated cost recovery system.*

Additional depreciation. The excess of the amount of depreciation actually deducted over the amount that would have been deducted had the straight-line method been used. § 1250(b). See also *Section 1250 recapture.*

Additional first-year depreciation. Before 1981, taxpayers could elect to deduct additional depreciation equal to 20 percent of the cost of new or used tangible depreciable property with an estimated useful life of six or more years. The maximum cost that qualified was $10,000 ($20,000 for married persons filing a joint return), and the basis for regular depreciation was reduced by the amount of depreciation claimed under this rule. § 179 before ERTA amendment. See also *Section 179 expensing.*

Adjusted basis. The cost or other basis of property reduced by depreciation allowed or allowable and increased by capital improvements. See also *basis* and *realized gain or loss.*

Adjusted gross income. A determination peculiar to individual taxpayers. Generally, it represents gross income less business expenses, expenses attributable to the production of rent or royalty income, the allowed capital loss deduction, and certain personal expenses (deductions *for* adjusted gross income). See also *gross income.* § 62.

Ad valorem tax. A tax imposed on the value of property. The more common ad valorem tax is that imposed by states, counties, and cities on real estate. Ad valorem taxes can, however, be imposed upon personal property (e.g., a motor vehicle tax based on the value of an automobile). §§ 164(a)(1) and (2).

Advance payments. In general, prepayments for services or goods are includible in gross income upon receipt of the advance payments (for both accrual and cash basis taxpayers). However, Rev.Proc. 71–21 (1971–2 C.B. 549) provides guidelines for the deferral of tax on certain advance payments providing specific conditions are met.

AFTR. Published by Prentice-Hall, *American Federal Tax Reports* contains all of the Federal tax decisions issued by the U.S. District Courts, U.S. Claims Court, U.S. Courts o   and U.S. Supreme Court.

AFTR2d. The second series of the *American Federal Tax Reports.*

Alimony payments. Alimony and separate maintenance payments are includible in the gross income of the recipient and are deductible by the payor. The payments must be made in discharge of a legal obligation arising from a marital or family relation-

ship. Child support and voluntary payments are not treated as alimony. Alimony is deductible *for* AGI. §§ 62(10), 71, and 215. See also *child support payments.*

Alimony recapture. The amount of alimony that previously has been included in the gross income of the recipient and deducted by the payor that now is deducted by the recipient and included in the gross income of the payor as the result of front-loading. § 71(f).

All events test. For accrual method taxpayers, income is earned when (1) all the events have occurred that fix the right to receive the income and (2) the amount can be determined with reasonable accuracy. Accrual of income cannot be postponed simply because a portion of the income may have to be returned in a subsequent period. The all events test also is utilized to determine when expenses can be deducted by an accrual basis taxpayer. The application of the test could cause a variation between the treatment of an item for accounting and for tax purposes. For example, a reserve for warranty expense may be properly accruable pursuant to generally accepted accounting principles but not be deductible under the Federal income tax law. Because of the application of the all events test, the deduction becomes available in the year the warranty obligation becomes fixed and the amount is determinable with reasonable certainty. Reg. §§ 1.446–1(c)(1)(ii) and 1.461–1(a)(2).

Alternate valuation date. Property passing from a person by reason of death may be valued for death tax purposes as of the date of death or the alternate valuation date. The alternate valuation date is six months from the date of death or the date the property is disposed of by the estate, whichever comes first. The use of the alternate valuation date requires an affirmative election on the part of the executor or administrator of the estate. The election of the alternate valuation date is not available unless it decreases both the amount of the gross estate *and* the estate tax liability. §§ 1014(a) and 2032.

Alternative depreciation system. A cost recovery system that produces a smaller deduction than would be calculated under ACRS. The alternative system must be used in certain instances and can be elected in other instances. § 168(g). See also *cost recovery allowance.*

Alternative minimum tax (AMT). The alternative minimum tax is imposed only to the extent it exceeds the regular income tax (in effect, the tax liability is the greater of the tax liability calculated using the AMT rules and that calculated using the regular income tax rules). The AMT rate (21 percent for the individual taxpayer and 20 percent for the corporate taxpayer) is applied to the alternative minimum tax base. The alternative minimum tax base is calculated by modifying taxable income for the following: (1) add tax preferences, (2) add certain adjustments, (3) deduct certain adjustments, and (4) deduct the exemption amount. §§ 55–59. See also *business untaxed reported profits.*

Alternative tax. An option that is allowed to corporations in computing the tax on net capital gain. The rate is 34 percent of net capital gain. An option that is allowed to the noncorporate taxpayer in computing the tax on net capital gain. The rate is 28 percent of net capital gain. For 1988 and after, the alternative tax will not produce a beneficial result unless regular tax rates are increased by Congress or unless the alternative tax rates are decreased by Congress. §§ 1(j) and 1201. See also *net capital gain.*

Amortization. The allocation (and charge to expense) of the cost or other basis of an intangible asset over the asset's estimated useful life. Intangible assets that have an indefinite life (e.g., goodwill) are not amortizable. Examples of amortizable intangibles include patents, copyrights, and leasehold interests. See also *estimated useful life* and *goodwill.*

Amount realized. The amount received by a taxpayer on the sale or other disposition of property. The measure of the amount realized is the sum of the cash and the fair market value of any property or services received, plus any related debt assumed by the buyer. Determining the amount realized is the starting point for arriving at realized gain or loss. The amount realized is defined in § 1001(b) and the Regulations thereunder. See also *realized gain or loss* and *recognized gain or loss.*

Annuity. A fixed sum payable to a person at specified intervals for a specific period of time or for life. Payments represent a partial return of capital and a return (interest) on the capital investment. Therefore, an exclusion ratio must be used to compute the amount of nontaxable income. The exclusion ratio is used until the annuitant has recovered his or her investment in the annuity contract. Thereafter, all of the annuity payments received are included in gross income § 72. See also *qualified pension or profit sharing plan.*

Appellate court. For Federal tax purposes, appellate courts include the Courts of Appeals and the Supreme Court. If the party losing in the trial (or lower) court is dissatisfied with the result, the dispute may be carried to the appropriate appellate court. See also *Court of Appeals* and *trial court.*

Arm's length transaction. The standard under which unrelated parties would determine an exchange price pursuant to a transaction. Suppose, for example, X Corporation sells property to its sole shareholder for $10,000. In testing whether the $10,000 is an "arm's length" price, one would ascertain the price that would have been negotiated between the corporation and an unrelated party in a bargained exchange.

Assignment of income. A procedure whereby a taxpayer attempts to avoid the recognition of income by assigning the property that generates the income to another. Such a procedure will not avoid the recognition of income by the taxpayer making the assignment if it can be said that the income was earned at the point of the transfer. In this case, usually referred to as an anticipatory assignment of income, the income will be taxed to the person who earns it.

Association. An organization treated as a corporation for Federal tax purposes even though it may not qualify as such under applicable state law. What is designated as a trust or a partnership, for example, may be classified as an association if it clearly possesses corporate attributes. Corporate attributes include centralized management, continuity of existence, free transferability of interests, and limited liability. § 7701(a)(3).

Attribution. Under certain circumstances, the tax law applies attribution rules to assign to one taxpayer the ownership interest of another taxpayer. If, for example, the stock of X Corporation is held 60 percent by M and 40 percent by S, M may be deemed to own 100 percent of X Corporation if M and S are mother and son. In such case, the stock owned by S is attributed to M. See, for example, §§ 267 and 318.

Audit. Inspection and verification of a taxpayer's return or other transactions possessing tax consequences. See also *correspondence audit, field audit,* and *office audit.*

Automatic mileage method. See *automobile expenses.*

Automobile expenses. Automobile expenses are generally deductible only to the extent the automobile is used in business or for the production of income. Personal commuting expenses are not deductible. The taxpayer may deduct actual expenses (including depreciation and insurance) or the standard (automatic) mileage rate may be used (24 cents per mile for the first 15,000 miles and 11 cents thereafter) during any one year. Automobile expenses relative to medical purposes and in connection with job-related moving expenses are deductible to the extent of actual out-of-pocket expenses or at the rate of 9 cents per mile (12 cents for charitable activities). See also *transportation expenses.*

B

Bad debts. A deduction is permitted if a business account receivable subsequently becomes partially or completely worthless, providing the income arising from the debt previously was included in income. Available methods are the direct charge-off method and the reserve method. However, except for certain financial institutions, TRA of 1986 repealed the use of the reserve method for 1987 and thereafter. If the reserve method is used, partially or totally worthless accounts are charged to the reserve. A nonbusiness bad debt deduction is allowed as a short-term capital loss if the loan did not arise in connection with the creditor's trade or business activities. Loans between related parties (family members) generally are classified as nonbusiness. § 166. See also *nonbusiness bad debts.*

Basis. The acquisition cost assigned to an asset for income tax purposes. For assets acquired by purchase, basis would be cost (§ 1012). Special rules govern the basis of property received by virtue of another's death (§ 1014) or by gift (§ 1015), the basis of stock received on a transfer of property to a controlled corporation (§ 358), the basis of the property transferred to the corporation (§ 362), and the basis of property received upon the liquidation of a corporation (§§ 334 and 338). See also *adjusted basis.*

Bonus depreciation. See *additional first-year depreciation* and *Section 179 expensing.*

Book value.   The net amount of an asset after reduction by a related reserve. The book value of accounts receivable, for example, would be the face amount of the receivables less the reserve for bad debts. The book value of a building would be the cost less the accumulated depreciation.

Boot.   Cash or property of a type not included in the definition of a nontaxable exchange. The receipt of boot will cause an otherwise tax-free transfer to become taxable to the extent of the lesser of the fair market value of such boot or the realized gain on the transfer. Examples of nontaxable exchanges that could be partially or completely taxable due to the receipt of boot include transfers to controlled corporations [§ 351(b)] and like-kind exchanges [§ 1031(b)]. See also *realized gain or loss* and *recognized gain or loss.*

Bribes and illegal payments.   Section 162 denies a deduction for bribes or kickbacks, fines and penalties paid to a government for violation of law, and two-thirds of the treble damage payments made to claimants under violation of the antitrust law. Denial of a deduction for bribes and illegal payments is based upon the judicially established principle that allowing such payments would be contrary to public policy.

B.T.A.   The Board of Tax Appeals was a trial court that considered Federal tax matters. This court is now designated as the U.S. Tax Court.

Burden of proof.   The requirement in a lawsuit to show the weight of evidence and thereby gain a favorable decision. Except in cases of tax fraud, the burden of proof in a tax case generally will be on the taxpayer.

Business energy tax credit.   See *energy tax credit—business property.*

Business expenses.   See *trade or business expenses.*

Business gifts.   Business gifts are deductible only to the extent that each gift does not exceed $25 per person per year. Exceptions are made for gifts costing $4 or less and for certain employee awards. § 274(b).

Business untaxed reported profits.   Such profits are a positive adjustment for purposes of the corporate alternative minimum tax. For taxable years beginning prior to 1990, the amount is one-half of the excess of pretax book income over the alternative minimum taxable income (AMTI). For taxable years beginning after 1990, the amount is 75 percent of the excess of adjusted current earnings over the alternative minimum taxable income (AMTI). §§ 56(c)(1), (f), and (g). See also *alternative minimum tax.*

C

Canons of taxation.   Tax criteria used in the selection of a tax base originally discussed by Adam Smith in *Wealth of Nations.* Canons of taxation include equality, convenience, certainty, and economy.

Capital asset.   Broadly speaking, all assets are capital except those specifically excluded by the Code. Major categories of noncapital assets include property held for resale in the normal course of business (inventory), trade accounts and notes receivable, and depreciable property and real estate used in a trade or business (§ 1231 assets). § 1221. See also *capital gain* and *capital loss.*

Capital contributions.   Various means by which a shareholder makes additional funds available to the corporation (placed at the risk of the business) without the receipt of additional stock. Such contributions are added to the basis of the shareholder's existing stock investment and do not generate income to the corporation. § 118.

Capital expenditure.   An expenditure that should be added to the basis of the property improved. For income tax purposes, this generally precludes a full deduction for the expenditure in the year paid or incurred. Any capital recovery in the form of a tax deduction would have to come in the form of depreciation. § 263.

Capital gain.   The gain from the sale or exchange of a capital asset. See also *capital asset* and *net capital gain.*

Capital gain or loss holding period.   The requirement for long-term treatment is that the asset be held for more than six months for assets acquired before January 1, 1988 and for more than one year for assets acquired after December 31, 1987. See also *holding period.*

Capital gain net income.   If the total capital gains for the tax year exceed the total capital losses, the result is capital gain net income. Note that the term does not distinguish between the long-term and short-term classifications. § 1222(9). See also *net capital gain.*

Capital loss.   The loss from the sale or exchange of a capital asset. See also *capital asset.*

Cash basis.   See *accounting method* and *cash method.*

Cash equivalent doctrine.   Generally, a cash basis taxpayer does not report income until cash is constructively or actually received. Under the cash equivalent doctrine, cash basis taxpayers are required to report income if the equivalent of cash is received (e.g., property is received) in a taxable transaction.

Cash method.   A method of accounting that generally reports income when cash is collected and reports expenses when cash payments are made. However, for fixed assets, the cash basis taxpayer claims deductions through depreciation or amortization, the same as is done by an accrual basis taxpayer. Prepaid expenses must be capitalized and amortized if the life of the asset extends "substantially beyond" the end of the tax year. See also *constructive receipt.*

Casualty loss.   A casualty is defined as "the complete or partial destruction of property resulting from an identifiable event of a sudden, unexpected or unusual nature" (e.g., floods, storms, fires, auto accidents). Individuals may deduct a casualty loss only if the loss is incurred in a trade or business or in a transaction entered into for profit or is a loss arising from fire, storm, shipwreck, or other casualty or from theft. Individuals usually deduct personal casualty losses as itemized deductions subject to a $100 nondeductible amount and to an annual floor equal to 10 percent of adjusted gross income that applies after the $100 per casualty floor has been applied. Special rules are provided for the netting of certain casualty gains and losses. See also *Section 1231 gains and losses.* See also *disaster loss.*

C corporation. A corporation that has not elected conduit treatment under § 1361. See also *S corporation status.*

Cert. den. By denying the Writ of Certiorari, the U.S. Supreme Court refuses to accept an appeal from a U.S. Court of Appeals. The denial of certiorari does not, however, mean that the U.S. Supreme Court agrees with the result reached by the lower court.

Certiorari. Appeal from a U.S. Court of Appeals to the U.S. Supreme Court is by Writ of Certiorari. The Supreme Court does not have to accept the appeal and usually does not (*cert. den.*) unless there is a conflict among the lower courts that needs to be resolved or a constitutional issue is involved.

Change in accounting method. A change in the taxpayer's method of accounting (e.g., from FIFO to LIFO) generally requires prior approval from the IRS. Generally, a request must be filed within 180 days after the beginning of the taxable year of the desired change. In some instances, the permission for change will not be granted unless the taxpayer agrees to certain adjustments prescribed by the IRS.

Change in accounting period. A taxpayer must obtain the consent of the IRS before changing his or her tax year. Income for the short period created by the change is required to be annualized.

Charitable contributions. Contributions are deductible (subject to various restrictions and ceiling limitations) if made to qualified nonprofit charitable organizations. A cash basis taxpayer is entitled to a deduction solely in the year of payment. Accrual basis corporations may accrue contributions at year-end if payment is properly authorized before the end of the year and payment is made within two and one half months after the end of the year. § 170.

Child and dependent care credit. A tax credit ranging from 20 percent to 30 percent of employment-related expenses (child and dependent care expenses) for amounts of up to $4,800 is available to individuals who are employed (or deemed to be employed) and maintain a household for a dependent child under age 13, disabled spouse, or disabled dependent. § 21.

Child support payments. Payments for child support do not constitute alimony and are therefore not includible in gross income by the recipient or deductible as alimony by the payor. Generally, none of the amounts paid are regarded as child support unless the divorce decree or separation agreement specifically calls for child support payments. However, if the amount of the payment to the former spouse would be reduced upon the happening of a contingency related to a child (e.g., the child attains age 21 or dies), the amount of the future deduction in the payment will be deemed child support for post-1984 agreements and decrees. § 71(c). See also *alimony payments.*

Claim of right doctrine. A judicially imposed doctrine applicable to both cash and accrual basis taxpayers that holds that an amount is includible in income upon actual or constructive receipt if the taxpayer has an unrestricted claim to such amounts. For the tax treatment of amounts repaid when previously included in income under the claim of right doctrine, see § 1341.

Claims Court. One of three Federal trial courts that consider Federal tax controversy. Appeal from the U.S. Claims Court (formerly to the U.S. Supreme Court) now goes to the Court of Appeals for the Federal Circuit. See also *trial court.*

Clear reflection of income. The IRS has the authority to redetermine a taxpayer's income using a method that clearly reflects income if the taxpayer's method does not do so. § 446(b). In addition, the IRS may apportion or allocate income among various related businesses if income is not "clearly reflected." § 482.

Closely-held corporation. A corporation, the stock ownership of which is not widely dispersed. Instead, a few shareholders are in control of corporate policy and are in a position to benefit personally from such policy.

Community property. The states with community property systems are Louisiana, Texas, New Mexico, Arizona, California, Washington, Idaho, Nevada, and Wisconsin. The rest of the states are classified as common law jurisdictions. The difference between common law and community property systems centers around the property rights possessed by married persons. In a common law system, each spouse owns whatever he or she earns. Under a community property system, one-half of the earnings of each spouse is considered owned by the other spouse. Assume, for example, H and W are husband and wife and their only income is the $50,000 annual salary H receives. If they live in New York (a common law state), the $50,000 salary belongs to H. If, however, they live in Texas (a community property state), the $50,000 salary is divided equally, in terms of ownership, between H and W. See also *separate property.*

Completed contract method. A method of reporting gain or loss on certain long-term contracts. Under this method of accounting, gross income and expenses are recognized in the tax year in which the contract is completed. Reg. § 1.451–3. Limitations exist on the ability to use the completed contract method. § 460. See also *percentage of completion-capitalized cost method* and *percentage of completion method.*

Component depreciation. The process of dividing an asset (e.g., a building) into separate components or parts for the purpose of calculating depreciation. The advantage of dividing an asset into components is to use shorter depreciation lives for selected components under § 167. Generally, the same cost recovery period must be used for all the components of an asset under § 168.

Condemnation. The taking of property by a public authority. The property is condemned as the result of legal action, and the owner is compensated by the public authority. The power to condemn property is known as the right of eminent domain.

Conduit concept.   An approach the tax law assumes in the tax treatment of certain entities and their owners. Specific tax characteristics pass through the entity without losing their identity. For example, items of income and expense, capital gains and losses, tax credits, etc., realized by a partnership pass through the partnership (a conduit) and are subject to taxation at the partner level. Also, in an S corporation, certain items pass through and are reported on the returns of the shareholders.

Constructive ownership.   See *attribution*.

Constructive receipt.   If income is unqualifiedly available, it will be subject to the income tax even though it is not physically in the taxpayer's possession. An example would be accrued interest on a savings account. Under the constructive receipt of income concept, such interest will be taxed to a depositor in the year it is available rather than the year actually withdrawn. The fact that the depositor uses the cash basis of accounting for tax purposes is irrelevant. See Reg. § 1.451–2.

Consumer interest.   Interest expense of the taxpayer of a personal nature (not trade or business interest, investment interest, qualified residence interest, or passive activity interest). TRA of 1986 provided that no deduction is permitted for consumer interest. However, the provision is not fully effective until 1991. § 163(h). See also *qualified residence interest.*

Contributions to the capital of a corporation. See *capital contributions.*

Convention expenses.   Travel expenses incurred in attending a convention are deductible if the meetings are related to a taxpayer's trade or business or job-related activities. If, however, the convention trip is primarily for pleasure, no deduction is permitted for transportation expenses. Likewise, if the expenses are for attending a convention related to the production of income (§ 212), no deduction is permitted. Specific limitations are provided for foreign convention expenses. See § 274(n) for the limitations on the deductions for meals. § 274(h).

Correspondence audit.   An audit conducted by the IRS by mail. Typically, the IRS writes to the taxpayer requesting the verification of a particular deduction or exemption. The completion of a special form or the remittance of copies of records or other support is all that is requested of the taxpayer. To be distinguished from a *field audit* or an *office audit.*

Cost recovery allowance.   The portion of the cost of an asset written off under ACRS, which replaced the depreciation system as a method for writing off the cost of an asset for most assets placed in service after 1980. § 168. See also *alternative depreciation system.*

Cost recovery period.   A specified period in the Code for writing off the cost of an asset under ACRS.

Court of Appeals.   Any of thirteen Federal courts that consider tax matters appealed from the U.S. Tax Court, U.S. Claims Court, or a U.S. District Court. Appeal from a U.S. Court of Appeals is to the U.S. Supreme Court by Writ of Certiorari. See also *appellate court.*

D

Death benefit.   A payment made by an employer to the beneficiary or beneficiaries of a deceased employee on account of the death of the employee. Under certain conditions, the first $5,000 of such payment is exempt from the income tax. § 101(b)(1).

Death tax.   See *estate tax.*

Declaration of estimated tax.   A procedure whereby individuals and corporations are required to make quarterly installment payments of estimated tax. Individuals are required to make the declaration and file quarterly payments of the estimated tax if certain requirements are met. In 1989, a declaration is not required for an individual if the estimated tax is reasonably expected to be less than $500.

Deductions for adjusted gross income.   See *adjusted gross income.*

Deductions from adjusted gross income. See *itemized deductions.*

Deferred compensation.   Compensation that will be taxed when received or upon the removal of certain restrictions on receipt and not when earned. An example would be contributions by an employer to a qualified pension or profit sharing plan on behalf of an employee. Such contributions will not be taxed to the employee until the funds are made available or distributed to the employee (e.g., upon retirement). See also *qualified pension or profit sharing plan.*

Deficiency.   Additional tax liability owed by a taxpayer and assessed by the IRS. See also *statutory notice of deficiency.*

Depletion.   The process by which the cost or other basis of a natural resource (e.g., an oil or gas interest) is recovered upon extraction and sale of the resource. The two ways to determine the depletion allowance are the cost and percentage (or statutory) methods. Under the cost method, each unit of production sold is assigned a portion of the cost or other basis of the interest. This is determined by dividing the cost or other basis by the total units expected to be recovered. Under the percentage (or statutory) method, the tax law provides a special percentage factor for different types of minerals and other natural resources. This percentage is multiplied by the gross income from the interest to arrive at the depletion allowance. §§ 613 and 613A.

Depreciation.   The deduction of the cost or other basis of a tangible asset over the asset's estimated useful life. § 167. As to intangible assets, see *amortization.* As to natural resources, see *depletion.* Also see *estimated useful life.* The depreciation system was replaced by ACRS for most assets placed in service after 1980 but still applies for assets placed in service before 1981. See also *recapture of depreciation.*

Determination letter.   Upon the request of a taxpayer, a District Director will comment on the tax status of a completed transaction. Determination letters are most frequently used to clarify employee versus self-employed status, to determine whether a pension or profit sharing plan qualifies under the Code, and to determine the tax-exempt status of certain nonprofit organizations.

Direct charge-off method.   A method of accounting for bad debts whereby a deduction is permitted only when an account becomes partially or completely worthless. See also *reserve for bad debts*.

Disaster loss.   If a casualty is sustained in an area designated as a disaster area by the President of the United States, the casualty is designated a disaster loss. In such an event, the disaster loss may be treated as having occurred in the taxable year immediately preceding the year in which the disaster actually occurred. Thus, immediate tax benefits are provided to victims of a disaster. § 165(i). See also *casualty loss*.

Dissent.   To disagree with the majority. If, for example, Judge B disagrees with the result reached by Judges C and D (all of whom are members of the same court), Judge B could issue a dissenting opinion.

District Court.   A Federal District Court is a trial court for purposes of litigating (among others) Federal tax matters. It is the only trial court where a jury trial can be obtained. See also *trial court*.

Dividends received deduction.   A deduction allowed a corporate shareholder for dividends received from a domestic corporation. The percentage to be applied in calculating the dividends received deduction is dependent on the percentage of stock ownership. If the stock ownership percentage is less than 20 percent, the percentage is 70 percent of the dividends received. If the stock ownership percentage is at least 20 percent but less than 80 percent, the percentage is 80 percent. If the stock ownership percentage is at least 80 percent, the percentage is 100 percent. §§ 243–246A.

E

Earned income.   Income from personal services as distinguished from income generated by property. See §§ 32 and 911 and the Regulations thereunder.

Earned income credit.   The earned income credit is 14 percent of earned income up to $6,500 (a maximum credit of $910) for 1989. If either earned income or adjusted gross income exceeds $10,240, the $910 maximum credit must be reduced by 10 percent of the amount by which the greater of earned income or adjusted gross income exceeds $10,240. Therefore, no earned income credit is allowed if either earned income or adjusted gross income is $19,340 or more. § 32.

Earnings and profits.   A tax concept peculiar to corporate taxpayers that measures economic capacity to make a distribution to shareholders that is not a return of capital. Such a distribution will result in dividend income to the shareholders to the extent of the corporation's current and accumulated earnings and profits.

Education expenses.   Employees may deduct education expenses if such items are incurred either (1) to maintain or improve existing job-related skills or (2) to meet the express requirements of the employer or the requirments imposed by law to retain employment status. Such expenses are not deductible if the education is required to meet the minimum educational standards for the taxpayer's job or the education qualifies the individual for a new trade or business. Reg. § 1.162–5.

Employee expenses.   The deductions *for* adjusted gross income include reimbursed expenses and certain expenses of performing artists. All other employee expenses are deductible *from* adjusted gross income. § 62. See also *trade or business expenses*.

Energy tax credit—business property.   A 10 percent to 15 percent tax credit is available to businesses that invest in certain energy property. The purpose of the credit is to create incentives for conservation and to penalize the increased use of oil and gas. The business energy tax credit applies to equipment with an estimated useful life of at least three years that uses fuel or feedstock other than oil or natural gas (e.g., solar, wind). §§ 46(a) and (b) and 48(l). See also *estimated useful life* and *investment tax credit*.

Entertainment expenses.   Such expenses are deductible only if they are directly related to or associated with a trade or business. Various restrictions and documentation requirements have been imposed upon the deductibility of entertainment expenses to prevent abuses by taxpayers. See for example the provision contained in § 274(n) which disallows 20 percent of entertainment expenses. § 274.

Estate tax.   A tax imposed on the right to transfer property by reason of death. Thus, an estate tax is levied on the decedent's estate and not on the heir receiving the property. §§ 2001 and 2002.

Estimated useful life.   The period over which an asset will be used by a particular taxpayer. Although such period cannot be longer than the estimated physical life of an asset, it could be shorter if the taxpayer does not intend to keep the asset until the asset wears out. Assets such as goodwill do not have an estimated useful life. The estimated useful life of an asset is essential to measuring the annual tax deduction for depreciation and amortization. An asset subject to ACRS is written off over a specified cost recovery period rather than over its estimated useful life.

Excise tax.   A tax on the manufacture, sale, or use of goods or on the carrying on of an occupation or activity. Also a tax on the transfer of property. Thus, the Federal estate and gift taxes are, theoretically, excise taxes.

F

Fair market value.   The amount at which property would change hands between a willing buyer and a willing seller, neither being under any compulsion to buy or sell and both having reasonable knowledge of the relevant facts. Reg. § 20.2031–1(b).

F.2d.   An abbreviation for the Second Series of the *Federal Reporter,* the official series wherein decisions of the U.S. Claims Court (before October 1982) and the U.S. Courts of Appeals are published.

F.Supp.   The abbreviation for *Federal Supplement,* the official series wherein the reported decisions of the U.S. District Courts are published.

Field audit.   An audit by the IRS conducted on the business premises of the taxpayer or in the office of the tax practitioner representing the taxpayer. To be distinguished from a *correspondence audit* or an *office audit.*

First-in, first-out (FIFO).   An accounting method for determining the cost of inventories. Under this method, the inventory on hand is deemed to be the sum of the cost of the most recently acquired units. See also *last-in, first-out (LIFO).*

Foreign earned income exclusion.   The foreign earned income exclusion is a relief provision that applies to U.S. citizens working in a foreign country. To qualify for the exclusion, the taxpayer must be either a bona fide resident of the foreign country or present in the country for 330 days during any 12 consecutive months. The exclusion is limited to $70,000. § 911.

Foreign tax credit or deduction.   Both individual taxpayers and corporations may claim a foreign tax credit on income earned and subject to tax in a foreign country or U.S. possession. As an alternative to the credit, a deduction may be taken for the foreign taxes paid. §§ 27, 164, and 901–905.

Franchise.   An agreement that gives the transferee the right to distribute, sell, or provide goods, services, or facilities within a specified area. The cost of obtaining a franchise may be amortized over the life of the agreement. In general, a franchise is a capital asset and results in capital gain or loss if all significant powers, rights, or continuing interests are transferred pursuant to the sale of a franchise. § 1253.

Fringe benefits.   Compensation or other benefits received by an employee that are not in the form of cash. Some fringe benefits (e.g., accident and health plans, group term life insurance) may be excluded from the employee's gross income and therefore not subject to the Federal income tax.

Fruit and the tree doctrine.   The courts have held that an individual who earns income from property or services cannot assign that income to another. For example, a father cannot assign his earnings from commissions to his child and escape income tax on such amounts.

G

Gift.   A transfer of property for less than adequate consideration. Gifts usually occur in a personal setting (such as between members of the same family). Gifts are excluded from the income tax but may be subject to the *gift tax.*

Gift tax.   A tax imposed on the transfer of property by gift. Such tax is imposed upon the donor of a gift and is based upon the fair market value of the property on the date of the gift. §§ 2501–2524.

Goodwill.   The ability of a business to generate income in excess of a normal rate on assets due to superior managerial skills, market position, new product technology, etc. In the purchase of a business, goodwill represents the difference between the purchase price and the value of the net assets acquired. Goodwill is an intangible asset that possesses an indefinite life and therefore cannot be amortized for Federal income tax purposes. Reg. § 1.167(a)–3. See also *amortization.*

Government bonds issued at a discount. Certain U.S. government bonds (Series E and EE) are issued at a discount and do not pay interest during the life of the bonds. Instead, the bonds are redeemable at increasing fixed amounts. Thus, the difference between the purchase price and the amount received upon redemption represents interest income to the holder. A cash basis taxpayer may defer recognition of gross income until such bonds are redeemed. For Series EE savings bonds issued after 1989, the interest otherwise taxable at redemption can be excluded if the bonds are qualified educational savings bonds. As an alternative to deferring recognition of gross income until the bonds are redeemed, the taxpayer may elect to include in gross income on an annual basis the annual increase in the value of the bonds. § 454.

Gross income.   Income subject to the Federal income tax. Gross income does not include income for which the Code permits exclusion treatment (e.g., interest on municipal bonds). For a manufacturing or merchandising business, gross income means gross profit (gross sales or gross receipts less cost of goods sold). § 61 and Reg. § 1.61–3(a).

Group term life insurance.   Life insurance coverage permitted by an employer for a group of employees. Such insurance is renewable on a year-to-year basis and does not accumulate in value (i.e., no cash surrender value is built up). The premiums paid by the employer on such insurance are not taxed to an employee on coverage of up to $50,000 per person. § 79 and Reg. § 1.79–1(a).

H

Head of household.   An unmarried individual who maintains a household for another and satisfies certain conditions set forth in § 2(b). Such status enables the taxpayer to use a set of income tax rates [see § 1(b)] that are lower than those applicable to other unmarried individuals [§ 1(c)] but higher than those applicable to surviving spouses and married persons filing a joint return [§ 1(a)]. See also *tax rate schedules.*

Hobby loss.   A nondeductible loss arising from a personal hobby as contrasted with an activity engaged in for profit. Generally, the law provides a rebuttable presumption that an activity is engaged in for profit if profits are earned during any three or more years during a five-year period. § 183. See also *vacation home.*

Holding period. The period of time property has been held for income tax purposes. The holding period is crucial in determining whether gain or loss from the sale or exchange of a capital asset is long-term or short-term. See also *capital gain or loss holding period.* § 1223.

Home office expenses. See *office-in-the-home expenses.*

H.R. 10 plan. See *self-employment retirement plan.*

I

Imputed interest. For certain long-term sales of property, the IRS can convert some of the gain from the sale into interest income if the contract does not provide for a minimum rate of interest to be paid by the purchaser. The application of this procedure has the effect of forcing the seller to recognize less long-term capital gain and more ordinary income (interest income). §§ 483 and 1274 and the Regulations thereunder. In addition, interest income and interest expense are imputed (deemed to exist) on interest-free or below-market rate loans between certain related parties. See also *interest-free loans.* § 7872.

Individual retirement account (IRA). Individuals with earned income who are not active participants in qualified retirement plans are permitted to set aside up to 100 percent of their salary per year (generally not to exceed $2,000) for a retirement account. The amount set aside can be deducted by the taxpayer and will be subject to income tax only upon withdrawal. Specific requirements are established for the withdrawal of such amounts, and penalties are provided for failure to comply. If the employee is an active participant in a qualified retirement plan, the IRA deduction is phased out once adjusted gross income exceeds certain amounts. Even if the IRA deduction has been completely phased out, the taxpayer can still make a nondeductible contribution. § 219. See also *simplified employee pensions.*

Installment method. A method of accounting enabling a taxpayer to spread the recognition of gain on the sale of property over the payout period. Under this procedure, the seller computes the gross profit percentage from the sale (the gain divided by the contract price) and applies it to each payment received to arrive at the gain to be recognized. §§ 453 and 453A.

Intangible drilling and development costs. Taxpayers may elect to expense or capitalize (subject to amortization) intangible drilling and development costs. However, ordinary income recapture provisions now apply to oil and gas properties on a sale or other disposition if the expense method is elected. §§ 263(c) and 1254(a).

Interest-free loans. Bona fide loans that carry no interest (or a below-market rate). If made in a nonbusiness setting, the imputed interest element is treated as a gift from the lender to the borrower. If made by a corporation to a shareholder, a constructive dividend could result. In either event, the lender may have interest income to recognize and the borrower may be able to deduct interest expense. § 7872.

Investigation of a new business. Expenditures by taxpayers who are not engaged in a trade or business incurred in the evaluation of prospective business activities (acquiring an existing business or entering into a new trade or business). If the expenditures are general, it is the position of the IRS that no deduction is permitted even if the investigation is abandoned because the taxpayer is not engaged in a trade or business. The courts, however, have permitted a loss deduction providing the expenditures were specific.

Investment indebtedness. If funds are borrowed by noncorporate taxpayers for the purpose of purchasing or continuing to hold investment property, some portion of the interest expense deduction may be disallowed. The interest deduction is generally limited to net investment income. Amounts that are disallowed may be carried forward and treated as investment interest of the succeeding year. Prior to 1991, the net investment income ceiling is increased by a statutory dollar amount that is being phased out (i.e., the phase out will be complete in 1991). § 163(d).

Investment tax credit. A tax credit that usually was equal to 10 percent (unless a reduced credit was elected) of the qualified investment in tangible personalty used in a trade or business. If the tangible personalty had a recovery period of five years or more, the full cost of the property qualified for the credit. Only 60 percent qualified for property with a recovery period of three years. However, the regular investment tax credit was repealed by TRA of 1986 for property placed in service after December 31, 1985. §§ 46–48. See also *recapture of investment tax credit* and *Section 38 property.*

Involuntary conversion. The loss or destruction of property through theft, casualty, or condemnation. Any gain realized on an involuntary conversion can, at the taxpayer's election, be postponed (deferred) for Federal income tax purposes if the owner reinvests the proceeds within a prescribed period of time in property that is similar or related in service or use. § 1033.

IRA. See *individual retirement account.*

Itemized deductions. Certain personal expenditures allowed by the Code as deductions *from* adjusted gross income. Examples include certain medical expenses, interest on home mortgages, and charitable contributions. Itemized deductions are reported on Schedule A of Form 1040. § 63(d).

J

Jobs credit. Employers are allowed a tax credit equal to 40 percent of the first $6,000 of wages (per eligible employee) for the first year of employment. Eligible employees include certain hard-to-employ individuals (e.g., youths from low-income families, handicapped persons). The employer's deduction for wages is reduced by the amount of the credit taken. For qualified summer youth employees, the 40 percent rate is applied to the first $3,000 of qualified wages. §§ 51 and 52.

K

Keogh plan.   *See self-employment retirement plan.*

L

Last-in, first-out (LIFO).   An accounting method for valuing inventories for tax purposes. Under this method, it is assumed that the inventory on hand is valued at the cost of the earliest acquired units. § 472 and the Regulations thereunder. See also *first-in, first-out (FIFO).*

Lessee.   One who rents property from another. In the case of real estate, the lessee is also known as the tenant.

Lessor.   One who rents property to another. In the case of real estate, the lessor is also known as the landlord.

Life insurance proceeds.   Generally, life insurance proceeds paid to a beneficiary upon the death of the insured are exempt from Federal income tax. An exception is provided when a life insurance contract has been transferred for valuable consideration to another individual who assumes ownership rights. In such case, the proceeds are income to the assignee to the extent that the proceeds exceed the amount paid for the policy plus any subsequent premiums paid. Insurance proceeds may be subject to the Federal estate tax if the decedent retained any incidents of ownership in the policy before death or if the proceeds are payable to the decedent's estate. §§ 101 and 2042.

Like-kind exchange.   An exchange of property held for productive use in a trade or business or for investment (except inventory, stocks and bonds, and partnership interests) for other investment or trade or business property. Unless nonlike-kind property is received (boot), the exchange will be nontaxable. § 1031. See also *boot.*

Limited expensing.   See *Section 179 expensing.*

Liquidation of a corporation.   In a complete or partial liquidation of a corporation, amounts received by the shareholders in exchange for their stock are usually treated as a sale or exchange of the stock resulting in capital gain or loss treatment. § 331. Special rules apply to the liquidation of a subsidiary under § 332. Generally, a liquidation is a taxable event to the corporation. § 336. Special rules apply to a parent corporation that is liquidating a subsidiary. § 337.

Low-income housing.   Low-income housing is rental housing that is a dwelling unit for low or moderate income individuals or families. Beneficial tax treatment is in the form of the *low-income housing credit.* § 42. See also *accelerated cost recovery system.*

Low-income housing credit.   Beneficial treatment to owners of low-income housing is provided in the form of a tax credit. The calculated credit is claimed in the year the building is placed in service and in the following nine years. § 42.

Lump-sum distribution.   Payment of the entire amount due at one time rather than in installments. Such distributions often occur from qualified pension or profit sharing plans upon the retirement or death of a covered employee. The recipient of a lump-sum distribution may recognize both long-term capital gain and ordinary income upon the receipt of the distribution. The ordinary income portion may be subject to a special five-year or ten-year income averaging provision. § 402(e).

M

Majority interest partners.   Partners who have more than a 50 percent interest in partnership profits and capital, counting only those partners who have the same taxable year, are referred to as majority interest partners. The term is of significance in determining the appropriate taxable year of a partnership. § 706(b). See also *accounting period* and *principal partner.*

Marital deduction.   A deduction allowed upon the transfer of property from one spouse to another. The deduction is allowed under the Federal gift tax for lifetime (inter vivos) transfers or under the Federal estate tax for death (testamentary) transfers. §§ 2056 and 2523.

Medical expenses.   Medical expenses of an individual, spouse, and dependents are allowed as an itemized deduction to the extent that such amounts (less insurance reimbursements) exceed 7.5 percent of adjusted gross income. § 213.

Mitigation of the annual accounting period concept.   Various tax provisions that provide relief from the effect of the finality of the annual accounting period concept. For example, the *net operating loss* provisions provide relief to a taxpayer whose business activities for different taxable years fluctuate in terms of profits and losses. See also *accounting period.*

Moving expenses.   A deduction *from* AGI is permitted to employees and self-employed individuals provided certain tests are met. The taxpayer's new job must be at least 35 miles farther from the old residence than the old residence was from the former place of work. In addition, an employee must be employed on a full-time basis at the new location for 39 weeks in the 12–month period following the move. Ceiling limitations are placed on indirect expenses (e.g., house-hunting trips and temporary living expenses), but no ceiling exists for direct moving expenses (e.g., expenses of moving personal belongings and traveling). § 217.

N

Necessary.   Appropriate and helpful in furthering the taxpayer's business or income-producing activity. §§ 162(a) and 212. See also *ordinary.*

Net capital gain.   The excess of the net long-term capital gain for the tax year over the net short-term capital loss. § 1222(11). See also *alternative tax.*

Net operating loss.   To mitigate the effect of the annual accounting period concept, § 172 allows taxpayers to use an excess loss of one year as a deduction for certain past or future years. In this regard, a carryback period of three years and a carryforward period of fifteen years are allowed. See also *mitigation of the annual accounting period concept.*

Net worth method. An approach used by the IRS to reconstruct the income of a taxpayer who fails to maintain adequate records. Under this approach, the gross income for the year is the increase in net worth of the taxpayer (assets in excess of liabilities) with appropriate adjustment for nontaxable receipts and nondeductible expenditures. The net worth method often is used when tax fraud is suspected.

Ninety-day letter. See *statutory notice of deficiency.*

Nonbusiness bad debts. A bad debt loss not incurred in connection with a creditor's trade or business. Such loss is deductible as a short-term capital loss and will be allowed only in the year the debt becomes entirely worthless. In addition to family loans, many investor losses fall into the classification of nonbusiness bad debts. § 166(d). See also *bad debts.*

Nonqualified deferred compensation plans. Compensation arrangements that are frequently offered to executives. Such plans may include stock options, restricted stock, etc. Often, an executive may defer the recognition of taxable income. The employer, however, does not receive a tax deduction until the employee is required to include the compensation in income. See also *restricted property.*

Nonrecourse debt. An obligation on which the endoser is not personally liable. An example of a nonrecourse debt is a mortgage on real estate acquired by a partnership without the assumption of any liability on the mortgage by the partnership or any of the partners. The acquired property generally is pledged as collateral for the loan.

O

Office audit. An audit by the IRS of a taxpayer's return that is conducted in the agent's office. To be distinguished from a *correspondence audit* or a *field audit.*

Office-in-the-home expenses. Employment and business-related expenses attributable to the use of a residence (e.g., den or office) are allowed only if the portion of the residence is exclusively used on a regular basis as a principal place of business of the taxpayer or as a place of business that is used by patients, clients, or customers. If the expenses are incurred by an employee, the use must be for the convenience of the employer as opposed to being merely appropriate and helpful. § 280A.

Open transaction. A judicially imposed doctrine that allows the taxpayer to defer all gain until he or she has collected an amount equal to the adjusted basis of assets transferred pursuant to an exchange transaction. This doctrine has been applied where the property received in an exchange has no ascertainable

fair market value due to the existence of contingencies. See also *recovery of capital doctrine.*

Options. The sale or exchange of an option to buy or sell property results in capital gain or loss if the property is a capital asset. Generally, the closing of an option transaction results in short-term capital gain or loss to the writer of the call and the purchaser of the call option. § 1234.

Ordinary. Common and accepted in the general industry or type of activity in which the taxpayer is engaged. It comprises one of the tests for the deductibility of expenses incurred or paid in connection with a trade or business; for the production or collection of income; for the management, conservation, or maintenance of property held for the production of income; or in connection with the determination, collection, or refund of any tax. §§ 162(a) and 212. See also *necessary.*

Organizational expenses. A corporation may elect to amortize organizational expenses over a period of 60 months or more. Certain expenses of organizing a company do not qualify for amortization (e.g., expenditures connected with issuing or selling stock or other securities). § 248.

Outside salesperson. An outside salesperson is one who solicits business away from the employer's place of business on a full-time basis. The employment-related expenses of an outside salesperson are itemized deductions unless reimbursed by the employer. If reimbursed, such expenses are deductible *for* AGI.

P

Partnerships. Partnerships are treated as a conduit and are not subject to taxation. Various items of partnership income, expenses, gains, and losses flow through to the individual partners and are reported on the partners' personal income tax returns.

Passive activity. A trade or business activity in which the taxpayer does not materially participate is subject to limitations on the deduction of losses and credits. Rental activities and limited partnership interests are inherently passive. However, relief from passive activity limitation treatment is provided for certain rental real estate if the taxpayer actively participates in the activity. The ceiling on the relief is $25,000. § 469. See also *portfolio income.*

Passive investment income. As defined in § 1362(d)(3)(D), passive investment income means gross receipts from royalties, certain rents, dividends, interest, annuities, and gains from the sale or exchange of stock and securities. Revocation of the S corporation election may occur in certain cases when the S corporation has passive investment income in excess of 25 percent of gross receipts for a period of three consecutive years.

Passive loss. Any loss from (1) activities in which the taxpayer does not materially participate, (2) rental activities, or (3) tax shelter activities. Net passive losses cannot be used to offset income from nonpassive sources. Rather, they are suspended until the taxpayer either generates net passive income (and a deduction of such losses is allowed) or disposes of the underlying property (at which time the loss deductions are allowed in full). Landlords who actively participate in the rental activities can deduct up to $25,000 of passive losses annually. However, this amount is phased out when the landlord's AGI exceeds $100,000. Passive loss limitations are phased in beginning in 1987 and will not be fully effective until 1991. See also *portfolio income.*

Patent.   A patent is an intangible asset that may be amortized over the asset's remaining life. The sale of a patent usually results in favorable long-term capital gain treatment. § 1235.

Percentage of completion-capitalized cost method.   A method of reporting gain or loss on certain long-term contracts. The Code provides that only in limited circumstances may the completed contract method be used. The options available to the taxpayer who is not eligible to use the completed contract method are the percentage of completion method and the percentage of completion-capitalized cost method. Under this latter method, the taxpayer must take into account 90 percent of the items with respect to the contract under the percentage of completion method. The remaining 10 percent can be taken into account under the taxpayer's normal method of accounting (e.g., completed contract method). § 460. See also *completed contract method* and *percentage of completion method.*

Percentage of completion method.   A method of reporting gain or loss on certain long-term contracts. Under this method of accounting, the gross contract price is included in income as the contract is completed. § 460 and Reg. § 1.451–3. See also *completed contract method* and *percentage of completion-capitalized cost method.*

Personal and dependency exemptions.   The tax law provides an exemption for each individual taxpayer and an additional exemption for the taxpayer's spouse if a joint return is filed. An individual may also claim a dependency exemption for each dependent, provided certain tests are met. The amount of the personal and dependency exemptions is $2,000 in 1989. Beginning in 1990, the $2,000 amount will be indexed for inflation. § 151.

Personal expenses.   Expenses of an individual for personal reasons that are not deductible unless specifically provided for under the tax law. § 262.

Personal property.   Generally, all property other than real estate. It is sometimes designated as personalty when real estate is termed realty. Personal property also can refer to property that is not used in a taxpayer's trade or business or held for the production or collection of income. When used in this sense, personal property could include both realty (e.g., a personal residence) and personalty (e.g., personal effects such as clothing and furniture).

Personal residence.   The sale of a personal residence generally results in the recognition of capital gain (but not loss). However, the gain may be deferred if the adjusted sales price of the old residence is reinvested in the purchase of a new residence within cer-

tain prescribed time periods. Also, taxpayers age 55 or older may exclude $125,000 of the gain from tax, provided certain requirements are met. §§ 1034 and 121.

Personalty.   All property other than realty (real estate). Personalty usually is categorized as tangible or intangible property. Tangible personalty includes such assets as machinery and equipment, automobiles and trucks, and office equipment. Intangible personalty includes stocks and bonds, goodwill, patents, trademarks, and copyrights.

Points.   Loan origination fees that may be deductible as interest by a buyer of property. A seller of property who pays points is required to reduce the selling price and therefore does not receive an interest deduction. See *prepaid interest* for the timing of the interest deduction.

Pollution control facilities.   A certified pollution control facility, the cost of which may be amortized over a 60–month period if elected by the taxpayer. § 169.

Portfolio income.   The term is relevant in applying the limitation on passive activity losses and credits. Although normally considered passive in nature, such items for this purpose are treated as nonpassive. Therefore, net passive losses and credits cannot be offset against portfolio income. Examples of portfolio income are interest, dividends, annuities, and certain royalties. § 469. See also *passive activity.*

Prepaid expenses.   Cash basis as well as accrual basis taxpayers usually are required to capitalize prepayments for rent, insurance, etc., that cover more than one year. Deductions are taken during the period the benefits are received.

Prepaid interest.   In effect, the Code places cash basis taxpayers on an accrual basis for purposes of recognizing a deduction for prepaid interest. Thus, interest paid in advance is deductible as an interest expense only as it accrues. The one exception to this rule involves the interest element when a cash basis taxpayer pays points to obtain financing for the purchase of a principal residence (or to make improvements thereto) if the payment of points is an established business practice in the area in which the indebtedness is incurred and the amount involved is not excessive. § 461(g). See also *points.*

Principal partner.   A partner with a five percent or greater interest in partnership capital or profits. § 706(b)(3). See also *majority interest partners.*

Prizes and awards.   The fair market value of a prize or award generally is includible in gross income. However, exclusion is permitted if the prize or award is made in recognition of religious, charitable, scientific, educational, artistic, literary, or civic achievement, and the recipient transfers the award to a qualified governmental unit or a nonprofit organization. In such a case, the recipient must be selected without any action on his or her part to enter a contest or proceeding, and the recipient must not be required to render substantial future services as a condition of receiving the prize or award. § 74.

Public policy limitation.   See *bribes and illegal payments.*

Q

Qualified pension or profit sharing plan.   An employer-sponsored plan that meets the requirements of § 401. If these requirements are met, none of the employer's contributions to the plan will be taxed to the employee until distributed to him or her (§ 402). The employer will be allowed a deduction in the year the contributions are made (§ 404). See also *annuities* and *deferred compensation.*

Qualified residence interest.   A term relevant in determining the amount of interest expense the individual taxpayer may deduct as an itemized deduction for what otherwise would be disallowed as a component of personal interest (consumer interest). Qualified residence interest consists of interest paid on qualified residences (principal residence and one other residence) of the taxpayer. Debt that qualifies as qualified residence interest is limited to one million dollars of debt to acquire, construct, or substantially improve qualified residences (acquisition indebtedness) plus $100,000 of other debt secured by qualified residences (home equity indebtedness). The home equity indebtedness may not exceed the fair market value of a qualified residence reduced by the acquisition indebtedness with respect to such residence. § 163(h)(3). See also *consumer interest.*

R

RAR.   Revenue agent's report, which reflects any adjustments made by the agent as a result of an audit of the taxpayer. The RAR is mailed to the taxpayer along with the 30-day letter, which outlines the appellate procedures available to the taxpayer.

Realized gain or loss.   The difference between the amount realized upon the sale or other disposition of property and the adjusted basis of such property. § 1001. See also *adjusted basis* and *recognized gain or loss.*

Realty.   All real estate, including land and buildings. Permanent improvements to a building (fixtures) become realty if their removal would cause significant damage to the property. An example of a fixture might be the installation of a central air conditioning or heating system to a building. Thus, personalty could become realty through the fixture reclassification.

Reasonable needs of the business.   See *accumulated earnings tax.*

Recapture.   To recover the tax benefit of a deduction or a credit previously taken.

Recapture of depreciation.   Upon the disposition of depreciable property used in a trade or business, gain or loss is determined measured by the difference between the consideration received (the amount realized) and the adjusted basis of the property. Before the enactment of the recapture of depreciation provisions of the Code, any such gain recognized could be § 1231 gain and usually qualified for long-term capital gain treatment. The recapture provisions of the Code (e.g., §§ 1245 and 1250) may operate to convert some or all of the previous § 1231 gain into ordinary income. The justification for recapture of depreciation is that it prevents a taxpayer from deducting depreciation at ordinary income rates and having the related gain on disposition taxed at capital gain rates. The recapture of depreciation rules do not apply when the property is disposed of at a loss. See also *residential rental property, Section 1231 gains and losses, Section 1245 recapture,* and *Section 1250 recapture.*

Recapture of investment tax credit.   When investment credit property is disposed of or ceases to be used in the trade or business of the taxpayer, some or all of the investment tax credit claimed on such property may be recaptured as additional tax liability. The amount of the recapture is the difference between the amount of the credit originally claimed and what should have been claimed in light of the length of time the property was actually held or used for qualifying purposes. § 47. See also *investment tax credit.*

Recapture potential.   Reference is to property which, if disposed of in a taxable transaction, would result in the recapture of depreciation (§§ 1245 or 1250) and/or of the investment tax credit (§ 47).

Recognized gain or loss.   The portion of realized gain or loss that is considered in computing taxable income. See also *realized gain or loss.*

Recovery of capital doctrine.   When a taxable sale or exchange occurs, the seller may be permitted to recover his or her investment (or other adjusted basis) in the property before gain or loss is recognized. See also *open transaction.*

Regulations.   Treasury Department Regulations represent the position of the IRS as to how the Internal Revenue Code is to be interpreted. Their purpose is to provide taxpayers and IRS personnel with rules of general and specific application to the various provisions of the tax law. Regulations are published in the *Federal Register* and in all tax services.

Related-party transactions.   The tax law places restrictions upon the recognition of gains and losses between related parties because of the potential for abuse. For example, restrictions are placed on the deduction of losses from the sale or exchange of property between related parties. A related party includes a corporation controlled by the taxpayer. § 267.

Research and experimentation expenditures. Three alternative methods are provided in the Code. The expenditures may be expensed in the year paid or incurred, deferred subject to amortization, or capitalized. If an election is not made to expense such costs or to defer the expenditures subject to amortization (over 60 months), the research and experimentation costs must be capitalized. § 174. Two types of research activities credits are available. These are the basic research credit and the incremental research credit. The rate for each type is 20 percent. § 41.

Reserve for bad debts.   A method of accounting whereby an allowance is permitted for estimated uncollectible accounts. Actual write-offs are charged to the reserve, and recoveries of amounts previously written off are credited to the reserve. The Code permits only certain financial institutions to use the reserve method. § 166. See also *direct charge-off method.*

Reserves for estimated expenses. Except in the limited case for bad debts, reserves for estimated expenses (e.g., warranty service costs) are not permitted for tax purposes even though such reserves are appropriate for financial accounting purposes. See also *all events test.*

Residential rental property. Buildings for which at least 80 percent of the gross rents are from dwelling units (e.g., an apartment building). This type of building is distinguished from nonresidential (commercial or industrial) buildings in applying the recapture of depreciation provisions. The term also is relevant in distinguishing between buildings that are eligible for a 27.5 year life versus a 31.5 year life for ACRS purposes. Generally, residential buildings receive preferential treatment. §§ 167(j)(2) and 1250. See also *recapture of depreciation.*

Restricted property. An arrangement whereby an employer transfers property (usually stock) to an employee at a bargain price (for less than the fair market value). If the transfer is accompanied by a substantial risk of forfeiture and the property is not transferable, no compensation results to the employee until such restrictions disappear. An example of a substantial risk of forfeiture would be a requirement that the employee return the property if his or her employment is terminated within a specified period of time. § 83. See also *nonqualified deferred compensation plans.*

Retirement of corporate obligations. The retirement of corporate and certain government obligations is considered to be a sale or exchange. Gain or loss, therefore, is treated as capital gain or loss upon the retirement of a corporate obligation rather than as ordinary income or loss. §§ 1271–1275.

Return of capital doctrine. See *recovery of capital doctrine.*

Revenue Procedure. A matter of procedural importance to both taxpayers and the IRS concerning the administration of the tax law is issued as a Revenue Procedure (abbreviated Rev.Proc.). A Revenue Procedure is first published in an Internal Revenue Bulletin (I.R.B.) and later transferred to the appropriate Cumulative Bulletin (C.B.). Both the Internal Revenue Bulletin and the Cumulative Bulletin are published by the U.S. Government Printing Office.

Revenue Ruling. A Revenue Ruling (abbreviated Rev.Rul.) is issued by the National Office of the IRS to express an official interpretation of the tax law as applied to specific transactions. Unlike a Regulation, it is more limited in application. A Revenue Ruling is first published in an Internal Revenue Bulletin (I.R.B.) and later transferred to the appropriate Cumulative Bulletin (C.B.). Both the Internal Revenue Bulletin and the Cumulative Bulletin are published by the U.S. Government Printing Office.

S

Scholarships. Scholarships are generally excluded from gross income of the recipient unless the payments are a disguised form of compensation for services rendered. However, the Code imposes restrictions on the exclusion. The recipient must be a degree candidate. The excluded amount is limited to amounts used for tuition, fees, books, supplies, and equipment required for courses of instruction. Amounts received for room and board are not eligible for the exclusion. § 117.

S corporation status. An elective provision permitting certain small business corporations (§ 1361) and their shareholders to elect (§ 1362) to be treated for income tax purposes in accordance with the operating rules of §§ 1363–1379. Of major significance are the facts that S status avoids the corporate income tax and corporate losses can be claimed by the shareholders. See also *C corporation.*

Section 38 property. Property that qualified for the investment tax credit. Generally, this included all tangible property (other than real estate) used in a trade or business. § 48. See also *investment tax credit.*

Section 179 expensing. The ability to deduct a capital expenditure in the year an asset is placed in service rather than over the asset's useful life or cost recovery period. The annual ceiling on the deduction is $10,000. However, the deduction is reduced dollar for dollar when § 179 property placed in service during the taxable year exceeds $200,000. See also *additional first-year depreciation.*

Section 1231 assets. Depreciable assets and real estate used in a trade or business and held for the required long-term holding period. Under certain circumstances, the classification also includes timber, coal, domestic iron ore, livestock (held for draft, breeding, dairy, or sporting purposes), and unharvested crops. § 1231(b).

Section 1231 gains and losses. If the net result of the combined gains and losses from the taxable dispositions of § 1231 assets plus the net gain from the involuntary conversion of nonpersonal use assets is a gain, the gains and losses from § 1231 assets are treated as long-term capital gains and losses. In arriving at § 1231 gains, however, the depreciation recapture provisions (e.g., §§ 1245 and 1250) are first applied to produce ordinary income. If the net result of the combination is a loss, the gains and losses from § 1231 assets are treated as ordinary gains and losses. § 1231(a). See also *recapture of depreciation.*

Section 1244 stock. Stock issued under § 1244 by qualifying small business corporations. If § 1244 stock is disposed of at a loss or becomes worthless, the shareholders may claim an ordinary loss rather than the usual capital loss. The annual ceiling on the ordinary loss treatment is $50,000 ($100,000 for married individuals filing jointly). See also *worthless securities.*

Section 1245 property. Property that is subject to the recapture of depreciation under § 1245. For a definition of § 1245 property, see § 1245(a)(3). See also *Section 1245 recapture.*

Section 1245 recapture. Upon a taxable disposition of § 1245 property, all depreciation claimed on such property after 1961 will be recaptured as ordinary income (but not to exceed the recognized gain from the disposition). See also *recapture of depreciation.*

Section 1250 property. Real estate that is subject to the recapture of depreciation under § 1250. For a definition of § 1250 property, see § 1250(c). See also *Section 1250 recapture.*

Section 1250 recapture. Upon a taxable disposition of § 1250 property, some or all of the additional depreciation claimed on the property may be recaptured as ordinary income. Various recapture rules apply depending upon the type of property (residential or nonresidential real estate) and the date acquired. Generally, the additional depreciation is recaptured in full to the extent of the gain recognized. See also *additional depreciation* and *recapture of depreciation.*

Self-employment retirement plan. A designation for retirement plans available to self-employed taxpayers. Also referred to as H.R. 10 and Keogh plans. Under such plans, a taxpayer may deduct each year up to either 20 percent of net earnings from self-employment or $30,000, whichever is less.

Self-employment tax. A tax of 15.02 percent (subject to a 2.0 percent credit) in 1989 is levied on individuals with net earnings from self-employment (up to $48,000) to provide Social Security benefits for such individuals. If a self-employed individual also receives wages from an employer that are subject to FICA, the self-employment tax will be reduced if total income subject to Social Security is more than $48,000.

Separate property. In a community property jurisdiction, separate property is that property that belongs entirely to one of the spouses. Generally, it is property acquired before marriage or acquired after marriage by gift or inheritance. See also *community property.*

Short sales. A short sale occurs when a taxpayer sells borrowed property (usually stock) and repays the lender with substantially identical property either held on the date of the short sale or purchased after the sale. No gain or loss is recognized until the short sale is closed, and such gain or loss is generally short term. § 1233.

Simplified employee pensions. An employer may make contributions to an employee's IRA in amounts not exceeding the lesser of 15 percent of compensation or $30,000 per individual. These employer-sponsored simplified employee pensions are permitted only if the contributions are nondiscriminatory and are made on behalf of all employees who have attained age 21 and have worked for the employer during at least three of the five preceding calendar years. § 219(b). See also *individual retirement account.*

Small business corporation. A corporation that satisfies the definition of § 1361(b), § 1244(c)(3), or both. Satisfaction of § 1361(b) permits an S corporation election, and satisfaction of § 1244 enables the shareholders of the corporation to claim an ordinary loss.

Standard deduction. The individual taxpayer can either itemize deductions or take the standard deduction. The amount of the standard deduction depends on the taxpayer's filing status (single, head of household, married filing jointly, surviving spouse, or married filing separately). For 1989, the amount of the standard deduction ranges from $2,600 to $5,200. Additional standard deductions of either $600 (for married taxpayers) or $750 (for single taxpayers) are available if the taxpayer is either blind or age 65 or over. Limitations exist on the amount of the standard deduction of a taxpayer who is another taxpayer's dependent. Beginning in 1989, the standard deduction amounts are adjusted for inflation. § 63(c). See also *zero bracket amount.*

Statute of limitations. Provisions of the law that specify the maximum period of time in which action may be taken on a past event. Code §§ 6501–6504 contain the limitation periods applicable to the IRS for additional assessments, and §§ 6511–6515 relate to refund claims by taxpayers.

Statutory notice of deficiency. Commonly referred to as the 90–day letter, this notice is sent to a taxpayer upon request, upon the expiration of the 30–day letter, or upon exhaustion by the taxpayer of his or her administrative remedies before the IRS. The notice gives the taxpayer 90 days in which to file a petition with the U.S. Tax Court. If such a petition is not filed, the IRS will issue a demand for payment of the assessed deficiency. §§ 6211–6216. See also *thirty-day letter.*

Stock option. The right to purchase a stated number of shares of stock from a corporation at a certain price within a specified period of time.

Stock redemptions. The redemption of the stock of a shareholder by the issuing corporation will be treated as a sale or exchange of the stock if the redemption is not a dividend. §§ 301 and 302.

T

Targeted jobs tax credit. See *jobs credit.*

Tax avoidance. The minimization of one's tax liability by taking advantage of legally available tax planning opportunities. Tax avoidance can be contrasted with tax evasion, which entails the reduction of tax liability by illegal means.

Tax benefit rule. A rule that limits the recognition of income from the recovery of an expense or loss properly deducted in a prior tax year to the amount of the deduction that generated a tax benefit. § 111.

Tax Court. The U.S. Tax Court is one of three trial courts of original jurisdiction that decide litigation involving Federal income, estate, or gift taxes. It is the only trial court wherein the taxpayer need not first pay the deficiency assessed by the IRS. The Tax Court will not have jurisdiction over a case unless the statutory notice of deficiency (90–day letter) has been issued by the IRS and the taxpayer files the petition for hearing within the time prescribed.

Tax credit for elderly or disabled. An elderly (age 65 and over) or disabled taxpayer may receive a tax credit amounting to 15 percent of $5,000 ($7,500 for qualified married individuals filing jointly). This amount is reduced by Social Security benefits, excluded pension benefits, and one-half of the taxpayer's adjusted gross income in excess of $7,500 ($10,000 for married taxpayers filing jointly). § 22.

Tax-free exchange.   Transfers of property specifically exempted from Federal income tax consequences. Examples are a transfer of property to a controlled corporation under § 351(a) and a like-kind exchange under § 1031(a).

Tax home.   Since travel expenses of an employee are deductible only if the taxpayer is away from home, the deductibility of such expenses rests upon the definition of tax home. The IRS position is that tax home is the business location, post, or station of the taxpayer. If an employee is temporarily reassigned to a new post for a period of one year or less, the taxpayer's home should be his or her personal residence and the travel expenses should be deductible. If the assignment is for more than two years, the IRS position is that it is indefinite or permanent and the taxpayer is therefore not in travel status. If the assignment is for between one and two years, the IRS position is that the location of the tax home will be determined on the basis of the facts and circumstances. The courts are in conflict regarding what constitutes a person's home for tax purposes. See also *travel expenses.*

Tax preference items.   Those items set forth in § 57 that may result in the imposition of the alternative minimum tax. See also *alternative minimum tax.*

Tax rate schedules.   Rate schedules appearing in Appendix A that are used by upper income taxpayers and those not permitted to use the tax table. Separate rate schedules are provided for married individuals filing jointly, head of household, single taxpayers, estates and trusts, and married individuals filing separate returns. § 1.

Tax table.   A tax table appearing in Appendix A that is provided for taxpayers with less than $50,000 of taxable income. Separate columns are provided for single taxpayers, married taxpayers filing jointly, head of household, and married taxpayers filing separately. § 3.

Thin corporation.   When debt owed by a corporation to its shareholders is large in relationship to its capital structure (stock and shareholder equity), the IRS may contend that the corporation is thinly capitalized. In effect, this means that some or all of the debt will be reclassified as equity. The immediate result is to disallow any interest deduction to the corporation on the reclassified debt. To the extent of the corporation's earnings and profits, interest payments and loan repayments are treated as dividends to the shareholders. § 385.

Thirty-day letter.   A letter that accompanies a revenue agent's report (RAR) issued as a result of an IRS audit of a taxpayer (or the rejection of a taxpayer's claim for refund). The letter outlines the taxpayer's appeal procedure before the IRS. If the taxpayer does not request any such procedures within the 30–day period, the IRS will issue a *statutory notice of deficiency* (the 90–day letter).

Timber.   Special rules apply to the recognition of gain from the sale of timber. A taxpayer may elect to treat the cutting of timber that is held for sale or use in a trade or business as a sale or exchange. If the holding period requirements are met, the gain is recognized as § 1231 gain and may therefore receive long-term capital gain treatment. § 631.

Trade or business expenses.   Deductions *for* AGI that are attributable to a taxpayer's business or profession. Some employee expenses may also be treated as trade or business expenses. See also *employee expenses.*

Transportation expenses.   Transportation expenses for an employee include only the cost of transportation (taxi fares, automobile expenses, etc.) in the course of employment when the employee is not away from home in travel status. Commuting expenses are not deductible. See also *automobile expenses.*

Travel expenses.   Travel expenses include meals and lodging and transportation expenses while away from home in the pursuit of a trade or business (including that of an employee). See also *tax home.*

Trial court.   The court of original jurisdiction; the first court to consider litigation. In Federal tax controversies, trial courts include U.S. District Courts, the U.S. Tax Court, and the U.S. Claims Court. See also *appellate court.*

U

Unearned (prepaid) income.   For tax purposes, prepaid income (e.g., rent) is taxable in the year of receipt. In certain cases involving advance payments for goods and services, income may be deferred. See Rev.Proc. 71–21 (1971–2 C.B. 549) and Reg. § 1.451–5. See also *accrual method.*

Unreasonable compensation.   Under § 162(a) (1), a deduction is allowed for "reasonable" salaries or other compensation for personal services actually rendered. To the extent compensation is excessive ("unreasonable"), no deduction will be allowed. The problem of unreasonable compensation usually is limited to closely-held corporations where the motivation is to pay out profits in some form deductible to the corporation. Deductible compensation, therefore, becomes an attractive substitute for nondeductible dividends when the shareholders are also employees of the corporation.

USTC.   Published by Commerce Clearing House, *U.S. Tax Cases* contain all of the Federal tax decisions issued by the U.S. District Courts, U.S. Claims Court, U.S. Courts of Appeals, and the U.S. Supreme Court.

V

Vacation home.   The Code places restrictions upon taxpayers who rent their residences or vacation homes for part of the tax year. The restrictions may result in a scaling down of expense deductions for such taxpayers. § 280A. See also *hobby loss.*

W

Wash sale.   A loss from the sale of stock or securities that is disallowed because the taxpayer has within

30 days before or after the sale acquired stock or securities that are substantially identical to those sold. § 1091.

Worthless securities.   A loss (usually capital) is allowed for a security that becomes worthless during the year. The loss is deemed to have occurred on the last day of the year. Special rules apply to securities of affiliated companies and small business stock. § 165. See also *Section 1244 stock.*

Writ of certiorari.   See *certiorari.*

Z

Zero bracket amount.   A deduction that was generally available to all individual taxpayers in arriving at taxable income. It represented the equivalent of the standard deduction for taxable years before 1987. A deduction was not taken by the taxpayer for the zero bracket amount because it was built into the tax tables and tax rate schedules. Because the amount was built-in, if the taxpayer itemized deductions, only the excess itemized deductions (amount of the itemized deductions in excess of the zero bracket amount) were deductible. TRA of 1986 repealed the zero bracket amount and replaced it with the standard deduction for 1987 and thereafter. The zero bracket amount for 1986 is presently used in the 10-year forward averaging calculation for lump-sum distributions. § 63(c). See also *standard deduction.*

APPENDIX D-1

Table of Code Sections Cited

[See Title 26 U.S.C.A.]

Table of Regulations Cited

APPENDIX D–3

Table of Revenue Procedures and Revenue Rulings Cited

APPENDIX E

Citator Example

ILLUSTRATION OF THE USE OF THE P–H CITATOR [1]

Background

The Prentice-Hall *Federal Tax Citator* is a separate multi-volume service with two loose-leaf current matters sections. Cases that are reported by the *Citator* are divided into the various issues involved. Since the researcher may be interested in only one or two issues, only those cases involving the particular issue need to be checked.

The volumes of the P–H *Federal Tax Citator* and the period of time covered by each are:

Volume 1 (1919–1941)

Volume 2 (1942–1948)

Volume 3 (1948–1954)

Volume 1, Second Series (1954–1977)

Loose-leaf, two volumes (1977 to present)

Through the use of symbols, the *Citator* indicates whether a decision is followed, explained, criticized, questioned, or overruled by a later court decision. These symbols are reproduced in Figure E–1.

Example

Determine the background and validity of *Adda v. Comm.*, 37 AFTR 654, 171 F.2d 457 (CA–4, 1948).

---

1. Features contained in the P–H *Federal Tax Citator* that do not appear in the CCH *Citator* include the following: (1) distinguishes between the various issues in the case, (2) lists all court decisions that cite the court decision being researched, (3) indicates the relationship (e.g., explained, criticized, followed, or overruled) between the court decision being researched and subsequent decisions, and (4) pinpoints the exact page on which one court decision is cited by another court decision.

FIGURE E–1

Prentice-Hall Citator Symbols*

COURT DECISIONS

Judicial History of the Case

- a affirmed (by decision of a higher court)
- d dismissed (appeal to a higher court dismissed)
- m modified (decision modified by a higher court, or on rehearing)
- r reversed (by a decision of a higher court)
- s same case (e. g., on rehearing)
- rc related case (companion cases and other cases arising out of the same subject matter are so designated)
- x certiorari denied (by the Supreme Court of the United States)
- (C or G) The Commissioner or Solicitor General has made the appeal
- (T) Taxpayer has made the appeal
- (A) Tax Court's decision acquiesced in by Commissioner
- (NA) Tax Court's decision nonacquiesced in by Commissioner
- sa same case affirmed (by the cited case)
- sd same case dismissed (by the cited case)
- sm same case modified (by the cited case)
- sr same case reversed (by the cited case)
- sx same case-certiorari denied

Syllabus of the Cited Case

- iv four (on all fours with the cited case)
- f followed (the cited case followed)
- e explained (comment generally favorable, but not to a degree that indicates the cited case is followed)
- k reconciled (the cited case reconciled)
- n dissenting opinion (cited in a dissenting opinion)
- g distinguished (the cited case distinguished either in law or on the facts)
- l limited (the cited case limited to its facts. Used when an appellate court so limits a prior decision, or a lower court states that in its opinion the cited case should be so limited)
- c criticized (adverse comment on the cited case)
- q questioned (the cited case not only criticized, but its correctness questioned)
- o overruled

* Reproduced from the Federal Taxes Citator with the permission of the publisher, Prentice-Hall, Inc., Englewood Cliffs, N. J. 07632

Solution

Turning directly to the case itself (reproduced as Figure E–2), note the two issues involved ("1." and "2."). For purposes of emphasis, these issues have been bracketed and identified as such by a marginal notation added to Figure E–2. The reason for the division of the issues becomes apparent when the case is traced through the *Citator*.

Refer to Volume 3 of the First Series (covering the period from October 7, 1948, through July 29, 1954) of the P–H *Federal Tax Citator*. Reference to the case is located on page 5505. This page is reproduced in Figure E–3.

FIGURE E–2

ADDA v. COMMISSIONER OF INTERNAL REVENUE   457
Cite as 171 F 2 457

ADDA v. COMMISSIONER OF INTERNAL
REVENUE.
No. 5796.

United States Court of Appeals
Fourth Circuit.

Dec. 3, 1948.

ISSUE 1

1. Internal revenue ⬥792

Where nonresident alien's brother residing in United States traded for alien's
benefit on commodity exchanges in United
States at authorization of alien, who vested
full discretion in brother with regard thereto, and many transactions were effected
through different brokers, several accounts
were maintained, and substantial gains and
losses realized, transactions constituted a
"trade or business," profits of which were
"capital gains" taxable as income to the
alien. 26 U.S.C.A. § 211(b).

See Words and Phrases, Permanent
Edition, for other judicial constructions
and definitions of "Capital Gains" and
"Trade or Business".

ISSUE 2

2. Internal revenue ⬥792

The exemption of a nonresident alien's
commodity transactions in the United States
provided for by the Internal Revenue Code
does not apply where alien has agent in
United States using his own discretion in
effecting transactions for alien's account.
26 U.S.C.A. § 211(b).

⎯⎯⎯⎯◆⎯⎯⎯⎯

On Petition to Review the Decision of
The Tax Court of the United States.

Petition by Fernand C. A. Adda to review
a decision of the Tax Court redetermining
a deficiency in income tax imposed by the
Commissioner of Internal Revenue.

Decision affirmed.

Rollin Browne and Mitchell B. Carroll,
both of New York City, for petitioner.

Irving I. Axelrad, Sp. Asst. to Atty. Gen.
(Theron Lamar Caudle, Asst. Atty. Gen.,
and Ellis N. Slack and A. F. Prescott, Sp.
Assts. to Atty. Gen., on the brief), for re-
spondent.

Before PARKER, Chief Judge, and
SOPER and DOBIE, Circuit Judges.

PER CURIAM.

[1, 2] This is a petition by a non-resident alien to review a decision of the Tax
Court. Petitioner is a national of Egypt,
who in the year 1941 was residing in
France. He had a brother who at that
time was residing in the United States and
who traded for petitioner's benefit on commodity exchanges in the United States in
cotton, wool, grains, silk, hides and copper.
This trading was authorized by petitioner
who vested full discretion in his brother
with regard thereto, and it resulted in profits in the sum of $193,857.14. The Tax
Court said: "While the number of transactions or the total amount of money involved in them has not been stated, it is apparent that many transactions were effected
through different brokers, several accounts
were maintained, and gains and losses in
substantial amounts were realized. This
evidence shows that the trading was extensive enough to amount to a trade or business, and the petitioner does not contend,
nor has he shown, that the transactions
were so infrequent or inconsequential as
not to amount to a trade or business." We
agree with the Tax Court that, for reasons
adequately set forth in its opinion, this income was subject to taxation, and that the
exemption of a non-resident alien's commodity transactions in the United States,
provided by section 211(b) of the Internal
Revenue Code, 26 U.S.C.A. § 211(b), does
not apply to a case where the alien has an
agent in the United States using his own
discretion in effecting the transactions for
the alien's account. As said by the Tax
Court, "Through such transactions the alien
is engaging in trade or business within the
United States, and the profits on these
transactions are capital gains taxable to
him." Nothing need be added to the reasoning of the Tax Court in this connection,
and the decision will be affirmed on its opinion.

Affirmed.

Figure E-3

» Adamson — Adler «   5505

ADAMSON, JAMES H. & MARION C. v
U. S., — F Supp —, 36 AFTR 1529, 1946
P.-H. ¶ 72,418 (DC Calif) (See Adamson
v U. S.)
ADAMSON, R. R., MRS., — BTA —, 1934 (P.-
H.) BTA Memo. Dec. ¶ 34,370
ADAMSON v U. S., 26 AFTR 1188 (DC Calif,
Sept 8, 1939)
    1v—Coggan, Linus C., 1939 (P.-H.) BTA
    Memo. Dec. page 39—806
ADAMSON; U. S. v, 161 F(2d) 942, 35 AFTR
1404 (CCA 9)
    1—Lazier v U. S., 170 F(2d) 524, 37 AFTR
    545, 1948 P.-H. page 73,174 (CCA 8)
    1—Grace Bros., Inc. v Comm., 173 F(2d)
    178, 37 AFTR 1014, 1949 P.-H. page 72,433
    (CCA 9)
    1—Briggs; Hofferbert v, 178 F(2d) 744, 38
    AFTR 1219, 1950 P.-H. page 72,267 (CCA
    4)
    1—Rogers v Comm., 180 F(2d) 722, 39 AFTR
    115, 1950 P.-H. page 72,531 (CCA 3)
    1—Lamar v Granger, 99 F Supp 41, 40
    AFTR 270, 1951 P.-H. page 72,945 (DC Pa)
    1—Herbert v Riddell, 103 F Supp 383, 41
    AFTR 975, 1952 P.-H. page 72,383 (DC
    Calif)
    1—Hudson, Galvin, 20 TC 737, 20-1953
    P.-H. TC 418
ADAMSON v U. S., — F Supp —, 36 AFTR
1529, 1946 P.-H. ¶ 72,418 (DC Calif, Jan
28, 1946)
ADAMS-ROTH BAKING CO., 8 BTA 458
    1—Gunderson Bros. Engineering Corp., 16
    TC 129, 16-1951 P.-H. TC 72
ADAMSTON FLAT GLASS CO. v COMM.,
162 F(2d) 875, 35 AFTR 1579 (CCA 6)
    4—Forrest Hotel Corp. v. Fly, 112 F Supp
    789, 43 AFTR 1080, 1953 P.-H. page 72,856
    (DC Miss)
ADDA v COMM., 171 F(2d) 457, 37 AFTR 654,
1948 P.-H. ¶ 72,655 (CCA 4, Dec 3, 1948)
    Cert. filed, March 1, 1949 (T)
    No cert. (G) 1949 P-H ¶ 71,050
    x—Adda v Comm., 336 US 952, 69 S Ct 883,
    93 L Ed 1107, April 18, 1949 (T)
    sa—Adda, Fernand C. A., 10 TC 273 (No.
    33), ¶ 10.33 P.-H. TC 1948
    iv—Milner Hotels, Inc., N. Y., 173 F (2d)
    567, 37 AFTR 1170, 1949 P.-H. page 72,528
    (CCA 6)
    1—Nubar; Comm. v, 185 F(2d) 588, 39 AFTR
    1315, 1950 P.-H. page 73,423 (CCA 4)
    g-1—Scottish Amer. Invest. Co., Ltd.,
    The, 12 TC 59, 12-1949 P.-H. TC 32
    g-1—Nubar, Zareh, 13 TC 579, 13-1949
    P.-H. TC 318
ADDA, FERNAND C. A., 10 TC 273 (No.
33), ¶ 10.33 P.-H. TC 1948 (A) 1918-2 CB 1
    a—Adda v Comm., 171 F(2d) 457, 37 AFTR
    654, 1948 P.-H. ¶ 72,655 (CCA 4)
    1—Nubar; Comm. v, 185 F(2d) 588, 39 AFTR
    1315, 1950 P.-H. page 73,423 (CCA 4)
    g-1—Scottish Amer. Invest. Co., Ltd.,
    The, 12 TC 59, 12-1949 P.-H. TC 32
    g-1—Nubar, Zareh, 13 TC 579, 13-1949
    P.-H. TC 318
ADDA, FERNAND C. A., 10 TC 1291 (No.
168), ¶ 10.168 P.-H. TC 1948 (A) 1953-1
    CB 3, 1953 P.-H. ¶ 76,453 (NA) 1948-2
    CB 5, 1948 P.-H. ¶ 76,434 withdrawn
    1—Scottish Amer. Invest. Co., Ltd., The,
    12 TC 59, 12-1949 P.-H. TC 32
ADDA INC., 9 TC 199 (A) 1949-1 CB 1, 1949
P.-H. ¶ 76,260 (NA) 1947-2 CB 6 with-
drawn
    a—Adda, Inc.; Comm. v, 171 F(2d) 367, 37
    AFTR 641, 1948 P.-H. ¶ 72,654 (CCA 2)
    a—Adda, Inc.; Comm. v, 171 F(2d) 367, 37
    AFTR 641, 1949 P.-H. ¶ 72,303 (CCA 2)
    e-1—G.C.M. 26069, 1949-2 CB 38, 1949 P.-H.
    page 76,226
    3—Koshland, Execx.; U.S. v, 208 F(2d)
    640, — AFTR —, 1953 P.-H. page 73,597
    (CCA 9)
    4—Kent, Otis Beall, 1954 (P. H.) TC
    Memo. Dec. page 54—47

ADDA, INC.; COMM. v, 171 F(2d) 367, 37
AFTR 641, 1948 P.-H. ¶ 72,654 (CCA 2, Dec
6, 1948)
    sa—Adda, Inc., 9 TC 199
    s—Adda, Inc.; Comm. v, 171 F(2d) 367, 37
    AFTR 641, 1949 P.-H. ¶ 72,303 (CCA 2) reh.
    den.
    e-1—G.C.M. 26069, 1949-2 CB 39, 1949 P.-H.
    page 76,227
    e-2—G.C.M. 26069, 1949-2 CB 39, 1949 P.-H.
    page 76,227
ADDA, INC.; COMM. v, 171 F(2d) 367, 37
AFTR 641, 1949 P.-H. ¶ 72,303 (CCA 2, Dec
6, 1948) reh. den.
    sa—Adda, Inc., 9 TC 199
    s—Adda, Inc.; Comm. v, 171 F(2d) 367, 37
    AFTR 641, 1948 P.-H. ¶ 72,654 (CCA 2)
ADDISON-CHEVROLET SALES, INC. v
CHAMBERLAIN, L. A. & NAT. BANK
OF WASH., THE, — F Supp —, — AFTR
—, 1954 P.-H. ¶ 72,550 (DC DC) (See
Campbell v Chamberlain)
ADDISON v COMM., 177 F(2d) 521, 38 AFTR
821, 1949 P.-H. ¶ 72,637 (CCA 8, Nov 3,
1949)
    sa—Addison, Irene D., — TC —, 1948
    (P.-H.) TC Memo. Dec. ¶ 48,177
    1—Roberts, Supt. v U. S., 115 Ct Cl 439,
    87 F Supp 937, 38 AFTR 1314, 1950 P.-H.
    page 72,292
    1—Cold Metal Process Co., The, 17 TC
    934, 17-1951 P.-H. TC 512
    1—Berger, Samuel & Lillian, 1954 (P.-H.)
    TC Memo. Dec. page 54—232
    2—Urquhart, George Gordon & Mary F.,
    20 TC 948, 20-1953 P.-H. TC 536
ADDISON, IRENE D., — TC —, 1948 (P.-
H.) TC Memo. Dec. ¶ 48,177
    App (T) Jan 14. 1949 (CCA 8)
    a—Addison v Comm., 177 F(2d) 521, 38
    AFTR 821, 1949 P.-H. ¶ 72,637 (CCA 8)
    1—Urquhart, George Gordon & Mary F.,
    20 TC 948, 20-1953 P.-H. TC 536
ADDITON, HARRY L. & ANNIE S., 3
TC 427
    1—Lum, Ralph E., 12 TC 379, 12-1949 P.-H.
    TC 204
    1—Christie, John A. & Elizabeth H., —
    TC —, 1949 (P.-H.) TC Memo. Dec.
    page 49—795
ADDRESSOGRAPH - MULTIGRAPH
CORP., 1945 (P.-H.) TC Memo. Dec.
¶ 45,058
    f-10—Rev. Rul. 54-71, 1954 P.-H. page
    76.453
ADDRESSOGRAPH-MULTIGRAPH CORP.
v U. S., 112 Ct Cl 201, 78 F Supp 111, 37
AFTR 53, 1948 P.-H. ¶ 72,504 (June 1, 1948)
    No cert (G) 1949 P.-H. ¶ 71,041
    1—New Oakmont Corp. The v U. S., 114
    Ct Cl 686, 86 F Supp 901, 38 AFTR 924, 1949
    P.-H. page 73,181
ADELAIDE PARK LAND, 25 BTA 211
    g—Amer. Security & Fidelity Corp., — BTA
    —, 1940 (P.-H.) BTA Memo. Dec. page
    40—571
ADELPHI PAINT & COLOR WORKS,
INC., 18 BTA 436
    1—Neracher, William A., — BTA —, 1939
    (P.-H.) BTA Memo. Dec. page 39—69
    1—Lyman-Hawkins Lumber Co., — BTA —,
    1939 (P.-H.) BTA Memo. Dec. page 39—350
ADEMAN v U. S., 174 F(2d) 283, 37 AFTR
1406 (CCA 9, April 25, 1949)
ADICONIS, NOELLA L. (PATNAUDE),
1953 (P.-H.) TC Memo. Dec. ¶ 53,305
ADJUSTMENT BUREAU OF ST. LOUIS
ASSN., OF CREDIT MEN, 21 BTA 232
    1—Cook County Loss Adjustment Bureau,
    — BTA —, 1940 (P.-H.) BTA Memo. Dec.
    page 40—331
ADKINS, CHARLES L., — BTA —, 1933
    (P.-H.) BTA Memo. Dec. ¶ 33,457
ADLER v COMM., 77 F(2d) 733, 16 AFTR 162
(CCA 5)
    g-2—McEuen v Comm., 196 F(2d) 130, 41
    AFTR 1172, 1952 P.-H. page 72,604 (CCA 5)

Correlating the symbols reproduced in Figure E–1 with the shaded portion of Figure E–3 reveals the following information about *Adda v. Comm.:*

- Application for certiorari (appeal to the U.S. Supreme Court) filed by the taxpayer (T) on March 1, 1949.

- Certiorari was denied (x) by the U.S. Supreme Court on April 18, 1949.

- The trial court decision is reported in 10 T.C. 273 and was affirmed on appeal (sa) to the Fourth Court of Appeals.

- During the time frame of Volume 3 of the *Citator* (October 7, 1948, through July 29, 1954), one decision (*Milner Hotels, Inc.*) has agreed "on all fours with the cited case" (iv). One decision (*Comm. v. Nubar*) has limited the cited case to its facts (l) and two decisions (*The Scottish American Investment Co., Ltd.* and *Zareh Nubar*) have distinguished the cited case on issue number one (g–1).

Reference to Volume 1 of the *Citator* Second Series (covering the period from 1954 through 1977) shows the *Adda v. Comm.* case on page 25. This page is reproduced in Figure E–4.

Correlating the symbols reproduced in Figure E–1 with the shaded portion of Figure E–4 reveals the following additional information about *Adda v. Comm.:*

- The case was cited without comment in two rulings and two cases: *Rev.Rul. 56–145, Rev.Rul. 56–392, Balanovski,* and *Liang.*

- It was followed in *Asthmanefrin Co.* (f–1).

- It was distinguished in *deVegvar* and *Purvis* (g–1).

- It was reconciled in *deKrause* (k–1).

Reference to the "Court Decisions" section of loose-leaf Volume 1 for the *Citator* covering the period from 1977 to the present shows that *Adda v. Comm.* was cited in *Judith C. Connelly* and *Robert E. Cleveland,* with each case limited to its facts (l). This page (10, 012) is reproduced in Figure E–5. Loose-leaf Volume 2 contains a "Supplementary Compilation" section and a "Current Monthly Supplement" section. Be sure to refer to these sections. Otherwise, very recent citations might be overlooked.

Except as otherwise noted, it would appear that *Adda v. Comm.* has withstood the test of time.

ADASKAVICH—ADELSON   25

ADASKAVICH, STEPHEN A. v U.S., 39 AFTR2d 77-517, 422 F Supp 276 (DC Mont) (See Wiegand, Charles J., Jr. v U.S.)

AD. AURIEMA, INC., 1943 P-H TC Memo ¶ 43,422
e-1—Miller v U.S., 13 AFTR2d 1515, 166 Ct Cl 257, 331 F2d 859

ADAY v SUPERIOR CT. OF ALAMEDA COUNTY, 8 AFTR2d 5367, 13 Cal Reptr 415, 362 P2d 47 (Calif, 5-11-61)

ADCO SERVICE, INC., ASSIGNEE v CYBERMATICS, INC., 36 AFTR2d 75-6342 (NJ) (See Adco Service, Inc., Assignee v Graphic Color Plate)

ADCO SERVICE, INC., ASSIGNEE v GRAPHIC COLOR PLATE, 36 AFTR2d 75-6342 (NJ, Supr Ct, 11-10-75)

ADCO SERVICE, INC., ASSIGNEE v GRAPHIC COLOR PLATE, INC., 36 AFTR2d 75-6342 (NJ) (See Adco Service, Inc., Assignee v Graphic Color Plate)

ADDA v COMM., 171 F2d 457, 37 AFTR 654 (USCA 4)
Rev. Rul. 56-145, 1956-1 CB 613
1—Balanovski; U.S. v, 236 F2d 304, 49 AFTR 2013 (USCA 2)
1—Liang, Chang Hsiao, 23 TC 1045, 23-1955 P-H TC 624
f-1—Asthmanefrin Co., Inc., 25 TC 1141, 25-1956 P-H TC 639
g-1—de Vegvar, Edward A. Neuman, 28 TC 1061, 28-1957 P-H TC 599
g-1—Purvis, Ralph E. & Patricia Lee, 1974 P-H TC Memo 74-669
k-1—deKrause, Piedad Alvarado, 1974 P-H TC Memo 74-1291
1—Rev. Rul. 56-392, 1956-2 CB 971

ADDA, FERNAND C.A., 10 TC 273, ¶ 10,133 P-H TC 1948
1—Balanovski; U.S. v, 236 F2d 303, 49 AFTR 2012 (USCA 2)
1—Liang, Chang Hsiao, 23 TC 1045, 23-1955 P-H TC 624
g-1—de Vegvar, Edward A. Neuman, 28 TC 1061, 28-1957 P-H TC 599
g-1—Purvis, Ralph E. & Patricia Lee, 1974 P-H TC Memo 74-669
k-1—deKrause, Piedad Alvarado, 1974 P-H TC Memo 74-1291

ADDA, INC., 9 TC 199
Pardee, Marvin L., Est. of, 49 TC 152, 49 P-H TC 107 [See 9 TC 206-208]
f-1—Asthmanefrin Co., Inc., 25 TC 1141, 25-1956 P-H TC 639
1—Keil Properties, Inc. (Dela), 24 TC 1117, 24-1955 P-H TC 615
1—Saffan, Samuel, 1957 P-H TC Memo 57—701
1—Rev. Rul. 56-145, 1956-1 CB 613
1—Rev. Rul. 56-392, 1956-2 CB 971
4—Midler Court Realty, Inc., 61 TC 597, 61 P-H TC 368

ADDA, INC.; COMM. v, 171 F2d 367, 37 AFTR 641 (USCA 2)
1—Pardee, Marvin L., Est. of, 49 TC 152, 49 P-H TC 107
1—Saffan, Samuel, 1957 P-H TC Memo 57-701
2—Midler Court Realty, Inc., 61 TC 597, 61 P-H TC 368

ADDELSTON, ALBERT A. & SARAH M., 1965 P-H TC Memo ¶ 65,215

ADDISON v COMM., 177 F2d 521, 38 AFTR 821 (USCA 8)
g-1—Industrial Aggregate Co. v U.S., 6 AFTR2d 5963, 284 F2d 645 (USCA 8)
1—Sturgeon v McMahon, 155 F Supp 630, 52 AFTR 789 (DC NY)
1—Gilmore v U.S., 16 AFTR2d 5211, 5213, 245 F Supp 384, 386 (DC Calif)
1—Waldheim & Co., Inc., 25 TC 599, 25-1955 P-H TC 332
g-1—Galewitz, Samuel & Marian, 50 TC 113, 50 P-H TC 79
1—Buder, G. A., Est. of, 1963 P-H TC Memo 63-345
e-1—Rhodes, Lynn E. & Martha E., 1963 P-H TC Memo 63-1374
2—Shipp v Comm., 217 F2d 402, 46 AFTR 1170 (USCA 9)

ADDISON—Contd.
g-2—Industrial Aggregate Co. v U.S., 6 AFTR2d 5964, 284 F2d 645 (USCA 8)
e-2—Buder, Est. of v Comm., 13 AFTR2d 1238, 330 F2d 443 (USCA 8)
2—Iowa Southern Utilities Co. v Comm., 14 AFTR2d 5063, 333 F2d 385 (USCA 8)
2—Kelly, Daniel, S.W., 23 TC 687, 23-1955 P-H TC 422
f-2—Morgan, Joseph P., Est. of, 37 TC 36, 37, 37-1961 P-H TC 26, 27
n-2—Woodward, Fred W. & Elsie M., 49 TC 385, 49 P-H TC 270

ADDISON, IRENE D., 1948 P-H TC Memo ¶ 48,177
1—Waldheim & Co., Inc., 25 TC 599, 25-1955 P-H TC 332
f-1—Morgan, Joseph P., Est. of, 37 TC 36, 37, 37-1961 P-H TC 26, 27
1—Buder, G. A., Est. of, 1963 P-H TC Memo 63-345
e-1—Rhodes, Lynn E. & Martha E., 1963 P-H TC Memo 63-1374

ADDISON, JOHN MILTON, BKPT; U.S. v, 20 AFTR2d 5630, 384 F2d 748 (USCA 5) (See Rochelle Jr., Trtee; U.S. v)

ADDRESSOGRAPH - MULTIGRAPH CORP., 1945 P-H TC Memo ¶ 45,058
Conn. L. & P. Co., The v U.S., 9 AFTR2d 679, 156 Ct Cl 312, 314, 299 F2d 264
Copperhead Coal Co., Inc., 1958 P-H TC Memo 58-33
1—Seas Shipping Co., Inc. v Comm., 19 AFTR2d 596, 371 F2d 529 (USCA 2)
e-1—Hitchcock, E. R., Co., The v U.S., 35 AFTR2d 75-1207, 514 F2d 487 (USCA 2)
f-2—Vulcan Materials Co. v U.S., 25 AFTR2d 70-446, 308 F Supp 57 (DC Ala)
f-3—Marlo Coil Co. v U.S., 1969 P-H 58,133 (Ct Cl Comr Rep)
4—United Gas Improvement Co. v Comm., 240 F2d 318, 50 AFTR 1354 (USCA 3)
10—St. Louis Co. (Del) (in Dissolution) v U.S., 237 F2d 156, 50 AFTR 257 (USCA 3)

ADDRESSOGRAPH - MULTIGRAPH CORP. v U.S., 112 Ct Cl 201, 78 F Supp 111, 37 AFTR 53
f-1—St. Joseph Lead Co. v U.S., 9 AFTR2d 712, 299 F2d 350 (USCA 2)
e-1—Central & South West Corp. v U.S., 1968 P-H 58,175 (Ct Cl Comr Rep)
1—Smale & Robinson, Inc. v U.S., 123 F Supp 469, 46 AFTR 375 (DC Calif)
1—St. Joseph Lead Co. v U.S., 7 AFTR2d 401, 190 F Supp 640 (DC NY)
1—Eisenstadt Mfg. Co., 28 TC 230, 28-1957 P-H TC 132
f-2—St. Joseph Lead Co. v U.S., 9 AFTR2d 712, 299 F2d 350 (USCA 2)
f-3—Consol, Coppermines Corp. v U.S., 8 AFTR2d 5873, 155 Ct Cl 736, 296 F2d 745

ADELAIDE PARK LAND, 25 BTA 211
g—Custom Component Switches, Inc. v U.S., 19 AFTR2d 560 (DC Calif) [See 25 BTA 215]
O'Connor, John C., 1957 P-H TC Memo 57-190

ADELBERG, MARVIN & HELEN, 1971 P-H TC Memo ¶ 71,015

ADELMAN v U.S., 27 AFTR2d 71-1464, 440 F2d 991 (USCA 9, 5-3-71)
sa—Adelman v U.S., 24 AFTR2d 69-5769, 304 F Supp 599 (DC Calif)

ADELMAN v U.S., 24 AFTR2d 69-5769, 304 F Supp 599 (DC Calif, 9-30-69)
a—Adelman v U.S., 27 AFTR2d 71-1464, 440 F2d 991 (USCA 9)

ADELSON, SAMUEL; U.S. v, 52 AFTR 1798 (DC RI) (See Sullivan Co., Inc.; U.S. v)

ADELSON v U.S., 15 AFTR2d 246, 342 F2d 332 (USCA 9, 1-13-65)
sa—Adelson v U.S., 12 AFTR2d 5010, 221 F Supp 31 (DC Calif)
g-1—Greenlee, L. C. & Gladys M., 1966 P-H TC Memo 66-985
f-1—Cochran, Carol J., 1973 P-H TC Memo 73-459
f-1—Marchionni, Siro L., 1976 P-H TC Memo 76-1321
f-2—Krist, Edwin F. v Comm., 32 AFTR2d 73-5663, 483 F2d 1351 (USCA 2)
f-2—Fugate v U.S., 18 AFTR2d 5607, 259 F Supp 401 (DC Tex) [See 15 AFTR2d 249, 342 F2d 335]

FIGURE E–5

ADAMS—contd.
f—First Amer. Bk. & Trust Co. v U.S., 43 AFTR2d 79-741 (DC Okla) [See 34 AFTR2d 74-5963, 504 F2d 75]
f—Howard, Jerry Eugene v U.S., 46 AFTR2d 80-5246, 80-5247 (DC Kan) [See 34 AFTR2d 74-5963—74-5964, 504 F2d 75-76]
f—Platt, John H., Jr. v U.S., 48 AFTR2d 81-6108, 519 F Supp 208 (DC Ill) [See 34 AFTR2d 74-5964, 504 F2d 75-76]
Cooper, E. Leon, M.D. v U.S., 49 AFTR2d 81-1040, 539 F Supp 120 (DC Va) [See 34 AFTR2d 74-5963, 504 F2d 75]
Moats, Robert L. v U.S., 52 AFTR2d 83-6237, 564 F Supp 1336 (DC Mo) [See 34 AFTR2d 74-5963, 504 F2d 75]
e—Fed. Home Life Ins. Co. v Ross, Kristin D., 53 AFTR2d 84-971 (DC Ga) [See 34 AFTR2d 74-5963, 504 F2d 75]
Verdung, Philip W. v U.S., 53 AFTR2d 84-1238, 84-1239 (DC Ill) [See 34 AFTR2d 74-5963, 504 F2d 75]
e—Latimer, Carl v U.S., 54 AFTR2d 84-5935 (DC Ill) [See 34 AFTR2d 74-5963, 504 F2d 75
n-1—Sotelo, Onofre J.; U.S. v, 42 AFTR2d 78-5011, 436 US 291, 98 S Ct 1808, 56 LEd2d 292
f-1—Neckles, Theodore v U.S., 42 AFTR2d 78-5808, 579 F2d 940 (USCA 5) [See 34 AFTR2d 74-5963, 504 F2d 75]
e-1—Rimbey, Harry D. v U.S., 42 AFTR2d 78-5816 (USCA 7)
1—First Nat. Bk. in Palm Beach, Exec. v U.S., 43 AFTR2d 79-904, 591 F2d 1149 (USCA 5)
e-1—Fidelity Bk., N.A. v U.S., 45 AFTR2d 80-973, 616 F2d 1185 (USCA 10)
e-1—Garsky, Jerome L. v U.S., 41 AFTR2d 78-927 (DC Wis)
e-1—Goodman, David v U.S., 42 AFTR2d 78-5516 (DC NJ)
f-1—Copperman, Nathan v U.S., 42 AFTR2d 78-5846 (DC NY)
e-1—Waghalter, Milton H. v U.S., 45 AFTR2d 80-412 (DC Tex)
f-1—Cella, Eugene A. v U.S., 45 AFTR2d 80-1073 (DC NY)
1—Rubrecht, Vincent v U.S., 48 AFTR2d 81-5494 (DC NJ)
e-1—Roth, Harold v U.S., 52 AFTR2d 83-5751, 567 F Supp 498 (DC NY)
e-1—Gray, Robert J. v U.S., 54 AFTR2d 84-5049, 586 F Supp 1130 (DC Kan)
e-1—Bradford, Virgil, In re, 52 AFTR2d 83-6247 (Bkt Ct Va)
e-1—Lucas, Donald Gaylord, In re, 54 AFTR2d 84-6291 (Bkt Ct Conn)
ADAMSON, A. E., TRUSTEE, 1981 P-H TC Memo ¶ 81,285 (See Petty R. M. & Allene A.)
ADAMSON, AUGUSTUS E. & BERNICE B., 1981 P-H TC Memo ¶ 81,285 (See Petty, R. M. & Allene A.)
ADAMSON, KENT A., 1982 P-H TC Memo ¶ 82,371
a—Adamson, Kent A. v COMM., 54 AFTR2d 84-6115, 745 F2d 541 (USCA 9)
e-2—Foster, Richard H. & Sara B., 80 TC 228, 80 P-H TC 120
ADAMSON, KENT A. v COMM., 54 AFTR2d 84-6115, 745 F2d 541 (USCA 9, 10-16-84)
sa—Adamson, Kent A., 1982 P-H TC Memo ¶ 82,371
ADAMSON, L. M., JR., TRUST, 1981 P-H TC Memo ¶ 81,285 (See Petty, R. M. & Allene A.)
ADAMSON, LARRY R. & FLORENCE A., 1973 P-H TC Memo ¶ 73,107
f-4—Vetrick, Joseph J., Jr. & Susan H., 1978 P-H TC Memo 78-393
ADAMSON, LARRY R. & FLORENCE A., 1977 P-H TC Memo ¶ 77,226
e-1—Raynor, Brian K., 1983 P-H TC Memo 83-2413
ADAMSON, LEE A., 1981 P-H TC Memo ¶ 81,285 (See Petty, R. M. & Allene A.)
ADAMSON, RAY P., 1981 P-H TC Memo ¶ 81,285 (See Petty, R. M. & Allene A.)
ADAMSON, SANDRA L., 1981 P-H TC Memo ¶ 81,285 (See Petty, R. M. & Allene A.)
ADCOCK, HOMER & DOROTHY, 1982 P-H TC Memo ¶ 82,206
e-1—Kauffman, Wilma G., 1982 P-H TC Memo 82-2193

ADDA v COMM., 171 F2d 457, 37 AFTR 654 (USCA 4)
1—Connelly, Judith C., 1982 P-H TC Memo 82-2866
1—Cleveland, Robert E., 1983 P-H TC Memo 83-1223
ADDA, FERNAND C.A., 10 TC 273, ¶ 10.133 P-H TC 1948
1—Connelly, Judith C., 1982 P-H TC Memo 82-2866
1—Cleveland, Robert E., 1983 P-H TC Memo 83-1223
ADDA, INC., 9 TC 199
1—Security Bancorp, Inc. v U.S., 48 AFTR2d 81-5514 (DC Mich)
4—Watson Land Co., 1983 P-H TC Memo 83-744
ADDA, INC.; COMM. v, 171 F2d 367, 37 AFTR 641 (USCA 2)
Security Bancorp, Inc. v U.S., 48 AFTR2d 81-5514 (DC Mich)
Watson Land Co., 1983 P-H TC Memo 83-744
ADDEO, ARTHUR J., Jr. & MARY, 1984 P-H TC Memo ¶ 84,493
ADDINGTON, WILLIAM H. & DONNA L., 1980 P-H TC Memo ¶ 80,046
a—Court Order, 10-20-81, 663 F2d 104 (USCA 5)
d—1981 P-H 61,000 (USCA 10)
ADDISON, ALBERT I., 1979 P-H TC Memo ¶ 79,317
e-1—Ridenour, Harry P., Jr. v U.S., 52 AFTR2d 83-5589 (Cl Ct)
ADDRESSOGRAPH-MULTIGRAPH CORP., 1945 P-H TC Memo ¶ 45,058
1—Buffalo Wire Works Co., Inc., 74 TC 938, 74 P-H TC 509
ADEE, ALLEN R., TRUST NO. 1 v U.S., 52 AFTR2d 83-6437 (DC Kan, 7-19-83)
ADEE, DONALD P., TRUSTEE v U.S., 52 AFTR2d 83-6437 (DC Kan) (See Adee, Allen R., Trust No. 1 v U.S.)
ADEE, JACK R., TRUSTEE v U.S., 52 AFTR2d 83-6437 (DC Kan) (See Adee, Allen R., Trust No. 1 v U.S.)
ADELEKE, JOEL & CATHERINE A., 1980 P-H TC Memo ¶ 80,479
e-1—Pike-Biegunski, Maciej Jan & Denise Nadine, 1984 P-H TC Memo 84-1123
ADELSON, SHELDON G. v U.S., 54 AFTR2d 84-5428, 737 F2d 1569 (USCA Fed, 6-28-84)
remg—Adelson, Sheldon G. v U.S., 52 AFTR2d 83-5211 (Cl Ct)
s—Adelson, Sheldon G. v U.S., 51 AFTR2d 83-574 (Cl Ct) 535 F Supp 1082
s—Adelson, Sheldon G. v U.S., 54 AFTR2d 84-5959 (Cl Ct)
ADELSON, SHELDON G. v U.S., 51 AFTR2d 83-574 (Cl Ct) 553 F Supp 1082 (12-27-82)
s—Adelson, Sheldon G. v U.S., 54 AFTR2d 84-5428, 737 F2d 1569 (USCA Fed)
s—Adelson, Sheldon G. v U.S., 52 AFTR2d 83-5211 (Cl Ct)
rc—Adelson, Sheldon G. v U.S., 54 AFTR2d 84-5959 (Cl Ct)
e-1—Mann, Guy L. Est. of, 53 AFTR2d 84-1304, 731 F2d 273 (USCA 5)
ADELSON, SHELDON G. v U.S., 52 AFTR2d 83-5211 (Cl Ct, 6-14-83)
remd—Adelson, Sheldon G. v U.S., 54 AFTR2d 84-5428, 737 F2d 1569 (USCA Fed)
s—Adelson, Sheldon G. v U.S., 51 AFTR2d 83-574 (Cl Ct) 553 F Supp 1082
rc—Adelson, Sheldon G. v U.S., 54 AFTR2d 84-5959 (Cl Ct)
ADELSON, SHELDON G. v U.S., 54 AFTR2d 84-5959 (Cl Ct, 9-12-84)
s—Adelson, Sheldon G. v U.S., 54 AFTR2d 84-5428, 737 F2d 1569 (USCA Fed)
rc—Adelson, Sheldon G. v U.S., 51 AFTR2d 83-574, 1 Cl Ct 61, 553 F Supp 1082
rc—Adelson, Sheldon G. v U.S., 52 AFTR2d 83-5211, 2 Cl Ct 591
ADELSON v U.S., 15 AFTR2d 246, 342 F2d 332 (USCA 9)
e—Dollins, Ronald Lee, 1982 P-H TC Memo 82-1733 [See 15 AFTR2d 248, 342 F2d 335]
e—Nichols, Marilyn L., 1984 P-H TC Memo 84-338 [See 15 AFTR2d 248, 342 F2d 335]
f-2—Gibbons, William, Jr. & Claralee J., 1978 P-H TC Memo 78-370
f-2—Macdonald, Glencora, 1980 P-H TC Memo 80-925

APPENDIX F

Comprehensive Tax Return Problems

Problem 1

1. George H. and Helen C. Brown are married and file a joint return. George is a CPA employed by Lambert & Co., CPAs. His Social Security number is 232–65–7801. Helen is a self-employed psychologist. Her Social Security number is 298–37–2234. The Browns live at 3405 Elm Street, Worthington, Ohio 43085.

2. George and Helen have two dependent children, Michael, age 14, and Gail, age 12. Michael's Social Security number is 333–11–4790, and Gail's is 333–11–4791.

3. George's salary for 1988 was $55,000. His employer withheld $9,860 for Federal withholding, $990 for Ohio withholding, and FICA (Social Security) of $3,379.50.

4. Helen is a self-employed family counselor. The name of her business is H.C. Brown Family Counseling, and her employer identification number is 76–1145967. The business is located at 321 Main Street, Worthington, Ohio 43085. She uses the cash method of accounting.

5. Helen collected $72,400 from clients during 1988. She conducts her practice in a rented office that is fully furnished, so she has no depreciable assets in her business. During the year, she incurred the following expenses:

Advertising	$1,800
Bank service charges	240
Dues and publications	650
Insurance	2,100
Legal and professional services	3,000
Rent on business property	9,600
Supplies	820
Travel	1,200
Meals and entertainment	700
Utilities and telephone	660

6. On March 1, 1988, the Browns acquired a duplex located at 680 Spring Street, Worthington, Ohio 43085 for $120,000. A professional appraiser estimated that the value of the land was $20,000. The Browns paid $24,000

down and negotiated a mortgage for $96,000. Both sides of the duplex were occupied, and both tenants continued as renters. Rent of $500 per month was collected from each tenant. The Browns actively participate in the management of the duplex. The following expenses were incurred during 1988:

Cleaning and maintenance	$1,800
Insurance	1,200
Legal and professional fees	580
Mortgage interest	9,600
Repairs	6,000
Property taxes	2,700

7. In July, George attended a two-week tax seminar in New York City. His employer paid the $1,000 seminar fee, but did not reimburse George for his other expenses. George spent $2,400 for transportation and lodging and $500 for meals.

8. George earned interest of $1,300 on a savings account at Worthington Savings & Loan. Helen earned $1,870 of interest on her account at Columbus Bank & Trust Co. They earned interest of $2,200 on a joint account at Ohio National Bank.

9. The Browns earned dividends on jointly owned stock as follows: $1,400 from General Computer Corporation; $540 from Acme Equipment Sales Corporation; and $1,000 from Genada Games, Inc.

10. George and Helen sold all of their stock in four different companies during the year. None of the companies paid dividends. Information pertaining to the stock is shown below:

Corporation	Date Acquired	Date Sold	Selling Price	Basis
Hite	12/21/78	03/14/88	$22,000	$14,500
Winters	02/16/88	11/23/88	10,000	11,500
Gray	04/28/86	05/10/88	5,000	7,400
Snow	09/11/87	02/02/88	2,400	2,000

11. The Browns incurred the following expenses during the year:

Medicines, doctors, hospitals	$ 6,770
Transportation and lodging for medical treatment	1,180
Eyeglasses and contact lenses	860
Estimated payments on state income tax	130
Real estate taxes on residence	2,700
Mortgage interest paid to Ohio Bank	13,200
Interest on car loan	1,120
Interest on credit cards	450
Child care expenses	4,000

12. Helen contributed $7,500 to her defined contribution Keogh plan.

13. The Browns made timely payments on estimated Federal taxes of $2,700 each quarter. If they have a refund due, they want it credited toward estimated taxes for 1989.

Requirements:

Prepare the 1988 Federal income tax return for George and Helen Brown. You will need Forms 1040, 2106, and 2441. You will also need Schedules A, B, C, D, E, and SE. If you use *WEST–TAX Preparer* software to solve the problem, the program will complete all forms and schedules except Form 2441. It will be necessary to complete Form 2441 by hand and enter the child care credit from line 8 of Form 2441 in the program on line 41 of Form 1040.

Problem 2

In December 1987, James D. (J.D.) McVey graduated from the University of Minnesota and immediately accepted employment with Union Valve Corporation, a West Virginia corporation that manufactures and distributes mining and drilling equipment. Under the terms of the employment agreement, J.D. was to assume responsibility (effective February 1, 1988) for the sales region comprising the states of Montana and Wyoming. Since Union Valve Corporation had not yet established an office in the region, J.D. was to conduct all business from his home. J.D. was expected to locate his home in either Montana or Wyoming, and he chose Searcy, Wyoming, due to its central location and available housing.

J.D. is 22 years of age and had been a full-time student at the University of Minnesota since his graduation from high school four years ago. He married Gloria, age 25, during his junior year in college. Gloria has custody of her child by a former marriage, Anthony, age 3.

During 1988 the McVeys had the following receipts:

1. Salary of $32,000 from Union Valve Corporation of which $2,403.20 was withheld for FICA and $4,100 for Federal income tax purposes (all reflected on Form W–2). Although J.D. received a bonus of $3,500 for his sales in 1988, such bonus was not declared and paid by Union Valve Corporation until February of 1989.

2. Commissions of $24,300 earned by Gloria from the sale of real estate from early June through December 31, 1988. Gloria operates this business out of the McVeys' apartment as a sole proprietor.

3. In 1988 the McVeys won $10,000 in a contest sponsored by a national chain of fast-food franchises. Although the winning ticket was registered in Gloria's name, she placed the proceeds in a savings account with Anthony listed as the owner. Interest on this account for 1988 amounted to $400, none of which was withdrawn.

4. Receipts of $4,200 from the lessee of property in Ypsilanti, Michigan. The property, a two-story brick house located in a residential area, was acquired by J.D. when his aunt died on December 21, 1987. As executor and sole heir of his aunt's estate, J.D. assumed control over the property on February 25, 1988. On March 1, 1988, he listed the house as being for rent but was not able to find a suitable tenant until late May. Under the terms of the two-year lease, the lessee was required to pay the following amounts: rent of $500 per month (beginning on June 1, 1988); the last month's rent of $500 in advance (the rent for May of 1990); and, a damage deposit of $200.

   The Ypsilanti property had a value of $150,000 and an adjusted basis to J.D.'s aunt of $50,000 on the date of her death. Gloria, who has had considerable training and experience in matters dealing with real estate, estimates that 20 percent of the value of the property is attributable to the land.

5. Cash of $500 received by Gloria from the estate of J.D.'s aunt. The amount was paid by J.D., acting in his capacity as executor, to Gloria in return for the services she performed in appraising estate assets. Indications are that the charge was reasonable for the services rendered.

6. Upon the final dissolution of his aunt's estate and after the payment of all expenses and taxes, J.D. received the following:

	Fair Market Value on Date of Death	Adjusted Basis to Aunt
Cash	$15,000	$15,000
Household furnishings	6,000	?
1957 Chevrolet convertible	12,000	3,200
Jewelry (mainly gold and silver)	8,000	?
Personal effects (e.g., clothing)	1,200	?

The dissolution and final distribution occurred on March 26, 1988. Under his aunt's will, J.D. was not entitled to any commission for serving as the executor of the estate. As executor, J.D. did not elect the alternate valuation date for the estate.

On June 26, 1988, J.D. received in the mail a check for $5,725 from the United Insurance Company. Unknown to him, J.D. was the designated beneficiary of an insurance policy on the life of his aunt. The policy had a maturity value of $5,000, and an enclosed statement from the company indicated that his aunt had paid premiums thereon of $2,600. Of the amount received, $725 was designated as being interest accrued since the date of his aunt's death.

7. On August 4, 1988, J.D. received $18,200 from the sale of the 1957 Chevrolet [see item (6) above]. Although the car was in good condition when his aunt died, it needed certain repairs to place it in top condition for resale. After J.D. received several estimates from mechanics who specialized in such restorations, he decided to do the work himself. In this connection, J.D. spent $2,400 on replacement parts and devoted considerable spare time to their installation. Based on the estimates received from the mechanics, the value of J.D.'s services was $2,100.

8. On September 25, 1988, J.D. sold his aunt's jewelry for $7,600.

9. Throughout 1988, Gloria received child support of $300 per month (for a total of $3,600) from her ex-husband. Gloria's ex-husband can prove that he furnished more than 50 percent of the support for Anthony.

10. Since beginning employment with Union Valve Corporation, J.D. has been covered under their group term life insurance policy. The policy applicable to J.D. provides for coverage of $100,000 and designates Gloria as the beneficiary.

11. Union Valve Corporation follows a policy of allowing its employees to choose between coverage in its noncontributory accident and health care plan *or* the receipt of an annual award of $1,500 in additional wages. For 1988, J.D. chose the medical insurance option. [Note: items (10) and (11) are not reflected in the salary information furnished in (1) above.]

12. Federal income tax refund of $140 received on March 6, 1988. In January of 1988, the McVeys filed a Form 1040A and a State of Minnesota income tax return for 1987 to recover some of the withholdings from Gloria's

wages from a part-time job, as the tax liabilities proved to be less than the amounts withheld. In addition to the Federal refund, a refund of $40 was received from the Department of Revenue of the State of Minnesota on March 20, 1988.

13. Dividends of $250 and interest on a savings account of $420. The dividends were received on Hansen Corporation stock owned by Gloria, while the interest was from a joint savings account at Searcy National Bank that J.D. established with some of the funds inherited from his aunt. None of the interest was withdrawn by the McVeys.

14. During 1988 Gloria had the following receipts involving the sales of marketable securities:

Asset	Date Acquired	Date Sold	Selling Price
100 shares of common stock in Yaxley Corporation	3/18/83	7/15/88	$5,200
500 shares of preferred stock in Zinstad Corporation	7/30/84	10/2/88	6,500

The selling price listed is net of brokerage commissions. In other words, it represents the amount Gloria actually received.

On March 18, 1983, on the occasion of her first marriage, Gloria received 100 shares of common stock in Yaxley Corporation as a wedding present from her father. The stock was acquired by her father on November 10, 1971, had an adjusted basis to him of $3,000, and had a fair market value of $3,800 on the date of the gift. No gift tax was due or paid as a result of the transfer.

Upon the receipt of a cash property settlement from her first husband, Gloria purchased 500 shares of preferred stock in Zinstad Corporation for $10,000. Shortly after purchase, she received a nontaxable two-for-one stock split.

15. In January J.D. received a check from Union Valve Corporation for $460 ($400 for travel and lodging, $60 for meals), which represented reimbursement for a trip he made to the home office in West Virginia. The trip for the job interview was made in November of 1987 and led to the offer of employment that J.D. later accepted. It was the understanding of the parties that the company would reimburse J.D. for reasonable expenses actually incurred. The $460 was not claimed as a deduction on the McVey's joint return filed for 1987, nor was the reimbursement shown on the Form W–2 (for 1988) sent to J.D. by the employer in early 1989.

16. A check for $645 received on March 19, 1988, from Union Valve Corporation, which represented reimbursement for some of the McVeys' moving expenses [see item (18) below]. This amount was included in the W–2 sent to J.D. for tax year 1988.

17. In February of 1988, a check for $420 received from Ajax Casualty Insurance Company which represented the amount due on a policy covering Gloria's 1980 model automobile. In December of 1987, J.D. totalled the automobile on the way to class. When the accident occurred, the car had an adjusted basis of $1,800 and a fair market value of $520.

During 1988 the McVeys had the following disbursements:

18. On January 12–13, 1988, the McVeys drove to Searcy, Wyoming, to find a suitable place to live. After two days of narrowing the alternatives, they leased an apartment [see item (20) below]. The return trip to Minneapolis took place on January 16–17.

    On January 30–31, 1988, the McVeys drove to Searcy with their personal belongings. As per the lease agreement, the apartment in Searcy was occupied by them on February 1, 1988.

    Expenses incurred in connection with the January 12–17 and the January 30–31 trips are summarized below.

	January 12–17 Trip	January 30–31 Trip
Meals while in transit	$ 50	$ 20
Meals in Searcy	60	25
Lodging while in transit	110	50
Lodging in Searcy	80	40
Trailer rental	—	210

The distance between Minneapolis and Searcy (one way) is 1,100 miles. In addition, the McVeys drove 140 miles looking for an apartment in Searcy during their January 14–15 stay. As noted in item (16), J.D.'s employer reimbursed the McVeys for $645 of the above expenses. Under company policy, however, mileage is not covered under the reimbursement plan in the case of new employees.

19. As a graduation present from his parents, J.D. received $3,000 for a down payment on a new automobile. On January 2, he purchased a new Buick station wagon for $15,000 through an automobile dealer in Montana with delivery in Detroit. Shortly thereafter, Gloria took a bus to Detroit and picked up the car (the dealer had provided Montana license plates). The reason J.D. used a Montana dealer was to avoid either the Minnesota or the Wyoming sales tax (Montana has no sales tax). The scheme backfired, however, when J.D. registered his car in Wyoming in early March of 1988. On that occasion, he was assessed and had to pay a Wyoming use tax of $600.

    Not counting the two trips mentioned in item (18) above, the station wagon was used as follows during 1988:

	Miles
Business	19,465
Medical	380
Charitable	900
Personal	8,326

In addition, J.D. spent $82 on parking while in business travel status.

20. On January 15, 1988, the McVeys leased a three-bedroom apartment in Searcy for one year (occupancy as of February 1). In addition to a $100 damage deposit, they paid the following amounts for this facility during 1988:

Rent ($400 per month)	$4,400
Utilities	1,320
Telephone	1,209

When they moved in on February 1, J.D. converted one of the bedrooms (approximately 20 percent of the total available floor space) into an office. The office was furnished with office equipment obtained from a local furniture-leasing concern. All lease charges were billed directly to Union Valve Corporation. The office was used exclusively for business, either by J.D. or by Gloria when she began her real estate activities in June.

The McVeys estimate that they use their phone 40 percent of the time for business.

Except for the lease charges on the office furniture, none of these expenses were paid by J.D.'s employer.

21. In order to facilitate her real estate operations, in June Gloria leased a used automobile for $210 per month. Lease payments by the McVeys during 1988 totalled $1,260. The car was used 80 percent for business and 20 percent for personal. Operating expenses on the automobile (e.g., gas and oil) were the responsibility of the lessee and amounted to $450.

22. During 1988, the McVeys incurred the following additional expenses in connection with their business activities:

	Gloria	J.D.
Dues to professional organizations	$ 75	$110
Expenses for attending professional meetings (e.g., business seminars)	150	—*
Subscriptions to professional journals	48	95
Entertainment (e.g., business lunches)	140	—*
Business gifts	200	—*

* These items were billed directly to Union Valve Corporation.

Except as indicated, none of J.D.'s expenses were reimbursed by his employer. All of these expenses are properly substantiated and satisfy the requirements of § 274 of the Code. Prior to Christmas of 1988, Gloria made gifts (worth $40 apiece) to each of five families that had purchased residential property through her during the year. The gifts were of such a nature that none of the cost was attributable to gift wrapping.

23. During 1988, J.D. paid the following amounts regarding the Ypsilanti rental property [see item (4) above]:

Repairs	$1,280
Management fee	350
Leasing costs (e.g., advertising)	240
Property taxes (not chargeable to the estate)	1,392
Special street-paving assessment	520

The special paving assessment was made by the City of Ypsilanti against all property owners in a four-block area. The assessment was made in December of 1988 for paving repairs and replacement that would be carried out in early 1989.

24. During 1988, the McVeys had interest expense as summarized below:

Montgomery Ward revolving account	$300
J.C. Penney revolving account	140
First National Bank of Searcy	460

The Montgomery Ward and J.C. Penney accounts were used to purchase clothes, toys, and certain household items.

The interest paid to the First National Bank of Searcy was for amounts J.D. borrowed to help pay for Gloria's dental work [see item (25) below].

25. Medical expenses paid during 1988 were as follows:

Payee	Amount
University of Minnesota Memorial Hospital	$1,875
Dr. Peter Lyons (diagnostician)	450
Dr. Richard Spain (radiologist)	370
Dr. Kenneth Wolford (general dentistry)	3,500
Dr. James Myers (orthodontia)	2,400
Bone and Joint Clinic of Searcy	750

The first three charges were incurred in December of 1987 and were the result of J.D.'s automobile accident [item (17) above]. Because J.D. was a student at the university, however, the parties involved allowed him to defer payment until 1988. No interest was charged for the privilege of late payment.

Due to a lack of funds while J.D. was a student, Gloria had been postponing some necessary dental restoration (e.g., crowns, bridges). She also needed braces to improve her appearance. These procedures were initiated and partially carried out in the last half of 1988 by Drs. Wolford and Myers working as a team. Although the orthodontia correction was only 50 percent complete by the end of 1988, the McVeys paid Dr. Myers the full amount that would be due. Full payment for orthodontia work before all of the services are rendered is not an uncommon practice.

As a result of an injury sustained while moving from Minneapolis to Searcy, J.D. began experiencing discomfort in his back. Ultimately, he went to the Bone and Joint Clinic of Searcy for a series of X-rays and orthopedic therapy. Although the McVeys were under the employer's medical insurance plan [see item (11) above], the expenses resulting from the December automobile accident occurred before J.D. became an employee. Unfortunately, the coverage of the plan does not extend to dental work. In late December, however, J.D. remembered about the plan and promptly filed a claim with Central Insurance Company (the carrier of the Union Valve Corporation plan) for the orthopedic charges. On January 22, 1989, J.D. received a check from the carrier for $650 (the policy had a $100 deductible feature for out-patient treatment). The McVeys do not keep a record of their drug expenditures.

26. Cash charitable contributions for 1988 include Searcy United Fund Campaign ($450), First Methodist Church of Searcy ($350), and the Italian Red Cross ($100).

Shortly after moving to Searcy, J.D. donated his aunt's personal effects [see item (6)] to the local branch of the Salvation Army.

Requirements
Based on the following assumptions, prepare a joint income tax return for the McVeys for calendar year 1988. The return should be in good form and should include all necessary supporting schedules.

Assumptions

   A. The McVeys use the cash method of accounting and the calendar year for tax purposes.

   B. Wyoming does not impose a state income tax. No state income taxes were paid or are due for 1988 to Minnesota or Michigan.

   C. Do not make assumptions not supported by the facts. For example, under (19) you must use the automatic mileage method allowed by the IRS because you cannot determine all of the operating expenses (gasoline purchases are unknown).

   D. Allocate the full office in the home expenses to J.D.

   E. Other relevant information concerning the McVeys and their affairs is summarized below:

- Gloria's social security number is 371–42–5207.

- J.D.'s social security number is 371–09–7846.

- In Minneapolis the McVeys lived at 1318 Queensbury Street (Apt. 12H), 55440.

In Searcy the McVeys live at 492 Commerce Street (Apt. 4), 82190.

The rental property in Ypsilanti is located at 789 University Drive, 48197.

   F. The McVeys made timely quarterly estimated Federal tax payments of $1,000 each quarter.

Problem 3

Roy C. Long (age 50) and Reba A. Long (age 48) have been married for 25 years and currently reside in a condominium located at 685 Palomar Drive, Decatur, Illinois 62525. They have two daughters, both grown and self-supporting. However, Reba's widowed mother (Lucille Armbrust, age 68) lives with them.

Approximately 15 years ago, Roy established his first liquor retail outlet. Over the years, the operation has been increasingly profitable and has grown to four stores, one of which has become particularly well known for its assortment of fine wines. Shortly after the start of the business, Roy requested and obtained approval from the IRS to change from the cash to the accrual method of accounting. Roy continued to use the cash method as to nonbusiness income and expenses. Roy decided to stay with the calendar year for reporting purposes as it ideally suited the nature of his business.

An unadjusted and partial income statement for "Roy's Emporium of Wines and Spirits" for 1988 contains the following information:

Sales		$1,877,150
Cost of goods sold—		
Beginning inventory	$ 305,000	
Purchases	1,300,000	
Less final inventory (based on year-end physical count)	(308,000)	1,297,000
Gross profit		$ 580,150
Other income—		
Proceeds from the condemnation of land and building	$ 185,000	
Refund from the cancellation of a casualty insurance policy	3,200	

Proceeds from the sale of scanner register	$ 8,000	
Proceeds from the sale of two manual type-writers and one calculator	100	196,300
Total income		$ 776,450
Other expenses—		
Depreciation	$?	
Bad debts	7,000	
Advertising	42,000	
Wages	287,000	
Taxes	51,115	
Insurance	18,000	
Rent	68,400	
Repairs	5,600	
Charitable contributions	500	
Chamber of Commerce dues	100	
Credit reports	860	
Telephone	8,200	
Utilities	19,600	
Armored car pick-up service	2,400	
Delivery expense	5,300	
Office supplies	3,800	
Fine for selling to underage customer	500	
Attorney's fee	2,233	
Employer contributions to H.R. 10 (Keogh) plan	43,050	
Leasehold improvements	32,000	597,658
Net income before depreciation and income taxes		$ 178,792

Further explanation concerning some of these items appears below:

1. Inventory is valued at the lower of cost or market. Losses due to spoilage and breakage are minimal and are not accounted for separately. Any shipping pilferage and other damage of merchandise is replaced by the suppliers. The purchases account, however, has not been adjusted to reflect the burglary to Store No. 1 on the night of March 13, 1988. On this occasion, merchandise (mainly vintage wines) purchased in 1988 with a cost of $9,800 (retail value of $20,200) was stolen. As to the loss, Roy filed a claim with Security Insurance Co. for $16,160. The claim was denied by the carrier on the grounds that the negligence of Roy's employees led to the loss. Roy promptly instituted court proceedings against Security Insurance Co., although his attorney had advised him that under the terms of the policies, the results of the litigation could go either way.

2. Roy was so upset as to the claims performance of Security Insurance Co. that on July 1, 1988, he cancelled the coverage on his business. The three-year policy was taken out on July 1, 1986, at a cost of $15,000, and the refund of $3,200 was the amount of the premium returnable under the terms of the contract for the remaining coverage of one year. On July 1, 1988, Roy replaced the coverage with a policy issued by the Safeguard Insurance Company. The policy cost $18,000 and provides protection from casualties for a three-year period.

3. Ordinarily, Roy's sales are on a cash-carry basis. With better customers, however, credit sales are permitted. Bad debts are reported under the specific charge-off method. During 1988, Roy wrote off 12 accounts, totalling $8,200, as being worthless. He did, however, recover $1,200 from an account written off and deducted for tax year 1987. The sales figure reflects credit sales for 1988 and includes amounts not yet collected.

4. In 1987 the city of Decatur instituted condemnation proceedings against the property where Store No. 1 was located; the city intended to use the property for a bus storage and repair facility. After considerable negotiations, an out-of-court settlement was reached on April 1, 1988, whereby Roy transferred title to the property for a price of $185,000 (its agreed-to fair market value). Information concerning the property is as follows:

Date of acquisition	December 18, 1983
Cost of acquisition	$100,000
Method of depreciation	Statutory percentage

As to both the cost of the property and the condemnation award, assume 10 percent is attributable to the land and 90 percent to the building.

On January 20, 1989, Roy reinvests $195,000 ($185,000 condemnation award plus $10,000) in a new warehouse. The warehouse will be used to store the extra inventory needed for Roy's liquor stores.

5. Being an innovative person who is interested in labor-saving devices, Roy decided to experiment with an automated checkout system. Pursuant to this objective, on August 1, 1986, he purchased a new scanner cash register for $22,000. The equipment was immediately installed in Store No. 3 and continued to operate until it was removed and sold to a supermarket on May 1, 1988.

Roy decided to abandon the experiment for several reasons. For one, much of the merchandise (particularly imported goods) stocked in his store did not contain the universal product code. More importantly, many of Roy's customers objected to the absence of price labels on each product. The scanner had an estimated useful life of ten years.

Bonus depreciation under § 179 was claimed for tax year 1986.

6. The manual typewriters and the calculator were acquired in 1977 at a total cost of $850 and, based on an estimated useful life of 10 years (no salvage value), were fully depreciated through tax year 1987. In computing the depreciation deducted, the straight-line method was used.

7. Of the $42,000 spent on advertising, $4,000 was for full-page ads in newspapers trying to influence the general public against a bill pending in the state legislature that would impose stricter gun controls. Roy, an avid hunter, is a member of the National Rifle Association and a firm believer in the right of citizens to possess arms.

8. Roy prides himself on full compliance with the state and local liquor control laws. In spite of this attitude, one of his employees became careless and was caught selling liquor to minors. Quite distraught over the possible effect on his reputation of a conviction and fine, Roy hired the best attorney in town to contest the proceeding. The effort proved fruitless and Roy was fined $500. The attorney was paid $2,233 for the services rendered. These amounts are reflected in Roy's unadjusted income statement.

9. The charitable contribution of $500 reflected on the income statement represents a cash gift to the United Fund in the name of the business.

10. The charge for armored car service provides for daily pickups of cash from all four retail outlets.

11. Taxes of $51,115 include the employer's share of the FICA tax, FUTA, ad valorem state and local taxes on business property, and various license fees.

12. Roy is not known for paying generous salaries to his employees, but he does provide coverage, at the rate of 15 percent, under an H.R. 10 (Keogh) plan instituted several years ago. The amount of $43,050 contributed to this plan in 1988 does not include coverage for Roy. Also, the $287,000 figure for wages does not include any sums Roy may have withdrawn from the business.

13. Anticipating the loss of the building through condemnation by the City of Decatur [see item (4) above], Roy located and rented another facility for Store No. 1. Although the location was ideal and the rent was reasonable, the condition of the building was not. Because Store No. 1 is Roy's greatest revenue producer (largely due to its selection of fine wines) and his pride and joy (the business started here), he felt compelled to improve the facility. The location was renovated at a cost of $32,000, with the improvements being completed and the premises occupied by April 1, 1988. Under the terms of the lease, Roy has the right to occupancy for 10 years with the option to renew for another 10 years. Roy estimates that the useful life of the improvements is 12 years. He is not certain as to whether the option to renew the lease will be exercised.

14. With the exception of the leasehold improvements to Store No. 1, Roy is not a believer in a heavy investment in capital for the business. In three of his stores, for example, all improvements (such as counters and shelves) were furnished by the lessors of the buildings and are reflected in the rents Roy pays. Depreciation information on the remaining assets is summarized as follows:

Asset	Date Acquired	Cost
Delivery truck # 1	2/1/87	$ 8,500
Delivery truck # 2	5/2/88	9,200
Refrigeration equipment	8/30/86	18,700
Office equipment	11/1/78	4,600

15. The delivery expense of $5,300 consists of the operating costs (e.g., gasoline, oil, tires) involved in the use of the two delivery trucks. It does not, however, include any depreciation [see item (14)].

16. Repairs to the leased buildings Roy uses in the business are his responsibility as a tenant. One item for $2,500 (included in the $5,600 total) was for the replacement of an air conditioning unit at Store No. 2. Although it was not his obligation, Roy had the work done because the landlord was out of town and customers were complaining about the lack of temperature control. Roy was reimbursed for this expense by the landlord in early 1989.

Roy and Reba had the following nonbusiness transactions for 1988:

17. Interest income of $18,465 on City of Decatur general revenue bonds.

18. Accrued (but undistributed) interest income of $18,500 on Roy's H.R. 10 (Keogh) plan.

19. Dividend income of $12,800 from Decatur Lumber Company, a locally owned corporation of which Roy owns 1 percent of the stock.

20. Fees of $2,400 paid to Roy for serving on the board of directors of Decatur Lumber Company.

21. On March 10, 1988, the Longs sold their home of 15 years for $280,000.

    Details concerning the sale and the property are summarized below:

Sales commissions	$16,800
Qualified fixing-up expenses	3,800
Original cost	50,000
Capital improvements (e.g., swimming pool, landscaping, central air conditioning)	20,000

    Ad valorem real estate taxes on the property for 1988 amounted to $3,695 all of which was paid on December 10, 1988, by the purchaser.

    On February 14, 1989, for a price of $162,000, the Longs acquired title to a new condominium which they occupied shortly thereafter.

    The sale of the house and the purchase of the condominium were due to the favorable real estate market and the desire on the part of the Longs for a smaller and less demanding place to live. The condominium is closer to Roy's businesses and requires less upkeep.

22. During 1988 Roy paid income taxes to Illinois as follows:

Prepayments for tax year 1988	$10,000
Amount due on April 15, 1988, for tax year 1987	3,000

    Roy estimates that he will owe additional state income taxes of $4,000 for tax year 1988.

23. On March 20, 1989, Roy mailed a check for $7,500 to the trustee of the H.R. 10 plan. This represented Roy's contribution on his own behalf for tax year 1988.

24. During 1988, the Longs made the following additional expenditures:

Interest on bank loans [the proceeds of which were used to purchase some of the City of Decatur bonds—see item (17) above]	$4,400
Interest on amounts borrowed against life insurance policies [the proceeds of which were used to help purchase some of the Decatur Lumber Company stock—see item (19)]	2,200
Premiums on life insurance policies [Roy is the owner and insured, and Reba is the beneficiary]	3,600
Ad valorem real estate taxes on the condominium [from the date of purchase through December 31, 1988]	2,800
Check mailed on May 1, 1988, to a local CPA for the preparation of the 1987 Federal and state income tax returns	1,200

25. In 1988 Roy transferred 200 shares of Decatur Lumber Company to the St. Mary's Catholic Church (Decatur) in satisfaction of the Long's church pledge of $4,000 for years 1988–1989 ($2,000 each year). The stock, acquired several years ago, had a basis of $10 per share and a fair market value of $20 per share on the date of the transfer.

26. As noted earlier, Reba's mother (Lucille) lives with the Longs who furnish all of her support. During 1988, Lucille's only source of income was Social Security payments in the amount of $2,850 and interest income from a savings account of $983. The interest income was not withdrawn, and the Social Security payments were deposited in Reba's savings account.

27. During 1988, the Longs made four timely payments of $15,000 each to the IRS. These prepayments of 1988 income taxes were based on the Federal income tax liability they incurred and paid for tax year 1987.

Requirements

Based on the following assumptions, prepare a joint income tax return for the Longs for tax year 1988. The return should be in good form and should include all necessary supporting schedules.

Assumptions

A. Although the return is being prepared as of its due date (April 15, 1989), you are aware that Roy has reinvested the condemnation proceeds [item (4)] in a new warehouse in early 1989.

B. Medical and drug expenses for 1988 are minimal and do not exceed the percentage limitations. The Longs do not carry any medical and hospitalization insurance.

C. Other relevant information concerning the Longs is summarized below:

   - "Roy's Emporium of Wines and Spirits" has an employer identification number of 93–4811838.

   - Roy's Social Security number is 540–44–6957, and Reba's is 542–02–3701.

   - As a business address, Roy uses the location for Store No. 3: 1340 Grizzly Drive, Decatur, Illinois 62525.

APPENDIX G

Table of Cases Cited

Davis v. Commissioner of Internal Revenue, 10-26
Davis, United States v., 4-22, 14-3
Delman, Estate of v. Commissioner of Internal Revenue, 5-28
Delp, Frank S., 11-4
Deputy v. du Pont, 6-6
Diedrich v. C.I.R., 14-2
Donruss Co., United States v., 2-20
Doyle v. Mitchell Bros. Co., 4-5
Dreicer v. C.I.R., 2-16
Druker v. C.I.R., 2-26
Dunn & McCarthy v. C.I.R., 6-6

E

Ebben, Leo G., 14-2
Edwards v. Cuba R. Co., 20-17
Eisner v. Macomber, 4-3, 5-27
Elot H. Raffety Farms, Inc. v. United States, 20-3
Erie Hill Rose, 11-10
Estate of (see name of party)

F

Farm Service Cooperative v. Commissioner of Internal Revenue, 2-42
Faulconer, Hunter, Sr., 6-34
Fausner v. C.I.R., 10-12
Fay v. Helvering, 8-9
Finkbohner v. United States, 2-20, 6-24, 8-9
Fischer, L. M., 4-11
Flint v. Stone Tracy Co., 1-2
Frank, Morton, 6-15
F.W. Woolworth Co. v. Commissioner of Internal Revenue, 2-8

G

Galt v. Commissioner of Internal Revenue, 4-16
Gee, George L., 10-40
Gelinas, Joseph T., 15-16
Ginsberg v. C.I.R., 20-42
Golconda Mining Corp. v. Commissioner of Internal Revenue, 2-42
Goldberg, Harry H., 6-22
Golsen v. Commissioner of Internal Revenue, 2-16

H

Hawkins v. C.I.R., 5-10
Heard v. C.I.R., 2-42
Helvering v. ___(see opposing party)
Henry, James A., 15-16
Henry Schwartz Corp. v. Commissioner of Internal Revenue, 2-41
Hillsboro Nat. Bank v. C.I.R., 6-8
Horst, Helvering v., 4-16
Hort v. Commissioner of Internal Revenue, 16-14
Horwith v. Commissioner of Internal Revenue, 19-30
Houlette, Richard T., 15-17

I

Illinois Terminal R. Co. v. United States, 6-31

J

James v. United States, 4-2
J. H. Baird Publishing Company, 15-26

K

Kahler, Charles F., 4-10
Keller v. C.I.R., 6-9
Kennedy v. C.I.R., 6-7
Kieselbach v. C.I.R., 5-26
Kintner, United States v., 20-3
Kirby Lumber Co., United States v., 2-41, 4-5, 5-29
Kluger Associates, Inc. v. Commissioner of Internal Revenue, 14-9
Korn Industries, Inc. v. United States, 18-15

L

Landfield Finance Co. v. United States, 5-5
Lang, Estate of v. Commissioner of Internal Revenue, 2-42
Latimer–Looney Chevrolet, Inc., 17-41
Lazisky v. Commissioner of Internal Revenue, 2-42
Lennard, Estate of v. Commissioner of Internal Revenue, 2-41
Lesslie, Thomas E., 11-31
Lewis, United States v., 18-9
Lindeman v. Commissioner of Internal Revenue, 5-15
Loco Realty Co. v. C.I.R., 15-11
Lucas v. Earl, 4-16
Lucas v. North Texas Lumber Co., 4-9
Lustgarten v. Commissioner of Internal Revenue, 18-24
Lynch v. Turrish, 14-2

M

Maid of the Mist Corporation and Affiliated Corporations, 2-42
Malat v. Riddell, 16-3
Mantell, John, 4-13
McWilliams v. Commissioner of Internal Revenue, 6-27, 14-19
Merchants' Loan & Trust Co. v. Smietanka, 4-2
Miller v. Commissioner of Internal Revenue, 2-8
Mitnick, Moses (Also Known as Eddie Lewis), 10-17

N

National Home Products, Inc. v. Commissioner of Internal Revenue, 18-56
National Muffler Dealers Ass'n, Inc. v. United States, 2-27
New Colonial Ice Co. v. Helvering, 6-2
North American Oil Consolidated v. Burnet, 4-9, 18-9

O

Old Colony R. Co. v. Commissioner of Internal Revenue, 11-12
O'Malley v. Ames, 14-3
Ostheimer v. United States, 4-57

Subject Index

Medical expense deduction, 11–3, 11–5
Moving expense, 10–7, 10–21, 10–22, 10–23, 10–24, 10–25, 10–37
Percentage limitation for meals, 10–6 to 10–9, 10–11, 10–40
Percentage reduction for meals, 10–6 to 10–9, 10–15, 10–19, 10–20, 10–21, 10–25
Recreation expenses, employer-paid, 10–8
Reimbursed expenses, 10–8, 10–11
Subsidized eating facility, 5–21, 5–22, 10–8
Substantiation requirements, 6–28
Tax home, 10–15, 10–16 to 10–17
Tax planning, 5–32
Travel expense, 10–7, 10–15, 10–26 to 10–27, 10–38
Value of meals, 5–24
Medical Expenses
 Allowed as itemized deduction for AMT, 12–14, 12–25
 Capital expenditures, 11–4 to 11–5, 11–29
 Charged on credit card, 11–29
 Child and dependent care credit alternative, 13–44 to 13–45
 Deductibility of, 6–4, 10–4, 11–2 to 11–4
 Deductible as alimony payments, 11–6
 Deduction versus credit, 13–44 to 13–45
 Defined, 11–2 to 11–4
 Dependency exemption, 11–7
 Of dependents, 3–6, 6–22
 Incurred for dependents, 11–3, 11–6 to 11–7
 Insurance premiums, 11–5 to 11–6
 Lump-sum payments of, 11–7, 11–29
 Meals and lodging, 11–3, 11–5
 Multiple support agreement, 3–36
 Nursing homes, 11–2 to 11–3, 11–29
 Paid on behalf of decedent, 11–7
 Paid on behalf of former spouse, 11–6
 Paid on behalf of nonspouse or nondependent, 3–36 to 3–37
 Paid by retirement plan distributions, 19–11
 Percentage limitations, 3–5, 3–28, 3–36 to 3–37, 11–2, 11–27, 11–29, 12–13
 Physical and dental examinations, 11–2
 Prepayment of, 11–28
 Preventive care, 11–2
 Reimbursed, 5–12, 5–14, 5–22, 11–7 to 11–8
 Special schools, 11–3 to 11–4
 Substantiation requirements, 11–29
 Tax planning, 11–27 to 11–29, 13–44 to 13–45
 Timing the deduction, 11–27 to 11–29
 Transportation expenses, 11–5, 11–29
 Year of deduction, 11–7
Medicare Supplemental Premium, 13–40 to 13–41
Member of Household, see Dependency Exemptions
Memorandum Decisions, see Citations
Mid–Month Convention, 9–15, 9–16, 9–17, 9–18, 9–42, 9–43, 9–44, 9–45, 9–47
Mid–Quarter Convention, 9–14, 9–18, 9–40
Military Benefits, 5–3, 5–17
Mining Exploration and Development Expenditures, 6–25, 12–7 to 12–8, 12–24, 12–26, 12–30
Minimum Tax, see also Alternative Minimum Tax, 4–5, 12–3, 13–25 to 13–26
Ministers of the Gospel, 5–16
Money Purchase Pension Plan, see Defined Contribution Pension Plan
Mortgage, see also Nonrecourse Debt
 Assumption of, 14–3

Credit for interest paid, 13–23, 13–24, 13–25, 13–27
Exceeding property's adjusted basis, 14–2
Interest on, 11–12, 11–15 to 11–16, 11–29 to 11–30, 12–15, 12–24
Loan origination fees, see Loan Origination Fees
Prepayment penalty, 11–16
Qualified residence, 11–12, 11–15 to 11–16, 12–14, 12–15
Second residence, 11–15, 12–15
Moving Expenses
 Buying and selling expenses, 10–23, 15–18
 Classification of, 10–22 to 10–25
 Deductibility of, 6–22, 10–20 to 10–21, 10–22, 10–37, 11–26
 Direct expenses, 10–22 to 10–23
 Distance test, 10–21, 15–17
 Dollar limits, 10–23 to 10–25
 Filing requirements, 10–25
 House-hunting trips, 10–23
 Indirect expenses, 10–23 to 10–24
 Itemized deduction, 6–22
 Meals, 10–7, 10–21, 10–22, 10–23, 10–24, 10–25, 10–37
 Reimbursed, 10–21, 10–22, 10–25, 10–39
 Tax planning, 10–39
 Temporary living expenses, 10–23
 Time test, 10–21 to 10–22, 15–17
 Transportation costs, 10–22 to 10–23
Multiple Support Agreement, 3–12 to 3–13, 3–36
Multiple Taxation, see also Double Taxation, 1–26 to 1–27, 11–8
Municipal Bonds, 5–25 to 5–26, 6–29 to 6–31, 20–4, 20–13, 20–37
Mutual Funds, 5–27

N

Negative Income Tax, 13–17, 13–27
Negligence Penalty, 1–22, 1–31
Net Capital Gains and Losses, see also Capital Gains and Losses, 3–32, 16–2, 16–19 to 16–24
Net Investment Income, 4–30, 11–13, 11–14, 12–15, 12–16
Net Operating Losses (NOL)
 Alternative minimum tax, 12–13 to 12–14, 12–25, 12–26
 Capital gains and losses, 8–20, 8–21, 8–23
 Carrybacks and carryovers, 1–28, 7–22, 8–18 to 8–20, 8–23 to 8–25, 8–26 to 8–27, 12–13 to 12–14, 15–25, 18–7, 18–9, 20–6, 20–7, 20–8 to 20–9
 Casualty losses, 8–19, 8–20
 Charitable contributions, 8–23, 8–25
 Computation of, 8–20 to 8–23
 Corporations, 8–20, 12–26, 20–5, 20–6, 20–7, 20–8 to 20–9, 20–11, 20–13, 20–15
 Deduction not allowed to partnerships, 20–34
 Depreciable property, 6–25
 Itemized deductions, 8–19, 8–20
 Personal and dependency exemption, 8–20, 8–23, 8–25
 Quick refund procedure, 8–20
 Recomputation of tax for carryback year, 8–23 to 8–25
 Refund claims, 8–20, 8–24
 Standard deduction, 8–20
 Tax credits, 8–23
 Taxpayer inequities, 8–18 to 8–19